ACROSS THE HIMALAYAN GAP

ACROSS THE HIMALAYAN GAP

An Indian Quest for Understanding China

Edited By
Tan Chung

Preface By
Karan Singh

Foreword by
Kapila Vatsysyan

GYAN

ISBN : 978-81-212-0585-6

Published, 2018

Published by

GYAN

Gyan Publishing House
5, Ansari Road
Daryaganj, New Delhi-110002
Phone: 011-47034999, 9811692060
www.gyanbooks.com
E-mail: books@gyanbooks.com

Printed at: G. Print Process, Delhi.

CONTENTS

		Pages
Acknowledgements		xi
Foreword	Kapila Vatsyayan	xiii
Preface	Karan Singh	xv
Introduction	Tan Chung	xvii

Indian Leaders' Speeches in Chinese Universities

1. **Prime Minister Rajiv Gandhi at Qinghua University, Beijing, 1988** 5
2. **Prime Minister Narasimha Rao at Beijing University, 1993** 13
3. **Vice-President K.R. Narayanan at Fudan University, Shanghai, 1994** 19

Indian Savants' Observations on China

4. **Raja Rammohun Roy** 27
5. **Gurudeva Rabindranath Tagore** 29
6. **Mahatma Gandhi** 35
7. **Pandit Jawaharlal Nehru** 45
8. **A.K. Coomaraswami** 53
9. **P.C. Bagchi** 57

Perspectives

10. **A Holistic Eye on Cultural Interface and Synergy** 71
    Kapila Vatsyayan
11. **The Critique of Modernity in India and China** 77
    Prasenjit Duara
12. **Enchantment and Disenchantment: A Sino-Indian Introspection** 91
    Ravni Thakur & Tan Chung
13. **Gandhi and Mao: National Identity for an Alternative Future** 105
    Mira Sinha Bhattacharjea
14. **Body, State and Cosmos: Mao Zedong's "Study of Physical Education" 1917** 117
    Patricia Uberoi
15. **A Sino-Indian Perspective for India-China Understanding** 133
    Tan Chung

16. **Unveiling Xuanzang and the Xuanzang Spirit** 149
Haraprasad Ray

17. **Towards an Understanding of Socialism with Chinese Characteristics** 155
Hemant Adlakha

Culture and Art

18. **Some Aspects of Jataka Paintings in Indian and Chinese (Central Asian) Art** 173
M.C. Joshi & Radha Banerjee

19. **India and China: Beyond and the Within** 181
Lokesh Chandra

20. **My Tryst with Chinese Art** 193
M.N. Deshpande

21. **Icons of Cultural Linkage** 197
D.C. Bhattacharyya

22. **Cultural Synthesis in the Buddhist Art of China** 203
Arputharani Sengupta

23. **New Revelations of Xinjiang Art** 213
Priyatosh Banerjee

24. **The Creation of Goddess of Mercy from Avalokitesvara** 217
Bagyalakshmi

25. **The Manichaean Input to Chinese Culture and Art** 227
Radha Banerjee

Socio-Political Changes and Economic Development

Socio-Political Institutions

26. **Development and Democracy: The Indian and Chinese Experience** 237
Manoranjan Mohanty

27. **Understanding "Human Relationships" in China** 243
Kamal Sheel

Economic Developments

28. **The Economic Ideas of Mao Zedong: Agricultural Transformation** 253
Utsa Patnaik

29. **Roads for Large Populations Towards Development and Prosperity** 261
S.P. Gupta

Gender Issues

30. **Change and Continuity: Orthodox Discourse on Gender Relations in China** 269
Ravni Thakur

Page

31. **Women and Family in India and China** 287
Bidyut Mohanty

32. **Women and Adult Literacy in China** 295
Shreemati Chakrabarty

History and Literature

Tagore and China

33. **The Controversial Guest: Tagore's 1924 Visit of China** 311
Sisir Kumar Das

34. **Tagore's Inspiration in Chinese New Poetry** 335
Tan Chung

Ancients on War

35. **Strategic Thinking in Ancient India and China: Kautilya and Sunzi** 357
Giri Deshingkar

36. **Arthashastra and Sunzi Bingfa** 365
V.R. Ragavan

Modern Chinese Literature

37. **The Lofty Height of a Writer: My Evaluation of Lu Xun** 367
Manik Bhattacharyya

38. **Comeback of Hundred Flowers in Chinese Literature: 1976-1989** 379
Sabaree Mitra

India-China Relationship

39. **Mao Zedong's Vision: China, The World and India** 395
Mira Sinha Bhattacharjea

40. **The Nehru Years Revisited** 403
Giri Deshingkar

41. **Retrace Indian Steps in the Agricultural Scene in China 40 Years Back** 415
S.K. Bhutani

Diplomats' Reminiscences

42. **Interwoven Memories About China** 423
K.P.S. Menon

43. **My Tryst with India-China Friendship—A Talk at IGNCA** 427
K.P.S. Menon

44. **Diary of an Old China Hand** 433
A.K. Damodaran

45. **Delicious Memories—A Talk at IGNCA** 437
A.K. Damodaran

46. **Walk out of the Dinner and Eat It—A Talk at IGNCA** 439
Brajesh Mishra

Page

47. Memories of An Indian Ambassador, 1987-1991 443
C.V. Ranganathan

48. A Young Indian Diplomat in China in the 1960s and 1970s 449
K.S. Rana

49. How I Arrived on the China Scene 459
Vinod Khanna

Better Understanding

50. How to Understand China? 473
V.V. Paranjpe

51. How to Understand Deng Xiaoping's China? 481
C.V. Ranganathan

52. Positive Agenda for Positive Action: Better India-China Understanding 487
Eric Gonsalves

53. Indian Policies Towards China—A Talk at IGNCA 491
Salman Haidar

54. Looking at China Across the Border 495
Dipankar Banerjee

55. India-China Relations: A Military Perspective 501
V.R. Raghavan

56. Three Agreements and Five Principles between India and China 505
Swaran Singh

57. Building Confidence with China 519
Swaran Singh

58. China Becoming a Superpower and India's Options 535
Sreedhar

59. The Importance of Understanding China 541
Surjit Mansingh

Contributors 447

ACKNOWLEDGEMENTS

When we first conceived this volume two years ago we had no idea that the baby would have been so fat as it is now. The two years of delivering it has taken off an extra ounce of fatness from all of us. It has been a long course of soliciting, praying, hoping against hope, ecstasy of receipt of intellectual properties, and, then, reading, typing, keying in, translating different software systems into our Apple Mackintosh (of which the spell check fails), checking, re-checking, re-re-checking, editing, discovering errors and unifying Chinese spellings, etc. Being its editor, I truly realize how limited is the capacity of one individual. It is only through collective hard work that such a fat baby can be born.

I have a very long list to offer my gratitude, but if I spell out, this page of "Acknowledgements" would become a thick "Who's Who". The readers have a chance to come across the names of all the contributors in a number of places so that I may be excused for not thanking them one by one. Here, I wish to say that only after we fail to obtain valuable writings from some eminent people did we treasure our success from other eminent personalities. "Time is money" that is why it is so difficult to have it dropped on one's begging palm. I would put more emphasis and say: "Time is gold". The value of gold that we are denied makes what we hold doubly treasurable. Many of the articles enshrining this volume belong to the "to be chewed and digested" category of Francis Bacon's classifications. As we do not have the resources to pay, we get them as labour of love. And love is what no money can buy. To be loved by so many is an immense reward to our own labour of love too. The book will perpetuate this noble love story.

But, I shall fail my duty if I do not thank Dr. Karan Singh who has never with held a "yes" to my demand. He inaugurated our Seminar on "India and China Looking at Each Other" held in September, 1996, and sent us his "Preface" just by the asking. Dr. Kapila Vatsyayan is always a friend, guide and philosopher to me. It was her inspiration that has created this book. Kapilaji, as the Academic Director of The Indira Gandhi National Centre for the Arts, has given us enormous moral and material support to our endeavour. Besides, we have also got an article in her name with her approval.

I should also thank Dr. Ravni Thakur for coming to our rescue when we were behind schedule. She is a China scholar and fluent in English. As Assistant Editor, she did free me from a lot of burden in proof reading. Besides, she also made editorial touches to some of the articles to enhance their quality. Because of time constraint, we could not implement many of her good suggestions.

Last but not least, I want to register my thanks to my colleagues of the East Asian Programme (EAP) unit of IGNCA. Dr. Radha Banerjee and Ms. Sudhanshi Vasudev have helped me in doing almost everything: from getting the intellectual properties to processing them including proof reading. Ms. Rajni Adlakha, my secretary, was very cooperative and uncomplaining when I involved her to share my over burden. We also had an excellent and dedicated helper in Mr. Dharam Vir Pandey. We depended on him for not only keying materials into the computer with great speed, but also for putting all materials into page-maker, etc. It was his unbounded zeal and many a sleepless night that have prevented this book from further delay.

TC

FOREWORD

Prof. Samuel P. Huntington of Harvard University was here in India last year, and many of us had pleasant interactions with him about the civilizational discourse which we, in India, have been very much concerned all along. The Indira Gandhi National Centre for the Arts (IGNCA), in the 13th year of its youth now, is an institution specially dedicated to culture and art, i.e. the best part of human civilization. As we take a holistic view, we not only treat different civilizations as various manifestations of a whole—the human civilization, but also do not endorse the "Us and Them" proposition as discussed in Huntington's world-famous book *The Clash of Civilizations and the Remaking of World Order*. "One harmonious world", to the Indian cultural mind, is no euphoria, but a dedication and commitment. To us, nothing is more important than the realization of the "Universal Civilization" in which each component is treating the other as an equal with respect and affection.

The East Asian Programme in our IGNCA was first called the "cell of Sino-Indian Studies" when it was started by Prof. Tan Chung in 1989. Even after this name-change (which means the expansion of its scope), Tan Chung and his colleagues in this unit still work on Sino-Indian Studies as the most endeared field—if not an obsession. For more than two years now the unit has undertaken this project of "India and China Looking at Each Other", and the present volume is the first fruit of this project. My congratulations to Prof. Tan Chung and his colleagues—those who have helped in bringing out this volume. Perhaps, never before has there been any work like this, and in the present volume readers can have a good view of how Indian intelligentsia have looked at China and what have been their concerns. I very much wish that this volume is circulated among the Chinese intellectuals, academicians experts and politicians so that they will gain a correct perspective about the "Indian perspectives" on China. Prof. Tan Chung, with cameras at the ready, is eager to capture the Chinese responses so that he and his team will produce a companion volume to this with a sub-title of "Chinese quest for understanding India". I wish him success in these discourses which, I venture to think, would help remove the apprehension in some quarters about the future clashes of civilizations. As Tagore, Nehru and many other Indian savants have said, if India and China can establish an ideal relationship of indepth understanding of each other, they will play a great role in promoting universal amity and harmony. For, our two countries not only have two-fifths of the world's total population, but these two human communities have carried with them two ancient civilizations and a thick cultural sediment of noble spirit and mental wisdom that would help to overcome the obstacles in the way of creating the Universal Civilization.

The present volume has an impressive list of contributors, some life-long China experts, others with immense information and insight about China. I welcome their contributions and thank their labour of love. Many of them, perhaps, have not had interactions with IGNCA before. Now that we have established our associations, I hope they will return to us again and again, and take interest in what we are doing in IGNCA. I also hope that this volume can attract many more readers who have never read our publications so far. Though in name ours is an institution of "arts", but it should be understood in the widest sense of the term. Our activities cover creative and critical, written and oral literatures, the oral, written, and visual traditions of a civilization, lifestyles and the interface between material and spiritual cultures. Our focus, of course, is on India, on all what she has achieved in the long history of her civilizational existence, but we always pursue an open-door policy, and go out and out to appreciate the cultural achievements of other countries and other civilizations on the one hand, and welcome with open arms input from individuals, institutions and other quarters outside India on the other. We have already started some contacts with China, with her culture and art, with her traditions and lifestyles, but we want to enlarge these contacts. Perhaps, this volume will bring us many more friends from India, China and other countries to help strengthen our activities in IGNCA in its multifaceted dimensions. In this volume, strategists and ex-diplomats focus their attentions on Confidence Building Measures and constructive cooperative relationship. To my mind, the best mutual understanding between different peoples and cultures does not crystal in the mind, but springs from the heart. Only when there is an indepth acquaintance and appreciation of each other's culture and art can there be the true smile from the heart.

With these words, I offer this volume to our readers and hope the pages are opened with appreciation and critique, resulting in wider participation in our civilizational discourse.

New Delhi
April, 1998

Kapila Vatsyayan

PREFACE

India and China between them represent the two oldest continuing civilizations in the world, covering more than one-third of the entire population of Planet Earth. This fact alone highlights the tremendous importance of inter cultural visits and studies between these two nations who have been neighbours ever since history began. Unfortunately, as a result of Western dominance, the ancient links gradually disappeared causing a vacuum which now needs to be filled. The seminar organised by the Indira Gandhi National Centre for the Arts recently was a welcome step in this direction, and the present volume will certainly be an important contribution towards developing a closer understanding between India and China. Hopefully it will be followed in due course by a companion volume entitled "Chinese Perspective on India".

It is well known that Buddhism, which was born in India, became the major cultural link between the two civilizations. China already had a flourishing Confucian tradition with which Buddhism interacted in a positive and non-confrontational manner. Among the many persons who carried the message of the Buddha to China was the famous scholar Kumarajiva who came from my home state of Kashmir. While it is generally known that the Buddhist influence spread from India to China, there is an inadequate appreciation regarding what we have received from China. Tea, porcelain, silk and printing are among the great gifts of China to world civilization.

We are shortly entering the third millennium A.D. For us in India and China, whose civilizations go back much further in time, the event may not be as exciting as it is to the West. Nonetheless, it does mark an important milestone in modern history. If the 19th century has been described as the century of Europe, and the 20th as the century of America, it is possible that the 21st century will be described as the century of Asia, in which China and India will inevitably be major players. A creative interaction between the Indic and the Sinic civilizations will be a major factor in this process.

It is my sincere hope that universities and other academic institutions in India will begin paying closer attention to India-Chinese relations—political, economic and cultural. The Indira Gandhi National Centre for the Arts has made a useful contribution in this direction.

Karan Singh

New Delhi
1st December 1997

INTRODUCTION

This book partially fulfils the target of our two-year old project entitled "India and China Looking at Each Other". The inspiration behind this project is the now well-known idea propounded by Dr. Kapila Vatsyayan, Academic Director of IGNCA, in the fall of 1990 at the Mogao Caves at Dunhuang, China, that Indians and Chinese stopped trying to know each others country's, politics, culture, history, society, etc. through the prism of the Western Hemisphere. Instead, they should look at each other directly. At that time, the learned circles in India had very little access to the Chinese scholarship particularly in the field of her culture and arts. Under the vigorous drive of Dr. Vatsyayan, IGNCA brought the Director of the Dunhuang Academy, Prof. Duan Wenjie, and his senior colleague, Prof. Shi Weixiang, to India, utilized their presence in New Delhi to hold an international seminar on "Cave Art of India and China" in 1991, and mounted an impressive exhibition of the Dunhuang paintings in the premises of IGNCA in 1991-92. Subsequently, we brought out the book *Dunhuang Art Through the Eyes of Duan Wenjie* in 1994 which has helped Indian scholars to peep into Chinese scholarly efforts in studying the marvellous Dunhuang art treasure.

Quite some water has flowed down the Yangtse and Ganga since Kapila Vatsyayan made the *looking-at-each-other* call eight years ago. However, academic endeavours are always behind the rapid changes in the world scene. Today, not only the India-China relationship has entered a new phase of constructive cooperation, but the international development portends an urgency that the two ancient and modern civilizations of India and China become more pro-active in uniting Asia, if not the world, in their endeavour of building up a harmonious and just world order while humanity marches into the 21st century. With such a situation in view, we launched the project of "India and China Looking at Each Other" to help accelerating the process of promotion of mutual understanding between India and China. We held a four-day seminar in November, 1995 on "India and China : Looking at Each Other", and a one-day seminar in September, 1996 on "Indian Diplomats' Reminiscences on China". The present volume can be viewed as a harvest-gathering — not only of crops sowed by these two seminars, but much more gleaned from the vast intellectual fields of a total of 40 Indian scholars and experts.

I must hasten to add that much as we would like to bring out a book which should represent the pinnacle achievement of Indian research on China, we know our limitations on two counts. For one thing, to do an extensive research on the past and existing Indian studies on China would take considerable time (at least a couple of years) which will unduly delay the publication of this book, and deprive us the advantage of timely gathering feedbacks—like the Chinese saying goes: without erecting the pole you won't see its shadow. Another factor is our mixed experience in knocking at the scholarly doors — and many, many times at some of these doors — to beg for treasurable intellectual properties. What is brought out before our readers is the maximum extent to which our persuasion has reached. Apart from such handicaps, we also wish to make the present volume a basic reference book so that it presents. in a nutshell, various dimensions of Indian scholarly interest on China. Thus, our emphasis is on inclusiveness, not selection and elimination. The immediate need in India and abroad, we think, is an overview about the Indian studies on China. The reference value of this volume has been strengthened by the important speeches made by Indian government leaders in China, by excerpts from the writings of the past Indian savants who have said many important things about China, all these which may not be readily available to the interested general public and research scholars. So, this volume has become a kind of parade, a kind of monitor about India's researches, perspectives, opinions, etc. on China. To both the Indian and foreign readership this volume might provide a mirror of the Indian thinking from various angles about her most important neighbour — China.

But, this volume is more particularly targeting at the Chinese readership. Presently, there is an increasing number of Chinese intellectuals who can read English. When there is something informative or worth telling the Chinese public, there will be interested experts to render them into Chinese and place them under the purview of the wider readership in

China. We very much hope the contents of this volume, wholly or partially, be communicated to the Chinese intellectuals, to the Chinese thinktank through whom even to the Chinese political leaders. We know that there is a desire on the part of Chinese high-ups to understand India, Indian psyche and Indian attitude towards China, but have not had enough feedback. Doubtlessly, without knowing India well even if China wishes to be India's best friend she will not know how to become. Understanding is the first step towards confidence building measures.

The same will be true for India to befriend China which cannot be achieved by mere goodwill and blind enthusiasm. In fact, it was this blind enthusiasm in the 1950s that has blown up the magnificent bubble of "Hindi-Cheeni Bhai Bhai" and led the Indian mood onto the arena of illusion and miscalculation. A true India-China rapprochement cannot and should not return to the "Bhai Bhai" days, and let sentiments once again overwhelm rational thinking and cold calculation. Hence, the Indian ruling elite and policy-makers need to know not only how China marches towards her future goals, but also how China and her elite think of India. We notice that although mutual understanding between the two countries has improved substantially, a wide gap between the mental reconstruction and ground reality still exists. In order to bridge this gap we need to supply the Indian perspectives on China to the Chinese, and collect the Chinese perspectives on India and make them available to the Indian intellectual public. This two-way flow of information is what exactly our "Looking At Each Other" project aims at. Thus, after this volume hits the stand we shall try to see it circulated in China. After it is read by Chinese intellectuals there is bound to be reactions and rejoinders etc. Our next agenda is to collect the feedback and bring out its companion volume which will be the "Chinese perspectives on India".

To this volume we have given the title "Across the Himalayan Gap". We hope that when we bring out its companion volume to reflect the Chinese perspectives on India such a title will appear outrightly out-dated. We hope we shall be in a position to declare the disappearance of the "Himalayan Gap" when we christen our next volume. Actually, even in the present volume, we see many Indians, past and present, already flying across the Himalayan gap of Sino-Indian understanding. Resorting to this title actually reflects three things: (1) our strong wish that this gap should be bridged, (2) our bringing out this volume to try to bridge this gap, and (3) a scaffold of the bridge already emerging in this volume. General Banerjee, one of our contributors, has suggested that when we "look at each other", we must not look "merely with our two open eyes, but also with our inner eye", i.e. the eye that "provides a deeper view and a degree of understanding". This summarizes our intention and hope. Of course, we are conscious of the probability that the perspectives reflected by this volume is a one-side view, looking at Chinese developments, historical and current, and also India-China relations only from the Indian vantage position and reflecting only the Indian psyche. It is for the Chinese readers of the volume (and readers all over the world also) to point out the gaps of understanding and what is missing from this volume. I am sure, after we gather the feedback from China (and abroad) many of our authors of this volume would like to re-respond to the Chinese (and other foreign) responses, would like to revise their opinions and conclusions, would like to argue, to debate. Then, intellectually, the relations between India and China would be enlivened, filled with candid exchanges of opinions, trading criticisms, learning how to understand each other with empathy and sympathy. Trading arguments and criticisms to the extent of exhaustion can preclude future trading of blows, and hammering misunderstanding can forge true understanding.

Through the process of doing this volume we have gathered some thoughts. First of all, we don't live in a static and changeless world. As Prime Minister Rao said in China in 1993 that "we are at the threshold of a new century." Of course, our concept of time need not be tied up with the round figures of the Christian calendar which we call the "Common Era". It is legitimate to argue that the year 2000 or 2001 will be as ordinary as any other year, and there is literally no threshold or gate for us to enter into the 21st century. However, from a general historical viewpoint, we see human evolution already arriving at the crossroad whether we acknowledge it or not. On one plane, the world has completed its journey through the course of Western domination that had begun two or three centuries ago. Even without conceiving any "Asian Century" there is no gainsaying that the Eastern Hemisphere has already wrested a lot of initiatives and dynamism from its erstwhile "better half" — the Western Hemisphere. The universal belief that the West is the upper limit of cultural, in particular, scientific and technological achievements is no longer sustained. The upcoming Eastern countries are contributing greater and greater to the material life of the world that is progressively reducing the human dependence on the Western, especially European industrial output. On another plane, along with the diminution of Western domination there is a change of cultural atmosphere with containment giving way to engagement, rivalry giving way to cooperation, nationalism giving way to globalization, superpower politics giving way to economic interface and synergy. Such a new phenomenon helps us to replace, once for all, the East-West-never-meet scenario by the holistic perspective of East-in-West and West-in-East scenario. Moreover, we are already inside the threshold of the third Revolution — Information Technology. Civilization and culture have become softer and softer despite the spectre of "Clash of Civilizations" courtesy of Harvard Professor

Samuel P. Huntington. Further more, human resources have become more precious than money and machine. Far-sighted seers have begun to attribute non-materialistic elements, like spiritual culture, ethos, dedication, morale, purposiveness, the spirit of sacrifice, and other qualities of the people as vital inputs to progress and economic growth. Considering all this epoch-making development at this crucial juncture of century/millennium-turning we must ask the questions: where will India and China stand? Any new challenge and new roles for the two nations to play on the global stage in the coming years?

When we stand at the threshold of a fast moving world we are reminded by what Jawaharlal Nehru said in 1952 that we should "look at the long perspective of history and try to peep into the future, ignoring for the moment our present discontent," and, then, see "the importance of India and China functioning with a measure of cooperation". This volume has provided us with an opportunity to review what Tagore and Nehru have said about the future development of humankind. Our contributors, particularly those who look at India-China relations from a global and futuristic perspective, have echoed in their writings that a new era has dawned in the horizon. Those who have focussed attention on historical developments have also shown a dynamic spirit, and we see their observations vibrating with excitement, reflecting a yearning for new concepts and refreshing perspectives. All this becomes a clarion call to us not only to partake in the excitement and ecstasy of threshold-entering, but to contribute our mite in fuelling a refreshing perspective on India-China relationship.

Secondly, as Ambassador Ranganathan has written in this volume, there is "need for Indians to develop the habit of an independent assessment" while we study China, "rather than depend on borrowed judgements made from different strategic viewpoints." Those of us who teach China or guide research on China in India have long felt the inadequacy of the international scholarship which was dominated by the US campuses. We were yearning for alternative perspectives and also started nursing them. Experience shows that apart from bias and prejudice (which have always been more developed in the developed world and stronger in the strong Western powers than in other countries and areas), it has been disadvantageous to look at Chinese developments from the Western cultural viewpoints than from the Indian.

While doing this volume we are all the more convinced that the time has come for us to develop either an Indian perspective or a Sino-Indian perspective in studying China. By Indian perspective we are translating Kapila Vatsyayan's advocacy into practice, we are taking a direct flight to China, not travelling via the Western Hemisphere. That is to say, we don't carry the extra burden of prejudice emanating from other quarters. This should not be construed as an anti-Western attitude, nor do we intend to exclude the Western Hemisphere from our academic pursuit even if it deals only with India-China interface. The Western Hemisphere has been, and will always be a great source of information and wisdom in all branches of scholarship, not excluding Chinese studies. This proposition, however, does not preclude establishing an Indian perspective on China. The absence of such a perspective, so long, has not only weakened an indepth Indian understanding of China, but also hampered further promotion of mutual understanding between India and China.

In conceiving and delivering this volume we have already experienced the birthpang of creating the Indian perspective on China. We already see Indian scholars, like Prasenjit Duara and his contemporaries in the USA, and Manoranjan Mohanty and a number of others in India, taking a lead in building up the Indian perspective — or a refreshing perspective with a dynamic Indian mind behind it. Prasenjit, in fact, is in an avant-garde position, and he has many decades to shape himself as a new tide in Chinese studies. His writings are an inspiration to those of us who have taught him at Delhi University, and will always be a guiding light and landmark for the younger generations of Indian (also foreign) scholars.

I have used the term "Sino-Indian perspective" which has found echo in this volume from other contributors as well. Readers may discover that when terms such as "Indian perspective" and "Sino-Indian perspective" enjoy limelight, there is always the "Western perspectives" lurking in the dark. Never mind the misnomer of "Western perspectives", its presence here as a kind of whipping boy only shows how eager on our part to blaze a new trail in Chinese studies in India. The whipping boy should not have figured if it had not come in our way. I have no intention to cast any aspersion on Western or US scholarship on China. If there is a situation of someone more equal than others, the others should be equally blamed than someone. Learning from other quarters is not the same thing as surrendering one's own judgement and, worse still, getting into the straitjacket laid by others. Indian scholarship on China can never prosper if it remains a faded carbon copy of the Western scholarship.

By "Sino-Indian perspective" we mean to take cognizance of the Sino-Indian interface from a holistic perspective. Jawaharlal Nehru has reminded us that even when Sino-Indian relations are not what they should be we still should see the "golden links" lining up the Indian and Chinese civilizations through history. Had such a Sino-Indian perspective commanded the governments of India and China and their ruling elites in the past the deterioration of India-China relations in the 1960s would not have taken place. Prime Minister Rajiv Gandhi, in his 1988 address, said significantly: "We are summoned by our past to the tasks which the future holds. We have a mutual obligation to a common humanity. India and China can together give the world new perspectives on a world order..." It is from such a height that we emphasize on the adoption of the Sino-Indian perspective, that the two peoples recognize each other as their cultural cousins, that they view each other with a serious indepth understanding of each other even at the time of hostility. Our diplomat-authors have given us a treat of their valuable experiences while serving in China or dealing with China in the Foreign Office in New Delhi during the overcast days. Some of the scenes are very moving conveying the truth through their anecdotes that the two great civilizations would never lose this Sino-Indian perspective—this tender feeling towards each other.

Thirdly, I think all the contributors in this volume agree with me that *we are quite conscious of what we have put in black and white being always overtaken by fast developing events and fast changing perspectives.* In order to avoid being judged out-dated we are always ready to revise and update our writings even if they have been well-researched with a lot of indepth and mature deliberation. Those who have joined in the discourse in this volume on India-China relations have amply suggested that the want of a dynamic perspective on the problems facing the bilateral relations in yesteryears may have jeopardized past relationship, and even when India-China discomfiture was stalemated there were initiatives on both sides to break the ice. Today, a sea change has taken place from the icy scenarios the 1960s and 1970s. And with every passing day something new is coming up in the internal developments of India and China as well as the international environment compelling a forward mood in the bilateral relations between New Delhi and Beijing. Moreover, the fleeting scenarios between Moscow and Beijing, Washington and Beijing, all the more foreclose any everlasting concepts/misconcepts, and unchanging mentality between our two capitals.

Often, Chinese diplomants and journalists who have been closely following reports and comments published in the Indian media, are joined by Chinese academia to nurse a feeling, if not misgiving, that even today the criteria of the 1960s and 1970s are still being applied to gauge Chinese motivations and schema. Such a feeling may get mitigated after reading this volume. For, the following pages do give to the Chinese and world public a glimpse of what we may describe as the matured views on China on the part of various Indian intellectuals. We hope that all the readers, particularly the Chinese readers, can give cognizance to this maturity, and the balanced approach in most of our entries. Wherever deficiencies still prevail they are due to the want of adequate information rather than a misunderstanding culture. When an Indian and a Sino-Indian perspective grow from strength to strength, and when perspectives and insights can keep pace with the fleeting scenarios, such deficiencies may get eliminated automatically. If this volume gets wide publicity in India and is being seriously read by all those who may, in future, be asked to report or comment on China they will no longer linger in the misunderstanding culture, and a facelift will appear in the China reportage in the Indian mass media. Yet, one must reconcile to the reality that by not looking at each other for a long time, the prevalence of the misunderstanding culture was but nature. And we have to allow a transitional course of transforming it into an understanding culture. This, once again, underlines the intention of bringing out this volume.

Fourthly, when we talk of the fleeting scenarios and impermanency of policies, equations, perspectives, and opinions etc., we know something will remain permanent and unalterable by any force of the world. Apart from truth, humanism, the longing for peace, the desire to befriend, the entities of India and China will remain on earth for as many millennia in the future as they have travelled in the past. While India and China's existence is permanent, so is India-China interface and synergy — never mind temporary set backs. In our volume we see current thinking echoing past wisdom of the savants on this point. As I pen these words, I read the new Indian Defence Minister, George Fernandes, quoting Edgar Snow that "the moment India and China become friends, the two would change the course of history," (*The Hindustan Times*, April 17, 1998, p. 12). The Minister has taken many by surprise, hence his observation is weightier than tons of positive assurances from known Indian friends of China. We feel greatly encouraged by the prospect that whatever conflicting ideologies and difference in political subjects, there is universal recognition of the importance of India and China coming together for the good of humankind. This is exactly what this volume is firmly committed to.

To return to Edgar Snow courtesy of George Fernandes, India and China were still to get a rightful berth in the commity of nations. Today, not only both the countries are celebrating (and about to celebrate) the golden jubilee of their Independence/Liberation, but our globe has already shrunk in size with many dominant powers of yore in shrunken strength and stature. India and China which are already "population supper powers" are only one step away from preeminence — dropping the prefix "population", i.e. converting population burden into valuable assets. The agenda of unity and comradeship between the two countries has already emerged by itself, and the earlier it is taken up the better for both the peoples and humanity as a whole. It is all the more reason that this book should be read by all sensible and forward-looking Indians and Chinese who will, then, turn this spark into a prairie fire—in constructive sense.

If the book can be likened to a feast, it is served in 8 courses. In the first course we have reproduced the three speeches made by different Indian leaders in different Chinese universities: Prime Minister Rajiv Gandhi's at Qinghua University, Beijing, in 1988; Prime Minister Narasimha Rao's at Beijing University, Beijing in 1993; and Vice-President (then, and now President) K.R. Narayanan's at Fudan University, Shanghai, in 1994. I need not remind our readers that, like other such speeches delivered in India and abroad, these contain a large dosage of input from the Ministry of External Affairs,. thus reflecting the Indian government's policies vis-a-vis China. A careful reading of them will get an insight into the basic attitude of the Government of India towards China: harking back to historical amity and cultural intercourses between two great civilizations, and looking forward to the days of future interface and synergy. Students on India-China relationship can read these speeches along with what Jawaharlal Nehru had said about China (which are quoted quite substantially in the second section of this volume) and see that India-China relations have been guided by a friendly approach, by and large, while the border dispute, the 1962 war, and the post-1962 India-China unpleasantry look like just an aberration.

In the second course, we try to exhibit the gems from the wisdom of India on China. Due to the constraint of space, the quotations are far from exhaustive, and what we have gleaned are titbits from the ideas of only six famous persons : Rammohun Roy (1772-1833), Rabindranath Tagore (1861-1941), M.K. Gandhi (1869-1948), Jawaharlal Nehru (1889-1964), A.K. Coomaraswamy (1877-1947), and P.C. Bagchi (1898-1956). These six savants either had a keen interest in Chinese history, culture and modern developments, or played a role in promoting India-China understanding. Many of the observations of these savants are sagacious and insightful. We have served on a silver platter the chopsuey of delicacies which are not available in ordinary restaurants.

Rammohun Roy's satire about "three Chinese converts" is pungently delicious. It was written apparently with a caricature of the want of sophistry on the part of Chinese intellect, but, after reading it carefully, one finds it, in reality, a sharp exposure of the Western prejudices against the Eastern peoples. While an angry Christian missionary calls names such as "astonishing depravity", "the depth of Satan", "benighted creatures", a smiling Chinese coolly quotes Confucius to teach the learned Westerner that "bad temper always turns reason out of doors". The concluding paragraph brings out the Chinese (and Eastern) contempt on the ideas that the bearers of White Man's Burden wish to impose on the oriental minds. Rammohun's satire, thus, has a close reference to the ideological encounter even today.

The quotations from Tagore are mainly from "Talks in China" in 1924, and the entire recorded speech that he delivered on the Bengali New Year Day, April 14, 1937 while inaugurating Visva-Bharati Cheena-Bhavana. Both his lecture tour to China and the founding of Cheena-Bhavana were great events in the annals of India-China relations. The importance of Tagore on India-China relations is not confined to what he said and wrote, but his spiritual influence on the Indian political leaders, particularly, Jawaharlal Nehru. When we review what Nehru said and did vis-a-vis China uptill the surfacing of the border dispute, we see unmistaken inspiration of Tagore.

"I consider myself a Chinese" said Mahatma Gandhi in 1947. Before he plunged into the Independence Movement in India he had been an active lawyer in South Africa, mainly taking up cases for Indians and Chinese against the apartheid regime. On the other hand, the name "Shengxiong" (literally "holy hero", the Chinese translation of "Mahatma") commanded universal love and admiration in China. A section of the Chinese political activists in the 1920s, 1930s and 1940s might not approve Gandhi's approach of "non-violence" in the freedom struggle, but even they joined others to willingly receive inspiration from the Mahatma in their own struggle for a free and liberated China. Gandhi's preoccupation with the domestic affairs of India prevented him from paying more attention to China. As he himself often expressed: his fighting for the independence of India was also for the freedom of China, and a free India would do all she could to render help to China's freedom struggle. Gandhi would honour his promise under any circumstance. Unfortunately, things went out of his control at the crucial juncture and his life, his inspiration and promise were cut short by the assassin's bullets in 1948.

Yet, the Mahatma did have important interactions with the Chinese leaders and others. He and Nehru had separate important discussions when the Chinese head of state, Generalissimo Chiang Kai-shek, visited India in 1942 with a sepecific purpose of talking to them. After the talks, Nehru and Gandhi discussed between themselves intensively about India's support to China in the latter's life-and-death anti-Japanese struggle, which resulted in Gandhi's solemn pledge to China (conveyed to the Generalissimo by his own writing) that even when he (Gandhi) was launching his anti-British agitations, he would see to it that they would not harm the interest of China. I think, this is not only a historic event, but symbolizing the fond affection of India for her neighbour and cultural cousin—China.

Quotations from Nehru on China is not an easy task. Few, if any, non-Chinese statesman in human history have spoken and written so much about China as Nehru did. This very fact proves that Nehru was a Sinophile. One cannot over-emphasize the point that historical events were unkind to Nehru, that not only his dream about a close comradeship between India and China after the Independence was destroyed by the cold war which placed India and China on opposite camps, but the 1962 war further destroyed his robust health, and cut short of his outstanding life and career. Objectively, it may be argued that Nehru himself should share a part of the blame for the deterioration of India-China relations as he was the sole China-policy-maker of Government of India. But, an indepth understanding of Nehru can convincingly conclude that Nehru was more sinned than sinning.

In this abstract section, we have also included some observations of Dr. P.C. Bagchi, India's greatest sinologist, and Dr. Coomaraswamy who has left behind a rich legacy on culture and art which is specially endeared to IGNCA. The quotations reflect the fairly deep interest and understanding of scholarly minds a couple of generations our senior.

Coming to our third course, i.e. the "Perspective" section, we are both gratified and disappointed for what we have obtained and what we have not. We were almost on the verge of getting some leading lights of academics and strategists to enshrine in our volume, but circumstances snatched away what had looked surely coming. Dr. Kapila Vatsyayan's contribution could have been much weightier if we could devise a system to record what she had already said and what she would be willing to say about Chinese culture and art from her insightful vision and abundant knowledge and information. We hope to make up this in our future publications as she continues to guide our work and academic pursuits.

We have already mentioned about Prasenjit Duara who is more than generous to let us have a piece which is going to be a chapter in his latest book. Again, we should have highlighted him more as his scholarship is truly epoch-making. The next joint article authored by Ravni and me is actually inspired by Duara, and an attempt to travel along the course in which he has taken the lead. It serves as a footnote to what Duara has done both in this volume and elsewhere, particularly in understanding India and China's response to the Western cultural influence and challenge in modern times. I hope these two articles will stimulate a wide scholarly participation in this discourse.

To Mira Sinha Bhattacharjea, Mahatma Gandhi and Chairman Mao are not just a historical phenomenon, but worthy of being placed on a much higher pedestal. Both Indian and Chinese civilizations have not only produced great saints, but also preserved a saint-worshipping culture. What she has said about Gandhi and Mao are not just the signals of her mind, but the flowers from her heart. Patricia, on the other hand, looks at Mao with a pair of pathologist's eyes — a kind of laboratory examination with sophisticate sociological expertise. She has also selected an unusual tissue from the now much reduced colossal Mao image for her biopsy. Both the materials and methodology of Dr. Uberoi are unique and refreshing.

The two pieces thereafter by Tan Chung and Haraprasad Ray tread on identical grounds of cultural studies which have not attracted enough attention from Indian scholars so far. Ray has highlighted the famous Chinese pilgrim, Xuanzang, to illustrate the Sino-Indian cultural interface that Tan Chung paints on a larger canvas, and both have under their employment the Sino-Indian prism. The two articles may be treated as tutorials for the inculcation of Sino-Indian perspective.

Hemant Adlakha is a young up-coming scholar whose passion lies in reaching an indepth understanding of China and promoting it among Indian academics. He picks up a current Chinese parlance of building up socialism with "Chinese characteristics". Though this very complicated and difficult topic might frighten away veterans, Hemant, in his relatively young experience and scholarship, has dared to crack the hard nut.

Through these eight articles we hope to initiate a discourse which focusses more on perspectives than on concrete issues. To quote the Chinese saying: "Zuiwengzhiyi buzai jiu" (The boozer's real enjoyment is not in the liquor) — inebriation brings in greater pleasure than the intake of alcohol. We are not just "perspective" drunkards, but it is the "perspective" which leads us into pastures and wonderlands that have not been frequented. There is so much between India and China which deserves scholarly attention, while the eight articles have not covered even a small corner.

Coming to the Fourth Section, the theme is "culture and art". We put it in priority to other sections not just to remind our readers that this volume is the creation of an insitution dedicated to the enquiries of culture and art, but we have a mission of attracting our readers to such fields before they are drawn into geo-political, geo-economic and geo-strategic considerations without sufficiently inhale the fragrance and fed with the beauty of civilizations. Today, humanity is trying to put the cold war discourses on the back-burner while the cold war mentality is hard to be laid to sleep. There is a vacuum in the mind which should be filled up by the glittering gems of civilizations. To reiterate what Kapila Vatsyayan has penned in her "Foreword", we cannot get international (particularly India-China) understanding crystalling in our mind, if it does not "spring from the heart". And "culture and art" is a heart-warming course before practical issues engaging our minds.

Prof. M.C. Joshi, Member Secretary of IGNCA, is a depository of information of art subjects, and after his visit to China in 1996, has shown enthusiasm in comparing details between Indian and Chinese, particularly Buddhist art. This is his first attempt in comparing Indian art with its Chinese counterpart in a small way. The same is the case of Prof. M.N. Deshpande whose information and insight about art and culture are without match. He was very kind to let us have a short account of his impressions about China even when he had many other assignments. Prof. Lokesh Chandra who is a living monument of Sino-Indian studies and cultural contacts has honoured us with an article to let our readers have a glimpse of his profound scholarship. Then, we have Prof. D.C. Bhattacharyya's article on cultural linkage with profound discussion, while Dr. Arputharani Sengupta's piece on Chinese Buddhist art has covered a vast canvas, bringing the Chinese scene under the purview of an Indian Prism. We are also fortunate to include an article contributed by Dr. Priyatosh Banerjee. As an octagenarian he is academically as active as people several decades younger. Both Bagyalakshmi and Radha Banerjee are closely associated with the East Asian Programme of IGNCA. Bagya gives a summary of what she is currently engaged in — preparing a comprehensive book on Guanyin, the East Asian symbol of supreme power of *Karuna* (compassion). Radha's article unfolds a religio-cultural movement which, though died down in the Western Hemisphere in a course of three centuries, had not only gathered inspirations from Buddhism on its way form West Asia to China, but also integrated in the popular "struggle ethic" in coastal China for more than a thousand years until yesterday.

The fifth course in this volume falls into four sub-divisions. In the "Socio-political Institutions" section, we have Prof. Manoranjan Mohanty discussing a very imporant issue of the relative growth between economic development and political democracy. Dr. Kamal Sheel chooses to investigate into the Chinese social phenomenon of "guanxi" (connections) and its influence on Chinese politics. In the section on "Economic Development", we have two pieces by Prof. Utsa Patnaik, and Dr. S.P. Gupta, both knowledgeable about the Chinese economic development among our leading academia. Gupta's was the paper for our 1995 Seminar without updating, Patnaik's was originally a paper for a seminar in the Institute of Chinese Studies even earlier. But their basic perspectives and insightful projections are always valid and instructive. Prof. Patnaik's piece, in particular, echoes with Prof. Mira Sinha's discussion on Mao as a visionary. The two Indian academicians' great admiration for a past Chinese revolutionary is itself a significant international phenomenon judging the intellectual trend in China today, trimming short historical memories to an un-Chinese extent.

We have three pieces on the "Gender" issue by Dr. Ravni Thakur, Dr. Bidyut Mohanty and Dr. Shreemati Chakrabarty. The vitally important topic relating to the conditions and fate of one fifth of humanity, i.e. the total number of women in India and China, has been focussed upon in these three articles.

Our sixth course on "History and Literature" is again divided into four sub-sections. First, there are two articles on "Tagore and China" by the Tagore Professor of the University of Delhi, Prof. Sisir Kumar Das, and myself. Originally, we were planning to jointly bring out a book on this topic. While that did not workout, we have this opportunity to put our writings together here which highlight Tagore's importance among Chinese intellectuals and writers. Tagore, as we have seen, is an inspiration to all of us who have adopted a Sino-Indian perspective in our discourses on India and China. The more Tagore is truly understood, the better will be the development of India-China relations.

In the next sub-section we have Prof. Giri Deshingkar's discourse on military strategy in the two countries, in addition to Lieutenant General V.R. Ragavan's rejoinder. The two pieces form a part of the proceedings of our 1995 seminar in which Prof. Deshingkar was the paper-presenter, and General Ragavan was the discussant. Since the philosophy of defence is almost absent in modern India (so also in China to a lesser degree), these two entries should arouse interest from more scholars and strategists of the two countries to continue this discourse.

In "Modern Chinese Literature", we have gathered two articles which are parts of the Ph.D. dissertations of Dr. Manik Bhattacharyya and Dr. Sabaree Mitra. Manik has initially given us a very long piece as he has had so much to say about Lu Xun, the cynosure of his eyes. Although he has to reduce the length after so much "ge'ai" (cutting off the parts which are endeared to himself), it is one of the finest appreciations and appraisals on Lu Xun which any Indian student of Chinese literature can pen. Sabaree's piece on a more current phenomenon in Chinese literary scene is informative and useful to literature-lovers.

In the last sub-division "India-China Relationship", we have selected two essays. The first is by, once again, Prof. Mira Sinha, who has placed Sino-Indian relations within the macro of Chairman Mao Zedong's world strategy. In the second article, Prof. Deshingkar, focusses on the Indian leader, Jawaharlal Nehru, and his impact on India-China relations. Both these articles were penned more than a decade ago. Their perspectives are, none the less still refreshing. The third article, written by a retired Indian diplomat, Ambassador S.K. Bhutani, is a very interesting account. That we have not put this article in section VII to which it also can belong is becasue of the special historical value provided by Bhutani.

In addition to Ambassador Bhutani, a good number of diplomatic friends have obliged us in sending in their contributions which is spread in both section VII and section VIII. In fact, the most delicious part of our "feast" lies here. I am immensely grateful to the contributors — or, should we say, the chefs of such delicious food for thought. Here they are: former Foreign Secretary and Ambassador K.P.S. Menon, Ambassador A.K. Damodaran, Ambassador Brajesh Mishra, Ambassador C.V. Ranganathan, Ambassador S.K. Rana, Ambassador Vinod Khanna, in addition to Ambassador Eric Gonsalves and Ambassador Salman Haidar, each of whom were, at one time or another, important actors in India-China relations. Years later when all the internal reports of the Ministry of External Affairs are throw open, the public will find how these names have been pro-active in India's tryst with China. All of them arrived on the stage when there were enormous misgivings, distrust, and unease on the diplomatic front between the two countries. But, after reading what they have penned after retirement with a hindsight, we are greatly impressed by the inner strength of the two great civilizations in enduring temporary discomforts, in seeing the bright sun behind the dark clouds.

In the "Reminiscences", we see the memory lane of Mr. K.P.S. Monon (I should have described him as "Menon Junior", because his illustrious father of the same namesake was India's first Ambassador to China before and after Independence; Menon senior was also Nehru's close advisor on foreign policy as he was appointed to the Foreign Office as a special secratary having a higher rank than the secretaries) which covered the territory of two generations of Indian diplomatic career in China. In time scale, the two generations trace back to the War capital Chongqing (Chung-King) in mid 1940s down to Beijing in the end of 1980s. Ambassador Menon returned from China just in time to be the Foreign Secratary to prepare for Prime Minister Rajiv Ghandhi's historic visit to China. His talk and article included in this volume have substantial historical values. In this section, we have a range of remembalance and anecdotage that begins with K.P.S. Menon's vast canvas and ends with Vinod Khanna's very personal reflections. To become an IFS officer during Vinod's time was like to qualify for Imperial Examinations in China in yesteryears. In Ambassador Khanna's diplomatic career we see an Indian youth's determined destination for China during the Nehruvian Era. Vinod's article will surely be the social-historian's delight. No, I should stop scanning the menu now so that our readers are keen to taste the delicious food themeselves with a sense of hunger.

While delicacies abound in this course awaiting the connoisseur, I must at least serve one on a platter as an appetizer. Ambassador Brajesh Mishra relates how he used to walk out from the Chinese banquet halls after enjoying all the courses, even the desserts. This was the period after the Bangla Desh Operation and Chinese leaders invariably showed solidarity with Pakistan by criticizing the Government of India, hence the walk out by India's Charge D'affaires. Premier Zhou Enlai (or some other Chinese leader) who always had a human touch thought that such unpleasant drama should not hurt the Indian diplomat's gourmet humour, so the speeches which had earlier been fixed between the second and third course was thoughtfully rescheduled to the end of feasting. Quarrelling for quarrel's sake should not intervene in the get-togethers of international community is the message that comes out so vividly from the reminiscences of ambassadors Mishra, Damodaran, and others.

Incidentally, Mishra was also the recipient of the historically famous "Mao Smile" in 1970. I remember, soon after that my father, Prof. Tan Yun-shan of Santiniketan, visited Delhi for some work, and Prime Minister Indira Gandhi received him in the Parliament House. I was present at the audience. Both Mrs. Gandhi and my father were not the talkative type, and silence always punctured their conversations on many, many occasions. This time, Mrs. Gandhi surprised us by eagerly asking about Chairman Mao's style, obviously wanting to know how serious was the "Mao smile" towards Brajesh Mishra. My father, then, explained the long Chinese diplomatic tradition of sending proper messages on selected occasions. I think, Mrs. Gandhi got the assurance from my father that it was a very serious and sincere "smile", and the opportunity should not be lost. I narrate this to supplement what Ambassador Mishra has said at our seminar which will be remembered as a valuable reference material. On the whole, the eight "reminiscenses" add up to a vivid recapitulation of the lifestyle of Indian diplomacy with special focus on the Beijing scene. It is a pity that none of them has brought out their memoirs to unfold the great treasuries of information and insight as the titbits of their reminiscences have assured us about this richness. Only Ambassador Ranganathan, has served the wrap-up of his tenure as the Indian envoy-extraordinary in China—a very fruitful fulfilment of diplomatic mission and India-China friendship and understanding with the crowning glory of Prime Minister Rajiv Gandhi's historic visit to China. Incidentally, his was the first Indian embassy manned by 100% Sinologue officers in Beijing which is quite a record. There is another record created by him as the first Indian ambassador delivering a formal address in a Beijing conference (of the Chinese Association of Dunhuang and Turpan Studies) in 1987 in eloquent mandarin (and I am eyewitness to it). All in all, the historical value of these reminiscenses will grow when their occurrences recede to the background in the passage of time. This, in turn, adds value and weight to our volume as a reference book.

We have designed our last section as the Finale which would have a couple of more contributions from eminent quarters had there not been circumstances in our disfavour. The ten contributions we have fortunately obtained are penned by two categories of authors: diplomats who have retired and strategists who never retire. To the first category belong Ambassadors V.V. Paranjpe, C.V. Ranganathan, Eric Gonsalves, Salman Haidar. To the second belong Major General Dipankar Banerjee, joined by his senior Lieutenant General Ragavan, Mr. Swaran Singh and Mr. Sreedhar, both from the Institute of Defence Studies and Analyses. Last but not least, we have Prof. Surjit Mansingh who had a diplomatic career but is an academia now in a premier university specializing in international affairs including strategy.

Paranjpe is a retired IFS officer who used to do English-Chinese interpretation for India's first Prime Minister-cum-Foreign Minister, Jawaharlal Nehru, when he talked to leaders like Chairman Mao Zedong and Premier Zhou Enlai. This article of his was published elsewhere, but, on public demand, we have included it in our volume. It not only contains valuable historical information that has been left out by official documentation of both governments, but gives valuable tips about improving India-China understanding.

I am always tempted to quote the important episode revealed by Paranjpe about Mao's farewell words to Nehru in 1954. Seeing Nehru off to the car after treating him to a private dinner, Mao held tight Nehru's hand and quoted ancient Chinese poet, Qu Yuan:

"O, sadness can't be sadder
Parting company in life time;
And gladness can't be gladder
Meeting with a new friend."

The two pieces written by Ambassadors Ranganathan and Gonsalves, are weighty materials that not only reflect the Indian perspective on China's development, but also the problems faced by the Government of India in dealing with China, pointing to the right direction for improving relations with China. Ambassador Salman Haidar's piece is the record of his talk to our 1996 Seminar when he was Foreign Secretary (the head of Indian Foreign Service). It is in the nature of spelling out India's policy by its chief executive, hence with self-explanatory importance. Both Generals Banerjee and Raghavan are ex-fighters in the China front who now turned into experts on Indian defence strategy including its China dimension. They have approached the topic from both a historical perspective and a future prospect.

Gen. Banerjee opened with a scene in the India-China front in the 1960s. "A blanket of snow covered the earth below my feet as I drudged slowly to the observation post," he wrote. Today, the retired general sits in an air-conditioned office to offer advice to "sane strategic planners" while tranquillity prevails where the general's footsteps have been buried by snow for three decades. Swaran Singh's two pieces are related to each other which can help understand the India-China task in building up the CMB (Confidence Measure Building) pertaining to the treaties signed between the two governments. Sreedhar's piece voices a genuine Indian concern which, if brushed aside, would stand in the way in the long-term engagement between India and China. We would wish Chinese responses to the issues raised in this article. Prof. Mansingh has written the last word for our volume, bringing out the importance of understanding China on the part of Indian specialists and general public. She has correctly pointed out the deficiencies in India's Chinese studies along with suggestions on their improvements.

On this constructive note, we now leave the readers to leaf through the book. It is a big meal with uneven portions, some sweet, some sour, some easy to digest, some difficult to swallow, some tender gravy, some hard substance. The book has a vast coverage of time and space, different facets, various disciplines, inter-and cross-disciplinary narratives and discourses. It tries to address to issues, appealing to beliefs of as wide a range as possible, yet weaving around a central theme — understanding between nations, particularly between India and China. It is a volume of paper and words that has the ambitions of the monkey-king, Hanuman (or his Chinese reincarnation Sun Wu Kong), to fly beyond Himalayan peaks, to reach the hands and hearts of as many Indians, Chinese, and other nationalities. We would be happy if its readership swells into five, six, seven digits. But, even if only a fraction of our dream is fulfilled, we shall deem our labour, as we look at the salt stains on our shirts, worth its salt.

New Delhi
April 25, 1998

TC

Postscript

On page xx, I have written that we were mentally prepared for the deliberations in this volume being overtaken by events. Merely two weeks after these words had been penned there arrived the Era of Pokhran II. The new turn of India-China relations makes it all the more obvious that the present volume should immediately meet its target readers and join other efforts from various quarters to bridge the Himalayan gap of understanding between India and China. Since there was already a delay in bringing out the book (which was originally meant to be a new year gift), we have decided against sending the contributions, particularly those that have a strategic angle, back to their authors for updating. Pokhran II has not only endorsed the purposiveness of our Project of "India and China Looking At Each Other", but even urges us to go ahead and complete our Mission Part II, i.e. gathering the Chinese perspectives on India to make our next presentation to our readership. We shall be getting busy for that. I personally feel that whatever dismay and suspicions existing, it would be easier and healthier for the Sino-Indian understanding of each other now that India and China are nuclear twins. But, this can be discussed only in another book.

Auguest 17, 1998

TC

INDIAN LEADERS' SPEECHES IN CHINESE UNIVERSITIES

INDIAN LEADERS' SPEECHES IN CHINESE UNIVERSITIES

领袖的讲演

1. Prime Minister Rajiv Gandhi's Address at Qinghua University, 1988
2. Prime Minister Narasimha Rao's Address at Beijing University, 1993
3. Vice-President K.R. Narayanan's Address at Fudan University, 1994

1

PRIME MINISTER RAJIV GANDHI AT QINGHUA UNIVERSITY, BEIJING

(DECEMBER 21, 1988)

I am delighted at this opportunity to visit this renowned university. It is a symbol of what modern China has achieved, a symbol of the Chinese pursuit of excellence.

Thirty four years ago, my grandfather, Jawaharlal Nehru, came to China as a messenger of peace and goodwill and found here a spirit of both peace and goodwill. Between India and China the spirit is now being rekindled.

The coming together of India and China in the early fifties was a development of historical international importance. Not only did it presage friendship between the two most populous nations of the world, counting between them a third of all humankind, it represented what was for the time an almost unique example of two great nations, with two totally different economic and social systems, coming together to give a practical demonstration of peaceful coexistence among different systems. Placed in the context of the epochal change brought about in the world by the independence of India and the liberation of China, among the most important events of the mid-point of the twentieth century, the friendship which Jawaharlal Nehru sought with China was a friendship that could fundamentally affect the destiny of humankind.

Apart from the immense potential for world peace and cooperation implicit in peace and cooperation between India and China, there was also the imperative of facing together the common problems with which both countries were confronted. We were both ancient civilisations, with memories going back into the deepest recesses of the distant past, who had both undergone a prolonged period of national trauma caused by the strangling of our freedoms, the parcelling out of our economies, the stultification of our social and moral progress. We both saw the liberation of our nations not so much as the culmination of a struggle but as the beginning of an opportunity to serve our people, build our economies, transform our societies and take our countries forward.

Through the period of our struggle for freedom and your struggle for liberation, India and China viewed developments in each other's countries with deep sympathy and understanding. Our great national poet, Rabindranath Tagore, started a Cheena-Bhavana (the House of China) at his Universal University, Visva-Bharati, at Santiniketan, of which I now have the honour to be Chancellor. Our involvement in your liberation struggle found expression in the immortal mission which Dr. Kotnis led to China. Jawaharlal Nehru envisaged friendship between India and China as a major pillar of the post-colonial world order.

India and China worked together for peace in Asia and the world when they first emerged from the thralldom of imperialism. Together we saw that the world order was vitiated by confrontation, by a lack of respect for the sovereign equality of nations, by intolerance of alternative national systems for the organisation of political, economic and social life. We saw that our newly won independence would be secure only in a world which had liberated itself from the assumptions and prejudices of the past.

A striking example of the persistence of past prejudice was the refusal to recognise the People's Republic of China, the culmination of the great revolution which had swept China. India was among the first to recognise the great and welcome change that had burst upon your country. Those who refused to recognise that the China of the Opium Wars had been consigned to the pages of history began menacing the new China from different directions and in different ways. Through this period of tribulation, India stood by China.

Another manifestation of the persistence of the old ways into the new era was the attempt which was made to restore the colonialisms that had crumbled during the Second World War. The attempt was doomed, but not before hundreds of thousands had perished in this dangerously reactionary endeavour. The agony was most long drawn out in Indo-China. India and China, representing the resurgent voice of resurgent Asia, worked towards ending colonialism everywhere, taking the world from under the shadow of the past into the sunlight of the new era.

Together, India and China articulated a new philosophy summed up in the Panchsheel, the Five Principles of Peaceful Coexistence: respect for territorial integrity and sovereignty; non-aggression; non-interference; equality and mutual benefit; and peaceful coexistence.

There have been many momentous events in the three and a half decades that have gone by since we jointly adopted these principles. We have had serious differences among ourselves, leading at one stage even to armed conflict. We have not always been of one view on international issues.

In contrast to the warmth of our friendship and a shared sense of purpose which marked our joint endeavours in the early years, the last thirty years or so have been a period of estrangement. Contacts between us have been sharply reduced. Information about each other has become the preserve of scholars instead of being the knowledge of people. A sense of persisting differences prevailed over the early sense of common perceptions and common goals. Despite this, India and China held similar views on a number of matters of international importance and India continued to support China on such crucial issues as the restoration to China of its rightful place in the United Nations system.

We have seen vast progress in each of our countries. Where once there was a China of famines and shortages, now there is a China self-reliant in feeding its people. Where once there was a China with but nascent industry, now there is a China looking with conviction and confidence towards becoming one of the world's major economic powers in the 21st century. At one time, China suffered from low levels of literacy, backward-looking social practices and rapid population growth. Now there is a China respected the world over for what it has achieved in giving education to its people, promoting social progress in different spheres of human endeavour, and making a remarkable effort at population planning.

India too has undergone a major structural transformation. We too have overcome our vulnerability to famines and food shortages and are now self-sufficient in foodgrains production.

Our industry has developed from its earlier fledgling stage. Today, we have a broad industrial base with a highly diversified industrial structure. In education, we have steadily increased our literacy rates and we aim at universal elementary education by the beginning of the next decade.

Social progress has been evident in such areas as the removal of untouchability, affirmative action in favour of disadvantaged sections of society, education for girls and the integration of women into the mainstream of the nation's progress.

Both our countries have given priority to the development of science and technology. Your achievements in space are truly remarkable and justly admired. You are doing important work in frontier areas of superconductivity, medicine and biotechnology. We in India are also working in these areas. We are among the few countries which have developed remote sensing satellite technology for the management of natural resources. We have made useful advances in many areas of industrial and defence electronics and material sciences. In telecommunications, we have developed our own digital switching system. Both of us have significant capabilities in the field of software development including work in the most sophisticated areas. There are possibilities of India and China undertaking joint research in critical areas of electronics.

While there is comparability and complementarity between what we have achieved, it is interesting that we have achieved what we have in ways that are remarkably different, one to the other.

The three pillars of India's modern nationhood are parliamentary democracy, secularism and socialism.

We have a multiplicity of political parties and elected legislatures at the Central and State levels, in addition to elected local bodies. Governments are formed by the party or combination of parties constituting a majority in the legislature and are, in turn, responsible to the legislature. At periodic intervals, normally of five years, the electorate renews or changes its mandate. Our system allows for different parties to come to power at different levels at different times. It also allows for different parties to rule at the Centre and in the States and in the local bodies at the same time. Equal rights are guaranteed by our Constitution and assured by our democratic process to all minorities, religious, ethnic, linguistic. Our judiciary is independent of the executive. Our press is free to report, comment and criticise. We believe that freedom of expression and the free exchange of views are not only intrinsically valuable but have also promoted stability in our society by furnishing safety values which forestall social and economic pressures before these trigger of an explosion. Democracy has enabled us to maintain a steady course through four decades of rapid change.

The second pillar of our State is secularism. It is a word with different connotations in different languages. We mean by secularism that the State in India does not interfere in the religious practices of its citizens, nor does it encourage the mixing of religion with politics. The State has no religion. At the same time, our State respects the religious sensibilities of our people, values the spiritual and cultural strength which religion imparts, and ensures full freedom of worship and propagation for all religions. Nearly twenty per cent of our population belongs to various religious minorities, the largest of these being the Muslims. All our religious groupings have a high and honoured place in our society, with the assurance that no section of our people will be discriminated against on grounds of religion. Special programmes have been put in place to assist minorities in need of special assistance.

Socialism in India is indigenous to our experience and our conditions. It is not a dogma. It is responsive to changing circumstances. It has had the resilience to develop with time. The focus of our socialism is the uplift of the poor, succour to the weak, justice to the oppressed and balanced regional development. To attain these ends, we believe the State must control the commanding heights of the economy, and that self-reliance should be the first principle of development. We stress that the pattern of progress must be so designed as to give all parts of the country equitable opportunities of growth and all sections of our people an equitable share of the fruits of development. Our emphasis on balanced regional growth and our accent on the reduction of social disparities have meant leavening the imperatives of growth with considerations of equity. Our socialism sees the thrust of the development effort as growth with social justice.

Our development strategy is one of planning for a mixed economy. The State sector is predominant in core and heavy industry and also in much of infrastructure, but most of light industry and all of agriculture is in the private sector. Our development objective is the modernisation and transformation of our economy with an overriding priority to the elimination of poverty. Planning in a democratic framework necessarily places great importance on evolving a consensus on goals and instruments. At times, this imposes constraints in the larger interest of democratic consensus and participation.

This strategy has served us well. We have succeeded in setting our economy on an accelerating growth path. Agricultural productivity and production have increased steadily and the vulnerability of agriculture to the weather has been reduced. Industry is now growing rapidly. We hope to accelerate our growth further in the next decade. Foodgrains output will be doubled over the next ten to fifteen years. Our Perspective Plan envisages the eradication of poverty and unemployment by the end of the century.

But many problems remain. Our rate of growth of population remains too high. While impressive increases in foodgrains production have been recorded in many parts of our country, the task ahead is that of spreading this Green Revolution to new areas and to new crops. We have to make our industry more efficient and competitive, with better products and higher quality. We believe that much sharper domestic competition is necessary to ensure this. It is also necessary, progressively, to open up our industry to the pressures of international competition.

To tackle these problems, we in India have taken, as you in China have done, new steps and new initiatives in economic policy, while remaining true to our basic principles. We have embarked on a process of planned liberalisation giving much greater autonomy to our public sector enterprises and greater flexibility to our private sector to invest, expand and upgrade technology. Indian industry has reached a stage where it must increasingly integrate with the world economy in terms of technology, quality and cost competitiveness. We are encouraging foreign investment where it can help our efforts to modernise. We are also trying to decentralise planning and decision-making to secure better results. This is especially important for our strategies of rural development. A key element of this strategy is increasing people's participation in the planning process.

In this context, your own bold experiments in economic reform are of special interest to us. They have already produced rich dividends for China. We believe we have much to learn from your experience. Some of what we are doing in India may also be of interest to you. No two developing countries are more similarly placed than yours and ours. Despite differences in philosophies of planning and methods of management. India and China can give and take a great deal from each other. We believe you share this view.

I represent a new generation in India. I was but a boy in the heyday of India-China friendship. I was still a young man when differences were converted into conflict. I have grown in a world which has not benefited but only been disadvantaged by estrangement between India and China. I have come to office with the firm conviction that, between ourselves, we must make a new beginning. I am heartened that the Chinese leadership is more than prepared to put behind us past rancour and past prejudices. I am heartened that we are both prepared not to be mired in the past. As we enter the last decade of this century, India and China are called upon to look forward, not behind, to reach out to new horizons, to seek new vistas of friendship and cooperation, to explore new paths of benefit to each other and of benefit to the world.

I do not believe our joint advocacy of peaceful coexistence was either a coincidence or an accident of history. It arose out of certain perceptions which had grown out of our historical experience. I would like to dwell a little on this.

The distinguishing characteristic of the civilisations of India and China is not so much their antiquity as their continuity. Nevertheless, specific interactions between our civilisations have not been continuous despite the thousands of years that our respective civilisations have run a parallel course of continuity. The exchanges were, perhaps, at their most intense during the period of the Three Kingdoms in China when there was much trade and travel between India and China, when Indian art influenced Chinese art, when the artifacts and products and technology of China came to India. For centuries, Indian ports were a regular point of call for Chinese ships. The prosperity of the Chola empire in southern India was largely based on their trade with China. Till today, the fishing nets of Kerala, on the south-west coast of India, are called Chinese nets and designed on the Chinese pattern. This phase in our mutual exchanges was bracketed by the accounts left behind by two of the greatest Chinese travellers to India: Fa Xian in the 5th Century, who visited our University at Nalanda, which housed a large Chinese community, and Xuan Zang in the 7th Century A.D., who was a guest at the court of our last great Buddhist Emperor, Harshavardhana.

It was the message of the Buddha that led to an awakening of awareness and an intensification of exchanges between our two great civilisations. It has given us insights into the human condition which are more profound and long-lasting than would be indicated by a mere cataloguing of when Bodhidharma sailed to Canton or Yi Jing came to India. Drawing on these insights, Jawaharlal Nehru declared here in Beijing thirty four years ago:

> "Fear and hatred and violence have darkened man's horizon for many years. Violence breeds violence, hatred degrades and stultifies. And fear is a bad companion."

It is perhaps such insights which enabled our two contemporary systems, so different from one another, to formulate common principle for the sustenance of the new world order which, together, we sought.

Another characteristic of our civilisations which perhaps led us towards the concept of peaceful coexistence was our millennial experience of synthesis. It helped us recognise that the modern world demanded understanding and respect for the diversity of political and economic systems the world over. While others sought to impose uniformity by persuasion or force, India and China spoke up for coexistence among different social and economic systems. It was an affirmation made by two ancient civilisations, now turned into two modern states, but following very different social and economic systems.

I am conscious of the fact that, although India and China were the architects of the Five Principles of Peaceful Coexistence, our own relations have not always conformed to these principles. We have had differences of perception and differences of opinion. Yet what must not be forgotten in a listing of differences is a listing of commonalities in our world outlook. There has been significant parallelism in the views expressed by India and China on a wide range of issues relating to world security, the international political order, the new international economic order, global concerns in regard to the environment and space, matters of momentous significance such as the Law of the Sea and the Antarctic Treaty, information and communication, culture and art. There are and have been differences but, considering the fact that India is a member of the Non-aligned Movement and China is not, that India is a member of the Group of 77 and China is not, that India is not a nuclear weapon power and China is, it is significant that there is such a wide area of commonality between our points of view and so much scope for further dialogue for the attainment of shared objectives.

Now, as the spirit of the mid-fifties is rekindled, the time has come to end our estrangement and make a new beginning. We must find an acceptable solution to the boundary question within a realistic time-frame. This can be achieved in an atmosphere of mutual understanding and mutual confidence. The border issue is a complex one, touching as it does upon the emotions and sentiments of our people. These aspects have salience in China too. We need patience, wisdom and statesmanship to resolve the issue to the mutual benefit of our peoples. The core of any solution that may emerge is mutual acceptability. We should jointly endeavour to find such a solution in order to put relations between India and China on a solid basis. We are determined to move in this direction. It is important that while we search for a solution, peace and tranquillity are maintained in the border areas. I have every hope that during this visit we will, together with our Chinese friends, build a better political climate for the solution of the border question.

Cooperation between India and China should be expanded significantly. Trade between us is far below the potential of our economies. Cooperation in science and technology is still to take off. I believe that economic, scientific, technological and cultural cooperation between the two countries will greatly contribute to better understanding between our peoples and our governments, and will indirectly help us in solving complex problems.

We are at an important conjuncture in world affairs. There is a palpable relaxation of tensions and evidence of dialogue replacing confrontation.

The people of Namibia are at long last on the verge of securing their freedom. Their struggle for independence has been a saga of courage and dignity. However, in South Africa, the abomination of apartheid persists. We demand comprehensive, mandatory sanctions against Pretoria under Chapter VII of the United Nations Charter, failing which we apprehend an unprecedented bloodbath in the struggle to end this iniquity.

There has been a radical turn of events in West Asia. A Palestinian State has been proclaimed. It has been recognised by both China and India and other peace-loving countries the world over.

We are glad that dialogue has begun between the United States and the Palestine Liberation Organisation. We extend our whole-hearted support to the three-point Palestinian Peace Initiative put forward by our brother, Chairman Yasser Arafat. The spirit of tolerance which he has evoked is in keeping with the traditions of Asia and the aspirations of our continent.

In Kampuchea, a solution appears to be emerging which could both end the conflict and forestall the resurgence of the forces of genocide. We would welcome cooperation among all concerned in fostering a just and equitable settlement in Kampuchea which will ensure the independence, sovereignty and nonaligned status of that country, free of outside interference and intervention.

In South Asia, a new dawn is breaking. South Asian regional cooperation has made a good beginning. Recent changes in Pakistan, with the emergence of a democratically elected government led by Prime Minister Benazir Bhutto, have opened up encouraging prospects for enduring friendship and goodwill between our countries, reflecting the natural affinities and affection which the people of India and Pakistan have for each other. In Sri Lanka, the Accord which I signed with President Jayewardene guarantees the unity and territorial integrity of that country and has brought respect, recognition and a meaningful devolution of powers to the Tamil minority. In the Maldives, our immediate response to the call for assistance from a friendly neighbour in his hour of need has ensured the triumph of the democratic will of the people of the Maldives against the forces of subversion and destabilisation. In Afghanistan, we are persuaded that strict respect for the Geneva Accords will lead to the emergence of a government based on national consensus, which can ensure the independence, integrity and nonaligned status of the country, provided only there is a complete cessation of all outside interference and intervention in the affairs of the country.

At this crucial turning point in contemporary history, we must assess afresh the work that India and China can do, individually and together, in fashioning the new world order which is emerging from the chrysalis of the old.

The two major nuclear weapon powers have agreed in principle that a nuclear war cannot be won and must not be fought. Mahatma Gandhi and Jawaharlal Nehru recognised this in 1945, in the immediate aftermath of Hiroshima and Nagasaki. It augurs well for the future of our world that this perception has now gained wider currency. We are encouraged that this principle has received practical expression in the form of a dismantling of intermediate nuclear forces and the initiation of a process designed to secure strategic arms cuts.

The moot question before us is whether these first ever steps of nuclear disarmament presage movement towards the elimination of all nuclear weapons. Or do these steps merely presage a marginal adjustment in global strategic deployment, perhaps even the shifting of the nuclear arms race into new and ever more dangerous dimensions?

In answering these questions, the task before us is not just to wait upon events but to influence them. India and China can together do a great deal to ensure that the moves which have now been initiated proceed in the only direction which promises sustained peace and sustainable development. To this end, our first step must be to resuscitate and revitalise our decades-old commitment to the Five Principles of Peaceful Coexistence.

There are two basic arguments which sustain nuclear weapons. The first is that as such weapons have been invented, they cannot now be disinvented. The second is the doctrine of deterrence which holds that it is only your capacity to destroy your opponent which forestalls your opponent from destroying you.

The danger of universal destruction through the use of nuclear weapons arises not so much from the fact of their invention as from an international system which concedes their need and legitimises their possession and use. It is the old order which resulted in the invention of these terrible weapons. We cannot disinvent these weapons but we can certainly alter the world order which has given them legitimacy and tolerated their continued existence.

As regards the doctrines of deterrence, they have not worked in the past because the balance of power is an inherently unstable balance, which all the parties concerned are all the time attempting to upset in their favour and to the disadvantage of others. For deterrence to be credible, there must be commitment to the use of the instruments of deterrence. But, in the era of nuclear weapons, the use of such weapons will only lead to global holocaust.

Therefore, nuclear disarmament requires not only the dismantling of nuclear weapons but, even more importantly, the dismantling of the mentalities which go with these weapons. We need to evolve generally accepted principles of international security to replace doctrines of deterrence. We need to evolve systems of conflict-resolution which forestall the resort to arms. We need to promote thinking about the world order required to sustain a world beyond nuclear weapons. Advance thinking on these matters is essential. Otherwise, even after nuclear weapons are eliminated, the danger will remain of the world slipping back into the nuclear arms race. That alternative process of thinking could best commence from the Five Principles of Peaceful Coexistence which India and China were the first to enunciate.

The alternative process of thinking cannot limit itself to security and the international political order alone. It must embrace economics, the environment, space and our common heritage.

As developing countries, India and China share common concerns about the functioning of the international economic order. The world economy continues to be characterised by inadequacies and imbalances which hamper development in the developing countries. India and China have been hurt much less than many other developing countries but neither of us can afford to be complacent. Both in the area of international finance and in the area of trade, there are disturbing trends which weaken established multilateral institutions and mechanisms. The world pays lip service to interdependence and cooperation but commitment to these concepts in practice is less evident. These trends are dangerous for the North as well as the South. We must reconstruct a consensus on international economic forums to bring about a new international economic order, based on a recognition of global interdependence. Without this, the new international political order would be of little comfort, difficult to attain and impossible to sustain.

In the last decade, political and economic changes have been leading to the emergence of a multipolar world. The European community seems to be firmly set on establishing an integrated European economy by 1992, though unresolved questions still remain. Japan has emerged as a major economic centre whose decisions influence the rest of the world. The inherent strength and vitality of the American economy, and especially their advanced technology, remain crucial to the international economy. The Soviet Union is restructuring its economy with profound global implications. How these power centres will act and react on each other and how they will impact on the developing world are matters for serious analysis. The intertwining of economic power and military strength could create new security concerns. It is all the more important then that we actively work for a new international order where questions of peace and security are settled through non-violent means.

Another area of international action in which fruitful cooperation between India and China is indicated could be in regard to the environment. We have both suffered the consequences of environmental degradation. We have both worked on programmes designed to make conservation an integral part of the development process. We have both recognised that the cost of preserving the environment is an essential component of the costs of development because, if these costs are not recognised and paid for now, degradation will exact a much higher price than conservation. There is much work we can do together, many lessons we can learn from each other, and something we can add to the world's repository of knowledge by conscious cooperation in the interests of sustainable development.

We are both committed to the peaceful uses of outer space. We have both protested against attempts to misuse space for military applications. We both believe that nothing could be more dangerous than the shifting of the nuclear arms race into this new dimension. We are also both concerned at space being converted into a garbage dump for the technology experiments of the advanced economies. Like the seas and the seabed, space too is a common heritage of humankind. It is a heritage which all of us must work together to preserve.

Between us, we are the repositories of some of the most significant treasures of human inheritance. We believe in international cooperation to preserve and promote the cultural heritage of humankind. When UNESCO came under siege, India and China were together on the same side in defending the organisation and asserting its vital role.

Now that the world is beginning to explore the possibility of coexistence in preference to deterrence, of cooperation in preference to rivalry, of interdependence in preference to beggaring the neighbour, of nuclear disarmament in preference to nuclear escalation, it behoves the original advocates of the Panchsheel — India and China — to set themselves up as an example to the world.

I see optimism in both India and China today; optimism about the progress our countries can make, optimism about realising our goals of development, optimism about the levels of cooperation we can reach, optimism about the work we can do together to restore our countries to their traditional position in the vanguard of human civilisation, optimism about the contribution we can make to rebuilding the world order nearer our hearts' desire.

We are summoned by our past to the tasks which the future holds. We have a mutual obligation to a common humanity. India and China can together give the world new perspectives on a new world order, which will ensure peace among nations and justice among peoples, equity for each and prosperity for all, freedom from fear and freedom from want, a world where we live together in happiness and harmony.

2

PRIME MINISTER NARASIMHA RAO AT BEIJING UNIVERSITY

SEPTEMBER 9, 1993

It is a great honour to be invited to speak at Beijing University, the foremost seat of education in the People's Republic of China. It is always a privilege to be amongst the faculty and students of an institution of learning with few parallels in the world. India's scriptures from times immemorial have perceived educational institutions as the epitome of the cultural and civilisational achievements of any society. As I commence my remarks, the words of the French philosopher Diderot about you, the Chinese people, come to my mind. He said and I quote:

> "These Asiatics are endowed with great antiquity, art, intellect, wisdom, policy and in their taste for philosophy and in their judgement they dispute the merit in these matters with the most enlightened peoples of Europe."

Others have described your society and your polity as a continuum which has existed for over 4,000 years as an unparalleled achievement in human history.

My people and my civilisation have also been so described by philosophers and historians. That out of the four or five thousand years of our continuity as civilisations, for nearly 2,000 years we have interacted with each other, provides the durable foundation for Sino-Indian relations.

Our remote cultural ties are best illustrated by the word "*chinambar*" (Chinese cloth) which occurs in Indian literature for many centuries. This means an old tradition of trade and commerce between the two countries. In addition to Faxian and Xuanzang Chinese marine travellers to India's Malabar Coast from olden times have left behind their impressions. So, it is with a deep sense of our historical and cultural closeness that I come to this gathering.

Speaking in a university with this history, one cannot but be aware of the larger forces that shape our lives. It is universities like "Beida" in China and Santiniketan in India which first contributed to the emancipation of thinking that was a necessary pre-condition to Asia's emergence half a century ago from the shadows of colonialism. This phenomenon, achieved through different means in India and China, resulted in similar ends. Both countries embarked upon an experiment without precedent in history, the rapid and fundamental transformation of large societies with strong indigenous roots. Both countries chose not to blindly imitate the path that had been travelled, much more slowly, by Europe during her mercantile transformation and industrial revolution. Our countries choose instead to modernise their economies and transform their societies in accordance with the ethos of our own peoples.

China chose one form of socialism, India chose another. Despite criticism by hindsight that abounds everywhere today, it is undeniable that the pioneering work of the fifties and early sixties in both countries laid the foundations for the rapid advances that we have recently been making. China has embarked upon a process of reform which has shown outstanding results over the last decade. India has more recently embarked upon economic reforms which have already begun showing results.

Though both China and India chose varied options, different socio-economic methods in their nation-building efforts, the objective was similar: the economic development of our societies and the well-being of our peoples. From having a predominantly agriculture-based economy, India today ranks among the important industrialised countries endowed with technological skills, trained manpower resources and a progressively modern economy. Our economy has been diversified and at the same time integrated in a way where different sectors of economic activity are being evolved in a balanced manner taking into account the factors of natural resources, demographic equilibrium and the norms of productivity and consumers' satisfaction.

For the first time in recent times people in India and in China are producing enough food to feed themselves. Grain import has become a sophisticated option in which secondary economic considerations are relevant. The spectre of mass starvation only too familiar to our forefathers for more than 100 years during the colonial and immediate post-colonial period, no longer haunts our peoples. This is no small achievement; it has been done by the creative application of modern science by millions of peasants assisted by teams of dedicated scientists and field workers in our countries. In a sense it is the continuance in the technological epoch of our separate traditions of farming developed over the centuries by our two civilisations in their specific, separate ways in indigenously developed methods of wider use of irrigation and also in the most economic utilization of natural fertilizers. This has enabled us today to pause for a moment and plan a more rewarding and richer pattern of life for our people. It is our shared aim to achieve in the 21st century the ambitions of great men and women who gave so much for their people, many millennia ago.

Over the last two years especially, we have embarked on a restructuring of our economy on the basis of de-regulation, liberalisation and modern management and marketing techniques. We have tried to build on the foundations laid during previous decades of economic development. The objective of the new reforms is to plan the economic future of India in a manner where the pressures of inflation and recession are resisted and where fiscal discipline and emphasis on increased productivity become practical norms. I must also point out that the processes of economic modernisation and reforms are being fashioned, taking into account all aspects of human existence and all ingredients which constitute the quality of life; the ingredients of literacy, health, shelter, required minimum incomes and environmental safety. That is what we call reform with a human face. And this is no idle expression.

Over and above all, our aim is to achieve an equilibrium between the encouragement of unfettered human endeavour on the one hand and the imperatives of distributive justice in a developing society on the other.

The choices made in the process are no doubt bold and impressive. But what is even more remarkable is the capacity that these two great nations with a heavy weight of history have shown to learn from their experiences and to adjust their thinking and policies to deal with reality. What gives me confidence for the future is this ability to learn from experience that both India and China have displayed since they became masters of their own destinies.

The world today stands at a new watershed. We all see the symptoms of the far-fetching transformations that the world is undergoing. The end of the cold war, the disintegration of the Soviet Union, the emergence of new centres of power and structural adjustment of the world economy are all results of fundamental shifts in ways of thinking, technology and in the balance of socio-economic forces at national and regional levels. I see these changes as leading inexorably to a world where prosperity, and in course of time power, are more equally shared among the nations. The question that faces our two peoples is: How shall we deal with this rapid process of change? At this crucial juncture in the changing international situation, the basic issues of peace, security and development are being approached with new terms of reference resulting from the pressures and changed attitudes that affect the whole world. We should deal with these issues with a vision of the universality of human endeavour, tempered by respect for socio-cultural diversities between different societies and civilisational entities, with a sense of justice and fair play. This needs great tolerance and the avoidance of confrontation and the willingness to cooperate. This is by no means an easy exercise. But the test of any ancient civilisation consists in doing precisely this, by innovating appropriate methods of survival and progress, without forsaking basic values which makes the real difference between life in all its splendour on the one hand, and mere physical existence on the other.

The need for a universal approach cannot be over-emphasised. No major problem facing humankind today — particularly today when the world, roughly speaking, is unipolar politically and multi-polar economically — can be resolved on a regional or subregional basis, except where it is conceived of as an integral part of a universal endeavour. Peace, Disarmament, Environment, Sustainable Development — each one of these requires a global approach and the context of a global order. I believe that the guiding principles for the creation of the new international political and economic order should be economic security and political justice for each country, for each society. For this purpose, urgent endeavours are required for achieving general and complete disarmament in a non-discriminatory manner. Immediate and cooperative action should be taken by the international community to preserve the ecological balance in environment, to nurture and sustain human rights, not on the basis of intrusive and unilateral stipulations or external pressures, but on the basis of values shared by all societies and also respecting the diverse social and cultural traditions which constitute the content and corpus of human rights in different societies. These efforts for dealing with significant issues have to be undertaken with the awareness that we live in a world of economic, social and ecological inter-dependence. No individual country or group of nations can address this issue single-handed. Our approach, of necessity, has to be based on a harmonising of varying perspectives, varied needs and diverse approaches

Our two countries are themselves emerging from certain aberrations in their relations into an era of normalcy and enhanced mutual understanding. We have taken several steps together in the last five years to improve communication and understanding between our governments, leaders and peoples.

Our trade has been growing, although there is much more that we can do in this area. We have resumed border trade last year, something that benefits the common man in both countries. These are, however, only small beginnings. I am confident that we have still to tap the full potential of the possibilities that exist for our two large economies to interact in the economic sphere. We could consider several modalities to realise this immense potential. Such cooperation in the economic sphere would not only lend further strength to our bilateral relations but would also contribute to economic cooperation in overall terms in Asia and in the rest of the world.

We have re-established Consulates in Bombay and Shanghai, and the numbers of our nationals visiting each other's countries have grown manifold. Equally significant is the fact that we have maintained the momentum of high level political dialogue between the leaders of our two countries. Your Premier was good enough to visit India in December 1991 and our President came to China in 1992. Even on issues that once divided us, we are agreed on the need for and the manner of, dealing with these questions. I am confident that if we both continue this process, our common border will continue to be a border of tranquillity.

Our bilateral relations are on the way towards achieving the stability, durability and good neighbourliness that both our peoples desire.

We, however, do not live in a vacuum, no matter how large the space that we occupy. India and China are both agents of change and are also subject to the changes that are sweeping the world. Now that we have found ways of dealing with our bilateral issues, perhaps the time has come for us to evaluate the new world order that is emerging and to evolve a vision and strategy for the benefit of peoples throughout the vast continent of Asia. A general agreement on India-China strategy and approach on a series of issues could be conducive to an Asian resurgence.

What should this Asian resurgence consist of? It must include a vision of rising above our historical memories and prejudices and narrower local interests to achieve the greatest good of the largest number. We are both dedicated to doing so within our societies. We have already shown the ability to conceptualise the principles that should guide international relations when we, together, evolved the Five Principles of Peaceful Co-existence, or Panchsheel as they are known in India. These principles remain as valid today as they were when they were drafted.

The question is whether these principles can be realised, and whether an Asian resurgence can be achieved, in the context of the larger international community to which we belong. An introspective response to this question can be no better than what Jawaharlal Nehru stated at the Asian Relations Conference on the 23rd March, 1947. He said:

"It was here (in Asia) that civilisation began and man started on his unending adventures of life. Here, the mind of man searched unceasingly for truth, and the spirit of man shone like a beacon which lighted up the whole world. It is this dynamic Asia from which great streams of culture flowed in all directions that I am talking about. The vibrance and creativity of the Asian peoples can surely realise the principles and objective which I mentioned."

Jawaharlal Nehru had a vision of Asia. He had also a vision of India and China in Asia and the world. This was not mere romanticism. His historically sensitive mind always went back to those early days when, in the first millennium of the modern era, our two civilisations, our two ways of thought, our different methods of articulating that thought came together in blinding flash of creative exuberance. The great Buddhist pilgrims and travellers who traversed the Himalayan passes did not achieve a mere feat of physical endurance of dedication to a great idea. They were among the great scholars in history who achieved an astonishing feat of cross-cultural and inter-linguistic communication. In four or five generations the great works of Buddhist philosophy, mythology and literature were translated from Pali and Sanskrit to the Chinese language. There are only two or three similar occurrences in the history of the human mind, the Greek-Arab encounter in Europe which led to the renaissance. I thought it necessary to mention this in moment of recapitulation of our long cultural dialogue. We have something to inspire us when we walk forward in our quest for a new understanding.

These memories are useful: All memories are useful if they are not permitted to rationalise present inaction. We, in our generation, know that we cannot afford to relax until the more than two billion peoples of our two countries, each man, woman, and child, has the opportunity to look forward to a decent life with dignity and freedom, not necessarily self-limiting luxuries. The resurgence of the Asian peoples after centuries of passivity is now beginning. We have learnt painfully to benefit from our mistakes to choose between difficult options in development, in security, and in the rights of the individual. The Asian resurgence which Nehru so fondly believed in, has still to come but, today, the objective conditions for such a resurgence are rapidly coming into being. In the last decade, Asia has shown that it can achieve socio-economic transformation rapidly, finding its own methods, without turning its back on the rest of the world. The question really is not whether Asia is ready for a resurgence. Asian resurgence is in fact already taking place. The need now is that Asian resurgence should expand into a vision of general happiness of the whole of humankind. In this vision there would be no place for hegemony or exploitation, whether inside or outside the Continent.

I do not under-estimate the difficulties that face us in such a task. Fresh challenges are appearing. Can our fragile global ecological system stand the strains of development and subsistence? What will be the pattern of growth required for sustainable development? When disastrous technologies have all but destroyed the Earth's ecological balance, how do we reverse the trend set by affluent countries? And if in the process, they swing to the other extreme and seek to choke off even the legitimate developmental needs of the developing countries, how can the latter resist the new suppressive process? How do we overcome the one-sided restrictions and limitations, sought to be imposed on our technologies and capacity for material and human resource development? These are questions that require the collective wisdom of humankind if satisfactory responses are to be found.

Twenty-two years have passed since the People's Republic of China assumed her rightful place in the United Nations. For twenty-two years before that India was proud to be among the forefront of Nations that urged early acceptance of this just and correct principle. Today, as we approach the half century marks of the world body, our two countries, the largest in the world must do everything possible to ensure that this institution works towards the full realisation of the immense human potential inherent in man — a potential that transcends political and economic arrangements, necessary as they are, but addresses also the far larger concerns of want and hunger, ignorance and disease, that still afflict so much of humankind. These preoccupations pauperise the worth of life. So, only a true liberation from these can allow our world to be truly a part of the free and liberated spirit of the century.

India and China have already made a beginning in cooperating in international fora on questions that relate to global environment. The agreement that we have signed during my visit provides that this cooperation, both bilaterally and internationally, will be intensified.

There are other threats to the emergence of a cooperative world order. They come from attempts to limit the ability of large numbers of humankind to harness modern technology and science to their own economic betterment. Discriminatory restrictive technology regimes, which seek to cloak perhaps commercial self-interest fall in this category. We, India and China, must work together with what we have for the benefit of our peoples.

Equally important is the need for real progress in nuclear disarmament. If there was any justification for the vast nuclear arsenals that certain powers maintain, that has long since ceased with the end of the Cold War. These inhuman weapons must be declared illegal; the world must embark upon a time-bound and firm programme for the complete elimination of nuclear weapons whether declared or clandestine. India has made proposals for a new international consensus on nuclear disarmament, and has listed the steps through which this can be achieved without affecting the genuine security interests of most countries.

Why is this an important area of human endeavour? Unless we secure peace, countries will continue to waste precious resources, talent and effort which could better be utilised to promote national well-being. India has long ago made a clear choice. I do not think that there is another instance where with security needs such as India's and remaining outside all alliance systems, any country spends as little as India does on defence.

But the greatest hurdle against the establishment of a cooperative world order is the assumption that there is only one way of running an economy. Both India and China are too large as economies, and too diverse in other respects, to be fitted into the strait-jacket of economic models that might have worked for smaller, homogeneous entities. You are seeking what you call a socialist market economy, developed with Chinese characteristics, which takes into account your own genius and conditions. The remarkable progress that you have achieved in this experiment is evident to the world. We too are seeking to free our economy while utilising the creative genius and energy of our people. Our results so far have been heartening. The prospect of our success seems to arouse unwarranted apprehensions. New advocacies to prevent the free exchange of ideas are being presented to developing countries. Our answer, in India, as a democracy, is that we should permit the circulation of ideas, out of which the country chooses and adopts what it thinks it needs. We are also sanguine about the wisdom of our people who will see through what is not in their interest no matter how attractively packaged.

It is in this circulation and exchange of ideas that universities have a major role and a historical responsibility. The ties between India and China were formed over a thousand years ago by the exchange of ideas, at a time when it was much more difficult to establish contact. One is humbled when one thinks of the dedication of Faxian who spent fourteen years travelling in order to bring back his precious load of books to China. Compared to him we are in a fortunate position, yet we do not accomplish even a fraction of what he did.

There is another tremendous benefit which these great monks gave us. Their travel chronicles provide one of the few available pictures of a situation in India at that distant time. So, when we meet here today in these hallowed precincts, we are only trying to recapture the first carefree rapture of that earlier encounter. In our own time, Rabindranath Tagore realized the significance of the university in international understanding. This was why he founded the Cheena-Bhavana, the house of Chinese culture, in his own university in Santiniketan, Visva-Bharati. One of its earlier students, Vasudev Gokhale, has written of how at this university, for "the first time after a lapse of a few centuries, a handful of Indians, sitting in an academic institution, attempted once more to break through the tough linguistic barriers that had estranged friendly neighbours."

Friends, we are at the threshold of a new century. There is an old saying that he who predicts the future is rash, even if he tells the truth. Despite this, I venture to say that Asia could come into its full stature and attain its full destiny in the coming century if India and China work together to make it so. Kautilya once said that the "welfare of a state depends on an active foreign policy." He was also clear that "strength is power and happiness is the objective." While strength is power and happiness is the objective, this purposiveness has to be tempered by a capacity for detachment and an inner willingness to believe in selfless endeavour. The great Chinese philosopher Laozi expressed this admirably when he said and I quote:

"All things in nature work silently; they come into being possessing nothing. They fulfil their functions and make no claim on things, all creatures alike do their work and then we see them subside. When they reach full bloom, each returns to its origin, returning to origins means rest, means fulfilment of destiny. This reversion is an eternal law and to know this law is wisdom."

If we are able to bear these maxims in mind in the conduct of our relations, we will be able to share a positive future of harmony and amity built on abiding foundations.

I once again thank the authorities of the University for giving me this opportunity of meeting you here. As the passenger to the next century approaching their destination, I wish you, to the fullest extent, the joy of adventure, the excitement of quest and the satisfaction of success, i.e., success in steering humankind in a safer and happier state, to the twenty first century.

3

VICE-PRESIDENT K.R. NARAYANAN AT FUDAN UNIVERSITY, SHANGHAI

OCTOBER 27, 1994

I am honoured, Mr. President, by your kind invitation to speak at the Fudan University. This is one of the premier academic centres of China with which my country has had very close relations. India's links with the east coast of China go back into history. It was the major route for trade and travel between our two countries across the seas. It was from these shores that Admiral Zheng He set sail in the fifteenth century on his epic voyages and visited my native state of Kerala on the west coast of India years before the Portuguese navigator Vasco da Gama landed at Calicut.

Standing before this illustrious audience today my mind goes back to the early days of creative interaction and exchange of ideas between our two ancient civilizations. Referring to the spread of Buddhism it has been said that in those days China was, probably, more influenced by India than India by China, which according to Jawaharlal Nehru, was "a pity because India could have well received with profit to herself, some of the sound common sense of the Chinese, and with its aid checked her own extravagant fancies." As a matter of fact it was not a case of one-way cultural traffic. India also got several new ideas from China and also certain products like silk, sugar and tea which were in a real sense "seeds of change" which transformed the habits and living styles of people all over the world as profoundly as religious and philosophical ideas. Besides it must be remembered that Buddhism itself got assimilated and Sinified making it almost indistinguishable in the Chinese cultural milieu. As Tagore said: "The truth we received when your pilgrims came to us in India and ours to you — that is not lost even now." It is thus that we can still appreciate the role played by the great pilgrim-scholars like Fa Xian, Xuan Zang, Kumarajiva, and Bodhidharma in the cultural cross-fertilization between India and China.

One significant feature of the encounter between Indian and Chinese cultures was that it was not a merely bilateral process but one that encompassed almost the whole of Asia, especially South East Asia. It was an encounter which did not result in a cultural clash but in peaceful coexistence and a degree of interpenetration. Of India Tagore once asserted that "here in India history is trying out a ceaseless experiment of uniting humanity together... We can refuse none, we shall accept all, even those who might have come to over-run and conquer us". May I here point out a historical fact. Except for the upheaval following the partition of India, an upheaval that was tragic but transient, and occasional communal clashes here and there, millions of people belonging to different faiths, racial origins and speaking different languages live, by and large, peacefully and harmoniously in our vast country. There has never been in the long history of India any religious wars like the Crusades and the Thirty Years War as in European history. So have India and China lived in peace and good neighbourliness for thousands of years except for a very brief but unfortunate and unnecessary conflict in the recent past.

I have recalled ancient history in the spirit of the Chinese saying "Use the past for the present". Before our independence Nehru once said that the friendship between India and China was "very precious to us, not only because of the thousands of golden links that have bound us in the past, but of the future that beckons to both of us". And after independence he remarked that we were harking back to our old friendship in order to promote understanding between the two countries helped by "the wisdom of the past".

During the long, dark night of colonialism India and China were separated from each other. But the leaders of India's freedom movement and China's liberation struggle reached out to each other across the colonial barrier. The first significant contact between the representatives of the Indian and Chinese nationalist movements was when Jawaharlal Nehru met the members of the Chinese delegation at the Congress of the League Against Imperialism at Brussels in 1927. Nehru was impressed with the Chinese delegates and wrote: "I was led regrettably to wish that we in India might also develop some of their energy and driving force at the expense, if need be, of some of our intellectuality." At Brussels the two delegations issued a joint declaration. From Brussels Nehru had urged the Indian National Congress to start a strong agitation in support of China's struggle and also for the withdrawal of Indian troops the British had sent to China.

The mass rallies and agitations conducted in India for the Chinese cause had reached the ears of the Eighth Route Army. In the 1930s there was some exchange of correspondence between Nehru and Mao Zedong and Marshal Zhu De. There was a letter dated November 26, 1937 from Zhu De to Nehru thanking India "in the name of the Chinese people and in the name of the Eighth Route Army in particular" for the mass rallies held in India in support of China. It was in this letter that the suggestion was made that the Indian National Congress might despatch a medical mission to China which was promptly organised by Nehru. The heroic story of Dr. Kotnis in the service of the Chinese people and in the cause of India-China friendship was thus a wonderful manifestation of people-to-people relations between our two countries when we were still a subject nation and you under imperialistic attack on your freedom and independence. Marshal Zhu De stressed this anti-imperialist solidarity in his letter when he stated that the Chinese were "fighting the battle of Asia...Our Struggle is your struggle."

On her part China had extended strong support to India's struggle for Independence from Britain. China pleaded with the Allied powers for granting freedom for India. The leaders, the press and the people of China expressed their, support to India's movement for Independence under the leadership of Mahatma Gandhi. When Nehru was arrested by the British the Chinese Communist Party, in a joint telegram to him, Mao Zedong, Zhou Enlai, Ye Jianying and other Chinese leaders said: "The Chinese people have been grateful for your warm kindness in campaigning for support for their cause of war against Japan. We deeply believe that you and the national leaders who have been struggling for the Indian people's liberation will soon be released and carry on your struggle now that all the people of India and the progressive personalities of the world are demanding your freedom."

It was this anti-imperialist solidarity, this concern for Asian liberation and world peace that expressed itself in our respective international policies after Indian Independence in 1947 and China's Liberation in 1949. That India was the second and not the first country to announce diplomatic recognition to new China was only because U Nu of Burma conveyed to Nehru that his country would like to be the first to announce its recognition. Today all of us look back upon the 1950s as some sort of golden age in Sino-Indian relations. It was the period when the Five Principles of Peaceful Coexistence were proclaimed jointly by our two countries which have now been accepted as the just and correct basis for regulating relations among nations. Premier Zhou Enlai's visit to India in 1954 and Nehru's visit to China the same year, and the cooperation between them at the Bandung Conference in 1955 exercised a distinctly new influence on Asian-African as well as international relations.

Writing in July 1954 Nehru observed: "The coming together of India and China, in spite of their differences, was a major event in Asia and perhaps even for the world." The leaders of China, I believe, had the same perception. However, it was a period when the cold war was breathing its hot air on both India and China. Nehru once gave expression to his feeling that the coming together of India and China was not to the liking of the great powers. It is interesting to recall that many years earlier Rabindranath Tagore with his poetic insight into politics observed that as China's strength grows and "when such a great strength as this obtains possession of the vehicle of the modern age — that is when it obtains mastery over science — then what force will stop it? .... So it is with good reason that the nations who enjoy wealth and abundance are afraid of the evolution of China and attempt to hold her back." Perhaps that approach prevailed to some extent with regard to India also which was the second populous country in the world and to the relations between the two countries in the colonial as well as in the cold war period. The world has now happily come out of that era and today it is up to us to determine our own destinies and raising our relationship in a world that is essentially pluralist and peaceful, not in any narrow and exclusive manner, but in full and free cooperation with all the nations of Asia, Africa, Europe and America.

Before I leave the age of cold war that is no more, let me recall a small but meaningful event of that time. As we know China was kept out of the United Nations during that period. I happen to have come across in the writings of Nehru that at the

China was kept out of the United Nations during that period. I happen to have come across in the writings of Nehru that at the 10th anniversary of the United Nations at San Francisco in 1955 the question of China taking its place in the U.N. was discussed. In his letter to the Chief Ministers of Indian States dated 20th July 1955 Nehru wrote: "Informally suggestions have been made that China would be taken into the United Nations but not in the Security Council, and that India should take her place in the Security Council. We cannot, of course, accept this as it means falling out with China and it would be very unfair for a great country like China not to be in the Security Council. We have, therefore, made it clear to those who suggested this that we cannot agree to this suggestion. We have even gone a little further and said that India is not anxious to enter the Security Council at this stage, even though as a great country she ought to be there. The first step to be taken is for China to take her rightful place, and then the question of India might be considered separately". This is relevant today when the question of the expansion of the Security Council is on the international agenda to provide adequate representation to the countries of Asia, Africa and Latin America.

The cold war had clouded and distorted the vision of most countries in the world. Now that we are out of it we have the responsibility to play a new role. In the discussions with Prime Minister Rajiv Gandhi on December 21, 1988 His Excellency Deng Xiaoping said: "China and India share a common responsibility to mankind". China has today forged ahead in economic development in a spectacular manner. It is one of the most important and dynamic economies of the world thanks to its audacious but careful experiment in "Socialist market economy". We look upon this development with admiration. India too has been pursuing a bold policy of opening up and liberalisation of its economy under the leadership of Prime Minister Narasimha Rao. During the brief period of three years it has yielded substantial results and attracted the attention of the world. The policy is to provide free play to productive forces and to entrepreneurship, open up to the world, attract foreign investment, remove bureaucratic shackles on the economy, and apply science and technology to the developmental process, all within the framework of the democratic system with special emphasis on the needs of the masses and the demands of social justice.

At this new and exciting stage of the economic development of our two countries there is great scope for us to exchange experiences, learn from each other and engage in cooperation on a scale that is unprecedented. In the thousands of years of our friendship and cooperation, cultural and political dimensions had dominated our relations. It is time we put some concrete and substantial economic and scientific-technological content into our historic relationship. During the last few years we have explored seriously and quite comprehensively the prospects of economic cooperation. Our trade is now reaching one billion dollar mark. But all this is not enough considering the size and the population of our two countries and our capabilities and potentialities. In my view greater priority has to be placed on the development of economic relations. That would be of benefit to both our countries, to the Third World and also to the developed countries which are goaded by the lure of our immense and expanding markets.

May I be permitted to quote again from His Excellency Deng Xiaoping. In December 1988 he observed during his conversation with the late Prime Minister Rajiv Gandhi:

> "In recent years there has been comment about the next Century being the Asia Pacific Century... I do not agree with this view point... Even if the far eastern region of the Soviet Union and western part of the United States and Canada are included, their population still comes to only about 300 million, whereas the combined population of our two countries is 1.8 billion. If China and India fail to develop, it cannot be called an Asian Century". This is the responsibility that we owe to Asia and the world. Since 1988 China has developed further and fast and is a member of the Asia Pacific Economic Cooperation. Can the next Century be that of the Asia Pacific without the now fast developing India with its 900 million people?" Mr. President, I have had the privilege of coming to China for the first time in July 1976. I was the first Ambassador of India here after a lapse of 15 years. I recollect that on presenting my credentials to the then Vice-Chairman of the National People's Congress, I handed over to him the Letter of Recall of my predecessor, Mr. G. Parthasarathi, saying that there has been slight delay of 15 years in sending that Letter of Recall. I added that perhaps 15 years were a very short time in history of the 2000 years of India-China relationship. I am glad to say that since 1976 our relations have developed gradually but steadily, gathering in the last few years a new momentum. High level exchanges have been taking place in rapid succession. In 1979 the then Foreign Minister of India, Mr. Atal Bihari Vajpayee, came to China. In 1988 the late Prime Minister Rajiv Gandhi visited, opening a new chapter in our relations, particularly

official visit in 1992. The present Prime Minister, Mr. Narasimha Rao, visited China in September 1993 when several cooperation agreements including the important Border Peace and Tranquillity Agreement were signed. From China also important personalities and delegations have visited India including His Excellency the Prime Minister Mr. Li Peng, the Foreign Minister and the Minister of Defence. May I recall here that even in the most difficult days the leaders of our two countries have held before them the vision of friendship and cooperation between India and China. On October 24, 1962 Premier Zhou Enlai wrote to Prime Minister Nehru: "I think we should look ahead and we should take measures to turn the tide". And Nehru wrote in response on October 27, 1962: "I agree with you that... we should look ahead... and make a serious attempt to restore the relations between India and China to the warm and friendly pattern of earlier days and even improve upon that pattern."

During the last few years both our countries have been engaged in serious attempts to develop our relations over a wide field — economic, cultural, technological, political and international. It is my perception, Mr. President, that India-China friendship and cooperation could be a notable feature of the 21st Century. It is a new world in which we are living, a world that is basically multi-polar and pluralist, a world in which there is a new system of modern states in this ancient continent of Asia, and in which the centre of politics and economics has been shifting to Asia and the Asia-Pacific. It is a favourable environment in which India and China can cooperate with each other, not in any sort of narrow and exclusive relationship, but in the context of world cooperation and world peace, and in accordance with the Five Principles and the principles of non-alignment and peaceful coexistence.

Mr. President and distinguished friends, I understand that the Fudan University was named after a saying from a Confucian classic which reads : -

"Brilliant are the sunlight and moonlight,
Again the morning glory after a night."

I can see the streaks of the morning glory in the eastern sky. Rabindranath Tagore said in one of his poems :

"In front lies the Ocean of Peace.
Into that ocean of peace, my friends, let us launch our boats."

Gandharva Couple, Ajanta Cave No.1, 7th Century Wall Painting.
(See Kapila Vatsyayan's article)

"Sudana Jataka" the Chinese Version of Visvantara Jataka, Mogao Cave No. 419 of Sui Dynasty (581-618).
(See M.C. Joshi's article)

Flying Figure, Mogao Cave No. 321.
(See Kapila Vatsyayan's article)

Dunhuang Wall Painting of Flying Figures, Mogao Cave No. 320.
(See Kapila Vatsyayan's article)

Wall painting from Miran, Xinjiang, 3-4th centuries, Courtesy of National Museum, New Delhi

Xue Yue Guanyin, Dazu Cave Northern Hill, around 11-12 Centuries ıtury.
(See Bagyalakshmi's article)

Manichaean Leaf from Khocho (Turfan) 8th Century A.D. 254 of the 5th Century.
(See Radha Banerjee's article)

"Shamaka Jatakạ", Mogao Cave No. 299 of Northern Zhou Dynasty (557-581).
(See M.C. Joshi's article)

Thousand arm thousand eye Guanyin, Courtesy of National Palace Museum, Taipei xpansive
(See Bagyalakshmi's article)

A Huge Map on the Wall, painted in the 10th Century, Mogao Cave No. 61, Detailing the expansive, Holy Abode of Manjusri called Wutaishan (Mount of five peaks) in Shanxi province (See Arputharani Sengupta's article)

" Sakyamuni preaching on the Vulture peak Mogao Cave No.17,18th century)
(See Àrputharani Sengupta's article)

The Chinese presentation of Sibi Jataka, Mogao Cave No. 254 of the 5th Century
(See M.C. Joshi's article)

Flying Celestials of Early Western Chalukya, 6th Century, Courtesy of National Museum.
(See Kapila Vatsyayan's article)

Ruru Jataka, Dunhuang Presentation, Mogao, Cave No. 237, 5th Century.
(See M.C. Joshi's and Arputharani Sengupta's articles)

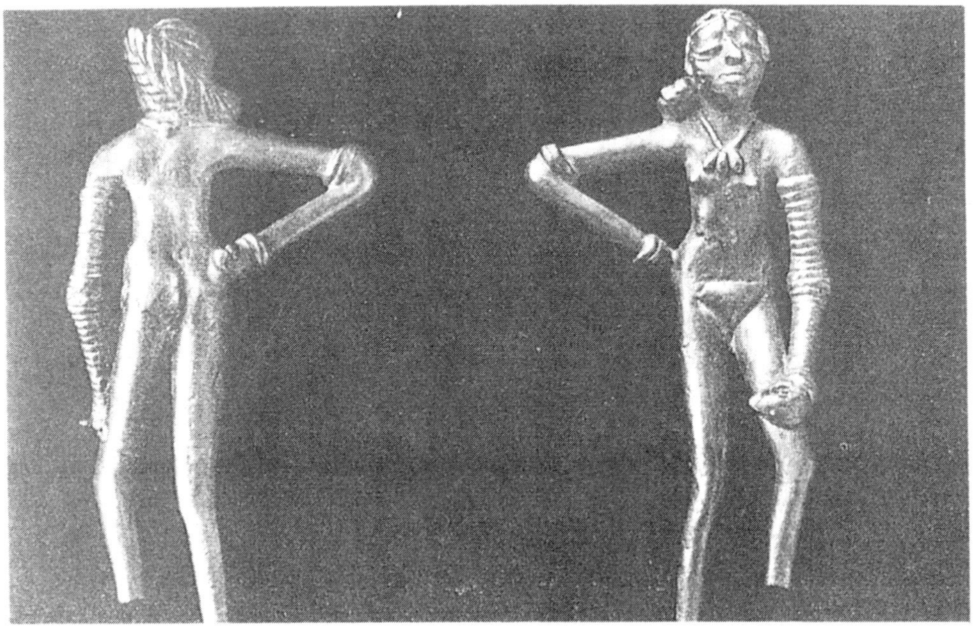

Front and back views of the dancing girl from Mohenjo-daro, bronze, Chalcolithic period, courtesy of National Museum, New Delhi

A Glimpse of the Ajanta Painting, Cave 2, Depicting Visvantara Jataka. (See M.C. Joshi's article)

Visvantara Jataka from Sanchi Stupa, Ist Century B.C.
(See M.C. Joshi's article)

Stone Sculpture of Flying Figure, Khajuraho, 11th Century.
(See Kapila Vatsyayan's article)

Vajravarahi Mandala from Yotkan of 10th Century.
(See Priyatosh Banerjee's article)

Hariti from Gandhara, 2nd Century.
(See Bagyalakshmi's article)

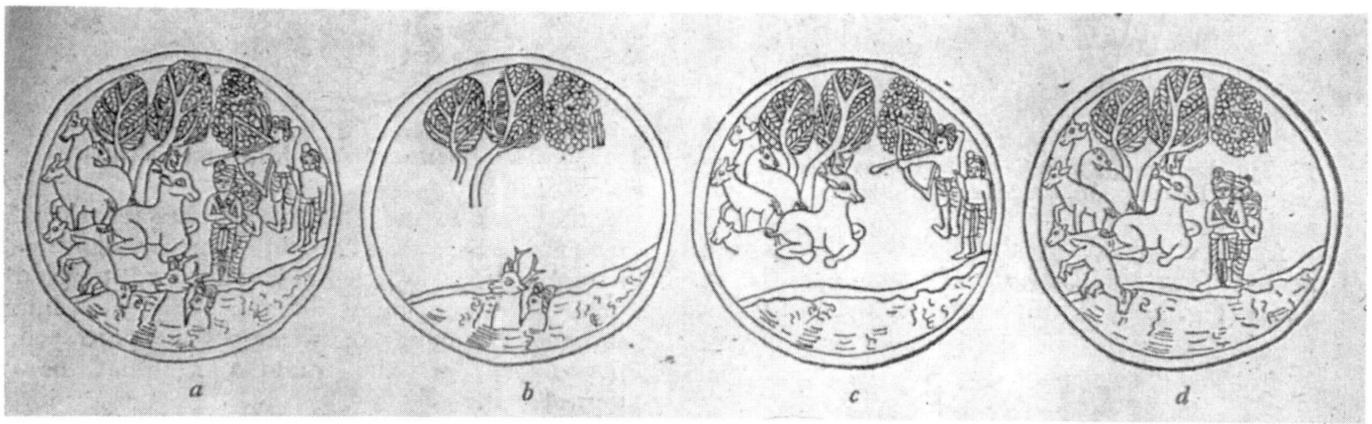

Ruru Jataka Medallion from Vedika, Bharhut, Courtesy of Indian Museum, Calcutta.
(See Arputharani Sengupta's article)

Wall Painting from Khotan on the Silk Road, 3-4 Centuries.
(See Arputharani Sengupta's article)

INDIAN SAVANTS' OBSERVATIONS ON CHINA

INDIAN SAVANTS' OBSERVATIONS ON CHINA

智者看中國

4. Raja Rammohun Roy
5. Gurudeva Rabindranath Tagore
6. Mahatma Gandhi
7. Pandit Jawaharlal Nehru
8. A.K. Coomaraswamy
9. P.C. Bagchi

4

RAJA RAMMOHUN ROY

A DIALOGUE BETWEEN A MISSIONARY AND THREE CHINESE CONVERTS

Missionary: How many Gods are there, my brethren!

lst Convert: Three.

2nd Convert: Two.

3rd Convert: None.

Missionary: Horrid! The answers are from the Devil.

All: We know not where you got the religion which you have taught us, but thus you have taught us.

Missionary: Blasphemers!

All: We have heard you with patience nor ever thought of crying out against you, how much so ever you surprised us by your doctrine.

Missionary: (Recovering himself and addressing the 1st convert.) Come, come, recollect: how can you imagine that there are three Gods?

lst Convert: You told me there was God the Father, and God the Son, and God the Holy Ghost, and by my Swanpan [Calculating instument] I find that one and one and one are three.

Missionary: O! I see your blunder. You remember but half the lesson. I told you also that these Three are One.

lst Convert: I know you did, but I thought you had forgotten yourself, and concluded that you spoke the truth at first.

Missionary: O no! You must believe not only that there are Three persons, each God, and equal in power and glory, but also, that these Three are One.

lst Convert: That is impossible. In China we do not believe contradictions.

Missionary: Brother! It is a mystery.

lst Convert: What is that, pray?

Missionary: It is — it is — I know not what to say to you, except that it is something which you cannot possibly comprehend.

lst Convert: (Smiling) And is it this that you have been sent 10,000 miles to teach?

Missionary: O the power of carnal reason! Surely, some Socinian has been doing the Devil's work in China.

But (turning to the 2nd convert,) how could you imagine, there are two Gods?

2nd Convert: I thought there were many more till you came and lessened the number.

Missionary: Have I ever told you that there are two Gods? (Aside.) The stupidity of this people makes me almost despair.

2nd convert: True, you have not said in so many words that there are two Gods, but you have said what implies it.

Missionary: Then you have been tempted to reason upon this mystery.

2nd Convert: We, Chinese, are wont to put things together and to come at truth by comparison. Thus you said there were three persons that were each perfect God, and then you said one of these persons died in one of the countries of the West, a long while ago; and I therefore concluded the present number to be two.

Missionary: Astonishing depravity! O the depths of Satan! It is in vain to reason with these poor benighted creatures. But (addressing the 3rd convert) perverse as you two brethren are, you appear worse than they: What can you possibly mean by answering that there are no Gods ?

3rd Convert: I heard you talk of three, but I paid more particular attention to what you said on the point of there being only one. This I could understand; the other I could not; and as my belief never reaches above my understanding (for you know I am no learned Mandarin) I set it down in my mind that there was but one God, and that you take your name of Christian from him.

Missionary: There is something in this; but I am more and more astonished at your answer — "None."

3rd Convert: (Taking up the Swanpan.) Here is one. I remove it. There is none.

Missionary: How can this apply?

3rd Convert: Our minds are not like yours in the West, or you would not ask me. You told me again and again, that there never was but one God, that Christ was the true God, and that a nation of merchants living at the head of the Arabian gulf, put him to death upon a tree, about eighteen hundred years ago. Believing you, what other answer could I give than "None"?

Missionary: I must pray for you, for you all deny the true faith, and living and dying thus, you will without doubt perish everlastingly.

1st Convert: Cong-foo-tse [Confucius], our revered master, says that bad temper always turns reason out of doors, and that when men begin to curse, the God Spirit of the universe abandons their hearts.

2nd Convert: You must be angry with yourself and not with us, for you have been teaching us at different times doctrines as contradictory as those of Cong-foo-tse and Buddha. The immortal emperor Sinchong has said that he is not to be numbered with wise men, nor to have a name in the hall of ancestors, who undertakes a voyage without making up his mind to its purpose, and preparing himself to give a clear and kind answer to the question of a stranger.

3rd Convert: These rebukes are just: but Ter-whangtee says, in his golden words, that mirth is better than rice. You came, it seems, to bring us a new riddle: but while we thank you, we beg to inform you that Kienlong, our late celestial emperor, has supplied us with a plentiful store, much more entertaining than yours; and when you can read as well as speak our divine language, we recommend to you his delectable history of the Mantchoo [Manchu] Tartar, that pretended to be inspired by the Grand Lama, but could never be made to comprehend the Swanpan.

(Cited from Jogendra Chunder Ghose (ed.), *The English Works of Raja Rammohum Roy*, Delhi: Cosmo Publications, first published in 1906, reprint 1982, Vol. IV., pp. 911-13.)

5

GURUDEVA RABINDRANATH TAGORE

1. TALKS IN CHINA, 1924 (Excerpts)

• "I have been given to understand that China never felt the need of religion. This I find hard to believe. People very often judge their neighbour's religion from their own narrow sectarian definition. I am sure that if it had been my good fortune to stay longer I should have been able to realise those deeper chords in the heart of China, whence to music of the spirit comes."

• "You have a temple near by where there is a picture, carved upon the rock, of an Indian monk or sage who came to this country centuries ago. What is most interesting about him is the fact that when he came here he felt that these hills were just like the hills with which he was familiar in his own motherland. It is said that this hill came flying from India to this place. But the real fact is that the hill which he had known in his own country had a Sanskrit name meaning the Vulture Peak. When he saw a hill here so like the one he had loved in India, he felt a great delight and gave it the same name.

When I came, I too saw your beautiful lake and the hills around. They did not seem at all strange, for your hills speak the same language as ours, your lake has the same smile as our lakes, your trees the same physiognomy, with only a slight difference, as our Indian trees. Therefore, when I find myself in the heart of nature here, I realise the unity of different countries in their outer aspect."

• "I know that many of you do not understand me, but something has drawn you to come and look at me. It is not because you expect any message from me, but, as I believe, because of some memory of that glorious time when India did send her messengers of love to this land, — not her merchants nor her soldiers, but the best of her children, — and they came bearing her gifts across deserts and seas."

• "In Asia we must seek our strength in union, in an unwavering faith in righteousness, and never in the egotistic spirit of separateness and self-assertion. It is from the heart of the East that the utterance has sprung forth: 'The meek shall inherit the earth.' For the meek never waste energy in the display of insolence, but are firmly established in true prosperity through harmony with the All.

In Asia we must unite, not through some mechanical method of organisation, but through a spirit of true sympathy. The organised power of the machine is ready to smite and devour us, from which we must be rescued by the living power of spirit which grows into strength, not through mere addition, but through organic assimilation. That we should borrow science from the West is right. We have a great thing to accept from the people of West, — their treasure of intellect, which is immense and whose superiority we must acknowledge. But it would be degradation on our part, and an insult to our ancestors, if we forgot our own moral wealth of wisdom, which is of far greater value than a system that produces endless materials and a physical power that is always on the warpath."

There was a time when Asia saved the world from barbarism. Then came the night, I do not know how. And when we were aroused from our stupor by the knocking at our gate, we were not prepared to receive Europe who came to us in her pride of strength and intellect. The West came, not to give of its best, or to seek for our best, but to exploit us for the sake of material gain. It even came into our homes robbing us of our own. That is how Europe overcame Asia.

We did Europe injustice because we did not meet her on equal terms. The result was the relation of superior to inferior; of insult on the one side and humiliation on the other. We have been accepting things like beggars. We have been imagining that we have nothing of our own. We are still suffering from want of confidence in ourselves. We are not aware of our own treasures.

We must rise from our stupor, and prove that we are not beggars. This is our responsibility. Search in your own homes for things that are of undying worth. Then you will be saved and will be able to save all humanity. Some of us, of the East, think that we should copy and imitate the West. I do not believe in it. What the West has produced is for the West, being native to it. But we of the East cannot borrow the Western mind nor the Western temperament. We want to find our own birthright."

• "But many will point to the weakness of China and India and tell you that thrown, as we are, among these strong and progressive peoples, it is necessary to emphasize power and progress in order to avoid destruction. And I would not have you deceived by the Sunday-school talk that no advantage is to be won by unrighteousness. In the words of the great ones of my people:

> *'With the help of unrighteousness men do prosper.*
>
> *With the help of unrighteousness men do gain victories over their enemies.*
>
> *With the help of unrighteousness men do attain what they desire.*
>
> *But they perish at the root.'*

• "We should know this, that Truth, — any truth that man acquires, — is for all. Money and property belong to individuals, to each of you, but you must never exploit truth for your personal aggrandisement — that would be selling God's blessing to make profit. Science also is truth. It has its own place, in the healing of the sick, and in the giving of more food, more leisure for life. But when it helps the strong to crush the weaker, to rob those who are asleep, that is using truth for impious ends and those who are so sacrilegeous will suffer and be punished, for their own weapons will be turned against them.

But a new time has come, the time to discover another great power, the power that gives us strength to suffer and not merely to cause suffering, the immense power of sacrifice. This will help us to defeat the malevolent intellect of brute greed and egotism, as in the pre-historic age intelligence overcame the power of mere muscle.

Let the morning of this new age dawn in the East, from which great streams of idealism have sprung in the past, making the fields of life fertile with their influence. I appeal to you to make trial of this moral power through martyrdom. Prove how, through the heroism of suffering and sacrifice, — not weak submission, — we can demonstrate our best wealth and strength. Know that no organization however big can help you, no league of prudence or of power, but only the individual with faith in the infinite, the invisible, the incorruptible, the fearless."

• "Now I am in China, I ask you, I ask myself, what have you got, what out of your own house can you offer in homage to this new age? You must answer this question. Do you know your own mind? Your own culture? What is best and most permanent in your own history? You must know at least that, if you are to save yourselves from the greatest of insults, the insult of obscurity, of rejection. Bring out your light and add it to this great festival of lamps of world culture."

• "Materialism is exclusive, and those who are materialistic claim their individual rights of enjoyment, of storing and possessing. You are not individualists in China. Your society is itself the creation of your communal soul. It is not the outcome of a materialistic, of an egoistic mind, — a medley of unrestricted competition, which refuses to recognise its obligations to others."

• I see that you in China have not developed the prevailing malady of the world, the lunacy of an unmeaning multiplication of millions, the production of those strange creatures called multi-millionaires. I have heard that, unlike others, you do not give great value to the brute power of militarism. All this could not be possible if you were really materialists.

It is true that you love this world and the material things about you with an intensity of attachment, but not by enclosing your possessions within the walls of exclusiveness. You share your wealth, you make of your distant relatives your guests, and you are not inordinately rich. This is only possible because you are not materialistic.

I have travelled through your country and I have seen with what immense care you have made the earth fruitful, with what a wonderous perfection you have endowed the things of every day use. How could this have been possible through a greedy attachment to material things?"

• "Our ancestors had a great ideal of the spiritual relationship between peoples, but there were no end of difficulties in their way; they could not carry their message in a comfortable manner. Nevertheless, a thousand years ago, they could speak in your language. Why? Because they realised the importance of the work in hand, — how invaluable was this bond of unity between nations, which could surmount the difference of languages. It is the one bond that can save humanity from the utter destruction with which it is threatened today, through the selfishness which is torturing mankind and causing misery in the world.

Is it not marvellous how these men at all arrived, and having come, translated their metaphysical ideas into Chinese, a language so utterly different from Sanskrit that the difficulties thereby encountered were far more insurmountable than the mountains they climbed, the deserts they traversed, the seas they navigated?"

• "If I could live among you, I could speak to you and you to me, and our thoughts would live through our close contact. They would bear fruit, not immediately, but in the process of time. Obstacles would vanish, misunderstandings would not be possible. Our relation would no longer be one-sided. We would work and produce together from the mutual contact of our hearts and minds. But our professors and schoolmasters demand lectures, from which no deep impression remains but only some faint outlines upon the memory, — merely events, which find their paragraphs in the newspapers, but do not leave their mark on the hearts of men.

The truths that we received when your pilgrims came to us in India, and ours to you, — that is not lost even now. We may feel that those ideas have to be adapted to the present changed conditions, and we cannot accept in their totality the thoughts and teachings of thousands of years ago. We may even grow angry over them, considering them mischievous, but we can never forget them completely because they were mutually assimilated to our lives. They are there for good or for evil, the result of a real meeting for which our ancestors paid.

What a great pilgrimage was that! What a great time in history! Those wonderful heroes, for the sake of their faith, risked life and accepted banishment from home for long, long years. Many perished and left no trace behind them. A few were spared to tell us their story, but most had no opportunity to leave a record behind. For such relics of theirs as have been spared to us, we should be thankful, as well as for something in them which we may call primitive because their primitive conditions of life had one great advantage, — the coverings were less."

• "I built my China on a basis of the great works of your great artists of the olden days. I used to say to myself: The Chinese are a great people. They have created a world of beauty. And I remember feeling angry with others who had scant respect for you, who could come to exploit and molest you, and who ignored the debt they owed you for your civilisation, for the great works which you had produced.

Of course we know that, such a vision, created from the best products of your history, and your past, does not represent the actual life of your people. Yet I firmly believe that it is from the ideal that we get to know the best aspects of the real, and that the complete life is given by these two seen together. I must admit it is difficult for a stranger to discover this innermost truth, but I believe I have caught glimpses of it.

One thing I have felt, and it has often been spoken of by foreigners whom I have met in your land. You are very human. I too have felt the touch of the human in you, and I have come, or at least I hope I have come, close to your heart. I myself am filled, not with a feeling of mere admiration and wonder, but with a feeling of love, especially for those persons with whom I have come into close touch. This personal touch is not an easy thing to obtain.

Some people say that you have the gift of accepting things as they are, that you can take your joy in a naked presentation of reality, which you value, not because it has any association with some thing outside itself, but simply because it is before you, attracting your attention. May be it is because of this gift that you have been willing to accept me as I am, not as a poet, not, as some foolish people think, as a philosopher or, as still more foolish people imagine, as a prophet, but as very much of an individual."

• "You have asked me to offer some frank criticisms on this day of my departure. I absolutely refuse to accede to your request. You have critics innumerable, and I do not want to be added to their ranks. Being human myself I can make allowances for your shortcomings, and I love you in spite of them. Who am I to criticise? We people of the Orient possess all kinds of qualities of which others do not approve, — then why not let us be friends.

You shall have no criticisms from me, and please refrain from criticising me in return. I hope my friends in China will not have the heart to probe into my failings. I never posed as a philosopher, and so I think I can claim to be let alone. Had I been accustomed to living on a pedestal, you could have pulled me down and damaged my spine, but since I have been living on the same level, I trust I am safe."

2. ADDRESS AT THE OPENING CEREMONY OF VISVA-BHARATI CHEENA-BHAVANA ON APRIL 14, 1937

The most memorable fact of human history is that of a path-opening, not for the clearing of a passage for machines or machine guns, but for helping the realisation by races of their affinity of minds, their mutual obligation of a common humanity. Such a rare event did happen and the path was built between our people and the Chinese in an age when physical obstruction needed heroic personality to overcome it and the mental barrier a moral power of uncommon magnitude. The two leading races of that age met, not as rivals on the battle-field, each claiming the right to be the sole tyrant on earth, but as noble friends, glorying in their exchange of gifts. Then came a slow relapse into isolation, covering up the path with its accumulated dust of indifference. Today our old friends have beckoned to us again, generously helping us to retrace that ancient path obliterated by the inertia of forgetful centuries, and we rejoice.

This is, indeed, a great day for me, a day long looked for, when I should be able to redeem, on behalf of our people, an ancient pledge implicit in our past, the pledge to maintain the intercourse of culture and friendship between our people and the people of China, an intercourse whose foundations were laid eighteen hundred years back by our ancestors with infinite patience and sacrifice. When I went to China several years ago I felt a touch of that great stream of life that sprang from the heart of India and overflowed across mountain and desert into that distant land, fertilising the heart of its people. I thought of that great pilgrimage, of those noble heroes, who, for the sake of their faith, their ideal of the liberation of self that leads to the perfect love which unites all beings, risked life and accepted banishment from home and all that was familiar to them. Many perished and left no trace behind. A few were spared to tell their story, a story not of adventurers and trespassers whose heroism has proved a mere romantic excuse for careers of unchecked brigandage, but a story of pilgrims who came to offer their gifts of love and wisdom, a story indelibly recorded in the cultural memory of their hosts. I read it when I was received there as a representative of a revered race and felt proud as I traced the deep marks our ancestors had left behind on their achievements. But I also felt the humiliation of our long lasting evil fate that has obscured for us in an atmosphere of insanity the great human value of a noble endeavour, one of the most precious in the history of man.

I told my Chinese hosts on that occasion: "My friends, I have come to ask you to re-open the channel of communication which I hope is still there; for though overgrown with weeds of oblivion, its lines can still be traced. I have not the same voice that my ancestors had. I have not the wisdom they possessed. My life has not attained that consciousness of fulfilment needed to make this message fruitful. We in India are a defeated race; we have no power, political, military or commercial; we do not know how to help you or injure you materially. But, fortunately, we can still meet you as your guests, your hosts, your brothers and your friends. Let that happen. I invite you to us as you have invited me. I do not know whether you have heard of the institution I have established in my land. Its one object is to let India welcome the world to its heart. Let what seems a barrier become a path, and let us unite, not in spite of our differences, but through them. For differences can never be wiped away, and life would be so much the poorer without them. Let all human races keep their own personalities, and yet come together, not in a uniformity that is dead, but in a unity that is living."

That has happened and friends are here from China with their gift of friendship and co-operation. The Hall which is to be opened today will serve both as the nucleus and as a symbol of that larger understanding that is to grow with time. Here students and scholars will come from China and live as part of ourselves, sharing our life and letting us share theirs, and by offering their labours in a common cause, help in slowly re-building that great course of fruitful contact between our peoples, that has been interrupted for ten centuries. For this Visva-Bharati is, and will, I hope, remain a meeting place for individuals from all countries, east or west, who believe in the unity of mankind and are prepared to suffer for their faith. I believe in such individuals even though their efforts may appear to be too insignificant to be recorded in history.

It might be supposed that in a world so closely knit by railways, steamships and air lines, where almost every big city is cosmopolitan, such special invitations for contact are superfluous. But, unfortunately, the contacts that are being made today have done more to estrange and alienate peoples from one another than physical inaccessibility ever did. We are discovering for ourselves the painful truth that nothing divides so much as the wrong kind of nearness. People seem to be coming in each other's way, dodging and trapping one another, without ever coming together. We meet others, either as tourists when we merely slide against the surface of their life, entering hotels only to disappear from their land, or as exploiters in one disguise or another. We are living in a world where nations are divided into two main groups those who trample on others' freedom, and those who are unable to guard their own; so that while we have too much of intrusion on others' rights, we have hardly any intercourse with their culture. It is a terrorised world, dark with fear and suspicion, where peaceful races in dread of predatory hordes are retreating into isolation for security.

I am reminded of my experience as we were travelling up from Shanghai to Nanking along the great river, Yang Tse. All through the night I kept on coming out of my cabin to watch the beautiful scene on the banks, the sleeping cottages with their solitary lamps, the silence spread over the hills, dim with mist. When morning broke and brought into view fleets of boats coming down the river, their sails stretching high into the air, a picture of life's activity with its perfect grace of freedom, I was deeply moved and felt that my own sail had caught the wind and was carrying me from captivity, from the sleeping past, out into the great world of man. It brought to my mind different stages of the history of man's progress.

In the night each village was self-centred, each cottage stood bound by the chain of unconsciousness. I knew, as I gazed on the scene, that vague dreams were floating about in this atmosphere of sleeping souls, but what struck my mind more forcibly was the fact that when men are asleep they are shut up within the very narrow limits of their own individual lives. The lamps exclusively belonged to the cottages, which in their darkness were in perfect isolation. Perhaps, though I could not see them, some prowling bands of thieves were the only persons awake, ready to exploit the weakness of those who were asleep.

When daylight breaks we are free from the enclosure and the exclusiveness of our individual life. It is then that we see the light which is for all men and for all times. It is then that we come to know each other and come to co-operate in the field of life. This was the message that was brought in the morning by the swiftly moving boats. It was the freedom of life in their outspread sails that spoke to me; and I felt glad. I hoped and prayed that morning had truly come in the human world and that the light had broken forth.

This age to which we belong, does it not still represent night in the human world, a world asleep, whilst individual races are shut up within their own limits, calling themselves nations, which barricade themselves, as these sleeping cottages were barricaded with shut doors, with bolts and bars, with prohibitions of all kinds? Does not all this represent the dark age of civilization, and have we not begun to realize that it is the robbers who are out and awake?

But I do not despair. As the early bird, even while the dawn is yet dark, sings out and proclaims the rising of the sun, so my heart sings to proclaim the coming of a great future which is already close upon us. We must be ready to welcome this new age. There are some people, who are proud and wise and practical, who say that it is not in human nature to be generous, that men will always fight one another, that the strong will conquer the weak and that there can be no real moral foundation for man's civilization. We cannot deny the facts of their assertion that the strong have their rule in the human world: but I refuse to accept this as a revelation of truth.

It is co-operation and love, mutual trust and mutual aid which make for strength and real merit of civilization. New spiritual and moral power must continually be developed to enable men to assimilate their scientific gains, to control their weapons and machines, or these will dominate and enslave them. I know that many will point to the weakness of China and India and tell us that thrown as we are among other ruthlessly strong and aggressive world peoples, it is necessary to emphasize power and progress in order to avoid destruction. It is indeed true that we are weak and disorganised, at the mercy of every barbaric force, but that is not because of our love of peace but because we no longer pay the price of our faith by dying for it. We must learn to defend our humanity against the insolence of the strong, only taking care that we do not imitate their ways and, by turning ourselves brutal, destroy those very values which alone make our humanity worth defending. For danger is not only of the enemy without but of the treason within us. We had, for over a century, been so successfully hypnotised and dragged by the prosperous West behind its chariot that, though choked by the dust, deafened by the noise, humbled by our helplessness, overwhelmed by speed, we yet agreed to acknowledge that this chariot-drive was progress, and that progress was civilization. If we ever ventured to ask, however humbly: Progress towards what, and progress for whom? — it was considered to be peculiarly and ridiculously oriental to entertain such doubts about the absoluteness of progress. It is only of late that a voice has been heeded by us, bidding us take account not only of the scientific perfection of the chariot, but of the depth of ditches lying across its path. Today we are emboldened to ask: what is the value of progress if it make a desert of this beautiful world of man? And though we speak as members of a nation that is humiliated and oppressed and lies bleeding in the dust, we must never acknowledge the defeat, the last insult, the utter ruin of our spirit being conquered, of our faith being sold. We need to hear again and again, and never more than in this modern world of head-hunting and cannibalism in disguise that: — By the help of unrighteousness men do prosper, men do gain victories over their enemies, men do attain what they desire; but they perish at the root.

It is to this privilege of preserving, not the mere body of our customs and conventions, but the moral force which has given quality to our civilization and made it worthy of being honoured, that I invite the co-operation of the people of China, recalling the profound words of their sage, Lao-tze [Laozi]: *Those who have virtue attend to their obligations; those who have no virtue attend to their claims.* Progress which is not related to an inner ideal, but to an attraction which is external, seeks to satisfy endless claims. But civilization, which is an ideal, gives us power and joy to fulfil our obligations.

Let us therefore abide by our obligation to maintain and nourish the distinctive merit of our respective cultures and not be misled into believing that what is ancient is necessarily outworn and what is modern is indispensable. When we class things as modern or old we make a great mistake in following our calendar of dates. We know that the flowers of Spring are old, that they represent the dawn of life on earth, — but are they therefore symbols of the dead and discarded? Would we rather replace them with artificial flowers made of rags, because they were made "yesterday"? It is not what is old or what is modern that we should love and cherish but what has truly a permanent human value. And can anything be more worthy of being cherished than the beautiful spirit of the Chinese culture that has made the people love material things without the strain of greed, that has made them love the things of this earth, clothe them with tender grace without turning them materialistic? They have instinctively grasped the secret of the rhythm of things, — not the secret of power that is in science, but the secret of expression. This is a great gift, for God alone knows this secret. I envy them this gift and wish our people could share it with them.

I do not know what distinctive merit we have which our Chinese friends and others may wish to share. Once indeed our sages dedicated themselves to the ideal of perfect sympathy and intellect, in order to win absolute freedom through wisdom and absolute love through pity. Today we cannot boast of either such wisdom or such magnanimity of heart. But I hope we are not yet reduced to such absolute penury of both as not to be able to offer at least a genuine atmosphere of hospitality, of an earnestness to cross over our limitations and move nearer to the hearts of other peoples and understand somewhat of the significance of the endless variety of man's creative effort.

6

MAHATMA GANDHI

July 24,1924

WAR AGAINST OPIUM

The White Cross is an international anti-narcotic society whose headquarters are in Washington. It appears to have branches all over the world. Its letterhead contains distinguished names as trustees or standing council. Its executive secretary, Mr. McKibben, writes a long letter urging me to secure India's cooperation in the White Cross crusade against opium. I cull the following passages from the letter;

> "The people of China resisted its invasion in two wars and in 1906 took the first opportunity in a century and a half to gain deliverance by pulling up or ploughing under the poppy on millions of acres. So long and so binding had been their enslavement that it was predicted that at any attempt to take opium away the Chinese people would rise in insurrection. Spence, an English writer, said in 1882 that "revolution would result if the Chinese Government would undertake suppression of the growth of the poppy, the quiet seaports would be turned into hell, streets would run with blood." So far were these dire forecasts from coming true that no action of the Chinese Government was ever so popular as its determined and successful campaign for poppy destruction. It became a fervent, sweeping, religious movement. In a thousand cities and villages old smokers stacked up their pipes in piles as high as the houses as a burnt offering to Heaven. Jubilant processions, music and banners, voiced the general thanksgiving, while women wept tears of joy that the century-old curse was lifed.
>
> Their rejoicings were short-lived. The British Government kept its promise to cease importing opium but, as has happened before and since, as you too well know, the Western world kept the word of promise to the ear but broke it to the heart. In place of opium there was poured upon devoted China a flood of morphine, heroin and cocaine, ten times worse. In this atrocity, I blush to say, the United States was a participant until a recent day. In consequence of chaotic conditions, military chieftains have now forced upon unwilling Chinese farmers, a renewal of poppy planting, excusing themselves because native opium is better than foreign morphine. Those who know China best believe that her fundamentally sound conscience will again respond when the nations give them support and will again rid their land of opium.
>
> It is universally recognized that no one nation can save itself. Opium products are so compact, so easily concealed and the wages of the traffic so enormous that, as long as the drugs are produced, they will find their consumers. The American Congress has accordingly appealed to all nations to unite in suppressing the opium poppy and the cocaine shrub, reserving only such amounts as are considered necessary in medicine and science. A Conference has been agreed on to meet in Geneva in November 1924, to put into effect this proposal. This Conference will be vested with authority whereby it may, if it will, inaugurate measures that will deliver the world from the menace.
>
> The question is now before the world, how may this Narcotic Conference be brought to act in the spirit as well in the letter of this mandate? Shall they meet the world's hopes or blast them? To you, Sir, I need not name one all-powerful agency that may be invoked, namely, the power of public opinion, the focussing of the world's conscience and conviction upon the meetings of that Conference.
>
> The organization of which I have the honour to be a representative, the White Cross International Anti-

narcotic Society, is seeking a voicing of public opinion and conscience, focussing it upon the November Conference in a way to move them irresistibly to use the opportunity providentially in their hands and rid the world of its greatest physical menace.

The experience of China should convince India that fears which have sometimes been expressed of "Oriental revolt" against "deprivation of opium" will prove groundless in India as they did in China. It is perhaps not strange that some representatives of the British Government in India fear that India is so wedded to opium that "serious consequences would follow any attempt to take it away". There is far less danger of this in India than in China. India has never become enslaved to the extent of China, even though its victims have largely been those on whom the whole future depends, namely the babies doped by their mothers day after day while the mothers are at work in the factories. Indian ladies, who are devoted social workers, say this practice is well-nigh universal. If "revolt" is apprehended, it would seem to a friendly observer most likely to be a revolt of the people against a Governmental policy which poisons to death the babies in their mothers' arms, or leaves them alive as if born old, pallid, emaciated, stunted, blasted in body and hopeless of future, the motive being that the Government might get the revenues 'which it needs'.

The world can never be delivered until India saves herself by ceasing to poison her own oncoming generations and by ceasing to pour her opium into the veins of other nations. For the sake of India and of the world, we lay before Mr. Gandhi and the people of India this our request for expressions of their mind such as will convince the coming Opium Conference that India both seeks deliverance from her own opium enslavement and joins hands for the redemption of the world. ...

Furthermore, may we ask what is the wish of the people of India as to who shall be their representatives and spokesmen at the Opium Conference? In previous meetings, have the convictions of India been accurately voiced? Whether sent unofficially or, as would be more fitting, clothed with full powers of representation, we would suggest that India send some of her best sons to speak for her that the world may know her mind. If in any way our organization can assist in bringing before the Conference the expressions of Indian conviction, we shall be at your service."

The White Cross may rely upon India's cooperation in its noble work. The All India Congress Committee (A.I.C.C.) has only recently unanimously passed a resolution which places on record its emphatic condemnation of the opium policy of the Government of India. If every poppy plant were rooted out, there would be no protest in the land against the act. The people will certainly rejoice when the whole of the revenue from intoxicating drinks and drugs is stopped, their sale absolutely prohibited except strictly as medicines to be sold by certificated chemists or druggists.

But unfortunately for us and the world, India's opinion is today represented by a Government that does not represent its people. At the forthcoming convention, therefore, it will not be the people of India that will be represented, but it would be the foreign rule over India that will be represented, in the interests not so much of humanity as chiefly of its revenue. Whether it would serve any useful purpose to send an unofficial representative, such as Mr. Andrews, truly representing the people, is a matter to be considered by the A.I.C.C.

Let us, however, see what the goal of the humanitarian crusade is. Miss La Motte has shown by unchallengeable figures that the world's production of opium is far in excess of its medical requirements and that so long as it continues, so long will the immoral and soul-destroying traffic in it continue in spite of efforts to the contrary. She has shown, too, that the Government of India is the greatest culprit in the matter. The goal cannot be reached till the Government of India honestly carries out the wish of the best mind of the world, immediately to reduce the cultivation of opium in its jurisdiction to the lowest term possible and without counting the cost. The Government of India alone has blocked the way and it is feared that it will do so again. And it will do so not because India wishes, but because she is helpless.

("War Against Opium", published in *Young India*, July 24, 1924, *Collected Works of Mahatma Gandhi*, Vol. 24, pp. 428-30.)

May 13, 1927

There was persistent agitation against the despatch of Indian troops from almost all the Indian public bodies. But I am sorry to have to confess that Indian public opinion is not powerful enough to carry in such matters weight with the Government. It has to be recognized that we are after all a fallen nation struggling to rise and therefore beyond wishing nations like you all success in their endeavour to attain full freedom, we can do very little indeed to help.

(Letter to Chinese Students Association, May 13, 1927, *ibid*, Vol. 33, p. 316.)

August 5, 1927

The sadness of the reminder is heightened by the fact that our mercantile fleet may at any moment be turned into a fleet warring against our own liberty or against that of nations with which India has no quarrel and with whose aspirations India may even have every sympathy, as for instance, China. There is nothing to prevent the Government from commandeering any one of the ships belonging to the swadeshi companies for carrying soldiers to punish China for daring to fight for liberty.

("Indian Shipping", in *Hindu*, Aug. 5, 1927, *ibid*, Vol. 34, p. 279).

August 27, 1938

DISCUSSION WITH HENGCHIH TAO*

GANDHIJI: I am exceedingly sorry to receive you when I am in distress. I may not break my silence even to speak to you. But of course you will say whatever you want to. You may speak, I may not.

Prof. Tao explained that he was a member of the People's Council of Action of all China. This was a body of 140 or 150 drawn from all parties in China, under which the whole of China was united to meet Japanese aggression..., under one supreme military command of Chiang Kai-shek ... Tao was happy that a Medical Mission from India was sailing to China as a token of India's sympathy, and he asked Gandhiji if he had any suggestions to offer in order to fight the war to a successful conclusion.

G. I do not know that I can throw any light on the problem at the present moment. My method is so radical that it is wholly inapplicable to your struggle. You cannot all of a sudden change the course of the struggle. A nation in arms cannot all at once give up arms and accept non-violence as its weapon.

Prof. Tao saw the difficulty and explained that the Chinese had not even time to think, the aggression was so sudden and so unprovoked. But he would like to discuss problems of national reconstructions. He had given up university work in order to take up peasants' education and he was deeply interested in the Wardha Education Scheme. "What exactly is the core of the Scheme?" he asked.

G. The central fact is some village craft through which the whole of the man or the woman in the child can be drawn out.

"But there was the difficulty of teachers," said Prof. Tao, and Gandhiji laughed. "We had the same difficulty. Would you have trained teachers to learn a craft or craftsmen to learn the art of teaching?" asked Prof. Tao.

G. The average educated man can be expected easily to master a craft. Our craftsmen will require much longer time to acquire the necessary general instruction than an educated man, say like you, can require to learn, say, carpentry.

"But," said Prof. Tao, "our educated man is after fat jobs and money. How can he be interested in this?"

G. If the scheme is sound and appeals to the educated mind, it must prove attractive in itself and thus wean the educated youth from the lure of gold. It must fail, if it does not evoke sufficient patriotism from the educated youth. There is one advantage with us. Those who have received instruction through the Indian languages cannot enter colleges. It is just possible that they will find the scheme attractive.

Prof. Tao was deeply interested in our present political struggle. How were we going to acquire power at the centre?

G. If we are true to our salt in the seven provinces, the accession of strength that will come to us will put us on the way to power at the centre.

T. But the power is being felt everywhere, and the Congress prestige has risen. Has it not?

G. The Congress prestige has risen. The people have become conscious of their power and strength. The Government also recognize this. My fear is that this power may throw us off our balance.

---

*"Hengchih Tao was famous Chinese educationist Tao Xingzhi (or Spelled as Hsing-Chih). — Editor

Prof. Tao reverted to the question of mass education. He made an attempt to describe the Chinese system of "relay" teachers whereby each man or woman who had learnt something had to pass it on to the next one he or she came across. Even the child, the "little" teacher, had to share his or her learning with his illiterate parents, and the Chinese through this system were liquidating illiteracy and ignorance on a mass scale.

G. I have no doubt that it can. I would like you to write for me a short note on how the "relay" teachers and the "little" teachers are taught, how they teach and with what result.

Prof. Tao said he would gladly comply.

Prof. Tao would not go without a message from Gandhiji for the people of China. He explained that even a non-violent message would be welcome.... They were engaged in a war of self-defence, but in other respects they were observing non-violence... On May 20 Chinese planes had flown over Japanese towns, and they might easily have spread death and destruction among the people of Japan in retaliation for the bombing of so many Chinese ports by Japan. But instead of raining bombs they rained handbills and leaflets showing the wrong of the war....

G. But the self-inflicted restraint won't last when the real stress comes. The temptation will be irresistible. I shall not be surprised. It is inevitable. There is no love in war. We have got to come to the conclusion that either there is to be complete non-violence or undiluted violence. Is not this enough message?

Prof. Tao wondered if someday the Chinese might expect to have Gandhiji in their midst.

G. I almost came to your country when those who had invited me had to stop me from going owing to the disturbances that had taken place. I do want to see peace reigning in your land during my lifetime. Nothing will please me better than to visit your great country someday.

(In *Harijan*, Aug. 27, 1938, *ibid*, Vol. 67, pp. 250-52.)

November 22-23, 1940

Just as you are engaged in a terrific life-and-death struggle, so are we. Yours is an ancient country and so is ours and although yours is a much bigger country than ours, ours is not by any means a small country and there is much in common between you and us. Speaking personally, I may inform you that I was in touch with the Chinese colony in Johannesburg and gave them legal advice. They were a colony of 1,200 and I came in closest touch with everyone of them and so the Chinese are not strangers to me by any means. Although you are engaged in a life-and-death struggle and so are we, the means we employ for regaining our freedom are different from the means you employ for retaining your freedom. This does not mean that I want to criticize the means you have adopted. The remedy you employ in self-defence is an age-old one. I am employing a remedy which is unknown to the world on the political field. But since you have come all the way from China merely to reciprocate the good wishes that Pandit Jawaharlal carried there, the only service I can render in my humble way is to put forward before you and, through you, the Generalissimo, the new remedy I am applying. I found it in South Africa in 1906, when all my resources were exhausted, in order to combat difficulties which might have meant the death of the Indian community in the Transvaal if we had not found this remedy. And since 1920, we have applied this remedy more or less successfully, perhaps with more success than otherwise, till at last the Congress has become a powerful body, and in a nutshell, it is this, viz., to be prepared to die as bravely as the bravest Chinese soldier, but without trying to kill your opponent or do the slightest harm to him, whether in offence or self-defence. If we succeed here in instilling into the mass mind bravery to die without killing, I think that not only shall we have regained our liberty without violence but we shall have presented to the world a remedy to do away with all wars. If I have succeeded in giving you the kernel of the movement, I would ask you to watch this movement with interest and bless it on behalf of China. More I cannot say until we have regained our liberty with these absolutely peaceful means.

You will see that it is not without a purpose that I have taken up the wheel at the present moment when, ordinarily speaking, it would be discourtesy to a guest to keep spinning when he comes. But I have taken it up both to demonstrate the process and to show you how, externally speaking, I derive all the power of peace from the spinning-wheel. You will have noticed that the spinning-wheel finds a central place in our national flag, and it is the one thing which establishes a living relation and identification with the masses of India.

Please carry my good wishes to the Generalissimo, to the Madame, his staff and all who are putting up a brave fight in self-defence and I wish you early peace.

(Talking to Tai Chi Tao, President of the Examination Yuan of the Chinese Government, Nov. 22-23, 1940, *ibid*, Vol. 73, pp. 190-91.)

October, 1941

If we cannot take the weavers in our fold nothing will get done. But we cannot go by mere faith. Today they are using mill yarn. We have to change this situation. We have to give them handspun yarn. My feeling is that the War is not going to end soon. No import of cloth will be possible. Prices of textiles will also rise. Only Indian mills will be manufacturing cloth for use in India. A time may come when they will not be able to supply all our requirement. Cloth in India will then become scarce. In China too such a situation had arisen. But the Chinese are a hard-working people. They started the charkha in every home and in their own way quickly solved the problem. Our method will be a little different but the effort required will be as much or more. A day may come when people will ask us for cloth. It would be a disgrace to tell them that we could not supply it.

(Speech at AISA Meeting, in *Khadi Jagat* (Hindi Journal), October, 1941, *ibid*, Vol. 74, p. 390.)

February 11, 1942

Dearest friend,

As you know I am living in a village out of touch with the outside world. I came to know of your arrival in my country side by side with the precious message from Pandit Nehru that you were coming to Wardha and to grace my cottage with your presence. And so I refrained from sending you a word of welcome. But to my great sorrow I have just learnt that you would not be able to come to Wardha and you would not think of letting me come to you. I must leave you to imagine my sorrow that although you are in my country I shall miss seeing you and your noble partner. We know each other through correspondence but much more through Jawaharlal Nehru. I have many ties with your country. I know that your's is a vaster country than mine. And I do not know that your's is not a more ancient culture than ours. I know what it is to lose one's liberty, having lost it for so many centuries. My whole heart goes out to you in your fight to preserve your own. May God crown your effort with success. The knowledge, that circumstances over which you and I have no control make it impossible for us to meet brings us closer in spirit.

(Letter to Generalissimo Chiang Kai-shek, Feb. 11, 1942, *ibid*, Vol. 75, pp. 306-307.)

February 13, 1942

Generalissimo Chiang Kai-shek, Delhi

It has caused me greatest grief to learn you and your partner cannot visit Sevagram where my wife and the little settlement were looking forward to receiving you. Failing this I would have gone anywhere to see you whilst you were on Indian soil. But I understand from Pandit Nehru that it could not be. I must be satisfied with being in spirit with you. All good wishes for yourselves and your country follow you.

(Telegram to Chiang Kai-shek, Feb. 13, 1942, *ibid*, p. 313.)

June 10, 1942

I say that the British power in India should go today for the world peace, for China, for Russia and for the Allied cause....

QUIT INDIA MOVEMENT may not interfere with the movement of British troops, but it is sure to engage British attention. It would be wrong of them to reject my proposal and say India should remain a slave in order that Britain may win or be able to defend China. I cannot accept that degrading position. India free and independent will play a prominent part in defending China. Today I do not think she is rendering any real help to China. We have followed the non-embarrassment policy so far. We will follow it even now. But we cannot allow the British Government to exploit it in order to strengthen the stranglehold on India. And today it amounts to that. The way, for instance, in which thousands are being asked to vacate their homes with nowhere to go to, no land to cultivate, no resources to fall back upon, is the reward of our non-embarrassment. This should be impossible in any free country. I cannot tolerate India submitting to this kind of treatment. It means greater degradation and servility, and when a whole nation accepts servility it means good-bye for ever to freedom....

I have waited long, and I can wait no longer. It is a terrible tragedy that 40 crores of people should have no say in this war. If we have the freedom to play our part we can arrest the march of Japan and save China.

It is fear of the Japanese that makes him [Rajaji] tolerate the British rule. He would postpone the question of freedom until after the war. On the contrary I say that if the war is to be decisively won, India must be freed to play her part today. I find no flaw in my position. I have arrived at it after considerable debating within myself; I am doing nothing in hurry or anger. There is not the slightest room in me for accommodating the Japanese. No, I am sure that India's independence is not only essential for India, but for China and the Allied cause.

India lying at the feet of Great Britain may mean China lying at the feet of Japan. I cannot help using this language. I feel it. You may think it startling and big. But why should it be startling? Think of 400 million people hungering for freedom. They want to be left alone. They are not savages. They have an ancient culture, ancient civilization, such variety and richness of languages. Britain should be ashamed of holding these people as slaves. You may say: "You deserve it!" If you do, I will simply say it is not right for any nation to hold another in bondage.

(Interview to Preston Grover, Wardha, June 10, 1942, *ibid*, Vol. 76, pp. 207-12.)

June 14, 1942

Dear Generalissimo,

I can never forget the five hours' close contact I had with you and your noble wife in Calcutta. I had always felt drawn towards you in your fight for freedom, and that contact and our conversation brought China and her problems still nearer to me. Long ago, between 1905 and 1913, when I was in South Africa, I was in constant touch with the small Chinese colony in Johannesburg. I knew them first as clients and then as comrades in the Indian passive resistance struggle in South Africa. I came in touch with them in Mauritius also. I learnt then to admire their thrift, industry, resourcefulness and internal unity. Later in India I had a very fine Chinese friend living with me for a few years and we all learnt to like him.

I have thus felt greatly attracted towards your great country and, in common with my countrymen, our sympathy has gone out to you in your terrible struggle. Our mutual friend, Jawaharlal Nehru, whose love of China is only excelled, if at all, by his love of his own country, has kept us in intimate touch with the developments of the Chinese struggle.

Because of this feeling I have towards China and my earnest desire that our two great countries should come closer to one another and co-operate to their mutual advantage, I am anxious to explain to you that my appeal to the British power to withdraw from India is not meant in any shape or form to weaken India's defence against the Japanese or embarrass you in your struggle. India must not submit to any aggressor or invader and must resist him. I would not be guilty of purchasing the freedom of my country at the cost of your country's freedom. That problem does not arise before me as I am clear that India cannot gain her freedom in this way, and a Japanese domination of either India or China would be equally injurious to the other country and to world peace. That domination must therefore be prevented and I should like India to play her natural and rightful part in this.

I feel India cannot do so while she is in bondage. India has been a helpless witness of the withdrawals from Malaya, Singapore and Burma. We must learn the lesson from these tragic events and prevent by all means at our disposal a repetition of what befell these unfortunate countries. But unless we are free we can do nothing to prevent it, and the same process might well occur again, crippling India and China disastrously. I do not want a repetition of this tragic tale of woe.

Our proferred help has repeatedly been rejected by the British Government and the recent failure of the Cripps Mission has left a deep wound which is still running. Out of that anguish has come the cry for immediate withdrawal of British power so that India can look after herself and help China to the best of her ability.

I have told you of my faith in non-violence and of my belief in the effectiveness of this method if the whole nation could turn to it. That faith in it is as firm as ever. But I realize that India today as a whole has not that faith and belief, and the Government in free India would be formed from the various elements composing the nation.

Today the whole of India is impotent and feels frustrated. The Indian army consists largely of people who have joined up because of economic pressure. They have no feeling of a cause to fight for, and in no sense are they a national army. Those of us who would fight for a cause, for India and China, with armed forces or with non-violence, cannot under the foreign heel, function as they want to. And yet our people know for certain that India free can play even a decisive part not only on her own behalf, but also on behalf of China and world peace. Many like me feel that it is not proper or manly to remain in this helpless state and allow events to overwhelm us when a way to effective action can be opened to us. They feel, therefore, that every possible effort should be made to ensure independence and that freedom of action which is so urgently needed. This is the origin of my appeal to the British power to end immediately the unnatural connection between Britain and India.

Unless we make the effort there is a grave danger of public feeling in India going into wrong and harmful channels. There is every likelihood of subterranean sympathy for Japan growing simply in order to weaken and oust British authority in India. This feeling may take the place of robust confidence in our ability never to look to outsiders for help in winning our freedom. We have to learn self-reliance and develop the strength to work out our own salvation. This is only possible if we make a determined effort to free ourselves from bondage. That freedom has become a present necessity to enable us to take our due place among the free nations of the world.

To make it perfectly clear that we want to prevent in every way Japanese aggression, I would personally agree that the Allied Powers might, under treaty with us, keep their armed forces in India and use the country as a base for operations against the threatened Japanese attack.

I need hardly give you my assurance that, as the author of the new move in India, I shall take no hasty action. And whatever action I may recommend will be governed by the consideration that it should not injure China, or encourage Japanese aggression in India or China. I am trying to enlist world opinion in favour of a proposition which to me appears self-proved and which must lead to the strengthening of India's and China's defence. I am also educating public opinion in India and conferring with my colleagues. Needless to say, any movement against the British Government with which I may be connected will be essentially non-violent. I am straining every nerve to avoid a conflict with British authority. But if in the vindication of the freedom which has become an immediate desideratum, this becomes inevitable, I shall not hesitate to run any risk however great.

Very soon you will have completed five years of war against Japanese aggression and invasion and all the sorrow and misery that these have brought to China. My heart goes out to the people of China in deep sympathy and in admiration for their heroic struggle and endless sacrifices in the cause of their country's freedom and integrity against tremendous odds. I am convinced that this heroism and sacrifice cannot be in vain; they must bear fruit. To you, to Madame Chiang and to the great people of China, I send my earnest and sincere wishes for your success. I look forward to the day when a free India and a free China will co-operate together in friendship and brotherhood for their own good and for the good of Asia and the world.

In anticipation of your permission, I am taking liberty of publishing this letter in *Harijan.*

(*Ibid,* Vol. 76, pp. 223-26.)

July 15, 1942

The Congress resolution itself hints at the possibility of a large number of Indians going over to the Japanese side— if they effected a landing on the Indian shores — as we now know happened in Burma, Malaya and for aught I know Singapore too. I am of the opinion that this might have been prevented at least so far as Burma is concerned, if she had been made independent. But it was not done. We know the result. We are determined so far as it is humanly possible to secure our independence, so that no Indian worth the name would then think of going over to the Japanese side. It would then become as much India's interest as the Allies' interest to resist Japanese aggression with all her might.

China never tried any experiment in non-violence. That the Chinese remained passive for some time is no proof that it was a non-violent attitude. For the first time in history non-violence instead of being confined to individuals, religious enthusiasts and mystics, has been brought down to the political field and been experimented on by vast masses of mankind. Just imagine, that instead of a few Indians, or even a million or so, all 400,000,000 Indians were non-violent, would Japan make any headway in India, unless they were intent upon exterminating all the four hundred million?

If India were to listen to me, she would give non-violent help to China. But I know that will not be. Free India would want to be militarist. She will then get all the material and men she needs — although it appears that China with her vast populations will not need men. Today unfree India cannot send a single person to China. I go further — free India can even plead with Japan and Japan will have to listen.

As we have said in our resolution all hopes have been dashed to pieces. The burden is shifted. But it is open to America, to Britain, to China and even to Russia to plead for India which is pining for freedom.

(Interview with foreign correspondents, July 15,1942, in *Harijan*, July 26, 1942, *ibid*, pp. 299-303.)

July 26, 1942

TO EVERY JAPANESE

I must confess at the outset that though I have no ill-will against you, I intensely dislike your attack upon China. From your lofty height you have descended to imperial ambition. You will fail to realize that ambition and may become the authors of the dismemberment of Asia, thus unwittingly preventing World Federation and brotherhood without which there can be no hope for humanity.

Ever since I was a lad of eighteen studying in London, over fifty years ago, I learnt, through the writings of the late Sir Edwin Arnold, to prize the many excellent qualities of your nation. I was thrilled when in South Africa I learnt of your brilliant victory over Russian arms. After my return to India from South Africa in 1915, I came in close touch with Japanese monks who lived as members of our Ashram from time to time. One of them became a valuable member of the Ashram in Sevagram, and his application to duty, his dignified bearing, his unfailing devotion to daily worship, affability, unruffledness under varying circumstances and his natural smile, which was positive evidence of his inner peace, had endeared him to all of us. And now that owing to your declaration of war against Great Britain he has been taken away from us, we miss him as a dear co-worker. He has left behind him as a memory his daily prayer and his little drum, to the accompaniment of which we open our morning and evening prayers.

In the background of these pleasant recollections I grieve deeply as I contemplate what appears to me to be your unprovoked attack against China and, if reports are to be believed, your merciless devastation of that great and ancient land.

It was a worthy ambition of yours to take equal rank with the great powers of the world. Your aggression against China and your alliance with the Axis powers was surely an unwarranted excess of the ambition.

I should have thought that you would be proud of the fact that great and ancient people, whose old classical literature you have adopted as your own, are your neighbours. Your understanding of one another's history, tradition, literature should bind you as friends rather than make you the enemies you are today.

If I was a free man, and if you allowed me to come to your country, frail though I am, I would not mind risking my health, maybe my life, to come to your country to plead with you to desist from the wrong you are doing to China and the world and therefore to yourself.

But I enjoy no such freedom. And we are in the unique position of having to resist an imperialism that we detest no less than yours and Nazism. Our resistance to it does not mean harm to the British people. We seek to convert them. Ours is an unarmed revolt against British rule. An important party in the country is engaged in a deadly but friendly quarrel with the foreign rulers.

But in this they need no aid from foreign powers. You have been gravely misinformed, as I know you are, that we have chosen this particular moment to embarrass the Allies when your attack against India is imminent. If we wanted to turn Britain's difficulty into our opportunity we should have done it as soon as the war broke out nearly three years ago.

Our movement demanding the withdrawal of the British power from India should in no way be misunderstood. In fact if we are to believe your reported anxiety for the independence of India, a recognition that independence by Britain should leave you no excuse for any attack on India. Moreover the reported profession sorts ill with your ruthless aggression against China.

I would ask you to make no mistake about the fact that you will be sadly disillusioned if you believe that you will receive a willing welcome from India. The end and aim of the movement for British withdrawal is to prepare India, by making her free for resisting all militarist and imperialist ambition, whether it is called British Imperialism, German Nazism, or your pattern. If we do not, we shall have been ignoble spectators of the militarization of the world in spite of our belief that in non-violence we have the only solvent of the militarist spirit and ambition. Personally I fear that without declaring the independence of India the Allied powers will not be able to beat the Axis combination which has raised violence to the dignity of a religion. The Allies cannot beat you and your partners unless they beat you in your ruthless and skilled warfare. If they copy it their declaration that they will save the world for democracy and individual freedom must come to naught. I feel that they can only gain strength to avoid copying your ruthlessness by declaring and recognizing now the freedom of India, and turning sullen India's forced co-operation into freed India's voluntary co-operation.

To Britain and the Allies we have appealed in the name of justice, in proof of their professions, and in their own self-interest. To you I appeal in the name of humanity. It is a marvel to me that you do not see that ruthless warfare is nobody's monopoly. If not the Allies some other power will certainly improve upon your method and beat you with your own weapon. Even if you will leave no legacy to your people of which they would feel proud. They cannot take pride in a recital of cruel deeds however skilfully achieved.

Even if you win it will not prove that you were in the right; it will only prove that your power of destruction was greater. This applies obviously to the Allies too, unless they perform now the just and righteous act of freeing India as an earnest and promise of similarly freeing all other subject peoples in Asia and Africa.

Our appeal to Britain is coupled with the offer of free India's willingness to let the Allies retain their troops in India. The offer is made in order to prove that we do not in any way mean to harm the Allied cause, and in order to prevent you from being misled into feeling that you have but to step into the country that Britain has vacated. Needless to repeat that if you cherish any such idea and will carry it out, we will not fail in resisting you with all the might that our country can muster. I address this appeal to you in the hope that our movement may even influence you and your partners in the right direction and deflect you and them from the course which is bound to end in your moral ruin and the reduction of human beings to robots.

The hope of your response to my appeal is much fainter than that of response from Britain. I know that the British are not devoid of a sense of justice and they know me. I do not know you enough to be able to judge. All I have read tells me that you listen to no appeal but to the sword. How I wish that you are cruelly misrepresented and that I shall touch the right chord in your heart! Anyway I have an undying faith in the responsiveness of human nature. On the strength of that is that faith which has prompted this appeal to you.

(Appeal to Japanese, being published by Japanese newspapers, *Nichi Nichi, Yomiuri, Miyako* in *Harijan*, July 26, 1942, *ibid*, pp. 309-12.)

September 10, 1942

The use of tea is said to have originated in China. It has a special use in that country. As a rule, one cannot rely on the purity of drinking-water in China and therefore it must be boiled before use to ensure safety. Some clever Chinaman discovered a grass called tea which when added to boiling water in a very small quantity gave it a golden colour.

(Gandhi thought, same like coffee and cocoa, tea was not required by human body.)

("Ray to Health" *Arogyani Chavi*, in Gujarati original rendered into Hindi, then, English, Sept. 10, 1942, *ibid*, Vol. 77, p. 14.)

October 11, 1942

...[A century] ago, what is known as the Opium War took place between China and Great Britain. China did not wish to buy opium from India. But the English wanted to impose it on China. India was also to blame, in that several Indians had taken opium contracts in India. The trade paid well and the treasury received crores of rupees as opium revenue. This was obviously an immoral trade and yet it went on flourishing. Finally, as a result of a mighty agitation in England, it was stopped. A thing of this type, which simply ruins people, should not be tolerated for a single minute.

(October 11, 1942, *ibid*, p. 17.)

April 29, 1945

I long for the real friendship between China and India based not on economics or politics but on irresistible attraction. Then will follow real brotherhood of man.

(Letter to Prof. Tan Yun-shan dated Mahabaleshwar April 29, 1945, *ibid*, Vol. 94, p. 199.)

November 5, 1947

I consider myself a Chinese.

(Gandhiji added, he was no stranger to the Chinese. He had lived among them in South Africa and many of them were in jail with him during the passive resistance movement there.)

India is a great friend of China. In Pandit Nehru, China has a guarantee of that friendship.

(Interview to Chinese delegation of *ibid*, Vol. 89, p. 476.)

7

PANDIT JAWAHARLAL NEHRU

January 16, 1929

Unfortunately little is known in India of the present conditions in China. It is generally assumed that China has gained her freedom from Western imperialism. A resolution congratulating China was passed by the National Congress although some of us pointed out the true facts and opposed the resolution.

(Letter to Soong Chingling, *Selected Works of Jawaharlal Nehru, henceforth, SWJN*, Vol. 4, p. 85.)

July 3, 1937

India and China — vast countries, but bigger than the size of these great countries are the problems that face them. Both are world problems of the first magnitude, and what happens ultimately in India or China is of great significance to the world at large. It is right, therefore, that we should know each other well and understand each other, for we may have much to do with each other in the future.

(Foreword for the Chinese translation of India and the World, J.N. Correspondence, N.M.M.L. i.e. Nehru Memorial Museum and Library.)

July 7, 1938

There are no two countries which have had so long and continuous a stream of culture...The world today, so advanced in many ways, is yet showing shocking deterioration of morality, and in arresting its spread, the countries like China and India with their great cultures have a mission.

(*SWJN*, Vol. 9, p. 56.)

July 31, 1938

All Asians are aware that the Heavenly Empire (China) is fighting for their common aim. The Indian sympathies for China are understandable, as China is nearest to us and our relations with her are thousand-years old.

(*Jawaharlal Nehru Papers*, pt. III sn 284, N.M.M.L.)

August 21, 1938

India's sympathy goes for China for a variety of reasons. Like China, India is aspiring and fighting for national freedom. The forces of national freedom in both countries extend to each other the hand of sympathy and suport....India has a fourfold task to perform: (1) She must ceaselessly condemn the despatch of Indian troops to China and demand their withdrawal as also that of Indian people attached to the British consulates in China; (2) she must organise an effective boycott of Japanese goods; (3) she must educate the people never to supply men and material to the British Empire in its wars; and (4) she must pay to China till it pinches. The ancient friendship of the two peoples of China and India must now be reinforced by the new *camaraderie* of the two freedom-loving nations.

(*SWJN*, Vol. 9, p. 209.)

December 27, 1938

...we have had innumerable great demonstrations in favour of the Chinese people, and the whole of India has felt at one with them in their hour of trial. To send you our sympathy is a poor enough gift when you have to face great trials and privations, even an account of which makes us shudder....I have the fullest faith in China's future and I am convinced that she will triumph over her present difficulties.

(Letter to Soong Chingling, *SWJN*, Vol . 9, p. 632.)

August 5, 1939

The two formidable powers in the world today are Russia and the U.S.A.... The two would-be mighty powers of the world are India and China.

(*SWJN*, Vol. 10, p. 117.)

August 29, 1939

The relation of China and India goes back to thousands of years. Many of our principles are similar and our gains and losses are complementary. The time is ripe when we should join hands and proceed on the path of freedom and progress.

(Translation of Hindi broadcast, Chungking, J.N. Papers, N.M.M.L.)

October 13, 1939

I wish we could do more to assist the China Defence League. At present however everything is in the melting pot here as elsewhere....in discussing the future of India and war aims and peace aims with the British Government, we have laid stress on a free China. We cannot expect the British Government to say anything which might create difficulties for them with Japan. But we do expect that they will not alter their China policy to the disadvantage of China.

(Letter to Soong Chingling, *SWJN*, Vol. 10, p. 552.)

January 17, 1940

In Kashmir I was not far from Chinese territory and my thoughts often went to China and what was happening there. There was Tibet, not far from us, and Chinese Turkestan, but mighty mountains stood as barriers between us."

Letter to Soong Mailing

(*JN Papers*, Vol. 13, p. 16.)

February 21, 1940

The magnificent way in which China has stood up to Japanese aggression has won for her the sympathy and admiration of India and of people throughout the world....The Chinese people, engaged as they have been for two and half years in a life and death struggle, have yet paid a great deal of attention to...constructive activities....

A recent instance shows how these industrial cooperatives deal with major problems. The magnificent road that has been built from Kunming to the Burma border is now one of the main routes into and out of China. This road brings China very near to Burma and India and along this road, and the railway that is being built alongside, will no doubt flow merchandise and all manner of goods. The economic intercourse between India and China will thus grow and the bonds that unite China and India will increase to their mutual advantage.

(*Ibid*, p. 561.)

December 23, 1945

It seems obvious to me that in the future India and China will necessarily come nearer to each other. By that I do not mean mere continuation of the ancient bonds, although they will of course be there. Taking an objective view of the world situation as it seems to develop, it seems inevitable that in their own interests, China, India and some other countries of South East Asia will have to hang together and develop together, not only culturally but economically as well, through the contacts of trade and commerce. They will not be able otherwise effectively to resist the aggression of the so called Western Powers. ...A strong and united China and a strong and united India must come close to each other. Their amity and friendship will not only lead to their mutual benefit but will also benefit the world at large.

(Presidential address at the Fifth Annual General Meeting of the Sino-Indian Cultural Society, held at Santiniketan)

1946

It was through Buddhism that China and India came near to each other and developed many contacts.

(*The Discovery of India,* Signet Press, Calcutta, 1946, p. 200.)

We have seen how the Chinese people, after seven years of horrible war, have not lost the anchor of their faith or the gaiety of their minds.

(*Ibid*, 1946, p. 87.)

The ancient wisdom of China and India, the Tao or the True path, wrote Tagore to Dr. Tai Chi-tao (Dai Jitao), was the pursuit of completeness, the blending of life's diverse work with the joy of living.

(*Ibid*, pp. 86-87.)

In India, as in China, learning and erudition have always stood high in public esteem.

(*Ibid*, p. 88.)

China and India have stood for certain ideals in human life for ages past. These ideals must be adapted to the changing circumstances of the world today. But they must remain to guide us in the future as they have done in the past. I trust that it may be given to our two countries to cooperate together in the cause of world peace and freedom and that neither of us, in good fortune or ill fortune, will loce our souls in the pursuit of some temporary advantages.

(*JN Papers*, pt I, Vol. 48, p. 55.)

January 20, 1946

The news from China that the civil war has ended and a basis of agreement arrived at to ensure the unity and the peaceful development of China has been received with the liveliest satisfaction in India. ...The major fact is that China has had the wisdom of compose its internal quarrel. This is a matter of major significance to India, to Asia and to the world. We all look to China to take and lead in the regeneration of Asia. ...If China and India hold together the future of Asia is assured.

(*SWJN*, Vol. 3 p. 336.)

September 7, 1946

China, that mighty country with a mighty past, our neighbour, has been our friend through the ages and that friendship will endure and grow. We earnestly hope that her present troubles will end soon and a united and democratic China will emerge, playing a great part in the furtherance of world peace and progress.

(Broadcast over All India Radio, Sept. 7, 1946, *Ibid*, p. 407.)

October 19, 1946

Although yet faltering like a patient getting up from the sickbed or a prisoner released from jail, India is today among the four great powers of the world, other three being America, Russia and China. But in point of resources India has a greater potential than China.

(Address to army Officers, Oct. 19, 1946, The Hindu, *ibid*, p. 311.)

November 13, 1946

In the previous summary Russians, Chinese and other nationalities are put in a class apart to whom visas should not be granted without prior reference. This, as I have stated above, is discrimination against some nations which will naturally be resented. We are trying to develop friendly relations with China and it seems odd that we should prevent the Chinese from coming to India except on official or very special business.

(Instructions to External Affairs Department, *SWJN*, 2nd Series, Vol. 1, p. 211.)

March 23, 1947

China, that mighty country with a mighty past, our neighbour, has been our friend throughout the ages and that friendship will endure and grow.

(Inaugural speech at the Asian Relations Conference, New Delhi, p. 4.)

We welcome you, delegations and representatives from China, that great country to which Asia owes so much and from which so much is expected.

Inaugural speech at the Asian Relations Conference, New Delhi,

(*Jawaharlal Nehru's Speeches* Vol. 1, p. 209.)

1947

What more wonderful journey there can be than to follow the old caravan routes right across Asia or from India to China via Turkistan and Sinkiang? I am filled with regret when I think that perhaps I shall never have the time or the oportunity to undertake this long, arduous and yet leisurely journey. For many years I have gazed at the map of Asia and traced these routes traversed by famous travellers. I have read many books about these travels and sought to satisfy thereby my own wander lust. Asia fascinates me, the long past of Asia, the achievements of Asia through millennia of history, the troubled present of Asia, and the future that is taking shape almost before our eyes. Perhaps if I actually visit many of the places in Asia, about which I have read so much, I would be disappointed, for the old glory has departed and often where a proud culture flourished only a backward desert now remains. It is more satisfying to see ruins which the imagination can fill as it chooses.

(Foreword to KPS Menon's book: *Delhi—Chungking,* in *SWJN*, Second series, Vol. 2, p. 406.)

July 3, 1948

It is more than 20 years since I had a glimpse of you in a Moscow hotel. Ever since then I had hoped and wished to meet you again, for to see you and meet you is to gain faith in the vital things of life, and sometimes one wants that faith very badly. You have been a beacon not only to China but to many people in other countries. I do not know if you would realise how much your radiant personality has meant to others. I wish I could come to China and meet you, for I fear you will not come to India. But why should you not come to India for a little while? It will be good for us and good for you also if I may say so. But whether we meet or not, I think of you often and the photograph you sent me long ago looks at me and cheers me up.

(Letter to Madam Sun Yat Sen, in *ibid*, Vol. 7, p. 661.)

(In her letter, to Nehru dated April 9, 1948, Soong observed : "India and China are like giant oxen, burdened with an irritating yoke of outside interference pulling against the weight of feudalism and exploitation". To this Nehru replied : "We had more than our fill of trouble and perhaps you have had more than your fill."—Editor.)

1949

From a world point of view, probably the most important event is the success of the Communist armies in China. Undoubtedly this is affecting, and will affect more and more in the future, not only the entire position in Asia but in the world. For us in India, it is of the utmost importance.

(Letter to the Chief Ministers, Art. 1, 1949, *ibid*, Vol. 10, p. 303.)

The policy of some of the Western Powers has been generally to suport the more conservative governments in South East Asia. This policy has failed. In China, even big scale suport by the U.S.A. has not succeeded in making any difference. Indeed, psychologically speaking, it has been a definite disadvantage. People in China have felt that the Chinese Government was becoming a stooge of foreign powers and have turned away from it. It may be said that the victory of the Communists in China is due less to their inherent strength than to the disintegration of the Nationalist Government and its exceeding unpopularity with all classes of people. It could not learn the lesson in time and so it is passing into history.

(*Ibid,* p. 305.)

May 14, 1949

What is hapening in China is of course of major importance not only to Asia but to the whole world and every step that we might take in regard to it has to be most carefully considered. Our desire has always been and is to retain the friendship of the Chinese people and to cooperate with them as far as possible. That will be our guiding principle.

(Letter to the Chief Minister, *ibid*, Vol. 11, p. 269.)

June 3, 1949

The question of Hong Kong will then no doubt arise and this may give rise to a lot of trouble. Undoubtedly Hong Kong is Chinese and must, some time or other, revert to China. I supose the U.K. Government must realise this, although they have a perpetual lease of Hong Kong. No Chinese government, Nationalist or communist, can agree to any foreign power holding on to Chinese territory.

(Letter to the Chief Ministers, *ibid*, Vol. 11, p. 275.)

June 4, 1949

The Chinese revolution, as I have previously pointed out to you, is one of the biggest changes and upheavals in history and it is going to have very far-reaching consequences. Those consequences cannot simply be judged in terms of communism. This Chinese revolution has been said to be a continuation of the revolution that started in China in 1911 when the Manchu dynasty was thrown out. Since then, for these long years, China has been in great travail and her millions have suffered terribly, and essentially all these ups and downs of forty-eight years have been parts of a major agrarian revolution. No one can say what the future of China will be. The country will still take a fairly considerable time to settle down in any form. Standards are very low there and communism by itself does not raise standards, though a better organisation of the agrarian system does relieve the burden on the peasantry to some extent. Ultimately standards can only be raised by greater production as well as proper distribution.

Competent observers, well-acquainted with the Chinese scene, say that the leaders of the Chinese communists are certainly one hundred per cent Marxists, but their interpretation of Marxism is not always in line with the present Russian interpretation. Apart from this it is always made to fit in realistically with conditions in China. I think it may be said with truth that in spite of the sympathy that the Soviet Russia has for communist China, the former has not viewed with favour many developments in China. Only four years ago, Soviet Russia, in a sense, disowned the communists of China by making a treaty with the Nationalist Government. It is also, on the whole, true that the Soviet Russia has not helped with any supplies to communist armies of China. Their supplies had largely come from Japanese dumps left after the War and from capture of American material given to the Nationalist armies.

The Chinese communist armies, therefore, have gained their success not with Soviet aid but relying largely upon themselves. Therefore they are not dependent on the Soviets, as many communist parties and groups in Europe have been. They have shown this independence on various occasions. Their leaders are undoubtedly able men and they have twenty-five years hard experience behind them. Neutral and even hostile observers have stated that their solution of the land problem is for the moment effective and has given satisfaction to the peasantry. Also that their administration has compared very favourably, both from the point of view of efficiency and integrity, with the administration of the Nationalist Government in China. All this leads to the conclusion that the agrarian problem is first in priority in large parts of Asia, including India.

(*Ibid*, p. 284.)

October 24, 1949

But there is one point about the Communist victory in China. It continues an agrarian revolution that has been going on for years all over Asia. In India we have been wiser. We have broken up the big estates and are bringing in a system of peasant ownership. We are giving compensation to the old owners at a tremendous cost because we think it is cheaper than violence. In China there are no concessions to this agrarian revolution which has been captured by the Communists. Whatever one thinks of the Communist victory, one cannot ignore this basic reality.

(Nehru's reply at the Press Conference at Ottawa, Oct. 24, 1949, *ibid*, Vol. 13, p. 404.)

December 18, 1949

In common with other Governments we cannot ignore realities. The Indian Ambassador at Nanking had been recalled to New Delhi to confer on the question of recognizing Communist China. The basic problem of China is agrarian and the solution of that problem will better the course of developments in China. The same aplies to India. We are putting an end to the big landlord system gradually. Thus one of the major upsetting features of Asia has been controlled in India because of the Government's policy of breaking up huge landlord estates and farming areas and distributing these among the individual farmers.

(Speech at the Verses Club, New York, Dec. 18, 1949, *ibid.* Vol. 13, p. 306.)

March 17, 1950

China is the country for which I have the greatest admirations. There have been big changes there. The honourable Member Mr. Hiren Mukherjee suggested that we emulate China. I will be glad to do so as far as I can but I would like to remind Mr. Hiren Mukherjee that till only a year ago, China was looked upon as a country where corruption, black marketing and every kind of evil prevailed. ...My point is that the situation in China today is not quite what it was a year ago. Perhaps, the People's Government of China is more effective that we are; let us by all means try to emulate them in this respect.

(*Letter to Chief Ministers*, Vol. 2 p. 25.)

December 7, 1950

...there are certain countries like India and China with pronounced national characteristics where history and tradition exert a profound influence on the course of events. I am sure there is a great deal of good in the tradition. We should have gone under but for that.

(*Ibid*, p. 240.)

January 12, 1951

Great nations have arisen in Asia with long memories of the past they have lived through and with their eyes fixed on a future of promise, ...China has taken a new shape and a new form. But whether we like that shape and form or not, we have to recognize that a great nation has been reborn and is concious of her new strength. China in her new-found strength, has acted sometimes in a manner which I deeply regret. But we have to remember the background of China.... We, in India, have had two thousand years of friendship with China. We have differences of opinion and even small conflicts but when we hark back to that long past something of the wisdom of that past also helps us to understand each other.

(*Ibid*, pp. 276-77.)

June 5, 1952

There is no reason, however, why we should not gradually develop these contacts with great nations like China and U.S.S.R. Both these countries are our neighbours and in the long run, we are bound to have greater dealings with them. Indeed, so far as India and China are concerned it becomes increasingly clear to me that the future of Asia depends very largely on our contacts and association. That does not mean that we should copy each other, to interfere with each other. It does mean a basic understanding that our association is essential for the peace of Asia and advantageous to both countries... If, however, we look at the long perspective of history and try to peep into the future, ignoring for the moment our present discontent, then the importance of India and China functioning with a measure of cooperation becomes obvious.

(*J.N. Papers*, Vol. 3, p. 5.)

Indeed it may be said that the three great world problems today are: the fate of capitalism, which means the fate of Europe and America, the future of India, and the future of China, and all three are inter-related.

(*SWJN*, Vol. 6, p. 12.)

November, 1954

I received an extraordinarily cordial welcome everywhere in China....I was greatly impressed by it. It was clear to me that this welcome represented something more than political exigency. It was almost an emotional upheaval representing the basic urges of the people for friendship with India.

Essentially our [Indian and Chinese] problems were alike that is vast countries and populations, cheifly agriculture, with low standards of living and the necessity to raise these standards by industrialization and agricultural reform. Even in regard to floods, we had similar problems. Our approach to the solution of these problems was not the same and yet there was much in common with it and we could profit by each other's experience, provided always there was a friendly aproach and no interference with each other.

(*Ibid*, Vol. 4, p. 85.)

Chairman Mao referred to the age-old association as well as to the new friendship between China and India. Both countries were struggling for peace. They had more or less common experiences in recent history and both countries needed to reconstruct their economies as both were industrially backward. The Chairman considered that India was industrially somewhat more advanced.

(*Ibid*, p. 78.)

The major impression I got was of a country smoothly running with enormous potential strength which was being translated gradually into actual strength.

Another impression that I gathered was of the essential Chineseness of almost everybody I met, from leaders to the public....

(*Ibid*, p. 86.)

I could not help feeling during my visit to China, even more than I have done before, how completely irrelevant was the idea that this great nation could be ignored or bypassed....The time has passed when they can be injured much by [isolating China and not allowing China to function in the United Nations]...It is the rest of world that is more likely to suffer from it.

(*Ibid*, p. 87.)

China was not a threat to any country and wished to live in peace with all other countries. But the U.S.A. did not permit her to do so and even brought pressure to bear upon England, France, and other countries to prevent them from co-operating with China.

(*Ibid*, p. 78.)

Chairman Mao dealt at some length with the past two World Wars and their revolutionary consequences. He pointed out that China had no atom bombs or any equipment of the latest type. But the U.S. and the U.S.S.R. had both. Ultimately it was the people who would count and who would be the deciding factors. He pointed out that the experience of both the World Wars was that the countries who started the war were defeated and those who were on the defence won. Another consequence was revolutions in some countries and the freedom of some colonial countries. Thus, if unfortunately another World War took place, disastrous as it might be, it would lead to the defeat of the aggressors and possibly other revolutionary changes might take place. He was not afraid of a war if it came, but he did not want it because of its disastrous consequences to the world and because it would come in the way of developing their countries. I was not fully in agreement with Chairman Mao's analysis, but I entirely agree with him that war must be avoided and every step which might lead to war should also therefore be avoided.

(*Ibid*, pp. 80-81.)

November 15, 1954

I was particularly interested in what was happening in China and I say that the most exciting countries for me today were India and China. We differ, of course, in our political and economic structures, yet the problems we face are essentially the same. The future will show which country and which structure of Government yields greater results in every way.

(*Letters to Chief Ministers*, Vol. 4, p. 73.)

8

A.K. COOMARASWAMI

From the Chinese point of view the primary function of art is to reveal the operation of the Spirit (chi) in the forms of life; in India it has been said that all songs alike, whether sacred or profane, refer to God, and that he alone is the true teacher who reveals the presence of the superlative Spirit (paramatman) wherever the mind attaches itself; in Islam, it is the music of the spheres that is echoed by the human voice and lute, and every lovely form whether of nature or art derives its beauty from a supermundane source. Needless to say that these conceptions of the world as a theophany are in no way distinguishable from those of the Platonic and Scholastic traditions. In other words, the beauty of the aesthetic surfaces, or that of the natural forms of which they may or may not remind us, is always a good, but not a final good; works of art are like nuts, to be stripped of their lovely material husk, if one would see the picture that is not in the colours, just as to find nature as she is in herself (that nature whose manner of operation is imitated in art) "all her forms must be shattered." The very purposes of art are ultimately iconoclastic; and it is precisely in this sense that anthropomorphic and naturalistic forms of art are least of all artistic, since it is no part of nature's way to imitate her own effects; and the artist is compared to be Divine Architect precisely in this respect, that he does not work by means of ideas external to himself, but "by a word conceived in his intellect," and judges of what things ought to be like, not by observation, but "by their ideas," which he must first of all conceive in imitable forms. The perfection of art is then indeed achieved when the intellectual operation, the art in the artist, by which he works, becomes itself the whole form of the work to be done, which then proceeds from the artist without calculation. And this is the significance of the Chinese "flight of the dragon," and disappearance of the artist himself. For if there be an ultimate perfection towards which all things tend, that of One the very forms of whose intellect are already lives, although not made by hands nor according to any external model — then to speak of a humanly "creative art" implies that the relative freedom and spontaneity of one who is in full possession of his art (i.e. in whom the form of the thing to be made already inheres in all its details), and the "life" of the work itself (which is likewise a reflection of its author's vitality), are truly imitations of this nature in its manner of operation and in its effects.

It is of the first importance, then, lest we misunderstand it entirely, to realize that the appearances presented by this art are not, or are only accidentally and incidentally, reminiscent of visual perceptions. There is no studying here from a posed model, nor any recording of transient effects of light. All of the themes that belong to "genre" are foreign to this art; the nude, for example, is never represented for its own sake, but only when the theme requires it, nor can this be explained by any moralistic considerations, where sexual symbolism is freely enough employed for doctrinal purposes. Even the Chinese landscape is not a "scape" in our sense, but much rather an allusive (and only for us elusive) conversation about the conjoint principles of existence. We must not fall into the common error of seeing in ancient folk, or Asiatic arts an inadequate attempt at that kind of descriptive workmanship which we tacitly assume to have been the goal of art whenever we speak of an "evolution" or "progress" in art. We must not flatter ourselves by saying that "that was before they knew anything about anatomy," or complain that "the" rules of perspective have been ignored, forgetting that our own medical and topographical preoccupations may not have interested those whom we are considering. We must not suppose that "composition" has here been determined only by a search for comfort, as with ourselves, but realize that in a significant art, composition is a matter of the logical relationships of parts, and that if the result is pleasing it may not be because pleasure has been pursued, but because there are principles of order that are common to thought and vision, or in other words because the truth, whether mathematical or metaphysical, cannot be otherwise than beautifully expressed. Not that all arts — even the most abstract — are not strictly speaking "imitative", but that in art, as distinguished from descriptive and scientific figuration, "similitude is with respect to the form," and mimesis is of that sort that assumes the existence of naturally adequate symbolisms, whether visual or aural, or geometrical or natural, since in this view of life analogies are assumed on all levels of reference; and this indeed is why apparently naturalistic forms, those for example of mountains, clouds, or animals, and likewise all human relations whatever, can as well as geometrical forms be used in the communication of other than merely physical meanings.

(From *The Asiatic Art*, New York by The New Orient Society of America, 1965, pp. 8-10.)

Indian influence extended to China, Korea and Japan, with Indian ideas generally and Buddhist forms of art specifically, by direct and indirect routes; overland through Khotan, and by the southern sea route and through Cambodia and Campa. In China, however, where an ancient civilisation had long previously attained to a high stage of consciousness, and had found expression in a solemn and cultivated art dating back to the second millennium B.C., and where, despite the settlement of Indian traders and priests, especially at Loyang [Luoyang], there was never any question of Indian social or political domination, the situation was far other than that of Farther India and Indonesia. The Indian element in the art of the Far East is nevertheless a considerable one; for here there was not merely the acceptance of an iconography and of formulae, but the assimilation of a mode of thought; so that we have to take into account effects both of the outer form of Indian art and of an inner emotional working of Indian thought.

A Chinese contact with Indian Buddhism was made in the first century, 67 A.D. and probaby earlier. Our knowledge of Chinese painting and sculpture in the third, fourth, and early fifth centuries is, however, so slight that we cannot seriously discuss the Indian, Iranian, and Hellenistic influences that may have been exerted at this time, except to point out that all are apparent in Central Asia. Between 357 and 371, however, we read of no less than ten embassies sent from India to China; and amongst Indians settled in China may be mentioned the priest Kumarajiva (383), and Prince Gunavarman of Kasmir, who is credited with Buddhist converts in Sumatra, is said to have painted a Jataka scene in Canton, and to have died in Nankin [Nanjing] in 431. In the contrary direction Fa Hsien [Faxian], travelling in 399-413 across Central Asia and entering India through the Panjab, spent six years in Magadha and Bengal, and returned home via Ceylon and Sumatra. It is certain that from at least the middle of the fourth century A.D., probably a good deal earlier, there was constant intercourse between India and China by the sea route; perhaps also by a southern land route through Burma, whereby the Indian water-buffalo was introduced to Chinese agriculture. Taking these facts into consideration with the difficulty of the northern land route, we might expect to find unmistakeable evidences of Indian influences in Southern China, as we do in Campa. Unfortunately we know very little about Chinese art in the third, fourth, and early fifth centuries. Some of the so-called Han tiles may date from this period, and it is interesting to find that while their decoration is not in general suggestive of India, some bear numerous representations of what would be called in India caitya-vrksas, not indeed railed, but rising from pedestals marked with diagonal lines; and still more curious, other representations of trees enclosed by and rising above the double roof of a surrounding building, just as in the numerous examples of Indian reliefs depicting temples of the Bodhi-druma. But if these forms are of Indian origin, it seems probable that they can only have been borrowed as decoration, and not as Buddhist symbols. There are really no tangible evidence of Buddhist influences in Chinese art before the fifth century.

From the period of the Six Dynasties, Southern China has yielded a few Buddhist bronzes, of which the earliest, dated equivalent to 433 A.D. has been described as quite in an Indian style. The oldest known Chinese Buddhist stone sculpture, of 457 A.D., and unknown proveniarce, is regarded by Siren as derived from the early Kusana type, Mathura Museum Nos. A 1 and A 2.

According to some, too, the Chinese pagoda is nothing but a transformed Indian stupa. More likely the pagoda has been developed from indigenous forms, though under the strong influence of Indian models of the type of Kaniska's "stupa" at Peshawar, which made so great an impression on all the Chinese pilgrims.

In the meanwhile had developed the art of the Northern Wei dynasty, best exemplified by the well-known sculptured caves of Yun Kang [Yungang] near Ta-Tung-fu [Datong]. This is a highly original art, Chinese more than Indian or Gandharan in feeling, and no more Indian in detail than must inevitably be the case with an art representing an Indian religion. This art and its more immediate offshoots represent the flower of Buddhist sculpture in the Far East. Its formal sources cannot be directly traced, but must be in the main Gandharan, Iranian and Indian; it is most nearly related to the earlier mural painting of Tun Huang [Dunhuang].

In the transition period, sculptures at T'ien Lung Shan [Tianlongshan] are compared by Siren with Mathura types of the fifth and sixth centuries, and ... some may have been the work of an Indian artist "well acquainted with the products of the great Mathura school". In the Sui period there is clear evidence of Indian, or perhaps rather, Indonesian design in the pedestals of Buddhist figures at Mien-Cheu, Sze-Chwan [Mianzhu county in Sichuan province].

With the establishment of Chinese unity under the short-lived Sui dynasty, and their immediate successors the T'angs (618-906), with the development of a cosmopolitan capital at Loyang, where resided a considerable colony of Indian merchants and priests, and with the active development, from the sixth century onwards, of the trade route across Central Asia, there was established a closer connection with India and the West by land. Fa Hsien, the first Chinese pilgrim, had reached India about 399; Sung Yun [Songyun] about 518; Hsuan Tsang [Xuanzang] travelled extensively in India between 630 and 644, and is recorded to have taken back with him to China not only books, but also images and relics; Iching [Yijing] travelled in India and returned to China via Indonesia ca. 671-695. In the contrary direction, Gunavarman of Kasmir, ca. 431, Bodhidharma of Southern India, ca. 529-36, of Buddhism in various Mahayana forms. In the eighth century China had direct political relations with Kasmir.

It is not surprising, then, that we find in the T'ang period a more mixed and less purely Chinese art developing, Indian (Gupta) and late Hellenistic elements crossing and intercrossing with the Chinese idioms of the Six Dynasties. There exist Chinese works of the T'ang period that could almost be thought to be Indian; just as there exist Indian and Cambodian works of late Gupta or early mediaeval date that seem to foreshadow Far-Eastern types.

Still more eclectic is the mixed Central Asian art of Tun Huang in the far west of China; this Central-Asiatic-Indian art, though its actual examples are the work of artisans rather than of great artists, forms the foundation of Chinese Buddhist art in the T'ang period; and is almost our only source of knowledge for T'ang painting.

Towards the close of the T'ang period the vitality of Chinese Buddhist art is on the wane; specifically Buddhist art is becoming exquisite, over-refined, and finally lifeless. But there comes into being in the Yuan and Sung [Song] periods another kind of painting, philosophical and poetic, which is essentially a product of a fusion of Taoist and Ch'an ideas.

In the meantime Chinese influence was extending westwards (Mongol period of Persian art) and in the contrary direction Tibetan Lamaism was spreading through Mongolia and China carrying with it all its apparatus of elaborate iconography, and ritual mysteries. M. Pelliot, indeed, has remarked that "a monograph ought to be prepared, dealing with the religious art in Hindu style which was favoured in China from the thirteenth to the fifteenth century".

A specific instance of the migration of a Nepalese artist is afforded in the case of A-ni-ko, who became Controller of Imperial Manufactures at the court of Kublai Khan in 1279, and made large numbers of images and paintings for his Chinese patron. One Yi Yuan became his pupil, "studying under him the making of Hindu images", and this Yi Yuan or Lieu Yuan in turn became the author of innumerable Buddhist figures set up in all the celebrated sanctuaries of the two capitals, Shan Shang-tu and Pekin [Beijing]. Nepalese artists, too, settled in Tibet, and there produced the bronzes and temple banners which are familiar to collectors. There is in fact a common Lamaistic art which extends, from the thirteenth century onwards, from Nepal through Tibet into China, of which the creations are iconographically similar, and only to be distinguished by the gradual change of style which corresponds to the local ethnic conditions.

(From *The History of Indian and Indonesian Art,* New York: Dover Publications, 1965: pp. 150-55.)

9

P.C. BAGCHI

CHINA AND INDIA COMPARED

If two different people like the Chinese and the Indians, who lived in different climates, spoke different languages, and possessed different traditions of culture and religion, could meet on a common platform and work harmoniously for a common civilization, the reason was probably much more deep-rooted than we are generally used to believe. The cultural and social ideals of the two peoples had many things in common. It is possible to discover a community between the two amidst the great diversities of expressions. The same reliance on some heavenly order, the same force of tradition, and similar social ideals characterized the two civilizations in the past.

T'ien and Varuna

The central point in the ancient religious belief of China was the conception of *T'ien* [Tian] "Heaven." The Heaven is the creator, the preserver as well as the destroyer of everything in the world. He is the august sovereign, full of majesty, who created and placed the people in their proper place. He is the guardian of the universal order. He controls the movement of the sun, the moon and the stars, the rotation of the seasons, and the ways of mankind. He sees everything and judges everything. He rules through a mandate which may be withdrawn in case those to whom it is entrusted do not preserve it according to his intentions. He is responsible for the security, prosperity and the good of mankind. Those who conform to his order never have to come to grief but those who violate it get destroyed. One of the old odes brings out his relations with man:

"May Heaven guard and keep you
In great security,
Make you staunch and hale,
What blessing not vouchsafed?
Give you much in increase,
Send nothing but abundance.
May Heaven guard and keep you,
Cause your grain to prosper,
Send you nothing that is not good.
May you receive from Heaven a hundred boons,
May Heaven send down to you blessings so many
That the day is not long enough for them all."

There is a god like *T'ien* in the Hindu pantheon of ancient times — he is the Vedic Varuna. Varuna who corresponds to Iranian *Ahura Mazda*, was the greatest Indo-Iranian god. In the Vedic hymns too he occupies the same position. The name meant "the Encompasser" and the god seems to have personified the entire shining heaven. He is conceived as the king of all, both gods and men, — the universal monarch. He sends the dawns, makes the sun cross the sky and causes the rain. He is the upholder of both the physical and the moral orders. He is the great lord of the laws of nature. He established heaven and earth. He dwells in all the worlds. He is the guardian of the whole world and the supporter of the earth and the heaven. By

Varuna's ordinances the moon and the stars move and shine. He regulates the seasons and the months. He is also the regulator of the waters that bring prosperity to the earth.

Varuna is also the moral governor. His anger is roused by sin, the infringement of his ordinances, which he severely punishes. He is a punisher of falsehood. He is an omniscient god and there is nothing in the world which he does not know. He is a constant witness of men's truth and falsehood. No creature can do, think, or devise anything without being noticed by him. So great and so powerful is the great god Varuna.

Varuna's order is called *rta*. He is the chief guardian of this order. He does not allow anybody, either god or man, to infringe this order.

T'ien-tseu and Rajan

According to old Chinese belief the Emperor was the sole trustee of the mandate of the Heaven and hence he was called — the Son of Heaven, *T'ien-tseu* [Tianzi]. But the trustee could not afford to be an arbitrary ruler. The mandate which he received from the Heaven was not a perpetual mandate. It could be withdrawn the moment it was misused. We have seen that the Heaven was considered as the omniscient and all-powerful sovereign who could not brook the infringement of the universal order of which he was the sole guardian. So the Son of Heaven, the sovereign on earth by the heavenly mandate, had to know the heavenly intentions and follow strictly the heavenly order. Tradition records the fall of Emperors who had failed to understand these intentions and neglected the path of virtue.

Hence the Emperors are often reminded of their heavy duties. One of the ancient Emperors is reported to have said: "August is the Emperor above. Raise your aspirations above common level. I shall like your distinction and humility. When virtue shines on earth it is the glory of the Heaven. The Emperor who follows Him well gets abundance of good. Great is the mandate of the Heaven. It is not perpetual. It is not easy to keep it. In ancient times the Emperors had days of prosperity and happiness so long as they conformed to the intentions of the sovereign on high. Consequently I also fear the judgment of the Heaven day and night and thus conduct myself." Thus a prince who aspires after the position of a true sovereign must make himself perfect. He should fulfill his duties towards his parents, should know the Heaven and the people. The manifold duties of the Emperor, the Son of Heaven, are set forth in the Great Law which is said to have been promulgated by the Emperor Wu-wang in the 12th century B.C. As it has many points of similarity with the duties of the king (*rajadharma*) as set forth in the law-books (*dharma-sastras*) it is better to give a full translation of the text. It is as follows:

"Firstly, the five elements. The first is water, the second fire, the third wood, the fourth metal and the fifth earth. The nature of water is to drench, and to flow down, that of fire is to burn and rise high. The wood lends itself to be bent and shaped. The metal obeys the hand of the worker and assumes different shapes. The earth receives the seeds and yields harvest. Water drenches, flows down and produces salt. Fire burns, rises high and produces bitter taste. Wood, bent and shaped, produces bitter taste. Metal obeys, changes its forms and produces acid taste. Earth receives seeds, yields harvest and produces sweet taste."

"Secondly, the five acts. The first is external bearing, the second speech, the third looks, the fourth hearing and fifth reflection. The external bearing should be composed, the speech conforming to reason, the looks perspicacious, the ears extremely attentive and the mind meditative and penetrating. A well composed bearing is respectful, a speech conforming to reason is well regulated, a perspicacious look conduces to prudence, and application to hearing is the mother of good counsels, and a meditative and penetrating mind attains the highest wisdom."

"Thirdly, the eight parts of administration. The first concerns the good (of the people), the second the commodities of life, the third sacrifices, the fourth public works, the fifth education, the sixth criminal law, the seventh hospitality and the eighth military service."

"Fourthly, the five regulators of time. The first is the year, the second the month, the third the day, the fourth the twelve zodiacal signs and the stars and the fifth the time calculation or the calendar."

"Fifthly, the highest perfection befitting an Emperor. Oh, Prince, by setting example of the highest perfection you will get the five blessings which you must divide among your numerous subjects. Your numerous subjects will imitate your sublime perfection and will help you to preserve it. When your numerous subjects do not create unrest and your ministers do not enter into a conspiracy against you it is the effect of the highest perfection of which you will set the example."

"Do not oppress the weak that has neither brothers nor children. Do not fear those who hold a high rank. Among the officers who are talented and who administer the affairs well, excite the desire to advance always in the path of virtue and your state will be flourishing. Men entrusted to govern are virtuous when they are affluent. If you do not know the means of enabling them to maintain good harmony in their families which are also yours, they will commit crimes. If you shower favours on those who do not love the virtue you will have to repent for having vicious men in your service."

"No partiality, no injustice, administer justice like a sovereign. No special and irregular affection, follow the principles which the sovereign teaches us by example. No special and unruly aversion, let us follow the way that is indicated by the sovereign by his example. Let us, all together, advance towards sublime perfection of which sovereign is the example. Let us reach, all together, this sublime perfection. The exposition of the sublime virtues of the Emperor, when developed, becomes the law of customs, the most perfect teaching."

"Sixthly, the three virtues. The first is uprightness and equity, the second firmness in the government and the third softness in the government. It is necessary to govern the quiet and peace loving men with an equitable uprightness, those who resist and refuse to obey with firmness and those who are docile and obedient with softness. It is necessary to govern with firmness those who stagnate in indolence and with softness those who distinguish themselves by their talents and good disposition."

"Seventhly, the examination of doubtful things. It is necessary to select and appoint soothsayers to ascertain the truth, some by means of the tortoise shell and some by means of the reeds. When you have doubts on an important affair, discuss it yourself, discuss it with your ministers and officers, consult the people and have the tortoise and the reeds consulted. If your undertaking is approved by yourself, by the tortoise, by the reeds, by your ministers and officers and by the people unanimously it will succeed."

"Eighthly, the different effects. These are rain, fair weather, heat, cold and wind as well as the periods. While all the five things come in sufficient quantity and each of them in time, all the plants prosper. If one of them comes too abundantly or fails to come it is calamity. There are beneficent effects also. The seriousness of the Emperor causes rain at the proper time, his good administration causes serenity of the sky, his prudence causes heat, his mental application causes cold, and his great wisdom causes the wind. There are also unfortunate effects. The inconsiderateness of the Emperor makes the rain last long, his errors the serenity of the sky, his indolence the heat, his hastiness cold and his stupidity wind. Let therefore the Emperor examine them every year, let the high nobles examine them every month and let the officers examine them every day. If nothing untowards happens then you will see that the grains have ripened, that the administration is intelligent, that the talented men are honoured and the families enjoy peace and happiness."

"The people are like the constellations (the Emperor and his ministers are like the sun and the moon). Some constellations like the wind, some the rain. The sun and the moon accomplish their revolutions and thus bring the winter and the summer. The moon goes round the constellations and brings the wind and the rain."

"Ninthly, the five blessings. The first is longevity, the second health, the third health and peace of mind, the fourth the love of virtue and the fifth a complete life. The six evils are: the first, a life shortened by misfortune, the second illness, the third sorrow, the fourth poverty, the fifth perversity and the sixth weakness (of character)."

Kingship was also largely regarded as a divine institution by the Hindus in ancient times. The Kings in the Vedic hymns associate themselves with the acts of the great god Varuna and consider themselves as the true representatives of Varuna on earth on whom the gods bestow their principal energies. Varuna is the *rajan*, king, *samraj*, universal monarch and the *ksatra*, the possessor of sovereign power on high. So also is the king on earth. He is the *rajan, samraj, ksatriya*. Varuna is the lord of *rta* or *dharma* — the cosmic law. The king on earth is also the protector of this law. Assumption of royalty was accompanied by a series of sacrifices beginning with *abhiseka* or consecration and ending with the *asvamedha* or the full consummation of the royal power. These sacrifices alone could establish complete unity between the gods and the kings and this unity was essential as authority was supposed to come from the divine guardian of the cosmic order. As the kings considered themselves the counterparts of the gods on earth, a moral sanction was necessary for their acts and this sanction could be procured by offering sacrifices alone that the divine intentions could be properly understood.

The position and the duties of the king are more fully described in the law-books (*dharmasastras*) as well as in the Great Epic (*Mahabharata*). The picture of the king as drawn in this literature is in every respect similar to that of the "Son of Heaven."

It is said that the king is a divinely appointed person. He combines in himself the essence of the presiding deities of the eight quarters of the earth, viz., Varuna, Indra, Vayu, Yama, Surya, Agni, Candra and Kuvera. He is not an ordinary man but the great god in the form of human being.

But this divinely ordained king cannot afford to be an arbitrary ruler. Acquisition of qualities, similar to those mentioned in the Chinese "Great Law," is the *sine qua non* of his assumption of royalty. He must be an embodiment of fatherly love, protection and care. He is the model for his people who rise with him or fall with him. "As is the king so is the people." Even the nature of the age is determined by the king's personal conduct. It is categorically said: "Let a man be purified in heart, let his folks and ministers reverence his acts and he is a king, the best of kings." He is responsible for the happiness of his kingdom. He must learn to control himself, overcome love and anger, and subdue his passions. The virtues of the king that became proverbial in the Epic and the Law-books are wisdom, breeding, self-respect, knowledge, courage, generosity, gratitude, and uprightness. The people suffer if the king is sinful and they enjoy prosperity if he is virtuous. He remains the custodian of the divine trust so long as he follows the path of virtue.

Ancestor Worship and Pitriyajna

The manes occupied a large place in the Chinese religion of early times. Next to the Heaven, their influence was considered as the most important in shaping the future of posterity. Sacrifices were offered to them periodically as it was by pleasing the departed ancestors that their children could expect to attain prosperity, longevity, happiness, peace, etc. Their way was considered as the straight road that was to be followed by their children. This is clearly stated in the old texts: "In the temples the musical instruments resound forcefully and harmoniously. The ancestors hear their sounds. They come down and bring with them all the blessings. They receive the offering through the intermediary of the personage that represents them. Through the mouth of the master of the ceremony they say: you will have a long life. You will have an endless life." At the end of the sacrifice, the sacrifice exclaims as if under a divine inspiration: "The representative of our ancestors has eaten and drunk. Wealth and happiness will be showered on us. Misfortune will never visit us."

Much about this sacrifice to the manes is said in the ancient odes preserved in the She-king, [Shijing]. These odes are often characterised by a simplicity and elegance that reminds us of the hymns of the Rig-Veda. One example from the fine translation of Arthur Waley will be sufficient to give an idea of this type of poetry. To take the Ode No. 204 addressed to the ancestors —

"Ah, the glorious ancestors —
Endless their blessings,
Boundless their gifts are extended;
To you too, their needs must reach.
We have brought them clear wine;
They will give victory.
Here too is soup well seasoned,
Well prepared, well mixed.
Because we come in silence,
Setting all quarrels aside,
They make safe for us a ripe old age,
We shall reach the withered cheek,
we shall go on and on.
With our leather-bound naves, our
bronze clad yokes,
With eight bells a-jangle
We come to make offering.
The charge put upon us is vast and mighty,
From heaven dropped our prosperity,

Good harvests, great abundance.

They come, they accept,

They send down blessings numberless."

Thus it was not merely for long life and prosperity that sacrifice had to be offered to the ancestors. Good harvests also depended on their kindness. That is why they had to be offered all the best things available — the first fruits, good food and drink, the best animal for sacrifice and so on. The details of the sacrifice are also available from the odes. Thus we are told that one person while sacrificing to his ancestors presented cucumbers, the hairs, the blood and the fat of an ox that was killed for the occasion. He offered perfumed wine as libation. The hairs of the animal were offered to prove that the animal was pure. Its blood was offered to show that the animal had been really killed. The libations of scented wine were given so that its smell could attract the ancestors to the sacrificial place. That fat was burnt for the same purpose.

The Pitris, the departed ancestors, occupied the same important place in the life of the Hindu as in the life of the Chinese. Sacrifice to the manes (*pitriyajna*) was the most important duty of the householder. No social and religious ceremony would be complete without an offering to the manes. In the Vedic hymns the Pitris are regarded as the companions of the gods. They live in the highest heaven and revel with the gods. They receive oblations along with the gods as their food. Sacrifice is offered to them with the hope that they would intercede for and protect their votaries. They have the power to injure their descendants for any sin committed against them and hence their favour is implored. They are capable of giving wealth, offspring and long life to their sons who follow their way. The way of the Pitris (*pitriyana*) is regarded as more important than the way of the gods (*devayana*).

The sacrifice to the manes figure even more prominently in the Hindu social and religious life of later times. It gradually became more elaborate. It had to be performed regularly not only in the appointed season of the year but also at the time of the important social ceremonies such as investiture with sacred thread, marriage, etc. It was considered that without imploring their favour none of these family duties could be properly fulfilled. In spite of considerable changes in the religious ideas the importance attached to the *Pitriyajna* in ancient times is still maintained in the Hindu life of today.

Taoism and Indian Thought

We have seen that according to the ancient Chinese belief it was of the utmost importance for the king and the people to ascertain the intentions of the *T'ien* (Heaven) and to work according to them for the preservation of the Heavenly order. The intentions of the Heaven were ascertained objectively by divination with tortoise shell and reeds at the time of the sacrifice. This was the traditional method. A subjective approach seems to have been discovered much earlier and it was further developed by a philosopher named Lao-tseu [Laozi].

Lao-tseu was an elder contemporary of Confucius and lived between 570 and 490 B.C. His personal history is not much known. He was most probably a librarian in the court of the Chou Emperors and it is said that while engaged in the study of the ancient archives there, he discovered his new philosophy. He has himself told us that his philosophy was not his own creation and that it was embedded in the old tradition. His credit was merely to discover it.

The word *Tao* has been differently understood. It is admitted by all that the word cannot be properly rendered into a foreign language. In the old texts it means : 'way', 'way of virtue', 'principles of wisdom', 'the way of perfection,' and so forth. *T'ien-tao* meant 'the way of the Heaven'. It thus came to be considered as the unique principle behind the appearance of things. It is both transcendent and immanent. That is the reason for which it lends itself to be realized subjectively. Lao-tseu believed that it could be realized by religiosity, fervour and mystic union with the principle.

Lao-tseu's philosophy is contained in a famous book entitled *Tao-to-king* [Daodejing]. Tao is defined in it as the eternal universal principle. It is said that it cannot be expressed or defined in language and that "if a name has been given to it, it is as a symbol, if not of its unfathomable essence, at least of the way in which it manifests itself on earth." The text further says:

"This principle which is enunciated is not that which always existed. The being that may be named is not that which always existed. Before all times, there was an ineffable and unnamable being. When he was still unnamable he conceived the heaven and the earth. He then became namable and gave birth to all beings. Man's knowledge of the universal principle depends on the state of his mind. The mind which is habitually free from passions knows its mysterious essence. The mind which is habitually full of passions knows only its effects."

The disciples of Lao-tseu while explaining the passage say that before all times there was a being who was self-existent, eternal, infinite, complete and omnipresent. It is impossible to name him and speak of him because human words apply to perceptible beings. But the primordial being was at the beginning, as after, essentially imperceptible to the senses. Before the origin of the world there was nothing beyond him. His essence alone existed at the beginning. This essence possessed two immanent properties — the *yin*, that is the state of concentration and *yang*, its expansion. Their exteriorization gave birth to the two perceptible forms of the heaven and the earth. The principle thus assumed a name. The tate of *yin*, the state of concentration and repose, is the real state of the principle. The state of *yang*, the state of expansion anJ action or the state of manifestation in perceptible beings, is its condition in time, a condition which is illusory.

To these two conditions of the principle correspond in the mental faculty of man the two states of repose and activity. As long as the mind is productive of ideas it is full of images. It is then moved by passions and recognizes only the effects of the principle. But when the cogitation of the mind stops and the mind becomes void and calm, it then becomes a pure and unstained mirror in which the ineffable and the unnamable essence of the principle reflects itself.

This principle is further defined in the *Tao-to-king* as the "true nature." The superior kind of wisdom consists in knowing this true nature of self. It can be attained by imposing one's own will on himself and in mastering his passions. It can be realized by renouncing all forms of conventional knowledge and worldly activities. In the words of Lao-tseu, a true sage "acts without acting, is busy without being busy, tastes without tasting, sees with the same eye the great and the small, much and little." These words of Lao-tseu are capable of only one interpretation. Man ought to realise the universal principle or the true nature of his self. This principle which is identical with the true nature cannot be defined by words, it has to be realized. Realization is possible only when the passions have been mastered, the worldly ideas and images have been removed from the mind and a perfect calm has been attained. The mind goes back to its real nature when it is completely clean and void. This cannot be attained through conventional knowledge. When it is attained, the mind undergoes a complete change. The man then moves in the world but not as others do. As he is then free from passions he acts but he is not moved by any of his actions; he looks at others but sees in them only one universal principle. He does not then distinguish this man from that man.

There is a practical side of this mysticism. The method by which the transcendental state can be reached is indicated by Lao-tseu in the following words: "Close your mouth and nostrils and you will run to the end of your days without any decay. To talk too much and to indulge in too many anxieties is to waste yourself and to shorten your life. To concentrate the rays of intelligence on the intelligence and not to allow the mental functions to disturb your body is to cover (or to protect) the body so that it may endure long." This method is set forth much more elaborately by his disciple Chuang-tseu [Zhuangzi] (380-320 B.C.?) in the following words: "One should retire to river banks or solitary places and abstain from doing anything just as those who really love nature and like to enjoy leisure do. To take in breath in a measured way, to evacuate the air contained in the lungs and to refresh it by fresh air lengthens one's life."

There is no doubt a close similarity between this conception of Tao and that of the Upanishadic Brahman. Like Tao, Brahman is also conceived as the unique reality behind the universe. He is eternal, omniscient and omnipresent. He is both transcendent and immanent. He is the cosmic *atman* while the individual *atman* or self is one with him. It is not possible to describe this Brahman in language. It is not possible to know him with our senses. It is only by purifying our mind, by *tapas* or by religiosity and fervour that we can realize him. The whole science of *yoga* was evolved as an expedient of this realization. It required complete concentration, expulsion from the mind of all impressions of the exterior world either through breath control or meditation in secluded places. Realization of the Brahman meant the establishment of perfect unity between the cosmic and the individual *atman*. This could be possible in a mind completely free from the grasp of the objective world. This realization also meant a going back or return to the original principle (*karana*). Further, in the Yoga texts it is clearly stated that *Prakrti* or the creative principle has two movements, outward and inward, and when its inward movement reaches completion, liberation is attained. The outward movement leads to the creation of illusory objects which bind down the mind to the objective world. These two movements are similar to the conceptions of the *yin* and the *yang*, the states of concentration and expansion inherent in the Tao.

The analogy can be carried even farther. But what has been said above makes it quite clear that the philosophy of Lao-tseu and the Upanishadic philosophy had some striking similarities. It is impossible to maintain that Tao was a borrowed conception. There is no evidence of any contact between India and China before the 1st century B.C. The ancient Taoism was by then a fully developed philosophy. Besides, we have seen that the conception of Tao was a logical development of some of the old Chinese religious ideas.

The similarity was due to a natural and inevitable development of similar religious ideas of a more distant past. As in

China so also in India the old religion gave rise to ritualism (*karma*) on the one hand and philosophy (*jnana*) on the other. In China the former was developed in the hands of the literati headed by Confucius who upheld the traditional and elaborate sacrifice to the *T'ien* and the manes, the divination, etc. The latter, the philosophical aspect, was developed by Lao-tseu and his followers. Lao-tseu had probably his predecessors. They advocated a subjective approach for the realization of the divine will. In India too the traditionalism was advocated and developed by the makers of the Law-books (*dharmasastras*) while the philosophical approach defined for the first time in the Upanishads was further developed in the various systems of later times.

(Form *India and China : A Thousand Years of Sina-India Cultural Contact*, Calcutta: China Press Limited, 1944, pp. 184-203)

CHINESE INFLUENCE ON INDIA

Cultural relations between India and China seem to have been mostly a one-way traffic. That is why no serious attempt has ever been made to discover any Chinese influence on Indian life and thought. In fact the impact of Indian cultural influence on China has been so heavy that the possibility of any Chinese influence on India has not occurred to anybody. Besides, from the Han to the Song period the number of Chinese scholars that came to India were much less than the number of Indian scholars that went to China.

It is always difficult to trace the influence of any foreign idea on ancient Indian thought. The ancient texts do not as a rule indicate the provenance of an idea even if it be borrowed. India, faithful to her time-honoured tradition, had no interest in the history of an idea. Her real interest was in the idea itself and in how far it could contribute to the advancement of her own cultural ideals. When an assimilation seemed possible the synthesis became so perfect that no trace of its foreign origin could be discovered.

It is however possible to trace certain Chinese influences on Indian life and thought at the very first sight. In material culture we had borrowed a number of Chinese things since very early times. Trade relations with China were as old as the time of Chang Kien [Zhang Qian]. Chang Kien speaks of these relations by the Burma road and refers to Chinese commodities imported from South-Western China by Indian merchants. Hiuan-tsang[Xuanzang], ... speaks of the introduction of peaches and pears in India from China in the Kushan period. Vermilion, I have suggested, probably came from China. Porcelain industry known in later periods in certain parts of India seems to have been introduced from China. It is well known that some varieties of silks(*cinamsuka*) came from China. Besides, plantations of tea and *leechee* were also introduced from China in comparatively later times.

What is however more important is the Chinese influence on certain types of literary compositions and mystic cults. Strictly speaking we never developed the tradition of writing history or historical annals in ancient times. There is reference to *Itihasa* in old texts but we do not know what sort of composition it really was. In some of the *Puranas* we get the list of ruling dynasties and the names of kings but there is no attempt to record the political events of any particular reign or give a chronological picture of the succession of rulers. It cannot be considered as a historical annal in the real sense of the term. Albiruni states that the Shahi rulers who claimed descent from the ancient Kushans possessed dynastic annals which were written on silk. These annals were preserved in the fort of Nagarkot but were destroyed during the Muslim invasion. These are probably the same records which Hiuan-tsang refers to as *ni-lo-pi-t'u* (*nilapitam*) which contained official annals and State papers. The colour "blue and yellow" evidently speaks of the colour of the silk on which the records were inscribed. It is needless to say that the custom of keeping such records on silk is Chinese. The Kushans had very intimate relations with China and it is quite likely that they introduced the practice of keeping State annals from that country.

Since early medieval times some of the Hindu States in India started appointing official annalists to keep historical records of the reigns of their rulers. This is first noticed in Kashmir and Nepal. The *Rajatarangini* and its supplement are systematic annals of the kingdom of Kashmir. The *Vamsavalis* of Nepal go back to about the 9th century. The treatment of historical data is more accurate in these Vamsavalis than in the Kashmir chronicles as they indicate the dates of the reigns and the events occurring during a particular reign. In the East the Ahoms introduced the practice of writing such annals which are called *Buranjis*. The practice of writing dynastic annals is so new to Indian tradition that one is tempted to attribute it to Chinese influence. In China alone this tradition was developed since very early times. In India it was followed mostly in the outlying kingdoms which were in close contact with China for several centuries.

The Indian Buddhist world used to take real interest in China and the Chinese. The Chinese records tell us that a king named Sri-Gupta had built a monastery at Bodhgaya for the use of the Chinese monks. We do not know who this Sri-Gupta was but he might have been connected with the early rulers of the Gupta dynasty. Hiuan-tsang was held in high esteem even long after his departure from India. A story reported by a Japanese Buddhist traveller in India in the 9th century says : "In large number of Buddhist temples in Middle India, Hiuan-tsang was represented in paintings with his hemp shoes, spoon and chop-sticks mounted on multicoloured clouds. The monks paid respect to the image on every fast day."

In the Brahmanical mystic literature, the Tantras, Maha-cina ("the Great China") occupies a very important place as being the seat of a special type of mystic cult called Cinacara or the practice of China. The object of this cult is a goddess called Mahacinatara. The cult was held to be so important that a great sage like Vasistha is made to travel to China to get his initiation to this cult. It is said that he got his initiation to this new form of mysticism from Buddha whom he found there practising the cult in the company of women. However mythological the account might appear, it seems to contain some historical truth. Its implication may be better understood from a comparison of later Taoism with certain forms of Indian mysticism.

Attempts to trace the philosophy of Lao-tseu to Indian sources have not achieved any positive result. Historical relations between China and India started much later than the times of Lao-tseu or even the time when the famous Taoist classic *Tao to king* appeared in its completed form. But the resemblance of Taoism with the ancient Indian philosophy was so striking that the Indian scholars who first went to China could not but be impressed by it. They found something of their own in the Taoist philosophy. The first Buddhist missionaries in China were sheltered in the Taoist temples and got mixed up with the Taoist priests. It is not unlikely that some of these priests on their return to India would make use of their knowledge of Taoism in developing their own philosophy. Kumarajiva who was a follower of Mahayana and a great exponent of the philosophy of Nagarjuna is reported to have written a commentary of the *Tao to king*. Some of his Chinese disciples made deliberate attempts at a synthesis of the *Madhyamika* philosophy of Nagarjuna and the Taoist philosophy.

In later times, specially in the T'ang period, India seems to have taken some interest in Taoism. Towards the middle of the 7th century, a king of Eastern India (Kamarupa, Assam) named Kumara also called Bhaskaravarman who was a follower of the Brahmanical faith, spoke of his keen interest in Lao-tseu and his philosophy to two Chinese envoys in India — Li Yi-piao and Wang Hiuan-ts'o [Wang Xuance]. He asked the latter for a portrait of Lao-tseu and requested the former to send him a Sanskrit translation of the *Tao to king*.

The request was communicated by the Chinese envoy to the Emperor and the latter immediately promulgated an edict by which Hiuan-tsang was entrusted with the work of the Sanskrit translation of the text in collaboration with Taoist scholars. The text was discussed and scrutinized during several days. The Taoist teachers were mixing up Buddhist technical terms as found in the *Abhidharma* and *Madhyamika* texts with Taoist terms but Hiuan-tsang was against it. He was of opinion that to use Buddhist terms in translating Taoist terms would lead to a misunderstanding of both the philosophies.

There was some difficulty in translating the word Tao. Hiuan-tsang proposed to translate the word as mo-k'ie—*marga* "the way" — but the Taoists would translate it as p'u-ti—*bodhi* "illumination". After a long discussion Hiuan-tsang succeeded in convincing his Taoist opponents that a correct translation of the word would be marga "the way". The Sanskrit translation was then completed without further hindrance.

There is however no information as to whether the translation was sent to the Indian king. The translation was completed in 647. Wang Hiuan-ts'o, we know, led three more missions to India, the first in 647 and the last two in 657 and 664. So occasions were not wanting for presenting the translation to King Bhaskaravarman. There are reasons to believe that the translation reached India and was introduced in the circle of Buddhist mystics who utilized it in their own way to develop a new school.

The school of Buddhism is called Sahajayana. Whereas some of its tenets can be traced back to the fundamental Mahayana philosophy, there are others which seem to be quite exotic. The literature of this school does not seem to be very old. It flourished mostly between the 7th and the 12th centuries and its oldest text the *Hevajratantra* may go back to the 7th century. The fundamental metaphysical doctrine of the school is called *Sahaja* or "the doctrine of Sahaja". Sahaja literally means "nature" and hence "the true nature" and it is not used in that sense in any other early Indian philosophy. The Sahaja is defined in the standard texts of the school thus: "The whole creation is bound by this Sahaja nature. It is neither positive nor negative. It has the character of emptiness. It cannot be defined in words. It is something to be realized by self." The method of realization involves Yoga — meditation, breathing exercises, postures, etc., and also a number of mystic practices in the company of women.

It is needless to go into a detailed comparison between the Taoist and the Buddhist Sahajayana practices here. Such a comparison will show a perfect agreement between the ideologies of the two schools. Hiuan-tsang's translation of the word Tao as *marga* was only a literal translation. It did not convey the metaphysical implications of the word and so a new and more appropriate translation was Sahaja. The author of the translation has been forgotten but he was without doubt an Indian Buddhist mystic.

A Vaisnavite sect of Eastern India called *Sahajiya* is in fact a later development of the Sahajayana school of Buddhism. It originated most probably in the 11th century. Its adherence to Vaisnavism is only superficial. Its mystic practices have much in common with the Buddhist mysticism of later times. It retains the doctrine of Sahaja, sets forth methods for its realization which are similar to the Buddhist and Taoist methods and uses technical terms which are similar to those used by the later Taoists and the Buddhist mystics.

Later Taoism therefore was known in India and was extensively utilized by the Indian mystics, whether Buddhist, Brahmanical, or Vaisnavite, in developing their doctrines. Both in India and China their practice was confined to secret societies.

(From *India and China: A Thousand Years of Sino-Indian Cultural Relations,* Calcutta: Saraswat Library, 1981, pp. 247-54.)

PERSPECTIVES

PERSPECTIVES

观察视角

10. A Holistic Eye on Cultural Interface and Synergy
Kapila Vatsyayan

11. The Critique of Modernity in India and China
Prasenjit Duara

12. Enchantment and Disenchantment: A Sino-Indian Introspection
Ravni Thakur & Tan Chung

13. Gandhi and Mao: National Identity for An Alternative Future
Mira Sinha Bhattacharjea

14. Body, State and Cosmos: Mao Zedong's Study of Physical Education
Patricia Uberoi

15. A Sino-Indian Perspective for India-China Understanding
Tan Chung

16. Understanding Xuanzang, and Xuanzang Spirit
Haraprasad Ray

17. Towards an Understanding of Socialism with Chinese Characteristics
Hemant Adlakha

KAPILA VATSYAYAN

10

A HOLISTIC EYE ON CULTURAL INTERFACE AND SYNERGY

Art is an index of culture. It has socio-political basis having correlation with the growth and nature of the culture of a particular group of people at a given time. The more a people progresses from its primitive life the more it evolves a complicated social structure which is reflected in its art, science and literature.

Every human race has passed several stages of life. Civilization grows out of the interactions of the cultures of different ethnic groups. The discovery of the Indus Valley Civilization shows that India was not isolated from the rest of Asia and this was also the case with China. In fact, the culture of a place is not purely self evolved. Cultures are typified in the mythology of different nations.

Culture is acquired by diffusion through various sources. The civilization of a people does not evolve always of its own accord. The more the histories of the growth of the present day nations are traced out, the more we hear of the interconnections of the cultures of different ethnic groups. From a holistic view this is the phenomenon of interface and synergy. The discovery of the Indus Valley Civilization has opened a new vista to the eyes of the Indians, that Indian civilization did not come out ready-made. It was the result of the interaction of many historical forces. India was never isolated in her long course of history. The new researches have proved that from the earliest period the culture of China came into contact with the West. These cultural contacts have been typified in Chinese mythology. In other words, the cultural goods of Western and Central-Asian civilizations have been introduced in different ages in China and these have been described as different epochs of Chinese history.

Cultural treasures are international in their character and they never remain as the monopoly of any specific nation. The best example of this is provided by the cultural remains of Central Asia (a large part of it lies now in the Xinjiang Uighur Autonomous Region of China). It was in the region where many races and peoples met and developed a composite culture. It was in the region where the language spoken was Indo-European, the religion was Buddhism, and the civilization, Indo-Iranian. The art of the region was also cosmopolitan bearing the stamps of Hellenistic, Iranian, Indian and Chinese traditions. This art serves as an index to the cultural condition of the people of this region. As the time passed the Hellenistic tradition disappeared and there occurred here the triumphal march of the Persian art, when Persia asserted her national independence under the Sassanian Dynasty from the 4th to 7th century AD.

With the advent of Islam, Persia lost its importance. The prestige of Iran fell low. At this stage Bamiyan which was an important centre of Iranian culture turned to India for inspiration and the art of Central Asia was revitalised by Indian art traditions and the Indian way of life assimilated by Bamiyan to this region. During this period the Gupta and Ajanta art exercised a profound influence on the art of the oasis towns of the Tarim basin specially in Khotan, Kumtura and Kizil.

Reverting to the undivided sub-continent of India, the first great achievements of Indian people in the field of art and culture are represented by the Indus Valley Civilization belonging to the chalcolithic period (around 2500 BC). This civilization was also known as Harappan culture. This culture indicates a distinct change from the hills to the organised urban communities. In this period iron remained unknown and copper was mainly used. The planned towns and houses with developed drainage system and well-laid roads show a high degree of urban development.

Excavations at Harappa have brought to light a large number of objects including statuettes, steatite seals with inscriptions (which are yet to be deciphered), terracotta female figurines with fan-like head dress and eloborate jewels, animal figures skilfully modelled, painted potteries, beads of different types and many other objects of utilitarian interest. The female figures show the popularity of the Mother-goddess cult in Harappan sites. A terracotta from Mohenjodaro is of special interest representing a toy chariot of which the forepart consists of the head of a horned ram and the rest, its body and tail, of a bird. This type of bird chariot we see from Basrah (Bihar) till the Gupta times. It is not impossible that the representations of the bird chariot in Chinese art of the Han period were derived from India.

The Harappan artists have shown special skill in carving animal figures. They are bold and spirited. Most of them show realistic treatment. Dancing girl in Bronze from Harappa is marked by its highly attenuated form. It appears that dancing as an art was widely practised by the Harappan people. Dance has been held in high esteem in the Indian society throughout the centuries as it is very popular even today. Dance is the most divine of all arts.

Harappan seals and several other objects would indicate that various types of religions, in addition to the mother cult, were prevalent in Harappan sites. They include the worship of snake, tree, phallic etc. The Siva-Pasupati cult was existent in Harappa in a rudimentary form as is evident from the well-known seal from Mohenjodaro that contains the representation of a figure in Yogic form surrounded by various animals. The seal was recovered from Mohenjodaro by Sir John Marshall. He has identified the seal as *Siva-Pasupati* who is also a *Mahayogi* (a great yogi or ascetic) and *Mahatapa* (one who exercised great austerities). This seems to be the archetype or precursor of the later Vedic Siva who has been hailed as an ideal yogi. This shows the interrelationship between the Indus culture and the Indian art and thoughts of the Vedic and later periods. Another instance of this kind of interrelations between the Indus culture and the later Indian civilization is indicated by the Mohenjodaro female figures and the goddess of Lauriya Nandangarh. Such figures, nude and steatopygus, occur frequently in the ancient world in the Neolithic times from Central Europe to the Gangetic valley. These figures represent the great mother. The female ideal and its creativeness play, as we know, an important part in Indian art. Thus the feminine idea of beauty, though canonised by Indian art later, goes back to a matriarchal society where the mother exercised her authority and was sanctified. Her exaggerated forms indicate the power of fertility, abundance and prosperity. Few other art in the world has preserved the ancient ideal of feminine beauty as Indian art has done. Here I am reminded about the magnificent feminine figures I saw at the Mogao Grottoes at Dunhuang—the Bodhisattvas, deities, flying figures etc. These pretty and graceful figures seem to have developed along the Silk Road, and reached their highest perfection at Dunhuang. Then, there is Guanyin, the Goddess of Mercy in the East, which had her enchanting feminine grace, dignity and authority arising from the scenic grandeur among the Yulin caves during the post-Tang creation, expanding in time and space into innumerable art symbols in China, Japan, and Southeast Asian countries that can rival the whole Indian tradition from Indus Valley to Gupta goddesses, to Tantric Taras, and to Durga and Kali of later periods. All such developments point to the unity of Asian and international art. Cultural movements transcend time and space, and cultural symbols transpose from one context to another, from one country's territory to another.

To understand Indian art it is necessary to acquaint oneself with the background which made its distinctive evolution possible. It is bound up with India's great past. That past has expanded and developed over an immense expanse of time and space. Through the ages many great events took place which have left their indelible impression on Indian culture and its character. Many tribes and races such as the Aryans, Parthians, Greeks, Sakas, Kushans, Huns, Turks and Mongols made this land their home. They brought with them their indigenous cultures and then merged with the races already here. This mingling of races and cultures and their absorption into what may be called the mainstream of Indian civilization proved to be a significant historical process rich with many possibilities.

The exact nature of relationship between the Indus Valley Civilization and early Vedic culture is yet to be worked out accurately as no appreciable form of art has come to light which can integrate the Harappan Civilization with Vedic India. It may however be possible that the Vedic Civilization too was perhaps a part of Chalcolithic civilization.

The regular history of Indian art begins with the Mauryan period (4th to 3rd century BC). The Magadhan kingdom which was rooted in the heart of India challenged successfully the Greek political expansion. Chandragupta Maurya, the founder of this dynasty, was responsible for creating an all-India empire. He entered into matrimonial alliance with the Greeks as he married the daughter of Selukos who inherited the eastern possessions of Alexander the Great. King Ashoka (grandson of Chandragupta Maurya) who preached the Buddhist doctrine erected many pillars surmounted by animal's capitals which are majestic in form and execution. The Ashokan pillars are marked by such high standard of polish peculiar to them. Some scholars hold that these pillars were executed by foreign sculptors like the Syrian Greeks. There are others who hold that Ashokan art is indigenous in origin and development.

We have two theories about the lion symbol of the Ashokan pillars. some say that lion was indigenous to India, others think it was a borrowed symbol from Egypt through West Asia. Interestingly, while the Chinese have the word for lion "shi" obviously borrowed from West Asian languages, the many stone lions that have been carved out in various historical periods, and have been guarding the imperial palaces and Buddhist shrine (I saw many of them in the Dunhuang caves) seem to have an Ashokan touch. Lion, after all, has been alien to the Chinese legendary animal kingdom doing duty of guarding ancient Chinese graves. They have strengthened the guards' brigade of Chinese palaces and shrines due to India-China culture synergy.

The Kushan kingdom was inhabited by various peoples, Bactrians, Tocharians, Iranians and Indians. According to Xuanzang's record, Kanishka who was the greatest of the Kushan kings had conquered also Kashgard and Khotan. The Kushans were selective in their religious outlook as is evident from their coins which contained representations of Indian Saivite and Buddhist gods including Buddha figures and Iranian and the Hellenistic deities which led to the growth of a composite culture.

The Kushan period is memorable for more reasons than one, first and foremost being the fact that Buddha came to be represented in anthropomorphic form for the first time during the Kushan rule albeit that the origin of the Buddha image is still a debatable subject. Secondly, the Kushan rulers took great interest in the expansion of the Silk Road trade which connected China with India and Western Asia: with the northern route running through Taxila, Kapisa, Kashgar, Kucha, Karashar, Kizil, Turfan, Hami and Anxi and the southern route through Yarkand, Khotan, Dandan-Uliq, Niya, Miran and Lopnor. The two routes finally met at Dunhuang on the western frontier of China. The diverse peoples of the Tarim basin used different languages: Sanskrit, Chinese, Syriac, Sogdian, Turkish, Tokharian and Khotanese though they were all greatly influenced by the Indian culture from Kashmir, Gandhara and Bamiyan under widespread influence of Mahayana Buddhism, whose devotionalism and compassion were entirely congruent with the needs of a fluid, cosmopolitian Oasis culture. The Mahayana stressed the ideal of the laymen thus bringing the religion closer to life. It aimed at Universal *Nirvana* rather than the personal salvation which was the goal of an Arhat. During the Kushan rule many monks went to China to preach Buddhism.

Under the Kushans flourished two important schools of art, one in Gandhara and other in Mathura. The Gandhara school was a hybrid product — a combination of Indian Buddhist theme, and modified Hellenistic art style. The Kushan school of Mathura was however founded on Indian tradition. It was earth-bound and voluptuous. Another contribution of the Kushans was that King Kanishka introduced the *saka* calendar which is still followed in India side by side with the Vikram era. The Kushan age was a peaceful, prosperous and dynamic epoch in Indian history.

The Kushans were followed by the imperial Gupta rulers (4th to 7th century AD) who carved out a vast empire comprising the whole of Northern Indian and a part of the southern peninsula. The Gupta Age is the golden age of Indian history. During this age, the art and literature reached their zenith. The Gupta emperors belonged to Brahmanical faith but they practised religious tolerence and made handsome grants also to the Buddhist shrines. The peace and tranquillity of the Gupta Age with its sufficiency of leisure for its refined nobility resulted in the efforescence of all kinds of art, painting, drama, literature and stories of love and adventure.

Cave art, an Indian invention which reached its zenith in Gupta period, expanded further afield along the Silk Road. If we liken Ajanta to the fountainhead of cave art, the river flows along the Silk Road to Bamiyan, to Turfan and Kizil, to Dunhuang, to the central and eastern part of Gansu (Binglingsi, Maijishan etc.), and further east to Longmen at Luoyang, and Datong near the Sino-Mongolian border. Ajanta and Datang form the two ends of the garland of magnificent cave art on the Eurasian continent. I am told that the thousands of scattered art caves in Gansu and Ningxia in northwestern China were even out-numbered by the carved sites in Sichuan province where the world's greatest Buddha statue is located. The Indira Gandhi National Centre for the Arts is privileged to be in collaboration with the Dunhuang Academy of China. We have hosted an international seminar of "Cave Art of India and China" and an Exhibition on the Mogao Paintings in New Delhi in 1991 in collaboration with the Dunhuang Academy, having the personal participation in these two historical events of Prof. Duan Wenjie. We have also brought out a volume on Dunhuang Art which is the only one of its kind in English literature. However, what the Dunhuang frescoes have revealed is a Brave New World in art, in cultural synergy and syntheses, in India-China interface which deserves much greater attention and India-China academic collaboration to unveil its magnitude and historical significance. My visit to Dunhuang and interactions with Prof. Duan Wenjie and his colleagues both in Dunhuang and in New Delhi have convinced me about the importance and urgency of strengthening in-depth studies on India-China cultural interface and synergy based on available source materials.

Whether one subscribes to the view that there is an Asian culture or even to something which could be called Asian art in contra-distinction to European art, it is obvious that there are certain underlying aesthetic principles which are manifested in the artistic traditions of many parts of Asia. The affinity is not only at the level of world view theme and content and shared faiths, but is also evident in certain stylistic conventions which are pervasive in the Asian continent and which can be clearly identified. This history can be traced back to the 2nd century BC and continues until the 15th century AD or sometimes later.

Indian scholars have an important role to play in the endeavour of in-depth study. In the sphere of cave art, much of the ideas, motifs, and styles originated from the Indian minds although they were developed, modified, and adapted by Chinese artists in Dunhuang and other places. Inspite of all the modifications and adaptations, the striking similarities in Indian and Chinese cave arts are evident. I wish to delve a little into the motif of India-China flying figures. To begin with, I wish to say that while in European art, angels are known and they are invariably winged, while except for a few notable examples in Sanchi and Bharhut and two examples in Burma (Myanmar) there are no winged angels in India and also in Dunhuang. I would like to call such a figure the flying messenger — a type of *Vidyadhara* or *Kinnara*. The motif is a pervasive intra-Asian phenomenon.

A conscious understanding of the movement of the body which could suggest the release from the ground or freedom from the gravity without either extending the upper limbs as wings of a bird or, in fact, conceptually or virtually losing contact with the ground, is evident from the Indian text of Bharata, namely, the *Natyasastra*. In Chapter IV it describes a variety of movements. One amongst these is the *vrscika karana*.

The most important feature of this *karana* is an extension of one leg, either sideways or forward or backward or crossing with the other leg. The cadence takes its name from this important feature, and all the cadences belonging to this category arrive in a moment of time at a pose which gives the impression of kneeling in static positions and flying in dynamic moments.

The *Natyasastra* lists nearly ten *karanas* of this variety such as the *nikuncita*, the *vrscika kuttila*, the *lata vrscika*, the *vrscika recita*, the *vrscika*, the *mayuralalita simharksita*, the *lalatatilaka*. To these could be added the three *karanas* which derive their movements from the *cari* position and which may be roughly grouped as the *bhujangatrasita recita* and *bhujangancita:* one more *karana* called the *vidyudbhranta* could also be added. The latter four form a distinct separate group which is characterised by a crossing.

In terms of *kinetics*, one has to understand this as a movement of the lower limb, either by using the whole leg as a unit or as two sections of the thigh and the calf with a break in line by an extension of flexion of the knee resulting in an acute or abtuse angle. The static leg is usually bent with the knee turning outward sideways, termed in the *Natyasastra* as the *ksipta* position in some contexts, and *nata* in others. The torso, the lower waist and upper chest can be treated in a variety of ways and so can the upper limbs, with a similar lower limb position: mainly it can be frontal or profile or a posterior view of the lower limbs and anterior view of the upper torso.

I mention such details because I think they can be kept as the basis for reference for anyone taking up the study of Dunhuang flying figures. I have seen some of them on the walls of the Mogao caves (of course, a lot more from published materials), and find that they have been developed into a special genre of art motif and style. No wonder that the flying figures have become virtually the logo of Dunhuang. Though the Dunhuang flying figures look much freer from the attraction of gravitation thus marking a departure from their Indian prototypes, they still bear the familiar characteristics as having been demonstrated in Indian cave art and elsewhere.

I may also mention, here, the close connection between dance and sculpture in the Asian and Indian artistic traditions. Any lay observer is aware of the similarity of approach and treatment of the human form in the twin arts. From the earliest times, the dancing figure inspired the sculptor and the sculpturesque beauty of line and form inspired the dancer: the connection was not just on the level of spirit and content but also concrete form. Indonesian, Cambodian, Laotian, Thai, Burmese and Ceylonese and some aspects of Chinese dance and sculpture leave the same impression. There is an awareness immediately of an intimate connection between the art forms in a region and amongst different traditions of dance and sculpture of the geographical area.

I can easily see the influence of the Dunhuang flying figures (though, in this case, the art form is chiefly painting, not sculpture) on modern Chinese dancing performances. When I was at Dunhuang in 1990, I met scores of art students (including dancers) from Beijing and other places of China who had taken a lot of trouble to journey to the Mogao Grottoes to assiminate the inspiration emanating from the flying figures. Dunhuang seems to have become the Mecca for Chinese dancers as the Konark Sun Temple having been for Indian dancers over a millennium or more.

While it is not possible to go into the fascinating and complex history of interaction between Indian and Asian artistic traditions, it would be worthwhile to understand the nature of this similarity and distinctiveness in the context of a specific motif, such as the *vrscika karanà* on account of its extraordinary popularity in the dance techniques and its continued depiction and portrayal in the sculptural mural and fresco traditions of South East Asia, and East Asia, particularly China.

In India, one of the first portrayals of this occurs in the context of the motif of the flying *vidyadhara, gandharva, mithuna,* dancing *kinnara* and other miscellaneous riches and corner figures. While it is true that most of them do not depict dance poses and very many of them have not been modelled with the dance in view, many of them can be classified as dance poses even if they occur on arches, niches and corners and fulfil a purely architectural function.

The sculptural representation of *gandharva* and *apsara* and of male and female forms flying are found in Indian art from the earliest times. Actually by the time Bharata codified movements of dance, a high degree of stylization must have already taken place to enable him to prescribe the rules for movements suggestive of flying, leaping and kneeling in many chapters of his work. The sculpture representation may well have preceded Bharata's codification.

Movements of flying could have been suggested in a variety of ways and an obvious one could be to take a leap in the air by losing or suggesting a loss of contact with the ground. In the absence of visible wings, Indian, Chinese and other Asian traditions cleverly use poses, cadences and apparels to inject dynamism into the flying figures to win cognizance from the viewers. There is mastery, even perfection, in the artistic treatment of the Indian and Chinese flying figures which is, at once, stylised and symbolic even with the impression of natural ease. In the Indian treatment the principle uniformally followed allows movement only of one leg and at no time is the forking of the legs allowed. This is virtually adhered to in all representations of the motif throughout the sculptural, pictorial and dance traditions of the region covering the Indian Sub-Continent and many countries of South East Asia and East Asia specically China, extending over a period of fifteen centuries and more. In Dunhuang, of course, this adherence to the principle is more liberal, but one cannot describe such liberalism as observance of the principle in contravention. Here, one observes the particular enthusiasm on the part of Dunhuang art creators to make the flying figures appear flying. This enthusiasm is shown particularly on the creation of the fluttering apparel almost always with long silk bands as if wings are added.

I do not intend to give the historiography of the art genre of flying figures in this study, but perhaps, I should trace its genesis to the *Vidhyadhara* from Ranigumpha, Udayagiri caves which is one of the earliest examples of the genre. A celestial figure carrying a tray of garlands is seen with one knee bent in front and the other leg extended at the back in an arch. The weight of the body is on the foot of the bent knee in front and the tray of flowers in one hand helps the forward thrust of the figure.

There is another example of a flying figure found in a portion of a frieze from the Ananta Cave at Khandagiri. The figures on either side of the arch are flying forms perhaps coming to worship the hood of the Naga: the torso of these figures leans completely forward in the direction of the front bent knee and the other leg extends backward; the foot is raised to a higher level than the knee so that it is vertically in line with the thigh and hip. We have other examples of flying figures from the Ramgarh hills and the stupas of Bharhut and Sanchi.

In the Karle caves, there are two reliefs of flying couples sculptured in arches. Although these figures have been identified as early examples of Mithuna, their poses also fall into the category of *vrscika karana* from the point of view of movement. They seem as if the precursors of the characteristic knee bend and the slight back flexion which was to develop into the beautiful and dynamic motifs of the flying figures seen on the arches of the stupas of Amaravati and Nagarjunakonda. In the Karli figures everything is restrained: a slight bend of the front kee balances the back extension of the other leg. It is this back extension which leads to the flowing curves of the Amaravati sculptures. Here their arms clasp suggesting a typical *pindi* and in one of the reliefs the female figure has a pair of *anjali hasta* above her head.

In the Amaravati and the Mathura sculptures the portraiture of flying movement has developed remarkably with grace and elegance. The artistry of the flying figures shown in the Amaravati, Nagarjunakonda and Mathura have reached their artistic zenith, and are hard to excel. I am not itemizing the numerous specimens at other places in India as the list is too long to be exhausted.

The flying figure is just one of the Indian cultural treasures that have been carried to China by the "Great Carrier" — Mahayana. It was, beyond doubt, created to help the disciples of Buddhadharma to expand their imaginations onto the worlds beyond the prosaic surroundings of the ancients. The invention of this motif helped strengthen the vivid depiction of the Heavenly Bliss of the Buddhist paradise. That this Indian invention and its aims and functions have been greatly appreciated and even more enthusiastically emulated by the disciples of Buddha in China are eloquently testified to at the Mogao Grottoes. Of course, we see at Dunhuang that this Indian genre had already undergone modifications and adaptations through its travel along the Silk Road. As a result, the Dunhuang flying figures bear more resemblance to their next-door sisters of kizil and other sites in Xinjiang than to their distant cousins at Amaravati, Nagarjunakond and Mathura. Dunhuang, indeed, has turned a new leaf in the history of the development of the art genre that is dedicated to the flying figures — a new genre of culture and art that serves the specific interests of socio-political development of China in the first millennium A.D.

I have already said that art is an index of culture. When we study the flying figures of India and China we automatically enter into the arena of India-China cultural interface and synergy. I hope this brief study induces research interest and dedications to this arena which is not only a fascinating field, but also a path not trodden by many scholars, particularly by the scholars of India and China who should have taken a lead in the study, and are culturally equipped for the task.

PRASENJIT DUARA

11

THE CRITIQUE OF MODERNITY IN INDIA AND CHINA

In recent years, the very idea of History has been much deconstructed and criticized (see for instance Anderson 1991, Duara 1995). The modern territorial nation and linear History are seen to have co-produced each other as the principal mode of belonging in the twentieth century. Individuals learn to identify with nation states that have supposedly evolved over a long history to reach the self-conscious unity of the two and are thus poised to acquire mastery over the future. The linear History of modern nation-states projects a territorial entity (the nation) backwards in time as its subject (or actor or agent) which evolves or progresses to the present and future. In projecting the presently constituted or claimed territorial nation into the past, national histories seek to appropriate for the present nation-state the peoples, cultures and territories which actually had scant relations with the old empires.

Here I will consider other narratives or discourses which have challenged this History of the nation in China and India. Because these alternative narratives have been largely ignored or marginalized in both nationalist narratives and modern scholarship, it is important to explore their critical potential.

These alternative narratives centre principally around the notion of "culture". The early usage of culture to oppose evolutionism can be found within Europe itself in the writings of Johann Gottfried Herder (1744-1803). Those figures in Asia whose alternative ideas I try to understand through the notion of culture were, perhaps, mostly unaware of Herder's usage, but the circumstances of its appearance in the two contexts have much in common. According to George Stocking, in the late 18th century Herder reacted against the cultural imperialism of French and Scottish Enlightenment conception of universal progress and the implicit hierarchy of cultural achievement. He emphasized the variety of national character, each national culture an expression of its own unique *Volkgeist*, all equally manifestations of the divine realizing itself in the spiritual development of humanity as a whole. To be sure, while Herder may be seen as a source of pluralism and anthropological relativism, his notion of culture never closed the back door to racialist evolutionism. Each national spirit evolved from an "internal prototype": Jews would retain the spirit of their ancestors, blacks could never acquire the "finer intellects" of the Europeans, and so on (Stocking 1987, 20). Thus, if "culture" presented an oppositional stance towards the Enlightenment discourse of "civilization", which since Hegel we have identified as History, it was also capable of re-calling this evolutionism as a supplement.

Within Asia this oppositional mode has also challenged linear, evolutionary conceptions. More often than not, like Herder's critique, these challenges have targeted one or more dimensions while reproducing other assumptions of the dominant narrative of History. Thus, Zhang Taiyan (1869-1936) and occasionally, Lu Xun (1881-1936) denied progress while accepting evolutionism (Ogata 1984), Rabindranath Tagore (1861-1941) and Liang Shuming (1893-?), each in their own way, denied comparability while accepting progress. Mahatma Gandhi (1869-1948) was one of the only significant figures to deny History in toto. The latter half of this essay will seek to understand the significance of Gandhi's thought as well as the mirror in which his total and determined opposition to History was reflected. Modern scholarship has not been particularly sympathetic to these critics of the Enlightenment project. For example, history text-books in America, India or China either ignore most of these figures, or, where they are unable to ignore them, as in the case of Gandhi, assimilate their actions and ideas into the narrative of national liberation or into a lesson on moral courage. There is a tendency to pass over the critique of modernity.

The dominant narrative of modern Chinese history in both China and the West is the narrative of modernization. This has been seen as a painful and uncertain process, which has nonetheless, inched towards a full modern consciousness in distinct phases. These phases are familiar enough and I will just outline them. The narrative begins with the Opium War of 1840 and the initial refusal of the imperial state and the mandarinate to recognize the challenges posed by the West. This was followed by the self-strengthening movement where Western learning was sought to be confined to practical matters designed to strengthen the empire, while Chinese learning was reserved for all essential matters — the classic *ti-yong* dichotomy[1]. With the increasing failure of the self-strengtheners to confront the military challenges of the late 19th century, segments of the literati and progressive bourgeoisie began to advocate institutional reform without challenging the basic principles of the Confucian imperial system. The exemplary representative of this phase is Kang Youwei (1858-1927) and his experiments during the 100 Days of Reform. The 1911 republican revolution challenged, of course, the traditional political system, but it was left to the May 4th movement of 1917-1921, to finally and systematically attack the very cultural underpinnings of the old system.

Of course, this simple linear narrative does not do full justice to the complex responses to modern discourses that emerged in the late 19th and early 20th centuries. Those who responded by questioning the project of total modernization in China, have been called conservative, although Benjamin Schwartz has observed that their responses are very modern (Schwartz 1976, 4). Particularly in the Chinese political context, they have been painted in negative colours as people opposed to the epochal trends of progress and freedom. I would like to extend Charlotte Furth's very useful distinction between two forms of "conservatism" or what I call questioning narratives of modernity in China (Furth 1976, 39-41). The first form is one which tried to separate culture from politics and thus was able to find compatibilities between science, rationality and traditional culture. In this form, culture was often subordinated to the needs of politics and technology. The second finds this distinction difficult to sustain because it sought to exalt spiritual culture over materiality. Thus, the values and ideals of this culture would necessarily shape certain essential aspects of political and material life.

Represented by the national essence school (*guocui*) of thinkers like Zhang Binglin (i.e. Zhang Taiyan) and Liu Shipei, the first type according to Furth, was concerned with the preservation of those cultural ideals seen as embodying the historical genius of the Chinese people (Furth 1976, 31-32; see also Chang 1987, 112, 150). As such, this school was not opposed in principle to modernity, but questioned its adequacy for the life of the nation and the individual. At its edges, I find that this nationalist critique tended to merge with formulations of the East versus West binary which depicted the East as the source of spiritual culture and the West as the source of material or scientific Western culture, both of which, however, were necessary for humanity. Thus the critique of History through culture, while mostly used to anchor the *nation* on alternative grounds, was also linked to a redemptive *universalist* model. Most of the critiques of modernity we encounter in both China and India are versions of this form. The ideas of Liang Qichao (1873-1929) on his return from Europe after witnessing the devastation of the First World War exemplify this model of (national) culture with aspirations to redeem the universe. Liang now believed that Chinese (and Eastern) civilization had a great responsibility towards the world to counter the destructiveness of Western civilization (Hay 1970, 137-140). This model received much patronage from visiting Western philosophers like Russell and Dewey and from its most ardent advocate, Rabindranath Tagore, whose pan-Asianism was deeply affected by his personal friendships in China. Although Tagore's last visit to China in 1929 was welcomed neither by the CCP nor the KMT (Hay 1970, 323-324), even the Kuomintang (KMT) leader Dai Jitao (Tai Chi-tao)(1889-1949) espoused the theme of Asian spiritual unity in the magazine *New Asia* during the early 1930s where he depicted Sun Yat-sen (1866-1925) as the father of a pan-Asianism focussed on China's cultural values. In Dai, anti-imperialism and the discourse of culture coalesced together into a popular Chinese image of the time which saw the entire society as a "proletariat responsible both for the Asian anti-imperialist struggle and for preserving the purity of Asian culture" (Mast and Saywell 1974; 98).

The second type of critique of modernity was embodied in what Furth calls the neo-traditional Confucianism of figures like Kang Youwei and Liang Shuming and was centrally concerned with the religious and spiritual questions. Although they were not necessarily opposed to modernity, they perceived the religious truths of Confucianism as occupying not only a separate, but a more elevated, plane than did science. In other words, this was a realm which embedded Truth that theoretically could not be judged by the standards of science or History. One may see this notion of culture in a Herderian light, but it is also continuous with the self-strengtheners' "ti-yong" formulation which regarded the moral goals of Confucianism as the ends of technological adaptation.[2] For 20th century Confucianists, culture could not be completely separated from politics since the religio-moral values of Confucianism could not but inform the polity and society. This was not true for the adherents of the national essence school because the culture they advocated was in some senses subordinate, or at least, adaptable to the requirements of modernity. They could choose the substance or content of culture to suit the requirements of the age in a way in which a Confucianist could not because he sought to carry over certain substantive values and orientation to the world.

Because he was inspired by the evolutionism of History, scholars have tended to regard Kang Youwei as operating essentially within its problematic. Certainly, he reveals some of the most unfeeling racial prejudices of evolutionism. In his vision of utopia in "*The Great Unity*"*(datong)*, Kang writes of the inferior races, which include all but the white and yellow races, that they will be decimated by the natural principle of the strong prevailing over the weak. For instance, the "fierce and ugly" races of India who die by many thousands in epidemics each year, will hardly be able to overcome the British; since the bodies of Negroes "smell badly", it is difficult for the racial barrier against them to be levelled. Those few of the black and brown races who are not annihilated will marry with the lighter races and will ultimately become amalgamated with the white people (Kang 1958, 142-3). And yet the intensity with which he subscribed to evolutionism should not blind us to another dimension of his thought which emphasized love and equality of all in the world. Chang Hao (1987) stresses the indeterminacy of Kang's ideas drawn from different Confucian schools, Buddhism as well as Western ideas. Thus Kang's evolutionism co-exists (not without tension, see Kang 1958, 41) with a moral quest and activism which derived from a Confucian "cosmic imperative" and his utopia is informed by the moral values of *ren* (benevolence, altruism). Indeed, if one views Kang not only as a political thinker, but as a philosopher and religious leader, as did his disciples like Liang Qichao, then we have to see his ultimate goal as the spread of Confucian moral and spiritual teachings in order to save the world. (Chang 1987, 21-65).

However, few Confucianists of the 20th century were practically able to realize this religio-moral vision in society, at least in a form that made it recognizably different from the modern vision of society. Were they perhaps content with Feng Youlan's (or Fung Yulan) suggestion that "the sage within is simply a man whose outer kingliness lies in the fact that he does what everyone does but understands it differently"? (Cited in Furth 1976, 41). Liang Shuming may have been among the few who insisted that the sage's actions in the world must be realized in the form of a Confucianist moral community. Liang's rural reconstruction institutes were inspired by Mencius: The elite were to be the teachers, responsible for leading the masses and for their ethical transformation. In this sense, the teacher was to aspire to be a sage; the central institutional agent of the government was to be the school; and the cadre were to be the spiritual hierarchy of dedicated students. He loathed the self-interested, competitive spirit of Western capitalism and attacked the Westernized educational system for creating a privileged class that had lost the tradition of the morally perfect *junzi* or "gentleman"(Alitto 200). He sought to re-organize society on the basis of the traditional ethical bonds through such hallowed institutions as the 11th century *xiangyue* (village compact), so that society and moral instruction "could make an indivisible whole" (Alitto 206). At the same time, like Kang, Liang Shuming never really parted with the evolutionist perspective. But it was an evolutionism that was re-worked to rid it of any value hierarchy. Of the three stages of Will that he wrote about, the Western stage, the Chinese stage and the Indian stage, each was equally validly concerned with the problems of humanity at the appropriate stage of development. Of course, as Alitto points out, none of this critique prevented him from identifying the essence of Chinese culture as an absolute value (Alitto 1979, 84).

Many of the same processes and tendencies can also be found in the 19th and 20th century history of India, but the narrative has not been emplotted in the same way. Here, the critique of modernity has almost as much visibility as the narrative of progress although the sting of the former has often been removed. We may see the narrative of progress as tied together at three points by the figure of Ram Mohun Roy (1772-1833) and the Bengal Renaissance, the moderate wing of the nationalist Congress Party at the turn of the century, and by Jawaharlal Nehru (1889-1964), first Prime Minister of India. But the shadow of a parallel process (not quite narrativized) of the critique of History allows us to see how the orderly succession of a linear narrative, as in the progression to modernity in Chinese historiography, may be bifurcated by relating each of these developments to a reaction or counter-movement in the parallel process.

The climax of the Chinese narrative represented by the birth of full modern self-consciousness in the May 4th movement, actually begins the narrative in the Indian case. The Bengal Renaissance of the first half of the 19th century championed by its initiator and central figure, Ram Mohun Roy upheld reason and individual rights against "superstition" and the hierarchy of caste and family. True, he held onto Hinduism, but this Hinduism was transformed into a unitarianism and the repository of reason. Moreover, by virtue of the very rationalistic methods whereby he sought to establish his case, he revealed himself to be a modernist and is popularly known in India as the "Father of Modern India". Ram Mohun and his followers advocated the improved status of women, the adoption of English language and scientific education in Bengal (Ray 1975, 14-15). Even more radical than Roy was the Young Bengal movement of the 1820s, a smaller-scale but more thoroughly iconoclastic movement of the Westernized Bengali youth led by the Anglo-Indian, Henry Vivien Derozio (1809-1831). Influenced by the philosophy of Hume and Bentham and radical thinkers like Tom Paine, they claimed to measure everything with the yardstick of reason. Their attitude to religion, which was informed by Voltaire, led them to denounce the Hindu religion with great fervour (Ahmed 1975, 99). For the Derozians as for the May 4th iconoclasts, the total rejection of the old was only matched by the total affirmation of the new.

As the 19th century drew on, however, the early form of radical iconoclasm against Hinduism and tradition in general subtly began to give way to more complex, if not always more nuanced, responses to modern ideas and practices. Bankim Chandra

Chattopadhyay (1838-1894) perhaps the most acclaimed man of letters in the Calcutta of his days, and who had once described himself as a member of the Young Bengal group (Raychaudhuri 1988, 203), articulated one such response to modernity which was to find many adherents among the intelligentsia of late 19th and 20th century India as a whole. Bankim acknowledged the significance and desirability of science and rationality. The West had achieved progress, prosperity and freedom because it had placed reason at the heart of its culture. But the West was superior only in the culture of material life, and had little to contribute to the spiritual aspect of life. Here it was the East that had the upper hand. Man was imperfect if he had developed only one side, especially the material. The perfect and complete man combined the religious truths of Hinduism with the love of reason. To be sure, figures like Chattopadhyay, just as much if not more than the Chinese, were affected by European Orientalists (Raychaudhuri 1988, 8) who, it might be said, projected a yearning for a "lost spirituality" into Oriental societies.

Bankim Chandra and other like-minded thinkers such as Aurobindo Ghosh (1872-1950) and Swami Vivekananda (1863-1902) occupy a place in the trajectory of opposition to modernity somewhere between the national culture group and the neo-traditional Confucianists. Like the former, Bankim recognized the significance and necessity of modern ideas: rationalism, progress, individualism. But his nationalism led him to claim that a purified and regenerated Hindu ideal was far superior as a rational philosophy of life than anything Western religion or philosophy had to offer. Like the cultural essence school, Bankim distinguished modernity from westernism, and claimed that modernity could become part of a transcendent Hindu cultural ideal. But in practice, the tensions in his thought led him to oppose reformers who advocated reform of Hindu customs and practices by appealing to the colonial state on the basis of enlightened reason. Bankim did not oppose reform in principle; but he believed that change would and should follow from the new moral consensus that would emerge from the rejuvenated national culture, or national religion as he preferred to call it (Chatterjee 1986, 73-79). Thus, as with Liang Shuming, politics and culture could never really remain separate: the religio-moral insight would necessarily shape the vision of the ideal society that had to be realized.

In the history of Indian nationalism, the early 20th century is seen as marking a political break between the extremists and moderates; between those who wanted immediate independence and would use agitational politics to achieve it and those who sought more gradual, constitutional modes to attain concessions ultimately towards independence. From the perspective of culture, this political break also fits, albeit imperfectly, with the incorporation within mainstream nationalism of a discourse of the nation founded in Hindu culture as opposed to the European model of civilizational progress for the colonies. The assumptions of the latter are captured in the Moderate critique of "the un-British rule of the British in India" to which Moderates like G.K. Gokhale (1866-1915) and Jawaharlal Nehru's father, Motilal Nehru (1861-1931), subscribed. Hindu nationalism was exemplified by Gokhale's fellow Maharashtrian, the extremist B. G. Tilak (1856-1920), who took nationalist rhetoric out of the lawyers' chambers and into the streets to mobilize Hindus during their communal festivities. Although Gandhi drew his ideas from a variety of sources and evolved a unique blend, he too drank deeply from this trope of "culture", of an irreducible (Hindu) spirituality as a foundation for his nationalism.

At this point, the Indian narrative of national modernization becomes complicated. We are at a cross-road: should we focus on Jawaharlal Nehru as the flowering of modern consciousness or on Gandhi who turns his back on History? We could by focusing on Nehru and the segment of the intelligentsia favouring the vision of a fully modern society which dominated certain strategic points of Indian public life through most of the independence movement, develop the narrative of emancipation. To be sure, even among this group, there were few who advocated the kind of break with history that we have seen in the May 4th or even among the Derozians. For Nehru the significance of traditions lay not in a transcendent spiritual or moral telos but in the historical development of the nation. All the great rulers of Indian history such as Asoka, the Guptas, Akbar and several of the Moghul emperors attempted to develop a political framework to unite the cultural diversity of the sub-continent. This History, while giving the Indian people their unique qualities, also placed them within the progressive and emancipatory project of the Enlightenment.[3]

Like the Chinese historians, Nehru saw the historical nation through the biological metaphor of growth and decline. The great heights of Indian thought, culture and science had been reached as early as the 11th century and subsequently entered a long dark period of rigidity and stagnation (Nehru 1960, 121-128). To be sure there were short cycles of creativity thereafter, especially during the reign of Akbar and some of the other Moghul emperors, but until the modern period which was uniquely the period of vigour and dynamism of the Europeans, there was no basic growth in India. From even this brief outline, we may see that Nehru displays an ambivalence regarding the question of a pre-formed national subject of ancient times. The end of creativity coincides roughly with the advent of the Islamic period, but individual Muslim monarchs are able to re-generate society periodically. Certainly there was no question of the *substance* of an ancient culture re-appearing in Jawaharlal Nehru's *Discovery of India*. That was left to Hindu nationalists of different stripes from the benign to the savagely vengeful. Even more than for the cultural nativists, culture and politics were separable for Nehru. Indeed not only were they separable, but culture occupied a distinctly subordinate position in relation to history. And as with the Chinese Marxists, a national culture may once have embodied (and will again embody) the supreme ideals of its age. Though not a Marxist, in the way in which Nehru sustained the ideas of the uniqueness of national culture within a modernist vision of History, he resembled the Chinese Marxists when they were not violently anti-historical. Perhaps we can place his ideas somewhere between the nativists and the Marxists in China.

But the narrative has to confront the figure and impact of Gandhi. He is perhaps among the most difficult political figures to understand in terms taken from modern discourses. My reading of Gandhi here owes much to works by Partha Chatterjee and Ashis Nandy. What were Gandhi's basic ideas about modern civilization? For Gandhi the religio-moral vision was so compelling that it could not brook the separation of politics and culture, a distinction regarded by true believers — whether Gandhi or the variety of religious fundamentalists that we encounter in the world today — to be a particular imposition of modernity itself. In *Hind Swaraj* published first in 1909, Gandhi launches a total indictment of modern civilization as it has developed in the West and subsequently brought into India. Gandhi pursues a line of argument that can also be found in the Western romantic tradition as well as in certain Hindu and Buddhist texts. His argument, however, is not founded upon a textual or scriptural tradition, but rather on a universalist moral philosophy. According to Gandhi, the modern organization of society which is designed to release its productive potential and produce increasing wealth and comfort for all, is ultimately self-destructive. Modern civilization actually makes the individual a prisoner of his or her own craving for luxury and self-indulgence, generates a destructive competitiveness and brings about poverty, inequality, and large-scale violence (Gandhi 1938, 24-27, 44-45).

Unlike the Marxists, who critiqued colonialism for its class character but praised it for unleashing new productive forces and technology in "stagnant, feudal societies", Gandhi criticizes precisely these productive forces. Modern machinery can only create the desire for more goods, it can never satisfy it. Worse, industrialism brings destruction, exploitation and disease to a society, and creates an especially exploitative relationship between the city and the village (Gandhi 1938, 68-70). If modern industrialism cannot find a place in Gandhi's religio-moral vision of society, nor can the modern state. For Gandhi, whose anarchism was influenced by Tolstoy, the critique of the modern state flows logically from his ideas about industrialism. The modern state was only necessary because of the needs of industrialism and the co-ordination of large-scale orgnizations. Parliamentary representation does not improve Gandhi's image of the state because representative politics is based on a competitive individualism. In the new independent India, the state could never be the appropriate machinery for the rejuvenation of village society and economy. More important, the state as a coercive agency *could not claim an inalienable authority* for that authority lay in the law of Dharma or moral duty which resided outside the state (Iyer 1973, 253-260). Only religion possessed that transcendent authority by means of which the existing establishment could be challenged.

Gandhi proposed a utopian society of largely autarkic village communities called *Ramarajya* (or the kingdom of Rama, the legendary sage-king). This was to be a patriarchy in which the ruler, by his exemplary moral qualities expressed the collective will. It is also a utopia in which the economic organization of production, arranged according to an idealized "varna" form of organization with a perfect system of reciprocity, would ensure that there would be no competition and differences in status. The ideal conception of *Ramarajya*, in fact, encapsulates the critique of all that is morally reprehensible in the economic and political organization of civil society (Chatterjee 1986, 92). The similarity of this vision to a Mencian conception of society is striking, but its similarity to a Maoist utopian vision is even more intriguing.

If we temporarily free Mao from the narrative of modernity and slice Chinese historical materials from the angle of a counter-narrative, we can make much sense of both Gandhi and Mao. Both were in search of alternative forms of community, alternatives to competitive — in particular, market — models of society implicit in the emancipation of idea. Although Mao held on to the notion of economic progress, their common concern for economic and politically autarkic communes, the loathing of urban domination, the mistrust of technological expertise, and the superiority of spontaneously self-governing communities over systems of representation, whether this was the Party or Parliament, confirmed for both the necessity of subordinating politics to a communal morality.

While History itself for Mao remained within the progressive linearity of the Hegelian-Marxist formulation, the question of human will as the counter-point to the automaticity of the unfolding of History remained unresolved, as it did in the formulation generally. According to Frederic Wakeman (1973), Mao's understanding of will provides an opening to influences from Chinese intellectual and moral traditions, including those from Wang Yangming to Kang Youwei. Wakeman is careful to note that this is not some timeless influence and he tracks it particularly through Kang Youwei's synthesis in the early part of the century which, although we have seen it to have been an incomplete synthesis, identified the telos of evolution as the morality of *ren*. We may see this pre-occupation in Mao's view in the fact that the ability to make History demanded the possession of a moral force, "a kind of revolutionary sincerity" or purity among individuals (Wakeman 1973, 324). Thus it is the irruption of an obscured genealogy of *ren* into the dominant narrative that moved Mao, perhaps despite himself, to subvert the telos of progressive History by the quest for a moral community.

Yet, Mao was not an anti-modernist while Gandhi most definitely was. Mao's communal utopia was not transcendent; indeed, it was immanent and, frighteningly, imminent. Gandhi's utopia was based upon a distinctly transcendent foundation and as such he was able to resist assimilation into the romantic critique of modernity. Chatterjee argues that European romantics critiqued science and rationality from within the Enlightenment discourse. They never called for the ultimate abandonment of Reason, but were rather torn between the demands of Reason and Morality, Progress and Happiness, Historical Necessity and Human Will. These tensions did not trouble Gandhi, as they did many other Indian thinkers and leaders including Tagore (Chatterjee 1986, 99-100). The foundation of Gandhi's views of society derived fundamentally from his composite religious vision of Truth, denying History, and defying the Enlightenment problematique of his age. But the nation was not denied; at least not for the moment. Having no anchor in History, or even in history (which has no permanent anchor), the nation would have to embody the transcendent Truth.

What makes it possible for someone like Gandhi and his ideas to occupy the supremely important place that they do in Indian society and history? It is most unusual to find the general acceptability and prestige accorded such anti-modern ideas among people educated in modern society in other parts of the world. The contrast is particularly striking in the comparison with China, both with the Republic of China (ROC) and the People's Republic of China (PRC). Although I have compared him with Mao, the comparison must break down with respect to Mao's ultimate adherence to the Englightenment project and his violent rejection of the past. Then, of course, there is the case of Liang Shuming who has been compared to Gandhi. Indeed, Liang liked to regard himself as a Chinese Gandhi. But the comparison with Liang Shuming is telling, because Liang's influence or prestige among China's intelligentsia is but a fraction of Gandhi's in Indian society.

To be sure, practically speaking, Gandhi accommodated, and was happily accommodated by, many modern forces, not the least of which was the emergent Indian industrial bourgeoisie, especially the house of the Birla. But regardless of whether or not his ideas are practised in India today, the relative prestige that they occupied itself needs explanation. Moreover, although we are often reminded that Gandhi's political and economic ideas are no longer, nor were they really ever, influential in India, they have existed as a strong oppositional force criticizing the establishment. Oppositional groups inspired by Gandhian ideas seek to critique the most extreme effects of modernity and provide ways, however meagre, of mitigating its most destructive results, whether they be the social costs of large-scale industrialism and urbanism, the untramelled growth of state power in the name of progress, or the unforseen devastation of the environment. In particular, the environmental movement, especially in India, has led to a resurgence of interest in Gandhi's critique of modernity. The critique of modernity may have been finally domesticated by Indian nationalism, but it has not disappeared.

I propose to undertake two strategies to explain the differences in the weight and influence of anti-modern ideas in India and China among the intelligentsia and elites more widely. I wish to underline that my strategies refer particularly to the ways in which these politically active elites — the designers of these new nation-states — represent themselves and their visions of political community; they do not refer to some abstract entity such as Indian or Chinese political cultures. The first strategy will seek the possible institutional anchors for such anti-modernist perspectives in the different political cultures of these elites. This strategy will provide us with the necessary but not sufficient condition to explain the difference. The second strategy considers the particular ideological conjuncture in which Gandhian ideas emerged and took root. This had much to do with the specific circumstances of imperialism and modes of resistance in the two countries: with Gandhian resistance to direct British rule and the Chinese response first to indirect imperialism, and then the military and ideological resistance to Japanese imperialism. The first strategy appeals to an argument for cultural difference in the way the elite was integrated with the polity, the second to differences in ideology and cultural strategies of resistance.

Lin Yu-sheng (1979) has argued that the totalistic iconoclasm of the May 4th movement was itself made possible by the organic unity between the cultural and political order in the Chinese imperial system. In this sytem, universal kingship integrated the cultural-moral order with the socio-political order. The collapse of this pivot in the system led to the collapse of the legitimating principle of this elite's cultural-moral order, which subsequently enabled the totalistic attack on the traditional order.[4] There is a remarkably symmetrical argument made for Indian society by the Indologist Louis Dumont. Dumont (1980) argues that it is religious ideas, especially of hierarchy and pollution, and the Brahmin priesthood that held together the entire system. Kingship and politics, although protecting religion, was fundamentally dependent upon religious ideas and the ritual activities of the Brahmin priesthood for their legitimation. So where, in Lin's account, the cultural and moral, as well as the more broadly social sphere, were dependent upon the imperial institution for their legitimation, in Dumont's view of India, politics and society depended upon religious institutions and ideas. Thus in India, "religion encompassed the political", whereas in China, it was the political which encompassed the religious (or moral culture).

Both views may be criticized for essentializing complex cultural traditions, for reducing the enormous diversity of China and India to simple, and some would say, simplistic principles. I have found some value in their formulations as ways of understanding how elites perceived and integrated themselves with political power. Thus in Lin's formulation, we may better think of the organic unity as a representation which informed the world-view of the literati elite and upwardly mobile segments of society; as for Dumont, we need to qualify his assertion about religion sanctioning politics by the extent to which this relationship was relevant to the self-understanding of different, particularly lower-class, groups. By understanding these formulations as specific elite representations rather than as timeless cultural principles, we may also see how differently these elite representations have shaped the emergent nations in the two societies as the new sources of sovereign authority. In the comparative study that follows I turn to a study by Arjun Appadurai of the history of a south Indian kingdom and temple community from the 18th until the early 20th century. For the Chinese materials I will use my own researches and other materials from the north China plain in the 19th and 20th centuries.

Appadurai's study of the Sri Partasarati Svami temple in Madras gives us a clear picture of how authority was constructed in this society. Before the British took over the area in the late 17th century, a triangular relationship obtained in the community between the kings, the sectarian priests of the temple and the temple community, the last of which also happened to be subjects of the kingdom. A set of transactions, material and symbolic, held the three together. Sovereignty lay actually with the deity of the temple. By providing royal gifts and protection (other patrons might grant more generous gifts, but could not provide protection) to the temple, the king, who demonstrated the highest form of service to the deity, came to share in the paradigmatic royalty of the deity. "By being the greatest servant of the deity, the human king sustains and displays his rule over men" (Appadurai 1981, 51). Thus, the authority of the rulers in the kingdom was, in practice, crucially dependent upon their patronage of the temple.

Behind the conferral of these ritual honours and critical to the link between the temple community and the king and the royal bureaucracy, were, of couse, the sectarian managers of the temple who were also the religious leaders of the community. While the king was granted the authority to be the ultimate arbiter in temple disputes, the actual day to day, managerial authority of the temple community lay with these leaders; and the monarch could not encroach upon the prerogative. As Appadurai puts it, "the ceremonial exchanges of honour between warrior-kings and sectarian leaders rendered public, stable and culturally appropriate an exchange at the level of politics and economics. These warrrior-kings bartered the control of agrarian resources gained by military prowess for access to the [symbolically] re-distributive processes of temples, which were controlled by sectarian leaders. Conversely, in their own struggles with each other....sectarian leaders found the support of these warrior-kings timely and profitable" (Appadurai 1981, 74).

With the expansion of the colonial British state and the growth of its control over the most intimate spheres of life, especially in the late 19th century, this particular interaction of religious and political structures of authority fell away and the triangular relationship was replaced by a state-civil society model of authority. At the structural level, the British dispensed with temples as the authoritative basis of rule in south India. Moreover, reversing the pattern of the past, the colonial administration sought increasingly to control the day-to-day affairs of the temple, thereby encroaching upon the authority of the temple leaders and generating enormous conflict and unending litigation. The historic process we have outlined was an effort at classic state building — whereby the state attempts to appropriate the authority of local communities — albeit in the colonial context.

What was the effect of this state-making upon the religious structures of authority? Needless to say, the old triangular relationship collapsed. Moreover, the authority of the sectarian leaders was being increasingly challenged. Yet, this temple and Hindu temples all over India continued to play a vital role in electoral politics, political mobilization, and politics in general. Control of temples continued to generate intense competition between local power-holders, their lawyers and publicists (Washbrook 1976). Cut off from state power, sectarian and Brahmin elites sought to reinforce their religious authority within the community and temple which continued to provide, as Appadurai argues, a last resort for working out political entitlement. Temple honours were not only valued cultural markers because they brought enhanced status to the recipient, but because they also brought control of temple resources, their followings and their allies. Thus the continued importance of religious institutions in the power and self-perception of an important segment of the Indian elite would ensure religious ideas a role in the emergent narratives of the nation.

Let us now consider the way in which religious and political structures of authority were articulated at the local level in

China, both before and after the process of modern state-making took hold. In the villages of north China during the late 19th and early 20th centuries, patronage and management of the religious sphere of activity — endowing and managing temple lands, building and repairing temples, organizing temple festivities, serving on temple management committees — clearly brought honour and status to those engaged in them. These activities were monopolized by the village elite, who in terms of leisure and resources, were best able to avail of them. In many villages these activities in the religious sphere provided the framework for managing the public affairs of the village, for instance, running the crop-watching association or the self-defence corps of the village. Morever, in some villages, temple committees also functioned as the ultimate tribunal to judge offenders in the village under the watchful eyes of the gods (Duara 1988, Ch. 5).

I have argued that the active role played by the village elite in the religious sphere was sanctioned by the cosmology of a universal bureaucracy headed by the emperor but composed of both earthly and godly bureaucrats mediating the relationship between spiritual and temporal worlds (1988, 134 -136). The activities of this universal bureaucracy provided a model for leaders to represent their authority and exercise their responsibilities. For whatever practical reasons the village elite performed their activities in the religious sphere, the bureaucrats' patronage of officially sanctioned gods and the gentry's sponsorship of both official and non-official gods communicated a clear message to them about the style and responsibilities of political leadership in society. It also alerts us to the way in which authority in the religious sphere at the local level was symbolically dependent on the pivotal role of universal emperorship and, more widely, on the ritual activities of the imperial bureaucracy. This is brought home most sharply when the modernizing state began to send a different message regarding the religious sphere in the villages and urged village leaders to transfer their allegiance from the religious realm to the more secular activities of the modern regime.

At the turn of the 20th century, the provincial adiministration of Zhili and Shandong under the initial leadership of Yuan Shikai (or Yuan Shih-Kai) sought to implement a series of modernizing reforms at the village level and target the old religious sphere as the source of "superstition" and also substantial resources. The success of this administration in appropriating temples and temple property was not inconsiderable (Duara 1988, 148 -155). This was due largely to cooperation by the village elites who saw new channels of social mobility in the schools, titles and programmes which came down to the village came from a national authority. These resources functioned to certify and bolster the authority of the village elite who monopolized official positions in this initial period (Duara 1988, 157). In other words, the rural elite turned out to be extremely adaptive and responsive to state demands: they were able to transfer their allegiances from the religious sphere to the secular relatively painlessly. They were able to do so because for them it had been the political within the religious that had been salient in the first place. The religious domain had ceased to be a factor in the political role of the elite any more.

What does this comparative excursus tell us about the greater prominence of critiques of modernity in India? Surely not the simplistic conclusion that religion is necessarily anti-modern. Religion, in and of itself, is scarcely incompatible with modernity as the increasingly popular role of religion in the US, Japan or Taiwan reveals. In China, the areas which have prospered most in recent years, such as the south and southeast coast, have also witnessed a massive religious revival. I believe it tells us that where elites locate their authority outside of the political power of the state, which often tends to be in organized religions, they are able not only to generate opposition, but also to articulate alternative narratives to the authoritative discourse located within this political power. Thus, a state-building programme in India did not foreclose, and may even have contributed to the expansion of a space within which certain elite groups could engage in an indigenous critique of the narrative of History associated with the colonial power. This is also how we can understand the force of Gandhi's resistance to granting moral authority to the state.

In China, since universal kingship encompassed the religious and moral order, the source of authority for local elites as well as intelligentsia resided principally in the political. We have seen how the pivotal role of the political shaped the allegiance of the elite at even the most local levels of rural society. The collapse of the political pivot which made possible the radical iconoclasm of the May 4th movement also de-legitimated critiques of the emergent order originating in the non-modern sectors of society. Non-modern and non-elite popular religious movements, such as those led by the Small Sword Society (see Duara 1995, Ch. 3), continued to flourish and challenge the hegemonic discourse especially as it pertained to popular religion. However, lacking links with the modern intelligentsia, they were unable to articulate a counter-narrative of dissent that was acceptable in the public domain.

The relative autonomy of religious authority in India enabled a man like Gandhi to be as influential as he was. But it would be a mistake to identify Gandhi entirely with the project of the 19th century Hindu elite who sought to found the nation in the idea of a "spiritual culture" in opposition to History. Stephen Hay has revealed how the entire 19th century Hindu renaissance was the work overwhelmingly of Brahmins in Bengal and South India. It was also largely the celebration of the high Brahminic philosophical tradition of the Vedas and the Upanishads. While at one level, Gandhi, a non-Brahmin, drew from this tradition, Ashis

Nandy (1987, 155-8) points out that at another level, he marked a break with this tradition because Gandhi's Hinduism affirmed the non-canonical and the folk. While this may make him similar to the Chinese nativists in search of traditional roots of a modern, national culture, yet we should recall that for Gandhi it was often the non-modern within these folk traditions that he valued. Gandhi's critique of modernity derived its legitimacy in substantial part from the popular, sectarian religious traditions which continued to play a vital part in Saurashtra, the area he came from. This corner of Gujarat was an area of eclectic and competing religious cultures including ascetic Jainism and Christianity and his family was strongly influenced by the devotional tradition of monotheistic Hinduism of *bhakti*. It was from this tradition that he derived his opposition to classical, caste-bound Hinduism and projected a religious nationalism based on non-violence and compassion. Most of all, the *bhakti* tradition gave him an orientation and style. By following in the path of *bhakti* teachers, walking about the land preaching his message, Gandhi, the latter-day saint, was able to reach out to the ordinary people (Rudolphs 158, 172).

If the continued meaningfulness of religious traditions among segments of the elite leadership of the national movement in India created a space and an audience for the critique of modernity, the substance of Gandhi's critique itself was not a necessary outcome of this space. The substance must be understood in the context of his encounter with colonial ideology. Ashis Nandy (1983) has argued that the psychological impact of colonial ideology is much more devastating and longer lasting than its political or economic effect. This impact is felt both in the colonized society as well as in the colonizing society. The justification of world colonization by Western powers required the construction of an ideology of rule that not only transformed the representation of the colonized peoples, but also recast the self-image of Western society as one that was quintessentially and definitionally the antithesis of the East. In the Indian context, the "natives" were marked variously as cowardly, effeminate, naively childlike, superstitious, ignorant and the like. In turn the West was characterized by the images of youthfulness, aggressiveness, and mastery, exemplified so well in the British public school. In doing so, it repressed many of the antinomian Dionysian features of Western society itself, such as femininity, childlikeness, passiveness, the positive qualities of age, at great psychological cost to this society. Nandy examines the crippling effects of this ideology on those at the interface of the encounter such as Rudyard Kipling, E.M. Forster and C.F. Andrews, on the one side, and westernized Indians such as Aurobindo Ghosh on the other.

Gandhi was among the very few elite Indians to successfully resist the colonial representation of the Indian. In my opinion, upper caste Hindu reformers tended to respond to the colonial psychological onslaught with a myopic defensiveness of a reconstructed Hindu spirituality (versus Western materiality) — itself an Orientalist representation, albeit with positive connotations. Partly in consequence of this defensiveness, Hindu elites have been much more closed to the kind of self-criticism that characterized May 4th intellectuals in China. Gandhi was able to break through this defensiveness and, according to Nandy, resist the linkages at the root of colonial ideology between progressive mastery at the heart of History on the one hand, and racism, hyper-masculinity and adulthood on the other (Nandy 1983, 100). His doctrine of passive resistance and non-violence sought to liberate activism and courage from aggressiveness and recognize them as perfectly compatible with womanhood. Keenly aware of the disfiguring effects of colonialism on the British themselves he pointed to the abandonment of true Christian values which, he believed, could never justify colonialism.

But (and this is not part of Nandy's argument) Gandhi appears to have taken a final step of equating the irrationality and immorality of colonialism with that of modernity as a whole. So deeply implicated were the categories of modern thought with colonial ideology that to accept the Western criterion of a true antagonist — to be a player in the game of "modernization" — would be to violate one's own being, to remain imprisoned within the deforming categories of the other.

Thus the sufficient condition enabling Gandhi's critique of modernity lay in the encounter with colonial ideology and his ability to provide a psychologically valid alternative to it in his nationalism, especially for a middle class caught awkwardly between two worlds. In China, the imperialist presence was of course widely resented and anti-imperialism was at the core of political movements for the first half of the 20th century. But the absence of institutionalized colonialism in most parts of China also meant that colonial ideology was not entrenched among both colonizer and colonized in the same way as it was in India and other directly colonized countries. The opposition to imperialism was chiefly political and economic and did not present the urgent need to root out imperialist ideology in the very self-perception of a people. It is interesting to speculate on the role and effects of Japanese colonial discourse in the early 20th century.

As far as I know, few scholars have taken up this subject seriously. However, work seeking to understand the Japanese construction of History and the Orient is beginning to emerge, most notably, Stefan Tanaka's *Japan's Orient* (see also James Fujii, 1993). At the centre of Tanaka's concern is the Meiji production of *toyoshi* (literally, Eastern History), a historical narrative of great consequence for East Asia. From our perspective, *toyoshi* combined linear History with the oppositional discourse of "culture" in a way that Japan could resist the hierarchies of universal History and thus establish its equivalence to the West and yet create its own superiority in relation to the rest of Asia, particularly China which came to be designated in this discourse as Shina. As the foundation of an alternative History, the East was idealized (or Orientalized) and for figures like Okakura Tenshin, Japan's mission lay in re-entering the Asiatic past and regaining the lost beauty of Asia. The dominant academic trend, however, tended to objectify Shina as Japan's past, as a temporal inferior, even while claiming some of the timeless qualities of Asiatic ideals as being embodied in modern Japan (Tanaka 1993, 19). While it is important to recognize the indeterminacy of *toyoshi* discourse and the fact that it inspired many Japanese to reach out to other Asians to build a positive future, nonetheless, there was, even amongst the most noble-minded of these figures, a paternalism towards Japan's Orient that seeded the violent appropriation of this discourse by Japanese imperialism (Tanaka 1993, Ch. 5).

From the outset, then, it would appear that Japanese colonial ideology took a different approach to its colonial subjects that would have made a Gandhian type of response inappropriate, if not meaningless. In proclaiming the establishment of the Greater East Asian Co-prosperity Sphere as the mission of Japanese rule in the 1930s and 1940s, the Japanese imperialists were appealing to the Orientalism of *toyoshi* which celebrated an Asiatic unity. Idyllic village communities based upon the spirit of age-old cooperation were to be the building blocks of the Japanese empire which was the only force capable of resisting the corrupting influences of Western capitalism. (Hatada 1976, 10-15) Although there was a world of difference between Gandhi and the Japanese imperialists, nonetheless, the basis of a critique founded upon alternative Asian values which Gandhi also espoused was arguably extremely suspect in China.

In a recent forum on my 1995 book, *Rescuing History from the Nation: Questioning Narratives of Modern China* (Bulletin of Concerned Asian Scholars, Vol. 29, July-October), John Fitzgerald comments on an earlier version of this paper. Fitzgerald examines the internalization of Western imperialist images of the smelly, wily, emasculated and inscrutable Chinese among a large number of Chinese novelists and politicians of the early 20th century, and concludes that the sources of Chinese and Indian self-images in Orientalism were perhaps not so different after all. His alternative view is that what was different was "the relative ease with which Chinese nationalists accepted the colonial representations of John Chinaman as the foundation for fashioning a 'new kind of people' ..." in contrast to Indian nationalists. I agree with Fitzgerald's judgement and believe that it advances our conclusion a step further. Apart from exceptional individuals like Gandhi, the self-image of middle-class Indians was made, in significant part, from both the positive and negative stereotypes of imperialist Orientalism. Yet Indian nationalism (and not necessarily the movement) tended to use the positive Orientalism as a shield to deflect serious self-examination that might have been provoked by the negative Orientalism. It still, however, begs the question as to why Indian nationalists found it difficult to explore and act upon this criticism.

Why this relative lack of "ease" among Indians, has, I sense as one with no expertise in psychology, to do with the presence or absence of everyday, colonial rulership, whether in India, Korea or Algeria. Although this does not hold for every person or even every group in the colonized society, the strongly dualistic or Manichaean relationship between colonialism and nationalism makes it very difficult for these nationalists and intellectuals to be self-critical in the May 4th way. The space for self-examination is often filled by a defence mechanism that sanctifies the self — or a part of the self. One might make the argument that this is the reaction of only bourgeois nationalists and it is true that they probably have a greater stake in the status quo than many others. But a cursory look at multicultural politics in contemporary America reveals a recognizably similar process that suggests that it might also have to do with the everyday confrontation of identities constructed as self and other. The ability to criticize the Self demands some distance from a powerful, objectifying Other, or perhaps it demands the Other principally as an internalized Self, which provides a curious autonomy from a real Other standing over the Self. At the same time, however, this self-criticism — while valuable as a practice — is, of course, no guarantee of liberation.

To return to the exceptional Gandhi. It is perhaps inevitable that, with widely varying degrees of destructiveness, all of our representations imply normative hierarchies which tend to marginalize and repress peoples and cultures. Is Gandhi relevant to understanding how and why to keep our dialogue open to the Other?

My answer is a yes and a no. Gandhi's contribution was to demonstrate that it may be possible to bring vast masses of people into the political mainstream without the same violent or wrenching transformation of their self-image that 19th century imperialism had produced among the intelligentsia; to locate the sources of self-empowerment (*swaraj*) not only in an external or elite discourse but within the best in their popular traditions; and to project an ideology that minimized the instrumentalization of the people with whom he worked. In these respects he also resembled grass-roots reformers in China like Jimmy Yan and Liang Shuming for whom the transformative impulse was balanced by the need to preserve the local as a value, even though he was much more politically popular than were they.

In preserving the local — here religious traditions in relation to the modernizing center — as a value, Gandhi was able to transform it into a space from which the dominant ideology of the state could be critiqued — a space similar in many ways to civil society in the West. We tend not to equate religious space with civil society because the enlightenment project was directed against the authority of the church. If, however, we may step aside from the history of modern Europe and seek our perspective from political developments for democratization in East Europe, Latin America, the Philippines and elsewhere, then we have to recognize that the critique of state and state ideologies has come from the authority provided by religious sources such as the Catholic church and Liberation Theology.

The narrative of emancipatory modernity in China has its power because it has elicited the commitment of both the Chinese state and the modern intelligentsia. Its gains for the Chinese people in many areas of life cannot go unappreciated. Moreover, despite my criticism of the Chinese intelligentsia's representation of the "people", I believe that the highly elitist Indian intelligentsia and bureaucracy (outside of the Gandhian *satyagrahi* and some activist groups) can learn much from Chinese egalitarianism. Yet the consuming commitment of Chinese intellectuals to the narrative of modernity has tended to produce a monologism in which gradualist reformers like Liang Shuming, Jimmy Yan, Tao Xingzhi and others (each of whom could perhaps have played the role of a Gandhi under different circumstances) have been marginalized. In the process, this narrative has obscured the vitality of popular culture, religion and their associational life, and de-legitimated the critique of modern ideologies originating outside of modern discourses. Despite the repeated persecution of the intelligentsia by the Chinese state, it is this shared narrative which has thrown so many of them repeatedly into the arms of the state and at the same time alienated both from the living cultures of the "masses" and of "tradition". While the state has made effective use of the narrative of modernity to expand its own powers, the Chinese intelligentsia has robbed itself of alternative sources of moral authority which it might have found in history and popular culture.

At the same time, Gandhi's success in politicizing the people was also limited by the fact that his politics were a meditation on the methodology of morality. We may think of his mission as the production of a self that was less epistemologically controlling, but *morally* self-aware and self-controlled. Indeed, such was his dedication to this disciplinary project, that it became its own totalization and took its own toll. This totalizing impulse is also reflected in his utopianism which was so radically oppositional that it reproduced the essentializing quality of modernity which he sought to fight. Thus by conflating colonialism with modernity as a single, given mode of being, he objectified it and did not attend to the *historical* tensions within that could unravel it. How would Gandhi have accounted for pacificist traditions in modern society, for the power of the environmental movement, for the increased visibility of androgyny, for the "age revolution"? Gandhi did not recognize that any de-construction of a system of ideas must also fall prey to this system. To put it more affirmatively, "it is a question of explicitly and systematically posing the problem of the status of a discourse which borrows from a heritage the resources necessary for the de-construction of that heritage itself" (Derrida 1978, 282).

In not posing the problem of his affiliation with that which he critiqued, Gandhi could not see that the transcendent Truth which his conception of the nation sought to embody was exactly parallel to the nation as the subject of transcendent History, an essence which remained even as all tangible histories were re-written, dispersed or died out. In seeking to banish History as the foundation of the nation, Gandhi banished historicity itself and ended up with a transcendental ideal, the more impossible to realize. As historians, our task is to displace History, but at the same time, to rescue history. We do so with the knowledge that the nation cannot be essentialized as a transcendent reality, beyond self-serving regimes and bickering interest groups. The nation exists as representations of community inseparable from these very groups pursuing their partialities but also embodying their larger aspirations in narratives of transcendence. As representation, the nation also conceals itself as a relationship of power which uses its political and rhetorical apparatuses to suppress alternative visions of community. The nation as representation and power has been well served by History and Truth. The real historical nation is an elusive relationship which can only be understood by marshalling all the resources that history has to offer.

Notes

1. Zhongxue weiti, xixue weiyong", i.e. "Making Chinese learning the substantive body while adopting the utility of Western learning", was the central policy of Chinese "Self-strengtheners" in the second half of the 19th century. Here, "ti" (the substantive body) and "yong" (utility) are symbols for Chinese values and Western values respectively.
2. Here I am differentiating myself from the Levensonian dichotomy which sees *tiyong* as an un-self-conscious expression of culture as telos, whereas "modern conservatives" are seen to manipulate or rationalize culture self-consciously. The instrumental use of culture was alive before the modern divide, and Confucian spirituality could also function as an alternative telos in the modern era (See Duara 1995, Ch. 3; also Chang 1987).
3. Nehru actually develops a variation upon the Hegelian progression of the universal "spirit of the age", which the modern Indian nation must once again realize.
4. Lin argues further that in the process of engaging in the totalistic attack, the May 4th revolutionaries reproduced the assumption of the very unity between culture and politics, seeking once again to legitimate culture by some other master narrative.

References

Ahmed, A.F. Salahuddin. 1975. "Ram Mohun Roy and his Contemporaries" in V.C. Joshi ed. *Rommohun Roy and the Process of Modernization in India* Delhi: Vikas Publishing House. pp. 89-103.

Alitto, Guy S. 1979. *The Last Confucian: Liang Shu-ming and the Chinese Dilemma of Modernity* Berkeley, Ca: University of California Press.

Anderson, Benedict. 1991. *Imagined Communities: Reflections on the Origins and Spread of Nationalism* London. (Revised and expanded version of 1983 text).

Appadurai, Arjun. 1981. *Conflict and Worship under Colonial Rule: A South Indian Case,* Cambridge, UK: Cambridge University Press.

Chang, Hao. 1987. *Chinese Intellectuals in Crisis: Search for Order and Meaning* (1890-1911). Berkeley and Los Angeles: University of California Press.

Chatterjee, Partha. 1986. *Nationalist Thought and the Colonial World: A Derivative Discourse.* London: Zed Books.

Derrida, Jacques. 1978. *Writing and Difference* trans. Alan Bass. Chicago: University of Chicago Press.

Duara, Prasenjit. 1988. *Culture, Power and the State: Rural North China, 1900-1942* Standford: Standford University Press.

__________ 1995. *Rescuing History from the Nation: Questioning Narratives of Modern China* Chicago: Chicago University Press,.

Dumont, Louis. 1980. *Homo Hierarchicus: The caste system and its implications* Chicago: University of Chicago Press.

Fujii, James A. 1993. *"Writing out Asia: Modernity, Canon, and Natsume Soseki's Kokoro"* in *Positions: East Asia Cultures Critiques* 1.1: 194-223 (Spring).

Furth, Charlotte. 1976. "Culture and Politics in Modern Chinese Conservatism." in Charlotte Furth ed., *The Limits of Change: Essays on Conservative Alternatives in Republican China* Cambridge, Ma: Harvard University Press.

Gandhi, Mohandas Karamchand. 1938 edition. *Hind Swaraj or Indian Home Rule* Ahmedabad: Navajivan Press.

Hatada Takashi. 1976. *Chugoku sonraku to Kyodotai Riron* Tokyo.

Hay, Stephen N. 1970. *Asian Ideas of East and West: Tagore and his Critics in Japan, China and India* Cambridge Ma: Harvard University Press.

Hayford, Charles W. 1990. *To the People: James Yen and Village China* New York: Columbia University Press.

Hegel, Georg W.F. 1956 *The Philosophy of History* trans. by J. Sibree. New York: Dover Publications.

Hsiao Kung-chuan. 1975. *A Modern China and a New World : K'ang Yu-wei, Reformer and Utopian, 1858-1927* Seattle and London: University of Washington Press.

Iyer, Raghavan N. 1973. *The Moral and Political Thought of Mahatma Gandhi* New York: Oxford University Press.

K'ang Yu-wei. 1958. *Ta T'ung Shu: The One World Philosophy of K'ang Yu-wei* Trans. from the Chinese with Introduction and Notes by Laurence G. Thompson. London: George Allen and Unwin Ltd.

Levenson, Joseph R. 1965. *Confucian China and its Modern Fate: A Trilogy* Berkeley and Los Angeles: University of California Press.

Lin Yu-sheng 1979. *The Crisis of Chinese Consciousness: Radical Anti-traditionalism in the May Fourth Era* Madison: University of Wisconsin Press.

Mast III, Herman and Saywell, William G. 1974. "Revolution out of Tradition: The Political Ideology of Tai Chi-tao" *Journal of Asian Studies* XXXIV. 1 (November): 73-98.

Nandy, Ashis 1983. *The Intimate Enemy: Loss and Recovery of Self under Colonialism* Delhi: Oxford University Press.

_________ 1987. *Traditions, Tyranny and Utopias: Essays in the Politics of Awareness* Delhi: Oxford University Press.

Nehru, Jawaharlal. 1960. *The Discovery of India* New York: Anchor Books.

Ogata, Yasushi. June, 1984. "Shinmatsu shinkaron no shisoteki isso to sono kaishu" (The status of evolutionary thought in the late Qing). *Todai Chu Tetsubun Gakkai Ho* No. 9, 1984. pp. 37-57.

Ray, Rajat K. 1975. "Introduction" in V.C. Joshi ed. *Ram Mohun Roy and the Process of Modernization in India* Delhi: Vikas Publishing House. pp. 1-20.

Raychaudhuri, Tapan. 1988. *Europe Reconsidered: Perceptions of the West in Nineteenth Century Bengal* Delhi: Oxford University Press.

Rudolph, Llyod I. and Susanne H. 1967. *The Modernity of Tradition: Political Development in India* Chicago: University of Chicago Press.

Schwartz, Benjamin. 1976. "Notes on Conservatism in General and China in Particular" in Charlotte Furth ed. *The Limits of Change: Essays on Conservative Alternatives in Republican China* Cambridge, Ma: Harvard University Press.

Stocking, George. W. 1987. *Victorian Anthropology* New York: The Free Press.

Tanaka, Stefan. 1993. *Japan's Orient: Rendering Pasts into History* Berkeley and Los Angeles: University of California Press.

Wakeman, Frederic Jr. 1973. *History and Will: Philosophical Perspectives of Mao Tse-tung's Thought* Berkeley and Los Angeles: University of California Press.

Washbrook, D.A. 1976. *The Emergence of Provincial Politics: The Madras Presidency 1870-1920* New York: Cambridge University Press.

RAVNI THAKUR & TAN CHUNG

12

ENCHANTMENT AND DISENCHANTMENT: A SINO-INDIAN INTROSPECTION

"The particular components of the cultures concerned at the time of encounter and circumstances of the encounter determine what one admires and emulates as well as what one detests and rejects."

— Tapan Ray Chaudhuri

We think it necessary to write this article to respond to Prasenjit Duara's initiative in re-understanding the historical evolution of India and China. In his refreshing book, *Rescuing History From The Nation*, Duara writes:

> "The history of China can no longer be innocently a history of the West or the history of the true China. It must attend to the politics of narratives...." (p. 26)

Duara has warned us against narrativizing Chinese History "in the Enlightenment mode". He also draws our attention to "the heterophony of the Chinese past" and "a Chineseness that is simultaneously Western and Chinese". He thinks the existing history, i.e. discourses of history are quite contaminated by attempts both to romanticize the Enlightenment on the one hand, and to eulogize the Chineseness.

After Edward W. Said, whose *Orientalism* raised the objection against "orientalizing" the Asian cultures, Duara is launching another movement to cleanse historical discourses, particularly pertaining to China. We think that this should not be a one-man show, and all like-minded Indian scholars should join in. This essay is essentially such an appeal. As the Chinese saying goes: "Jiaowang guozheng" i.e. when you right the wrong you tend to overdo. When Said raises his campaign against "Orientalism", he also becomes suspect of indulging in Occident-baiting. When many other scholars participate in the movement initiated by Duara the movement will become cacophonic and heterophonic and its sum-total will come closer to a holistic perspective. This is the starting point and motivation of our essay.

We agree not to romanticize Enlightenment. Nevertheless we need to examine the Enlightenment and what it has brought along to Asia, specifically to India and China. As honest historians, we should see enlightenment in an objective manner — avoiding the either pro- or anti- extremes. Confucius said: " Don't do to others what you don't like others to do to you." Even if History (value added historical discourse) and Enlightenment (abusing its name to stigmatize non-Western civilizations) have wallowed in unjust excesses, this should not make them naked targets of tit for tat. Moreover, what we are concerned with, what we wish to re-understand in modern discourse, started with the discourse of the enlightenment. So must we start with it too.

Enlightenment is primarily a cultural historian's broad definition of a particular historical period (roughly 18th century onwards)[1] during which intellectual, cultural and artistic endeavours in Europe (and consequently in other parts of the world) was guided by a specific world-view. Two major themes in philosophical thought played the dominant role. First, in political philosophy, the development of the social contract theory from Hobbes to Locke to Rousseau, became a part of everyday talk, leading in turn to the theory of the "Rights of man". Here, of course, both the French Revolution and American Independence became examples. The second most important theme was the increasing prestige of "Science" and consequently "knowledge based on empirical observation" rather than holy texts. Hence Darwin's philosophy of Evolution is discursively the most important. These two major themes, of course, had their offshoots in literature and art, but it is in the questioning of religious dogma and tradition that these philosophical currents found a place in unfamiliar and entirely different cultures.

Kant's much quoted work, *What is Enlightenment,* says: "Sapre Nude!"[2] Dare to know! Be guided by your own understanding! This is the watchword of Enlightenment. (Schwarcz, p. 1) Appealing to reason and through it to knowledge was one of the most powerful ideas of the 19th century that found many sympathetic ears in India and China. By the end of the 19th century, most of the authors and philosophers associated with the project of Enlightenment such as Kant, Darwin, Hume, Paine, Voltaire, Rousseau, Mill, Bentham, Adam Smith etc. had been translated into Chinese and were accessible to Indians in English versions.

The Enlightenment project worked in two ways simultaneously when it came in contact with non-western countries. At one level it constructed the non-western world as the "other" of Enlightenment. At another level, because colonialism was also the product of Enlightement, it worked as a new "enchanted" world-view. The reality of colonialism was to shape the relationship the intellectuals of India and China were to develop with the project of Enlightenment. A comparable process can be identified in India and China which, to use Adorno's words, is at once an enchantment and a disenchantment.[3]

To regard Enlightenment as the mother of coloniolism is over-simplification. Enlightenment, after all, had its human dimension, and stood on the side of the oppressed against the oppressors. However, one finds it difficult to ignore the analytical framework of dialectical materialism that a superstructure must spring up from the base, that Enlightenment was the mindset of the bourgeoisie who, after transforming themselves from the oppressed into masters of their own destiny, tended to become greatest oppressors humankind had ever seen. The bourgeoisie loved Enlightenment when opportunities shied away from them. After a fundamental turn in their favour they saw super-profit, Enlightenment began to suffer schizophrenia. On the one hand, it continued to engineer progress and enlightenment at home. On the other hand, it could not tolerate any equal, let alone superioı, abroad. Britain which was far ahead of others in championing modernization and Enlightenment at home, had a very contrary attitude in seeing socio-economic modernization in her colonies. This had a greater impact in India and China.

China and India came in contact with western ideas of enlightenment not simultaneously (China many deades later than India), but contemporaneous with their respective degradation of national sovereignty and self-respect (India many decades earlier than China). However, there was a qualitative difference in the two degradations of India and China. In the case of India, it was the irresponsibility of the East India Company which handed over India to the British Crown like a bankrupt gambler mortgaging his ill-gotten asset to the money lender. The East India Company was both landlord (of India) and merchant rolled into one. The post-1857 revolutionary scene saw India being turned over from one landlord to another. This scenario was described by Jawaharlal Nehru (1889-1964) in these words:

> "The feudal landlords and their kind who came from England to rule over India had the landlord's view of the world. To them India was a vast estate belonging to the East India Company, and the landlord was the best and the natural representative of his estate and his tenants." (Nehru, p. 308).

The Chinese scene, however, from the British angle again, was not the handover of tenants from a company to the sovereign government, but the progression of an act of forcing opium into China's throat by the likes of Jardine and Matheson (and, of course, the East India Company) onto the followup action by waging the Opium War against China on the part the British government. After that, Sino-British relations were conducted by the British "Gun-boat Diplomacy" and the Unequal Treaty System. Britain adopted a policy of "after gaining an inch, then demand a foot" (*de cun jin chi*) in her aggression against China. This scenario differed greatly from what was painted by Nehru apropos of India's becoming a stable British colony. Here, one should not ignore India's position as a periphery-cum-sub-centre in Britain's controlling-periphery-by-periphery global strategy, and India's being used as a spring board in Britain's expansion in the Eastern Hemisphere. For instance, all British wars against China were fought by Indian troops. This put China's semi-colonial state several degrees lower than India's colonial status.

Another glaring difference in the Sino-Indian comparison lies in India's being under the umbrella of one colonial power in contrast with China's being aggressed by almost every power on earth, from Great Britain to tiny Austria. Japan which had always been an obscure neighbour, suddenly behaved as a lord with growing ambitions to enslave China. As Sun Yat-sen declared in 1894 at the founding of "Xing-Zhong Hui" (Association for China's Resurgence):

> "A magnificent China is today treated as dirt by neighbours, and her dignified culture falls into contempt in the eyes of foreigners. ... Today, we are encircled by great powers, under the close watch of the tigers and eagles who have long been covetous for our rich minerals and affluent products, and who vie with one another in nibbling and swallowing, in cutting us like a melon or a bean."[4]

In both countries, this search for tools with which to understand the plight of their countries was facilitated by the new class of urban intelligentsia who had access to the world-view of the Europeans. Pannikar points out that several categorizations have been used for describing the people who were at the forefront of intellectual history in this period. In both India and China, they have been variously described as social reformers, marginal men, cultural brokers, westernizers, and compradores. (Pannikar, p. 63). In the case of China, Chow Tse-tsung points out that the major force behind the dissemination of western ideas was the increasing number of students who went on to study in Europe and America by the end of the 19th century (p. 12). The early formation of the intellectual community was in the growth of national organizations and societies and magazines brought out by these societies. This process is also common to both India and China.

British colonialism in India must be viewed from a holistic perspective. India was brought under a universal context although she could see the good things of modern civilization only through the glass windows. Through moral humiliation and economic exploitation Indian intellectuals still had enormous curiosity towards the extended horizon brought by the country's new conquerors. They had their first flush of romance with western ideas, and saw the positive in British rule over India. As Pannikar points out, "The notion of divine dispensation — enabled the intellectuals to welcome and legitimize the colonial presence. That British rule could be an instrument not so much of exploitation and oppression, but of socio-political transformation, was an articulation of this consciousness." (p. 32) This perspective led first of all to an attack against "tradition".

Apart from the initial romaticization, the Indian intellectual response to Enlightenment continued to grow from the fellow-feeling as long as India was a part (not quite degraded) of the British Empire — even long after her Independence. The "Brown Englishman" scenario is a historical reality which should be assessed both positively and negatively. When Nehru referred to the early Hindu reformers, Ram Mohun Roy, Dayananda, and Vivekananda, he described them drinking "from the rich streams of English literature". (p. 363) The Indian "educated class", said Nehru, had "admiration and acceptance of almost everything western". (pp. 354-55).

Tapan Raychaudhuri in his study of Bengali intellegentsia points out that, "Implicitly the Bengali intellectuals examined afresh the two components of their own culture — the indigenous and the acquired." (p. 22). Pannikar points out that 19th century Indian intellectuals were firm believers in the efficacy of Enlightenment as a panacea. Like Chinese intellectuals, they traced the sources of all ills in Indian society to the ignorance of the masses and the weight of traditional thought and learning.

In India, we see Liberalism replacing pre-colonial sensibilites and ideas. Mill, Spencer, Rousseau and Paine were popular amongst Indian intellectuals. The idea of liberty was first absorbed in Bengal through the work of Derozio. (Raychaudhuri, p. 13) The journals published at this time by the students of Hindu College in Calcutta between 1828-43 were influenced by the ideals of the French Revolution. More importantly, as Pannikar points out, Britain was viewed as the champion of these principles. As Rammohun Roy (1772-1883), one of the most famous of the early Indian reformers put it thus:

> "A nation of people not only blessed with the enjoyment of civil and political liberty but also interested in promoting liberty and social happiness, as well as free enquiry into literary and religious subjects among those nations to which their influence extends."

The age of Ram Mohun Roy is sometimes described as the "Indian Renaissance", and later Indian intellectuals, like M.N. Roy (1887-1954), admired the courage of the "fathers of indian Renaissance" to attack the "time-honoured but enslaving social customs and prejudices" perpetuated in India. M.N. Roy argued, further that India might have a great civilization but it would be ridiculous to think that "the Theory of Relativity was already announced in the Vedas, and that the world should learn its science from ancient India." Ancient Indian cultural achievement should not blind modern Indians from the reality that "the world has gone ahead." Meanwhile, "Indian history was stagnant" hence her "cultural superstructure" failed to develop.[5]

Here again, one notices the enchantment with the self-defined project of Enlightenment which is felt by Indian intellectuals. They see Britain as the saviour of their country and hope that the popularization in western thought in India will free the country from its superstitious and irrational past. Above all, modern British institutions such as the Parliament and the legal system were praised by most Indians of this period. This admiration is what led them to accept British rule.

We must point out that just like there was a schizophrenia in Enlightenment, it was also there in the Indian response to Enlightenment. In other words, enchantment and disenchantment may not be a fixed sequential order. They occurred in simultaneity, or in chicken-and-egg interrelationship. Vivekananda (1862-1902), the Mencius to spiritual leader, Ramakrishna (1836-1886), found it necessary to attack Disenchantment before he propounded Enchantment. He said:

> "We talk foolishly against a material civilization. The grapes are sour. Material civilization, nay even luxury, is necessary to create work for the poor. Bread! Bread! I do not believe in a god who cannot give me bread."

(Ravinder Kumar, pp. 137-38).

Jawaharlal Nehru could synthesize enchantment and disenchantment as if to effect a mental healing of schizophrenia. He wanted India "to function in line with the highest ideals of the age we live in, though we may add to them or seek to mould them in accordance with our national genius." (p. 593) And he defined the highest ideas as "Humanism" and "Scientific Spirit". In Nehru's agenda of "modernization", he saw both advantages and disadvantages of modern science to an old civilization. The advantage lies in the enlargement of "man's understanding and control of many things", thus de-mystifying Nature and preventing the exploitation of religious priests. The disadvantage lies in the want of holistic perspective in western science. This is dangerous to a human: "The very forces science has released overwhelm him and carry him forward relentlessly, and often an unwilling victim, to unknown shores." (p. 594) It was this danger that made Nehru conscious about the importance of synthesizing spiritualism with materialism, "to find a harmony between the world of fact and the world of spirit". (p. 593)

Nehru's discourse on tradition versus modernity quickly travels from the stage of enchantment to that of disenchantment. He wrote in *The Discovery of India*:

> "Today, in the world of politics and economics there is a search for power and yet when power is attained much else of value has gone. Political trickery and intrigue take the place of idealism, and cowardice and selfishness the place of disinterested courage. Form prevails over substance, and power, so eagerly sought after, some how fails to achieve what it aimed at." (p. 595)

Here we notice Nehru's lament about the disappearance of "idealism" which, as we have cited a little while ago, he thought was the aspiration of the modern age. In other words, he had seen "high idealism" in Enlightenment, but also discovered the dangerous trend of Enlightenment in generating materialism sans spiritual nobleness, in leading the human being astray, in creating a world madly in quest for power.

Nehru's disenchantment was echoed by Rabindranath Tagore (1861-194) (or the other way round) in much stronger language. Tagore's "last birthday address" was on "crisis of civilization". In this address, Tagore almost summarized the entire process of metamorphosis of an Indian intellectual mind from enchantment to disenchentment journeying through western civilization. He thought so "firmly rooted in the sentiments" of Indian leaders fighting for Independence was the Indian "faith in the generosity of the English race". Tagore admitted: "I was impressed by this evidence of liberal humanity in the character of the English and thus I was led to set them on the pedestal of my highest respect." He, then, narrated what he saw in Japan and USSR their rapid industrialization which, then led him to resent British imperialists' sacrificing "the welfare of the subject races to their own national greed". He lamented that while many other countries were "marching ahead", India alone "smothered under the dead weight of British administration, lay static in her utter helplessness." This was "the tragic tale of the gradual loss of my faith in the claims of the European nations to civilization."(Ghose, p. 186)

Tagore said all this in 1941 when the mad, mad world was caught by the World War II, and he squarely blamed the western civilization for it:

> ".... the demon of barbarity has given up all pretence and has emerged with unconcealed fangs, ready to tear up humanity in an orgy of devastation. From one end of the world to the other the poisonous fumes of hatred darken the atmosphere. The spirit of violence which perhaps lay dorment in the psychology of the West, has at last roused itself and desecrates the spirit of Man."(*Ibid*, p.188)

In the above, we have sweepingly surveyed the progression of the Enlightenment discourse in India and see even a man like Tagore who had so much absorbed the western civilization into his "Visva-bharati" (the universal commonwealth) thus integrating his intellectual being into the western Brave New World, uttering such harsh words against the western civilization. Even while doing that, he still had faith in the Englishmen. He remarked : "if I had not known them, my despair at the prospect of western civilization would be unrelieved."(*Ibid*, p.168) A westerner may easily exhibit his bias against other civilizations and cultures, but we cannot accuse either Tagore, or Nehru, or other Indian intellectuals for incurable prejudice against the west while they censured western civilization. Nor can anyone say that Tagore and Nehru were bearers of the Brown Man's Burden in the same manner did the bearers of the White Man's Burden. In fact, we should go a step further to say that though of Indian descent, Tagore and Nehru were, by and large, a part of the modern age, a part of the western civilization, cherishing the "highest ideals" of the west. They themselves had recognized this, and had no regret for being so. Therefore, in Tagore and Nehru we do have the romanticization of the Enlightenment, of the western civilization, of the good guys among the Englishmen. Their critique of the western civilization does not pose as a dichotomy to their romanticization of it. On the other hand, neither Tagore nor Nehru had the pretension of discoursing in "pure" Indian history, because their romanticization of the Indian tradition gets along very well with their romanticizing the western civilization. We have to adopt a holistic perspective to understand this phenomenon.

II

Although China was brought under the ambience of western civilization in a quite different manner as did India, there was undoubted enchantment of the West to the Chinese intellectuals from the initial stage a century ago uptill today. Duara has pointed out the important phenomenon of Liang Qichao (1873-1929) who, for the first time in Chinese intellectual history, wrote "the history of China in the narrative of the Enlightenment" — a "History in the linear mode". (p. 33) Duara is also insightfully sensitive to Liang's basic conviction that "a people without a linear History will soon be forced off the stage of History because they have no means of forming groups and writing against others who will aggress upon them." (p. 35) This, we feel, is quite refreshing from the Indian viewpoint. Liang Qichao's discourse has a strong dosage of social Darwinism which is, by and large, absent from Tagore's and Nehru's. This is easily understood. While Tagore and Nehru, were born a part and parcel of the elite of the western world, no patriot in China in modern history had such a mental setting. Duara has noted Liang's departure in the discourse of History from his mentor and leader of the Reform Movement, Kang Youwei (1858-1927). This was because of Kang Youwei's identifying himself as one of the last mohicans of the Confucian scholars and a part of the ruling elite of Chinese socio-politico-cultural traditon. On the other hand, Liang Qichao, though also a Confucian scholar like Kang Youwei who had already passed the second stage of the Imperial Examination and was separated from imperial appointment by only the last exam, had opted out of the exalted company of the Chinese mandarins. Such an option enabled him to identify himself with the peril faced by China in the natural selection of social Darwinism.

We have already alluded to the two different historical backgrounds leading to India and China's respective intercourses with Enlightenment. It can, perhaps, be said that India was firmly brought onto the lap of Enlightenment by her colonial master, while China had no such *good* fortune. Sensible Chinese intellectuals, beginning from the anti-opium hero Commissioner Lin Zexu(1785-1850), started to peep into Enlightenment through the impressive show of British gun-boat diplomacy. As Mao Zedong humorously observed in his "On the people's democratic dictatorship" that inspite of Chinese eagerness to enlist themselves as pupils of the West (he mentioned even the Taiping rebellion leader, Hong Xiuquan, 1813-1864), it "was very odd" that "the teachers always committed aggression against their[Chinese] pupils"[6]. Such an oddity persisted from Hong Xiuquan to Sun Yat-sen's time, making the Sino-Western intercourse basically an equation between the rapacious teacher and the pitiable student. Such an equation naturally could not be stably maintained. Ram Mohun Roy could insightfully grasp this in his satire, "three Chinese converts".[7] Like their Indian counterparts, Chinese patriotic intellectuals in the late 19th and early 20th century, too, were in disarray, caught between enchantment and disenchantment. But, on the whole, the western observers gained an impression of China's less submissive response to Enlightenment than India. The massive anti-Christian riots in China towards the end of the 19th century were often cited as convincing evidence. Scholars, led by John King Fairbank, interpreted this Chinese defiance in terms of "Sinocentrism"a proposition which has been contested amongst Indian scholars.[8]

Duara has joined Levenson and others to delve into the depth of Chinese concept of race, nation in terms of the subtle difference between "nationalism" and "culturalism". But, one thing worth remembering is the peculiar circumstances in which patriotic Chinese intellectuals of the 19th and 20th centuries found themselves. In the past, a Chinese intellectual (particularly an ambitious one) could choose between three alternative life styles. First, in a lawful native mood, he tried to either become distinguished (as a Mandarin), or become rich, or become both if the going was good; otherwise he retired to his village to read and rhyme while carving out a livelihood by ancestral inheritance or by selling his intellectual property. The second alternative was to join and even lead a mass rebellion, playing the time-honoured Chinese game of "cun ze wei wang, bai ze wei kou", i.e. if you win, you become King; and if you lose, you are branded as a bandit. The third alternative was to flee from his native place in times of natural or human calamities. Some, by their special gift and extra-hard working, could also succeed in life even abroad. As livelihood was held much more important than any other aspect of a typical Chinese human being, culture only came as a convenient supplement rather than an incurable obsession.

Levenson and others have wondered why the Chinese never exhibited strong nationalist feelings in history like the Europeans, and arbitrarily filled the Chinese vacuum with an imaginary "culturalism". Over-playing Chinese "culturalism" gives the impression that the Chinese are abnormal human beings with an extra cultural gene inside them. If this was really the case, we shall not be able to explain why in the Chinese reactions to western culture they went much further than other Asian nations to attack their own cultural traditions. Therefore, one must see that they are a down-to-earth practical people primarily guided by the interest of their personal and family survival and career advancement. Culture became their secondary considerations only. And it is absolutely arbitrary and distorting to put Chinese people in the extra cultural gene family. The formulation of "culturalism", which should not have been conceived by any scholar who has an indepth understanding of the Chinese psyche, may, perhaps, serve a purpose to turn China into a whipping boy in chastening imperialist aggression.

When ambitious Chinese intellectuals like Liang Qichao, Sun Yat-sen(1866-1925) began to exercise their options among the three alternatives we have alluded to a little while ago, they found a shocking perspective that not only was there no paradise on earth because of the presence of conquerors everywhere, but the Chinese race was placed in a precarious situation of degradation to the lowest extent possible. In other words, China was being driven to the state of total extinction, and Chinese were being led to the destination of the Jews or even the black African slaves. It was this crisis that made Liang Qichao, Sun Yat sen etc. embrace social Darwinism and used the fear of natural selection to instil a mental urgency among the Chinese. Of course, they did so not to turn the yellow race into a world conqueror but to save the Chinese nation from degradation. Such a strong thrust survived in Sun Yat sen, Chiang Kai-shek, Mao Zedong and Deng Xiaoping, and is manifest in the Chinese ethos in the mainland, in Taiwan, in Hong Kong, in Southeast Asia, in North America — wherever Chinese may settle. If the non-Chinese community develop a feeling of unease today, they should trace the genesis of this fervour and see that much as some Chinese may like to be on top of the world, a new community of Yellow Man's Burden carriers have not emerged. Some have already noticed the behaviour of the Chinese *nouveaux riches,* particularly those on the Mainland. The majority of them do not show ambition of their western counterparts to expand wealth endlessly without saturation. Conversely, the new emergent consumerist appetite in China shows far greater voracity than that prevails in North America and elsewhere in proportion to people's income and production capacity. Such a phenomenon precludes a Chinese emulation of the 19th century type of European super-profit-chasing and global conquest.

Our discussion seems to have gone a little beyond what we originally intended, but it is important to see how strongly the Chinese have reacted to the "sub-colonial" scenario of Sun Yat-sen's coinage. (Sub colonial position is worse than the colonial position.) History, of course, cannot be written by ifs and buts. But, if China were in the same position as India during the 19th and early 20th century, i.e. as a stable colony under one master who practised a kind of "responsible colonialism"[9],the Chinese response to the Enlightenment would have, perhaps, been exactly the same as the Indian response.

When we compare China's response to the western challenge with what India did, we see the exposure of two Chinese traits. First, Chinese surpass Indians in more-royal-than-the-king style of internalizing foreign influences. Second, the Chinese readiness in modifying traditions, adapting traditions to changing times is greater than that of their Indian counterparts.

In the past, we have the Chinese enthusiasm in embracing Buddhism and be its flag-bearer long after Buddhism had gone out of fashion in its own motherland — India. Today, we see the younger generations in China much more westernized than their counterparts in India although few of the Chinese understand western languages equally well as the westernized and non-westernized Indians. Lu Xun, in his *Ah Q zhengzhuan* (the True Story of Ah Q), created a category called *Jiayang guizi* (the pseudo-foreign-devil). This reminds us of the Chinese Christian converts' being branded as *Ermaozi* (the secondary foreigner) during the anti-Christian riots in the end of the 19th century. Much of the popular hatred against the "Secondary Foreigners" was because of the latters' more-royal-than-the-king behaviour, using the deterrent image of the foreign conquerors to bully the natives. Lu Xun's Pseudo-Foreign-Devil is a caricature for such a behaviour. But, on closer examination we find an autobiographic note in presenting this notorious role by the author.[10] Lu Xun, in this way, was an unrepentent Pseudo-Foreign-Devil who advised Chinese youth to read only foreign language books. A typical reflex of Lu Xun's Pseudo-Foreign-Devil trait is his essay *Moluo shili shuo* (A Treatise on Mara/Demoniac Poetry Power). After praising Byron, Shelley, Pushkin etc., Lu Xun concluded: "Now, let us take up a search among Chinese writers, can we find any spiritual fighter? Can we find any sincere voice which can make our compatriots perfect and strong? Can we find any warm voice to render assistance to get us out of cold and barrenness?" Finally, he lamented that there was no voice of any sage to break the depression of China.[11]

We have, earlier quoted M.N. Roy's praise for Ram Mohun Roy who had many more courageous Chinese counterparts like Liang Qichao and fellow-campaigners of the 1898 "Hundred Days' Reform" (some of whom were executed). M.N. Roy, on the other hand, was a greater radical than Lu Xun. But, Lu Xun's writings on the whole are not as charitable to the reformers/ revolutionaries of his own country as M.N. Roy to his Indian seniors. In Lu Xun, his generosity to foreign progressive trends and his stinginess towards native progressive trends were two sides of the same coin. To view him in totality, Lu Xun was consciously playing the destructive role not because he wanted to destroy everything Chinese, but he was targeting at the young radical readership — trying to create a disillusionment among them for "Chineseness" so that a better China might emerge. Such an approach reached its maddening height during the Cultural Revolution (1966-69) which was, as Mao Zedong reiterated, guided by Laozi's philosophy of *Bupo buli* (no destruction, no construction). Paradoxically, it is the Hindu holistic perspective to project the God of Creation (Brahma), God of Destruction (Siva), and God of Preservation (Vishnu) as a three-in-one deity. It was Lu

Xun and Mao Zedong who unwittingly employed this destruction-construction dialectics to the pursuit of socio-political reinvigoration.

Lu Xun's greatest enemy (both ideologically and practically) was the "guocui" (national quintessence) school. In his campaign against the exponents of National Quintessence (those who thought Chinese civilization was great even during the time of China's national crisis), he was joined by a close friend Chen Duxu (1880-1942), founder of the Communist Party of China and founder-editor of *Xin Qingnian* (New Youth). In an editorial of the magazine, Chen wrote:

> "Speaking of conservatism, we indeed do not know which of our traditional institutions may be fit for survival in the modern world. I would rather see the ruin of our traditional 'national quintessence' than have our race of the present and future extinguished because of its unfitness for survival... The world continually progresses and will not stop." (Chow Tse-tsung, p. 46)

Here, again, the key words of the Enlightenment discourse are easy to find — progress and survival. It is in order that China should progress that Chen wants to do away with tradition which is, in turn, identified as unfit for progress. This dichotomy between an unfit old world and a dynamic new world is common to most of the contributors to *New Youth* such as Hu Shi, Li Dazhao, Cai Yuanpei, the then President/Vice-Chancellor of Beijing University.

Along with a plea to do away with out-moded tradition, Chen Duxiu and Hu Shi (1891-1962) tried to cultivate the spirit of individualism in China. Hu Shi stimulated the spread of individualism by introducing Ibsen to China. Hu Shi asserted that: "society destroyed individualism". This criticism was extended to the Chinese family system and its strict moral codes of conduct. Chen Duxiu published Samuel F. Smith's *America a hymn to freedom.* (Chow Tse-tsung, p. 295). The current of liberalism prevalent in China was on the whole influenced by Rousseau's concept of general will. Rousseau was popularized in China by Liang Qichao at the beginning of the 20th century. Other popular Western authors and their works introduced were John Stuart Mill and his *On Liberty,* Adam Smith and his *The Wealth of Nations,* Montesquieu's *L'esprit des Lois* and several other works all of which emphasise reason and rule of law. Along with this was the attitude of scientism, which was described by Duara as "the view which places all reality within the national order and deems it knowable by the method of science." (p. 87). This was the call which led China to rebellion against all things old including classical language. In fact, the *Baihua* (colloquial/ plain) language movement was one of the major reforms initiated during this period. (In fact, the May Fourth Movement which was supposed to be the foster-mother of the Communist Movement in China, ended as a strong drive for colloquial language and literature.) Intellectuals and students started talking and writing in modern Chinese as against the stilted formality of the classical style. This brought about not just a vernacularization of language but also of values. (Schwarcz, p. 73)

India and China's different reactions to the Enlightenment finally crystallized in their respective attitudes towards "tradition". While concentrating on her struggle for Independence, all social forces had to unite which gave India no opportunity to wage the kind of communist revolution that saw victory in China in 1949. The result was that, as Nehru put it: "India has to struggle with traditionalism in the shape of some aspects of Hinduism, caste, etc...."[12] Nehru often talked about India's road to modernization as that of China minus an "R" letter — China's being "revolution", and India's, "evolution". We think such a fundamental difference in approach deserves an intensive study if we wish to have an idepth understanding of India and China's modernization courses. Much has been said about India's "non-violent" tradition against China's pursuit of a violent revolution. There must be deeper socio-political factors than the presence or absence of force, belief or non-belief of "non-violence". After all, violence was not totally absent in the long course of India's Indenpendence movement, and her post-Independence socio-economic advancement.

The social status of the two countries' respective modernization engineers could be a factor. However, social science studies have graduated from the Marxist formulation of China's having a proletariat-peasants movement in contrast to India's bourgeois and petty-bourgeois reform. Prof. Ravinder Kumar thinks of a broad-based "social vision" being the dynamic force in India, and practically all the Indian strata wished to correct the anomaly created by British colonialism "whereby the Indian economy was drawn into a subordinate relationship with the economy of Great Britain" — developing a cash-crop and food-grain rural economy while allowing only commerce to grow in urban India, subjecting Indian industries under bondage. It was such a situation that created the Bengali intellectual awakening. (p. 140) Judging by this analysis, China, before 1949, had experienced an entire century of rural stagnancy and near bankruptcy. It was pauperization and destitution that had driven China's national awakening onto the warpath — destroying the rural share-cropping system.

III

Lu Xun, in the same essay on "Mara Poets", made a derogatory observation on India, lamenting that the great Indian civilization which had created the *Vedas*, the epics of *Ramayana* and *Mahabharata*, and the poems of Kalidasa, declined in race and human power, literary achievement was ruined. This dawn of civilization was transformed into a "shadowy state" (*ying guo*).[13] Indeed, when Chinese intellectuals felt threatened about national survival in the 19th and early 20th centuries, they were fond of quoting the Indian example — an example of "*wangguo nu*" (slaves without their own country). This was rather harsh, but it was meant as a shock treatment for the sick Chinese mentality rather than an attempt to malign a neighbour for whom Chinese had had greatest affinity and admiration. Lu Xun had another occasion to comment negatively on India when he recommended the youths to read less Chinese books. He commented: "When I read Chinese books I feel quiescent and distanced from the real human life. When I read foreign books — with the exception of India — I feel in touch with human life, and want to do some work."[14]

Liang Qichao, in his loud advocacy for Reforms in 1898 also cited the example of India, and attributed her becoming a British colony to her conservative tradition and changelessness since she was the most ancient civilization.[15] Both Lu Xun and Liang Qichao referred to India because of the close-neighbour effect. Such a close-neighbour effect is also reflected in the responses on civilization by Tagore, Nehru and others. We have already alluded to Lu Xun's habit of not being charitable to his compatriots who should have deserved a compliment or two for their endeavour to modernize China. Now, it seems that he was equally uncharitable to the contemporary Indian modernizers, but, we were told by Prof. Wang Shijing, famous biographer of Lu Xun (who was so gracious to have come to New Delhi all the way from Beijing to attend the Seminar we organized at the Jawaharlal Nehru University to commemorate Lu Xun's birth centenary in 1981), that Lu Xun had a great admiration for Tagore. When Lu Xun lectured at the Hong Kong YMCA on February 16, 1927, he said: "Let us think about what are the nations that don't have their voices. Do we hear the voice of Egypt? Do we hear the voice of Annam, of Korea? Apart from Tagore, do we hear other voice of India?"[16] So, here we find a rare occasion of Lu Xun's praising Tagore while painting a dismal picture of Asia.

Tagore, on the other hand, adopted a very China-friendly attitude from his youth. Dr. Kalidas Nag, Tagore's long-time secretary, wrote:

> "The earliest so-far-traced reference to Tagore's interest in Asian affairs is to be found in his Bengali article on *Death Traffic in China* protesting vigorously against the inhuman Opium trade of the European merchants. The article was published in 1881 before the foundation of the Indian National Congress.... when he read that brilliant vindication of Eastern idealism by Professor Lowes Dickinson in his *Letters of John Chinaman*, Tagore was the first to popularize the book in Bengali through his essay, *Chinamaner Chithi* (1905-06)."[17]

To Tagore, and here the holistic perspective dominates, the fate of India and the fate of China were interconnected. He felt indignant when China was aggressed upon. The same was the mindset of Nehru. Nehru's innumerable statements gave away his admirations for the bravery of Chinese people in fighting the Japanese aggression. Nehru's condemnation of the Japanese aggression was only outstripped by Tagore's correspondence with the Japanese poet Yone Noguchi in 1938. Noguchi initiated the correspondence in the hope of neutralizing Tagore and, through Tagore, the high-ups of the Indian public, but what he received was the outright condemnation of Japan and whole-hearted sympathy towards China from the Nobel laureate. Tagore explained that when he protested against "Westernization" during his lectures in Japan, he hoped the "land of Bushido" (Japan) would do nothing to imitate the Western "moral cannibalism"; now that Japan, too, was ruined "by their own war-lords run amok", destroying "the inner spirit of chivalry of Japan". Tagore said candidly rejecting an invitation to visit a Fascist Japan:

> "You know I have a genuine love for the Japanese people and it is sure to hurt me too painfully to go and watch crowds of them being transported by their rulers to a neigbouring land to perpetuate acts of inhumanity which will brand their name with a lasting stain in the history of Man."[18]

Tagore had admired Japan for her modern awakening and capacity to stand up before the western conquerors of the world as equals. But, Japans' being converted into the 8th or 9th imperialist aggressors of the world (being the only non-western new comer) pained Tagore, albeit his hope for a genuine Asian resurgence in true humanist spirit was not diminished. When Tagore condemned English irresponsibility towards India in his "crisis in civilization", he also criticized them in failing their "responsibility towards China in the Far East". When he expressed hope for the future he said: "Perhaps that dawn will come from this horizon, from the East where the sun rises"(Ghose, p.188, 189), obviously having China in mind also. Nehru, in his discourse on modern civilization in *The Discovery of India*, referred to China as "static", and wished both India and China learnt from the west, much as Liang Qichao mentioned India and China in the same breath. When Nehru stressed on the importance of spiritual value, he quoted the sayings of Confucius and Laozi (or Lao Tzu) to strengthen his argument. (p. 595-96)

As defeated nations by western imperialism, both India and China lost their independent initiatives to unite the two peoples together. Indian and Chinese modernizers could watch the social changes taking place in each other's countries through half open windows before Independence and Liberation. However, after more than a century of reacting to the challenge and beneficial influence of Englightenment, both India and China have advanced on the road of modernization in a similar manner. One significant change in the two ancient civilizations is the pro-active role of the youths who, for many thousand years, had been suppressed by a patriarchal tradition that dominated both India and China. In India, the organization of "Young Bengal", formed in the early 1830s, was dominated by youths. Members of this organization published journals (in Bengali) such as *Bigyan Sar Sangraha* and *Gyan-anvershan*. In China, there was the *New Youth* magazine which, like its senior Indian counterparts, was devoted to the propagation of Enlightenment and criticism of tradition. There was also the "Young Turk" movement in India which was to mobilize help and moral support for Turkey during the Balkan wars of 1912 and 1913. The movement was not wide spread. But it, once again, highlighted the pro-active role of the youth in a cultural tradition that used to subject the young firmly under the guidance of the seniors.

In China, the assertion of the younger generation has been even greater than India. For one thing, all the pioneers in the socio-political movements were young in age. Liang Qichao became a prominent leader behind Emperor Guangxu's "Hundred Day" reform edicts (1898) at the age of 25. When Sun Yat-sen started revolutionary activities in Hawaii in 1894, he was only 28, and those who supported him were almost all in their twenties and thirties. Huang Xing (1874-1916), the Commander-in-chief of the 1911 Revolution started organizing armed rebellion at the age of 30. Another fellow-revolutionary, Cai E (1882-1916), was a young man of 33 when he aborted Warlord Yuan Shikai's dream of becoming the emperor in 1915. Mao Zedong (1893-1976) was one of China's earliest conscious Marxist in his thirties, and became the world-famous "red star over China" at 42. Thousands of communist martyrs perished in their twenties and thirties which laid the foundation of the People's Republic of China. Lu Xun used to describe China as a "stern-eyed society" (*deng yanjingde shehui*) in which the son was forbidden to take any initiative under the stern-eyes of the father. When the son became a father, he did the same to his sons, forgetting how much he had resented at the receiving end of the stern-eyes. Lu Xun did not analyse why the sons could not break away the vicious "stern-eyed" circle. But it was Enlightenment which has freed China from such a strong patriarchal tradition. Similarly, Tagore, Gandhi, Nehru, Subhas Chandra Bose etc. all represented the assertion of Indian youths when they came to the limelight. Both India and China are countries full of youthful dynamism and vigour thanks to their interaction with western culture.

There has also been a sea change in both the countries about the status of women. This change has arrived through a long course of advocacy, struggle and reform. While in China, Yan Fu (1853-1931), Kang Youwei and Liang Qichao advocated education for women and an end to foot-binding, in India one of the first campaigns launched by the Bengali intelligentsia of this period was the demand to ban Sati (widow burning) and allow widow remarriage. In China, the campaign to improve the lot of women was part of a general reform of the family system. At the turn of the century, Yan Fu and other reformers, followed later by Chen Duxiu and other revolutionaries, argued that the old family system was inappropriate for China's needs in the modern times. In 1916, Chen Duxiu suggested that a new family system with freedom to each individual member be put in place. Writers such as Lu Xun, Hu Shi, Zhou Zuoren (1885-1968) and others called for the right of female education and the need to bring women out of confines of their houses. They even attacked the system of one-sided chastity. After the May Fourth Movement of 1919, girls started participating in the reform movement and the women's movement started in right earnest.[19]

The campaign against Sati in India was started by Ram Mohun Roy in 1818. In advocating the abolition of sati, Ram Mohun based his arguments on scriptural authority as well as on humanitarian grounds. (Pannikar, p. 89). Pannikar points out that, "In a sense the debate over sati was the beginning not only of a regional, but also of a national' intellectual community. It raised two questions: first, the relevance of scriptural sanction as a precondition for changing the social norms in vogue; secondly, the desirability of state intervention in socio-cultural matters." (p. 90)

Similarly, the debate about widow remarriage started as early as1835 and was already a much discussed issue when its most famous advocate, Vidyasagar published his treatise *Marriage of Hindu widows* in 1856. In all public discussions that occurred on this subject, the main question remained whether scriptural sanction was possible for these issues. Along with anti-sati and widow-remarriage, there was the even more important aspect of gender equality, recognizing women's potential to be equal to that of men.

Traditionally, India was less male-chauvinistic than China. This is proved by the existence of numerous goddesses in Indian legends in contrast to the paucity of them in early Chinese mythology. There was the interesting phenomenon of a woman, Wu Zetian, becoming a "Son of Heaven" (emperor) in Chinese history in the 8th century. She could do so only with the invocation of Buddhist sanctity. Another interesting phenomenon was the emergence of Guanyin who was supposed to be the Chinese version of Indian Bodhisattva Avalokitesvara, but turned out to be the most influential Goddess of Mercy in the East upto this day. This sequence of first a female replacing the male of China's "Son of Heaven", and then, an Indian male deity underwent sex metamorphosis in China all connected with Buddhism augured well for the women's liberation in this otherwise extremely male-chauvinist civilization. However, the evil institution of foot binding might have implicated Buddhism because the bound feet of high-class women were to match with those of the Boddhisattvas, whose footsteps on the ground looked like just a lotus petal. Today, China has stolen the thunder of even many western countries by projecting a phenomenon popularly known as *yinsheng yangshuai*, i.e. the thriving of women in contrast to the decline of men. In the field of sports in particular, it is the female athletes and sportspersons who have bagged most of the international honours for China. In comparison, the facelift of women's physical and mental potential and achievements in various fields are much greater in China than in India. Conversely, women from Communist China in North America and other countries are less stable in character and in marital faithfulness, and more vulnerable to bad influences and immorality than their counterparts from India, and from Taiwan, Hong Kong, Singapore, and other Asian countries also. Westernization has worked more fiercely in China than in India in both the benign and malignent directions so far as women are concerned.

What Duara has placed in the same category of Gandhi's *Ramarajya* is the *Datong* idealism by a modern Chinese scholar Liang Shuming (or Liang Souming). Liang discoursed on "Eastern and Western Civilizations and their philosophies" from 1921 onwards till he died recently. His work is appropriate here because he was a student of both Indian philosophy and Neo-Confucianism. Liang classified world civilization into three(which Duara has also alluded to). He used Schopenhauer's concept of "the will" as the basis of his division. The first was western civilization since the Renaissance. This civilization was based on what he called "the Will" going forward to seek satisfaction. It emphasized rationality, knowledge and the conquest of nature. The second was the Chinese way where the will did not go forward or backward but sideways. This way led to adjustment with circumstances rather than change. In Indian civilization Liang saw a case of atrophied will. The Indian did not go forward or adjust, he just became spiritual. This was the third way in which spiritual life and religion were fully developed but material conditions remained abject. (Chow Tse-tsung, p. 329) However, Liang went on to criticize western civilization as a dead end because here man had become a slave to machines. He advocated a combination of eastern and western civilizational ethos as the way forward. Liang's analysis of Indian civilization seems to hold true if we notice that in their encounter with western thought, Indian intellectuals always leave a space for spirituality.

Indian and Chinese intellectual's fascination with the ideals of Enlightenment did cause a sea change in their world views. The discourse of enlightenment also provided them with powerful and sharp tools of analytical reasoning that the intellectuals first used to question and criticize their own civilizations and later to condemn the continuing exploitation by the West. Here we notice a similarity and divergence in the way Indian and Chinese intellectuals worked. While in India, the growth of modern nationalism led to the demands first for reform under British rule and then for total withdrawal of the British, in China the very same growth of nationalism led to the emergence of the Communist Party as the final arbitrator of the political future of China. Both countries are thus staking a claim for a modern nationhood as different from that of its colonial masters.

Raychaudhuri points out that a distinctive product of Indian nationalism was its analysis of the economic problem, especially poverty (p. 15). Naoroji's *Poverty and Un-British rule in India* is the classic statement on this problem. The writer, like the other nationalists of the period, was to use precisely the arguments of Enlightenment to plead for a resurgence of native industry and manufacture. He was also to focus on the exploitative policies of the British in India and point out the drainage of resources systematically taking place. Another writer, Chandernath Basu also questioned the principles of *laissez faire* and pleaded for policies which would lead to the industrialization of India.

In China too, the admiration for the west turned into anti-western positions as the material conditions of Chinese society deteriorated throughout the 1920s and 1930s culminating in the civil war between the Communists and the Kuomintang factions. Here, too, the criticism of the west's economic exploitation and imperialism was to be at the forefront of the growing search for a new alternative for the nation.

One of the first intellectuals in China to turn his back on the Western project was the xenophile Liang Qichao. He, as we have noted, had been loud in advocating western ideas. After the first World War, Liang travelled to Europe and got himself disillusioned. Writing home from Europe he noted that:

"The Europeans have dreamed a vast dream of the omnipotence of science; now they decry its bankruptcy. This is a major turning point in current world thought." (Chow Tse-tsung, p. 328).

Ultimately, the project of westernization had to contend with another major pull in China, that of nationalism. Like in India, this new nationalism was a product of western thought and yet it was also the basis from which to criticize the West. This is perhaps best exemplified by the Communists who made use of Marxism and combined it with elements of tradition which allowed them a critical overview of both western history and their own history. One of the main critics of the west was Qu Qiubai (1899-1935), a leading communist in the early years. Writing in the early 1930s, Qu said:

"There is no cause left over from the May Fourth...China's cultural movement must now follow the needs of the revolution. Intellectuals and students must now take off the mantle of the May Fourth! What is needed and what ought to be is that they all gather under the banner of anti-imperialism." (Schwarzc, p. 287).

As the war with Japan escalated in the late 1930s and was followed by the massacres of Chinese people in Nanjing and other places, Qu's point of view gained many adherents. The disillusionment with the west was further strengthened by the awareness of the racist ideology of the westerners in China. Like in India, there were several places where "dogs and Chinese" were not allowed entry. After this period, those intellectuals who continued to champion European ideas and ways were looked down upon as "slaves to foreigners who had lost their peopleness and Chineseness." (Schwarzc, p. 288). With the victory of the communists in 1949, this criticism against the Enlightenment project as represented by the May Fourth intelligentsia reached its zenith.

In India too, along with a criticism of British economic policy, the Indian intellectual view of the British, and consequently of Europe was to suffer a jolt with the growth of racism in the latter part of the British rule. Ram Mohun Roy himself had been insulted by certain Englishman for not showing proper deference. The growing number of educated professionals, lawyers, doctors, journalists and other intellectuals, who had imbibed the ideas of the Enlightenment and been through British educational institutions were no longer willing to be second class citizens in their own country. This critique of the West is perhaps best represented by Gandhi in India and Mao in China, both of whom turned their backs to western products and western thought.

When we mention Mao and Gandhi we virtually step beyond the framework of our discourse on enchantment and disenchantment. On the part of Mao, he made two significant advances along the direction of modernization. First, he stood the champions of western Liberalism on their heads by embracing the propositions of Karl Marx who was the most ferocious critic of the western civilization. Then, after embracing Marx, he immediately stood him on his head by formulating his "Mao Zedong Thought" which was, in a way, the departure from the western modernization trends. Not only theoretically did Mao try to smuggle in the dynamism of "peasantry" to usurp the Marxian proletarian determinism, but in the political activities of the People's Republic of China to which Mao was the supreme ruler there were a series of outlandish directives and approaches that baffled all the ideologues of historical and dialectical materialism, culminating in the Cultural Revolution and the "Gang of Four" agenda of willingly opting "socialist" poverty, ignorance and backwardness by rejecting "bourgeois" prosperity, enlightenment and advancement.

Gandhianism in India has some resemblance to Maoism in China albeit there is no consensus among Indian social scientists, even among the Gandhian followers about the true nature of Gandhianism. One commonality between the two is self-reliance, and another is the reiteration of spiritual value. Duara has equated Gandhi's *Ramarajya* idealism with the Chinese *Datong* utopia (p. 233) although Mao seldom championed this utopia which was distinctively Confucian. Tagore, however, christened his university with his utopian idealism of "*Visva-bharati*" and Tan Yun-shan (1898-1983) formulated a Sino-Indian utopia, by writing "Datong" into the aims and objectives of the Sino-Indian Cultural Society of which Tagore was the President of its Indian chapter from 1934 to 1941, which position was taken over by Nehru in an honorary capacity. We should add that "Datong" and "Taiping" are similar ideals and there could be the input of "*Mahasamata*" in the Taiping utopia.[20]

We have alluded to Nehru's reference to the "highest ideals" of the modern age, while Nehru seemed to have distanced himself from Gandhi's *Ramarajya* utopia. Being highly suspicious about anything which had a religious overtone, Nehru did commend Albert Einstein's observation that "the serious scientific workers are the only profoudly religious people." (p. 593) Nehru also added a footnote: "Fifty years ago, Vivekananda regarded modern science as a manifestation of the real religious spirit, for it sought to understand truth by sincere effort." (ibid) Thus, both Gandhi and Nehru went along the road of modernization by reiterating spiritualism, although there was a degree of difference in their respective reiteration.

This brief discourse about some narratives reflecting Chinese and Indian responses to the call of nation building, crisis management, and international cultural interface and synergy can help historians from India and other countries to re-examine History, and join the efforts of Professor Prasenjit Duara and other scholars in arriving at a deeper understanding on the development of Asia, particularly India and China. This has assumed even greater importance as Harvard University professor Samuel P. Huntington has drawn the contours of the "clash of civilizations" in the post-Cold War world. First of all, we cannot but agree with Huntington that "Human history is the history of civilizations. It is impossible to think of the development of humanity in any other terms."[21] The popularity of Huntington's new discourse is bound to draw greater scholarly attention to civilizational behaviours. There is no doubt of the Cold War inheritance and Superpower arrogance in the Huntington paradigm. But, the threat of a doomsday prospect (which is what Huntingtonism boils down to) is much more civilized than the threat of nuclear armament and that of information-based warfare. Secondly, while world civilization is becoming more democratic, equitable and holistic, Huntingtonism seems to revoke the ghost of White Man's Burden, and social Darwinism of the worst kind. Incidentally, Huntington has also discussed China's "response to the West and Modernization" and seems to have picked up from Prof John King Fairbank's waste-paper basket the following proposition:

> "Unlike Japan, China's rejectionist policy was in large part rooted in the Chinese image of itself as the Middle Kingdom and the firm belief in superiority of Chinese culture to those of all other peoples."[22]

Huntington has a very naive way in looking at the Sino-Indian cultural interface in history, as he observes:

> "China's absorption of Buddhism from India, scholars agree, failed to produce the 'Indianization' of China. The Chinese adopted Buddhism to Chinese purposes and needs. Chinese culture remained Chinese... The Chinese have to date consistently defeated intensive Western efforts to Christianize them."[23]

The thrust of these observations is not as ridiculous as the anti-China mind behind them which could arrive at the following outlandish and shocking conclusion:

> "The United States, Europe, Russia, and India have thus become engaged in a truly global struggle against China, Japan, and most of Islam."[24]

again,

> "With the West, Russia, China, and Japan devastated [in the war] ... the way is open for India, if it escaped such devastation even though it was a participant, to attempt to reshape the world along Hindu lines."[25]

We don't want to turn our essay into a shadow-boxing with Huntington, but just to quote Huntington to highlight the importance of indepth understanding of civilizational intercourse which Prasenjit Duara has piloted. To return to what we have quoted at the very outset, i.e. Duara's aim to stear clear from romanticizing either the West or China, Huntington has opened another prospect of demonizing both — even India is being implicated. Should we now — the scholars of India and China — join Duara and try to draw the contours of *Ramarajya* and *Datong* for the future destiny of humanity, or let Huntington and company push civilizations to a mutually injuring clash — enabling India to build a Hindu temple on the global debris? We look forward to answers and more answers!

Notes

1. On the basic philosophy and critical criteria of the Enlightenment philosophy, see Earnest Cassirer, *The Philosophy of the Enlightenment*, Princeton, 1951.
2. Immanuel Kant, "What is Enlightenment" in Hans Reiss (ed.), *Kant's Political Writings*, London, 1970, p. 54.
3. Adorno and Horkheimer essentially developed the notion of disenchantment of the self away from traditional religious moorings as one of the consequences of the Industrial Revolution. We have used the concept here to express the complicated relationship that existed between the Indian and Chinese intellectuals and the project of Enlightenment.
4. Cited in Wu Tsu-hsiang, *Sun Yixian Xiansheng Zhuan* (Biography of Sun Yat-sen), Hong Kong: Far East Book Company, 1982, Vol. 1, p. 114.
5. *M.N. Roy, "Indian Renaissance"* in Verinder Grover (ed.), M.N. Roy, New Delhi: Deep & Deep Publications, 1991, pp. 101-103.
6. *Selected Works of Mao Tse-tung* Vol. IV, Beijing/Peking: Foreign Language Press 1969, pp. 412-13.
7. See Part II, the first piece quoted in this volume.

8. Tan Chung has led this contest, and his *Triton and Dragon* has been widely read and appreciated by teachers and students of Chinese history in the Indian universities.
9. Tan Chung coined the words of "responsible imperialism" and "irresponsible imperialism" in his discourse on the "unequal treaty system". (See Tan Chung, pp. 250-58).
10. Tan Chung, "Ah Q or Superman? An appraisal of the appraisals of Lu Xun", in *China Report*, Vol. XIII, Nos. 2&3 (March-June), 1982, pp. 25-26.
11. See *Lu Xun Quanji* (Collected Works of Lu Xun), Beijing: People's Publishing House, 1981, Vol. 1, pp. 63-100.
12. Nehru's Presidential address at the general body meeting of the Indian Institute of Public Administration in New Delhi on April 6, 1957. See *Jawaharlal Nehru's Speeches*, Vol. 3 (1953-1957), New Delhi : Publications Division, 1983, p. 165.
13. *Lu Xun Quanji*, Vol. 1, p. 63.
14. *Ibid*, Vol. 3, p. 12.
15. Liang Qichao, "Lun bubianfazhi hai "(on the harm of non-reform), in *Wuxu bianfa* (the 1898 Reforms), reference materials compiled by the China Historical Society, Shanghai: People's Publishing House, 1957, Vol. 3, p. 12.
16. *Lu Xun Quanji*, Vol. 4, p.15.
17. Kalidas Nag, *Discovery of Asia*, Calcutta: The Institute of Asian African Relations, 1957, p. 9.
18. See *Poet to Poet*, Santiniketan: Sino-Indian Cultural Society, 1938, *passim*.
19. For details, see Ravni Thakur's article in this volume.
20. See Tan Chung's article "Sino-Indian Perspective" in this volume.
21. Samuel P. Huntington, *The Clash of Civilizations And The Remaking of World Order*, paperback, Penguin Books, 1997, p. 40.
22. *Ibid*, p. 72.
23. *Ibid*, p. 76.
24. *Ibid*, p. 315.
25. *Ibid*, p. 316.

References

Chow Tse-tsung (1960), *The May Fourth Movement: Intellectual Revolution in Modern China*, Stanford: Stanford Unversity Press.

Duara, Prasenjit (1995), *Rescuing History from the Nation: Questioning narratives of modern China*, Chicago: The University of Chicago Press.

Ghose, Sisirkumar (ed.), (1966), *Tagore for You*, Calcutta : Visva-Bharati.

Kumar, Ravinder (1983) *Essays in the social History of Modern India*, New Delhi: Oxford University Press.

Pannikar, K.N. (1994) *Culture, Ideology, Hegemony: Intellectuals and Social Consciousness in Colonial India.*, New Delhi: Oxford University Press.

Raychaudhuri, Tapan (1988), *Europe Reconsidered: Perceptions of the West in Nineteenth Century Bengal*, Delhi: Oxford University Press.

Schwarcz, V. (1986), *The Chinese Enlightenment: Intellectuals and the legacy of the May Fourth Movement of 1919*, University of California Press.

Tan Chung (1986), *Triton and Dragon: Studies of Nineteenth Century China and Imperialism*, Delhi : Gian Publishing House.

MIRA SINHA BHATTACHARJEA

13

GANDHI AND MAO: NATIONAL IDENTITY FOR AN ALTERNATIVE FUTURE

By Way of Explanation

M.K. Gandhi and Mao Zedong continue to be highly controversial political figures even decades after they have faded away from the political scene. Questions of a fundamental nature regarding their political roles and philosophies still surround them. For instance: Was Gandhi a saint, a religious and ethical teacher, or a wily politician? Was he really an uncompromising opponent of modernity? Was Mao more Chinese, less Marxist? Did his "thought" contribute to the relevance and enrichment of Marxism in the changed world of the 20th century? Or was it a denial of ideological fundamentals? Did their philosophies and praxis have significance beyond the historical time and the national space in which they lived and worked? It is therefore necessary to begin by outlining my approach to an understanding of these two men as well as the whole integrated complex of thought and action that together constitute the historical role they played.

I regard Gandhi and Mao as the most outstanding of the many remarkable men that Asia, and perhaps the world, has known in this century. The ideas they advocated and the methods they used were unique and novel. They cannot be appreciated in their fullness if they are located within the narrow confines of the nation, its culture and history, or even of the spiritual knowledge and intellectual traditions on which they drew. The historical context in which they functioned was of course, national. But, what they opposed and the objectives they set for their national struggles were global and holistic. To explain: Both men struggled against and rejected not merely the colonizing or invading power (Britain for Gandhi and Japan for Mao) but the system as each perceived it that these powers represented. This was western civilization, industrialization or modernisation as Gandhi termed it. Or, imperialism, colonialism and capitalism, as Mao called it. The phenomenon both opposed was, to put it loosely, the West.

Although Gandhi and Mao approached this phenomenon from widely different if not mutually hostile perspectives, both understood it as being exploitative, oppressive, violent and dehumanizing. Both also perceived the West (qua system) as rapidly becoming hegemonic across the globe, ready to draw in all post-colonial newly independent nations. This was the only and seemingly inevitable future for all nations, including their own, which they rejected. It was, however, a desirable and tempting future for many, replete as it was with the promise of progress, modernity, and national strength. Gandhi and Mao advocated instead, a value-centred alternative future, and experimented with new type political and economic institutions and social relationship as interrelated parts of an equally holistic and integrated system. Neither, however, specially Gandhi, had a road map or detailed blue print of the alternative future. For Mao, there was the example of the Soviet Union which, however, he did not follow, and which, in later years, he treated as a "negative" not positive example.

Both men, I argue, perceived their national political circumstances in essentially similar ways. One was that the challenge of the West qua system, confronted the nation in both the outer (external) and inner (domestic) spheres of national life. This in turn dictated the dual objectives that each set for his national struggle: independent statehood, and an end of the dominant-subordinate equation that characterized the colonizing/aggressor power and the nation in the outer sphere. And, in the inner sphere, the objective was to catch up with modernity and the modern world. In the 20th century modernity, it can be argued, was a historical necessity and not a matter of choice specially for large entities like India and China. To these objectives that were common to all newly independent countries, Gandhi and Mao added the objective of guiding the country towards rejecting the West and envisaging an alternative future.

The other was the national condition of India and China. The two countries were continental in size and population; with a diversity of nationalities, religions and, in India, languages. They were rural, poor and in the main, pre-modern in every aspect of national life, including an underdeveloped sense of the national self in modern political terms.

It was towards these ends that the two leaders aroused a proud and self-reliant nationalism among the masses, and used a political idiom that borrowed heavily from popular tradition and culture. Both based their national struggles on the peasant and the countryside; gave priority to agriculture; to collective and manual labour over the machine, whether tractor or factory; to traditional but improved means of production (the spinning wheel and the hoe). Both also rejected the intellectual traditions and educational systems of the West as a package, and borrowed selectively what was useful. Simultaneously, however, both stressed the need for the masses to acquire features of modernity like punctuality, efficiency, objectivity, rationality, individual rights and of course technology.

Gandhi and Mao also, in broadly similar fashion, attempted to convey a picture of their preferred alternative societies to the masses. They did so again, in cultural and pre-modern terms. Gandhi spoke of the future as *Rama Rajya* and Mao of *Tatong*. These terms were invested with radically different content and meaning which, yet again, was conveyed to the people in startlingly similar ways. For one, the method of political struggle was itself a teaching/learning experience which, over the long term, helped generate a new political culture, as did participation in productive work and, of course, formal instruction. The preferred mode of conveying the new meaning to the people for both, was personal and leadership example. It was also perhaps the most effective.

It was towards these ends within view Gandhi and Mao in fact conceptualised and constructed a culturally rooted, poor peasant national identity. This contrived identity not only reflected the national condition, it formed the basis of a new national unity and the focus of policy. Even more, it contained the seeds of its evolution over time into a future identity as *satyagrahi* for Gandhi, and the proletariat for Mao, appropriate to their envisaged futures. Each personified this complex identity by his personal identification with his nation and its poor peasant. At the same time, each also personified the evolving identity of the *satyagrahi* or true proletariat immanent in it.

Images are powerful things. The images of Gandhi and Mao as nationalists and peasant leaders are still powerful enough to discourage any serious considerations of the universalist dimension of the national identities they constructed, and of the alternate systems they advocated not for their nations alone, but for all humankind.

The essay that follows, is a preliminary attempt at examining how Gandhi and Mao came to construct such complex national identities and why these identities have been rejected by both societies.

I

The life and personality of Mahatma Gandhi were such as to create a series of indelible images each symbolic of the man, of his political role, and of his larger message. Four such images are evocative and compelling.

One is of the quiet withdrawn ascetic working his *charkha* in deep empathy with the peasant. The second is of the spindly legged leader, at the head of a ragged band of equally spindly legged followers, marching to the sea to defy the mighty British Empire, by the simple mundane act of making salt from sea water. The third is of a determined, half-naked fakir striding proudly up the steps of Buckingham Palace. The fourth, is again of a Gandhi working his *charkha*. But this time, withdrawn into grey silence in Calcutta, face turned away from the Independence Day celebrations in Delhi. All four images unmistakably establish Gandhi's identity as an Indian, as one of India's dumb millions. This is the Gandhi Nehru described in 1944 as "the great peasant, with a peasant's out-look on affairs and a peasant's blindness to some aspects of life..."[1] who nevertheless, symbolized the nation and awakened it to life, hope and courage.

The last image, for Nehru at least, was symbolic perhaps of Gandhi's "peasant blindness" to some aspects of life, modernity, industrialization and machine magic, which was the Congress choice in 1947, denying the Gandhian alternative. This last image conveyed in a manner that words cannot, the depth of Gandhi's depression over the Congress decision to accept partition, which for him was an evil and a "sin" — and the failure of his chosen heir, and of the nation, to walk him towards *swaraj*.

All four images convey without ambivalence, Gandhi's Indianness, an identity that has never been seriously questioned either by his political opponents or by his followers. Gandhi was, in appearance, in dress, in the political vocabulary and in the political symbols he adopted, as well as in the methods of political action that he innovated, deeply and rootedly Indian. He was not uncertain of his Indianness as was Nehru and, in Gandhi's view, the westernized Indian, "a queer mixture of East and West, out of place everywhere, at home no where" as Nehru described himself.[2]

Yet only the last image conveys also Gandhi's universalism in its inability to celebrate only a transfer of power from British to Indian hands, and the rejection of his alternative future. This nation-transcending identity however, has never been seriously examined and explored. On the contrary it has been more often rejected and denied by locating him exclusively in Hindusim and as a discrete Indian. Yet Gandhi's refusal to celebrate independence or to regard it as the end goal of the struggle he had led, his sojourn in Noakhali and in riot-torn Calcutta, taken together with his major post-independence activity, testify to his commitment to the goal of *Purna swaraj* as analternative future for all nations and for humankind as a whole. In short, Gandhi's identity with all mankind and indeed with all forms of life, has not been recognised in his own country. This is ironic for Gandhi's concern for all forms of life has been universally acknowledged. Recognition of the universalism of Gandhi's message came even during his lifetime — from Leo Tolsoy as early as 1910 and, decades later, from Albert Einstein who regarded Gandhi "as the only truly great political figure of our age". "The veneration in which Gandhi has been held throughout the world" he wrote, "rests on the recognition, for the most part unconscious, that in our age of moral decay he was the only statesman who represented that higher conception of human relations in the political sphere to which we must all aspire with all our powers... It is my belief that the problem of bringing peace to the world on a supranational basis will be solved only by employing Gandhi's methods on a large scale."[3] In later years, Gandhi's method of non-violent political revolution inspired movements as varied as those of Martin Luther King in the US, of Czeck students during the Prague Spring; of the Vietnamese bonzes; and the Eritrean rebels whose motto was "Gandhi in one hand and the gun in the other" and even of a section of Chinese students who demonstrated at Tiananmen in 1989. That Gandhi's universalist identity was visible through his Indian idiom in politics is also affirmed by the number of non-Indians who were drawn to work with him from his earliest days in South Africa upto his death. Indeed, it is possible to assert that Gandhi's identity as a universalist thinker is more relevant and commanding today than is his identity only as an Indian nationalist.

The same seems to be broadly true of Mao Zedong the other great Asian personality of this century. Like Gandhi, the Chinese peasant identity he represented was widely valued and acknowledged through the years of the national struggle, but has lost its appeal and relevance in today's China. But, unlike Gandhi, Mao's universalist or Marxist image has also suffered largely because of the collapse of the communist experiment worldwide. It has, however, still more vitality and universal appeal than does that of Stalin or even of Lenin.

In Mao's case however, despite his deliberate choice of Marxism-Leninism as the fount of his ideas and practice, his Chineseness was never in doubt. A year after Mao's death, Wang Gungwu assessing Mao wrote: "No one surely could mistake Mao for anyone but a Chinese."[4] Like Gandhi, Mao's Chineseness resided in his appearance, in his dress (the blue jacket of the peasant), his language, in the symbols and methods of political action that he innovated. And, above all, like Gandhi, it resided in his identification with the peasant. Unlike Gandhi, Mao's identity as peasant was more spontaneous and natural. He came from peasant stock and had not been denaturalized by western education and culture as had Gandhi. Consequently, Wang Gungwu observed that "Mao never wasted time worrying about his Chinese identity or about the decline and fall of Chinese civilization. He was effortlessly and supremely confident about being Chinese almost the way Churchill was about being English, and never suffered the agonies and self doubts, which paralysed so many of his generation."[5] Mao could therefore, he said, take a foreign ideology like Marxism-Leninism to the Chinese people "as if it were the most natural thing for him to do."[6]

Again, like Gandhi, since Mao's Chineseness was never in doubt, its imprint on the borrowed ideology was proudly acclaimed in the sinification of Marxism. In turn, despite Mao's self-identification as a Marxist, the seriousness with which he undertook theoretical explorations and innovative practices of Marxism (and his deliberate attempts to uproot the Confucian basis of Chinese culture), provoked wide debate on whether or not Mao was a Marxist. In the late 1960s, as Sino-Soviet relations worsened, Moscow and the CPSU, as the explicators of Marxist doctrine, placed Mao firmly in the category of a chauvinist Chinese with a feudal mentality thus challenging his Marxist identity. "Mao thought" was condemned as being parochial, as having no universalist theories, by Soviet theoreticians. Within China, Mao's post-1958 Marxist innovations were condemned by his domestic political opponents as "mistakes" having no relevance to Marxism or to China or to its economic development. The tragic Cultural Revolution was Mao's last attempt to revitalise the struggle for liberation at least within China, and to put the Chinese and world revolution back on the right tracks. If Gandhi turned his back on the achievement of independent statehood for India in August 1947, and even on the Congress Party a few months later by advising it to disband itself, then Mao, it may be said, turned his back on all the achievements of the Chinese Communist Party and the Chinese state over some 35 years, by calling upon the people to "Bombard the Headquarters" at the start of the Cultural Revolution.

Like Gandhi, Mao, it seems, was prepared to plough a lonely furrow, to risk sacrificing the political future of China, if necessary, for the cause of making revolution world wide.

As political leaders and thinkers, Gandhi and Mao had dual objectives, dual concerns and they followed, therefore, dual strategies. They walked politically, to borrow a Maoist phrase, on two legs. Gandhi's striving throughout his life, was to seek and "do truth", just as Mao's was to pursue his socialist truth and, in like manner, to "do socialism", or in his words to "make revolution". For both each individual act and policy therefore had to be illumined by, and reflect this search. Each act had also to contain the seed or the germ of its own enlargement into an ever higher dimension of "truthful" (for Gandhi) and "revolutionary" (for Mao) life, that would lead to the desired future. Few, if any, of their acts were finite or limited in purpose, meaning and symbolic significance. It would however be incorrect to assume that the two great leaders began with the gift of certitude about the desired future. Instead, each acknowledged the experimental and tentative nature of his search and of his truth and liberating action. The only certitude both had was that of what should not be. For Gandhi this was what he variously termed as modern, western or industrial civilization best epitomized in Imperial Britain and its political, social and economic institutions. For Mao it was "capitalism" best epitomized in western imperialism, and after World War II, in the United States and its social and economic institutions. It is important to emphasize here, that both Gandhi and Mao were opposed to the *systems* that colonialism and imperialism represented not merely to the country that was the nation's imperialist enemy i.e., to British colonisation of India or to Japanese aggression in China. For both it was not the British and Japanese nation or people that was the enemy or the other. It was their system and the values and policies it advocated and adopted. The fact of colonisation and aggression only provided the occasion, the external condition, and the basis for invigorating their oppressed countrymen into collective struggle for national independence as the first major step towards the higher goal of *swaraj* or socialism. Thus from the earliest their separate political activity was conducted at two distinct levels of objectives, method and organisation. The one, independence, was limited in time to the short run, and in space, only to the nation. The other, namely *swaraj* or socialism, extended into epochal time and encompassed all of humankind.

On his return to India, Gandhi worked through the Indian National Congress and its leaders for political independence from British rule. It was for the attainment of this objective tht he was to name Jawaharlal Nehru as his heir, in acknowledgement of Nehru's national standing. Mao, in Yanan, was as unaware of Gandhi's political thought and action, as Gandhi was unaware of his. The two great leaders were distant neighbours. But, in 1937 when the second united front with the KMT was formed, Mao like Gandhi, also worked for China's national liberation from Japanese aggression through the KMT and its leader, Chiang Kai-shek, acknowledging thereby the national following that Chiang could command. Both, as history and even their successor regimes testify, were successful in the way they worked this strategy. In 1947 India and in 1949 China emerged into nationhood and independence. India's post-independence leaders acknowledged Gandhi's contribution and leadership gratefully, and enshrined him as the father of the nation. In China, after the death of Mao, Deng Xiaoping and his comrades continued to praise Mao for his leadership of the national liberation movement, even as they proceeded to diminish his Marxist contributions.

Both leaders were at that time and for a considerable time thereafter, minor or side currents within the mainstream of the national movements of their countries and within, as it were, their parent parties, the Congress and the KMT. Both however, honed and trained their own corps of followers distinct from what I have called their parent parties: Gandhi, through his constructive programme trained *satyagrahis* and Mao, in Yanan, trained and disciplined the communist party. These were their "troops" in the struggle for the higher goal of *swaraj* for Gandhi and socialism for Mao. For both leaders, however, there could be no sharp divide between the two broad goals. It would be incorrect therefore to describe them as first stage and second stage goals. Instead they were for both Gandhi and Mao, umbilically linked parts or aspects of a whole. To explain: It was said earlier that for both men each individual act even in the struggle for independence contained the seed or the germ of its own enlargement into ever higher dimensions of *swarajist* or socialist life. Thus the method, the programme and the leadership of the movement for the attainment of political independence were to be the womb and guarantors of this later enlargement. For Gandhi the effort was to transform the Congress from within, to commit it to the use of "truthful and non-violent means, and to the service of the dumb semi-starved millions who inhabited India's 700,000 villages. Towards this end, he tried to transform the Congress by giving it a mass (peasant) base, a four anna membership, as well as *khadi*, the livery of the empowered poor, and to have the Congress employ Hindustani instead of English, and make it the common language of the people.

That was in 1920 when the special session of the Congress held in Calcutta, which seemed to usher in a Gandhi era in Indian politics. Writing his *Autobiograpy,* Nehru recalled how "the whole look of the Congress changed; European clothes vanished and soon only *khadi* was to be seen; ..... the language used became increasingly Hindustani... and there was a growing prejudice against using a foreign language in our national work, and a new life and enthusiam and earnestness became evident in Congress gatherings.[7] It was then that Congress and with it, India, adopted the Indian identity that Gandhi had so carefully constructed, and made it their own. Two years later violence broke out at Chauri Chaura. This and many other happenings made Gandhi realize that neither Congress nor its leaders like Nehru had been converted to his philosophy of non-violence, that the majority were uncomfortable with the identity he had created. It seemed likely then that they would not share in the struggle and sacrifice for *purna swaraj.* Gandhi then withdrew organisationally from the Congress to train his *satyagrahi's* for carrying the struggle beyond independence to *swaraj* with, without, or even against an untransformable Congress. Nevertheless Gandhi continued to work with the Congress and to influence its decisions in the direction of adopting only non-violent methods of struggle even if it did not accept his philosophy, and towards a compromise form of system that he called "parliamentary *swaraj.*" However, the manner in which independence was finally accepted by Congress, namely its *voluntary* acceptance of the partition of India on religious grounds, destroyed that identity and unity of the Indian nation and the Indian people which he had so deliberately constructed and of which he had made himself the living symbol.

II

Gandhi's own Indian identity was slow to evolve. The process began when he was a young boy, and reached its loin cloth, sandalled image only in middle age. As a child he ate the forbidden meat because, as he confessed in his autobiography, "he wished to be strong and daring *and wanted my countrymen also to be such, so that we might defeat the English and make India free.*"[8] Little is known of his childhood experiences to explain this early sense of nationalism, of country and nation. We may safely presume that political nationalism was in the Indian air, as it were, as was its corollary, the urge for political freedom. The Englishman in his strength and stature (five cubits tall), remained the model for the young nationalist to emulate. This was further reinforced in London when he encountered the resident British and found them to be highly principled and tolerant. So Gandhi's first response was to become "a proper Englishman" in dress, in manners and in accomplishments. Yet he remained a hungry vegetarian for he had vowed, under maternal pressure, not to eat meat. Vegetarianism however soon became a matter of faith and belief for Gandhi began to redefine the meaning of strength. In articles that he wrote for the *Vegetarian* he set out to prove that Indians, though vegetarians, were "as strong, if not stronger than Indian meat eaters and for that matter, even Englishman ...."[9] He also abandoned the attempt to become a fancy English gentleman and began to advocate the virtues of simplicity and frugality. Gandhi's ideal type from then on was that of a strong sturdy vegetarian "shepherd," who led an outdoor life in harmony with nature. Where Gandhi derived this idea from is not known. Just as I have been unable to explain why, suddenly, Gandhi became aware of salt as a heavily taxed article, a burden on the poor millions of India, and therefore an act and a symbol of the great injustice of colonialism and of the ruling British. Gandhi never lost sight of these ideas. Rather, they came to provide the first rough sketch of the Indian identity that he was to conceptualise, construct, and assume over the coming years in South Africa and complete in India.

His years in London were evidently a period when Gandhi experienced deep confusion about his identity, and what it meant to be an Indian. This was also the period in which he became aware of his ignorance and of his very limited knowledge of things Indian. Thus, when asked by Quaker friends to compare the English version of the Gita with the original, he was ashamed at having to confess that he was neither familiar with its text, nor could he read Sanskrit. In similar fashion, it was a Conservative member of Parliament whose advice led him to read Indian history and to familiarise himself with Indian customs before he began to practise law in India. It was also in London that Gandhi discovered religion and was strongly drawn towards Christianity. He joined the Theosophical Society but resisted conversion on the plea of his ignorance about the religion into which he had been born. It was perhaps only a deep innate sense of national pride that precluded him from being converted. Thus began his search for his Indian roots, and a discovery of India quite unlike that of Nehru, for it was more an exploration of the meaning of India and of being Indian.

This exploration took the form of learning about Hindu, not historical India; of studying not his provincial language, but Sanskrit, the classical language of India and of its great philosophical writings; of finding a way to live and practise law, ethically and honestly. He returned to India a compulsive social reformer, beginning first with his own family. He introduced all manner of reform -- though still on western lines — including physical exercise, dietary changes, the wearing of shoes and of European instead of Indian dress and so on. Unable to compromise with the moral corruption he saw all around him, and even in the profession that was supposed to ensure justice, he failed miserably as a lawyer. His only success was to draft a memorial for a poor Muslim farmer whose land had been confiscated, for which he charged no fee. Nevertheless the debts he had accumulated had to be met, so Gandhi escaped to South Africa when the opportunity arose.

In South Africa, Gandhi's life was soon dominated by the world of politics, and the relationship between imperial Britain and its subjects. I have said elsewhere that he *experienced* South Africa in that he reacted with deep humiliation to racial discrimination as its social practice and its official policy. Even the rich established traders of Durban did not, he found, react to "conditions which implied grave insult" because, as Gandhi observed, "they did not mind such things being habituated to them."[10] Gandhi had arrived in South Africa when anti-Indian feeling was on the rise and the law described the Hindus as "semi-barbarous Asiatics or persons belonging to the uncivilized races of Asia, who were therefore not legally entitled to the rights enjoyed by the "civilized"[11] The worst sufferers were the Hindus, the only Indian group to be called "Asiatics". The Mussalmans, though Indian, declared themselves to be Arabs, the Parsees claimed to be Persians, and the Indian converts (who were largely waiters), to be Christian, and were therefore not, by legal definition, "Asiatics" and uncivilized. Only the Hindu was called a "*coolie*", with all what that term denoted. Gandhi, to his distress discovered that there was no "Indian" community, for none of the 150,000 Indians in Natal, was aware of his identity as an Indian.

Gandhi had gone to South Africa only on a year's contract and was reluctant to undertake practical action to rectify this state of affairs. Nevertheless, he used his time to investigate the Indian condition in South Africa and to impress upon the traders the gravity of the problem as he saw it. He also wrote letters to the newspapers to establish insult, to protest insult to the traders, and to create a sympathetic public opinion by appealing to the much admired British system of justice and to Christian values. he also advised the traders to organise themselves. And, when his farewell party turned into a working committee meeting because of the proposed government move to defranchise even the propertied traders, Gandhi decided to stay on and to fight.

As Gandhi constructed the problem, he perceived it to be principally one of identity. Many years later at his famous trial in Ahmedabad, Gandhi would say that it was in South Africa that he discovered that as a man and an Indian he had no rights. *"More correctly I discovered that I had no rights as a man because I was an Indian."*[12] The identity imposed on them, that Gandhi felt had to be rejected by those of Indian origin, was that of the Hindu as *coolie* who was by legal definition therefore, uncivilised. Even Gandhi himself, respected in London and Bombay, was regarded as a *coolie*, being Hindu, though he was *a lawyer trained at the Inner Temple*. Gandhi therefore swiftly drew up a strategy of petitions to the Natal Legislative Assembly and to the Secretary of State for the Colonies in London. The very first petition rejected the *coolie* identity and claimed a new identity for all Indians. It began with the sentence "Your petitioners are *British subjects*". This phrasing placed all Indians as British subjects, under British protection even from Natal's colonial legislation. The sanction for claiming this identity was derived from the Queen's Proclamation of 1885 which promised "our subjects, of *whatever race or creed* be freely and impartially admitted to office in our service...." Indians in South Africa, Gandhi argued, were first subjects of the British Empire because the Indians of India were its subjects, and were as such resident in South Africa. Gandhi was to convert this claimed identity into a statement of political fact not open to infringement or compromise. This petition, according to Gandhi, sowed "the seed of the fight for *national self respect*"[13] of the despised Hindu and Indian in far away South Africa.

His activity thereafter took on that rounded character so characteristic of all Gandhi's political action. He used this identity to fuse the divided, apathetic and demoralised Indians, into a self aware and united community. He built ties between this new community and India as the mother country; and made both the Congress and the British Indian government aware of his struggle against what he called "national injustice". Simultaneously he insisted that the Indians as British subjects, should demonstrate their loyalty to the Crown, and as Indians, should organise themselves. So the Natal Indian Congress was established and the rich traders became its mainstay, the Christians its translators and the indentured labourers, the only real *coolies*, its mass base. Under his direction, the Natal Indian Congress became a "teaching shop." Its members learnt to speak up, to question, to participate in discussion and decision making. They were introduced to Indian history and culture to counter the charge of being uncivilized, and were educated in election procedures, hygiene, sanitation, keeping accounts, recording proceedings and punctuality. In short, the members were being forged slowly but deliberately into a *modern* Indian community united across religion, language, social status and caste. And, when famine broke out in India, the Natal Indian Congress (NIC) collected donations for "the starving poor" in India, thus forging links with the motherland. Gandhi also committed the NIC, meaning the rich traders, to serve and support "the poor and the helpless" meaning the indentured labourers or *coolies*, with whom they had little in common. This was perhaps his first experiment with political trusteeship. A few years later, when the strategy of petitions needed to be strengthened with more direct political action, the wealthy traders would become "*coolies*." They sold vegetables from door to door, like *coolies*, in support of the indentured. Later, Gandhi would lead his long march of the indentured to defy the Transvaal laws, *dressed in the loongi* of the *coolie*, the identity he was now ready to assume.

During his stay in South Africa, Gandhi returned to India several times. In 1902 he attended the Congress session at Calcutta. Each visit seemed to confirm the extreme degree of alienation of the Indian, particularly the educated Indian, from his cultural and religious roots. The dirt and filth he saw all around seemed to him to symbolize the extent to which Indians had lost both national and personal self respect. He was disappointed at the manner of functioning of the Congress, at the lack of seriousness and of debate, the disinterest of the only national party in the plight of the South African Indians, and so on. Each time on his return to South Africa, he tried to ensure that the NIC would not develop on the same lines, or function as Indian National Congress did.

Almost exactly a century ago, in 1894, Gandhi began an intensive search for the Indian identity that was to lead him back to Hinduism. There was a certain deliberateness about his pursuit of this interest, for Hinduism did, not at that time, influence or form an important part of Gandhi's personal life nor of his public and political life. He made the *Gita* his book of daily reading, but not as prayer. Instead, Gandhi sought in it a way to integrate personal morality with social and political morality and found this to lie in its emphasis on duty. This exploration into Hinduism was, for Gandhi, both a personal and a political exploration in search of his own identity as an Indian and that of India as a nation. For Gandhi there could be no divide or distinction between the India he represented in his person and the Indian nation which he sought to identify in contemporary terms. The interface that he sought between his inner and his outer lives, came about through his own interpretation of Hinduism and of the *Gita*.

In his private life Gandhi sought to do his duty. He assumed responsibility for all his actions and for those of his followers; discovered what he called the "true" practice of law and later of journalism; began to dispossess himself of worldly, material good including a petty life insurance; took the vow of sexual abstinence; and experimented through political organisations and the farms he founded to live the alternative life style, "the life of the tiller of the soil and the handicraftsman". His, it will be recalled, was the model of the strong Indian, that he had advocated as a student in London. His public life rested on unpaid service to the community; on invoking God — as morality not religion, to bind the multi-religious Indian community to its vows and promises; on transforming all organisations he created into institutions based on service to the most needy and deprived; to make trusteeship the commanding principle; and above all to make the various groups of Muslims, Parsees, Hindus and Christians aware of a single shared identity, as Indians. And, as Indians, to empower them to struggle against the prevailing racial injustice through what I have called elsewhere, "truth action". These developments both resulted from and resulted in a growing disenchantment with western/English/modern/industrial civilization, which reached its apogee in the years from 1908-1909. It was expressed in a small booklet that he wrote hurriedly on his voyage back to India, called *Hind Swaraj*.

Gandhi's years in South Africa were years of intense learning and unlearning, of experiment in the individual and collective practice of his moral and political philosophy, in the shape of "truth action" or satyagraha. In the process, he borrowed from the counter currents of western thought particularly from Tolstoy, Ruskin and Thoreau, as well as from the leaders of the

Indian national movement. However, Gandhi acknowledged no religion, no ideology and no guru as his own. Only Gokhale came close to being his mentor but even then Gandhi made his differences with Gokhale quite evident. By the time he returned to India in 1915, Gandhi had adopted an identity for himself and constructed one for India that bore little resemblance to any identity advocated by other Indian leaders. The *Ramarajya* he invoked was a national construct not a historical fact. It symbolized *swaraj* a society based on truth and truth-action, on non-violence, high personal morality, and a commitment to selfless service. This society, as Gandhi envisaged it, would be comprised of free individuals (*satyagrahis*) able to act individually against injustice, who contributed their labour and who, above all, were in harmony with nature and all living things, willing to die rather than compromise with untruth and violence. In brief, what Gandhi did was to construct a revolutionary identity for India and the Indian, which would convey the essence of its long civilization, the realities of India as it struggled against colonisation and subjugation, and the India that he would like it to become.

Gandhi derived this national identity from two sources. One was his unfolding understanding of the external condition, that is of the world of politics dominated, as he saw it, by British power and western civilization. As this understanding was enlarged by his experience of oppression, injustice, racialism and, above all, by Christian hypocrisy, the identity he constructed comprised all its dialectical opposites. It was displayed in 1930, in Gandhi's most perfect act, the Dandi March, that symbolically pitted the unarmed, hungry, oppressed but courageous peasant, against the armed and rapacious British lion. It was as backdrop to this act that Gandhi had announced his disillusionment with British imperial principles and policies and his metamorphosis into a non-violent non-cooperative west-rejecting rebel and nationalist, at his trial in 1922. Political independence and *swaraj* became his declared goals, long before the Congress resolved to demand independence, not dominion status in 1930.

The second source of the identity that Gandhi constructed for India, was his perception of the domestic Indian reality, its dominant Hindu culture and its Hindu majority, its communal, and provincial divides; its diversity of language and custom, the excrescence of the caste system and of untouchability, its moral decay, its apathy, its cowardice and its loss of a sense of self. The recovery of the Indian self became his principal objective for which he provided an image and identity that bypassed the western educated Indian to extol the peasant still untouched by western civilization. His economics and his emphasis on rural development too were derived from his perception of the Indian reality. "The economics and civilization of a country, where the pressure of population on land is greatest, are and must be different from those of a country where the pressure is least. Sparsely populated, America may have need of machinery. India may not need it at all. Where there are millions upon millions of units of idle labour, it is no use thinking of labour-saving devices."[14]

This composite national identity was not a past or present reality. It was both Gandhi's preferred or reinvented reality as well as the ideal type to which he, at that time aspired. In sum, he reinvented the Indian nation as a civilizational unity of many religions and many languages, proud of its tolerance of diversity and of community, capable of *ahimsaic* action, of forging a global alternative to western civilization, that would be life sustaining not life destroying. He was fond of repeating "if we are to make progress [towards *swaraj*] we must not repeat history but make new history". And, to make new history, to make the imagined identity a present reality, the central tasks he listed were to ensure Hindu-Muslim unity, eradicate untouchability and promote *khadi*.

This identity as mentioned earlier energised the Congress and the masses and ushered in the short-lived Gandhi era. By the mid-1930s Gandhi had begun to part ways organisationally and programmatically with the Congress. Rather it may be more accurate to say that Nehru and the Congress majority became increasingly intolerant of Gandhi's higher level goal of *swaraj*. The one remaining link was the shared objective of achieving independence. But the manner in which this came about — through partition — destroyed the very basis of Gandhi's preferred identity for the Indian nation, namely unity between Hindu and Muslim.

Jinnah's two nation theory became, after 1947, the new reality to which Gandhi began to respond by constructing a new Indian identity, a new political programme and new symbols which would, at the same time, convey his larger message to India and to the world. This was the problem to which he addressed himself after 1947. Gandhi resumed writing in the *Harijan* and began a series of articles which should count amongst his most serious writings. He wrote on what he called "things of eternal value," to be woven into "a system of ethics and morals suited to the present day." But the truth-action he undertook in those critical years before his assassination was, as in Noakhali, individual not collective. This was symbolic of his altered appeal — to the individual in independent India not as before independence, to the national collective. It was, in brief, the identity of the solitary individual — as a variant of Gandhi's example of the solitary *satyagrahi*, willing and prepared to pit himself against the organised power of his own state, that for him could still link the altered present to a *swarajist* future.

III

Mao in China followed a broadly similar circuitous route before he came to conceptualise and construct an identity for the Chinese nation and people. He began, like Gandhi, with rebellion against injustice and an early sense of injured nationalism. Unlike Gandhi, however, he rebelled against his father and left home. His early reading consisted mainly of classics and old romances about peasant rebellions. In the course of his studies he came across a pamphlet that opened with the sentence "Alas, China will be subjugated!". It bemoaned the loss of outlying areas of the Chinese empire like Korea, Taiwan, Indo-China and Burma to the western imperialists, and left a lasting impression on Mao. He also learnt of the advances in western technology that introduced railways, telephones, steamship etc. and wanted to have them for China, and he read biographies of the great leaders of the west. From all this he drew the conclusion that China had to be made rich and strong and free of imperialist control. From then on India, as a full colony, became the negative example of a fate that must not befall China. Mao like Gandhi, manifested a strong sense of nationalism even in early youth, and also a spirit of social reform. He supported the 1911 revolution that destroyed the old imperial system, admired Sun Yat-sen and joined the regular army briefly. Then followed the formative years of his intellectual development, his interest in the relationship between ethics and good government, in attacking old social customs and traditions and in the self-cultivation of mind and specially of the body. "... when the body is strong" he wrote, "then one can advance speedily in knowledge and *morality*..."[15] (emphasis mine). In 1918 at the age of 21, Mao went to Beijing where he worked as a library assistant at Beijing University. There he was exposed to socialist ideas, to parliamentary democracy and to anarchism. He recalled being confused, still "looking for the road". His only certainty was that he knew he was anti-imperialist and anti-militarist. On his return to Changsha a year later, he had already settled on the socialist idea and at the same time had instincively identified himself with the poor and the hungry, especially the peasant. Equally instinctively he sensed that a great union and a great progressive force was latent in the masses of the Chinese people. All this led him to help found the Communist Party in 1921 that was committed to opposing both the imperialists and the militarists.

Nevertheless, Mao's uncertainty about the road and the method of revolution continued. With hindsight the reasons for this persisting uncertainty are not too difficult to identify. For one, the "anti-imperialism" that was, written into the first and second manifestos of the CPC (1922) was in the context of China's times, a mewling bloodless abstraction which was given rather short shrift. In vulgar imitation of Soviet Russia, the manifesto referred to "anti-imperialism" more as an ideological slogan than as a dominant and oppressive national reality. Czarist Russia, it may be recalled, was not a victim or object of imperialist aggression: it was itself imperialist. For the Bolsheviks, therefore, "anti-imperialism" was directed only somewhat vaguely against "world imperialists", and more urgently against Czarist imperialist policies — at home in relation to non-Russian nationalities, and abroad to Czarist expansionism, particularly in China. "Anti-imperialism", as included in the CPC manifesto, blindly followed this formulation. It conveyed little of the gravity of the imperialist onslaught that China had suffered since the Opium Wars. It resonated even less, with the contemporary and growing menace of expanding Japanese aggression.

Moreover, for the Comintern and for all Marxists including the young CPC, nationalism was suspect. It was regarded as the "handmaiden" of the bourgeoisie, the dynamic only of the bourgeois democratic revolution. The leadership of the Chinese revolution which was democratic and national was consequently gratuitously entrusted to the KMT by the CPC. Thus, while it supported the "bourgeois" revolution led by the KMT, the CPC in keeping with Comintern orthodoxy, awaited the right historical moment when, as the vanguard of the proletariat, it would be called upon to conduct China's proletarian revolution. For almost fifteen years thereafter, that is, for as long as it held to this understanding imperialism and of its own historical role, the CPC was unable to register success, or to discover that its awaited historical opportunity had arrived or was about, to arrive. The CPC, needless to say, had no solutions or answers to the central political question in China namely, how to save China, for the simple reason that it did not pose the central question as a national question. Mao's confusion therefore persisted. Some decades late he was to describe his dilemma thus:

> "When I joined the Communist Party, I knew that we must *make revolution*, but against what? And how were we to go about it? Of course we had to make revolution against imperialism and the old society. I did not quite understand what *sort of a thing imperialism was*, still less did I understand how we could make

revolution against it. None of the stuff I had learned in thirteen years was any good for making revolution. I used only the instrument language."[16]

In those intervening years, the revolution and the CPC failed in its repeated attempts at formenting urban insurrections and suffered a major defeat at the hands of the KMT in 1927.

Around that time Mao began a long journey of investigation away from party and Comintern orthodoxy, to seek answers to *what* "making revolution" was all about, *who* would "make revolution", and *how* it was to be made. In order to do so, he moved from the realm of the "idea", to that of China's objective situation, that is to its contemporary social and political realities. This led to a unique Maoist understanding of the concrete substance of domestic and external aggression and of the strong linkages between them. His investigation into domestic oppression resulted in his discovery of peasant unrest and revolutionary ferment in Hunan in response to the multiple oppression of the peasantry. From the specific investigations he conducted in Hunan in 1927, Mao generalised an entire Chinese countryside with revolutionary potential. He concluded that without the peasantry, and more specifically, without the poor peasant, there would be no revolution of the oppressed. As for external aggression, Mao found evidence of it writ large across China: It pointed to Japanese imperialism as the aggressor at a time when the western imperialists seemed to be in retreat. It was through these twin "discoveries" that Mao came, as he put it, "to understand the objective world of China". Working thereafter from inside out, from Chinese reality to the Marxist idea, from CPC practice to CPC theory, Mao summarised the revolutionary experience of those fifteen yeras, and gradually arrived at the "correct line", that is, at the strategy and tactics for "making revolution." The conclusions he drew from his discoveries of the *what, who* and *how* of "making revolution" came to form the basis of his strategy of revolution and what has been called his Sinification of Marxism.

In brief, Mao concluded that Japanese aggression posed the principal danger as well as a new threat to China in that Japan, unlike the western imperialists, was determined to control the *whole* of China and to transform it into a *colony* like India. Anti-imperialism for the CPC unlike for the CPSU could not therefore, remain an abstract slogan; it codified the hegemonic reality of China. He argued that his new danger had fundamentally transformed class relations within China, making resistance to Japanese imperialism a *national* and not a *class* issue. The CPC's past experience of unsuccessful urban insurrection and his discovery of the revolutionary potential of the peasantry, led Mao to transfer the locale of the revolution from the cities to the countryside. But, in those early years, it was still with the objective of setting up *Soviets*, on the model provided by the Soviet Union.

The theoretical question that Mao faced thereafter, was how to link together the two dominant features of China's "objective world": an oppressed therefore revolutionary peasantry, and a nationwide anti-Japanese struggle, and how to do so without denying the ideology he had espoused, that is, while pursuing the goal of "making revolution". By relying on his perception of China's "objective world" and by rejecting Soviet/Comintern, CPC orthodoxy, Mao was to stumble upon and so discover the "key", as he put it, to "making revolution".

The essential features of Mao's strategy are well known. They are: controlled guidance of peasant revolution, to direct it not only against "feudal elements" and "militarists" as the direct oppressors of the peasantry, but also against them as *natural allies* of Japanese imperialism; the call for a nationwide struggle against Japanese aggression; the innovative strategy of the united front from above; the legitimation of Chiang Kai-shek and the KMT as leaders of the united front in the *national* war of resistance; the separate but simultaneous training and honing of the CPC and the Red Army in Yanan, for later seizure of power from the KMT; and finally the establishment of intimate, inseparable and critical linkages between the outside world (including the imperialists) and the Chinese struggle and the call for building a parallel international united front against Japan (or Fascism).

It was also at this time that Mao undertook a reconstruction of the concept of China as a "single multinational state", and of the Chinese nation as "a union of all nationalities", including the Han. No longer was the party to promise statehood and self-determination to the various nationalities of China as it had done in the Ruijin Constitution of 1931. Instead, Mao began to posit a larger unity — that of the "people" — which included all, regardless of ethnicity or social class, who supported the struggle against Japan. Mao's reconstructed China was presented as a country with a "rich revolutionary tradition", but which was "semicolonial and semifeudal" and for whom imperialism was the most ruthless enemy". Japanese imperialism in China was thus cast as the most important contemporary reality, a non-national external factor that threatened the *entire* Chinese people and the Chinese state. Accordingly, the principal goal of the Chinese Revolution was redefined as resistance to Japan and not just the struggle against militarist and anti-democratic forces within China.[17] Hence, the high ideological CPC objective of conducting a pure or orthodox proletarian revolution led by the working class to usher in socialism was also scaled down. Thereafter the task of the CPC was to resist Japan and complete the national and democratic revolution that had so far been entrusted to the KMT. Thus by the mid-thirties, the CPC, under Mao, was no longer content to patiently await conditions for a proletariat-led revolution: It was to use the struggle against Japan to *create the conditions* for this eventuality to come about. In Mao's new strategy this called for direct CPC participation in the national struggle and the later leadership of the national democratic revolution, and its transmutation into a movement of *national liberation*. From about that time the enlarged meaning given to the term "national liberation, and the revolutionary role assigned to it by Mao and the CPC, were to differ from Soviet usage and practice. These differences were to persist and to be reflected in CPC strategy and policy, even after the PRC came into being.

The identity that Mao — a self confessed Marxist, conceptualised for China as a nation, and the revolutionary role he assigned to the peasantry, bear greater similarity to the identity that Gandhi created for the Indian nation and people, than they do to those envisaged by his contemporaries whether Marxist or not. Neither identity was cast in class terms as it had been in 1922. Nor did it take the urban worker as its model, even as the future was envisioned in proletarian terms. Mao, in fact, displayed some of the same distrust of China's urbanised workers and the urban educated as Gandhi did of the westernised urban Indian. Many years later, Mao was to describe the peasantry as being "poor and blank" thus suggesting that it was neither "contaminated" by the ideas of western liberalism nor by the mainstream Soviet and CPC doctrines on "making revolution". The Long March was the most symbolic of Mao's revolutionray acts: It pitted the ragged, ill-fed, ill-equipped millions of Chinese peasants, against the better fed, better equipped forces ranged against them. The images of the peasant as representing China and as revolutionary, were then fused into a composite identity that symbolised the essence of being Chinese with the potential of becoming socialist. At that time, this identity seemed both true and relevant to China's situation. Like Gandhi again, Mao based his strategy of development -- political, social and economic, on the villages. The commune that he innovated in 1958 can be imaginatively regarded as the experiment in the field of Gandhi's governing idea of a self reliant, multifaceted, multiproductive, self governing (in the main), and peaceful village community. For Gandhi this was the unit of a future *swarajist* society that would expand from the village to the nation, and beyond to the world, consisting of fully enlightened *swarajist* individuals. The communes that Mao advocated in 1958 were similarly to be the building blocks of a future socialist society, which would also expand beyond the geographic, cultural and racial frontiers of the nation to the whole world. For both men, liberation or salvation could never be for just the individual or his small national community: It required the salvation of all humankind. Like Gandhi again, Mao laid great emphasis on changing the way the people perceived themselves, their reality and their future, and of the importance of changing their ways of thinking, their value systems and their social relationships. The tragic Cultural Revolution that Mao embarked upon in later years, was intended to bring about just such a transformation, not only of party leaders and cadres, but also of the people, by "touching their souls" because, as Mao once put it, "you have to be reborn to be a communist."

Unlike the struggle led by Gandhi, the revolution led by Mao was an armed struggle, undoubtedly dictated by the Chinese political reality but also by his ideology. It is always interesting to speculate how a Gandhi transplanted into Mao's China would have perceived and responded to the situation: As Mao did, or by Sincising *satyagraha*? Mao, in a quite literal sense, armed the oppressed Chinese peasant and created the legendary Red Army as the people's army. Simultaneously, however, he placed the army firmly under civilian/political leadership and control and disciplined the soldier to till the soil, work the machine, and serve the people. It is possible to see in Mao's writings his preference for the use of non-violent means whether for overcoming the enemy or for changing society and the individual. Also through his writings runs a concern for ethical values and a socialist truth to be discovered beyond, and perhaps inspite of, Marxist doctrine. That he regarded all orthodoxies as man-made and therefore open to reinterpretation and further development, is suggested by philosophical statement that new contradictions would arise even in a socialist society.

After his death Mao, like Gandhi in India, has been hailed as the father and liberator of the nation. The present leadership however has abandoned all empathy with this long term goal of "making revolution" as he envisaged it. The culturally rooted peasant revolutionary identity that he created for the nation and the people and which he attempted to realise in political life, after 1958, is no longer resonant with the economic policies and political goals of today's China. This identity has instead faded into history as has that of the Indian nation created by Gandhi. This loss of a revolutionary identity symbolised in the persons of these two leaders, has resulted in two things. One is its replacement by an emergent elitist identity in keeping with that of the modernised west. The other is the metamorphosis of the nation into the state in both countries. India and China have become or are in danger of becoming what I have described elsewhere as "ordinary" countries, fast becoming integrated into that system that Gandhi and Mao had opposed. They are no longer making or are even concerned with making what Gandhi called "new history".

Notes

1. Jawaharlal. Nehru, *An Autobiography* (London: John Lane The Bodley Head, 1939), p. 253.
2. *Ibid.*, p. 597.
3. Albert Einstein, "On Peace - And Gandhi", in Norman Cousins (ed), *Profiles of Gandhi* (Delhi : Indian Book Company 1969), p. 99.
4. Wang Gungwu, "The Chinese", in Dick Wilson (ed.) *Mao Tse-tung in the Scales of History* (Cambridge: Cambridge University Press, 1977), p. 273.
5. *Ibid.*, p. 274.
6. *Ibid.*, p. 275.
7. Nehru, *op. cit.*, pp. 65-68.
8. M.K. Gandhi, *An Autobiography* (Ahmedabad: Navjivan Trust, 1929), p. 15.
9. *Ibid.*
10. *Ibid.*, p. 78.
11. *Collected Works of Mahatma Gandhi,* (New Delhi : Publications Divison, 1975) Vol. 1, p. 19.
12. A.G. Noorani, *Indian Political Trials* (New Delhi : Sterling Publishers, 1976), p. 193.
13. Gandhi, *op. cit.*, p. 104.
14. M.K. Gandhi, "Two Civilizations" in the *Harijan,* 11 May, 1935.
15. Stuart Schram, *The Political Thought of Mao Tse-tun,* Harmondsworth: Penguin, 1969, p. 152.
16. "Talk on Question of Philosophy" with Kang Sheng and Chen Boda, 18 August 1964, in Stuart Schram (ed.) *Mao Tse-tung Un rehearsed* (Harmondsworth: Penguin, 1969), p. 20.
17. See "The Chinese Revolution and the Chinese Communist Party" (1939), in *Selected Works of Mao Tse-tung* (London: Lawrence and Wishart, 1954), Vol. III, pp. 72-101.

PATRICIA UBEROI

14

BODY, STATE AND COSMOS: MAO ZEDONG'S "STUDY OF PHYSICAL EDUCATION" (1917)

Quotations :

(i) Whenever I look at our educated youth, I see that they have not the strength to catch a chicken, nor mentally the courage of an ordinary man. With pale faces and slender waists, seductive as young ladies, timorous of cold and chary of heat, weak as invalids — if the people of our country are as feeble as this in body and mind how will they be able to shoulder burdens and go far? [From an essay by Chen Duxiu in *New Youth* (1915)][1]

(ii) Who does not know how poor is the health of our citizens? Our youth appear as apparitions with sunken cheeks, hollow eyes and dried up scaly skin. Yes, the very same youth on whose shoulders is placed the burden of protecting the nation, religion and society.... Are these youth, with their skeletons of dried, brittle bones, up to the task? (From a popular book on Indian wrestling)[2]

I. LOOKING AT EACH OTHER/REFLECTING ON ONESELF

The two colophons to this paper belong to two different territorial spaces, to two different moments in historical time. They share the idea that the degeneracy of the nation is witnessed in, and inscribed upon, the unfit bodies of "youth" — of young *men* to be precise. And they share the hope that youth, by individually re-forming their unhealthy bodies, would be able to bring about national regeneration.

This mode of connecting fit individual bodies with the health and strength of the nation — what a recent writer has felicitously termed "somatic nationalism"[3] — is a conspicuous feature of discourses of the body in modern times. As has often been observed, such discourses are also typically, if not invariably, endorsed by the authority of modern science.[4]

Somatic nationalist discourses and practices originated in the west, and were distinctly inflected, at the point of their origin, by the western (and Christian) cultural milieu. That, after all, is a matter of history. But as one looks back now from the vantage of the turn of the century, one can appreciate how speedily and successfully somatic nationalism became an unquestioned feature of a shared global grammar of modernity, manifested through many local varieties.

Nonetheless, the historical priority of the Western experience of modernity, and of the West's own social scientific reflection on this experience, have made it the measure against which all other varieties appear as deviations from an established norm, as evidence, perhaps, of the lingering residue of indigenous "tradition". Even from the "South" we tend to regard each other only through the prism of Western modernity. We rarely look at each other in order to rethink theories of modernity. And we rarely look at each other in order to better reflect upon ourselves.

This essay analyses a particular text of modern Chinese somatic nationalism and its wider context of production in the light of familiarity with some comparable materials from South Asia. The aim is not a *direct* comparison of the two discourses, but a confirmation from two different culture areas of the possibility of alternative somatic modernisms. Albeit inexplicitly, the exercise questions some received theories of the relations of body and society under modernity. It also suggests that a global/local rather than a west/non-west perspective on bodily practices could also enable the recovery of alternative somatic nationalist ideologies within the modernising history of the West as well.

II. SOCIAL BODIES

In a rather chatty and unfinished essay on "body techniques", now regarded as a foundational contribution to the two fields of the anthropology of the body and semiotics, the French sociologist Marcel Mauss had sought to show the extent to which society inscribes itself on human bodies. His examples were rather mundane and anecdotal: styles of swimming and running had been modified in his own lifetime; 8,000 spades had had to be changed every time a French division replaced an English one — and vice versa — in the trenches during the First World War because the French and English had different techniques of digging; and so on. While the human body belongs to the world of nature, it is also, Mauss insisted, a "technical object" whose use is learned in everyday practice. That is why "the way in which... men know how to use their bodies" differs from society to society, and according to age, sex, status, means and fashion.[5] To this proposition contemporary writers have added the reminder that the body is also man's "first and most natural classifier and source of symbols"..., "an important means of metaphorical expression and symbolic communication".[6]

For Mauss, apparently, body techniques, like the Saussurean "sign", were more or less arbitrary, constrained only by human physiological limitations, and possibly also by an evolutionary trend towards greater efficiency of motion. However, more recent social science writing has sought to chronicle a "political anatomy" of the body in which bodily techniques and perceptions are linked more purposefully with history. In particular, Michel Foucault has argued that the rise of modernity has required the "disciplining" of "docile" bodies, even as it (paradoxically) democratised the polity: the former process was merely the "darkside" of the latter.[7] Foucault was referring here not only to societies or historical periods which have been notoriously regimented, politically or in their productive practices, or to domains of activity for which regimentation would appear self-evidently essential (like the army), but to a generalised condition of "domination" in post-Enlightenment society where "docility" is linked inextricably with "utility". This new mechanics of bodily discipline and surveillance contrasted significantly, qualitatively and quantitatively, with the earlier disciplinary methods of monasteries, armies and workshops, of regimes of slavery, servitude and vassalage. The important discontinuity in Foucault's perception was with practices of monastic asceticism "whose function was to obtain renunciations rather than the increase of utility and which, although they involved obedience to others, had as their principal aim an increase in the mastery of each individual over his own body."[8] In other words, *the disciplining of others* and *regimens of self-discipline* were posited as two qualitatively different forms of bodily discipline and, in Foucault's scheme, assigned to different historical formations.

Foucault's formulation has had a powerful impact on social science studies of the branches of knowledge (such as psychiatry, penology, public health and pedagogy) and typical institutions (hospitals, asylums, prisons, public schools, etc.) through which human bodies are (mostly non-coercively) disciplined in modern times. But it allows of only a single historical trajectory, itself arguably moderated by the mind/body dichotomy of post-Enlightenment Europe.[9] It thereby forecloses the conceptual possibility that a different cosmology may enable the construction of alternate understandings of the relation of body and society in modern times.

My article attempts a new reading, interpretation and reflection upon Mao Zedong's first published work, an essay on the theme of physical culture.[10] It seeks, first, to shift the focus away from the spare facts of Mao's psycho-biography, which have usually provided the terms of reference for analysis of this essay (see Section III), and to locate the text within the wider conceptual universe of revolutionary discourse of the May Fourth era.[11] In this, following procedural and conceptual leads from semiotics and literary analysis, particular attention is paid to the metonymic linkages and metaphoric relations that are articulated in this text and other writings of the period[12] (Sections IV and V). Finally, in a somewhat more speculative manner, Mao's advocacy of physical culture is considered in a wider, comparative framework as a type of somatic response to the challenge of western imperialism (Section VI). There has been a burgeoning literature in recent years on the phenomenon of "somatic nationalism".[13] However, in this paper I draw for comparative purposes mainly on materials from South Asia. This choice of a field of comparison has been partly occasioned by serendipitous acquaintance with writings by Joseph S. Alter on the north Indian wrestling tradition and on "yoga therapy";[14] and partly purposeful, in recognition of the interesting parallels, and also discontinuities, in the somatic responses of India and China to the modern world.[15] I should concede at the outset, however, that my reading of Mao's essay on physical culture in the light of the collective consciousness of the May Fourth period and of general somatic nationalist responses to imperialism rather discounts the original and creative role of Mao as author: This is a problem inherent in the methodology adopted. But I hope, nonetheless, that this paper might also provoke fresh reflections on the theme of somatic nationalism.

III. "A STUDY OF PHYSICAL EDUCATION"

Mao Zedong's essay, "A Study of Physical Education" (*Tiyu zhi Yanjiu*), appeared under the pseudonym "Twenty-eight Stroke Student" (Ershibahua Sheng), referring to the number of brush strokes required to write the Chinese characters for his name, in the April 1917 issue of the revolutionary journal *New Youth* (*Xin Qingnian*).[16] Until fairly recently, "A Study of Physical Education" was the only complete and authentic pre-1923 Mao text available to scholars in the west, though this deficiency has since been remedied.[17] It is this, above all, that accounts for the special interest that has been shown in this text which is, in itself, a relatively undistinguished piece of writing. It was not prominently positioned in the particular issue of *New Youth* in which it appeared; it was written — for some reason — under a pseudonym, though Mao was already known as a student leader and political organiser in his native Hunan; and it was devoted to a theme which would surely have appeared rather stale and hackneyed against the heady backdrop of *New Youth*'s collective attack on Confucianism on the one hand, and the beginning of the famous "Literary Revolution" on the other.[18] In fact, there is every reason to suspect that, had Mao not achieved the status he ultimately did, the text would have attracted little attention. As it is, however, it is seen to provide significant insights into the multifarious "influences" to which the young Mao had been exposed in the early May Fourth period, that is, prior to the effective introduction of Marxism into China; and into those aspects of Mao's thinking, embedded in his personal biography, that were later to find reflection in the specifically "Maoist" recension of Marxism-Leninism.

Notwithstanding its subject matter, presented in a very down-to-earth manner with practical suggestions for beginners, "A Study of Physical Education" is not an easy text to read. Replete with allusions to Chinese history and the classics, it is written in a classical literary style much less transparent than that used by many of the better-known *New Youth* writers, even before the vernacular movement had got properly under way. (*New Youth* "officially" switched to the vernacular language at the beginning of 1918.) Perhaps Mao, more than these others, needed to establish his credentials as a literary stylist, for this was his first published work and that, too, in a journal that had already achieved national standing. Besides, unlike most of the *New Youth* luminaries, Mao was not "to the manner born" in the literati-gentry class and was supposedly rather sensitive on the question of his relatively humble social origins.

"A Study of Physical Education" has been interrogated with two paramount questions in mind. In the first place, it has been considered important to identify the *sources* of Mao's thought, and specifically to locate them in *either* the eastern *or* the western traditions. According to an influential paradigm in Sinological studies, Chinese intellectuals of this period were torn between their intellectual commitment to the necessity for change and their emotional commitment to Chinese values,[19] a dilemma ultimately resolved only by the "anti-Western Westernisation" that Marxism-Leninism happily provided. In this light, the question that interests most of the interpreters of Mao's essay is simply this: Where, at this point in time, just prior to the introduction of Marxism into China, did Mao personally stand on the continuum of opinion from radical iconoclasm through to conservative traditionalism?

The second question was provoked by the history of Mao's emergence as the pre-eminent Chinese Communist leader through a series of intra-party ideological struggles: Was Mao truly a "materialist" in his outlook, as his hagiography and Cold War paranoia proclaimed? Or was his Marxism merely skin-deep, over-laid on an essentially "idealist" foundation? Both these questions were magnified from the time of the Sino-Soviet dispute and the Great Leap experiment, when Mao appeared to be reaffirming the indigenous and unorthodox roots of his Marxist theory and practice, and then through the Cultural Revolution, his "second childhood" (or adolescence), recapturing the essential, idealist Mao of the May Fourth period.

New Youth (founded in September 1915), the journal in which Mao's essay appeared, is widely identified with the high tide of "All-out Westernisation" in early twentieth century China. In the name of "science" and "democracy", this journal had spearheaded an attack, first, on aspects of the Chinese national character; and then, more explicitly on Confucianism. The young Mao, according to his own account, was an enthusiastic reader of *New Youth* and an admirer of its two leading contributors, Hu Shi and Chen Duxiu. Under their influence, as he later explained, rather apologetically, to Edgar Snow, "my mind was a curious mixture of ideas of liberalism, democratic reformism and utopian socialism. I had somewhat vague passions about "nineteenth century democracy", utopianism and old-fashioned liberalism, and I was definitely anti-militarist and anti-imperialist."[20]

None of these self-confessed western influences is readily discernible in "A Study of Physical Education". Jesus and Mohammed are mentioned in passing, along with Confucius and Buddha, while Germany and Japan are cited briefly as examples of nations which had successfully introduced programmes of physical education. For the rest, Mao's sources and references were all Chinese, and scarcely "revolutionary" at that. Again there was little evidence in this essay of the strident anti-Confucianism that marked many of the other writings of this period. Mao was, it is true, unusually attracted to the heterodox traditions in preference to orthodox Ju Xi Neo-Confucianism, but his essay contained nonetheless a number of quotations from Confucian texts and a couple of not-unflattering references to Confucius himself. Mao's catalogue of worthy exemplars also mentioned a number of Confucian scholars and statesmen, the criterion for their inclusion being, it appears, their positive attitude to the body and to the practice of the martial arts on the one hand; or, philosophically speaking, a preference for movement rather than quiescence as the supreme principle of heaven and earth.

But while Mao justified and sought to legitimate his programme of physical education and its underlying philosophy by reference, in particular, to the scholar-patriots of the seventeenth century who had fought against Manchu rule and to statesmen such as Zeng Guofan who had helped to crush the Taiping rebellion in the nineteenth century, the project for physical education was itself a westernising and anti-Confucian endeavour, associated with Treaty Port culture, with the "returned students" (especially those from Japan), and with the Chinese anarchists — with persons, as Schram has noted, politically and socially on the margins of mainstream Confucian society. Certainly, it would have been regarded as unbecoming to the dignified image of the Confucian scholar-gentleman to practise physical culture with the vigour that Mao and his friends displayed. Inspired by the example of his favourite teacher, Yang Changji (later Mao's father-in-law), whose discipline of taking cold water baths, even in the Peking winter, was believed to have led to his premature demise,[21] Mao and his friends took their commitment to physical culture very seriously indeed:

> "In the winter holidays, we tramped through the fields, up and down mountains, along city walls, and across the streams and rivers. If it rained we took off our shirts and called it a rain bath. When the sun was hot we also doffed shirts and called it a sun bath. In the spring winds we shouted that this was a new sport called 'wind-bathing'. We slept in the open when frost was already falling and even in November swam in the cold rivers. All this went on under the title of 'body training'."[22]

While this measure of practical involvement in physical culture may well have been unusual, even among the more radical students and advocates of physical education and military training, it should be noted that the general programme for physical education was perfectly in accord with the orientation of *New Youth* at the time, in continuity with the earlier nationalist and radical discourse. The journal had already published a number of appraisals of German methods of military training, and had often pointed to the physical weakness of Chinese youth as a chief contributing factor in the national decline. As Chen Duxiu put it in a famous article which is thought to have influenced Mao's own effort (see the first of the two colophons to this paper), a weak, timorous and effeminate generation of Chinese youth could hardly be expected to "shoulder burdens and go far".

In short, then, the attempt to evaluate "A Study of Physical Education" according to scales of "westernising" or "traditionalist", "revolutionary" or "conservative", appears to be quite inconclusive: it seems that it was all these at once. That is, while the theme of the essay places Mao in the company of the anti-traditionists, its language, presentation and thinking appear to be firmly grounded in a Chinese thought world.[23] This was understandable, Schram has argued, because the May Fourth generation was essentially a transitional one, betwixt and between.[24] Other writers would add that Mao (because of his relatively humble background or his particular personality type?) had his feet quite firmly placed on the Chinese soil and could in no sense be labelled an "alienated intellectual" like some of the leading iconoclasts of the *New Youth* coterie.

Similarly one should note here, lest the theme be lost sight of, that "A Study of Physical Education" also fails to disclose either a clearly "idealist" or a "materialist" orientation. This was not necessarily because Mao was confused or muddled or ideologically still unformed (awaiting his "conversion" to Marxism), but, as I hope to show here, because his was a *different*, and essentially *non-antagonistic*, understanding of the body-mind relationship. It was a cosmology and theory of embodiment in terms of which the idealist/ materialist dichotomy makes little sense.

IV. AN ALTERNATIVE READING

The alternative reading of "A Study of Physical Education" that I propose through the following two sections of this paper assumes that at some level, or in some way, Mao and the other writers of *New Youth* were co-participants in a shared universe of discourse, whatever may have been the manifest differences in the style, presentation and content of their individual arguments.[25] A brief resume of the text will be followed, first, by an examination of its metonymic or narrative structure — the logic of its argument — against the background of the revolutionary discourse of *New Youth*, and then by a consideration of the central metaphor that informs and structures the text. This metaphor asserts that the human body, the state and the cosmos share a relationship of resemblance for the reason that they are all similarly constituted of a balanced opposition of analogous qualities. Actually, this metaphor is barely hinted at in the text itself: its full significance is apparent only in the light of the wider universe of revolutionary discourse in which it pertained and was completed.

"A Study of Physical Education" opens with the following, extremely forthright, statement of the problem:

"Our nation (*guo*) is wanting in strength (*li*). The military spirit has not been encouraged. The physical condition of [our people] (*minzu*) deteriorates daily. This is an extremely disturbing phenomenon. The promoters of physical education have not grasped the essence of the problem and therefore their efforts, though prolonged, have not been effective. If this state [of affairs] continues, our weakness will increase further."[26]

Mao then goes on to explain that remedying this state of affairs is, in the first instance, a matter of self-consciousness or awakening (*zijue*), that is, of a subjective transformation, after which objective results should follow. In other words, programmes of physical education can succeed only if motivation comes from within. They cannot be imposed from without.

Traditions of physical education and the degree of emphasis on body-building and the martial arts differ from country to country, Mao continued, but their commonality is the idea of the compatibility and complementarity of physical education with moral and intellectual training. This compatibility is rooted in the obvious fact that the mind has no existence without the body:

"Physical education complements education in virtue and knowledge. Moreover, both virtue (*de*) and knowledge (*zhi*) reside in the body (*ti*). Without the body there would be neither virtue nor knowledge. Those who understand this are rare. People stress either knowledge or morality. Knowledge is certainly valuable, for it distinguishes man from animals. But wherein is knowledge contained? Morality, too, is valuable; it is the basis of the social order and of equality between ourselves and others. But where does virtue reside? *It is the body that contains knowledge and houses virtue* (emphasis in original).[27]

Unfortunately, Mao said — and it was a theme that he would reiterate throughout his life — the Chinese education system pathologically overemphasises book learning, and undervalues physical training. Curricula are so heavy, even for primary school children, that they would appear to have been designed simply 'in order to exhaust the students, to trample on their bodies and ruin their lives'.[28]

This is sheer nonsense, for the only calamity that can befall a man is not to have a body (*shen*). What else is there to worry about? If one seeks to improve one"s body, other things will follow automatically. For the improvement of the body, nothing is more effective than physical education. *Physical education really occupies the first place in our lives. When the body is strong, then one can advance speedily in knowledge and morality, and reap far-reaching advantages* (emphasis in original)."[29]

Mao was insistent that it is quite wrong to believe, as many Chinese do, "that the mind and the body cannot be perfect at the same time, that those who use their minds are deficient in physical health and those with a robust body are generally deficient in mental capacities."[30] On the contrary, since knowledge is gained through the senses and the senses are located in the body, a good physique, brought about through physical culture, enhances knowledge and creates the stamina required for study. It also, importantly, "harmonises sentiments" (*tiao ganqing*), in the sense of creating emotional equipoise,[31] and strengthens the will (*yizhi*) and capacity for endurance:

"Those whose bodies are small and frail are flippant in their behaviour. Those whose skin is flabby are soft and dull in will (*xinyi*). Thus does the body (*shenti*) influence the mind (*xinli*). The purpose of physical education is to strengthen the muscles and the bones; as a result knowledge is enhanced, the sentiments are harmonized, and the will is strengthened. The muscles and the bones belong to our body (*shen*); knowledge, sentiments and will belong to our heart (*xin*). When both the body and the heart are at ease, one may speak of perfect harmony. Hence physical education is nothing else but the nourishing of our lives and the gladdening of our hearts."[32]

There are a number of subjective (*zhuguan*) and objective (*keguan*) reasons, Mao goes on to say, why students dislike physical education. Subjectively, they are not really convinced of its value; but, even when they are convinced, there are many who feel embarrassed to exercise, in public or in private: "Flowing garments, a slow gait, a grave, calm gaze — these constitute a fine deportment, respected by society. Why should one suddenly extend an arm or expose a leg, stretch and bend down?"[33] The objective reasons are (*a*) the long-standing Chinese cultural preference for literary over military accomplishments (or, as Mao puts it more philosophically earlier in the essay, for "tranquillity" and "contemplation" over "movement" [*dong*]); and (*b*) the half-heartedness of official attempts to promote physical education. Changing the objective factors is a more difficult proposition because it means changing others, whereas changing the subjective factors means merely changing oneself. In Mao's opinion, changing oneself is both more important and also, of course, more immediately practicable.

Continuing in this characteristically pragmatic vein, Mao insisted that it does not really matter which of the many methods of exercise and health regimens one follows. Any one of them will do for, according to Mao, they all have the single function of improving the circulation of the blood (*xuemai liutong*). However, some important general points should always be borne in mind: (*a*) exercising, by whatever regimen, needs to be done *regularly*; this, in itself, creates interest and pleasure and gives rise to a feeling of a well-being; (*b*) exercise must be done with full *concentration*, not absent-mindedly; and (*c*) exercise must be "*savage*" (*man*) and "*rude*" (*zhuo*),[34] in contrast to the genteel deportment expected of the Confucian literatus, and described so graphically in the passage cited earlier.

With these general principles and rationalisations in mind, Mao then goes on to describe in practical detail, and to invite his readers' reactions to, the regimen of exercises that he himself had found beneficial. This appears to be an eclectic and idiosyncratic routine. No allegiance is claimed to any traditional training practices of the Chinese martial arts, but at the same time its solitary and individual nature distances it from the western drill and mass gymnastics programmes which, in Mao's opinion, had so far been quite ineffective in the Chinese context. This is consistent with Mao's assertion that it is better to rely on and seek to discipline *oneself*, rather than others, the self-awakening of the individual being the first step in any effective project of reform.

The exercises Mao recommends are grouped into six sections: exercises for the arms; for the legs; for the torso; for the head and neck; massage (literally, "slapping", *daji*) for all parts of the body, to quicken the circulation of the blood and improve muscle tone; and all-round exercises such as jumping and deep breathing. Interestingly, there has been to my knowledge no secondary commentary on the specificities of these exercises in themselves, and no attempt to tease from this regimen a theory of the body or of the body-mind nexus. Schram"s English translation of "A Study of Physical Education" leaves out the exercise regimen altogether — no doubt an understandable editorial decision in the context in which it was published. But his extensive French commentary also pays no attention to the exercises themselves, except to comment that the exercises are, with some exceptions, inspired by "western gymnastics",[35] the clinching argument for this proposition being Mao's very unConfucian recommendation for exercising in the nude! No significance has been attached, for instance, to Mao's several statements that the basic aim of all exercise regimes is to improve *the circulation of the blood* — not, as in contemporary body-building ideology, to build sheer *muscular strength* or a beautiful body for display. That is, though the object of the regime of exercise is to create a strong body, its strength lies in inner balance and control, and in the moral firmness and mental fitness that accompany such bodily discipline.[36] Nor is there any comment on the principle of lateral symmetry between left and right, conspicuous in the instructions, or on the implications of the numerical symbolism of sets of three, five and ten repeated actions. In fact, altogether a very *instrumental* understanding pervades the commentary on the text,[37] quite contrary to Mao's own theory of embodiment, and implicitly discounting the sincerity of his assertion that vigorous, regular and concentrated exercise produces in the subject a feeling of pleasure, a total sense of physical and mental well-being, and emotional equipoise above the reign of fickle passions.

V. FROM METONYMY TO METAPHOR THE METONYMIC AXIS: HEALTHY BODIES, A STRONG STATE

The metonymic structure of "A Study of Physical Education" is encapsulated in Mao's opening sentence which draws a clear metonymic connection between the physical condition of the Chinese people, individually and collectively, and the viability of the nation-state.

- The logic of Mao's argument goes as follows:
- individual Chinese are physically weak
- the whole Chinese people is physically weak
- the nation-state is weak in the face of its enemies
- If youth can be made self-conscious of this causal connection, and begin the practice of
- physical culture with discipline and perseverance
- they will individually become strong, and
- the people as a whole will become strong, and
- the nation will prosper.

This, it should be noted, was a thoroughly conventional mode of argumentation. It had been usual in Chinese reformist and revolutionary writings, ever since China's defeat in the Sino-Japanese war of 1894-95 and with added momentum after Japan's notorious "Twenty-one Demands" of 1915, to begin by drawing attention to China's conspicuous weakness in the face of western and Japanese imperialism, to attribute this debility to one or another national failing or deficiency and to suggest a remedy, endorsed by modern science,[38] in the light of the experiences of those very same nations that were responsible for China's loss of political sovereignty. Conventionally, the first step in remedying this situation was perceived to be the awakening of individual and collective self-consciousness (*zijue*). Mao's opening gambit captured this "formula" to perfection!

Mao's chief commentators have all accepted this metonymy at its literal face value. Indeed, their interpretation is given force by the notable emphasis that Mao places on the martial spirit and the martial arts (at places he seems to identify physical culture with the martial arts), and by his admiration for the scholar-patriots of the seventeenth century who had fought against Manchu rule. The commentators have similarly accepted in a literal sense the other main causal arguments in the essay: (*a*) that the development of the body takes precedence over the development of the mind (*xin*, the root of knowledge and virtue) because it is the body that "houses" the mind and that makes possible its existence; and the seemingly converse and rather circular argument (*b*) that the development of the body strengthens the will, which is the root of all positive action (including the practice of physical culture!). As already noted, a great deal of scholarly energy has subsequently been devoted to determining whether or not Mao was at this time, as he later confessed to being,[39] an "idealist", or whether, as his communist biographers have sought to show on the basis of evidence external to this text, he had already manifested "a precocious penchant for dialectical materialism".[40]

The burden of much contemporary writing on metaphor and metonymy, following early leads by Roman Jakobson,[41] is that while the two figures may be usefully distinguished on several grounds and for various purposes, metonymy may also transmute into metaphor, and vice versa. Following this line of argument, I suggest here that the metonymic or causal connection that Mao states so clearly in this essay (that is, between the physical condition of the Chinese people, individually and collectively, and the viability of the nation-state) may be *re*-read as a powerful and resonant metaphor in the light of the collective discourse of *New Youth*. This metaphor posits that the connection between the individual person and the state is the fact that they are — or certainly ought to be — *similarly constituted of a dialectical relation between spirit and form, congruent with the relation of spirit and matter that is believed to underlie all existence.*

In "A Study of Physical Education", Mao is challenging his readers to concede the self-evidence of this proposition, and to accept its practical consequences.

This section briefly examines the underlying metaphor of "A Study of Physical Education" as revealed and completed through reflection against the political rhetoric of *New Youth*. The description is based on a study I had earlier made of the thought-world of the Chinese New Culture Movement.[42]

In the Neo-Confucian ontology to which, I believe, the *New Youth* writers were intellectual heirs, the central ontological question was to find a solution to the existential problems posed in Buddhist thought between *li* (principle) and *shi* (affairs), that is, between the metaphysical and the experiential realms of being. Though there was no single and uncontested answer to this "existential predicament" (as Thomas Metzger has called it),[43] all schools of Neo-Confucianism were united in two fundamental ideas: (*a*) belief in the mutuality and reciprocity of both realms, whatever their relative emphases; and (*b*) faith in the potentiality of Man, through his own striving, to bring his mortal world into conformity with the organising principles of the cosmos.

In a parallel way, the *New Youth* ontology dichotomised. Being into two opposed realms or levels, that of immanent reality, which is permanent (*chang*) and absolute (*juedui*), and the impermanent (*wuchang*) and relative (*xiangdui*) level of manifest phenomena. These two levels were seen to be equally and reciprocally constitutive of reality in the sense that the Absolute exists only by its manifestation in phenomena, while manifest phenomena exist only in relation to the Absolute. As Chen Duxiu put it in the same essay from which we had occasion to quote earlier:

> "The philosophers of India all believed the phenomenological world to be an illusion and Brahma the only true reality.... It is true that according to modern science, the data of the senses are deceptive and phenomena impermanent. In this sense the [Buddhist] theories are correct. But one must understand that while the data of the senses are deceptive, the material world itself is real; phenomena are impermanent, but matter (*shishi*) endures. The multitude of phenomena change in an instant — this is impermanence; but atoms and species eternally perpetuate themselves — this is permanence. If atoms and species never perish, the world is without end. If the world is without end, living things have no end. If living things have no end, then history has no end.... The individual in the world is like a cell in the human body. The new and the old, the dead and the living, follow

in an endless and inescapable cycle. Matter endows descendants (i.e. the atom is indestructible); spirit bequeaths history (i.e. the species are indestructible). Though the life of the individual cannot be prolonged, the life of the whole body cannot be destroyed."[44]

A second type of linkage between the two levels of Being posited in the *New Youth* ontology was that of the homology or congruence of their respective structures, and it is to this aspect especially that I seek to draw attention here. It was asserted that the whole of creation in time and space expresses an underlying unity of "spirit" (*jingshen*) and "matter" (*wuzhi*), while similarly, at the level of experience, all living phenomena, including man and his institutions, should ideally reflect a unity of "spirit" (*jingshen*) and "form" (*xingshi*): the alternative was a pathological state of alienation. This theory of the mutuality of "spirit" and "form" in all manifest existence paralleling the relations thought to be operative at the metaphysical level, provided the conceptual frame in terms of which the *New Youth* writers interpreted their present position and delineated their political and social goals. For whensoever "spirit" and "form" were perceived to be in a dissonant relation, therein was created man"s obligation to restore them to a condition of balanced unity in accordance with the archetypal principles of the Absolute. Obviously, at any one point in time, the achievement of balance might necessitate a corrective overemphasis on either one or the other aspect of existence, spirit or form, depending on the immediate circumstances.

Thus, for instance, when discussing the realm of politics, the *New Youth* writers insisted that the contemporary crisis stemmed from the fact that the revolution in the "state form" from monarchism to republicanism had not been matched by an appropriate change in the "spirit" or "psychology" of the people. That is why, at this point in time, a cultural revolution was deemed to be the most urgent and important of current political tasks. As the political scientist, Gao Yihan, wrote in *New Youth* a few months before Mao Zedong published his piece on physical education:

> "The previous revolution was a revolution in form (*xingshi*). The present revolution is to be a revolution in spirit (*jingshen*). The revolution in the political system has already been understood and put into effect by our countrymen. But the revolution in political spirit and education has not yet come into being among our people. This will commence from [this year], 1917."[45]

Mao, of course, made a similar statement when discussing the problems involved in the implementation of programmes of physical education in China. He maintained that in these programmes, too, there had been a change only in form, without the correspondingly necessary change in subjective attitudes. In a way, this was the problem he had started out from.

Regarding the balance of mind and body, however, the situation was deemed to be quite the reverse, for it was felt that Chinese culture, under the influence of Confucianism, had consistently overemphasised the spiritual aspect (the cultivation of man"s mental and moral faculties) at the expense of the physical.[46] This, again, was a pathological situation, with predictably disastrous consequences. "In the strong races", Chen Duxiu had written in "The Objectives of a Modern Education",

> "...animalism (*shouxing*) and humanism (*renxing*) develop simultaneously. Other races preserve only animalism, or care only for humanism at the expense of animalism — these are the decadent and weak peoples. What is the special virtue of animals? Their will is tough; they struggle and do not admit defeat; they are strong in body and spirit and stand up to nature; they are self-reliant and not dependent on others; they are sincere and straightforward, not false and hypocritical. The white races have colonized and conducted business all over the earth — this is due to their animality. The Japanese now have hegemony in Asia — this again is because of their animality".[47]

It was not really the case, then, that Mao Zedong was at this time a budding materialist, while the other *New Youth* writers were still prisoners of "idealism". In respect to human institutions, Mao and the *New Youth* writers were alike agreed that the "formal" aspect of existence had been overemphasised to the detriment of the "spiritual" (i.e., that cultural change had failed to accompany institutional change), while in the domain of man there was a general consensus that his physical development should now be correctively emphasised to restore imbalances perpetrated by the Confucian tradition. The total picture that emerges, however, is one that reasserts the principle of harmonious balance, with a preference for the spiritual aspect of being as the *initially activating* or transformative element of the dualism whenever a dynamic perspective was required. In other words, where the emphasis was on process more than on structure, the spiritual aspect of being would have special significance. Change in spirit might activate change in form, but the reverse determination — from outside in, from "objective" (*keguan*) to "subjective" (*zhuguan*) (to use the neologisms favoured by Mao) — was not conceived possible!

There was thus no inconsistency whatsoever in Mao Zedong's posing as a champion of physical education while simultaneously claiming to be an "idealist" and taking enormous pride in a mark of "one hundred plus five" out of 100 for an original essay on "The Power of the Mind".[48] Emphasis on physical culture to counterbalance a pathological imbalance of mind and body was necessitated not just by the familiar causal argument of *mens sana in corpore sano*, which he manifestly put forward, but, more importantly, by the metaphor that linked the body, the polity and the cosmos in a dialectical vision of human and cosmic order.

VI. VARIETIES OF SOMATIC NATIONALISM

Social Darwinism and Eugenics were two exceedingly influential turn-of-the-century sciences whose implicit function was the rationalisation of imperial domination.[49] This rationalisation was achieved by the projection of western (and in China also Japanese) dominance as the outcome of a natural law whereby the fittest of persons, of peoples and of nations were historically destined to prevail over those less fit.

The rise of such theories, as Foucault has sought to show, coincided with new modes of social and economic organisation and new social institutions for "disciplining" human bodies. The creation of strong and healthy bodies through various forms of discipline and through the emerging practice of "sports"[50] was believed to be directly linked to the enhancement of national power, as well as producing the moral fibre and character that destined some to rule over others. This line of thinking not only rationalised the imperialist project to itself, but was also internalised by the reforming and nationalist elites among the colonised peoples, who came to see their subjection as partly self-deserved — unless or until they could appropriately reform their bodies. In India, nationalist leaders of various hues — M.K. Gandhi, Bal Gangadhar Tilak, Madan Mohan Malaviya, Moti Lal Nehru, etc. — were all advocates of physical culture and, as is well known, mass drill remains a prominent feature of the training of cadres of the right-wing Hindu organisation, the RSS.[51]

Similarly in China at the turn of the century, physical training in line with British, Japanese or Prussian models, was introduced in the schools and military academies, and was widely advocated by reformist and nationalist leaders. Justifying these programmes, a clear link was drawn between individual/personal physical fitness and national military prowess.

There was also a gendered aspect to the psychology of colonialism, as scholars like Ashis Nandy, following Edward Said, have pointed out.[52] This took the form of an imputation of effeminacy to the subject races in general, Orientals in particular.[53] Again, this was a thesis both propagated by the colonial powers and internalised by colonial subjects. Mao's sarcastic description of the deportment of the Chinese literati — though not quite as explicit as Chen Duxiu's earlier mockery of China's educated youth (with "pale faces and slender waists, seductive as young ladies, timorous of cold and chary of heat, weak as invalids"[54]) — nonetheless still evokes the Orientalist stereotype. National renovation through physical culture was in this sense conceived as a process of what one might call "re-enmasculinisation" — of individuals, and of the people as a whole.

Writing in 1917, Mao clearly accepted the Social Darwinist type of argument that China had lost its sovereignty and succumbed to imperialist pressures because individual Chinese were physically weak, effeminate, lacking in will power and ruled by fickle passions more than by reason. Physical education was posited as the initial step in rehabilitation, and it implied, in the first instance, an inversion of the Chinese value system and the principles of social structure that these values endorsed, which privileged those who worked with their minds over those who worked with their physical strength. In a similar way, the north Indian wrestling tradition, grappling with more elemental concerns, negates the principle of caste hierarchy that structures Hindu society, and even seeks to surmount the communal divide;[55] or competitive sports in Europe and America allow some individuals from lower classes to win higher social status, even transcending the race barrier.

However, as a number of studies have shown, attempts to reform the nation and resist external pressure through bodily discipline may take various forms and find justification in several different understandings of embodiment, of sexuality, of masculinity, and of the relation of the individual to the social body. Mao Zedong's 1917 essay on physical education represents *one type* among the several varieties of somatic nationalist thinking, and is interesting for the light it throws on this general phenomenon. It also has wider comparative and anthropological relevance for its reflection on the way in which the individual, healthy male body can serve as an icon, allegory or metaphor to represent the well-being and regeneration of the national society.

Mao's early essay, "A Study of Physical Education", provides a counter-view to interrogate a theoretical position of wide currency in contemporary social science. Derived from the work of Michel Foucault, in particular from his writings on penology (already referred to in Section II), this suggests that the essence of modernity lies in the institution of increasing controls over, and intervention in, the management and surveillance of docile and passive human bodies. This is a process which permeates society and social institutions, and which is also reflected in methods of physical training and health culture.

As in other countries, one type of modernist discourse in China, well represented also in the columns of *New Youth*, has taken this position, advocating state-sponsored and institutionalised mass programmes of physical education. Though he does not explicitly repudiate such programmes, Mao nevertheless maintained that they had been quite ineffective in improving the physical status of the Chinese people, whatever may have been their impact elsewhere; and it was important in his view to understand the reasons for this failure. This was his starting point in this essay which, while accepting the proposition that healthy bodies constitute the basis of a strong nation, nonetheless sought to suggest a different mode of discipline and a different type of relationship between the disciplined body and the state.

As we have seen, Mao's theory of physical education — and this is true of many theories of physical culture, the martial arts and the performing arts in other times and places — views discipline as first and foremost a question of *self-discipline*, and not of disciplining *others*. Creating a strong and healthy body is primarily a matter of "self-consciousness", of the will to self-reform. The regimen of exercise (perhaps also of diet and of continence?[56]) is an individualistic one, self-imposed, self-monitored and self-directed; it is also not intended primarily for display. Rather, it seeks to put the individual, through the experience of his own body, in touch with wider cosmological principles.

Notwithstanding the references to China's declining military power, with which Mao begins his essay, and the celebration of the "rude" and "savage" component in human nature, "A Study of Physical Education" does not evince the psychology of hyper-masculinity that Nandy, and subsequently Mrinalini Sinha, have regarded as typical of both metropolitan and colonial elites under the regime of imperialism. More than masculinist aggression against others, Mao seeks the realisation of an harmonious state of balance between the mental and the physical aspects of the person.

In such an understanding, the relationship of the individual body to the social body is that of an exemplar, not that of a "cog in a wheel", the passive object of external discipline. Obviously, at a commonsensical level, disciplined individual bodies should aggregate to make a strong nation, but in fact the relationship Mao assets is akin to the principle of "sympathetic magic" (in Frazerian terms) such that an individual who has achieved balanced self-control and has realised within himself the principle of harmony and well-being is necessarily in tune with the sources of social and cosmic order as well.[57] The relation, in structural terms, is both metonymic and metaphoric, both causal and analogical.

Foucault would presumably have assigned Mao's theory of ascetic self-discipline, in terms of its bodily practice, to a pre-modern historical formation. Others might do so on grounds of its cosmology.[58] Indeed, as we have noted, commentaries on Mao's intellectual development have identified it with the pre-Marxist "prologue" of his career as a twentieth century revolutionary leader, or with the pathology of his "second childhood" during the Cultural Revolution. There is imputed also a measure of contradiction, if not of schizophrenia, in Mao's emphasis in this essay on individual self-consciousness, for this seems to be at odds with his proven ability as an organiser (of *others*, that is). For instance, remarking on the importance Mao accords in this essay to "conscious action as opposed to a mere mechanical execution of orders" (Foucault's "docility") Schram observed in 1967 that this "patently contradicts the emphasis on *organization* that Mao also exhibited even before he had thoroughly assimilated the Leninist principles of democratic centralism". "For half a century", Schram went on to say, "Mao has been torn by the conflict between an ideal of spontaneity and the will to impose the discipline necessary for effective action. This contradiction still [i.e. in 1969] persists in the China of the Red Guards".[59] Elsewhere, in a more generous mood, Schram characterised such contradictions as evidence of Mao's natural bent for "dialectical" thinking.

But, whatever its roots in indigenous somatic theories and cosmologies, comparative evidence suggests that the type of understanding of bodily discipline articulated in Mao's essay should be considered as one of a *range* of different types of twentieth century somatic nationalism. These different formulations may be polarised as alternatives within a single universe of discourse, or they may simultaneously coexist in the somatic theories of a single individual.[60] That is, somatic nationalism *may* be manifested in hypermasculine aggression and in organised physical training programmes — as, for instance, among Bengal reformist and terrorist groups, and the RSS — but it may *also* take the form of self-discipline and controlled masculinity, where self-perfection has a definite (if ineffable) relation with national well-being. The exercise regimen of the north Indian wrestler is informed by this sort of "utopian somatics",[61] and it may surely be recognised also in Gandhi's famous "experiments with truth".[62]

A considerable literature has emerged in recent years on the identification of the nation with the female (the maternal) body. Imperial power is likened to the rape of the mother, and indexes the impotence and emasculation of her sons, who are unable to protect her. Much less has been written on the inverse equation: the healthy *male* figure as icon, allegory or metaphor for the regenerate nation.[63]

Whatever may have been Mao's ideas on the "woman question", an issue very much in the air through the May Fourth Movement,[64] there was no evidence in his essay of a conceptualisation of the female body as signifier of the nation — whether as the victim of imperialist aggression or as the focus of patriotic resurgence and regained national honour. It was the unhealthy male body which signified China in its present condition of corruption and degeneration — at least in the revolutionary literature we have been examining — while the fit, healthy and harmoniously balanced male body was constructed as the icon of a rejuvenated nation.

How resonant this imagery has been was brought home to me recently, quite coincidentally, while reading the biography of a young Chinese woman from a professional intelligentsia family, who had been "sent down" to the countryside during the Cultural Revolution. Thus stigmatised, she had sought to prove her worthiness for revolutionary citizenship — *somatically* — by transforming her female body into a fit, healthy, male one. She describes these efforts in language strongly reminiscent of Mao's description of his youthful "body-training" (see Section III above):

> "As I matured physically, I developed a craving to become more and more like a boy. I tried to read all the biographies of great men I could find and strove to strengthen my willpower.... When a roaring gust of wind rose, I would stay for hours on end where it blew the strongest. I would swim in the river during the coldest spell in winter. Years later, when I was assigned to settle down in a rural area, I continued to torment myself so as to harden my willpower....
>
> I was challenging my own fate and my 'gender status'."[65]

This denial of her female body was made all the more poignant by the fact that her coming to womanhood occurred at the very moment when, hidden in the crowds, she watched her "counter-revolutionary" father being paraded down the street to jeers and abuses.

But that is an aside....

Viewed in the context of "somatic nationalism", the question of whether Mao's essay on physical education was Chinese or western in its inspiration appears somewhat misplaced. It was just a typically and globally twentieth century product. Somatic nationalist theories, along with the systems of knowledge that endorsed them and the related bodily disciplines, were part of the shared intellectual ambience of elite and reformist groups in the east and west alike, dialectically interrelated in a world system of nations.

As to the question of whether this text should be considered evidence of the author's philosophical orientation as an idealist or as a materialist, Mao's theory of embodiment and of the body-mind nexus renders this question unintelligible. On the other hand, the essay certainly contributes to the comparative understanding of alternative conceptualisations of bodily well-being (balance, not sheer strength), of masculinity (self-control, not aggression), of the purpose of body-building (to improve the circulation of the blood rather than to promote muscular overdevelopment) and of the relation of the individual healthy body to the state and the cosmos (analogy of structures, rather than direct causality).

Notes

1. Chen Duxiu, *"Jinride Jiaoyu Fangzhen"* (The Objectives of a Modern Education), *New Youth (Xin Qingnian*, Tokyo Daian edition, 1962), Vol. 1, No. 2, p. 118.
2. Quoted in Joseph S. Alter, "Hanuman and the Moral Physique of the Banarasi Wrestler", in Bradley Hertel and Cynthia Ann Humes (Eds.), *Living Banaras: Hindu Religion in Cultural Context* (New York: State University of New York Press, 1993), p. 142.
3. See Joseph S. Alter, "Somatic Nationalism, Indian Wrestling and Militant Hinduism" (ms).
4. See e.g. Frank Dikotter, *Sex, Culture and Modernity in China: Medical Science and the Construction of Sexual Identities in the Early Republican Period* (London: Hurst & Company, 1995).
5. Marcel Mauss, "Body Techniques", in *Sociology and Psychology: Essays by Marcel Mauss* (trs. Ben Brewster) (London: Routledge and Kegan Paul, 1979), pp. 97-119.
6. Roy F. Ellen, "Anatomical Classification and the Semiotics of the Body", in John Blacking (Ed.), *The Anthropology of the Body* (London: Academic Press, 1977), p. 356.

7. Michel Foucault, *Discipline and Punish: The Birth of the Prison* (trs. Alan Sheridan) (New York: Vintage Books, 1979), p. 222.

8. *Ibid.*, p. 137.

9. For a similar comment, see Joseph S. Alter, "The Body of One Color: Indian Wrestling, the Indian State, and Utopian Somatics", *Cultural Anthropology*, Vol. 8, No. 1, 1993, p. 49. Cf. also McKim Marriott, "Constructing an Indian Ethnosociology", *Contributions to Indian Sociology*, n.s., Vol. 23, No.1, 1989, esp. pp. 1-3.

10. *"Tiyu zhi Yanjiu"* (A Study of Physical Education), *Xin Qingnian (New Youth)*, Vol. 3, No. 2, April 1917. Though Mao's term *tiyu* is usually rendered in English as "physical education", and indeed encompasses organised physical training within the education system, his understanding of *tiyu* is certainly much broader than this. Huang I-shu (personal communication) has suggested that the term "body-building" would be a more apposite rendering in the present case.

11. My model for this enterprise is Lucien Goldmann's classic study of the tragic vision of Pascal and Racine: *The Hidden God: A Study of Tragic Vision in the Pensees of Pascal and the Tragedies of Racine* (London: Routledge and Kegan Paul, 1964).

12. Here I have been influenced by some writings on the deployment of literary tropes in non-literary texts, especially in reference to the production of ethnographies. See, for instance, James Clifford and George Marcus (Eds.), *Writing Culture: The Poetics and Politics of Ethnography* (Berkeley: University of California Press, 1986). See also Hayden White, *Tropics of Discourse: Essays in Cultural Criticism* (Baltimore: The Johns Hopkins University Press, 1978), esp. ch. 3; S.E. Hyman"s literary reading of Darwin, Marx, Frazer and Freud, *The Tangled Bank: Darwin, Marx, Frazer and Freud as Imaginative Writers* (New York: Atheneum, 1959); Darko Suvin's analysis of the imagery of Marx's *Grundrisse*, "Transubstantiation of Production and Creation: Metamorphic Imagery in the *Grundrisse*", *The Minnesota Review*, n.s., No. 18, 1982, pp. 102-15; and Marc Angenot and Darko Suvin, "L'implicite du Manifeste: Metaphores et Imagerie de la Demystification dans le "Manifeste Communiste"", *Etudes Francaises*, Vol. 16, Nos. 3-4, 1980, pp. 43-67.

13. See, for instance, the literature cited by Joseph S. Alter in his paper, "Somatic Nationalism, Indian Wrestling and Militant Hinduism", *loc. cit.*

14. In addition to the papers already cited (notes 3 and 10), see: Joseph S. Alter, *The Wrestler's Body: Identity and Ideology in North India* (Berkeley: University of California Press, 1992); also "Celibacy, Sexuality and the Transformation of Gender into Nationalism in North India", *Journal of Asian Studies* 53, 1994, pp. 45-66; "The Celibate Wrestler: Sexual Chaos, Embodied Balance and Competitive Politics in North India", in Patricia Uberoi (Ed.), *Social Reform, Sexuality and the State* (New Delhi: Sage, 1996), pp. 109-131; "Seminal Truth: A Modern Science of Male Celibacy in North India", *Medical Anthropology Quarterly*, Vol. 11, No. 3, 1997, pp. 275-98; and "A Therapy to Live by: Public Health, The Self and Nationalism in the Practice of a North Indian Yoga Society", *Medical Anthropology*, Vol. 17, pp. 309-35.

15. John Rosselli had earlier pointed to the similarity between late nineteenth and early twentieth century Bengali nationalist movements for physical education, and developments elsewhere (China, Japan and Europe), citing specifically Mao's article on physical education. See John Rosselli, "The Self-image of Effeteness: Physical Education and Nationalism in Nineteenth Century Bengal", *Past and Present*, No. 86, 1980, pp. 121, 132. The late Niharranjan Ray had drawn my attention to many commonalities between the writings of the *New Youth* group and those of early Bengali nationalists and social reformers.

16. Tokyo Daian edition, 1962, pp. 145-55. A complete French translation of Mao's essay, along with explanatory notes and an excellent introduction, was published by Stuart Schram, *Mao Zedong: Une Etude de l'Education Physique* (Paris/The Hague: Mouton), and an abbreviated English translation in Schram's anthology, *The Political Thought of Mao Tse-tung* (Harmondsworth: Penguin Books, rev. ed., 1969), pp. 152-60, where it stands as the "pre-Marxist" "prologue" to Mao"s career as a Marxist revolutionary. Other sources for this period include Mao's surviving school notebooks, textbook annotations and correspondence, selectively reported by Li Rui in *Mao Zedong Tongzhi di Chuqi Geming Huodong* (Beijing: Zhongguo Qingnian, 1957); Xiao San (Emi Siao), *Mao Zedong Tongzhi de Ertong Shidai, Qingnian Shidai yu Chu Qi Geming Huodong* (Mao Tse-tung: His Childhood and Youth) (Bombay: People's Publishing House, 1953); and Siao-Yu (Xiao Shudong), *Mao Tse-tung and I were Beggars* (London: Hutchinson, 1961).

17. See Robert A. Scalapino, "The Evolution of a Young Revolutionary — Mao Zedong in 1919-1921", *Journal of Asian Studies*, Vol. 42, No. 1, 1982, pp. 29-61. Of general interest also is Roxane Witke, "Mao Tse-tung, Women and Suicide in the May Fourth Era", *China Quarterly*, No. 31, 1967, pp. 128-47.

18. For details on the anti-Confucian and "new literary" movements, see especially Chow Tse-tsung, *The May Fourth Movement: Intellectual Revolution in Modern China* (Cambridge, Mass: Harvard University Press, 1960), chs. 11 and 12; Maurice Meisner, *Li Ta-chao and the Origins of Chinese Marxism* (Cambridge, Mass: Harvard University Press, 1967), esp. ch. 2; and Jerome Grieder, *Hu Shih and the Chinese Renaissance: Liberalism in the Chinese Revolution, 1917-1937* (Cambridge, Mass: Harvard

University Press, 1970), esp. Pt. 2. For a structural semantic analysis of the changing contents of *New Youth* through the May Fourth period, see Patricia Uberoi, "A Cognitive Study of Revolutionary Discourse: *New Youth* and the Chinese New Culture Movement", Ph.D. dissertation, University of Delhi, 1980; and " 'Science', 'Democracy' and the Cosmology of the May Fourth Movement", *China Report*, Vol. 23, No. 4, 1987, pp. 373-95. See also Lawrence Sullivan and Richard H. Solomon, "The Formation of Chinese Communist Ideology in the May Fourth Era: A Content Analysis of *Hsin Ch'ing-nien*", in Chalmers Johnson (Ed.), *Ideology and Politics in Contemporary China* (Seattle: University of Washington Press, 1975), pp. 117-60.

19. See particularly Joseph Levenson, *Confucian China and its Modern Fate: A Trilogy* (Berkeley: University of California Press, 1968).

20. Edgar Snow, *Red Star Over China* (Harmondsworth: Penguin Books, rev. ed., 1972), p. 174. Mao's claim here to have been "anti-militarist" during the May Fourth period perhaps needs some explaining, since it appears to contradict his obvious admiration of martial virtues and his concern for China's military self-strengthening. It should be recalled that the context was the rise of warlord regimes after Yuan Shikai's attempted monarchical restoration movement. Under the circumstances, many Chinese intellectuals, including possibly Mao, had come round to the view that China might be best suited to a federal system of government, and that attempts to achieve hegemonic control over the whole of China were bound to be unsuccessful.

21. Hsiao Yu (Siao-Yu), *Mao Tse-tung and I were Beggars*, p. 41. Yang Changji was a teacher of ethics, philosophy and education at the First Provincial Normal School in Changsha, where Mao studied from 1913 to 1918. With a sound background in the classics, and some ten years" study abroad in Japan, England and Germany, it was Yang who introduced Mao to the writings of the *New Youth* group, and who was probably instrumental as an intermediary in getting Mao's essay on physical culture published in the journal. See Stuart Schram, *The Political Thought*, p. 28; *Mao Tse-tung*, pp. 38-40, 42; and *Mao Zedong*, pp. 28-29.

22. Snow, *Red Star*, pp. 172-73. As is well known after Mao's much-publicised swim in the Yangtze river in July 1966, river-swimming continued to be Mao's special test of his physical powers of endurance. See Li Zhisui, *The Private Life of Chairman Mao* (London: Chatto and Windus, 1994), p. 463.

23. Schram, *Mao Zedong*, pp. 32, 38. Rosselli, interestingly, asked the same question in reference to the late nineteenth century Bengali advocates of physical culture. He concluded that they should be described neither as "traditional" nor as "western". A better summation of their intent, according to Rosselli, would be "purifying", a reaction to British imputations of "licentiousness" against Hindu culture. See Rosselli, "The Self-image", pp. 125, 131.

24. Schram, *Mao Zedong*, p. 37.

25. See note 12. From this perspective, the question of whether or not or to what degree Mao was influenced by the so-called "radical iconoclasts" is not negotiable: it is assumed that he *was* one of them. Of course, whether these iconoclasts were really what they seemed may be another matter!

26. Mao Zedong, "*Tiyu*", trs. slightly modified from Schram, *The Political Thought*, pp. 152-53.

27. Mao, "*Tiyu*", p. 146; trs. Schram, *The Political Thought*, pp. 153-54. Schram, quoting Benjamin Schwartz, notes that the "triptych" of "virtue", "knowledge" and "body" may have been borrowed from Herbert Spencer via Yan Fu's translation (*Mao Zedong*, p. 37).

28. Mao, "*Tiyu*", p. 146; trs. Schram, *The Political Thought*, p. 154. Over forty years later, Mao was still voicing the same grievance against the unhealthy bookishness of the Chinese educational system. For instance, in his remarks on the Spring Festival day in 1964, Mao is reported to have said, "There are too many classes, doing untold harm to the students. Primary and middle school children and university students live under tremendous tension every day. The equipment and lighting are bad, and as a result there are more and more near-sighted children." In Jerome Ch'en, *Mao Papers* (Bombay: Oxford University Press, 1971), p. 93. "Half the classes ought to be cut. Confucius taught only six subjects — propriety, music, archery, riding, poetry and history (*shu*); yet he trained such disciples as Yen [Hui], Tseng [Seng], and Meng [Mencius]. It will not do for children to have no cultural recreation, swimming and physical exercise" (Ch'en, *op. cit.*, p. 93). "The present system strangles talents, destroys young people. I do not favour it. Too much reading. The examination system fights [the students] like enemies. It is murderous and must be stopped". Ch'en, *op. cit.*, p. 94. Note that nineteenth century Bengali proponents of physical culture similarly castigated Bengali bookishness, which they saw as leading to "indigestion and brain fever" and "feeble development of muscles", that is, somatic imbalance. See Rosselli, "The Self-image of Effeteness", esp. p. 124.

29. Mao Zedong, "*Tiyu*", pp. 146-47; trs. Schram, *The Political Thought*, p. 154.

30. Mao Zedong, "*Tiyu*", p. 148; trs. Schram, *The Political Thought*, p. 156.

31. Mao Zedong, "*Tiyu*", p. 149. Indian wrestlers feel similarly about their discipline. See, e.g., Alter, *The Wrestler's Body*, ch. 5; and other writings by Alter cited above.

32. Mao Zedong, "*Tiyu*", p. 150; trs. Schram, *The Political Thought*, p. 158.

33. Mao Zedong, "*Tiyu*", p. 151; trs. Schram, *The Political Thought*, p. 158.

34. Mao Zedong, "*Tiyu*", p. 153; trs. Schram, *The Political Thought*, p. 160.

35. Schram, *Mao Zedong*, pp. 31-32. It will be clear from my own exposition here that I do not agree with Schram on this point. Even a brief glance at writings on the principles and practices of forms of traditional Chinese medicine (e.g., *qigong* therapy) and martial arts (such as, *taijiquan*) suggests several common points of emphasis: for instance, on left-right symmetry; on the necessity for mental concentration and perseverance in the routine; on the dialectic of quiescence and motion; on the importance of the smooth circulation of the blood; on the desirability of emotional equipoise; and on the principle of balance. See Zhang Mingwu *et al.* (Comp.), *Chinese Qigong Therapy* (Jinan: Shandong Science and Technology Press, 1988); Yang Zhenduo, *Yang Style Taijiquan* (Beijing: Morning Glory Press, 1991). See also Li Zhisui, *op. cit.*, p. 256. I do not have the technical competence in either field to pursue these comparisons further here in relation to Mao's essay. For an interesting paper exploring the religious, cosmological, medical and humoral ideas underlying the practice of a South Indian (Kerala) martial art, see Philip B. Zarrilli, "Three Bodies of Practice in a Traditional South Indian Martial Art", *Social Science and Medicine*, Vol. 28, No. 12, 1989, pp. 1289-1309.

36. See Alter's several discussions of the Banarsi wrestlers' contrast of the dicipline of the *akhara* and the modern style body-building gymnasium, in *The Wrestler's Body*, pp. 50-57. Alter links this with the "body-mind synthesis" that he sees as characteristic of "the regimens of health and exercise practised in India — yoga, vyayam, dietetics — [which] exert control over the body not only through a physical mechanics of muscular training and organic chemistry but also through a disciplined regimentation of what we [westerners] would call the subjective mind" (*ibid.*, p. 93). Commentators on Chinese martial arts similarly contrast the muscular/attacking styles and styles like *taijiquan* in which "strength" derives from "using the mind, not force".

37. A similar instrumental approach has sought to detach Gandhi's use of non-violent protest and hunger strike as political techniques from, for instance, his dietary concerns, vows of silence, and practice of *brahmacharya*.

38. See D.W.Y. Kwok, *Scientism in Chinese Thought, 1900-1950* (New Haven: Yale University Press, 1965), Benjamin Schwartz, *In Search of Wealth and Power: Yen Fu and the West* (Cambridge, MA: Harvard University Press, 1964); also, Frank Dikotter, *Sex, Culture and Modernity in China, op. cit.*

39. Snow, *Red Star*, p. 174.

40. Li Jui, *Mao Zedong*; Schram, *The Political Thought*, pp. 38-39.

41. Roman Jakobson and Morris Halle, *Fundamentals of Language* (The Hague: Mouton, 1956); see also Claude Levi-Strauss, *The Savage Mind* (Chicago: Chicago University Press, 1966), 150n.

42. See the items cited in note 19. See also "Suicide, Incest and Cannibalism: An Anthropological Exegesis of a Modern Chinese Short Story", *Social Analysis*, Vol. 16, pp. 60-78.

43. Thomas A. Metzger, *Escape from Predicament: Neo-Confucianism and China's Evolving Political Culture* (New York: Columbia University Press, 1977), p. 77.

44. Chen Duxiu, "*Jinride Jiaoyu Fangzhen*", p. 115.

45. Gao Yihan, "*Yijiuyiqi Nian Yuxiang zhi Geming*" (The Revolution We Hope for in 1917), *Xin Qingnian* (Tokyo Daian edition, 1962), Vol. 2, No. 5, p. 401.

46. Recall the well-known Mencian aphorism: "Those who labour with their minds [*xin*] govern others; those who labour with their physical strength [*li*] are governed by others." Mao himself admitted to the influence of this mind-set when, serving as a soldier in the provincial army, he had nonetheless thought it beneath his dignity as an intellectual to be seen carrying water (or anything else) for himself. See Schram, *Mao Tse-tung*, p. 34. The theme was later to dominate Mao"s strategies for politically reforming class enemies, especially wayward cadres and intellectuals. See, e.g., Li Zhisui, *op. cit.*, pp. 252-53, 390.

47. Chen Duxiu, "*Jinride Jiaoyu Fangzhen*", p. 118. See also notes 2 and 45.

48. See Hsiao Yu, *op. cit.*; Schram, *The Political Thought*, pp. 25-26.

49. On Social Darwinism, see particularly Schwartz, *In Search of Wealth and Power*, Ch. 4; and Kwok, *Scientism in Chinese Thought*, Frank Dikotter's recent book on theories of sexuality in the Republican period has interesting material on the influence of

evolutionist and eugenicist ideas in this period. *(op. cit.* especially Ch. 4) also *The Discourse of Race in Modern China* (London: Hurst and Company, 1992).

50. See Pierre Bourdieu, "How can One be a Sportsman?", in *Sociology in Question* (London: Sage Publications, 1993), pp. 117-31.

51. See Alter, "Somatic Nationalism"; also *The Wrestler's Body*, Appendix.

52. See Ashis Nandy, *The Illegitimacy of Nationalism* (Delhi: Oxford University Press, 1994), pp. 30-31, 42; and *The Intimate Enemy: Loss and Recovery of Self under Colonialism* (Delhi: Oxford University Press, 1983), Pt. I; also M.S.S. Pandian, "Gendered Negotiations: Hunting and Colonialism in the Late Nineteenth Century Nilgiris", in Patricia Uberoi (Ed.), *Social Reform, Sexuality and the State* (New Delhi: Sage, 1996), pp. 239-63.

53. See Edward Said, *Orientalism* (London: Routledge and Kegan Paul, 1978); also Mrinalini Sinha, *Colonial Masculinity: The "Manly Englishman" and the "Effeminate Bengali" in the Late Nineteenth Century* (Manchester: Manchester University Press, 1995).

54. Chen Duxiu, "*Jinride Jiaoyu Fangzhen*", p. 118.

55. For instance, Alter, *The Wrestler's Body*, pp. 22-23, 116-19, 195-97, 217-18.

56. Mao had told Edgar Snow that he and his friends in Changsha had no time for trivialities like love and romance, or the "ordinary matters of daily life" — food, for instance — but preferred to talk only of large matters — the nature of men, of human society, of China, the world, and the universe!" (*Red Star*, p. 172). This observation was metonymically linked in Mao's autobiography with his practice of physical culture at that time (pp. 172-73). Commenting on this passage, Schram rather primly observes that, though Mao and his friends may have eschewed discussions of everyday trivialities, Mao's attitude to women was somewhat more complex: "chaste he may have been, as the Chinese are in general, but his love for Yang Kai-hui [his second wife, daughter of Yang Changji] and his marriage — his fourth — in 1939 to a beautiful actress, suggests another of the numerous contradictions in his personality", i.e., that of a "lover of women" (*amoureux*) *vs.* "ascetic" or "spartan Puritan". See Schram, *Mao Zedong*, pp. 34-35, 42. Schram's conjecture finds support in the recent, not uncontested, revelations of Mao's personal physician, Li Zhisui. Li recorded, in some detail, Mao's proclivity in his later life for young women (and for rich cuisine), and his anxiety over sexual performance, along with his continued interest in the exemplary practice of feats of physical endurance, and his resistanceto taking medicines. See Li, *op. cit.*, pp. 103-24, 463; also Tan Chung, "The Elusive Mao: Reading between the Lines of Memoirs of Doctors and Others", *China Report*, Vol. 32, No. 2 (1996), pp. 159-89.

    On the question of sexual continence it may be noted that the manual of *qigong* therapy referred to in note 36 specifically warns against "excessive sexual intercourse" which "consumes the essence of life": "a person must not seek the temporary pleasure of sexual life at the expense of his life-long happiness!" (pp. 93, 221). One is reminded again of the north Indian wrestler's ideal of *brahmacharya* (continence), which defines true strength as the control and containment, not the expenditure, of male seed. See in this regard Alter, "Seminal Truth", *op. cit*; and Dikotter, *Sex, Culture and Modernity in China, op. cit.*

57. Cf. Tan Chung's interpretation of Mao in the light of Chinese Buddhism's "Bodhisattva tradition" (*op. cit.* pp. 178-79).

58. In *Sex, Culture and Modernity in China*, Frank Dikotter postulates an "epistemic rupture" in Republican understandings of bodily practice, expressed in terms of a contrast between "imperial cosmology" and the modern biological sciences as the grounding of somatic discourse. I would prefer to see the change not in terms of an opposition of imperial cosmology / modern science, but as an opposition of Confucian cosmology/ scientistic *cosmology*, the latter being, perhaps, more "new wine in old bottles" than a major epistemic break (see Uberoi, "A Cognitive Study of Revolutionary Discourse", *loc. cit.*). But arguing this case would take us too far afield.

59. Schram, *The Political Thought*, p. 23.

60. Cf. Dikotter's discussion (*op. cit.*, p. 165) of the "polarity" in nationalist discourses on sexuality "between a relatively independent individual based on the idea of self-regulation, and the coercive intervention of civil society, justified in the name of the collective health of the nation."

61. Alter, *The Wrestler's Body*, Ch. 10; and "The Body of One Color", *op. cit.*; also "A Therapy to Live By", *loc. cit.*

62. See, for instance, Bhikhu Parekh, *Colonialism, Tradition and Reform: an Analysis of Gandhi's Political Discourse* (New Delhi: Sage Publications, 1989).

63. On the nation conceived as the maternal body, see, e.g., the references in Alter, "Celibacy, Sexuality and the Transformation of

Gender into Nationalism in North India", *op. cit.*; also Christiane Brosius, "Mapping the Nation", in Pooja Sood (Ed.), *Mappings* (New Delhi: Eicher Gallery, 1997), pp. 15-19.

64. See Elizabeth Croll, *Feminism and Socialism in China* (London: Routledge, 1978); Roxane Witke, "Mao Tse-tung, Women and Suicide in the May Fourth Era", *loc. cit.* Several commentators on the political iconography of India in the 1990s have, however, noted the muscular enmasculinisation of Ram as icon of regenerate Hinduism.

65. Li Xiaojiang, "My Path to Womanhood", in Committee on Women's Studies in Asia (Ed.), *Women's Studies, Women's Lives: Theory and Practice in South and Southeast Asia* (New Delhi: Kali for Women, 1994), pp. 103-4.

TAN CHUNG

15

A SINO-INDIAN PERSPECTIVE FOR INDIA-CHINA UNDERSTANDING

I

Ramapithecus, the direct ape ancestor of humanity, was first discovered in 1932 at Rama at the Indian foothills of the Himalaya (now lying within Pakistan). In recent years, a large quantity of fossils of this species has been discovered in Yunnan, while this Chinese province has acquired a new reputation as the "homeland of Ramapithecus", in addition to its honoured place as the homeland of the earliest apeman in China called Yuanmou Man (discovered at the Yuanmou County of Yunnan). These archaeological discoveries indicate that the trans-Himalayan regions covering both India and China (and neighbouring areas) form an important cradle of human civilization. The civilizations of India and China are the twins emerging from this cradle. This is the starting point of my proposition for a Sino-Indian perspective.

After being born in the same cradle the two ancient civilizations (India and China) have followed separate courses of development which is but natural. With different lifestyles the two peoples have emerged as two separate socio-cultural systems almost entirely different from each other, at least on the surface. We have to treat India and China as two separate cultural entities even if they were initially from the same cradle of human origin. We have to gather different sets of information about their growth and development. Also we have to employ different modes in retrieving the information. This point needs to be looked into.

Unlike the traditional good Hindus who were keen to liberate themselves from the sentient dust so that they could go to Heaven where everything would be spiritual and non-materialistic (not eating real food to free the heaven from toilets), their Chinese counterparts were very particular in carrying a part of their worldly enjoyments to the after-life world. Their good descendants obliged them by burying the choicest treasures along with their dead bodies. As a result, apart from natural resources, the underground China is the richest repository of artifacts on earth. Hence, China has the largest archaeological industry of the world today. When we reconstruct Chinese history, we are able to take advantage of the archaeological discoveries of the last five decades which have virtually revolutionized our understanding of China. Indian historians are not so fortunate in enjoying such a rich archaeological harvest as their Chinese counterparts have been enjoying in the last half a century, and will also enjoy in the future years.

The Chinese descendants of Ramapithecus have travelled through the footsteps of the Yuanmou Man (who lived 1.7 million years ago), Lantian Man (who lived about a million years ago), Beijing (Peking) Man (who lived 2-700,000 years ago). Their successors were made of many other specimens of early apemen discovered at various places inside the country. On the one hand, there is almost no blank spot within the present territory of China where traces of pre-historical human ancestors are missing. On the other hand, all the various specimens of early apemen discovered within the Chinese domain show some kinship with one another, enabling historians to claim their belonging to one integral human stream in the evolution on earth.

Yellow River was known as the "cradle of Chinese civilization" because of ample archaeological evidence already known in many centuries. There were three early neolithic civilizations. The earliest was the Yangshao Civilization (which existed for about two thousand years around the period from 5000 to 3000 BC) springing from the middle stream of the Yellow River. Yangshao had two younger sisters: Majiayao Civilization (which existed around 3-2000 BC) along the upper stream, and Dawenkou Civilization (which lasted a couple of thousand years, and transformed itself into Longshan Civilization around 2600 BC) along the lower stream. Majiayao Civilization was succeeded by Qijia Civilization (which existed around 2000 BC) in the same locale, while Longshan civilization replaced both Yangshao and Dawenkou civilizations in the middle and lower streams and lasted uptill the third or second millennium BC.

Longshan Civilization spread over a much larger canvas, reaching the sea coast and the bank of the Yangtse River which, we are certain now, is another cradle of Chinese civilization. Recent archaeological discoveries inform us about the Hemudu Civilization (which existed as a living reality on earth around 4800 BC lying in the lower stream of the Yangtse along the sea coast concentrating on Jiangsu and Zhejiang provinces), Liangzhu Civilization (which was alive around 3300-2250 BC), Qingliangang Civilization (with a vintage of about 6,000 years belonging to the upper Neolithic), Majiabang Civilization (having a dating around 4750-3700 BC).

These details serve the Chinese historians to refute the earlier international premise that Chinese civilization originated from Central Asia. I wonder whether Indian historians would like to do the same. But, even without touching the contentious points about the Aryans and Dravidians it may not be out of order to treat the Indian civilization essentially as a continuous indigenous growth, no matter how much external influence it has absorbed into its cultural fabrics. Then, we have a picture of two great civilizations grown side by side just like the twins coming into their own manhood in proximity.

Such a scenario rules out any separatist approach treating the two civilizations as total strangers in their formative millennia. It is just illogical to assume that the two civilizations of such gigantic dimensions in such geographical proximity would treat each other as untouchables in the entire course of history of thousands and millions of years. Moreover, we find common things in Indian and Chinese legends like Chinese Pangu's (the creator of Heaven and Earth) bearing resemblance to Indian Purusa. These legends depict Indian and Chinese landscapes symbolic as the transformations of the bones and fluids of Purusa and Pangu (mountains made of their bones, and rivers made of their fluids). Chinese knew Kunlun as early as Indians knew Himalaya. According to a Tang scholar of the 7th century, Daoxuan (596-667), "Kunlun" and Himalaya were one and the same.[1] Many scholars suspect the Chinese legend of "Xiwangmu" being a goddess of Indian origin, albeit it is difficult to convince others without historical evidence. How to get historical evidence to prove the travel and transfer of legend is the innate difficulty of cultural studies.

II

If we regard India and China as cultural twins from the same cradle, it is important to find the cultural affinity of the two civilizations. One common symbol is the powerful snake whose legendary image is known as *Nagaraja* in India, and *Long*/Dragon in China. In Chinese Buddhist literature, these two symbols have merged into "*Long*". (Chinese translators, like the famous pilgrim Xuanzang, rendered the supernatural *Naga* in ancient Indian texts into *Long*/dragon on purpose.) Ancient Chinese heard about the magical power of Indians to call rains whenever they wanted. Some Indian Buddhist monks, like Vajrabodhi and Amoghavajra etc., demonstrated such a power by playing with the symbol of *Naga*/Dragon. We have records of Indian monks presiding over imperial rain-invoking ceremonies when China was visited by severe drought in the years 366, 726, 772 and 889, the last occurred in independent Yunnan — the state of Nanzhao.[2] Both India and China were *agrocultures* (I have coined the term to replace the tongue-twister "agricultural culture") for which rain-fall assumed great importance. The imaginary powerful *Nagaraja*/Dragon symbol definitely had a connection with it. We can describe the two civilizations as Snake-Power Twins before the advent of Buddhism in China.

I have taken this proposition of *Naga-Long* twinhood to the academic fora both in China and in Taiwan, and have encountered violent opposition. My opponents argued that *Long* had had its independent existence for five-six thousand years, that China was always the Homeland of Dragon, and the Chinese were famous for being the "Progenies of Dragon" (*Longde chuanren*). Even the idea of a part of the social functions of the dragon symbol might originate from India was unacceptable because it hurt the Chinese pride in their thousand years of affinity with *Long*. This, in a way, underlines the daunting task of popularizing the Sino-Indian perspective among Chinese (and also Indian) scholars while studying the history and culture of India and China. The Sino-Indian perspective involved here is to treat Chinese and Indian cultures not as two separate entities developing in isolation, but as the two faces of the same culture developing in diffrerent socio-cultural surroundings constantly benefited by interface synergy. The mystification of the supernatural power of snake in India and *Long* in China was the product of agroculture of both the countries. While we don't have concrete evidence for the Indian input in the imagination of the pre-Buddhist Chinese *Long*, we certainly can trace the Indian influence on the Buddhist (and post Buddhist, if you wish) Chinese

Long. For one thing, the artifacts that symbolize *Long* created in pre-Buddhist China are by and large free from the fierce look that typifies the Buddhist *Long* (like the Chinese say, "*zhangya wuzhua*", i.e. baring its teeth and waving its claws) which clearly demonstrate the inner social function of *Long*/Dragon as the guardian of the imperial system. It is in this function that we clearly see the Indian contribution.

To recapitulate what I have spelt out elsewhere, during the pre-Buddhist period, even as late as the Han Dynasty, the Dragon/*Long* was treated as a "beast" *(chu)*. The famous Han scholar, Wang Chong (27-97?), cited Chinese traditions like *Long* being reared so that people could eat its liver.[3] But, in Indian legends, Siva was a *Naga*, Buddha was also a *Naga*, and the Indian traditions of *Nagaraja* performing the role of a guardian-angel for the God/Buddha and the sacred treasure. It was this message which was driven home in Chinese oral culture as well as literary tradition. Only after absorbing this cultural function from the Indian *Nagaraja* did the Chinese *Long* become a close companion of the Chinese imperial families in all dynasties from Sui-Tang till the Manchu. Another clear Chinese borrowing from India is the "Dragon-King" (*Longwang*) from the Indian *Nagaraja*. China scholars have found that this cult of *Longwang* has settled deeply in China's socio-cultural chemistry as many penetrating studies, like that of Prasenjit Duara, who has included *Longwang* in his projection of the "cultural nexus of power" in China.[4] *Longwang*/Dragon King is undisputably the symbol of Sino-Indian cultural twinhood that demonstrates the existence of Snake-Power Twins of India and China.

As culture advanced, the Snake-Power Twins transformed themselves into a new and higher stage of relations. This was brought about by the "Great Carrier" Mahayana — here I use the Sanskrit word from a non-religious perspective, viewing it as the carrier of a large treasure of Indian culture to China in the name of Buddha. Before I delve into the Sino-Indian cultural synergy wrought by the Buddhist evangelic movement, let me take up the early Sino-Indian contacts from the firm ground backed by historical evidence. We are in a position to say that Indians were among the earliest foreigners to know about the Chinese silk, and also to engage in its international trade long before the famous "Silk Road" between Luoyang and Rome became a thriving international phenomenon. The first foreign words for Chinese silk were "cinamsuka" (Chinese silk dress) and "cinapatta" (Chinese silk bundle) enshrined in Kautilya's *Arthasastra* which goes back to the 4th century BC. There was the famous "Chinese discovery of India" in the 1st century BC by Zhang Qian (also spelled as Chang Ch'ien), personal envoy of the powerful Han Emperor Wu (reigning from 140 to 87 B.C). When he was sent to Central Asia to conclude alliances against the Hun tribes, he saw silk fabrics, the products of the southwestern Chinese province Sichuan, in the market place of "Daxia" (probably Afghanistan or north of it). He was told that the fabrics were re-exported by the Indian merchants to the hinterland of Central Asia.[5]

When Yunnan was annexed into the Han Empire in the 1st century AD, the Chinese authorities found that among the foreign settlers there was an Indian community named "Shendu" (perhaps a corruption of "Hindu") that was "Indians" or "India." But, the Chinese knowledge about "Shendu" went back to as early as the pre-Han days (3rd century BC) according to some ficticious historical accounts. India also loomed large in the broad rubric "xiyu" (western regions), because if we glean the data from all early Chinese narratives about Xiyu, we definitely find the depictions of India. Another ambiguous rubric is "Daqin" which was connected with India in two ways. First, India was trading with "Daqin" (denoting Roman Empire) on the sea. Second, ancient Chinese confused Europe with India and other far-away lands which they had had contacts through the sea. For instance, the Chinese records attributed elephant-teeth and rhinoceros as products of Daqin (while these were clearly Indian specialities not produced in Europe). Thus when the Han records say that Daqin was keenly interested in Chinese silk it actually indicated a triangular route of the Chinese export of silk reaching India, and also Europe via India. In 166 AD, the Chinese recorded the arrival of an embassy probably sent by the Roman Emperor, Mareus Aurelius Antonius, in the Han court. The Roman embassy arrived by sea and landed somewhere near the present Guangdong Province in southern China, and journeyed to the Han capital, Luoyang, by road. The embassy made a present to the Chinese emperor which contained ivory, rhinceros' horn (a precious ingredient for Chinese medicine) and the shell of hawksbill turtle, all products of India.[6] From these accounts, we see fairly brisk contacts between the two great civilizations across great distance either through Central Asia overland, or over the sea. This would not exclude the direct trans-Himalayan contacts as well. Only when there were contacts could legends travel between the two civilizations.

I now return to the legend of *Longwang* which forms a part of the "cultural nexus of power" in China. *Longwang* provides an interesting academic phenomenon of historical development of mythology through which an imaginary symbol has been transformed into material social power. Such a transformation is no strange phenomenon in India as well. When foreign and native tourists see historical sites in India and China they are fed with a lot of information originated from legends packaged as historical data. This commonality between India and China speaks of their shared richness of cultural traditions, and also their common possession of unscientific cultural temperament. But, as scholars of cultural studies, we scientifically recognize religion as a component of culture although religion is not science. A historian makes a scientific observation that Buddhism was spread to China, and, as a result, Chinese created some holy shrines on their soil. So, when we look at the cultural map of China we see the sanctification of mythology in China's day-to-day life as if it forms a part of China's historical development. Let me spell out a little.

Among the legends of Yunnan, there is one recorded in the *Gazetteer of Yunnan Province* compiled during the Ming Dynasty (1368-1644). A "Cock's Foot Hill" (*Jizushan*) at Binchuan County in the province was obviously christened after the Sanskrit *Kukkutapadagiri* — the name of the hill only 50 kilometres away from the bodhi tree under which Gautama Buddha attained his enlightenment. The Yunnan legend claims that Jizushan, too, was the place where Lord Buddha had practised asceticism. A mystic fragrance would greet a visitor, says the legend.[7] Here, the duplicating effect of culture was at work. Ramapithecus split into two groups and settled on both sides of the Himalaya, Kukkutapadagiri begot its double, and Lord Buddha pursued his enlightenment twice — once in ancient Bihar (Magadha), and another time in ancient Yunnan! My observation here is a mix between archaeological findings and legends, but it is an objective assessment of the cultural reality in between the Indian and Chinese civilizations. Many, particularly the people of Yunnan, have accepted the mix as a cultural heritage.

Let me give another example. In Chinese historical and semi-historical documents: there are places called "Shang Tianzhu", "Zhong Tianzhu", and "Xia Tianzhu" which literally mean, "Upper India", "Middle India", and "Lower India". These three names actually indicate just a few square kilometres in Hangzhou City in Zhejiang Province in eastern China. How has such a mix-up come about? It is because of a legend that was the making of an ancient Indian Buddhist monk-scholar "Huili" (whose real identity is lost). In 326, this monk from western India came to Hangzhou. After seeing a hill in this area (in the vicinity of the scenic West Lake), he authoritatively proclaimed that the hill had been flown to China from Magadha (Bihar)! The Chinese believed him and, henceforth, called the hill "Tianzhushan"(the "Indian Hill") and "Feilaifeng"(the "Peak that has flown here from India").[8] It was this legend that has contributed to the existence of "Upper", "Middle" and "Lower" India on the Chinese map.

Rabindranath Tagore, who undertook a tour in China in 1924, was informed about this legend when he visited the spot at Hangzhou. He made a significant observation: "[T]he real fact is that the hill which he [Huili] had known in his own country had a Sanskrit name meaning the Vulture Peak [*grdhrakuta*]. When he saw a hill here so like the one he had loved in India, he felt a great delight and gave it the same name." Tagore added: "This man [Huili] ... not only discovered a resemblance between the hills here and those of his own land, but found his unity of heart with the people of this country."[9]

Chinese legend-makers have claimed that four Indian Bodhisattvas have settled in China: Avalokitesvara at Mount Putuo in Zhejiang Province, Manjusri at Mount Wutai in Shanxi Province, Samantabhadra at Mount Emei in Sichuan Province, and Ksitigarbha at Mount Jiuhua in Anhui Province. Now, these legends have gone beyond their originally designed substance of oral literature. They have been utilized by people of China today, particularly the tourist departments, as facts confirmed by cultural traditions as well as by history and geography. China's being a tourist attraction today (so is India) contrasts greatly to, say, America's attraction. Millions of tourists go around China climbing mountains and reaching very remote corners of the country not only to appreciate natural scenery, but also pay homage to historical memories — visiting a Tang monastery, a Song pagoda, or a Northern Wei cave etc. Ninety per cent of these historical memories are associated with the spread of Buddhism in China. When we see architectural wonders being built hundreds and more than a thousand years ago in the remote corners of China to commemorate the arrival of Buddhism we know that in historical times immense human activities were attracted to these places surmounting many folds of difficulties than the tourists do today — being beckoned by legends and mythology. In other words, legends became an important investment in China's cultural splendours. This is her gain as the Buddhist-twin of India — the country that has invented Buddhism.

It turns out that though India invented Buddhism she benefited much less from this invention as compared with China. For Buddhism, it had a horizontal development, and for some time it was as if all the roads were leading to China — eminent monk-scholars, scriptures, artifacts, and legends. To the Chinese, the four great Buddhist Bodhisattvas (as alluded to just now) had left India for good, but not the Buddha. No Chinese account, however daring, has the audacity to claim that Buddha is no longer residing in India. Indian mythology, i.e. the Tantric traditions, however, reached a very daring and pro-China conclusion proclaiming China as the country where the true Buddha lives. The Tantric literature *Taratantra* in the section entitled "Rudrayamala", described an Indian ascetic, Vasistha, having failed to obtain *siddhi* (divine power) in India, travelled to China — the "land of Atharvaveda" where he saw Buddha having an indulgence in meat, wine and women. Vasistha emulated such behaviours of Buddha and "attained final liberation".[10]

All this shows that Buddhism has injected a special dynamism in our studies of the history of India, China and India-China relations, and should force us to adopt the Sino-Indian perspective. What we have cited above are indications of the non-demarcation of an international boundary between India and China in the cultural arena. As the Chinese say: "Ni zhong you wo, wo zhong you ni." (There is me in you, and you in me.) so is there India in China and vice versa. I should think that such a holistic phenomenon surely exists independent of Buddhism, but it is Buddhism which has made the phenomenon so obvious. The study of legends has served to sharpen our awareness of this holistic vision which is the essence of the Sino-Indian perspective I am discussing.

Let me move from legend to historical records which is a strong Chinese turf. According to a recent study the term "Zhongguo" (now the Chinese name for "China") appeared 178 times in all written documents before China's unification in 221 BC. "Guo" in the bisyllable denoted "country", or "state", while the other syllable "zhong" denoting "centre". (This has given rise to the international term "Middle Kingdom", and also the international stigma of "sinocentrism".) But, politically China was not one state when these terms appeared. A detailed investigation of these 178 concepts proves that they mean different things in various contexts, and were anything but the suggestion that China lay in the centre of the universe. One scholar felt that "zhongguo" arrived as a symbol of a kind of unity in diversity.[11] This shows clearly that the progenies of the Ramapithecus north of the Himalaya started an endeavour in the hinterland of present China to build up a commonwealth sharing a common cultural development. Such a commonwealth would not exclude communities from various directions who might not be the direct descendants of the trans-Himalayan Ramapithecus. It can be said that in ancient India, the same movement towards establishing a commonwealth was in action culminating in the establishment of the Maurya and Gupta empires.

To continue with the historical employment of the "Zhongguo" terminology. Chinese Buddhist scholars, from the early centuries of our common era onwards, attached to it a new signification, i.e. India. Daoxuan, in *Shijia Fangzhi* (Gazetteer of Sakyamuni World) wrote :

> "When we discuss terminology we generally say zhongguo' is the western regions [xiyu], its another name is 'Central Tianzhu' [Central Heavenly India]. Sages of this land reiterate that the western country is Zhongguo."[12]

Here, Daoxuan was citing the ancient Indian signification of "Madhyadesa" for Magadha. That he had no hesitation in transposing the Chinese term "Zhongguo" (Central state) to Magadha, the heartland of Buddhist India (in modern Bihar) may indicate his absolute loyalty to Buddha, but also indirectly reflects the open-mindedness among Chinese intellectuals of his times. He, further, in the same text, cited a debate taken place in the court of Emperor Wen of Song (reigning from 424 to 453 AD). In the presence of the emperor, Buddhist monk-scholar Huiyan out-smarted learned scholar He Chengtian by saying that in summer in India there was no shadow which proved that India was the real "zhongguo". The emperor was pleased to hear that and offered an appointment to the monk.[13] Once again, it was the Chinese ruler's being convinced, (in this case, that India, not China, was the central state and lay at the centre of the earth) that should be noted than monk Huiyan's going overboard to compliment India.

We notice that *Shijia Fangzhi* was a famous Chinese book penned in "High Tang", i.e. when Tang Dynasty attained highest power and prosperity, while Tang Dynasty is generally regarded as the "golden period" of China's cultural development. During such a period, Chinese Buddhist writers, Daoxuan and many others, used the term "Zhongguo" only to signify India, while calling China "Dongtu" (Eastern Land). In non-Buddhist literature during Tang one seldom comes across (if ever) the term "Zhongguo" — and denoting China. But, terms like "Tianzhu" (Heavenly India), and "Xitian" ("Western Heaven" also denoting India), are replete in Tang literature. The conclusion drawn from this phenomenon is the absence of narrow feelings of nationalism, which explains how the name of India attained a special status of respect and intimacy when Chinese imperial power reached its zenith in the ancient period. Beyond doubt, this cultural intimacy was more because of the sharing of Buddhist culture as the two civilizations graduated from the stage of Snake-power Twins to a higher stage of Buddhist Twins.

III

The importance of Buddhism to Chinese history cannot be over-exaggerated, and is certainly unique in the arena of international intercourse and synergy. Buddhism entered China around the beginning of the Eastern Han Dynasty (if not earlier), and was steadily gaining momentum during the post-Han period. One reason of its increasing popularity in China was the losing of control by the guiding imperial ideology, i.e. Confucianism. Intellectuals became disillusioned about its moral authority seeing the moral corruption of the ruling elite. Also, the want of epistemological depth in Confucianism drove people to other schools of thought for greater inspiration. This gave rise to an intellectual wave during the 3rd and 4th centuries which is termed "Xuanxue" (metaphysical studies). The basic inspiration to this new wave was provided by the teachings of Laozi (also spelled as Lao-Tzu) (6-5th centuries BC) and Zhuangzi (also spelled as Chuang-Tzu) (369?-286?). Incidentally, the themes like "Dao", i.e. Tao, and "Wu" which was something similar to the Indian concept of "Sunya" much talked about in the discourse of Metaphysical Studies paved the way for Chinese intellectuals to appreciate the teachings of "Abhava" (non-existence) and other tenets of a foreign religion that was Buddhism. "Dharma" was initially translated into "Dao" in Chinese, and stories about Gautama Buddha's being the reincarnation of Laozi[14] were circulated widely which were tacitly accepted by the early Chinese Buddhists for the sake of integration of the Indian religion into Chinese mainstream culture.

Another important factor for Buddhism to find smooth conversion in China was the country's undergoing a process of integrating various foreign ruling families and their alien ethnic customs and habits and ways of life. The foreign rulers during the period of Sixteen Kingdoms (304-639 AD) drove hard to remove the concept of alienness (the concept of "Hu") from the Chinese minds. Promoting Buddhism greatly facilitated this task.

A third factor is that, Buddhism which stood essentially for Peace, Equality, Compassion and Spiritual Nobleness became an attractive twilight in the horizon before a China that was ravaged by war, cruelty, selfishness, and power struggle. Buddha was called "Pingdengwang" in Chinese literature which term is the Chinese translation of "Mahasamataraja" (King of Equality) of ancient Indian concepts. China has, thus, imported the concept of "equality" (*pingdeng*) not from the French Revolution (as it was generally believed), but from India (from the Buddhist movement). I have put forward the theory (and written elsewhere) that Buddhism gave birth to a "Struggle Ethic" to balance the ideological loner of the Confucian "Harmony Ethic", and injected a new dimension of "mahasamata" (great equality) into the Chinese idealism "Taiping" which used to denote "great harmony and peace".[15]

As K.M. Panikkar has pointed out, cultural influence is always a two way traffic.[16] China's being indebted to India and vice versa is a worthwhile research topic that has been initiated by Bagchi, Tan Yun-shan, Ji Xianlin, etc. It is an endless field for modern scholars. While trying to counter the opinions of Hu Shih (a pioneer of the May Fourth Movement), K.M. Pannikkar made a striking observation that the eminent Indian monks went to China "to influence and not to be influenced".[17] While not entirely agreeing with sich am analysis, I think, those who have been engaged in the study of the history of India-China relations do find an asymmetric scenario of Chinese culture's being far more influenced by India than vice-versa. Such an asymmetry must be looked at from some new angles.

First of all, I think we should not conceive Buddhism as an Indian cultural conquest of China. From a holistic perspective we must treat the entire course of the history of Buddhism as a Sino-Indian joint venture. We must see the interrelation between China's being heavily converted into a Buddhist country and the fading away of Buddhism in India — the cradle of its birth. When we interconnect these two developments we get a picture of Buddhism leaving India for China, and eventually settling down there. Why did Buddhism leave India? Because the development of Mahayanism which transformed an originally self-purification movement (a movement replacing *Atmagraha* or ego-clinging by *Dharmagraha* or truth-clinging as vividly described by Prof. Feng Youlan/Fung Yulan of Beijing University) into a universal cosmology. Such a universal cosmology could prosper only when there was a universal empire on earth which existed only in China, not India. I am oversimplifying a little to say that after the Gupta period, the socio-political development in India was not conducive to the evangelism of Mahayana which had virtually eclipsed the "Hinayana" schools of teaching.

Secondly, we should turn to China to see that while the imperial system was declining in India during the 6th and 7th century, this was the period that China succeeded in reviving the Empire. When the Sui and Tang rulers of China, and even their precursors like the Liang Emperor Wu (reigning from 502 to 549) and Topa Wei Emperor Xiaowen (reigning from 471 to 499) in divided China, took up such a revival, they discovered the deficiency of the Han imperial political legacy and diligently searched from the Indian civilization what could cement the new imperial system in China. The result was a happy marriage of the Mahayana imperial cosmo-political ideology with the socio-political reality on the soil of China. What I want to highlight is that Mahayanism was not merely the dogma propounded by Nagarjuna, Asanga and Vasubandhu, but the entire socio-political spiritualism which helped China to give her universal imperial system the second lease of life from the 6th century upto 1911. We all know that if we want to study Mahayana Buddhism we have to use Chinese literature as its depository of tenets. If we want to make our study relevant with its socio-political context, we must focus on Chinese history, instead of Indian history. So, it is clear that Mahayanism as a historical cultural movement has reached its zenith in China, and such a zenith was the creation of Chinese efforts assisted by Indian and Central Asian monk scholars. In the Chinese efforts we see a substantial input from the lay Chinese ruling elite whose utmost interest or ultimate aim was not to develop Buddhadharma in China, but to strengthen the Chinese imperial system. This explains why in China so many Buddhist monasteries and temples bear the word "guo" (state), and so many of them prided themselves on the receipt of imperial patronage and attention. While Taoism as a religion (different from the purely academic Taoist philosophy) was seldom patronized by any Chinese dynasty, Confucianism was never a religion in the strict sense of the term. But, Buddhism was embraced by the ruling elite of China for a much longer duration than those of any country. And the symbiosis between Buddhism and the Chinese political order can compare with any theocracy of world history. Yet, never was China a theocracy per se. Such a symbiosis is truly remarkable which invigorated both the Chinese political system and Buddhism. This, all the more, requires us to look at the Indian influence on China from the angle of Chinese dynamism. This Chinese dynamism and the beneficial Indian influence complemented each other in the past, and may still remain a positive factor in China's political development in the present and future.

Finally, we have a picture of not more Indian cultural influence on China, but more Chinese pro-active input to synthesize the two great civilizations. Returning to Pannikkar's observation about Indian Buddhist preachers' arriving in China "to influence and not to be influenced", the actual picture is that they, eminent among them like Kumarajiva, Bodhidharma, Amoghavajra etc., had taken China as their own country and tried to build the Tusita utopia on her soil. In contrast no Chinese Buddhist monks participated in such extraordinary altruistic international synergy (in India), hence the creation of the asymmetry. It is clear here that the two civilizations had decided to experiment cultural synergy only on Chinese soil — to marry Mahayana universalism in the mind with Chinese universalism on the ground. To conceive this Sino-Indian joint venture as a one-way traffic is out of order.

All I have alluded to above is an intercultural discourse, not comparative studies. Keeping to the lane of interculturality means not to deviate from the holistic perspective which is the soul of our Sino-Indian perspective. If we allot "X" to India, and "Y" to China as their representative symbols, the holistic perspective prevents us from separating X entirely from Y. In other words, we are seeing the totality of the cultural development of XY, not X and Y. If we see X, that is the X dimension of XY, so do we see its Y dimension. The X dimension is only a different ramification of the Y dimension, not a separate entity independent of the existence of Y. While the Indian deities have many faces, India and China are likewise bound by such a scenario: each is only one facial ramification to the deity, and both are connected with each other by an interfacial relationship. Logically, I cannot see how the cultural development of India and China going beyond this interface scenario, but to build up a comprehensive and convincing historiography requires further research efforts.

Even before building up this holistic historiography, we can try to illustrate in a disjointed manner. For instance, we see the magnificent Indian architecture of the 16th century built on stones, and we associate the reign of Akbar to its architectural magnificance. One striking feature of the architecture of the Akbar period is the prominence of pillars, beans, brackets, and arbours (with pillars supporting an umbrella-shape roof without walls) which are not structurally essential, but more functioning as decorative adornment. We know that pillars, beams, brackets and arbours belong to the wooden architectural tradition. While pre-16th century India was conspicuous in her absence of such a tradition, China was the greatest wooden edifice civilization in all centuries until recent times. The phenomenon of arbour is intriguing. While there was hardly any such architecture in ancient India, the forts and palaces built by Akbar and his successors exhibit them plentifully on top of the buildings. Again, arbour has always been an important ingredient in Chinese architecture, particularly palatial complexes. Not being a student of architecture, nor having studied it in any detail, I cannot proclaim with confidence but only wish to submit that with a great wooden architectural tradition so close to India, and with the ethnic affinity of the Moghul rulers with Timur who was a Chinese emperor of the Yuan Dynasty, one cannot imagine that the Chinese architectural styles were not reflected in the 16th century Indian edifices — hence the interesting phenomenon of constructuring stone forts and palaces by Akbar and other rulers and their aristocrats with a wooden-architectural outlook and arbour adornment.

I walk on a slippery ground while making the above submission, but return to safer turf to examine the interface scenario projected by the cultural development in China. A usual fallibility in cultural studies is to hook the cultural phenomena with socio-religious labels. People first conceive fixed categories, e.g. Confucianism, Taoism, Buddhism etc., and fit cultural phenomena into preconceived straitjacket. In this way the transfer, transformation and transposition of cultural symbols and concepts slip away from scholarly grasp. For instance, there was a very interesting text entitled *Taipingjing* (Canon of Taiping/Grand Peace/Grand Justice) composed in the 2nd Century A.D. Though this text which was absorbed as a part of the Taoist scripture during the 11th century may have been doctored repeatedly in the course of nearly a thousand years, it reveals a substantial development of a Chinese cosmology having a parallel existence with the orthodox Confucian cosmo-political ideology. The *Taiping Canon* begins with a mystic observation of "Santong zhuanlun, you qu you lai" (When the three systems turn their wheels, they go away then come back). The "three systems" (*santong*) was a native Chinese concept which denoted heaven, earth and humanity, but "turn the wheels" was obviously an adoption of the Indian idiom of turning the "dharmacakra" (by Buddha). Inside the text there are many allusions, such as the sage-god's being conceived when the holy mother had a dream, nine dragons having descended to baptize the new born, the sage's abandoning home to cultivate enlightenment at the age of 27 etc., which obviously lift a leaf from the Indian legend of the Buddha. There are other allusions like "renru" (which is the Chinese translation of Sanskrit *Ksantyrisi*), "shenguang" (Chinese reference to the Buddhist symbol of *devabha*, i.e. the halo), "tianyu" (an adaptation of the Indian concept of *naraka* or hell) etc. that further illustrate the input of Indian cultural elements.

What is more important is that the *Taiping Canon* has a focal theme of the causative interactions between human behaviour and the mood of Heaven and Earth, as well as the humanization of Heaven and Earth. Heaven is likened to father, and Earth, mother, hence, Heaven and Earth are the parents of all beings of the world. Heaven is capable of being happy, angry, getting sick. Humanity, particularly the saints, are capable of sharing the body, heart, emotions, reasoning, love, hatred, and ways/roads of Heaven and Earth.[18] *Taipingjing*, thus, was the first Chinese discourse that has adopted such a holistic perspective in viewing Heaven, Earth and Humanity, as if the three systems were not only symbiotic, but also interchangeable. Obviously, such a refreshing discourse could not be 1the outcome of developing the native Chinese thinking without absorbing exotic elements from a foreign cosmology. Just as I have earlier suspected the borrowing of a close-neighbour wooden architectural tradition by the 16th century Indian palace edifice, it is now equally logical to submit that the close-neighbour Indian cosmological tradition has made the discourse in *Taipingjing* so refreshing. Some scholars have recognized the extreme importance of this *Taiping Canon*, while others hesitate to quote it because of its being doctored. Granting all the likelihood of impurity this document suffers, its main thrust in totality points to a refreshing Chinese world-view that had attained maturity from the time when Han ruling ideology (call it Confucianism if you like) was on the decline.

Here is just a glimpse of the cross-cultural effect between India and China. This cross-cultural effect was developed along side the close-neighbour effect. There is a Chinese story that during ancient times there was a beautiful woman, the Western Shi (*Xishi*), who had a close-neighbour, the Eastern Shi (*Dongshi*). Western Shi was all charm and grace, but she came out of the house with an expression of illness and pain. The Easter Shi, however, was of robust health. She felt jealous that when both of them were in public the bystanders all cast their admiring eyes on Western Shi, none cared to look at her. She concluded that the source of her neighbour's attraction was sickness. So, Eastern Shi started making a feint of feeling sick and pain in public which immediately drew ridicule from the bystanders. I relate this story not to equate any country with Eastern Shi, but to illustrate that in a close-neighbour scenario, cultural influence is automatic and spontaneous, also with compulsion. Such a close-neighbour effect has acted between India and China for all times to come, in the past, present, and future.

Returning to the new perspective of the three-in-one harmonious and symbiotic relationship between Heaven, Earth and Humanity, it is clear that such a refreshing cosmology was bound to be absorbed by the mainstream ideology of China. Han Yu (768-829), the great orthodox scholar of the Tang Dynasty said to be "anti-Buddhist" (actually not so), in a memorial to the Emperor, observed: "Your Majesty's *dao* [ruling virtue] merges with Heaven and Earth. Your Majesty's benevolence penetrates all animals and plants."[19] Such a formulation by a mainstream Chinese/Confucian scholar synthesizing Heaven, Earth and Humanity, extending the holistic perspective to all animals and plants (*dongzhi*) sounds quite outlandish to orthodox Chinese discourse of the pre-Tang periods. Its connection with the refreshing *Taipingjing* cosmology cannot be ruled out.

I have noted the *Taipingjing* reference to Heaven as father and Earth as mother. We have the famous Tang Dynasty authority and commentator of the "Thirteen Classics" of Han Confucianism, Kong Yinda (574-648), making a refreshing interpretation of the ancient Chinese conception of "Tianzi" i.e. the "Son of Heaven" (a designation for the Emperor) as "fu tian mudi, ziyang xiamin" which may be translated as "Heaven be the father and Earth be the mother, while they and their agent the Emperor nurture the subjects as their children."[20] Such a definition sounds quite revolutionary to Han dynasty and pre-Han Chinese imperial thinking. Viewed together, Kong Yinda and Han Yu have given enough notice about the changing Chinese ruling ideology, and such a change, as I have shown, benefited from the close-neighbour effect and cross-cultural effect with India.

I have, a moment ago, hinted at the fallability of dividing Chinese culture into water-tight compartments of Confucianism, Taoism and Buddhism. Buddhism, of course, is a religion which has its exclusive existence. So has been Taoism. But, outside these two religious institutions cultural symbols, concepts, art, literature have moved, travelled, transformed, transposed, transplanted in a free and dynamic world in China. To stick labels like "Confucian", "Legalist", "pro-Buddhist" or "anti-Buddhist" etc. seems totally meaningless. Even more important is the phenomenon that Confucian scholars (like Kong Yinda and Han Yu) had expanded their vision beyond Confucianism, beyond the boundaries set by the ancient Chinese philosopher Confucius (551-479 B.C.) and his Vivekananda, Mencius (372?-289 B.C.). Confucianism, in fact, cannot be easily defined in the same manner in which Buddhism is bound by definable religious symbols and regulations. Confucianism, being not a religion, is deficient in such symbols and regulations. If we insist on using the Confucian label, then Kong Yinda and Han Yu were neo-Confucians, and they were followed up by neo-neo-Confucians, and neo-neo-neo-Confucians endlessly. Thus, we see in "Neo-Confucianism" a misnomer that has been imposed by foreign scholars on Chinese culture. This misnomer never occurs in Chinese discourses because its Chinese equivalent never exists.

If we, for a moment, discard this misnomer and see what had transpired we discover the climax of Sino-Indian cultural synergy. We know that the so-called "Neo-Confucian" movement that emerged during the Song Dynasty consisted two mainstreams: (1) "Lixue", i.e. the "Li" school propounded by the two brothers, Cheng Hao (1032-1085) and Cheng Yi (1033-1107), and (2) "Xinxue", i.e. the "Xin" school propounded by two chief exponents Lu Jiuyuan (1139-1193) and Wang Shouren (better known as Wang Yangming) (1472-1528). However, the fountain-head of these two streams was Zhang Zai (1020-1077) whose observations reflects an eclectic mind that had absorbed Indian cultural quintessence to enrich Chinese philosophical visions.

I am no expert of Zhang Zai's philosophy which has been studied quite intensively by modern scholars from the "Neo-Confucan" perspective. Let me, for a change, point out certain Sino-Indian cultural synthesis in Zhang Zai's thinking. In the first place, Zhang categorically said that he wanted to grasp the fundamental truth of the universe for which he had delved into the discourses of Confucians, Buddhists, of Laozi (or Lao-tse) the contemporary of Confucius, and Zhuangzi (or Chuang-tse). He criticized all their epistemological findings, but created a new concept of "Taixu". The term was first coined by Zhuangzi as a mystic state beyond human reach and realization. But, the Buddhists also had "Taixu" or "Taixukong" denoting the realm which an *Arhat* ascends to after *nirvana*. By Zhang Zai's time, the Buddhist "Taixu" had stolen the limelight from Zhuangzi's coinage. The latter was beyond human comprehension, while *Sunyata* (which was what "Taixu" had conveyed) occupied the focal place in Buddhist epistemology. What Zhang Zai did was to adopt *Sunyata* to make it the starting point of his new epistemology.

Another obvious adaptation of Zhang Zai was his famous book entitled *Jingxue Liku* which may be translated as "The Cave of Reasoning in the Study of Classics". The book examines Chinese cultural traditions from various aspects, and there is no doubt about the author's dedication to the study of Chinese classics (call them Confucian if you like). But the title has enshrined the Indian concept of *Guha* (cave) which was so important a symbol in Indian classic, the *Vedas*, the *Upanisads*, and the Buddhist scriptures, as the house of god, of treasures, of enlightenment. Zhang Zai had thus put his discussion on classical Chinese traditions into "Liku" (cave of truth). He must have known that the Indian "cave" (*guha*) was always related to *Vyoman*, i.e. Heaven, so, Zhang Zai, in fact, had borrowed the Indian symbol *Guha* to lend support to his theory about "Taixu", taking a leaf from the Indian *Guha-Vyoman* binary.

An interesting Sino-Indian synergy is the perpetuation of "Devananda" in its Chinese equivalent "Letian" (*Le* for *ananda*, and *tian* for *deva*) One of the first Chinese "Confucian" elite to highlight *devananda* was Bai Juyi (772-849) who titled himself as "Letian Jushi", i.e. *Devananda Upasaka*, and in Tang poetry, the name Bai Letian (Bai Devananda) was equally known as Bai Juyi, Zhang Zai revived this "Devananda" spirit by observing "Shang da ze letian" (When we reach the height of wisdom, we become *devananda*". This should also be noted as a cross-cultural effect on the influential Song scholar.[21]

Zhang Zai made many significant observations which had always kept the Indian symbols of *Sunyata* and *Guha* in mind. He said:

"Xu (sunyata) is the source of *Ren* (highest virtue as spelt out by Confucius and Mencius)."

"*Xu* (Sunyata) gives birth to *Ren*, and *Ren* is accomplished in *Li* (Reasoning)."

"The sage reaches the extreme of *Xu (Sunyata)*, that is why he can choose goodness and refines himself. When the *Xin* (heart) is not in the state of *Xu* (like a *guha*), it will be obstructed."[22]

The last quotation has, in fact, taken a leaf from the Buddhist theory of "Bodhicitta", which is translated into Chinese as "Putixin" (the heart of Bodhi). In Buddhism, "Xin" (heart or mind) occupies a central place, and the Vairocana Buddha is called "Xinwang rulai", which literally denotes the "King of the Heart/*Xin*". There are 60 categories of Xin (heart), one of which is "Kuxin", the "cave-heart". Here, we see another meaning of Zhang Zai's title of "Liku" (cave of reasoning) which signifies his own heart, "Xin".

Now, it becomes easier to understand the second mainstream of the new cultural movement during the Song Dynasty, viz. the "Xinxue" (the School of Heart). Lu Jiuyuan, who propounded it along with his two brothers, equated "Xin" with "li" which reminds us about Zhang Zai's title "liku". Wang Shouren, expounded this to attribute "Xin" as the fundamental essence of the universe. His advocacy of "liangzhi" (the benign knowledge) is not just the adoption of Mencius' coinage of the term, but has placed the *Xinxue* school in the same mould of the Buddhist advocacy of *Bodhicitta.*

Looking at the first mainstream i.e. the "Lixue" (the School of Reasoning), we see the founders of this school putting more input to Zhang Zai's basic propositions about Li/Reasoning, which he described as the embodiment of the Confucian "Ren", and the child of *sunyata*. "Li" was never a vital symbol in Chinese discourse during the pre-Song period, but the Buddhist preachers used it as an important expression. There was the pre-Mahayana school which was termed "Xiaocheng" (Hinayana) with a derogatory connotation. Then, in addition to *Xiaocheng* (Hinayana) and *Dacheng* (Mahayana), a third school emerged to complete the Buddhist *Triyana*, i.e. "*Licheng*". I don't know what its Sanskrit equivalent is, but *Licheng* is the "true Bodhisattva teaching" or the "teaching of Pratyeka Buddha". The Buddhists also developed two distinct realms: "*Lijie*", the Realm of *Li*, as distinguished from "Zhijie", the Realm of *Zhi*/wisdom. Along with this distinction come the two categories of *Mandala* : the one prefixed with "Li" is the *Garbhadhatu Mandala*, while the other prefixed with "zhi" is the *Vajradhatu Mandala*. Obviously Zhang Zai's fundamental symbol "Li" drew greater inspiration from the Sino-Indian Buddhist discourse than any native Chinese or Confucian discourse. Zhu Xi (1130-1200), who personified the climax of the "School of Li", developed Zhang Zai's "Li" into a new category of "Tianli" (Heavenly Li) which was one of the opposites of his dichotomous formulation of "Tianli" versus "Renyu" (human desire). Here, Zhu Xi has let the cat out of the bag, and his *Tianli-Renyu* dichotomy is not fundamentally different from the Buddhist discourse of maximizing the influence of *dharma* and minimizing the ramification of *maya* (desire) — that is all what Buddhism is about.

At the risk of over-simplification, we can categorize the so-called "Neo-Confucian" movement as the binary of a "Li" school which had absorbed the dynamics of the *dharma's* campaign against *maya* and also the Indian dynamics of *siddhanta* (which is *Li* in its Chinese translation), and another "Xin" school which was to expound *Bodhicitta* by camouflage. Some historical accounts written by modern Chinese scholars on the evolution of philosophical schools in China have put Han Yu and Zhang Zai in the anti-Buddhist category which, as I have spelt out, is a totally wrong conclusion without any indepth understanding of Sino-Indian interface.

I now integrate the discussions in this section into the previous section to show that Sino-Indian cultural interface not only created a distinctive Buddhist mainstream in Chinese culture, but also extended the cross-cultural effect into the so-called "Confucian" mainstream which ultimately became Sino-Indian cultural input to the development of China's ruling cosmo-political ideology. From the thinking of Zhang Zai we can detect a new element of holistic perspective integrating Heaven, Earth and Humanity almost identical to what was advocated in *Taipingjing* which took its final shape during the time of Zhang Zai. The difference between Zhang Zai's writings and *Taipingjing* lies in the fact that while the latter was virtually an underground literature with extremely limited circulation among the exalted circles, the former joined the writings of past sages, including Confucius and Mencius, to become the exalted learned discourse, and curricula for the candidates of the Imperial Examinations. Thus, even if the input was minute and subtle, its impact would be great. This makes it worthwhile for us to glean more from Zhang Zai's observations:

"Heaven and Earth share their virtues, sun and moon shine together."

"Sages integrate among all other people while their own entities disappear, thus peace prevails over the universe."

(This contrasts with the Confucian saying: "The gentleman makes peace but does not integrate with others.")

"When the in-group and out-group are integrated, and when the self and all beings are equal, the essence of Tao is grasped."

"There should be equality and justice between two, not partiality towards self."

"When the heart is in the state of *Sunyata*, equality and justice can be achieved, then it is relatively easy to see the right and wrong, then one knows what one should do and what one should not."[23]

From these quotations we see pre-Han concepts of "heping" (peace), and "gongping" (equality and justice) being revived which was but natural as the Buddhists were loudly campaigning "*santi*" (peace) and "*samata*" (equality). Late Prof. Feng Youlan (also known as Fung Yulan) of Beijing University points out that the finest philosophical tradition be summed up by the following words of Zhu Xi which, actually, originated from the mind of Zhang Zai:

"*Wei tian di li xin,*
Wei shengmin li ming,
Wei wangsheng ji juexue,
Wei wanshi Kai taiping."[24]

(Oh, setting up the heart for Heaven and Earth,
For the life of the living masses;
Let the forgotten learning of past sages
Revive and continue for ever,
Let our posterity enjoy
The Grand Equality and Harmony.)

Here, I have translated the Chinese word "taiping" into the "Grand Equality and Harmony" because this is the nearest signification of the term. It is the "taiping" which has united the idealism of the so-called "Neo-Confucianism"with *Taipingjing*, the canon which was supposed to be that of Taoism. And this idealism of Taiping is a ramification of Sino-Indian cultural interface.

I have alluded a little earlier to the "Struggle Ethic" of Chinese culture which was inspired by Buddhism. Now, we find that "taiping" the "Mahasamata" idealism of the "Struggle Ethic" has also been absorbed into China's Harmony Ethic. Infact, the great Manchu ruler, Emperor Kangxi (also known as Kang-hsi) (reigning between 1661 and 1721), admired Zhu Xi so much that he got the *Collected Works of Zhu Xi* republished as an imperial edition, with himself writing its "Preface". For seven hundred long years after Zhu Xi had enshrined the bisyllabic "Taiping" in his works with the golden letters, and two hundred years after Emperor Kangxi had owned these two golden letters in his "imperial edition", no Chinese had tried to translate this Taiping idealism into practice until there rose a scholar whose mastery of Zhu Xi and other classical writing failed to earn him a place in the ruling elite of China. The scholar was Hong Xiuquan (also spelled as Hung Hsiu-Ch'uan) (1819-1864), a drop-out from the Imperial Examination System (*Keju*) who led millions of peasants of south China to arms and established an ephemeral rebel regime named "Taiping Tianguo" (The Celestial Kingdom of Taiping). As I have written elsewhere, this Taiping Movement had many Indian cultural input in it.[25] I may just add here that though the Taiping regime was revolutionary, it still circulated Confucian classics with slight modifications. Hong Xiuquan composed a poem "Jian" (Sword) in 1843, many years before he rose in arms in (1851) which says:

"I hold the sword to bring stability to my country,
The universe is one family where we drink the dew of harmony
... ...
Tigers leap and dragons fly in a brave new world,
Unification in *Maha-Samata* (*taiping*) creates bliss and mirth."[26]

Hong Xiuquan's Edict issued in Nanjing in 1860 in the name of "Tianwang" (Chinese translation of "Deva-Maharaja") says: "Delivering people from misery and save people's lives", "let everyone obey the real Tao and enjoy the bliss of *Taiping*". Prime Minister Hong Rengan in his "Edict on New Governance" issued about the same time or later says: "We obey the Mandate of Heaven and unite us with the heart of Heaven above".[27] I point out all this to show that even the Taiping rebellion (1851-1863) that marked the climax of China's Struggle Ethic can still be regarded as a part of her Harmony Ethic — on the road to realize the Taiping utopia. The uniting factor of China's Harmony Ethic with her Struggle Ethic had surely an input of Sino-Indian cultural synergy.

V

Hong Xiuquan's entry into this discourse has already brought my survey of the Sino-Indian Buddhist Twinhood to the 19th century. People might wonder whether I have over-emphasized the importance of Buddhism which was virtually forgotten in India in the second millennium. This may be true, but, as I have said earlier, there was the second upsurge of Buddhism, the making and thriving of Mahayana Buddhism in China with mass Chinese intellectual participation under extensive patronage of Chinese rulers. As I have discussed just now this second upsurge also established a spiritual linkage between the Buddhist mainstream and the Chinese non-Buddhist mainstream. It was a kind of Sino-Indian cultural interaction by proxy — on Chinese soil, through Chinese exponents of Indian Buddhist culture. It must be pointed out that although the second millennium ushered in many centuries of Islamic domination to be followed by a Christian-Western domination in the last three hundred years in India, we still should treat India as a country of Buddhist and Brahmanic cultures. Therefore, the continuity of Sino-Indian Buddhist Twinhood lasted well beyond the end of the first millennium if we look from a historical perspective.

Unfortunately, such a historical perspective has evaded even scholars who have been sensitive to the Sino-Indian cultural interface and synergy. K. M. Pannikkar echoed Dr. P.C. Bagchi's views that contacts between India and China through Buddhist monks virtually ended in the 11th century. But, we know that an 85 year old Indian monk of the Nalanda Monastery by the name "Suddhasri" journeyed to China to pay homage to Manjusri's shrine at Mount Wutai through the sea with seven disciples during the Jin (Nurchen) Dynasty in the 12th or 13th century. Three of the disciples died on the way while another three turned back. But, Suddhasri and his disciple Buddhasri reached Wutai.[28] That the reference to them is passed down by the imperial documentation network (not by Buddhist historiography as in most of the earlier cases) shows the continuity of Buddhism-friendly political atmosphere in China then. Both of them stayed back and breathed their last in China in all probability. In the 14th century, there were some eminent contacts which too were recorded in the official documents. There was an eminent monk, Dhanabhadra, who was a former prince of Magadha. He travelled extensively throughout China, and became an important missionary and spiritual *guru* both in the imperial Yuan (Mongol) court and in Korea. I visited the site where he had erected a temple in Chuxiong County in Yunnan Province named Shizishan (Hill of the Lion) which is now a thriving tourist spot in his memory.[29] An anecdote about Dhanabhadra occurred during the great famine in Beijing (the Yuan capital) in 1359. When asked by the Crown-Prince how to find relief, the Indian monk showed a magical anticipation of supplies of foodgrains and advised the rulers not to panic. His prediction about the arrival of grains from the sea came true.[30]

There were two eminent Indian monks by the same name of "Pandita" who had made their marks in China during the 14th century. In the beginning of the century, "Dharmasri Pandita" had established his ashram in Hangzhou. He was both loved and respected by the Yuan officials and the Chinese people. The officials of the Zhejiang Province built a large temple for him.[31] In the 1360s, there arrived another Pandita from Magadha. He saw the overthrow of the Mongol government, and the establishment of a new Chinese dynasty — the Ming Dynasty which was founded by Zhu Yuanzhang, a one time Buddhist monk who eventually turned into the leader of the revolutionary peasant force. This peasant ex-monk emperor not only received Pandita, but granted a title to him, appointing him as the overall head of all the Buddhist temples in China. Pandita also gave lectures to the emperor on Buddhadharma.[32]

It was also a wrong impression that Buddhism was not patronized in China after the Song Dynasty. The Mongol and Manchu rulers were devotees of Buddhadharma, particularly reverential to Tibetan Buddhism. The National Palace Meseum in Taipei still preserves among its Manchu palace treasures the imperial copies of Buddhist sutras written in Sanskrit, Tibetan, Manchu and Han scripts. From the 6th century onwards upto the end of imperial China in the present century there had always been Buddhist temples within and around the Chinese palaces frequented by the imperial families for the blessings of the Buddha.

Buddhism has revolutionized Chinese way of life in many ways. It has created new institutions and conventions from burning incense to burning the dead people, from chanting charms to chanting scriptures (which, in turn, helped Chinese to discover the tone-phonemes in their tongues). For more than a thousand years Chinese have been celebrating two festivals in the new year, one on the first day of the first month, and another 15 days later because Chinese learnt that in the "country of Buddha", i.e. India, the month commenced on the full moon which was half a month later than the Chinese practice. And the mode of celebration of the second festival (called "lantern festival") is the imitation of Diwali. Again, we have an instance of duplication.

While Buddha has assumed the highest position among all foreign gods in China, the highest native Chinese god, the Jade Emperor (*yuhuang dadi*) is the duplication of Indra. Bodhidharma (in China from 520? to 536? till his death) took a seat directly in the Chinese heaven after his demise. The Chinese pantheon, in fact, is crowded with Indian personalities. China has the dubious honour of having the maximum numbers (numbering thousands) of Buddhas. According to Chinese oral literature, even the Indian monkey Hanuman (Chinese name "Sun Wukong") is a Buddha with the title of "Ever Victorious Buddha in Fighting" (*Douzhansheng Fo*).[33]

I have alluded to earlier the cartographic phenomenon of Indian/Buddhist names occupying spaces on Chinese territory. Now, even the spiritual/religio-superstitious spaces of the Chinese culture have this Indian domination. This becomes strikingly similar to the Southeast Asian scene which has evoked the rather controversial proposition of "Indianization". There exists a Chinese saying which must be a thousand years old that:

> "All good words of the world have been Buddha's sayings
> Most of the famed mountains are in the monks' possessions."
> (*Shishang haoyan Fo shuojin, tianxia mingshan seng zhanduo.*)

This saying complements what I have just said and makes it a phenomenon of triple Indian domination on Chinese cultural space: the pantheon, the map, and the good sayings. "India in China", thus, is a well-proven proposition while the Sino-Indian Twin-hood in Buddhism has been expanded into the larger cultural and even material life of China.

Perhaps, no one, in modern times, has been so deeply moved by the spirit of Sino-Indian Buddhist brotherhood as Rabindranath Tagore. After commending the "great pilgrimage" between the Indian and Chinese civilizations during their Buddhist twin-hood, Tagore initiated a modern endeavour to bring back the golden period. He appealed: "It is our duty today to revive the heroic spirit of that pilgrimage following the ancient path which is not merely a geographical one but the great historical path that was built across the difficult barriers of race difference and difference of language and tradition, reaching the spiritual home whose man is one in bonds of love and co-operation."[34] While Tagore saw "civilization in crisis", he also saw the dawn "from the East where the sun rises". He continued: "A day will come when unvanquished Man will retrace his path of conquest, despite all barriers, to win back his lost human heritage."[35]

Tagore who was a synthesis of East and West had a clear vision that humanity was leading down the garden path if the cultural heritage of India and China (also of other Asian countries) was to become entirely subservient to the Western materialist obsession embracing conquest as its hall mark. No one can accuse Tagore as an obscurantist and none did. It is, however, true that the enlightened movement launched by Tagore and others to use the traditional tonic to make up the congenital deficiency in morality and human values in our modern world has not achieved enough results to see the "sunrise from the East". The unenviable fact is that both India and China are still groping for the right direction of their cultural development. India is knocked in an endless debate between the modernists and the traditionalists unaware of the stealthy manipulation of the "modernizers"—those who equate westernization with modernization, and leave no stone unturned to replace native values by western ones. In China, the "modernizers" had already enjoyed a field day (which contributed to the Tiananmen episode of 1989), and the country now is trying to stear her way clear from the extreme courses of a "whole-hog westernization" (*quanpan xihua*) and "new Confucianism". This is the juncture when both the ancient civilizations need to take stock of their civilizational strength and weakness in order to plunge into the new century and new millennium which are only two years away. A holistic Sino-Indian perspective will help this stock-taking and promote the quest for the correct parth of modernization in India and China.

Modern technology and the arrival of the new information era has greatly reduced the distance between India and China. While the ancient Chinese, like Xuanzang and others, had to take a perilous journey to India to acquire materials and wisdom in quest of truth, today everything is available for the asking. The Himalayan barrier between the two countries has finally vanished. After all, it was from this Himalayan cradle that the first Indian and first Chinese were born. The cradle still stands there as an eternal symbol of Sino-Indian twin-hood. Let this be the constand reminder to the two countries when they march into the future.

Notes

1. Daoxuan did a remarkable research in the 7th century to prove this. See his *Shijia Fangzhi* (Gazetteer of Sakyamuni World), reprint, Beijing: Zhonghua Bookshop, 1983, pp. 8-11.
2. Information gleaned from various historical accounts by Prof. Geng Yinzeng of Beijing University. Details will appear in the forthcoming book by Geng Yingzang & Tan Chung on *A Chronology of India-China Interface* (tentative title) to be brought out by IGNCA.
3. Yhere is a Chapter entitled "Long zu pain" (the elusive dragon) in Wang Chong's writing *Lun Heng* ((On Balance), considered to be one of the earliest Chinese works written with a rational, materialixtic spirit.
4. See Prasenjit Duara, *Culture, Power, and The State: Rural North China, 1900-1942,* Stanford University Press, 1988, pp. 31-35.
5. This famous episode was included by Sima Qian (145 or 135-87? B.C.), China's Herodotus, in *Shiji* (The Records of A Historian), the first of China's 24 Dynastic Annals, *juan* 116 & 123.
6. *Hou-Han shu* (The Second Annals of Han Dynasty), *juan* 88.
7. Information supplied by Yunnan Tourism officials. I haven't cross-checked the Ming Dynasty Gazetteer of Yunnan *(Yunnansheng zhi).* However, this Jizushan is a well-known Buddhist shrine in China.
8. Archival source of the legend is *Fozu tongji* (History of Buddhist system compiled by monk Zhipan of the 13th century), *juan* 36. But, this is a well established tradition universally accepted by the scholars of Tang Dynasty from the 7th century onwards, if not earlier.
9. Rabindranath Tagore, *Talks in China,* Visva-Bharati, 1925, pp. 60-62.
10. Cited from Benoytosh Bhattacharyya, *An Introduction to Buddhist Esoterism,* Delhi: Motilal Banarsidass, 1980, pp.155-6.
11. Jiang Yihua, "Lun India yilai zhongguode guojia yishi yu zhong-wai guanxi yishi" (On China's concept of state and concept of Sino-foreign relations in modern times), in *Xinhua Wenzhai* (Xinha Digest), Beijing, No. 9, 1997, p. 63.
12. Daoxuan, *op. cit.*, p. 7.
13. *Ibid.*
14. In the famous legend known as "Laozi hua hu" (Laozi reincarnated in foreign land) which must have emerged in the early centuries, and was codified in a Taoist text entitled *Laozi hua hu jing* (The sacred Book of Laozi's Reincarnation in Foreign Land) penned by Taoist priest, Wang Fu, in the 3rd century. The Tang emperors had proscribed it and ordered the destruction of its copies but could not prevent it from secret circulation.
15. See Tan Chung, "Buddhist Incense to Chinese Mass Rebellion : A study of the Boxer Rebellion of 1900" in *Triton and Dragon: Studies on Nineteenth-Century China and Imperialism,* Delhi : Gian Publishing House, 1986, pp. 567-90.
16. See K.M. Panikkar, *India and China,* Bombay: Asia Publishing House, 1957, p. 63.
17. *Ibid,* p. 64.
18. The complete text of the *Taiping Canon* is now restored. See Wang Ming (comp), *Taipingjing hexiao*(Restoration and annotation of Taipingjing), Beijing: Zhonghua Bookshop, 1960, passim.
19. Ma Tongbo (ed.), *Han Changli wenji xiaozhu* (Annotated edition of the collected works of Han Yun), Hongkong: Zhonghua Bookshop, 1972, p. 426.
20. *Liji Zhengyi* (True meanings of the Book of Rites), *juan* 4, Kong Yinda's discourse on "Jun tianxia yue tianzi".

21. *Zhang Zai ji* (collected works of Zhang Zai), Beijing: Zhonghua Bookshop, 1978, p. 35.
22. *Ibid*, p. 325.
23. *Ibid*, p. 33-34, 273, 280, 285.
24. In the concluding part of the revised edition of Feng Youlan's *History of Chinese Philosophy*. See Feng Youlan, "Zhongguo zhexuede diyun jingsheng" (The fundamental spirit of Chinese Philosophy), in *Zhongguo Wenhua* (Chinese Culture), No. 5, 1991, pp. 9-11.
25. See Tan Chung, *Triton and Dragon*, "Chinese peasant war for Taiping dreams", "A new look of peasant rebellion in China", pp. 443-528.
26. See Tan Chung, *Classical Chinese Poetry*, in "Classics of the East" Series, Calcutta: The M P Birla Foundation, 1991, p. 501, with slight modification of the translation.
27. See Jin Youfu et al (comps), *Taiping tianguo shiliao* (Historical source materials on the Taiping Celestial Kingdom), Shanghai: Zhonghua Bookshop, 1955, p. 51-52, 96.
28. Ji Yun et al (comp), *Xu wenxian tongkao* (Supplementary to *Wenxian tongkao* or General Reference Book of Official Documents), published by Manchu government in 1747 which revised the 1586 version of the same title compiled by Wang Qi, *juan* 254, "xianshi" (fairies and Buddhists).
29. Documents about Dhanabhadra will be published by the Yunnan Academy of Social Sciences, Kunming, soon.
30. Information supplied by Prof. Geng Yinzeng.
31. Ditto.
32. Ji Yuan, *op. cit.*
33. Tan Chung, "The Golden Monkey", *The India Magazine*, Vol. 13, Dec. 1992, pp. 82-88.
34. Tagore's message to the Chinese friends in general dated April 23, 1934. See *Twenty Years of Visva-Bharati Cheena-Bhavana*, Santiniketan,1957, p. 37.
35. Tagore "Crisis in Civilization", in Sisir Kumar Ghose (ed), *Tagore For You*, Calcutta: Visva-Bharati, 1966, p. 189.

HARAPRASAD RAY

16

UNDERSTANDING XUANZANG AND THE XUANZANG SPIRIT

People in India remember Xuanzang (also spelled as Xuanzhuang, Hsuan Tsang, Yuan Chuang or Hiuen Tsang etc.) primarily for his *Records of the Western Regions during the Tang Dynasty* (*Da Tang Xiyu Ji*), as if the pilgrim-scholar came here only to write a travelogue after his return to China, thus doing grave injustice to this great "Master of the Tripitakas"(*sanzang*). In order to correct this let me first refer to the popular Chinese novel *Xiyouji* (Pilgrimage to the West) which was processed into a jewel of Chinese literature by Wu Cheng'en (1500? - 1582?). This novel which was quoted by Jawaharlal Nehru in *The Discovery of India* as "Monkey" (p. 207) was not the creation of its author's imagination. A historical perspective should treat this novel as the climax of the development of the Xuanzang legend for 900 years beginning from the day he returned to the Chinese capital as national hero, and his subsequent achievement in China to raise the status of Buddhism to that of a "State Religion" so to say. Stories about Xuanzang's undergoing the perilous journey to reach India and his subsequent return to China with the Buddhist sutras were in circulation among the masses in a typical Chinese fashion even when the Tripitaka Master was still alive. The erection of Dayan Pagoda (the "Pagoda of the Great Swan", likening Xuanzang's return to a migratory bird) at the imperial capital Changan in 652 to commemorate Xuanzang's historic return by the imperial government was the creation of the monument of Xuanzang and the starting point of the Xuanzang legend. In subsequent post-Tang dynasties, fantastic Xuanzang stories were told, retold, performed, written, re-written umpteen times till they became *Xiyouji* — China's equivalent of *Ramayana*. In the novel *Xiyouji*, Xuanzang acquired two supreme images: (1) being the purest of human beings whose flesh could make demons immortal; (2) entering the Heaven as a new incarnation of the Buddha. The novel has immortalized Xuanzang's pilgrimage to India which has been well known in China for many centuries as "Xitian qujing", i.e. "Obtaining Truth from the Western Heaven". So, the eulogizing of Xuanzang's pilgrimage also immortalized the image of India as the "Western Heaven".

Xuanzang has since become a historical monument, a legend, a semi-deity, a man of many parts : Buddhologist, traveller, philosopher, translator, as well as an outstanding messenger and promoter of culture among the nations of Asia. His outstanding feats have been eulogized not only in China, but also in India, Korea, Japan, Vietnam and other countries. Xuanzang has become a household name both in China and India. He has left for us an extremely rich cultural heritage in the fields of theory, science of translation, history, geography, folk customs, cultural intercourse and commerce.

Xuanzang was born in 600 in a family of scholars in Henan province. He learnt the Confucian classics. Having been converted to Buddhism at a young age, he went to Sichuan (in which the main city, Chengdu was a seat of Sanskrit learning then as it is today), and other places in China and in India to acquire knowledge of Buddhism from the renowned scholars like Silabhadra. About Xuanzang's pilgrimage to India we are not quite sure when he started the journey (either in 627 or in 629). But, he returned from India to China in 645 for sure. He left his country being chased by a government warrant of arrest (for violating the imperial ban on travelling abroad imposed by the new Emperor Taizong who usurped the throne in 626). When he returned, a red carpet reception was laid for him. All this added colour to his historic pilgrimage. He was soil bound, and finally returned to his motherland, although his Indian colleagues entreated him to stay on in India. In his accounts and lectures he often mentioned Confucianism and Taoism, and even translated into Sanskrit the Taoist text, *Daodejing* at the request of the Kamarupa king Bhaskara Varman, whom Xuanzang mentions as "Kumara Raja". Xuanzang must have been pained at heart to see the ignorance among the Indians about China except some at the royal courts. His translation of *Daodejing* was a very thoughtful endeavour to introduce Chinese philosophy and culture to the Indians. But alas, this translated text in Sanskrit is lost to us.

At the time of Xuanzang, Buddhism was firmly established in China. Before his departure for India, he studied Hinayana and Mahayana texts, specially the latter. He had mastered the treatises on epistemology (*Vijnanavada*), particularly the "Compendium of Mahayana" (*Mahayana-samgraha*) of Asanga which had already been translated into Chinese three times. Through the translations of the treatises of this school done in the 6th century by Paramartha, Xuanzang had come to know about the existence of the *Yogacarabhumisastra* (Treatise of the Lands of the Practice of Yoga) concerning the seventeen stages of spiritual progress, a monumental compendium of the epistemological school, also known as Yogacara (Practice of Yoga). Paramartha had translated a fragment. Xuanzang wanted to study the Sanskrit original. He eventually took it home from Nalanda, and translated it after his return to China between 646 and 648 AD, and circulated his translation under the title *Yujia Shidi Lun.*[1]

Xuanzang devoted his life to a conscientious and scrupulous study of the Buddhist texts and translated into Chinese 75 treatises into 1,335 fascicles of Buddhist classics, bringing systematically the *Vinayas, Sutras* and *Sastras*, and other discourses to China. He developed the indigenous Chinese school of consciousness, and founded the *Weishi* (*Vijnanavada*) sect. His theories and thoughts were also disseminated abroad by foreign scholars.

There were a host of great Indian Buddhist scholars like Kumarajiva (AD 344-413 or 350-409), Buddhabhadra (359-429), Dharmaksema (385-433), Paramartha (499-569), Bodhiruci I (5th to 6th century), Bodhiruci II (died 727), Amoghavajra (705-774), and many others who worked tirelessly to expound the *Dharma* to the Chinese elite as well as the laity, and also translated Buddhist literature from Sanskrit into Chinese. They were actively supported by the Chinese ruling class, and a great number of Chinese intellectuals of whom Faxian (337?-422?), Xuanzang and Yijing (635-713) were the finest examples. We observe in this scenario a Sino-Indian intellectual joint venture in the creation of a new spiritual order. Fed with ancient Indian symbols and imageries, the entire undertaking went through a long process of hard work and internalization, and, finally became an integral part of Chinese heritage.

Before embarking on his pilgrimage, Xuanzang was already adequately equipped with the knowledge of the latest developments in Buddhist philosophy, but it was his insatiable urge for higher learning that inspired him to come to India, so that he could enrich the Chinese Buddhist culture with additional treasures that had not been available in China. He also wanted to collect the texts and take them to China for rendering them into Chinese for dissemination of the right kind of Dharma. He, thus, set the model for modern students: To deepen your knowledge in a particular branch of science or art, by obtaining it from the place of its origin. This is particularly important for present Indian China scholars who have not firmly cultivated the habit of studying first-hand source-materials.

Xuanzang is regarded as one of the best scholars of Buddhism for all times. Some of the works translated by him are among the largest, namely, "The great Sutra of the Perfection of Wisdom" (*Mahaprajna-paramita sutra*) in 600 *juans* (fascicles), translated in 659, "The Treatise of the Lands of the Masters of Yoga" (*Yogacaryabhumisastra*) in 100 *juans*, translated in AD 646-648 and "The Great Exegesis" (*Mahavibhasa*) which is a compendium of the scholastic scriptures of the Sarvastivada school of Hinayana. Although a Mahayanist by faith, Xuanzang's ideal was to possess a perfect knowledge of all the trends represented by various Buddhist schools, particularly of the Sarvastivada school, a very elaborate system, whose knowledge is essential for an understanding of the intricacies of the Buddhist doctrine. He studied the different treatises of *Sarvastivada-Abhidharma* with the most competent teachers in India.

Xuanzang was fully aware of the fact that a knowledge of the non-Buddhist systems of philosophy was essential for a thorough understanding of the Buddhist doctrine, and also to refute the arguments of the opponents. The result was his translation of *Dasapadarthasastra* (The Treatise on the Ten Elements), a *Vaisesika* treatise by Candramati or Maticandra whose Sanskrit original is lost. We are grateful to the pilgrim that this valuable treatise is preserved for us in his Chinese translation.

Xuanzang's *Cheng Weishi Lun* (completed in AD 659) is the translation of a commentary on Vasubandhu's *Trimsika* (Thirty Verses), a basic text of the Vijnanavadasa school. It repudiates all belief in the reality of the objective world, maintaining that citta (*cittamatra*) or vijnana (*vijnana-matra*) is the only reality. The work represents the views of the ten masters among whom Sthiramati and Dharmapala represented the schools of Valabhi (West India) and Nalanda (East India) respectively. Being the disciple of Silabhadra of Nalanda, Xuanzang naturally adopts the views of the Nalanda school as final. Xuanzang has preserved, through this work, records of inestimable value which otherwise would have been lost forever. In the 1930s the great scholar-explorer Rahula Sankrityayana started re-translating this work into Sanskrit with the help of a Chinese scholar, but unfortunately, the task remained incomplete

The establishment and development of various sects of Buddhism underwent significant evolution in China. In the Wei and Jin periods (AD 220-420), Buddhism of the South (that now practised in India, Sri Lanka and other South and Southeast Asian countries except Vietnam) emphasized the theoretical sides, while Buddhism of the North (that is now practised in East Asia including Vietnam) honoured *Chan* (*dhyana* - meditation). During the years of Sui and Tang (581-907), Buddhism followed the path of unification, most sects upholding the cultivation of both *ding* (*samadhi* — self hypnotisation) and *hui* (*jnana* - knowledge) simultaneously with the enlargement of both *chan* and *yi* (theory). It was at this time that the *Tiantai* sect reached its zenith synthesizing both Southern and Northern Buddhism.

Meanwhile, the continuous inflow of Buddhism resulted in the formation of the *Faxiang* sect (*Weishi —Vijnanavada*). This sect created by Xuanzang inherited its theory from the teachings of the two sects of Indian Mahayana Buddhism (*Dacheng*). In the early Tang period *Faxiang* or *Weishi* coexisted with the *Sanlun* (the Three Madhyamika Treatises School) and Tiantai (named after Mount Tiantai) sects.[2] But *Faxiang* which preserved the true Indian Buddhist theories survived only for a short time. In its place came the new sects which were adopted to fit with the social milieu of China. They were the *Huayan* and the *Chan* sects that began to flourish during the reign of Empress Wu Zetian (684-704).[3]

Xuanzang's pilgrimage to India has set a brilliant example of internationalism and interculturalism. No wonder this pilgrimage for obtaining authentic scriptures has been kept alive for more than a thousand years in China as an idiom of "qujing" (to "obtain scriptures"). Today, this bisyllable hangs on the lips of every Chinese who show sincerity of learning from other cultures. Such a culture may be called the Xuanzang tradition. To India, Xuanzang's pilgrimage yields an additional benefit. This benefit can be quantified by the total times of mention of Xuanzang's name in the introductions engraved on stones and metal put up by the Archaeological Survey of India at the sites of ancient Indian monuments. As accurate information about these monuments have not been passed down by their creators, the archaeological authorities of India have found in the name of Xuanzang the best historical witness. Xuanzang has led other Chinese chroniclers of fill in a good number of blanks in ancient India historiography. One can imagine what darkness Indian historians would have to grapple with had Xuanzang's pilgrimage not taken place, or had he not left his immortal account *Da-Tang xiyuji*. Here, we have a case of Xuanzang's helping the posterity of his Indian gurus, colleagues, and friends to revisit the living and doings of their ancestors even after more than a millennium.

China is the first country in the world to have espoused translation work as a serious task of scholarship. Starting as an individual enterprise, the cause was very soon promoted by the Chinese emperors for centuries through the establishment of regular Translation Bureaus. In the history of translation of the Buddhist texts which were the firsts in the world to be ever translated, the task was given great importance both during the Sui (581-618) and Tang (618-907) dynasties. A Translation Society was organized at high levels at the Daxingshan Monastery in the capital, Changan. Indian scholars played an important role in translation work. For instance, Narendrayasas of the Sui dynasty spent four years translating 23 volumes. Prabhakaramitra in the Tang Dynasty finished 35 volumes in three years.[4]

Before Xuanzang, translation of Buddhist scriptures was always piloted by Indian scholars who often did not have good command of Chinese; they were aided by the Chinese who, in turn, were not conversant in Sanskrit. As a result, the interpretation was often both rigid and insipid. There had been long discussions over centuries about the merits and demerits of literal translation and free translation. Kumarjiva (AD 344-413), for example, strongly argued for free translation. Aided by the Chinese scholars his translations were both elegant and fluent, but they were not always faithful to the originals.[5]

Xuanzang combined both these methods for the first time. He sponsored a new period of translation initiated by the Chinese themselves. With his great learning and profound command over Sanskrit, Xuanzang's interpretations avoided all the defects of the earlier period. When Xuanzang directed his translation-work, his assistants used to listen to his expositions of the scriptures. While being faithful to the meanings of the original words, his translations were both fluent and elegant. Among other numerous translations, he had rendered the abstruse theories of *Mahaprajnaparamitasutra* into 600 fascicles of natural and fluent four-word poems, and made the presentation of the doctrine more vivid.[6] Here is a case of transcreation which marks the pinnacle point of translation.

Before starting his epoch-making venture in transcreation, Xuanzang considered the propriety of following Paramartha's method which sometimes omitted repetitions and made certain additions. After thoughtful deliberations he resolved to exercise some liberty in order to make the original meaning clear while retaining the beauty of the language. Along with his disciples, he followed a method of translation which was a departure from that followed by Paramartha. Xuanzang's method subsequently came to be known as the "New Method". Thus, the pedantic tendency found in the translation of Paramartha and his disciples was replaced by freedom-cum-faithfulness of Xuanzang and his school. The method of Paramartha came to be called the "Old Method".[7]

As of today, besides five complete Vinayapitakas which were mostly translated from Sanskrit, some being rendered into Chinese from local dialects, there are also Chinese translations of shorter texts belonging to the various Vinaya schools, such as the Pratimoksa or "the Rules of ordination" of the monks and the nuns, and numerous other miscellaneous texts including the commentaries on the Vinayas called *Vibhasa* and *Matrika*. The Pali Vinayapitaka in Chinese belongs to only one school, whereas the Chinese collection is the richest collection of the Vinaya literature known so far. Thus it provides us with the greatest opportunity for the study of the ancient Vinaya literature.[8]

A comparison of the Vinayapitakas in Chinese translation with their Pali counterparts often yields new and significant insight. The accounts in the Chinese Vinayas are often more complete than those in the Pali Vinayas and shed more light on many aspects of early Indian life and society. They are also the source of information on the doctrinal schism between the various Buddhist schools. According to P.C. Bagchi, "In fact a study of the Chinese Vinayas is indispensable if we want to reconstruct the history of the early Buddhist church in India."[9] The scholars of Buddhism and Chinese Language should now pay attention to these fundamentals about Sino-Indian studies so that our understanding of India-China cultural synergy firms upon Xuanzang and other Buddhist masters of China and India.

For a long time Buddhism played the role of a great medium of cultural exchange between India, China and the neighboring countries. The scholar-monks from India and China made outstanding contributions to the friendly intercourse between both the countries. Xuanzang's work "*Records of the Western Region*" has always been held in high esteem by the Indian historians as a mine of data. Cunnigham, the great archaeologist always carried a copy of the translation of this travelogue during his archaeological survey throughout India. It is presumably during this period (Tang dynasty) that the art of paper-making was introduced from China to India, and Indian medicine, astronomy, calendar and phonetics were extensively in use in China, and produced indelible impact on almost all aspects of Chinese life and culture.

It is possible to surmise that being of foreign origin, paper did not find a permanent place in India's academic domain, as it was thought to be sacrilegious to use an object of foreign origin for use in writing sacred scriptures. Hence, use of palm-leaf (*bhurja-patra*) continued even after the advent of paper in India. In the realm of literature, Chinese *bianwen* (a literary style by mixing prose and poetry, like the *Campukavya* in India) had its source directly from the Buddhist texts, and influenced greatly the advancement of Chinese literature in the succeeding age. But, this Bianwen literature has been enshrined on paper for more than a thousand years which has served a wonderful purpose of keying into memory in black and white what the Tang monks used to speak, chant, sing, and perform in sound and body language. Xuanzang who had carried a rich stock of mythological stories from India to China must have given a fillip to this new genre of Chinese literature.

The shining example of Xuanzang as a trans-cultural bind between India and China can never be over-emphasized:

> "One does not know what most causes wonder in the translations of Xuanzang: the rapidity with which they are executed, the rigor of the terminology, or the erudition and penetration shown by this scholar, who was the only one in China to combine a first-rate Chinese culture with a perfect knowledge of Sanskrit."[10]

These weighty commendation were offered by the famous French Sinologist, Paul Demieville (1894-1979). Such a high appreciation of Xuanzang's achievement can come only when the commentator himself becomes highly conversant in Sanskrit and classical Chinese.

Taking a cue from Demieville, we should regard Xuanzang as a cultural giant whose one foot was firmly planted in Chinese soil and another in Indian soil. That such a cross-cultural giant could emerge is mighty evidence the India-China cultural interfaceand synergy. Xuanzang and many eminent monk-scholars of China and India were instrumental to carve out the contours of this image between India and China. Other names in mind are Kumarajiva, Bodhiruci I (in China in the first half of the 6th century), Bodhiruci II (as alluded to earlier). and Amoghavajra (705-774). Xuanzang's difference from these eminent

Indians lies in the fact that he was translating Buddhist scriptures virtually single-handedly, while his senior and junior colleagues above mentioned had a brigade of Chinese scholars to assist them. In other words, none of the eminent Indians possessed his easy facility with both Chinese and Sanskrit. This amphibious habituation between two great cultures is exemplified by Rabindranath Tagore (1861-1941) who could saunter in the gardens of English and Bengali literatures and pluck their flowers freely. But, we need a modern Xuanzang who can do as Tagore did half a century ago in the gardens of Chinese and Indian literatures. And this was exactly what Xuanzang did 1,300 years ago. If China could produce such a great Sino-Indian cultural amphibian (like Xuanzang), India surely can. If India could produce an Indian-English cultural amphibian (like Tagore), she surely can produce another Indian-Chinese cultural amphibian. That we have not yet produced one proves only our weakness in the desire, not capability.

The year 1998 celebrates the birth centenaries of two great savants in Sino-Indian Studies and India-China cultural affinity: Dr. P.C. Bagchi (1898-1956) and Prof. Tan Yun-Shan (1898-1983). Dr. Bagchi was a shining example of an Indian quest for indepth understanding of Chinese civilization. He came on the cultural scene at a time when most of the educated Indians were either ignorant about or indifferent to the legacy of multifaceted Chinese heritage and its importance to Indian history. The life and work of him are convincing examples of what a perfect Sino-Indologist stands for and to what extent an Indian can advance as a frontline Sinologist, if given the will power. Had there not been the sudden death to this savant (over burdened by performing the duty of running a premier university of India, i.e. Visva-Bharati), we would have seen many more decades of fruitful research in Sino-Indian studies, and bequeathed with a richer heritage from Bagchi's generation of India-China amphibious cultural habituation. Dr. Bagchi's example serves to strengthen my conviction that India, too, can produce her counterpart of Xuanzang, and can carry the Xuanzang spirit to her cultural and academic endeavour in forging a greater understanding between India and China.

Hetuvidya (*yinming* i.e. theory on causation) is an important part of Yogacara system based on Dharmalaksana school founded by Xuanzang, an offshoot of the Vijnanavada philosophy of Dharmaraksita. Xuanzang systematically introduced *Hetuvidya Sastra*, as a result of which it was in fashion in China for a time, but was forgotten later. In modern China, with the publication of more than a dozen books and seminar papers, the development of studies on *Hetuvidya Sastra* is being promoted simultaneously with the revival of Xuanzang studies.[11] This is encouraging for the Indian scholars of Buddhism with a sound knowledge of Sanskrit who can take advantage of the situation so that both India and China can benefit through cooperative research programmes.

Many new archaeological and literary discoveries over an extensive area running from China to India through Central Asia have broken new grounds and shed new light on the material and spiritual culture of the past. If we combine and integrate the results through the cooperation of all concerned scholars, we shall then be doing yeoman's service to ourselves as well as to our countries. The locations given in Xuanzang's travelogue require to be re-investigated. The social system, the class relations, inter-sect rivalry and conflict require to be studied *de novo*.[12] This list is far from complete, but can induce Indian scholars to take the first step. If Xuanzang can be likened to a torch-bearer, it is time now that modern scholars in India and China carry the same torch to shine upon the path so that India and China can march forward towards the utopia of *sukavati*.

Notes

1. P.C. Bagchi, *India and China, A Thousand Years of Sino-Indian Cultural Contact*, Calcutta; China Press, p. 151.
2. For an idea about the main sects of Chinese Buddhism, see, P.V. Bapat (ed.), *2500 Years of Buddhism*, New Delhi, The Publications Division (Government of India), 1956, pp. 124-31.
3. Song Jiayu, *Tangdai Fojiao yu Tangdai Shehui* (Buddhism and Society during the Tang Dynasty), Beijing, 1978, p. 4.
4. Wang Yarong, "Lun Tangdai chuqi de Fojing Fanyi" (A study of the translation of Buddhist scriptures in early Tang Dynasty), in Huang Xinchuan, Ge Qianjun (eds.), *Xuanzang Yanjiu Wenji* (Collection of Essays on Xuanzang Studies), Zhengzhou, 1995, pp. 265-77.
5. Qu Junfeng, "Xuanzang fashi zai fanyi shiyeshangde gongxian" (Xuanzang's contribution to the cause of translation), in *Ibid*, p. 115.

6. For a few rare examples of Xuanzang's translation, see, Wu Baihui, "Yin sanxiangde Fanwen yuanwen he Xuanzangde yifa" (The Sanskrit original text of 'Three aspects of reason' and its translation by Xuanzang), in *Ibid*, pp. 131-33.

7. P.V. Bapat, *op. cit.*, p. 247.

8. P.C. Bagchi, *op. cit.*, p. 138.

9. *Ibid*, p. 139.

10. Quoted by Kamaleswar Bhattacharya in his, "Xuanzang's contribution to *Buddhology*, A non-Sinologist's observations", Huang Xinchuan, *op. cit.*, p. 467

11. Gao Zhennong, *"Shilun Xuanzang xueshuo zai jindai Zhongguode fuxing"* (Revival of Xuanzang's doctrine in Modern China), in *ibid*, pp. 223-38. The author has given details of organisations engaged in Xuanzang studies.

12. A humble beginning has already been made in this regard by the present writer through three articles. The first of them, "Geographical Notes on Xuanzang's travel in the East and Northeast India has been published in *Roop-Lekha*, Journal of A.I.F.A.C.S., New Delhi, vols. lxiv-lxvi (March, 1997), pp. 28-33. The other two are awaiting publication.

HEMANT ADLAKHA

17

TOWARDS AN UNDERSTANDING OF SOCIALISM WITH CHINESE CHARACTERISTICS

Introduction

"Modernisation", "development" and "democracy" are terms without which no study of the newly independent countries of the 'Third World' could be considered complete after the Second World War. Similarly "globalisation", "market economy" and "civil society" have become the key words following the end of the Cold War. It is common knowledge that on the one hand liberal western Europe encouraged former ex-colonies and semi-colonies to emulate western models to achieve modernity. On the other hand, there were countries which achieved national liberation and won revolutionary victories and opted for the socialist model as the alternative road to realise the goal of economic modernisation. However, sooner than everyone's expectation, barring few exceptions, both these models were found unfit by the ruling elite of the developing countries in Africa, Asia and South America. Over four decades of experimenting with modernisation theory as prescribed by the west and the political elite, a large number of developing countries have developed their underdevelopments, and the number of people without jobs has increased manifolds, in addition to widespread poverty, corruption and institutionalised crime.

The picture is no longer rosy amongst the countries which espoused socialism earlier. The initial successes achieved by the governments of these countries through their various people-oriented policies and programmes, and sincere efforts in providing social justice to their people, have gradually receded in response to hostile forces of world bank institutions and non-cooperative international financial market. The failure of western patterns of modernisation has its genesis in the powerful west, whose fundamental aim was to create and control overseas markets rather than help develop the economy of the underdeveloped regions of the world.[1] It is paradoxical that the eventual failure of the Soviet Union and several other socialist regimes have strengthened the claims of the capitalist world that there is only one road to modernity. However the fact remains that no single model is ideal for all nations to follow. Given different social, political, historical and cultural conditions, the only viable way is to chart out one's own model for development, rather than becoming a "carbon copy" of modernity. This is exactly what the new leadership of the People's Republic of China (PRC) had in mind when it decided to embark on the path of a bold, radical and pragmatic economic restructuring nineteen years ago.

However one may like to look at it, the Chinese experiment can neither be branded as a typical socialist model of transformation, nor an approach that has cast socialism to the wind. The Chinese Communist leadership has been able to do so on the strength of its success in devising with theoretical finesse the ideological justification for what it calls "modernisation with Chinese characteristics". Contrary to what is generally perceived outside China, the theory of building "socialism with Chinese characteristics" evolved gradually amidst all kinds of opposition and resistance from within the Party. In the first place, a proper historical perspective demands that modern history of China should not be cut asunder into the Mao Era and the post-Mao Era. Behind this "Chinese characteristics" we still see the ingredients of "seeking truth from facts", "China in the primary stage of socialism", "adherence to the proletarian dictatorship", "adherence to the primacy of socialism", "supremacy of the leadership of the Communist Party", "adaptation of Marxist principles to the conditions of China", etc. — all old wine of the Maoist heritage. One should acknowledge Deng Xiaoping's contribution to the new line of thinking in developmental strategy — "achieving prosperity for all the people of China, but allowing a section of them to get rich first", "reform and open door", "socialist market economy" etc. — but this contribution is built on the foundation-stone of Mao Zedong Thought, not a thunder-burst out of the blue, nor something emerging from a vacuum. In other words, Deng's new strategy is the revised version of the Maoist strategy, not something *de novo.* A source of historical distortion seems to have come from Chinese official quarters. Jiang Zemin, Deng's chosen successor, made the following observation in his speech at Deng's condolence meeting :

> "Comrade Deng Xiaoping was a great Marxist, a great proletariat, statesman, militarist and diplomat, long-tested communist soldier, chief architect of China's reform and open door and socialist modernisation construction, and founder of the theory of building socialism with Chinese characteristics." [2]

Mao's name is missing in this vital context about "building socialism with Chinese characteristics", as Jiang has put it. Can we draw the conclusion that it was never Mao's central theme to build socialism according to Chinese characteristics, or such a concept was totally unknown in Mao's development philosophy? I don't think we can. Let me quote a few specimens from the now quite forgotten one-time world-famous adage of Mao:

> "There is no such thing as abstract Marxism, but only concrete Marxism. What we call concrete Marxism is Marxism that has taken on a national form, that is, Marxism applied to the concrete struggle in the concrete conditions prevailing in China, and not Marxism abstractly used." [3]

> "Marxism-Leninism is a theory that Marx, Engels, Lenin and Stalin created on the basis of actual fact, and it consists of general conclusions derived from historical and revolutionary experience. If we have only read this theory but have not used it as a basis of research in China's historical and revolutionary actuality, have not created a theory in accordance with China's real necessities, a theory that is our own and of a specific nature, then it would be irresponsible to call ourselves Marxist theoreticians."[4]

> "Russian history has created the Russian system. They support only the Bolsheviks. In this way they have created the Russian state, which is entirely necessary and reasonable for them. ... Chinese history will create the Chinese system." [5]

I am not saying that the post-Mao period is exactly the continued development of the period when Mao Zedong Thought had its supremacy. Deng had pursued a new post-Mao policy which was described as the "second revolution" of modern China which, I think, is a faithful description. But in no way can Deng's theory of "Chinese characteristics" be viewed as the discontinuation of Mao Zedong Thought (not Maoism). As Deng himself proclaimed in 1976 after the smashing of "Gang of Four":

> "We need to revive Mao Zedong Thought, uphold Mao Zedong Thought, and also need to develop Mao Zedong Thought."[6]

But, was Deng really committing himself to continue with the basic tenets of Mao Zedong Thought or it was merely a publicity tactic to win support and legitimacy in order to regain a leadership position within the Communist Party of China (CPC)? Nevertheless, we cannot deny him the credit of fulfilling his commitment to further develop Mao's theory of "early stage of socialism" (*chuji shehuizhuyi*). A young Chinese historian, Wang Zhanyang, who specialises in contemporary political history of China, establishes the link between Deng's theory of "Chinese characteristics" and Mao Zedong's policies of national development in his recently published 700 page long book, *Mao Zedong's Strategy for Nation Building and Reform and Open-door in Contemporary China.* The book, many Chinese historians claim, has in many ways filled a void both in the study of Mao's Thought and in investigating the theory of building socialism with Chinese characteristics. According to Wang Zhanyang, "the central core of Comrade Deng Xiaoping's thoughts, is his theory of building socialism with Chinese characteristics. This theory, at one level, has been derived by Comrade Xiaoping from China's concrete conditions, while, at another level, if observed in accordance with the spirit of seeking truth from facts and its fundamental theoretical content, it is also directly linked with Mao's theory of early stage of socialism, is the direct continuation and development of this theory of early stage of socialism."[7]

Twenty years ago, when the reorganised CPC leadership announced the drastic revision of Mao's socialist developmental paradigm, both admirers and opponents among the observers of the PRC were caught unawares. Within China there were mixed reactions of "relief" and "disbelief": Relief because the long-awaited respite from continual political turmoil ultimately arrived; [8] disbelief because this arrival had come sooner than many had expected. Interestingly, observers outside China also expressed "relief" and "disbelief" but in an entirely opposite sense. Disbelief because Maoist "Chinese model" was the object of admiration in the West and the ideal model for emulation in the Third World (for Marxists and Socialists)[9], as an alternative "third way" to achieve economic growth and cultural prosperity. For many others, the end of "politics in command" (*zhengzhi guashuai*) in China was a relief as the new model of market-friendly policies was seen as China's attempt to end its "self-imposed" splendid isolation from the rest of the world. China is all geared up to defy all odds and persist with the efforts to turn the dream of creating a new modern, strong and socialist China into a reality. Rhetoric apart, there is the fact that "neo-authoritarian" PRC regime is going to achieve the unique task of building a China based on its very own socialist characteristics. This is a challenge to the classic argument put forward in the 1960s by Martin Lipset that modernisation, development and democracy cannot exist unless they co-exist. Lipset argued: "only economic modernisation and political democracy can create a modern and diverse society."[10] Whereas inside China, as the Party elite and intellectuals are openly admitting the impact of reform in the economic structure in social, cultural and political spheres, their concerns regarding China's future as reflected in the Chinese debates bear a fundamentally different character. As the western political elite over the long run is quite hopeful of dealing with a reform-minded, liberal-democratic Chinese leadership. In fact, many are even underpinning their hopes on dealing with a China no longer ruled by the CPC. In sharp contrast, the focus of debates within China is not in search of a civil society or to create conditions for a multi-party democracy.

Ever since the CPC decided to launch the historic Reforms at the Third Plenum of the Eleventh Central Committee in December 1978, there has been a sea change in China and the country has had a face-lift in its socio-political, cultural and economic life. This achievement, however, is earned at the expence of the reputation of and confidence in Marxism. The scale and intensity of debates thus generated both within and outside China have been astonishing. While success is justification enough, and the Marxist circles in China and abroad are singing hymns to the Chinese success, the non-Marxists are widely divided in viewing the Chinese experiment. Some think that China has been won over to the "Capitalist Camp", others remain sceptical as the Chinese reforms are only confined in the economy not in the political structure. There is also a blurred vision for those who are obsessed with ideological clarity, unable to decide whether China is in the family of "She", viz. Socialism, or in that of "Zi", viz. Capitalism. But, such a blurred vision has not prevented the emergence of China as a respectable member of the commity of nations, and a developing country with much better living conditions than the rest in the same category. Not surprisingly, the accolades which were being showered upon China by the world media and the European and American corporate houses in the early phase of the country's efforts to bury the ghost of "Cultural Revolution" in the late seventies and early eighties are now being abandoned. At a time when the developing nations were caught up in the fierce infighting and a cut-throat competition with each other in order to woo multinational finance capital, foreign investments kept flowing into China freely and easily, and then, there was suddenly a threat of the end of it. Whereas the key factors far behind China's impressive gains in the previous decade were attributed to trade, foreign direct investment (FDI), and high rate of domestic savings, in the 1990s the successive annual reports of the World Bank and the International Monetary Fund have been prescribing a larger role for the market forces in China's financial system, in the labour market and in particular in the State owned enterprises (SOEs). If China chooses to puzzle the scholars who are all keen to show allegiance to great thinkers of social sciences of the western world and hold Chinese wisdom in contempt, the ball is not in the Chinese court. However researchers in the western hemisphere may like to ridicule the Chinese pattern of development, the Chinese themselves find in their own twists and turns a straight road to the future. This entails a proper perspective on our part to understand what is meant by "Chinese characteristics".

Today, China is integrating herself into the "mega-circulation" of the world economic development. The world economy is a pyramidal structure with "hi-technology" products at the apex and labour intensive products forming the vast base. Today, on the one hand some agricultural products have acquired "hi-technology" status, manufacturing processes for consumer goods is being eliminated progressively from the developed countries. Even in the developing world, hi-tech can be acquired, and the production process can be upgraded to compete with that of the advanced world. This is the rhythm of the world economic development today. China fully understands that these persistent demands are being used as leverage to catapult the country into international financial market or what is now called "globalisation". Experts in China are well aware of the heavy costs such as the weakening of the State and eventually of political control slipping out of the hands of the CPC, if they are to meekly succumb to these outside pressures. China's communist elite, are therefore, absolutely clear on the prominent and overwhelming role of the State in China's economic development strategy. The "self-reliance" as professed during the days of Mao has now become self-reliance by using foreign funds and technology both wanting in China. Moreover, the breathtaking pace at which socialist China is moving towards achieving its set target of becoming a middle-level advanced industrial nation by the year 2050 has set the alarm bells ringing. Some, in the USA at least (if not in the entire western world), regard the year 2030 as "doomsday" because that would be the year the Chinese GDP (or actual economic strength) would rise to the top position, beating USA to the second place. In other words, the above scenario is nothing else but a true manifestation of the growing disenchantment of the financial and the political elite in the west, including the intelligentsia, with a China obdurately refusing to give up its search for an alternative developmental paradigm. It is in this background, with globalisation having made a clean sweep across the world, we in India should focus on how the Chinese themselves view their country's battle to survive and succeed in what they feel as a hostile, unfriendly world.

At a glance, it is quite evident that in communist China today, the vehement opposition towards capitalism witnessed in the past has receded. What remains unclear, however, is whether this drastic change is merely a tactic or a long term strategy. At one level, the ardent advocates of a market economy and liberal democracy outside China are congratulating themselves for bringing China into the international market. At another level, within China the concerns are growing as a result of the CPC's failure to resolve the inevitable conflicts between the state and market. One such failure was globally televised in the late eighties, to the discomfiture of the communist regime. Perhaps many more "failures" will follow.

All kinds of euphemisms are being employed to describe China's efforts to accommodate itself within the world market network. But to the disappointment of many, China continues to cling strongly to its socialist integrity, at least in name if not in spirit. Contrary to the views of those who have proclaimed the eastern European "Velvet Revolution" as the "end of history", the Chinese have displayed a unique sense of audacity in rejecting pro-market "civil society". It is to the credit of the CPC that it could realise long before its counterparts did in Eastern Europe and the Soviet Union, the need to introduce new elements in the rigid, bureaucratic and excessively centralised political and economic structure. At a time when in western countries the new social movements were threatening to clip the growing interference of the state and the mighty market forces in order to save civil society; and in Poland — followed immediately in other parts of central and eastern Europe — new popular movements were beginning to challenge the corrupt, inefficient ruling groups, the CPC took a bold initiative by introducing radical economic reforms. These reforms, first launched in the rural sector in the late seventies, gained ground immediately and took firm roots by the early eighties. It was on the basis of this early success of rural reforms, the then Chinese leadership became emboldened enough to embark upon an enormous ambitious plan of building a new socialist China with its very own characteristics.

Furthermore, much to the dismay it caused outside China, the CPC declared its undaunting faith in Marxism-Leninism at a time when internationally socialist theories were being dubbed as irrelevant and outdated. Inside China, the policy of building socialism with Chinese characteristics was seen as an alternative path for modernisation — an alternative to both the Soviet planned economy and the western model of free economy. Although it is not clear what particular model the new CPC leadership had or still has in mind, it may be argued that the alternative paradigm it is attempting to construct should be viewed more in cultural terms than economic. No wonder, it took the CPC nearly ten years to move ahead in its experiment with the institutions of market economy with an ideological veneer i.e., Socialist Market Economy (SME).

Conventional wisdom believes that the older a civilisation, the harder and slower it becomes in bringing about a change in the thoughts and the value systems of its people. Notwithstanding the advent of modern age and profound impact of the institutions of modernity in global terms, in an uneven manner though, the dominant view today is that the inherent element of timelessness in ancient societies does not allow these societies, such as China, to change rapidly. So, they say that the West alone can have the privilege of experiencing a much more rapid and all encompassing change. This vantage position which the developed nations of the western world enjoy today is indeed the result of the material gains achieved over the past two hundred years or so of the colonial rule. Ironically, it (the West) claims that its success and progress in economic, technological, political, social and cultural terms is linked to its so-called superior institutions over their counterparts in the much older civilizational spheres.

It is in this context that the rapid pace at which China has been moving ahead (rather leaping forward) in the last few decades has caused some worries in the advanced world. Indeed, no alternative pattern of development (in the post-colonial societies) has yet evolved that could be subscribed for societies which have not followed the trajectory of the Industrial Revolution and Renaissance for reasons beyond their control. China's performance in economic and social terms in particular has been causing concern in the western nations as they see it as a challenge to their own formula of industrialisation (read westernisation) which they have forced upon the developing world. It is in this backdrop that we should deal with the complexities and riddles presented by China's development mode. I describe it as complexities and riddles because that is the way in which we, the captured audience of the overarching yet invisible arm of the world media — both in print and in electronics — perceive the home of one fifth of humanity hatching another "Yellow Peril" of sorts. Our intention here is not to paint the West as the villain of the piece. Conversely our purpose is to highlight the painstaking efforts Chinese people have been making to cope with the challenges thrown by population growth and underdeveloped production capacities internally and by the do-or-die scenario externally — with "free-market" and "globalisation" posing as another round of Neo-imperialist menace to China and other parts of the developing world.

Back Ground of Reform Strategy

Very briefly, we will look into the history of the background in which the new reform strategy was evolved. China is a country of over eight hundred million rural people, of which several million are still living in poverty and hunger. It is this fundamental problem that is facing the CPC that cannot be ignored by anyone willing to understand China today. In December 1978, when the CPC under a new ruling group led by Deng Xiaoping decided to do away with what was known as Maoist developmental paradigm and implement a new set of pragmatic economic policies, the idea was not to abandon Marxism but to chart out a new path that will further consolidate the basic doctrine of socialism. People of China had put their faith in Deng's call to "modernise" China because they were able to see in it the blue-print of a strong and prosperous socialist China. Outside experts chose to interpret these developments as the so-called shift in the party line from "politics in command" to "economics in command". Experts in China however were of the view that this was only consistent with the CPC position of further promoting the development of the relations of production from a lower to higher level. The so-called shift was caused by two factors. Firstly, to rectify the past mistake of defying the law of nature in the economic sphere and therefore avoid reoccurrence of mass political campaigns, or political movements (*Zhengzhi yundong*), such as the Great Leap Forward (GLP) and the Great Proletarian Cultural Revolution in the future. Second, to gradually establish a socialist legal system that will ensure "rule of law" (*fazhi*) and not the "rule of individuals" (*renzhi*). This is in sharp contrast to how rapidly growing communist China is viewed differently by the advocates of the so-called "China-threat theory". A strong and modern China in the near future is perceived by many as a dangerous power which would go to any extent to maintain its expansionist status. While the PRC's achievements in terms of providing social justice along with the material needs to its vast population is ignored sans "democracy", "freedom" and "human rights".

"Modernisation" is a highly political and contentious term. In fact, just as a matter of general interest, it is not easy to find in Chinese an expression similar to this English word. The term gained popularity as a development model in the late sixties, thanks to political science and sociological studies carried out in the American universities in order to subjugate newly independent Third World societies. During this period, modernisation theory emerged as the most influential approach in comparative politics. One basic premise of the modernisation theory was to encourage the newly independent and other Third World countries to follow the Western/American model as the ideal one for achieving economic and social development, as against the command economies of socialist countries like China, Cuba, North Korea and some other countries of Africa and Asia. The fundamental postulation of the modernisation theory in the sixties and seventies was that all systems will inevitably need to move to liberal democracy. I am not delving into the merits/demerits of the theory, suffice here to note that the Chinese leaders have shown little interest in it. As Yu Gongmei observes: "after the World War II several newly independent countries mechanically followed the social, political and economic systems of the western First World with the American model as the ideal, however, the outcome was just opposite of what they had desired. Indeed some of these countries did achieve an overall economic growth within a very short period, but communal clashes, racial disturbances, religious killings, civil wars, power-struggles, political coups and all kinds of bloody chaos have become the order of the day in these societies. Western liberal democracy has failed to deliver to the Third World countries the expected economic prosperity, social harmony and happiness. Thus it is clear, countries with different historical, social, economic and cultural conditions should not go the developed countries' way to achieve modernisation."[11] The current thinking in China is that in the past, particularly during the decades of the sixties and seventies, China made the mistake of not following the fundamentals of the classical historical materialism, i.e., the level of the productive forces can only be promoted through the continuous enhancement of the relations of production. In other words, experts in China are saying that the process of modernisation was stalled during those decades as theorists in China had failed to realise the need to further develop new relations of production. It is now being argued that given the relatively backward state of the productive forces in the country, transition to "full" socialist relations of production had proceeded too quickly.[12]

Although modernisation did find a place in the Chinese socialist developmental discourse in the early fifties itself, both the term and the concept however were conceived and interpreted differently by the then leaders of China. According to them, the aim of socialist modernisation programme was to enable economically backward China to bring about an advanced technological revolution and quickly catch up to the highest world standards in economy, science and technology. As early as 1954, Zhou Enlai had clearly advocated the goal of turning China into a strong and modern socialist nation. Sometime later, Zhou once again declared, "we must modernise our agriculture, industry, national defence and science and technology in order to establish our fatherland as a strong socialist country, the key to achieve this goal lies in realising modernisation in science and technology. ... We are far behind the advanced world standards ...we must strive hard to overtake and move ahead, we will overtake and move ahead".[13]

It is in this context, when Deng Xiaoping raised the goal of socialist modernisation goal, he did not merely repeat the slogan first raised by Zhou in the 1950s. Instead, Deng went a step further by re-emphasising the Marxist viewpoint that "science and technology is the primary forces of production". Deng declared: "The great historical responsibility the people of China have on their shoulders is to achieve the target of total modernisation in agriculture, industry, national defence and science and technology within the twenty first century and thus establish a strong, modern, socialist China. ... Under the dictatorship of the proletariat, if we don't carry out modernisation, we won't be able to raise the level of science and technology, we won't be able to develop our social forces of production, the national potential won't be strengthened, we won't be able to enhance the material and cultural standards of our people, so, we will fail to fully consolidate our socialist political and economic systems and therefore we will fail to safeguard the security of our nation."[14]

In present-day China, economic growth is viewed as the key to the country's socialist modernisation drive, which in turn depends on political stability. In sharp contrast, westerners are obsessed with pushing China into the liberal modern world with the establishment of "modern" political and economic institutions such as parliamentary democracy and free market etc. After the Tiananmen episode, it (the west) has, by and large, lost all hope of China's turning the western way, as was pointed out by Jie Chen and others in a recent study on the degree of popular support for the "authoritarian" government in communist China. They claim, before 1989 most western observers of China were quite optimistic about the prospects of the post-Mao reformist regime, however, after the Tiananmem crackdown, the mood among China scholars turned overwhelmingly pessimistic.[15] It is needless to point out that, these pessimistic notions were the result of the conventional western wisdom that economic reforms in communist China over a decade have created (new) social, cultural and economic forces that are seriously challenging the monopoly of the CPC.

Unlike the commentators and China experts in the West, Chinese do not suffer from any such disillusion regarding the aims and goals of the PRC's vigorous modernisation initiative. Nowhere in the Chinese debates has one come across pronouncements like the changes in China's economic structure means the end of socialism and the restoration of capitalism. Instead, the line of thought in China is that the strategy of the economic reform is aimed at improving the level of the productive forces. It is for this reason that modernisation as a goal is the crucial factor for the legitimacy of Chinese Communist Party. As Liang Lidong and Huang Zhengchao have argued, "China's modernisation drive is being promoted through the policies of reform and open door as a result of the basic contradiction prevailing in society today. Reform is the conscious readjustment of mutually unsuitable elements existing between production relations and productive forces on the one hand, and between superstructure and the economic base on the other. Open Door is the timely tapping of material resources, information and energy. Stable, steady progress of reform and open door policies will inevitably continue to liberate and develop productive forces, the absolute truth of the continuous development of productive forces in turn will decide the relations of production. Reforms will promote growth, growth will lead to stability."[16]

Theoretically, China's current modernisation programme is not new, but it has acquired a fresh look since the early eighties. In practice, three things come to mind that distinguish China's new modernisation initiative spearheaded by Deng Xiaoping from the previous attempts under Mao and Zhou. The new elements are, in order of priority: political stability at home, peaceful international environment and greater interaction with the world economy. The above three factors formed the basis of what Deng termed as modernisation with Chinese characteristics. Since the Third Plenum of the Eleventh Central Committee of the CPC held in December 1978, Deng had been consistently advocating stability as the foremost condition for China's modernisation. At a time when "bourgeois liberalisation" seemed to have grappled China, particularly a section of the urban elite, Deng promptly warned the Party of the dangers of untimely movements such as the "fifth modernisation" and their potential threat to political stability, social order and the smooth implementation of the task of socialist modernisation. Deng's concern (or obsession) for maintaining stability and order had its origins in the lessons learnt from nearly twenty years of social disorder that had prevailed in the Chinese society between 1958 and 1976-78. When summing up the lessons of the past, Deng said in a speech at a special meeting of cadres on January 16, 1980: "The experience of the Cultural Revolution has already proved that chaos leads only to retrogression, not to progress, and that there must be good order if we are to move forward. Under China's present circumstances it is clear that without stability and unity we have nothing. ... Since our people have just been through a decade of suffering, they cannot afford further chaos ..."[17] Deng very well knew that this stability could only come from the Communist Party and therefore, in 1979, he reiterated the need for upholding the Four Cardinal Principles: upholding the socialist road, upholding the peoples' democratic dictatorship, upholding the leadership of the CPC and upholding Marxism-Leninism and Mao Zedong Thought. Deng made it absolutely clear, "to achieve Four Modernisations, these are four basic prerequisites."[18]

In all of Deng's pre-Tiananmen(1989) statements the stability factor was always his primary concern ever since he had embarked on the path to catapult China into economic high growth zone. In January 1980, while speaking before the Party cadres belonging to the Central Committee on the current situation and the tasks facing the CPC, Deng dwelt on the need to maintain political stability and unity. He said: "without political stability and unity, it would be impossible for us to settle down to construction. This has been borne out by our experience in the more than 20 years since 1957, and especially by last year's. Now we have achieved — or basically achieved — political stability and unity. Comrades at various posts must jointly take responsibility for preserving and developing it." [19] Then again, barely a month had passed when speaking at the Third meeting of the Fifth Plenary Session of the Eleventh Committee of the CPC, Deng declared: "while working with complete dedication for the four modernisations, we must, with equal dedication, preserve and develop a political situation marked by stability, unity and liveliness."[20] Deng's overemphasis on political stability and unity within the Party has always remained a key element of his theory of building socialism with Chinese characteristics. All the ingredients of what is now known as the socialist market economy or in other words the Chinese type of socialism are found in Deng's pronouncements and writings from the late seventies to the early eighties. What is significant here is the fact that political stability and order have always figured prominently throughout his observations. And the reason for this is not difficult to discern. When in 1979 Deng first made public his grand plan of quadrupling China's 1980 GNP by the turn of this century, he knew quite well that without stability it would be impossible to achieve in a backward Third World country like China. Added to this was the other unique factor of China being a socialist country. Gradually he developed his modernisation plan of"three stages" or as it is called in Chinese, "*san bu zou*" (walking in three steps). The first step being to double the per capita GNP of 1980 by the year 1990 and provide the basic needs to all people of China; the second, to double the GNP of the 1990 level by the year 2000 so that the people of China can enjoy moderately comfortable living standards; and third, to raise China's per capita GNP to reach that of the middle level developed countries by the middle of the next century. This three-stage development strategy was formally approved and adopted at the CPC's 13th Congress. In his report to the Congress, Zhao Ziyang, the then General Secretary of the CPC argued: "China is in the primary stage of socialism. The socialist revolution in China has occurred in a backward country. Because our socialism has emerged from the womb of a semi-colonial, semi-feudal society, with the productive forces lagging far behind those of the developed capitalist countries, we are destined to go through a very long primary stage. During this stage we shall accomplish industrialisation and the commercialisation, socialisation and modernisation of production, which many countries have achieved under capitalist conditions."[21]

Although Zhao was removed from the Party's post in the aftermath of the 1989 students unrest, the Party continued to adhere to his argument of continuously developing new relations of production to promote the growth of the productive forces. Jiang Zemin (Zhao's successor as the CPC General Secretary) in his first address to the Party after assuming his post, made it clear that the above argument of developing the productive forces was the core element of China's socialist reform process. In a speech marking the 40th anniversary of the establishment of the PRC, he said: "socialism is a system that requires constant development and improvement on its own basis. To base ourselves on Chinese reality, sum up our practical experience and —

in accordance with the actual level of our social productive forces and the objective needs for further development, purposefully readjust the part of the production relations which does not conform with the productive forces, and readjust the part of the superstructure which does not conform to the economic base — this is what we mean by socialist reform."[22] The message Jiang was conveying to the Party's rank and file and the people of China in general was that leaders may come and go but the basic line of the Party to achieve the goal of the socialist modernisation through reform and the open door strategy would remain unchanged. Observers outside China, including India, it seems, are divided into two opposite groups in their views on China's achievements. One group is of the view that the rapid growth of China symbolises her blazing a new trail in taking her economy along the right path of giving a facelift to a poor and developing country. The other group consists of cynics and we have a specimen of cynicism here: "whether one regards it (China's economic successes) as a theoretical coup or a practical joke, there is no doubt about the audacity of the capitalist-roaders in Beijing as they try to make Karl Marx look more and more like Adam Smith".[23] Within China, however, the commonly held view is that of prudent optimism. It is the consensus within China that the thirst of popular aspirations could not have been quenched by the overflow of rhetoric, and the CPC had the formidable task of taking China forward along the road of improving living standards while remaining committed to the other goals of socialism. The overall response of Chinese society to undesirable phenomena like income disparity, corruption, a bureaucracy that is suffocating and high-handed etc., is by and large appreciative, expectant, and tolerating. Perhaps, it is due to the melange of China's traditional and contemporary political culture that despite being "backward", people of China have shown a remarkable sense of responsibility in giving unconditional but not uncritical support and willingness to participate in the programme of rebuilding the nation after long, chaotic and turbulent years of the Cultural Revolution.

The Search for "Civil Society"

Following the instant collapse and disintegration of "state socialism", first in East Europe and subsequently in the erstwhile Soviet Union, which were swept away by the liberal, reform wind in favour of "free market" and civil society, intellectuals in the west started devoting too much attention to the study of a "nebulas civil society and public sphere" in China. Suddenly, social science studies in the western academia were filled with enthusiasm in search of a different political culture in China which in their reckoning has been emerging since the reform started. As a result of huge inflows of international finances into China and increased exposure of a rigid, tightly enclosed Chinese society to previously unknown foreign (read western) culture, the focus of these new studies was on public assembly and free association in places such as discos, Karaoke, bars and Macdonald restaurants, on the role of pro-reform, liberal intellectuals, and on consumerism as a new communication medium for the spread of "individualism" and so on. The high point for these studies on the presence of a "civil society" in China in some form or the other was what is now universally known as the "historic" happenings at the Tiananmen Square in 1989. A review of the writings enshrined in books and research papers and newspaper articles which flooded the market following the "democracy movement", reveal how voguish the theme of "civil society/public sphere in China" had become.

By the early nineties, "civil society" was the new agenda in China studies. In 1994, during my one-week stay at the Nankai University in Tianjin, I attended a day-long Seminar on "Contemporary Political Culture in China" organised by the Department of History. At the seminar, Professor Ge Quan, a young scholar of contemporary Chinese political history, while reacting to western scholars' premises about the emergence of a new "democratic" political culture in China as a result of the economic reforms, remarked: "An increasingly high number of western scholars, including those who have switched over to China studies from other fields of studies, engaged in research ranging from avant-garde literature and art to anthropology and post-Marxism proves the high priority China has come to acquire in the academia outside China. However, the ultimate aim of all such studies seems to be, regardless of the historical factors of time and space, to employ all available theoretical frameworks and methodological approaches to locate the birth of a civil society in the so-called Beijing Democracy Movement. For these scholars, what matters the most is, the decade-long market reforms have finally succeeded in the realisation of a nascent civil society in China." Similar sentiments are echoed in the vast amount of political literature now available in China. These Chinese scholars argue that the notion of civil society is being forced upon China as if it can be easily exported and implanted everywhere. Notwithstanding the CPC's unexplained stoic silence on the sudden disintegration of the communist parties and "state socialism" in the countries of the erstwhile "socialist bloc" and the former Soviet Union, Chinese experts and analysts have been closely studying the post-communist developments in these societies. Continuing social and financial insecurity for the large majority of the population, widespread unemployment and an overall decline in all aspects of life in these countries has shown that dreams of "freedom", "democracy" and "prosperity" as promised by the so-called civil society were in fact the agents for "free market" and "westernisation of culture".

Particularly alarming for the Chinese elite has been the moral, cultural and social crises in Russia today. The free market therapy has actually plunged the Russian society into a situation where national and cultural identity is facing the threat of elimination. These bitter realities of embracing "civil society" has forced Chinese intellectuals to seriously consider the question of compatibility of democracy with China's polity and national sovereignty. It is therefore not surprising to see the failure of Chinese intellectuals and pro-democracy elements to come out with any theoretical alternative or a viable Solidarity-style public protest movement. Some Chinese scholars attribute this failure to the vast dissimilarities in terms of historical traditions, social structure, economic levels and natural conditions, between China and the erstwhile "socialist bloc". Many others, including those who once were strongly advocating for eastern European-type "civil society" (*gongmin shehui*) in China, gradually realised that any move to initiate change in China's political structure sans high levels of economic growth is bound to be a disaster like the situation in Russia today. It is in this context that we should understand the arguments of those within the CPC who raise accusing fingers at pro-liberal reformers. Also, many young Chinese intellectuals, who are not falling prey to the thesis of East Asian Confucian cultural model based on market economy, are arguing that the neo-Confucianists are aiming not so much at reviving China's traditional past, as at "denationalising" and "de-Chinafying" it.

To return to the western premises, we have Clement Stubbe Ostregaard, Craig Calhoun, Thomas B. Gold etc. who first applied concepts such as "public sphere", "civil society" to provide an alternative understanding of the 1989 People's Movement in Beijing. In an article published just five months after the June Fourth episode, Ostregaard, a China specialist from Denmark, claimed that a civil society had been developing in China for some years as a result of the economic reform process which has succeeded in effectively reducing the all pervasive power of the Party-State.[24] Craig Calhoun was the first scholar who relied upon the public/private space theory of Habermas to point out that the 1989 Protest Movement was an attempt towards establishing a public sphere (*gonggong kongjian*) in China outside the control of the State.[25] Not that such new theoretical formulations went unchallenged. But the nature of the objections and disagreements with the above postulations had much to do with the tools of analyses than the desired end results. Frederick Wakeman dismissed the above assertion by arguing that for Habermas, as in the case of Marx, the emergence of "public space" as a communication sphere to protect civil society against the state was inextricably connected with the strong bourgeois rule. According to Wakeman, such a linkage alone fixes both ideal types in a particular historical setting, and if we allow ourselves to be hobbled by teleology, then neither concept is going to fit the Chinese case very well.[26] Despite such strong theoretical reservations, it is surprising how the popularity of the civil society argument got a further impetus by a series of new projects taken up by social historians, particularly in America, who had earlier emphasised the traditional bases of civil society and public sphere in China. This new generation of social historians had in the early 1980s begun tracking down the roots of civil society in the late imperial or, as they prefer to call it, pre-modern China. Notable among these scholars are David Strand, Martin K. Whyte, William T. Rowe, Mary Backus Rankin and Prasenjit Duara. According to one western scholar, a distinct pre-modern civil society existed in the late nineteenth, early twentieth century China in the form of corporate groups and voluntary associations like guilds, neighbourhood associations, clans and lineage, surname associations, and religious groupings in the form of temple societies, deity cults, monasteries and secret societies. Perhaps the most important common phenomenon of these organisations was that these were formed outside, or independent of, the state.[27]

Undoubtedly, the purpose of these studies was to emphasise the close link between an autonomous public space as present in the late Qing and the early Republican China and the reappearance of these incipient elements of semi-official, semi-autonomous collectively owned business enterprises within the interstices of a China reeling under the market reforms. The Stone Corporation, the Institute for the Study of the Development of Agricultural Economy, and the Institute for the Study of Reforms in Economic Structure etc., are some such quasi-official enterprises and semi-NGOs who were not only actively behind the 1989 students demonstration but also recognised as instrumental in "reviving" the Habermasian private sphere. At a broader level, if this was so, then why is it that any form of public protest against the State prior to 1989 in China, say the Tiananmen Movement of 1976, is not accepted by the same scholars as similar to a "civil society" or "public sphere" phenomenon? If a mass public protest directed against the "authoritarian" state or against a brutal, repressive ruling clique can be considered as part of a civil society culture (the reference here is to the 1989 Beijing Spring Movement) then even the Cultural Revolution had certain signs of independent, autonomous public protest culture. It is in this sense, one may argue, the public or private sphere theory of

Habermas conceived out of a given historical context loses its relevance when applied to China, as has been the case in the recent western scholarship on interpreting "political culture" in contemporary China.

For most, if not all, sociological studies on the contemporary social life in China from 1956 to 1978 suggest that Chinese people during this period were subjected to political sufferings more than economic hardships. Some recent studies on the life in China during the 1980s and 1990s also reflect that the majority among Chinese, particularly in the rural areas, continue to live in most deplorable conditions. In other words, what needs to be emphasised is that twenty years before and twenty years since the economic restructuring process began, in both phases, millions of Chinese have had to live in most austere and adverse conditions no matter whether the CPC was following the policy of "politics in command" or "economics in command". In the first phase, social instability was caused by the ultra-left political mistakes, while in the second phase which is still unfolding, it is the rapid pace of economic liberalisation which is the cause of social instability. If the pre-reform decades were politically catastrophic, then the post-Mao period has witnessed the great divide in urban and rural fortunes. Before, it was the urban segments of the population who were forced to live uprooted life as a result of organised migration from urban into rural areas. Now, it is the turn of millions of rural Chinese to rush into the cities to market their unorganised cheap labour. Some foreign observers and experts see market forces having succeeded in distancing China away from Marxism while pushing it towards the desired goal of a new political culture similar to the western bourgeois liberal democracy, civil society and human rights. For quite some time, the western political elite was quite hopeful of dealing with a reform-minded, liberal-democratic Chinese leadership. Many even dreamt of doing business with a China no longer ruled by the CPC. A section of the western expertise on China began to pray for the death of Deng in the hope that moderate leaders would have to yield to the demand for political reforms. Such a hope was also denied when Deng passed away in early 1997, and the rumoured challenges to Jiang Zemin (considered as a hard liner by many) were a non-starter. Now, western optimism for China's "modernisation" has to pin hope on the post-Jiang era which would not dawn at the fag end of the 20th century. The deadly enemy to this hoping against hope lies in the misconception in the hope itself.

The Language of Political Discourse in China

As noted in the beginning of this paper, the language of political discourse in China is fundamentally different. At one level, key political terms in the western political narrative such as political behaviour, governance, parliamentary or representative democracy, civic culture, public and private sphere/space and so on, have yet to enter into the mainstream political writings in China. At another level, the problem is related with the difficulty of translating the terms into speakable Chinese. Let me further elaborate this point. It will be incorrect to consider this language barrier as peculiar to Chinese. For the main issue here is not merely finding an appropriate Chinese expression which will be genuinely true to the original meaning of the term. The larger issue is that of different cultural and political implications as a consequence of the tension that will thus be generated between traditional etymological beliefs and the alien, modernist concepts.

In simple words, what we are talking about here is not the issue of just simply translating the networks of meanings from one language/culture into the other, but we are essentially emphasising on the challenges the new translation strategies would be posing to the existing philosophical concepts. In other words, the difficulty lies in translating across etymologies.[28] Let us take up some terminology. The first time the term "civil society" was employed in the contemporary political discourse in China was in the mid-eighties when liberal, pro-reform intellectuals and scholars started questioning the authenticity and validity of the officially circulated Chinese translation for the German original term of "Burgerliche Gesellschaft" — *shimin shehui.* Taken literally, it means: urban (shi), people (min), social (she), and association (hui). These scholars argued, the term actually should have been translated as "citizen's society" *(gongmin shehui)* since *burgerliche* in German meant "citizen" (citiyon) and not just "bourgeoisie" (burger). In an article published in *Tianjin Shehui Kexue* (Tianjin Social Sciences) in April 1986, Shen Yue, the first Chinese scholar to raise the controversy, unearthed the concept of "towns people's right" (*shimin quanli*) from Marx's writings and claimed that Marx had used the term "towns people" as an economic concept and it included both the bourgeoisie and the proletariat for people who had come to the cities or towns in search of work. The basic characteristics of the towns people, according to Shen's interpretation, apart from residing in the urban areas, was their participation in market economic activities.[29] Thanks largely to the liberal attitude of the CPC towards intellectuals and ideological debates, Shen was described by many as lucky to have escaped the wrath of the anti-reform hard-liners within the Party. What surprised many in China was the subsequent re-run of the entire article in CPC's mouthpiece *Renmin Ribao* (People's Daily) on November 24, 1986. Many observers outside

China, interpreted this development as the first official acknowledgement by the CPC of the use of the term civil society. However, it is a fact that till date no party document or policy statement has ever employed such a term. Some analysts described this as the CPC's ambiguity and weakness to enter into such hypersensitive ideological debates. Finally, in the aftermath of the 1989 "counter-revolutionary" students movement, contrary to the claims by foreign observers that the liberal views and the pro-liberal urban elite were being put under severe censorship, Shen Yue again attracted the attention of Chinese political scientists when his second article on the same theme was published in the leading journal of academic debates, *Zhexue Yanjiu* (The Journal of Philosophical Research) in 1990.[30] This time, however, Shen did not have to wait for others to respond. Xi Zhaoyong, a professor of political philosophy at Nanjing University, joined issue with Shen Yue. Although Xi agreed with Shen that the German term "burger" could mean both *citizen* and *bourgeoisie*, he, however, asserted that in most cases Marx and Engels had used it to mean the bourgeoisie.[31]

At the same time, against the backdrop of the *failed* democracy movement of 1989, many Chinese scholars who were now residing in western Europe and America — the most prominent being the "dissident" Chinese intellectual Liu Binyan — who were inspired by the events in Eastern Europe joined China scholars in the west to continue their efforts to smuggle in an analogue for the eighteenth century bourgeois public sphere in order to explain the use of such symbols as the "Statue of Liberty" in the Tiananmen public demonstrations. Unlike in English where the terms "civil society", "public sphere" and "public space" are all seen as coterminous, in Chinese the main difficulty is to distinguish them in translation. The term "shehui" (society), according to some studies, does not even have a history of more than a hundred years or so.[32] It is a twentieth century Chinese borrowing from Japan and was imported by the Chinese intellectuals who had gone to Japan in search of modern information and wisdom. True, the two components of the term, *she* and *hui*, are of Chinese origin. But *hui*, as noted earlier, meaning "association" at once invited suspicion of connections with rebellious, secret societies. Similarly, *she* traditionally had a very limited scope connoting a "community" or "organisation". Interestingly, the word which is borrowed from Japanese, where in a reversed word order (*huishe*) it becomes a "company" or "organisation". This reversed word order in Chinese used to connote a clandestine or secret society. Arising from such semantic differences as well as difficulties there have emerged seven various translations for "civil society" in contemporary Chinese literature. They are: (1) *shimin shehui:* literally "the society of city people", (2) *chengshi shehui:* literally "the society of the cities", (3) *gongmin shehui:* literally "the society of the citizens of the country" — a "dissident" Chinese formulation, (4) *minjian shehui:* literally "the society not associated with the government" — a Taiwanese formulation,[33] (5) *qunzhong shehui:* literally "the society of the masses" (as a pre-stage to civil society), (6) *pingmin shehui:* literally "the society for ordinary people" (in describing issues of Eastern Europe)[34] and (7) *shehuizhuyi shimin shehui:* literally "the socialist society of urban people" (meant to be a socialist brand of civil society). The last translation epitomises a distant confluence of Chinese socialist mood with that of western liberal mood. Yu Keping, a senior researcher with the Contemporary Research Centre, attached to the CPC Central Committee Editorial and Translation Bureau, has been writing extensively on the theme and has succeeded in adding a totally new dimension to the entire debate in China over the possibility of civil society in the future.

Several other political terms and concepts which are now regularly being referred to in the Chinese political debates, are posing a great difficulty to the authors and readers alike. Chinese term *guojia* is the common denomination for "state", "country" and "nation" while, "public domain", "public sphere" and "public space" all are translated as *gonggong kongjian* or *gonggong lingyu.* In 1994, I also met at the Tianjin Seminar, Professor Liu Zehua, a noted Chinese historian, who specialises in traditional Chinese political culture and is also known for his vehement opposition to bourgeois-liberal notions of democracy. Professor Liu, likened the current use in China of the above terms to the latest consumer goods coming from Europe and America and the rage created by them among the urban nouveaux riche. He pointed out: "less than a decade ago no one in China's academic circles had heard of 'civil society', 'public space', 'free domain' etc. But now the use of such terms has become a fad among the university elite." However, Jurg Habermas who is credited in the west as the founder of the "communication theory" and public and private space theory in 1960s, has not yet been translated into Chinese, said Liu.

At the level of theory, scholars in China are yet to engage themselves in the discourse on civil society. It is true that the notion has found a place in political debates in China. But oddly enough, intellectuals and the urban intelligentsia do not seem to be very enthusiastic about the concept. On the basis of what they see in the experiences of miracle-making (but now in crisis) smaller nations in East and South-east Asia, they do not envisage the validity or applicability of the civil society concept in the case of China. Many Chinese simply dismiss the western prognosis on civil society becoming a reality in China in the near future.

They regard civil society a "magic bag" (*bai bao dai*) or, in other words, a ragbag into which anything in the name of civil society can be stuffed. Not surprisingly, therefore, no major study exclusively devoted to the study of the origin and growth of civil society in general, and its application to China in particular, has been updated in China. The only article that deserves our attention is by two political scientists who supported a theory of benign interaction between civil society and the state, by claiming that the role of the state in regard to civil society has two aspects. First, the state must recognise the independent civil society and provide institutional and legal guarantee and a legitimate field of action for it. Secondly, the state should carry out necessary interference and regulation over civil society.[35] The co-authors of the article, Deng Zhenglai and Jing Yuejin, engage themselves with the Hegelian state/society dichotomy and hold the view that society is subordinate to the state. However, both Deng and Jing, fail to address the issue of how "civil society" is to be viewed contemporaneously in China's context. For example, in an economically backward society in China, will civil society be created from above by the state or will it rise as a challenge to the state from below?

Notwithstanding China's different cultural traditions, there is reason to believe that once she is totally immersed in the globalisation of economic development she will not be able to maintain a totally separate identity if the rest of the world, or the majority of nations are inclined to adopt a model of "civil society" even if there is going to be unity in diversity in their experimentation. In other words, the harmony between the State, the collective and the individual will be regulated by a more or less uniform standard when the future world implements inter-cultural and interface synergy. If the Chinese experiment can find something superior to the western model, many third world countries will follow suit, which, in turn, will force western social scientists to accord recognition to the "Chinese model" and modify their theories about human evolution and modernisation. If this is not to be the case, China will have to conform to the majority socio-political trend, or face sharp contradictions between the ruling system and the subjects, particularly the forward-looking social elite. It is encouraging that more and more social scientists in China are showing increasing interest in understanding the crucial role of the government in a society which is undergoing transformation from a traditional, rural society into modern, industrial nation.

Conclusion

To sum up, we see that Western mainstream China scholars discredit the CPC's insistence on stability instead of bold political reform. Their conviction about the increasing Chinese demands for democratisation in the future may also be an error.[36] This contradicts sharply with the dominant mindset in China that political pluralism or multi-party democracy are not the vital and pressing issues for the country. Commentators in China believe, that the country is passing through a transitional phase, hence has to grapple with problems of corruption, increasing crime, widening income disparity and misuse of political power etc. A new framework will take time as China travels along the uncertain terrain of building socialism with Chinese characteristics. But to describe these efforts as "crisis of faith in the existing ideology" or "the death of Marxism in China" will be a gross mistake. We must give the benefit of doubt to the Chinese ruling elite and their intellectual resources, and allow them to take their time to meet the mainstream of world evolution. If China can blaze a new trail to show a better formula of socio-political transformation than what the west has imposed on the Third World countries, it will be all the more welcome.

Here, I must draw public attention to the current Chinese discourse on the future of China from a cultural view-point. There is optimism among a section of Chinese intellectuals that a kind of renaissance is taking shape in China which is described by the famous Professor of Philosophy of Beijing University, Zhang Dainian, as embarking on a new road of Chinese modernisation by rejecting the two other alternatives of either a whole-hog westernisation or a restoration of traditional Confucian order. Sources of such optimism have its roots in modern Chinese history, particularly in the experiences accumulated over the past one hundred years during which China has emerged a strong, sovereign socialist country. Professor Zhang rejects both bourgeois liberalisation and conservative Confucian renaissance models as inevitable death-traps. In an aritcle re-printed in *Xinhua Wenzhai* (Xinhua Digest) recently, Professor Zhang and Wang Dong, co-authors of the article, firmly declare that only by following the overall path of creating socialism with Chinese characteristics can Chinese civilisation achieve modernisation. The article goes on to list down ten major contributions that the new China would be making in the history of the world civilisation in the next century. Professor Zhang calls them "Ten Creations", they are: (1) creating a strong, democratic, civilised new and modern socialist China, (2) creating a new culture with Chinese type of socialism based on a high degree of unity of the material and spiritual civilisations, (3) creating a new type of structure based on socialism with Chinese characteristics: a new type of market economy — a new type of democratic polity — a new type of scientific culture, (4) creating a trans-century Chinese wave of "structural reform" "take-off economy" "national unity" and "cultural renaissance", (5) creating a new road and new pattern of socialist modernisation with Chinese characteristics, (6) creating a modern, reformed Chinese nationalism, (7) creating a new value system based on socialism with Chinese characteristics, (8) creating a new methodological body enriched with the spirit of the times as well as the oriental essence, (9) creating a modern revival of new Chinese civilisational forms and (10) creating a modern, new type of subjectivity, blended with a new world culture of the twenty-first century.

Professor Zhang thus refutes Huntington and school who are vociferously propagating the so-called "clash of civilisations" and "China threat" theories, by arguing that such theories are born not out of ignorance but out of prejudices. Zhang Dainian and Wang Dong conclude their essay on a note of optimism regarding future of China as well as a peaceful, non-hegemonic, multi-centered world order in which there will be harmony between eastern and western cultural systems and value concepts. This happy note gives hope to foreign, especially Indian, China watchers to expect a new China emerging in our new millennium which is only two years away. While "Chinese characteristics" are exclusive Chinese property, its universal lesson will not be lost once China succeeds in breaking away from the western imposition of "modernisation", in proving it wrong that "all roads lead to Rome or Westminster or Washington". We, in India, are particularly interested in the Chinese defiance against the western cultural hegemony, and will watch with keen interest how far they succeed. Perhaps, a close comparison of the two nations' experiences can benefit each other, and help strengthen the "Chinese characteristics" in their long march towards the socialist goal as well as create an Indian awareness for "Indian characteristics" in our own socio-political evolution.

Notes

1. Touraine, Alain. (1997) *What Is Democracy?* Tr. David Macey. See the Introduction. p. 8, (Colorado & London : Westview Press).
2. *People's Daily* (*Renmin Ribao*) February 25, 1997, Beijing.
3. Mao Zedong. *Selected Works of Mao Tse-tung,* Vol. 2, Peking: Foreign Language Press, 1953, 195.
4. Mao. *Selected Works*, Vol. 4, p. 31.
5. Mao, *Selected Works*, Vol. 3, pp. 283-84.
6. *Deng Xiaoping wenxuan (Selected Works of Deng Xiaoping 1976-1982)*, People's Publishing House, Beijing, 1983, p. 261.
7. Wang Zhanyang (1993) *Mao Zedongde jianguo fanglue yu dangdai Zhongguo de gaige kaifang,* (The State building policies of Mao Zedong and the current reform and opening up of China), Guilin People's Publishing House, p. 643.
8. Lee, Sarel (1976) *Subterranean Individualism: Contradictions of Politicisation*, in *Telos*, No. 32.
9. Holmes, Leslie (1997) *Post-Communism: An Introduction* (London: Polity Press).
10. Lipset, M (1960) *Political Man: The Social Basis of Politics* (London: Heinemann).
11. Yu Gongmei (1993) *Zailun zai shenhua gaige zhong xunqiu zhengzhi wending* (Again on seeking political stability in intensifying the Reform), in Wu Daying and Yu Gongmei (eds.) *Reform and Open-door versus Political Stability* (Beijing : Chinese Publishing House of Democratic Legal Sysytems).
12. Xiao Zhen (1981) *Beijing Review,* August 10-17. As cited in Paul Bowles and Tony Stone, "China's Reforms: A Study in the Application of Historical Materialism"; *Science & Society,* Vol. 55, No. 3, Fall 1991, pp. 261-90.
13. *Selected Writings of Zhou Enlai* (1984) Vol. 2, (Beijing: People's Publishing House).
14. *Selected Works of Deng Xiaoping* (1983) (Beijing : People's Publishing House).
15. Jie Chen, Yang Zhong and Jan William Hillard. (1997) "The Level and Sources of Popular Support for China's Current Political Regime", *Communist and Post-Communist Studies*, Vol. 30, No. 1, pp. 45-64.
16. Liang Lidong and Huang Zhengchao. (1993) "On maintaining political stability in China's modernisation process", in Wu Daying and Yu Gongmei (eds.) *Gaigekaifang yu zhengzhiwending(Reform and Open-door versus Political Stability)* Beijing: Publishing House of Democratic Rule of Law, China.

17. *Selected Works of Deng Xiaoping: 1978 - 1982.*(1983) p. 237, Beijing: Foreign Languages Press.
18. *Ibid.* p. 172.
19. *Ibid.* p. 236.
20. *Ibid.* p. 261.
21. Zhao Ziyang. (1987) "Advance along the Road to Socialism with Chinese Characteristics" *Beijing Review*, 30: 45, November 9-15.
22. Jiang Zemin. (1989) *Beijing Review* , 32 : 41, October 9-15.
23. Lal, Sham. (1997) "The Ironies of Independence", *Biblio*, Vol. II, Nos. 7-8, pp. 8-9.
24. Gu Xin. (1995) "A Civil Society and Public Sphere in post-Mao China? An Overview of Western Publications" in *China Information.*
25. *Ibid.*
26. Wakeman, Frederick Jr. (1993) "The Civil Society and Public Sphere Debate: Western Reflections on Chinese Political Culture", in *Modern China*, Vol. 2, April.
27. Walder, A. (1989) "The political sociology of the Beijing upheaval of 1989", *Problems of Communism.*
28. Wang Hui, Leo Ou-fan Lee and Michael M. J. Fischer (1994). "Is the Public Sphere Unspeakable in Chinese? Can Public Spaces (gonggong kongjian) Lead to Public Spheres?" In *Public Culture*, Vol. 6, University of Chicago.
29. Shen Yue (1986), "Bourgeoisie rights should be translated as towns people's rights", in *Tianjin Shehui Kexue*, (Tianjin Social Sciences) Vol. 4.
30. Shen Yue (1990), "An examination of towns people's society" in *Zhexue Yanjiu* (Philosoplical Studies), Vol. 1.
31. Xi Zhaoyong (1990), *An examination of "examination of townspeople's society", Zhexue yanjiu,* Vol. 5.
32. See *Public Culture*, Vol. 6, 1994.
33. Ibid. p. 601.
34. *Dushu* ("Reading" magazine), Vol. 1, p. 12, 1997 Beijing: Sanlian Publishing House.
35. Deng Zhenglai, " Civil society versus the state: an academic appraisal", in *China Social Sciences Quarterly*, Vol. 5, Spring, 1993. Hong Kong.
36. Zhang Dainian and Wang Dong, Zhonghua wenmingde xiandai fuxing he zonghe chuangxin, (The modern resurgence and composite innovations of Chinese civilization) *Xinhua Wenzhai* (Xinhua Digest), No. 8, 1997.

CULTURE AND ART

CULTURE AND ART

文化藝術

18. Some Aspects of Jataka Paintings in Indian and Chinese (Central Asian) Art
M.C. Joshi & Radha Banerjee

19. India and China: Beyond and the Within
Lokesh Chandra

20. My Tryst with Chinese Art
M.N. Deshpande

21. Icons of Cultural Linkage
D.C. Bhattacharyya

22. Cultural Synthesis in the Buddhist Art of China
Arputharani Sengupta

23. New Revelations of Xinjiang Art
Priyatosh Banerjee

24. The Creation of Goddess of Mercy from Avalokitesvara
Bagyalakshmi

25. The Manichaean Input to Chinese Culture and Art
Radha Banerjee

M.C. JOSHI & RADHA BANERJEE

18

SOME ASPECTS OF JATAKA PAINTINGS IN INDIAN AND CHINESE (CENTRAL ASIAN) ART

An important linkage between the Ancient art of India and China is provided by Buddhist narrative episodes especially the Jataka tales detailing the previous lives of Buddha. Each story ends with a moral illustrating the Buddhist ideal of Dharma and self-sacrifice in diverse forms. The tradition avers that these stories were narrated by Buddha himself during the course of his sermons to drive home the message that by constant practice of virtuous deeds or *Paramita* (the highest virtue) one reaches the status of the "Enlightened One". In these tales, the pre-Enlightened Buddha was designated as the "Bodhisattva" — a lay creature on the path of Enlightenment, in the form of a humam being, or animal, birds, fish etc.

Paramita consists of a host of spiritual values such as *dana* (liberality), *sila* (moral precepts), *kshanti* (forebearance), *virya* (energy), *prajna* (knowledge), and *satya* (truthfulness). By means of vivid story-depiction the Bodhisattva, through the Jataka tales, sought to inculcate virtuous living amongst his followers rather than insistence on doctrinal dogmas triyng to create a new faith at the level of the commoner. The Jataka stories demonstrate the exemplary behaviour on the part of one whose highest example was the accomplishment of highest knowledge.

Thus Bodhisattva as depicted in the Jatakas was an aspirant after knowledge who wanted to rise through a chain of good deeds and virtuous living to the exalted status of Buddhahood. The original concept of the Jatakas support the belief in rebirth and the principle of Karma. Despite their Buddhist affiliation, the genesis of the Jataka stories is shrouded in obscurity. No doubt, they were reduced to writing (in Pali) of a much later date after the passing away of Buddha, but they seem to have been a part of India's archaic oral tradition which was presented in a Buddhist context with necessary modifications in the early historical periods. The evidence preserved in early Buddhist art of Bharhut and Amaravati reliefs and other sites shows that by about the second century B.C., their narrative forms were more or less standardized. The Jataka stories in Bharhut reliefs bear inscribed captions probably with a view to educate those Buddhist worshippers who were visiting the sacred sites, urging them to follow the righteous path. The Jatakas are numerous, nearly 500 or so referring to significant events relating to the lives of the Bodhisattvas constructively preparing for a higher goal leading to perfection of knowledge.

The Jatakas unfold, with great artistry and convincing power, the entire panorama of ancient Indian life, laden with scenarios of passion and compassion, wickedness and benevolence, reward and punishment, life and death. There is also a fluent sculpturing of the Jataka tales for the sheer delight of story-telling which has indeed emigrated from India far beyond her boundaries to enliven and enrich the art and culture of the country that adopated it. The Jataka stories became a favourite subject with artists in ancient India, Ceylon, Central Asia, China, Nepal and Tibet. These stories exercised a great moral influence on the people, establishing a firm conviction that merit would result from performing virtuous acts of courage, liberality, fortitude, nobleness and self sacrifice.

The Pali Jatakas are the 10th book of the *Khuddaka Nikaya*. They had attained popularity among the students of religion and culture on accout of their noble contents, apart from furnishing valuable information on the social, political and religious life of the people in ancient India. It is interesting to note that each story opens with a preface which describes the circumstances in the life of the Buddha which led him to tell the story of his past lives. The Jataka stories depict the long series of encounters in life faced by the Enlightened One in his previous lives when he existed as a Bodhisattva. At the end of every story there is a brief summary in which the Buddha identifies the different persons in the story.

The Jataka narratives rose from the oral literature of Madhyadesa (the "middle country") coinciding with the areas of Harayana, Uttar Pradesh and Bihar. Some of the tales are also found in a modified version in the *Pancatantra, Kathasaritsagara,* etc. while in some other cases they have parallels in the *Mahabharata, Ramayana, Puranas* and a few episodes mentioned in the religious literature of Jainism. The Northern Indian flavour of the Jataka tales is evident. Many Jatakas occur in the *Mahavastu* in prose as well as in verse written in mixed Sanskrit. A careful study of the Jatakas shows that the stories are highly edifying and have various purposes to serve. However, the proto-Mahayana schools like Sarvastivadin Buddhists also added certain sacred episodes based on earlier traditions called "Avadanas" which are also represented in arts. Yet, the Jatakas never lost their significance. According to *Saddharmapundarika Sutra,* Buddha himself admitted that he had been utilizing *sutras, gathas* and Jatakas to highlight his teachings. (Il. 45)

Aryasura's *Jatakamala* (meaning "the garlands of birth stories") written originally in execellent Sanskrit is a very important text for the study of Jatakas, which were adopted from the Pali versions belonging to the canonic literature of the Theravada school. The *Jatakamala* was affiliated to the Northern (Mahayanic) Buddhism. Perhaps there was more than one *Jatakamala.* Somendra, the son of the reputed medieval Kashmiri writer Ksmendra (author of the *Avadana Kalpalata*), observes: "There exist many Garlands of Birth Stories of the Jina by Gopadatta and other teachers, who, discarding the usual order of the *Avadanas,* gathered tales and told them at length in elaborate prose (gadya), interespersed with verse, holding themselves free as to the proportion of the two styles, which they made interchange. They all treat of the praise of the right path, but owing to their profoundness, are hard to understand."

The *Jatakamala*, written in the purest Sanskrit in good lengths, is a selection of 34 Jatakas with the avowed object of arousing the true faith in the minds of the readers. Aryasura, its author, was a gifted writer. His 34 episodes were selected from such birth stories which had had a long circulation before his times in India. Sura says that the tales penned by him were faithfully adopted in writing from the oral traditions, but there were also omissions of certain insignificant details so that the elegance of style and the concentration of thought content were achieved. For instance, Jujuka, the Brahmana in the Visvantara Jataka, is simply referred to as a Brahmana here. About the author of *Jatakamala*, i.e. Aryasura, no firm identity has been established so far. Taranath identifies him with Asvaghosha. In all likelihood, Aryasura must have lived before 460 AD, as we find the painted verses from *Jatakamala* in Ajanta depicting Kshantivada Jataka in Cave II which itself has been dated to the latter half of the 5th century A.D.

Jataka stories adorn many ancient Indian monuments including Bharhut and Sanchi during second and first century BC, in Amaravati and Goli during 2nd and 3rd century A.D., and also in the caves of Ajanta from 2nd century B.C. to fifth century AD and elsewhere during the later periods. The Chinese pilgrim, Faxian, while visiting Ceylon around AD 412 saw at Abhayagiri depictions of the 500 various presentations of the Bodhisattva during his various births. Xuanzang, another Chinese pilgrim of the 7th century, mentioned stupas erected in honour of the Bodhisattva whose deeds were related in the Jatakas. We now take up four Jataka stories and discuss their places in Indian and Chinese art. Painted parallels of Ajanta Jataka scenes are available in the Chinese Central Asian art especially at Dunhuang, Kizil, Miran, etc. bringing out various adapations of original Indian Jataka stories in localized versions.

In the murals of Ajanta presently, nearly twentyfive Jataka stories have been found painted in addition to two avadanas. A few Jatakas like Sama, Sibi, Hamsa and Saddanta Jatakas have been painted in more than two caves. To some extent the painter had followed Aryasura in regard to Jatakas like Visvantara, Sibi, Matsya, Hamsa, Ruru, Kapi, Ksanti, etc. but with modifications whenever required. The Sibi Jataka in cave No.1 follows the archaic Brahmanical (Mahabharata) version while its depiction in cave No.17 remains faithful to Jatakamala with certain additions of details to highlight the story. The portrayal of Shyama (Sarvan) and Saddanta Jatakas in cave No.10 (dated 2nd/1st century B.C.) follows the Pali version, so also are the paintings of most of other Jataka stories in later caves of the 5th century A.D. Yet it is evident that the artists who created these Jataka painting had also drawn inspiration from other available sources of information as well as their own imagination.

It is worth mentioning that in eastern Central Asia the artists worked at Kizil seem to have drawn inspiration from the art of Ajanta. especially in the case of the representation of the Jatakas and Avadanas. Scholars have invited our attention to the fact that many of the Jatakas and Avadanas depicted in Kizii correspond to those painted in Ajanta, like Mahisha Jataka, Visvantara Jataka, the Sibi Jataka, the Maitribala Jataka, the Ruru Jataka, the Vanara or Kapi Jataka, the Hasti Jataka, the Purna Avadana, and Shyama, etc. There is however, some difference in the mode of delineation of the Jatakas, in Ajanta and Kizil. While at Ajanta mostly the stories are depicted in various scenes in spatial arrangement according to the different settings of the Jatakas, in Kizil only the most dramatic part of the story is generally delineated. There are however some exceptions in illustrating only the central idea of a Jataka.

Syama or Samaka Jataka: Amongst the older Jatakas at Ajanta which has parallels outside is the Shyama or Samaka Jataka in the cave No. 10, a caitya hall narrating the story of Bodhisattva as Shyama who tirelessly served his blind hermit parents. The Jataka highlighted the role of an ideal son dedicated to the service of his aged father and mother setting an inspiring example for the common people. The details are as follows.

In one of his previous births, the future Buddha was born as Syama who was a model of filial piety. His old and blind parents lived as hermits in a remote part of the Himalayas. Syama was their sole support. One day when Syama went to a pool to fetch water for his parents he was struck by an arrow of the king of Benares who came there hunting deer in the forest.

Indra was deeply impressed by Syama's filial piety and restored him to life. In China this story is known as Samaka Jataka which mentions that the king of Kapilavastu (instead of Varanasi according to the Indian tradition) went to the forest. While hunting, he killed near a stream a hermit boy. When the king came to know that he killed the boy. He went to the boy's parents and told them about what had happened and led them to where Samaka was lying. Samaka's agony moved the heaven and earth. Out of campassion a god placed an elexir into Samaka's mouth and the poisonous arrow dropped from his body; not only the boy was resurrected, but the eye-sight of the blind parents was also restored. A few scenes of this Jataka are also found in Cave No.17 at Ajanta. In Cave No.10 (Ajanta) four incidents of Jataka tale are extant: (i) the King with his retinue shooting an arrow towards Sama; (ii) The king grievously repentent on his accidental mistake; (iii) Sama's blind parents wailing upon the wounded body of their son in the hermitage; (iv) Sama's resurrection to life.

In Cave No.17 a surviving painting shows Sama carrying his blind parents, and the king carrying the body of Sama, and then Sama preaching to the king (after he was resurrected to life) like a true Bodhisattva.

The story of Syama has also a Brahmanical version in which the hero is Sravana Kumar instead of Syama. The dedicated son, Sravana was accidentally killed by King Dasaratha of Ayodhya on a royal hunt. Unlike the Buddhist version, the boy was not resurrected to life. The blind parents wept loudly and cursed the king.

Xuan Zang who was in India (629-645 AD) mentions in his description of Gandhara a stupa about ten miles from Pushkaravati (Charsada) which was then believed to mark the site of the Syama Jataka, the story has been represented in the art of Sanchi, Gandhara and Ajanta. The Indian (Syama) story had a wide appeal because of the fact that it depicts Syama's love and adoration for his blind parents, an ideal which is of great social interest. The representation of the story in Sanchi is a beautiful composition depicting the forest scenery. In Gandhara several episodes were grouped in a single frame. The boy with a pitcher on the shoulder indicates that he is going to collect water for his old parents. The figure of the king in his hunting dress is represented twice. On the banks of the pool are shown cattle and deer and beyond them to the right the blind hermit and his wife are seated awaitng the return of their son who has gone to bring water for them. This representation is a mixture of forest scenery and human pathos.

The Chinese have translated "Syama" into "Shamo", and "Samaka" into "Shang Mo Jia". But the more popular name for "Samaka" or "Syama" is "Shanzi", its first syllable being the transliteration of "Syama", while its second syallable "zi" being no different from the suffix used for Confucius, Mencius, Laozi and other ancient thinkers. This fact shows that in China's oral (and also written) literature, Syama has reached a stature of saints. Also, the story of Sama has been elevated to the status of Sutra — there is the popularity of the text entitled *Shanzi Jing* (literally, the Sutra of Sage Sama).That Chinese tradition gives greater eminence to Syama Jataka than to other Jataka tales was because of the importance of filial piety which was a corner-stone of the cardinal norms of the Chinese society. The story of "Shanzi" was a household word in China, having crossed the boundaries of Buddhism. It has become a part of China's own spiritual tradition.

The depiction of Syama Jataka has appeared in the Dunhuang caves and the Xinjiang grottoes. In Cave No. 299 of Mogao there in a long horizontal panel decorating the gorgeous ceiling depicting: (1) the palace of the king, (2) the king's hunt, (3) the king chasing a deer along a stream, (4) the king killing Syama by mistake, (5) Syama being buried, (6) Syama's blind parents being informed about the tragedy, and (7) the resurrection of Syama. In comparison. the Xinjiang cave painting is much simpler, showing only the killing of Syama.

This and other portrayals of Syama Jataka at Mogao caves, Dunhuang, are elaborate and vivid. The final scene which shows the blind parents embracing their son's body and wailing in anguish represents poignantly the grief of parting. The tragic tale ends on a happy note with the solution of Buddha's magical power resurrecting Samaka. The painting composition is tightly structured with a clear focus on the theme. People's activities are interwoven with the landscape — hills, trees and the streams — making it a realistic representation. It has been inferred by scholars in China that the story was intended to convey the idea of loyalty to the authorities in addition to piety to parents. At Ajanta (Cave No.17) there is a painting of another story of an elephant devoted to his blind parents, almost on the same theme, narrated through Matriposaka Jataka.

Visvantara Jataka: The most famous Jataka common to Buddhist art of India and China is Visvantara or Vessantara Jataka (in Pali) from early times. The tale emphasises the importance of dana or offering charity and gifts. According to the story in the kingdom of Sivi, there was a king named Sanjaya and he had a son Visvantara whose generosity became a household word in the country and everyone rushed to him to solicit something. Visvantara tried his utmost not to disappoint anyone. One day he even gave away the auspicious white elephant, the harbinger of rain which was a national treasure, to a neighbouring kingdom which had suffered the visitation of draught. People in his own kingdom were indignant at his excessive generosity and demanded his banishment. On the order of his royal father Visvantara left for the forest with his wife and two children. During the course of the journey he first gave away his horse, then the chariot. He even parted with his two children to a Brahmin (Indra in the guise of an old Brahmin demanded them from him). As if this was not enough, he even gave away his wife. The king of gods, Sakra (i.e. Indra) finally reunited him with his children, wife and father, and he returned to his kingdom welcomed by everyone.

Visvantara represents the last existence of Gautama Buddha as Bodhisattva. As a result of his meritorious deeds during the previous births Gautama attained enlightenment and became Buddha. The Bodhisattva embarks on his journey from supreme sacrifice to supreme knowledge as Buddha. He accepts all hardships of his banishment with joy. While Visvantara is in the jungle no beast or bird of the forest does any harm to each other, and there is perfect harmony and friendship among all species till Visvantara bids goodbye to the forest to come back to his kingdom.

Visvantara personifies the highest virtue of sacrifice, the spirit of renunciation and equanimity to fulfil *dana paramita.* His story became the favourite piece for story-tellers, and was the poets' ready reference and the artists' delight. With the help of poets and artists *dana paramita* became a universal tradition of ancient India.

The Visvantara narrative is found sculpted in the art of Bharhut, Sanchi, Gandhara, Ajanta, Amaravati, Nagarjunakonda, Goli and Ajanta in India, and in Miran and Kizil in Chinese Turkistan and Dunhuang and many other places in China. In Sanchi, the depiction is to be found on the lower lintel of the northern gateway of the great stupa. The episodes runs from right to left on the central portion of the outer gateway of the lintel, beginning at the right end. If we go throgh the Visvantara relief at Goli we are confronted with a completely sequential frieze, of which only the left end has been lost. The story is here presented in sequence from left to right. In the first scene that has survived, Visvantara, accompanied by a large retinue is riding at the city gate on the state elephant. The favourite presentations of Visvantara Jataka mainly highlight two places, viz, the forest and the palace. Narratives of the happenings in the palace and the city are arranged in the upper register and the forest scenes are in the lower register of the corridor wall of cave No. 17 of Ajanta. This combination has resulted in a powerful impact on the spectators, touching the inner chord of the hearts of the people.

The Visvantara Jataka seems to have been very popular in Central Asia as in India. A. von Le coq discovered a very elaborate depiction of this Jataka at Kizil. The greed of the black Brahmin beggar and the trepidation of the sons before they were gifted away by the compassionate Bodhisattva are vividly, poignantly and dramatically presented in a 7th century painting in one of the caves. The representation of Jataka in Miran is also elaborate. The manner of delineation of the Jataka in Miran shows beyond doubt the extension of Gandharan style to the eastern part of Xinjiang. Further it is intersting to note that there is a short

Brahmi inscription on the thigh of Visvantara's elephant which has been interpreted as being equivalent to Roman Tita. It shows that there were itinerant Roman artists who had moved to Central Asia to execute Buddhist temple art. The Amaravati sculpture as in the Miran paintaing very vividly shows the agitation of the people for the banishment of Visvantara. In both the places the king is seated on a throne with his right foot placed on a footstool and the hand is placed on the thigh.

On the left of the illustration at Miran it depicts the offering of the elephant by Visvantara and on the right his gifiting away the cart and the bull. But one significant thing to note is that the Amaravati panel omits Visvantara's taking leave of his father — the scene which is the vital link in the Central Asian painting.

In the Ajanta painting we find Visvantara taking leave first of his mother, Phusati and then his father king Sanjaya. The queen mother is shown seated on a throne, and Visvantara, kneels down before her with his hands joined in adoration. There are three maids depicted in three different poses below the queen and the prince. By the side of the queen there are a female chauri bearer and two more maids, holding ornaments probably for the prince to enable him to offer gifts according to his heart's desire. Visvantara is shown again near the feet of his father seated on the throne. The face of the king betrays anxiety. Here also Visvantara kneels down with folded hands. In both the places he is shown bedecked in jewellery and crown. The artist brings out very successfully the nobility of Visvantara's character, i.e. his respect for his parents and obedience to his father's wishes on the one hand and the anxiety of his parents and an overspread gloom in the palace because of the impending banishment of Visvantara on the other.

When one compares the details of the Ajanta painting with those of the Central Asian fragments one hardly fails to recognise the identity of their subject matter. It is interesting to note that though the other parts of the story are found depicted in many sculptures and paintings, this particular incident of Visvantara's taking leave of his father before going on exile survives now only in Ajanta but also in the Central Asian fragments.

The Visvantara Jataka occupies a pride of place in the Dunhuang Jataka paintings, albeit it is there assuming the identity of "Sadana Jataka" (named after the great river). The popularity of Sadana Jataka began probably with the founding of the Sui Dynasty by an emperor who was one of the most devout Buddhist rulers in Chinese history. Particular attention should be given to the painting of the "Sudana story" in cave No. 419 of the Mogao Grottoes, Dunhuang. When the Director of the Dunhuang Academy, Prof. Duan Wenjie, visited us in 1991, he brought the life size copy of this painting executed by none other than himself, which was 111.5 cm in height and 359.5 cm in length. The original was painted during the Sui Dynasty at the turn of the 6th-7th century. The painting was almost a copy of the Ajanta "Visvantara Jataka" filled with the details about his gifting away the white elephant, his exile journey, his giving away the horse (hence he had to pull the chariot by hand like pulling a ricksha), then parting with the chariot, then the children, then the wife. The painting also showed God Sakra reinstating him to his Kingdom and his being welcomed back by the king and his people.

In comparison, while the Sudana story painted in cave No. 419 at Dunhuang did not highlight the restoration of the two sons to the prince, the Ajanta cave No.17 painting of Visvantara Jataka illustrated in the central portion the payment of a large sum of coins by king Sanjaya to the Brahman, Jujaka, for the return of the two grandsons.

Ruru (Deer) Jataka: The Ruru Jataka narrates the story of the Bodhisattva's birth as a deer, often regarded as sacred and innocent in India, particulary in the Buddhist tradition. There are other Jatakas mentioning the Bodhisattva's birth as deer or stag two of which are also illustrated at Ajanta (Cave No. 17) — the Nyagrodha-Mriga and Sarabha-Mriga Jataka. In the Ruru Jataka story which has been portrayed in various sites in India and outside we see a deer being betrayed by an ungrateful man who should feel indebted to the deer for saving his life from drowning. Instead, the man reveals the deer's secret hideout to the king, which leads to the deer's being captured. The turning point comes when the deer appeals to the conscience of the king by exposing the treachery of the man. The king finally corrects the wrong doing and gets the deer freed. It is a very interesting and moving story. The artists have depicted the various consecutive events of the story with great feeling.

Incidentally, in China we have the very popular story of the nine-coloured deer. The Mogao Grottoes in its Cave No. 257, have preserved a wall painting of the vintage of Northern Wei (439-534 AD) which is 60 x 595 cm. in size. The reproduction of the painting was also exhibited in New Delhi at the IGNCA ground in 1991 along with other reproductions. The painting gives a detailed account of how the nine-coloured deer first saves a man from drowning. Then, the man discovers this marvellous animal and reports it to the queen who is a greedy person eager to capture the wonderful deer. The sequence of the painting goes on to show the capture of the deer because of the man's leading the queen's hunters to his secret hideout. In the centre of the painting is the conversation of the deer with the king revealing the treacherous deed of the man, as well as the sequential end of the deer's being freed, and the man's being punished.

Thus, we see that this story about the nine-coloured deer is a slight variation of the Ruru Jataka. In its Indian version, the deer (actually the deer-king) is a golden deer — while its Chinese counterpart is a deer of nine-colours. We know that the Chinese use numbers to describe things often in a figurative manner. They generally use the word "five-colours" to mean multi-colour, and there is no "six-colour" in Chinese vocabulary. Here, the usage of "nine-colour" is purported to indicate rarity. In this Chinese story, the deer is just such a rare treasure that one hardly comes across in daily life. This conforms to the theme of the Ruru Jataka. Why has the Chinese version preferred to depict it as the "nine-coloured" rather than the "golden" deer is not clear to us. But, we know that to the Indians gold is the highest value of treasure. In real life also there is greater treasuring of gold in India than in China which is a country that does not produce much gold. Another departure of the Chinese version is that instead of the king's desiring to possess the deer (as is in the Indian version), it is the queen who is greedy (in the Chinese version). But, both the versions end with the king's listening to the appeal of the victimized deer and performing justice. We know that according to the Chinese political tradition the king cannot be devious and is always the arbitor of justice. If the Chinese had to adopt the Ruru Jataka in its totality it would have compromised the image of such an arbitor. So, the changed detail (putting the blame on the queen, but never the king) is out of political considerations. There is another deviation in the Chinese story's ending with the treacherous man's being punished which is not mentioned in the Indian Ruru Jataka. We must add that the reproduction we saw in the IGNCA exhibition in 1991 was executed by no other person than Prof. Chang Shuhong, the legendary Founder-Director of the Dunhuang Research Institute (now the Dunhuang Academy) who had passed away about five years ago. It was a marvellous painting which cannot be surpassed in skill, colour scheme and characterization. This painting joins its original inside the Dunhuang cave to rank as real masterpieces that human efforts can create. They are not only the finest depictions of the Jatakas one has ever seen, but can be considered as among the greatest paintings of China — even of the world.

Sibi Jataka: The kingdom of Sibi produced many virtuous kings of whom was the son and successor of King Ushinara. This new Sibi king was known for his philanthrophy among his other virtues. One day, Indra and Agni came to test this. The two deities disguised themselves as a hawk and a pigeon. The hawk started chasing the pigeon who fell on King Sibi's lap trembling with fear. The hawk demanded the king to surrender the pigeon as its prey. This the king refused, as he decided to protect the poor thing who had taken refuge under his protection. After much argument the hawk agreed to leave the pigeon alone if the king would offer a piece of flesh from his own body which was equivalent to the weight of the pigeon. The king was more than happy to make such a sacrifice. Strangely, after endlessly cutting off his own flesh from different parts of his body and putting it on the scale, the king found that the pigeon still overweighed. Then the king threw his entire body to the scale even then he could not equalise the weight of the bird. At this point the hawk and the pigeon revealed their true identity and offered boons to the king for his unbounded charitable spirit. There are many versions of the Sibi Jataka and the one narrated above is found in the *Mahabharata* also. In the *Jatakamala* the story of Sibi is somewhat different. Indra came as a blind person to king Sibi and asked him to donate one of his eyes so that he could regain his sight partially. Sibi, however, offered both eyes for the complete restoration of the blind man's sight. The ready willingness of king Sibi to sacrifice both his eyes moved Indra into revealing his true form and going away after giving boons to the king. A stone slab from Nagarjunakonda depicts a scene from Sibi Jataka wherein the story quite resembles that of king Sibi of the *Mahabharata* in which the king is required to tear out flesh equal in weight for the pigeon. There is a man standing with a balance in the hand while the king is engaged in cutting flesh out of his body. There is a panel from cave No. 17 at Ajanta, showing warriors with weapons, flags and buntings, rejocing in the capital and eulogising the King's virtuous deeds.

In the above we see that there are two versions of Sibi Jataka in Indian literature: one is King Sibi's parting with his own eyes , and another his willingly having his flesh cut off in order to save the dove. The Chinese have bifurcated these two according to the narratives of the scriptures. The king who sacrifices his eyes is named "Kuaimu Wang" (the king with happy eyes) which is the Chinese translation of Sanskrit "Sudhira". The Chinese name for "Sibi" is "Shibi" which transcribes the Sanskrit sound. A very interesting painting in Mogao Cave No. 275, illustrated during the period of Northern Liang (421-439), is a panel of the size of 76.5x 312.5cm. The panel has five Jataka tales in a roll horizontally arranged. The picture on the extreme right is the story of King Sudhira's donating his eyes to a blind Brahman. The next picture on its left depicts King Sibi's sacrificing his flesh.

The copy of this panel was exhibited in IGNCA in 1991-92, and the artist who copied it, Prof. Shi Weixiang, was also a guest of IGNCA at the time.

There are a number of paintings pertaining to the story of King Sibi (sacrificing his flesh) inside the Dunhuang caves. Two paintings came to the IGNCA exhibition. Apart from the Northern Liang painting mentioned just now, there is another in cave No. 254 in the Mogao Grottoes of the vintage of Northeren Wei of the size of 122.5 X 164 cm. Once again, this was copied by Prof. Duan Wenjie. The painting makes an excellent depiction of the king who occupies the central place. The pigeon stands on his lap in a pitiable shape. Surrounding this central scenario are the other details of the story. There is the hawk, and also the scale. The cutting of flesh and other details are also in the painting. The central figure of the painting, i.e. King Sibi, is ably presented as a kind-hearted Bodhisattva without any fear of self-sacrifice. The illustration has brought out the enlightened Bodhisattva spirit to the fore which is exactly what the Jatakas have aimed at.

The Jatakas have provided just one of the innumerable platforms for India and China to unite their minds and hearts. The examples shown above exemplify the echoes of the two great civilizations — India and China. There is a vast field for scholars of both the countries to inquire into the India-China cultural interface and affinity. When more Indian scholars join in this endeavour there will be greater results of purposeful research. During our visit to China (myself accompanied by Prof. Tan Chung) in 1996, we discovered the keen expectation on the part of our Chinese brethren — to interact and exchange with their Indian counterparts. It is hoped that Indian scholars do not disappoint them. We must not think that by so doing we do them a favour. It is a good opportunity for us to learn as well. The more we understand the Chinese cultural development, the more we know better about our own neighbours. The art treasure like what is preserved in the Mogao grottoes is the cultural heritage of China, India, and the entire humanity. The rich information and insight stored in this treasure must be further explored for the benefit of our understanding of India's cultural past. Let us join with fellow archaeologists, art historians and scholars of other disciplines in China to launch a joint venture for the good of human knowledge and wisdom as well as international amity, peace and harmony. Just as the Jataka stories have been invented to promote all such ideas and ideals in our mundane world, so should we be inspired to carry it further so that more and more human beings are turned into the good examples of Bodhisattvas.

References

Banerjee, P, *New Light on Central Asian Art and Iconography*, Abha Prakashan, New Delhi, 1992.

Banejee, Radha, *Ashtamahabodhisattva* (The Eight great Bodhisattvas in art and literature), Delhi, 1994.

Ghosh, A (ed), *Ajanta Murals*, New Delhi 1967.

Griffithe, J, *The Paintings in the Buddhist Cave temple of Ajanta*, London, 1896-97.

Kern, H (ed), *The Jatakamala by Aryasura*, Boston, 1883.

Marshall, J and Foucher, A, *The Monuments of Sanchi*, Vol, II-III, Calcutta, 1940.

Mishra, Jagadish Chardra, *Jatakamala (Bodhisattvavadanamalaparaparyaya) of Aryasura*, (with Hindi presentation), Varanasi, 1987.

Mitra, Debala, *Ajanta* (tenth edition), New Delhi, 1992.

Ning Qiang, Cong Yindu dao Zhongguo — mouxie bensheng gushi goutu xing chengde bijiao" (From India to China — A Comparations of some Jataka story illustrations), in *Dunhuang Yanjiu* (Dunhuang Studies), No. 28 (1991), pp. 3-12.

Zhao Xiurong, "Shilun Mogaoku 275 ku beibi gushihuade fojing yiju" (A tentative study on the Jataka story paintings on the northern wall of Cave No. 275 of the Mogao Grottoes), *ibid*, pp.13-27.

Tan Chung, *Dunhuang Art through the eyes of Duan Wenjie*, IGNCA, New Delhi 1994.

Yazdani, G, *Ajanta* (text and plates), Vol. I-IV, (Oxford, 1930-55)

LOKESH CHANDRA

19

INDIA AND CHINA: BEYOND AND THE WITHIN

The last twentythree centuries have seen a continuing cultural interflow between the Western Paradise that is India and the Celestial Kingdom that is China. The rustling breeze of Buddhist fragrance has awakened the mindscape of both countries, endowing them with the web of thought, the harmony of art, the magnificent colour of murals and sculptures, incarnating a new life and sinking into the sensitivities of our peoples deep-reaching muscles of mystery, draped in the intimacy of the mind. The first contacts were made by Buddhist scholars from India who appeared in the Chinese capital in 217 BC under the Qin dynasty. Contacts during the Qin dynasty are a fair possibility as the Sanskrit word for Cathay is Cina, as such was the dynastic name Qin heard by the Indians.

Voltaire (1694-1778), the unrivalled French writer and philosopher, was impressed by the "sublime ideas" of the Indians about the Supreme Being. His enthusiasm for Asian civilisation and Eastern wisdom was shared by Sir William Jones. Jones followed the standards set up by the French philosopher; and he read him assiduously. Voltaire admired the political organisation of China and her ethics based on Reason. He found in China a great civilisation which owned nothing to the Graeco-Roman or Christian tradition. The Chinese managed their affairs of state more rationally and without Christianity. The German philosopher Leibnitz too had established the Berlin Academy to open up interchange of civilisation between Europe and China. The more the Europeans investigated China the more they found India to be its roots, in fact India is the Greece of Asia, the birthplace of philosophical ideas with overwhelming influence on art and poetry.

The *chinoiserie* of the 18th century led to revealing the fabulous bonds of China with India. In their study of China, French scholars started to unravel Central Asia and India. Jean Pierre Abel-Remusat published a history of Khotan in 1820 and his French translation of the travels of Faxian (319 AD) through Central Asia, Afghanistan and India appeared posthumously in 1836. By his labour, it became evident that Chinese sources were fundamental to the understanding of Indian history. In fact, the Indian pronunciation of this first great Chinese pilgrim derives from Abel-Remusat's transcription, like that of his illustrious successor Xuanzang. The travels and biography of the latter were again translated by a French scholar, Stanislas Julien in 1853-58. The biography of Xuanzang after his return to China as summarised by Julien 132 years ago is still our main guide. Indian scholars rarely have access to this French work and are thus deprived of detailed knowledge of the academic achievements of Xuanzang after his return. Julien was again the first to point out that Sanskrit literature had been translated into Chinese on a gigantic scale for a thousand years. In his Sino-Sanskrit concordance of Buddhist works, published in 1849, he gave the Sanskrit titles of Chinese Sutras from a Chinese catalogue of 1306. Thus he injected a new dimension into Indic studies.

Names of Indian savants and sages, deities and divine beings, titles of works and toponymns abound in Chinese chronicles, hagiographies, canonical texts and other historical treatises. Complete Sanskrit texts of hymns are also extant in Chinese transcriptions. These hymns have sunk their roots deep into the lipping adoration of the Chinese. To decipher Sanskrit from them, Julien wrote *Methode pour dechiffrer* et *transcrire les noms sanscrits qui se rencontrent dans les livres chinois* in 1861. Even after the passing of 130 years it remains our only guide, though in dire need of updating and enlarging.

Silk across the sands: Roman ladies of rank, draped in see-through muslin cottons of India and in shining silks and brocades of China, were the eyeful rage of Imperial Rome. Silk was imported from China, where its production began as early as the New Stone Age (third millennium BC). The oracle bone inscriptions of the Yin dynasty contain Chinese characters for mulberry, silkworm, thread and woven fabric. The consort of the Yellow Emperor 2640 BC made sericulture fashionable by herself cultivating mulberry trees, raising worms and reeling silk. The *Nihongi* states that this fabulous fabric was introduced in Japan around AD 300. The Roman empire at Rome and later at Constantinople realised the potentialities of silk. Emperor Justinian had two Iranian monks, who were living in China to smuggle silkworms to Constantinople in the hollows of their bamboo canes in about AD 550. In the 19th century steeped in Classical antiquity, it was but natural that a German geographer called the ancient way from Changan [Xian] to Rome: *Seidenstrassen* or the Silk Route. This Eurocentric nomenclature emphasised the commercial aspects of the route. After all, the Greek word serikos for "silk" is derived from seres "Chinese", that is the Chinese fabric. As children, we saw the Chinese cycling around the streets of Lahore and peddling silk. China and silk were interlinked in our minds. However, Prof. Raghu Vira who was well acquainted with the glorious history of China mentions that the Chinese were a symbol of the Confucian Classics, great artists and architects, painters and sculptors of exquisite skills. Buddhist icons in the flat and in the round, bearers of profound thought of Buddhism, a vast segment of the world's cultural heritage, and a people who had preserved thousands of Buddhist sutras whose Sanskrit originals had been lost in India, the land of their origin. The Chinese paintings in our home and the Shanghai and Taisho editions of the Chinese Tripitaka covering a whole wall of the residence left a deep impression on my growing mind. In later years when I took up the study of Central Asia, silk and sutras came to mind again as two characteristics of the Chinese and of the Sutra Route.

To the Chinese, Central Asia was the way to the Western World of India. Across the vast stretches of desert, in the void of the self, they heard the echo of "I am the Truth". Travelling and traveller became one, one with the eternal. The waterless deserts were the void of the self. The traveller trod not with his feet, but with his heart on wings. Courage tore the terror of the terrain, and despair turned to hope in the supreme quest of a beyond without shores. The drop departed from its native home found a shell and became a pearl. The desert and oasis became an embodiment of Buddhist teaching, according to Takayasu Higuchi, "The desert symbolises hell and the oasis paradise, or in the broader parameters of Buddhist philosphy everything flows and nothing is permanent". Yijing speaks of the hardships and perils that had to be braved to reach India: "No doubt, it is great merit and fortune to visit the Western country (India) in search of the Dharma but at the same time it is an extremely difficult and perilous undertaking.... Many days have I passed without food, even without a drop of water. I was always worried and no spirit was left in me.... If, however, a monk happened to reach India after such perilous journey, he would find no Chinese monastery there. There was no fixed place to settle down. We had to move from place to place like a blade of grass swept by the wind." The monk Xuankui, who could not come to India as he suffered from illness, wrote: "My heart goes to the sacred land of Buddhist temples. I dream to move in the land of the Buddha. Will that auspicious day ever come, when with the help of a cup or bowl only, I shall be able to cross and reach India? Shall I be able to witness the magnificent flow of Dharma in India?"

Heavenly horses: Though the route has been named by the Europeans, it was not opened by them as a communication system for silk. At the end of the second century BC, the Han emperor Wu sent Zhang Qian to *Xi-yu,* the Western World. His return to Changan in 126 BC was the opening of a regular road, as the Chinese realised the importance of other cultures. Xenophobia and the concept of Barbarians underwent change. Nomadic tribes traded silk with Central and Western Asia. The main purpose of the journey of Zhang Qian was defence: to find the whereabouts of the Hun barbarians who had been a major menace to Han China. The thorough-bred "heavenly horse" (*tian ma*) was imported from Dawan to improve breed of horses during the Han dynasty. Zhang Qian was amazed to see in Bactria staves or walking sticks made of bamboo of *Qiong* and cloth of *Shu*, both from Sichuan. The Bactrians had purchased them in India. This subsequently led the Chinese to the discovery of Yunnan. An ancient trade route ran from Sichuan through Yunnan into North Eastern India, thence to North Western India and then to Iranian lands. Silk-horse barter was a feature of Western Han. The Han Emperor Wu twice despatched troops under the command of General Li Guangli to obtain fine horses across the Tianshan mountains from the West. The new breed reinforced the military capability of China to such an extent as to eliminate the Huns and to expand their power as far as Korea. The Imperial Mausoleum of Western Han in Yangjinwan has thousands of clay figures of war horses. Kasyapa Matanga, the first Indian teacher in China in the first century AD, stayed at the *Baimasi* or White Horse Monastery. The word "white" can refer here to the colour of the horse or the horse of the "white" people. The ethnicon of Kucha was "white" and *svetadvipa* "white land" refers to an area beyond North Western India. The white horse is at the base of the modern economic miracle of Japan. At the end of the Second World War, General MacArthur rode the sacred white horse of the Emperor of Japan to seal the newly won victory, and offered the equivalent of Marshall Aid to Japan. The Japanese responded: "No aid, only trade. We will work hard and grow rich." The white horse became the heavenly horse that led Japan to unprecedented economic heights.

Music, milk, paper, rice, fruits: In 138 BC Zhang Qian, the envoy of the Chinese Emperor, took back musical instruments and Mahatukhara melodies from India to the Chinese capital Changan. The son-in-law of the Emperor Wu wrote 28 new tunes based on this melody which were played as military music. Along with Buddhism, the Tokharians of the route introduced milk to China. The Chinese ideograph pronounced *lak* in ancient times, which meant various kinds of fermented milk products, was a loan from Indo-European (Latin lactic). The peach and pear reached India in the reign of Kaniska and hence they were known as *cinani* . Paper had been manufactured out of silk in Han times, but with the introduction of Buddhism Indian cotton also became a component of paper, as is evident from the old lexicon entitled *Gujin Ciku* where the silk radical of the character *zhi* for silk is replaced by the cotton radical, after the invention by Cai Lun. Cotton cultivation had been introduced from India to China in the second century BC. The Japanese word *uruchi* is derived from the Sanskrit *vrihi.* It seems to have arrived via North Western India where Greek and Roman influences were dominant. Rice is *oruza* in Greek and Latin (oryza), both derivatives of *vrihi.* The knowledge of rice came to Greece from the expedition of Alexander and the mention of *oruza* by Theophrastus (c.320-300 BC) dates almost from the lifetime of Alexander who died in 323 BC. The Japanese is so close to the Greek form that its origin can be connected with a variant of *vrihi* that was prevalent in North Western India, from which the Greek and Japanese forms are derived. The peach and the apricot were introduced to Rome in the first century AD through Iran, via Armenia, Greece and Rome. In AD 647 the king of Gandhara in North Western India sent the "Buddha-land vegetable" to the Chinese court.

Graeco-Roman elements: The three Tathagatas of the past, present and future, in China and Japan are: Dipankara, Sakyamuni, and Maitreya. Xuanzang localises the cult of Dipankara the Tathagata of the past at Nagarahara (modern Jalalabad in Afghanistan). His names, translated into Chinese by various pairs of characters meaning "Constant Light", "Universal Light", "Blazing Torch", show proximity to the Iranian light cult. The sitting posture of Maitreya, with his feet hanging down the seat in European fashion, are a feature of North Western India, where Iranians, Greeks, Romans, Scythians, Kushans, and Tokharians jostled with the Indians.

The continued political presence of the Achaemenians, Parthians, Seleucids, Indo-Greeks, and Kushans had a far-reaching impact on the cultural hegemony of North Western India. It rendered the *osmosis* of Iranian and Hellenistic ideas into Buddhism. The king-cult or emperor-worship was prevalent in Iran, Greece and Rome. The deification of kings was a solemn act of legislation in Greece even before Alexander crossed over into Asia. It was transplanted into Rome. Images of deified kings were installed in temples in live physical dimensions or in heights of multiples thereof to express greater loyalty. The loyalty of the provinces to Rome was gauged by the veneration which they felt for the person of the Emperor, whom they were prepared to treat as a god. The practice of offering divine honours to Augustus began in the East soon after Actium and in the course of his reign penetrated to all parts of the Empire.

The *renzhongxiang* have been a puzzle to Japanese, Chinese and European scholars (for instance, Yoshimura Rei, Roshana Hokai *renzhongxiang no kenkyu, Bijutsu Kenkyu* 203.125-39). They were personalities in statues. These were life-size sculptures, made to the breadth of the donor's finger (*angula*). There are several instances of them in the Buddhist world. The proportions of a Tibetan Buddha are those of the Prince of Shalu (Zhva.lu) or the image of an Avalokitesvara has the same size as Sontsengampo, the first emperor of Tibet. These portrait-statues of the royalty were an expression of sanctified power. The Sanskrit word *pratima* means a portrait-statue done to (*prati*) the measures (*ma*) of the donor. The *Daibutsu*, larger than life-size, were an extension of this principle: the colossal Maitreya statue at Darel seen by Faxian, the two images at Bamiyan, the 27 metre high standing Maitreya at the Binglingsi caves are royal enterprises. They remind us of the colossi in the Graeco-Roman world. The colossus of Apollo astride the entrance of the harbour of Rhodes was the most celebrated in Greek antiquity, 120 feet high, made by Chares in 250 BC. Colossal statues of deities and emperors were erected all over the Roman empire to impress the might of Rome on the people. Zenodorus was summoned by Nero to Rome and there he made a statue 106 feet high to represent the emperor but dedicated to the Sun. In the eighth century, Rocana of Nara, symbolised imperium. Emperor Shomu ordered, in AD 743, the construction of the gigantic statue (*daibutsu*) of Rocana, 16 metres in height, at the Todaiji monastery, in his attempt to unify the nation in an awareness of its power, to consolidate the sovereignty of nation in a harmony of the emperor and his people on the deeper spiritual levels of a shared awareness: it was a "Grand National Temple". Portrait-statues or colossi in China and Japan go back to North Western Indian prototypes which were cognate to Roman concepts of imperial power expressed as cult images.

The portents of sweating, weeping, shaking, light-emitting images from the Jin (AD 265-420) to the Northern Qi and Northern Zhou (AD 550-81) dynasties are sensitive not to individual worshippers but to the body politic. Their forerunners were the state cults of Greece and Rome. The Roman historian Livy records sympathetic sweating while Hannibal was in Italy at a critical stage of the Second Punic War. Livy and St. Augustine cite that Apollo of Cumae lamented publicly when the Greeks were worsted by the Romans in three successive wars of the second century BC. Just as the safety of ancient Troy depended on the statue of Pallas, the Buddhist images in China were also palladia. It is an indication that the Graeco-Romanised peoples of North Western India were active intermediaries not only in the trading of silk, but also in the transmission of the sutras. The role of the Graeco-Roman world in the conditioning and in the transferring of Buddhism across the Sutra Route, deserves a close study.

From Jade beauties to flying devis: The Chinese were fascinated by jade beauties and by the music and dances of the Central Asian peoples. The Zhou (1027-256 BC) got music of the Western Barbarians and played it on special occasions to vaunt their political might. The first three masters of Buddhist psalmody (*bombai*) in China were Kuchean, Scythian and Sogdian. In AD 384 Lu Guang brought music from Kucha as triumphal booty.

The Mogao Caves at Dunhuang and the Yulin Caves have extensive representation of flying goddesses some of whom hold musical instruments. Beginning with Northern Wei (386-534) they came down to the Yuan dynasty (1271-1368). They emerge from the Pool of Seven Jewels in the Pure Land of *Sukhavati*. They dwell in heaven and refrain from taking meat and wine, but collect the sweet nectar of different flowers and scatter blossoms from the sky to make the world fragrant. With no robes above the waist, they fly in the air in their flowing scarves. The flying celestials at Dunhuang with long silk scarves trailing out gave rise to the "Scarf Dance". Their hand and body postures are strongly reminiscent of the Indian style of dancing.

In 568 Emperor Wu of the Northern Wei married a Turk princess of the A-she-na family. The princess brought in her train the musicians of Kucha. Since then we find the music of Kucha, Kashgar, Bukhara and Samarkand in Northern Zhou.

The concupiscent statues of goddesses at Nau Bahar in Bactria established the equation "ideal beauty = Buddhist image" in the East Iranian world. Even when Buddhism had faded away, early Persian poetry continued to cultivate abstract mental forms poignantly recalling ideas of the grace of Buddhist statues. Ayyuqi writes of his beautiful heroine that "she was... a Buddhist statue in a temple full of offerings". Further on, we find the crescendo in stanzas 2138-42 where she is addressed as *Bot* (Buddhist statue), then *lo'bat* (statuette), and finally as *naubahar*, the Buddhist monastery which was well-known for its graceful statues in Iranian literature upto the time of Yaqub in the 13th century. No wonder that the metaphor of the *Bot* "Buddhist statue" is constant in early Persian poetry.

The Annals of the Sui and Tang dynasties record Iranian dances and musical instruments. Prosperity flowed into the Tang capital Changan, an international centre of politics, trade and culture, as it was the eastern most terminus of the trans-national Silk Route. Chinese poets speak of citizens of Changan enjoying wine served by Barbarian women in the taverns. Some of the finest murals at Dunhuang are of dancing goddesses in the joyous tenderness of their vibrant movements. These dancing angels are Indian for they wear no raiments above the waist. Dunhuang Caves show three types of female dresses: the flowing drapery of Chinese ladies, the tight wear of Central Asian beauties and the sensuous elegance of the bare bodies of Indian belles who bid the onlooker to accompany them into worlds of luminous beauty.

In the reign of Kaniska bilateral relations entered a new phase in economic, political and cultural domains. Kaniska as the greatest of Kushan emperors symbolised his international status by the adoption of four titles: Devaputra or son of Heaven from China, Shaonana Shao or King of Kings from Persia, Kaisara or Caesar from Rome, and Maharaja of India, signifying the imperial dignity of the four superpowers of the time: China, Persia, Rome, and India. He played a major role in the dissemination of Buddhism to China. The policy of cultural internationalism enunciated by Asoka found its prime efflorescence in the reign of Kaniska. Xuanzang relates that Kaniska defeated the Chinese in Central Asia and Chinese princes were sent as hostages. Territories were allotted to them in Panjab which were known as *Cina-bhukti*, an area that Xuanzang visited in the seventh century. Now it is a village Chiniyari near Amritsar, and Chiniot from *Cinakota*. The Chinese princes introduced two new fruits to India: the peach and the pear. They came to be known respectively as *cinani* and *cinarajaputra* which means "Peach the Chinese Princess" and "Pear the Chinese Prince".

The Yuechi rulers presented Sanskrit texts to the Chinese court in 2 BC. The Han Emperor Ming dreamt of a golden person. On enquiry from his courtiers he learnt that He was the Buddha. He sent ambassadors to the West (i.e. India) to invite Buddhist teachers. They returned with Dharmaraksa and Kasyapa Matanga. They arrived on white horses laden with scriptures and sacred relics. The first Buddhist monastery was built for them on Imperial orders and it came to be known as "The White Horse Monastery" (*Baimasi*). They wrote "The Sutra of 42 Sections" to provide a guide to the ideas of Buddhism and to the conduct of monks. This monastery exists to this day and the cenotaphs of the two Indian teachers can be seen in its precincts.

The translation of the first Sanskrit sutra into Chinese is by An Shigao in the middle of the second century. He was a Parthian prince turned Buddhist monk. He had abdicated the throne in favour of his uncle to take up the robes. A number of his translations have survived. He founded a school of translation of Sanskrit texts into Chinese, which was hailed by the Chinese literati as "unrivalled". Among his associates were *bhiksus* from Sogdiana (corresponding to modern Samarkand and Bokhara) known as *Uttarapatha* or "Northern India" in Chinese historical works. The name of Kang Seng-hui from Sogdiana stands out as a master of Sino-Indian literature and as one who preached in South China in a systematic manner. He even translated a short Ramayana into Chinese.

Kumarajiva, born of an Indian father and a Kuchean princess, educated in Kashmir and Kashgar, was a scholar of great reputation. He reached Changan in 401 and worked till AD412. He translated 106 works into Chinese. Most outstanding is his Chinese translation of the Sanskrit text entitled *Saddharma-pundarika-sutra*, known for short as the "Lotus Sutra". He is one of the most outstanding stylists of Chinese prose. He is the only Indian whose Chinese diction has been hailed over the centuries by Chinese men of letters.

The Lotus Sutra is at once a great work of literature and a profound religious classic, containing the core and culmination of Buddha's ageless teaching of compassion and the way to achieve liberation from suffering. For more than fourteen hundred years, it has been a rich source of themes for art. Generations of monks, nuns, and lay believers confident in the sutra's promise of spiritual reward for those who revere it and pay it homage have made opulent transcriptions of it, fashioned lavishly ornamented caskets for its preservation, and commissioned votive art depicting its narratives and religious teachings. The range of artistic expression inspired by the Lotus Sutra is astonishing.

The path of sutras: This route is the first and foremost pathway of texts and translators, of sutras and schools of thought, of the triumphs of Buddhism as the mental and material culture of East Asia. The development of Buddhist temple architecture, new stylistic features in Chinese that arose from translations of Buddhist texts, the Buddhist plurality of inhabited worlds as opposed to the Chinese earth-centred world view, and various elements of cultural transmission, opened up Sinocentrism to wider horizons. The several people inhabiting the route participated in the cultural exchange for a millennium. The earliest and most celebrated of the masters was the Parthian An Shigao who organised the first translation team, after his arrival at Luoyang in AD 148. An Xuan (AD 181), Tian-ti (AD 254), An Faxian, An Fajin (AD 281-306) are other Parthians who translated Sanskrit works. From Gandhara came Jnanagupta who translated the Kannon chapter of the Lotus Sutra (AD 561-78).

Kubha or Kabul, the capital of modern Afghanistan, sent the largest number of scholars whose Chinese translations are found in the *Tripitaka*. In AD 383 Gautama Sanghadeva arrived at Luoyang. Vimalaksa was another teacher of Kabul who was a great master of *Vinaya*. He was a teacher of Kumarajiva at Kucha and he came to China in AD 406. Sanghabhuti from Kabul translated three works in AD 381-85. In AD 404 Punyatara of Kabul translated the *Sarvastivada-vinaya*, together with Kumarajiva. Buddhayasas (AD 403-13), Dharmayasas (AD 407-15), Buddhajiva (AD 423), Dharmamitra (AD 424), Gunavarman (AD 431), Buddhatrata, Buddhapala (AD 676), Prajna (785-810) were from Kabul who took part in the translation of *vinaya*, *vaipulya* and other texts. The Chinese monk Zhiyan went to Kabul to obtain Sanskrit texts. He was a companion of Faxian on his journey to India. The Brahmana Wutao of Lampaka (Lamghan in Afghanistan) translated a *Dharani* of Amoghapasa in AD 700.

From Udyana or Swat, Vimoksasena came to China in AD 541. He was a descendant of the Sakya family of Kapilavastu. Narendrayasas (AD 557-68), Vinitaruci (AD 582), Meghasikha (AD 705), Danapala (AD 980) were from Udyana. Danapala translated 111 works, which are found in the *Tripitaka*.

Dharmanandin (AD 384) and Mitrasanta (AD 705) were monks from Tukhara. Yijing saw a Tukhara monastery in Eastern India, which had "been built long before by the people of that country for the accommodation of the Buddhist monks from Tukhara. The monastery was very rich and had an abundant supply of all necessities and comforts of life. No other monastery could surpass it in this respect."

The Yueh-chih were the earliest non-Indian translators of Sanskrit texts into Chinese. Lokaksema came to Luoyang in AD 164 and worked till AD 186, and has left 12 translations including the longer *Sukhavati-vyuha* (Nj 25) and *Aksobhyavyuha* (Nj 28). He is the third translator of sutras after Kasyapa Matanga and Dharmaraksa. He was followed by a Yueh-chih householder Qian in AD 220 who taught the heir apparent of the Wu dynasty. The *Tripitaka* has 49 works by him, which include the *Prajnaparamita* of 10,000 verses, the longer *Sukhavati-vyuha* and *Vimalakirti-nirdesa*. The greatest of Yueh-chih masters is

Dharmaraksa whose family had lived at Dunhuang. He was born around AD 230 at Dunhuang. He came to Luoyang in AD 266. He translated several sutras of the *Vaipulya* class for the first time. Ninety of his work: survive in the *Tripitaka*. He was called the "Bodhisattva from Dunhuang", and he contributed the most in the conversion of China to Buddhism, and made Changan the foremost Buddhist centre in China. A tireless itinerant preacher and ingenious translator, he integrated Buddhism in the intellectual and spiritual life and gave China its classics of Mahayana. He translated the Lotus Sutra for the first time, which later became the most venerated and fundamental scripture. He got Sanskrit manuscripts from Kashmir, Kucha, Khotan. His collaborators included two Kucheans, a Yueh-chih, a Khotanese, a Sogdian, and Indians. Various nationalities on the Sutra Route climaxed in his person. In AD 373 a Yueh-chih householder Shih-lun translated four works.

The first Kuchean monk who translated sutras at the White Horse Monastery in AD 257 was Yan. In AD 307-12 came Srimitra who translated the *Mahamayuri*. Towering over all is Kumarajiva whose translation of the Lotus Sutra is a marvel of transcreation. He translated a number of *Prajnaparamitas*. Sanskrit manuscripts used to come to China from Kucha, for instance, the *Avaivartika-cakra-sutra* was brought to Dharmaraksa by a Kuchean envoy. Sujiva, a member of the royal house of Kucha, came to China in AD 568 and introduced the seven keys of Indian music: *sadharita, kaisika, sadja-grama, sadja, sadava, pancama,* and *vrsabha.*

The Sogdian Kang Zhu translated a *sutra* at Luoyang in AD 187. In the next decade, came another compatriot Kang Meng-Xiang who translated at Luoyang six works, including a life of the Buddha, in AD 194-99. Half-a-century later Kang Sengkai Sahnavarman translated some works at the White Horse Monastery in Luoyang in AD 252. Kang Seng-hui the eldest son of the prime minister of Sogdiana, came to the capital of the Wu kingdom in AD 241. In 251 he began his work of translation. In AD 396 Kang Daohe translated a *sutra*, which is lost. Yijing gives a bio-sketch of Sanghavarman of Sogdiana who came to China around AD 656. He was ordered by Emperor Gaozong to go on a pilgrimage to India. In Chinese texts Sogdiana is a part of Northern India, Uttarapatha in Sanskrit, or its Chinese translation "Northern India" which extended from North-western India upto Sogdiana. This usage was common in India and China. Northern India in Chinese texts refers to north-west India, and regions beyond, in fact to the dominions of the erstwhile Kushan empire or Kusansahr.

While the Sogdians and their language had disappeared, European expeditions have discovered fragments of Sogdian texts near Dunhuang and in the Turfan depression. They reflect Chinese Buddhist literature from which they are predominantly translated. Majority of the translations date from the Tang dynasty's dimination in Central Asia (about AD 650-750).

Yijing speaks of the nobility and purity of the monk Changmin in the following words: "He sacrificed his life for the good of others. He was pure like a mirror, he was priceless like the jade of Khotan". Khotan was famed in China for its jade and *sutras*. In the eloquent panegyric of Visa Samgrama (P 2787) Khotan is called *Ratna-janapada*, "the Land of Jade". Zhu Shixing, the first Chinese to leave his country in quest of *sutras*, chose to journey to Khotan, famous for Sanskrit originals. He undertook this arduous journey in AD 260 and succeeded in locating the Sanskrit text of the *Prajnaparamita* in 25,000 verses. He had a copy made at Khotan. In AD 282 he sent his Khotanese disciple Punyadhana together with the Sanskrit manuscript to China. Written on birch bark leaves it was preserved in a Chinese monastery till the sixth century. In AD 291 the Khotanese Moksala and the Indian layman Zhu Shulan started its translation. It was given the title *Fangguangjing* "the sutra of the emission of light". True to its name, it was to play a dominant role in the formation of Buddhist thought in East Asia. In AD 296 the Khotanese Gitamitra arrived at Changan with a copy of the same scripture. In AD 401 the Chinese pilgrim Faxian spent three months at Khotan and speaks of the flourishing community of Mahayana. In the beginning of the fifth century Zhi Faling found the text of a shorter recension of the Avatamsaka sutras at Khotan. It was translated by Buddhabhadra in AD 422. In AD 689-91, the Khotanese monk Devaprajna translated six works. Siksananada of Khotan rendered several works, of which 16 are found in the Tripitaka. Reigning Empress Wu (684-705) sent a special envoy to khotan for the Sanskrit text of the *Avatamsaka* and organised its translation along with Siksananda for five years (AD 695-99). In AD 721 Zhiyan, a son of the king of Khotan, translated four works. Khotan was in the forefront of the transmission of Sanskrit sutras to China. A bilingual Sanskrit-Khotanese conversation roll, the only one of its kind, was discovered at Dunhuang. The conversation has the following sentences:

> "Have you equipment for the road or not.
>
> I do not like equipment for the road. A horse or two and I shall go.
>
> Have you books or not?
>
> I have some.

What is the book?

Sutra, Abhidharma, Vinaya, Vajrayana.

Among these what book (i.e. title) is there?"

This conversational piece is a clear indication of the frequent transmission of Sanskrit sutras from Khotan to China.

The standard Chinese expression for travelling monks means that they went primarily "to obtain the doctrine." The oldest Sanskrit manuscript of the Lotus Sutra in existence today, the so-called Kashgar manuscript, is a manuscript from Khotan and it has a colophon in the Khotanese language giving the names of donors and benefactor relations. History lives. We also know that Hyecho, a famous Korean monk of Siils returned from India via Anxi near Dunhuang in AD 723.

Khotan established its hegemony over the Southern Central Asian states in the first century AD by breaking the power of Yarkand (*Sha che*) and extended its authority upto Kashgar. Yarkand is mentioned in the Kasika commentary on the Sanskrit grammar of Panini. It had brilliant academic traditions. Kumarajiva was initiated into Mahayana by Suryasoma, the royal prince of Yarkand. Kumarajiva confessed that when he studied the Hinayana texts he considered stone to be wonderful and had not recognised gold.

Dao'an, the great master of "Fundamental Non-being" (ben-wu) was fully conversant with the concepts of emptiness versus phenomenal existence, or the relation between "Absolute Truth" and "Worldly Truth" as expounded in the Prajnaparamita. It reminds us of the convergence of the spiritual and the secular, or better their symbiosis, in the ideas of President Ikeda-san. They are the live hues of sensibility of the dawning century of an open society. Dao'an used to explain the entire text of Moksala's *Fangguangjing* twice a year at Changan. To enable him to complete and correct his understanding on many points, he obtained a Sanskrit original of the Astasahasrika from Turfan in AD 382. Turfan introduced systematisation of Abhidharma, till then unknown in China. The king of Turfan sent his royal priest and Abhidharma-expert Kumarabodhi to Changan in AD 382, as a member of a tribute mission to the Chinese court. The pilgrim Yijing mentions two monks of Turfan, Pi'an and Zhi'an who boarded a ship to India. They fell sick on board and died.

China has many grottoes that rival Ajanta in their synthesis of Indian suppleness, Hellenic elegance and Chinese grace. The Yungang caves were excavated between AD 414 and AD 520 under Wei rulers. Fiftythree caves remain till this day and contain over fiftyone thousand statues. It is one of the largest groups of stone cave temples in China. After the first Wei capital Datong was transferred to Luoyang in 494 work commenced on Longmen. Sculpting went on for 400 years till the Tang dynasty. It has around 1,00,000 statues; the highest is 55 feet high. It is a treasure-house of China's heritage of sculpture.

On the ancient Han frontiers, in the vast deserts of Inner Asia lies the sandy city of Dunhuang, the "Blazing Beacon". In this tiny oasis are the sacred grottos of *Qian Fo Dong* or "Caves of the Thousand Buddhas"(also named "Mogao caves"), carved into a rocky cliff rising aside a meandering rivulet. The walls of these caves are covered by murals of surpassing beauty, with the largest array of authentic paintings extending over several dynasties: a task of sixteen centuries. It has ever been the sacred oasis, one of the glories of Buddhism. A stone tablet of the Tang dynasty states that the first "Cave of Unequalled Height" was constructed by an Indian monk in AD 366, increasing upto 460 caves as faith continued to inspire radiant visions.

Mogao Caves: The Sutra Route is an age-old witness to the mingling of many ancient cultures of the Chinese, Iranians, Tokharians, Graeco-Romans, and Indians. The outstanding achievements of mankind are strewn along this path which culminates at Dunhuang, with its golden sands and blue skies. The first town was established here as a midway stop of the travel route in the first century BC at the time of the Han dynasty. It has seen Zhang Qian the Han ambassador to befriend the tribes of the West, Xuanzang the prince of pilgrims to procure sutras, Marco Polo on his return to Europe, and others, too many to specify. Ancient ballads tell the sad and lonesome life of Chinese soldiers on these remote borders of the west. The prosperity and stability of the country under Emperor Wu (AD 265-90) favoured the development of international trade and cultural exchange with improved agricultural techniques and irrigation. In the middle of the third century it became a main commercial centre with a mixed Chinese and Barbarian population.

At the grottoes of Dunhuang Pelliot went through 16,000 manuscripts crouched in a tiny space, working by the light of a candle or in his own words: "a philologist travelling at the speed of a racing car." He selected all the rolls that were of any importance for their contents or for their antiquity authenticated by dated colophons. The Pelliot Collection at Paris is a repository of historical data that will be under investigation for another century. Local legends in Central Asia claim that three hundred towns lie buried beneath the desert with great treasures protected by demons. The number 300 reminds of the *Tri-ratna* of Buddhism.

The Buddhist past of Serindia obliterated by the onslaught of Islam and abandoned to the all-devouring sand is being brought to light by a devoted band of scholars in Paris. The hand-written notes of Pelliot have been translated into Chinese at the Dunhuang Institute, such is their importance. The photographs of the chapel interiors taken by the Pelliot Mission have formed the principal basis for the international study of Dunhuang art. Dunhuang was the occidental bastion of China, the gateway to the Indo-Iranian and Roman worlds. It was the sentinel of a trail whence China gave the pear and peach to India, orange, rose, peony and chrysanthemum to the West. The first ever moveable printing types were found by Pelliot at Dunhuang and are dated by him to about 1300. This discovery is so momentous that even *Webster's New international Dictionary* records it under the entry "Type". Paul Pelliot's Notes on Marco Polo are a mine of information on historcial geography and on the etymologies of place-names which reveal lost dimensions. For instance Bokhara, with its modern Turkman form Buhara, is derived from Sanskrit *vihara* through its Sogdian, Uighur and Mongolian form *buqar*, a city whose skyline was dominated by the spires of Buddhist monasteries and hence this name. The city retained its sanctity and importance even after Islamisation. It was here that the first of the seven Sunni Imams, known as Imam Bukhari (810-70), was born in the 9th century. His collection of 7,000 *hadith* constitute the *Sahih* or true compilation which is regarded as the most authentic book of traditions by the Sunnis, held sacred only next to the Quran. What a dissembling coincidence that the Imam of Delhi is Imam Bukhari.

Divine musical instruments are played to which heavenly angels or apsaras dance in *Sukhavati* the resplendent Western Paradise of Amitabha. The flying goddesses from cave 321, which belongs to the golden age of Early Tang (618-741 AD) are unique. The sensuous tenderness of the body, the delicate flowing lines of drapery, the joyous colours, garments vibrating with the rhythm of space: mirror the vigorous culture of Serindia. Bearing in their hands trays of fruits and flowers, arrested as it were in their stately flight for a moment, they seem to bid the onlooker to accompany them into worlds of luminous beauty.

Chan was carried to China by Bodhidharma, the youngest son of a king of Kanchi and a follower of Prajnatara's eminent line. Palm leaves inscribed by Prajnatara have survived in Japan. Bodhidharma reached China early in the sixth century after long peregrinations. He had an audience with the noted patron of Buddhism, Emperor Liang Wu (502-550) of South China. He pointed out to the Emperor the futility of establishing monasteries, copying *sutras* and supporting monks. The historicity of Bodhidharma has been controversial. The first mention of Kanchi is in "*The Record of the Transmission of the Lamp*" compiled in 1002. The *Chan* tradition says that their doctrine was transmitted by an uninterrupted succession of twenty-eight Indian patriarchs: from Mahakasyapa the disciple of the Buddha, to Bodhidharma who brought it to China. Bodhidharma handed down the doctrine to Huike (traditional dates: 487-593), and from him through four other Chinese patriarchs to Huineng (639-716). Bodhidharma finally transmitted the "Seal of Mind" to Huike, who had cut off his arm to express the deep sincerity of his resolve. In the Kozanji ink scroll of the Six patriarchs of the Bodhidharma lineage, Huike kneels down in front of him. Blood gushes forth from the stump of his left arm, and the knife and the cut-off arm lie next to him on the ground. According to late accounts Bodhidharma crossed the Yangtze on a reed, and spent nine years in meditation in front of a rock wall at the Shao-lin monastery.

Bodhidharma had said that Daofu had acquired the skin, the nun Zongchi the flesh, and Taoyu the bone, and that Huike had penetrated into the marrow (the essence) of the doctrine. Like this statement, mist surrounds the evolution of the legend of Bodhidharma, which is as controversial as he himself must have been in life. The tradition is consistent in pointing out that he was a prince of Kanchi. His association with Tamil-speaking Kanchi is confirmed by the Japanese form of his name: Bodai-daruma, shortened to Daruma. The Tamil form is Bodhi-daruma; a modern painting at the Kanchi Seminar on *Dhyana* and Tantric Buddhism held on 10-15 March 1986, had the caption Bodi-daruma. The Japanese name Daruma goes back to an ancient popular name of the master. moreover, the tradition that the doctrine was transmitted from Mahakasyapa to Bodhidharma appears to have a basis. It seems that the modern Kacchapesvara Temple at Kanchi was a Buddhist sanctum in ancient times dedicated to Mahakasyapa the first patriarch of *Dhayana Buddhism.* To this day there are some Buddhist sculptures in this temple. The tradition of twenty-eight patriarchs of *Dhyana Buddhism* can be of Indian origin.

There are three basic scriptures of *Chan* (i) *Lankavatara-sutra*, (ii) *Vajracchedika Prajna-paramita* and (iii) the *Hymn to nilakantha Lokesvara.* Bodhidharma took Gunabhadra's translation of the *Lankavatara-sutra* as its scripture, as it was the only available Chinese version at the time.

The "Record of the Succession of the Dharma-treasure", a history of *Chan* Buddhism discovered from the Dunhuang Caves, says that the first patriarch of the *Lankavatara* as representing the Dharma-treasure was Bodhidharma who revealed the inner meaning of the *Sutra.* The connection of Bodhidharma and *Lankavatara* is thus intimate. *Lankavatara* can refer to Kanchi. It is stated in the life of Xuanzang by Huili: "Kanchipura is the sea-port of South India for Ceylon, the voyage to which takes three days". Further, subtle nuances point to Kanchi as the native place of Bodhidharma and as the home of *Chan.* The tea ceremony ends with the banging of the lid on to the teapot. When I enquired of my Japanese host, Prof. Chikyo Yamamoto, he said: "Master Bodhidharma used to slam the lid in times of yore". How Indian! I was sure once again: It must go back to Bodhidharma.

Chan adepts reject the written word and claim an unwritten doctrine, transmitted from mind to mind, where the heart of man directly sees into its own nature. Yet, when Huineng was invested as the Sixth Patriarch, the corridor was painted with scenes from the *Lankavatara*, besides the paintings of the Five Patriarchs Transmitting the Robe of Bodhidharma and the Dharma as a testimony for future generations. Bodhidharma had sanctioned the lineage of five Chinese Patriarchs of *Chan* in a *gatha* that ran: "one flower with five petals is unfolded". In its earlier phases *Chan* Buddhists were mainly a kind of *Lankavatara* sect. The teachings of *pratyatma-gati-gocara* of the *Lankavatara* provide a philosophical basis for the transcendental intuition of *Chan.* In the *Lankavatara*, Buddha tells Mahamati to attain a state of inner realisation (*pratyatma-gocara*) and when one has *pratyatma-jnana* one is enlightened. The *Lankavatara* is unique in emphasising that life is experiencing truth: seeing must be living and living seeing. The *Lankavatara* certifies the existence of the Buddha-mind in each of us and provides *Chan* in doctrinal base. The *Lankavatara* forbids meat-eating and recounts eight reasons for abstaining from meat. To take the lives of animals and eat their flesh is like eating our own. Eating meat is spiritual pollution. To this day, food in *Chan* monasteries is vegetarian. While *Chan* stands on its own, the *Lankavatara* confirms it and is also its philosophical essence.

The *Lankavatara* was highly philosophical and abstruse to the Chinese. During the time of the Sixth Patriarch Huineng the emphasis shifted to the *Vajracchedika* which was more understandable than the recondite *Lankavatara.* Besides meditation, painting was the other forte of *Chan. Prajnaparamita* lent itself admirably to the tenor of *Chan* painting. The *Chan* masters of Mid Tang were distinguished by their non-conformist techniques of painting. Wang Mo "Ink Wang" painted landscapes starting from configurations of ink splashes, the manner of *Chan* painters who delighted in expressing their sincerity in trans-logical forms like a "one stroke" Bodhidharma (Jap. Ippitsu Daruma by Shokai Reiken 1315-1396). The dictum *rupam eva sunyata sunyata eva rupam* of the *Vajracchedika inspired Chan* art which vanished into nowhere, with its diaphanous water colours and empty spaces interfering with the coherence of thought and form. A painting shimmered in meditation. *Chan* was deeply steeped in the *Prajnaparamita* philosophy of *sunyata.*

The *Mahaprajnaparamita-sutra* is called "the king of sutras which protect the state". *Sutras* have been copied, chanted and expounded with the belief that the merit of these acts would stop calamities in the state and attain peace and security.

The fifth chapter of the *renwangjing* is entitled *Huguo* (Japanese *Gokoku)* "protecting the country". Tathagata says: "You, sixteen Great Kings, must practise the Rite of Protecting the Country, and you must keep, read and explain this *sutra.* If in future ages the kings of countries wish to protect their kingdoms and to protect their own bodies, they too must act in the same way."

The Tang dynasty established an extensive empire and under it Buddhism reached its apogee by the induction of *Vajrayana* texts. The grandeur of their ritual ensured unprecedented popularity in the imperial household, in the great families of the realm as well as among common people. *Sutras* were used for "the benefit and advantage of the state". The logistic problems involved in distant military campaigns in Central Asia were resolved with success through Vajrayana rituals. It would suffice to cite the strategic military role of Vajrayana rituals of Vaisravana who was venerated in China and Japan as a god of war. T1248 by Amoghavajra gives a *dharani* entitled *Dharani of Devaraja* of the north. Vaisravana watches over armies for protecting the *Dharma*: If one pronounces this *dharani* before an image of Vaisravana which represents the Devaraja under his terrible aspect, he sends his third son Nada to the side of those who direct their troops for the protection of their country; or still, if one covers the armour plate of his image with the powder of gold and offers him perfumes, flowers and other offerings while pronouncing the *dharani* a hundred thousand times, he himself takes the command of his celestial troops and goes to support his devotee, to whom he assures victory; or furthermore, if one recites non-stop day and night he delegates his heir-prince Dokken at the head of celestial troops; or still one can suspend his image on a staff and carry it as a banner fifteen paces in front of the army which will render the enemy ineffectual. The *Vaisravana-kalpa* (T 1247) by Amoghavajra, specifically consecrated to Nada, adds in the colophon that during the "grand troubles of the Five Kingdoms", one tried in vain during eight months all sorts of other ceremonies. Only the rite prescribed in this text proved efficacious for stabilising the country. It refers to the troubles which burst forth in Central Asia at the end of the reign of Emperor Xuanzong during the Tang dynasty and by the "Five Kingdoms" are intended the five foreign peoples who besieged the city of Anxi. The incident is reported in details in the "*Ritual of Vaisravana*" by Amoghavajra (T 1249). In AD 742, the Five Kingdoms of Seiban=Tibet, Daiseki=Arabs, Koko=Sogdians, and others besieged the city of Anxi. On the second day of the second moon, a report was presented to the Emperor demanding relief troops. The Emperor said to master Yijing: "Master! the city of Anxi is besieged by Arabs and others and it requires troops. But as it is situated at a distance of 12,000 leagues, it will take eight months for my troops to arrive there, and I do not know what to do". Yijing replied: "Why does Your Majesty not invoke to your aid the Devaraja of the north, Vaisravana with his celestial troops". "How can I invoke him?" "By the intervention of the Serindian monk Amoghavajra". The Emperor sent word to this monk who invited him to provide an incense-burner and follow him to the monastery. The monk pronounced a *dharani* from the *Renwangjing* (tr. by Amoghavajra) 27 times. The Emperor then saw hundreds of soldiers in arms and the monk explained to him that they were the troops of Dokken the second son of Vaisravana, who had come to take charge before departure for Anxi. In the fourth month he received a report from Anxi, declaring that, on the very day of the ceremony they saw appearing in the north-east of the city, the envelopings of an obscure haze, of giants dressed in armour plates of gold. They heard an uproar of drums and of horns, and experienced a violent trembling of the earth. The troops of the Five Kingdoms, frightened, retired to their camps, where rats of gold gnawed the strings of their bows and of their traps. A voice in the sky enjoined to spare the old and the feeble, who could not flee away. Then Vaisravana manifested himself in person on the northern gate of the city. They drew his image which was appended to the report addressed to Emperor".

The first Tang Emperor Gaozu (AD 618-627) received from Fu Yi his seventh memorial in AD 626 requesting a ban on Buddhism. His Councillor Peiji reminded him: "O Your Majesty! formerly when you raised the righteous armies, you promised before the Three Jewels that you would open the doors of the profound school (Buddhism) if you were enthroned. Now, the world has come under your benevolent administration and you possess the wealth of the four seas. If you want to accept the words of [Fu] Yi, it will affect your past virtues and foster what is evil in you." Thus, profundity of Buddhism lay embedded into the very foundations of the Tang state. A natural consequence was the quest for Tantric texts in India and elsewhere, their translation into Chinese and the efficacious utilisation of their ritual. It led to the progressive development and continuous spread of *Tantras* in China, spurred on by periodic Chinese reverses in Central Asia.

In AD 629, or the first month of the third reignal year of Emperor Taizong (AD 627-649), an Imperial edict ordered Buddhist monks to recite the *Renwangjing* in the national capital on the 27th of every month to pray for the welfare of the nation. The government undertook to supply all the materials for the ceremonies.

Armies, manuscripts and scholars are allies in China. In the beginning of the seventh century after a military expedition to Champa, the Chinese army returned with a rich booty of 1,350 Buddhist manuscripts among other things. They were all of Indian origin.

During the Tang dynasty Indian astronomers served on the Imperial Board for the purpose. Three Indian astronomical schools of Gautama, Kasyapa and Kumara were known at Changan in the seventh century. More accurate calendars were prepared anew by Indian astronomers. Sanskrit mathematical works were translated into Chinese which are lost.

In the seventh and eighth centuries, scientific works were known as "Brahmana books" in China. Books with the prefix "Brahmana" dealt with astronomy, calendrical science and mathematics. Unfortunately, since all were subsequently lost, one cannot now estimate what they had contributed. It is certain, however, that during these two centuries Brahmana scholars were employed in the Astronomical Bureau at the Chinese capital. Kasyapa Xiaowei, who was there shortly after AD 650, was occupied with the improvement of the calendar, as were most of his later Indian successors. The greatest of them was Gautama Siddha who became President of the Board. It seems that these brahmanas brought an early form of trigonometry, a technique which was then developing in their country.

Though most of their writings failed to survive, something more should be said here of these Indian astronomers and calendar-experts of the Sui and Tang. The story begins with the books of Brahmana astronomy such as the *Polomen tianwenjing*, mentioned in the Sui Shu bibliography, but long lost. These must have been circulating about AD 600. During the following two centuries we meet with the names of a number of Brahmana astronomers resident at the Chinese capital.

The first was Gautama Lo, who produced two calendar systems in AD 697 and AD 698, but the greatest was Gautama Siddha who compiled the *Kaiyuan Zhanjing* about AD 729, in which a zero symbol and other innovations appeared. It is a work of great importance often mentioned. In any case the paradox remains that we owe to the Brahmana Gautama Siddha the greatest collection of ancient and mediaeval Chinese astronomical fragments.

Vajrayana masters, Subhakara, Vajrabodhi and Amoghavajra, arrived in China and translated the major texts of their school into Chinese during the reign of Emperor Xuanzong. Hence it is important to evaluate the varied dimensions of his glorious rule.

Himself a poet, the Emperor welcomed poets like Li Bo (701-762), and Du Fu (712-770). Existing forms of poetry were brought to the highest perfection in the period. The Tang dynasty was to be most famous for its poetry. "Poets and painters contributed to the elegance of his magnificent court ceremonial." The Tang lyric poetry was inspired by the cosmic reverie of Taoism and the universal impermanence of earthly things, evoked by Buddhism. It is very apparent in the poems of Li Bo. A clear prose style of the essayists developed. "New forms of sentences make their appearance in prose writing, with new pictures and similes brought from India through the medium of Buddhist translations."

In the domain of painting lay the principal achievement of Tang. The six fundamental laws of painting laid down by painter Xiehe were drawn from the Indian *sadanga* canons. Central Asian monks were continually pouring into China as decorators of Buddhist temples. The famous Tang painter Wu Daozi was strongly influenced by Central Asian techniques. As a pious Buddhist he painted pictures for temples. In such an environment the *mandalas* must have been welcome as new visual types of a complex and hence advanced idiom in Buddhist painting. Sculptures in stone and bronze, excellent fabrics, finest lacquer, high quality porcelain had the active encouragement of the Emperor.

The administration was strong, and schools were established in every village. Fond of music the Emperor founded a Music School in 714 to train musicians in the fashionable foreign-influenced music. The Emperor selected an elite of 300 best musicians and trained them personally in the Agreeable Spring Court of the Imperial Pear Garden. The Emperor is honoured as the patron saint of the theatre. The members of the Left Jiaofang school were dancers, those of the Right were singers. The Buddhist scenes of song and dance at Dunhuang evoke memories of foreign dancers who are bare on the upper portion of the body: "Women ceased to veil themselves as of old."

A few hundred Indian teachers went to China from the first to the twelfth century. They have bequeathed a legacy of about 3,000 works translated from Sanskrit into Chinese. We may mention a couple of them: Gunavarman a prince of Kashmir who reached Nanjing in AD 431; Buddhabhadra, born at Nagarahara, claimed direct descent from Amrtodana, the uncle of Lord Buddha. Nagarahara is modern Jalalabad. He died in China in AD 429. Bodhiruci was from south India. A Chinese envoy came to the Chalukya court in AD 692 to invite Bodhiruci. He reached China in AD 693 by sea and translated Sanskrit works. One of the last outstanding Indian teachers in China was Dharmadeva of Nalanda. He was received by the Chinese Emperor in AD 973.

The Chinese pilgrims to India like Faxian, Xuanzang, Wang Xuanze, Yijing, and others have bequeathed historic records which are invaluable for the understanding of the cultural and political history of India. Yijing has left short bio-sketches of 60 eminent Chinese monks who visited India. In 964, three hundred Chinese monks started for India, to pay Imperial homage to the holy places. They set up five Chinese inscriptions at Bodhgaya. One of the inscriptions ends: "I now make use of the eulogy of the marvellous excellence of the three bodies and the sculptures that I have executed of the extraordinary acts of the Thousand Buddhas, in order to secure the prosperity of the glorious sovereign of my country and to offer to him for many years a holy longevity." Edouard Chavannes brought to light these five Chinese inscriptions at Bodhgaya, the only ones in India. They were erected in the 10th and 11th centuries to pay imperial homage of China to the holy places of India in moving language. Unswallowed by devastating centuries, they are with us still: alas! cenotaphs to the splendid creativity of a millennium smothered by fundamentalism. Chavannes translated into French the lives and voyages of over sixty Chinese pilgrims to India written by Yijing. His translation of the voyage of Songyun to Udyana and Gandhara (518-22) and of the itinerary of Wukong (751-90) are primary sources for Indian history. For wider dissemination they deserve to be translated into English. The four volumes of his *Cinacents contes et apologues*, running to over 1600 pages, are a treasury of Indian story literature, extracted from the Chinese *Tripitaka*. It is a *sine qua non* for the history of our literature and for our folklore. Like several other French classics on Indology and allied disciplines, it needs to be done into English.

Indian scholars were honoured guests as late as the Ming. Pandita Sahajasri led a twelve-member Indian Buddhist delegation to China. He was received by the Yuan and Ming emperors in 1364 and 1371. He was from a *ksatriya* family of Kapilavastu. His status and privilege placed him in a position to soften the autocratic temper of the emperor. Recently a blue and white jar of the Xuande period (1426-1435) has been discovered with Sanskrit mantras all around: *diva svasti svasti madhyandine*... It seeks good fortune by day, by midday, by night: at all times.

The long and time-honoured contacts have been matured over time, reverberating in a subtle interweave of thought, ritual, legend and art. They are symbolic of the depths of our hearts. India and China were linked by a route of thought, the way of cultural exchange, the Sutra Route and not only the Silk Route. Ideas, imperia and emporia; intellectuals, generals and traders; monks, marshals and merchants; cassocks, armour and silk were all pilgrims on this route bringing together many races in companionship. Fabrics, fruits, vegetables, and technologies enriched life. This spirit of an "open society" was the bridge of dreams floating under an open sky.

M.N. DESHPANDE

20

MY TRYST WITH CHINESE ART

Before I started my dialogue book I had undertaken the study of the Svatamber Jain Canon under my late revered teacher H.D. Sankalia. This first introduction to a monastic religion was the first step that ushered me into further studying of Buddhism. It was in August 1944 that I had the opportunity of going to Taxila (where flourished in ancient times an important Buddhist University) to join the Indian School of Field Archaeology started by Sir R.E. Mortimer Wheeler to learn new excavation technique. On my way to Taxila, I availed myself the opportunity to study the Buddhist relics of Kushana period at Mathura and the Indo-Greek art of north-west India in the museum at Lahore. During my three months long training in the new techniques of archaeology I had the good fortune of visiting the monasteries in and around Taxila. I could study the stupa and Vihara architecture, iconography along with the rich collections of Buddhist antiquities in the Taxila Museum. These opportunities opened my eyes and gave me a new vision of Buddhist art and architecture.

As luck would have it, I was absorbed in the Archaeological Survey of India and had sample facilities to study Buddhist monuments in the Deccan such as the caves at Karle, Bhaja, Bedsa, Kanheri and Junnar together with Buddhist centres like Balabhi in Saurashtra as well as Jain caves in that area. It was in the year 1950 that I had the good fortune of being posted at Aurangabad and could study extensively the caves of Ajanta-Ellora, Pitalkhora and Aurangabad caves and obtaining a deeper understanding of the Buddhist art and philosophy. The Buddhist art of Western India commences around the middle of 2nd century BC and reached full development along with sculpture and paintings right from the 6th century AD. It was in the 1970s that I could visit Bamiyan (Afghanistan) and study Gandharan art, etc. in Kabul Museum through the relics preserved therein.

I travelled a long way as a professional archaeologist till I became the Director General of the Archaeological Survey of India from which post I retired. Amidst the innumerable professional opportunities and hazards, I had the pleasure to have a peep into Chinese art, particularly Chinese Buddhist art through books and exhibits. I developed a great fascination towards the culture and art of our great neighbour — China, but had no opportunity of visiting that great country.

Fortune smiled on me when I reached my seventies. The Indira Gandhi National Centre for the Arts (IGNCA), New Delhi, under Dr. Kapila Vatsyayan started a collaboration with the Dunhuang Academy of China. Prof. Tan Chung of Jawaharlal Nehru University was an honorary consultant of IGNCA and he was the man in charge of the collaboration. In 1991, IGNCA had some very important programmes in the Indian capital. It first organized an international seminar on "Cave Art of India and China", and, then, put up a very impressive exhibition of the wall paintings of Mogao Grottoes. For these two events, the Director and a life-long curator of Dunhuang art, Prof. Duan Wenjie, visited New Delhi and stayed for a month along with his senior colleague, Prof. Shi Weixiang. Dr. Vatsyayan was so kind to put me on the job to organize the Seminar on "Cave Art of India and China", which had the honour of Dr. Shankar Dayal Sharma, then, Vice-President of India, to preside over the concluding session. Through the participation of work for the Seminar and also for the Exhibition, I began to have my tryst with Chinese art, as it were.

In August, 1994, Dr. Kapila Vatsyayan asked me to join the IGNCA delegation to China to participate in the international seminar at Dunhuang. During that seminar, I and Prof. Tan Chung helped the Dunhuang Academy to organize a follow-up seminar on "Cave Art of India and China". I also had the rare privilege to go around to see the fascinating wall paintings of the Mogao Grottoes.

Before proceeding to China I had worked on the Kanheri Grottoes near Bombay, its 100 caves making the biggest Buddhist cave art in India. I also worked on the seven groups of caves at Junara. But the Dunhuang cave art is so enormous with 45,000 square metres of wall paintings and 2,415 stucco statues of Buddhas and Bodhisattvas spread among 492 caves, just beyond comparison with what we have in India. When I entered the Dunhuang caves in the company of Prof. Tan Chung, Dr. Radha Banerjee and Dr. Baghyalakshmi, all from IGNCA, I felt as if I was having a miniature *Vishva Rupa Darshana* (cosmic vision). In fact, the moment I saw Dunhuang Caves I fell in love with it, and I wished that I was not of the age of 74 but at least two or three decades younger, so that I could have enough energy to work on it. Hence, I offer my sincere advice to my young scholars among Indian archaeologists and art historians to make it their career to study Dunhuang and to have an indepth comparison of this wonderful art treasure with its Indian counterpart.

Because of the agglomeration of sand and earth in the hill, the Mogao caves were not suitable for exquisite sculpture. But the creators of Dunhuang art, lasting as long as a dozen centuries, converted the environs into magnifient canvases for frescoes. In many caves, I saw everywhere, exceptd the floor, being covered with excellent paintings without an inch of space to spare. In some Sui and Tang caves of the vintage of 7th, 8th centuries I saw how the space of the cave was fully utilized. On one side of a cave there is a kind of stage on which there are stucco statues. The Buddha sits in the centre, with the two main disciples, Kasyapa and Ananda, standing on both sides as if to escort him. Then, the Buddha-disciples trio are flanked by two Bodhisattvas, mostly Avalokitesvara and Manjusri. Some times, even this quinquepartite group is flanked by two warriors at the extremes. In Ajanta, we have the Buddha flanked on the one hand by a Padmapani, and on the other by a Vajrapani. The Chinese seemed to have treated Padmapani a grade higher than Vajrapani, hence the Vajra warriors stand a degree further away from the Buddha than the Padmapani doubles.

In the background, there is always a fine painting which usually depict the life story of the Buddha. There is Mayadevi's dream of the elephant and Prince Siddhartha's leaving the palace. Prof. Tan Chung pointed out some strangle figures painted just at the back of the Buddha statue, and told me that the Dunhuang scholars generally identified these as the "thunder gods". I looked at the scenario and the picture of the Ajanta "Maravijiya" (victory over the devils) came to my mind. I said they could be symbols of the *mara* (devil). After saying that I hastened to add that when painting the story of the Buddha, four episodes are must: Mayadevi's dream leading to the birth of the Prince, the Prince's departure from the palace in search of bodhi (enlightenment), Buddha's overcoming the seduction, detraction, and threat of the devils — the "Maravijiya" — and, finally, his attaining the enlightenment. "Where is the 4th episode, then?" asked Prof. Tan Chung. Yes, nowhere is it painted on the wall. Suddenly I discovered that the sitting Buddha statue was in *Bhumisparsha mudra*, with his right hand touching the ground. So, here it was. How cleverly this composition was constructed, I thought, combining background wall painting with foreground stucco statue! Later, Prof. Tan Chung repeatedly told this little "discovery" to fellow seminarists many of whom felt it a new revelation. Prof. Tan Chung, then, observed that many of the already fixed identifications in Dunhuang art which had all been done by the Chinese scholars (some with suggestions from European scholars many decades back) could be re-opened for fresh reconstruction and reidentification. And a fruitful exercise of this kind had to involve Indian experts. I felt inclined to agree with him. Indeed, Chinese can learn many things from their Indian counterparts and vice-versa. There is a need for increasing contacts and exchange of expertise between the two peoples.

The Dunhuang experience was a golden moment in my life and this has set me thinking how Buddhist thought and culture were received in China in the beginning of the Christian era. About 500 hundred years earlier the royal prince Siddhartha had left his palace and became a *paribrajaka* and wandered from place to place, and teacher to teacher to find out the key to the elimination of *dukkha*. China was a similar country as India and her saints had also pondered over such humanistic problems. Confucius (551-497 BC) had left identical teachings. Laozi believed in individual salvation, and his Tao was so similar to Buddha's *dharma* that the early Chinese Buddhists used the word "dao" to translate "dharma". Also, Laozi's "wuwei" could be compared with Buddha's "sunyata".

Buddha embarked on a radical path and he wanted all his fellows to take to ascetic life. He did not encourage philosophical discussion or theorising about metaphysical problems because at the roots of human misery was *maya* (desire) and greed. Once the eight-fold path (right view, right aspiration, right speech, right action, right livelihood, right effort, right mindfulness and right meditation) is achieved the human problems are solved. He had no god to appease nor any sacrifice to perform. His teaching was entirely ethical in nature and he believed in substantiality of life. Prof. R.B. Pandey puts this in a very profound sentence, viz. "as logic sprang full grown from the head of Buddha". He did not ask any of his disciples to think of him as their guide, the disciples should follow the Dharma that he had practised, and only his doctrine could guide the people (*Majjhima Nikaya*).

Kapilavastu was the place where Buddha was born. The place name tells us that this was perhaps the place from where the sage Kapila had propounded the *sankhya* philosophy, having *gyana* and *yoga* as the two important elements of his philosophy. Buddha likewise laid emphasis on *Samayaka gyana* and meditation. In *Majjhima Nikaya* he demonstrated inhalation and exhalation and asked the monks to practise it with intensitiy. He had even asked his son Rahula to practise cultivation of mindfulness and achieve tranquillity of the body and control of the mind, and freedom from thought and transforming the consciousness into impermanence of illumination (*bodhi*). The monasteries like Dunhuang came into existence from 4th century AD and there must be a very vigorous period to digest when Indian Bhikshus spread Buddha's message of compassion for the happiness and welfare of beings. This organized ethical religious code was gladly accepted by the Chinese people and their rulers. From the 4th century onwards we find that Buddhist monks from China came to India for study. Among them the names of Faxian and Xuanzang are well known. They carried home with them hundreds of Buddhist manuscripts which were translated into Chinese by learned and dedicated Bhikshus, like Kumarajiva, Bodhidharma, Paramartha who went from India to China to propagate the new faith. The glowing account of how Xuanzang lived at Nalanda city and returned to his country having acquired complete mastery of the tenets of Buddhism is fascinating.

The other important factor leading to dissemination of Buddhism outside was the spread of Indian art and painting side by side with Buddha dhamma itself. Ajanta was the fountainhead of inspiration. It was during the days of Ashoka that calculated efforts to spread Buddhist religion started in earnest. Ashoka had sent his son Mahindra and daughter Sangamittra to Ceylon and, perhaps, some artists from Kashmir went to China from Central Asia and planted the roots of Indian art there. But in China, not only Indian but Sogdian and Greek elements also intermingled and created an art vocabulary which needs to be studied indepth by Indian art historians and archaeologists.

It is very necessary to train our scholars with good grounding in Pali and Buddhism to learn Chinese and spend years in Chinese universities, studying sculpture, paintings and architecture on the one hand, and Buddhist scriptures on the other. This should be a long term project. If the Indian scholars are expected to have a firm grounding in Chinese Buddhist art, they should endeavour to follow a long course of study extending over many many years to acquire specialisation. The study of Buddhism is gaining popularity in the universities of United States and Europe, India should not lag behind in this academic pursuit. With the revival of Buddhism in India, China and other countries it is all the more necessary that a very concerted effort is made to study ancient Buddhist texts and Buddhist art in both India and China.

D.C. BHATTACHARYYA

21

ICONS OF CULTURAL LINKAGE

Buddhist iconographical texts often refer to *Mahacina* as the source of some distinct form of the iconography of the images of divinities. For instance, in the *Sadhanamala* there is the description of a form of the goddess Tara, composed by one *Sasvatavajra*, which the latter refers to as the *Mahacinakrama* form[1], Both in the text of the *Sadhanamala* and in the colophon; *Mahacinakrama* evidently implies that the iconographic form concerned was popular in the geographical dispensation of *Mahacina*, and, as the suffix *Krama* indicates, the composer of the *sadhana* introduced the aforesaid popular form to the Indo-Nepalese Buddhist pantheon. This will mean that *Mahacina* was a land of much iconographical potential holding authenticity and prestige.

An interesting illustrated manuscript of the *Astasahasrika-Prajnaparamita*, dated A.D. 1015 and now in the collection of the Cambridge University Library, there are several illustrations of Buddhist divinities along with inscribed labels not only disclosing the identity of the relevant images, but also associating most of them with a topographical placement. A parallel version of this manuscript, but bearing the date A.D. 1071, is there in the holding of the Asiatic Society, Calcutta. Interestingly, this manuscript contains the illustration of a male divinity with the accompanying inscribed label reading: *Mahacine Manjughosah.*[2] The inscription may have either of these two meanings: (i) Manjughosa (a well-known form of the Bodhisattva Manjusri) while he was at *Mahacina;* (ii) Manjughosa as he is known in *Mahacina*. In both the interpretations, *Mahacina* evidently bears a geographical connotation, and that being the case, the second of the above interpretations seems to be more valid because the objective of the *Astasahasrika-Prajnaparamita* manuscript concerned ostensibly was to prepare a visual documentation of the distinctive iconographical forms of divinities which had acquired celebrity at the various shrines and centres of Buddhism.[3]

The expression *Mahacina* definitely refers to a land that could be regarded as "Greater China", and not the "mainland" of China. Stael Holstein discovered from the lamaistic establishment, *Pao-hsiang Lou* (*Buaxianglou*), in the city of Peiping (Beijing) in China as many as 787 Buddhist bronze images belonging to the pantheonistic community of Chinese Buddhism. These objects of visual representations were studied, along with a series of photographs from three manuscripts in Chinese, admirably by Walter Eugene Clark, and he published the valuable materials in two volumes under the title of *Two Lamaistic Pantheons.* Clark recovered the Sanskrit names of the images from their Chinese counterparts. These materials not only throw significant light on the inter-relationship between Indian and Chinese Buddhist iconography, but also offer information of much relevance in the history of Buddhist iconography in general. It is interesting to note that Clark's list of images contains the names like *Cina Tara* and *Cinakrama Tara*,[4] and none of the images bears the epithet *mahacinakrama*. It seems that the topographical epithets *cina* and *mahacina* were two distinct connotations.

That *cina* and *mahacina* referred to two separate geographical concepts is known from various other sources. Here we can refer to a glaring evidence to put the point across. In the *Laghukalacakrarajatantra-Tika* there is the prescription for the composition of the canonical texts in the languages, and perhaps also in the scripts, prevalent in the respective lands. It has the following categorical statement: *Tatha bhotavisaye yanatrayam bhotabhasaya likhitam / cine cinabhasaya / mahacine mahacinabhasaya.*[5] Here three distinct geographical territories, viz., *Bhotavisaya, Cina* and *Mahacina,* are mentioned. This leaves no doubt that *Cina* and *Mahacina* are two separate entities in terms of the geo-cultural identities. *Cina* is positively the present-day China, and *Mahacina* is the land where Chinese culture commuted notwithstanding the orthodoxy of the geo-political boundary. In that case, what is known as Central Asia or the Chinese Turkistan should really be that land referable by the expression *Mahacina* or Greater China.

However, there is a wrongly upheld belief that *Mahacina* stands for Tibet. In the above-mentioned statement of the *Laghukalacakrarajatantra-Tika,* there is the mention of a land called *Bhotavisaya* which is distinct from *Mahacina* and *Cina.* The *sadhana* No. 127 of the *Sadhanamala* is ascribed to the authorship of Nagarjuna, and, as per the further information given in the colophon, the iconographical concepts delivered in the *sadhana* concerned are derived from the tradition of the *Bhota* country *(aryya-nagarjjunapadaih bhotesu uddhritamiti)*.[6] In this *sadhana* there is the description of three different presentations (2-, 4-, and 8-armed) of the Ekajata form of the goddess Tara. Since all these presentations are quite distinct from the form of the Mahacinakrama Tara of the *Sadhanamala*, referred to earlier, it seems that *Bhota* and *Mahacina* represent two distinct geo-cultural entities. *Bhota*, in fact, is Tibet and Bhutan forming one cultural unit. The contribution of the Tibet-Bhutanese tradition of *Bon-Po* culture is of much significance in the evolution of Tantric Buddhist iconography and rituals.[7] In the above-mentioned colophon statement of the *Sadhanamala* the reference evidently is to Tibet *(Bhota)*, and not to Central Asia *(Mahacina)*.

That *Bhota* is Tibet, and *Mahacina* is Central Asia or other than Tibet, can be known from other authorities as well. It is well-known that the Lamaistic form of Buddhism is primarily pertinent to Tibet. In a Nepalese Buddhist work entitled *Tantratattvasamuccaya*, there is an interesting observation which is as follows: *Nepaladese sakyanam sasvatatantram / bhotadese lamanam kambojatantram / cinadese cininam pitatantram / mahacinadese vratyanam misratantram / simhaladese naganam sthaviratantram* / etc.[8] Here the people of the *Bhota* country is associated with the *Kambojatantra*, and they are called as the *lamas*, and they seem to be distinct from the *vratyas* who are associated with *Mahacina* and with the *Misratantra*. The ascription of the *Kambojatantra* to *Bhota* or Tibet is interesting because Amritananda, the residency Pundit in Nepal in the nineteenth century under Brian Hodgson, associates the Lamaistic Buddhists (of Tibet) with the *Kambojadesa* in the following statement in his *Dharmakosa-Samgraha: Asmakam nepaliyanam bauddhanam mate evameva / athaca kesancit kutracit kincidbhedo bhavisyatyeva / paranca kambo jadesiyairlamabhidnanair bauddhairnaiti riti/* etc.[9] In fact, cultural nomenclatures differed not merely on the change of time, but also on the personal interpretation of the individuals looking at a culture.

However, it is pertinent to mention that the reference to any culture does not necessarily imply its relevance only to the political boundary of the country of its origin. It is understood that because of the predominantly Chinese cultural traits, the presence of which is not the result of any force or motive, the vast land of Central Asia has been referred to by the ancients as *Mahacina* or Greater China, and as Chinese Turkistan by the present-day chroniclers. It is true that it is almost impossible to single out the Chinese features from the cultural complex of Central Asia. But the fact remains that the overall Chinese ethos there cannot escape notice. Minute and detailed analysis shows that the Indian, Persian, Turkish, and Mongol elements are also present there in various modes and manners. Central Asia seems to be the land where various cultures seem to have stepped out of their respective playgrounds in order to revel in a composite game of give and take.[10]

In view of the stepping out from the boundaries of the orthodoxy, and because of the participation in activities bereft of the consideration of who contributes what, Central Asian culture has been referred to by the *Tantratattvasamuccaya*, mentioned above, as *misratantra*, i.e., the amalgamated system, and the people involved in it as the *vratyas* or the disconnected ones. Once one steps out of the protected realm of orthodoxy, one gets disconnected from the concerns of the mainstream culture. That is exactly what might have happened with the mendicants, monks, and itinerant travellers and merchants traversing Central Asia through the so-called Silk Route. In their every footstep in the journey between China and India through Khotan, and in the reverse travel, they got themselves distanced from the culture of the land of the origin, and they adapted themselves to the other itinerant cultural traits that they happened to meet *en route*. Being disconnected or distanced from the mainstream culture, they verily were the *vratyas*, and because of their adopting alien cultural traits during transitory meetings with fellow itinerants, they imbibed a mixed culture which admittedly can be called the *misratantra*. It is in the fitness of things that the *Tantratattvasamuccaya*, referred to above, has characterized the culture of *Mahacina* or Central Asia as the *misratantra* followed by the *vratya* people.

The composite character of the art and iconography of the Central Asian centres cannot escape notice. Several interesting examples illustrating this point can be cited. In a number of drawings and banner paintings from Dunhuang one notices the representation of a bearded male figure holding in one of the hands a *stupa* or *caitya*-like item.[11] The represented divinity has rightfully been identified as one of the directional guardian deities *(maharajika* or *dikpalas)* referred variously as Vaisravana, Jhambala, Dhanada or Kubera in the Buddhist and Brahmanical parlance. But the ascription of a *stupa* or a *caitya* as an attribute in the hand of any aspect of this divinity is not supported either by the Buddhist or Brahmanical texts. In the *Pratimalaksana* of the *Visnudharmottara*, however, Vaisravana-Kubera is associated with a *sibika* or a conveyance of the palanquin type.[12] It is interesting to note that both Ravana and Kubera, the two sons of the sage Visrava, and both of whom are known as Vaisravana, are associated with the celebrated divine chariot known as *Puspaka*, as per the *Kiskindhya-Kanda* of the *Ramayana*. A *caitya* or a *stupa* does not bear the sense of a conveyance, but the gradual transformation of the concept of a chariot (*a la* Puspaka) into that of a palanquin *(sibika)* in course of time cannot be ruled out as an impossibility. Although the *caitya* or *stupa* primarily has funerary connotation, one should not miss its relevance to the concept of a journey — the Great Journey or *Mahaparinirvana*, to be precise, in the Buddhistic tradition. The interpretation of a divine chariot (*Puspaka*), originally associated with Vaisravanas (sons of Visrava of the *Ramayana*) to that of a *caitya* or *stupa* of Vaisravana-Jhambhala of the Buddhistic contexts is indeed an ingenuity of the Central Asian artists.

Another interesting example of the metamorphosis of a visual symbol in Central Asian art should also be referred to here. In a very interesting article entitled "The Sun and Moon as gods in Central Asia", Professor Hans-J. Klimkeit has made the following pertinent observations: "... sun and moon are not only symbols held in the hands of Buddhicised Hindu deities, as in the case of the Mahesvara figures of Dandan Ulik, near Khotan, or symbols adorning the figure of a Buddha, as in the case of Maitreya with his lunar symbolism or the tattoed Vairocana from Khotan. At least along the northern silk route there had been indigeneous deities who were assimilated to the growing circle of gods incorporated into Central Asian Buddhism."[13] Following Klimkeit's disclosure, the present writer investigated into the possible meaning of the sun-and-moon symbolism in the Brahmanical and Buddhist contexts, and it was revealed that the motif represented the concept of the complementariness of the male and female principles — the *purusa* and *prakriti* in the Brahmanical context, and the *prajna* and *upaya* in the Buddhistic parlance.[14] In the *Sadhanamala* and *Nispannayogavali*, the Buddhist deities are often referred to as seated on the *candrasana* and *suryasana*. The real meaning of these terminologies are explained in the *Kalacakratantra-Raja* where it is made clear that these imply the male and the female principles *(prajnopayabhede bhavati hi kamalam candrasuryasanam ca)*.[16]

The simultaneous presence of the sun and the moon as attributes in the hands of Buddhist deities in Central Asian art, in fact, is the visual interpretation of the concept of *Yuganaddha* or the complimentariness of the male and female principles which, in the Tantric Buddhist viewpoint, is the comprehension of the concept of *prajnopaya viniscayasiddhi*, i.e., achievement lies in the coordination of the end *(prajna)* and means *(upaya)*. Although the artists of Central Asia were detached from the culture of the mainstream, it is interesting to note that they did not forget the intrinsic concepts of the theology that sustained their roots. The iconological interpretation of a profound ideology upheld in the mainland culture is a unique example of how the artists of Central Asia were simultaneously traditional and contemporary. In the trials and travails of a series of adoptions and adaptations, they lived with a visual language that satisfied their inner urge, and, at the same time, was communicatively relevant to the people around hailing from miscellaneous cultural stocks.

A unique banner painting from Dunhuang has been noticed with unusual iconographic features. It represents Avalokitesvara in the standing posture. It is captioned in the *Catalogue* of the Dunhuang banner paintings as "*Kuan Yin a neuf tetes et six bras*,"[17] i.e., Avalokitesvara with nine heads and six arms. A common form of this divinity shows him with eleven heads; nine heads for him is doubtless unusual. In view of this, the *Catalogue* describes the representation as an "aberrant form."[18] The illustrated iconographic form needs a descriptive analysis for its proper appreciation in terms of a subtle cultural amalgamation.

The figure shows its principal serene face singularly disposed. Overhead this there are three tiers of subsidiary faces: five in the lowest tier surmounted by two and one at the upper two tiers in the succeeding order. All the heads, excepting the topmost one, wear bejewelled tiaras. The head at the top shows a monk (Buddha)-like knot of hair, making it conspicuously that of a separate personality. It is apparent that the painting illustrates a divinity not with nine heads, as claimed in the *Catalogue* citation, but with eight heads, while the topmost head is that of a *Jina*, perhaps of Amitabha, the usual sire *(kulesa)* of Avalokitesvara. In that case, the paintings depicts an eight-headed and six-armed form of Avalokitesvara.

Of the six hands of the deity, the two uppermost hands exhibit the sun and the moon motifs, a common feature of Central Asian representations of Avalokitesvara. The two middle hands on both the sides display the *abhaya* pose with an entwined lotus stalk in each of them. The lowest right hand holds the water vase, while the left shows the rosary. Six-handed forms of Avalokitesvara are not rare in Buddhist iconography, both in the textual and artistic dispensations. But the simultaneous presence of eight heads and six arms in a form of Avalokitesvara is not a common phenomenon. The image seems to hold some special meaning put to it by the artist who might have desired to represent a concept that he had inherited from the varied sources to which he had a privileged access.

One of the possible interpretation of the image could be that it represents Avalokitesvara as the saviour from eight great perils *(astamahabhaya)*, just like his consort Tara who also is known to have an *Astamahabhaya* form. But in neither of the forms of Avalokitesvara and Tara in such a concept there is the provision for the representation of the deity with eight heads. Avalokitesvara representing such a concept is usually shown flanked by panels depicting the eight perils that he is supposed to rescue the devotee from.[19] In a similar role, his consort Tara is described in the texts as being surrounded by eight subsidiary goddesses *(astadevyantarale tu bhavayet tararupini).*[20] In other words, in the latter dispensation, altogether nine (one central and eight subsidiary) divinities are represented, as could be seen in the labelled illustration in the manuscript of the *Astasahasrika-Prajnaparamita*,[21] referred to above.

The present representation of Avalokitesvara from Dunhuang does not bear much proximity to the *Astamahabhaya* concept either of Avalokitesvara or his consort Tara. However the *abhaya* pose in the middle hands, both right and left, in the image does bear a predominant sense of protection against fear *(abhaya)*. In view of this, the image is likely to be associated with the concept of Avalokitesvara as the saviour from eight great perils, although with an unconventional visual rendering.

But the image could perhaps be read in a different perspective. In the *Nispannayogavali* there is the reference to the *digdevas* (divinities of the cardinal directions) and *vidigdevas* (divinities of the subsidiary directions)[22] complementing the principal deity. The concept ostensibly represents the all-pervasive character of the divinity. It is not unlikely that the Dunhuang image under discussion represents the omnipresence of Avalokitesvara, visualised through making the image as an eight-headed one. Such an interpretation, although seemingly contrived, is endorsed by the fact that the concept of Avalokitesvara as *digadhisa* (lord of the directions) and as relevant to all the six seasons (*sadritusu bhaktavatsalah*) is known in the Nepalese Buddhist tradition.[23] A *dharani* manuscript contains both these concepts in diverse contexts. Although the astral content of the Dunhuang image of Avalokitesvara, envisaged by the sun and the moon as the attributes in the hands, is a typical Central Asian feature, it is tempting to read in the image a distanced note of conceptual sharing. The six hands of the image could perhaps be a notional reminiscence of the six seasons to which Avalokitesvara has been equated, as in the aforementioned *dharani* tradition. Avalokitesvara indeed is an all-pervasive and timeless divine presence in the Buddhistic tradition. It is not likely that some creative genius of an itinerant Central Asian artist visualized a form which is unconventional, but not at all irrelevant.

Although detached from the mainstream culture, the Central Asian artist had good grasp of the inherited and adopted traditions. He had a good comprehension of things to enable him a selective view of any visualization. That is why he was able often to conceptualise an expression with a preferential visual vocabulary. For instance, in the numerous caves at Kizil in Central Asia there are representations of some major Buddhist *Jataka* tales in the pictorial form. Interestingly, most of these paintings depicting the *Jatakas* have a selective representation of the story with only a single panel[24]. Invariably the most representative episode of the narrative containing the core of the dramatic intent has been chosen by the artist to convey the message intended. This shows that the artist as well as the viewer mentally resusciated the episodes not painted in the caves. Many of the same Jataka tales are represented in the paintings at Ajanta caves. But there the narrative runs into a number of panels dealing with episodic details.

In fact, brevity is the essence of Central Asian art, and it is characterized by a unique sense of composite participation by artists belonging, either by inheritance or by adoption, to diverse racio-cultural affiliations. The art of the region has therefore to be appreciated as a uni-voiced echo of a cultural diversity in which individual contributions are made redundant.

Notes

1. *Sadhana* No. 101 of the *Sadhanamala*, Vol. I.
2. Saraswati, S.K. *Tantrayana Art: An Album*, Calcutta, 1977, p. LXXXV and coloured illustration No. 238. Also see P. L XXIX and coloured illustration No. 217 from the Ms. dated A.D. 1071 bearing the inscription: *Pancasikhaparvate vagirattah. Vagiratta* obviously a scribe's error for *Vadirat*, a form of Manjusri which is akin to the Manjughosa form. *Pancasikhaparvata* might bear a reference to the multi-peaked mountaineous region of Central Asia alluded to in the other Ms. dated A.D. 1015 as *Mahacina*.
3. These priceless documents have been studied by various scholars of whom the most distinguished is Alfred Foucher. See his pioneering work *Etude sur l 'Iconographie Bouddhique de l'Inde*, Vols. I & II, Paris, 1900 and 1905.
4. Clark, Walter Eugene, *Two Lamaistic Pantheons*, 2 Vols, Cambridge Mass., pp. 218 and 282.
5. Manuscript No. G. 4727 in the collection of the Asiatic Society of Calcutta, quoted in H.P. Shastri's *Descriptive Catalogue of Sanskrit Manuscripts in the Government Collection under the care of the Asiatic Society*, Calcutta, 1917, p. 77.
6. *Sadhanamala*, Vol. I, p. 267.
7. See Per Kverne's "A Bonpo version of the wheel of Existence", *Tantric and Taoist Studies*, ed. Michel Strickmann, Bruxelles, 1981, p. 274 ff.

8. Ms. No. *Ta*.32, folio 11B, in the collection of the Darbar Library, Kathmandu, Nepal.
9. See H.P. Shastri's above-mentioned *Catalogue* (note 5 above), p. 193.
10. For interesting discussions on Central Asian Culture, see P. Banerjee's *New Light on Central Asian Art and Iconography*, Delhi, 1992.
11. *Bannieres et Peintures de Dunhuang conservees au Musee Guimet*, Paris, 1976, No. 191.
12. *Pratimalaksana* of the *Visnudharmottara*, ed. and translated by D.C. Bhattacharyya, New Delhi, 1991, pp. 53-54.
13. Klimkeit, Hans-J. "The Sun and Moon as Gods in Central Asia", *Bulletin of the South Asian Religious Art* (SARAS), Reading (U.K.), No. 2, April, 1983, pp. 11-23.
14. Bhattacharyya, D.C. "Metamorphosis of a Central Asian Motif", *Buddhist Iconography*, Tibet House, New Delhi, 1989, pp. 149-53.
16. E.G., *sadhana* Nos. 13, 16, 17, 19, 22 etc. of the *Sadhanamala*.
16. *Sri Kalacakratantra-Raja*, ed. Biswanath Banerjee, Asiatic Society, Calcutta, 1985, p. 104.
17. See *Musee Guimet Catalogue* (mentioned in note 11 above), illustration No. 92.
18. *Ibid.*, p. 174.
19. For instance, in the illustration No. 53 of the *Musee Guimet Catalogue* mentioned above. Also, in the Kanheri cave of India Avalokitesvara as the savior from eight Great Perils is represented as being flanked by the eight panels depicting the Perils.
20. This characterisation of the goddess Tara is contained in the *sadhana* No. 99 of the *Sadhanamala* dealing with the *Astamahabhaya* form of the goddess. See p. 207 of the latter.
21. Saraswati, *op. cit.*, coloured illustration Nos. 131 and 132. For an elaborate discussion on this motif in manuscript illustration, see D.C. Bhattacharyya's "The Transformation of the Ardhanarisvara Image in Buddhist Art", *Buddhist Art And Thought*, ed. K.K. Mittal and A. Agrawal, New Delhi, 1993, p. 47 ff.
22. *Nispannayogavali*, ed. B. Bhattacharyya, Baroda, 1949, p. 23.
23. A *Dharani* Ms., dated in the Nepali *Samvat* 711 (*varse candraditya-matrikayam*), which is equivalent to A.D. 1591, contains these concepts of Avalokitesvara. This Ms. belonging to a Buddhist monk named Mahendra Sakya which could be consulted by the present writer during his visit to Kathmandu in Nepal in 1975. Although comprehensive notes from this Ms. were taken at that time, the monk did not allow any of the documents at his disposal to be photographed.
24. Schingloff, Dieter "Tradition of Indian Narrative Painting in Central Asia", Aksayanivi, ed. G. Bhattacharya, Delhi, 1991, p. 163 ff.

ARPUTHARANI SENGUPTA

22

CULTURAL SYNTHESIS IN THE BUDDHIST ART OF CHINA

World civilizations are replete with cultural syntheses, but Sino-Indian synthesis does not have many parallels. There were international highways through which culture travlled. Mahayana (which literally means the "Great Ferry") was an important vehicle in the India-China intercourse. How culture travelled would not be as easily detectable as the visible cargo. The more remote the time, the greater is the difficulty in detecting such movement. We can only note, not scientifically analyse, how the Chinese had the legend of *Pangu* who looked like a copy of the Indian *Purusa.* Then, the Chinese Kunlun might be exactly the Indian Himalaya. China in the remote past was not strong in worshipping female deities. Yet, there was "Xiwangmu", more than three thousand years old who was doubtlessly a goddess, and described in *Shanhai Jing* (Book of Mountains and Seas) in an outlandish manner — a testimonial of her foreign origin. Chinese scholars begin to consider the possibility of her being the Chinese duplicate of *Uma* (and "Wangmu" might be the corruption of "Uma").

Central Asia became a melting pot of Indian, Persian and Roman art and culture, which in turn travelled eastwards to China by way of the oases of the Tarim Basin and the neightbouring areas. Thus the diverse influence of popular and courtly cults, Taoist and Confucian elements intermingling with influences from the east and west brought in vigour and the immense variety to Chinese art styles and subject matter. The scope of narrative painting increased with the wall paintings of the Buddhist sutras in the shrines. There is literary evidence to show that Buddhist monastic community was in existence in Central China by AD 65. During the second century there was also a flourishing Buddhist community in Katigara from where the new faith spread northwards into South China and Sichuan. However, Buddhism was merely one among many popular cults when the Han Dynasty came to an end in the midst of chaos in AD 221. During the four hundred years of stress and uncertainty, between the fall of the Han Dynasty and the rise of the Tang, Buddhism grew to a tremendous wave that spread the new doctrine to every corner of China.

Mahayana was the form of Buddhism which took root in China and this is inseperable to the cult of Amitabha Buddha and the Lotus Sutra. To understand how much it differed from the Theravada Buddhism, we have to pause for a moment to consider the life and teachings of the Buddha. The generally accepted dates of the historical life of Gautama Buddha is 566-486 BC. His legendary life spans several births, both human and animal. The Bodhisattva's life story of previous births known as Jatakas, prepared the way for his Buddhahood. His last historical life is mixed with legend and miracle. He was miraculously conceived and delivered as the prince of the Sakya clan ruling on the border of Nepal. He was predicted to become either a Universal Monarch or a Buddha, the Enlightened One.

Buddha, who was venerated for having reached the superhuman state of non-being, was indicated only through symbols. The aniconic form of the Buddha are his foot-prints, the stupa, the umbrella, the Bodhi tree, the *dharma chakra* and an empty seat. Incidents from the life of Buddha are portrayed with appropriate devices, such as a riderless horse to indicate Gautama's farewell to his horse and groom when he resolved to renounce the world. A pair of deers symbolise the Buddha's sermon in Vaisali. Thus the Buddhist sculptures prior to Mahayana Buddhism has an incomparable structure of high complexity. The aim of the aniconic Theravada Buddhism is to preserve the pristine quality of *nirvana* attained by the Buddha. The Buddha, in the Sunyata state remained disembodied for more than five hundred years.

After the Buddha's death the task of maintaining the Doctrine fell upon the monastic order that functioned with the support of the merchant class, casteless in the Indian society. Patronage was also extended by the emperors who were conscious of its values as a unifying force. But the doctrine of renunciation of all desires in order to break the chain of rebirths remained a difficult proposition to the common people. Towards the end of the era, the monks without the cohesion of a central authority progressively retreated into monasticism with the belief that Sunyata (emptiness) is nothingness. They regarded the striving for *nirvana* in the human death as the ideal of the return of a life to nothingness.

During the first century AD, Emperor Kanishka I recalled the monks from retreat and convened the fourth Buddhist Council in Kashmir. What transpired as the result of the dialogue is revolutionary in nature. The perfection of the Wisdom Sutra, formulated in about 50 AD, infused new life to Buddhism. The arguments in the Sutra poses Classic logic that emptiness is not reached by the negation of matter; for emptiness is the fundamental truth that brings matter into being. The later postulations developed in the Lotus Sutra left no place for misunderstanding: The true cause of illusion is the preoccupation with the self that clings to material things. Therefore, emptiness is actually selflessness. As a corollary to selflessness the virtue of compassion for others developed, exemplified by Amitabha Buddha of Mercy and Compassion.

The phenomena of Amitabha drastically changed Buddha's original doctrine: the renunciation of the world to break the chain of rebirths. In the popular cult of Amitabha, the *nirvana* of the canonical sutras is replaced by a Paradise in which even sinners can find eternal happiness in Paradise, by virtue of repention. The Lotus Sutra of Amitabha proclaims that the Buddha nature is imminent in all beings. The reality of life is reflected in the doctrines taught by Amitabha in sermons and parables. Thus The Lotus Sutra became a rich source of inspiration and the artists in Central Asia delighted in painting Amitabha's Western Paradise and varieties of conscious life from the Sutra.

After presenting Amitabha Buddha as worthy of worship, the historic Buddha receded to the state of eternal Omniscent Supreme Being. The way of Amitabha Buddha and the transcendent Buddha were followed by the numberless Bodhisattvas of limitless benevolence who choose to come time and again to this world to help and guide mankind. The Bodhisattva Avalokitesvara completes the Buddha trinity and they are surrounded by a host of Bodhisattvas, angels and fierce guardians and devotees. In the assimilation of the syncretic-doctrine the iconography underwent several tranformations in China.

During the first century AD, Gandhara art gave form to Buddha for the very first time. The style is Graeco-Roman and the Buddhist iconography has no anticedence. There is no evidence of the halo in Indian art prior to Gandhara art and the anatomical realism in human form is contrary to Indian aesthetics. In Mathura we find an earnest attempt to soften this stark realism by presenting Buddha's all revealing body as if through a veil, symbolising the transcendent quality of the Buddha. But it was Gandhara art which travelled to China by means of portable shrines, narrative scrolls, votive stupas and small-scale Buddhist reliefs.

The earliest examples of Gandhara art in Central Asia is to be found in Miran. The unique paintings of Miran in Gandhara style have no counterpart in India. Among the clusters of stupa shrine, two yielded paintings that miraculously survived on large segments of plaster flakes. Part of the restored murals are in the British Museum and the National Museum in New Delhi, while fragments of the Vessantara Jataka are preserved only in photographs.

Shrines enclosing stupas is an early development. Free-standing square, rectangular, circular and apsidal structures have hardly survived. The square shrine in Miran contained a stupa in the centre. On the circular base of the solid mound, about four feet above the floor was a delicately painted dado of winged angels. Dated second century, the seven Cherubims are startling in their resemblance to Christian iconography and classical style. In fact, the broad treatment of form and colour is derived from Graeco-Roman mosaics. The wide gaze of the angles occupy the level to catch the eyes of the worshipper during the circumbulation of stupa in the centre. The adaptation of the form to the particular structural conditions is a western tradition.

The tempera painting on stucco plaster recovered from the south-east corner of the passage contains part of the composition depicting a Buddhist theme. The scene is a procession of monks following the Buddha, identified by the halo, the top knot and the hand raised in blessing. The features, including the moustache, have close resemblance to Gandhara sculpture. The technique employed in modulation by means of shading is derived from the blocking of form in tonal planes familiar to Roman mosaics. That the technique is derived from the art of mosaic is re-inforced by the manner in which the flat background is squared into small cubes. Other details, such as the brownish-red ascetic robe of Buddha and the chouri bearer among the monks are copies of the source in India. But the wide, expressive eyes are stylistically different from those painted in Central Asia or in Ajanta.

A stupa shrine nearby has similar dado of angels painted on the square wall of the passage. The undulating swag dado, familiar in Gandhara art, frames realistically painted youthful busts. The bejewelled girls adorned with flowers, gracefully play on a guitar or carry decanter and cup. The secular theme and the style give the impression of a Bachanial mural in the Eastern province of the Roman Empire.

The mural on the peripheral wall indicates that much care was taken in the consideration of the composition. In the curve of the swag the emblamatic portrait of prince Vessantara is included and is placed immediately below the Jataka scene of Prince Vessantara making an offering of the wish-granting white elephant. The form and style is Gandhara and details such as the ritual objects in the hands of the prince and the stylised treatment of the folds of his garment are of particular interest.

The 18 feet long mural on the peripheral wall starts on the south-eastern wall. The Jataka unwinds from the left of the entrance with the scene of the pious prince riding out of the palace gate, banished by his father. Before him a "classical quadriga" carries his equally pious wife and two sons. Then the scene shifts to the forest where the prince on foot presents his miraculous white-elephant to four Brahmin mendicants. Cutting across the broken segment of the wall on the northern side, the scene shows the royal couple in their jungle retreat and then moves forward to the happy conclusion of their return to the palace. The short Kharoshti inscription above the mural, on the right side of the entrance, identifies Prince Vessantara in the painting.

According to Stein, the mural is painted in "true pompeian red". But inspite of the Roman motifs, forms and colours the mural appears to be a collaborative effort, for there is a distinct Indian aesthetic discernible in the portrayal of Prince Vessantara. The technically sophisticated method of modelling in the Buddha group is not repeated here. Also, the representation of the elephant contains the charm for which the Indian artists are known for. In subsequent portrayal of the elephant in Central Asia we notice an inability to capture this particular style. Another characteristic of the Indian style is the two dimensional rendering of form, where even landscape assumes a decorative pattern that retains the two dimensional picture plane.

The mural is signed by the artist on the thigh of the white elephant, with a short inscription in Kharoshthi. The name of the artist is Tita. According to Abbe Boyer, the French scholar, "Tita" is the Roman name Titus in Sanskrit. Titus is a popular Roman name of the period. The swag motif and details in the swag also point to Roman origin. Among the puttis carrying the swag are figures wearing the "Phyrygian" cap that is an unmistakable copy of the Persian god Mithra, worshipped throughtout the Roman Empire. Yet, among the bare footed monks in the mural above the dado of the girl with a pitcher, is a starburst; an ancient symbol for the sun that was used as the main decoration on personal items owned by the Mecedonian kings. The stylised 14 point star in the mural is a symbol of light and if it bears a reference to the cup held by the girl in the dado; the cup could mean the "water of life". As religious symbols, "to light the darkness" and "water of life" have origins outside the Buddhist philosophy.

The iconography in the Miran mural is quite complex. The presence of the Persian god Mithra among Roman forms, incorporated in a Buddhist narrative, indicates the changes that were taking place in the evolution of the two religions. The Church of the first five centuries is to be understood in its ancient setting in the pagan Graeco-Roman world. Here, Christianity inherited the Jewish prohibition of images but due to the pagan background, the early Christians regarded the pagan idols as indeed animated by spirits. In order to hold fast to their faith and witness its unique claims Christians had to stand against the pagan symbols. Yet, during its early development, Christianity often got mixed up with mystery cults and foreign religious current in the Roman world. It was not uncommon to find Jesus identified with Mithra, Orpheus or Hermes and the kinship to Buddha being even more obvious, it is not surprising for a synthesis to take place at this point of time and place. The mural in Miran is characteristic of the confluence of several streams in Central Asia. As observed by Stein "inspiration from the contemporary art of the Roman Orient" is obvious. One of the pictorial traditions that would have definitely served as a model for the artists in Central Asia is the Graeco-Roman tapestry. A piece of woollen tapestry which was used in a burial was found at the Lou-lan site, abandoned at the end of 3rd century AD. It represents the head of Hermes with Caduceus. The tonal variations produced on the face of Hermes by means of woven strands of wool approximates the modelling technique employed in the Buddha group in Miran. A similarity is also seen in the rendering of the wide staring eyes. Evidence points to the settlement of people from the Roman Empire. Some of the fragments of wood carving recovered from a ruined house in Lou-lan have decorative motifs which include composite classical figures and laurel wreaths linked together.

In Miran, the ruins of a temple near the stupa-cluster has a substructure of niches framed by attached columns. The capital of the half columns is an adaptation of classical design derived from Bactria or Syria. Originally the niches contained huge seated images that were modelled out of clay mixed with hay. The ingenious use of available material in the second century and the resemblance to Gandhara style make them prototypes to the stucco sculptures in the cave shrines. The temple was in all probability a combination of masonary and wooden structure. It should be noted that the stupa shrine in Miran with the Prince Vessantara mural, was once decorated in fine gilded wooden carvings.

It is remarkable, during the long history of Chinese art, human form did not find expression; unless as a mask during the Shang Dynasty (1766-1111 BC) or a decorative adjunct as in the bronze table leg of the Zhou/Warring States (481-221 BC) period. It was only during the Han Dynasty (206BC - AD221) that sculptural representation of human form appeared in the reliefs of funerary chapels. The colossal mortuary sculptures in stone on the Spirit Road of Han tombs have few human figures compared to the impressive avenue of fantastic animals. These and the battalion of terracotta attendants in underground burial chambers are distinct affirmation of faith in guardian spirits and immortality. In contrast to these indigenous forms are the iconic Buddhist sculptures that seem to have developed almost simultaneously during the Han period. These distinct and separate streams rarely meet. Yet, the fierce guardians in the pantheon is a Chinese invention which derives from local cult.

Mahayana Buddhism in China is a driving force which introduced the human form as the primary mode of communication to spread the faith. During the early Han period, relief sculpture and painting as pictorial language, is primarily meant for funerary purpose. A surprising range of style and technique is apparent in painting. The fluid brush strokes of the painted brick from the tomb near Luoyang and the steady line drawing of funerary banner from the Mawangdui tombs from Changsha, are respectively Confucian and Taoist in principle. While both portray customs and manners of the contemporary Han period of mid-2nd century BC, the funerary banner is esoteric, its symbolic content is pre-Buddhist. More than thirteen varieties of fantastic birds and animals frame human dwelling in clearly defined planes, where the spirit world dominates the earthly life. The Chinese dragon portrayed in the banner and in the funerary banner and in the sculptures of the Spirit Road is a benign guardian, unlike the Dragon King in the Buddhist Sutra. In the Sutra, Amitabha Buddha rescues the young daughter of the Dragon King but the dragon eventually transforms into a powerful guardian in Buddhist iconography. In the Chinese culture the auspicious symbol of the protective dragon is enduring. If the symbolic structure of the Sutra of the Dragon King's Daughter is analysed, it will be found that its origin lies beyond India and China, hence its lack of relevance to both the cultures. However, it is evident from the Western Han sculptures and paintings, that a transmission of form and technique is taking place even before the advent of Mahayana Buddhism. To a large extent the Silk Road played a role in bringing the world closer to the Han Empire.

The pre-Han art in China is remarkable for the absence of any painting or sculpture. Especially remarkable is the lack of human figure in its formal expression. The Chinese sensibility to form, scale and decoration is apparent even without any reference to human form. All forms of decoration remained essentially two dimensional. Sculpture as such played only a minor role and throughout most of Chinese history, animals have been the preferred subject for sculptors. An important tradition of sculpture based on the human figure began as Buddhism reached China from India during the first century AD. Even then, Chinese artists practised sculpture only when commissioned for a Buddhist or ceremonial purpose. And it is in painting, even more clearly than in sculpture, we notice the incorporation of Indian tradition, particularly in the form of story-telling.

In India, the narrative form in painting precedes that of sculpture, though very few remain prior to 15th century. According to ancient literature scroll or pata paintings have been made in various parts of India. The word "pata" means woven cloth in Sanskrit, and originally cloth was used as the support. The narrative scroll, believed to be admired by Gautama Buddha, is a particular kind known as "Charana Chitta". According to the commentary of Buddhagosa of the first century A.D., the scroll contained picture panels placed one below the other in a vertical format or arranged horizontally. The format of the horizontal bars in the gateway of The Great Stupa of Sanchi is probably the earliest example of the narrative scroll transferred to stone. The analogy is strengthened by the scroll-form of the terminals on the cross-bars. The ancient tradition is a living form among the patachitrakars of India.

The narrative scroll is integral to story-telling. In the Buddhist world, the scrolls helped to spread the doctrine through the portrayal of the life of Buddha. They were painted by itinerant monks who recounted the stories in rhythmic prose-verse. Through the lively interaction of the visual and performing arts, communication became more effective, particularly when Buddhism was taken to China. Through the scroll painting, narration gained greater appeal due to the musical intonation of the recital that gave time the necessary structure, as the visual unwound in sequential story script. Transmitted thus, the narrative scroll tradition of India found outstanding expression in the Buddhist art of China.

Several narrative scrolls from the walled-up chapel, from the Caves of the Thousand Buddhas in Dunhuang, are now in the collection of the British Museum, London. The vertical scrolls, dating between 5th to 8th centuries AD, are painted on silk gauze in mineral colours. In a typical scroll, each frame is a square surrounded by a dark frame. The border is left unadorned so that the focus is on the "Still." An interesting invention is a narrow vertical band on the "Still" that alternates from right to left on each successive panel. The alternation helps the eye to follow the passage of the sequence. Though the band is mostly plain, some carry calligraphy. The inclusion of inscribed cartouche is a Chinese invention. So also is the iconography of billowing cloud form to indicate a dream sequence or a supernatural occurrance. In some of the scrolls the cloud form breaks through the frame, linking the narrative from one panel to the other. The quality of serenity in the traditional linking of figures by facial expression and gesture is noticeable even within the small frame. The inclusion of landscape and architectural setting to create an illusion of depth to each of the picture plane is noteworthy.

The adaptation of the scroll form for wall murals leads to several original methods in China. Quite often the traditional frame structure is dispensed with for the sake of pictorial composition. In Dunhuang Cave No. 257, the painter uses an unusual device in the composition of the Deer King Jataka, in which each episode is placed within an individual space created by the topography of the landscape. As a result, the various episodes, seperated by time and space, are integrated in a harmonious manner. The integrative function of landscape in painting is a Chinese innovation which reaches greater achievements in later periods.

The Deer King Jataka in the Northern Wei (386-532 AD) style starts from the foreground on the left, where the Deer carries the youth across the river on his back. In the next episode the youth kneels before the Deer in gratitude, and the Deer wanders off into the landscape after the boy's departure. The landscape is quite barren, except for the diagonal series of hills that rise and fall like the dragon's teeth, holding within its jaw the various episodes. The interplay of series of diagonals create a dynamic pattern.

At the mid point in the narrative, the story shifts to the extreme right and progresses towards the left to culminate on the Deer King once again. This sudden shift in the direction of the narrative is made possible due to the wide-angle vision of the wall mural. The other part of the story is on the right. It depicts the king and the queen seated in an architectural setting. They wear distinct clothes fashionable during the period. In postures and gestures the scheming enchantress, the queen, desires the "nine-coloured" pelt of the Deer King. The ungrateful youth stands in the court with the plan to betray the secret dwelling of the Deer King. As the story progresses towards the left to the approaching danger, the sleeping Deer King is awakened by his friend — the crow. The Deer King confronts the wrong-doer with great dignity. Thus the story culminates in the centre with a moral. The development of the Chinese art tradition is a judicious assimilation where the representation of space and volume on the ground plane and around each figure is Chinese in character. The vertical or horizontal narrative scrolls of India find a new expression in the Chinese mural, giving rise to a new genre in landscape painting.

In Dunhuang the Deer King is represented several times in aid of the narrative. It is derived from narrative technique perfected in India several centuries earlier. The technique of continuous narration, such as the Ruru Jataka from Barhut, involves a composition in which various episodes of the story which happened at different places and different time are represented in a single composition. In the Indian version, the story takes place in a forest near the river Ganga where the golden ruru or stag lived. The three successive episodes are represented on the same medallion. The story starts in the foreground, where the son of a merchant, in the act of drowning himself, is rescued by the golden stag, which carries him to the bank on his back. The second episode, on the right upper half, shows the ungrateful youth pointing out the stag to the King of Benaras, who has promised reward to acquire the magical deer seen in a dream by his queen. The king is seen in the act of taking aim with his bow to shoot at the deer. The climax in the centre shows the king, having dropped the bow, listening with awe and admiration to the eloquent sermon of the deer on the merit of right conduct. The contrite youth stands behind the king. The innovation in the technique is due to the constraints posed by the restricted medium, which in turn leads to a distinct structure in pictorial composition.

A mural painting from Kucha, now in the Museum Volkerkunde, shows how the Indian narrative tradition and Buddhist iconography is transmitted to Central Asia. The mural shows a picture canvas being held up to the viewer. The mural is painted in an illusionistic technique quite sophisticated in its rendering. The naturalism in the portrayal of the man holding the cloth is maintained by the modulation of form in colour while the nature of the white cloth and the drawing is rendered in stark lines. The wall painting integrates in a harmonious composition four incidents in the life of Buddha. The composition of the narrative follows a plan that moves from lower left to the upper left and then from lower right to the upper right. The format appears as if a vertical scroll is cut into half and spliced together to form a rectangular panel. The story follows an anecdotal sequence of Buddha's birth, enlightenment, first sermon and ultimate nirvana. Remarkable achievement, especially in style and technique reveals an impressive pattern of continuity and level of skill drawn from India. The iconography is derived from Gandhara art, for the earliest representation of a rich legendary life-cycle of Buddha is found in Gandhara. The portrayal of the Buddha proportionately larger in scale is a convention derived from Indian sources. This device is consistently used in the portable shrines and the sculptures of Central Asia as well.

Painting traditions from India contributed much to the Chinese compositional techniques, particularly in the strip narrative, for both mural and scroll paintings. The influence is particularly evident in large compositions, both of crowded scenes and of single figures. A complex compositional technique evolved in the Paradise scene, beloved of the Amitabha sect. In the Dunhuang mural paintings of the Tang period (618-907 AD), the composition follows the traditional format of the Buddha in the centre seated on a lotus throne. He is surrounded by Bodhisattvas and disciples. The Paradise radiates from the centre, expanding into palace and temple compounds with pleasure gardens, where crowds of mortals sing, dance and attend discussion and preaching. The scene is resplendent with magical happenings. The composition employs aerial view of buildings in isometric projection, a method developed in the west. The assimilation of linear perspective from one source is combined, as it were, with the Indian mode of figure composition. The integration of the two results in the peculiar Chinese style. In the landscape, each architectural rendering is a cameo seen from above whereas the figures are seen at eye level. To achieve focus on areas of interest the artist resorts to distortion of scale. Thus the scene sparkles with the supernatural even when it incorporates the real. These large compositions, though religious in nature are often extraordinary study of pure landscape. The Buddhist murals thus ushers in a new tradition of Chinese landscape painting.

Large, single-figure painting was also popular at this time. In terms of surviving evidence, the nearest we can come to such works are the votive banners in silk, painted or embroidered. In the silk painting of the 8th century, the Paradise of Amitabha shows the Buddha, holding a crystal globe and seated on a lotus throne under a canopy decorated with flowers. The lotus throne wafts on the curlings of waves, echoeing the blue of the Buddha's hair, framed by a pronounced halo. The Buddha is surrounded by four Bodhisattvas and six monks. Among the two donors shown in the realm of the mortals on the lower plane, the woman on the left of the picture is intact, while only the hat remains from her missing male counter-part to the right. In the centre of the lower level there is a doorway, symbolising the entrance to Amitabha's Paradise. Since it is a Tibetan invention, the silk painting is a testimony to the cultural exchange that took place when Tibetans occupied Dunhuang in 759 AD. In Tibetan Buddhist paintings, this gateway is painted like a patch of cloth under the lotus throne of Buddha. Or the entrance is indicated by a square or oblong piece of silk appliqued in the middle of the lower border to denote the heavenly entrance. The Tibetans in turn acknowledge Nepali and Kashmiri influence besides that of India in the Tibetan *Thankas*.

The painting of the Paradise of Amitabha also shows synthesis of the Ajanta style. The outlines of the drawing suggests rounded plasticity and the continuous fine contour line that guides the composition. The application of colour is decorative rather than atmospheric and the two dimensional picture plane is retained. The pavilion structure is not rendered in linear perspective, instead it is conceived in terms of an overall design. Particularly pronounced is the influence in the ornamental nature of the foliage, jewelry design and the mode of highlighting the features, such as the nose, chin, cheek and forehead.

The use of white in Dunhuang art in the general scheme of painting is a unique feature derived from the Ajanta murals. While the white in the ground is left unpainted in details such as the waves beneath the lotus seat, colour is applied in thin wash in several areas so that the white ground of the cloth shines through. The luminosity thus achieved is harmonised with the rich brightness of pigments applied thickly on top of other pigments. The usage of the lime white is identical to the Ajanta style to decorate a dress or parts of architecture. White is also used as an underpainting to give a burnished luminosity to the jewelry and as a highlight on nose and forehead. It is also used as an accent in the mural, painted predominantly in bright pigments applied flat with very little variation in tonal values.

At this point it is pertinent to take note of the description of the making of Tibetan *Thankas*, to which the silk painting bears a close resemblance. The rules for the preparation of devotional Buddhist paintings on cloth has endured from antiquities. According to literary sources the cloth meant for painting is dipped in lukewarm water with glue and lime and then stretched on a thin frame made of wood or bamboo to dry. The surface is then rubbed several times with a smooth stone and sprinkled with lime water until it becomes ready for painting. The main guidelines are then drawn: the border, a central perpendicular line, the two diagonals intersecting at the centre and other lines according to the figures to be sketched. These lines map out the perfect symmetry and balance that constitute the serenity of the Buddhist icon. Following the guidelines a faint drawing of the main figure is made with a pencil which in turn is brushed with a thick brush dipped in black ink. Thereafter the painting begins. The background is painted first followed by the clothes of the main figures. The day of commencement of the painting and the time of drawing the eyes are fixed for an auspicious day according to the astrological considerations.

Comparable to the painting on silk is the embroidery of the Buddhist icon, both of which were votive offerings from Cave No.17 in Dunhuang. Donated by traders and pilgrims, the silk embroidery, which is contemporary to the silk painting, shows remarkable similarity in form and style. The 241 cm high embroidered cloth is divided into three zones, vertically and horizontally. Amitabha Buddha stands on a lotus in the centre and is enclosed within two concentric mandorlas. Above him is a jewelled canopy on either side of which are two angels borne aloft by clouds. Known as "xiangyin shen", the flying figures literally mean gods of fragrant music. Beneath the Buddha's feet is a rectangular strip of appliqued cloth, symbolising the entrance to the heavenly abode filled with "fragrant music".

Chinese Buddhist art reflects on the ways in which religious, literary, social as well as cultural practices were conceptualised. The Buddhist iconography was adopted and adapted to fit native systems of belief. The Buddhist legend too underwent tremendous transformation and the stories of magical *Hetuprataya* contributed greatly to this. The "Jing Bian" or illustrations of sutras are meant to communicate the Buddhist doctrines. Other important themes are the life story of Buddha, Jataka tales and the rewards of Amitabha's Western Paradise or Pure Land. The scenes of great splendour of Paradise contrasted with images of the tortures of hell awaiting evil-doers provided dramatic interpretation in Chinese paintings.

Buddhism was instrumental in developing the "renwu" or the human figures genre, which is one of the four disciplines of Chinese paintings. There emerged a number of great masters in portrait-painting who, without exception, achieved their fame by painting Buddhas, Bodhisattvas and other Buddhist figures. They were Wei Xie (3rd-4th century) and contemporary Zhang Mo, Gu Kaizhi (346-405 AD) and contemporary Dai Kui, Lu Tanwei (d.485?), Zhang Sengyao (6th century AD) and contemporary Yang Zihua. There were many famous painters from foreign countries. Cao Zhongda (original foreign name lost) was not only a class in himself, but created the "Cao style" with very refined depictions of the Buddha's and Bodhisattvas' costumes as if his figures had just emerged from water. While Cao Zhongda had hailed from Central Asia, another painter had settled down in China during the same period by the name of "Sengjia Fotuo" originally from Central India (his Indian Buddhist name must be Sanghabuddha). This was not only the century of great portrait artists in China, but one of them Xie He (also Hsieh Ho), was both an artist and also an art theoretician. The Six Principles, popularly known as "Liu-Fa" propunded by Xie He in 490 AD, set a standard for criticism of painting in China. Xie He's codification closely follows the Indian canons. Yashodhara's commentary reads:

"Jayamangala on the Kamasutra has been in practise from the ancient times."

Rupa bhedah Paramani Bhava Lavanuayojanam
Sadrisyam, Varnika bhangam iti citrani shadangakam

The correspondence between the Indian and Chinese canons can be seen in the following analysis.

1. The *Bhava* and *Lavanya* contribute to life giving critical element in painting. The vitality or spirit is transferred from the artist to his brush. In the Chinese the reverberance of life breath is *Qiyun.*
2. "Lavanya" by itself means an aspiration to beauty of form.
3. "Rupa Bheda" corresponds to the appearance of the object, whereas *Jin* is the true reflection of the object in the depiction of form.
4. "Pramanani" is the depiction of form through a study of the underlying structure. *Bi* is the structure laid by the brush.
5. "Varnika Bhangam" is naturalism through the application of descriptive colour and thereby the rendering of form.
6. "Yojanam" is organisation in a pictorial composition.

While all the above canons can be transcribed into Xie He's rules, his sixth principle, "Transmission and Perpetuation" or the copying of old master's works, is unique to Chinese tradition. Transmission by means of copying is dictated by conditions in which Chinese art developed from the first century onwards.

Before Buddhism was introduced to China, the experience of the Chinese artists was limited to animistic symbols and composite animal forms, mostly in two dimensional decorative pattern applied to ritual objects. The portrayal of human form and the medium of sculpture and painting are striking by their very absence. When the religious art of Buddhism came to China, the Chinese artists had to copy the human form in sculptures and paintings with great diligence to master the form and technique which was unknown to them until then. Records show that Cao Buxing, artist of the Three Kingdoms, was one of the earliest painters to copy Buddha's form. Since sculpture is not an expressive art in China as in many other cultures, Xie He's Six Principles have played an important role in the subsequent development of Chinese painting.

Dunhuang, since Han and Jin times, was the gateway to the west. Being on the cross-roads it absorbed several cultural cross-currents. If Buddhism brought Indian art to China, trade and political turmoil in the Roman Empire brought other people with a pantheon of anthropomorphic gods and a rich mythology. Synthesised with the native system of belief, Buddhist legends underwent tremendous transformation. Buddhist art too absorbed diverse influences and different styles evolved simultaneously or at different times in various sites. Apart from India the predominant influence is from Rome and Middle East, particularly that of Thrace, Syria and Persia. Roman influence can be seen in the development of linear perspective and atmospheric rendering of space. The shrine paintings of China employ the Pompeiian mode in the isometric projection of buildings and landscape as a setting for human activity. The scientific observation of the environment derived from the west underwent a spiritual transformation in Buddhist art and ultimately became a unique Chinese medium to express the poetic Taoist principles by means of mysterious landscapes.

The first few centuries of the Christian era was particularly charged with missionary zeal. Therefore it is not surprising that Mahayana Buddhism absorbed Christian doctrines in the Lotus Sutra. Of particular interest is the phenomena of Amitabha Buddha and his Western Paradise. The particular form of Amitabha's sermons from the Vulture Peak and his way of teaching through parables the distinction between good and evil has no anticedence in India or in China. Certain conclusions may be drawn from the pivotal role played by the fourth Buddhist Council convened by Emperor Kanishka-I in Kashmir during the first century AD and the ensuing dialogue that resulted in Mahayana Buddhism and the Buddhist art of Gandhara. In fact the Roman penchant for portraiture has left in Gandhara sculptural proof of the Roman presence and several iconography which are puzzling in their form have origins in the Graeco-Roman world of early Christianity.

The syncretic doctrine of Mahayana Buddhism gained popularity as Pure Land Buddhism due to the preachings of *Saddharma-pundarika* or the Lotus Sutra. Amitabha Buddha preaching at Vulture Peak is a motif representing the Lotus Sutra in its entirety, even though several parables find representation. The iconography of Vulture Peak also represents the Western Paradise on Mount Potalaka in which Amitabha presides. The imaginative compositions of allegories and parables interweave within splendid paintings of paradise. The new genre of painting on the Lotus Sutra brought forth favourite artistic themes, such as the The Revelations of the Eternal Life of the Thathagata, The Compassion of Avalokitesvara, Supernatural Deeds of King Resplendent's Two Sons, The Seven Major Parables, The Attainment of Buddhahood by the Daughter of the Dragon King etc. The Appearance of the precious Stupa, Children Making A Stupa, The King Saving the Sage Asita and the Ordeals of the Bodhisattva Sadaparbuta, and other narratives having special appeal are those that illustrate the magical power of Buddha in coming to the rescue of suffering people, such as: Sumati Burning Incense to Evoke Buddha's Blessings and Conversion of 500 Robbers. There are also narratives related to but not specifically mentioned in the Sutra which find expression in painting. Of particular interest is the miracle of the fire pit that turned into a lotus pond when Rahula was thrown into it to prove that he was Sakyamuni's son. Several such stories of persecution, including that of Bodhisattvas is rather surprising in Buddhism which is known for its peaceful co-existence.

In general the teachings of the "Twenty-Eight Chapters of the Lotus Sutra" appear either in the upper part of the picture area or in the centre, creating a focal point within a large space, while amplifying scenes, such as narratives and parables in the surrounding areas. The illustrations are arranged from top to bottom on the picture plane. Cameos representing the Lotus Sutra are incorporated into a pictorial composition. But the iconography does not follow a structure in the selection and arrangement of the themes, except those from the Sutra narratives, are usually composed with landscape as a background. By being anecdotal, no attempt is made to create a composition in terms of sequential arrangement. The artists' main concern appears to be the overall design that interprets spiritual experience by means of bold areas of colour and abstract meandering patterns of rhythmic lines.

The murals in the shrines are gigantic compositions that spread across the wall several square metres in area. The distinguishing feature of the Buddhist murals is the unique treatment of space. By the very magnitude of size the murals cannot be seen all at a time. The composition is laid out in such a manner that several units having different messages combined to form the whole. The apparent inconsistency of scale and the intentionally ambiguous treatment of space becomes meaningful when experienced part by part. The cue to this movement is given by the movement of the figures and the rhythmic lines that connect one area to another. It is common knowledge that these paintings were meant to spread the Buddhist doctrine. It should not have been difficult for a Buddhist monk, well acquainted with the narrative, to interpret the visuals to the passing traders and pilgrims. Often several narratives are running parallel to each other, intermingling freely or turning one area common to both the stories. The painting of the Vulture Peak in Cave No.61 in Dunhuang has the typical "multiple view point" so that even while considering a part of the mural, one has to scan the painting in a holistic cultural perspective keeping in view all relevant events.

Cave No.61 of Dunhuang belonging to the short period of the Five Dynasties (907-960 AD), shows a follow-up of the paintings of the splendid paradise of Amitabha Buddha of the Tang Dynasty. Though the painting lacks the richness and magnificence of Tang patronage, it is poignant in its expression of a period of stress and unease. The Vulture Peak combines illustration of several chapters of the Sutra that covers an area of fifty square metres. The viewers' attention is drawn to the upper right corner where the billowing mass of writhing forms emerge as dragons, reminiscent of the familiar Kui pattern on the Shang bronze vessels. That this is the "Wish-fulfilling Jewel Mandala" is strengthened by the hand that emerges out of the swirling cloud in the lower plane. The disembodied hand turns in a protective gesture towards the dark cloud of dragons above. The dragons and the cloud pattern teach that Buddhahood can be attained through the intervention of Amitabha who saved the young daughter of the evil "Dragon King", expounded in the Devadatta Chapter of the Sutra.

Beneath the hand of Buddha a stupa mound is held aloft in a cloud that trails across the land, carrying the viewers' eyes to a bridge that spans a river that materialises out of the mist. There are three men on a hillock, observing the vision of the "Wish-fulfilling Jewel Mandala" from the other side of the bridge. The narrative moves to the left where a man in a boat floating in a mysterious river that flows around the compound walls of palaces. The Sutra of Innumerable Meanings speaks of a boat in which bodhisattvas carry people across the river of life and death to the Shore of Supreme Enlightenment. It is interesting to observe that the "River of Life" encircles each and every building in the composition. In the foreground, two men stand beyond a small shrine near the boat and look upwards. Their glance is carried further upwards by the flight of birds in symmetrical formation on either side of the Vulture Peak. Above the Vulture Peak curlings of clouds spread across the horizon, separating the mortals below from the realm of the immortals above. The imagery derives from the esoteric schools that has developed during the Tang period. Their mystical speculations and complex images and symbols probably encouraged the use of calligraphed cartouches within the composition to be more explicit to the uninitiated.

With an intention to reveal the Eternal Life of Thathagata, each part of the painting has significance. The parable of the Magic City in the Third Fascicle of the Sutra has created on the wall-painting, the two storeyed palaces raised high on plinths and encircled by walls pierced by a gate tower which is five storeys high. The two men standing on the grounds of the building on the right represent "The Parable of Farming". The multiple viewpoint characteristic of Chinese painting takes the viewer on a gliding tour of the panorama. The scanning vision takes us into every compound, made possible by the isometric projection of the buildings seen from above. In contrast, the shifting viewpoint zooms in on figures seen at eye level, irrespective of their position in the picture plane.

The visionary nature of the Buddhist paintings combined with Taoist beliefs instilled forever in Chinese painting the quest for the "manifestation of the spirit residing in every form". Nature is transcribed not through observation but by means of spiritual introspection. The Five Dynasties painting of the Vulture Peak is energised by "the effortless flow of the interacting forces of nature". The symbolic and spiritual content of the Sutra are conceptualised in an imaginary landscape. Spiritual harmony nourishes the mountains, hillocks, swirling clouds and the water waves that rise and fall and flow in a unifying rhythm that permeates the whole universe.

References

Albert von le Coq, *in Zerman Bilderatlas Zur Kunst and Kulturgeschichte.* (Composite Character of the Art of Central Asia), Austria, 1977.

Bussagli, Mario, *Painting of Central Asia*, Skira, 1963.

Harle, J.C., *The Art and Achitecture of the Indian Subcontinent*, Penguin, 1987.

Marshall, John, *The Buddhist Art of Gandhara ...*

Herzfeld, Ernst, E. *Iran in the Ancient East*, Oxford University Press, 1941.

Rosenfield, John.M, *The Dynastic Arts of the Kushans*, UCLA, 1967.

Stein, Aurel, *On Ancient Central Asian Tracks*, India, 1984.

Stein, Aurel, *Exchange of Cultural Influences: Dunhuang—Chinese Turkistan*, India, 1900-1916.

Sullivan, Michael, *The Arts of China*, UCLA, 1967.

Tregear, Mary, *Chinese Art*, Thames and Hudson, 1993.

Whitfield, Roderick and Farrer, Anne, *Caves of the Thousand Buddhas: Chinese Art from the Silk Route*, The British Museum, 1990.

Zwalf, W., *Buddhism: Art and Faith*, The British Museum, 1985.

Kurata, Bunsaku and Tamura, Yoshiro, *Art of the Lotus Sutra*, Kosei Publishing Co. 1987.

Tan Chung, *Dunhuang Art Through the Eyes of Duan Wenjie*, IGNCA, New Delhi, 1994.

PRIYATOSH BANERJEE

23

NEW REVELATIONS OF XINJIANG ART

It is my great pleasure to make a short contribution to this immense and valuable volume which, I am sure, will promote India-China understanding. When we work on the art of Xinjiang ("Chinese Turkistan", as it was conventionally known), we find that our information multiplies, new revelations can be harvested. Let me illustrate this below.

The plaque in question was collected from Yotkan (Xinjiang Uighur Autonomous Region of China) by the famous explorer, Sven Hedin and is now housed in the Ethnographische Museet, Stockholm, Sweden. So far as my knowledge goes, the theme of the plaque which is of great iconographic interest does not seem to have been identified as yet by any scholar. We are, however, very thankful to Dr. Joanna Williams who has reproduced it in her article *The Iconography of Khotanese Painting,* published in *East and West* (New series Vol. 23, March-June, 1973, Fig. 70), though she has offered no remarks regarding its identification. Stylistically, the plaque can be attributed to 9th-10th century AD.

The plaque presents a very intricate composition in the form of a *Yantra* or *Mandala* consisting of two intersecting triangles one of which points to the top or apex and the other to the bottom. Inside the first triangle is portrayed a female divinity dancing in *Pratyalidha* pose over a corpse. She is surrounded on all sides by various subsidiary deities. At the bottom of this diagram or *Yantra* is a *purna-kumbha*, (i.e., a jar filled with sacred water and foliage) with a passant lion at one side and a pig at the other.

The main deity which dances over a corpse as mentioned above is somewhat damaged at the face, the lower portions of the legs and few other places, rendering it difficult to understand some of her details. It is very difficult to make out the contents of the face of the deity which was perhaps like that of a sow.

The deity has two arms. Her right hand which is raised seems to hold a *vajra* with the *tarjani* (the pose of the raised index finger in a menacing attitude) and the left holding a *khatvanga* (a staff surmounted by a *vajra* or *kapala* or *trisula*). She wears a garland of skulls. Around her are her attendant deities shown at the corners of the triangles. Further, on either side of the tip of the second triangle (i.e., the triangle which points to the bottom) are two female divinities. The pair at the left includes a kneeling deity with the hands raised and looking up to the principal deity of the Mandala. Her accompanying figure sits with her legs pendent, and a staff held in her right hand. Similarly, the other pair at the opposite side consists of two female figures, one kneeling and looking up to the main deity and the other deity sitting with her legs pendant and holdinig a circular object which may be called a kapala.

Now with the above background we may discuss the question of the identification of the theme the plaque represents. In our present task we have to depend largely upon the *Sadhanamala* (the Buddhist iconographic texts, containing the procedure of worship) edited by Benoytosh Bhattacharyya, Baroda, 1924. It is interesting to note that the general features of the main female deity of the present *Mandala*, dancing in *Pratyalidha* pose agree to the description of the *Vajravarahi* of the two-armed variety as is apparent from the following Dhyana specimen:

Atmanam Bhagavatim Vajravarahim dadimbakusuma-prakhyam dvibhujam ekananam trinetram muktakesam sanmudramudritam digambaram pancha jnaanatmikam sahajananda svabhavam dakshinena vajra- tarjanikaram-vamena-karotaka-khatvanga-karuampratyalidha-padakranta-bhairva-kalaratrikam-sardramunda-malamkritagatram-sravadrudhiram-pivantim bhavayet.

"The worshipper should conceive himself as goddess *Vajravarahi* whose complexion is like the pomegranate flower, who is two-armed, one faced and three-eyed, has dishevelled hair, endowed with six auspicious symbols, is nude, whose essence is the five knowledges, who is of the nature of *Sahaja* pleasure, who shows in the right hand the *vajra* together with the *tarjani*, and bears the *khatvanga* in the left, who stands in *pratyalidha* attitude (i.e. the left leg outstretched while the right leg slightly bent and placed behind),who tramples upon the fierce Kalaratri represented as the corpse, decked in the garlands of wet heads and who drinks of the blood trickling therefrom." (Benoytosh Bhattacharyya, *Indian Buddhist Iconography*, Baroda, 1924, pp. 103-104).

On the basis of the above quoted *sadhana*, I am inclined to hold that the central figure of our ivory plaque is *Vajravarahi* with her companions (namely Dakini, Lama, Khandaroha and Rupini).

In the *Chakrasamvara Mandala* the attributes of *Vajravarahi* are explained as follows: "She is one faced to indicate the essential sameness of all things and with two hands, because truth is two-fold, absolute and relative...She is naked with dishevelled hair because she has been set free from illusions that hide the essence of things. She wears a girdle adorned with portions of skulls because she bestows supreme bliss and with her right hand in the gesture of menace (*tarjani Mudra*). She clutches the vajra and terrifies the demons of the ten points of space." (Kazi Dawa Samdup, *Sricharasamvara Tantra*, Aditya Prakashan, New Delhi, 1987, p. 24.)

The Mandala under discussion is placed on a circular pedestal decorated with beads or lotus petals. Below the pedestal is a Purnakumbha with sacred water and foliage shown at the bottom. On its left is a rampant lion, on a lotus base at the left and a seated pig at the right.

Purna-kumbha is an auspicious symbol, used in all forms of Indian worship, Hindu, Buddhist and Jaina. In *Jaina Ayagapata* (tablet of homage), it occurs invariably as one of the eight auspicious symbols. The *Purna-kumbha* in a mandala signifies the *abhisheka* ceremony, i.e. the consecratory rite. As we know from the Tantra, the *Pranapratishtha* of the deities (the infusion of life in the deities) is performed over it.

Now the presence of the pig in association with the Purna-kumbha, signifies beyond doubt that the plaque is a representation of the *Vajravarahi Mandala*.

The *Purna-kumbha* is an attribute also of another Buddhist deity called Marichi who has three faces, one of which is that of a sow. It is interesting to note that a Marichi figure from Khiching (Orissa) bears behind her head a *Purna-kumbha* with foliage. Dr. Debala Mitra who has illustrated this figure in her book "Buddhist Monuments of India' does not seem to have noticed this Purna-kumbha motif.

The Mandalas are generally shown as circular or square in shape. But the Tantra texts describe Mandalas also as geometrical diagrams as our ivory plaque.

Geometric symbolism was an important part of Hindu ritualism too. In this connection Havel notes: "The principal object of worship in Vaishnava temple in Southern India is the *Sudarsana Chakra*, Vishnu's discus which symbolises the creator's mind or the first thought of the Supreme Being when the desire of creation moved him to manifest himself. It is represented as a circle of fire with four projecting points of flame. On one face of the chakra sits the lion incarnation of Vishnu in yogi pose enclosed in an equilateral triangle. On the other face are two similar triangles, one standing on its apex and the other on its base, symbolising respectively the evolutionary and involutionary cosmic power. This is the mystic symbol of the Universe known as King Soloman's Seal."

In Japanese Buddhism the Mandala of two sections symbolises the *Vajradhatu* and *Garbhadhatu*. The Buddha mind is generally represented as a triangle of flame pointing downwards. The symbol occurs on the breast of *Variochana Buddha*. (William Edward Soothill and Lewis Hudus, *A Dictionary of Chinese Buddhist terms*, Oxford, 1931, p. 250 a).

This ivory plaque shows clearly the fact that Tantric Buddhism was popular in Yotkan (Khotan region) in the ninth-tenth century AD. This form of Buddhism originated in India. It became in course of time very popular in Tibet, Nepal, and Central Asia.

It is difficult to ascertain whether the ivory plaque in question was a local product of Yotkan or it was taken there by a pilgrim or trader. Whatever it may be, the Khotan region was an important centre of Tantric Buddhism during the early medieaval period, as we know from other sources also. Even if not a local product, the object might have come to Central Asia in response to a local demand.

BAGYALAKSHMI

24

THE CREATION OF GODDESS OF MERCY FROM AVALOKITESVARA

Bodhisattva Avalokitesvara/Guanyin occupies a unique place in the Mahayana Buddhist pantheon. Buddhist sutras speak of several bodhisattvas but it is Avalokitesvara/Guanyin who is revered and adored by followers of both Hinayana and Mahayana Buddhism and by all art lovers. He/she has acquired a status equal to the Buddha and sometimes his importance surpasses even the Buddha's. The Westerners know the deity as the Chinese goddess of love and compassion. If Buddhism has been the greatest contribution of India to world religions, the transformation of Indian Avalokitesvara to Guanyin-the Goddess of Mercy — is the creation and contribution of China to the Buddhist world. Despite three major setbacks suffered by Buddhism in Chinese history, the symbol of Guanyin, the goddess of mercy however had continued to prosper and flourish and has rightly been called the "cult of half Asia".[1]

In the *Mani Kambum* it is related that Bodhisattva Avalokitesvara emerged as a ray of white light from the right eye of Amitabha after the latter had given himself up to earnest meditation and hence regarded as his spiritual son. The Bodhisattva brought forth the prayer "Om mani padme hum", "Oh! the jewel (of creation) is in the Lotus!"

The Avalokitesvara/Guanyin formulation has not been free from controversy, almost from the inception. The Chinese word "Guanyin" is an abbreviation of "Guanshiyin" which denotes "seeing the voice of the world" if rendered literally. Is this meant to be a translation of Avalokita, Avalokita svara or Avalokitesvara? The name Avalokita means "viewed", "beheld" and can be used in the masculine, feminine and neuter genders. Avalokita-svara means the hearer of voices of the suffering beings while Avalokitesvara conveys the existence of a Lord who is omniscient in observing all the activities, including sufferings of humanity. Such a deity can be called as the lord who looks in every direction or "Regarder of cries of the suffering beings". Kumarajiva's and Xuanzang's translations as Guanshiyin, Guanzizai continued for some time but it was the term Guanyin which found favour ultimately.

Though many Sutras have spoken the greatness of the Bodhisattva, it is in the *Saddharma pundarika Sutra* (*Miaofa lianhuajing*) -- jewel among the Mahayana Sutras -- where Avalokitesvara's virtues have been extolled in a special chapter. The chapter itself became so important that it was treated as a separate sutra called the *Avalokitesvara Sutra*. The importance of the *Avalokitesvara Sutra* came to be known when a King fell ill and he was asked to recite this particular Sutra. The King was cured and thus faith in the Sutra was generated and the Bodhisattva too gradually came to occupy the central stage.

The popularity of Avalokitesvara is due to the personification of *karuna* (compassion) and *prajna* (wisdom). While wisdom makes the Bodhisattva close to the human minds, compassion makes him/her close to the human hearts. All other deities possess these two qualities to a certain degree, but for Avalokitesvara/Guanyin, being their perfect representation, it is easier for him/her to assimilate the attributes of other Brahmanical deities like Brahma, Vishnu and Siva thus becoming the most powerful of all spiritual powers, the father and mother of all.

Avalokitesvara who is a male Bodhisattva in India was transformed into a goddess in a Chinese male oriented society. A preliminary statement can be made here, that sinicization of Buddhism led to the creation of the Goddess of mercy with Chinese characteristics from a male deity with Indian characteristics. What brought about this change in the gender of this Bodhisattva and why? This transformation of a male deity from India into a female Goddess of mercy in a strongly patriarchal Chinese society both at the terrestrial and celestial levels has surprised many. Celestial because for any woman to gain entrance into the Paradise of Amitabha, she should shed her female form and assume a male form. For a female divinity to have grown in the terrestrial level in a male dominated society, and to have given rise to a cult is equally strange. It is not that there were no goddesses prior to the introduction of Buddhism in China. Only they were not as important.

The transformation does not appear to have come about suddenly. The male Bodhisattva was gradually given an ambiguous form so that people saw what they desired to see. If we examine the iconographic representations of the goddess in China and elsewhere, the paintings and statues of this Bodhisattva initially did not reveal this change. The female anatomy was conspicuously absent, but from a graceful body structure one could feel the feminine element. At the same time the male characteristics of moustache and beard were also visible in the form of tendril like lines. Even these vanished in the sculptures of the Dazu caves where they appear to be completely female.

Dreams, Visions and Legends of Guanyin

Dreams, visions, naturally formed images, efficacy, configuration of multiple images, pilgrim sites, legends, miracles, configuration of multiple images, folklore and last but not least, the reign of Empress Wu Zetian of Tang Dynasty, appear to be the factors which contributed to the creation of the Goddess of Mercy. Although they seem to be exclusive of each other they are in fact interlinked, making it a process of "cause and effect" for the evolution of the goddess.

The "creation of Goddess of mercy" symbolic of maternal love and infinite compassion can be traced to the 5th century and not as late as 11th or 12th centuries as made out by many scholars. The encyclopedic *Fayuan zhulin* which was compiled in 668 mentions that Guanyin manifested himself in feminine form in AD 479 to rescue his devotee Peng Zujiao from chains. There was another instance when that Bodhisattva had manifested himself in the female form to heal the "dissolute and emaciated Northern Qi emperor Wen Cheng (reigning 561-65 AD). With the translation of the *Cundi devi dharani Sutra* in the seventh century, the feminine aspect of Guanyin in the form of Cundi-Avalokitesvara (*chun tie-guanyin*), "mother of seven kotis of Buddhas" was established in China.

In the annals of Tianzhu, Guanyin is said to appear in the form of a woman in white in the dream of Qian Liu (852-932 AD), the founder of the Wu Yue kingdom, and told him that his kingdom would survive the chaotic Five Dynasties period for he was compassionate and averse to killing. She also told him that he could find her on Mount Tianzhu in Hangzhou. Later, when he became the king he dreamt of the same lady who asked him for a place to stay and promised to be the tutelary deity of his kingdom. Upon inquiries the king found out that the only white robed Guanyin image was in the Tianzhu Monastery and the image housed in the Monastery was that of the feminine white-robed Guanyin.

In the year AD 939, it was said that while meditating, monk Daoyi saw a bright light coming from the stream. When he looked up he found a wooden piece with a strange fragrance. He gave the wood to a local artisan for making an image of Guanyin. The artisan cut open the wood and found a ready-made "naturally formed image" of the deity. The bodhisattva's face was compassionate and beautiful. The artisan planned to keep this image and make one from ordinary wood. But Guanyin appeared in the dream of Daoyi and warned him of the deception. The artisan had to part with the ready-made image. Some years later Daoyi had another dream in which a "white-robed person" told of the arrival of a monk from Luoyang the following day and that he, Daoyi should ask him for the relic of the Buddha that was amongst the latter's possessions. The next day the monk came and Daoyi asked for the relic. The monk saw the image and was greatly moved and offered the relic to be installed in its crown. Guanyin himself is said to have appeared as a white-robed person in Daoyi's dream and predicted about the monk's visit.[2]

Visions of Guanyin as a beautiful lady to vision-seeking pilgrims added another dimension to the popularity of the goddess. The Chaoyin dong (Cave of Tidal Sound) in Mount Putuo is the foremost place where the pilgrims had visions of the Bodhisattva. With the passage of time places like the Diamond Boulder and the Purple Bamboo Grove were also regarded as Guanyin's preaching sites. The *Fozu Tongji* has the following passage from the *Cao-an lu* (Record of a grass hut) written by Nanhu Daoyin during the period 1165-73 AD:

> "Mount *Pu-to* is in the great ocean. It is situated southeast of Jin [Ning-po], about a thousand kilometres by the water route. It is no other than the mountain called Potalaka that is declared by the *Hua yen* Jing to be the 'isolated place at the end of the ocean' where kuanyin Bodhisattva lives. It is also no other than the Mount Potalaka that is declared by the *Dabei Jing* to be the place where the palace of Kuanyin in which Sakyamuni Buddha reveals the heart-seal of the Mantra of Great Compassion is located. The Cave of Tidal Sound is on the island. Ocean tides pound in and rush out day and night making deafening noises. In front of the cave is a stone bridge on which pilgrims stand facing the cave to pray. If they are sincere, they

sometimes can see the Great Being sitting leisurely. Or they will see Sudhana come forward as if to welcome them. Other times one will see the pure vase of green jade or the Kalavinka bird flying as if performing a dance. Some six or seven li from the cave there is a large monastery. Merchants, diplomats and tribute bearers sailing to and from the various countries in the Eastern Sea would come here to pray for safety. Those who are reverential and sincere all receive protection without fail."

It was the Cave of Tidal Sound where Guanyin appeared to pilgrims as mentioned in the early accounts of the island. From the Song dynasty onwards, important officials and well known persons who visited the islands wrote about it. A collection of poems and essays left by the visitors are collected in the island gazetteers. Besides important people, ordinary pilgrims and even illiterate ones have also helped by word of mouth repeating stories they had heard or marvels they had themselves witnessed. Stories were of great help in making Guanyin a goddess. Emperor Wenzong of Tang (AD 827-39) loved to eat clams. Fishermen on the southeast sea coast were burdened with the task of supplying clams to the emperor. One day a huge clam was served that could not be opened by a knife. When the emperor knocked on the shell the clam opened by itself and inside was a portrait of Guanyin. The emperor was astonished and preserved the shell in a sandalwood box. He consulted a Chan master who explained to him that the appearance was to kindle his faith so that he would be judicious and love the people. The Lotus Sutra says that for those who need to be saved by the Bodhisattva, Guanyin appeared as a Bodhisattva to preach the dharma. The emperor said that he had seen the form but had not heard the preaching. The Chan master asked the emperor if he believed what he saw and the latter replied in the affirmative. The master said that if there was faith then the emperor had already heard the preaching. From that day onwards the emperor stopped eating clams and ordered the installation of Guanyin images in the monasteries of the country.

Guanyin with the fish basket is based upon the legend of a Chan believer and his daughter Lingzhao who was believed to be a manifestation of Avalokitesvara carrying a bamboo basket. The story goes thus — In the year AD 817 of the Tang dynasty a beautiful girl in the countryside was much sought after for marriage by eligible young men. As the number of men who were eager to marry her was large, she adopted a novel method for selecting a suitor. She put forth a condition that she would marry the person who would memorize the Guanyin chapter of the Lotus Sutra in one night. Twenty men succeeded in doing this but because there were still too many for the marriage, she again made a request that these twenty should learn by heart the *Vajracchedika Sutra* overnight. Once again there was a sizable number of men who had achieved the feat. The girl's third condition was that he who memorized the entire Lotus Sutra in just three days could marry her. A man named Ma Lang was the only one who could accomplish this and so the marriage was to take place. Just as the marriage ceremony was to commence the girl took ill and died. Soon after the burial an old priest visited Ma Lang and requested him to dig up the grave. The coffin contained only pieces of golden bones. The old priest said that the girl was a manifestation of Guanyin who had come to lead people to salvation. After saying this the old man too vanished. From then on the people of the district became Guanyin devotees.

The Legend of Miaoshan[3]

Over the years, the story of a girl (actually Guanyin) who successfully resisted her father's attempt to get her married, sought her own destiny while bringing succour to the suffering people grew into a legend. Many variations of this story have also been extant from time to time as the Chinese reincarnation of Guanyin. The most popular text however is the one written by the Buddhist monk Puming of the Tianzhusi after a vision he experienced in 1103. The version given by Yu Chengxue can be summarised as follows:

"Guanyin was born with the name of Miaoshan, the youngest daughter of King Miaozhuang. From her childhood, she followed the precepts of religion. When she came of a marriageable age, the King sought a husband for her. Guanyin defied her father. Persuasions and threats from the king had no effect on the girl's resolution not to marry. In anger, the King sent her away to the White Sparrow Monastery with instructions that she should be compelled to obey. The nuns tried their best and ill treated the girl to make her submit. This only strengthened her resolve. Since the nuns failed, the King set fire to the monastery. While all the nuns died, only the girl who sat erect reciting sutras survived. The King sent for his daughter in the hope that she would change her mind. But finding her resolute, the king ordered her execution. As she was about to be beheaded, the sword broke into two and a tiger from nowhere bore her away to a forest. She remained unconscious for sometime and then dreamed that two boys in black carried her to the Underworld. Here she met Yama who attended her with great respect. She saw all the sinners and other suffering beings. She recited sutras on their behalf and they were delivered. When she awoke evil beasts and venomous dragons were struggling to harm her. But when she took refuge in a hermitage an old man gave her mountain peaches to eat and led her to Xiangshan where she made her dwelling. She pursued religious cultivation for some years. One day from afar she saw that the King was sick, not responding to treatment. She took the form of an aged monk and told the King that he could be cured only by the arms and eyes of his closest kin. The King asked the monk for advice once more and the monk said the "holy elder" on Xiangshan would grant him his wishes. The holy elder, who was none other than Miaoshan severed her own two arms and her two eyes and handed them over to the envoys. The King was advised to meet the holy elder. When the king met the holy elder, she was indeed without arms or eyes and the body was covered with streams of blood. The King was grieved and was also startled to find that the elder resembled Guanyin — and was his third daughter. The King besought heaven and earth to make his daughter whole again. Soon, the holy elder had arms and eyes by the thousand. And then Miaoshan bowed before him and urged him to practise good deeds to which the King readily agreed."

The story of Miaoshan in various forms had found an immense appeal and had a wide circulation. This legend no doubt offered women in China a role model to defy parental marriage arrangements while observing the path of piety.

At another level, the legend of Miaoshan had many important lessons for the women. First is the filial piety which Miaoshan exhibited. Instead of resenting the wicked persecutor, she returned to her father when he was seriously ill. There is an element of sacrifice in giving up her arms and eyes. And above all, it had a great appeal to women as it symbolized the independent female spirit and the willingness to suffer in the face of pressures from the family.

Configuration of Images Into Female Guanyin

Although Chinese mythology had been dominated by male gods and masters, the presence of female divinities has always been a part of Chinese folk belief. Amongst them can be recognized four divinities whose collective popularity extends from ancient times to the present. They are *Nuwa*, the legendary creatress of humans, *Xiwangmu* the Queen Mother of the west, Guanyin the Goddess of Mercy and Tianhou the Empress of Heaven. These four divinities have an interesting and significant relationship and collectively they represent a continuing "spiritual potency" and significance to the masses, religious and political groups.

Nuwa was most revered as the mother goddess. She created the first human beings, the nobles from yellow soil and base men from straw. She battled against floods and destroyed monsters. Nuwa not only created beings but also constantly changed shape, an attribute associated with Guanyin too.

Xiwangmu is represented as a beautiful lady attended by the "Daughters of Jade". It is to be noted that in the early versions of the legend both Nuwa and Xiwangmu looked rather alien to the natives of China but by and by were totally integrated into the superstructure of ruling hierarchy and rationalized in the popular belief of the oral literature. But the Buddhist divinity Guanyin which was foreign in origin appeared to have overtaken both these feminine divinities as well as Tianhou.

Forgiveness, mercy and compassion in the Chinese context were seen as primarily feminine characteristics. During the Tang Dynasty Guanyin has been portrayed as a Goddess and a companion to Amitabha, Lord of the Western Paradise. This led to Guanyin's association with the Western Paradise and thence to the sharing of the characteristics with the Taoist Queen Mother of the west —*Xiwangmu*. Later the characteristics of goddess *Tianhou* were also absorbed by Guanyin and the latter was looked upon as a goddess of sailors and a protectress of those at sea.

Shuiyue Guanyin (Guanyin of Moon and Water)

The concept of the Shuiyue Guanyin arose from the eminent Tang poet Bai Juyi's poem "*Ode to the portrait of Shuiyue Guanyin*" expressing his devotion for the "Moon's reflection in Water form of Guanyin" (*Shuiyue Guanyin*). The poem reads as follows:

"Floating in water,
Clean and pure,
As if hiding

In the white light.
When I set my sight
All egos are vanishing.
Your disciple Bai Juyi
With devotion under your feet.
You are my cynosure
Life after life forever."

The poem was represented in a painting by the famous Tang artist Zhou Fang. Although it is one of the thirty three forms of Guanyin, it is not based on the scriptures. The Dunhuang manuscript *P. 2055* mentions that Zhai Fengda copied the Sutra for the Shuiyue Guanyin as a mark of wishing good luck to his late wife. But unfortunately the original is no longer to be found. There is no documented base for the Sutra in Buddhist Scriptures and it is difficult to ascertain whether this sutra was from India or the creation of the natives. It was after about a century that the artists of Dunhuang took a fancy to the concept of the Shuiyue Guanyin.

Songzi Guanyin

Songzi Guanyin (Guanyin who gifts sons to mothers) is another form of Guanyin and regarded to be a Chinese creation — at least adaptation. The Lotus Sutra states that a woman desirous of a male child should only pray to Avalokitesvara and her wish is granted. The concept of Songzi Guanyin may have its origin in the Indian goddess Hariti. Hariti, a Hindu goddess was said to be originally an ogress. The legend, according to *Samyuktavastu*, said that once Hariti decided to capture and eat up all the children in Rajagriha. All the children disappeared and there were bitter lamentations. The bereaved parents went to the Buddha and requested him to make Hariti harmless. Buddha remained silent but the next morning after his round with the begging bowl asking for alms he went to Hariti's abode and finding the five hundredth and the youngest son Priyankara there. He hid him inside his begging bowl. On her return Hariti found that her favourite son was missing and asked the remaining 499 sons for the whereabouts of the youngest one. They had no knowledge of the Buddha's act. In great despair Hariti started hunting for him till her search brought her to the Buddha where after paying her respects to the Buddha she asked about her son. The Buddha replied that she must first promise to follow his precepts and give the people of Rajagriha assurance of security to which she readily agreed. The Buddha then converted her, and she in turn became the "Protectress of Children".

At a conceptual level "child giving" was not restricted to Guanyin alone but was a function of earlier goddesses also. But the very same role seems to have been appropriated by Guanyin subsequently. In another instance Songzi Guanyin is said to be associated with Yaoji, the Taoist goddess, daughter of Xiwangmu. In this form the "Princess of Fairy Clouds watches over women in their confinement and cares for them during their childbirth."

Alice Getty has cited the case of "Songzi Guanyin" who was looked upon as "Dispenser of Fecundity" and for whom there was an extant cult of those desiring children.[4] She agrees that Songzi Guanyin was the female form of Avalokitesvara with a child in the arms as a symbol of the quality of "Giver of Children". The transition to the female form with its flowing robes was therefore a "natural convergence".

The conclusion that could be drawn is that in Chinese society even an "imported deity" like Guanyin was subjected to "profound transformation" expressive of the underlying need for mythical feminine symbols in the context of dominant hierarchy. The local folk traditions seem to have accepted the female transformation consistent with the traditions of local goddesses. Guanyin seems to have absorbed all the local beliefs and traditions in a big way.

Can it be said that Guanyin became more popular in China as her all pervasive qualities offered solution to the problems faced by women in China particularly in a sociological order fixed by Confucian ideals and carried on for centuries? There appears to be some force in this argument. Barbara Reed in her study has said that in popular Chinese beliefs, the blood of both menstruation and child birth is spiritually polluting.[5] Guanyin responds to women because of their sex and is said to possess power to save women from sexual attacks, physical, emotional and social suffering.[6]

The thirty three manifestations of Avalokitesvara/Guanyin in the *Saddharmapundarika* became popular cults in Sui (581-617) and Tang (618-907) dynasties. These manifestations according to Prof. Lokesh Chandra indicate the assimilation of Indian and indigenous deities and beliefs and is a continuing process.[7] "The incorporation of Buddhist goddesses into Guanyin and the natural propensity of women towards feminine forms, not to speak of several other factors led to Guanyin in female form becoming dominant in China especially after the Tang and more often the Song Dynasty".

The Dunhuang murals bear witness to the trend of painters making the images of Bodhisattvas more feminine and worldly in order to "please the viewers". The thirty three manifestations of Guanyin kindled the imagination of painters resulting in a plethora of Guanyin images. Besides the painters, perhaps the whims and fancies of the common people also played an important role in depicting Guanyin as a goddess.

Very many legends interwoven with local folklore on the miraculous powers of Guanyin are extant in China. The iconographic models of Guanyin seen in various manifestations all over China and in places where overseas Chinese are in large numbers is a testimony to its popularity and the faith the people have in the powers of Guanyin.

Certain generalized observations can be made from the depiction of Avalokitesvara / Guanyin and the ideas and concepts that were sought to be conveyed by the extant images. These include:-

- Avalokitesvara in the desire to help humankind assumed different forms and it is no surprise that Avalokitesvara / Guanyin symbolizing divine womanhood was considered to be most appropriate.
- Compassion and mercy were considered as special attributes of women.
- If we are to be guided by the early Mahayana texts, it does not matter whether god is depicted in male or female form or in an asexual form, as the ultimate reality is in nothingness "Sunyata".
- The depiction symbolized and popularised certain myths and legends associated with Guanyin. Helping the sea farers, "giving children", Guanyin with a fish basket[8] identified the deity with the common people who yearned for children.
- Guanyin in the course of Chinese history absorbed the magical powers and attributes of existing indigenous divinities and such a changeover took place without any tension in the then prevailing social or religious order.
- The transformation of Guanyin into a female form should be seen in the overall context of Sinicization. Such transformations were not restricted to Guanyin alone. Maitreya was transformed into a totally new form of a "laughing Buddha", a practice still prevalent in China and Southeast Asia. Such transformations have evolved, perhaps to fit in certain prevailing ideals then dear to the Chinese, like having an offspring, prosperity etc.

The French Sinologist Maspero has suggested an explanation for the transformation of Avalokitesvara into a female form. Mahayana Buddhism had always considered enlightenment as the conjunction of wisdom and compassion. Symbolically, in Tantric Buddhism, wisdom is considered to be male and compassion female. With the introduction of Tantric Buddhism in 8th century made popular by many Tantric masters who were active at that time, all the Buddhas and Bodhisattvas were provided with female consorts.

The evolution of Guanyin as the goddess of mercy has been explained by John Blofeld as related to Tara. Tara is looked upon as "a beautiful female divinity able to manifest herself in twenty-one different forms for the sake of succouring sentient beings." Tara has two main functions : to rescue human beings from woes, to assist them in ridding themselves of the delusions binding them. Blofeld believes that these are the same functions of Guanyin also. According to him such an attractive being supported by Buddhist texts would not have been overlooked by the Chinese unless they had some other means of portraying compassion. The Chinese have always been disposed to envisage friendly divinities in idealized human form, and the beautiful Tara now as a sweet faced matron, now as a winsome maiden would have been very appealing. As Guanyin the Bodhisattva of compassion could not be ignored, the mediator and the artists would have hit upon the idea of visualizing Guanyin in a form similar to Tara's and he cites three early paintings where the posture and mudras were akin to Tara's. These images belong to an era "where the forms of Tara and Guanyin began to merge".

In his book "Hinduism and Buddhism" Sir Charles Eliot states that the creation of female Guanyin was probably "facilitated by the worship of Tara and Hariti, the latter is frequently represented as caressing a child." In his view the Chinese religious sentiment required a Madonna and it is not unnatural if the god of mercy who is reputed to assume many shapes and to give sons to the childless came to be thought of chiefly in a feminine form.

The Wu Interregnum

An aspect that needs to be examined is the Chinese history during the Sui times. Yang Jian the founder of the Sui Dynasty, and who ruled as Emperor Wen was born in 541 in a Buddhist temple. Until the age of 12 he was brought up by a Buddhist nun whom he fondly called as the preceptor (*A-che-li*, Acharya in Sanskrit). Emperor Wen's queen Wen Xian came from a devout Buddhist family and was herself an ardent Buddhist who used to arrange Sutra reading in the palace in the evenings. Emperor Wen and his queen earned the name of *ersheng* -- Twin-Sages. In the year 602 the empress died. The empress had been a strong influence on the emperor. On her death the court historian promptly declared her a Bodhisattva. In view of the strong influence of the empress on the administration and the spread of Buddhist ideology it is possible that the Bodhisattva-ization of the empress could have marked the beginning of feminization of Bodhisattva.

Another remarkable example of feminine eminence a hundred years later was Empress Wu Zetian. Although according to the Confucian beliefs having a woman rule would be as unnatural as having a "hen crow like a rooster at daybreak", during the most glorious years of the Tang dynasty a woman did rule and ruled successfully. Women of this period enjoyed more freedom. They did not bind their feet nor lead submissive lives. Being born into a rich and noble family Wu was taught to play music, write and read the Chinese classics. When she was only thirteen she was recruited to the court of Emperor Taizong. When she was just an obscure imperial lady, she was loved by the young prince who later became Emperor.

On the death of Taizong, Gaozong retrieved Wu from a nunnery back to the palace. Wu, who was twenty seven years of age worked her way into the inner circle of the Emperor and by her ruthless manipulations became the favourite concubine of Gaozong. In time she gave birth to the sons he wanted and succeeded in deposing Gaozong's wife Empress Wang. As mother of the future emperor of China she became very powerful.

Emperor Gaozong was a weak character both physically and intellectually. Wu on the other hand proved to be a genius in sorting out the knotty problems of the Tang Empire. When the emperor suffered a crippling stroke she took over the administrative duties of the court and a position equal to the emperor. Just as the Sui Emperor Wen and his wife Wen Xian were called then, Wu and Gaozong became *er-sheng* (twin sages). Actually, beneath the surface of this "*twin-sagehood*" of Gaozong's ruling machinery there was only one authority i.e. Empress Wu.

In order to challenge Confucian norms against ruling by women, Wu began to elevate the position of women. She had scholars to write biographies of famous women. She said that the ideal ruler was one who ruled like a mother does over her children. Inspite of her ruthless climb to power, her rule proved to be benign. After the death of Gaozong she became the first (and eventually the only one) female "Son of Heaven" in Chinese history. Some of the titles that she arrogated to herself were "Sacred Emperor of the Golden Cakra", "*Shengmu*" (Holy Mother), "Her Majesty from the Phoenix Throne", etc.

During her reign Empress Wu placed Buddhism over Taoism as the state religion. She invited the most gifted scholars to China and built Buddhist temples and cave sculptures. Chinese Buddhism achieved its highest development under her reign. The Fengxian temple is the largest and most representative grotto at Longmen. It is said that after Wu Zetian was conferred with the title of empress she donated a year's worth of money ordinarily used for cosmetics to build this temple in order to enhance her prestige. The seated Buddha in the centre of the temple is a huge statue and has the appearance of a kind and gentle woman. It could be because Wu had donated the money to carve this particular Buddha hence the womanish face. Similarly the concept of *Shengmu* (Holy Mother) was also Wu's creation. As she was keen to be deified she had many statues cast to her liking. The impetus given by her for making innumerable images in female form resulted in the popularization of Guanyin as a goddess. As proof of this, one has to see the statues in the caves of Dazu (named after one of Empress Wu's reign eras) especially of Shengmu and several Guanyin images which have a distinctly royal bearing and feminine looks. Perhaps this was an important reason for scholars like Kenneth Chen to place the beginning of feminization of Guanyin to the Tang period.

Many scholars have sought to prove that *Pandaravasini* (clad in white) was the precursor to the White-robed Guanyin and have thus tried to explain the feminization of Guanyin. There is also the suggestion of transformation of Tara into the female Guanyin. But there is no evidence of Tara being transformed into female Guanyin or that *Pandaravasini* is actually White-robed Guanyin. Absence in intermediate figures in space and time indicative of a gradual evolution from either Tara or *Pandaravasini* into Guanyin the goddess in China is the strongest evidence against such a hypothesis. An important aspect that negates the above theory is that the emergence of "White-robed Guanyin" in China was after a gap of four to five centuries after the appearance of Tara in India. If the colour white symbolised purity, Guanyin could have been shown dressed in white holding a white lotus seated or standing on a white lotus base and there was no need for sexual transformation.

The entry of Tantric Buddhism gave rise to a bewildering variety of forms of Guanyin in the beginning. All varieties of forms from strongly masculine to feminine and the ambivalent forms of Guanyin were noticed in the Buddhist pantheon of China. This indicates people's unquestioned faith in such forms and various miracles seen in many Chinese texts played a decisive part in carrying on worship of the different beautiful female forms of Guanyin. In fact such representations were codified by many legendary miracles experienced by people and more so by women who looked upon the Goddess for alleviating their sufferings and get them their wishes.

The Influence of Cult Sites

It can be said that the Guanyin cult took root in China only when Guanyin became associated with certain sites and when people began to go on pilgrimages to these places. The deity's popularity in China led to the growth of cultic centres in various places. Miracles firmly anchored the Bodhisattva to these sites resulting in a rich fare about the almighty Goddess of Mercy in oral literature.

The first centre for Guanyin was Xiangshan. The Xiangshan monastery had an image of the 1,000 armed and 1,000 eyed Guanyin in Dabei Pagoda (Pagoda of the Great Compassionate one). It was described as being made in person by a human manifestation of Dabei.

Tianxiansi has an image of Guanyin which was also made by human manifestation of Dabei. Tianxiansi was a nunnery. In the era of 618-628, when the nuns wanted to have an image of the great Compassionate One painted on the wall they were in need of a good artist. In response to the call, a couple accompanied by a young girl arrived there and the girl who did the painting was apparently a manifestation of Guanyin.

Determining the sex of the Bodhisattva Guanyin (only in China) depends on the founding myths of pilgrimage sites. Pilgrimage sites vary in importance for two reasons. In some sites Guanyin may have appeared in person and performed miracles for common benefit. Some other sites may already have a miracle working image of Guanyin and thus become very well known to people all round. The Dabei pagoda near Xiangshan monastery belongs to the first category.

The Chronicle of the Upper Tianzhu tells us the "spontaneously found" image of Guanyin which turned out to be a discovery by monk Daoyi. From this account it appears that the image housed in Upper Tianzhu Monastery must have been the feminine white robed Guanyin. The white robed Guanyin became very popular from the 10th century onwards after Putuoshan became famous as Guanyin's abode and the iconography of white robed Guanyin began to be increasingly merged with that of Potalaka Guanyin.

Interest in the images and portraits of Guanyin and efforts to preserve and disseminate them were important mechanisms in linking Guanyin to a Goddess. Depiction of Guanyin in a like manner in different media undoubtedly helped its universal acceptance. Gazetteers have recorded tales of visions of Guanyin in Putuo shan in the female form with acolytes *Longnu* and *Shan Cai*. Shrines and pilgrimages form a hen-and-chicken chain-reactions to make the Guanyin cult an everlasting living culture in and outside China.

Conclusion

In India, Avalokitesvara was the product of assimilation of important Hindu deities, while in China the symbol absorbed all the characteristics and functions of indigenous goddesses as well as Buddhist goddesses like Tara and Hariti.

The Buddhist pantheon in China over a period of time had adopted many symbols some originally from India and later many other characteristics which are purely Chinese. The emergence of Moon and Water depiction of Guanyin is one such example which indicated absorption and assimilation. Another feature has been the introduction of *yin* symbols (for example - moon, water, vase) from the *yin-yang* polarity of Chinese thought. The assimilation process was then complete. If the symbols were to indicate certain ideas of the artist (not necessarily of the perceiver), the icons of Avalokitesvara in India, Nepal and China including Tibet give rise to innumerable interpretations. The introduction of tantric Buddhism gave yet another dimension to the whole concept with a variety of new and esoteric divine forms.

Guanyin images have thus undergone considerable expansion in China and have exceeded the boundaries of Buddhism. The deity was no longer an exclusive Buddhist religious symbol but had become a popular cultural hero/heroine to both Buddhists and non-Buddhists. Buddhist influence spread to other non-Buddhist realms in the daily life and culture of the Chinese though the period cannot be specified. Therefore the multiple images of Guanyin should be seen as the multireligious and cross-cultural symbol which was definitely feminine with many additional attributes.

The mighty support given by Empress Wu to Buddhism helped the Empress to promote herself as a compassionate Bodhisattva. It could be safely said that the female form gained momentum during her time underwent a long process of transformation gradually and steadily that Guanyin came to be accepted universally as a goddess. Many legends and folklore helped in popularising the goddess. The story of Daoyi's discovery of a piece of fragrant wood floating in the water near South Wutai mountain led to the first occurrence of Baiyi Guanyin while the Upper Tianzhu Monastery in Hangzhou undergoing a major revival. The Baiyi Guanyin enjoyed widespread popularity from the tenth century onwards. Paintings and statues, tales and myths of Guanyin temples from Northern Song (960-1127) were proof of the importance of the Baiyi Guanyin and the emergence of Putuo Shan as a famous Guanyin site.

Through multi-cultural engineering, the East Asians ultimately settled for an Avalokitesvara in the form of Guanyin, a graceful and powerful feminine symbol to demonstrate most effectively the quintessence of the Bodhisattva – Absolute Compassion.

Notes

1. C.N. Tay, "Kuan-Yin, the cult of half Asia"., *History of World Religions*, Vol. 16, No. 2.
2. Susan Naquin and Chun-fang Yu (ed), *Pilgrims and Sacred Sites in China*. University of California Press, 1992.
3. Glen Dudbridge, *The Legend of Miao-shan*, Oxford University Publishers, 1978.
4. Alice Getty, *The Gods of northern Buddhism*, Dover Publications, 1988.
5. Barbara Reed, "The Gender Symbolism of Kuan-yin Bodhisattva," *in Buddhism, Sexuality and Gender*, Sri Satguru Publications, Delhi 1992.
6. This is not restricted to Chinese society alone. This belief is also prevalent in India. In China in a popular tale associated with Putuo island, Guanyin rescues a menstruating girl in need.
7. Lokesh Chandra, *The Thousand armed Avalokitesvara*, IGNCA/ Abhinav Publications, New Delhi, 1988.
8. The Chinese word for fish is *yu* and is phonetically identical with the word meaning abundance. According to Wolfram Eberhard in the book *Hidden symbols in Chinese life and thought*, this symbolizes wealth. A picture showing a child with a fish would mean "May you have an abundance of high-ranking sons."
9. Maspero H."The Mythology of Modern China," in J. Hackin (ed.), *Asiatic mythology*, New York, 1932, pp. 352-58.

RADHA BANERJEE

25

MANICHAEAN INPUT TO CHINESE CULTURE AND ART

Years ago, Indians used to talk about China's insularism, and the "Middle Kingdom" looking down at all foreigners as "barbarians", obviously taking the other quarter's disinformation with a pinch of sugar. Gradually, as our direct channel of information from China opens up, we see a Taj Mahal being hidden behind high walls. The garden of art in China is a fascinating field with such magnificent varieties catching the eye. Here, I propose to deal with one of the varieties — the Manichaean art and culture. With the opening up of the Silk Road trade as a result of explorations in Central Asia by Zhang Qian (the Ambassador of Han Emperor Wu), many religious ideas and art motifs and other things came to China from the West in the 2nd and 1st centuries B.C. Among them mention may be made of Buddhism, Zoroastrianism and Manichaeism. The history of Buddhism and Zoroastrianism in China is well known. Little attention, however, is paid to Manichaeism and the manner in which it spread to the east including Chinese Turkistan (now Xinjiang, i.e., the "new territory" in its Chinese name) and China, particularly the coastal provinces.

Manichaeism was propounded by a cultural reformer called Mani who was born in 216 AD in Cteshipon in Babylonia which was then part of Persia. Mani proclaimed himself a prophet and the messenger of god in Babylon, although he was not of Babylonian origin, but an Iranian descendant. His father, Patik (*Pattikos* in the hellenized form) was a native of Hamadan, and his mother, Maryam was a member of the princely family related to the ruling Arsacid Dynasty. The name Mani is perhaps of Semitic origin, and the term *Manichaios* is a hellenization of the Aramaic *Mani Hayya*, Mani the Living. In Manichaean texts this epithet is often given to transcendental and benevolent things or beings. Mani is also called *Mar* (*Aram*, i.e. lord). His Chinese name, "Mo-mo-ni", is a version of *Mar Mani* -- Lord Mani. The environment in which Mani spent his youth accounts for the strong elements of eclecticism and syncretism that were his teachings. Mani was brought up in a liberal atmosphere. His father, by temperament, was inclined to mysticism, and was devoted to the study of the religious sects.

Mani was an exceptionally gifted child and he inherited his father's mystic temperament. It is said that communications of a supernatural character came to him. He travelled far and wide including Turkistan (*cin*), India, Iran etc. with many disciples to carry out evangelism. After forty years of travel he returned with his retinue to Persia and converted Peroz, King Shapur's brother to his teaching. The Zoroastrian priesthood, however, hatched plots against Mani by poisoning the ears of the king. After a brief period of hiding Mani was captured and crucified at the age of 65.

Manichaeism may be regarded as a ramification of Gnosticism. Central to the Manichaean teaching was dualism, conceiving the world and all its creatures in the Great Divide between the good, represented by Light, and the bad, represented by Darkness — and Mani personified Light or was the God of Light. Mani had thus adopted Zoraster's dualistic doctrine of the fundamental struggle between light and darkness, soul and matter. He also drew from the teachings of the gentle and humane Buddha certain lessons for the conduct of life to be acceptable everywhere by mankind. This eclectic character was the strength and the basic nature of Manichaeism.

Mani lifted a leaf from Buddhism. He divided his followers into two categories. First, the Elect or Perfect, who led a life of celibacy and extreme austerity, exemplifying the highest standard of life, and who dedicated themselves to the task of preaching the doctrine. Women as well as men were received into the order. The Elect wore white robes, which covered their bodies entirely. Even the hands were not to be seen unless they had to work — then they need not be covered. Various types of headgear, which indicate the specific ranks of their bearers, were worn in addition to the uniform white robe. There is an interesting painting from Chotscho, that shows a high priest with a distinctive headgear which evidently belonged to the Elect.

The head is encompassed by a solar disc and the crescent moon laid around it. Mani was venerated among the Uighurs as *Kun ai tangri, esun-moon-godi.* The symbols of sun and moon occupy an important place in Manichaean cosmology and these two celestial bodies emit spiritual light and enlightenment. The second category of Mani's followers comprised the Auditors or Hearers as the laymen of the community were called. Both the elects and hearers are disciplined by Mani's ten commandments. Manichaeism keeps seven seals for its emblem. Four of these were doctrinal, comprising: (1) Love for the god-patriarch; (2) Faith in the sun and moon as the great orbs of light; (3) Reverence for the divine elements in Primal Man; and (4) A recognition of the inspired office of the great revealers of religions. The other three seals were of a moral and ethical nature relating to the standards to be observed in day to day life.

Manichaeism was a typical trans-regional and trans-cultural religious movement. Paradoxically, the writings of Europe from Britain (including the *Encyclopaedia Britannica*), Russia and other countries hardly mention the influence of Buddhism on Manichaeism. But, the scholars of China and Japan have highlighted this influence. We know that when Mani preached in Turan in India, the local people took him as the Buddha. The Manichaean documents in Sogdian script also described Mani as Buddha. All this points to the hybrid character of Manichaeism which was preached east of Iran as different from its other stream that penetrated into Europe and northern Africa. We, therefore, can divide the Manichaean religio-cultural movement into two: (1) Western Manichaeism and (2) Eastern Manichaeism. Western Manichaeism did not survive long. By the end of the 6th century there was hardly any trace of it in the Roman Empire. But, Eastern Manichaeism was quite tenacious, lasting beyond the first millennium of our common Era.

Modern enquiries on Manichaeism in China was sparked off by the discovery by Sir Aurel Stein in 1907 of several Manichaean texts in Chinese along with many thousands of Buddhist scrolls from cave No 17 of the Dunhuang Grottoes. The Stein collection of Chinese manuscripts (now housed in the British Museum, London) comprise some important Manichaean manuscripts viz., the Confessional for the Hearer, The Hymns in praise of Mani and Manichaean deities and saints, and a Compendium of the teaching of the Sect. The example of Sir Aurel Stein was followed by Professor Paul Pelliot of France. He was an eminent scholar conversant in Chinese language. During his expedition in Central Asia he paid a visit to the Dunhuang Grottoes and took away from there academically valuable Chinese manuscripts including Manichaean documents to Paris (which are housed in the Bibliotheque Nationale). Among these documents there is a small fragment of Manichaean text containing a summary of rules for the Manichaean religious organization.

Chinese scholars have begun to trace the genesis of Manichaeism in China and discovered the presence of its culture as early as the post-Han period, around the 4th century. In *Jin Shu* (Annals of Jin Dynasty), there are two references which deserve our attention. There was a man named Liu Hong in Luoyang who gathered more than a thousand followers to his *Guangming* (light) belief which could be Manichaeism. (*Jin Shu, juan* 86). Another man Hou Ziguang, also of the Jin Dynasty, said he was the son of the Buddha coming from a foreign country named *Daqin*. He also gathered several thousand followers and proclaimed himself the "Great Yellow Emperor". (Ibid, *Zaiji* 6). He also could be a Manichaean convert having acquired his belief either in Europe (which was called *Daqin*) or in Asia Minor.

The most intriguing thing lies in the two Dunhuang manuscripts collected by Pelliot which were the fragments of the *Laozi hua hu jing* (The Canon about Laozi's reincarnation in a foreign country). In the first *juan* (fascicle), it mentions that 450 years after the passing away of Laozi, he flew to a neighbouring country in a gust of air of *ziran guangming dao* (the natural and bright Tao) passing through the *Sunyata*, and was born as a prince. Then, he left the palace and joined Tao, assumed the title of *Momoni* and turned the *Dharmacakra* (the wheel of truth). Then, he preached *erzong* (Two doctrines) and *sanjie*(three worlds). This discovery sparked off a warmth of interest among Chinese scholars who made inquiries about the text of *Laozi hua hu jing* which was authored by a Taoist priest, Wang Fu, during the Jin Dynasty in the 4th century AD. Here, Wang Fu seemed to be using the information from Manichaeism to achieve his aim — making belief that Buddha was an incarnation of the ancient Chinese philosopher, Laozi, who was revered as the patriarch of Taoism.

When was Manichaeism introduced to Central Asia is still a subject of speculation. While we concede Central Asia as the necessary conduit for Manichaean religion and culture to reach Chinese soil, there is also evidence of this religio-cultural movement retracing its footsteps to arrive at Xinjiang from the hinterland of China. In 755 there occurred the An Lushan rebellion against Emperor Xuanzong (reigning from 712 to 755) who fled from the capitals of Changan and Luoyang. The Tang government asked Uighur for help in quelling the rebels. The Uighur troops liberated Luoyang and Changan in 757 but did not withdraw until the following year. During his stay in Luoyang the Uighur ruler Mou Yu made the acquaintance of Manichaean monks probably of Sogdian origin. They must have made some impression on him, because when he vacated the city he took four monks with him. Shortly after this the Khaghan declared Manichaeism as the state religion of the Uighur empire. The whole story is narrated in the famous trilingual inscription of Karabalghasun. This is the first and only time in the history of Manichaeism that it reached such a high status of a state religion. Most of the Uighur nobles became converts to Manichaeism. Archaeological discoveries and systematic studies on the cave temples in Eastern Turkistan throw considerable light on the Manichaean religious and cultural activities in this region. Many Manichaean manuscripts were recovered from Turfan. They show that Manichaeism was widespread in Turfan during the 7th to 10th centuries. This is supported by the statement of the Arabic geographer, Tarim ibn Bahral-Mutawadi who came to Central Asia some time between the 8th and 9th centuries. He had observed that there were many followers of Manichaeism in Northern and Eastern Xinjiang. Another geographer Jahiz (9th century) has recorded that nine Uighur tribes were converted into Manichaeism by the eighth century.

Some fragments of a Manichaean book written in Turkish mention that in 803 the Khan of Uighur Kingdom went to Turfan and sent three Manichaean Magistrates to pay respects to a senior Manichaean cleric in Mobei. A Manichaean hymn of the 8th century from Turfan written in Middle Persian mentions that most of the Khan's kinsmen were devoted to Manichaean faith. The Manichaean manuscripts found in Turfan were written in three different Iranian scripts, viz. Middle Persian, Parthian and Sogdian script. These documents prove that Sogdia was a very important centre of Manichaeism during the early mediaeval period and it was perhaps the Sogdian merchants who brought the religion to Central Asia and China.

During the early 10th century Uighur emerged a very powerful empire under the influence of Buddhism with some Manichaean shrines converted into Buddhist temples. However, there was no denying the historical fact that the Uighurs were worshippers of Mani. The Arabian historian Al-Nadim informs us that the Uighur Khan did his best to project Manichaeism in the Central Asian kingdom (of Saman). Chinese documents record that the Uighur Manichaean clerics came to China to pay tribute to the imperial court in 934. The envoy of Song Dynasty by the name of Wang visited Manichaean temples in Gaochang. It appears that the popularity of Manichaeism slowly declined after 10th century in Central Asia.

Manichaean art is religious in nature, and devoted to the propagation of Manichaean doctrines. Mani, as is attested to by all oriental sources, was an accomplished artist, who utilized his artistic talent in decorating his canonical works using art for the popularization of his religious ideas. He despatched scribes and illuminators along with his missionaries to strengthen evangelism. According to his own testimony: the pictures illustrating his writings were to complete the educated people's instruction, whilst rendering the message easier to understand for others. It is generally held that in the matter of illustrating his instructional treatises he adhered to the tradition which was already evolved in the Gnostic circles. There were a good many rich Jews in Mesopotamia, thus, it is quite possible that they encouraged the production of costly manuscripts, and Mani made use of them to prepare his own illustrated sermons. Being an Iranian, Mani must have been influenced by the Parthian-Syrian art idioms of Dura-Europos in the execution of his art works.

Though Manichaeism spread in many countries, the majority of Manichaean art examples have survived only in Eastern Tukistan where the followers of this religion received a wide support from the Uighur royal families during the 8th-9th centuries. Of all the sites in Eastern Turkistan, Kharakoja seems to have been the most important centre of Manichaean activities. Manichaean art of the region can be divided into two broad categories, viz. the wall paintings and miniatures. Their existence and importance have hardly attracted scholarly attention. We are much indebted to the arduous efforts on the part of German explorers, A von Lecoq and his colleagues. It is from an old temple complex that A von Lecoq (a well known Turkologist from Germany) discovered first in 1904-5 water-colour painting of a Manichaean high priest surrounded by a number of his clergy all clad in white Sacerdotal clothes characteristic of the Manichaean monastic order. The portrait of the high priest is shown in his monastic robe with a rectangular piece of embroidery covering a part of his bosom. His tall white cap is also embroidered with gold. His face is oval, nose acquiline, but eyes small and rather slanting, typical of the manner in which Chinese artists depict a Westerner. The nimbus of the figure contains the crescent and sun disc symbols. This extraordinary nimbus and the impressive costume create the impression that the figure is very important and perhaps a portrayal of the prophet Mani. As I have alluded to earlier sun and moon symbols occupy an important place in Manichaean cosmology. The discovery of this picture disproves the old theory that the Manichaeans had no churches and shrines embellished with paintings.

Another mural fragment from Khoco portrays three Manichaean women on a blueblack ground which is also a piece of fine artistic work. These three women closely resemble each other. Their hair is parted in the middle and falls over the back and shoulders. Their headgear consists of a roll of white cloth tied in a bow behind the ears. The fragmentary condition of the painting makes it difficult to ascertain whether they represent lay women or deities.

Karakhoja[1] (Khoco) fragments have yielded many illustrated Manichaean manuscripts distinctive by their contents as well as their artistic qualities. We may first take up here for discussion the Manichaean Leaf, bearing the Berlin Museum No. Mik III, 4979. One side of it depicts a church ceremony, with a high ranking Manichaean priest in full vestments (but the picture of his head is lost). A red embroidered stole is wrapped around his neck and shoulders. The stole bears a pattern of red lozenges on white background. The priest kneels down with his right leg before a man in full armour who is probably a Uighur king with three attendants. To the priest's left two Manichaean elects stand behind in white garments along with a layman, probably an auditor.

In the foreground of the picture there is Ganesha along with the Hindu trinity consisting of Visnu in Varaha incarnation, Brahma, bearded and pot bellied, and the three-eyed Siva. Facing them on the left are seated two Iranian Manichaean gods. Below these deities the leaf is damaged but paintings of flowers and ducks can still be made out. The artist who has drawn this picture, it seems, is equally conversant with the Hindu and Manichaean pantheons. The Hindu deities depicted here correspond to their descriptions given in the Indian *Shilpasastra*. The scene perhaps tries to suggest that Mani had been in India and borrowed Indian religious ideas to enrich the Manichaean pantheon which is hinted by the Manichaean tradition. Even if he was never in India, his having come into close contact with Indian culture (including Hindu deities) is beyond doubt.

The miniature on the other side of the leaf depicts a religious celebration, the famous feast of Bema commemorating the martyrdom of Mani. This celebration took place every year in the Spring, for, according to St. Augustine, Mani died in March. In the centre of the picture, there is a red dias standing on a blue carpet. In front of the dias is a three-legged golden bowl containing melons, grapes, etc. as offering. Further forward stands a table bearing loaves of wheat bread in the shape of the sun disc and crescent. Again the miniature depicts several rows of different ranks of the elect many of whom have their names written on their white robes. The auditors (the hearers or lay worshippers) by their side can be distinguished by their high conical black hats.

Equally interesting is another Manichaean leaf (bearing No. MIK III 6368) in the Berlin collection. On one side of the leaf there is a two part picture divided vertically by a narrow band of writing in the middle. The picture shows priests arranged in two rows, one above the other. They wear black hair and tall hats. Each priest kneels at a low desk and each has a sheet of white paper in front of him. In the background are two flowering trees, one on either side. On one of the trees sits a golden bird. The other side of the leaf shows two splendid creepers, with inscriptions in black and red ink. The top of the leaf originally contained many musicians of whom only one vina player is extant. The floral designs and beautiful colours of this fragment are worth noticing.

In addition to the above there are several other fragments from a Manichaean book in the Berlin Museum collection. One of them contains the head of a woman with a beautiful face and a white hat. While another fragment shows the head of a man with usual white hat and sharp feature of a Uighur Turk. He has a well groomed moustache and beard. This type of face occurs later in Persian miniatures too.[2]

These mural fragments and miniatures illustrate various episodes and ceremonies pertaining to the Manichaean faith. They throw abundant light on the rites, rituals and costumes of the Manichaean priests and lay worshippers. Since the Manichaean religion is now extinct these murals and miniatures constitute a valuable source for the study of Manichaean religious life and art styles which are predominantly Iranian in character.

Manichaean art has left its mark also in the cave art of Central Asia. All the three temple complexes of Turfan, i.e. Toyuk, Bezeklik and Sangim, contain many Manichaean grottoes which have been studied in great details by Prof Chao (Zhao) Huashan of the Bejing University. According to his researches, the main and side chambers of the Toyuk Grotto No. 2 contain pictures of the Manichaean treasure trees accompanied by envoys of light, and of the meditations of the disciples, etc. These pictures are repeated also in the Toyuk Grotto No 7.

The Bezeklik temple complex too has many grottoes devoted to Manichaean subjects, like the veneration of the divine tree, portraits of Mani's followers in Persian dress, as well as a sketch of a Manichaean temple (Grotto No. 38 B. according to the classification of Professor Chao Huashan). From some of these Bezeklik caves there have been discovered also Uighur inscriptions which help in the dating of the caves.

At Sangim, Prof Chao could visit only two Manichaean temples which he termed as the Northern Temple and the Southern

Temple. They also contain many pictures depicting the Manichaean subjects such as the Tree of Life, the Tree of Death, the Orchard of Treasure Trees, etc.[3] We know from Manichaean texts that at the core of the Manichaean creed was a dualist doctrine that postulated two kingdoms: the Kingdom of Light (*guangming wangguo*) and the Kingdom of Darkness (*hei'an wangguo*). These two kingdoms are represented by two trees as mentioned above. There is an explanation of the nature of these two trees in the Book of Giants (*Juren shu*) that says: Virtue is expressed by Light or by the Tree of Life which occupies the East, the West and the North, while to the South there is the Tree of Death. The *Kephalais* (Essentials of the Faith), an ancient Manichaean manuscript written in Coptic discovered in Egypt during the 1930s explains that these two trees are the Tree of Virtue and the Tree of Evil. The trunk of the two trees twist around each other in two places. The relative positions of the two trees also illustrate the Manichaean doctrine of three moments i.e. the Initial Moment; the Median Moment, and the Ultimate Moment.

According to the *Compendium of the Teaching of Mani: the Buddha of Light,* a Manichaean temple has five sections containing a lectorium, a hall for instruction, a hall for prayer and penitence, a hall for preaching, and a monk's hospice. In these five halls, monks and their followers lived together, engaged in spiritual cultivation and character improvement. According to Prof Chao, the imposing Northern Mosque in Sangim typifies the Manichaean temple.

From the chronological point of view the halls are divided into two periods. In the former period, the layout has several features: the main chamber is relatively wide, the side chambers are also quite spacious, but the prayer and penitence hall is rather small. The frescoes of the first period, can be placed in the early seventh century specially the painting of the Grotto No. 2 of Toyuk. The boar heads of this period are surrounded by a ring of white circles set in black, resembling a string of pearls imitating Persian motifs of the Sassanian period. Toyuk grottoes show two portraits of donors wearing striped cloaks with their hands raised. Prof Chao Huashan has described this dress as that of Macedonian aristocracy. At that time Macedonia was an important centre of Manichaean faith. The Manichaean grottoes of the second period (9th century) are distinguished by the presence of the Uighur script and their large scale showing the might of the Uighur empire.

Manichaeism was very popular in China during Tang Dynasty (618-907), the documents of which period yield various names like *Moni, Momoni, Momonifa* (law of Mani), *Xiao moni* (small Mani), *Da Moni* (great Mani), *Moni shi* (Mani priest) etc. After Tang, these names disappeared, and Manichaeism was popularly known as *mingjiao* (the Bright Religion). During the Ming Dynasty (1368-1644), the government could not tolerate a non-government organization using the imperial title "Ming", hence, Manichaeism was banned, and its activities went underground. As I have alluded to earlier, during the post-Han period of political instability, Manichaeism arrived in China and was utilized by rebel leaders to mobilize followers. Such a phenomenon developed after the Song Dynasty (960-1279), particularly along the coastal regions where secret societies and rebellions sprang up by leaps and bounds. Even during the Song Dynasty there was the interesting occurrence in the two coastal provinces of Zhejiang and Fujian which is known as *chicai shimo* (literally, "eating vegetables and serving the devil"). In *Fozu Tongji*, which is an important historiography of Buddhism in China compiled by Buddhist scholars during 1258-1269, there is an account which categorically identifies these vegetarian followers of the "devil" as belonging to the Association of *Mingjiao*, i.e. the new Chinese name for Manichaeism. The account says that the leader wore a headgear of violet colour, while the followers wore white costumes. They worshipped the white Buddha.[4] Many of these followers demonstrated their rebellious spirit and were quelled by the Song government. After that, all subsequent governments were supressive against Manichaean activities, albeit the Manichaean followers' tenacity in their faith and in their organized activities.

The Quanzhou county of Fujian province was a place that used to have Manichaean activities from Song Dynasty onwards. This was also the place where there was an Indian community during the Tang and Song (and even afterwards), and where the remains of a Hindu temple have been found. Whether the presence of the Indian community and the Manichaean activities there had any connection with each other we are not able to ascertain. Historical reference alludes to a Manichaean temple built at Quanzhou in 1148. Archaeological excavations at the ruins of this temple at Huapiao Hill in this county have yielded several tens of broken pieces of black porcelain bowls of Song vintage, one of which bears the letters "mingjiaohui" (Association of the Bright Religion).[5]

In the Quanzhou Museum of the History of Maritime Intercourses (*Quanzhou haiwai jiaotongshi bowuguan*) there is a carved Buddha of the Mani Light which was recovered from the ruins of the Mani temple (of Song Dynasty) at Huabiao Hill. The sculpture is round in shape, resembling a sun. While a Buddha-like deity fills the circular sculpture, the deity wears a Chinese Buddhist robe and with a typical Chinese face. The design in the background depicts sun rays emitting from the deity. This very interesting artifact deserves close examination. It looks like that the *Mingjiao* followers were worshipping an alternative Buddha who, they might have wished, would bless the poor masses for a change — unlike the usual prevalent Buddhas in China who had been quite monopolized by the rich and high-ups. That Manichaeism came all the way from the Western Hemisphere to China to make the noble ideas and ideals serve the down-trodden is a fascinating historical phenomenon. I hope my brief account stimulates more Indian scholars to study it in collaboration with Chinese scholars.

In conclusion, Manichaeism was a religio-cultural movement that had a very significant influence on Chinese development. It is clear that its activities both helped spread the popularity of the Buddha and competed with the Buddhist institution to the extent that the Manichaean followers were maligned as "vegetarian followers of the devil". As the Manichaean culture was internalized by the oral literature of the common people the movement has lost much of its distinct traces as well. This, however, should not inhibit us from making further inquiries about this fascinating movement which also bears a dimension of Sino-Indian interface if only indirectly.

Notes

1. *Along the ancient Silk Routes: Central Asian art from the West Berlin State Museums,*The Metropolitan Museum of Art, New York, 1982.
2. *Ibid.*
3. Chao, Huashan, "New evidence of Manichaeism in Asia: A description of some recently discovered Manichaean temples in Turfan" in *Monumenta Serica*, No. 44 (1996), pp. 267-315.
4. *Fozu Tongj* (Chronology of the reign of the Patriarch Buddha), *juan* 48.
5. See Zhuang Weiji, "Quanzhou Monijiao Chutan" (Tentative studies on Manichaeism at Quanzhou) in *Shijie Zongjiao Yanjiu* (Journal of Studies on world Religion), Beijing, No. 3, 1983, pp. 72-82.

SOCIO-POLITICAL CHANGES AND ECONOMIC DEVELOPMENT

SOCIO-POLITICAL CHANGES & ECONOMIC DEVELOPMENT

社會政治經濟發展

Socio-Political Institutions

26. Development and Democracy: The Indian and Chinese Experience
Manoranjan Mohanty

27. Understanding "Human Relationships" in China
Kamal Sheel

Economic Developments

28. The Economic Ideas of Mao Zedong: Agricultural Transformation
Utsa Patnaik

29. Roads for Large Populations Towards Development and Prosperity
S.P. Gupta

Gender Issues

30. Change and Continuity: Orthodox Discourse on Gender Relations in China
Ravni Thakur

31. Women and Family in India and China
Bidyut Mohanty

32. Women and Adult Literacy in China
Shreemati Chakrabarty

MANORANJAN MOHANTY

26

DEVELOPMENT AND DEMOCRACY: THE INDIAN AND CHINESE EXPERIENCE*

One of the cruel ironies of today's world is that India which is applauded as the world's largest democracy has the largest number of poor and destitute in any country, and China which has achieved, a steady rise in people's living standards and has also acquired the status of a world power has failed to develop democratic institutions and practices. It is also interesting to note that despite the absence of liberal democratic freedoms the West has a deep fascination with China which is reflected not only in the tourist inflow to China but also in the flow of foreign investment and government good will. Operation of democratic institutions such as free and fair elections, existence of competitive politics and dissent do not particularly attract either Western tourists or Western capital to India. On the contrary the geopolitics of South Asia has been governed by the US and other Western countries as compared by India's pre-eminent position and therefore they have followed by an large a policy of containment of India vis-a-vis its neighbours. The functioning democratic system of India has had little effect on their policy.

The experience of India and China have put the theory of democracy to a severe test. Two old questions need to be asked again about democracy. In addition, two new questions have to be raised.

Do formal political institutions and practices constitute democracy or does it involve appropriate socio-economic conditions which enable citizens to exercise their political rights. On this issue India scores poorly with nearly forty per cent of its people below what is statistically called a "poverty line". China has asserted that it is engaged in creating better living conditions for its people after overthrowing semicolonial and semifeudal domination. Today, however, this dichotomy between economic and political conditions of democracy is seriously questioned. Their mutual dependence is emphasised. Therefore both India and China have to achieve yet more conditions of democracy.

The other familiar question relates to equality and freedom. Western liberal democratic theory asserts the priority of freedom over equality even though the radical stream in liberalism stresses that gross inequalities are detrimental to the exercise of freedom. On this criterion pre-Reform China scored higher marks than India. Social inequalities were reduced in China to a very large extent with the abolition of landlordism and formation of cooperatives and Communes and also takeover of the bourgeoisie owned industries by the state. The wage system was directed towards promoting equality and limiting income differences within the six point grade system. In India too there were a number of measures taken in the early decades following independence to curb monopoly in industry, abolish zamindari system and carry out land reforms. In both the countries the stress on equality declined in the 1980s and almost disappeared in the 1990s. In the past decade or so equality has been a low priority in both China and India. The "equalitarianism", "theory of eating from the iron rice bowl" and such ideas of the Cultural Revolution were severely criticised by the Chinese reformers as being obstacles to the development of the productive forces. The perspective of the present day leadership in China is to "allow some people to get rich first" so that the general level of growth is raised steadily. In India the introduction of the Structural Adjustment Programme promoted the ideology of profit and the egalitarian programmes of social transformation took the back seat.

The two new issues arise from the great democratic upsurges of the past few decades, namely the social movements such as the women's movements, the environmental movement, the autonomy movement and the human rights movements. One question posed by them is to concretise freedom as freedom from multiple forms of domination so that freedom to realise the

*Paper Presented to the 1995 seminar on "India and China Looking at Each Other".

potentialities of the human being is advanced. Patriarchal domination continues substantially in all the countries of the world as evident from the deliberations at the Fourth World Congress of Women in Beijing and as documents in the 1995 *Human Development Report.* China and India have only marginal difference among them. As to ethnic self-determination there has not yet been a scientific measurement. But both the countries have fairly centralised regimes and both have regions manifesting popular discontent. The caste hierarchy and disabilities in India are targets of public attention and social action. There is no comparable social problem in China though new forms of social stratification have emerged in the recent years.

The other issue is response of the modern state to these expanding democratic demands. All ruling elites would like to have an appearance of being popular and responsive to the demands of the various unprivileged groups. And they engage in innumerable measures of legitimation to create a climate of acceptability among the people. Thus the modern state is coercive, responsive and legitimative at the same time. For this purpose it has developed sophisticated systems of management of society, complex methods of propaganda and innovative techniques of manipulation. Today the technology of repression and the vast networks of communication allow the formal democracy to continue while the citizens remain helpless. There is a new authoritarianism in the modern societies including those of the West which make the basic notion of democracy nominal. The tragedy is that while failing on the scores of either political or socio-economic freedom both India and China have fast accumulated the resources of modern authoritarianism. These tools include modern capitalist preoccupation with consumerism promoted through advertisement. Sensate entertainment that commercialises culture in the global scale on the one hand and building up security forces of all kinds to suppress democratic movements on the other. It is this process which is strengthened by the forces of capitalist globalisation. The alliance of Western capitalists and the native elites has intervened to assimilate the rest of the third world into the Western model of capitalist political economy. The alternatives which the socialist revolutions and the anticolonial struggles had presented have been defeated in course of the battles of the recent decades. The socialist experiments adopted the same economic goals as capitalist systems and failed to promote socialist democracy. The anticolonial struggles such as India's which centred on the comprehensive concept of *Swaraj* failed to institutionalise after Independence.

The result was the crisis of the state and crisis of development in the third world to tackle which the elites leaned on the West. Thus today on the one hand there is an expanding demand for multidimensional freedom while on the other hand there is a an advancing tide of global hegemony by the capitalist West. The experiments in India and China are caught in this historical conjuncture.

With these comparative notes let us look at the democratic prospects in China.

The Communist Party of China's Perspective on Democracy

Has democracy receded as a goal in contemporary China? In recent years the proclamations of the Chinese leadership have articulated their policy perspective in terms of "reform, development and stability". The pressures from the Western countries on the human rights issue have had only marginal effects on the course of political development of China. The Chinese communist leaders have frequently asserted that stability in politics and society is an essential condition for China's economic growth and they would not take any risk that might disrupt that process.

Yet development of "socialist democracy" has been reiterated in every session of the National People's Congress (NPC) and also the Congress of the Communist Party of China (CPC) as an important goal. And above all, the constitution of China declares that the goal is to "turn China into a socialist country with a high level of culture and democracy". This statement constantly accompanies the well known objectives such as "four modernisations", and turning China into a "medium level developed country" by the middle of the twenty-first century. In other words, there is a continuing commitment to promoting democracy in China, but at the same time there is an unambiguous refusal to hasten up the process of competitive politics or expression of serious dissent in China.

To understand this contradiction let us try to ascertain to what extent do contemporary Chinese leaders share the Western notion of democracy.

Having been a product of the May Fourth Movement of 1919, the Communist Party of China was bound to uphold the ideal of democracy. After all the favourite slogans of the Chinese intellectuals then were pop promoting "Mr. Science" and "Mr. Democracy." At the same time the Bolshevik Revolution had provided the main inspiration for the foundation of the Communist Party of China and thus had prompted it to challenge the civilization. China's elite was also looking for its own ways of building a new society. It is this back drop in which we have to understand Mao Zedong's theory of New Democracy. Distinguished from bourgeois democracy of the West and socialist democracy of the USSR it was an anti-feudal, anti-colonial revolution based on the united front of four classes— workers, peasants, petite bourgeoisie and national bourgeoisie who constitute "the people" (*Renmin*). This created a system of people's democracy. It was both a class concept and a mass concept covering some ninety per cent of the population of a society the rest being the enemies.

The nature of the Chinese revolution and the operation of the People's Democratic Dictatorship after 1949 had a common organisational principle, namely, "mass line". It meant "from the masses, to the masses". The revolutionary strategy of the Communist Party of China during the 1937-1949 period relied heavily on the support of the masses and the same approach was sought to be implemented during the period of rural transformation, from land reforms to the People's Communes. People's involvement and active participation were essential aspects of Communist Party of China's political line under Mao Zedong's leadership.

The Cultural Revolution was conceived by Mao as a great experiment in socialist democracy. Masses were called upon to undertake ideological debates and orient all activities towards socialist goals of building an alternative participatory moral-political order serving the interest of the working people. It challenged not only the bourgeois notions of liberal democracy but also the elitist centralised system that had evolved in the Soviet Union since the days of Stalin.

It is the practice of the Cultural Revolution which invited a strong reaction from Deng Xioaping. The mass upsurge during the Cultural Revolution degenerated into conditions of anarchy, large scale and arbitrary persecution and institutional collapse. The Third Plenum of the Eleventh Central Committee of the Communist Party of China in December 1978 decided to "change the focus from class struggle to economic construction". Since then the approach to democracy in the Communist Party of China under Deng's leadership has been centred on this. The "one focus" and "two points" framework which governs the policies of the reform period in China has clearly affirmed this line of thinking. The perspective entails that the two points namely (1) "Reform and Open Door" and (2) Four Cardinal Principles have to promote economic development. (The Four Principles relate to adherence to socialist road, leadership of the Communist Party of China, People's Democratic Dictatorship and Marxism Leninism Maozedong Thought).

The contemporary approach of the Communist Party of China to democracy has three components. Firstly, the Chinese state has to continue to be a people's democratic dictatorship where freedoms are allowed within the stipulated terms defined by the Communist Party. Secondly, the basic economic and social conditions of life of citizens must continue to improve as material foundations of democracy. Third, institutions, law and processes of accountability must gradually evolve to enhance the quality of democracy. This perspective carries the class perspective into a new framework of promoting economic development. It has an element of power sharing vertically as well as horizontally especially accommodating the aspirations of minority nationalities.

This perspective is reflected in political practice in various spheres in present-day China. The Tiana'nmen Square demonstrations were crushed by the Chinese armed forces to reestablish the point that the dictatorship had to be maintained to ensure stability. Deng Xiaoping himself called it "a counter revolutionary rebellion". Those who wanted political freedoms in China along Western lines were condemned as proponents of "bourgeois liberalisation". Demonstrations and oppositional activities continue to be banned in China thus inviting strong criticisms from the western liberals that China was yet to develop "civil society".

In the same way the Chinese leaders claim that their concept of human rights includes right to basic needs of life, right to development and right to national sovereignty which are as important as right to freedom of expression and other civil liberties. This is how "stability" is regarded as a necessary condition for economic development. At the same time the Communist Party of China leadership has stressed the importance of building institutions and operating them with regularity and according to procedures. They wish to avoid by all means the anarchy and factional strife of the Cultural Revolution.

Thus the present approach to democracy in China is grounded in the historical experience of last hundred and fifty years since the Opium War. China wanted to get out of the humiliation suffered under colonial domination, so achievement of national honour in the world became a major political objective of all the leaders in twentieth century. All of them wanted to end poverty and destitution in China and build a prosperous economy comparable to the advanced western nations. They also wished to realise "People's rights" or curb feudal and other forms of socio-political domination within the country. Nationalism, Development and Democracy were the three themes which run through the ideas and politics of Sun Yat-sen and his Three People's Principles, Mao Zedong and his New Democracy and Deng Xiaoping and his Theory of building socialism with Chinese characteristics.

Thus democracy is not an isolated principle or ideal. As a system of self determination it is part of an integrated perspective involving values of nationalism, social justice and people's welfare. Democracy is not a mere procedural arrangement of elections and judicial process. It is at the same time connected with socio-economic rights of people. It is this approach which has unfolded concretely in recent policy measures in China.

While the Chinese communist leaders reject the western approach to democracy they are sensitive to certain global trends which uphold democratic values and norms. They cannot ignore the fact that this century has been a century of great democratic upsurge. The anti-colonial struggles, social revolutions and new social movements together have expanded human consciousness and urges for freedom. All countries including the liberal democratic and industrialized countries of the West are restructuring their systems to promote women's rights, rights of minorities, indigenous people, cultural identities, socially oppressed groups such as dalits in India. Besides, institutional guarantees of justice, participatory decision-making and accountability are demanded all over the world. Whereas the western powers would claim to assimilate all these demands within the capitalist framework other voices seek new kinds of democratic transformation that facilitate multidimensional liberation in all parts of the world.

As a part of this process the Chinese leaders have taken a number of steps to promote democratic changes in China during the reform period.

Democratic Practices

The constitution of People's Republic of China passed in 1975 was replaced by a new one in 1982 which bore greater resemblance with that of 1954. It dropped some of the Cultural Revolution elements and spelt out in detail the composition and powers of national, provincial and local institutions. Since 1978 the National People's Congress has been elected every five years and met annually to discuss the national budget and major policy matters. The Standing Committee of the National Peoples Congress meets almost every month to formulate laws and regulations. During the last fifteen years many laws have been made covering social, economic and administrative matters including foreign trade, taxation and criminal procedure which were left to discretions of Communist Party of China units earlier. Thus institutional functioning has improved considerably in China during the reform period.

Important decisions including appointment of Premier have been put to vote and that Li Peng's reelection as Premier in 1993 was not supported by more than one third of the National People's Congress Deputies, was also part of the published proceedings. Upto the County level the number of candidates has been more than the number of posts thus having an element of choice before the electors. At the *Xiang* (Township) and *Cun* (Village) levels there is a three dimensional division of power between Party, the Administration and enterprise management.

The role and status of the non-communist parties has acquired greater significance. The Chinese Peoples Political Consultative Conference (CPPCC) National Committee discusses all important policy drafts and gives serious suggestions. There are many appointments upto the Minister and Vice-Governor level from among non-communists. The mobilisation of patriotic forces of China and among overseas Chinese to build a prosperous motherland on a "united front" basis has facilitated this process. The non-communist forces do not treat this "united front" as a communist tactic but as a serious endeavour to build a prosperous China where they also make major gains for themselves.

The Communist Party of China functioning itself has changed its organisational mode. Opponents of Deng's line are removed from office, but not prosecuted as was the case in the earlier years or harassed by political campaigns as during the Cultural Revolution. There is much greater inner-party democracy in the Communist Party of China Politbureau and Central Committee at present leading to many compromise formulations involving Chen Yun (till his death) and Deng. Though Deng has ensured that proponents of his line alone are lined up in the Communist Party of China, People's Liberation Army and the government to succeed him.

The Prospects

The present-day theoretical framework in China centres around the concept of "socialist market economy" and "building socialism with Chinese characteristics" which were articulated in the fourteenth Congress of Communist Party of China in 1992. One of the characteristics is the role of the state in regulating the market for macro-economic coordination and for achieving socialist objectives of reducing disparities. In other words, firm political control by the Communist Party of China is a basic feature of China's political economy designed by Deng Xiaoping. The successor generation of leadership with Jiang Zemin "at the core", as they put it, seems to be committed to this line of thinking.

Visitors to China who interrogate Communist Party of China cadres on political issues are often told that they have tried to have two guarantees so as to prevent a Soviet type of collapse. One is the legitimacy of the reforms from which practically every household in China has benefitted and which has raised China's status in the world, making Chinese citizens proud of their country's economic achievements. Second is the strict political control and vigilance by the Communist Party of China which ensures stability and peace and concentrate all efforts on economic construction. Such an approach was evident from the assumption of top state, army and party — all in one person, namely Jiang Zemin as Party General Secretary, President of Peoples Republic of China and Chairman, Military Affairs Commission. At lower levels too — as in the Wuxi rural area where I have done field work — in many *cun's* the Director of a Village Committee and the Secretary of the Party Branch and Manager of the Industrial Company was the same person. This was the reversal of a trend of differentiation of the party and the government from enterprise management which had been operative in the 1980s.

This combination of market economy with political authoritarianism is likely to continue for the foreseeable future in China because of three reasons, two domestic and one external. The two domestic reasons are: First, the policies are popular in the country for they are raising people's standard of living everywhere. Second, a large measure of consensus exists among the Chinese elites, the victims of the Cultural Revolution who are in power and the beneficiaries of reforms, the managers, technicians, entrepreneurs, foreign returned experts. These are the forces who are in control in all spheres including the government, the army and the party. The structure of interests in contemporary China unites politics and economy so solidly that backed by patriotism this elite has a relatively smooth sailing course. The external impetus comes from the business corporations in the Western countries who find it easier to deal with clearcut authorities in authoritarian regimes rather than chaotic situations of conflict as in India. They find great merit in the East Asian model of market economies led by authoritarian regimes as in South Korea. In fact, China is developing close economic relations with the ASEAN countries which is likely to reinforce the present model in its own territory. Above all, the overseas Chinese whose investment in China has been a major accelerator of China's growth have shown more interest in China's economic development and rise as a major world power rather than in her democratic transformation.

This external factor has been unchanged despite the mobilisation of democratic opinion by the exiled Chinese intellectuals after the Tian'anmen episode. Their efforts to link up with dissidents in China and organise support campaigns for human rights have failed to influence either business groups or Western governments. Delinking of the annual renewal of Most Favoured Nation status in trade relations with China by US President Clinton a couple of years ago was an indication of this. The Chinese government makes occasional gestures like post-conviction deportation of Harry Wu earlier. But on the whole, China remains unmoved on its political line.

But such a model has its inherent contradictions. Market economy is considered a canon of liberal democracy in the age of capitalism. In China it may have achieved economic growth but has caused serious social inequalities. If the proportion of income disparity in a village like Hela in Wuxi was 1 : 10 in 1979, it was 1 : 10,000 in 1993 as per the data collected by me. In addition to inter-household inequality the disparity between regions has grown further. Coastal provinces such as Jiangsu and Guangdong are prospering very fast while inland areas such as Shaanxi and Ningxia remain far behind even though they too are developing steadily. The social differentiation among classes is increasing both in rural and urban areas, between rich peasants and poor peasants in the countryside and business persons, managers and ordinary workers in the city. The problem of the unemployed, migrant workers and the floating population is a serious source of social instability and discontent in China.

Yet another source of tension in the polity is the new milieu of competition in profit-making. With autonomy available to enterprise managers they try all possible methods to obtain business contracts within the country as well as from foreign investors. This has led to corruption and criminalisation in large scale. Ideological commitment having receded, the cadres are out to fulfil economic targets in one way or the other. Since 1993 the Communist Party of China has launched a massive campaign to curb corruption with summary trials of corrupt officials and heavy punishments, in addition to making apeals in the name of socialist morality. But still the trend remains unabated.

The culture of consumerism has emerged as a dominant trend in contemporary China. The austerity and simplicity of the Mao era was given up as outdated and an economic constraint on market development. So production and sale of consumer goods was emphasised as a part of the new economic path. This brought into China western goods and services, western life style and cultural practices. The Special Economic Zones may have been a source of much profit-earning for the PRC, but they were also the channels for the introduction of corrupt practices including smuggling and prostitution. The Communist Party of China has from time to time attacked such "cultural decadence" and "spiritual pollution". But it has failed to restrain the tidal wave of westernised consumerism. During the celebrations of the birth centenary of Mao Zedong in 1993 this theme was discussed in many fora. Still the leadership did not wish to stress this theme lest it led to a "reemergence of a left cult".

It is this objective social situation which is bound to lead to political protest and challenge to the prevailing system. Some may do it in defence of the Chinese revolution and legacy of Mao Zedong. Some who are inspired by western liberal democracy may use all opportunities to demand greater political freedom. Yet others while accepting the need for reform in the old style socialist system may challenge the present trend of capitalist development under Communist Party leadership and seek fuller democracy under a humane and participatory socialist system. They may cherish a vision of socialist freedom which secures material, cultural and political conditions of freedom in the course of building socialism. But none of these forces has the strength that can shake up the present regime. With domestic achievements and external support the Deng Xiaoping path for China is going to continue well into the twenty-first century.

KAMAL SHEEL

27

UNDERSTANDING "HUMAN RELATIONSHIPS" IN CHINA

The phenomenal growth of local enterprises in China is marked by a simultaneous increase in the role of social networks and corruption. It is said that for entrepreneurs and rural enterprises corruption has become an indispensable means of operation (Rocca 1992). Why is it so? How should one explain the paradoxical phenomenon of corruption and growth? What role does the particular nature and pattern of rural economic growth, evinced by the process of informalization, play in the rise of social networks and corruption?

The most essential characteristics of informal economy, is that it is a process of income generation activity that is unregulated by the institutions of society, in a legal and social environment in which similar activities are regulated. Its dynamism stems from its subversion of formal, bureaucratic and legal processes of production and distribution through informal, personalized, and extra-legal formats of arrangements. The informal economy is thus about linkages. Its deeper social embeddedness within the broader pattern of human interaction differentiates it from depersonalized and limitless competition of political economics of respectively the state plan and the free market. As a more socialized economy, defined by norms of primary communities and individualized choices of families or of individual participants, its reproduction and expansion, Shanin writes, is characterized by "lesser significance given to money-wages nexus vis-a-vis barter, inter-family and intra-family cooperation, self consumption and such considerations as patronage and clientelism, kinship loyalties and factional hostilities." (Shanin 1988: 114).

In the growth of local enterprises in China, the play of such social networks as family, clan and lineage connections or *guanxi* (literally, "relationship/connections")cannot be denied. This often manifests itself in economic efficiency and better productivity on the one hand, and informal and extra-legal practices or corruption and graft on the other. Thus, while they account for the widespread corruption and normalness, they are also the source for the success and growth of new income generating activities. As Helen Siu writes it would be naive to expect local wisdom and entrepreneurship to flourish if and when these irrationalities are removed (Siu 1989 :196). In fact such "irrationalities" may be seen embedded in the particular pattern of economic growth in rural China, of which social networks and norms are an integral part.[1]

Guanxi, Yan (1996) explains, is a uniquely Chinese normative social order which is based on the particularistic structure of relationship as characterized in Confucian ethics. In its primary form, that is based on primary relations familial, kinship, and communal as opposed to the voluntarily constructed — *guanxi* provides one with a social space and at once incorporates economic, political, social and recreational activities. Incorporated within *guanxi* is the notion of *renqing* (human feeling) which maintains moral obligations, emotional attachments and stable reciprocity over a long period of time. Yet, it is, Yan writes, "not a static structure but a dynamic process embedded in social interactions in everyday life, all of the relational boundaries in one's *guanxi* networks have to be defined and redefined repeatedly through active participation in social exchanges." (Ibid:4). In its extended form, *guanxi* refers to the cultivation of myriad forms of new short-term and instrumental connections outside the framework of primary relations for mutually beneficial purposes. Here it "ceases to be a total social phenomenon; instead, it has become a web of single-stranded connections, each of which has a special function in advancing one's personal interest." (Ibid: 23). "The distinction between the primary and extended forms of *guanxi*, while recognizing the different practices between villagers and urbanites, takes into consideration all possible links between rural and urban, between old and new and between past and present." (Ibid: 25). Its specific nature is dependent upon historical socio-cultural context of a region.

Explaining the role of *guanxi* in Chinese socio-cultural order, Mayfair Yang terms the collection of practices in the realm of personal relationship and social exchange in society as the Chinese gift economy, or the art of *guanxi*. According to Yang the gift economy consists of the personal exchange and circulation of gifts, favours and banquets, and the art in *guanxi* exchange "lies in the skillful mobilization of moral and cultural imperatives such as obligation and reciprocity in pursuit of both diffuse social ends and calculated instrumental ends." (Yang 1989: 35). She notes that in the contemporary political and cultural economy of China, the gift economy along with the state redistributive economy and the resurgent petty commodity economy is one of three distinct and contesting modes of exchange. "The gift economy thus does not arise in a vacuum, nor is it a totally independent mode of exchange lying completely outside of state distribution. Rather, it poaches on the territory of another mode of exchange, seeking the right occasions to strike and divert resources to its own method of circulation. In the process, it alters and weakens in a piecemeal fashion the structural principles and smooth operation of state power." (Yang 1994:189). In this fashion, it challenges the official power and subverts the dominant mode of economy.

Yang, however, correctly cautions us not to conflate informal economy with the "gift" economy. Both have their own distinct forms. They follow their own rules and operational logic. But they are not mutually exclusive in the sense of representing separate institutions of functions (political, economic, religious, etc) of social structure; rather their techniques traverse institutions and are intertwined within them." (Yang 1989: 27). This distinguishes what is deeply socially rooted and acceptable and what is "invented" and may or may not still be acceptable. To be more precise, it points to one form of "gift giving" as socially acceptable and to the other as socially inappropriate or corruptive part of informal economy.

Conversely, it would however be equally wrong to equate the informal economy exclusively with venality. As noted above, its reproduction depends upon entering into both formal and informal social exchange within a given context. What is important to note here is that the informal economy transgresses boundaries of the existing moral economy in the same fashion as it did of the command economy. This transgression may make some of its activities acceptable and some condemnable for not being exclusively geared towards both "diffuse social ends" and "calculated instrumental ends" but only the latter. Also, such transgression may indicate reconfiguration or extension of existing social networks and relationships in a novel form within the specific historical context of China, with its characterization as positive and/or negative functional-roles or its viewing as the return of the suppressed traditional or pre-capitalist values.

To the extent that the growth of local enterprises depend upon circumvention or subversion of the formal command as well as moral economy, its articulation results in informalizing social relationship through redeployment of existing socio-cultural norms and through restructuring, recycling, or "invention" of tradition. Multiple forms of socio-economic arrangements are thus generated at the fringes of command (as well as moral) economy. Sneaking into the territory of formal networks, these arrangements blur the boundaries of formal and informal, and old and new or reconfigured social relationship. In such a situation, *guanxi* may be established by revitalizing or reconfiguring such traditional institutions of society as family, village or communal units. It may also come about, as Rocca writes, through linkages to the newly reform-introduced culture of consumption, ostentation, opulence and individual enrichment. (Rocca 1992). Such extension or hybridization of *guanxi* may result in the primacy of means-end feature of such an instrumental web of personal connection. Alan Smart however correctly observes that the instrumental features of *guanxi* need not be overemphasized at the expense of ignoring the involvement of long-term trust and emotional attachment in such relations. He writes "manipulation and exploitative use of gift exchange is made possible only by the existence of forms of gift exchange that attach priority to the relationship as opposed to the immediate instrumental objectives." (Yan 1996: 24). Reconfigured or new routes to establish *guanxi* networks thus provides the possibility of blurring or extending the meaning of primary form of *guanxi* itself. But in both forms, its role in subverting the formal or state structure cannot be denied.

The imperative for the use of *guanxi* in both its primary and extended form emanated from the post-Mao institutional changes which vigorously promoted industrialization and marketization. In the Maoist period of collectivization, Anagnost notes, "the village resembled, in certain striking ways, the closed corporate communities of the Latin American highlands. With the recent policies, however, the avenues to wealth within the village have become increasingly dependent on the individual connections that extend outside the local community." (Anagnost 19849: 214). During the era of communes, production brigades, and production teams, collectives controlled almost all means of production. No independent production function was alloted to the peasant households. Moreover, the state's policy of socialist egalitarianism promoted "the big iron rice bowl" and discouraged individual differences in talent, knowledge and experience replacing the principle of "to each according to his work" in income distribution. In this context, the post-Mao decollectivization and the contract responsibility system provide peasant households autonomy over their production activities making them independent commodity producers. Yet, the new ethic of entrepreneurship or the policy of "getting rich first" within a socio-political structure characterized by the control of the bureaucratic party-state over the essential resources requires full play of *guanxi* for its efficient access for income generation.

In the particular context of the growth of rural enterprises of China, the play of *guanxi* networks in both its primary and extended forms may be observed in interpenetrating and diffusing the boundaries between the state, capital and labour. We therefore use the distinction between the primary and extended forms of *guanxi*, as suggested by Yan, with possibilities of overlapping between them, in explaining their respective roles in the reproduction and expansion of local enterprises.

Guanxi In Its Primary form and Its Impact on Rural Enterprises

Guanxi based on horizontal family, clan and communal networks accounts for multiple arrangements necessary for the rise of local wisdom and entrepreneurial spirit or ethic. Its imperatives rise not because local governments have lost their leading role in the countryside as a consequence of the post-Mao reform but because peasant households have emerged as independent production units — contesting and encroaching socio-political and economic resources controlled by the state. Relative autonomy to their process of production and distribution facilitated their use of multiple socio-economic arrangements available to them to coopt, incorporate or control the local bureaucracy. Clan and lineage networks thus have sprouted in the post-Mao era to fill the void vacated by the state. One thus, witnesses, restoration of clan/lineage/community temples and ancestral halls, dormant after the Communist Revolution and often destroyed during the Cultural Revolution. The ubiquitous clan registers — which traditionally established rights and privileges of a household within social, cultural and territorial boundaries of clans, have resurfaced. The local peasants often pay between 10 to 30 yuan per male in each household for registration. A family with many children even contribute more than 100 yuan for this. The role of clans in local feuds and conflicts as well as mutual assistance in production have increased. It is said that during hardships in their daily lives, peasants now mostly turn to clansmen for help and security. A study notes that "with the founding of new China, the power of clans came under destructive attack and disappeared from the scene for a time. In recent years, however, clan power has once again raised its head in rural communities, and is continuing to grow." (JPRS 14 January 1992: 79). It laments the rise of such potentially damaging force as a feudal remnant in rural communities. The study report, however, notes that "we must realize clearly that the resurgence of clan power in China's rural communities at the present stage is the resuscitation of an old force in the process of rural economic system reform. To a certain extent, it temporarily meets certain needs of rural residents by arousing once again the clan kinship feelings that were suppressed in the past. In some aspects of production and daily life, this fills a void left in the collective economic organization." (Ibid: 82).

The rise of *guanxi* networks based on clan and other horizontal social institutions thus provide an alternative means to carry out production and fulfil other local socio-economic needs. As such, it subverts constraints imposed by the state and opens avenues for the growth of local enterprises. It interferes in the state's collection of taxes, control of resources, and transmission of information. Describing the rampant phenomena of "petticoat influence" and "relationship networks" in rural communities, Chen Youngping notes that now:

> "When township and town leaders select cadres, they appoint only relatives; when they appoint or nominate village organization cadres, they favor fellow clansmen; they place trusted followers in important agencies or in positions where a profit is to be made; and whenever a clansman or his children break the law, they intercede on their behalf .... Because an overwhelming majority of township and town cadres are villagers from certain natural village who grew up locally, they have thousand and one tie to the clan groupings in the natural villages and a strong clan consciousness... As a result, clan power, as well as the strengthening of the patriarchal clan system concept that stems from it, has permeated government agencies. Thus the corrosive influence of cadres on clan powers and the clan system concept intensifies the corruption of Party style and the social atmosphere." (Chen 1992: 81).

It is therefore not surprising when a town cadre in the township government remarks that presently in the appointment or nomination of a rural organization cadre, not only is it necessary to take into consideration whether a person's work performance is adequate, but one must also take into account whether the clan he represents is influential; otherwise it will be impossible to move ahead with work. (Chen 1992:81).

In rural economic life also, the clan power have permeated the rural collective economy. Clan takeovers of rural enterprise, or the clear trend towards such clan takeovers are becoming frequent. Chen's (1992) survey of five villages found that between 1986 and 1987 several small collective enterprises were established with antiquated equipment thrown out by the larger urban industries. Each had not more than 15 workers. In all, the plant personnel were appointed jointly by the higher authority and village organizations. All these enterprises, however, soon lost money. In 1988, the plant manager contract responsibility system was introduced with the right of appointment to village organizations. Managers were granted autonomy in hiring staff and workers. They in all cases hired their relatives or clansmen, managed their enterprises in patriarchal fashion, and turned these ventures into profitable income generating activities inspite of the general slump in the economy.

For example, the Maotao Village Plastics Plant produced plastic packing boxes for food products with an output value of 150,000 yuan per year. This plant, it is noted, had only seven staff members and workers, four of whom were directly related to the plant manager, including a daughter, a younger sister, the younger sister's husband, and a niece. The other three staff members and workers were fellow villagers that the plant manager trusted. The plant manager said: "Members of one's own family are easy to get along with. They have a family feeling about the plant, and they do not quibble about how much money they make." That such family style village enterprise is able to succeed so well in prevailing economic slump makes people treat him with increased respect. (Chen 1992: 82).

Small and medium size enterprises in rural China are usually embedded in the local kinship system. "Even in enterprises where production socialization is advanced," a study notes, "the family style mode of production is still widely followed. In such activities as putting together optimum work team and project contracting, the hiring of relatives and contracting of family members are extremely common." (Yang 1991: 80). According to Yang, reasons for this "clannishness" in enterprises lie in its capacity to recruit and retain labour. In remote areas, enterprises have no recourse to recruit outside workers and their own workers have problems finding marriage partners. The survival and expansion of enterprises thus require hiring children of its own workers, most of whom are married within the locality itself. Poorer enterprises as well as those with low status and hard work, e.g., welfare, environmental, public health, and construction enterprises, are also forced to look inward for recruiting workers for the above reasons. On the other hand, better endowed enterprises like those of high-tech, "three capital sources", foreign trade, and high status, naturally attract a large number of workers with those already having "connections" there succeeding. In both types of enterprise, "clannishness" thus tends to increase. Such clannishness help enterprises recruit labour and thrive. But it also results in the abnormal movement of labour, weakening labour market, promoting dependency, and discouraging talent, education and experience.

The play of inter and intra family cooperation, its capacity to control the self consumption, its abilities to provide access to opportunities and resources, and its subsumption of exploitative labour relationship or hostilities within bonds of complicity indicate the myriad ways in which *guanxi* networks promote income generation and expansion of informal sector. Yet, these also account for the rise of local protectionism, parochialism or creation of what Chinese call "kingdoms", factional hostilities and exploitation.

Extended *Guanxi* and Its Impact on Local Enterprises

In the second instance, *guanxi* in its extended form relates to instrumental-personal ties which often manifests itself in corruption. As such, the *guanxi* networks facilitate informal sectors to bypass formal rules and regulations to gain access to essential resources, subsidized credit, state-contracts, tax benefits to keep its price advantages and maintain its income generation activities. They create the basis for the informalization of privilege or the bureaucratic corruption, and more broadly informalization of social, political, and economic norms.

Guanxi in the specific context of the informalization of privileges, Lee writes, "refers to informal relationships among official and cadres. Such *guanxi* operates outside the formal structure of the Party-state. *Guanxi* is concerned with an expectation of reciprocity on a face to face setting. It carries some pejorative meaning in the sense that it may not be legally acceptable, or at least is not regarded as proper." (Lee 1990: 35). It accords preferential treatment as against established conventional norms to those "outsiders" who come into its networks. It creates spaces in normal formal channels, opens so called "back doors", and accommodates the "other" into the threshold of dominant interests. One of the factors accounting for the growth of local enterprises, Oi notes, is the privileged access to selective allocation through connections and "going through the back door." (Oi 1995: 1142). A report on the problem of enterprises thus similarly notes that as the government directly controls enterprises through measures such as directive planning, materials distribution, and pricing control, enterprises are forced to look for ways out of their production operation difficulties through asking help from "mayors" instead of seeking markets. (JPRS 20 March 1992: 28).

The practice of the gift-giving or money transactions without establishing personal relationship (i.e., as established in the norms of the person or office) for exclusive one time economic benefits may be called institutionalized corruption. Their descriptions in the Chinese press, however, reflects the thin boundary between the un-institutionalized and institutionalized corruption and its heterogeneous forms. For example, one of the economic crimes of local enterprises was noted to be "seeking opportunities to make a fortune by holding dinner parties and giving gifts." It explains that "some people in rural enterprises profit themselves under the name of holding dinner parties and giving gifts. To link up with a large factory, a small town factory of 40 employees spent 23,000 yuan on gifts, about 40 percent had nonstandard receipts." It was less the custom of gift giving for the enterprise benefits than the one time collective swindling of money to make personal fortunes which was more objected to. Similarly, a 1996 report finds public funded entertainment doing far greater harm than public funded wining and dining, and notes that in spite of the state regulations against it the practice has continued in many overt and covert ways. (FBIS-CHI-96-021 31 January 1996: 17).

A study of economic crimes of rural enterprises notes its most serious manifestation in "the unlawful possession, embezzlement, diversion and waste of collective property by employees through the use of power and position." (JPRS-CAR-92-002 22 January 1992: 81). It raises objection to the personal swindling of money by the managers of enterprises but remains mum on the swindling by the collective. On the other hand, a provincial report from Shandong lamented excessive corrupt practices by the collective enterprises. Its four month audit unearthed financial irregularities of 510 million yuan in the form of tax evasion and breaching of provincial regulations; the total amounted to 8 percent of the national fund in question. It informs that "in the industrial and commercial circles, and in some administrative institution, the phenomenon of fiddling around with the books, retaining sales income and profits that should be handed over to the government, issuing lavish bonuses in cash or in kind, giving gifts or dinners, and giving and taking bribes are widespread." (SWB 11 January 1989).

Another document on "unhealthy tendencies" details "evil practices of using certain loopholes or weak links in reform to seek personal gains or selfish interests for a certain unit." For example, state organizations, functionaries, and enterprises illegally buying up state materials in order to resell them at a profit to the benefit of individuals but to the detriment of the public, the reform, and the state construction plan. Listed in corruption are also cases of giving unauthorized promotion in work or grade in a haste to disrupt the wage reform and cadre system of state functionaries; using one's position and powers to accept bribes, extort money from other people, smuggle or trade smuggled goods, illegally remit or withhold foreign exchange, evade taxes, and embezzle state financial and material resources in violation of law and so on. (Quoted in Myers 1989: 195).

Such list may go on longer and longer. References of the stupendous growth of corruption abound in the current official reports. Scholars have noted its multiple forms and variety (Ostergard and Petersen 1991; Oi 1989; Myers 1989; Sands 1989). Without digressing into a discussion of corruption, it may be noted that precise demarcation between *guanxi* and corruption, because of its thin boundaries, requires examination of particular local contexts.

In fact, multiple forms and ways of gift giving and bribery make the distinction between the two difficult. They are extended under the names which are perfectly legitimate and have the sanction of both state and society. It is reported that bribes are now offered under more than thirty names, such as letter of appreciation, information charges, rebates, handling charges, fees for hard work, etc. All these are permitted by the state in the economic sphere. The bribes are also offered as gifts in the name of celebrating a festival, marriage, funeral, moving to a new house, loans, and various other occasions of life-cycles which have traditional social sanctions and are part of the normative social order. Informalization of such formal channel of state legitimated fee-payment and socially sanctioned gift-giving lead to the ambivalent meaning of such practices. Its ambivalence makes the prosecution difficult. The Chinese Law Newspaper thus laments that people and enterprises do not inform authorities of offences that take place.

"Concern about good-will" maintaining *guanxi*, a report says, "is becoming more and more intense in China's cities and countryside nowadays, and the giving of 'good-will gifts' is also getting worse." (JPRS-CAR-90-027 13 April 1990).[2] Its survey in 1988 of the Yiyang prefecture, Hunan province, reflects that peasants spent 170 yuan per person per year or close to one third of their earning for good-will gifts. In Shenyang, city residents paid close to one fourth of their income for the gift-giving.[3] Yan's study of the cost of cultivating *guanxi* in Xijia village, Heilongjiang province found that the majority of peasants there spent more than 20 per cent of their household income for gift giving. Of the families surveyed, 31 per cent of them spent between 301 to 500 yuan, and another 31 per cent between 501 to 700 yuan per year for gifts with the average cash income per household in 1990 being around 2,500 yuan. 21 percent of families even spent more than 701 yuan and only 17 per cent extended less than

300 yuan as gifts. (Yan 1996: 11). Such astronomical proportion of the household budget going for the cost of cultivating *guanxi* not only reflects its necessity and importance for a peasant household but also its increasingly extended uses. Under such circumstances, it is indeed difficult to determine when and at what point this practice left the threshold of gift-giving and turned to bribery.

Noting this phenomenon, a report indicates that formerly, when relatives or friends married in a rural village, the well-wishers coming to the wedding brought with them several *jin* of rice or noodles, or they carried a basket of eggs, melons, or fruit, or possibly even a chicken in order to partake of the wedding meal. Later on, this "escalated" to where sending 5 or 10 yuan was considered "generous". By 1987, a peasant in the Zhujiang delta region of Guangdong province had to send a gift worth at least 20 yuan, and "during the past two years, the price of the gift has 'gone up' tremendously." (JPRS-CAR-90-027 13 April 1990: 57). The Rural Socio-Economic Survey Team of Jiangling County in Hubei province notes that within a year, from 1988 to 1989, the cost of "red expenses" (i.e., wedding expenses) have registered a 40 per cent rise from 6,368 to 8,964 yuan. According to the Beijing Municipal Statistical Bureau survey, the average cost of marriage in 1989 was found to be around 12,000 yuan, increasing 2.06 time from over 5,948 yuan spent in 1986. In Shanghai, and richer areas like Wuxi and Wenzhou, the wedding cost have crossed 10,000 yuan long back.[4]

Marriages are also getting marked by ostentious display of wealth. Until 1988, colour television sets, refrigerators and tape recorders were the only luxury items that a young couple in the countryside desired as the wedding gifts. Now, "these three luxury items have become 'necessities' at marriage time, 'otherwise the marriage is off!' How shameful when other people see that there is not even a television set, refrigerator, and such for the wedding!" (*Ibid*: 55).[5] Gold has become popular and is used for rings, earrings, necklaces, and brooches. At wedding feast, large denomination bank-notes are used to make tiny boats in the shape of gold ignots to float on the soup served with each guest receiving one as a gift. Or, notes are used to form "Double Happiness" character suspending in the main room as a mark of honour. Some couples get their nuptial chamber decorated in a style which is neither Chinese nor western but costs more than 30,000 yuan. Not unlike marriages, funeral ceremonies and other ritual too are marked by conspicuous consumption. For example, a young entrepreneur in Nanxi zhen, Siu notes "singlehandedly financed the funeral of his grand father, providing 40 banquet tables for the mourners. According to friends, this generation skipping in funeral finance was brash and unconventional act, but good for business all the same." (Siu 1989: 201).

As far as marriages are concerned, it is reported that more than 50 per cent of the wedding expenses in Beijing and Wuhan comes from parents and relatives' gifts. In Hubei, a survey reflects that 77 percent of expenses were borne through assistance from parents or gifts from friends and relatives.[6] Poor or less influential households, not able to afford such "red expenses", raise the money by taking loans from everywhere. It is noted that 23 per cent of rural wedding preparations are now paid for with loans and the situation is no better in cities. Gifts and loans from relatives (near and/or extended) and friends indicate occasions when money tranactions may facilitate building up of *guanxi* and may in many instances cross the fringes of gift-giving to acquire the status of bribery.

Similarly, the process of informalization provides avenues for hybridization or extension of *guanxi* networks through the recycling of available socio-cultural resources or invention or reinvention of tradition. This manifests itself in revitalization of festivals, ceremonies, religion or even creation of pseudo socio-cultural organizations. Helen Siu's fine description of the recycling of chrysanthemum festivals in Xiaolan village in Guangdong province demonstrates the need to attract potential investors to the area resulted in staging the festival and historically such recycling facilitates the onward percolation of a state culture to make local society. In the context of post-Mao reform policies, the chrysanthemum festival, she writes, "was organized by the town government with a different order of magnitude... The cadres in Xiaolan felt that staging the chrysenthemum festival was useful and appropriate as an event to show the overseas Chinese, potential investors in the new era of economic reform, that the government was liberalizing in earnest. Addressing the festival largely to the regional and the lineage associations overseas, the organizers shrewdly played the 'politics of native roots'. The festival was unmistakenly a local government event and to celebrate it in the traditional style, former landlords and 'literati types', knowing the art of cultivating chrysenthemum, were sought out to train apprentices." (Siu 1990: 785).

Rise of religion, cults, new scientific and technological organizations are all symptoms of the informalization process encroaching and subverting the formal structure for diverse needs arisen from heterogeneous activities for income generation. They point to the hybridization of *guanxi* networks. Noting the activity of new scientific and technological organizations at the township level, a CPC report from Jiangsu remarks that these "have arisen everywhere in response to the peasants' quest for wealth, and their organizational power far exceeds that of party and government organs. Nearly 100,000 associations have been established throughout the country for the study of specialized technology, and they claim over 3 million members. Now that the Party's rural economic policies have brought further deregulation, this force will 'sweep the plains like a praire fire'." (Wang Shulin, 1993: 4; see also Wang and Yang 1991: 85-90). Religion, it is noted, is gaining power and has become a social force intervening in party and government organs. In a country in Northern Jiangsu, the number of protestant Christians has arisen from mere 1,500 in 1979 to over 20,000 in 1991 with 35 percent of members belonging to the younger generation. (Wang 1993: 4). Negatively, there are instances of rising of gangs, cults like the temporarily expanded Mao cult in 1989 and later, and other such pseudo tradition based on associations which are still illegitimate, unaccepted, and rejected but their dangerous potentials are difficult to discount.[7]

Multiple forms of arrangement evolving out of the process of informalization thus can be seen as directed towards either/ or both "diffused social ends" and "calculated economic ends", overlapping often to serve diverse needs for the reproduction and growth of local enterprise. In this sense, the phenomenal rise in gift giving, ostentatious display of wealth in marriage and other social occasions, and the resurgence and elaborate restructuring of the traditional social and cultural practices indicate the imperative of establishing *guanxi*. Its significance in creating informal space in pursuit of entrepreneurial spirit and attaining the objective of income-generation or profitability cannot be denied.

Finally, the resurgence of these pre-capitalist relationships need not be taken as the return to precapitalist forms of production. It should be seen more as one of the many forms of relationship in the process of production and distribution in which both new entrepreneurs and the local governments enter for their local enterprises. Old forms thus continue but acquire new meanings in a changed historical context. The post-Mao rural reform, characterized by the informal economy of growth thus do not indicate a return to pre-capitalist mode but a novel mode of production.

Conclusion

Seeming paradoxes and "irrationalities" evident in the growth of local enterprises in China's rural areas thus are necessary parts of the operational logic of the process of informalization. If fact, in contemporary China, what usually appear as paradoxical or irrational in the context of accepted patterns of either socialist or capitalist economies can be better comprehended as the motor force of economic growth integrally linked with the informal economy. The contemporary assertion of entrepreneurial spirit is rooted in such factors as accretion of a strong state with active market forces, reconfiguration of labour relations on the basis of local and personal considerations with attendant degradation and exploitation, and the rising phenomenon of "*guanxi*" -- substituting and rearranging vertical relationship of production with horizontal networks of social exchange alongwith "adaptive mechanism" available within a particular socio-cultural realm. Such successful instances of growth indicate that what unlocked the energies and creative potentialities of people was neither the "state getting out of economy" nor the emergence of pure market relationship but their convergence within a unique set up of history and culture to which economic activity is embedded. It is thus likely to produce a process of growth in which parochialism, protectionism, venality, new social actors divided on the basis of gender, generation, and clan or ethnic ties or their riches would be as much embedded in socio-political and economic activities as the authoritarian state interventionism, "capitalist" values and market practices, and freedom for entrepreneurial initiatives.

Notes

1. In fact, finding the ambiguous nature of property rights in China, economists like Weitzman and Xu emphasize the need to look at the particular characteristics of the Chinese culture to explain the phenomenal growth of local enterprises.
2. Much of the ensuing discussion is based on survey reports on contemporary wedding expenses published in JPRS-CAR-90-027 13 April 1990 : 54-57.
3. The survey found out that this figure amounted to 31.2 percent of peasant per capita earnings nationwide in 1988 and 35.5 percent of peasant per capita consumption for the same year. The figure for the city residents was equivalent to 28 per cent of per capita earnings in the cities nationwide for the same year, and 49 percent of city residents' per capita consumption nationwide for the whole year. All in all, these figures reflected about one third increase from that of 1987.
4. It is reported that "betrothal gifts" sought by the bride's family now account for many kinds such as meeting gift, visitation gift, holiday gift, sharing gift, wedding anouncement day gift, registration gifts, bride's departure gift, threshold crossing gift (i.e., bride crosses the threshold into the groom's family), bride escort gift, matchmaker's gift and so on. There is almost an unending list

of gifts and gift-giving occasions bearing many different names according to particular customs of different localities that are increasingly becoming a part of the marriage rituals.

5. A report of the Jiangling Rural Survey Team in Hubei province indicates that in 1989 "more than 85 percent of rural newly wed households had a television set, a refrigerator, and a taperecorder purchased at a cost of approximately 5,000 yuan. In addition were payments for gold rings, an electronic keyboard, and a motor-cycle for which the newly wed households paid between several hundred and more than 1,000 yuan.
6. In a bizzare and extreme example, a report mentions that in order to make a wedding extravagant, a young man in Wuhan, his mother and father, brothers and sister spent some 10,000 yuan of the family's savings accumulated over a period of more than ten years. When this was still not enough, the retired father had to take a "second job" driving a pedicab "searching for extra income" by toiling at the train station and pier. In less than three days after the son's raucous wedding, the father died of fatigue. (JPRS-CAR-90-027 13 April 1990: 57).
7. Noting the growth of Mao cult and fortune tellers, a student commented that "after abondoning deification, so many citizens are prostrating themselves anew at the feet of a series of newly fabricated gods whom they are beseeching to dispel disaster and repulse evil, not getting out of the strange clutches of the "gods" after all. "Just what does this show! So many fearsome gods!" Raising the cultural level of the people is the key to China's modernization (Shi Fu 1990: 85).

References

Anagnost, Ann."Prosperity and Counter Prosperity: The Moral Discourse on Wealth in Post Mao China". *Marxism and Chinese Experience: Issues in Contemporary Chinese Socialism,* edited by Arif Dirlik and Maurice Meisner. New York: M.E. Sharpe, 1989, 210-234.

Beijing Review May 15-21, 1995.

Blecher, Marc."Development State, Entrepreneurial State : the Political Economy of Socialist Reform in Xinji Municipality and Guanghan County." In *The Chinese State in the Era of Economic Reform,* edited by Gordon White. London: Macmillan, 1991.

Blecher, Marc. "Sounds of Silence and Distant Thunder: The Crisis of Economic and Political Administration." In *China in the Nineties: Crisis Management and Beyond,* edited by David S. Goodman, and Gerald Segal. Oxford: Oxford University Press, 1991.

Brodsgaard, Kjeld Erik and Strand, David. *Reconstructing Twentieth Century China: State Control, Civil Society, and National Identity.* Oxford: Oxford University Press, 1996.

Chang, Chun and Yijiang Wang. "The Nature of Township-Village Enterprises." Paper presented at the "International Conference on Property Rights of Township-Village Enterprises (TVEs) in China," Hangzhou, China, August 7-9, 1994.

Chen, Aimin. "China's Rural Enterprise Development: Some Structural and Regional Characteristics." Paper presented at the "International Conference on Property Rights of Township Village Enterprises (TVEs) in China," Hangzhou, China, August 7-9, 1994.

Chen Yongping, "Resurgence of Clan Influence in Rural Areas", *Shehui* (Society), 9 (20 september 1991): 6-9, Shanghai [JPRS-CAR-92-001 14 January 1992: 79-83]

China Daily, "Rural industry gives boost to Nations' Economy". Beijing, February 25, 1992.

China Today, October 1994.

China Today, May 1995.

Christiansen, Flemming. " 'Market Transition' in China: The Case of Jiangsu Labor Market, 1978-1990". *Modern China.* 18: 1: 72-93, 1992.

Feng Tongqing. "Workers and Trade Unions under the Market Economy : Perspectives from Grass Roots Union Cadres." Translated in *Chinese Sociology and Anthropology* 28: 3 (Spring 1996).

Green Report. Annual Report on Economic Development of Rural China in 1993 and the Development Trends in 1994. Beijing: China Social Sciences Publishing House.

Guo Jian. "Grey Mentality — An Undercurrent in Reform." *Tangtai,* (Present Times), 25 (15 April 1993: 56-57) [JPRS-CAR-93-040 18 June 1993: 29-30].

Hart, Keith. "The Informal Economy." In *A Dictionary of Economics,* edited John Eatwell et. al. London: Macmillan, 1987.

Huang, Philip. *The Peasant Family and Rural Development in the Yongzi Delta 1350-1988.* Stanford, California: Stanford University Press, 1990.

JPRS-CAR-92-002. 22 January 1992. "Economic Crimes Committed by Rural Enterprises" in *Zhongguo Shehuibao,* (Daily of Chinese Society), Beijing (1 Nov. 1991): 3.

Lee, Peter Nan-shong. "Bureaucratic Corruption during the Deng Xiaoping Era", *Corruption and Reform.* 5: 29-47, 1990.

_____" The Chinese Industrial State in Historical Perspective: From Totalitarianism to Corporatism." In *Contemporary Chinese Politics in Historical Perspective,* edited by Brantly Womack. Cambridge: Cambridge University Press: 153-179, 1991.

Lemarchand, Rene. "The Political Economy of Informal Economies", Paper presented in Yale Agrarian Studies Program, 1991.

Li, David. "A Theory of Ambigious Property Rights in Gray Markets and the Chinese Township and Village Enterprises." Paper presented at the "International Conference on Property Rights of Township-Village (TVEs) in China," Hangzhou, August 7-9, 1994.

Liang Hsueh-chu. "Small Fish Eat big Fish: Changes in the System of Ownership." *Jiushi Niandai* [The Nineties] 11 (1 Nov. 1992 : 36-39), Hong Kong [JPRS-CAR-93-003 22 January 1993: 28-32].

Mao, Shu-yun."The Chinese Discourse on Civil Society." *The China Quarterly* 137 (March 1994): 180-193.

Mei Zhusong."Township Enterprises Face 10 Challenges in Market Economy." *Nan Pei Chi* (North and South Poles), 272 (18 Feb. 1993:58-60), Hong Kong [JPRS-CAR-93-028 5 May 1993: 26-28].

Migdal, Joel S. "The State in Society: An Approach to Struggles for Domination." pp. 7-34 in *State Power and Social Forces: Domination and Transformation in the Third World,* edited by Joel S. Migdal, Atul Kohli, and Vivienne Shue. New York: Cambridge University Press. 1994.

Myers, James T. "China: Modernization and 'Unhealthy Tendencies'." *Comparative Politics* 21:2 (193-213), 1989.

Nee, Victor and Su Sijin."Economic Growth in China: the View from the Villages". *Journal of Asian Studies* 49 (February 1990): 3-25.

Nee, Victor and Frank W. Young. "Peasant Entrepreneurs in China's 'Second Economy'. An Institutional Analysis." *Economic Development and Cultural Change,* 1991.

Oi, Jean, The Fiscal Reform and the Economic Fundations of Local State Corporatism in China". *World Politics* 45 (October 1992).

_____ "The Role of Local State in China's Transitional Economy." *The China Quarterly* 144 (December 1995): 1132-1149.

Portes, A., Castells, M., and Benton L.A., (eds.) *The Informal Economy: Studies in Advanced and Less Developed Countries.* Baltimore: John Hopkins University Press, 1989.

Putterman, Louis. "Dualism and Reform in China." *Economic Development and Cultural Change,* 1992.

_____"The Role of Ownership and Property Rights in China's Economic Transformation." *The China Quarterly* 144 (December 1995): 1047-1064.

Riskin, Carl. "Small Industry and the Chinese Model of Development." *The China Quarterly* 73 (March): 77-98, 1971

_____ "Where is China Going?", in *The Chinese Economy and Its Future: Achievements and Problems of Post-Mao Reform,* edited by Peter Nolan and Dong Fureng. Cambridge: Polity Press, 1990.

Rocca, Jean-Louis. "Corruption and Its Shadow: An Anthropological View of Corruption in China." *The China Quarterly* 130 (June 1992): 402-416.

Sachs, Jeffrey. "Ownership Reform in the TVEs." Paper presented at the "International Conference on Property Right of Township-Villages (TVEs) in China", Hangzhou, August 7-9, 1994.

Sands, Barbara. "Market-clearing by Corruption: the Political Economy of China's Economic Reforms." *Journal of Institutional and Theoretical Economics.* 145: 1 (116-20), 1989.

Scott, James. *Domination and Arts of Resistance.* New Haven: Yale University Press, 1990.

Shi Fu "Mao, Fortune-Telling Fads, Signs of Social Malaise" in *Daxuesheng,* (University Students), 3 (10 March 1990): 10-11 [JPRS-CAR-90-048 5 July 1990:84-85].

Siu, Helen. *Agents and Victims in South China.* New Haven: Yale University Press, 1989.

____"Socialist Peddlers and Princes in a Chinese Market Town." *American Ethnologist* 16 (May 1989).

____"Recycling Tradition: Culture History, and Political Economy in the Chrysanthemum Festivals of South China". *Comparative Study of Society and History,* 1990.

Wang Shulin, "Counter Strategies for Diminished CPC Power in Rural Areas" in *Dang Xiao Luntan* (Forum of Party Schools), 11 (November 1992): 58-61, Beijing [JPRS-CAR-93-012 16 February 1993:41].

Wang Xiaoyi and Yang Weimin, "Social Changes in Rural Areas" in *Shehuixue Yanjiu* (Studies in Sociology), 2 (20 March 1991): 15-20, Beijing [JPRS-CAR-91-041 23 July 1991: 85-90].

Wang Zhanghui,"Township Public Finance and Its Impact on the Financial Enterprises and Peasants in Mainland China", *Issues and Studies,* Vol. 31:8 (Auguest 1995).

Weitzman, Martin L., and Xu, Chenggang. "Chinese Township-Village Enterprises as Vaguely Defined Cooperatives." *Journal of Comparative Economics* 18: 121-145, 1994.

White, Tyrene. "Political Reform and Rural Government." In *Chinese Society on the Eve of Tianamen,* edited by Deborah Davis and Ezra F. Vogel: 37-60, 1990.

Yan Xiaofeng et. al. "Differentiation and Integration of China's Social Structure at the Present Stage." *Zhongguo Shehui Kexue,* (Social Sciences in China), 4 (10 July 1990: 121-30) [JPRS-CAR-90-069 7 September 1990: 42].

Yan Yunxiang,"The Culture of *Guanxi* in a North Chinese Village", *The China Journal,* No. 35 (January 1996): 2-25).

Yang Guan,"On Enterprises Becoming 'Clannish'", *Shehui* (Society), 4 (20 April 1991): 42-45, Shanghai [JPRS-CAR-91-043 29 July 1991: 78-81].

Yang, Mayfair Mei-hui. "The Gift Economy and State Power in China". *Comparative Study of Society and History,* 1989.

_____ *Gifts, Favors, and Banquets: The Art of Social Relationships in China.* Ithaca: Cornell University Press, 1994.

Young, Susan. *Private Business and Economic Reform in China.* New York: M.E. Sharpe, 1995.

_____ "Uncertain Property Rights and Individual Entrepreneurship in Rural China." Unpublished manuscript, 1996.

UTSA PATNAIK

28

THE ECONOMIC IDEAS OF MAO ZEDONG: AGRICULTURAL TRANSFORMATION

The People's Republic of China which was established in 1949 under the leadership of Mao Zedong, is today a rapidly developing nation of a billion people; on present trends it is poised to emerge as the largest economy in the world in about two decades (by the year 2015), overtaking both Japan and the USA. The counter-revolution in the USSR and its rapid economic and social collapse since 1990 under the regime of "market reforms", lends a special interest to the sharply contrasting scenario in the world's largest remaining socialist state. The question inevitably arises: what were the characteristics of that growth strategy which permitted rapid development during the three decades 1949-79; and what is the relation of that strategy to the apparently very different policies the Chinese planners themselves call "socialist market economy", which seems to be compatible with continuing rapid development — so far — in China?

This article will not go into a description of the trends after the policy changes of 1979, some acquaintance with which on the part of the reader, is taken for granted. It argues rather that a strong and broad basis for China's rapid growth on all indicators — not only economic but also social welfare indicators, currently termed "human development" — was laid in the quarter century before 1979, as part of the Maoist strategy from the early fifties of raising the rate of capital formation sharply, and of pursuing a policy of balanced growth on the basis of the use of a range of techniques of varying capital intensity. The essential institutional prerequisite for following this strategy was comprehensive land reforms followed by the formation of co-operatives and later the communes. The main thrust of the argument of this article will be that despite all the hyperboles and encomiums, as well as the criticisms and the anathematisation of egalitarianism, the real and rational content of Mao Zedong's contribution to the economic and social development of new China continues to be insufficiently appreciated by economists; in particular it is argued that there was an important element of innovation in the Maoist strategy of reaping the full advantages of surplus labour in rural areas, on a scale hitherto never attempted, and that this was a major component of the sharp rise in the rate of capital formation in the economy as a whole without any undue restriction of the rate of rise of mass consumption.

Actual Economic Surplus and Its Contribution to Investment

In a backward economy which is launching on a modern industrial growth path, the initial problem is not that the existing economic surplus is too small, but that the specific forms in which the economic surplus is produced and appropriated, are not forms which are conducive to a high rate of investment.

The main forms of surplus are land rent, usury interest and commercial profit, and only a small part is capitalist profit. In short, the economy and its agrarian sector in particular is dominated by landlords, moneylenders and traders, while the capitalists are few. The former groups may invest their surpluses "productively" from their individual point of view since they get a return by rackrenting petty tenants, squeezing debtors through high interest and so on, but their surpluses are not invested productively from the social point of view for such "investment" does not of itself add to productive capacity and to output. These types of return represent income transfers from one large group of people who lack property, to another small group of people who monopolise property in the form of land or money capital, and who are not greatly interested in improving productivity. (The landlords generally consume their surplus or use it in rent yielding or non-agricultural investment, traders by definition are not interested in increasing production, and usurers are interested in transferring peasant assets which are collateral to loans, to themselves.) The problem then is, how to transform these socially unproductive forms of surplus into socially productive forms, leading to a rise in asset formation and hence in incomes. Both in China and India, countries with a long established agrarian production, the economic surplus actually produced around 1950 in the agrarian sector could not have been less than between a quarter to a third of the net domestic product contributed by that sector, while the unproductive part was about two-thirds of the total surplus.

Historically, the answer to the problem of transforming the forms of surplus, has taken two distinct paths in the sphere of agrarian relations. The first path has been the revolutionary and, hence, socially broad-based, democratic one of abolishing the categories of rent and interest by seizing the landed property of rentiers without compensation, namely confiscating it, followed by a free and egalitarian distribution to the peasants, and writing off all outstanding loans. Given their improved status, the peasants then evolve capitalist production "from below". The second path has been the conservative, socially elitist and narrowly based one of preserving landed property substantially, perhaps taking over a small part after paying compensation to the landlords, and distributing the land thus acquired through the market, by selling to those who can afford to pay. This method automatically limits the redistribution to a minority with money, and excludes the majority of the poorer peasants who need land most. Here, capitalism of the landed elite is promoted at the expense of a broadbased peasant capitalism.

In Asia, the conservative path is exemplified by the Meiji land reform in Japan during 1869 to 1873, which abolished the feudal right to rent-cum-tax of the nobility (*daimyo* and the *samurai*) only by paying them compensation, namely, the capitalised value of their rents as cash and bonds; and then taxed the farmers heavily to finance the compensation. In Japan, the democratic path is exemplified by the land reform implemented by the US occupation regime in conjunction with the Japanese authorities in 1945, under which all land with lords in excess of 1 *cho* (2.45 acres) was acquired and distributed at a nominal payment to the tenants, while non-resident landlords were not allowed to keep even 1 *cho* but had to surrender all their land.[1] The insistence of the US occupation regime in Japan at that time on the most comprehensive land reform ever in the post-war period, arose from the perception that the twin pillars of Japanese militarism rested on the *zaibatsu*, and the prevalence of petty tenancy as opposed to owner occupation. The revolutionary path, on the other hand, was exemplified by the confiscation and free distribution of land in Soviet Russia after 1917, and by the land reform in China after 1949. In the latter two cases the egalitarian and free distribution of land to peasant households was thought of as the successful completion of an essentially capitalist task of doing away with feudal property, and as a transitional phase to the eventual establishment of production cooperatives or collectives, in which individual ownership of the material means of production would be replaced by cooperative and collective ownership of enlarging greatly the size of the unit taking decisions and undertaking production and investment.

An interesting study by Lippit highlights the contribution made by land reform in China directly to resources for financing industrial development.[2] For the year 1952, the total of incomes obtained by the propertied classes in rural areas by way of land rent, usury interest and profit, is estimated to amount to 16.9 per cent of the value added (net income) in agriculture, to which is added the tax contributed by the owner-operators which was another 2.1 per cent of the net income, giving a total of 19 per cent of value added in agriculture as the estimate of surplus, or 9.39 billion yuan at 1952 prices. (This is almost certainly a substantial underestimate given that illegal taxes and traders' commissions which are also a part of surplus, were not taken into account possibly owing to the absence of the relevant data.) Of this total which became available to the peasants with the radical land reform entailing the removal of the rent, interest and taxation burden, a little more than half or 4.9 billion yuan was mopped up by the new government via the new revised rates of tax and through controlled terms of trade; while the remainder or 4.5 billion yuan was retained by the peasants and raised their average income.

Thus the peasants benefited, and at the same time the new state had access to resources released by the refom: this transfer from the agrarian sector to the state, expressed as a percentage of total gross and net domestic investment in the economy in 1952, amounted to 34.7 per cent and 44.8 per cent respectively, according to Lippit, which is certainly very substantial. This reveals the direct contribution of the land reform to development finance. However, by its very nature it was a one-shot stimulus to the economy; maintaining the new higher rate of investment, and raising it further over time, would not come about automatically but had to be planned for. The increased income of peasants after the reform could, in principle, have been saved and invested; but given the abysmally low standard of living of the majority of peasants under the old system it is very likely that it would be wholly consumed, for on a per family basis it worked out only to about 55 yuan in 1952. Egalitarian land reform, while removing the incubus of a parasitic landlord and taxation system, did not thus, of itself promise a rapid rise in productive investment, therefore in the resulting output growth rate and, hence, in the ability of agriculture to provide the monetised food and raw materials needed by growing industry. In effect, poverty was now being equitably shared.

It is well known that despite its much larger geographical area than India, the cultivable area has always been less in China, and cultivation practices perforce considerably more intensive. With its longer history of agricultural surplus based society than India, the availability of cultivable land per household was only three-fifths of the Indian level in 1950, though more intensive practices by way of larger application of labour days and of manures per unit area allowed the Chinese farmers to produce higher yields and also higher output per head of population. Raising productivity further when yields are already high is a far more difficult proposition than when they are low to begin with: for there is little technical "slack" left to be taken up. Any raising of yields and of labour productivity needed large investments in extending irrigated area and reclaiming land. Each farming household individually lacked enough surplus funds for investing in fixed capital, particularly the irrigation systems and infrastructure which were a precondition for higher production; nor did individual households have much tax paying capacity, while the collection of small taxes from millions of households posed a formidable problem in terms of cost and feasibility for the government, if the old structures of exploitative intermediation were not to be revived. An enlargement of the scale of producing units, say, by forming every 100 households into a cooperative on the other hand would by itself cut the problem of tax collection to 1 per cent allow the fiscal potential of this sector to be tapped.

According to the socialist perspective, land reform in itself was a bourgeois measure taking society no further than had the French Revolution nearly two centuries earlier; land reform constituted a necessary condition for further institutional change towards cooperation. The urgency of pooling peasant efforts for the purpose of investment was all the greater given the fact that the level of environmental degradation and deforestation in China was far higher as compared to, say, in India at that time, and had been aggravated by nearly forty years of commercial exploitation, civil war and external invasion before 1950. Countering the massive problems of large-scale deforestation, soil erosion and land degradation could not be realistically done on an individual basis but required the pooled effort of many hundreds of households on local projects. The abysmally low standards of public sanitation and health care, the prevalence of epidemic diseases from snail infested canals and mosquito infested water, called for a massive collective investment effort towards cleaning up the environment and initiating a health care system to provide service to those who needed it regardless of their purchasing power.

Potential Economic Surplus Arising from Under-Employment, and Its Mobilisation

So far we have discussed the problem of mobilising *the actual economic surplus* produced as part of the existing level of output in the economy, for the purpose of investment. There was another source of economic surplus which could be tapped for the purpose of capital formation, however, and this was what we term the *potential surplus* inherent in the existence of unemployment and underemployment of labour, particularly rural labour. This is usually referred to as "surplus labour" in literature; this term has produced much confusion, with the neo-classical economists linking the existence of surplus labour to inefficiency in production and zero "marginal productivity" of labour. It should be made clear at the outset that when we refer to underemployment giving rise to a potential labour surplus which can be used for capital formation, this has nothing in common with the neo-classical concept of surplus labour. A simple numerical example will illustrate the concept of potential economic surplus arising from underemployment. In rural India as well as in rural China various estimates placed this surplus at between a quarter to one-third of the total labour-force.

Let us consider a stylised example of a small village in the post-reform period, comprising 30 farming households which are identical with respect to the size of family (5 members), the number of workers per family (2 workers), the area cultivated (0.5 ha each), the equipment possessed, and the labour days worked per annum (150 per worker and hence 300 per family) to produce the only crop — rice (two quintals per family). We assume that the most intensive known cultivation practices are being used to produce this output. For the time being we abstract from the seasonality of production and assume that labour time requirements are spread evenly over the year. The total number of workers in the village are 60 and they put in a total of 9,000 work days in the year to produce a total gross output of 600 quintals of rice (which corresponds to say, 500 quintals net output after deducting one-sixth by way of seed, animal feed and spoilage).This amount of work is essential for producing this amount of output, that is, there is no inefficiency in the system and reducing the total labour days would also reduce total output. (Neo-classical economists, on the other hand, think of a situation where the total labour days input can be reduced without reducing output, that is, there being a difference between the actual labour input and the necessary labour input, this difference being "surplus labour". Such a situation we are assuming does not exist by saying that there is no inefficiency.)

We assume that this 500 quintals net output distributed over the village population of 250 (giving 2 qtl per head) yields enough calories for working health, but it does not provide an adequate desired income for the village population even while the workers are, by definition, underemployed since each worker can get work only for 150 days in a year of 365 days. Clearly, worker would like to work more and even for a higher income, if possible. How much more? We do not know; in the absence of this knowledge we can provisionally adopt a work norm, say of 5 days a week or 250 days a year (allowing additionally for an annual two-week holiday), which given the opportunity each farm worker might be prepared to put in. The total required labour input of 9,000 days can thus be potentially performed by only 36 workers (9,000 divided by 250) instead of the 60 workers engaged, thus releasing 24 workers (60 minus 36) from rice production, for various other kinds of capital formation projects like irrigation which are needed to raise incomes in the long run. Since food output would be maintained at the earlier level, with 36 workers remaining in rice production working harder at 250 days to maintain the total labour input of 9,000 days, each of the 24 workers released could continue to be fed at the earlier average rate of 2 quintals rice per annum while they, too, worked at the rate of 250 days on capital formation projects. Thus, as far as the maintenance cost of labour is concerned, the capital formation would be costless. In this sytem, the potential labour surplus in terms of days is 100 (250 minus 150) per worker, or 66.7 per cent of the days actually worked. In terms of workers too, the potential labour surplus is 24 (60 minus 36) or 66.7 per cent of the total work force.

However, in practice, it is almost impossible to actually release workers for projects as long as the individual holdings are retained; pooling of production becomes a necessary precondition for converting the potential surplus into an actual one. This is because labour surplus exists in units of labour days while workers are indivisible and the withdrawal of workers necessarily has to be in discrete units of persons; one cannot withdraw half a worker from a farm. Suppose that the 30 farms in the earlier example continue to operate separately, then releasing 24 "surplus" workers means taking away not four-fifths of a worker from each of the 30 farms, which is impossible, but taking away one worker each from 24 farms. This at once means that there will be a farm specific labour shortage; the required labour input per farm of 300 days on these 24 farms can no longer be put in by the remaining single worker without over-working and violating the work norm; labour would have to be hired, obviously from the other 6 farms from which no one has been withdrawn, but no matter how underemployed the workers on the other 6 farms might be they would not work free for another farmer and wages would have to be paid. For the workers remaining behind to work harder, as well as maintain the withdrawn worker out of farm net output, and additionally pay out wages, would not be a rational outcome. Additionally, there is the question of who owns the new assets created; if the state owns it, the state cannot ask people to work in creating the assets without paying wages; if it tries to finance the wages by taxing the producers in rice-culture, they will not continue to work harder than before.

In short, the normal operation of the labour market cannot deal with this problem and "costless" capital formation becomes impossible. Essentially, what is required for costless capital formation is a system of "deferred wages", that is, everybody agreeing to work harder without an immediate rise in income, for by its very nature an asset creating project has a certain gestation period and cannot yield immediate income. Everyone has to agree to work harder now for a higher income in the future. But, how to operate such a system within the atomistic private property where it is not clear to whom the new assets will belong? As long as there is no system for ensuring that there are incentives for people to work harder without immediate payment, they will not work harder and the potential labour surplus will remain just that, with no practical use for new capital formation. All these issues were discussed threadbare by economists in the course of the sixties and seventies in India, and the consensus which emerged was that despite the majority of empirical estimates showing a labour surplus of one-fifth to one-third of the existing labour force in different regions, mobilising this surplus for costless capital formation was virtually impossible as long as everything else was unchanged. Only the completely landless labour would freely move to project work.

In China, however, "everything else" did not remain the same: the atomistic small scale units of production, the individual small farms, in which the surplus labour time was unproductively embedded, were done away with and the production pooled in larger units. It is precisely in permitting the pooling of surplus labour time and, hence, in enabling the effective mobilisation of the potential labour surplus in the form of discrete units of workers for capital formation, that the strength of the cooperatives and the communes lay. The pooling of production in the advanced cooperatives (comprising around 200 to 300 households) and later the much larger communes (about 3,500 households) did away with the practical problems of the withdrawal of workers for project work in discrete units, for as soon as production was pooled a smaller number of people working more days per year could not only put in the same total labour time in crop production as before, but indeed raised output further if the initial underemployment was severe, releasing others for projects of material and human capital formation.

At the same time, the egalitarian distribution system ensured that the withdrawn workers had access to the same basic standard of life as others (even though the project work they were doing actually yielded nothing to begin with), by giving them the same right to draw grain and necessities rations as the workers in crop and sideline production actually producing these necessities; and by allotting them work points for project work, against which they could claim a share in the remaining collective income. A policy directive ensured that up to 70 per ent of the grain output was to be distributed equally regardless of work points earned. In such a system the local availability of grain itself was crucial and a logical corollary was that all regions should grow grain.

In fact, even though the well known theory of socialist distribution was "from each according to his ability, to each according to his work", in practice the Maoist egalitarian strategy involved a deviation or went beyond this principle; what was being actually implemented was "from each according to his ability, to each according to his basic need's. This was by no means a utopian or unrealistic strategy; on the contrary, it was the only practical system which could have permitted the large-scale mobilisation of surplus labour which took place, and which served to raise the rate of capital formation to levels which have not been accurately estimated by economists to date. "Linking remuneration directly to work on the basis of household functioning would have meant that project workers would have got nothing and indeed could not have been any thing short of a disastrous policy at this stage, for what would have been induced into project work at all, except under similar systems of wage and other outlays by the state financed by inflationary credit and deficit financing, as were being operated in mixed economies like India at the time. Incidentally, all existing estimates of capital formation in China during 1955 to 1978 are underestimates because they ignore the non-monetised investment of labour which we are discussing; even those few estimates which try to take into account project labour, undervalue it because agricultural productivity is inadequately estimated.

A reading of the writings of Mao Zedong during the crucial period of the transition to the advanced cooperatives reveals the awareness of the labour mobilising potential of the cooperatives.

In 1954, commenting on a piece written by another author, Mao said,

> ".... under present conditions of production there is already a surplus of roughly one-third of labour power. What required three people in the past can be done by two after cooperative transformation, an indication of the superiority of socialism. Where can an outlet be found for this surplus labour power of one-third or more? For the most part, still in the country-side. ...The masses have unlimited creative power. They can organize themselves to take on all spheres and branches of work where they can give full play to their energy, tackle production more intensively and extensively, and initiate more and more undertaking for their own well being."[3]

In the event, the masses were not entirely left to decide on the undertakings to be locally initiated, but rather local adaptations and variations were to take place within a broad overall policy of promoting undertakings in the following groups : physical capital formation via land reclamation, hill terracing, afforestation and irrigation; infrastructure (roads, bridges and buildings); energy; rural sidelines and industries; and human capital formation (public sanitation, clinics and schools). The possibilities were certainly nearly limitless at this time given the existing abysmally low levels of material, educational and health development in the countryside. On land reclamation and afforestation Mao Zedong stressed the need for *"state organised land reclamation by settlers ... — the plan being to bring 400 to 500 m. mu of wasteland under cultivation in the course of three five year plans"*. He went on to say:

> "I think the barren mountains in the north in particular should be afforested, and they undoubtedly can be. Do you comrades from the north have courage enough for this? Many places in the south need afforestation too. It will be fine if in a number of years we can see various places in the south and north clothed with greenery."[4]

Mao Zedong confidently expected, even within the advanced cooperatives and before collectivisation, that the annual labour days employed per worker would rise substantially and that female participation rates would also rise as more rural undertakings were established, existing labour surplus thereby mobilised and increasing supply elicited:

> "Before the cooperative transformation of agriculture, surplus labour-power was a problem in many parts of the country. Since then many cooperatives have felt the pinch of a labour shortage and need to mobilise the masses of the women, who did not work in the fields before, to take their place on the labour front.... For many places the labour shortage becomes evident as production grows in scale, the number of undertakings increases, the efforts to remake nature become more extensive and intensive, and the work is done more thoroughly."[5]

Further, he goes on to say:

> "Things in this country also show us that an outlet can be found in the villages for rural labour power. As management improves and the scope of production expands, every able-bodied man and woman can put in more work-days in the year. Instead of over one hundred workdays for a man and a few score for a woman as described in this article the former can put in well over two hundred workdays and the latter well over one hundred or more."[6]

In fact, according to P. Schran's data from official sources, the annual number of days employed per person in rural China rose from 119 to 189 during 1950 to 1959, with most of the increase seen after 1955 during the shift to the advanced cooperatives.[7] (see Table below) The importance of the virtually costless capital formation entailed in mobilising surplus labour, can hardly be exaggerated:

Peasant Labour Day Inputs In Chinese Agriculture

Year (days)	*Average Days (billions of days)*	*Total Annual*
1950	119.0	26.489
1951	119.0	26.835
1952	119.0	27.168
1953	119.0	27.537
1954	119.3	28.155
1955	121.0	29.439
1956	149.0	38.084
1957	159.5	41.518
1958	174.6	47.474
1959	189.0	58.420

Note: The sharp increases from the large-scale mobilisations for rural water conservancy in the winter of 1955-56 and 1957-58 are reflected above. The estimates cited for 1959 appear somewhat improbable as demobilisation was seen throughout the year.

Source: Peter Schran, *The Development of Chinese Agriculture 1950-1959,* p. 75.

More than anything else it served to raise sharply the rate of investment in the economy; the official estimates almost certainly understate the real extent of rise since the unmonetised part of investment, which we have been discussing, has not been included. In rural areas, capital formation could be measured, and was often expressed, not in value terms but in terms of physical indicators like the volume of earth shifted in reclamation and terracing work, the number of irrigation reservoirs constructed, the miles of canals dredged, etc. Further, the rate of investment was raised sharply without imposing cuts in consumption on particular segments of the population, owing to the egalitarian distribution system. The rate of rise in real consumption of both peasants and workers during 1958-59 to 1978-79 was certainly slow, as might be expected since the trade-off in this early stage of industrialisation was between a higher rate of investment at the expense of a lower rate of consumption rise, in order to secure a higher rate of future consumption than would be the case with the alternative scenario of a higher rate of consumption now. But the egalitarian strategy essentially distributed the burden equitably.

The timing of the shift to the large-scale communes was not a happy one; it coincided with a run of very poor harvests complicated by floods in some parts of the country and attacks of pests in others. There was a very substantial downward deviation of output from the trend during 1959 to 1963, and this has complicated the evaluation of the shift ever since. There is a severe problem of causal identification here: it is arguable that even without the institutional change to communes, output would have fallen anyway, for agricultural output is subject to cyclical patterns of movement; India saw a severe downturn a few years later, in 1964-65, with no institutional change. Many scholars who are disposed to criticise the idea of large-scale collective production have, however, tended to place the main burden of the output decline on the shift to the communes; this in our view is not a tenable position. What is probably true is first, that the decline which would have taken place anyway, was exacerbated by the initial severe management problems entailed in the shift; and second, too much grain was procured during 1959-61 by the government which was unrealistic in expecting too immediate an impact on productivity of the shift to large-scale production. Given that output had actually fallen rather than increased, this led to a severe decline of rural availability of foodgrains, and an avoidable rise in crude death rate in rural areas.[8]

The egalitarian distribution system, paradoxically, must have served to mask the real impact of the food availability decline of 1959-61 since, unlike the case in a class society, this decline was no longer concentrated on particular narrow segments of the population, and therefore did not take the dramatic form of able-bodied poor people of working age showing extreme emaciation and death by disease and starvation. It was spread out much more evenly over the population of a given affected area than would have been the case even fifteen years earlier, and probably the decline in nutrition would have affected vulnerable groups like the very old, the very young, and parturient women the most. We do not believe that there was a sinister conspiracy of silence regarding the "famine"; rather, there was a genuine problem of appreciating the magnitude of the impact of availability decline in an egalitarian society. Along with a rise in the overall crude death rate, which emerged statistically much later as the numbers were put together, there also appears to have been a dramatic decline in the birth rate during 1958-60. This is perhaps not difficult to understand, for labour power was being mobilised almost on a war-for-production footing, and women were being extensively drawn into the work force at this time. In this initial period of the "Great Leap", household activities like cooking and child minding were also briefly socialised with the establishment of communal kitchens and creches to free women for labour, and mobility increased greatly as women moved to project work. With such a reversal of the old patterns of life and work amounting virtually to social dislocation, it would not be surprising if the decision to have children was postponed, reflected in a fall in the birth rate. The decline was sharp enough for the rate of natural increase to become negative in the year 1960. From 1962 the birth rate again jumped to unprecedentedly high levels as though the postponed decisions were now being taken, resulting in a marked "bunching" of births.

Some scholars have used a very dubious method of arriving at grossly unrealistic and inflated "famine deaths" during this period (1959-61) by taking account not only of the higher crude death rate (which is a legitimate measure) but also counting the "missing millions" as a result of the lower birth rate, as part of the toll. There is a great deal of difference between people who are already there, dying prematurely due to a sharp decline in nutritional status, and people not being born at all. The former can enter the statistics of "famine deaths" according to any sensible definition of famine, but people who are not born at all are obviously in no position to die whether prematurely or otherwise. The exaggerated figures of 30 million or more "famine deaths" in China are arrived at after including the missing millions because they were not born and, indeed, were not conceived at all. On this logic we would have to talk about large scale "famine deaths" in Western Europe during two World Wars owing to the fall in the birth rate. Instead of consistent application these academically dubious concepts are reserved, apparently, for exclusive application to the developing economies. More responsible estimates place excess mortality in China between 10 to 13 million during the 1959-61 period if the increased crude death rate during these years is compared to the level of 1958. The excess toll of this order is bad and is a permanent blot on the otherwise impressive record of welfare gains in the Maoist era. The highest level of the crude death rate in China's famine in 1960 which was 25.43 per 1,000 [9] was incidentally, *lower* than the "normal" average crude death rate during 1955-60 in eighteen developing countries; while the "normal" Indian crude death rate was very close at 24.6 per 1,000 during the same period, 1955-60. Needless to say, no one talks of "famine" in these developing countries or even in India — a good example of academic inconsistency.

After weathering the crisis of the 1959-61 period the commune system settled down, management problems were gradually overcome and the full benefits of large scale operation combined with continuing mobilisation of labour for material and human capital formation, were realised up to 1978. The crude death rate resumed its steep decline with the public sanitation campaigns and the provision of an elementary but effective rural health care system, which dramatically lowered infant and child mortality levels, while illiteracy declined more steeply than in any other developing country. Rawski has shown that the agricultural productive base was transformed, with the use of modern industrial inputs (fertilisers, fuels, cement) and fixed capital use (irrigation and drainage equipment, tractors, power tillers and other farm machinery) growing at over 20 per cent per annum during the fifteen to twenty year period before 1978. The winter works programmes provided employment for 2 to 2.5 months in the year during the seventies to workers numbering 50 million in the early seventies, rising to 100 million during the three years preceding 1979; this accounted for 30 per cent of the labour force. The winter works covered terracing, land reclamation, earthworks, irrigation works and the energy sector. By the late seventies, the average annual employment per worker in rural areas increased up to 250 days, compared to around 190 days in 1959.[10] This was a very creditable achievement given the fact that the work force was larger not only owing to growth but also to a large rise in the female participation rate.

After the policy regime shift in 1979, the employment generation and collective capital maintenance and new capital formation programmes received a severe setback as decollectivisation proceeded; the re-emergence of a serious unemployment problem in rural areas has been one consequence of the reversal of the Maoist development strategy.

Ultimately the rate of development of a society, not only economic growth as conventionally defined but also improvement in human welfare, depends on the rate at which it can invest in material as well as human capital formation. This essay has shown that the fundamental innovation of the Maoist development strategy, of which egalitarianism was an essential component, lay in converting an apparent liability into an asset: by directly transforming under-employed surplus labour into capital at minimal extra cost, a firm basis was laid for agricultural productive trnasformation which fed into industrial growth, as well as for the gains in human development indicators.

Notes

1. T. Nakamura, *The Post War Japanese Economy : Its Development and Structure*, Tokyo: University of Tokyo Press, 1981.
2. V. Lippit, *Land Reform and Economic Development in China: A Study of Institutional Change and Development Finance* Whiteplains: IASP, 1974.
3. Mao Zedong, *Selected Works,* Beijing: Foreign Languages Press, 1978, p. 269.
4. *Ibid,* pp. 197-219.
5. *Ibid,* p. 268.
6. *Ibid,* p. 270.
7. Peter Schran, *The Development of Chinese Agriculture 1950-1959,* Chicago: University of Illinois Press, 1969.
8. Carl Riskin, *China's Political Economy: The Search for Development since 1949,* New York, Oxford University Press, 1987.
9. *Ibid.*
10. T.C. Rawski, "Agricultural Employment and Technology", in R. Barker, R. Sinha and B. Rose (Eds.), *The Chinese Agricultural Economy* (Colorado: Westview Press, 1982).

S.P. GUPTA

29

ROADS FOR LARGE POPULATIONS TOWARDS DEVELOPMENT AND PROSPERITY*

In this paper I like to discuss the experiences of large populous economies in respect of growth and development. In general, they are notably different in many respects from the small/medium sized economies. Among the developing countries we can broadly identify seven most populous countries starting from China, India, USSR, Indonesia, Brazil, Nigeria and Argentina in the descending order. These countries between them cover 51.5 per cent of world population and in contrast a meagre 9.2 per cent of world Gross Domestic Product [GDP] measured at 1990 US dollar in 1994. Further, when their share in the world population decreased from 51.94 in 1980 to 51.51 in 1994, their share of the world GDP increased from 7.9 per cent to 9.2 per cent over the same period. This shows that although they started with a big handicap of a very low per capita GDP in 1980 compared to the rest of the world, their achievements in regard to GDP per capita are marginally better.

If you measure their population growth rate between 1980 and 1994 it comes to nearly 1.6 per cent as against 1.8 for the world overall. Of course world population growth averages the high growth of sub-Saharan Africa (above 3.0 per cent) and some Latin American and South Asian countries, alongwith a very low growth of developed countries. Among the 7 big populous countries the population growth rate is lowest in USSR followed by China and is the highest in Nigeria. In terms of GDP growth of this group of seven, the growth rate was 4.9 per cent between 1980 and 1994 as against a growth rate of 3.6 per cent, for other small and medium developing countries and 2.8 per cent of global growth between 1980 and 1990 and 1.96 per cent between 1990 and 1994. The developed countries witnessed a growth rate of 2.73 per cent in the 1980s and 1.58 per cent in the 1990s. This clearly shows that the overall growth rates and growth in GDP are much higher in the larger developing countries compared to other developing and developed countries. But inspite of this comparatively high growth, its per capita income is lower than that of other developing countries, mainly because of its large population.

Among the seven countries, we have chosen the first two most populous countries, China and India. Interestingly, these two countries together show the highest growth rates among the most populous seven large economies, India growing at 5.2 per cent between 1980 and 1994 China 9.6 per cent between 1980 and 1994. As against this, USSR is showing a negative growth and Nigeria has grew by only 2.3 per cent over the same period. Indeed, among most populous economies the success story comes mainly from China, India, Brazil and Indonesia of which again three are from the Asian sub-continent.

If we examine their individual growth performance, Brazil's growth has accelerated very recently, reflecting its liberalisation policy since 1992; China's growth trend started much earlier since the reform of 1978. But it accelerated significantly from 1991-92. For Indonesia the growth accelerated from 1985 coinciding again with their economic liberalisation activities. Nigeria and USSR are showing a deterioration in recent years. USSR's negative growth is explained by their problem of transition to a market economy. For Nigeria their new economic policy seems to have failed to show any positive impact.

There is often a generalization that all success stories of large and small developing countries can be explained by the growth of world trade and opening up of these economies with market based deregulation. But from any indepth scrutiny one finds that the reform package under the broad heading of "liberalisation" is very different from country to country. There is no standard recipe of a "reform package". Also their country specific applicabilities are not "neutral" to the factor endowment or initial conditions of any country as is often propagated by many economists. Indeed, the failure to appreciate the need for country-

*Paper presented to the 1995 seminar on "India and China Looking at Each Other."

specific adjustment has left a large number of economies in Africa from the main stream of fast growth. Here, in the case of China and India, I shall try to bring out certain specific development features which are relevant mostly for large populous countries. These are mainly in the area of regional imbalances and problems of backward areas — which get increasingly bypassed by a market economy oriented growth process. Indeed, the increasing regional imbalances observed both in China and India under market-oriented reform, are also applicable to most other populous countries. Similarly, in large countries, the problems of centre-state financial relations are coming more and more into sharp focus. The "new economic policy" in these countries asks for stability of the macro economic balances by centralised control and at the same time looks for micro level incentives (i.e. at the grass root) which are possible only by increasing decentralization and private sector involvement. Here an inherent conflict is coming out between the centralized role of the Government and the decentralization autonomy of the provinces/states. These two features are common in most large countries, given the diversified availability of factor endowment unevenly distributed spatially. These problems are much less in small economies like Hong Kong or Singapore. The wide spectrum of diversified factor endowment also encourages predominance of any import substitution lobby. In this respect, even the United States with its large diversified factor endowment is not an exception where there is a very strong lobby for the protection of domestic sector. To some respect this applies also to some of the European countries. Therefore, in the growth process of large populous economies there is a continuous debate on the role of domestic investment versus foreign direct investment. The general experience of most large countries tells that success is more visible in those countries where domestic saving and domestic activity have largely supplemented foreign direct investment and enterprise. The present high saving ratios of China and Indonesia are telling examples. The recent declining savings ratio of India is, therefore, a cause for concern among most economists. Another special feature of large populous countries is that they have large geographical coverages. This bring to focus the importance of transport, communications and spatial management of investment allocations. Also, the problem of rigidity or restriction in inter-regional movement, adds to the transaction cost in production in these economies.

Both in China and India a large majority of the population lives in rural areas and is engaged in rural activities. Hence, in their developmental activity, agriculture comes as a focal point. Finally, population policy in a populous country also became the key development objective. China's success can be ascribed largely because of its effective population control.

In the pre-reform days, both in China and India top priority was given to equity, removal of poverty, increasing the social aspects of standards of living. This, however, was attempted in China under a total state-controlled economy and in India with the public sector playing a dominant role along with the market forces. Both the economies adopted a strategy of import substitution and heavy industry growth. China over time, realized that maintaining high standards of living is becoming difficult unless efficiency in resources use is increased. The attempt to maintain equity through forced saving and administered directives resulted in social unrest, which came to a breaking point after the controversial Cultural Revolution. The key objective of present reform in China is to bring incentives back in the economy by increasing the role of the market with minimum changes in their political institutions. This is defined in China as an experiment in a socialistic market economy.

In India, because of heavy import substitution leading to increased inefficiency in production, the generation of a surplus for maintaining the tempo of equity measures and social development become impossible. This led to heavy borrowing, culminating in a balance of payments crisis. To meet the crisis, the new economic policy in India has been initiated.

China started her new economic policy much earlier, from 1978, but experienced acceleration from 1992. Compared to China, India started very late. Although the deregulation of the India economy started in mid 80s, the new economic policy in fact came into force from June 1991. However, at the beginning of her reform process the general indicators of social development were much lower than in China. Therefore, the concerns among economists about the social cost of transition were comparatively less in China, as compared to India.

(A) China's Key Economic Reform Strategies

Unlike India, China was not forced to undertake reforms by any economic, political or social crisis. Rather, Chinese leaders, in spite of the significant achievements in China's pre-reform era, in the elimination of mass poverty and substantial gains in the health, education and quality of life of the people, realised that the economy was becoming increasingly costly in terms of supression of personal consumption and that sustaining the past strategy will not be possible.

To reform the economy internally, the household responsibility system was put into effect in the countryside. Later on, in 1984, reform of the economic system had begun in the cities. During the process of economic reform, the Chinese Government stressed persistently on the role of commodity economy, while promoting the market mechanism under the guideline of macro-economic adjustment and control. Simultaneously, as part of socialist market economy public ownership was allowed to co-exist with the market. The socialist market economy consists of five key links such as the modern enterprise system, unified and open market, sound macro-economic adjustment and control, reasonable personal income distribution and multi-level social security system.

In order to open the economy to the outside world, as early as in 1980 four Special Economic Zones (SEZs) namely, Shenzhen, Zhuhai, Shantou and Xiamen were opened up. In 1984, fourteen coastal cities were opened up as a further step. In 1985, three delta areas along the Yangtze River and Pearl River and in the southern part of Fujian province as well as several other places were opened up. In the following years, Hainan Island, Pudong New Area in Shanghai, five big cities along the Yangtze River, eighteen provincial capitals and a part of inland and border cities were opened up. These zones were created initially as experimental stations to adjust and watch their operations vis-a-vis open market interactions.

There are four consistent themes in the Chinese approach to reform: gradualism, partial reform, decentralization and self-reinforcement of reforms. In almost all areas of reform, implementation has been spread over time, often several years and usually after experimentation. Such experiments were carried out in designated reform areas and after the results of trials were observed, these were then spread to other parts of the country. By using the gradual approach and by not subjecting the state sector to major shocks, China has succeeded in avoiding severe social costs during its transition. China's economic reform strategy can be examined under four major heads: Agricultural reform, Rural enterprise reform, State enterprise reform and Trade liberalisation.

1. Agricultural Reform

Agricultural reform started with the introduction of the household responsibility system and abolition of communes in agriculture and with this, Chinese authorities laid a firm foundation for reforming other sectors. Prior to 1979, agricultural production was organised according to communes that consisted of brigades and production teams. Detailed production planning decisions were made by higher level authorities and often did not take into account the local conditions. Remuneration for workers was based on the total income of the commune and was not closely linked to individual productivity. However, farmers generally were allowed to have private plots of land and to market their production from them at rural trade fairs.

The inefficiency of the agricultural sector prior to the reform was reflected in slow growth of production. To improve agricultural performance, the Government initiated reforms in the rural areas in 1979. The size of private farm plots was increased, diversification of production was encouraged and rural free markets for agricultural products were allowed to grow. Experiments were conducted with various methods of giving individuals greater autonomy and by 1984 the household responsibility system had emerged as the dominant arrangement. Under this system, right to use collectively owned land was contracted out to farm households for a fixed period. The household was responsible for meeting a share of the production teams mandatory state procurement quotas, taxes on agricultural output and contributions to collective services. After meeting these obligations, the household was allowed to dispose of its output either by selling to the state at negotiated prices or in the rural free markets.

The household responsibility system, together with increases in the relative prices of agricultural products, unleashed substantial productivity gains and resulted in a diversification of agricultural production. The growth rate of agricultural output averaged nearly 8 per cent a year during 1979-84, compared with a growth of less than 2 per cent a year in 1958-78. However, it declined to about 4 per cent per annum during 1985-93.

2. Rural Enterprise Reform

Since 1979, restrictions on non-agricultural activities in the rural areas have been relaxed and enterprises in these areas have been allowed to sell their products at market prices. As a result, a large number of individually or collectively owned enterprises were established or expanded in townships and villages. These township and village enterprises (TVEs) absorbed significant amount of the surplus labour that emerged as agricultural efficiency increased following the implementation of the household responsibility system. Competition in input and output markets is generally tougher for the TVEs than for state enterprises and their budget constraints are harder, reflecting their less easy access to subsidies and credit. Consequently, they have proved to be more flexible and more responsive to changes in market conditions than their counterparts in the state sector. The TVEs have made an important contribution to China's development by providing competition for state enterprises and creating an environment for the development of entrepreneurial expertise.

The rapid growth of the TVEs has led to a dramatic change in the economic landscape, particularly in the countryside, where they were estimated to total about 19 million and to employ more than 100 million workers in 1992 out of a total rural labour force of about 430 million. They contributed to about half of rural GDP and accounted for about one-third of the country's total in 1992.

3. State Enterprise Reform

In the pre-reform period, State enterprises were centrally controlled via the plan; leaving enterprise managers little or no room for initiative with respect to production, pricing, marketing and investment. Enterprises transferred all their surplus funds to the State, while losers were covered by budget subsidies. Investment funds and some working balances were provided to the enterprises through the Government budget in the form of grants; the banking system supplied additional working capital. Wages were paid according to a centrally approved wage scale and age was a major determinant of wage differences among worker. Under this system, enterprises were not held responsible for their financial results; instead, their main responsibility was to fulfil quantitative output targets established by the plan. Enterprise managers therefore had little incentive to improve efficiency and productivity.

The focus of enterprise reforms has been on increasing incentives by enhancing the enterprise decision-making authority and by providing them with greater financial resources, while making them more responsible for their own profits and losses. Following some experimentation, the Government in 1983 initiated a changeover on a national scale from profit transfers to income taxation and by 1986 profits of almost all enterprises were subject to taxation rather than being fully remitted to the Government. Since 1986, the Government has started to reduce interference in the day-to-day operations of the enterprises through the introduction of contracts for large and medium-sized enterprises. Under this contract responsibility system, targets were specified for an enterprise over a three- or four-year period for its performance, its production quota to the state and financial obligations to the Government. About 90 per cent of the enterprises had signed management contracts by 1988.

To accompany these changes, a bankruptcy law was enacted in 1986 and become effective in 1988, but until recently it was hardly used against state-owned enterprises. In 1988, the authorities also enacted an Enterprise Law, which seeks to transform the SOEs into fully autonomous legal entities that are responsible for their own profits and losses. Detailed regulations giving effect to the broad provisions of the law were issued in July 1992.

While reforms contributed to a pick up in the growth of output by the state enterprises, their share in total industrial production fell from 81 per cent in 1978 to less than 50 per cent in 1993, reflecting the greater dynamism of non-state enterprises and the serious problems that continue to affect the efficiency of state enterprises. Price controls persisted, production quotas for sale to the state remained part of the contracts, the SOEs had access to certain quantities of cheap raw materials, credit was readily available for investment and the budget continued to provide support for loss-making enterprises. It shows the unfinished nature of the reforms which is jeopardizing the macro-economic management. SOEs are contributing to a rapid rate of credit expansion, which reflects the mounting demands on the state budget to cover enterprise losses and low revenue buoyancy. To address these problems, the authorities during 1991 announced some 20 measures, 12 of which were to improve the operations and external environment of the SOEs and the others were aimed at facilitating the operation of market forces on the SOEs. Some measures, such as reducing mandatory planning, were a further step towards market economy.

Another important experiment in SOEs reconstruction is the shareholding system boosted by the establishment of stock exchanges in Shanghai and Shenzhen. Except for large enterprise in strategic sectors of the economy such as defence and high technology, most SOEs could eventually be converted into shareholding companies with the State retaining a significant share.

About 70 per cent of the losses of SOEs are policy-induced, mainly because of price control and if these enterprises are to be financially independent, it is necessary to liberalise the prices of the goods and services they produce.

4. Trade Liberalisation

Prior to 1978, China's foreign trade was handled exclusively by 12 stateowned foreign trade corporations (FTCs) organized along product lines. These corporations procured and traded the quantities directed by the central plan and all profits and losses which did not have direct access to foreign markets were given production targets under the plan for supply to the

FTCs. Through this trade plan, balance of payments was controlled.

Under the reforms, the FTCs were progressively given greater autonomy and made more accountable for their operations, while the administration of the system was decentralized and provincial authorities were given authority to establish their own FTCs. By 1989, most local branches of national FTCs had become independent entities responsible to the local authorities for their financial results, bringing the number of FTCs to about 4,000.

Starting in 1991, a number of new measures were taken to liberalize trade, in part stimulated by China's efforts to make its trade conform to international practices in the context of its application for re-entry into the WTO. All direct budgetary export subsidies to foreign trade corporations were eliminated from January 1991, and export tariffs on mineral ores were reduced. Import duties were reduced on a number of commodities and China's customs duty regulations were replaced with the harmonized commodity description and coding system. In April 1992, the import regulatory duty was eliminated and in October 1992, it was confirmed that the import substitution regulations had been terminated. In addition, under a memorandum of understanding with the United States, China announced its intention to publish many internal trade regulations to increase the transparency of the system. Other trade-related measures included a revision of the patent law to bring it into line with international conventions and various steps toward establishing legal conventions and practices for the conduct of external trade.

During the early stages of reform, various arrangements were tested for sharing foreign exchange with the objective of improving incentives for exports. A retention system was evolved, under which exporters surrender their actual foreign exchange and are issued retention quotas by the State Administration of Exchange Control (SAEC) equivalent to a portion of such earnings. Through 1990, a complex set of regulations had been developed that allocated foreign exchange differently according to industrial type and provincial location. In 1991, a significant simplification occurred under which a uniform retention rate for enterprises was set throughout the country and standard formulas were established for sharing foreign exchange between the centre and the localities. During the early 1990s, experiments with cash retention have been undertaken (notably in Hainan, Shanghai and Shenzhen).

In December 1991, all domestic residents were allowed to sell foreign exchange at the swap rate at designated branches of banks; since then, there has been virtually no restriction on the sale of foreign exchange in the swap centres. However, restrictions remain on purchases and for about three months in early 1993, the authorities attempted to cap the swap market exchange rate. This effort was abandoned when it became evident that most transactions were being driven into the black market.

With the new exchange arrangements in 1986, the official exchange rate was in effect pegged to the US dollar. There vere two devaluations in 1989 (21 per cent) and 1990 (9 per cent) and in 1991, small frequent adjustments in the official rate were made. By April 1993, the real effective exchange rate of the official exchange rate had depreciated 33 per cent more than in 1986 and 70 per cent more than in 1980. The authorities have indicated that the ultimate goal is unification of the exchange rates and convertibility of the currency.

(B) Indian Economic Reform Strategy

In India there were several attempts to liberalize or reform the system of economic management. In 1980, India began to adjust the long-pursued economic policy which stressed on development of state-run heavy industry and import-substitution. The main contents of the new economic policy consisted of measures such as to relax the control on private enterprises and foreign capital, to open industries (e.g. aluminum making, machine-tool building, chemical industry, chemical fertilizer, electricity, pharmaceutical etc.) which had been monopolized by the public sector, to foreign and private capital. It also raised the proportion of private capital in the planned investment from 45 per cent in the Fifth Five-Year Plan (1974-79) to 46 per cent in Sixth Five-Year Plan (1981-86). India's competitiveness had weakened because of its technological backwardness. In order to change the situation, the Indian Government revised the policy of import substitution to provide incentives to export and reducing the protection on imports.

In the 1980s, the Indian Government stressed on reorganization of low-efficient state-run enterprises and partial disinvestments, further relaxations of the control of private enterprises and foreign capital, introduction of a competitive mechanism, reduction of protection for domestic industries, promotion and importation of advanced technological equipment from abroad etc.

In July 1991, India had introduced a series of economic reform measures. These measures were initiated with the purpose of macro-economic stabilization mainly by a sharp reduction in the deficit of the public sector in the Central Government budget. The Government continuously attempted to reduce the ratio of fiscal deficit in GDP by reducing public expenditure, increasing taxation, abolishing part of commodity price subsidies and a partial privatization of public enterprises. In addition, a new trade and industrial policy was announced. The new industrial policy abolished the system of industrial licences, opened nine of the 17 industries which are monopolized by the state to private enterprises, the proportion of foreign equity was raised from 40 per cent to 51 per cent. It also eliminated licensing requirements for private domestic and foreign investment in certain industries and relaxed the restrictions under the Monopolies and Restrictive Trade Practices Act on expansion, diversification, mergers and acquisitions by large firms and industrial houses. The power sector, which had been a monopoly of the public sector, was opened to private, domestic and foreign investors. Regulations on pricing and distribution of steel were lifted. Domestic and foreign investors were invited to invest in the production, refining and marketing of oil and gas and in certain segments of the coal industry. A National Renewal Fund was established to assist workers who might be laid off during the process of modernizing, restructuring or closing uncompetitive firms in the public and private sectors. The Committees appointed by the Government to look into the functioning of the financial sector insurance and the tax system have submitted their reports. Another committee has formulated guidelines for the privatization of public enterprises.

The new trade policy deregularised export and relaxed control over import of advanced technological equipment. In order to promote exports and link India with the world markets, the Government has reduced tariffs many times. In February 1993, the rupee on trade account was declared to be fully convertible. In terms of policies related to foreign capital, the important measures which have adopted since 1992 include: foreign institutions are permitted to buy shares issued by Indian companies; the development of many kinds of minerals has been opened to foreign capital in accordance with the revised law of mineral products and India signed the convention of protection for foreign investment.

(C) Results of Economic Reform

In this section, I would like to explain the diverse economic results of the two countries over the last 14 years. The annual growth of Gross Domestic Product (GDP) in China during 1980-92 was 10.1 per cent as compared to 5.2 per cent for India. China had a per capita Gross National Product (GNP) of US$ 609 in 1992 compared with US$ 310 for India, with an average annual growth rate of 7.6 per cent and 3.1 per cent respectively. In specific sectors, especially in agriculture, the Chinese have made considerable progress with a growth rate of 5.4 per cent compared to India's 3.2 per cent during 1980-92. In regard to industry, China recorded an average annual growth rate of 11.1 per cent in comparison with India's 6.4 per cent during the same period. In the 1992-94 period, the Chinese economic growth rate has been very high at about 13 per cent per annum. In the case of India, the growth rate has been about 4 per cent in the same period. The annual rates of inflation during 1980-92 was 6.5 per cent in China. In the last two years (1992-94) the inflation rates have reached double-digit levels in China. India's inflation rate during the same period of 1980-92 was 8.5 per cent and has continued to be in the range of 8 per cent in the 1992-94 period.

Savings and investment ratios to GDP have been significantly higher in China. Gross Domestic Savings as a proportion of GDP in 1992 was 38.7 per cent for China compared with about 23.10 per cent for India. The Gross Domestic Investment ratios were 37.7 per cent and 23.6 per cent correspondingly. The figures for Foreign Direct Investment (FDI) shows that China has been much more successful than India in attracting GDI. Foreign Direct Investment in China was about US$ 95.6 billion from 1979 to 1994. In the case of India, FDI, which was negligible in 1991, has picked up substantially to reach a level of US$ 3.0 billion in the period of 1991 March to 1995 June.

In regard to foreign trade, the increase in exports and imports since 1979 has been extremely rapid in China. In fact, China's foreign trade grew even faster than the rest of the economy. The trade turnover rose from US$ 38 billion in 1980 to US$ 236 billion in 1994. The annual export volume in 1994 reached US$ 121 billion and the import volume was US$ 115.7 billion. India's export, on the other hand, witnessed an average annual growth rate of 5.9 per cent during 1980-94. India's trade turnover in 1994-95 was US$ 54 billion only.

The ratio of China's exports and imports to its GDP has also risen rapidly since 1978. In the fourteen years of reform and open door policy from 1978, China's ratio of exports to GDP rose sharply from 5.31 per cent to 19.58 per cent, while for India this was 5.6 per cent to 7.6 per cent. As a result of China's phenomenal expansion in foreign trade, its share in GDP rose from 13 per cent in 1980 to a high of 37 per cent in 1991. In India, the share of trade in GDP fluctuated within a narrow range of 18 to 20 per cent. Thus, not only did China's exports grow faster than India's in dollar terms, they also grew faster in relation to domestic growth. While India's share in world exports declined from over 2 per cent in the early 1950's and stabilised around

0.5 per cent, China more than doubled its share from 1 per cent to 2.7 per cent between 1980-end 1994.

China-India: A Comparative Outlook

There is a major difference between Chinese and Indian reforms. In India, agricultural land has always been in private hands and the organization of production consisted overwhelmingly of small owner-operated farms. Since Indian agriculture was never communised, it did not have to be decommunised. Further, Indian Government has proposed no significant agricultural reforms. Thus, the spectacular growth in output and productivity that China has experienced since 1978 after the household responsibility system has no counterpart in India, where the growth in total factor productivity is more gradual. In China, production of food grains rose from 163 million tons in 1952 to 450 million tons in 1993. In India, output of food grains was 51 million tons in 1950-51 and 177 million tons in 1992-93.

The contrasting achievements of India and China can also be seen in terms of important social parameters which show the position of China to be better than that of India. While life expectancy at birth in India is still as low as 59 years, the Chinese figure is 10 years more (69 years). In fact, mortality is two and a half times as high in India (79 per thousand live births in comparison with China's 31). China is well ahead of India as far as the elimination of health deprivation is concerned. Another important area in which the contrast is extremely sharp is basic education and literacy. In China, the proportion of rural population below the poverty in this period, and the magnitude of reduction has been much more modest: a fall from 55 per cent in 1977-78 to 42 per cent in 1989-90. China has done much better than India in this respect. This is mainly due to the high rates of growth of output and real income in China, which have helped to reduce poverty and to improve living conditions.

Concluding Remarks

The economic reform processes in China and India have been marked by extensive decentralization and deregulation, adjustments in the exchange rates, reduction in tariffs, financial sector reforms and modernisation of industry. In China, however, there is a distinctly discriminating "area-based" policy where zones have been provided with faster liberalisation measures, more favourable incentive packages and easier access to FDI. These then act like windows to establish contact with the rest of the world. This is warranted because China had no significant experience in the operation of a private sector market economy. In India, there has been only a limited effort at establishing special economic zones, primarily oriented towards exports. Since India too was a relatively closed economy in the pre-reform period, the successful way China has used the SEZs to open up the rest of the economy should be a lesson for India. For, in terms of achievements, the Chinese approach has induced a much better response than the Indian economic reform policy.

Both India and China have a major role to play in the future international economic scenario. But, they face a number of similar short and long-term economic problems. The Chinese economy is at present "overheated" and needs to contain its inflation and prices. It also has to streamline its centre-state relations and institutional framework for the conducive use of indirect, market-based instruments of economic management by the Government. India also has a problem of inflation, but in contrast to China's problems of "too much growth", her problem is one of "too little growth". Market-based economic management in India is in a much better shape but it too has a centre-state problem, though of a different kind : the problem of percolation of economic reform to the grass-roots because of some rigidity in the constitutional allocation of funds and revenue sources between the Centre and the States. India needs more decentralization whereas China's central authority is trying to revive its lost control on many provinces. Both economies have problems of building up an infrastructure base and containing growing inequality, both spatial, and between rural and urban areas. In the long run, China has the most challenging problem of establishing compatibility between its reform strategy and political structure and economic institutions. India is fortunate in this respect as her political institutions are closely geared to a democratic market-based system.

RAVNI THAKUR

30

CHANGE AND CONTINUITY: ORTHODOX DISCOURSE ON GENDER RELATIONS IN CHINA

"Gender relations" as a category is meant to capture a complex set of social processes. Flax puts it succintly when she says, "Through gender relations two types of persons are created: man and woman. Gender relations so far as we have been able to understand them have been relations of domination. That is gender relations have been more controlled by one of their interrelated aspects -- "the man" (Flax, 1990: 45). The continuity and commonality of this motif can perhaps best be understood by complementing gender theory with a perspective of both domination and change. Here the work done by Bourdieu is both seminal and useful.

Bourdieu, following the line of reasoning already laid down by Marx, Gramsci and Weber, argues that dominant discourses exercise power through the production of specific set of discourses. Bourdieu calls the relationship between "orthodox and heterodox" discourses (Bourdieu 1990).

Orthodoxy can, in a sense, be seen as representing a certain cultural continuity with regard to social relations. It is a discourse which, at any given moment, tends towards conservatism and towards preserving the status quo on a given subject. Dominant patterns of social relations are not always maintained by an exercise of repressive power but acquire power by a sort of consensus. Such consensus is based on which Bourdieu calls "habitus" or the accepted aspect of social relations which structure the disposition of agents.[1] In a sense, all orthodoxy attempts to do is to conserve this state of habitus and maintain a status quo vis-a-vis social practice. With regard to gender discourse, for example, changes in the material position of women do not imply that every aspect of gender discourse will change. Certain elements or gender discourse remain in doxa and mediated through social practice, are accepted by both sexes.

Orthodox discourse in China today is based on the ideology of Marxism and its specific vision of male and female roles. I shall argue that this "new" orthodoxy is in turn based on a more traditional habitus which is specific to China. This is partly because socialist orthodoxy has been imposed upon a more traditional orthodoxy in an authoritarian manner, succeeding in suppressing traditional elements rather than fundamentally changing them. Traditional ideas about women are then pushed underground and operate in a more complex fashion. Here we have a situation where heterodox discourse can turn into orthodoxy when it receives the backing of the state and its institutions.

By the time that the Communist Party of China was formed in 1921, discourse on gender relations had already experienced certain changes. Because of this, the Communist Party was forced to distinguish itself from two other discourses, both of them grounded on different conceptions of gender relations. The first was a more traditional discourse on the position of women, which derived its legitimacy from the Confucian classics. The second was the nationalist and liberal position, which was influenced by western ideas and became popular in China at the turn of the nineteenth century. I will first briefly discuss these two positions before turning to an examination of the way the Communist Party redefines gender relations.

Early Orthodox Discourse: The Construction of a Habitus of Gender Relations

Several scholars have pointed out the inferior position of women in traditional China. Chinese society in Confucian terms was a patriarchal society with strict rules of conduct. The underlying principles of governing rationale were the teachings of

Confucius (551-479 BC). The traditional ideal woman was a dependent being whose behaviour was governed by the "three obediences and four virtues." The three obediences were obedience to the father before marriage, the husband after marriage and the son in case of windows. The four virtues were propriety in behaviour, speech, demeanour and employment (O'Hara 1945). Education for women was intended to inculcate these virtues. Among the most recommended books of instruction for women were the *Nu jie (Precepts for Women)*, the *Nu er jing (Classic for Girls)* and the *Lie nu zhuan (Biographies of Eminent Chinese Women)*. All these books were supposed to furnish women with knowledge about how they should conduct themselves in society. The *Nu jie* is attributed to Ban Zhao (AD 0001), a famous women scholar and historian. These books gradually became the governing principles for female behaviour, especially among the elite.

All these books stressed the importance of the family for women and their seclusion within the household. Women were denied participation in any of the government or local community institutions. Discussing the reason for women's general degradation in China, Helen Snow makes the same point when she says:

> "The distinctive weakness of the position of Chinese women was due to the fact that property could not be transferred by marriage.... A Chinese woman was valuable in her own right only as a hostage or as a source of domestic labor power. She did not exist as a mother in her own right and had no legal control over her children." (H. Snow 1967: 48).

Alongside their lack of property rights, women were controlled by a firmly entrenched system of patriolocal marriages[2] and the related norm of female chastity. This rigid sexual morality was, and remains, a key link in the subordination of women. Particularly in the Song dynasty (960-1279AD), with the revival of neo-Confucian ideals, these ideas became even stronger and more widespread (Tianchi Martin-Liao 1985). A combination of these factors ensured that girls were seen only as burdens and temporary members of the natal family. Any investment in a daughter's well-being was considered a waste of money. Women's oppression was, thus, firmly rooted in China's feudal marriage system.

A husband could also repudiate his wife for seven reasons, originally contained in the *Li Ji* rule of conduct. These were: (1) disobedience of her husband's parents; (2) failure to bear children; (3) adultery; (4) jealousy; (5) loathsome disease; (6) garrulousness; and (7) theft (H. Snow 1967: 50). Such traditional laws served to make women in China extremely vulnerable and forced them to accept the position of subservience accorded to them in traditional discourse (Young 1973; Wolf 1978; Croll 1978).

Another obvious symbol of the confinement and subordination of women was the custom of binding the feet of young girls. This custom is said to have started in the Tang dynasty (618-906), in the later seventh century. The scores of classical poems written about the delicacy of the female foot and the walk that it ensured, testify to the important role played by this custom in terms of norms and standards of female beauty (Levy 1966).

However, in the light of what several scholars have noted, it needs to be stressed that the Confucian ideal of womanhood was mediated by the material position of the women. In general, the pressure and confinement of upper-class women was far greater.[3] Wolf points out that peasants could not afford the luxury of secluding their women (Wolf 1978: 161). Women, especially in the southern Chinese provinces of modern-day Fujian and Guangdong, often participated in field labour, and certain groups, such as the *Hakka*, were known for not binding the feet of women. This area of China also had a tradition of forming sisterhoods (*jiemei hui*) or support groups of women, including those who had refused to get married (Topley 1978).[4] Thus, these strict codes of conduct were in no way uniform.

Another scholar of Chinese history, Joanna F. Handlin, shows how even among the gentry the Confucian norms of behaviour for women were not rigidly followed. As she says: "The principles of female subordination and *li* designed to order society, tell us more about how the upper class thought women should behave than how they really did." (1975: 13). Focussing on a sixteenth-century Confucian scholar, Lu Kun, who attempted to admonish women towards good behaviour, she points out that by the end of the sixteenth century a whole range of female behaviour was visible in urban centres. In fact, she sees Lu Kun's admonitions as an attempt to counter the existing situation rather than as a representation of the reality of women's lives or, as Handlin puts it, "a dialectic between the actual and the real." (Handlin 1975: 15). Such a perspective is useful, for it raises the question of the actual interaction between women and society.

These examples are cited here to show how orthodox discourse is forced to construct itself in relation to a variety of other discourses. It also allows us to look at the means through which women do acquire a certain degree of power and autonomy. Wolf has suggested that within the family women accumulated power over time by building on their "uterine ties" or ties developed through giving birth to sons. In her later years, it is this close relationship that will ensure that a woman exercises power over her family and over her son's future family and her daughter-in-law. Wolf goes on to explain that women also found ways to exercise power through village gossip, a means by which the community of women could make their husbands lose face (Wolf 1978). Snow also notes that "gossip" was a weapon deployed very skilfully by women, and in certain cases men were forced to take refuge in monasteries or flee the village to guard their honour (H. Snow 1967: 50).

However, rather than seeing these examples as instances of female power as such, one could argue that this was the only way women could survive an otherwise abominable situation. It does not change women's power relationship in terms of gender relations. They exercise effective power only against their own sex, thereby further ensuring the legitimacy of male power structures, or an acceptance of doxic forms of identification. In fact, traditional folktales abound with stories of tensions between mothers-in-law and daughters-in-law, both of whom seek to preserve and build a power base within the family.

Thus, although it was possible for women to acquire a modicum of power in their old age through having given birth to sons, in terms of discourse, women remained clearly subordinate to men. In her own right, a woman had no power or legitimate position. In the final instance, she remained dependent on the good will of her husband and son. It was this real vulnerability of women that made the "women's question" (*funu wenti*) one of the burning issues of late nineteenth and twentieth century China, and provided the first instance of an organised and systematic heterodoxy on gender relations.

Repudiating Tradition: The Emergence of the Women's Question

Bourdieu argues that in times of crisis (here he implies social, economic and political crisis) prevailing systems of classification become a target of confrontation (1977; 1990). By breaking down objective structures of social relations and their institutions, the basis of prevailing orthodoxy becomes weaker, thus allowing critical opposition to emerge as a real possibility (1977: 169). This is clearly visible in the way gender relations became a field of conflict and a discourse to be contested in early twentieth century China.

Several scholars of Chinese history have pointed out that the issue of women's rights was first raised, though indirectly, by the intellectuals of this period. Their primary concern was nationalist, a natural response to the humiliating defeats that the Qing empire had suffered at the hands of the western powers. Having come into contact with western cultures, these intellectuals were interested in discovering why China had been easily defeated and what could be done to make it into a strong nation. This nationalism led them to advance a charter of reforms which included improving the position of women (Chow Tse-tsung 1960; Rankin 1975; Croll 1978). The main issues taken up by the reformers of this period were footbinding and the education of women.

By the end of the nineteenth century, several anti-footbinding associations had been set up. The custom was castigated as cruel and indicative of the low status of women in Chinese society. Part of the concern of these reformers was that the custom of footbinding made China appear culturally backward in the eyes of foreigners (Croll 1978). The pressure exerted by these reform groups finally succeeded in getting the Dowager Empress to pass an edict in 1902 which requested the gentry to "influence their families to abstain from the evil practice and by this means abolish the custom forever" (Levy 1966: 20). The main feature of this reform movement, however, is the almost negligible role played by Chinese women themselves. The movement as a whole did not penetrate very far into rural areas and remained restricted to the upper classes even in urban areas. It was only when this demand for "natural feet" was combined with the demand for women's education that Chinese women were to emerge as reformers in their own right.

Behean, in her research on the issue of early female education in China, notes that Shanghai was in the vanguard of the new movement to establish women's education. Although schools run by missionaries had come into existence a few years earlier, the first modern girls' school was established in Shanghai in 1897, and was associated with the reform movement of 1898. In 1997, an official nation wide system of elementary schools for girls was established and over the years their number continued to increase (Behean 1975: 381).

It is clear from the above that importance was being attached to education as a first step towards the improvement of the position of women. However, it was limited to urban women from a bourgeois or "respectable" background.[5] This was partially responsible for the "middle class" and urban nature of the initial feminist movement in China. On the other hand, the importance of female entry into formal education in China is demonstrated by the role played by female students in the various political movements that were emerging. Literacy served as an integrative mechanism for women, allowing them to acquire skills through which they could become self-supporting. It was within the confines of the new schools that the "woman's movement" (*funu yundong*) first emerged (Croll 1978).

The immediate and most noticeable impact of female education in China was the appearance of a number of magazines or journals for women.[6] Several of these were founded and run by women students who had left China to study abroad. During this period, Japan became a major centre for Chinese intellectuals interested in reforming the customs of their country. By 1997, there were about a 100 Chinese women students in Japan. Most of them were influenced by the patriotic sentiments of the male student community. However, along with espousing patriotism, women also spoke up for female equality (Liu Mei Ching 1988). The first journal to be published in China specifically devoted to women's issues was called the *Funu zazhi* (*Women's Journal*) edited by Chen Xiefen (Rankin 1975). The main focus of all the articles addressed to women was to motivate them to participate in the national movement. That women responded to these calls is evident from the number of women who participated in the anti-Manchu movement, the most famous being Qiu Jin (1875-1909).[7]

After the downfall of the Manchu empire in 1911, China declared itself a republic based on parliamentary democracy. Sun Yat-sen (1866-1925) was briefly the president of this first republic. This period saw the rapid acceleration of suffragette politics, when several women's organisations sprouted and women started campaigning for the vote. Major cities such as Nanjing, Beijing and Shanghai saw women barricading government offices and demanding the vote (Croll 1978: 66-7). This focus on specific women's demands was different from the pre-Republican issues which were identified more with nationalism than with feminism. This is evident in the kind of articles appearing during this period, stressing the need for women to become independent persons in their own right (Croll 1978: 82).

The high point of the early women's movement occurred during the May Fourth movement of 1919.[8] Listing the numerous effects of the May Fourth period, Chow says: "The movement also accelerated the decline of the old family system and the rise of feminism. And above all, the authority of Confucianism and traditional ethics suffered a fundamental and devastating stroke and new Western ideas were exalted." (Chow Tse-tsung 1960: 2).

It is not strange that during this time men were often prominent as champions of women's rights. Many of them, such as Chen Duxiu, Li Dazhao and others who participated in this new culture movement, were to raise the issues of women's subordination in the magazines they edited and in the essays and stories they wrote.[9] Another important indicator of the changing attitudes of the urban intelligentsia on the "women question" is the way women characters in fiction were dealt with. This period saw the birth of many young writers such as Lu Xun, Mao Dun, Guo Moruo, Ba Jin and Ding Ling, to name a few. All of them focus on the condition of women in their works and advocate male-female equality (Hsu 1981). The influence of Ibsen's plays in this period also testifies to the importance of this issue. Ibsen's play *A Doll's House* was translated into Chinese as early as 1918, immediately causing a great stir and leading to the emergence of cases of "Chinese Noras" (Schwarz 1975; Eide 1985; 1987). Lu Xun later wrote a rejoinder to this phenomenon of China's Noras in an article entitled, "What Happens after Nora Leaves Home?" (1923). He stresses the necessity to link women's emancipation, with their economic emancipation, as otherwise "they would only change one cage for another" (Lu Xun 1923: 86). The Chinese Communist Party was to focus on this need for women's material emancipation as the founding principle of its own discourse on the woman question.

The Communist Party and the Women's Question, 1921-49

The underlying emphasis of this position was the need to draw women into productive labour and organise them along class lines.[10]

The leadership of this task called "woman work" (*funu gongzuo*) was given to Xiang Jingyu.[11] Xiang was of the opinion that envisaging a separate women's movement was a political error and that the women's movement had to be part of the general communist revolutionary movement. The directives regarding women's participation in the Communist Party seemed to have followed a Soviet strategy of assigning the few available female cadres to organising women's groups at the grassroots level. These organisations, among other things, were responsible for holding demonstrations on Women's Day, 8 March. As Leith notes: "Throughout the twenties, March 8 continues to be a focal point for mobilizing women. By 1926, the movement had grown to such proportions that 10,000 gathered together in Canton, 800 in Hunan." (1973: 53).

Despite the initial success of a communist-led women's movement, a 1926 Party resolution noted that several problems remained. The movement was not really able to penetrate the masses. Many of the volunteers were more romantic than realistic and several of them had problems identifying with their constituents (Maloney 1980). Although the Communist Party succeeded in widening the context of the women's movement, its chief concern remained a focus on class struggle and, therefore, on women workers.

By 1927, the Communist Party had become a force to be reckoned with in urban areas. The Nationalists, encouraged by the imperial powers and its own fledgling bourgeoisie, found it expedient to check this growing working-class movement. They unleashed a white terror of unprecedented proportions during which thousands of communists and their sympathisers were killed (Cheneaux 1968). The centrality of "gender" as a factor in propaganda is testified to by the vociferous statements made against the alleged attempt of communists to change gender roles and morality. Diamond (1975b) comments on the use Nationalist propaganda of the period made of the woman's question. Rumours circulated about "naked women" who freely cohabited with men and lacked all morality. Stories were told of communist cadres forcibly cutting the hair of women. Such propaganda was essential to justify the mass executions that were carried out. Cai Chang, one of the women leaders of the period, recalls how: "More than 1,000 women leaders were killed... When girls were arrested in Hunan they were stripped naked, nailed on crosses and their noses and breasts cut off before they were killed.... It is actually true that if a girl had bobbed hair she was subject to execution as a communist in Hunan and Canton." (H. Snow 1967: 242).

Among those caught was Xiang Jingyu who was executed in March 1928 (Luo Qiong 1986: 87). Such brutal repression of the early labour movement and the women's movement forced the communists into the hinterland and the countryside became the mainstay of the Party in China. This move was also responsible for changing the face of the women's liberation movement.

In his *Report on an Investigation into the Peasant Movement of Hunan, 1927,* Mao Zedong points out the close link between a struggle against the feudal gentry and patriarchal ideas. This much-quoted paragraph explicitly denounces the system of male superiority in China. As Mao puts it:

> "A man in China is usually subjected to three systems of authority (political authority, clan authority and religious authority). As for women, in addition to being dominated by these three authorities, they are also dominated by the men (the authority of the husband). These four authorities — political, clan, religious and masculine — are the embodiment of the whole feudal-patriarchal system and ideology, and are the four thick ropes binding the Chinese people — particularly the peasants." (Mao Zedong 1956: Vol. I, 44).

Further on in the same article, Mao stresses the importance of organising women and sees their participation in anti-feudal struggles as part of the process of rural transformation which the Party desired. This particular text of Mao is of importance because it shows both the importance the Party attached to the issue of women's liberation, and the analysis maintained about its role within the overall revolution.

As the Communist Party strengthened its position in the countryside, it instituted several reforms that were to affect the position of women positively and radically. Davin notes that: "One of the greatest achievements of the Chinese Communist Party has been the change brought about in the lives of Chinese women in the rural hinterland." (1976: 243). Practical policies to deal with the situation of women were first applied in the Jiangxi Soviet (1927-34). These were the Land-reform law and the Marriage law.[12] These two documents were later to serve as the basis of the laws promulgated in the Yan'an period (1934-47). Although constant warfare and generally unstable conditions made the implementation of any policy a hazardous matter, women were granted equality with men at all levels (Davin 1976; Stranahan 1976; Maloney 1980).

The major focus of mobilisation for women during the 1930s, however, was to motivate them to contribute to the anti-Japanese war effort. Kay Ann Johnson points out that the work among women was felt to be necessary because in many cases women exercised a strong influence on the decision of the male members of the household to join the Red Army. To ensure a successful recruitment strategy, the Party soon realised the necessity of enlisting the support of the whole family (Johnson 1983: 52).

Separate women's organisations were also set up and special attention was supposed to be paid to women's work. Mao sums up the Party position when he says: "Women make up half the population. The economic position of women and the special oppression suffered by them not only shows the need felt for revolution but also implies that they represent a force to determine the success or failure of the revolution." (Luo Qiong 1986: 88).

Stranahan quotes unverified Chinese sources to list a figure of about 130,000 women who were members of one or another association. Of these, 70,000 were said to attend meetings regularly and joined in work projects (Stranahan, 1976: 35).

Several measures were also adopted to train women cadres and a special school called the School for Women Cadres (*Nu Ganbu Xuexiao*) was also set up (Price 1975). However, Janet Price (1975) notes that the number of women who actually participated in this and other cadre schools was extremely small and their responsibilities were limited to propagating the tasks outlined by the Party. Nevertheless, great emphasis was placed on women taking the lead in educating children and other women.

Women cadres already familiar with Party policy were trained to set up village cooperatives and women were encouraged to take up spinning, weaving and other such tasks (Davin 1976: 37). In areas where men had been drawn into the army, women were also encouraged to participate in agricultural production (Johnson 1983: 65). Periodic efforts were made to bring women into the political process though, here again, a strict sexual division of labour seems to have existed. There were very few women in leadership positions. Women who did emerge as leaders such as Cai Chang and Deng Yingchao through Party work were almost automatically assigned to women's work and women's bureaus.

A critical analysis of the early Party position: The initial period of the Communist Party's engagement with the "woman's question" demonstrates the limits of change in gender relations. While the Party attempted to question a traditional orthodoxy, and at this stage the lack of institutional legitimacy gave its discourse the flavour of a heterodoxy, it was unable to question the deep-seated habitus of gender relations. This is specially noticeable in the case of Party policy on intra-family relations. Once the Party had shifted its base to Yan'an, its position on the role of women was quite clear. Several directives on women's work pointed out the need for caution and care. Although the fundamental position of the Party — that women's participation in production was the way to female liberation — did not change, caution and unity were the operative words in its dealings with gender contradictions.

The struggle for women's rights in marriage and divorce was considered potentially divisive, especially since this affected the very constituents which the Party was seeking to win over. These were the poor and the middle peasants. If the marriage law was actually enforced, in some cases the peasants would lose not only their wives but also their lands. Numerous other incidents document the compromises that the Party made with rural patriarchy and traditionalism in order to further the aims of its "general revolution". Women who were interested in pushing forward issues of family reform were seen as divisive and accused of espousing separatism over the interests of the general revolution.

Stranahan records numerous incidents during the Yan'an days when women's interests were successively sacrificed in the name of unity and family harmony. Women who came to the women's bureaus with complaints about ill-treatment from the family were, in the 1940s, encouraged not to divorce or create dissension; instead, they were told to go home and attempt to raise their own political consciousness and that of their spouses (Stranahan 1976: 45-6), as well as to be productive and contribute to the general war effort against the Japanese. Cai Chang's words in the early 1940s seem to sum up the position of the Party: "Our current slogans for work in the woman's movement are no longer 'freedom of marriage' and 'equality between men and women', rather they are 'save the children and establish an abundant and flourishing family so as to cause each household to become a prosperous one'." (Johnson 1983: 75).

The most famous critique of this period is that of Ding Ling (1908-85), the *grande dame* of Chinese letters. Ding Ling came to Yan'an in 1937 after having escaped from a KMT prison. She was already famous as a controversial and daring woman writer in Shanghai. On arrival in Yan'an, she was made editor of the Party's propaganda magazine. Helen Snow recalls that many Party members at Yan'an were aghast at Ding Ling's reputation as an avant-garde feminist and by her attitudes towards free love and marriage (H. Snow 1968).

Ding Ling made an open critique of the double standards of the Party on the male-female issue, not only in her stories such as *When I was in Xia Village (Wo zai xiacun de shihour)* but also in her article published in the *Jiefang Ribao* (Liberation Daily), on 8 March 1942. According to Ding Ling, women were encouraged to take on new roles as Party activists and yet fulfil their obligations as housewives and remain responsible for the family. The result was that women were faced with unsolvable contradictions and were viewed with contempt irrespective of what they did. As she says: "They were damned for what they didn't." If women did not marry they were ridiculed, if they did, they were criticised for paying too much importance to family matters. She went on to say that male leaders should talk less of theory and more of actual practice. In the end, she made a pointed reference to the discriminatory attitude of the Party. She said that if the opinions she was putting forward had been those of a male leader, they would have been read with great seriousness; unfortunately, being a woman her opinion will probably be dismissed (Feuerwerker 1982: 32). Ding Ling was not wrong in her prognosis. Not only were her opinions and criticism dismissed, she found herself at the receiving end of a great deal of criticism, led by Mao himself (Feuerwerker 1982; Goldman 1971).[13]

Less scathing critics of the Communist Party have pointed out that it was not necessarily deliberate Party policy to uphold patriarchy. Instead, they argue, the compromises made by the Party regarding the woman's question were a result of the circumstances it faced in its drive to gain control of the Chinese countryside (Davin 1976). In the light of the historical evidence cited earlier, we see a dynamic relationship between Communist Party policy and the practice of gender relations. The early attempts to bring women into communist politics did exhibit a certain radicalism.[14] The Party, in its attempt to construct a policy on women's issues, ignored questions of female sexuality and intra-family relations. It is here that the Party succumbed to a habitus on gender relations. Its member's understanding of social relations was mediated by their sense of habitus, a habitus which for centuries defined a strict code of male-female positions and relations. The understanding of male-female relations continued to be overshadowed by those elements which remained in doxa, and constituted the unsaid, taken-for-granted and therefore "natural" difference of gender dispositions. It was these "natural" dispositions of men and women which made the issue of sexual morality and the general sexual division of labour difficult questions for the Party.

On the whole, the period leading up to the liberation of China in 1949 can be characterised as one in which the specific interests of women, and of a revolution in gender relations, were constantly compromised and relegated to become secondary issues. It would be correct to say that the Party lost a great opportunity to effect real change, and had it acted on its own revolutionary laws for female equality, problems that persist today would have been minimised to a large extent.

Institutionalising a new Orthodoxy: Women in Post-revolutionary China

October 1 1949 saw the establishment of the Pecple's Republic of China (PRC). This victory gave the Party the power to exercise effective control over the limits of discourse formation on most subjects. Through control of the channels of the production and dissemination of information, that Party was able to project its own ideas as the legitimate and correct way of approaching all social relations. It is in post-revolutionary China that we see clear and direct links between an institutionalisation process and the construction of an "orthodoxy".

The Communist Party, during its early years, was interested in extending the reforms that had been implemented in the liberated areas tc the rest of China. Its policy on women was put into practice with the creation of the All China Women's Federation (hereafter ACWF) in April 1949. In fact, during the period immediately following liberation, great attention was paid to the creation of women's organisations and youth organisations. Their purpose was to ensure that specific sectors of the population could be brought under the umbrella of the ACWF (Andors 1981). Its aims and goals were laid down in the Central Committee circular on women's work towards the end of 1948.[15]

The period immediately after liberation, 1950-53, saw the most radical implementation of the Marriage Law and the Land Reform Law. A series of campaigns via posters and so on were initiated to popularise the Marriage Law which had been proclaimed in 1950. According to Johnson, the basic premise of the campaign was "the belief that ideological propoganda could succeed in changing traditional attitudes towards women." (1983: 100). Efforts were made to educate and influence mothers-in-law to show them the necessity of supporting the reforms and for improving relationship with their daughers-in-law. However, in no instance was the family as an institution questioned (Davin 1976: 97; Eber 1989).[16]

Considerable effort was put into making divorce more acceptable to the population. In the early stages, when divorce courts were set up at local level, divorces were generally initiated by women and granted on anti-feudal grounds. A 1950 report on divorce claimed that 50 per cent of divorce application came from those between the ages of twenty-five and forty-five (Croll 1978). Although reform in the urban areas proceeded relatively smoothly, in rural areas it sometimes led to tragic results. There were incidents of women being forced to commit suicide or being killed because they demanded divorce (H. Snow 1967). By the late 1950s, however, the policy of granting easy divorces was changed and social stability again began to be cited as a goal.

Women were also encouraged to participate in production. The new Labour Law of the PRC declared that women were equal citizens and had equal rights to participate in production. Giving women land in their own names was only the beginnning of the process of social change. Since then, the marked improvement in the lives of Chinese women compared to their pre-liberation situation has been acknowledged by most writers on the subject.

However, while the legal and political measures adopted by the PRC definitely created a millieu for female equality, the actual implementation of reform remained uneven. The reforms did not go far enough in terms of changing male-female relations, especially within the family and marriage. Thus, the "intimate personal" lives of women remained constrained by the ideas of the natural sexual division of labour. Although the number of women involved in factory work and those entering white-collar services rose, the practice of ascribing "suitable female" tasks to them also increased. Thus women started to dominate in light industry and as junior teaching staff (Andors 1981).

During the land reform period in the countryside, the aim was to bring women into production by giving them land in their own names. However, in many cases the situation remained unchanged because women lacked the necessary skills to till their own lands. The best choice for women seemed to have been to lease the land to their male kin (Diamond, 1975a: 26). Croll further comments that since marriage remained patrilocal in nature, women tended to leave their land to their father or brother to manage (1978: 12).

During the first five-year plan, controversy also arose over the role of housewives. It was found that housewives felt socially despised because they did not engage in productive labour.

It is interesting to note that although the official press, eg. the woman magazine *Zhongguo Funu* (Women of China) tried to legitimise and in places even encouraged women to be housewives, the question of housework actually being productive labour never entered the debate. As Croll suggests, all the household activities undertaken by women were never quantified or even considered to be productive (1978: 12). Instead, women's status as dependents was stressed and campaigns such as the *Wu Hao* or Five Goods were inaugurated. This was supposed to politicise housework by showing its revolutionary worth. Women were told that they could contribute to society by ensuring that they kept the morale of their working husbands high and maintained harmony in the house (Davin 1976: 169). For working women, on the other hand, the problem remained that of the double burden. Although they had achieved a degree of status and social respect, little attempt was made to handle the contradictions of their position. Efforts to provide social services in the form of creches and canteens did not change the fact that housework was seen as a female task (Sidel 1974; Stacey 1983).

The initial post-liberation period, for women, was thus, fraught with contradictory demands. The Party was forced to waver from its own ideological understanding of women's liberation as being dependent on participation in what it defined as productive labour, and once again bowed to historical expediency, attempting to shelve the contradiction that occurred in terms of female equality and economic growth.

The Great Leap Forward and the Cultural Revolution: Women as Labour Heroines

The Great Leap Forward (GLF) launched in 1958,[17] and the collectivisation drive in rural areas that followed, saw a revival of the theme of women's participation in production. The GLF envisaged a rapid transition to socialism by mobilising masses of people to contribute to the production of goods (MacFarquhar 1983; Brugger 1981). Andors sees GLF policy towards women as a logical outgrowth of its attempt to mobilise mass labour as a development strategy (Andors 1975: 34). Women were encouraged, both in the rural areas and in the urban areas, to participate in labour.

Initially, women were supposed to take over those tasks which men vacated in order to participate in many small-scale rural industrialisation projects. They were freed from household duties through the creation of community childcare centres and canteens. In many rural areas, grandmothers and older women of the community were encouraged to look after children so that mothers could work (Hemmel and Sindjberg 1984). The benefits of female participation in labour were enormous, and many observers have recorded the positive impact that this had on women. According to Sidel (1974), an additional benefit of the GLF was to expand the inadequate healthcare system in rural areas. On the other hand, this drive to encourage women's participation in paid labour also bought certain contradictions to the fore, testifying once again to an unchanged habitus of gender relations.

The most obvious of these was the consistent devaluation of women's labour in the new sysem of wages in work-points. The maximum number of work-points available was ten. Women on average were never given more than six or seven work-points even where they performed tasks similar to those of men. The explanation put forward for this was that women were not reliable in their work due to the demands of childcare. What it actually showed was a continuing belief in female inferiority and resistance to the idea of women working in the fields. Tasks consistent with traditional female roles, such as spinning and weaving, were more easily accepted but traditional prejudices against women working in the fields still existed (Davin 1976; Croll 1978; Andors 1981).

In urban areas housewives were encouraged to join urban communes and neighbourhood committees. These in turn organised co-operatives of various sorts. Women were also asked to undertake jobs being made available in the light industrial sector because men were drawn into other work. Women especially older women, were also drawn into the service industry, such as childcare. This period saw an increase in childcare facilities and kindergartens available to working women, especially in state-run factories (Chan 1974; Davin 1976; Andors 1981).

When analysing the rhetoric on female liberation that emerged during this period, Andors comments that the measures which were conducive to women's emancipation were incidental to the policies being implemented. The goal of rapidly creating socialist institutions and of catching up with the West raised the issue of conflict between women's equality and socialist construction. Andor's reading of the situation also holds true if we examine the fact that policy changes after the Great Leap Forward rescinded many of the measures that had been used to encourage participation by women in wage labour. The cuts appeared first in the welfare services, such as rural creches and canteens.

The major conflict concerned women's primary responsibility in the period of socialist transition: were they to be dependents and helpers of their spouses or revolutionary and productive activists (Andors 1976: 101)? This conflict became more apparent because women were already visible in the field of production and a few had even emerged in leadership positions. Sheridan (1976), in an examination of the background and lives of young women leaders in China, notes that most of the women who had achieved political and social status in China and had been appointed members of the National People's Congress (NPC), were women workers who had risen from the shopfloor through a demonstration of skills in the production process. As Sheridan points out, the histories that she deals with show "the interlocking of several roles — political roles, family roles, and roles as workers" (1976: 60). Thus, in reality, women were constantly occupying multiple roles. In fact, what we notice is the addition of a new role for women — that of worker — on top of their existing family roles.

The onslaught of the Cultural Revolution in 1966[18] and the large-scale disruption that it brought to aspects of family and social life, also saw the disbanding of the All China Women's Federation (Croll 1977). Strong criticism was directed at the editors of the magazine *Zhongguo Funu* (Women of China), pointing out that during the early 1960s they had over-emphasised the role of women in the family while downplaying their role in production.

The most significant campaign to concentrate on the role of women in society was the Anti-Lin Piao and Anti-Confucius Campaign (*Pi Lin Pi Kong*) of 1972. It began with a critique of Lin Piao and was later extended to include an attack on Confucian moral values. The campaign, directly attributed to Jiang Qing the wife of Mao Zedong, named Confucian feudal values as the ideology of the oppressive ruling classes. A number of "Confucian statements" were attributed to Lin Piao who was then cast in the role of chief villain. Several derogatory statements he had made about women were criticised, and the occasion was used to compaign for female equality (Croll 1977).

Under the general guidelines of opposing discrimination against women, women and youth groups at local levels held meetings and implemented educational campaigns to fight the old attitudes towards women. Some of the specific issues raised concerned discrimination against women at work and the failure of men to participate in house-work; even the issue of encouraging matrilocal mariages in order to undermine the patriarchal family system was raised (Croll [ed.] 1974). As the campaign progressed, newspapers and periodicals carried articles which featured examples of women who proved the fallacy and biases of feudal discourse. These women were held up as role models and communist heroines (Croll, 1977; Johnson 1983: 194-297).

Interestingly enough, it was this campaign, coinciding with the heyday of the women's movement in the West, which led to claims of "patriarchy kowtowing in China" (Stacey 1979). The Chinese women's movement was cited as an example of the superiority of the socialist system where women's right were concerned (Eizenstein 1979; Weinbaum 1976). However, with the downfall of the Gang of Four following the death of Mao Zedong in 1976, policies have again changed in China. In typical fashion, so have the new role models being presented to women.

Re-emphasising Femininity and Motherhood: The Post-Mao Years

The economic and political changes that have occurred in post-Mao China have affected all levels of Chinese society and have led to the emergence of new guidelines and directives for women.[19] Although the ideological underpinnings of women's roles remain grounded in the previous notions of female equality, there is a striking difference today between the much publicised ideology of equality and the practise of female subordination. The new policies introduced by the Chinese government under the name of the "Four Modernisations" have once again brought the contradictions between the issues of female equality and the government's goals to the fore (Davin 1988).

The main policy change of the post-Mao period has been the introduction of the "household responsibility system"; in rural areas and the "industrial responsibility system" in urban areas (*Zeren zhi*). All these measures have been encouraged under what is called breaking the "big rice pot" (*da guofan*), a system of guarantees under which all workers, irrespective of performance, had a right to an average wage (Leung-Wing-yue 1988, Piehe. 1991, Christiansson 1989).

Women's contributions to the programme of modernisation have been outlined in Party directives to women's organisations and in journals specifically addressed to women (Jiang Tingsheng 1987). The repudiation of Cultural Revolution policies has meant that the ideological emphasis on confronting feudal attitudes towards women which were highlighted in the anti-Confucian campaign, have all been put on ice. Images of women which encouraged them to enter new avenues and emphasised their roles as labour and peasant heroines who could do all that men could do are a thing of the past. Today, there are new issues and new ideas regarding what women should expect under socialism.

The reconvened All China Women's Federation took over its old task of propagandising the aims of the Party vis-a-vis women. As in previous years of Party policy on the woman question, women are first and foremost called on to do their duty by working for socialism (Chang Jiaqin 1988). The Fifth National Women's congress, held in 1983 and attended by about 2,100 delegates, laid down the tasks of the women's movement for the next decade. A major policy document published in the aftermath of the conference emphasised women's roles as mothers and within the family. Women are seen to be responsible for childcare and the ideological care of the younger generation. Further, the lack of reference to any sharing of these tasks between men and women ensures that women remain primarily responsible for childcare. However, the document also stresses the government's commitment to defend the rights of woemn and children.

Besides childcare, women also remain largely responsible for house-work. A recent study of family life in urban China notes that women perform more than 70 per cent of all household labour. This naturally limits their access to job-training and other avenues for increasing their skills. In an interview with a journalist from *China Reconstructs* a working mother compares herself to a juggler: "Catching the 'ball' of her work for the country's socialist modernisation and snatching at the second ball of running a household" (Tan Manni 1980: 10).

This is corroborated by evidence from an extensive urban survey carried out in selected cities in which Whyte found that women do most of the cooking, cleaning and childcare (1984: 224). Though the government has shown a constant awareness of this fact, the modern solution is to encourage the production of consumer goods such as washing machines and refrigerators which will lighten the domestic loads of women (Robinson, 1985:44). Although domestic appliances certainly make life easier, women's responsibility for these tasks does not change. Mao Zedong's often cited comment that washing machines do not liberate women has today been turned on its head.

The continuing double burden caused by an entrenched sexual division of labour leads to inequality in other spheres. Dalsimer and Nisnoff note how the policies introduced in post-Mao China have created conditions which impose sex-differentiated roles on women in production (1984:32). Women find themselves forced into the service sector and into teaching. In 1982, women workers dominated in the broad fields of cotton textiles, finance and trade where they formed 60 per cent of the above force; they made up 50 per cent of the total labour force in light industry (*Women of China* 1983: 8). In 1990, women made up 37.6 per cent of the total employed in China. Out of this, only 20.5 per cent are employed in administrative jobs in the state sector (Pei Qing, 1992:20). Overall wages and material benefits to workers used to be higher in the state-owned sector. This sector also has subsidised services such as transportation, housing, schools and health-care facilities. Dalsimer and Nisnoff note, for example, that at the Changchun automobile factory, a state-owned enterprise, a dozen nurseries were provided whereas the embroidery factory in the same city with a 90 per cent female labour force only had a modest childcare centre on top of the factory (1984:27).

Apart from sex segmentation in different types of industries, there is sex discrimination within industries as well, especially as far as wages are concerned. While men are distributed throughout the eight-grade wage scale in the factories, women are more often found in the lower grades. In the Dalian ship-building works for example, one woman was reported at grade 7 and another at grade 5, while the other women workers were clustered in the lower grades (Dalsimer and Nisnoff 1984: 25). A similar bias seems to be occurring in the allocation of bonuses. A *Workers' Daily* commentary, "Attention Should be Given to Unequal Rewards between Men and Women", reported that after smashing the big rice pot, discrimination against women had again surfaced: "For example, women workers have the same, or even a greater workload than their male counterparts, but when it come to allocating bonuses some people would say, 'she is after all a woman and cannot compare to her male comrades'." (Leung Wing-Yue 1988: 85). Leung Wing-Yue also quotes a Chinese survey which found that over 60 per cent of redundancies caused by economy drives in factories during the second half of 1987 were of women (1988: 86). The same bias is reflected in the recruitment, training and promotion of women cadres (*China Daily*, May 1983, p. 3).

The chief reason given for discrimination against women is the fact that their household duties often make them neglect their jobs. Further, women's right to paid maternity leave also influences management decisions. These attitudes have become even stronger in recent years because most factories now enjoy the right to hire and fire employees. In certain cases, discrimination has been so acute that even graduates from Beijing University have been refused jobs. These incidents are a startling demonstration of how protective legislation for women can become a cause of discrimination against them. As Tan Manni points out: "Labour protection benefits for women often push them into unfavourable positions." (1983: 23).

Such acts of discrimination are also leading to the re-emergence of an argument which had been previously discredited in China. This is the demand that "married women" return home and give up their jobs in favour of men. An article in *China Reconstructs* quotes some husbands as saying: "Send our wives home and subsidise us with their wages. Then we are freed of household chores, we can do better at our jobs." (Tan Manni 1983: 23). Some working mothers echoed this demand and said: "I think I should give up my own career for the sake of my husband and family." (Tan Manni 1983: 23). Ideas such as the above represent a desire on the part of women to revert to older forms of habitus and show the way dominant values work through consensus and acceptance rather than by force.

However, it is interesting to note that the ACWF has come out strongly against the raising of such demands. It has pointed out the necessity for women to continue working and has reiterated the links between women's liberation and their participation in production. The Tianjin Women's Federation carried out a survey among working women which noted that the tasks women needed most help with are childcare and shopping. Of the 1,000 women interviewed, 797 wished for help with shopping (Tianjin Women's Federation 1985: 100). This is not surprising since a large urban population makes shopping a fatiguing task at the best of times (1985: 19).

Along with active discrimination in the job market and education, other forms of exploitation of women are also now prevalent. Women are victims of sexual harassment and physical violence. In recent years, the Chinese press itself has carried cases documenting the gravity of the problem (Dai Qing and Luo Ge 1988). Prostitution and pornography have become rampant in urban areas and numerous rackets dealing with the abduction, buying and selling of women have been exposed (Pearson 1989). There is evidence that patriarchal practices have resurfaced in rural China available from several sources. Female infanticide, much publicised in 1983-84, is only the extreme form of this tradition. The *People's Daily* of 23 March 1983 carried a letter from twenty-three women from Anhui province who had all suffered because of giving birth to baby girls. The letter describes how they were abused by their husbands and not allowed access to contraceptives until they gave birth to a son. The women write: "We cannot understand why 32 years after liberation, we women are still so heavily weighed down by such backward feudal concepts .... We long for a second liberation."

The official press in China has typically blamed feudalism as the cause of such practices. More critical analysis have seen the reemergence of this practice as tied to the way state policy has indirectly colluded with feudal ideas. The twin policies of the rural household responsibility system and the one-child family-planning policy are partially to blame (Croll 1983). Evidence suggests that reversion to the household as the main unit of rural production has led to peasants strongly desiring sons. This demand for labour conflicts directly with the government's one-child policy. Since a daughter is seen as a source of labour which is lost to the family on her marriage, women who give birth to girls are maltreated, and baby girls are killed. Croll notes that in some places the ratio of baby girls to baby boys was 1:4 (1984: 20). In 1990, women formed 48.4 per cent of the total population as compared to 48.7 per cent in 1982 (Pei Qing 1992: 20), showing the impact of female infanticide during the intervening years.

Croll also points out the danger of women's labour disappearing under that of the "household" in rural areas. Despite the many success stories quoted in the Chinese press, she adds a cautionary note:

> "Current policies returning production to the household are marked by the near omission of any substantive analysis of the household and the relations of production and exchange within it. In the absence of such discussion which defines the distribution of labour and rewards within the household, it is likely that the gender hierarchy will be reproduced in production and the individual contribution of women be camouflaged by the family wage." (Croll 1983: 126).

Women's labour may also be intensified now that they are expected to work on sideline occupations, help with agriculture and take care of the household's basic needs (Hopper 1984).

However, it should be pointed out that the ACWF has made certain efforts to combat the most overt forms of discrimination against women. It has carried out educational campaigns among women and has tried to popularise women's rights through an emphasis on the law. Fran Williard, for example, notes that complaints about mothers-in-law, humiliation by husbands who had mistresses, arranged marriages, physical and mental maltreatment, financial non-support and other forms of inequality were aired at tables managed by women lawyers and Federation members (1985: 14). Again, one notices that the problems as such have not changed despite decades of propaganda and favourable legislation. They are the problems against which women fought at the turn of the century.

While, on the one hand, the ACWF champions the equality of women, on the other hand, it also contributes to dominant notions of female roles and images. The way the Federation has dealt with the issues of "love and marriage" is a case in point. Since marriage is seen as the aim of all women, to be "left on the shelf" is considered a state to be pitied. Consequently, it is seen as the duty of social organisations such as the Women's Committees, the Neighbourhood Committees and Youth Organisations to arrange opportunities for young people to meet and get married. Marriage bureaux have also been set up to serve as officially sanctioned matchmakers. While marriage is seen as a natural way of life, the requirements of what counts as an eligible spouse have changed. These reflect the increased consumerism that is visible in urban areas (Tan Manni 1983: 12).

Another significant change in post-Mao China has been the encouragement given to consumerism through the means of advertising. Chinese cities today are littered with advertisements related to household goods from washing machines to tape recorders. As in other countries, advertisements in China use female models, and posters of smiling women standing in front of well-stocked fridges are commonplace. Alongside this, fashion and cosmetics have become important and the hairdressers, and beauty parlours are always full. Such trends mark a significant departure from the ideas of frugality and simplicity that China tried so hard to propagate earlier. They also reveal the resurgence of older notions of femininity, proving that a change in economic or political relations does not automatically imply a change in the way an orthodoxy on gender relations incorporates elements of long-standing cultural tradition.

Another aspect of post-Mao China that needs to be stressed is a remarkable fluidity in the opinions and discourses on the question of women. Harriet Evans, in a study of how popular magazines available in China deal with the sex-gender issue, notes: "Sensationalist, macho and violent stories, printed ostensibly to teach a moral lesson, are found alongside advice to young mothers about how to calm babies who cry too much." (1989: 12). She further notes that other semi-official magazines such as *Women's Forum (Funu luntan)* tend to discuss more topical issues like marriage problems and love matters and give advice on how best to handle these (Evans 1989: 12). These discussions represent a new emphasis on the more traditional nature of female roles in China today. They also represent a range of possibilities that have emerged with the loosening of Party control over publishing.

Though there has been a definite rise in conservatism on the question of women, hitherto unknown feminist voices have also been heard. Several women within the ACWF itself have taken consistent stands against the resurgence of sexism. They have pointed out that for women to be able to compete with men, they need access to job-training facilities and scientific knowledge. As a report by the Anhui Provincial Women's Federation says:

> "Lenin once pointed out that the working class should seek its own emancipation, as should working women. We feel that the same can be said of women becoming capable and qualified people in every field. Provided they are determined to break through the confines of conventionalism, work with persistence and diligence, and overcome obstacles in their path, women can certainly make something of themselves." (Anhui Provincial Women's Federation 1985: 33).

The report then goes on to list subjective and objective factors behind the subordination of women. It also demands that more women should be accepted as cadres in the Party. It points out that, at the provincial level, women form only 23.2 per cent of cadres and the figure decreases sharply among senior ranks. Women account for only 7.2 per cent of cadres at the county levels and 6.2 per cent at the prefectural bureau level (Anhui Provincial Women's Federation 1985: 35).

Despite such efforts on the part of the Federation, post-Mao China is a place where conventional ideas about women have resurfaced. As usual their problems have been subordinated to the immediate policy aims of China. The contradictions that are beginning to emerge between the gender-specific interests of women and the modernisation programme are expected to get worse unless an attempt is made to redress these trends.

Conclusion

An analysis of Chinese policy towards women, and the shifts and changes in the issues that are perceived as women's issues, shows that the crux of the problem has remained the contradiction between women's reproductive roles and their participation in wage labour. While the Chinese Communist Party has constantly expressed support for female liberation, this support has been conditional on women's specific interest not conflicting with the overall interests of the Party. The persistence of "feudal" values about women imply that economic liberation, though an important necessity for female liberation, is not sufficient in itself.

China's case demonstrates that gender relations remain an aspect most resistant to change. The rigid sexual division of labour upon which a habitus of gender relations is built is not only hard to change, but is tenaciously maintained despite changes in economic circumstances. In China one of the most fundamental beliefs remains: that of women's natural role as mothers and providers of the emotional and nurturance needs of their families. As shown, although the status of women in China has changed enormously, this automatic assumption continues to receive tacit support from the government. Their domestic responsibilities and their reproductive roles are seen as aspects which make women different from men, a biological difference which is seen as imbuing them with "natural" characteristics.

The persistent sexual division of labour and the failure to alleviate the domestic burden of women has merely resulted in the addition of new roles on top of women's previous roles, rather than a redefinition of male and female roles, resulting in the exhausting double burden faced by women. The government's limited efforts towards dealing with the specific demands faced by women justifies the charge made by feminists that the policies of socialist states towards women are constantly subordinated to the productivist goals of these states. An analysis of the continuing forms of female subordination, and the way in which socialist policy itself condones male-female inequality, is postponed. Every time the issue emerges from doxa, a new orthodoxy is constructed around it by emphasising one or the other role of women rather than attempting a fundamental restructuring of gender relations. This constant displacing of the women's question is often hidden by the formal equality that women have acquired, and behind the accession of women to previously unconventional occupations (Molyneux 1981b: 36).

The Communist Party, especially in the rural areas of China, first confronted feudal ideas about women in China as a heterodoxy, challenging a Confucian orthodoxy with its discourse of female equality. In the Chinese case it is interesting to note that the Party recognises the importance of ideological change, in fact it positively emphasises it, but it refuses to touch certain aspects of gender relations. These are the sexual division of labour and the consequent belief that women are naturally suitable for certain tasks. That is why the mobilisation of women for tasks which are a natural extension of their familial roles is no contradiction. The discourse of the Party becomes a new discursive alignment of old elements.

This is not an attempt at a deliberate policy by the Party. The Chinese case demonstrates that although the "wider limits" of the discourse on women are extended, certain elements remain behind. This also allows us to form an alternative hypothesis to that of Stacey and others who argue that the Party as such is patriarchal. Further, if we see discourse on gender as premised on those areas which the Party does not see as real contradictions, we can also understand women's own support and participation in the ranks of the Communist Party. They not only actively propagated the Party line but also believed in it. Like the Party, they were convinced that the contradictions between their gender-specific interests would be detrimental to the goal of national and class liberation. It is this aspect of Chinese policy on women that allows us to say that the new orthodoxy on gender relations is a curious mix of patriarchy and socialism, where the tensions between women's productive and reproductive roles remain unresolved. It also shows us the importance and power of discourse and the role that discourse plays in the mystification of the material subordination of women.

Another significant aspect of socialist rhetoric on gender relations is the protectionist discourse within which state support for female equality is couched. Women are constantly identified as those who need to be "protected", on par with children. Women's rights are enshrined in the constitution as a gift of the Party rather than as something won by women through struggle and because women deserve to be equal. This discourse of protectionism has been visible ever since the women's question first appeared as a necessary part of a charter of social reform. The stalwarts of the early reform movement are all men, with the exception of a few token women. In the socialist phase of the revolution, those women who emerged as leaders were automatically assigned to female tasks, which were seen as secondary to the overall goals of the revolution. This protectionist discourse of the Party is also what made it suppress the more radical and independent discourses which emerged within the women's movement during the period of the May Fourth movement of 1919. The Party cannot afford to allow competing discourses, which link questions of female subordination to intra-family relations and pose the problem as a contradiction between the interests of men and women. This would undermine the Party's legitimacy as the arbitrator of social relations.

The structural subordination of the ACWF, as a mass organisation is a natural consequence of this protectionist bias. This protective strategy serves a double function, for it also ensures that women who do act in their own interests outside the avenues provided for them, are successfully marginalised and discredited as divisive. The need for an independent women's organisation is removed if the Party constantly proclaims to support and protect the interests of women. Whenever this protectionism offered by the state and its organisations fails, the Party blames feudal ideology rather than examining the limitations and drawbacks of its own strategies and policies. Feudal ideology, in other words, becomes a convenient scapegoat for the tensions that emerge when the gender interests of women come into conflict with state policy.

Because of the Party's compromises at various levels, and the way women are defined as dependents, power relations between the sexes have changed very little over time. At the material level, women remain unequal to men in all areas of social life. At the level of discourse, this inequality is hidden behind an ideology of equality. Any analysis which seeks to examine the position of women in China, then, has to start with debunking this myth of equality which is maintained by orthodoxy. The ideology of equality through state protectionism ensures that the emergence of an independent women's organisation which will consistently champion women's rights is an uphill task.

While orthodoxy and its contents can be examined through the way the state presents its position on the woman's question, we also need to find a way of assessing what women make of these representations of themselves, and how they represent themselves in alternative ways. Women throughout different periods have responded to the demands made on them in different ways. While many have accepted the demands uncritically, others, as exemplified by Ding Ling, have tended to look critically at their position in society. The post-Mao years, with the loosening of control at various levels, further demonstrate that the state does not have a monopoly on the production of a discourse on women. Though it attempts to construct an orthodoxy, in practice, several discourses coexist.

This heterodoxy, in the Chinese case, contains different discourses, some seek a return to a position that existed before the CPC came to power and are echoes of conservative ideas about women; others seek radically to question all elements of a traditional and socialist orthodoxy. While the former justify and support discrimination against women by seeking to contract the limits of change that have occurred, the latter seek to widen the limits of discourse.

Strands of heterodoxy can also be spotted in different places. Within the Women's Federation, for example, there has been a growing acceptance of the existence of female subordination rather than pretending that the problems of women have all been taken care of. Although the ACWF is structurally limited in its propagation of female equality, it has highlighted and criticised incidents of blatant discrimination against women. Independent women's voices have also been heard through university student groups such as the Guangdong University students who have started a journal specially devotes to publicising cases of discrimination against women. Some of the more critical women writers are also part of this more independent critique of gender relations. A few women's studies programmes have also been set up in universities (Shen Zhi 1987).

In the final analysis, discrimination against women can be eradicated only if what is taken for granted about male-female relations is questioned; not by a revival of an earlier conception of male-female relations, as is happening in China today, but by a radical questioning of their relation. It is this apparent fit of women's natural roles with their objective circumstances that seems to provide a motif of continuity within the changing discourse on Chinese women.

Notes

1. Bourdieu defines habitus as "At once a system of models for the production of practices and a system of models for the perception and appreciation of practices. There the habitus implies a sense of one's place" and also a sence of other's place (Bourdieu 1990: 131)
2. The role played by patrilocal marriages has been examined by several scholars. In the case of China see, Freedman (1970).
3. This feature of feudal society leads one to argue that dominant or orthodox discourse in pre-capitalist societies attempts to control only those it classifies as its "representatives". The adherence to morals and values is, in fact, one of the bases on which the upper classes distinguish themselves from the general mass of the population.
4. While sisterhoods are a positive and successful example of resistance to social pressure, they existed only in south China. For many young women the only means of resisting forced marriages was suicide, a very common happening in traditional China. See Wolf (1978).
5. Croll has an interesting quote to prove the class bias of these early reformers. She quotes from the prospectus of one of the schools opened by a number of wealthy merchants: "In opening schools for girls we are reverting to the illustrious custom of the three dynasties. In order to open up the intelligence of the people, we must certainly make women free and afterwards customs can be changed.... It is the intention of the school to make no distinctions of rank but since in the future, pupils from the school will be leaders and teachers in other schools, only respectable families will be admitted." (Croll 1978: 52).
6. See Liu Mei Ching (1988) for details about the content of women's journals in Japan during this period.
7. Qiu Jin is often seen as the heroine of this period. She came from a gentry family, with liberal parents. She divorced her husband and left her children in order to study in Japan. There she came in contact with members of the *Tong Meng Hui*, an association set up under the leadership of Sun Yat-sen, later the president of Republican China in 1911. Qiu Jin participated in their activities and in 1906 returned to China to work and propagate revolution. She was arrested and executed by the Manchu government in 1909 when she and her co-conspirators planned the assassination of a high official (Croll 1978: 65).
8. The actual incident that started widespread demonstrations all over China was the protest of 4 May 1919 against the enforcement of the Versailles Treaty, from which the movement draws its name.
9. As early as 1916, Chen Duxiu suggested that a new family system was essential if women were to be liberated. The magazine *New Youth*, of which Chen was editor, ran regular columns on the subject from 1918 onwards. See Chow Tse-tsung (1960).
10. The leaders of the communist movement in China accepted the analysis outlined above because by the early 1920s women workers had emerged in large numbers in the urban areas of China. Further, Honing (1986) in her study of women textile workers in Shanghai points out that women were severely exploited and worked long hours under miserable conditions.
11. Xiang Jingyu was the only woman in the first politburo of the Chinese Communist Party. She studied in France with Zhou Enlai and returned to China in 1922 to participate in Party work. She was one of the few women who were part of the decision-making apparatus of the early Communist Party. She was appointed director for women's affairs by the Party in 1923. Xiang was especially against the early feminists, regarding them as middle-class women attempting social charity. This prejudice against feminists was to continue and the word "feminism" (*nuxing zhuyi*) came to be seen as pejorative. See Leith (1973).
12. The Soviet Land Law of 1931 provided for the distribution of land among hired hands, labourers and peasants regardless of sex (Stranahan 1976: 21). This was an historic landmark in China, for before this women had never had the right to inherit property. The second important piece of legislation in this period was the promulgation of the Marriage Law in 1931 (*Zhonghua Su-wei-ai gong he guo hunyin tiaoli*). This law listed three basic principles: free choice of marriage, legalisation of divorce and the position of children. See Delia Davin (1976).
13. In today's light, it is interesting to note that similar critiques have been made by female guerrilla fighters from Cuba and Zimbabwe. Women recall that on their return to "normal" life they were seen as "strange, loose women, while the men were welcomed back as heroes of the revolution". See Molyneux (1981 a).
14. A good example of the radicalism of certain of the women's organisations during this period is documented in William Hinton's *Fanshen* (1966), a history of how revolution and liberation occurred in the Long Bow village. Hinton records the steps that the

local women's organisation took against those men and mothers-in-law who continued to mistreat wives. He records how the "eat bitterness" (*chiku*) campaigns worked in practice.

15. The circular evaluated the experience of women's work in the liberated areas and pointed out the shortcomings that had existed. Commenting on the central task of women's work, the circular stated: "The orientation of womanwork in the liberated areas should still be based on mobilising and organising women for an active part in production.... In the first place women must be given equal rights and position with men, and in the countryside get and keep in equal share of land and property and learn to look upon labour as glorious." (Davin 1976: 203).

16. After the law was proclaimed, a survey of marriages in the rural countryside listed the different types of marriage as following: free marriage, arranged marriages where the couple were allowed to meet each other before the marriage, and arranged marriages where the couple had no choice. Of these three forms, free marriage, where the couple married by their own choice, was both the least common and the ideal that the Party encouraged (Davin 1976: 96).

17. The Great Leap Forward was a campaign launched in 1958 at the behest of Mao. It was the first large-scale attempt by the Party to collectivise rural landholdings under the famous Commune experiment. For details on the compaign and its effects, see MacFarquhar (1983).

18. The Cultural Revolution was launched in 1966. Its main aim was to attack what Mao termed the revisionist and rightist tendencies within the Party. He specifically called upon students to attack the leadership. Called the Red Guards (*Hongweibing*), students from all over China participated in mass campaigns against the top leadership. For details on the movement as a whole, see Robinson (1971).

19. Post-Mao China has witnessed major changes in the organisation of social and economic life in China. For details on the policy changes initiated in this period, see Feuchtwang et al. (eds.) (1988).

References

Andors, P. "Woman and work in Shenzhen", *Bulletin of Concerned Asian Scholars* 20 (3, 1988, pp. 22-42.

— "The Incomplete Liberation of Chinese Women", *China Now* 113 (Summer), 1985, pp. 8-12.

— *The Unfinished Liberation of Chinese Women 1949-1981.* Bloomington: Indiana University Press, 1981

— "Socialist Revolution and Women's Emancipation: China during the Great Leap Forward", *Bulletin of Concerned Asian Scholars* 8(l),1975, pp. 33-43.

Anhui Provincial Women's Federation, Office of Investigation and Study "How Women Can Become Achievers", *United Newsletter of Social Science* 12, 1985, pp. 32-91.

Behean, C.L. "Feminism and Nationalism in the Chinese Women's Press, 1992-1911", *Modern China* I (4), 1975, pp. 379-416.

Beijing Review "Is Women's Lib out of Date?", *Beijing Review* 50 (15 December), 1986, 7.

Brugger, B. *China: Radicalism to Revisionism 1962-1979.* London: Croom Helm.1981.

Chan, A. "Rural Chinese Women and the Socialist Revolution: An Enquiry in the Economics of Sexism", *Journal of Contemporary Asia* 4 (2), 1974, pp. 197-209.

Cheneaux, J. (1968) *The Chinese Labor Movement, 1919-1927.* Stanford, CA: Stanford University Press.

Chow Tse-tsung (1960) *The May Fourth Movement: Intellectual Revolution in Modern China.* Cambridge, MA: Harvard University Press.

— *Chinese Women Since Mao,* London: Zed, 1983.

— "Women in Rural Production and Reproduction in the Soviet Union, China, Cuba and Tanzania", *Signs* 7(2), 1981, pp. 361-99.

— *Feminism and Socialism in China.* London: Routledge and Kegan Paul, 1978.

— "The Movement to Criticize Confucius and Lin Piao: A Comment on the Women of China", *Signs* 2(3), 1977, pp. 721-26.

Dai Qing and Luo Ge. "Nuchong Hunfan", *Zhongshan* 2, 1988, pp. 33-49.

Dalsimer, M. and Nisnoff, L. "The Implications of the New Agricultural and One-Child Family Policies for Rural Chinese Women", *Feminist Studies* 13(3), 1987, pp. 583-607.

— "New Economic Readjustment Policies: Implications for Chinese Working Women", *Review of Radical Political Economics* 16, 1984, pp. 17-43.

— *Women, Work: Women and the Party in Revolutionary China.* Oxford: Clarendon, 1976.

Davin, D. "Women in the Chinese Countryside", in M. Wolf and R. Witke (eds), *Women in Chinese Society,* 1975, pp. 234-61.

Diamond, N. (1975a) "Collectivization, Kinship and the Status of Women in Rural China", *Bulletin of Concerned Asian Scholars* 7(1), 1975, pp. 25-32.

Diamond, N. "Women under the Kuomintang Rule — Variations on the Feminine Mystique", *Modern China* I (I), 1975, pp. 3-45.

Eide, E. *China's Ibsen: Ibsen to Ibsenism.* Monograph no. 55. Copenhagen: Scandinavian Institute of Asian Studies, 1987.

Eisentein, J.R. (ed.) *Capitalist Patriarchy and the Case for Socialist Feminism.* New York: Monthly Review Press, 1979.

Evans, H. "Chinese Women: The Public and Private Face", *China Now* 130,1989, pp. 36-38.

Feuchtwang, S., Hussain, A. and Pairasult, T. (eds.) *Transforming China's Economy in the Eighties: The Rural Sector, Welfare and Employment.* London: Zed, 1988.

Feuerwerker, Y. *Ding Ling's Fiction: Ideology and Narrative in Modern Chinese Literature.* Cambridge, MA: Harvard University Press, 1982.

Flax, J. "Postmodernism and Gender Relations in Feminist Theory", in L. Nicholson (ed.), *Feminism and Postmodernism.* London, New York: Routledge, 1990, pp. 39-62.

Freedman, M. (ed.) *Family and Kinship in Chinese Society.* Stanford, CA: Stanford University Press, 1970.

Handlin, J.F. "Lu Kun's New Audience: The Influence of Women's Literacy on Sixteenth Century Thought", in M Wolf and R. Witke (eds), *Women in Chinese Society,* 1975, pp. 13-38.

Honing, E. *Sisters and Strangers: Women in the Shanghai Cotton Mills, 1919-1949.* Stanford, CA: Stanford University Press, 1986.

Johnson, K.A. *Women, the Family and Peasant Revolution in China.* Chicago: University of Chicago Press, 1983.

Kang Keching. "Extract of Speech Given at the Fifth National Women's Congress", *Beijing Review* 38 (19 September), 1983, pp. 5-6.

Lan Chengdong. "How to Assess the Social Phenomenon of Increasing Divorce Rates"(*'Zeyang kandai lihun shuaishang sheng zhiyi shehui xianxiang'*) *Social Science (Shehui kexue)* 3 (March),1985, pp. 41-43.

Lang, O. *Chinese Family and Society.* New Haven, CT: Yale University Press, 1946.

Leith, K. "Chinese Women in the Early Communist movement", in M. Young (ed.), *Women in China,* 1973.

Levy, H.S. *Chinese Footbinding: The History of a Curious Erotic Custom.* New York: Walton Rawls, 1966.

Liu Mei Ching. *Forerunners of Chinese Feminism in Japan.* Ph D thesis. University of Leiden, 1988.

Luo Qiong. *Zhongguo Funu Yundongshi* (A History of the Chinese Women's Movement). Beijing: People's Publishing House, 1986.

Maloney, J. "Women in the Chinese Communist Revolution: The Question of Political Equality", in C. Beckin and C. Lovett (eds), *Women, War and Revolution.* New York: Holmes and Meiser, 1980.

Molyneux, M. "Women in Socialist Societies: Problems of Theory and Practice", in K. Young, C. Wolkowitz and R. McCullagh (eds), *Of Marriage and the Market: Women's Subordination Internationally and its Lessons.* London: Routledge and kegan Paul, 1981, pp. 55-90.

O'Hara, A. *The Position of Women in early China: According to the Lieh Nuchuan 'The Biographies of Emininent Chinese Women'.* Washington CD: Catholic University America, 1945.

Pearson, V. "Behind the Steel and Glass the Oldest Profession Flourishes", *China Now* 130, 1989, pp. 18-19.

Pei Qing "Les femmes Chinoises participent activement aux affaires publiques", *Beijing Information* 10 (9 March),1992, pp. 20-22.

Price, J. "Women and Leadership in the Chinese Communist Movement, 1921-1945", *Bulletin of Concerned Asian Scholars* 7(1), 1975, pp. 43-48.

Rankin, M. "The Emergence of Women at the End of the Ch'ing. The Case of Ch'iu Chin", in M. Wolf and R. Witke (eds), *Women in Chinese Society,* 1975, pp. 39-66.

Robinson, J.C. "Of Women and Washing Machines: Employment, Housework and the Reproduction of Motherhood in Socialist China", *China Quarterly* 101, 1985, pp. 32-58.

Saith, A. (ed.) *The Reemergence of the Chinese Peasantry.* London: Croom Helm, 1987.

Sheridan, M. "Young Women Leaders in China", *Signs* l2(1), 1976, pp. 59-58.

Sidel, R. *Families of Fengsheng: Urban Life in China,* Harmondsworth: Penguin, 1974.

Snow, H. *Women in Modern China.* The Hague: Mouton, 1967.

Stacey, J. *Patriarchy and Socialist Revolution in China.* Berkeley: University of California Press, 1983.

Stranahan, P. *Yan'an Women Under the Communist Party.* China Research Monograph no. 27. University of California, Centre for Chinese Studies, 1976.

Tan Li. "Reforms Improve Status of Women", *China Daily,* 25 October, 1984.

Tan Manni. "So that Women can Work without Worry", *China Reconstructs* 3 (March), 1983, pp. 8-11.

Tianchi Martin-Liao. "Traditional Handbooks of Women's Education", in A. Gerstlacher et al. (eds), *Woman and Literature in China,* 1985, pp. 165-89.

Tianjin Women's Federation, "The Quality of Chinese Women Must Be Improved and Socialization of Household Labor Speeded Up", *Labor and Personnel* 5, 1985, pp. 18-22.

Topley, M. "Marriage Resistance in Rural Kwantung", in A. Wolf (ed.), *Studies in Chinese Society,* 1978, pp. 247-69.

Weinbaum, B. "Women in transition to Socialism: Perspectives on the Chinese Case", *Review of Radical Political Economics* 8(l), 1976, pp. 34-59.

Whyte, M.K. "Sexual Inequality under Socialism: The Chinese case in Perspective", in J.L. Watson (ed.), *Class and Social Stratification in post-Revolution China.* Cambridge: Cambridge University Press, 1984, pp. 198-238.

Widmer, E. "The Epistolatory World of Female Talent in Seventeenth-century China", *Late Imperial China* 10(2), 12989, pp. 1-41.

Williard, F. "The Mark of Gender", *Feminist Issues* 5(2),1985, pp. 3-12.

Wolf, A. (ed.) *Studies in Chinese Society.* Stanford, CA: Stanford University Press, 1978.

Wolf, M. *Revolution Postponed: Women in Contemporary China.* London: Methuen, 1985.

Xiao Zhou "Virginity and Premarital Sex in Contemporary China", *Feminist Studies* 15(2), 1989, pp. 279-91.

Young, M. (ed.) *Women in China: Studies in Social Change and Feminism,* Ann Arbor: University of Michigan Press, 1973.

Yuan Liangsan and Jin Nan "Women's Work, Society's Responsibility", *Beijing Review* 49 (December), 1986, pp. 18-20.

BIDYUT MOHANTY

31

WOMEN AND FAMILY IN INDIA AND CHINA

Patriachies in both the countries have been subjected to strong cross-cultural currents for centuries together. However, Confucianism in China and Brahminism manifested in the *Manusmriti* in India treat women with discrimination which are dominant idiologies. Of course, Buddhism preaching equality between sexes did prevail in both the countries but have only a tangential impact on the patriarchy.

In the present century both the countries have undergone catalytic events namely the Freedom Struggle in India and a Political Revolution in China which tried to include women in the mainstream of those events. With the introduction of Structural Adjustment Programmes in both the countries some of the feudal values have reemerged, though it is our contention that the situation will not slide back to the original dark age due to the presence of the women's movement and awareness among men and women. In the subsequent sections we will discuss the social and economic status of both the countries to show that the Chinese women are a shade better than their counterparts in India.

Social Status of Women

India: The family and society at large consider women as second class citizens. The rituals relating to birth and marriage reflect a son-preference.[1] A related phenomenon of son-preference in the modern context is the amniocentesis test to abort the female feotus. This unfortunately is more prevalent in urban India. The sex selective test has increased the male-female ratio between 1981 and 1991 in a significant manner (Murthi, Guio & Dreze, 1997). The prevalence of dowry has increased a great deal and has spread to the low caste groups which earlier practised bride price. So much so that the ideal Kerala practice of husbands staying in wives houses has changed to demanding dowry. This phenomenon of taking dowry has increased considerably after the young men started going to Gulf countries and needed a lot of money to buy tickets and other things. Another important point with regard to marriage practices is that the majority of the marriages are arranged by parents. Love marriages are not encouraged even in urban areas though acute violence against women in recent years compel the parents not to consider arranged marriages particularly in the metropolitan cities like Delhi and Bombay etc. The assumption that the urban population are more modern in outlook and hence the traditional bias would get reduced there is proved wrong.

Other indicators of slow changing social mores are the characteristics of matrimonial columns of the leading English dailies, and advertisements in other media. For example the majority of the matrimonial ads show the preference of brides from the same castes and should absolutely be of fair complexion. The same bias for fair complexion also gets reflected in the range of cosmetic and more specifically a brand of face cream called "fair and lovely". It seems that the sale of this brand of cream gets sky rocketed just before the onset of the marriage season. If this is so in the urban areas it would be even truer in the rural areas.

In spite of Sharda Act which was passed in the 1950s to raise the age at marriage, child marriage particularly in North India is quite prevalent though the average age at marriage for females has increased to 18. Child marriage gives a very long span of reproductive age telling upon the health of the women as we will see a little later. This also gets reflected in terms of intra-family distribution of food, access to basic education and health care.

In the 1970s there was a discourse on whether women get adequate nutrition according to their needs or are they discriminated against. Some felt that women do sedentary work and hence require less calories. However, if we examine the work schedules of both men and women it is noticed that women are working for longer hours than men. But according to social norms they get less food.

In so far as access to health care also generally women do not get the best treatment when they fall ill. In addition the consciousness of being ill is more manifest among men than among women who always voluntarily suppress their ailment. (Kynch and Sen, 1983).

The size of average household has marginally declined from 5.55 to 5.51 in the last decade with a sharp decline in urban India during the same period indicating a high fertility and son-preference in the rural area particularly in North India. The total fertility rate for India as a whole is 3.7 in 1991.

The large size family shows that parents live with married sons since facilities are few for old age homes and taboos are attached if the parents stay separately or with married daughters. While it is important to look after old people, it is also true that in-laws interfere in every sphere of life of the daughters-in-law. As a result the norms of having large families, son-preference, discriminating attitude towards daughters get perpetuated.

On the front of literacy the picture is equally bleak. As per 1991 census only 39 per cent of the women population are literate. In other words more than 60 per cent women are still illiterate reflecting the low priority given to female literacy. The per centage of illiteracy is much higher (64 per cent) in the older age groups.

Another important pointer towards the discrimination against female child is the increasing sex ratio (males per 1000 females) over these years, in the age group of 0-6 years even though the child mortality rates for males and females in the age group of 0-4 years have narrowed down in the eighties. The explanation as alluded to earlier, lies in the fact that selective abortion is taking place in the urban areas of almost all the states. (Raju and Premi 1994).

In other age groups also women do not fare well compared to Chinese women. For example the maternal mortality rate is quite high in 1990 amounting to 570 per 100,000 births (Human Development Report, 1997), one of the contributory factors being only twenty per cent of the births are attended by the health personnel even as late as 1990.[2]

Generally women live longer than men after the reproductive age is over. Coupled with that the total fertility has declined. Hence the life expectancy at birth for females shows a shade higher than that of males, being 61.4 and 61.1 years respectively in 1994 (Human Development Report, 1997). However, the full potential of biological advantage accrue to women especially after the reproductive age has been denied to Indian women partly because a majority of women deliver their babies at home in North India and do not get best medical treatment when they are ill. (Dreze and Sen, 1995). Thus we find that the social status of women in India, though with regional variations, is low as indicated by the indices like high sex ratio, high maternal mortality, low literacy rate etc.

China: Socially Chinese women have come a long way from the picture depicted in the famous novel *Good Earth* by Pearl S. Buck. They no longer have to bind their feet to be able to walk like swans. One, of course, notices some women born before 1949 having tiny feet.

A spectacular achievement of the women of China has been in the field of education. For example in contrast to India's performance as we have mentioned before 68 per cent of China's adult females are literate.[3]

The life expectancy at birth for females is 71.1, according to Human Development Report 1997 and is higher by 4 years than that of males.[4] This is at par with some of the developed countries. Low maternal mortality rate namely, 90 per 100,000 live births and also low per centage of home delivery of babies (20 per cent in 1990) contribute to the longevity of women at a later age. (Human Development Report, 1997). It may be mentioned here that even though the health care needs of the mothers of the future workers have been taken care of, the work hazards of the women workers have not been attended to.

With regard to adult female literacy rate China has done exceedingly well since 71 per cent of its female population are literate by 1994. No wonder the infant mortality rate has been reduced to 31 per 100,000 live births in 1992, (Dreze and Sen, 1995) indicating a link between literacy and health care of the children. It is also important to mention here that the total fertility rate (1.7) has declined to the replacement level and has been fluctuating around that since 1990 which is comparable with the economically developed countries [5] (Lin Fude, Liu Jintang, 1997). This was made possible by many factors such as reduction in the span of reproductive cycle due to late marriage, low infant mortality rate, nuclear family, high female literacy and involvement in economic activities.

We have already noticed that the infant mortality is low and hence the desire to have more children will be less, provided son-preference syndrome does not influence the desire. Similarly, the link between female literacy and small family norm is also well established. At this point the famous Marriage Act, 1950 should also be discussed in brief to establish its link with low fertility rate. The Act provided women with a number of opportunities including treating them at par with men in the family, valuing their household work socially, encouraging them to be workers rather than being reproductive agents only.

In other words the Law tried to destroy the centuries old notions of family where patriarchy ruled supreme. It did yield significant results namely the age at marriage for females increased from 18.52 in 1950 to 25.5 in 1992 in rural area. In urban area the levels are even higher. Couples arranged marriages are less both in China than in India (Sha Jicai, Xiong Yu, 1997) and theoretically the decision of child bearing also rests with the wife.

Since the social pressure in the form of parent's desire for large family or the demand of dowry is apparently absent, Chinese family can opt for small family norm without feeling guilty about it.

The Marriage Law 1950 which entrusted so much power to women including taking initiative for divorce in a tradition-bound society, inevitably had serious consequences also. This increased the Divorce rate at a rapid rate at the initial stage though it has been declining now. A more traumatic consequence of this Law was that a large number of women committed suicide due to unbearable social pressure. Yet another negative impact of this Marriage Law is that it could not restructure the familial relationship between husbands and wives. The families still wanted to have male children. The one-child policy of the government made this situation more complex. The rural areas witnessed large scale female infanticide in order to have one male child. As a result the sex ratio (males per 100 females) at birth is higher than that of the developed countries. In 1982, for example it was 108.47. (Li Chengrui, 1992). According to Li, the phenomenon of high sex ratio can be explained in the following manner. First of all the racial influence leads to more male children to be born than female children. But the more important fact is the social practice of drowning female infants particularly in rural areas (*ibid*). This reflects the patriachal mentality, since sons are preferred particularly in the rural areas to carry out family names and worship the ancestators etc. Monica Das Gupta and co-authors (1997) also noticed that the juvenile sex ratios are high and have been increasing reapidly since 1960 in China fuelled by fertility decline and availability of sex-selective technology. They also noticed that the influence of son-preference decreased along with urbanisation. But they do not recommend urbanisation a panacea for this evil. On the other hand they feel that attitudinal change towards female child will play much more important role in reversing the trend. (*ibid*)

The discriminating attitude gets reflected in not sending girl child to school in some areas. It is also interesting to note that the political dramas written after 1949 Revolution showed the heroic deeds of women but they were never given the supreme command in any scenario (Julia Kristeva, 1977).

On the whole however, the situation of Chinese women is much better than that of India in so far as family and society are concerned though it requires many more years for the Confucian traditional patriarchy to be replaced by a new culture in favour of women.

Economic Status

India: Low social status of women gets reflected in low economic status also. We have noticed before that about 61 per cent of the Indian women are illiterates as per 1991 census. Accordingly, most of the women work in unorganised sector either in agriculture or in household industries. This in turn does not get captured in "statistical purdah" created by existing concepts and the methods of measuring labour participation that creates invisibility of women's contribution to National Income of the country (Gopalan, 1995). For example, the census defines work as gainful economic activities but activities done for domestic consumption are not considered as work. So we find that as late as 1991 only 22 per cent of total female population are considered to be workers in contrast to 52 per cent of the male population though the rural areas show slightly higher female work participation rate namely, 27 per cent, than that of the total rate. As expected the urban area has failed to provide much avenues for female workers as is evident from the statistics. (Premi and Raju, 1994).

In this context it is interesting to note that the recorded female participation rates varied across the states inversely with the influence of dominant patriarchal values except perhaps in Kerala. For example Uttar Pradesh, Bihar, Punjab and Haryana recorded female participation rates much below than the national average namely 22 per cent. But the states like Mizoram, Meghalaya, Manipur recorded much higher rate i.e., above 35 per cent which are not influenced by the patriarchal values of the North. Also Maharashtra which has undergone several social movements and is witnessing a different pattern of development compared to Punjab and Haryana has 33 per cent female work participation rate in 1991.[6]

Sectoral division of work participation rate is also available from various sources. For instance, in 1981 about 94 per cent of female work force and 89 per cent of male work force was working in the unorganised sector. In 1991 on the other hand the share of male work force has increased by 1 per cent whereas that of female work force has increased by two per cent. (Gopalan, 1995)

The Census also gives nine-fold classification of main workers in different industrial categories which can be further aggregated into primary, secondary and tertiary activities. The most important feature of this classification is that about 81 per cent of the total female workers are engaged in primary sector consisting of agriculture, live stock and mining in 1991. This per centage is very high in rural area namely 89.5 per cent which shows a marginal increase as compared to the 1981 situation. In contrast the per centage of male workers in the primary sector is 63.4 in 1991 and lower than that of females in rural areas by 8 per cent (Premi and Raju, 1994). It should also be noted that the per centage of male workers in the primary sector has declined between 1981 and 1991 and that of service sector has increased. But in case of female workers there has been a "feminisation" of primary sector. Several explanations have been offered to analyse this phenomenon. First of all, the Green Revolution has created some opportunities for women in agriculture. Secondly, the growing middle class has withdrawn male children from work and is sending them to schools leaving behind the girl child to slog in the field. Finally, whenever development generates more lucrative job opportunities, the men workers try to grab it first. With regard to the female industrial work force we notice another feature. The National Sample Survey Organisation has detailed industries into 384 divisions. It is interesting to find that women workers concentrate only in a few industries such as rearing of poultry, manufacturing of beedies (indigenous coarse cigarettes), matches and cotton spinning etc. all in the low skill and low paid categories. (Gopalan, 1995)

Since the female literacy rate is low (39 per cent in 1991), the per centage of women employees in Central and State governments is much lower than that of men (the per centage being 7.50 and 34.91 respectively in 1990). (Gopalan, 1995)

The gap between male and female wage rates show that for the same type of work women workers get lower rates *vis-a-vis* men workers. For example a male construction worker gets Rs. 31.58 per day but a female worker gets Rs.18.27 in a rural setting. The gap however, narrows down slightly in the urban area but it is still too glaring. (Gopalan, 1995). However, it is to be mentioned that different state governments have passed laws to give equal wage rates for men and women for doing similar kind of work. With regard to the impact of Structural Adjustment Programmes on Women's Work which was introduced in 1990, no systematic study has been done. But most of the women work in the unorganised sector. It is likely that in some cases their demand for certain specific activities such as electronic goods may increase. But in other cases they will be eased out first, if recession sets in the economy. More lucrative jobs will be taken up by men and market may perpetuate unequal status for women.

Thus we notice that the low status of women in the society gets reflected in low status of employment opportunities which gets reinforced by lack of land rights to women in India. In the next section we will see how have the Chinese women fared in so far as the economic empowerment is concerned.

China: Unlike Indian leaders who did not recognise the value of domestic work done by the women on the eve of the Independence in 1947, the Chinese leaders realised this value and championed the visibility of domestic work after 1949. This realisation led to the formulation of certain economic policies which enabled women to take part in the job market. Again since it was realised that women are the carriers of tradition and feudal values, the government not only formulated the policy but also implemented it with all sincerity.

As a result the share of female employment to total employment increased from 7 per cent in 1949 to 44 per cent in 1994 which is higher than the world average of 34.5 per cent (China's White Paper on Women, 1994). In other words 72.33 per cent of the total female population over the age group of 15 are employed in 1992.

So much so that the Human Development Report 1997 remarked in the context of feminisation of poverty that "China has made enormous progress in gender equality" *vis-a-vis* other developing countries. With these general remarks let us discuss the sectoral distribution of female employment as revealed by the statistics.

According to the While Paper on Women (1994), women are employed predominantly in "industry, agriculture, building, transport and communications, commerce, public health, education, party and government organs and social organisations". Even though it is quite vague in classifications the enumeration of these sectors indicate that women have access to almost all the fields. However, in so far as the nature of the job is concerned we find that women workers constitute only 34.4 per cent of the total persons employed in scientific and research job. Similarly the financial and insurance establishments employ 21.6 per cent female workers and the government establishments have 37 per cent of total jobs for women. (White Paper on Women 1994). We also have data on the per centage of female workers in soft sectors such as public health, sports and social welfare namely 50 per cent and in commercial consulting and other public service establishment it is 45 per cent (quoted in Agarwal, 1997).

The population census of 1990 also gives occupational breakups in terms of the above category. It is important to notice that the farm sector still employs the largest per centage of female workers namely 76 per cent which is higher than that of male workers by 7 per cent. Next in the order is the industry which employees 13 per cent women workers and 14 per cent of men workers. Industry as an occupational category however, is not defined clearly. Perhaps the township enterprises have been identified as industries which have been set up in the rural areas and out of a total of 100 million workers women workers constitute 40 per cent. According to some sources, the per centage of women workers to total workers is much higher in certain industries namely food, clothing, knitwear, toy and electronic industries as well as the traditional handicraft sector (Agarwal, 1997).

In the cities also the women participation rate increased more than that of men in certain sectors namely, public health, sports, catering etc. between 1982 and 1990 (Agarwal, 1997). The data regarding the sectoral composition of work force was also given in the 1982 Census. A comparative analysis of two sets of figures shows that nothing much has changed in the span of eight years. The census authorities commented that the proportion of women working as heads in various government organisations in 1990 increased by one per cent point. However, men work force in this sector constituted 90 per cent of the total. (Women and Men in China 1990). With regard to the wage rate men and women workers are supposed to get the same wage rate for identical kind of work. But the White Paper of 1994 notes that "due to current differences in cultural and professional composition, some real income gaps still exist between men and women". According to a survey conducted in 1990 it was revealed that women receive only 77.4 per cent of monthly income of men. In rural areas it is slightly higher i.e., 81 per cent of what their male counterparts get.

It is time now to focus on the impact of Structural Adjustment on Women. As a result of increasing private investment more women than men have become unemployed. In some places the private companies refuse to employ women on the ground that they have to be given maternity leave. The women are also encouraged to retire at the age of forty five (Rai, 1994). It is also interesting to note the comments of China Association for Labour Studies (1995) on the new trend of women's employment in the wake of Structural Adjustment Programme. The Association observes: "Guidance has been provided to enable women, in light of the industrial restructuring to shift to the tertiary sectors both *suitable for women in terms of their physical characteristics and favourable to bring their advantages into play.*" (italics are mine) It is worth commenting that the so-called anti-patriarchal state has brought the element of femininity to characterise their economic activities.

Similarly with respect to poverty also the Human Development Report 1997 observed that women in China constitute the bulk of the poor. More than 80 per cent of dropout children in 1990 were girls and the number of illiterate women was twice as much as illiterate men. In addition women in China are deprived of land rights also. Thus it is noticed that on the labour market front women's role is more visible and acknowledged also compared to that of India. But the patriarchal notion of femininity being suitable to only specific activities is becoming more evident in the wake of the market intervention.

Conclusion:

Both China and India situated on both sides of the Himalayas have experienced centuries old civilisations with underlying partriarchal ideas. The present century witnessed two catalytic events in India and China which tried to involve women in the mainstream. In India however, the post-independent government did not make sustained effort to visibly enhance women's contribution. As a result, after the freedom movement was over women were still treated as second class citizens. Even after the anti-dowry laws were passed the incidence of dowry death has still been on the increase. Son-preference has still dominated the Indian psyche. Women are still discriminated against with regard to access to food and health care. The sex ratio over the years has increased and reached the highest point of 107 in 1991. Similarly the low status of women and girl child got reflected through low literacy rate.

In India, the reality of the low social status of women, evidently prevents their work from getting its due value. The total work participation rate of females in 1991 is only 22.27. In rural areas it is slightly higher namely 26.79 than the total rate. Sectoral distribution indicated that 95 per cent of the female workers are concentrated in agriculture although the service sector also absorbed more women than the manufacturing sector which is the least women-friendly. As expected the wage rates for equal amount of work are not the same for males and females. But one positive thing has occurred in India namely women's movement which started in 1975. It not only has changed the academic curriculum at the university level, but also has influenced the policy perspective of the government leading to 33 per cent seat reservations in the local level political institutions along with other things. This in turn has brought about one million women to public life for the first time.

In contrast to the Indian situation, the political revolution of 1949 in China created situations in which the social and economic roles of women were much sought after. The leadership's resort to breaking the feudal values created a frontal attack on the bastion of such values namely, the family. As a result, grudgingly though, the patriarchal regime conceded some ground. The Marriage Law of 1950 was passed which raised the age of marriage and put emphasis on the mother's and child's health. The maternal mortality declined. Literacy increased. Women's participation in economic activities increased considerably.

Like the nine lives of the cat, the patriarchal regime bounced back after the reforms had started. Women could not get out of the agricultural sector and made only a modest gain in the service sector. Because of the one child policy female infanticide particularly in the rural areas have started reappearing. Women workers are most vulnerable to retrenchment. They do not enjoy equal pay for equal work. Their retirement age is lower than that of men though their life expectancy is higher than men by four to five years.

Unlike India, the interventions through women's movement started very late i.e., after 1990 though the oldest women's organisation (All China Women's Federation) came into being in 1949. After 1990, the women study centres have been set up in different universities and have taken up the gender issues more actively. Thus we find the status of Chinese women better than that of Indian women though both the sister countries have to take long journey before they reach the goal of equality and justice.

Table 1: Some Basic Statistics Showing Female Capabilities in India and China 1990 and 1991

	India (1991)	*China (1990)*
1. Sex Ratio females per thousand males	93	94
2. Adult literary rate	36.1	68
3. Life expectancy at birth (years)	59	71
4. Total Fertility rate	3.7	2.0
5. Births attended by trained health personnel (rates)	34	84
6. Pregnant women aged 15-49 with anaemias (1975-91)	88	n.a.
7. Maternal Mortality per 100,000 live births	570	95

Sources: 1. Richard Jolly (1997) *Human Development Report* (Oxford University Press, New Delhi).

2. J. Dreze and A. Sen (1995) *India: Economic Development and Social Opportunity.* (Oxford University Press Delhi).

Table 2: Women and Political and Economic Participation India and China in 1990 and 1991

	India	China
*1. Gender Empowerment measure rank (GEM)	86.0	28.0
2. Approximate Earned income share (per cent)	25.7	38.1
3. Labour force as per centage of total population (15 and above age group)	31.0	45.0
4. Farming, forestry, animal husbandry etc.	81.0	76.0
5. Industry	8.0	13.0
6. Tertiary	10.8	11.0

*Gender empowerment measure rank is calculated taking women parliamentarians, administrators and managers, professional and technical workers and earned income share. So lower the value higher the rank. However if we include the women in politics at the grassroots level with 33.3 per cent reservation, the rank of India's GEM will increase.

Source: 1. *Human Development Report, 1997*

2. M.K. Phemi and S. Raju (1994) *Gender in work force participation in the 1991 in India.* Submitted to UNIFEM (Unpublished).

3. Department of Social Science and Technology Statistics State Statistical Bureau (1995) *Women and Men in China: Facts and Figures* (Statistical Bureau, PRC Beijing).

Notes

1. The birth rituals relating to male child are different from that of female child. Similarly in traditional marriages, girls have to sacrifice symbolically their maiden identity. There are of course regional variations namely the southern regions wanted to eliminate the supremacy of Brahminism. However, in so far as the practice of dowry is concerned even these states have allowed the practice very conveniently. Again women in South India in general, and those of Kerala in particular, have some links with land and their social status is relatively good vis-a-vis their North Indian sisters.
2. In the state of Kerala on the other hand 92 per cent of the deliveries take place in the medical institutions in 1991 (Dreze and Sen, 1995).
3. It is interesting to note that one of the Indian states namely Kerala has achieved a spectacular result in terms of female literacy. About 86 per cent of the females (7 and above) are literate according to 1991 census.
4. In the respect of life expectancy also Kerala is well ahead of China i.e., 74.4 in 1990.
5. Dreze and Sen (1995) on the other hand, have reported that the total fertility rate is 2 and Kerala has still lower rate compared to China (1.8).
6. Kerala which has done superbly well on the literacy front has recorded very low work particpation rate of females in 1991. This can partly be explained by the presence of Gulf money sent by the male migrants. Other factors could be deliberate concealment of the work status for getting unemployment dole, and demographic transition etc. (Premi and Raju, 1994).

References

China Association for Labour Studies (1995). *Woman and Employment in China.* (Beijing).

Chinese Government's *White Paper on Women* (1994). Reproduced in *China Report* (1994) 30: 4.

Das Gupta, Monica, Jiang Zhenghua Xie Zhenming Li Bohua (1997) 'The status of Girls in China.' in *23rd IUSSP General Population Conference; Symposium on Demography of China,* China Population Association Beijing, 1997.

Dreze, Jean and Sen, Amartya (1995). *India Economic and Social Development* (Oxford, University Press Delhi). Government of India (1995) *Country Report* prepared on the eve of Fourth World Congress of women, Beijing (Department of Woman and Child Development, New Delhi).

Gopalan, Sarala. *Women and Employment in India,* Har-Anand Publications, Delhi 1995.

Gulati, L and Rajan, I. 'Gender issue in work force participation on Kerala' unpublished state report for IASP - UNIFEM Project on *Gender Issues in 1991 Census,* Thiruvananthapuram : CDs. 1993.

Jolly, Richard, *Human Development Report,* Oxford University Press, New York 1997.

Kynch, Jocelyn, and Sen Amrtya. 'Indian Women: Well-being and Survival', *Cambridge Journal of Economics,* Vol. 7, 1983.

Li, Chengrui, *A study of China's population,* Foreign Languages Press, Beijing, 1992.

Lin Fude and Liu Jintang 'China's Fertility Transition and the Prospect of Population Situation' 1997 in 23rd IUSSP General Population Conference, Symposium on Demography of China, China Populatlion Association, Beijing, 1997.

Mohanty, Bidyut 'Women and Panchayati Raj and Seventy Third Amendment Act', *Economic and Political Weekly,* Vol. 52, 1995.

Murthy, Mamta Guio, Anne Catherine and Dreze, Jean 'Mortality Fertility and Gender Bias in India: A district level analysis" in Sen, A and Dreze J (ed.) *Indian Development Selected Regional Perspective,* Oxford University Press, Delhi,1997.

Premi, M.K. and Raju, Saraswati (1994) *Gender issues in work force participation in the 1991 Census in India.* A report submitted to UNIFEM (Unpublished).

Raju, S and Premi, M.K. 'Decline in Sex Ratio: Alternative Explanation Reexamined', *Economic and Political Weekly,* April 25, 1992.

Rai, S. 'Gender Issues in China: A Survery', *China Report,* Vol. 30, No. 4, 1994.

Ritu Agarwal, *Gender Justice and Economic Reforms in India and China: A Study of the Country Papers Presented at the Fourth World Congress on Women in Beijing,* M. phil. Thesis submitted to Delhi University (unpublished), 1997.

Sha, Jicai and Xiong Yu. 'An Analysis on Family status of Contemporary Chinese Women', in *Symposum, 1997.*

State Statistical Bureau, *Women and Men in China facts and figures* China Statistical publishing House, Beijing, 1995.

SREEMATI CHAKRABARTI

32

WOMEN AND ADULT LITERACY IN CHINA

Developing countries have, in the last few decades, attached a lot of significance to the role of education in the development process. Education, both formal and non-formal, must play a crucial role in development programmes if they are to be meaningful. The International Council for Adult Education held a conference in Dar-es-Salaam in 1976 where issues and problem areas pertaining to adult education were identified.[1] Women were seen as a definite target group for the simple reason that all over the world literacy rates amongst women are lower than among men. If women are indispensable to the development process, literacy among women must increase. Therefore, governments and planners in several developing countries have made efforts to enhance literacy rates and educational levels among women both as a welfare measure and a developmental necessity. However, spreading literacy among adult women has been a complex, difficult and time-consuming task in all these countries. In tradition-bound societies like India, China and Bangladesh, the task has not been an easy one. This article looks at literacy and education among women in pre- and post-liberation China. I have considered the women-specific problems that promoters of adult education in China have faced after the country's liberation in 1949. I have also highlighted the endeavours of the state to overcome these problems. In the end I have attempted to compare the Mao period (roughly 1949-76) with the post-Mao (reform) era (1977-78 onwards) in terms of the state's commitment to remove illiteracy among women.

This article is based mainly on the following sources: (i) primary material available in Chinese collected during my visit to China between October 1992 and March 1993; (ii) secondary material in the English language; and (iii) information gathered through interviews which I conducted in China between December 1992 and February 1993. The interviewees included literacy workers, activists in the area of women's development, academics and officials.[2]

Women's Education in China

Although from an advanced civilisation which attached great importance to education, women in traditional China were deprived of its benefits as it was primarily a male domain. While embroidery, stitching and various other household skills were given importance for women, skills in sports, martial arts and dance eluded them due to the cruel custom of foot-binding.[3] These skills were, however, confined to the rich, i.e., the gentry. Since education was also family- and clan-oriented, occasionally women acquired reading and writing skills. We do hear of a few exceptionally good women poets and artists. Peasant women, whose knowledge of agriculture was profound, remained completely illiterate and deprived of any formal or non-formal schooling. The notion that "a talentless woman is virtuous" (*nuzi wucai bianshi de*) became almost an established tradition in China.

With the impact of Western influences from the second half of the 19th century, the concept of education for women began to change gradually. The introduction and encouragement of missionary schools for both the sexes, and more particularly for those who converted to Christianity, saw girls going to school on a formal basis. Undoubtedly, the number of such girls was very small both in absolute terms and in comparison with boys. Nonetheless, it was a landmark in the development of women's education because for the first time girls were leaving the confines of the home and attending classes in schools on the same footing as boys (Lewis 1974).

Women's literacy and education received a boost with the May Fourth Movement.[4] This movement, among other things, was also the first women's liberation movement in China as its leaders called for the overall emancipation of women. Education was seen as the primary tool for emancipation. Many women's organisations were active during this period; as a concession to their demands, in March 1921 girl students were, for the first time, admitted to Beijing University. By 1922 co-education became common. The Chinese Communist Party, which was formed in 1921, set up its Women Department and entrusted it with the task of organising women workers. Since the low level of women's education was a hindrance to political indoctrination, the Chinese communists began to emphasise on female literacy. In the period 1931-34, when the communists set up bases in the province of Jiangxi and later at Yanan in north China, they continued to maintain their emphasis on literacy and education, particularly for women with a poor peasant background, who comprised nearly half their constituents. The education policy of the base-area government of Jiangxi was to enhance, by every means, the education level of the workers and peasants. For this purpose, every possible political and material support must be given to the masses. Reports say that following implementation of this policy in 1933 in 2,932 towns, there were 6,462 night schools and 2,388 literacy classes. As a result, some 250,000 workers and peasants — both men and women — benefited (Zhongda 1987). Women's associations as well as peasant associations under the Communist Party played an active role in the gigantic task of spreading literacy in the countryside.

Detailed statistics on rural women's literacy levels in the pre-1949 era are not available. A survey of rural areas carried out by John L. Buck in the 1930s found that only 2 per cent of the female population aged 7 years and above had ever attended school and that only 1 per cent could read a common Chinese letter, while among males 45 per cent attended school and 30 per cent were able to identify commonly used letters (Buck 1937: 373). Another more recent study points out that the rise in the literacy levels of females began in the early 1940s and accelerated through the decade. The study further notes that until 1982 there were two periods when progress peaked — the first time in 1951-57, during which period female literacy grew at the rate of about 3.5 per cent per year, and the second time more briefly during 1970-74 when literacy grew at about the same rate. Between these peaks lies a period which includes five yeras of negative growth (1960-64) caused by the famine, and a period of accelerating production (1965-69). The study reveals that the immediate post-Mao period (the first four years only, as this study is based on China's 1982 Census) saw a de-acceleration to a zero growth rate. The famine of 1959-62 is seen as a watershed for education; it also most adversely affected rural women's education (Lavely et al. 1990). However, the fact remains that in the post-1949 period there was a rapid rise in female literacy as is evident from the 1982 census. For instance, among women aged 55 to 59, 90 per cent were illiterate; among those aged 15 to 19 years only 15 per cent were in the illiterate category (*ibid.*). Tables 1 and 2 show the literacy levels of women in both rural and urban areas and compare the same with those of men. From these figures what is still not clear and not possible to discern is the contribution of adult literacy programmes in quantitative terms. Nonetheless, the role of these programmes continues to be important as the drop-out rate among girls is still quite high. According to official Chinese sources, as cited in a research paper, nearly half the enrolled girls do not complete primary school (Rosen 1992: 257).

It was only with the liberation of China in 1949 that a massive literacy drive, encompassing almost all of China, could be launched. In the 1950s, in the first phase of adult education, "it developed in all walks of life, including cadres and staff members of central and local government institutions at various levels, workers and staff members of factories, mines and other industrial enterprises, members of rural cooperative teams, craftsmen of cities and towns and urban residents, etc. Most of them went to night schools and literacy classes." (Rosen 1992: 16). Reports say that a large number of women attended these classes but we have no figures to say what percentage of the total number of students were women. No doubt women greatly benefited from these classes. At liberation, female illiteracy rates were as high as over 90 per cent. Since then, as mentioned earlier, there has been a sharp increase in the number of women with access to education.

Table 1: Percentage of Illiteracy by Age and Sex: China 1982

Age Group	*Females*	*Males*
15-19	14.7	4.2
20-24	23.3	5.7
25-29	36.1	9.6
30-34	40.3	13.2
35-39	43.4	14.2
40-44	57.3	22.4
45-49	74.5	32.2

50-54	85.2	40.6
55-59	89.7	47.5
60+	95.4	60.9

Source: *Census of China 1982.* Chinese Academy of Social Sciences, Almanac 1986, pp. 314-15.

Table 2: Illiteracy in Urban and Rural Areas in China (1982 Census)

per 100 per cent		Urban			Rural	
Age Group	*Male-Female*	*Male*	*Female*	*Male-Female*	*Male*	*Female*
12 Plus	16.4	8.9	24.6	34.8	21.1	18.4

Sources: Raja Roy Singh, 1986. *Education in Asia and the Pacific: Retrospect and Prospect.* Bangkok : UNESCO, p. 92, cited in Huang Shiqi. 1992. 'Nonformal Education and Modernization', in Ruth Hayhoe (ed.), *Education and Modernization:* The *Chinese Experience.* Oxford: Pergamon, p. 147.

For example, in 1952, the proportion of girls among primary school pupils was only 28 per cent. By 1988 the figure had risen to 45.6 per cent. In the age group 7 to 11 years, 95 per cent of the girls were enrolled in school. The proportion of female to male teachers increased as well, rising from 17.1 per cent in 1952 to 41.5 per cent in 1988. More women were also participating in literacy and continuing education programmes (*Basic Education and National Development* 1991: 65-66). The employment rate for women also rose during this period. Table 3 shows the trends of female employment based on a sample survey conducted in 1987.

Table 3: Female Occupations

Form of Employment	*Per cent Female*
All Occupations	44.5
Professional and Technical	44.3
Government, Party, Mass Organisation, Enterprises, Institutions	12.3
Office Workers, Clerical	29.8
Commerce	45.8
Service workers	50.9
Labour, Farming, Forestry, Animal Husbandry, Fishery	47.4
Industrial workers, Transport and related jobs	35.8
Others	41.7

Source: *China Statistical Yearbook,* 1988. Based on 1 per cent Sample Survey, 1987.

Obstacles to Women's Progress

While it is true to say that women's literacy in China has made great strides, compared with its own past as well as with several other developing countries, the task is not complete and a lot still remains to be done. The problems therefore need to be looked into and analysed. Problems such as a large population, vast territory — much of which is rough and mountainous, — underdevelopment and poverty, are some of the general factors affecting the spread of literacy and are applicable to both men and women. Here, however, I shall focus on women-specific problems, and for this I have relied largely on my informants as many of them have first-hand knowledge of the situation, particularly in remote areas.

According to most of my informants, the primary cause of women's illiteracy is the continuation of traditional and outdated ideas. Women have been treated like slaves in China for centuries and their position still remains low in the minds of people in rural areas. The poorer the region, the lower is the status of women, remarked one literacy activist. In the minority areas the situation is bad because women are treated as unequal to men. Women themselves hold traditional notions about their position and many avoid attending classes intended for them. Areas where the message of communism has not penetrated are particularly problematic, according to my informants.

In some cases where women themselves have risen above the traditional bias, resistance comes from families, mainly husbands and mothers-in-law. The resistance is stronger in cases where the husband too is not literate. From the data available it appears that this is the second most important reason for continued illiteracy among women and therefore a block to the dissemination of literacy. According to informants, this resistance is also based on the outdated beliefs that a woman's place is inside the house, and that literacy and education are of no use to her.[5]

Household responsibilities are considered the third most significant reason which keeps women away from attending literacy classes and continuing with their studies. Not only older women but young girls too are expected to do household chores and are left with no time or energy to do anything else. That household work is the sole responsibility of women, is a long established practice, and I was told that although husbands share housework with wives in the urban areas, in rural China this is rare. Moreover, in rural and specially backward areas, modern household gadgets are not common, a fact that makes household chores tiresome and time-consuming. Also, large-sized families hinder women from finding time to attend classes. Small families are a more recent phenomenon.

Farm work, in addition to family responsibilities, is identified as another cause which keeps rural women away from literacy classes or forces them to relapse into illiteracy. In rural areas men have more free time for other activities than women. This is because, in many households menfolk still stick to the conventional arrangement that indoor chores are women's work even if they are full-time farm workers. Women themselves accept this, particularly in backward or relatively poor areas and make no effort to change it. Literacy workers and activists find it most difficult to make much progress in these areas.

Women cadres belonging to and working in remote parts of China (which are often inhabited by minority nationalities)[6] complain that in addition to distances, local customs and beliefs compound the difficulties to the spread of literacy. The sensitivity of the local populace, once hurt, is very hard to heal. Superstitions and false beliefs are the result of illiteracy and backwardness, and literacy is difficult to spread in the context of such backwardness — this vicious circle frustrates many an activist. Few enjoy working in backward areas over a length of time. An activist belonging to the Zhuang nationality and working with people of her own ethnic background, said that it was most difficult to convince people to have small families not withstading the fact that large families hinder education and literacy of the mother and the girl child. Paucity of funds is also a major problem. Precise statistics for expenditure on adult women's literacy are not available. However, the overall recurrent expenditure on education has been kept stable at 9 to 10 pre cent of state expenditure since 1983 (Henze 1992: 110-29). No one openly admitted that the state did not provide enough money to sustain literacy campaigns and programmes over a long period of time. Whenever I asked activists, officials or academics about what more, in their opinion, is needed for the successful implementation of the spread of literacy (I normally asked this question at the end, when interviewees were expected to say anything they wished to add), almost all of them said that more money is needed from the government — local or central. Although community resources have gone a long way in spreading literacy in China (some primary schools are completely run on local resources in the rural areas), it appears that there is need for more funding which, the concerned people feel, only the government is capable of providing.

Another problem which was not directly addressed but became quite evident was the shortage and low morale of personnel require to carry out literacy programmes. Finding a breed of dedicated, full-time literacy workers who would willingly face all hardships in exchange for limited gains is as difficult in China as anywhere else. In the early post-liberation phase, during the period of euphoria which the new system gave rise to, this was not so difficult. The All-China Democratic Women's Federation (now the All-China Women's Federation), the peasant associations, trade unions, Communist Youth League, etc., were able to provide full-time cadres, both professional and voluntary, for this gigantic task. With the passage of time this became more and more difficult. Fluctuations in the political scene made the implementation of many plans and programmes erratic. Depending on which way the wind was blowing, the activists found their contributions either rewarded or overlooked. During the period of reforms (i.e., since 1978), the difficulty has been even greater. The need to get rich fast and lead a comfortable life with all the modern amenities seems to have engulfed all of China. In this context it is worth noting that social workers in the form of literacy activists are dwindling in number. Young people looking for jobs have been shunning opportunities to work as literacy activists.

Massive Literary Campaigns

During the pre-reform period which can also be called the Mao era (i.e. up to 1978), massive propaganda campaigns were carried out to encourage literacy drives. The targets were both the prospective beneficiaries of the literacy programmes as well as potential literacy activists. The All-China Women's Federation adopted the task of publicising the relevant issues in its journal *Zhong Guo Funu* (Women of China) in the 1950s and the first half of the 1960s. This journal ceased publication during the Cultural Revolution (1966-76). Some issues of this journal carried several pieces on the state's efforts to promote literacy and education among women, mainly in the remote and poor areas. The articles or news reports also highlighted women's endeavour to acquire literacy and persevere in their efforts despite adverse circumstances in an often hostile environment.

One such case discussed in the journal is that of the suburb, Xiao Miao, in Tian Men county in Hubei province. Here, an evening school was started to spread literacy and technical education among the general population. Some 207 such schools had been started in the county. In a few cases the whole family, including husbands, wives, mothers-in-law, daughters-in-law, grandfathers and grandchildren, studied in the same class. The total number of female students was 2,314 (almost 50 per cent of the male students). Whatever theoretical knowledge the women gained in the evening would be put into practice the next morning and tried out in "the experimental field." Very often male heads of families objected to the idea of women working in experimental fields as it affected their income. Sometimes, cooperatives refused to sell fertilisers to women because they felt that they would not know how to use them effectively. Women, the report says, overcame the problems and managed things well. For example, they sold eggs to raise money for fertilisers, but never felt inclined to give up their literacy classes. In three years' time, Xiao Miao had many women technicians, and women's production per unit of land was higher than men's. Hard work and eagerness to learn brought success to these women, the piece concludes (*Zhong Guo Funu* 1958).

Propaganda campaigns aimed at literacy activists as well as prospective beneficiaries were carried out through radio (and later television) broadcasts, film shows, posters, banners, etc. Leaflets, flyers and booklets too were printed for free distribution. Peasant literacy textbooks printed in large numbers were widely distributed. These books varied from province to province and at times from county to county as local conditions had to be taken into account. In an article on anti-illiteracy campaigns in China, Wang Yanwei (n.d.: 6-7) of the Division of Peasant Education, Bureau of Worker-Peasant Education, Ministry of Education of China, stresses the importance of reading the "Peasant Literacy Textbook". He cites the example of Hu Ailiang, a woman member of Litan commune of Ming Qian county, Hunan province. She had a plot for growing cotton. The output per *mu* (1 *mu* is approximately one sixth of an acre) was only 10 kg because she did not have knowledge of scientific farming. She consulted with the agro-technical centre of the commune and asked why the yield was so low despite the rich soil, sufficient fertilisers and hard work. The technician handed her a book entitled "Scientific Management of Cotton Plots" but she returned it saying that she was unable to read, and remarked, "Although agro-technique is a treasure, an illiterate like me cannot possess it". Wang says that from then onwards she actively attended literacy classes. Several months later she was able to read the "Peasant Literacy Textbook". Eventually she could also read and understand writings on agro-technical know-how. A year later she applied her knowledge to the plot of land and it resulted in a bumper crop: eight times more than the previous yield. Wang Yanwei provides another example of a woman who joined literacy classes after a personal crisis. This happened in Tungwan commune, Wu Suan county in the Guangxi Zhuang Autonomous Region. A board on the edge of a grassland read, "Keep your cattle off this grassland because insecticide has been sprayed on it". The woman who could not read took her cow there, which died soon after eating the grass. This incident not only brought this particular woman to the literacy classes but also many others who were alarmed by this incident.

Mao Zedong Thought

During the pre-reform period (1949-1978), literacy was stressed for the dissemination of political propaganda as well. All those familiar with Chinese politics of the post-liberation Mao period are well aware of the significance of massive propaganda campaigns, on some issue or the other engulfing all of China fairly frequently. Implict in all these campaigns were Mao's political ideas, which the Communist Party and all its front organisations zealously spread. Although Mao's thoughts were propagated orally, campaigns were more effective through the print media; therefore the emphasis on literacy could not be underestimated. In fact, zealous propaganda of the Mao period helped the spread of literacy all over China. The urge to spread the thoughts of "the great helmsman, revolutionary and teacher", as his followers liked to call him, made many a Party cadre turn into a voluntary literacy activist. Similarly, this zeal created among many an illiterate peasant or worker the desire to become literate, to be able to read, and be enlightened on the subject of Mao's greatness. The Chinese government also invested a lot of money in bringing out printed materials. The little *Red Book*, which was more popular than the Bible had been in the Christian world, was printed in millions during the Cultural Revolution.[7] For the younger Chinese of that period it was fashionable to be in possession of the *Red Book* and to be able to pull it out at an instant's notice in any situation and read out the relevant (in the readers' opinion) passages aloud. The environment of the Cultural Revolution made literacy a political necessity. Despite the negative aspects of propaganda, one can say with a certain amount of assurance that it gave a boost to the spread of literacy. In post-reform China, as I saw and was told, the absence of such zeal has adversely affected the dissemination of literacy.

As far as women's literacy is concerned, Mao's thoughts and the publicity given to his *Red Book* did help. Study sessions were common since the Great Leap Forward (1958) and continued up to 1976. These sessions involved intensive reading and discussions of Mao's thoughts, and used to be held at all levels: commune, brigade, team, village and neighbourhood. It was more or less compulsory for all members, regardless of gender, to attend and "fruitfully participate" in such meetings, "struggle sessions" or re-education classes. The impact of politics on literacy classes was quite visible and direct. Contents of the texts or primers were loaded with praises for Mao and /or Mao's Thoughts. The intensity of these overtly politicised sessions varied from time to time. During the radical phases (the Great Leap Forward and the Cultural Revolution), it reached a peak.

After attaining a basic level of literacy, women read Mao's works and discussed them. It was said that during the Great Leap Forward the political awareness of the people had increased, although to bring about more awareness among (rural) women it would require a long time and was "a very difficult and complicated task and Marxism-Leninism and Mao's works will play a very important role to fulfil this task". According to an article titled "Vigorously Study Chairman Mao's Work" published in *Zhong Guo Funu* (1960), since the Great Leap Forward women have come out of the world of the household and arranged time to study as they "want to understand the problems". The article claims that since 1958, because of the Great Leap, "illiteracy has been wiped out", and the people's dream of studying further has become a reality. Despite their household responsibilities, women are taking an interest in education and the acquisition of skills. "The conditions are ripe for learning". This report obviously hides the truth, as by 1958 there was hardly any rural region which had achieved complete literacy. What is significant about this report is that, without saying so, it highlights the importance of political propaganda in the spread of literacy, particularly reading and writing skills. For example, the report mentions the achievements of the women of Feng Tian area during and after their study of Mao's works. It says:

> "The women's organization of Feng Tian has also played an important role. The women cadres took initiatives to study the Theory [of Mao's Revolution] and formed a vital team along with other women. They continuously mobilized more and more women to participate in the studies. They also imparted training to women to become (political) theory instructors. They also helped women to solve their problems so that they could come to study. All these efforts created enthusiasm for studies among women and strengthened the movement to study Mao's work." (*Zhong Guo Funu* 1960).

At another place it talks about women who have just acquired literacy and mentions that the "more the study, [the] more they love to study, [the] more they read, [the] more they do it wth enthusiasm", and keep themselves busy the whole day.

Literacy Workers

Political stability enables China's literacy movement to penetrate, sometimes with impressive results.1 Open meetings were held in every village when strategies to implement literacy programmes were discussed. Prospective participants in the programme along with teachers would discuss matters together to figure out the most effective method. Groups of literacy activists along with party cadres visited homes to sort out matters with each family. Discussions involved mothers-in-law and husbands as opposition to women attending classes came mainly from one of these categories. Literacy activists encouraged husbands to help in household chores so that wives could make it to classes. Mothers-in-law were also advised to support and help. My informants told me that convincing husbands in rural areas to help in domestic matters is most difficult. Household work continues to be looked down upon by men in rural China. "Things are improving", some said, "it is not as bad as it was in earlier times". They added that many among the younger generation were trying to overcome the "feudal ideas of male domination and superiority". In the village of Shi Ba Li Dian (about 18 km from Beijing), I was taken to a model peasant household. It was a weekday; the mother, who worked in rural enterprise was out working, the two girls were at school and the peasant father took care of the household all by himself during the day, throughout the off-season. This case was, however, almost an exception.[8]

The literacy workers, while counselling husbands and in-laws, stress the benefits of education. Families are told that women's literacy and education will add to their dignity and also make women more self-confident, which in turn would lead to the acquisition of skills useful to their families, society and socialism. What would the response have been if, in the course of persuasion, the economic aspect were excluded and stress were laid only on factors like dignity or determination? The informants said that they had never tried this tack but admitted that "beneficial consequences" must ordinarily include perceived economic advantages or else the target group would not give an encouraging response.

Some of the more concrete measures adopted in the literacy drive for women include "spare-time classes", night schools, and "door-step education", all of which have been tried at different places with different degrees of success. "Spare-times classes" provide flexible school hours to peasant women who work in the agricultural sector. Some of these "spare-time" classes would be open for 16 hours a day and students could walk in whenever they had free time and took lessons from teachers who would be available for them. I tried to get more information on what I thought was a novel way tc impart literacy — as I thought implementing this method would not be easy. I failed to learn much about it, which makes me think that its incidence is exceptional.

Door-step education is a system by which the student does not go to school but the school comes to her. Textbooks would be assigned to different households, and schedules would be planned in advance following discussions between members of the family, cadres and teachers. This scheme also allowed a great deal of flexibility and helped those women with small children and/or elderly relatives to look after. For other reasons as well, such as to avoid walking during advanced stages of pregnancy, to nurse a baby or to save time, many women prefer door-step classes. As pointed out to me, a positive fall-out of this system was that the teacher often became very close to the families and was "like another family member". The influence of teachers has often been so deep that the "targets" not only achieved literacy but improved themselves with more knowledge and skills. In other words, the desire to learn and a quest for knowledge emerged as personality traits.

Education Targeting Women

Winter schools, off-season schools and mobile schools were other innovations that facilitated the spread of literacy among women. In cold and mountainous areas, where agricultural work was intensive in the summer, women found it hard to attend classes during the peak season, and were therefore expected to enrol in these schools. As 40 per cent of China is mountainous, the number of such schools was not small. Mobile schools were particularly useful where people had to walk long distances over rough terrain or when classrooms were in short supply, or when the teacher did not live in the vicinity and came into the countryside from a nearby town or city.

Despite these measures, women's family responsibilities consistently remained a handicap; mothers of young children — of infants in particular — often kept away from classes. To resolve this problem, a variety of creches were introduced. The most effective and popular of these have been the cooperative creches. Here, women pupils share the responsibility of looking after each other's children. When one group attends classes, another looks after the children and vice versa. This saves the trouble and funding required to set up a nursery and pay day-care workers. This system of cooperative creches first began informally in a village in Hebei province and because it proved to be successful it was replicated in areas where women's literacy was taken up in earnest.

Other steps included classes exclusively for women although classes for both men and women together was the norm. My informants pointed out that in more "culturally backward" (i.e., conservative) areas, the idea of women attending classes with men was frowned upon. This seemed to be true of minority nationality areas and other remote regions as well. I wanted to know if Chinese Muslims had a problem on this account. The communists had always upheld the idea of co-education as opposed to the missionary system of separate convents for girls. Since the segregation of women in orthodox Islamic communities is commonplace, I wanted a clarification. The answer I got was "may be".[9]

In addition to these practical measures, the adult educators of China have evolved other methods too, which I thought were effective and worth emulating. For instance, husbands were encouraged to help wives in sustaining their literacy skills. Basic literacy would be imparted by the literacy worker/teacher and the husband had to carry on from there and make sure that the literacy levels reached by their wives did not decline. Similarly, children attending formal schools were encouraged to teach their mothers and grandmothers at home. Where husband and wife were both illiterate, they were both expected to acquire literacy together and later mutually help each other to maintain their levels of proficiency. To ensure that the husband-turned-teachers and child-turned-teachers were doing their job with interest and seriousness, a check on them was made periodically.

A system of rewards exists at all levels to extend recognition to individuals who turn out to be good students or teachers. During the pre-reform period, material incentives were not encouraged, so one frequently heard of "model literacy workers" and "model students". Anyone who selflessly and with a deep sense of devotion spread or acquired literacy was regarded to have shown a commitment towards socialism and Chairman Mao. Such a person was called a model and others would be urged to emulate him/her. The press, radio and television would give them and their achievements enjoy wide coverage. They would be asked to share their experiences with others and help those who were not so successful in improving their performance. After their accomplishments were widely publicised leaders and cadres would urge the rest of society to "learn" from them. This type of recognition was most heard of during the days of the Cultural Revolution.

Reform Period

In the reform period, ideological or non-material rewards of the earlier era were stopped. Literacy activists as well as beneficiaries have been offered cash prizes, medals (made of expensive metal), raises in salary, promotions, farm implements, draught animals and so forth, in addition to certificates and commendations. Wide publicity is given to such people. While talking about this, one of my informants told me about an unfortunate incident which smacked of the continued existence of feudal and backward ideas. A poor peasant woman (in a village in Gansu province) was judged the best student in her literacy class and was invited to receive a prize at a public function organised by the county authorities. At the meeting she shook hands with the village head and also sat next to him. This offended her husband so much that he beat her up after she returned home. The husband was outraged by the fact that his wife did not mind being seen publicly with another man even if the formalities of the occasion demanded it. On hearing of this case, the local Women's Federation brought the man to book and he had to apologise to his wife. The informant who narrated this story was trying to highlight the complexities and difficulties which cadres have to face because rural China still does not grant equality to women.

All those involved in fields related to adult literacy are well aware of the importance of post-literacy work because the tendency to relapse into illiteracy is quite common. To prevent this a series of steps have been adopted in China. Government checks the enduring effect of the campaign and discovers new problems. The Adult Education Bureau of Beijing, for instance, expects neo-literates to be able to read *Beijing Ribao* (Beijing Daily) when its investigation team goes in and around the city to check the level of literacy as part of its post-literacy work. According to officials, post-literacy measures take more time and effort. For women, visits to their houses by officials are not rare although in most cases periodic tests are organised by literacy workers which are held at the village primary schools. Often, the atmosphere at home is not conducive to the maintenance of their new skills. To overcome this problem skills are taught and training is given so that literacy is useful in daily life. Booklets in simple language dealing with harvests, crops, pig-raising, fish ponds and vegetable growing are distributed periodically. Women who have difficulty in reading these are advised to take the help of literacy workers.[10]

Those with high literacy levels are encouraged to study more, so that after completing basic education they are sometimes able to go for higher education. The Radio and Television University set up in the 1960s caters to the needs of many such beneficiaries of literacy programmes. In the post-Mao period the Central Radio and Television University (CRTVU) expanded greatly and by 1984 more than 600,000 students had enrolled in it (Hawkridge and McCormick 1983).

Handbooks on hygiene, child care and family planning are also made available to women, particularly the younger ones. In a few cases the family planning, health and literacy worker is the same person. This streamlines the work and makes it more effective, according to a few informants. For example, in some places the literacy activist who teaches women to read also writes out a leaflet as a family planning worker in which she explains the various methods of contraception, their side-effects and advantages, etc. The newly-literate women are expected to read them on their own and discuss them with the family planning worker. In the process the women's reading skills are enhanced. I was told that women do make a great effort to read these, as this so directly affects their lives.

Diminishing Priority

The overall view I have of China's efforts to expand literacy is that it is fairly commendable. Of course I am well aware that much of this information was not verifiable. I had to rely greatly on the informants' views and analyses. There was not much divergence in their opinions as most of them would reiterate the government's point of view. Moreover, the Chinese have not officially singled out women as a special target in their literacy drives. Women-specific policies in the literacy campaigns do not really exist. One has to discern the gender aspect in it through some effort. I had to rely a great deal on Women's Federation activists and officials who provided me with some of the required information. However, even before starting my research trip in China, I believed that post-Mao reforms with an emphasis on a market economy, would have had some adverse effects on literacy campaigns, especially on women's literacy. But it was difficult for me to ask directly as no one would give me a straight answer. However, through more indirect and informal ways I was able to determine that on adopting a liberal economy, adult literacy in general and women's literacy in particular has taken a back-seat. "Get rich quick" seems to be the general philosophy although it is not quite expressed that way.

The spread of literacy, it appears, is not a top priority in the government agenda. Earning money has become an end in itself. The nature of the reforms is also such that it tends to take people away from literacy classes. For example, the production responsibility system (which entails going back to family farms) now applicable to almost the entire Chinese countryside, after the dismantling of communes in the early 1980s, has created a greater demand for labour at farms and homes. Women and their family members find this more lucrative than attending literacy classes, which brings in no direct income. "Money is more important than education", one elderly activist said in an unguarded moment. The state supports the idea of non-formal education through the CRTVU but few have any idea have the time for it. Another informant admitted that it was far easier to convince people to get over traditional beliefs and persuade women to attend literacy classes than dissuading them from their money-earning ventures to save time to reading and writing. Official Chinese views will, however, give us a different interpretation. For instance, one author, while saying that literacy had dropped in China from 80 per cent in 1949 to 43 per cent in 1959, also says that:

> "During the long period of 15 to 16 years from the late fifties to the mid-seventies, the country was in the grip of political movements coming one after another, and economic development suffered severe setbacks. As a result, adult education, both general and technical, was regarded as heresy and it virtually came to a complete halt. It was only in 1976 when the ten-year nation-wide internal disorder was finally terminated, and especially after the Third Plenary Sessions of the Eleventh Congress of the Communist Party of China which decided to shift the stress of the whole Party of economic construction, that adult education could be restored and developed systematically again." (Yao Zhongda 1987: 17).[11]

The role of the Women's Federation has also changed with the reforms. The dedication of committed social workers was not quite visible to me. Professional women (engineers, academicians, scientists, etc.) have joined the organisation in large numbers and among the jobs they assign to themselves, literacy work hardly figures. From my conversations with many top officials of the Women's Federation I got the idea that women are encouraged to start their own businesses and become successful entrepreneurs. This seems to be in tune with the policies of the government. Education, which had always been the domain of the government and funded through public resources is now gradually beginning to rely on private funds. Among a large section of the Chinese academia, privatisation of education seems to be the ultimate aim. However, people agreed when it was pointed out that even if higher education gets some funding from private resources, literacy cannot be left to private funding alone as both the government and the community must play a vital role in this essentially welfare measure. On being directly asked as to how the literacy and basic education campaigns could become more achievement-oriented, almost everyone stressed the role of the government in providing both direct funding and creating other resources. The official viewpoint, however, undermines the importance of literacy campaigns and restructures adult education in order to be more development- and profit-oriented rather than welfare-oriented (Guan Shixiong 1987: 197). No longer is the problem of women's illiteracy addressed as seriously as before, nor are anti-illiteracy drives given the importance they deserve.

The impact of the new economic reforms on welfare-related activities, particularly women's welfare, appears to be adverse. This has been confirmed by many authors who are concerned with gender studies connected with China (e.g., Croll 1983). As far as the spread of literacy is concerned, the Mao period saw more advances. Women had to leave their homes to attend political classes along with men, and in the process learned to read. The communes and brigades saw this as their responsibility and this decentralisation of literacy work helped in the dissemination of literacy. Public funding (government and community) also supported literacy activists who therefore did not have to worry about looking for alternative sources of livelihood to sustain themselves and their campaigns.

The Chinese are also aware of the adverse effect of the reforms on women, and as a consequence passed a law in 1992 on the protection of Rights and Interests of Women. Article 18 of this law states:

> "People's government at various levels shall, in accordance with relevant provisions, incorporate the work of elimination of illiteracy or semi-literacy among women into plans for illiteracy elimination and post-elimination education, adopt organizational forms and working methods suitable to women's characteristics, and organise and supervise the relevant departments in the implementation of such plans."[12]

This is clearly a recognition by the state of its obligations towards the people to fight illiteracy.

The Girl Child

Recently, the Chinese have also expressed concern regarding the problems of the girl child. It is widely believed that if the girl child is made the target, then the problem of illiteracy among adult women will ultimately disappear. With this goal in view, the Eighth Five-Year Plan of China (1991-95) has specially targeted the four backward provinces of Ningxia, Guizhou, Gansu and Qinghai to promote primary education among girl children. It should be pointed out that regional variations in terms of development and hence education and literacy are quite remarkable in China. The Lingnan region (in south China) has always had a better literacy rate than the north China plain (Lavely et al. 1990). An experimental and research project sponsored by UNESCO in coordination with the State Education Commission is studying the problems of education of girl children in the above-mentioned, less developed and mainly minority-inhabited areas. The aims of the project are: to devise ways and means by which primary education would become universal; to remove illiteracy; and to eliminate unequal educational opportunities for men and women by the end of this century. The researchers in this massive project are evolving various methods to operationalise the policies and decisions.

Regarding their own perceptions on the issue, my informants, by and large, agreed that the economic reforms have not been particularly helpful towards illiterate and poor women in the backward areas, but they are hopeful that as wealth will finally "trickle down", these areas will benefit; widespread literacy and more education will be part of this benefit. Within two or three decades, said an informant, literacy drives will become irrelevant, as China would reach "100 per cent literacy like Japan". The compulsory education law of 1986 [13] (education was always compulsory but a law to enforce it was passed for the first time in 1986) as well as the law on women just quoted will take care of this. In the next generation there should be no illiterate adult women. My attention was drawn to Article 17 of the 1992 law on women's rights which states:

> "Parents or guardians must perform their duty of ensuring that female school-age children or adolescents receive the compulsory education. When parents or other guardians fail to send female school-age children or adolescents to school, the local people's government shall admonish or criticize them and, by adopting effective measures, order them to send their school-age female children or adolescents to school, with the exception of those who, on account of illness or other special circumstances, are allowed by the local people's governments not to go to school. The governments, society and schools shall, in the light of actual difficulties of female school-age children and adolescents in schooling, take effective measures to ensure that female school-age children or adolescents receive compulsory education for the numer of years locally prescribed."[14]

This law if translated into action will eradicate illiteracy among Chinese women and that would be a red-letter day in the history of the Chinese women's struggle for emancipation and empowerment. The Chinese experience, moreover, could also be valuable for other populous, developing countries like ours.

Conclusion

The socio-cultural features of the two countries — India and China — being fairly similar, each can gain from the other's experience. The rural situation, in particular, has many striking similarities in the two societies. In both societies traditional ideas have been the main hindrance to the spread of female literacy and also to problems like time-consuming household responsibilities and the burden of large families (in China's case due to the small family norm, women of the younger generation have relatively small families, but joint families are still common). Men in rural India, as in rural China, do not share household chores with their wives. In China the existence of communes along with common kitchens, mess halls as well as nurseries and day-care centres, freed both men and women from household work. However, such an organised commune system existed for barely two years, i.e., 1958-60. After this brief period very little socialised household services existed for Chinese women. (By the early 1980s, communes were totally dismantled.) Even taking these difficulties into account, the Chinese have a better record of female literacy in comparison with India. This is essentially due to the effective means and the novel methods invented and applied by the Chinese government and the Communist Party. Unlike India, China has so far not involved non-governmental organisations (except the UN and its agencies in welfare and developmental projects). Non-formal education is an area where NGOs in India have put in a lot of effort. It may be worthwhile for them to try out Chinese methods of disseminating literacy among rural women. Without widespread female literacy in rural India, programmes for health care, family planning, rural industrialisation and so on cannot hope to achieve much.

Notes

1. B. Hall and J.R. Kidd (eds.), *Adult Learning: A Design for Action* (Oxford: Pergamon) 1978, cited in Gordon Selman, 'Adult Education: An Awakening Force' in Chris Duke (1987: 67).
2. I went to China as a post-doctoral fellow under the India-China Bilateral Cultural Exchange and was there from October 1992 to March 1993. I was affiliated to the Beijing Normal University. I would like to express my gratitude to the Education Department of this University and particularly to Dr. Shi Jinghuan, Deputy Dean and Associate Professor, who did all that was possible to help me in my research. Thanks are also due to Ms. Zhu Weiqing, Graduate Students at BNU, Professor Sun Xiaomei of the Women's Cadre Training College, Beijing, and Anita Sharma, friend and colleague at Delhi University, for their help at different stages of this work. In addition, I would like to thank Mr. Ramachandran of UNICEF, Beijing, and Mr. and Mrs. P.N.G. Subramanian (India's Consul-General and his wife) for their help during my stay in Shanghai.
3. Foot-binding was a very cruel custom prevalent among the wealthy classes of north China. Girls from a tender age had to have their feet bandaged tight every night for years till their feet became deformed and remained small. The justification was that small feet looked beautiful and were an added qualification for marriage. Since the turn of the century, this oppressive custom was attacked by revolutionaries and progressive elements. In 1905, it was declared illegal but the practice continued for some more time in the countryside and among conservative sections.
4. The May Fourth Movement was an intellectual upsurge which engulfed urban China from 1915 onwards, although the name comes from the incident of 4 May 1919, when students of Beijing University as well as others protested and demonstrated at Tiananmen Square against some proposed provisions of the Treaty of Versailles. Anti-imperialism was a crucial component of this movement and it also marked the beginning of a women's liberation movement (see Chow Tse-tsung 1960).
5. Literacy workers connected with the All China Women's Federation, researchers at the Shanghai Institute of Human Resources Development, and students of the Women's Cadre Training College, Beijing, constitute my sources on this subject.
6. Minorities comprise 8 per cent of China's population; the majority 92 per cent are called the Han. The former occupy approximately 60 per cent of the land as well as the frontier regions. For an informative work on China's National Minorities, as they are officially called, see Dreyer (1976).
7. The Cultural Revolution was Mao's last effort to take China away from the capitalist road. Among the well-known works on the subject are, Hong Yong-Lee (1978) and Butterfield (1982).
8. In urban China, it is common for husbands and wives to share all household chores. I have observed this myself.
9. China has about 8 million Muslims who inhabit major parts of Gansu and Xinjiang provinces as well as the Ningxia Hui Autonomous Region.
10. information gathered from Ms. Zhang, Deputy Director at the Beijing Adult Education Bureau, during interviews in December 1992.
11. Deng Xiaoping announced the reforms at the Third Plenary Session of the Communist Party's Eleventh Central Committee in December 1978. These have had far-reaching consequences and hence the Third Plenum has become a historic event.

12. Called "Law of the People's Republic of China on the Protection of Rights and Interests of Women" (adopted at the Fifth Session of the Seventh National People's Congress on 3 April 1992).

13. A copy of the unpublished proposal (in Chinese) entitled "Present Situation and Problems of Girl Child Education in Villages and its Counter-measures" was provided to me by Dr. Shi Jinghuan of the Beijing Normal University.

14. Text of the 1986 Compulsory Education Law is available in a volume called *Educational Laws and Regulations of the People's Republic of China 1949-1989* (Beijing, 1991).

References

Basic Education and National Development: Forty Years of Chinese Experience. Shanghai Institute of Human Resource Development and UNICEF, 1991.

Buck, John L. *Land Utilization in China.* Nanjing: University of Nanjing Press, 1937.

Census of China (Chinese Academy of Social Sciences, Almanac 1986), *1982*

China Statistical Year Book, Beijing: Foreign Languages Pres, 1988.

Croll, Elizabeth. *Chinese Women Since Mao.* London: Zed Books, 1983.

Dreyer, June T. *China's Forty Millions: Minority Nationalities and National Integration in the People's Republic of China.* Cambridge, Mass.: Harvard University Press, 1976.

Duke, Chris (ed.) *Adult Education: International Perspectives from China.* London: Croom Helm, 1987.

Hawkridge, D. and R. McCormick. "China's Television Universities", *British Journal of Educational Technology*, 14(3): 1983, pp. 160-73.

Henze, Jurgen. "The Formal Education System and Modernization", in Ruth Hayhoe (ed.), *Education and Modernization : The Chinese Experience*, Oxford: Pergamon Press, 1992, pp. 110-29.

Lavely, William, Xiao Zhenyu, Li Bohua and Ronald Freedman. "The Rise in Female Education in China: National and Regional Patterns", *China Quarterly*, 121 (March), 1990, pp. 61-93.

Lewis, Ida Belle. *The Education of Girls in China* (Teacher's College, Columbia University, Contribution to Education No. 104). San Francisco: China Materials Center (reprint), 1974.

Rosen, Stanley. "Women, Education and Modernization", in Ruth Hayhoe (ed.), *op. cit.*, 1992. pp. 255-84.

Selman, Gordon. "Adult Education: An Awakening Force" in Chris Duke (ed.), *Adult Education: International Perspectives From China.* London: Croom Hel, 1987.

Shiqi, Huang. "Non formal Education and Modernization", in Ruth Hayhoe (ed.), *op. cit.*, 1992, pp. 141-82.

Shixiong, Guan."Developing a Socialist Adult Education System in China", in Chris Duke (ed.), *Adult Education: International Perspectives From China*, London: Croom Helm, 1987, pp. 196-200.

Tse-tsung, Chow. *The May Fourth Movement: Intellectual Revolution in Modern China.* Cambridge, Mass.: Harvard University Press, 1960.

Yanwei, Wang n.d. "People's Participation and Mobilization: Characteristics and Measures of Anti-Literacy Campaigns in China", in *Adult Education in China and Tanzania* (Post-M.A. Diploma Papers-V), Department of Adult Education and Extension, University of Delhi.

Yong-Lee, Hong *The Politics of the Chinese Cultural Revolution: A Case Study.* Berkeley and Los Angeles: University of California Press, 1978.

Zhong Guo Funu (Women of China). "Zai wenhua jixu yexiaoli" (At the Night School of Culture and Technical Knowledge), No. 7, 1958.

________. "Vigorously Study Chairman Mao's Works", No. 2, 1960.

Zhongda, Yao. "Adult Education Theory and Development in China", in Chris Duke (ed.), *op. cit., 1987*, pp. 13-18.

HISTORY AND LITERATURE

HISTORY AND LITERATURE

歷史与文学

Tagore and China

33. The Controversial Guest: Tagore's 1924 Visit of China
    Sisir Kumar Das

34. Tagore's Inspiration in China's New Poetry
    Tan Chung

Ancients on War

35. Strategic Thinking in Ancient India and China: Kautilya and Sunzi
    Giri Deshingkar

36. Arthasastra and Sunzi Bingfa
    V.R. Ragavan

Modern Chinese Literature

37. The Lofty Height of a Writer: My Evaluation of Lu Xun
    Manik Bhattacharyya

38. Comeback of Hundred Flowers in Chinese Literature: 1976-1989
    Sabaree Mitra

India-China Relationship

39. Mao Zedong's Vision: China, The World and India
    Mira Sinha Bhattacharjea

40. The Nehru Years Revisited
    Giri Deshingkar

41. Retrace Indian Steps in the Agricultural Scene in China 40 Years Back
    S.K. Bhutani

SISIR KUMAR DAS

33

THE CONTROVERSIAL GUEST: TAGORE IN CHINA

"I say that a poet's mission is to attract the voice which is yet inaudible in the air; to inspire faith in the dream which is unfulfilled; to bring the earliest tidings of the unborn flower to a sceptic world."

—Tagore: "First Talk at Shanghai", Talks in China (1924)

The *Jiangxueshe* (Beijing Lecture Association) invited Rabindranath Tagore in 1923 to deliver a series of talks. This Association, established in September 1920, was one of the many institutions that mushroomed in China in the wake of the May Fourth Movement. Its main objective was to invite foreign scholars and to arrange lectures by them for Chinese intellectuals. The Association had earlier invited John Dewey (1859-1952), Bertrand Russell (1872-1970) and Hans Driesch (1862-1941). They spoke to a limited number of scholars, but their lectures were more or less well received and Russell certainly made a great impression on Chinese intellectuals. The Association intended to invite Rudolf Euken and Henry Bergson but did not succeed. The invitation to Rabindranath Tagore created an unprecedented uproar which eventually culminated in strong hostility against him as well as against Liang Qichao (1873-1929), President of the Association, by the radical student circles and some ultra left-oriented political leaders. This essay examines the background and the possible ideological reasons for this hostility which made Tagore the most controversial guest in twentieth century China.

Sources of information about the Chinese response to Tagore are varied and divergent. Both Leonard Elmhirst and Kalidas Nag, who accompanied Tagore to China, maintained diaries but they are yet to be available to the general reader. The little that is known about the contents of those diaries do not contain much to shed light on the motivations of the concerted attack against the poet. A few publications from the Visva-Bharati at that time, however, offer valuable information about the poet's sojourn in China, although they contain precious little about the Chinese criticism of Tagore.[2] Four years after the death of the poet, Kalidas Nag edited a slender volume, *Tagore and China* (1945) which gave some more information. The most detailed and valuable work on the subject is the revised version of the doctoral thesis of an American scholar; Stephen Hay, published under the title *Asian Ideas of East and West* (1970). Hay has gone through a large mass of material — contemporary newspapers both in Chinese and English, unpublished diaries and private papers of many scholars, including those of Elmhirst and Nag and presented a detailed story in an immensely readable style and dramatic manner. Despite his sophistication of approach and elegance of presentation, Hay holds Tagore primarily responsible for the "failure" of his visit, which Hay thinks, was prompted by Tagore's desire to play the role of a prophet rather than a poet. He also projects the idea that Tagore went to China to propagate an ideal of the Orient, an ideal of one Asia and the cause of spiritualism against the materialism of the west. According to Hay, Tagore did not realise that the idea of the Orient was a gift of the western Orientalist, which was more a myth than a reality. Every Asian country had its own version of the Orient and Tagore's idea of Asia was different from that of the Chinese. Tagore's idea of a spiritual rejuvenation of Asia was rejected by both young and old. The former with crude vehemence and the latter with gentle indifference. Had he not gone to China as a prophet and a spokesman of Indian spirituality Tagore would not have met such humiliation. Tagore left China with bitter feelings, Hay thinks, rejected by all the students, the scholars, the politicians and the poets and the artists.[3]

It is difficult to locate all the lectures that Tagore delivered in China. Some are available in abridged form, and others in distorted form. A few were reproduced in the *Visva-Bharati Bulletin* and *Visva-Bharati Quarterly*. Most of them, however, are to be found in Tagore's *Talks in China*, published soon after his return from China in 1924. But for some reasons not known to us, Tagore banned the circulation of that book and published a new edition, drastically revised, the following year. Although these two books have the same title, and the same material to a great extent, they differ radically in their arrangement. Certain parts of the essays included in the 1924 edition were not only deleted in the 1925 edition, but the essays were rearranged under five headings : "Auto-biographical", "To My Hosts", "To Students", "To Teachers" and "Leave-Taking". The two essays "Civilization and Progress" and "Satyam" included in the 1924 edition, were included in the new edition without any change, but three lectures "At a Buddhist Temple", "To the Japanese Community at China" and "At Mrs. Bena's, Shanghai" have been omitted. In fact, a comparative study of these two texts shows that there have been changes of a very serious and radical nature. Tagore took great pains to delete all the information that was included in the first edition about places where the lectures were delivered, and also several perceptive passags. The reasons for such changes are not known. Although *Talks in China* is one of the significant writings of Tagore in English, it never received the attention it deserved either from Tagore scholars in Bengal or students of India-China relations. It is quite interesting to note that it was never translated into Chinese although quite a number of Tagore's other works were translated into Chinese and were well received.

Many articles that appeared during Tagore's visit to China in different newspapers and journals are difficult to locate, some of them are already lost or destroyed. A volume entitled *Lun Taige'er* (On Tagore), containing many articles on Tagore written by various Chinese scholars and political activists during the period between 1921 and 1924, published by Zhang Guangliang of the Institute of South Asian Studies of the Chinese Academy of Social Sciences at Beijing in 1983 provides interesting materials[4]. The long article by Ji Xianlin, the Director of the Institute and an eminent scholar, also the President of the Comparative Literature Association of China, is particularly valuable as it gives a scholarly analysis of the factors responsible for the controversy about Tagore's visit. According to him, the hosts of Tagore were political "reactionaries", who wanted to make use of Tagore to enhance their own political image and to find support for their ideology. The other reason, suggested by Ji Xianlin, is the inherent duality in Tagore's work and philosophy. Tagore was an anti-imperialist and intensely patriotic, but he was also a religious poet and a mystic. His poems and songs did inspire the Indians in their struggle against foreign rule, his poems and short stories indeed breathed a universal spirit, but strands of escapism were also apparent in his writings. The Chinese admirers of Tagore wanted to present him as a mystic without any concern for human suffering, as a writer engrossed in a world of dream and ethereal beauty without any understanding of the present reality. This interpretation of Ji Xianlin is partly prompted by a desire to tone down the severity of the Chinese protest against Tagore and partly based on Mao Dun's criticism of Tagore, which we will discuss later.

It is quite evident that the hostility that Tagore faced in China was partly because of his hosts, all of whom were targets of severe criticism by the radicals of that time. But that does not explain the extent of Chinese fury against a foreign guest. Tagore set foot in China on 12 April 1924 but the debate about him had started from September 1923, i.e., almost within a few weeks of the announcement of his visit. A group of poets and intellectuals, some of whom were abroad at that time, came out openly to criticise Tagore's thought and writings, which they considered a great threat to the Chinese youth. They made occasional references to Tagore's hosts but the references were generally oblique. The severity of the radical intellectuals criticism of Tagore makes one think that either they felt Tagore's influence on the Chinese youth was already quite pervasive and that it must be stemmed immediately, or there was a strong possibility of the Chinese youth being swayed away by the presence of Tagore. In either case it makes little sense. Krishna Kripalani wrote that "Tagore was hardly known in China" when he was invited there, and implied that the controversy that was generated was because of the ignorance of the Chinese intellectuals. Facts, however, are different. Soon after the news of the award of the Nobel Prize to Tagore reached China in 1913, a Chinese scholar named Qian Zhixian wrote an article in the *East*, in which he portrayed the poet as one dedicated to his motherland and to the welfare of the mankind.[5] Many young Chinese studying in the USA, England and in Japan, were familiar with the writings of Tagore. Guo Moruo, Hu Shi and Xu Zhimo, for example, read Tagore in English when they were abroad. And many more at home who could read English came under the spell of the *Crescent Moon and Gitanjali*. Tagore's works were translated into Chinese as early as in 1915 and his first translator was Chen Duxiu, one of the founders of the Communist Party of China. In the second issue of the influential journal *Xin Qingnian* (New Youth), edited by him, Chen published translations of four poems from *Gitanjali* (Nos. 1, 2, 25 and 35) with a note that Tagore was a mystic but also a mentor of the Indian youth.[6] It was around this time when Guo Moruo, who accepted Tagore as his hero, wrote the following poem in which he quotes the poet:

"The lead grey roofs of the fishermen's cottages
Gleam darkly with a circle of red flame
Now crimson ... now redder
Now orange ... now gold
It is as ever the white radiance of the moon.
On the seashore of endless world's children meet
The infinite sky is motionless overhead and the
restless water is boisterous.
On the seashore of endless world's the children meet
with shouts and dances.
Again I sit on the broken hulk on the shore
My little Ah-ho
Joins with a troop of children,
They play together on the sands.
Reciting this poem of Tagore
I go and play with them
Ah, if only I could become a pure child."[7]

In 1916 *Dongfang Zazhi* (The Eastern Miscellany), the oldest and most widely circulated Chinese journal, published one of the lectures of Tagore delivered in Japan. This lecture might have created an impression in China that Tagore was a sharp critic of modern western civilisation and a man of spiritual temper. But the other dimensions of Tagore's personality could not be totally unknown to the Chinese reading public as several young writers of promise had translated his poems, short stories and plays. *Gitanjali* was translated, though not the whole of it, and published in various journals (apart from the *New Youth*) by Zheng Zhenduo, Zhao Jingshen, between 1920 and 1923. In 1923 Zheng Zhenduo published his translation of *The Crescent Moon.* Its publisher, the Commercial Press, came out with a second edition of this translation the following year which competed with another translation of the same book by Wang Duqing published by the Taidong Press of Shanghai.

Translations of Tagore's stories began to appear in Chinese magazines from 1917, if not earlier; *Funu Zazhi* (Women's Magazine) published two stories of Tagore, *Chuti* (Home Coming) and *Dristidan* (Vision) in 1917. *Chuti* was translated three times before Tagore visited China, and Kabuliwala was translated six times; four of the translations appeared in journals before 1924. At least four plays — *Chitra, Sannyasi, The Cycle of Spring* and the *Post Office* — one novel (*The Home and the World*) and two volumes of essays (*Personality and Nationalism*) were available in Chinese translations. It is difficult to obtain detailed information about all the translators but some of them, Wang Duqing, Xu Dishan, Qu Shiying, Zheng Zhenduo, Bai Xiang and Shen Yanbing (more well known as was Mao Dun), were promising writers of that time. Wang Duqing (1898-1940), one of the founders of *Chuangzao she* (The Creation Society), was educated in France and was a fine poet. Xu Dishan (1893-1944), primarily a scholar and famous essayist, studied Indian philosophy at Oxford. He visited India in 1925 to study Sanskrit and Buddhist philosophy. Qu Shiying (1900-1976) was a teacher at the Peking University and Zheng Zhenduo (1898-1958), one of the founders of the Literary Research Society and editor of *Xiaoshuo Yuebao* (The Fiction Monthly), was a popular writer and a scholar of Chinese literary history.[8] It is important to remember that *Xiaoshuo Yuebao* with which Mao Dun and Zhou Zuoren were associated, published at least eight stories, three plays and a large number of poems of Tagore — many of them translated by Zheng Zhenduo — before 1924.

It is interesting to note that some of the critics of Tagore's China visit, like Chen Duxiu and Shen Yanbing, were among the Chinese translators of Tagore, and pioneers in introducing Tagore to Chinese readers. Their earlier admiration for Tagore's literary achievement prevented them from criticising him as a writer even when they expressed their reservations about inviting Tagore to China. There was, however, a strong belief that Tagore was invited to China to help Liang and his associates, particularly Zhang Junmai who had co-authored the work *Das Lebensproblem in China und in Europe* (1922) with Eucken. To refute the allegation Zhang had to make an announcement that he was unfamiliar with Tagore's thought before he had met him. "I have come to know that his heart is full of love and beauty", he wrote about Tagore, and added that, "Mr. Tagore and I have no connection with each other, and ... he definitely did not come to China to assist me."[9] That Zhang felt obliged to make a statement like this is an evidence of the bitterness that existed between Liang and his friends on the one hand, and those who opposed him on various issues since the last few years. Since 1917 a wind of change was blowing through the country. Its significant impact on intellectual activities was first felt on the Chinese language and literature. Hu Shi (1891-1962), a fine scholar of philosophy and literature and an ardent follower of John Dewey's pragmatism, started a movement in favour of *bai hua*, the language spoken by the common man, as against the time honoured literary speech *wenyan*.[10] He received support from Chen Duxiu and was successful in radically transforming Chinese cultural life. The debate initiated by Hu Shi was prompted by a desire of the future development of the Chinese language to make it an effective instrument of modernisation of the Chinese life.[11] The use of the people's speech in place of the antiquated literary language not only forged a closer relationship between writers and readers, but also led to a tremendous increase in the number of publication of newspapers and magazines. Translations from foreign languages also received a tremendous boost, which opened up a window to the world. The forces behind the language reform were but one aspect of a wide intellectual fermentation. They slowly extended to other areas challenging the validity and utility of the older tradition. A group of intellectuals, most of them educated abroad, criticised the traditional values, including Confucianism and welcomed western thought and technology to activise the dormant energy of China. The May Fourth Movement was the culmination of the people's anger and humiliation provoked by the Versailles Treaty of 1919, following which the intellectuals started becoming polarised on various social, philosophical and political issues. Chen Duxiu and his friends associated with the journal *Xin Qingnian* (New Youth) called for a total rejection of Confucianism. If China were to find a place of honour in the world, then the decadent culture of China sustained by Confucianism must be replaced by a twin ideal — Mr. Science and Mr. Democracy. This iconoclastic approach to the past had to be accepted in order to ensure progress.

Liang Qichao who had staged the "Hundred Days Reform" coup d'etat along with his mentor Kang Youwei in 1898, had a radical image in his younger days and was the hero of Mao Zedong in his youth.[12] He was the first in China to write on Karl Marx and had a profound impact on the Chinese youth through his writings on Rousseau and the French Revolution and by his scathing attack on Confucianism. In his early life he established an association, the main aim of which was to acquaint the younger generation with the various facets of western thought. But in 1919 when he went to Paris as a representative of China, there was a change in him. He was disillusioned by war-torn Europe. This was further intensified by his meeting with Bergson. Following this there was a shift in his position in respect of his attraction towards Europe and he became a critic of the technological civilisation of the west and blind faith in science. He wrote at that time: "millions of people on the other shore of the ocean are worrying about the bankruptcy of material civilization, sorrowfully and desperately crying for help, waiting for your aid, our ancestors in heaven, the sages and the older generation are all earnestly hoping, you will carry out their task. Their spirit is helping you."[13] The Chinese youth reacted to this appeal in two divergent ways. The majority found it unacceptable but some intellectuals, the most distinguished of whom was Liang Shuming, supported Liang Qichao. Liang Qichao's shift in position evoked sharp protests from the young Marxists, particularly Zheng Zhenduo, Zhou Zuoren, and Mao Dun. Chinese cultural tradition was at its peak and polarisation between the Chinese intellectuals was almost complete.

In February 1923 when Zhang Junmai, a disciple of Liang Qichao, emphasised the necessity for a reassessment of the Chinese civilisation, Mao Dun and Chen Duxiu declared unequivocally the worthlessness of the Chinese tradition and rejected his cautious note for a selective approach to one's ancient heritage. People belonging to various literary circles, too, were sharply divided on issues such as the role of literature in society. Xu Zhimo was happy about his acquaintance with I A Richard, C K Ogden, Lowes Dickinson, E M Forster and Katherine Mansfield, and deeply in love with Lin Huilin, the beautiful daughter of Lin Changmin (a friend of Liang Qichao and a member of the short-lived cabinet in 1917), Xu Zhimo's friend Qu Qiubai on the other hand was completely dedicated to Marxian ideology. When Qu Qiubai met Xu Zhimo and his circle of friends he felt they belonged to a world of dreams blissfully ignorant about the surrounding reality. It was also the time when Guo Moruo declared, "We are men on the revolutionary path and our literature of today can only justify its existence in its function of hastening the realization of social revolution... Now is the time for propaganda, and literature is its instrument."[14]

Hu Shi, the non-communist liberal, who also played the role of a host to Tagore, was a sharp critic of Liang Qichao's view of western civilisation. He believed that the civilisation which substituted machines for human labour was more spiritual than civilisations which continued to use men as beasts of burden. When Liang Shuming was defending Confucianism, Hu Shi was criticising *Kongjia* (Confucius and sons). But when the debate between the two was continuing, Chen Duxiu attacked not only the supporters of the ancient traditions but also Hu Shi, his one time intimate friend. It must be remembered that Hu Shi initiated the new literary movement with the support of Chen. After his return from the USA, he joined Peking University as a Professor of English and Philosophy. At that time he was extremely popular among the younger generation for his defence of Huxley's agnosticism and the pragmatism of John Dewey. He was a friend of Lu Xun and was universally regarded as one of the pioneers of modern Chinese poetry.[15] Hu Shi, a scholar by temperament, devoted more time to scholarly pursuits than to political debates.[16] However, despite his prominent role in the cultural reforms, his involvement in abstract philosophical problems and refusal to participate in the left movement also made him a target of attack of the members of the Communist Party, which ridiculed him as an inhabitant of the ivory tower of academic life. This was the man who evinced an interest in Tagore during the latter's visit to China in 1924.

Another person who expressed enthusiasm about Tagore's visit in abundant measure was the young poet Xu Zhimo (1895-1931). Elmhirst met him and Qu Shiying, a young philosopher and educationist, in April 1923 and discussed the possibility of Tagore's visit. They reported the discussion to Liang Qichao and Zhang, and both of them responded to the proposal heartily. For Xu Zhimo it was a great occasion. He was in Cambridge at the time when Tagore's reputation in England was at its zenith. A lover of Shelley and Keats and of Katherine Mansfield, Xu Zhimo responded passionately to Tagore's poetry for its sophisticated grace and universality. *The Crescent Moon* haunted him throughout his tempestuous life tragically cut short at the age of thirty.[17] He founded the *Xinyueshe* (The Crescent Moon Society) in 1923, launched a monthly journal in collaboration with his poet friend Wen Yiduo in 1925, called *The Monthly Crescent Moon*, and three years before his death he established a publishing house — The Crescent Moon Publications. But his view of literature isolated him from the group of writers represented by Guo Moruo and others. As early as in 1921 Guo had declared:

> "I am a proletarian
> Because but for my naked self
> I possess no other private property."[18]

Xu Zhimo's enthusiasm about Tagore was interpreted rightly or wrongly as an oblique criticism of Marxist view of literature. Liang Qichao, Hu Shi, Xu Zhimo, Zhang Junmai, Liang Shuming, despite broad differences among them, were thought to be members of a group opposed to the newly organised Marxists, and since they were the people to take an interest in Tagore, the poet appeared to have posed a threat to the radicals. They must have thought that while the influence of Dewey and Russell was limited to an extremely small circle, Tagore being a poet and playwright, already popular in China, had greater potentiality of influencing a larger audience. Therefore, he must be opposed.

Before sailing for China, Tagore told the press that when he received the Chinese invitation he felt that it was an invitation to India herself and as her humble son he should accept it. He hoped that his visit would re-establish the cultural and spiritual links between the two civilisations: "We shall invite scholars and try to arrange an exchange of scholars. If I can accomplish this, I shall feel happy."[19] These words were more than pleasantries, they were perfectly natural for the man who had always nourished great love for China and who visualised a centre of learning where the whole world would meet as if in a nest.

Tagore's knowledge of China was not confined, as it has been alleged by some of his critics, to a superficial acquaintance with Confucianism alone. It is true he said in China, "I had in my mind my own vision of China, formed when I was young, China as I had imagined it to be when I was reading my Arabian Nights, the romantic China, as well as the China of which I had caught glimpses when I was in Japan."[20] But any one familiar with Tagore's works in Bengali knows about his awareness of the suffering people of China since the early years of his literary career. His articles *Chine Maraner Byabasay* (The Death Trade in China) published in the Bengali magazine, *Bharati in 1881; Samajbhed* (Social Differences) written in 1901; and the famous *Chinemaner Chithi* (Letters of a Chinaman) based on Dickinson's *Letters of John Chinaman* published in 1898 are eloquent evidence of his knowledge of and interest in Chinese affairs. *Samajbhed* was based on an English article entitled "Tiger China and Lamb Europe" (published in *Contemporary Review*, London) about the western barbarity perpetrated against China. Tagore wrote that the present turmoil in China began with the intrusion of Christian missionaries in that country, who in their arrogance refused to recognise the necessity and the significance of diversities in a social system. Civilised Europe, Tagore observed, also refused to adhere to the principles of Christianity, and disrupted an ancient civilisation with its brute force to perpetuate its self-interest. In this essay as well as in "Letters of a Chinaman" Tagore emphasised the role of religion in Oriental civilisation, particularly the

Indian and Chinese. But what he considered to be the most heinous crime committed by the British was their role in the opium trade. The bulk of the opium imported into China was produced by the East India Company in India,[21] and thus the British made India, against her wishes, a party to the nefarious proposition. An optimist to the core, Tagore, however, believed that China would eventually discover her hidden strength to protect herself from the onslaughts of the west.

Numerous references to Chinese civilisation and contemporary Chinese life and political turmoils are scattered in the writings of Tagore, and all these comments and observations indicate his anxiety for the Chinese people. It will be wrong, therefore, to think that Tagore had an idealised or distorted vision of China when he visited that country. What he did not have was adequate information about the changing political scene after the May Fourth Movement and a clear understanding of the ideological regroupings of the Chinese intellectuals. Nor did he realise the intensity of the repugnance for Confucianism and aversion for a moribund feudal culture in China among the younger generation, and the strong possibility of his being misunderstood in an atmosphere of seething internal strife. The controversy about him started long before he set foot on Chinese soil. The theory proposed by Hay that Tagore's role as a prophet was mainly responsible for the controversy and disrespect shown to him appears to be untenable in view of the fact that a powerful group was determined to oppose him as soon as the news of his visit to China was announced.

Zheng Zhenduo, the editor of *Xiaoshuo Yuebao* (The Fiction Monthly) who had been translating Tagore since 1920, published two special numbers of the magazine in 1923 devoted to Tagore. In September that year he wrote a highly emotional editorial welcoming the poet:

> "Tagore is due to arrive in China shortly. He may reach China by the time this issue of our magazine reaches our readers.
>
> I can imagine Rabindranath Tagore in his flowing Indian garment touching the Chinese soil after a long and arduous journey. We welcome him with respect and affection. He comes through arcades made of emerald-green leaves of pine; he stands on the podium covered with fresh flowers, and we wait in folded hands for him, our hearts swelling in joy, to listen to his words.
>
> Indeed, that is how we should extend our welcome to him, even when no felicitations are adequate to express the minute fraction of our devotion and gratitude for him ...
>
> There are not many in the world today who deserve our felicitations. Among the few there are, Tagore is one and Tagore is the most deserving. He has given us love and light, he has given us consolation and solace. He has shown us light in midst of darkness; he is our dearest brother, an intimate friend and a comrade. In this strife-torn world of today he has created a paradise of poetry, beautiful and noble, whose gates are open to all men. It is like the light and warmth of the sun for all without any distinction.
>
> The West, if not the whole world, is engulfed today by blood-red clouds and is under the grip of a tornado of fierce envy. Each nation, each country, each political group looks at the other in anger, each sings the songs of revenge and dances wildly with the music of steel and guns. Each in greed like that of a poisonous dragon wants to swallow the whole world. How many lives have been lost, how many homes destroyed, how many fountains of jades and pearls dried up, how many green fields turned red in blood and how many woodlands consumed by fire! Only one man — Tagore — stands like a colossus, his one foot rests on the crest of the Himalayas and other on the Alps. In a voice as powerful as thunder he spreads the message of peace and love.
>
> The bright dawn of the future will emerge from the darkness of East. The angel of peace is on the move: he waits for us to respond. At times his voice gets stifled but his music vibrates with hope for ever ....
>
> He comes, he comes with precious gifts for us. He brings the paradise of his poetry, he illumines the surrounding darkness and reveals the essence of life and the world."[22]

Zheng Zhenduo's effusive admiration for Tagore was well matched by that of Xu Zhimo whose article welcoming Tagore was also published in the same issue of *Xiaoshuo Yuebao*. Xu who had just returned from a pilgrimage to the holy mountain

Taishan entitled his essay *Taishan richu* (Sunrise on Mount Taishan). It was a clever use of the syllable "Tai" which refers to the name of Tagore ("Taige'er" being the Chinese transliteration of "Tagore") and an attempt to identify Taige'er with the holy mountain. "My eulogy for Tagore's visit to China is the illusion I had at the time of sunrise," wrote Xu, "on Mount Taishan." The illusion he had on the mountain was of his transformation into a giant with uncombed long hair and outstretched arms. Then Xu's descriptive essays turn into poetic prose :

"The hand of the giant
points to the East —
What is there
What is unfolded by the East?
There in the East is the magnificent glowing vision
There in the East is brightness, great and pervasive.
He appears, arrives, he is here!
Let us sing
let us praise
it is the resurrection of the East
it is the victory of light..."[23]

The giant with uncombed long hair, his vision dominates the unbounded sea of clouds, which gradually dissolves into an universal ecstasy. His heroic hymns now resound all the four corners of the world.....

In another article entitled "Taige'er lai Hua" (Tagore's Visit to China) in the same issue of *Xiaoshuo Yuebao* wrote:

> ".... would it not be an event worth pondering that a man of the East has own universal admiration and acclaim on account of his personal achievement, and such a man is not a product of Japan, a country known for its military power and material prosperity, nor of China, a country which enjoys political independence, but of India, a subjugated country?"

Xu continued,

> "What would be the place of Tagore in world literature we cannot determine now. Whether he has made original contribution to poetry, whether his thoughts represent the renascent India or whether his philosophy is distinctive or not are questions which we cannot answer now. But we are certain about the greatness of his character. His poems and songs, his thought and work all may be forgotten or outdated. But his personality that emerges through all strifes and struggles is a memorial for all time.... We welcome him warmly because his harmonious and elegant personality can bring us immeasurable solace, open the imprisoned fountain heads of our heart, guide us in our endeavours, correct our abnormalities, temper our insolence and impudence, sharpen our nostalgia for the ancients, expand our compassion and love, and lead us into a perfect dreamland."[24]

Zhang Wentian (1900-1976), joined the Communist Party in 1925 and eventually played a crucial role to help Mao Aedong assume Party leadership at Zenyi in 1935 before the historic "Long March" — also wrote an article, "Poetry and Philosophy of Tagore", in the same journal,[25] in an equally exalted manner. A few excerpts from the article are presented here:

> "Tagore is a great poet and a great philosopher. His poetry contains his philosophy, while his philosophy is his poetry.
>
> In his *Cycle of Spring*, Tagore says, 'We, the poets, liberate mankind from the yoke of desire.' The function of true art is a thoroughfare leading to freedom.
>
> Art is not instruction. It gives joy, not advice. But this joy is different from physical enjoyment. It is spiritual joy.
>
> In the eyes of Tagore, both materialism and idealism are two extremes and both are erroneous. 'I believe

there is a latent vitality in the beauty of a small flower which is more powerful than the mightiest canon. I believe that in the voice of a bird, nature expresses itself with a power which is more powerful than the thunder.'

Tagore shows an ardent love for Nature, and regards all aspects of nature as manifestations of beauty. He does not love nature for its own sake, he considers nature as a part of God.

Many people deny Tagore the greatness of a poet because he does not stick to forms. In fact forms are but vehicles of fantasy and one of the means of self-realization ... Indians never admire forms for the sake of form.

Tagore is a true inheritor of the Indian sages. His writings evoke many possibilities of spiritual life. His songs already a part of the national literature of the Indian people are created with words and ideas full of vitality. His words delight our ears while his ideas penetrate into our hearts. His poetry diffuses radiance upon our hearts as they do to his own people. O Tagore, the poet of the Indian people, you are the poet of the entire humanity ......"

Some of the observations of Zhang Wentian were directed against the critics of Tagore, particularly against Wen Yiduo. Wen was in the United States from 1922 to 1925 but the news of Tagore's visit to China appeared so ominous to him that he wrote an article "Taige'er piping" (Criticism of Tagore) in *Shishi Xinbao* in 1923. Wen Yiduo (1899-1946) began his education in the traditional manner by studying classics. Only during his college years he developed an interest in English Romantic poetry. During the May Fourth Movement he was involved in political activities, prepared posters and propaganda leaflets though later he did not indulge in politics any more. He spent more than three years in the USA where he studied painting, and when he returned home in 1925 he was hailed as the pioneer of the formalist movement in Chinese poetry. Some of his early poems, such as "West Coast", "The First Chapter of Spring", "The Tears of Rain" and "The Red Candle", are examples of his power of creating close-knit stanzas and dazzling images. Being trained in the classics, Wen was concerned with the growing influence of Tagore on modern Chinese poetry and was partly responsible for restoring orderly poetic structure against the tide of free verse. In 1926 he wrote his famous essay "The Form of Poetry" wherein he asserted, "No game can be played without rules; no poem can be written without form." His greatest objection against Tagore was formlessness (*meiyou xingshi*). "Tagore's poetry not only has no form," he wrote, "one can also say that it has no contours. That is why his poetry is characterized by monotony. If we read the corpus of his verse from start to finish we are left with the impression of Pimpo, colourless, amoebae." These words remind one almost inevitably of Goethe's criticism of Indian art and sculpture. But Wen's sense of form was mechanical and external, which depended on strict metrical rules and sentence patterns. He never cared to remember that he had read Tagore's works in prose translation and did not enquire about the nature of their forms in the original. Many Chinese poets familiar with Whitman mistook Tagore's English renderings as a new variety of free verse. Wen's classical taste and love for rigour made him averse to any flexibility of metre. Wen's criticism of Tagore, however, went beyond the external formal features:

"The greatest fault in Tagore's art is that he has no grasp of reality. Literature is an expression of life and even metaphysical poetry cannot be an exception. Everyday life is the basic stuff of literature, and the experiences of life are universal things. Therefore, the palace of literature must be built on the foundations of life. Metaphysics is far from life, therefore, to make good literature. Literature becomes all the more difficult to express through the experiences of life. If the metaphysical poet lacks a good grasp of reality, I fear that he will forfeit his qualification as a poet."[26]

Similar charges were made quite frequently against Tagore even by his compatriots and Tagore took great pains in making them realise that his poetry did, indeed, express itself "through the experience of life". Wen thought that Tagore had no love for mundane existence and was interested only in life beyond the world. Wen wrote:

"Tagore's thought is no longer the thought of India because he is influenced by the West. He proclaims 'deliverance is not for me in renunciation'. But this western thought in him is only superficial and the underlying essential Indian thought is impaired. He longs for death much more than he sings hymns for life. From an artistic viewpoint, he is no more than an unknown traveller in this world. His language is replete with abstractions. It is the dialect of some other world, not the slang of the present world of ours."

Wen started with a misconception that Tagore's poetry was an echo of ancient India and wherever he found evidence of a life affirming attitude in Tagore he dismissed it as superficial and irrelevant. One may argue for and against Tagore's grasp of "reality" but to describe his poetry as life negating — "We long for our own home villages in the same way Tagore longs for his other world" — is a gross misunderstanding to say the least.

One feels that Wen's criticism of Tagore is lopsided. He said at the very outset of this article that he would join others in "Welcoming Sir Rabindranath Tagore" who was a "distinguished guest" to China. Then he added that he must address "ourselves — particularly our literary circles", and started with a criticism of Tagore's thought. He wrote that an artist howsoever successful would have his demerits and Tagore was no exception to this rule. He admits that "Tagore can always point out some truth somewhere unexpectedly", and observes that his "poetry is elegantly pretty" and "the greatness of Tagore's poetry lies in his philosophy." But his criticism was rooted mainy in his anxiety about Tagore's strong impact on the young poets. "Our new poetry is already hollow enough, fragile enough, rational enough, and formless enough. With the impact of Tagore it will develop from bad to worse and finally become hopeless in future. I wish to draw the attention of our literary circles to this fact."[27] This is a confession that the detractors of Tagore (or rather the opponents of Tagore's China visit) were driven to criticising him not because of their genuine disappointment with his literary achievement but because of China's internal politics. Wen obviously meant the experiments with free verse and the sudden influx of short verses or aphorisms in China on the model of *Stray Birds.*[28] Guo Moruo in his criticism of Tagore, which I will discuss later, also expressed his displeasure with the popularity of *Stray Birds* which he thought was a product of the influence of Japanese Haiku. Not only Bingxin, but poets like Yu Pingbo and Zhu Ziqing were also attracted towards short verses, obviously under the influence of Tagore.

Once Guo Moruo distinguished two major types of poetry with the help of the metaphor of a bay. "I think the mind of the poet", he wrote, "is like a bay of clear waters. It is calm as a mirror reflecting the myriad phenomena of the universe. But once the wind starts, the waves start to surge and all the phenomena of the universe move within it." The surging waves becoming the vigorous type of poetry like *Divine Comedy, Faust and Paradise Lost*, and the song of Li Bo and Du Fu. The ripples of the waves become the "quiet and lucid" type of poetry of Guofeng of Zhou times, the short lyrics of Wang Wei, and the *Crescent Moon* poems of Tagore.[29] Although by nature Guo had greater affinity with the poets of the first group, he came under the spell of Tagore, the Tagore of the *Crescent Moon* in particular.

In October 1923 when the Tagore controversy was slowly gaining momentum, Guo came out with an article criticising the *Fiction Monthly* for lacking in serious analysis of Tagore and demanding a clear exposition of Tagore's from his host.

> "Why should we invite Tagore? Certainly not to demonstrate our geographical proximity to the Asian poet, not because he is a Nobel laureate, or a knight of the British empire (Guo forgot that Tagore had denounced his Knighthood) or a world famous poet and a reputed orator in Europe?... What is our expectation from him? Has any one tried to understand his thought and has any one told us about it?..... We do not have any clear idea about his thought nor do we have any genuine urgency to listen to him. It is going to be like children playing with dolls and making Tagore an object of pity."

It may be noted that Guo jumped into the fray of the Tagore controversy not on his own but his leftist friends persuaded him to lend his support to the criticising campaign so that the vast youth of China should not be swayed to the conservative camp. Guo had such special feelings for Tagore that he hastened to announce that if anyone thought he was anti-Tagore it would be a mistake. Having made this clear he started his reminiscences. The supposedly anti-Tagore article paradoxically turned out to be an account of Guo's nostalgia for the good old days when he was under Tagore's spell:

> "I first came to know the name of Tagore in 1914. In January of that year I had gone to Japan for the first time. The literary fame of Tagore was at its zenith at that time. In September I entered the preparatory class of the first year of college. I was living with a relative. One day he came with a few sheets in English and told me that they were poems of an Indian poet. They were *Baby's Way, Sleep Stealer,* and *Clouds and Waves.* I read them with great amazement. First, these poems were written with such simplicity, second, the prose style, and third, they were so fresh and lucid. Since that time the name of Tagore became deeply imprinted in my mind. I wanted to buy all his books but they were not easily available in Tokyo as they used to be sold out as soon as they appeared in the market. It took me one year to acquire a copy of the *Crescent Moon.* When I got the book, I felt exuberant like a child.

I think spiritual feelings are products of man's loneliness and suffering. At that time I was far away from home, my mind heavy with the painful memories of a broken marriage. The world before me appeared strange and mysterious. The time between 1916 and 1917 was the most critical and tempestuous in my life. At times I was haunted by the idea of committing suicide, at times I thought of renouncing the world and become a monk .... I used to ask myself whether to accept the world with confidence or to surrender totally to fate. It was at that time I read *Gitanjali, Gardener, The King of the Dark Chamber* and *One Hundred Poems of Kabir.*

I still remember when I got those books in the autumn of 1916 at the Kang Shan library I felt I found my 'life of life', my 'fountain of life.' I used to rush to the library as soon as the classes were over. Sitting in a half-lighted corner I would read a book silently till my eyes becoming moist with tears of gratitude and my body surging gently with joy, the joy of *nirvana.*

But was the attraction of this world more powerful or was I weak? Neither did I commit suicide nor did I become a monk. My son was born in 1917. Just before his birth I asked for some material help from my spiritual master, Tagore. I made a selection of poems from his three books—*The Crescent Moon, The Gardener,* and *Gitanjali* — and sent their translations to a publisher at Shanghai. Tagore was then not widely known in China. My manuscript was rejected by the Commercial Press. I approached another publisher, Chung Hua, and I failed again .... My spiritual ties with Tagore were snapped .... I thought Tagore was a noble man, a sage, and I was an ordinary mortal of little worth. His world was different from mine. I had no right to be there."[30]

In this essay Guo observed that Tagore's thoughts were pantheistic. He had merely cloaked the traditional spirit of India with a western garb. Guo evinced an interest in Tagore (as well as in Goethe) because of his love for pantheism. He discovered pantheism not only in Goethe and Tagore but in the Chinese tradition as well. In a poem *Three Pantheists* (1919) he wrote:

"I love my country's Zhuangzi
Because I love his pantheism
Because I love his making straw sandles for a living

I love Holland's Spinoza
Because I love his pantheism
Because I love his grinding lenses for a living.

I love India's Kabir
Because I love his pantheism
Because I love his making fishnets for a living."

But there was a change in his ideology. He came to believe that the philosophy of historical materialism was the only way to solve the problems of the world. Without a change in the economic structure the poor would continue to suffer and the leisured class, to which Tagore belonged, will talk of the reality of Brahma, the dignity of the soul and the delight of love and use them as opium and wine for the intoxication of the masses. He suspected a sinister design behind the invitation to Tagore.

"If Tagore comes to China as a tourist we welcome him. But if he is invited for some purpose then I cannot but bandy words with his hosts. We wonder about Tagore's being invited to China this time. Is there any particular part of Tagore's thought that is admired by his hosts and what would they demand from him?"

He warned "we hope Tagore will not be a puppet of Beijing and Shanghai." A the same time Guo found it rather unpleasant that his one-time spiritual master should be visiting China without his expressing even a token of welcome. He remembered how Tagore had changed his "poetic style" after visiting Japan. He suggested Tagore should ride on the waves of Yangtze, see the expanse of the Dongting Lake, pass through the precipitous Wu Gorge, ascend the Emei mountain, so that the "heroic nature of our country" might contribute something to his writings. This, perhaps, he thought would be "our only repayment to our indebtedness to him."[31]

Some western scholars regard Guo Moruo as a severe critic of Tagore. They have overlooked the fact that Guo used the world *baoda* (to repay one's indebtedness) in his "severe criticism" of Tagore. Keeping in mind Guo's deep feelings for Tagore one might feel that the use of the word *baoda* is very significant. This article was an evidence of his spiritual communion with Tagore, it was also an evidence of the historical reality that the two had to part ways. In the context of China's socio-political milieu, a man of Guo Moruo's talent and temperament would never admire Tagore. In 1924 Guo had drifted far from Tagore.[32]

Tagore sailed from Calcutta on the Japanese ship *Atsuta Maru* on 21 March 1924. At Hong Kong, the Private Secretary to Sun Yat-sen met Tagore with an invitation from Sun. Since the days of the unsuccessful Reform Movement (1898), the best minds of China gathered round Sun Yat-sen and in 1924 he was certainly the most respected leader in the country. Sun requested Tagore to pay a visit to Canton. He wrote:

> "It is an ancient way of ours to show honour to the scholar. But in you I shall greet not only a writer who has added lustre to Indian letters but a rare worker in those fields of endeavour wherein lie the seeds of man's future welfare and spiritual triumphs."[33]

Tagore thought he was already late and did not want to delay his arrival in North China any further. Little did Tagore realise that when he would reach North China he would be chastised for his delay. His critics announced he was late indeed by a thousand years.

Tagore reached Shanghai on 12 April where he met Xu Zhimo who was to act as Tagore's chief interpreter, Zhang Junmai, and Qu Shiying. The following afternoon Tagore delivered his first speech to a small and select gathering, in which he made it absolutely clear that he was neither a prophet nor a philosopher.

> "For centuries you have had merchants and soldiers and other guests; till this moment, you never thought of asking a poet. Is not this a great fact — not your recognition of my personality, but the homage you thus pay to the spring times of a new age? Do not, then, ask for a message from me. People use pigeons to carry messages; and, in the war time, men valued their wings not to watch them soar, but because they helped to kill. Do not make use of a poet to carry messages."[34]

In this very lecture he said:

> "I am not a philosopher, therefore keep for me room in your heart, not a seat on the public platform. I want to win your heart, now that I am close to you, with the faith that is in me of a great future for you, and for Asia, when your country rises and gives expression to its own spirit — a future in the joy of which we shall all share."

Tagore repeated on several occasions that he was a poet, not a philosopher or a prophet. In his welcome address to Tagore, Liang Qichao said, "Rabindranath Tagore wishes to make it known that he is not a religious teacher or an educationist or a philosopher, he says that he is only a poet."[35]

This clearly indicates that Tagore did not have any particular mission, as suggested by some of the critics, except to re-establish, what he called, "the spiritual relationship" between India and China. It is not that he did not talk about the unity of Asia, the spirituality of the East or the materialism of the west. He did talk about all these issues quite forcefully and unambiguously. He had been talking about these issues all his life.

Two days after Tagore's arrival in Shanghai, Mao Dun wrote an article entitled "Our Expectations from Tagore" in the journal *Juewu* (Consciousness):[36]

> "The poet-saint of India has arrived at last. No sooner did the noble poet dressed in a flowing saffron robe and a red cap, set foot in Shanghai, the gateway of western imperialism, than was he welcomed with thunderous applause. But if one examines the nature of this welcome one notices at least a few discordant notes within it.
>
> An opponent of the western culture and a champion of the East has arrived. Now, certainly he will show us the way and point out our mistakes. China will find out its way to liberation. This is the hope of our scholars infatuated with spirituality and Orientalism.

On the other hand a group of young lovers of literature thinks, 'in this strife-storm world Tagore has created a paradise full of beauty and grace and tranquillity, an abode for the angels of poetry'....

We too respect Tagore. We respect him because he is pure in heart. We respect him because he feels for the oppressed and the underdogs. We respect him because he is on the side of the peasants. We respect him particularly because he is a poet of patriotism, he is a source of inspiration for the Indian youth in their struggle against British imperialism. And that is why, we, too, welcome Tagore.

But we do not welcome the Tagore who loudly sings the praises of the Oriental civilization, nor do we welcome the Tagore who creates a paradise of poetry that has made our youth intoxicated and self-complacent. We welcome the Tagore who works for the upliftment of the peasantry (though we do not support his methods), the Tagore who passionately sings, 'March alone'.....

We believe that the Chinese youth is generally traditional in his outlook, he is weak because of his poor understanding of the reality. The Chinese youth has kept his eyes closed and he is dreaming of a paradise for souls overlooking the 'thorns of life'. He thinks he can escape from the reality by achieving a few moments of bliss. We do not want this feeling to grow, nor do we want any further stimulus that leads our youth towards 'emptiness', anything that tempts him to believe that 'everything can be achieved by doing nothing.'

And that is the reason why we expect these two things from Tagore:

1. We hope Tagore will understand the weakness of the modern Chinese youth. Because they are afraid to face the reality, they want to escape into a world of illusion... In this sickening atmosphere we need someone who can give strength to them; someone who can encourage them to face the reality and to struggle with it.
2. We expect Tagore to oppose the imperialism of the West. He, with his intense patriotism, will be able to demolish the slavish admiration for the West prevailing among a group of people in China.

We believe in the power of poetry and we admire the works of Tagore, which are expressions of a long and untiring struggle. We also join our voice to the chorus of welcome to the great poet. We want to tell the youth of this country that it is their duty in inviting Tagore who works for the peasant, the Tagore who inspires patriotism and the Tagore who urges the Indian youth to oppose British imperialism. We also want the youth of China to know that the gift we expect from Tagore is not a spiritual realization of life, not an empty *Gitanjali*, but a gift of those words that arouse agony and enthusiasm, words such as 'March alone'..."

Within five days of the publication of Mao Dun's impassioned appeal Yun Daiying (1895-1931), one of the founders of the Communist Party of China, who was the editor of *Xin Qingnian* (The New Youth) and also the director of the department of propaganda of the Communist Youth League, wrote, "We will not attack Tagore personally out of any malice. But there is a possibility that he will be used by others. We, therefore, have no option but to oppose him."[37]

Howsoever well-intentioned and cautious these words of Mao Dun and Yun Daiying, the militants did not think it wise to wait any longer. A group of students began to distribute leaflets against Tagore in Shanghai on 17 April, three days after his arrival in China, and were very active at the meeting at Nanjing on 20 April.

What did Tagore speak at Nanjing? Did he try to tempt the youth to believe in an empty spirutalism? Dit he sing loudly the praises of the ancient civilizations of the Orient? Tagore addressed a gathering of thousand students who listened to him without any interruption. Tagore said, "You are here with the gift of your young life which like the morning star, shines with hope for the unborn day of your country's future. I am here to sing the hymn of praise to youth, I who am your poet, the poet of youth."[38] He reminded them of the fairy-tale of the princess taken captive by a giant, who was rescued by a young prince. He expanded the metaphor by identifying the princess with the human soul and the giant with machine. He appealed: "I ask you, my young princes, to feel this enthusiasm in your hearts and to be willing to rescue the human soul from the grip of greed which keeps it chained." Tagore went on to describe the different stages of man's progress and concluded that a "combination of brute and intellect has given rise to a terror which is stupid in its passion and yet cunning in its weapons; it is blindness made efficient and, therefore, more destructive than all other forces in the world." He declared:

> "But a new time has come, the time to discover another great power, the power that gives us strength to suffer and not merely to cause suffering, the immense power of sacrifice ... Come to the rescue and free the human soul from the dungeon of the Machine. Proclaim the Spirit of Man and prove that it lies not in machine guns and cleverness, but in a simple faith."

It is unnecessary to go into the details to Tagore's itinerary which included visits to several educational institutions and Buddhist organisations. But his visit to Qufu to pay homage to the tomb of Confucius as well as his meeting with Qi Xieyuan, the warlord controlling Jiangsu, Jiangxi and Anhui must have raised many eyebrows. His meeting with the deposed Emperor Puyi at the Forbidden city,[39] first time by any foreigner since 1912, added fuel to the fire of criticism that had been spreading. Before he reached Beijing, Tagore must have come to realise the feelings of antagonism towards him, though he was not aware of the magnitude and intensity of these feelings.

In the first public meeting at Beijing, near Zhonghai, the Middle Lake of the Imperial Palace, where Liang Qichao introduced him formally to the leading intellectuals of China, Tagore mused again on his favourite theme, faith in the spiritual perfection of life. In a talk to the boys and girls at Beihai, another scenic spot of the erstwhile palace, he talked about Asian unity, but admitted that "We have a great thing to accept from the people of the West their treasure of intellect, which is immense and whose superiority we must acknowledge." In the same breath he reminded his audience that "it would be degradation on our past; and an insult to our ancestors, if we forget our own moral wealth of wisdom, which is of far greater value than a system that produces endless materials and a physical power that is always on the warpath."[40]

This lecture could have been easily misconstrued as a defence of Liang's views on the western civilisation. Tagore certainly did share his view of the western civilisation and the role of science without abandoning what was best in one's own traditions. Tagore said very emphatically, "We must accept truth when it comes from the West ... unless we accept it our civilization will be one-sided, it will remain stagnant. Science gives us the power of reason, enabling us to be actively conscious of the worth of our own ideals." One section of the Chinese intellectuals, however, was determined by then to oppose Tagore at all cost. His words fell on deaf ears.

Liang in his welcome address explained the reasons for inviting Tagore. He reminded the audience that Tagore came from a "country which is our nearest and dearest brother — India." He talked about the history of India-China relationship from the ancient days in the fields of religion and philosophy, music, painting and architecture, sculpture, drama and poetry, astronomy and calendar, medicine and education. "Rabindranath Tagore is as important to us as Asvaghosha," he said, ".... and we hope the influence he is going to exert on China will not in any way be inferior to that of Kumarajiva and Cheng Ti." Despite the storm of hostility that was gathering momentum, Liang spoke with emotion, "the responsibility that we bear to the whole mankind is great indeed, and there should be, I think, a warm spirit of cooperation between India and China."

This speech was important if only because it was the first clear statement coming from Liang stating the main objective of Tagore's visit to China. He expected Tagore's visit to China would re-establish the age-old contacts between the two civilizations. Tagore on his part repeatedly emphasised that his mission was to find out ways to re-establish the ancient contacts between India and China. He talked of an Asian unity but not with any political motivation. "In Asia we must seek our strength in union, in an unwavering faith in righteousness, and never in the egotistic spirit of separateness and self assertion."[41] If he mentioned Asia in particular it is because of his disillusionment with the war-ravaged Europe and partly because of his attitude towards the Westophiles both in India and China. But he never failed to affirm that the ideals of his institution, Visva-Bharati, stretched beyond all national frontiers. "No one nation today can progress," he said, "if the others are left outside its boundaries. Let us try to win the heart of the West with all that is beast and not in revenge or contempt, but with goodwill and understanding, in a spirit of mutual respect."[42] He mentioned that Visva-Bharati represented that ideal of cooperation, of the spiritual unity of men and he made a fervent appeal to his Chinese "brothers and sisters" to take part in it, and thus fulfil a mission that began many centuries ago. It is a travesty of truth to say that Tagore went to China to talk only about Asian brotherhood and to criticise the west.

In the next meeting on 26 April, Liang repeated his welcome address at the National Normal University obviously to stress that his invitation to Tagore was to provide an occasion to renew the relationship between the two countries and to establish a really "constructive scheme of cooperation." Tagore, now more or less aware of the opposition to his visit, came out openly to respond to his opponents:[43]

> "I even heard some were opposed to my coming, because it might check your special modern enthusiasm for western progress and force. True, if you want a man who will help you in these things you have mistaken in asking me. I have no help to give you here: you already have ten thousand able teachers: go to them."

But he warned: "those who would have you rely on material force to make a strong nation, do not know history, or understand civilization either. Reliance on power is the characteristic of barbarism; nations that trusted to it have already been destroyed or have remained barbarous."

This interpretation of history-reliance on power and the concomitant disaster — whatever be its worth, was undoubtedly a forthright condemnation of some of the leading politicians of Tagore's time. Tagore had anticipated some of the arguments of his opponents. If power was so vicious and dangerous, how was it that the western countries were at the zenith of prosperity? Why was it that India with her rich spiritual heritage had been turned into a nation of hungry millions? "But many will point to the weakness of China and India," Tagore said, "and tell you that thrown as we are among the strong and progressive people, it is necessary to emphasize power and progress in order to avoid destruction." Tagore's words failed to convince his critics. He said, "Even at the cost of martyrdom and insult and suffering we must continue to believe in peace and love and kindness and idealism." It is not that his opponents did not believe in the value of peace and love and kindness and idealism but they were more concerned about ways to relieve the people of their suffering and humiliation. Tagore declared that:

> "My enemies may dominate and slay my body, but they cannot make me adopt their methods or hate them. The devil helps in the sphere in which he is master, but we must reject such aid if we want to save our life from utter destruction. Seek righteousness even though success be lost."

These were noble words, words spoken with force and truth of experience. But the idea of "righteousness" based on certain principles, which Tagore believed to be valid for all time, appeared too vague and nebulous to the section of the Chinese youth committed to building a new China. Tagore's words were of little use for them.

But Tagore was certainly not a puppet in the hands of Liang. He did not speak against material progress as such, nor did he eulogise poverty. What he urged was to take lessons from western civilization which was at the cross-roads of history. Power and material progress, Tagore asserted, could not be the ultimate goal of any civilization. Had there been a straightforward dialogue between Tagore and his critics much of the differences could have been resolved. Tagore's frequent use of the terms "the soul" and the "spirit" made his critics more and more suspicious about his designs. They attacked him with greater ferocity.

In a meeting at the Navy Club, Tagore spoke for the first time about his literary career, the revolutionary role he had played in the growth of Bengali literature, the attempts he had made to modernise its style and the experiments he had carried out to break new grounds in respect of themes and forms and metres. He spoke about his songs, that they "have found their place in the heart of my land" and that "the folk of the future, in days of joy or sorrow or festival, will have to sing them." Tagore claimed "this too is the work of a revolutionist."

Hu Shi, who pioneered the movement towards the modernisation of the Chinese language and successfully replaced the rigorous and obsolete classical style by the vigorous and natural *baihua*, immediately recognised the points of similarity between the experiments of Tagore and those of modern Chinese writers. Lin Changmin who was also present at the meeting spoke about the limitations of contemporary Chinese poetry caused by oversophistication and of the unsuccssful experiments to overcome the constraints of conventions. China was waiting for new poets, he said, "poets of revolutionary temper" who could break the chains of traditions. He described Tagore as an "arch-revolutionary" who could inspire Chinese poetry of the future.[44] In his reply Tagore, too, described himself as a "revolutionary" not to please his host but bcause he was just that. His audience in China had no opportunity to know — and Tagore did not tell them either — that in September-October of 1923 when the controversy about the news of his visit to China was raging he was busy writing a play — *Rather Rashi*. One of the characters in it is a poet. That poet says: "We obey the rules of rhythm, because there can't be music without it. We know that only Beauty can guide the ship of Power. You have faith only in austerity — austerity of cannons and of guns. That is the faith of the cowards and the weak." Precisely that was what Tagore meant when he declared himself a "revolutionary."

Mei Lanfang (1894-1961), an outstanding Beijing Opera artist who visited the Soviet Union early in life, in one of his articles on Tagore,[45] mentions an incident worth recalling. When he was in Hangzhou, Tagore was presented with a seal on which were inscribed three words —*Tai ge er.* Tagore was reported to have said that the two important ceremonies in the life of an Indian child were *namakarana* (naming) and *annaprasana* (taking of rice). The word *Tai* which happened to be the first letter of Tagore's name, was the name of one of the five sacred hills of China. Tagore said, "I thought as if I too, following the footsteps of Buddha, had got the right of access into the life and into the experience of the Chinese people. My life had got entwined with theirs."

The similarity between the name of Tagore and the Mount Taishan is a mere coincidence. He, however, was given a Chinese name, and that too on his birthday. The Crescent Moon Society arranged a function to celebrate the sixty-fourth birthday of the poet. In the presence of 400 distinguished citizens, Liang Qichao presented the poet with a stone-tablet inscribed on it in beautiful calligraphy: *Zhu Zhendan*, a Chinese name for Rabindranath. Contrary to the common practice of phonetic translation of foreign words, Liang chose *Zhen* which means a sudden flash out of the cloudy sky, implying the thunder god *Indra*, and *dan* (literally, *dawn*) indicating the sun, to translate the word Rabindra. Zhu is a shortened form of *Tianzhu* (meaning "heavenly India"), traditionally used as a surname for all those who came to China from India in ancient times. Liang said on this occasion:

> "The two characters, *Zhen* and *dan* have profound symbolic significance. Zhen means a sudden shock out of the cloudy atmosphere and dim sky. Then there is clearness. The beautiful sun which had just appeared in Japan emerges of the horizon (that is what the character *dan* signifies). What a scene! The original meaning of "Rabindranath" is contained in it. There would be no more apt rendering of the world than Zhendan. In ancient times from Han to Jin dynasty, all eminent monks arriving from the west had Chniese names. In most of the cases their sunames represented countries from which they came. All those who came from India had the surname *Zhu* ... Today our respected and beloved Indian poet celebrates his sixty fourth birthday. With all sincerity and great joy I offer him this name *Zhou Zhendan*, which joins both countries.[46] I wish that with this name, a token of our warm affection for him, our love will remain imprinted for ever in his heart. I wish the revival of the old friendship between the Indian and the Chinese peoples in this person whose name is *Zhu Zhendan*."[47]

Hu Shi offered the poet a scroll containing a poem of his own, *Parinaman*, as a memento of the close historical and cultural relationship between China and India. He hoped that the relationship would be renewed through the visit of the Indian poet. Tagore also spoke with emotion about Sino-Indian friendship. After the speeches were over, *Chitra* was staged in which both Xu Zhimo and Lin Huiyin played the roles of the god of love and princess Chitra respectively.

Present in the audience on this occasion was the most celebrated Chinese writer Lu Xun. His views on the value of tradition were radically opposed to those of Tagore and there is very little evidence of his familiarity with Tagore's writings. Most probably he was present at the birthday celebrations at the instance of his friend Hu Shi. In a letter to Hu Shi dated 27 May 1924 he mentioned about this function at the auditorium of *Xiehe* (Concord) and described Tagore's speech as a "grand discourse."[48] Three years later in his famous speech delivered at the Hong Kong YMCA he said that all the ancient civilisations of the world, Chinese and Egyptian included, had lost their voices. Nor was there any voice in Annam and Korea. There was only one voice still living and that was the voice of Tagore in India.[49] On the occasion of the birthday celebration of Tagore, however, Lu Xun was far from happy with Tagore's hosts. They tried to create a mystical atmosphere with burning incense. Some of them appeared with "Indian caps" on the stage. That also repelled Lu Xun. He wrote in disgust: "The way Xu Zhimo introduced the poet was as if he was a living god."[50] Later he wrote, "had not Xu Zhimo and his friends tried to idolize Tagore, our youth would not have felt so alienated from the respected poet."[51]

Tagore arrived at Zhenguang, the largest theatre hall in Beijing, the next morning to deliver his first formal lecture under the auspices of the Beijing Lecture Association. Tagore took this opportunity to make a strong rebuttal against his critics who considered him "out of date in this modern age". In India, Tagore said, he had been often condemned as "too crassly modern", as some one who had "missed all the great lessons from the past." He noted with a touch of sadness, "For your people I am obsolete, and therefore useless, and for mine new fangled and therefore obnoxious." He asked, why had he been so continually suspected to be contraband — smuggled on to the wrong shore of time? This also gave him an opportunity for introspection and to tell his audience about his background and his relation with the forces of social change in India. He talked about the movement launched by Rammohun Roy to reform the religious life of Bengal, of the literary movement initiated by Bankim Chandra Chatterji, and also of the "national movements" which gave confidence to the people in asserting their own personality. And all these movements, he asserted, were revolutionary in character. These movements, as all great human movements are, according to him, were related to some great ideal — the ideal of revelation of the spirit in man. If he was criticised as a pedlar of dreams and spirituality or as an obsolete specimen of the past, his reply would be : "the revelation of spirit in man is truly modern, I am on its side, for I am modern." He concluded his talk with an open challenge to his critics: "If you want to reject me, you are free to do so. But I have my right as a revolutionary to carry the flag of freedom of spirit into the shrine of your idols — material power and accumulation."[52]

These words were spoken with anger but not without conviction. Tagore did realise that the propaganda against him was too well-organised to be ignored. And the best thing for him was to face it with courage. This, however, provoked his critics to launch a counter-attack with greater ferocity. Next morning a group of young men was seen distributing handbills before he started his second lecture. He announced that he was combining two lectures into one.[53]

In this lecture Tagore used the story of "Jack the Giant Killer" to identify the monstrosities of modern civilisation with the giant, and the spirit of life with Jack. He had been condemned as a reactionary and a fanatical conservative, he mentioned, by men who had confused ideas about modernity and progress, and were unable to distinguish between truth and superstition:

> "I preach the freedom of man from the servitude of the fetish of hugeness, the non-human. I refuse to be styled an enemy of enlightenment because I do not stand on the side of the giant who swallows life, but on the side of Jack, the human, who defies the big, the gross, and wins victory at the end."

Soon after the lecture Tagore inquired about the contents of the leaflets he saw being distributed in the hall. His embarrassed hosts gave a brief and diluted version of the contents. Tagore, however, was not satisfied. Thanks to a group of Japanese visitors, he came to know of the full text what was actually a series of victriolic indictments against him. Even before he came to know of this, he wanted to talk to his critics; Hu Shi promised to arrange a meeting which did not take place.

The leaflets charged Tagore with the attempt to "indoctrinate" the Chinese youth. It was also alleged that he wanted China to go back to her inhuman ancient civilization and that he reproached the Chinese youth for their attempt to improve the material conditions of their society; his theory of soul and Brahma preached inaction and passivity and his defence of the spiritual aspects of the Chinese civilization was actually a defence of the barbarity of the ruling class throughout the ages.[54] Tagore felt that "these people are determined to misunderstand me" and decided to deliver only one more talk.

Word spread quickly. Nearly 2,000 young men and women came to listen to him on 12 May. Xu Zhimo delivered an eloquent speech on Tagore's thought and personality:

> "He advocates creative life, spiritual freedom, internal peace, educational progress, and the realisation of universal love. But they say he is a spy for the imperialists, an agent of capitalism, an exile from the endowed people of conquered country, a madman who advocates foot binding! There is filth in the hearts of our politicians and bandits, but what has this [to] do with our poet? There is confusion in the brains of our would-be scholars and men of letters, but what has this to do with our poet?"[55]

Hu Shi also appealed to the audience to listen to the gest with courtesy and toleration. Tagore in his speech, again asked his audience not to confuse between westernisation and modernisation. All that was western was not necessarily modern. All that was western must not be accepted uncritically.[56]

The lecture series came to an abrupt end. Tagore left Beijing for the Western Hills but he returned to the city after four days to attend a farewell party. On the morning of 18 May there was an unexpected gathering of students at the National Peking University. Withdrawn and dejected as he was, Tagore spoke with pain: "What do you want from me? ... You may call me uneducated, uncultured, just a foolish poet; you may grow great as scholars and philosophers, and yet I think I would still retain the right to laugh at your prudent scholarship." He regretted that he could not present himself as his true self. Had they known his poems, they would not have come to listen to his lectures, but his poetry. Then he went on, as if he was talking to himself.

"I have come to the secret of existence in some other way — not through analysis, but as the mother's chamber can be approached by a child. I had kept the spirit of the child fresh within me; because of this I have found entry to my mother's chamber wherein a symphony of awakening light sang to me from the distant horizon, in response to which I also sing, because of this I stand close to you, the young hearts of a foreign country whom my heart recognises as its fellow voyagers in the path of dreamland."[57]

These words must have had their desired impact on the young minds. Tagore realised that the gap between him and his audience was not unbridgeable. He could speak effectively and beautifully through his poems and plays, but "languages are jealous" and "poems are not like gold or other substantial things that are transferable."

Tagore was certainly happy to watch his play *Sannyasi* staged at Taiyuan, the capital of Shanxi — where he went soon after his unpleasant stay in Beijing — before an audience of 3,000 men and women. Here he met General Yan Xishan, known as the Model Governor, who expressed enthusiasm in Tagore's programme of Sino-Indian understanding. His critics, however, were still active and spared no opportunity to malign him. On his way to Shanghai, Tagore stopped at Hankou. In the course of his lecture there he met a vociferous group which shouted "Go back slave from a lost country" with such fury that friends of Tagore ran towards him to prevent the possibility of a physical assault. "My enemies may dominate and slay my body" Tagore said at Beijing, "but they cannot make me adopt their methods, or hate them." He remained composed and true to his faith. That very afternoon he spoke again on the same theme: moral force and physical power, to another audience at the nearby town of Wuchang. Voices of opposition dogged him till the day he left the shores of China.

A farewell meeting was arranged in the same garden in Shanghai where the Chinese had welcomed Tagore only a few weeks ago in April. The tempestous trip had ended and the poet was exhausted and tired. When his host Zhang Junmai requested him to offer some frank criticism of China Tagore declined to do so. He said,

"I absolutely refuse to accede to your request. You have critics innumerable, and I do not want to be added to their ranks. Being human myself, I can make allowances for your shortcomings, and I love you in spite of them... I have done what was possible — I have made friends."

Tagore did not criticise anyone but at the same time he rebutted the charges of his opponents with a gentle irony:

"Some of your patriots were afraid that, carrying from India spiritual contagion, I might weaken your vigorous faith in money and materialism. I assure those who thus feel nervous that I am entirely inoffensive; I am powerless to impair the career of progress, to hold them back from rushing to the market place to sell the soul in which they do not believe. I can even assure them that I have not convinced a single sceptic that he has a soul, or that moral beauty has greater value than material power. I am certain that they will forgive me when they know the result."[58]

These were his last words in China. On 30 May 1924 Tagore sailed from Shanghai to Japan.

Lu Xun complained that Xu Zhimo and his group had projected Tagore as a living idol and that had alienated him from the younger generation. Such criticism must have reached Tagore's ears too. He said in his farewell speech:

"There are so many who would deprive me of the contact of reality by trying to turn me into an idol. I feel certain that God himself is hurt because men keep their daily love for fellow beings in their homes, and only their weekly worship for Him in the Church. I am glad that my young friends in China never made these mistakes but treated me as their fellow human being."

Several intellectuals, however, felt unhappy with the nature of remonstrance against Tagore. Mao Dun, Qu Qiubai, Yun Daiying — all of them criticised certain aspect of Tagore's thought but all of them had special regard for him. But the movement that they initiated went beyond their control and assumed a proportion they had hardly anticipated. Mao Zemin (1896-1943), the younger brother of Mao Zedong, found Tagore's poems endearing and his essays and short stories delightful, although he considered Tagore's thought an impediment to the development of the youth of China. Qu Qiubai rated *The Home and the World* very high as a work of art, and thought it was unfair to criticise Tagore personally. A month after Tagore had left China, Zhou Zuoren, the brother of Lu Xun felt obliged to denounce the anti-Tagore agitation in strong terms, though he was totally indifferent to Tagore's works. He wrote: "Its (Oppose Tagore Movement) followers think they are scientific thinkers and Westernizers, but they lack the spirit of scepticism and toleration. Actually they are still the kind of Orientals who persecute heretics. If Eastern civilisation contains poisons of the worst kind, then this sort of authoritarian fanaticism is one."[59]

Five years later Tian Han, the author of the national anthem of China, admitted that the opponents of Tagore were mistaken. And the irony of fate is that Tagore who was considered anti-modern, anti-progress, reactionary and obsolete by the young communists, was also dreaded by the Shanghai District Kuomintang in 1929 for his views. The Kuomintang District office had issued instructions to all public situations that year when Tagore stopped at Shanghai on his way to Japan, not to welcome the Indian poet whose doctrines were "just as dangerous and poisonous as those of Karl Marx."[60]

It is worth quoting a few passages from an article [61] by Tan Chung as it summarises the main features of the anti-Tagore agitation led by Chen Duxiu during Tagore's stay in China:

> "*Xiangdao*, the first mouthpiece of the Chinese Communist Party followed Tagore's itinerary in China with short snippets written by Chen Duxiu and an unidentified pseudonym, "Shi'an", in 10 one-paragraph comments (a total of about 600 words) from 23 April to 10 July 1924. Chen Duxiu was an exponent of the May Fourth Movement and had the dubious honour of being the founder of the Chinese Communist Party only to be expelled by it after six years. Interestingly, he was probably the first to translate Tagore into Chinese....
>
> However, Chen Duxiu and his colleagues viewed Tagore's proceedings in China in 1924 with dismay. In the first place, as Shi'an confessed, they were concerned that such a giant figure as Tagore would bring unhealthy ideological influences to the youth of China on whom the Chinese Communist Party depended to launch a great revolution. It was for this reason that the *Guide Weekly* published in April 1924 an article written by the party leader Qu Qiubai to comment on Tagore's perception of the state and criticised his "Oriental culture". The article ended with a sarcastic remark : "Thank you, Mr. Tagore! But we have already had too may Confuciuses and Menciuses in China!"
>
> By the end of May, when Tagore was leaving Shanghai, Shi'an remarked that they had over-estimated Tagore's spiritual influence, and noted that the poet had not lived up to his saintly reputation and had mixed with unworthy companions such as the deposed Chinese emperor, diplomats of the imperialist powers, Buddhist monks and female Buddhist followers, and the well known Beijing Opera maestro, Mei Lanfang. He also quoted someone in Beijing commenting that Tagore was "no poet, but a politician." He observed that Tagore never talked about poetry during the entire course of his visit. Shi'an also quoted the advice of the eminent Kuomintang leader, Wu Zhihui, "Tagore, Compose your poems. When you can't manage someone else's country don't discuss world affairs." Chen Duxiu viewed Tagore's peace movement as advice to the Chinese to be servile to the imperialists.
>
> Tagore's spiritualism became an object of the duo's attack. Shi'an commented that the "representative of Oriental Culture" in Tagore had degenerated into a "heartless" person when he hobnobbed with ex-Finance Minister, Liang Qichao, forgetting about the starving millions of the world. Chen Duxiu wanted to expose the hypocrisy of Tagore's "spiritual life" by pointing out that Tagore accepted donations in Hong Kong for Visva-Bharati. Shi'an contested Tagore's self-proclaimed opposition to materialism and challenged the poet to distribute the money he received with the Nobel prize among the Indians who had no food and clothing.
>
> According to some critics, Tagore's mission to China had failed. But what was his mission? If we believe Tagore, his mission was to explore the possibility of cooperation between India and China. At the farewell address in Beijing Tagore said that he had accepted the Chinese invitation with a hope to "reopen the ancient channel of spiritual communication once again." The response of the Chinese intellectuals, however, was not warm. Lu Xun wrote sarcastically in November 1924 that Tagore's visit was like a giant bottle of superior scent which 'fumigated several gentlemen with literary and metaphysical flavour.' But soon after he left, 'We have seldom seen the Indian caps on our Cinasthana poets' heads any more nor were there news dispatches about Tagore'. While Chen Duxiu and Shi'an were obviously uncharitable to Tagore, Lu Xun's sarcasm revealed some truth about the whole controversy which was actually between two groups of

Chinese intellectuals. Not only was he an international figure of repute but Tagore had cast his "magical spell" (*moli*) — as described by some contemporary Chinese commentators — on some young intellectuals long before he had set foot on Chinese soil. The whole episode resembled the appearance of a comet in ancient China. Whenever it was sighted the comet became the central topic of speculation with baseless rumours about the possible fall of the government or the break out of a natural calamity. For Chinese political astrologers Tagore had assumed the proportion of a comet, which in a way is an acknowledgement of his importance in modern intellectual history of China."

Ji Xianlin has tried to give a more or less authoritative assessment of the controversial Tagore visit to China in his article "Tagore and China" (*Tiage'er yu Zhongguo*). He makes the following points:

1. It can be asserted that some interested groups in China wanted to play up Tagore's visit for the "backward influence" (*luohou shili*) lobby despite Hu Shi's contradiction. The Chinese hosts of Tagore never projected his anti-feudal and anti-imperialist dimensions.
2. At a time when class struggle was intensified in China the wrong projection of Tagore would naturally have a negative effect. And Tagore on his part "cannot but share the responsibility of not expressing his views in a balanced manner. He had over-stressed the role and significance of the Oriental culture and severely criticized the materialistic culture of the West in his China speeches." At no point was it clarified to his audience that Tagore never negated western modern science and technology and that he had appealed to the Indian people to acquire them.
3. There was a duality in Tagore's character and writings. "He had one face, that of a sage and another that of a warrior." He could lead a secluded life in the countryside and create poems out of his meditations amidst nature, but when he had seen the demoiac designs of the fascists, the militants and other devils he flared up with anger and created poems and essays as sharp as swords. It was the lapse of his hosts to project both sides of the poet. And that is why Lu Xun blamed the "Cinasthanis (Chinese) clad in Indian caps" (i.e., the hosts of Tagore) for their failure.
4. On the whole, however, Tagore's visit was a success as it promoted Chinese translations of his works and enlarged the area of their influence on Chinese life and it certainly strengthened the friendship between the two countries and reopened the avenues of Sino-Indian cultural intercourse.[62]

Despite all misunderstandings and hostilities, Tagore, too, felt "some path has been opened." He talked of his institution where men of different countries speaking different languages could come together. His mission was to establish 'the spiritual unity of man." In his final lecture in China he said, "I have done what was possible — I have made friends.' An anecdote related by Bing Xin in 1981 is worth recalling: "In 1924 when Tagore visited China, I was a student in the USA. Later I heard this from one who was with him at that time. When Tagore was leaving Beijing somebody asked him: 'I hope you have not left anything.' Tagore shook his head gently and said in a sad voice, 'Nothing except a portion of my heart!'"[63]

Since 1912 Tagore had visited many countries and everywhere he spoke on a few recurrent themes with remarkable consistency. During his first visit to America (1912-13), for example, he delivered lectures on "World Realization", "Self Realization" "Ideals of the Ancient Civilization of India" and "The Problem of Evil"[64]. On his second visit (1916-17) he spoke mostly against the cult of nationalism. On his third visit he spoke about the meeting of East and West and his religious experience. Any one familiar with *Sadhana* (1913), *Nationalism* (1917), *Personality* (1917) and *Creative Unity* (1922) will hardly find any departure from the basic issues in his *Talks in China*. His essential faith in the spiritual unity of man, his deep-rooted prejudices against materialism, his passionate attraction towards nature and veneration for the forest civilisation of ancient India and some of the doctrines of the *Upanisads* regulated all the activities of his life. "Men have been born in this world of nature, with our human limitations and appetites, and yet proved that they breathed in the world of spirit", wrote Tagore in an essay, *"The Second Birth"* included in *Personality*, and this had been a guiding thought for Tagore. Regarding Western civilisation he thought that the West with its "cult of power" and "idolatry of money" had in a great measure reverted man "to his primitive barbarism, a barbarism whose path is lit up by the lurid light of intellect."[65] He condemned the West, not because he was anti-progress or anti-science, but because he found that the "ideal of whole" had lost its force there, and he had seen in the recent events of history how individuals "freed from moral and spiritual bonds" found "a boisterous joy in a debauchery of destruction." He may have found a few sympathetic listeners in the West but in the long run he had to accept the fact that his was a voice in the wilderness. His Chinese experience was not basically different from his experiences in America, Europe and Japan. The hostility in China was more pronounced and well organised but that does not mean that Tagore was not criticised in other countries or that his ideas were welcomed. Stephen Hay in his summing up of Tagore's impact on Chinese youth writes that "nothing the Indian poet said could divert these ardent patriots from their pursuit of a new and more viable political order." Tagore certainly did not oppose the pursuit of "a new and more viable political order" either in China or in any other country. The enthusiasm with which Tagore hailed the new social experiments in Soviet Russia — "The cry of the Russian Revolution is also the cry of the world" — gives lie to all suspicions about Tagore, that he was impatient with the younger generation of China for their radicalism. Tagore's message was ignored by China and by the west and indeed also by his own country. It was not because it was false but because it was too demanding. China did not accept John Dewey or Bertrand Russell either but there were no organised demonstrations against them. In the case of Tagore, the leaders of the new generation perceived Tagore to be a serious threat and hence there were loud protests. Tagore in his capacity as an artist and thinker could only warn against the course of the modern civilization. He carried out his responsibility splendidly without fear or hesitation. When others did not respond to him, he marched alone.

Hay has tried to give an impression that Tagore asked the Chinese to "accept another wave of cultural influence from India" and the "possibility that China might contribute to an equal degree to the development of Indian culture."[66] Tagore mentiond several times that scholars from India came to China, and Liang certainly talked about Indian influence on Chinese thought. But it is ridiculous to suggest that Tagore persuaded China to "accept another wave of cultural influence from India." He asked for a closer relationship, a better understanding, not for a one-sided flow of thought. Comparing Chinese civilization with others Tagore found in it (particularly in its literature) a "spirit of hospitality" and he felt he had "drunk from its cup some draught of *amrita*, of deathlessness, because of which we who come from another land feel at home in this land of ancient civilization."[67] In his first "public lecture" he said how he had been fascinated by the quality of Chinese poetry: "I have not seen anything like it in any other literature that I know of."[68] Tagore did not ask the Chinese to accept another wave of Indian influence but to join him in his experiment of building institutions based on "the ideal of the spiritual unity of all races." He was fascinated by individualities of any race: "Let all human races keep their own personalities," he wrote, "and yet come together, not in a uniformity that is dead, but in a unity that is living."[69] Tagore mentions a picture, carved upon a rock, of an Indian monk whom a Chinese was offering food. Tagore saw in it "a most beautiful piece of symbolism." It was a symbol, he thought, of love and hospitality, not of domination or hegemony.

Tagore raised two basic questions, one about the relation between tradition and modernity, and the other about the usual identification of modernisation with westernisation. Since the May Fourth Movement, China was also concerned with these questions and Chinese intellectuals came out with different answers. If the essence of the ancient Chinese civilization was responsible for China's material degradation, as it was thought by many, it was most natural to question its relevance. If materialism was so degrading, as claimed by Tagore, his audience had a right to ask for the ways and means to reduce human suffering. Tagore did not give any practical programme, nor could he convince any one how to reconcile the spirit of the ancient culture with the forces of modernisation. He only intensified the crisis by raising questions. These questions could be ignored for some time, but not for all time. These questions were important not only for China but for India as well.

"I have done what was possible — I have made friends", said Tagore before leaving China. He continued to do what was possible for him. He devoted much of his energy in the last decade of his life to establishing Sino-Indian contacts. *Cheena-Bhavana* was founded in 1937; it flourished under the guidance of Tan Yun-shan, a native of Hunan province and a school-mate of Mao Zedong. The great Chinese painter Xu Beihong came to Santiniketan in 1940. Tagore urged Indians to learn the Chinese language and history and painting to live up to the spirit of the symbolism he witnessed in China: an Indian monk accepting offerings from a Chinese. It is significant that in 1941, six months before his death, Tagore celebrated the day he was given the new name "Zhu Zhendan" in a poem concluding with the sentence: "Wherever we find friends there begins a new life."

Notes

1. For details see Chow Tse-tsung, *The May Fourth Movement* (Stanford, 1959), p. 187f.
2. *Visva-Bharati Bulletin*, "Rabindranath Tagore's Visit to China", No. 1, Pt. I, "From Calcutta to Peking", May 1924, Pt. II, "In China", June 1924, p. III.
3. For a critical review of this book by Subir Ray Chaudhuri, see *Jadavpur Journal of Comparative Literature*, Vol. IX. Xu Zhimo who was Tagore's interpreter in his entire China visit, left behind his translations of the three speeches delivered by Tagore, i.e., his first speech in Shanghai (13 April), his speech in Beijing (1 May) and farewell speech in Shanghai (22 May). These translations were published in *Xiaoshuo Yuebao* in 1924 and are now included in *Xu Zhimo Quanji*, Vol. IV, pp. 189-216.
4. These materials were used in the Bengali work by Sisir Kumar Das and Tan Wen, *Bitarkita Atithi* (Calcutta: Prama, 1985); and also in Sisir Kumar Das, "Hostility During China Visit", *The Statesman*, 8 May 1985.
5. For this piece of information I am indebted to Ni Peigeng of the Institute of Foreign Literature of the Chinese Academy of Social Sciences, and Hua Yuqing of the Department of Chinese, Hangzhou University.
6. This journal which became the mouth piece of the Communist Party of China later, published Tagore's "On the Sea Shore" from *The Crescent Moon*, in Vol. V, No. 3, 1918. It was translated by Liu Bannong.
7. Quoted in Jonathan Spence, *The Gate of Heavenly Peace* (Penguin, 1981), pp. 257-58. Lines in italics are from the English edition of Gitanjali.
8. Zheng Zhenduo was the first Chinese biographer of Tagore. His biography of Tagore, *Tai Ge'er Zhuan*, was published in 1926.
9. Published in *Chen-Pao*, 31 May 1924, quoted in Hay, *op. cit.*, p. 214.
10. See Wm. Theodore de Bary *et al. (eds.)*, *Sources of Chinese Tradition* (Columbia University Press, 1960), Ch. XXVIII, pp. 820-24, 825-29.
11. See Amitendranath Tagore, *Literary Debates in Modern China*, 1918-1937 (Tokyo: The Centre for East Asian Cultural Studies, 1967), p. 37f.
12. For useful study of Liang see, Joseph R. Levenson, *Liang Chi-ch'ao*(Berkeley : University of California Press, 1970).
13. Quoted in Chow Tse-tsung, *op. cit.*, p. 328.
14. *Guo Moruo Wen-ji*, No. 7, p. 185, quoted in Julia C. Lin, *Modern Chinese poetry* (Seattle and London, 1972), p. 221.
15. Julia C. Lin, *ibid.*, p. 35f.
16. Hu Shi became quite a politician in his later life, and even became Taiwan's ambassador to the USA. For Hu Shi's life and thought see Sung Peng-Hsu, "Hu Shih", in Donald H. Bishop (Ed.), *Chinese Thought* (Delhi, 1985), pp. 364-91.
17. See Leo Ou-fan Lee, *The Romantic Generation of Modern Chinese Writers* (Harvard University Press, 1973), p. 124f.
18. Prefatory Poem to *Goddesses* (trs. David Roy), Kuo Mo-jo : *The Early Years* (Cambridge, Mass., 1971), p. 143.
19. Kalidas Nag (ed.), *Tagore and China* (Calcutta, 1945), p. 34.
20. *Talks in China* (Visva-Bharati, 1925), p. 116.
21. See Witold Rodzinski, *A History of China*, I (Oxford : Pergamon Press, 1979), p. 246-49.
22. *Lun Targe'er, op. cit.*, pp. 35-40, (Translated with the help of Tan Chung and Tan Wen.)
23. *Xu Zhimo quanji* (Essays), (trs. Tan Chung), Vol. IV, pp. 174-75.
24. *Ibid.*, pp. 166-68.
25. *Xiaoshuo Yuehao*, Vol. XIII, No. 2, 1923.

26. Quoted by Patricia Uberoi, "Tagore in China", *China Report*, Vol. X. No. 3, May-June 1974, p. 39. Patricia's translation is adopted with slight modifications. Also see Uberoi, "Tagore in China : A Chinese *Poet's* View", *Indian Literature*, Vol. XVI, Nos. 1-2, 1973.
27. *Wen Yiduo quanji*, Vol. III. p. 445 (trs. Tan Chung).
28. Bingxin or Xie Bingxin (1902-68) was a Chinese poetess who admitted her indebtedness to Tagore in the preface of her book *Stars.*
29. *Guo Moruo Wenji*, 7 : 12 trs. Lin, *op. cit.*, p. 203.
30. *Ibid*, 7 : 12, also included in *Lun Taige'er*, p. 66f. (Translated with the help of Tan Wen.)
31. *Lun Taige'er*, p. 72.
32. "The literature of yesterday is an unconscious sacred recreation for the aristocrats who hold supremacy in life. Like the poems of Tagore and the novels of Tolstoy, I feel as if they are only offering alms to the hungry ghosts." Guo Moruo's letter to Cheng Fangwu in *Zhonguo Xin Wenxue daxi*, Essay, Vol. I. p. 219.
33. Quoted in Hay, *op. cit.*, p. 147.
34. "First Talk at Shanghai", *Talks in China* (hereafter *TC*), (1924), p. 19; TC (1925), p. 59.
35. *TC* (1924), p. 13; *TC* (1925), p. 19.
36. 14 April 1924. Quoted in *Lun Taige'er, op. cit.*, pp. 73-77. (Translation with the help of Tan Wen.)
37. I am indebted to Tan Chung for giving me this piece of information. Italics mine.
38. "To Students at Nanking", *TC* (1924), pp. 26-31; "To Students II", *TC* (1925), pp. 80-86.
39. Many years later Tagore remembered this visit in his *Galpa Salpa*, a collection of stories for children: "There was a wonderful palace in the city of Beijing."
40. For the full text of the talk, *TC* (1924), pp. 33-39; *TC* (1925), pp. 65-69.
41. "To the Boys and Girls at Pei Hai" (Beihai), *TC* (1924), p. 36; *TC* (1925), p. 66.
42. *Ibid.*
43. For the full text see "First Public Talk in Peking", TC (1924), p. 79f; "To My Hosts, V", TC (1925), p. 73f.
44. "At the Scholar's Dinner, Peking", Mr Lin's Opening Speech, *TC* (1924), pp. 57-67. This has been left out in *TC* (1925). For Tagore's reply see *TC* (1924), pp. 9-69; *TC* (1925), "Autobiographical II", pp. 33-43.
45. "Yi Taige'er" (Reminiscences of Tagore), *Renmin Wenxue* (People's Literature), May 1961. (Translated by Tan Wen.)
46. In the past Indians called China "Cinasthan" which was in turn transliterated into Chinese as *Zhendan.* Liang Qichao in his speech rather mistakenly asserted that the word *Zhendan* was the transliteration of the word *Cina.*
47. This speech was quoted by Mei Lanfang in his article "Yi Taige'er".
48. *Lu Xun Quanji*, Vol. XI, p. 427.
49. "Wushengde Zhongguo" (The Voiceless China), *Lu Xun Quanji*, Vol. IV, p. 15.
50. *Ibid.*, Vol. V, p. 57.
51. *Ibid.*, Vol. V, pp. 585-86.
52. "First Public Talk in Peking", *TC* (1924), p. 94; *TC* (1925), p. 33.
53. The lectures are "The Rule of the Giant" and "Giant Killer". The combined talk was published *in Visva Bharati Quarterly*, July 1926. Needless to say, they were not included in *Talks in China*. In a letter to Pratima Tagore, on his way to China, Tagore wrote that he had to write six lectures, of which two he had written on the boat. The lecture delivered on 9 May, i.e. the first formal lecture,

was undoubtedly written a few days before that date. In all probability the two lectures written on his way to China were never delivered.

54. For the full text see Hay, *op. cit.*, pp. 170-71.
55. "Taige'er",*Chenbao* (Morning Daily), 19 May 1924, quoted in Hay, *op. cit.*, p. 193.
56. "Judgment", *Visva-Bharati Quarterly*, October 1925.
57. *TC* (1924), pp. 134-37; *TC* (1925) "To Students I", pp. 78-79. The 1925 edition omits the first part, as well as a few passages, in the original talk.
58. *TC* (1924), pp. 95-101; *TC* (1925), pp. 114-40.
59. Quoted in Hay, *op. cit.*, p. 199.
60. *Ibid*, p. 323.
61. Tan Chung, "Tagore in China", *The Sunday Statesman, Miscellany*, 20 July 1986, pp. 2-3.
62. Tan Chung has summarised the essay of Ji Xianlin.
63. *Lun Tai ge'er, op. cit.*, pp. 180-81.
64. All of them are to be found in *Sadhana. The Realisation of Life* (1913).
65. "The Modern Age", *Creative Unity* (1922, reprinted Macmillan, 1980), p. 121.
66. Hay, *op. cit.*, p. 242.
67. "Reply to the Scholars, Peking", *TC* (1924), p. 60; "Autobiographical II", *TC* (1925), p. 34.
68. Tagore's admiration for Chinese poetry found its most eloquent expression in his controversial but seminal article "Adhunik Sahitya" (included in *Sabityer Pathe*, 1937). The English translation, "Modern Poetry", in Amiya Chakravarti (Ed.), *A Tagore Reader* (Boston, 1961), pp. 241-53. In support of his view of modernity he quotes from Li Bai and adds, the joy of a natural and detached way of looking at things belongs to no particular age. It belongs to everyone whose eyes know how to wonder over the naked earth. It is over thousand years since the Chinese poet Li Bai wrote his verses, but being a moderner, Tagore looked upon the universe with freshly opened eyes.
69. "To Students at Hangchow", *TC* (1924), p. 25; "To My Hosts II", *TC* (1925), p. 65.

TAN CHUNG

34

TAGORE'S INSPIRATION IN CHINESE NEW POETRY

The arrival of Tagore in international literary scene just preceded China's New Cultural Movement in the wake of the student demonstrations on May Fourth, 1919, which is thus known as the May Fourth Movement. An important thrust of this movement was to launch a new literature called "*baihua wenxue*" (colloquial literature). While it was relatively easy to develop a new colloquial prose literature because of the existence of famous classical novels the language of which was already colloquial enough to serve as a model, the task of building up a new poetry was hard as there had been no genre of colloquial poetry in Chinese literature to be emulated. Tagore was a godsend to the pioneers of China's new poetry.

That Chinese poetic genii should focus their attention on Tagore is easy to explain. First, Tagore won the Nobel Prize by his masterpiece of poetry, and his *Gitanjali* and *The Crescent Moon* have won ovation in the poetic circles of the world even including Britain — the leader of modern poetry at that time. Second, Tagore was a fellow-Asian, hence his symbolism sounded more familiar and attractive to Chinese writers. Third, Tagore's example of being a writer of a humble, defeated culture risen to the fore-front of world literature was all the more inspiring to those who were searching for a new form of Chinese poetry in order to create a new Chinese culture so that the nation could keep abreast with the modern world. Fourth, Tagore's visit to China in 1924 and the "Tagore wave" created by this visit also contributed to the writers' enthusiasm in emulating Tagore.

Tagore's influence on Chinese intellectual trend was highlighted by the rise of a new school within the New Cultural Movement — the "*Crescent Moon* School" (*xinyuepai*). That this *Crescent Moon* School had its own special distinction can be illustrated from the correspondence of two liberal intellectuals, Luo Longji and Hu Shi. Luo wrote to Hu on May 5, 1931 that he had read an article in a daily newspaper of Shanghai — *Minbao* (People's newspaper) which was "supposed to be a leftist paper" — in which it said : "Today in China three ideologies hold the triangular balances: (1) Communism, (2) the "Crescent Moon" school, and (3) the Three Principles which refers to the ideology of Kuomintang." After reporting this Luo expressed his surprise that "I have never thought the 'Crescent Moon' could have such an importance."[1] Of course, to depict *The Crescent Moon* School as a counter-weight between the two giant rivals of Kuomintang and the communists appears to be an exaggeration out of proportion. However, the newspaper article does reflect the importance of the *Crescent Moon* School in China's intellectual life of that time. The *Crescent Moon* School was essentially a stream of literary trend. More precisely, it was a forum of a group of poets who had imbibed a measure of influence of Tagore, hence their not objecting to be branded by the title of a Tagore anthology. This School, however, had the association of Hu Shi, who was also a leader of the May Fourth Movement and an outstanding liberal intellectual who appeared to have kept aloof of the political contention between Kuomintang and CPC at that time. This might be the source of the above-cited exaggerated account of the standing of *The Crescent Moon* School. Tagore's admirers among Chinese intellectuals cannot be slighted.

The real force behind The *Crescent Moon* School, of course, was not Hu Shi, But Xu Zhimo (Elmhirst's "Shu Tsemou") (1886-1931) who acted as a host and interpreter to Tagore during the latter's China visit in 1924. Xu wore an Indian cap in the Tagore functions. He also converted a room in his Shanghai residence into Indian style where there were no tables nor chairs, but only carpets and cushions. His friends were quite shocked to see Xu Zhimo "rolling on the floor".[2] Xu died young by a tragic accident which cut short a career of great poetic talent. If he had lived as long as many of his contemporaries had lived, his role in the history of modern Chinese literature would have been greater than what is known. So also, Tagore's influence on China's new poetry would have been more pronounced than what is known.

In Xu Zhimo, there was a mini-version of Tagore. Rich, talented, romantic, exposed to progressive ideas but not plunging into the political activities. Not unlike Tagore in his young days, Xu Zhimo had tender feelings for fellow-beings, was inclined towards the charm of Nature, but knew how to make the best in material life. He was a potential Chinese Tagore being wiped out in his formative stage by ill fortune.

Among all authors in China's new poetry, Xu Zhimo and Xie Bingxin have held out as poets cast in the typical Tagorean mould. One of Xu's last poems composed in the end of 1930 was a poem dedicated to Hu Shi (his friend, philosopher and guide) entitled *"Aide linggan" (Inspiration of love)*, which is at once a replica of *Gitanjali*. This is a long prose poem in communion with the invisible spirit. It ends with a typical Tagorean touch:

"Now I really, really can die. I want you
to embrace me this way until I go away, until
my eyes open no more, until I fly, fly, fly
to the outer space, scatter into sands, scatter
into light, scatter into wind. Oh, sorrow,
but sorrow be short, sorrow be transient;
happiness be long, love is immortal!"[3]

This flight of Xu Zhimo's "inspiration of love" is going the same direction of Tagore's *Gitanjali*. In the end of *Gitanjali*, Tagore takes off:

"Like a flock of homesick cranes flying
night and day back to their mountain
nests let all my life take its voyage to
its eternal home in one salutation to thee."[4]

A search for idealism is an eternal theme in Tagore's poems. "In desperate hope I go and search for her in all corners of my room; I find her not." (*Gitanjali*, poem 87) Xu Zhimo's poetry joins such a search:

"She isn't here.
Where is she?
She stays in the shine bright
of clouds white.
Stays in the moon crescent,
distant and quiescent.
She stays in the lotus of the valley
ever open timidly.
Stays in the flower that reveals
from inside the lotus seed.
She stays in the adolescent heart
where prayers are sent forth.
Stays in its naive artlessness.
She isn't here.
She is in the quintessence of Nature."[5]

In this poem entitled *Where is she*? Xu Zhimo gives enough indications that his search for her is exactly Tagore's search. There are the "crescent moon", the "lotus", the "adolescent heart", the "naive artlessness", and the "quintessence of Nature" — all Tagorean symbols of idealism.

Tagore was fond of roses. Whether Xu Zhimo had the same love for roses we do not know. But, in interliterariness there is the phenomenon which I call the "telepathic transference of imagery". For instance, the use of the garland is a part of daily life in India, while the practice was totally absent in China. Yet, we notice that in modern Chinese poetry (as well as in prose) the symbolism of garland is not infrequently resorted to by writers. We have no doubt that this is an Indian import — an import of the imagery without its material entity. In poetic inspiration there is always the tendency of going for the unreal and abstract. The ancient Chinese poets had a favourite symbolism in the "celestial gate" although no one had ever been there. The "Cupid's arrow" is another foreign import into Chinese literary vocabulary but very few Chinese writers who use this symbolism have ever seen any drawing of the winged angels as depicted in the Roman legends, let alone ever experiencing such a weapon. In this way, we find Xu Zhimo experiencing the Telepathic Transference of Imagery from Tagore by indulging in the symbolism of the roses in his poem "Qing si" (Death of love) which is another unmistaken echo of Tagore:

"Oh, roses, red roses that conquer all
other beauties. The thunder storm of last night,
that is the signal of your birth.

The smile of your cheeks, that is
brought, from Heaven. Alas, the world
is too mundane to give them eternal residence.
Your beauty is your destiny!
You approach near me. Your enchanting
colour and fragrance have conquered another
soul — I am your captive!
You smile over there. I tremble over here.

I have caught you in my palm —
I love you, roses!
Colour, fragrance, flesh, soul, beauty, charm —
all grasped in my palm.
I tremble over here, you — smile.
Oh, roses! I can't tolerate your destruction, I love you!
Petal, corolla, stamen, thorn, you, me, —
How delightful ! — all merge into one; a mess of
redness, both hands soiled in fresh blood,
Oh, roses, I love You!"[6]

Of course, Tagore would not have been so abrasive, blunt and outspoken. Tagore seldom talked about "blood" in his poems, particularly associating blood with beauty and love. "I am your captive" is a Tagorean theme, but Tagore would say it differently: "Thou hast taken every moment of my life in thine own hands. Hidden in the heart of things thou art nourishing seeds into sprouts, buds into blossoms, and ripening flowers into fruitfulness." (*Gitanjali*, verse 81) The flowers, the Creator, Nature, men, "you", "me", these are the eternal bonds between Tagore and Xu Zhimo.

Singing hymns was poet Tagore's obsession. So did Xu Zhimo take it as a poet's duty. But, we see sometimes the Chinese disciple's sense of rebellion against this Tagorean sainthood in poetry. This comes out clearly in Xu's piece "words of groan" (*Shenyin yu*):

"I would have wished
To sing hymns about
This marvellous cosmos.
I would have wished
To forget, the sorrow
Which in mankind grows.
Like a red sparrow
who no worries knows.
Singing in the morn,

Jumping at even twilight.
If SHE had been by my side,
Like wind gently flies,
I would have wished
To sing my poem,
Like the flowing stream,
Would have wished
To place my heart at ease,
Like the fish in the lake.
But, today, my heart boils
As if burning oil.
How can I have the leisure
To care for my muse?
Oh, God!
Won't you return
HER life and freedom
For one day even?!"[7]

Xu Zhimo's poetry, in a sense, provides a development of the Tagorean muse across the Himalayas, which is the phenomenon of horizontal continuity in interliterariness. Like the transplantation of vegetation which develops new features in a new habitat, the Tagorean elements were bound to transform when they grew in China's new poetry. As the above poem of Xu Zhimo indicates, the young Chinese poet could not preserve the cool of his Indian mentor, even if he wished to emulate Tagore to perfection. But, Xu, never probably, had the pretension of doing so. For, his was a turbulent universe. His country was in turmoil where no Santiniketan could have existed. But, this could not spiritually separate Xu Zhimo from Tagore. Even in the boiling pot of his life, Xu had his longing for Tagore and his Santiniketan. This is what we can make out from his piece entitled "*Tianguode xiaoxi*" (News from the Celestial Kingdom), which reads :

"Lovely Autumn scene! Silent leaves fallen
gently, gently, dropping on this narrow path.
Within the fence, a whisper of tiny kids' laughter.
Clear sizzling sound the quietude of huts surround,
as if birds in the valley receiving the morning happily,
driving away stale stagnation of the night,
beginning, the unbounded brightness.
A momental ecstasy surges like the epiphyllum,
My mood is open, I forget my love for Spring.
The fear, doubt and anguish of life, melancholy and hurry —
I have the vision of the Celestial Kingdom amidst
the innocent kids' laughter!"[8]

Xu Zhimo was in India, and did visit Santiniketan. In this poem we a visid depiction of Tagore's "*Abode of Peace*". What had Xu in mind when he talked about the "Celestial Kingdom" we do not know. In Chinese tradition the paradise often points to the direction of India — the Kingdom of the Buddha. In any way, Xu Zhimo's depicting a quietude and a innocent kids' laughter bear the closest resemblance of Tagore's "Santiniketan". The two poets are in communion with Nature and peace and ease of mind.

The Crescent Moon School had its own publishing house — *The Crescent Moon* Bookshop in Shanghai — which was run by Xu Zhimo and some relatives and friends. In 1931, the bookshop published China's own Crescent Moon anthology entitled *Xinyue shixuan* (Selected poems of *The Crescent Moon*) edited by Chen Mengjia, who was himself a poet. The anthology formally launched the poets of *The Crescent Moon* School, and symbolized the sprouting of Tagore's seed in China's new poetry. As this was one of the earliest anthologies of modern Chinese poems, it had a pioneer role in the development of modern poetry in China. The anthology is a selection of eighty poems from eighteen authors. Apart from Xu Zhimo, a well-known poet, writer and scholar, Wen Yiduo (1899-1946) also contributed. In the initial stage, Wen Yiduo was one of the three pillars of *The Crescent Moon* Society, along with Xu Zhimo and Hu Shi. But, later Wen grew tired of Tagore and moved closer to the radical left. He was one of Tagore's critics on the eve of Tagore's visit to China. But, his "Criticism of Tagore" penned in 1923 did not prevent him from contributing to the Chinese Crescent Moon anthology in 1931. Further more, among the six pieces contributed by Wen Yiduo, half are the *Gitanjali* type of prose poems. "*Yige guannian*" (An idea) begins thus:

> "Your profound mystery, your beautiful lie,
> your stubborn interrogation, your golden ray,
> a little endeared meaning, a flame,
> a wisp of illusory call, who are you?"[9]

The poem also contains a few lines which look like Wen Yiduo's conversation with Tagore. First, there was Tagore:

> "When I sit on my throne and rule you with
> my tyranny of love, when like a goddess
> I grant you my favour, bear with my pride,
> beloved, and forgive me my joy."
> (*The Gardener,* verse 33)

Then Wen Yiduo replied:

> "Oh, tyrannical spirit, you have conquered me.
> Have you conquered me? You magnificent rainbow
> — the memory of five thousand odd years. You
> move not. Now I want to try how to hug you tight.
> — You are so tyrannical, so pretty!"[10]

The Chinese *Crescent Moon* anthology does not carry Wen Yiduo's piece of "Mori" (The end) which is at once the echo of Tagore's piece of the same title in *The Crescent Moon.* Here is Wen's voice: "I set up a fire in my heart, waiting quietly for a distant guest." "The guest is already before me, I close my eyelids and follow the guest's steps."[11] Again there is Sino-Indian communion between Wen Yiduo and Tagore with the former wishing to "follow" the latter like a disciple.

All poets deal with the theme of life's voidness. There is the yawning gap between illusion and reality. All poets share the sense of regret of not having the right choice of the timing of their life and death. Thus they hang in the balance in men's awkward existence. In this respect, Tagore's mood is usually more gracious, while Wen Yiduo cannot bear the human dilemma without scorn. Here, there is scope to compare the two ways of life. Tagore, in his desperate moment cries out: "Oh, dip my emptied life into that ocean, plunge it into the deepest fullness. Let me for once feel that lost sweet touch in the allness of the universe." (*Gitanjali,* verse 87) To this Wen Yiduo echoes:

> "Let me be drowned in the waves of your eyes!
> Let me be burnt dead in the furnace of your heart!
> Let me drink to death in the wine of your music!
> Let me be stifled to death in the fragrance of your breath!"[12]

Here Wen Yiduo approaches death with a Tagorean romanticism which even out-shines that of the Indian master.

We can have another round of comparison. Like the above verse of Wen titled "*si*" *(Death)*, the 86th verse of *Gitanjali* is exclusively devoted to the theme of "death". In the verse, Tagore describes the call of the messenger of Death: "The night is dark and my heart is fearful — yet I will take up the lamp, open my gates and bow to him my welcome." "I will worship him with folded hands, and with tears. I will worship him placing at his feet the treasure of my heart. He will go back with his errand done, leaving a dark shadow on my morning; and in my desolate home only my forlorn self will remain as my last offering to thee." Forever at peace with life and death. Tagore conducts his feelings with controlled emotions. Wen Yiduo, on the other hand, feels annoyed at the idea of death in another poem (in contrast to the above romantic feelings enshrined in his poem "Death"). He cries:

"Death, if you want to come, come quickly,
come quickly to cut short the boundless pain!
Haha! death, there your cruelty lies,
when I want you you come not,
like life, when I need him not, he exists!"[13]

However, like Tagore, Wen Yiduo is prepared to obey the dictates of destiny. He sings in his piece "Death":

"If you award me with joy,
I shall die with joy.
If you award me with pain,
I shall die with pain,
Death is my only demand on you,
Death is my utmost offering to you."[14]

In the same piece "Death", Wen Yiduo has paraphrased Tagore : "Oh, soul of my soul, life of my life".[15] This reminds us *Gitanjali*, verse 4 : "Life of my life, I shall ever try to keep my body pure". There are many other skilful adaptations of Tagore by Wen Yiduo. For instance, Tagore sings : "I know not how thou singest, my master! I ever listen in silent amazement." (*Gitanjali*, verse 3) Then, Wen Yiduo emulates in his poem "Mei yu ai" (Beauty and love):

"Oh, that giant star, the companion of the moon!
You have tied my eye-sight for no reason.
The bird in my heart stops its songs immediately,
because it, has heard your silent celestial music."[16]

Tagore sings in *Gitanjali* (verse 68): "The sunbeam comes upon this earth of mine with arms outstretched and stands at my door the live long day to carry back to thy feet clouds made of my tears and sighs and songs." Wen Yiduo imitates in his piece "*Shijiande Jiaoxun" (Lessons of time*): "The sun comes upon my bed, frightens away the spirit of dream. My worries of yesterday vanish, those of today haven't come yet."[17] In the same poem Wen Yiduo resorts to the Telepathic Transference of Imagery by singing: "At the moment time is all smile to me. I pray to him with folded hands : 'Grant me endless period!' "[18] Here again is an echo of Tagore: "I will worship him with folded hands, and with tears." (*Gitanjali*, verse 86). It remains doubtful whether Wen Yiduo had ever prayed with folded hands. There is another puzzle in Wen's poems when at two places he mentions burning the sandal-wood in offering[19] which is a common Indian practice but, was hardly in vogue in Wen Yiduo's time at least, if Chinese had ever indulged in such extravagant ritual even during the heyday of Buddhist conversion, simply because sandal-wood has always been a luxurious rarity in China. The truth is that Wen Yiduo has just acquired such Indian life details as poetic symbols. Why has he chosen to do it should be attributed to Indian cultural influence either through Tagore or through his profound knowledge of China's Buddhist past.

To Tagore poetry is the very devotion to God/Truth. Offering songs to God is the essence of Tagore's poetic life. "I am here to sing thee songs. In this hall of thine I have a corner seat." "When the hour strikes for thy silent worship at the dark temple of midnight, command me, my master, to stand before thee to sing." (*Gitanjali*, verse 15). In his master-piece, "*Hongdou pian" (The red bean*), Wen Yiduo is seized by this Tagorean passion:

"I have sung various songs,
Only forgetting to sing you.
But my songs should become newer, prettier.
These last sung prettiest ballads,
every word a bright pearl,
every word a warm tear.
Oh, my queen!
These are my humble presents to atone my sins,
These I kneel down and offer at your feet."[20]

Tagore's poetry is the reincarnation of happiness. When he wrote to Andrews in 1915, Tagore said: "I know I am Eternal, that I am *ananda-rupam*, my true form is not of flesh or blood, but of joy."[21] One of the highest embodiments of joy is Tagore's verse 58 of *Gitanjali*:

"Let all the strains of joy mingle in my last song
— the joy that makes the earth flow over in
the riotous excess of the grass, the joy
that sweeps in with the tempest, shaking and
waking all life with laughter, the joy that sits
still with its tears on the open red lotus of
pain, and the joy that throws everything it has upon the dust,
and knows not a word."

Wen Yiduo in his piece "Lessons of time" conceives "happiness" as "the only truth of life".[22] He has another short poem exclusively on "*Happiness*" (*Kuaile*) which sings:

"Happiness kisses my soul,
My world suddenly turns into paradise,
fully occupied by soft and charming angels."[23]

Rabindranath being named after the "sun" and the "thunder", his poetry carries a strong impact of the brilliance of the celestial fire-ball. In *Gitanjali* alone the powerful symbolism of the sun shines upon all the lines. "O thou holy one, thou wakeful, come with thy light and thy thunder." (verse 39) "O my sun ever-glorious!" (verse 80) "I came out on the chariot of the first gleam of light". (verse 12) "Thy voice pour down in golden streams breaking through the sky". (verse 19) "All the lights ablaze, golden pennons flying over thy car". (verse 41) "Under the golden canopy of thine evening sky". (verse 87) Verse 57 is specially devoted to the sun:

"Light, my light, the world-filling light, the eye-
kissing light, heart-sweetening light!
Ah, the light dances, my darling, at the centre
of my life; the light strikes, my darling, the chords
of my love, the sky opens,
the wind runs wild,
laughter passes over the earth.

The butterflies spread their sails on the seat,
of light lilies and jasmines surge up on the crest of
the waves of light.

The light is shattered into gold on every
cloud, my darling, and it scatters gems in profusion.
Mirth spreads from leaf to leaf, my darling, and
gladness without measure. The heaven's river has
drowned its banks and the Mood of joy is abroad."

Wen Yiduo was one the Chinese modern poets who had been infected by Tagore's powerful sun imagery. Like Tagore, Wen conceived the sun as the symbol of treasure and brightness. In his poem "*Chun'guang*" *(Spring light)* Wen sings:

"Suddenly a sheet of sun-light flashes before my eyes,
from my eyes fly out thousands of golden arrows,
my ears bear witness to the flapping sounds of wings,
as if a group of angels hovering in the sky..."[24]

Wen's poetry further personifies the sun. In his poem "*Qiuse" (Autumn colours*), Wen sings:

"Morning sun-light beams at the world.
its smile produces gold...."[25]

Wen Yiduo depicts the sun-set in the evening with interesting scenarios. In his poem "*Huanghun" (Dusk*), Wen sings:

"The sun tires out for the day,
earning a safe and sound dusk.
its face reddens with joy,
running straight towards the valley like mad."[26]

In another poem, Wen depicts: "The sun sets, responsibility closes its eyes." In yet another poem, he complains, "The evening sun hands the poet over to the annoying night."[27]

Wen Yiduo has two poems with the sun in their captions. One poem is "You swear by the sun" which is a mockery of the fidelity of love which is also one of *The Crescent Moon* poems. Another is "*Taiyang yin" (Song of the sun*). This was composed when Wen was a student in the U.S.A. It is a Tagorean poem but quite different from the piece written by Tagore already quoted. There are twelve stanzas of the poem. The first stanza complains about the ruthless revolution of the sun which painfully pierces the heart of the poet. The second stanza depicts the sun's scorching power. The third stanza wishes the sun running faster to free the poet from suffering the slow torture of life. The fourth stanza likens the sun to the golden bird, and wishes to ride on it so that the poet can see his home place once a day. The fifth stanza expresses the poet's nostalgia as the sun comes to him from the East. The seventh stanza expresses the poet's fellow-feeling that the sun is a vagabond like the poet himself. The eighth stanza describes the sun as a restless self-strengthening body. The tenth stanza defines the sun as the fire of life which gives the Eastern Hemisphere its enthusiasm and the Western Hemisphere its wisdom. In the twelfth and final stanza the poet wishes his home not situated on the earth, but stays in the heaven.[28]

Another interesting poem of Wen Yiduo is entitled "*Huangniao" (Yellow bird*) which is also a depiction of the sun implicitly. The sun that is the yellow bird is seen by the poet as a brilliant fire bow shooting its arrows like mad. He also likens the sun to an ambitious bird. The poem ends with the hope that the sun builds up a palace of art to let the poet — a soul losing his bearings — to have an early chance to settle down.[29]

A similar poem included in the Chinese *Crescent Moon* is "*Luori song*" (*Hymn to the setting-sun*) written by a lesser known poet, Zhu Da'nan. The poem depicts the sun as a golden bird which emits vicious flames, but is forced to retreat, behind the western mountains. The frogs are celebrating the victory in forcing the sun to exit.[30] If Wen Yiduo has already reduced Tagore's powerful symbolism of the sun to a half pitiable figure, Zhu Da'nan has brought it further down to the symbol of defeat. It is not difficult to understand the Chinese poets' resentment of the sun's vicious heat, particularly its harm during drought. Paradoxically, in India, and in Tagore's Santiniketan as well, the sun is a much more vicious fire-arrow-shooting-monster than in any part of China. Yet, Tagore should have never complained against the sun besides eulogizing its light and life-giving power. This speaks out the contrast of Indian idealism with religious devotion against the Chinese pragmatism with down-to-earth lifestyle. This explains the impact of transposition of symbolism to a different cultural *milieu.*

Another Crescent Moon poet worth mentioning was Shao Xunmei who also cast his poetry in the Tagorean mould. His "Nuren" (Woman) in *The Crescent Moon* anthology is also a *Gitanjali* type:

"I adore you, woman, I adore you like
I adore a small poem of a Tang master
— you tie my words with your warm and smooth
even-tones and crispy uneven-tones.
I disbelieve you, woman, I disbelieve you like
I disbelieve a ring of magnificent rainbow
— I don't know whether it's for me that you
blush, or for another hot dream?"[31]

There is one little lovely poem of Shao Xunmei which is not included in the Chinese *Crescent Moon anthology*. The poem begins thus, with the first line repeating its title:

"I am a lamb.
You are a pasture.
I eat you, I sleep in you,
I eat you, I sleep in you.
I also offer myself to you."[32]

The chemicals of this little poetic crystal must have come from the following lines of Tagore's *Stray Birds*: "The artist is the lover of Nature, therefore he is her slave and her master." (verse 86) "The great earth makes herself hospitable with the help of the grass." (verse 91) "The woodcutter's axe begged for its handle from the tree. The tree gave it." (verse 71) Thus, the Tagore-Shao affinity is established.

All the above illustrations prove the strong input of Tagorean inspiration in the Chinese Crescent Moon School. In the first place, we cannot imagine the emergence of a school named after Tagore's work without the poets' having really inspired by *The Crescent Moon* and other works of Tagore. Secondly, Tagore's popularity in China way back in the 1920s was testified to by Xu Zhimo and Wen Yiduo. Xu Zhimo wrote in 1924 that out of every ten new-wave poems in China eight or nine bear the imprint of Tagore's influence, and that the teenage school pupils were fond of reading Tagore's works in Chinese translations.[33] Wen Yiduo supplemented Xu Zhimo's testimony by saying in 1923 that "almost every word of Tagore has been *transported* to Chinese language". (Italic added).[34] Of course, what Wen Yiduo meant was that Tagore's works available in English had a good many takers by Chinese translators because the language of Tagore was simple and his meaning deep. Even in his critical article of Tagore, Wen Yiduo respected Tagore as a great philosopher, but did not think much of Tagore's artistic achievement. Here again, Wen Yiduo was not aware of and could not read Tagore's works in Bengali. Even then, the Chinese new-wave poets had already found a lot of food for thought in the available English translations of Tagore. Hence, there is little surprise that the new Chinese poets in the 1920s and 1930s had echoed so much of Tagore's ideas and imagery.

One revolutionary change which the *avant garde* poets of China have introduced in the new poetry (apart from the use of colloquial language) is the adoption of Tagore's style of prose-poem which is *the* style of *The Crescent Moon* anthology. There is yet another significant revolution courtesy of Tagore's influence. In early Chinese poetry the focal point is "I" and "me" which is supplemented by "she/he" and "her/him", but seldom "you". In the few Tagore anthologies which had wide circulation in China, like *Gitanjali, The Crescent Moon. Stray Birds*, the poet has highlighted "you" which at once strengthens the purposiveness of the muse. The Chinese *Crescent Moon* poets were quick in adopting this Tagorean style. That is why many pieces written by them both inside *The Crescent Moon* anthology and outside it look like taking a leaf out of Tagore's *Gitanjali* and other works. We have already had examples of Wen Yiduo in this respect as an illustration of this point. We can have more examples of this kind. A typical *Gitanjali*-type of poem in The *Chinese Crescent Moon* anthology is "Zou" (Go) composed by Rao Mengkan. The verse has four lines of prose form with the second and fourth lines rhymed, and same number of words both in the first and third lines, and in the second and fourth lines. This shows that the poet wished to give it a distinct verse form while adopting the technology of the prose-poem liberalization. The poem reads:

"I have spent efforts to make a boat for you,
I have been praying for wind day and night.
Only after you utter that soft word 'go',
You will find the boat in full sail alright."[35]

Shao Xunmei's piece "Jihou" (Seasons) in *The Crescent Moon* anthology provides another example of the Tagorean *You*-poem:

"When I first met you you gave me your heart
with a Spring morning in its inner part.
When I met you next you gave me your words,
words in which the fiery Summer do nurse.
We met again and you gave me your hand,
hand that has Autumn's falling leaves inland.
Our last meeting takes place in my short dream,
there's you and the Wintry wind to redeem."[36]

Once again, the poem shows the author's care for rhyme and metric uniformity. But, it is the Tagorean framework with a little finishing. Yet, the top-most Tagorean poem in the anthology is the opening piece "Wo denghou ni" (I wait for you) composed by Xu

Zhimo. If translated with skill this poem can merge into Tagore's works without any trace of its foreign origin. It is too long to quote in full. But, glimpses of it can be provided below:

> "I gaze at the evening outside my window,
> like a longing for my future.
> The quake in my heart blinds my hearing.
> ....
> I wait for your steps, your smiling words,
> your face, the soft silk of your hair, waiting for all what is you.
> ....
> I demand you so forceful that pains my heart.
> I demand your flame-like smile, your pliant waist, the
> flying stars in your hair and at the corners of your
> eyes. I fall into the air of intoxication.
> Like an island, floating helplessly among the green
> pythons of sea waves...
> ....
> No frozen expectancy and prayer can shorten
> a tiny inch the distance which
> separates you and me! The yellow dusk outside
> my window has stiffened into night's blackness.
> Icicles hang on the boughs. Birds pawns away
> their chirping. Silence is this cosmos
> in uniform mourning atire."[37]

Can these lines not comparable to those penned by Rabindranath?

Affinity with Tagore could not be surpassed by the poetry of Xie Bingxin, a poetess of modern China, who was as famous as other leading writers. Xie Bingxin, or Bingxin, was particularly impressed by the *Stray Birds*, which made her compose *Fanxing* (Crowded stars) in 1921 and *Chunshui* (Spring water) in 1922 — twin Chinese replicas of *Stray Birds*. Let us see some specimens of the poetess' masterpieces:

> "Crowded stars twinkling —
> The deep blue outer space,
> can you hear their conversations?
> In silent tranquillity,
> in dim glimmer,
> they sink deep into singing eulogies to each other."
> (*Fanxing*, verse 1.)

> "Out of my window the strings of the harp are struck,
> Oh, my heart!
> How is it so deeply entangled in the echoes!
> There is the limitless sound of the trees,
> there is the limitless brightness of the moon."
> (*ibid.*, verse 21.)

> "Flowers and stones lying beside the rails!
> Only in the flicker of this second,
> I and you
> a chance meeting in the limitless life,
> and also an eternal parting in the limitless life.

When I come again,
among the millions in our species,
where to find you?"
(*ibid.*, verse 52.)

"Oh, father!
Please come out and sit under the bright moon,
I want to listen to your talk about your sea."
(*ibid.*, verse 75)

"Oh, sea,
Which star has no light?
Which flower has no fragrance?
Which tide in my mind
has no clear sound of your waves?"
(*ibid.*, verse 131.)

"The flower at the corner of the wall!
When you are proud of yourself,
heaven and earth will shrink."
(*Chunshui*, verse 33.)

"Little pine tree,
let me keep you company,
the white clouds above the mountains have thickened!
(*ibid.*, verse 41.)

"Infant,
in the trembling of his cries
there is infinite mystic language,
brought from the earliest soul
wish to the world tell."
(*ibid.*, verse 64.)

"Spring arrives with hesitation
on this solemn altar —
amidst the unbounded indifference,
I can only hand a silk of Spring mood
to the insignificant weed
hidden in the cleft of the stairs.
(*ibid.*, verse 88.)

"Creator —
if in the eternal life
there is only one promise of extreme happiness,
I will demand this with utmost sincerity:
'I lie in the bosom of mother,
mother lies in the boat,
boat lies in the ocean of lunar brightness.' "
(*ibid.*, verse 105.)

"Under the green bower
I sit in deep thinking ——

Oh, poetic mood like floating silks!
Just as faint Spring light
draws you out,
The sound of the gardener's scissors
cuts you asunder."
(*ibid.*, verse 147.)

"Farewell, Spring water!
Thanks for your gentle Spring flow
carrying away lots of my thoughts."
(*ibid.*, verse 182.)[38]

There is, indeed, the Tagorean touch in these lines, soft-spoken, tender feelings, the poetess' finding complete harmony with Nature, trying to keep away the discordant notes of life from the symphony. In this sense, Xie Bingxin's inheritance from Tagore was greater than all *The Crescent Moon* poets putting together. While *The Crescent Moon* poets have learnt from Tagore's technique, Xie Bingxin alone imbibed Tagore's poetic soul. In Xie Bingxin's poems, Tagore's voice is transformed into Chinese language and female softness. Her anthologies of *Crowded Stars* and *Spring Water* were exceedingly popular in the 1930s and 1940s, particularly among younger readers. This indirectly spread the Tagorean message of harmony and peace among Chinese intellectuals.

Yet, we have not introduced the Chinese writer who had received the maximum influence from Tagore. His name was Guo Moruo (1892-1978), whose stature in the cultural scene of modern China can match with that of Tagore in modern India. Guo Moruo had a fruitful career of creative writing. He was almost as versatile as Tagore, was a poet, play wright, historian, archaeologist, educationist, and political activist. His position in the early decades of the People's Republic of China was like that of Gorky in the Soviet Union. He held the Presidency of the Chinese Academy of Sciences for life, a rare distinction to match with the eminence of Zhou Enlai who was the first Premier of the People's Republic till his death. During the Cultural Revolution, Guo Moruo, again like Zhou Enlai, was almost the lone eminent intellectual who could save his skin. The reason was that Chairman Mao Zedong had a binding love and respect for him. The two often composed classical poems together which figured as great cultural events in Communist China. No one could imagine that such an eminent career would not have been there at all if Tagore had not written *The Crescent Moon.*

It was more than a coincidence that when Guo Moruo arrived in the modern world in search of a career, Tagore had just arrived as a Nobel laureate. Japan played an important role in connecting these two. How Tagore's writings had entered the life of Guo Moruo has already been illustrated in the preceding essay by Sisir Das. Guo Moruo and Tan Yun-shan (founder-director of Visva-Bharati Cheena-Bhavana), were the two unique Chinese intellectuals who had Tagore entering into their life at a crucial juncture. Tan Yun-shan would have followed his radical Hunan school-mates to France (and, then, to Marxism most likely) had he not met Tagore in Singapore in 1927. That eventful meeting with the Indian poet transformed his life and career into that of a "modern Xuanzang". Guo Moruo never met Tagore. And unlike Tan Yun-shan, Guo was destined to embrace Marxism in any way -- Tagore or no Tagore. Yet, if there had not been Tagore we might not have heard of Guo Moruo at all. thus, I think the Tagore-Guo affinity is an equally historic example as the Tagore-Tan affinity both of which deserve to be highlighted in any discourse of Sino-Indian cultural relationship.

As has already been pointed out, Tagore entered Guo Moruo's heart when Guo stood at the cross-road of life. Between 1916-17, Guo was alternately seized by the desire of committing suicide or becoming a monk. The wreckage of his mind is described by a poem of classical style composed by him in 1916 entitled "*Ye ku" (Weeping at night*). The poem also outlines tne reasons which drove him to the brink of suicide. We can take a look of them:

"My soul has left my empty body to remain.
I suffer the torment of not reaching my end.
I have a country which exists only in name,
devastated by increasing wars in vain.
I have a home to which I cannot return.
Old and decaying health are my people's condition.
I have my love which is as good as broken.
A bird without a nest is what now I am."[39]

An interesting episode was Guo Moruo's composing two poems on the theme of suicide at about the same time. One poem written in the classical style, entitled "*Xunsi" (Seeking death)* was definitely composed in Okayama in 1916. The other poem written in new style entitled "*Side youhuo" (Enticement of death*). Guo gave the years of 1916 and 1918 as the possible time of the latter's composition.[40] A comparison of the two poems can help us reconstruct the turning point in Guo Moruo's life, as well as the moral influence exercised by Tagore on Guo Moruo. First, the poem of the classical style which surely was an earlier composition than the other, is a narrative of his going out of the house to end his life. But, he won't know where he should go, and he sighed repeatedly as he proceeded. As life was hard to live, death became relatively easy for him, he thought. He had ambitions to become a tiger, but ended in surviving like a dog. However, he still had his country and family in mind, and decided to endure longer in mankind. When he returned to the house, he saw his Japanese wife all in tears.[41]

The other poem on suicide written in the modern style is a product of entirely different psyche. The poem reads:

"I have a small knife
standing by the window beaming at me.
She says to me with a smile:
Moruo, don't burn your heart!
Come quickly and kiss my lips,
I can get rid of your worries.
Blue, blue sea waves outside my window
yelling at me with unceasing roar.
She calls me and says :
Moruo, don't burn your heart!
Throw yourself quickly into my bosom,
I can get rid of your worries."[42]

While in the first poem Guo Moruo was still under the impact of the threat of suicide, in the second poem the situation changed. The threat of death remained, but the poet's mentality had undergone a transformation. He had become a Tagorean poet, a poet-philosopher. In the poem he looked at the threat of death in a romantic spirit. His understanding of the meaning of living was tinged with a philosophical attitude. Yes, there is the enticement of death, but a philosopher who sees clearly the empty promise in that will not fall into the trap. The composition of this poem "*Side youhuo*" thus became the turning point of Guo's life. He had acquired strength to endure the torture of life, for he realized now that death was no solution to the problems which he had been facing. After composing the poem, both the knife and the sea became harmless to his life as he had decided not to be enticed, hence they would not pose as threats to him any more.

Guo Moruo himself wrote in his 1923 reminiscence that in the darkest years of his life, he had tried solutions by reading the writings of Chinese philosophers like Zhuangzi and Wang Yangming, by daily chanting the Old and New Testaments, by practising meditation with very little effect. It was only after reading Tagore's *Gitanjali, The Gardener, Raja* (The king of the Dark Chamber), and the Hundred Poems of Tagore from the Ukayama Library in 1916 that he had suddenly discovered "the life of life", and the "fountain of life". When he was reading Tagore, a "tranquil sadness" emerged within and outside his body. "I was enjoying the joy of nirvana", said Guo.[43] So, it was Tagore who had removed the threat to Guo Moruo's life and enabled such a great career to blossom to its natural end.

Interestingly, Guo Moruo himself put a foot-note to the poem "Side youhuo" in these words: "This was my earliest poem, probably written in the Summer of 1918,"[44] I have mentioned a little while ago that Guo had in another place noted that he had written this poem in 1916 along with some other poems. We know that Guo had started composing poems in the classical style many years earlier than his sojourn in Japan (his earliest poems published dated 1913 written in his home province). There is a mistaken statement about this poem of the *Enticement of Death*. But, if we try to understand Guo's psychology, we can take him as saying that this was the first (or one of the first) new poem he had composed. The mistaken note also helps us to see that considerable importance had Guo Moruo attached to this piece. In an autobiographical work entitled *Geming chunqiu* (*Revolutionary annals*), Guo Moruo divided his creative literary career into three phases. The first phase was conceived by him as the period of the influence of Tagore up till 1919, followed by two later phases when he was influenced by Whitman and Goethe respectively.[45]

· Guo Moruo's spiritual tryst with Tagore is one of the finest stories in interliterariness. But, the story has never been fully discovered, let alone being properly told. The scholarly distortions which have been discussed in Prof. Das' preceding essay have made it more imperative to restore the true historical perspective. In the first place, let us acknowledge Guo Moruo's abundant gratitude for Tagore. In a poem of Guo which has already been noticed widely, there was Guo's implicit acknowledgment about his mentor. The poem was composed in 1920, entitled "*Anshang" (On the shore*) which takes a leaf out of Tagore's "On the seashore" from *The Crescent Moon*. In the third verse of the poem, Guo directly used the Chinese translation of the Tagore poem of the following lines:

> "On the seashore of endless worlds children meet.
> The infinite sky is motionless overhead and the
> restless water is boisterous. On the seashore of
> endless worlds the children meet with shouts and dances."

Incidentally, these lines which were originally written in Bengali were used twice by Tagore as a part of both *Gitanjali* (verse 60) and *The Crescent Moon*.[46] Their featuring in the poetry of Guo Moruo[47] as an integral part of an original poem in Chinese language has thus created a record of the same lines living in the original poems of three languages — Bengali, English and Chinese. Only Tagore, who is the only author of two national anthems of the world (that of India and Bangla Desh), can create such a record. But, Guo Moruo's being instrumental to such an interliterary miracle also deserves recognition. This was Guo Moruo's special style of thanking the one who had meant so much to his life.

Guo Moruo openly acknowledged his indebtedness to Tagore in two other poems. In "*Chen'an" (Good morning)*, he affectionately calls :

> "......
> Good Morning! My young Motherland!
> ......
> Good Morning! The Great wall!
> ......
> Ah, Ah! Russian, how I admire you in awe!
> Good Morning! Poineer, how I admire you in awe!
> Good Morning! The Snowy Pamir!
> Good Morning! The snowy Himalaya!
> Good Morning! Rabindranath of Bengal!
> Good Morning! Academic friends of Santiniketan!
> Good Morning! Ganga!
> The sacred light flowing in Ganga!
> Good Morning! Indian Ocean! Red Sea! Suez Canal!
> ......
> (In the next half of the poem, he saluted the "Pyramid on the Nile", "Leonardo da Vinci", "Poets of Ireland", "Washington", "Lincoln", "Whitman" — after repeating the last name three times, then, "Whitman so expansive like the Pacific.")

Here, we can see that the foreign country enjoying the top place of honour was India, while the person enjoying maximum mention was Whitman — the American poet. But Tagore was far from eclipsed because of the graphic and vivid descriptions of Santiniketan (as "Ziran Xueyuan", i.e., "the Ashram of Nature"). Himalaya, Bengal, Indian Ocean, particularly, the Holy Ganga.

We note that "good morning" was not a traditional Chinese greeting, and what Guo Moruo had adopted in translating it, i.e. "Chen'an", is no longer in currency in Chinese language. I doubt whether it was ever a popular usage at all. So, the caption of the poem does reflect Guo Moruo's daring progressive mentality, not hesitant in embracing new ideas, new symbols and new lifestyles. It is, thus, important that he included Tagore and Tagore's India in the newness of his intellectual being.

There was another poem which Guo composed in 1922 entitled "Xianshi" (Offering of poetry) which was clearly Guo's expression of his gratitude for Tagore. The poem ends thus:

"Thou are my invisible teacher!
I emulate thee with vigour.
I weave my heart, my tears
into a chain of transient pearls.
I deck thy feet with it, my devotion to offer."[48]

Not only has the title of the poem taken a leaf out of *Gitanjali*, but the quoted lines are an obvious adaptation of verse 83 of *Gitanjali* which reads:

"Mother, I shall weave a chain of pearls
for thy neck with my tears and sorrow.
The stars have wrought their anklets
of light to deck thy feet, but mine will
hang upon thy breast."

It is, thus, not without foundation that we speculate the motivation of Guo's little *Gitanjali* being the offering of his affections for Tagore — the "invisible teacher" of his — in the same poetic manner as Tagore had offered for his invisible God. Guo was giving Tagore a Tagorean salute.

Ge Baoquan, a famous Chinese expert in translations and one who knew Guo Moruo well, wrote an article on "*Tagore and China" (Taige'er he Zhongguo*) in 1983 in which he also noticed the profound influence of Tagore on Guo Moruo. He wrote: "The first phase of his [Guo Moruo's] poetic creation belonged to Tagore's style." — a conclusion based on Guo's own admission as we have seen earlier. Ge Baoquan also quoted Guo Moruo to say that "After being addicted to Tagore, it is unavoidable to be under his impact."[49] Our task should be to find out the ramifications of Tagore's impact on Guo Moruo's early poetry.

I have a moment ago quoted Guo Moruo's little *Gitanjali* which was the poet's tribute to Tagore in 1922. In 1925, Guo Moruo composed his full *Gitanjali*, a collection of 42 verses with the same title "*Xianshi*" (Offering of poetry). In the introducing poem there are lines which at once convey a Tagorean touch:

"I have plucked you, this branch of plum blossom.
I keep you in the vase and worship you with devotion.
I have been a bee on pilgrimage,
inhaling your pure fragrance.
Oh, if anyone thinks I am bewitched,
I can also show my sting.
Tell me, who doesn't love flowers,
even when he emulates their silence."[50]

We can quote a few lines more like we have done earlier to Xie Bingxin's *Fanxing* and *Chunshui* to illustrate the Sino-Indian poetic communion between Guo Moruo's *Xianshi* series and Tagore's *Gitanjali*:

"You sit by my side wordless.
I feel shy to gaze because of them.
You bury your head, not turning your eyes.
Might be there's inhibition in your feeling.
Although my hands are hidden in my sleeves,
my soul has already embraced you.
There's no crime in doing so. I am sure.
When white clouds hug it, there's no damage to the moon's beauty."
(*Xianshi*, verse 8.)

"My flower must always blossom for you sake.
My constant youth has now come back.

I treasure not the grace of saintly poets,
nor do I lament living in the sea of sorrow.
(*ibid.*, verse 18.)

"Oh, girl, since you are the angel of Spring,
why so miserly with your gentle breeze,
and make me constantly hugged by freezing ice,
unable to blossom exuberant flowers."
(*ibid.*, verse 29.)

"The youth that will not come again, oh,
you are blown to the desolate country.
The mirror who knows no mercy, oh,
Why must you cast cold sarcasm on me!"
(*ibid.*, verse 39.)

"I dig for myself a deep ditch.
I come into it and lie on its bottom.
I bury myself with some sands and stones.
How do I know that people will come and trample on
the head of my dead body?"
(*ibid.*, verse 40.)

"Only a branch of withered flowers remain ——
the flowers which you have offered to me in vain.
The branch that covers my heart
is now dry and lifeless.
I now realize why you had given me the flowers ——
that being the ceremony of your presentation to me."
(*ibid.*, verse 41.)

"Oh, it's a pity I read not the end of your letter.
An unexpected joy shocks open my dreaming eyes.
I wake up to look around the four sides.
A broken vase falls before my grave."
(*ibid.*, verse 42.)[51]

We see in these extracted lines the familiar Tagorean dedication, purity of love, quiet submission and profound melancholy. Guo Moruo's theme of the poem is the paradise lost of his love for a woman who, for some mystic reasons beyond the poet's grasp, has failed to respond to his love. In the end, the poet has the consolation that she remains alone and not to be possessed by anyone else. The poem, in a way, reflects Guo Moruo's bitter experiences in love-seeking in early life. Yet, he was in the state of mind of a Tagorean idealist, unable to come to grip with the ruthless reality of life. What Guo Moruo attempted to create in his imitation *Gitanjali* was a kingdom of idealism for which he did not mind dying as a martyr. Love should remain pure, while dedication should have its deserved awards. It was the idealism of Tagore being reflected in Guo Moruo's mind.

There is another poem of Guo Moruo entitled "Shide xuanyan" (Manifesto of poetry) which also belongs to the *Gitanjali* realm, but with a mood drastically different from the one quoted above. Let the poem be cited in full:

"You see, I am so honest and candid.
I haven't an iota of artful quality.
I love those workers and peasants.
They bare their feet, their bodies.
I also bare my feet, my body.

I hate the class of the affluent.
They are beautiful. They love beauty.
Silks, scent, jewels on their entire bodies.
I am poetry. This is my manifesto of poetry.
My class is the proletariat.
Yet I am still a little too shaky,
have to be tempered to be steady.
Have just recovered,
maybe,
My spirit still not like steel.
That day will come, I believe
You see me roar like a tempest."[52]

Here is an interesting poem. The poem was composed in 1928, only three years after Guo Moruo had composed his imitation *Gitanjali*, "Xianshi". Yu Dafu, a friend and fellow-traveller like Guo Moruo, wrote an editorial note while publishing the latter poem in 1926. The note says that it was he (Yu Dafu) who published the poem against the willingness of Guo Moruo. Why did he do so? Said Yu: "I think it unimportant about the socialization of a poet. It is not necessary that vocables such as pistol, bomb, or hundred times of reiteration of "revolution" should occur in a poem to qualify it as a really revolutionary piece. When you artlessly reveal your real emotions, when you emit your volcanic warmth to make the readers of your poem share your sorrowful weep and joyful laughter you have fulfilled the sacred duty of a poet."[53] To Yu Dafu, both the poems of Guo Moruo, i.e., the lamentation of his lost love in "*Xianshi*" and the candid admission of his affinity with the proletariat in "*Shide xuanyan*", qualify as revolutionary poems, and perform the duty of awakening the fine sentiments of humanity all the same. That makes it easy to explain why a weeping Romeo in "*Xianshi*" in 1925 could become a roaring proletariat in "*Shide xuanyan*" in 1928. Is there any relevance of Tagore in this transformation? Yu Dafu, it seems, had already anticipated this transformation when he praised the noble sentiments of the weeping Romeo. We have earlier tried to establish the affinity between Guo Moruo's "Xianshi" and Tagore's *Gitanjali*, Yu Dafu has helped us to identify this affinity as the quality which can spread sympathy and empathy among men. Guo Moruo's manifesto of poetry instantly calls to mind Tagore's words in *Gitanjali* (verse 10):

"Pride can never approach to where
thou walkest in the clothes of the
humble among the poorest, and lowliest,
and lost.

My heart can never find its way to
where thou keepest company with the
companionless among the poorest, the
lowliest, and the lost."

What Tagore expressed above and what Guo Moruo expressed in his *Manifesto of Poetry* are identical in nature: it represents the desire of an intellectual to integrate himself into the world of the downtrodden. This was, perhaps, why Guo Moruo captioned his piece in such a way as if to link *Gitanjali* with the famous *Manifesto of the Communists*, a link between the influence of Tagore in him with that of Karl Marx who was Guo Moruo's later love. The linkage seems to suggest beyond doubt that Guo Moruo's falling in love with Marxism did not result in his negating his tryst with Tagore's spiritualism. This serves to contradict a feeling among Guo's contemporaries that any influence from Tagore was bound to neutralize the revolutionary potential of a Chinese youth. Guo Moruo's own growth process has proved that a Tagorean poet could become a communist writer.

Marian Galik (a famous Hungarian China expert) has pointed out the identity in Guo Moruo's poem "*Bieli*" *(Parting)* with Tagore's "*The Astronomer*", one of the pieces in *The Crescent Moon*, with both the poets longing to catch the moon.[54] Indeed, as *The Crescent Moon* had formed such an important part of Guo's life it was but natural that the moon, particularly *The Crescent Moon*, figured frequently in Guo's poetic creations. He had a poem entitled "*Xinyue*" (*Crescent moon*) composed in 1921, another entitled "*Xinyue yu baiyun*" (Crescent moon and white clouds) composed in 1919, another entitled "*Yuexiade sifenkesi*" *(Sphinx under the moon light)* composed probably in 1921 but published in 1922, yet another entitled "*Dui Yue*" *(Facing the moon)* composed in 1928. The moon also figures in many other poems which do not bear its name in their titles. Of interest is Prof. Galik's observation that in Guo's poem *Parting*, he also expressed his desire to get hold of the sun which, according to Prof. Galik, "does not figure in Tagore's poem", i.e., *The Astronomer*.[55] Galik, then discusses Guo's being attracted by the symbolism of the sun by suggesting that Guo's eulogizing the solar universe was an expression of his under the impact of Omar Khayyam, Whitman, Rodin and Millet.[56] I don't wish to contradict Galik's observation, but want to return to my earlier premise that one of the impact of Tagore on China's *avant garde* poets was the focus on the sun imagery. If my earlier premise can stand, then we can also count Tagore's influence on Guo Moruo's sensitivity to the solar glory in his poetry. Indeed, this sensitivity of Guo Moruo even surpasses that of Wen Yiduo, which we have illustrated earlier. To Guo Moruo the sun not only involved the solar universe, but was a hallowed symbolism like what Tagore had conceived. In an emotional poem entitled "*Taiyang mole" (The sun has set)*, Guo describes the light-waves of the sun as a force wanting to sweep clean the devils from the Heaven. The poem ends with the following lines:

"There is angry roar like tranquil thunder
which lumbers suddenly in my ears:
'We are all suns, you and I
away the darkness we drive,
and the devils we cleanse.
We hold our own torches,
march forward, march forward!' "[57]

There is Indianness in the metaphors of the above cited lines. Good overcoming evil is a permanent theme of the Indian ethos which the Indians annually commemorate in the Victory Festival (Diwali) every Autumn. The Chinese word "*mo*" which was the ancients' transliteration of the Sanskrit word *mara* (devil). Guo Moruo's likening the sun to the force of dharma (truth) which overcomes mara resurrects the ancient Chinese, particularly the Tang poetic symbolism transposing the image of the Buddha to that of the golden sun. The Tang poetic *jinlun* (golden wheel) was synonymous to "Buddhism", "sun", and "Tang imperial role". What made Guo Moruo revive this ancient theme must be due to his special feeling for Sino-Indian cultural affinity out of his admiration and affection for Tagore.

There is another element in Guo Moruo's metaphors for the sun which highlights Tagore's influence, i.e., Guo's emphasis on "light" — a favorite Tagorean theme. "We meet amidst the red light."[58] "The unbounded Nature has formed a sea of light."[59] "The sun in the sky, the light in my heart."[60] In his poem "*Taiyangde lizan" (Saluting the sun)*, Guo Moruo rhymed:

"Oh, sun! please light up my whole life
into a red current of blood!
Oh, sun! Please light up my entire poetry
Into the golden foams in flight! "[61]

These lines also highlight another aspect of Guo Moruo's solar metaphor, i.e., the internalization of the solar symbol into the poet's own being, which is more likely an Indian influence than Western. Similar sentiments were expressed by Guo Muruo in his poem *Haizhouzhong wang ri chu (A view of sunrise from the ocean liner)*:

"Oh, sun!
....
Please do sing me the triumphal song!
Today, my battle with the sea gains victory!"[62]

In another poem *Yu hai (Bathing in the sea)*, Guo expressed his sentiments thus:

"My blood shares the movements with the sea waves.
My heart burns together with the fire of the sun."[63]

In another poem Guo even exclaimed: "Oh, sun, our teacher."[67] All this does have a Tagorean touch as they are certainly the echoes of verse 57 of *Gitanjali* which sings these words:

"Light, my light, the world-filling light,
the eye-kissing light, heart-sweetening light!

Ah, the light dances, my darling, at the
centre of my life....
The light is shattered into gold on every cloud..."

Even the last line of Tagore found an echo in Guo Moruo's "The clouds are dyed in golden colour."[65] and "Innumerable golden rays are racing from my eyes towards the sun."[66] After hearing Tagore singing: "O my sun ever-glorious!" (*Gitanjali*, verse 80), Guo Moruo replied: "Oh, sun! If you don't shine upon me into thoroughly bright, I shall return not!"[67] These are sufficient illustrations of the spiritual communion between Tagore and Guo Moruo.

The Communion between Tagore and Guo Moruo also indicates the influence of pantheism in the two poets. While India is the native land of pantheism and Tagore imbibed it as a natural inheritance, Guo Moruo imbibed pantheism only through Tagore. The typical work of Guo Moruo which reflects his pantheist mood is the long poem *Fenghuang niepan* (The nirvana of the phoenix) in which Guo sang:

"One of all, harmony.
All of one, harmony,
Harmony be you, harmony be me.
Harmony be him, harmony be fire.
Fire be you.
Fire be me.
Fire be him.
Fire be fire."[68]

In Guo Moruo's own reckoning as stated in his poem "*Sange fanshenlunzhe" (Three pantheists*), the source of his pantheism came from three persons: (1) ancient Chinese philosopher, Zhuangzi, (2) Dutch philosopher, Spinoza, and (3) Indian philosopher, Kabir.[69] There is no mention of Tagore. Yet, Guo Moruo did digest Tagore's pantheist nourishment which can be demonstrated by comparing his poem "Diqiu, wode muqin!" (Earth, my mother!) with Tagore's *Gitanjali*. First, Let us listen to Tagore:

"Thy sunbeam comes upon this earth of mine
with arms outstretched and stands at my door
the livelong day to carry back to thy feet
clouds made of my tears and sighs and songs."
(*Gitanjali*, verse 68.)

"It is the same life that shoots in joy through the
dust of the earth in numberless blades
of grass and breaks into tumultuous waves
of leaves and flowers.
It is the same life that is reckoned in the
ocean-cradle of birth and of death, in ebb and in flow."
(*Ibid.*, verse 69.)

Now, listen to Guo Moruo:

"Earth, my mother!
I think everything in the universe is your incarnation.
Thunder is the deterrent sound of your breath,
Snow and rain mark the flying of your blood.
......
I drink a glass of water that is the sweet dew from Heaven.
I know it's your milk, the livelong juice of mine.
......
My soul is your soul."[70]

Both Tagore and Guo Moruo had a tryst with pantheism in these lines. Being an emulating force of Tagore, Guo certainly imbibed the Tagorean pantheism in conceiving the earth as his mother with all her mortal incarnations.

We have sufficiently spelt out Tagore's influence on the early poems of Guo Moruo, a writer of considerable importance and influence in shaping the new Chinese literature. Of course, Guo's poetry grew in its growing departure from the pantheist mood and the Tagorean style, committing deeper and deeper in the contemporary political struggle which Tagore had kept aloof from. However, as we have already alluded to earlier, a conclusion cannot be drawn that Guo had to necessarily discard Tagore's influence to throw himself whole-heartedly in the "revolutionary literature" movement which Guo himself was a driving force behind. While many of his contemporary radical friends viewed Tagore as a negative spiritual force, Guo Moruo never joined others in criticizing *The Crescent Moon* or *Gitanjali*. In fact, no patriotic spirit in any poem could surpass what was expressed in verse 35 in *Gitanjli* which reads:

"Where the mind is without fear and the
head is held high:
Where knowledge is free;
Where the world has not been
broken up into frangments
by narrow domestic walls;
Where words come out from
the depth of truth;
Where tireless striving stretches its arms towards perfection;
Where the clear Stream of reason
has not lost its way into
the dreary desert sand of dead habit;
Where the mind is led forward by
thee into ever-widening thought and action —
Into that heaven of freedom, my Father,
let my country awake."
(*Gitanjali*, verse 35.)

When Guo Moruo read these lines, he would not have been led away from loving Tagore and loving his own country. Incidentally, when Guo Moruo sailed back from Japan, and when his boat was touching the shore of Shanghai in 1921, he rhymed:

"Oh, the abode of peace,
the country of my parents!"[71]

Just when he was physically on the soil of his motherland, his mind and heart flow to Santiniketan (the abode of peace). Patriotism and Tagorean idealism were frozen in Guo Morun — the young Chinese poet who was destined to write, along with many others, the new poetry, new literature, new partiotic epic of a modern China. Nothing more vividly symbolic than this freeze to connect Tagore to the new chapter of China's spititual and literary awakening!

Notes

1. Luo Longji to Hu Shi, in *Hu Shi micang shuxin xue* (Sections of Hu Shi's correspondence from his private collections) by Liang Xihua (ed), Hong Kong, 1982, I, p. 368.
2. Liang Shiqiu, "Guanyu, Xu Zhimo" (About Xu Zhimo), in *Liang Shiqiu xuanji* (Selected works of Liang Shiqiu), Hong Kong, p. 128.
3. *Xu Zhimo quanji* (Collected works of Xu Zhimo), Hong Kong, 1983, Shiji (poetry), Vol. 1, p. 435.
4. *Gitanjali* Macmillan, 1953, p. 94.
5. *Xu Zhimo quanji*, Poetry, Vol. I, pp. 137-38.
6. *Ibid*, pp. 121-22.

7. *Zhongguo xinwenxue daxi* (Grand collection of China's new literature), shiji (poetry), Shanghai, 1935, p. 330.
8. *Xu Zhimo quanji*, Vol. I, pp. 47-48.
9. Chen Megjia (ed), *Xinyue shixuan* (Selected poems of *The Crescent Moon*), Shanghai, 1931, p. 50.
10. *Ibid*, pp. 50-51.
11. *Zhongguo xinwenxue daxi, op. cit*, p. 256.
12. *Wen Yiduo quanji* (Collected works of Wen Yiduo), Beijing, 1982, Vol. III, p. 241.
13. *Ibid*, p. 240.
14. *Ibid*, p. 241.
15. *Ibid.*
16. *Ibid*, p. 232.
17. *Ibid*, p. 230.
18. *Ibid.*
19. In his poem "Fengbo" (Trouble) and another poem "Youxi zhi huo" (Disaster of games), in *ibid*, p. 234-38.
20. *Ibid*, p. 292.
21. Sisirkumar Ghose (ed), *Tagore for You*,Visva-Bharati, Calcutta, 1984, p. 109.
22. *Wen Yiduo quanji*, Vol. !II, p. 230.
23. *Ibid*, p. 232.
24. *Ibid*, p. 183.
25. *Ibid*, p. 274.
26. *Ibid*, p. 229.
27. *Ibid*, p. 235, 253.
28. *Ibid*, pp. 268-70.
29. *Ibid*, p. 251.
30. *Xinyue shixuan*, pp. 242-43.
31. *Ibid*, pp. 103-4.
32. *Zhongguo Xinwenxue daxi, Poetry*, p. 373.
33. *Xu Zhimo quanji*, Vol. IV, Pt. II, p. 164.
34. *Wen Yiduo quanji*, Vol. III, p. 369.
35. *Xinyue shixuan*, p. 68.
36. *Ibid*, pp. 105-6.
37. *Ibid*, pp. 3-10.
38. *Zhongguo xinwenxue daxi, Poetry*, pp. 136-38.
39. *Guo Moruo quanji* (Collected works of Guo Moruo), Beijing, 1982. *Wenxue bian* (Literature), Vol. II, p. 429.
40. See footnotes of *ibid*, Vol. I, p. 130, 138.
41. *Ibid*, Vol. II, p. 430.

42. *Ibid*, Vol. I, p. 137.
43. Zhang Guangling, *Lun taige'er*, (On tagore), Beijing 1983, p. 63.
44. *Guo Moruo quanji, Literature*, Vol. I, p. 138.
45. Marian Galik, *The Genesis of Modern Chinese Literary Criticism* (Bratislava, 1980), pp. 40-41.
46. *Collected Poems and Plays of Rabindranath Tagore* (MacMillans, 1936), p. 51.
47. For Guo's poem "Anshang", see *Guo Moruo quanji, Literature*, Vol. I, p. 152.
48. *Ibid*, p. 173.
49. In *Nanya Yanjiu* (South Asian Studies), published by the Institute of South Asian Studies of the Chinese Academy of Social Sciences and Peking University, No. 3, 1983, p. 59.
50. *Guo Moruo quanji, Literature*, Vol. I, p. 259.
51. *Ibid*, pp. 267-68, 279, 290-291, 300-302.
52. *Ibid*, pp. 374-75.
53. *Ibid*, p. 304.
54. Marian Galik, *Milestones in Sino-Western literary confrontation (1898-1979)*, Wiesbaden, 1986, p. 51.
55. *Ibid.*
56. *Ibid*, pp. 52-53.
57. *Guo Moruo Quanji, Literaturre*, Vol. I, p. 332.
58. *Ibid*, pp. 329-30.
59. *Ibid*, p. 91.
60. *Ibid*, p. 56.
61. *Ibid*, p. 100.
62. *Ibid*, p. 160.
63. *Ibid*, p. 70.
64. *Ibid*, p. 329.
65. *Ibid*, p. 159.
66. *Ibid*, p. 100.
67. *Ibid.*
68. *Ibid*, pp. 44-45.
69. *Ibid*, p. 73.
70. *Ibid*, pp. 81-83.
71. *Ibid*, p. 161.

GIRI DESHINGKAR

35

STRATEGIC THINKING IN ANCIENT INDIA AND CHINA: KAUTILYA AND SUNZI*

This paper is meant to be only an exploratory comparison between strategic thinking in India and China in ancient times. For one thing, the problem of dating individuals, events and texts in Indian history is a formidable one. In China, on the other hand, it is much less of a problem, although the dates for Sunzi were in dispute for a long time. Interpolations in texts are common in both traditions but the oral tradition in India as opposed to the tradition of writing in China presents greater difficulties in reconstructing Indian texts. But the more serious difficulty in comparing the Indian and Chinese streams of strategic thinking stems from the strong "religious" base of Indian thought. In contrast, Chinese thinking has an unmistakable "secular" base. An off-shoot of the "religious" element in India was the social organisation it produced. Warfare in India was almost exclusively the preserve and even the duty of the *ksatriya varna* (warrior class) which was hereditary, although specific instances of the priestly *brahman varna* can be found thinking about and engaging in warfare. In China, although the *shi* (scholar-gentlemen) were trained in the military arts among other scholarly subjects, they did not constitute a hereditary group.

I

The absence of a "religious" base in Chinese thinking does not mean that the role of ethics in war was neglected. The Confucian school, particularly Mencius and Mozi not only emphasized ethical principles in warfare, they were opposed to war as such. But with the rise of the state of Qin and its expansion, the Legalist school of Shang Yang and Han Feizi gradually eclipsed the Confucian opposition to war. And although Legalism was theoretically abandoned when the Qin dynasty was overthrown by the Han (in 207 BC.), "State Confucianism" as adopted by the Han thinkers did not oppose war in the manner of Mencius. From Western Han onwards, realpolitik dominated Chinese strategic thinking. Whether the Marxist-Leninist base in Chinese strategic thinking in our century marked a partial return to "ethical" principles is a question beyond the scope of this paper.

It is probably a comment on the limits of ideology when it comes to applying it to practical matters that despite the strong "religious" base of Indian thinking, a strong school of *realpolitik* also appeared in India side by side with it. Thus, ancient Indian thinkers produced two schools of war, diplomacy and interstate relations; the *dharmayuddha* (ethical warfare) school; and the *kutayuddha* (devious warfare) school. The two schools were, however, not mutually exclusive. The practitioners of each school was informed by the principles and methods of the other and practised them. (In China, they were very nearly mutually exclusive). The best example of this is the great *Mahabharata* war in which one can see both schools of thought in operation; in this war the victory went to the practitioners of the *kutayuddha* school although the war itself has always been described as *dharmayuddha*. In the other epic war, the *Ramayana*, although both streams of thought were at work, the victory went to the *dharmayuddha* (righteous/ethical) school. And in the case of the wars fought by Emperor Ashoka, while all of them were presumably won by the methods of *kutayuddha*, after the conquests Ashoka himself turned a complete pacifist. This was the case with an individual (which is what has earned him fame) but in Indian thinking neither school ever completely replaced the other. At the level of rhetoric, the concept of *dharmayuddha* always reigned supreme. But in practice *kutayuddha* was often the norm. The defeat of Indian kings at the hands of foreign conquerors has been attributed by many to the loss of traditions of war-making, particularly that of *kutayuddha*. This is probably why, at present in modern India, the *kutayuddha* school seems to be in the ascendant,

*Paper presented to the 1995 seminar on "India and China Looking ar each other"

although even there the righteousness of the cause always dominates the rhetoric.

In ancient times, India was populated by numerous tribes. Some indigenous and others who had migrated into the subcontinent. (Some scholars have questioned this theory lately). They were culturally and technically unevenly developed and there was constant warfare among them, particularly between the immigrants and the natives. The wars were fought over territory, for lifting cattle (the chief form of wealth), for capturing women (the immigrants arrived with few women of their own), for honour and status, for self-aggrandizement in all spheres and sometimes out of anger, envy, fear or just display of heroism. While such warfare over centuries produced tribal rituals of warfare, codes of chivalry and heroism, technology of warfare and, of course, the all important hereditary group of warriors, the *ksatria varna*, it did not yield any body of thought which can be called strategic thinking which remains the major characteristic of Chinese thinking, particularly since the 4th century BC. Such thinking started with the establishment of well-recognized kingdoms/states as political entities possessing standing armies, administrations, laws and social order capable of supporting war.

Shaurya (heroism) continued to be valued as the virtue of an individual warrior but to this was added the concept of *neeti* (ethical principles) in the conduct of warfare. The belief grew that without neeti, war became merely a display of animal-like ferocity. For a victory based on principles (*dharmavijaya*), the king and the warriors had to observe certain codes in warfare. These codes were incorporated in the *Dharmashastras* (loosely translated as *Books of Law*). Warfare carried out according to the codes was also called *prakashayudha* (illuminated or open warfare). There was nothing secret about it. Preparations for such a war were made openly in the full knowledge of the adversary.

There was no element of surprise and there were strict rules about seasons of warfare, the duration of combat was restricted to daylight hours and rigid codes about close combat between warriors were observed. In all this, there was no room for strategy or tactics; only the numbers of warriors, their skills and the quality of weaponry counted. But, at the same time, diplomacy played an important role in building alliances for war and in making decisions about whether or not to go to war. The Chinese case around the time of Sunzi was quite different; set-piece battles were a thing of the past.

Inevitably, in actual warfare, the principles of righteous warfare were often set aside by individual warriors or their commanders. In fact, such was the sweetness of victory that some kings waged war for reasons of self-aggrandizement. The victory achieved for such selfish reasons came to be classified into two categories *aasurvijaya* in which the enemy's territory was annexed, enemy kings and commanders were bodly punished after the war, enemy cities were destroyed and the women were carried away as war booty. The second category produced *lobhavijaya* or victory out of covetousness or greed. This did not need waging a ruthless war of destruction but one for gain in terms of territory, wealth, women and so forth.

Only *kutayuddha* (devious warfare) could produce victories aimed of self-aggrandizement. Although the form was repeatedly denounced by ancient sages, it was nevertheless practised with increasing frequency until by the time of Emperor Ashoka, it came to be accepted as a norm. From practice, codification of devious warfare was only a short step. Several thinkers like Brihaspati and Shukracharya are known to have done this. But a comprehensive codification was undertaken by Kautilya, the great strategist of the Mauryan period.

The term *koota*, in the context of hunting, was used for a trap or snare. Consequently, in the context of warfare, it came to mean ensnaring or trapping the enemy. This included the use of magic spells and such other occult methods. (Sunzi decidedly rejected that use.) And when it came to weaponry prevalent in those days, it included the use of poisoned arrows, fire arrows and such other unauthorized weapons which could bring about destruction of men and property on a large scale. Other methods included poisoning of the enemy's water sources, attack by stealth, enticing the enemy into an unfavourable position, bribery, assassinations and attacks at night.

Almost every single war described in the epics and the puranas incorporated at least some of these forbidden methods. Sometimes, only one side is said to have done this. In the *Ramayana*, for example, the *raksasa* side is said to have resorted to *koota* methods. In the numerous wars fought between the devas and aasuras the latter are always accused of having used unethical methods. In general, it seems that such methods we attributed to the side which was technologically superior but nevertheless lost the series of wars in the end. The didactic message of these classics was that righteousness always emerged victorious. A few epics like the *Agni Purana*, however, condoned the use of *koota* methods by the weak as a last resort.

One prominent characteristic of the Hindu reading of reality is that the good is always mixed with or accompanied by the evil. Human nature is the product of a variety of influences (*karma*) from the previous births and the present life. So the same human being contains both righteous and unrighteous impulses, even the most ideally righteous person may occasionally commit unethical acts in the interests of larger righteous causes. Thus, in the *Ramayana,* Lord Rama, the most perfect human being known, nevertheless kills Vali, a brother of his ally, by deceit. In the *Mahabharata*, Lord Krishna, himself a major God in the Hindu pantheon, advises and resorts to all kinds of trickery in the service of the weak but righteous side in a dispute over a kingdom. Hindu classics always uphold the rhetoric of righteousness or dharma but condone and often justify lapses from the codes.

In this essay, I want to focus on the thinking of two strategic thinkers, Kautilya and Sunzi. Kautilya (also known as Chanakya and Visnusharman), who comes closest to the thinking of Sunzi as is available to us in his *Art of War* (*Bingfa*). Like Sunzi, Kautilya also rose as a strategic thinker in a period of constant warfare; both realized the importance of studying war as an important aspect of statecraft. However, Sunzi does not seems to have played any role in helping any particular state of his time to establish its hegemony over others. Kautilya on the other hand is said to have single-handedly engineered the victory of the Mauryas by destroying the Nanda power and to have put Chandragupta Maurya on the Magadha throne.

II

Kautilya's thinking on statecraft as a whole is available to us in the great classic *Arthashastra* (AS hereafter) which may be translated as the "Science of Politics and Administration". Unlike the *Bingfa* (BF hereafter), it covers a much broader range of subjects. But in this essay, we will discuss only those sections which deal with war and external affairs.

The AS recommends that a state should base its defences on the fort (*durg*) and the army. Of the two, it regards the fort to be more important since it allows the king to survive a siege and practise his diplomacy from that base. The army is, of course, important in defence matters but it can be completely lost on the battlefield leaving the king without any protection. In contrast, the BF totally rules out sieges as being expensive and wasteful.

For the defence of the state against enemies, the AS prescribes at least four bases, one each in every cardinal direction. These should preferably be natural defensive points such as mountains, water, desert, forests and the like. But in the state capital, a man-made fort is regarded as essential. It should have moats, ramparts and parapets for soldiers to shoot from. Wooden walls are ruled but as a fire-hazard. In the approaches to the fort, traps should be laid for the enemy. Inside it, it should be guarded by four types of formations comprising elephants, chariots, cavalry and infantry, each led by several commanders so that the loss of one or more to the enemy does not leave the formations leaderless. The fort should, of course, be well-stocked to withstand a siege but should have secret escape routes if the situation became desperate. As we shall see, Sunzi's thinking is very different.

The troops should, naturally, be from the warrior castes as far as possible. Lower *varna* are acceptable but the highest *varna*, Brahmins, are ruled out because of the peculiar Indian social system. The enemy can put Brahmin troops out of action simply by prostrating before them and prostrating persons, by law, could not be killed. The infantry can be a standing force or it can be raised for the particular war. But other branches, e.g., elephants, cavalry etc., must be standing formations led and trained by specialists. The army of an ally can be used but captured enemy soldiers should be used only with caution.

The AS prescribes a detailed hierarchy of officers. The *Senapati* or Chief-of-Staff is the highest officer, his station is at the rear. The lower commanders (*nayakas*) actually lead the troops in battle. Daily rigorous training must be the norm. Frequent inspections are required to keep the troops fighting fit. As for weapons, there should be a special office for acquiring them and storing them safely. Each weapon is to be marked with the king's insignia and strict inventories must be maintained to guard against loss.

Three main types of weapons are prescribed and seem actually to have been maintained in ordnance depots. The first category consisted of battlefield weapons such as bows and arrows, spears, swords, daggers, shields etc. The second type comprise those for defence of the fort such as stones, catapults and bows and arrows. The third type is meant for attacking enemy fortifications which includes scaling equipment as well as flaming arrows and other incendiary weapons. The AS puts a great deal of faith in magical practices such as casting spells.

In Kautilya's time, warfare was limited only to certain seasons. Generally it was avoided during the rainy season. The AS generally upholds this practice but says that the time for launching a war should also depend on the terrain which would become the battlefield.

It also prescribes that the type of troops to be deployed should be determined not only by the terrain but also by the disposition of enemy troops. The book lays down elaborate rules for establishing camps during the march against an enemy.

Although the AS puts a great deal of emphasis on devious warfare (*ktayuddha*), it prescribes that if a king has a clearly superior force and other factors are favorable, he should engage in open and rule-bound warfare (*prakashayudha*). Obviously in Kautilya's mind, a certain amount of odium continued to be associated with devious warfare. For it involved among other things attacking the enemy when he was vulnerable, feigning retreat to draw out the enemy into a trap, using elephants to break up closed ranks, attacking one flank and then the other, tiring out the enemy with one's inferior troops first and then attacking with superior ones, laying ambushes, attacking at night to deprive enemy soldiers of their sleep and then attacking them during the day with fresh troops, attacking the enemy troops when they were facing the sun and so forth. All such tactics are routine now but they were regarded as exceptional in Kautilya's time.

The AS, therefore, goes into great detail about the "conventional" warfare of its time. It prescribes standard battle-arrays (*vyuha*) which have a centre, two flanks and two wings. Each component of the *vyuha* is conceived as being of equal strength containing between 9 and 21 units; each unit in turn, should be based on an elephant or a chariot with five horsemen and 15 infantrymen in front and rear. There are four basic types of battle-arrays: the staff (in-line) array, the serpent (*wavy*) array, the circular array and the loose army. The choice is determined by the terrain and the enemy's troop disposition.

Great emphasis is placed on reserves behind every battle-array; this is where the king stations himself. The AS shows preference for mountains or forts to station the reserves. With the reserve force, there should be physicians and medicaments to treat the wounded, and field kitchens run by women. The women are also trusted with the task of "encouraging" the troops.

Before the beginning of action, the king should address his troops and emphasize that he is one of them. Next the Chief-of-Staff (*senapati*) should also address them and announce rewards for acts of bravery. (For example, killing the enemy king earned the reward of 10,000 coins and there were lesser rewards for other acts). Whatever loot the soldiers captured would be theirs but the Chief should also announce gratuities at the end of the war. It was the task of the officers to report acts of bravery by men fighting under their charge.

Whatever the form of warfare, the AS is scrupulous about one principle: not to cause harm to the subjects of the enemy king. So, when laying a siege to the fort, the people inside must be assured of their safety and be allowed to leave the fort for safe places. If territory must be annexed — it was usually not annexed -- only the king was forced to become an ally or a vassal — the people are to be won over through all means. Their customs must be respected and their gods must be revered by the new king. After the war, carrying away loot is forbidden. If the king was reduced to vassalage, he still retained control of the territory and the army and was not obliged to help his sovereign militarily.

It needs to be emphasized that the AS does not only speak about making conquests. It also discusses the strategies and tactics for the prevention of conquest by others. This is why a large portion of the book is devoted to statecraft and administration of the state.

But whether in conquering others or in preventing conquest, the AS takes conflictual relationship between states as the norm. So, management of these occupies an important place in Kautilya's thinking. It is almost certain that a large number of ideas he propounds came to him as received wisdom. And after him these ideas were appropriated by different texts as their own.

Kautilya's major contribution, in contrast with that of Sunzi, comes from his sense of political geography. The AS envisages the "international" arena, the *mandala*, as comprising 12 types of kings/states. It classifies them as follows: 1. The would-be conqueror, at the centre of the mandala. 2. The enemy whose territory borders on that of the would-be conqueror, i.e., the hostile neighbour. 3. The ally whose territory lies immediately beyond that of the hostile neighbour. 4. The enemy's ally who is the neighbour of one's won ally. 5. The ally's ally who is territorially distant. 6. The ally of the enemy's ally who is also territorially distant. Types 7 to 10 follow the same sequence but to the rear of the would-be conqueror. The last two types are No. 11, a neutral king/state neighbouring both the would-be conqueror and his/its enemy but is stronger than both. And 12, the king who is totally indifferent towards all other kings/states but is more powerful than the would-be conqueror, his enemy and the neutral king/ state.

All the advice in the AS is directed to the would-be conqueror (*vijigisu* or one desirous of victory). The underlying assumption is that neighbors always turn hostile. Another assumption is that a common enemy creates allies. But the categories of enemy and ally are not fixed. Under certain conditions, allies can become friends and vice-versa. The 12 types classified by the AS are possible combinations; they are not to be taken as the permanently existing actual situation in a mandala.

Kautilya assumes that except for the neutral and "indifferent" kings/states, all others in the mandala are of equal strength. So, in a concrete situation, the mandala gets divided into two more or less equal blocs, with one block-leader seeking to establish hegemony over all the others. The strengths of blocs being equal, diplomacy, strategy and tactics assume great importance in attaining hegemony.

The AS does emphasize the role of diplomacy but shows no preference for it over war. This is simply because one important component of the society of his time was the warrior group whose very existence was tied to fighting. Diplomacy, for Kantilya, was for winning allies, delaying war if one was vulnerable and for making postwar arrangements for a new order.

According to the AS, relations with other kings/states are to be established and carried out through *dutas* or ambassadors. It prescribes three types of ambassadors: the plenipotentiary, envoy with limited negotiating powers, and one who is only a messenger. It recommends that ambassadors should be stationed in all foreign states on a permanent basis and that they should enjoy what we call "diplomatic immunity" in modern parlance. In contrast to modern diplomatic norms, however, the AS expects the ambassadors to engage in spying, acts of sabotage and most importantly be active in securing defections from the enemy's army.

Kautilya distinguished between six major approaches to foreign policy. The first is a policy of maintaining peace with another state which is based on a treaty detailing the terms and conditions. The second is the policy of hostility which should be followed if one is stronger than the enemy. The third approach is one of inaction: It is most suitable when states are of equal strength. The fourth is outright invasion but this policy is recommended for the very strong. For the very weak is prescribed the fifth approach, i.e., seeking shelter with another king and wait for better days. The sixth and the last approach recommends a policy of peace with one king/state while maintaining hostility towards another; such a dual policy is possible if help is available from another state to fight the enemy.

The AS, naturally realizes that one may become the object of such policies by another king/state. So the enemy may force peace by a treaty on oneself. If that happens, Kautilya advises that one should drag one's feet in fulfilling the treaty obligations and wait for an opportunity to overthrow the enemy. If the treaty demands a hostage, for example, one should offer an inferior person. But if the enemy demands one's son as a hostage, the king should offer himself so that the son can plan to overthrow the enemy and rescue the father.

The AS describes many kinds of treaties, with or without various stipulations, temporary and long-term ones, sincere and dishonest ones. The aim is always to outsmart the adversary. It also discusses in great detail not only the six broad approaches outlined above but also their combinations. Even the necessity of surrender is not overlooked but it is always for buying time.

War-making is only one among the means to attain one's objective of hegemony. The other means are friendship and bribery to be employed against weak kings. Yet another two means to be deployed against the strong are splitting (the enemy's strength and alliances) and coercion (which includes war). The difference between the means and approaches/policies is that the means can be employed against domestic as well as foreign opponents whereas the policies can apply only to other kings/ states.

By way of broad strategy, the AS recommends that the would be conqueror should first go at the hostile neighbour and with the new power acquired, he should next tackle the neutral king/state. If he succeeds, he should proceed against the most powerful "indifferent" king. That would complete his hegemony over the mandala as a whole, for the rest would fall in line. But if there are no neutral or "indifferent" kings, the conqueror should first tackle his enemies and then secure the allegiance of the enemy's allies. In the event there are only two other states, one hostile and the other friendly, the would-be conqueror should crush the neighbouring state regardless of whether it is hostile or friendly and then proceed against the other. Finally, if there are a number of neighbouring states, they should be tackled one by one gaining strength in the process.

It goes without saying that Kautilya underlines all his strategies with the requirement that the would-be conqueror must satisfy himself that he enjoys superiority in such essential aspects as troop morale, war materiel and above all strategic advice. At the same time, the king must take precautions against insurrection within his own kingdom while he is away at war. So the AS recommends that a reliable Regent should be appointed and one-third of the army left behind for internal security. The most likely rebel leader should be taken by the king on his expedition. (The AS, as may be expected, also discusses how an insurrection should be planned and executed.) Finally, the AS elaborately discusses how gains and losses from an expedition against others should be estimated beforehand.

Kautilya wrote a practical handbook and therefore does not indulge in any theory of a good society, good actions etc. This is why to the modern mind he comes across as a totally amoral and cynical practitioner of strategies of war. Most Western comment on the AS is therefore negative in the extreme. In India, however, the book has never evoked any such negative response. This seems largely because despite the odium attached to *kutayuddha*, in all epic wars, the righteous side always emerged victorious. *Kutayuddha* always remained a kind of side-show. The second reason, I think, is that the AS was appropriated by other *shastras* and the *puranas* (or epics) in which the moral/ethical side of all human actions was abundantly stressed; so, devious and cynical practices came to be considered secondary, situational and answering only the needs of exigencies.

III

Sunzi was a product of the Warring States period (403-221 BC). At that time China was divided into numerous states, each with its own standing army. There was constant warfare among them. This allowed a number of "sages" (*Zi*) to travel from one state to another to offer advice on military matters to the kings. There is some doubt about whether such a person actually existed or whether what has come down to us as Bingfa (BF) was a compilation of the sayings of several strategists. For the purpose or this essay we will treat the BF as having been authored by Sunzi who may have lived in the 4th century BC.

If BF is to be summarized in one sentence, it would be: "The supreme art of war is to subdue the enemy without fighting". Sunzi cautioned the kings and their commanders not to place reliance on sheer military power. He exhorted them to resort to minimum killing and destruction of the enemy. They were to take all intact or as nearly intact as possible.

All this called for very high level skills of diplomacy and devising stratagems of deceit, bribery and extensive use of spies (one's own, from among the enemy's subjects and double spies, i.e., the enemy's spies won over). The army was only an instrument to deliver the *coup de grace* to an enemy previously made vulnerable through other means like subversion and causing a rift between him and his allies. Sunzi himself did not believe in magic weapons and asked the kings and commanders not to resort to them. In contrast, Kautilya favored their use.

Since most kings in Sunzi's time were prone to resort to war to satisfy their whims and greed — they lived unbelievably luxurious lives — Sunzi repeatedly asked them not to resort to military adventures. War was an important element of statecraft and had to be studied with seriousness. No war should be undertaken without drawing up detailed plans which were tailored to the situation of the enemy. In any case, wars must be short, swift and decisive. "There never has been a protracted war which has benefited a country" he said. He was especially aware of the economic consequence of war, particularly the inflation of currency during and after a war.

Sunzi firmly believed that only benevolent and righteous rulers could win wars. Rulers had to have unstinted support of their subjects behind them. By implication, he believed that such benevolent rulers had no fear of internal insurrection, a subject on which Kautilya has much to say.

The BF does not convey the impression that Sunzi had any imperial designs in mind for the ruler he was advising. The BF does use the word *ba* (hegemonic) but it seems to mean a more powerful ruler than others. In fact, the Legalists (Shang Yang, Han Feizi and Xunzi) who were empire-builders for the Qin state do not seem to have benefited much from Sunzi's teachings, except perhaps for battlefield tactics. When the Qin state ultimately established the first empire, its Emperor ordered that all classics before him (except works on technology) should be burnt. He did not spare the BF.

In contrast to AS, the BF has a very limited view of political geography. Sunzi is aware that the enemy may have allies but he basically speaks of bilateral responses to and initiatives vis-a-vis the enemy. He distinguishes between overall strategy (what should one do about the enemy?) and military strategy (how to win a war if one decides to wage one). He has little to say about the former question but is extremely detailed and meticulous about the second.

Both BF and AS share the importance of the terrain and weather while they differ sharply on the importance of numbers of soldiers and weapons. BF does discuss the use of different kinds of weaponry in some detail but the emphasis is clearly on tactics of mobile warfare. China did not then have cavalry, as India did, but AS nowhere speaks of using it for outflanking the enemy. In contrast, BF treats the main (*zheng*) force as a way of intimidating the enemy but actually resorting to the extraordinary (*qi*) force for attacks on the flanks and the rear of the enemy.

The primary target of the attack is the mind of the enemy commander. Is he rash? Is he quick-tempered? Does he have too delicate a sense of honour? It so, one must plan one's strategy accordingly. Sunzi rules out sieges and frontal attacks except to surprise and cause disarray. He always recommends the "indirect approach." One should attack only when one can win. But one must never hesitate to withdraw to conserve oneself and to entice the enemy to a battlefield favourable to oneself. Given enough rope, Sunzi seems to say, the enemy will hang himself.

The only constant thing about war is constant change of the situation. In fact, a good commander must take the initiative to create change and then to manipulate it. But the foremost method in warfare is deception. When capable, feign incapacity, when active, feign inactivity, when near the enemy, make it appear to him that you are far away. When you are far away, lead him to believe that you are near. Feign disorder and strike the smug enemy. Pretend inferiority and encourage his arrogance. When the enemy is strong avoid him.

As for tactics, when one has ten to the enemy's one, surround him and take him intact; when one has 5:1 superiority, attack and disperse him. But if only double his strength, seek to divide him. If equal to the enemy's strength, one can engage him but this requires great skill. If weaker, withdraw. In no case attack his elite troops. If you surround the enemy, leave an escape route; otherwise he will fight desperately. Keep him under strain and wear him down. BF is full of such aphorisms and modern commanders will at once recognize them. Kautilya has aslso mentioned many of the same tactics. BF is much shorter than AS and does not deal with "international relations" or administration of the state.

Unlike AS, BF (despite all known copies having been burnt by Emperor Qin Shihuangdi) was studied and extensively commented upon almost continuously over the next two millennia. Since late 19th century it has also been used as an important text book in Japanese military academies. There are many scholars and strategists in the West who believe that Mao Zedong's military thinking was based on Sunzi's BF but Mao denied that he had read BF before he came up with his own military doctrines. The two certainly differ on the subject of protracted war although they agree on several tactics.

IV

We finally come to an overall comparison between *Bingfa* and the *Arthashastra.* Both works display great clarity of thought and a strong sense of realism. Neither advocates protracted war or total war although both are convinced that war is a constant reality for the state and therefore must be studied and executed seriously. At the same time, both Sunzi and Kautilya make it abundantly clear that war is much more than just a fight among men; reliance on sheer military power does not assure victory. What we today call "software" is much more important than the "hardware". Thus strategy and tactics become supremely important elements and they must be practised in tandem with diplomacy.

The authors of both works were great practitioners of *realpolitik.* As such they do not indulge in moralizing or theorizing about the ends of power. Kautilya does pay lip-service to the upholding of a righteous social and political order, but Sunzi does not do that beyond saying that popular and just rulers can mobilize their subjects for victory more successfully than unpopular and unjust ones. Beyond this concession to righteous principle, both focus their attention on the goal: the achievement of victory over others through any means appropriate for the occasion. These include obtaining accurate information about the enemy's plans and actions to frustrate them. Both strongly advocate measures to break up the enemy's alliances and his internal structure in order to isolate and demoralize him. Both recommend indirect and devious approaches with deception at all levels playing the central role. Oddly enough, despite such single-mindedness in achieving victory/hegemony, both Kautilya and Sunzi are concerned about minimizing the economic costs of war as well as minimizing civilian casualities.

A closer comparison will, no doubt, bring out more similarities as well as differences between the two thinkers. Kautilya, it appears, is far more concerned about preventing conquest by others and far more in acquiring vassals than is Sunzi. Similarly, he also shows more sensitivity about internal security than does Sunzi. Above all, whereas Sunzi focuses somewhat narrowly on war, Kautilya has a much broader set of concerns taking in all aspects of statecraft, of which war is just one. But he applies himself to that one aspect with just as much concentration as Sunzi does.

Despite the great similarities -- almost identities -- between the two, there remains one major difference which has to do with the different social systems of India and China. As mentioned earlier, Sunzi's thinking may be summed up in one sentence: The victory is one where the enemy is subdued without fighting. Such a sweeping doctrine would have been inconceivable for Kautilya because that would have devalued the entire hereditary warrior *varna.* For this class, it was a disgrace to die anywhere except on the battlefield. So, a world without war was even theoretically inconceivable so long as one was within the established order. But a world without war was not only conceivable but eminently desirable for those outside the fold i.e., the Buddhists and the Jainas. Emperor Ashoka established the Magadha empire as a warrior informed by the thinking embodied in the *Arthashastra,* but having done that he saw the futility of it all. That wisdom made it impossible for him to continue as a warrior. And since he ceased to believe in the creed of warriors, his rightful place was outside the "Hindu" fold, in the path of the Buddha.

But among the rulers in India, Ashoka was an exception. China did not produce an Ashoka. The Indian rulers after Ashoka, Buddhists and Jaina ones included, waged wars as did the different rulers in China when the empire split up from time to time and they applied the concepts of AS and BF. However, in our own century, the Kuomintang in China and the armed forces in India wholly copied the western concepts of warfare almost to the last detail. Mercifully, they ignored one commandment of Clausewitz: "To introduce in the philosophy of war a principle of moderation would be an absurdity. War is an act of violence pushed to its utmost bounds". In our own times neither India, nor Pakistan nor China has resorted to Clausewitz's concept of "total war". Is there a civilizational lesson in this?

References

Samuel B. Griffith, *Sun Tzu, The Art of War,* New York 1963.

V.R Ramchandra Dikshitar, *War in Ancient India,* Delhi, 1987.

R.P. Kangle, *The Kautilya Arthasastra* (Vol. 3), Delhi, 1988.

P.V. Kane, *History Of Dharmasastras,* (Vol. 3) Poona, 1946-54.

K.A. Nilakantha Sastri, *Age of the Nandas and the Mauryas,* Banares, 1952.

Romila Thapar, *Ashoka and the Decline of the Mauryas,* Oxford, 1961'.

G.D Bakshi, *Mahabharata,* A *Military Analysis,* Delhi, 1990.

VR RAGHAVAN

36

ARTHASHASTRA AND SUNZI BINGFA*

An attempt to understand the strategic outlook of two great nations like India and China would require an examination of many strands of history. One most important strand would be the written account of the way the nations were protected from external and internal threats to their existence. India and China produced a unique pair of treatises, which allow us to examine strategic thoughts that guided their policies. The classical treatises of *Arthashastra* and *Sunzi Bingfa* are specially suited to this examination, by the range, scope and emphasis of their outlook.

Arthashastra and *Sunzi Bingfa* offer fascinating insights into the approaches to statecraft by two wholly different civilisations. It is nevertheless better to study them on their own terms instead of looking for commonalities. *Arthashastra* was conceived and named as the Science of Wealth. It focussed on creation of wealth as the means to ensure the well being of the state. *Sunzi Bingfa* is what might be called the Science of Decisive Results. The first covers a wide gamut of state-making activities. The second, while specifically directed towards winning a war, is indicative of the philosophy that should govern the activity of the state. The two classics were products of their times. In China, it was the period of Warring States , when various kings were contesting for supremacy within the pale of Chinese civilisation with nomadic horsemen threatening the frontiers. The Great Wall had yet to come up in its integrated shape and victory in war was seen as the best way to ensure the safety of the state. In India it was the time of post-Buddha warring kings. Alexander had visited, conquered a part of India and left behind strong satraps to rule the seized lands. These not very dissimilar circumstances nevertheless produced two contrasting doctrinal approaches to managing the state's security.

In the western world, by the end of the 4th Century BC, the mighty armies of Persians (Darius) and Greeks (Alexander) had come and gone. The new model armies of the Romans had already created an empire. Hannibal's campaign over the Alps with elephants had been conducted in 216 BC. Warfare had become an organised enterprise in all its aspects, viz., financing, organising, recruiting, tactics, generalship, logistics and training. In China and India, prior to the 5th Century BC, warfare had remained ritualistic, either based on unorganised masses crashing into each other, or of feudal knights battling individually according to the rules of personal combat, e.g., the probity of *Prakasha yudha.* Chivalry and the warrior's code took precedence over results. King Porus' regal answer to Alexander on how a defeated king be treated is indicative of the attitudes that guided warfare. In China the King (Duke) of Song in 638 BC declined to attack till the enemy army was fully arranged and such a civility made him lose the battle. Mao Zedong was fond of saying, "We are not the Duke of Song." Around the 5th Century BC, warfare had started getting organised into a method. By the 4th Century, warfare in both countries had become a "directed" affair.

In China, the King of Zhao had introduced the first major military reforms by 307 BC, by replacing the chariots with cavalry. By 299 BC the *Shangjun Shu* (sometimes also called *Book of Shangjun*) had been compiled. It formalised the views of the Legalists as opposed to the Confucian traditionalists. It saw war as inevitable and which must be won. It went on to say, "A wise ruler understands that he can attain surpremacy in the under-heaven only by victory and therefore obliges his people to serve in the army." The theory of proportional dependence of a state's power on its military success became the classic contribution of the *Shangjun Shu* . The period of Warring States ended by 221 BC. *Sunzi Bingfa* gave a sharper edge to the *Shangjun Shu* and made war the first priority of the state: "War is a matter of vital importance to the state; the province of life

*Comment on Giri Deshingkar's paper in the previously mentioned Seminar, November, 1995

and death; the road to survival or ruin. It is mandatory that it be thoroughly studied."

A comparable emphasis on the military aspect of state policy did not emerge in India. The *Arthshastra* focussed on preservation of the state through alliances, and the elaborate and almost esoteric "Mandalas" by which to determine inter-state relations. It thus emphasised balance of power — a much maligned outlook today in India. Kautilya's India looked at war as a feature of the state's life, something to be lived with, almost as if one puts up with a chronic illness with the help of palliatives. The army was just one of seven elements that constituted the state (king, ministers, land and people, towns and cities, treasury, forces, allies). War was treated as any other state enterprise and not considered vital as in *Sunzi Bingfa.* Bulk of the army was made up with the help of guilds (*shrenis*). The *mandala* approach was applied even to the regular army. The army chiefs and other generals were given the full treatment of spies, surveillance and mutual suspicions. The location of the army was decided by the need to keep it divided and not on operational needs. Compared to *Sunzi Bingfa*, war in *Arthashastra* was more an ongoing effort instead of a climactic, decisive act to shatter the present and shape the future. The perils of indecisive and therefore protracted wars from which no country ever benefits, as advised in *Sunzi Bingfa*, were never quite understood in Indian strategic thought. It was to cost India dear throughout its history, and even in the modern post-Independence period. Even in recent times Mao Zedong emphasised protracted war as the people's means to defeat the stronger forces of a state. *Arthashastra* does not mention protracted war at all. Perhaps living in a protracted state of conflict had made the rulers and peoples inured to it.

Historical and state factors played a not insignificant part in the evolution of the contrasting strategic emphasis on matters of the nation's safety. Even in the age when the king was synoymous with the state, India and China as kingdoms looked at threats to the state differently. Chinese convictions about it being the civilised centre, or middle, against the barbarian periphery, led to the military emphasis of *Sunzi Bingfa.* India had by then absorbed numerous military and civilisational invasions. A culturally accommodative state had emerged which is reflected in the *Arthashastra's* emphasis on alliances and spheres of influence.

Sunzi Bingfa emphatically related power to military strength. This special emphasis on the military as the indicator of national power, continues to weigh heavily in Chinese thought in modern times. Mao's immortal quote on political power growing out of the barrel of the gun, reiterates that emphasis even more tellingly than *Sunzi Bingfa.* Kautilya's *Arthashastra* viewed good counsel and correct judgement as the constituents of power and as more useful than military might. One also wonders in the light of the history of the time, if Kautilya was not more concerned with the intellectual and moral qualities of Indian leadership of his time than their personal valour! Along with power the relative importance given to decisive action is another area of divergent outlook. *Sunzi Bingfa* places a high premium on decisive, even deterrent action. There is a clear preference for action directed towards decisive results. The story of the author of the Chinese classic, actually beheading a few concubines of the King of Wu while teaching them drill, to show how obedience is to be obtained may be apocryphal, but is indicative of the ruthless emphasis on decisive results. The *Arthashastra* is almost managerial in its outlook on managing the affairs of the state.

The present may seem remarkably as a continuation of the past, if Indian and Chinese policies for the management of internal and external threats are any indication. *Arthashastra* and *Sunzi Bingfa* really cannot and should not be compared but used as insights into the two great civilisations' inspirations of state policies. They provide very useful clues to each other's outlook on the role of the state. More than that, they offer pointers to the future management of relations with each other. At the turn of the second millennium, when the need is more of interdependence than confrontation, *Arthashastra* and *Sunzi Bingfa* offer as good an understanding of what was done in the past, as of what can be achieved in the future. India and China will do well to learn from both the classics.

MANIK BHATTACHARYYA

37

THE LOFTY HEIGHT OF A WRITER: MY EVALUATION OF LU XUN

When Lu Xun (1881-1936) died the entire nation was engulfed in grief and he was honoured by the people as "the soul of the nation". Mao while commemorating Lu Xun's first death anniversary called him the sage of modern China. Lu Xun's works have been considered as an encyclopedia of Chinese society and his essays as a whole have been compared with the popular romance *A Dream of Red Mansions, (Honglou meng)* which is worth reading a hundred times.[1]

Why Lu Xun and his works have become a widely accepted topic of research is not only because of his remarkable contribution in the field of literature but also his views which provide authentic clues to facilitate our accessibility into the complex social reality of the time. The literary images in his writings were not merely faithful reflections of the real life characters but were moulded and created by him with certain specific messages. Lu Xun's contribution in the field of language and literature is enormous, thus, most of the commentators have viewed the greatness of Lu Xun primarily from the angle of literature. However, the point that he played an important role in the overall historical development of Chinese society, which was highlighted by Mao, has not been examined in depth.

I have the honour of knowing Mr. Wang Shijing, the biographer of Lu Xun, and accompanying him in Delhi and Agra when he came to participate in the special seminar commemorating Lu Xun's birth centenary organized by Jawaharlal Nehru University in 1981. This acquaintance has converted me into a fan of Lu Xun, so to speak. In the last seventeen years I have been obsessed with the reading of Lu Xun, who was also the topic of my doctoral research. I was overjoyed when Prof. Tan Chung asked me to do this article. However, the limited space he allotted to me inhibits me from pouring out all my admirations and assessments on this great writer of our century. Suffice it here to highlight a few aspects.

I

To begin with, let us see how mythology and scientific spirit have interwoven into a curious mix in Lu Xun. In the pre-scientific era, the longer the history of a civilization the greater wealth is its mythology. China belonged to this accumulative process. The massive absorption of Indian culture through the vehicle of Buddhism had doubly increased the treasury of legends and mythology before the birth of Lu Xun. When he grew old enough to appreciate cultural phenomenon, Lu Xun was marvelled by the mythological world that had surrounded him. To the older generations, the mythology in the cultural soil of China was not just a natural growth, but was deliberately planted by the guardians of morality to lead people to shun immorality and evil designs, and to be god-fearing. Lu Xun's generation was much less god-fearing than their seniors as they grew up in the fresh air of scientific spirit. Thus, to Lu Xun, spirits were not to be feared, but deserved appreciation about their creation, their attraction, and their value as cultural ingredients.

A Brief History Of Chinese Fiction (Zhongguo Xiaoshuo Lueshi) is a pioneering work in which Lu Xun traced the origin and evolution of Chinese fiction. His observations based on meticulous examination of the history of fiction writing are refreshing, showing an authentic understanding of the literary genre so far neglected by Chinese scholars. He considers mythology as the source of fiction. His comments on scarce and scattered mythological sources in China are insightful. He discovers the historically evolved characteristic features of Chinese fictions and observes that the same has never been recognized as superior literary work by most of the major schools of thought. The prose writing of historical and philosophical nature contained references to the life and activities of mythological and legendary figures, and great poets were inspired by myths and legends and made considerable use of mythology. Apart from being a part of historically recognized literary genres, mythology had no independent place. Fictions or stories therefore had no official recognition too. Ironically, the supernatural and outlandish themes and characters of gods, demons and spirits remained the subject matter of Chinese fictions throughout and enjoyed immense popularity among the people. Lu Xun believes that the motive of creating fantasies and extraordinary scenarios in far remote times was nothing but a positive and natural reflection of literary activities. He finds the relationship between mythology and embryonic religious thought somewhat natural and logical though both had originated from the primitive need of maintaining psychological balance of mind while living in a chaotic and hard life. *Shan Hai Jing* (the Book of Hills and Seas) is the oldest book of geography which contains quite a few legends. *Huainanzi* is another book enshrined with myths. *Zhuangzi* is a book written by the famous thinker of its namesake and his disciples in the Warring States (475-221 B.C.) period that contains a number of legends though it is essentially a work of philosophy. *Chu Ci* (the Songs of Chu) is a collection of poems compiled by Liu Xiang during Western Han Dynasty (206 B.C.-24 A.D.). It has poems written by Qu Yuan and Song Yu of Warring States period and Xiao Shan and Dong Fangsu of Han Dynasty. The book is rich in extensive mythological references. The tradition of mythology and fairy tales continued through ages by direct or indirect references in poems and even in philosophical and historical works. This shows that there was no dearth of imagination and fantasy in the social reality of China. The tradition established by poets like Qu Yuan continued by poets such as Ruan Ji, Tao Yuanming, Li Bai, Li He, Su Shi and essayist Zhuang Zhou (i.e. Zhuangzi). *Xi You Ji* (A Pilgrimage to the West) and *Liaozhai Zhiyi* (Extraordinary Events from The Leisure Study) are works about strange and fanciful happenings. The spirit of mythology and fictitious episodes was experimented by Lu Xun by giving a modern version of it in his *Gushi Xinbian* (Old Tales Retold).

Lu Xun considers the reason of indifference towards myths as the absence of a strict division between gods and ghosts in the written traditions of China. There are quite a number of ghosts who could become deities and worshipped by the people. Since there was absence of proper demarcation between men and gods in ancient China, religion could not be fully institutionalized. Myths and legends lost their due place in the history of literature. However, religious elements whether as metaphysical or mystical questions or as ritualistic cults were all along at work in the evolution of Chinese culture. The age of mythology and the realm of gods and spirits have remained lively in the minds of people through popular stories. "Wushi" or the position of priesthood was an important official status and "Wujiao" or Shamanism was a kind of primitive religion which was replaced gradually by "Shiguan" or official historian and by the system of recording history.[2] The indigenous religious system of Han people had four basic activities: ancestor worship, worship of heaven, divination and sacrifice. The inscriptions on oracle bones of Shang Dynasty (1523-1027 B.C.) were the earliest records of divination on important matters such as harvest, war, peace, natural calamities etc. Confucianism, the chief school of thought, which gradually developed into secularized ethical and political ruling ideology could not but reflect on such religious or spiritual matters.

The demarcation line between celestial and worldly characters remained confused and the attraction of such other-worldly strange stories were well relished by the common people while not entertained by the historians. This romantic source of the mythology nevertheless inspired creative minds through ages. Lu Xun's interest in the origin and evolution of civilization of humankind in general led him to examine other traditions. He was aware of the rich and profound source of Indian mythology. His knowledge of deities and demons of Indian tradition was acquired from Buddhist literature. The Buddhist tradition remained a popular yet separate tradition in China. Deities and demons of Buddhist texts were an integral part of the popular cultural tradition. It has been mentioned that Lu Xun acquired a religious name after he was dedicated to a monastery. His grandmother and his maid-servant used to narrate stories of nature, animals, fairies and popular myths. The deities and supernatural characters in folk operas were intensely watched by child Lu Xun. The hanging woman, different images of Wuchang, Mulian's rescue of his mother, the colourful description of Yama, the king of death etc. were Lu Xun's favourites.[3]

Lu Xun was brought up in a traditional atmosphere and gradually became aware of the splendid cultural heritage and ancient history. He studied Confucian classics and the time-honoured historical and philosophical texts. China's tradition of preserving a recorded history of the past and strict restriction on reading fictions made him more and more averse to classics. He became curious to know more about the mythological past and the origin of Chinese civilization beyond the limited references of myths and legends in historical texts. Fantasies and stories with supernatural characters always fascinated child Lu Xun. Later when he grew up he studied various aspects of human life and activities in the primitive and pre-historic stage of human civilization particularly that of China.[4] The rich and glorious past that he inherited through well-preserved historical evidences not only made him inquisitive about the origin of Chinese civilization but also made him feel proud about his own cultural heritage. His inquiries into the mythological life of China enabled him to make certain valuable observations on early religion, psychology and culture. With such insights acquired from his study of the past he could reflect on the contemporary life and society. The profound understanding of and a deep emotional attachment he had with various mythological images can be seen as an intrinsic element of his work. Mythology contains the life and achievements of human experience reflected in such characters who had uncommon and supernatural capabilities and who were able to understand the mystery of the nature through their long and arduous encounters with various phenomena. They have been eulogized or worshipped through ages as heroes, gods or as semi-gods. Among various mythological characters who are known popularly in China are Pangu and Nuwa and their stories concerning the origin of the earth, Kuafu and Houyi, the two heroes with indomitable determination: (Kuafu who tried to reach the sun and died, Houyi shot down nine suns and left only one for the earth), Lady Chang E and her consumption of the elixir in the absence of her husband and as a result her lonely flight to the moon, in addition to stories of semi-legendary kings such as Yao, Shun and Yu and other mythological characters such as Fuxishi, Shennongshi, Youchaoshi, Zhuanxu, Huangdi's (the Yellow Emperor) protracted war with Chiyou (the tribal chief of Jiu Liu race), and the eventual victory of Huangdi supposed to be the patriarch of the Chinese race.

Lu Xun's profound interest in mythology and his priding himself on belonging to a great civilization enriched by legends made him write his essay "The Power of the *Mara* Poetry". He traced back the literary creation in great civilizations of the world. He compared different civilizations such as Indian, Judaic, Persian, Arabic, Russian, and reflected on comtemporary China. While he admired outstanding literary works like the "*Four Vedas*", *Ramayana*, *Mahabharata* and the plays of Kalidasa of Indian civilization, he did not hesitate to criticize such mentality of boasting one's past glory. He was puzzled that while creative minds could attain such perfection in their literary and artistic endeavour this could not deliver the people from their miserable conditions.

It is significant that Lu Xun used the Sanskrit word "*Mara*" (in Chinese "moluo") in the caption of the essay, and made it clear about his longing for the *Mara* power. We know that the Indian mythology eulogises the power of *Mara* (demon) while on the other hand, Indian orthodox tradition advocates *Dharma* vanquishing *Mara* which is perpetuated in the annual celebration of the Festival of Rama's Victory over Ravana. Both the strains of Indian civilization have been internalized by the Chinese culture which is reflected in the alternate Chinese sayings of "Dao gao yichi mo gao yizhang" (when *Dharma*/Truth rises for a foot *Mara*/Evil rises for ten feet" and "Mo gao yichi dao gao yizhang" (When *Mara*/Evil rises for one foot" *Dharma*/Truth rises for ten feet). In this seesaw battle between *Dao* (truth) and *Mo* (the abbreviation of *Moluo*) in Chinese culture, Lu Xun obviously stood on the side of Mo/mara and was determined to stand Chinese tradition on its head. Lu Xun liked his essay about the power of *Mara* poems and often congratulated himself for having written it when he was very young. In the postscript of the *Fen (Grave)* series (1926), he expressed his dislike for most of his essays except the reference to the life and works of the *Mara* poets.

China's defeat at the hands of the Western powers and even Japan (a small country in China's eastern neighbourhood) administered an exogenous shock on the Chinese civilizational pride and complacency. Like the Indian response to the Western challenge, the Chinese intellectual elite of whom Lu Xun was a part evinced a keen interest in learning from the Western civilization while, at the same time, began a serious introspection of their own traditional values. Lu Xun was at the forefront of a section of Chinese intellectuals who launched a frontal attack on Chinese culture. This created a complex image of Lu Xun who was both a patriot and a motherland-baiter, having loyalty to both native and foreign cultural assets. Perhaps, the geo-social environment of his birth place, Shaoxing, was a contributory factor. Shaoxing had been known as "the home of retribution and erasure of shame".[5] People of Shaoxing put up heroic wars of resistance at the end of Song Dynasty (960-1279) against Jin (Nurchen) conquerors, and at the end of Ming Dynasty (1368-1644) against the Qing (Manchu) conquerors. Shaoxing has been the native place of revolutionaries, most notably Qiu Jin (1879-1907) who were in the front rank in taking up arms against the Qing rule in the early twentieth century. Little wonder why Lu Xun was so bold in absorbing ideas from new revolutionary sources. He remained sincere in that process of absorption throughout. The crisis in the post-Opium War China created a situation that was marked by degeneration, helplessness and a complexity of being proud of the past glory and sensitive to the national defeat at the hands of foreign intruders (including the Manchu). Lu Xun was born in such a critical time. It was not so difficult for him to consciously extricate himself from that pervasive sense of helplessness, but it was a formidable task to do so in his sub-conscious mind. The emotional attachment with the cultural ethos which had nurtured him and the fear of the disintegration or even the extinction of the nation disturbed the equilibrium of his mind. He was in the gradual process of being disillusioned with the tradition and his confused mind being refreshed by new ideas and scientific achievements emanating from the West. During his four-year stay in Nanjing the most significant inspiration he drew was from the Darwin's theory of evolution through the book *Evolution and Ethics* in which Yan Fu's ideas were also revealed. Lu Xun was deeply influenced by Yan's advocacy of evolution and natural selection.

Europe during the post-Industrial Revolution period experienced a series of remarkable achievements in different branches of science. The vigorous movement in favour of scientific method and empirical investigations gave rise to a host of new philosophies and theoretical formulations. The old concepts about the origin of the universe, nature, man, religion became ridiculous and new concepts and values replaced them in a very short span of history. The triumph of science became unchallenged. Even the religion became the subject-matter of scientific study. Philosophical questions about the reality, nature, man, god, mind, matter and ideas dealt with by earlier philosophers became the target of attack from the thinkers of positivism, denying the intelligibility, logics, rationality beyond materialism.

Lu Xun was carried away by such amazing human achievements and wrote few essays in response to such developments in early twentieth century. He expressed his keen interest in science and his concern for the progress of humankind in general. In "Shuo ri" (On Radium) he welcomed the discovery of radium by Madame Curie. He observed that the discovery of radium, a substance which emits light, was a great scientific discovery which demystified the beliefs of the past and also dealt heavy blow to the existing theories particularly the Newtonian theories of physics. He thought the discovery would provide revolutionary inputs in human thought. "Ren zhi lishi" (History of Man) introduced the biological theories to the Chinese. He explained the theoretical formulation of Ernst Heinrich Haeckel (1835-1919), the German biologist and a follower of Darwinism. Lu Xun systematically explained the different stages of the theory of evolution from the early Greek thought to the interpretation by Thomas Henry Huxley. He mentioned Pangu's legend of opening the heaven and separating the earth from it and Nuwa's legendary creation of humans on earth (with mud and hay). He compared the Chinese mythological scene with the western notion of creation by Noah and Moses. All this, according to him, was obstacle to the scientific understanding of the universe. He mentioned a number of scientists and thinkers who contributed to the demystification of human creation. He mentioned their works and was confident of the rapid and lasting impact of the theory of evolution on humankind and its contribution to removing the misconceptions about the origin of man.

Paradoxically, while he was denouncing the myths of his own country, he was fascinated by those of another continent. Lu Xun's enthusiasm in portraying the Themopylae episode in "Sibada zhi hun" (the Soul of Sparta) was indicative of the deep influence of the spirit of valour and patriotism of Spartan warriors. He wanted to invoke such a spirit of sacrifice from ancient Greek in the minds of the Chinese youth. The idea of inspiring the youth with an indomitable spirit of courage and ambition can be seen in Lu Xun's frequent references to Greek mythological images in many of his writings. The story of Prometheus, the prototype of Greek mythology, who stole fire for men from heaven and was punished with eternal torment, was a sourse of inspiration to Lu Xun. His own intense desire to bring such a revolutionary spirit from alien sources in an apparently lifeless and stagnating environment of China was reflected in many places.

There is no denying of Lu Xun's tilting to the exotic cultural phenomenon. He tried his utmost to infect his compatriots with this preference. But, he did it on purpose. Curiosity to the exotic eventually leading to xenophile was but human nature. But, he wanted to lead the Chinese xenophile towards a positive direction — to inhale inspiration from foreign cultures to cure the Chinese inertia and stagnancy. In fact, this tactics of Lu Xun was immensely successful. The Chinese youths liked to read Lu Xun because there were always sparks in his stories, his expressions, his literary persuasion. If one read Lu Xun one would not lie relaxed for long. In his works of art, you would see Lu Xun suddenly jumped up, and threw a stone into the still pond of your mind. Many young students, particularly those who had battened on the toil and moil of the poor, were initially keeping a respectable distance from Lu Xun's writings — picking up lighter and easily digestive stuff instead. However, they ultimately could not resist the assault of Lu Xun on their conscience and consciousness. They began to see the mockery of reality that when there was not even a single desk in China which did not tremble in the national crisis, still writers were churning out romanticism of the "Mandarin-Duck and Butterfly School" which was a constant target of Lu Xun's critique. Thus, Lu Xun played a role of constantly awakening the sleepy souls, curing their mental morbidness. While Lu Xun might be a xenophile he made his readers grow as patriots.

II

The incident of watching a newsreel in Japan which changed his mind is well known. The slide showed a crowd of strong and healthy Chinese enjoying the execution by the Japanese authority of a Chinese spy who was working for the Russians. The utter apathetic attitude of his compatriots to a victimized fellow-countryman worked as a stimulus in his mind. After the incident he dropped his original idea of becoming a physician, he writes: ".... this slide convinced me that medical science was not so important after all. The people of a weak and backward country, however strong and healthy they might be, could only serve to be made examples of or as witnesses of such futile spectacles; and it was not necessarily deplorable if many of them died of illness. The most important thing, therefore, was to change their spirit; and from that time on I felt that literature was the best means to this end, I decided to promote a literary movement."[6]

When Lu Xun was in Japan he often used to discuss with his friend Xu Shoushang three interrelated questions: how to have a human being with an ideal character? What was most wanting in China's national character? And what was the root cause of it?[7] On another occasion when Xu Shoushang asked him to be the first teacher of his son Lu Xun taught the child two Chinese characters "tian" (heaven) and "ren" (human).[8] The image of an ideal man and the problem of China's national identity was the key theme of Lu Xun's works. While he was influenced by Darwin's theory of evolution, western humanism and individualism, he never forgot his close acquaintance with the rural life and the peasants he had lived and played with during his childhood.

When Lu Xun was in Japan, the Dean of the Kobun College asked Chinese students to go to the Confucian Temple at Ochanomizu to pay respects to Confucius thinking that the Chinese students were all disciples of Confucius. Lu Xun was amused, "Do I still have to worship him here?"[9] He knew many had similar reaction to this. He recalled his days in Japan and his disappointment with Confucian social doctrine. He expressed his views on the classics and Confucius specially on the follower of Confucianism and their attempt to revive the teaching of classics and worshipping of Confucius. Yuan Shikai and other warlords after 1911 revolution were keen in such a revival of the ways of the sages in the twentieth century. But the people in general already began to believe that the traditional wisdom and the spiritual strength accumulated through the thirteen classics and worship of Confucius could in no way prevent China's humiliating defeat at the hands of foreigners. The Qing (Manchu) government spent enormous amount of money and energy to get foreign books translated while the whole education system of learning classics, writing stereo-typed eight-legged essays etc. was abolished in early twentieth century. In his essay "Confucius in Modern China" he not only attacked those adherents of Confucius and their ulterior motives behind their cult of Confucius, but also exposed these selfish and conservative forces by using the expression "brick to knock at the doors to fulfil their political ambitions". He made a distinction between the power-crazy politicians and the common people of China. The ordinary Chinese were never interested in the sage. Only those in authority admired and worshipped Confucius. Lu Xun writes: "We may say that the sages' luck took a turn for the better after his death. Because he could no longer pontificate, various authorities started whitewashing him in various ways till he was raised to awe-inspiring heights. And yet, compared with the later imported Sakyamuni Buddha, he cut rather a sorry figure. True, every county had a Confucian temple, but this was always a lonely, neglected place where the common folks never worshipped. If they wanted to worship they looked for a Buddhist temple or a shrine to some deity. If you ask ordinary people who Confucius was, of course they will answer 'A sage', but this is simply echoing the authorities."[10]

We have already observed that Lu Xun in his postscript for the *Grave* expressed that though he was brought up in classical education and learnt Confucian classics he never felt that these classics had something to do with him. His criticism of the tradition was a political task. He considered the burden of tradition in China a challenge awesome and formidable, so he prepared himself for a long and strenuous ideological confrontation with the traditionalists. His target was the Confucian ideology of his time, which evolved from the history and was the core of the old order. Therefore, his critique of Confucianism was penetrating, thorough and tenacious. The question of having any meeting point with the followers of Confucianism therefore did not occur, nor occupy any place in Lu Xun's literary communication. While talking about Confucius' neutrality on the existence of supernatural beings he writes: "Confucius was truly great, for though he lived at a time when witchcraft was rampant, he refused to follow the fashion and speak of ghosts and spirits. The pity is he was a little too clever. 'Sacrifice to your ancestors as if they were present' he said, 'Sacrifice to the gods as if the gods were present'. He simply used the device he had employed in editing the *Spring and Autumn Annals*, adding the words 'as if' in a slightly caustic way."[11] In fact Confucius refrained from discussion of supernatural beings, and he expressed his inability to understand fully the human affairs and life and thus took a rational stand of not being able to understand or even contemplate on death and supernatural existence.[14] Lu Xun comments, "Now Confucius was an extremely shrewd old gentleman. Apart from this question of having his portrait printed, it seems he possessed considerable subtlely and knew it did not pay to wreck things openly. Thus he simply refrained from discussion, and would on no account attack anything. And so, quite rightly, he became the sage of China, for his way is great and all embracing. But for this there might be someone else — not named Confucius — worshipped in the temples today."[13] Lu Xun's views on the ruling Confucian thought were construed with an intense desire to change the cultural behaviour of China. Confucian thought was a formidable and stumbling block on the way of doing that. He never failed to distinguish the difference between the socio-cultural behaviour of the common folk and the cultural elite. "Junzi" (the gentleman) was Lu Xun's stigma to ridicule the hypocrites, i.e. the so-called followers of Confucian ideas. He criticized the cruelty, hypocrisy, anti-people elitist attitude of such type of people. It is true that he was indignant towards ignorance, superstitions and utter indifferent attitude of the toiling masses but gradually he was able to discover the virtue of simplicity and innocence of China's common people. This made him mercilessly criticize the upper-class gentlemen and the so-called literate section. He felt the growing urge to grasp such subtleties in the behaviour of the people. He gradually realized the way in which people had been decieved by the age-old tricks of the ruling ideology.

Lu Xun's disagreement with the values of the feudal culture inflicted a sense of insecurity and loneliness upon his mind for some years, ".... this sense of loneliness grew from day to day, entwining itself about my soul like some huge poisonous snake."[14] It was only after the outbreak of the October Revolution which regenerated in him the second phase of his literary career. The May 4th movement made a deep impact on his mind and he regained his lost hope. The anti-feudal and anti-imperialist political spirit and the voice against the Confucian orthodoxy provided a concrete ideological guidance to his literary practice. His target of criticism was the dominant culture which was based on the Confucian-Mencian morality and ethical values. Reformers like Kang Youwei (1858-1927) and Liang Qichao (1873-1929) were not in favour of any fundamental change and were eager to impose the so-called cultural heritage as China's national identity on the majority of the people without considering the ongoing changes in the social, political and economic life of China. The champions of the national essence faced the crisis created by the infiltration of ideas from modern industrialized societies.[15] They realized that the native culture without royalty and the Confucian orthodoxy was inadequate to meet the challenge of the time. Their sense of insecurity and fear of losing identity forced them to uphole an extremely rigid and conservative line.

Lu Xun attacked the entire edifice of Confucian social doctrine. "Wo zhi jie lie guan" (My Views on Chastity), "Women xianzai zenyang zuo fuqin" (What is Required of us as Fathers Today), "Nuola zouhou zenyang" (What Happens After Nora Leaves Home) were some of his major essays in which he criticized the views of Confucian scholars on women, children and political system. He argues that the orthodox ideas such as chastity of women, filial piety of the children, autocracy, patriarchal authority, and treating children, young and women in a discriminatory way denying them any rights or freedom etc. are against the laws of nature. He writes: "We have no means of ascertaining what happened in China in remote antiquity; but by the end of the Zhou Dynasty the retainers buried with their masters included men as well as women, and widows were free to marry again. It appears then that this custom died out very early. From the Han to the Tang Dynasty no one advocated chastity. It was only in the Song Dynasty that professional Confucians started saying: 'Starving to death is a small matter, but losing one's chastity is a great calamity.' "[16] "New Year Sacrifice" narrates the plight of a widow. The theme of the story is based on the fate of a widow who remarries and meets a situation of either being captured by her former husbands' ghost and carried off to hell or condemned by the whole world. Eventually she becomes a beggar who is turned away by everyone and dies a total wreck. Lu Xun comments: "Only a society where each cares solely for himself and women must remain chaste while men are polygamous could create such a perverted morality, which becomes more exacting and cruel with each passing day."[17]

On how to emancipate children he observes: "The emancipation of children is something so natural that it should need no discussion, but the elder generation in China has been too poisoned by the old customs and ideas ever to come to its senses. For instance, if a crow caws in the morning, young people think nothing of it, but the superstitious old folk will be in a flutter for hours. It is most pathetic, but they are fast curing. Thus the only way is for those who have seen the light to start by emancipating their own children. Burdened as a man may be with the weight of tradition, he can yet prop open the gate of darkness with his shoulder to let the children through to the bright, wide-open spaces, to lead happy lives hence forward as rational human beings."[18]

In "Dengxia manbi" (Some Notions jotted down by Lamplight) Lu Xun summed up the history of China by saying that there were two types of periods the Chinese experienced: the periods when the Chinese longed in vain to be slaves and the periods when they succeeded in becoming slaves for a time.[19] So the spirit of the Chinese people has been to survive in a relationship not between two equal men but between a master and a slave. In the same essay he mentioned the ten grades in human relationship. The lowest were slaves who had no subjects below them. Lu Xun comments that even the slaves should not feel bad for they have wives and children who rank even lower. And there was hope for the children too for they would have wives and children below them to boss over. So this was the domain of slaves without a voice in protest. Lu Xun made a sarcastic reference to the romantic eyes with which foreigners looked at China. Bertrand Russell smiled when some Chinese sedan chair bearers smiled at him at the West Lake. Lu Xun comments: "....if chair bearers could stop smiling on their faces, China would long since have stopped being the China she is. The hierarchy handed down since ancient times has estranged men from each other, they cannot feel each other's pain; and because he can hope to enslave and eat other men, he forgets that he may be enslaved and himself be eaten... to say nothing of the women and the children whose cries are drowned in the senseless clamour of the murderers."[20] He calls upon the youth: "Feasts on human flesh are still being spread even now, and many people want them to continue. To sweep away these man-eaters, overturn the tables of these feasts and destroy this kitchen is the task of the young people today."[21]

In the preface to the Russian translation of "The True Story of Ah Q" Lu Xun expresses his doubt about his ability in creating a national soul of modern China.[22] He realizes the existence of a high wall separating two individuals from knowing each other. The so-called sages of China were really clever as they divided men into ten categories in a strict hierarchy of human relationships. Even the human body was classified into different categories making one's feet inferior to hands. Lu Xun comments that the defect in the creation of living is the human's inability to feel pain of others.

Lu Xun's condemnation of the Confucian tradition reached a new high in his *Kuangren Riji* (*A Madman's Diary*) in which he observes:

> "In ancient times, as I recollect, people often ate human beings, but I am rather hazy about it. I tried to look this up, but my history had no chronology and scrawled all over each page are the words: 'Confucian Virtue and Morality', since I could not sleep anyway, I read intently half the night until I began to see words between the lines. The whole book was filled with the two words — 'Eat people' ".[23]

The abnormal society was a consistent concern in this satirical fiction of Lu Xun. "Medicine" (*Yao*) is another story based on a similar theme but articulated in a more mature way. The plot is based on a common social background in which the man-eating-man mentality could grow. The execution of the revolutionaries at the end of the Qing Dynasty was very common and a fun-seeking crowd always gathered to enjoy such killing in public. More to it is the story's severe criticism of the Chinese superstition believing that eating fresh human blood could cure TB (which was a deadly disease in China in the olden days). Though Lu Xun did not say in so many words in this story, he surely was leading his readers to draw the horrifying conclusion of a China permeated with a man-eat-man culture. In *New Year Sacrifice* (*Zhufu*) Xiang Lin's wife, a diligent, honest and kind-hearted woman becomes the victim of the society. Her death symbolizes a social reality in which she is slowly devoured both physically and spiritually. Once again, the central theme of a cannibal society looms large behind the plot. On the one hand, you have people believing in benediction, but, on the other, such social paraphernalia introduces apartheid before god (forbidding a widow to touch the worshipping vessels thus driving her out of the domain of spiritual society), and such a cruelty is practised by "kind" people — certainly not wicked at heart — so that the readers can see the evil hand of the socio-cultural system which was the real villian in the destruction of human lives and souls.

I have highlighted these famous short stories of Lu Xun not just to repeat the now much hackneyed viewpoint eulogizing Lu Xun as a great revolutionary writer which he certainly was. What I wish to propound is the perspectives that can facilitate a deeper understanding of this unique modern writer who, like an Indian saint, won't pass this world very frequently. The first perspective with which we should look at these outstanding short stories of Lu Xun is the unique "character-engineering" of Lu Xun's fictions. They are all simple stories without much of a plot, without those twists and turns that characterize English fictions and those of other languages. The attraction of his stories lies in the characterization of the heroes and heroines of his stories. If these heroes and heroines were not there, there would be nothing left in the stories, not even worthwhile philosophizing on life and other matters (with the lone exception of the "Mad Man's Diary"). In other words, characterization is the soul, in the golden treasury of Lu Xun's stories. This has, I think, set a trend for modern Chinese fiction, particularly the "revolutionary" category of Chinese fiction — making character-engineering the main pillar of fiction creation. Secondly, following what I have just said, Lu Xun's characterization is uniquely Lu Xunian and hard to emulate. His characters are very ordinary — too ordinary to be chosen as great fiction material. Yet, they make such a great impact on the readers that ordinary characters don't. In other words Lu Xun has made the ordinary people extraordinary by an artistic process — like moulding mud into an idol. This artistic process, strangely, is prosecuted with very little effort — few words, almost no adjectives. For example, his "Zhufu" shuns elaborate building up, with no detailed descriptions of the looks of Xianglin's wife, of the master and mistress who employed her. Lu Xun just strings up a few sequential happenings and earns enormous sympathy for Xianglin's wife — the unfortunate maid servant. The master and mistress are apparently faceless characters in the story. But, Lu Xun has, in effect, pronounced an unwritten verdict on them, making the readers feel that they are objectively instrumental to driving an innocent and kind hearted maid mad and finally destroying her physically. I should add my last perspective to say how wonderful is a writer like Lu Xun who has had medical training. For, he is an artist made of pathological mastery. Lu Xun's unique success in the genre of fiction by contributing only a dozen short and very short and even very pedestrian stories lies in his pathological power to diagnose social illness. In this respect, one feels that Lu Xun should have devoted more time and greater energy in the creation of this new genre which I term as "pathological fiction". If he had gone on creating such characters like "Kong Yiji", "Ah Q" and "Zianglin Sao" he would have contributed much more not only to Chinese literature, but to China's modernization process. China had too many socio-cultural diseases and too few writers like Lu Xun to treat them with the literary medicine, while Lu Xun, the one talented pathological expert in literature, did not concentrate on such a highly valuable service to his country (and to the human kind as a whole). Here, I may sound a little uncharitable, but it only reflects my profound admiration for Lu Xun's genius, particularly his unparalleled pathological-literary genius, and my strong wish that other such writers emerge in large numbers to make human society healthier.

III

I should now take up Lu Xun's masterpiece, "True Story of Ah Q" which is a subject that deserves endless appreciation, critique, and extended reference onto other disciplines. Like the appearance of the writer, Lu Xun, the appearance of "True Story of Ah Q" is a rare historical phenomenon. The "True Story" and Lu Xun become symbiotic. Without the "True Story" Lu Xun's stature would have been reduced. Again, the Ah Q story, like its author, is never free from controversy. The critic Qian Xingcun considered Ah Q's image successful only in pointing out certain weaknesses of the Chinese people thus it was only a portrayal of morbid national character. He questioned the philosophical perspective with which Lu Xun wanted to depict Ah Q as a universal image of the Chinese reality. Qian observed that both Ah Q and his ideas were limited to the period of 1911 revolution, which did not exist any more. He concluded that Ah Q's image has already become extinct. There was no longer any need for being infatuated with the human skeleton. Ah Q's ideas along with his body should be buried.[25] However, another will-known critic He Qifang defended Lu Xun's artistic creation of an image like Ah Q. According to him literary characters too are being set in some social context. Lu Xun intended to expose the weaknesses of the Chinese nation but he could not find a single abstract representative which would embody common national vices. Therefore he could not restrict himself to writing only about Ah Q's ringworm scars, his tactics of winning psychological victory but had to depict the class relationship in rural China, characters other than Ah Q, how he was exploited, how he changed his attitude towards revolution etc. Moreover he wrote about the unsuccessful revolution by clearly pointing out to the fact that Ah Q was not only barred from participation in the revolution but also faced a tragic end at the hand of authorities created by the revolution.[26] The success of the story thus lies not only in that he created a character like Ah Q but primarily in the fact he so faithfully captured the contradictions in the society of rural China. It was a process in which Lu Xun gradually understood the complexity of the social reality and the difficulty in expressing critical views on the existing social and political institutions. He realized the futility of having any notion of changing the system by using current literary forms. Any expression which did not conform to the prevailing linguistic behaviour was simply unacceptable and denounced at the popular level. Such was the nature of the forces of conservatism in the literary field. A new word may attract immediate and vehement protest from the public. The vocabulary of that linguistic behaviour was ritually learned and inherited by the scholars. If anyone dared to break such "taboos", he/she would invariably become a social dissent. But Lu Xun presents that complexity in a different way:

"Ah Q who 'used to be much better off', man of the world and a 'worker', would have been almost the perfect man had it not been for a few unfortunate physical blemishes. The most annoying were some patches on his scalp where at some uncertain date shiny ringworm scars had appeared. Although these were on his own head, apparently Ah Q did not consider them as altogether honourable, for he refrained from using the word 'ringworm' or any words that sounded anything like it. Later he improved on this, making 'bright' and 'light' forbidden words, while later still even 'lamp' and 'candle' were taboo. Whenever this taboo was disregarded, whether intentionally or not, Ah Q would fly into a rage, his ringworm scars turning scarlet. He would look over the offender, and it were someone weak in repartee he would curse him, while if it were a poor fighter he would hit him. Yet, curiously enough, it was usually Ah Q who was worsted in these encounters, until finally he adopted new tactics, contenting himself in general with a furious glare."[27]

It is generally felt that the more you read this Ah Q story the greater becomes your empathy and sympathy, your intense feelings about culture, about society, about civilization etc. If you are well acquainted with the Chinese socio-culture, and if you have been nurtured by this culture such identities would magnify manyfolds. From the above quotation, one almost sees the contours of the Chinese culture which underwent a process from first discovering its weakness to feeling ashamed, and then frightened by it, and to ultimately making an effort to hide it, not just from other's views, but from its own consciousness so that it can pride itself on being great, on being capable of turning adversity into triumph. "You are Ah Q!" or "Don't be Ah Q!" has acquired the significance in China of a "national warning". *The True Story Of Ah Q,* thus, is a very effective medicine that has cured modern China from complacency and conservatism, that has fulfilled Lu Xun's personal ambition of using literature to cure China's civilizational malaise. Of course, it is a bitter pill for the Chinese civilization to swallow. But, after swallowing it, China has become pro-active in shedding its civilizational obesity, although many Chinese intellectuals would not grant this credit to the Ah Q story or to its author. Both Lu Xun and his masterpiece — the Ah Q story — are a great instrument of polarization, dividing their commentators into opposite camps, begetting whole-hearted admirers as well as severe critics. But, I feel this great masterpiece of modern Chinese literature — the Ah Q story — deserving greater attention and more indepth study than so far has been done.

When Chinese leaders discussed in 1949 whether the famous song "The Marching Song of the Volunteers" (*Yiyongjun jinxing qu*) should be adopted as the National Anthem of the new-found People's Republic of China (PRC), whether it was proper to retain such a line that "The Chinese nation has arrived at the most dangerous times", Premier Zhou Enlai said that there was no harm that such a warning remained to remind the citizens of the new Republic so that they would never become complacent in the future years. I think it is this criterion which should help us judge whether the "True Story Of Ah Q" remains great for all times to come. To begin with, I would go to the extent of diluting what I have observed just now about the Ah Q stories having cured the Chinese malaise. Yes, this can be established to ascertain what Lu Xun has achieved. But, such an assertion should not blind us from the reality that the socio-cultural malaise which China has accumulated in the course of many millennia could not have been cured by one short novel. Even if we think there was a temporary cure there is no guarantee that the disease would not recur. The "Ah Q Spirit" and the "Spiritual Victory" have not been wished away. We see leaders of China, who had been inspired by Lu Xun, by the Ah Q Story to throw their lot with the revolutionary course, betraying their innate Ah Q Spirit off and on long after the establishment of the People's regime. They used to paint a rosy picture of sorts when internal and external situations were very critical. Even today, one cannot be sure that the ghost of "Spiritual Victory" is not haunting the psyche of Chinese policy-makers and others, otherwise the Chinese official media would not have been so repetitive in issuing the warning "buke diaoyi qingxin" (cannot be complacent).

Another lasting relevance of the Ah Q Story is the existence of "Jiayangguizi" (the Pseudo-Foreign Devil). During the centuries of Western domination, "Foreign Devils" was a spectre that China had been troubled, frightened, and obsessed with. Such an overall international-internal situation gave rise to a new sub-strata which was culturally a cross-breed between the "Videshi" (foreign element) and "Swadeshi" (national element). This was actually an important sub-strata to help China to absorb Western cultural influence conducive to her modernization. However, they also intentionally or involuntarily played the role of "Ruling Periphery" that helped the western colonial powers to "rule the periphery by periphery". Lu Xun's "Pseudo-Foreign Devil" in the Ah Q Story puts him in the negative role — suppression of the revolutionary zeal of the masses. The Ah Q Story aided by the role of the Pseudo-Foreign Devil also viewed Dr. Sun Yat-sen's 1911 Revolution in a dubious light. What may be pointed out is that the description of this Pseudo-Foreign Devil was quite reminiscent to Lu Xun himself with two autobiographical references: his hair without the pigtail, and his walking stick nicknamed the "Civilized Stick" (*Wenminggun*). Chairman Mao said in a number of occasions the need to help the down-trodden (like Ah Q) to rebel against the Pseudo-Foreign Devils who did not allow the masses to join the revolution. We can even suspect Mao's being obsessed with such a scenario that he showed undue hostility in his political guidance over the governance of the PRC culminating in the persecution of many a foreign returned "Super Intellectuals" (*da zhishi fenzi*). Today, the social trend in China is again overturned with insinuations that the Pseudo-foreign Devils are back, and the Ah Qs have returned to the position of square one. All this only reflects the lasting relevance of Lu Xun.

The indomitable spirit of changing oneself and his environment was Lu Xun's quality. The change is not a natural phenomenon in human society, one had to make conscious effort in making changes. This ideal of social change with human perspective and dynamism had to be cherished and continuously strived for. It should be realized in dogged manner, continuously and in an imperceptible way, specially in countries like China where a huge population with a strong ideological hang over from the ancient times is awaiting to be awakened in a long period of time. Lu Xun gives the concrete method by quoting Han Feizi's art of horse-racing. One should not be ashamed even if one comes in last, "not to try" comments Lu Xun would be disastrous, ".... those runners who fall behind yet still press on to their goal, together with those spectators who do not laugh at them, will some day be the backbone of China."[28]

There has been an attempt, though veiled, undertaken by Lu Xun in his writings in general, and more visibly in the Ah Q story to conceptualize an image representing the ideal reflection of Chinese culture from a single individual. His search for the reflection of positive and dynamic qualities of Chinese culture in every Chinese was simply a matter of academic obstinancy. The sincerity he had and the perfection he gradually achieved in his communication was a rare example. His critique of tradition which developed through an all-embracing and assiduous study had outlived his time in providing us with a certain framework for human communication.

Lu Xun's writings were not the product of leisurely mind. His hatred for the art for art's sake was expressed by him on many occasions. His firm conviction of using literature to transform the national spirit never wavered. His spirit of engaging himself in understanding the essence of Chinese civilization and the contemporary mood of the people was so sincere and unique which remained unparallel in the history of modern China. He clearly dissociated himself from the advocates of classical language although he himself was trained almost thoroughly in the traditional education. He criticized vehemently the Confucian views and distanced himself from them. His voice against the so-called moribund national characteristics was unequivocal. He laid bare the selfish intentions of the so-called reformers and pseudo-progressive people. He overstepped almost all traditional rules and norms and advised publicly the young Chinese to read less or not to read Chinese books at all. He welcomed foreign ideas and theories and was enthusiastic in absorbing anything new. His fearless attitude to face all odds and criticisms while putting forward his views squarely was exemplary. As if the entire edifice of the so-called tradition began to crumble by an unforeseen cyclonic storm, Lu Xun remained steadfast, determined and sober-minded while returning the weapons thrown at him by his critics for years. He remained relentless in facing all sorts of abuse, slanders, innuendoes and allegations. Passionate patrioism, firm conviction in truth, and earnest desire to see a fundamental change in China were three basic aspects of Lu Xun's intellectual search. Concepts such as "man", "freedom" and "national identity" kept him engaged in a life-long inquiry into various types of texts. He hardly spared any opportunity of making himself exposed to new ideas and gradually realized that the passion for the country and the people was not enough to understanding the complex and intricate reasons working behind the changing reality. Affinity with mythological and romantic literary traditon of China was evident yet his spirit of grasping the hidden laws of the nature and the reality was profound. He questioned the validity of the divine source of imperial political power and therefore disapproved any experiment with the constitutional monarchy. He clearly expressed his support to the political leadership of Sun Yat-sen and the ideology of revolutionary democrats and highly evaluated Sun Yat-sen's role in the democratic process of China. He always cherished the genuine revolutionary spirit of great personalities of his time and respectfully acknowledged the contribution of revolutionary pioneers such as Zhang Taiyan, Sun Yat-sen and Li Dazhao. The struggle with his own self as well as with the existing intellectual and cultural perceptions continued for a long time and remained in ideological realm. On the other hand, Lu Xun remained the target of virulent attack by the established men of letters and the conservative political forces when he was alive. The price was too heavy for an individual to pay as it were. Even the so-called progressive and revolutionary writers of the time grossly misunderstood his views. The fame became an unbearable burden and made his nights sleepless. The struggle in real life of withstanding baseless allegations, abuses, and unhealthy and biased literary criticisms made his ideological stand clearer and firmer in a long course of fighting tenacity, tolerance and strong conviction.

Lu Xun, in his habitual offensive mood, stood on the opposite side of the Chinese tradition of pitying "the dog that has fallen into water" (*luoshui* gou) leading to his advocacy of a ruthless culture of "beating the dog that has fallen into the water". Ironically, he sometimes found himself at the receiving end of such a culture. He was blacklisted by the dominant publishing houses, and had to change pseudonym a hundred times to avoid detection and earn a pitiable existence of a guerrilla writer. This fact, perhaps explains for his high level of achievement and philosophical insights. The true understanding of culture through such a long-drawn trivial communication took a concrete and distinct shape in his writings. His writings of this stage which contained mostly such trivial matters became significant and meaningful. He not only showed sober-mindedness, tolerance and above all a healthy mental capacity but also exposed those so-called representatives or "gentlemen" of Chinese culture.

Lu Xun's legacy was thus formed through a process in which genuine, lively elements of Chinese culture of a particular time were discovered, classified, revived and re-established. The irrelevant, distorted and harmful elements as were propagated by such champions of the so-called national essence and those modernists under the influence of the West became too evident. The lack of seriousness, the utter failure of understanding of the true spirit of tradition and of the dynamics of culture apart from their hypocrisy, aristocratic pride and snobish attitude have been documented in Lu Xun's words. This was the significance of his role in specific historical context. He made the great masses of the people of an ancient civilization aware of their times, helped them in a painstaking attempt to regain thier self-confidence as a nation, and as a healthy, positive and constructive part of the global civilization without losing the distinctive native cultural identity. Lu Xun all along was engaged in conceiving of a comprehensive image of modern man and the problem of China's national characteristics. In such a philosophical attempt to grasp the deterministic laws of man's psychological and cultural behaviour Lu Xun eventually was able to construct a specific and commonly accepted features of national cultural behaviour and thus was successful in pointing out to the emerging universal pattern of human culture. He had a creative writer in the realm of literature but gradually broke his link with his own domain and laid the foundation of studies on culture with an inter-disciplinary approach. Particularly in his later stage of communication he became so much preoccupied with a routine interaction specially with his critics that a complex yet unique system of practical political thought evolved. In this aspect Lu Xun transcended the social-cultural theme to a political task. This was a concrete and easily visible role of a trail-blazing revolutionary which Lu Xun played in the process of criticizing and rejecting the old culture and paving the way for the new culture. It was not merely a task of rejuvenating a dying culture but recreating out of a mammoth structure a precise and healthy value system suitable for the time.

Notes

1. Li Zehou, *Zhongguo jindai sixiangshi lun* (A History of Modern Chinese Thought), People's Publishing House, Beijing, 1979, p. 439.
2. See Fan Wenlan, *Zhongguo Tongshi* (A General History of China), 5th ed. Peoples' Publishing House, Beijing, 1978, Vol. II, pp. 310-13.
3. Lu Xun's specific reference to Indian mythology can be seen in "Moluo shili shuo" (The Power of *Mara* Poetry), *Lu Xun Quanji (LXQJ)*. Vol. I and "Po e-sheng lun" *LXQJ*, Vol. 8.
4. Lu Xun's views on the origin and evolution of language, literature and other aspects of Chinese civilization and his references to the mythological past can be seen in many of his writings mainly in *"A Brief History Of Chinese Fiction*", "A Layman's Remarks on Writing", *LXSW*, Vol. IV, "Two or Three Things Chinese", *LXSW*, Vol. IV.
5. See Wang Shijing, *Lu Xun Zhuan (*Biography of Lu Xun*), Beijing*, 1978, p. 2.
6. "Preface to *Call To Arms*", *LXSW*, Vol. I, p. 35.
7. Xu Shoushang, *Wangyou Lu Xun Yinxiangji* (A collection of impressions of my late friend Lu Xun), p. 19.
8. *Ibid*, p. 91.
9. "Confucius in Modern China", (*Zai Xianzai Zhongguode Kong Fuzi*), *LXSW*, Vol. IV, p. 184.

10. *Ibid. LXSW*, Vol. IV, p. 185
11. "More Thoughts on the Collapse of Lei Feng Pagoda" (*zai lun leifengtade daodiao*), *LXSW*, Vol. II, p. 115.
12. Confucius himself strictly refrained from commenting on supernatural things. Some of his observations are often quoted to show his dislike for such matters like "wei zhi sheng, yan zhi si" (one does not even understand this life, how can one think to understand the life after death?), "wei neng shi ren, yan neng shi gui" (one is incapable of serving the interests of living beings how can one expect to serve the interests of dead spirits?) and "zi bu yu guai 1i luan shen" (The Master never talked about strange and unknown things).
13. "More Thoughts on the Collapse of Lei Feng Pagoda", *op. cit*, pp. 115-16.
14. "Preface to Call To Arms", *LXSW*, Vol. I, p. 36.
15. The champions of national essence or Heritagists considered cultural heritage of feudal China mainly Confucian and Mencian tradition as national essence of China. In order to maintain the feudal system they wanted to preserve national essence and vehemently opposed the New Culture Movement during the 1920s and 1930s. Such views were later expressed in *Xueheng* monthly published between 1922 and 1933.
16. "My Views on Chastity", *LXSW*, Vol. II, p. 19.
17. *Ibid*, p. 21.
18. "What is Required of us as Fathers Today", *LXSW*, Vol. II, p. 57.
19. "Dengxia manbi", *LXQJ*, Vol. II, p. 157.
20. *Ibid.*
21. *Ibid.*
22. *LXQJ*, Vol. 7.
23. "*A Madman's Diary*" (*Kuangren riji*), *LXSW*, Vol. I, p. 42.
24. See "Moluoshili shuo", *LXQJ*. Vol. I, p. 80.
25. Qian Xingcun, "Siqulede Ah Q shidai" (The Ah Q is dead and gone), *Wenxue Yundongshiliao Xuan*, (Selections of historical data of Literary Movement), Shanghai, 1979, Vol. II, p. 57.
26. He Qifang, "Lun Ah Q" (On Ah Q), *Renmin Ribao (Peoples' Daily)*, 16th Oct. 1956. p. 7.

SABAREE MITRA

38

COMEBACK OF HUNDRED FLOWERS IN CHINESE LITERATURE: 1976-1989

Mao Zedong was a writer of his own right which fact is eclipsed by his political career, particularly as the supremo of the people's Republic of China from 1949 to 1976. His influence on the development of Chinese literature was immense, including the negative effect of the Great Proletarian Cultural Revolution which sparked off from the literary realm and targeted writers in a big way (Though the villain of the piece was his wife, Jiang Qing). The Cultural Revolution and the Anti-Rightist Movement preceding it completely killed the prospects of a refreshing idea of turning the Chinese literary realm into a garden of blooming flowers. To quote Mao's formulation, it was "*Baihua qifang, baijia zhengming*" (Let hundred flowers bloom, and hundred schools contend). The letter "bai" (hundred) need not be taken literally to mean the exact number indicated. It is a Chinese euphemism to mean "a lot", even "innumerable". Thus, we see in Mao's "hundred flowers" scheme a great vision of enlivening the Chinese literary scene, even if the destroyer of the vision was the visionary himself.

The brilliance of Mao's "blooming garden" vision should be viewed from a historical perspective. There is a dichotomy between "Great Tradition" and "Little Tradition" in every civilization, but in China we find a creative society in literature, both written and oral (i.e. "folk" literature), on the one hand, and a very suppressive regime which frowned at writings which either threatened the ruling moral authority (mainly Confucian oriented), or were considered subversive in political content. This was the reality of "imperial China". During the Republican period, although there was much greater literary freedom, there was not much real encouragement given to literary works from the top. The May Fourth Movement was an unprecedented freedom struggle on the part of Chinese writers to demolish the repressive regime. In fact, the Chinese communist movement was virtually a younger brother of the May Fourth Movement, albeit it overgrew its elder brother hundred times. The birth of the People's Republic of China brought some of the erstwhile freedom fighters in literature to the position of authorities. Had Mao allowed them a free hand in developing literature, it would have ushered in an unprecedented blooming in the garden of Chinese literature. Thus, we see Mao Zedong playing a double role in the 1950s. On the one hand, as an ideological prophet and guide, he occasionally frightened literary and other creators, like his criticism on "*Wu Xun Zhuan*", the film that depicted a typical Confucian good man Wu Xun. On the other hand, there was his launching of the "Two Hundred" (Hundred Flowers and hundred Schools) movement which was truly brilliant.

The Cultural Revolution (1966-1969) was followed up by another seven long years of the reign of terror by the Gang of Four headed by Jiang Qing over Chinese writers. Following the fall of the Gang of Four and their subsequent arrest, a sense of relief was evident among the masses particularly the intellectuals and writers. It brought to the fore a renewed hope, which was strengthened by the political changes culminating in the Third Plenum of the Eleventh Central Committee of the CPC in December 1978, seeing Deng Xiaoping and his associates in control of power both in the Party and in the State. The most important agenda of the new leadership consisted of economic development and modernization of China. This leadership was pragmatic enough to realise that if the drive for economic development and modernization was to be successful, the co-operation of the intellectuals was essential. This realization was soon reflected in the leadership's attitude towards knowledge and the intellectuals who were the repository of knowledge. For instance, Deng Xiaoping's talks and speeches delivered over 1977 and 1978 indicate that the leadership was stressing the importance of knowledge and intellectuals in general, and science and technology, and scientific and technical personnel in particular. The intellectuals, who had been the targets of all the major political campaigns during the Mao Era, were grossly demoralized and apprehensive, and therefore lacked initiative. As a result, the new leadership, some of whom were genuinely in favour of greater intellectual autonomy (even though within a given framework) started a series of confidence-building measures to engage the co-operation of the intellectures.

In the sphere of literature, the first step in this confidence-building process was the Fourth National Congress of the All-China Federation of Literary and Art Workers,[1] held jointly with the Third National Congress of Writers in October, 1979. While discussing the role of literature and art, Zhou Yang said in his report to the Congress:

> "To eulogize and to expose...are the two aspects of a question. The crux of the matter is what stand to take, what to eulogize and what to expose. Literary and artistic works must portray the bright side of the life of the people and also expose the seamy side of society. Socialist literature and art perform the task of both criticism and self-criticism. We should not criticize our enemies only but should also take a critical attitude towards ourselves and our endeavours; otherwise, we cannot make progress."[2]

This defence of critical realism by Zhou Yang was a definite departure from Mao's literary doctrine which was being reviewed and modified to adopt to the new socio-political environment of the post-Mao Era.

The confidence-building measures coupled with the series of changes introduced in December 1978, not only gave an impression of China moving forward but also had a far-reaching effect on almost every sphere of Chinese intellectual life. What resulted was a comparatively favourable atmosphere for intellectual activity. The Chinese literary scene responded by displaying unprecedented vitality and variety. The literature that took shape had such new elements hitherto unseen in socialist China. These elements had a gamut of literary, social and political dimensions and thus, cannot be judged in terms of literary parameters alone. Nevertheless, these elements were so distinct that they became significant features of this new body of literature in so much that the post-Mao literature can justifiably be given the status of New Literature. Therefore, the attempt will be to first identify these new elements and then examine their social, literary or political dimension. Whereas some of these elements were common to both poetry and prose, others were distinctive characteristics of either poetry or prose.

Poetry

Poetry of the realist school continued in the post-Mao era. Majority of such works and their authors remained within the limits of current literary policy. Poetry of the type which had sung for the revolution and the new socialist life during the 40s, 50s and 60s, now sang for modernization. Full of didacticism, a lot of these poems were run of the mill, boring and sounded almost like rhymed political slogans. One such poem had the following lines:

> "The fresh blood of the revolutionary martyrs
> is sprinkled,
> In exchange for today's new constitution,
> Protect democracy, protect people's rights,
> Advance the Four Modernizations."

But starting from 1976 two new trends became prominent in poetry. The first is the poetry of protest, which emerged closely linked with the downfall of the Gang of Four and Democracy Wall, and the second being the poetry of the modemist school which has been termed "obscure poetry" (*menglong shi*) in China. These two streams often intermingle. Those involved in them were mostly younger writers.

During the Democracy Movement of late 1978, there was a profusion of wall posters expounding views on various political and social issues, advocating different roads of China's development and modernization, petitioning for justice and democracy, protesting against the tyranny of the Gang of Four during Cultural Revolution and expressing hopes for the future under the new leadership. Innumerable poems appeared on the Democracy Wall. The genesis of this poem-wave goes back to April 5th, 1976, when on the occasion of the Qing Ming Festival (Pure Brightness Festival, a Chinese traditional festival of ancestor worship) a huge crowd of Chinese ordinary citizens assembled in Tiananmen Square to pay homage to the memory of the late Premier Zhou Enlai and to protest against the extremist policies of the Gang of Four. The crowd not only placed wreaths on the Hero's Memorial, but also posted poems on the Memorial eulogizing Zhou Enlai and his policies.

In the Democracy Movement poems were also circulated in the form of booklets and published in unofficial magazines[3] entitled *Today, Explorations, Grass on the Plain, The People's Forum, The Spring of Beijing, China's Human Rights, Science,*

Democracy and Law, Dandelion, Harvest, April 5th Forum etc. The concerns of these poems were more or less the same as the wall posters, but had a more vivid tone of protest and that is why these poems have often been referred to as poetry of protest. Most of these poems are not outstanding aesthetically, albeit they are replete in patriotic emotion and noble sentiments. I cite some specimens below:

(a) *subtle political allegory*

Trust the Future by Shi Zhi

"......
The eyes of the people who trust in the future
Make me firmly believe in the future myself
Their eyelashes bat off the dust of history
Their pupils pierce the years of writings

No matter what people think about our rotting flesh
That sadness of a lost way, that pain of defeat

......
I strongly trust people fairly to assess
Our countless explorations, errors, successes,
failures,

......
Friend trust firmly in the future,
Trust in unyielding effort,
Trust in the victory of youth over death,
Trust the future, trust life."[4]

(b) *subtle imagery:*

Frozen Land by Meng Ke

"The funeral crowd floats past, a white cloud,
Rivers slowly drag the sun.
The long, long surface of the water, dyed golden.
How silent
How vast
How pitiful
That stretch of withered flowers."[5]

(c) *with strong ideological (socialist) flavour :*

An Eternity of Deeds and Misdeeds by Tai Chi

"......
Mao Zedong
Son of the Shaoshan plain,
Giant of the Chinese Revolution.
The people praised you
The evil and crafty made you, into a god.
Demon, devil and witch,
Blocked out our sun with fog
It's time to peel off your god like gloss
And give back to the people the leader they had."[6]

(d) *obscure poetry:*

Notes From the City of the Sun by Bei Dao

"......
Freedom
Float
Torn scraps of paper
......
Art
Millions of shining suns
are reflected in a broken mirror
......
Labour
Hands. Enfold the globe
......
Faith
A flock of sheep spill beyond the limits of their

pasture
the shepherd still plays his same old tune.
......
The Motherland
She was engraved on a bronze shield
which leant against a partition in a museum."[7]

But it is not the literary style or the aesthetic skill that set the poetry of protest apart from the mainstream of poetry in socialist China. What is most significant about them is that they symbolise a political act, politicisation of popular sentiment expressed through the medium of literature. No matter what the theme of the poem was, be it the misery of people dying in cold or of hunger or love for one's close ones or anything else, the feelings were always expressed in a greater political context. There are two aspects of this political act: (1) the need to express, and (2) the opportunity of expression.

The need to express must have been absolutely overwhelming in all walks of life all those who felt it necessary to rhyme — workers, peasants, intellectuals and so on. The poetry of protest indicates a widespread sense of anger, frustration, anguish and disillusionment as a result of a decade long Cultural Revolution compounded by numerous earlier political campaigns affecting almost every sphere of human existence. These feelings probably had reached that threshold where the very act of expressing became a need of utmost urgency. It is this urgent need that transformed socio-political consciousness into concrete spontaneous expression, thus making it a political act.

The other aspect is the point in history when consciousness was transformed into an act of expression. It was a period, which has since been named "*Beijingzhi chun*" (the Beijing Spring) when the stranglehold of politics became relaxed following the demise of Mao Zedong and the downfall of the Gang of Four. It was also a period when the political atmosphere was comparatively relaxed and tolerant. Therefore, free expressions in various forms, including literature, suddenly exploded which was unthinkable in the past. This combination of the long suppressed sentiments and the relaxed atmosphere became conducive to the emergence of poetry of protest.

The so-called "obscure poetry" and the controversy surrounding this genre came to the fore in 1979. In contrast to the poetry of the socialist realist school, the "obscure poetry" had the following features:

The poems were short in length, sometimes as short as one word, as in the case of "Life" by Bei Dao.

"Title of the poem: "*Shenghuo*" (Life)
Content of the poem: "Wang" (Net)"[8]

They were much more symbolically subtle and indirect compared to the long poems over-burdened with explicit slogans. Many of them also possessed a crisp political allegory. e.g., Gu Cheng's "One Generation":

"One Generation
The black night has given me black eyes,
Yet I use them to search for light"[9]

The most impressive feature of these poems is their experimentation with images, as in Gu Cheng's:

"Feeling":

"The sky is grey
The road is grey
The building is grey
The rain is grey
In this blanket dead grey
Two children walk by
......
One bright red
One pale green."[10]

Imagism, which was considered avant-garde in the 1910s among the Anglo-American poets, was very much a part of Modernist poetry in Taiwan in 1960s. Since then, the Taiwan poetry has graduated from its modernist phase. But most of these contemporary young poets of mainland China had not been exposed (at least till 1979) to either Western or Taiwanese Imagism.[11] This seems to indicate that the modernist phase in poetry had only just begun in 1979 in socialist China -- echoing the Crescent Moon School of the 1920s and 1930s.

Apart from the concentrated colour imagery, other features of Imagism, like the montage — the juxtaposition of images or sharp, perspicuous imagery -- were also being employed by some young poets. While the juxtaposition of images have no explicit linguistic connection, the perspicuous imagery often jolts readers by sudden metaphoric transference. "Curve" and "A Walk in the Rain" by Gu Cheng are examples of these two methods respectively.

Curve

"A bird in the gusty wind
Deftly changes direction
A youth tries to pick up
A penny
The grapevine in fantasy
Stretches its tentacles
The Wave in retreat
Arches its back."[12]

A Walk In The Rain

"Clouds that are grey
Can no longer be washed clean.
We open the umbrella
And simply paint the sky black"[13]

These young writers of "obscure poetry" have often been dubbed unhealthy and unpatriotic in the first place, and then, unappreciated for being obscure and difficult to understand. In an article which inaugurated the debate and criticism, a senior poet Gong Liu described these poems as "disgraceful" and "denigrating". Referring to the following lines by Gu Cheng:

The junk in mourning
Slowly passes by
And unrolls the dark-yellow shroud."[14]

Gong Liu commnets:

> "The Chinese people grow from the milk of the Yangtse and the Yellow River. Who, upon seeing these two rivers, is not proud of the glory of the motherland's landscape? Who has ever heard of Indians disparaging the Ganges, or Egyptians the Nile? Even Americans compare the Mississippi to a motherly river."[15]

According to him it will logically follow that such poems are unhealthy because it is a subjective impression of the Cultural Revolution and its aftermath hence with bourgeois or petit-bourgeois individualism.

The charge of difficulty and obscurity laid by the older poets and critics is probably not so much of a criticism against difficulty but more so against their content. Because all the "obscure" poets have been concerned with the Cultural Revolution and some of their poems are as critical and political as some trends in prose, like "scar literature". e.g., "China, My Key is lost" by Liang Xiaobin:

"China, my key is lost.
More than a decade ago,
I ran wildly along the red boulevard,
And cheered in the rural wilderness,
Later,
My key was lost
......
The sky is starting to rain again,
Oh my key,
Where might you be?
Wind and rain must have eroded you, I suppose,
And you are already very rusty;
No, I don't really think so,
I want to search stubbornly,
Hoping that I can recover you."[16]

This is probably one of the best political poems after 1949. The political allegory is unmistakable. It has succeeded in conveying a political message, hence not obscure. There is a dark innuendo, a sense of loss and sadness and yet a strong hope. While the "scar literature" has been received positively and encouragingly, such poems have been criticized.[17] Shu Ting's reaction to this discriminatory treatment is:

> "I believe that creative writing and literary criticism should be allies; the task force of poetry is now invading forbidden areas and is in need of artillery support... [It is not convincing] that fiction be allowed to write about the "wounds" but poetry forbidden to deal with the sighs; or to stress that everything is fine now and poets need only joyfully sing the praises of spring; or to discuss the problems of youth and condemn the depression, helplessness, and bewilderment of the young people without attacking the social factors that cause this mental state."[18]

Defence of these young poets and their works have come from Sun Shaozhen, Xie Mian, Xu Jingya, Gu Cheng and Ai Qing, on the issue of free verse. Of them Sun Shaozhen is the most unorthodox and courageous. In a symposium organized by the magazine *Poetry*, attended by critics and representatives of well-known journals, he argued that "art has its internal laws of development" and therefore literary criticism "cannot focus just on the reflection of life and ignore the art of poetry".[18] In March, 1981, Sun published an article entitled "New Aesthetic Principles Are Rising",[19] in which he evaluated these so-called "obscure poetry" as indications of the rise of some new aesthetic principles in socialist China. The main points of Sun's articles are:

• Instead of direct glorification of life, these poets are engaged in exploring "the secrets of life already dissolved in the heart and mind".

• They are keen on the expression of the "self", because they believe that "the individual should enjoy a higher status in society, since it is people as individual who creates society". Sun regarded the sense of alienation and melancholy in some of these poems as a reflection of the distortion of human relationships, a legacy of the Cultural Revolution.

•Contemporary poetry must change usual reading habits and liberate readers from the "stubborn grips of artistic convention".

Of these, it was the second principle of Sun Shaozhen that not only touched a raw nerve but hit off a separate debate on the question "expression of self". The pro-Maoist literary critics have always viewed this concept as an idea that contradicted the collective role of literature in a socialist society. On this issue, the opinion of the young poets has been most representatively elaborated upon by Gu Cheng:

> "The old kind of poetry has always propagandized about a 'non-individual' 'I' or 'self', an 'I' that is self-denying and self-destructive, an 'I' that is constantly reduced to a grain of sand, a road-paving pebble, a cog-wheel, a steel screw. In short, never a person, a human being who can think, doubt, and have emotions and desires.... In short, a robot, a robot 'I'. This kind of 'I' may have a religious beauty of self-sacrifice, but, as an 'I' who has eradicated his most concrete individual being, he himself finally loses control and is destroyed. The new kind of 'self' is born on this heap of ruins."[20]

PROSE

The literary developments in post-Mao Chinese prose are much more complex than poetry. There are complex interactions between themes, literary styles and artistic skill that in their various intricate combinations have opened up an exciting vista unprecedented in socialist China. Needless to say that this complexity makes it difficult to classify literary works in terms of any single given parameter. Let me try to bring out the striking features of post-Mao prose.

In the liberalized atmosphere following the fall of the Gang of Four, a new trend emerged in literature, that revealed the tyranny of the Gang of Four and the trauma suffered by people during the Cultural Revolution in particular and all past political campaigns in general. This new trend in literature, called the Scar Literature (*Shanghen wenxue*) were mostly written by writers in their late thirties and forties and were published in state-sponsored literary journals and newspapers. Scar Literature criticized past mistakes and exposed the darker aspects of socialist society. In contrast to the officially approved "socialist realism" or "revolutionary romanticism" of the Mao era in which the writers were supposed to only extol the shining achievements of socialism, Scar literature saw a return to the "critical realism" of the May Fourth Movement tradition and thus marked a new phase in Chinese socialist literature. What is more important is the fact that whereas the "critical realism" of the May Fourth period was directed at feudal social order and political bankruptcy and compromise of the Republican government, in the Scar Literature it was directed against the past mistakes and misdeeds of a regime and system still in control of the country. Not only there is no such precedence of such type of open literary expression of discontent (except of course the odd political allegories like "*The Dismissal of Hai Rui from Office*" by Wu Han in early 1960s), but even a wave of such expression was impossible in the past. Considering the period when Scar Literature dominated the scene, the causes of its emergence were of course the same as those of protest poetry.

The Scar Literature was named so after the short story called "Scar"[21] by Liu Xinhua. It portrays the story of a young woman who is forced to abandon her "counter-revolutionary" parents during Cultural Revolution and who in turn is abandoned by the young man she loves because of her tainted family background. Following the publication of "Scar", many real-life stories of family tragedy were printed as fiction all over the country. For the most part of 1977 and 1978, Chinese literature was dominated by Scar Literature with broadening themes depicting many aspects of psychological and emotional wounds suffered by the people in the past. Scar Literature came to be the symbol of popular anger directed at the Gang of Four and past campaigns and political persecutions.

One feature that was common in Scar Literature was a kind of formula of a victim, wrongly accused during the Cultural Revolution or at some earlier political campaign, the victim's steadfast belief in socialism and love of motherland in spite of persecution, the extent of persecution, attack on extremist political belief and its inhuman treatment of people and veiled attack on Mao's theory of continuous class struggle. Most of the works suffer from lack of subtlety. As in the case of Dai Houying's "*Man, Oh Man!*"[22] (*Ren Ah Ren*) in which the author was too eager to proclaim the cause of humanism to avoid naked accusations. This work, like many others in the post-Mao period, became famous not so much for its merits but for the author's courage and official disapproval. Some noteworthy works of Scar Literature are "The Homeroom Teacher" by Liu Xinwu, "The Transcript" by Liu Jinlan, "Three Professors" by Cao Guanlong, "The Gap" by Lao Hong, "At middle age" by Shen Rong and "Man, Oh, Man" by Dai Houying.

In the first phase, criticism was limited to the past experience and almost all the "scar" stories expressed hope and confidence in the future under the new leadership. But, they gradually extended to other issues like mindless dogmatism, abuse of power and privilege, corruption, prison conditions and so on. Encouraged by the call of the Third Plenum of the Eleventh Central Committee in December, 1978, in which writers and intellectuals were urged to "liberate thought", the dimension of venting suppressed complaints grew wider and wider. So much so that a literary exploration got underway in 1979 to probe into social problems beyond the making of the Gang of Four.

The literature published from 1979 to mid-1981 has been called "New Realism Literature" by Helen F. Siu and Zelda Stern.[23] This "New Realism Literature", like the Scar Literature, was published in state-sponsored literary magazines. What differentiated "New Realism Literature" from Scar Literature was that it dealt with issues of the post-Mao Chinese society and in terms of exposure, it was much more daring and specific. The "New Realism Literature" has sometimes been referred to as "exposure literature" in China and by the very implication of the term, includes not only the extended Scar Literature but critique of social abnormalcy, e.g. plays like "*If I were Real*"[24] and film scripts "*In the Archives of the Society*"[25] and "*Unrequited Love*",[26] in addition to a host of reportage. Maoist orthodoxy had sanctioned "exposure" only in the case of the enemy and therefore this kind of "exposure" is politically incorrect by the standard of the Chinese socialism, thus placing this new genre in the position of undesirable rebellion. There was a visible watershed, if not Great Divide, between the "socialist realism" and "critical realism" in Chinese literature.

Here is a question of exposing and reforming from within which may be analyzed in the context of Engels' evaluation of Balzac. Engels concluded, "That Balzac thus was compelled to go against his own class sympathies and political prejudices, that he saw the necessity of the downfall of his favourite nobles and described them as people deserving no better fate...that I consider one of the greatest triumphs of Realism...".[27] This means that, in spite of a writer's class interest, his truthful portrayal can result in underlining certain shortcomings and wrong tendencies in his own class. This is something which can possibly happen under realism, a style that has been viewed as supreme in traditional Marxist literary thought. Therefore, the "exposure" that results from truthful portrayal by writers of extended Scar Literature (dealing with post-Mao socio-political issues), is nothing but a classic case of literature performing its rightful role. Shaped by a special form of social consciousness, literature, in turn, is trying to influence social reality by revolting against certain unacceptable tendencies in the system.

Reportage (*Baogao wenxue*) is a journalistic report written in literary style and based on true events and concrete facts. The pace-setter of this style undoubtedly was Liu Binyan. His "Between Monsters and Men"[28] was a pioneering work that exposed the corruption within the party with stark vividness. It earned him immense popularity for his unflinching courage in using literature to redress social and political injustice. "Between Monsters and Men" has since then been regarded as a landmark in the resurgence of Critical Realism.

equally remarkable is the play "*If I were Real*" which deals with the sensitive issue of nepotism and abuse of power by the party officials, while the film script "*Unrequited Love*" portrays the horror of deification and blind dogmatism that tramples humanism and patriotism under foot. Hu Yaobang while admitting that writers had a right to be concerned with real problems, criticized "*If I were Real*" for choosing an exception to generalise about the Party and thus for giving an incorrect perspective.[29] "*Unrequited Love*" was criticized in April 1981, two years after its first publication. The author was charged with the violation of "Four Cardinal Principles" and with unfavourable comparison of socialist China with capitalist America.[30] Criticism of "*Unrequited Love*" was the first hint of the campaign against "bourgeois liberalization" in literature and art that was to come later.

An important concern that surfaced in Chinese literature in the first half of 1980s involved questions of universal human nature, humanism and alienation. The theme of universal human nature came to be manifested as a more humanised interpretation of Marxism which acknowledged the existence of nobleness and compassion in politically "wicked" characters. On the other hand, humanism was portrayed by characters that were humane towards their "class enemies" and recognized the human qualities of the "class enemies". This kind of exploration of complex human nature is reminiscent of the "middle man" theory of early 1960s in China when Shao Quanlin, Zhou Yang, Zhao Shuli and others advocated characters of flesh and blood who would have their inner contradictions and defects of character in spite of their faith in Communist ideology. Here is a typical observation:

> "Even characters who treat Communist ideology as the highest principle have inner contradictions and inner defects....We must not shirk the difficulties...of contradictions and struggles in life.... Cheap optimism can only oversimplify life."[31]

In the experimentation to study the multiple facets of human nature and human situations, many works written in the first half of 1980s were crude in skill and contrived in plots. Typical of this trend are Li Yingru's "*Miaoqing*", Zhang Xiaotian's "*Luxuriant Grass on the Plain*", Yu Mei's "*A, man...*", Liu Xinwu's "*Ruyi*" and Li Ping's "*When the Last Rays of the Sun Grew Dim*".

Though some of these works generated a lot of controversy after their publication and were criticized as unhealthy, they expressed a certain optimism concerning human nature. Other works of this period focussed on distorted humanity and alienated existence of individuals and in so doing made use of "psychological realism" to bare thoughts and consciousness of the characters. There is a certain parallel between the prose of this kind and "obscure poetry" both in literary style and in the treatment of themes. These prose pieces, like most obscure poetry, grasp the complexities of the inner feeling with a subtle sophistication.

The best in this category are "*On the Same Horizon*"[32] and "*Dreams of My Age-group*"[33] by Zhang Xinxin. By the astute use of imagery and symbolism, she relentlessly excavated the inner world of individuals and complexities of relationships. Though, she denies being a Modernist, her style and method are reminiscent of Western modernism.

Around the time when the concerns like human nature, humanism and alienation were emerging as a trend in literature, some literary theoretician like Wang Ruoshui had started discussing the relevance of these concepts in contemporary China. Wang Ruoshui was of the opinion that alienation can exist in a socialist society as well as a capitalist society. Apart from being influenced by Western and Eastern European Marxists, Wang based his arguments on Marx's early writings and said that alienation can exist in any system that produces forces which oppress people. He argued the Chinese socialist system since 1949 had produced personality cult, irrational economic policies bureaucratic indifference, corruption, privileges, selfish individualism, all of which had diminished human worth, alienation was inborn. He called for an ideological change to counter the repressive dehumanized manifestations of socialist China, which in turn would end alienation. He said "it is highly necessary to prevent these servants of the people transforming themselves into masters of the people".[34] In this call for revival of humanism, he regarded alienation as a negative manifestation in the socialist system which normally should have enhanced human worth. He also added that principles for revival of humanism could be found in Marxism and thus reiterated his faith in socialism. In other words, he stressed the need to reject the orthodox model of socialism, one that was established in Soviet Union and China where all the initiatives always came from top. Because "not every word and deed of the leaders absolutely and undoubtedly conforms to the people's interests" and "leaders sometimes can make mistakes".[35]

Wang Ruoshui's perceptions on humanism and alienation must have been shared by numerous writers who composed "obscure poetry" or produced works like "*On the Same Horizon*". It seems that when Wang analyzed the complex social phenomenon in a theoretical framework was perceived by these young practitioners of literature as they tried to mirror their living experiences. An interesting thing to note is the fact that some of these very young writers themselves are somewhat alienated from the system and thus illustrated the negative dehumanizing manifestations spelt out by Wang Ruoshui. The significance of Wang's argument on the existence of alienation in socialist society is that it indicates the emergence of a new class within a supposedly classless society and the polarization of the society, creating a ruling elite which has become indiffernt towards the masses and divorced from their interest. In their eagerness to assume the role of the guardians of socialism, they simply intoxicated themselves in the wine of priviledge, putting the people out of their minds.

This concern for humanism and alienation by both theoreticians like Wang Ruoshui and literary practitioners like the "Scar" writers and the implications of some negative manifestation as analyzed by them resulted in their becoming the targets of the Campaign against Spiritual Pollution launched in late 1983. Meetings were held all over the country, articles were published in leading newspapers and journals, castigating "spiritual pollution" that included not only the alienation discourse but also concepts such as modernism, individualism, existentialism etc. People who were associated with these concepts, either through theoretical analysis or literary expression, were deemed to have wanted to undermine orthodox ideology with "degenerated" Western ideas.

Incidentally, the post-Mao period and the Reform-induced free economy resulted in a marked increase in erotic elements and sexual themes in Chinese literature which was immediately frowned upon by the conservatives in the Party. Depiction of sexual relations and erotic scenes, however, were largely hidden in lyrical euphemism and in most works they were only subservient to socio-political themes.

Apart from the comeback of "yellow literature" which had taken a long vacation out of Mao's China, some of these works gave a wide variety of survey of status of women in traditional and contemporary Chinese society in terms of women's sexual dependence on men and their social conditioning linked to this dependence. Some works of this genre worth mentioning are "*Chaste Women*" by Gu Hua, "*A Long Night in Spring*" by Ye Nan, "*Madam Hei*" and "*Tiangou*" by Jia Ping'ao and "*Woman is the other half of Man*" by Zhang Xianliang. Of these, the works by Jia Ping'ao and Zhang Xianliang have succeeded in taking a more objective and sensitive view of the issues raised rather than flippantly sensationalising the potentially sensational themes. Specially the "*Woman is the Other half of Man*"[36] has taken an integrated look at the human reality, leaving behind an interesting study of psychological realism even after the immediate socio-political relevance is completely exhausted.

Needless to say that these issues must have existed in the Chinese society for a long time. In socialist China as love could be portrayed only by shared political belief and revolutionary enthusiasm until some years back, the general notion of sex could only be implied under the canopy of marriage. The fact that these issues were finally brought out boldly into the open literature can probably be attributed to (a) a conscious admission that such issues are social phenomena, and (b) an exposure to a variety of sociological concepts which could be identified with the contemporary social reality and through foreign literature and academic readings. Of course, the comparatively relaxed intellectual climate where such themes could be given expression is a decisive factor. The re-emergence of such themes is significant because it is linked with the continuous effort of the writers to broaden the scope of literature.

Another trend during 1985-86, was the preoccupation with innovation and technique. The inspiration for this trend could be a changed perception of human existence, i.e., human existence could be perceived not only in the framework of socio-political environment, as was the case so far since May Fourth Movement, but also in individualistic and psychological frame of reference. It is this changed perception which in turn may have emerged in the form of subjectivity, and irrationality and a yearning for the exotic. Mention must be made of "*Ah Mei in Pensive Mood on a Sunny Day*" and "*My Affairs in That World*" by Can Xue, "*You Have no Choice*" and "*Blue Skies and Green Seas*" (specially mentioned for the technical innovations) by Liu Suola, "*Coming-Going Back*" and "*Woman, Woman, Woman*" by Han Shaogong, '*King of Trees*' and "*Winds and Streams Everywhere*" by Ah Cheng and "*Scarlet Sorghum*" by Mo Yan. Though this trend in general is a revolt against realism, the works are too few and diverse to be placed under a single genre. Some of these works have been acclaimed. However, innovations in general have been received with little enthusiasm by most, including the liberals.

I should say that this trend of the subjective, illogical and irrational perceptions of human existence was reminiscent of certain features of "obscure poetry". Like "obscure poetry", this kind of expression of "self" is symbolic of a rejection of the past (both in terms of society and literature) and of the alienated distorted existence in the present.

The debate on the concept of alienation exploded again when Liu Binyan's "The Second Kind of Loyalty"[37] was published in 1985. In this work of reportage, Liu contrasted the loyalty of Lei Feng brand which unquestioningly followed the dictum of the Party and Mao in everything and, in Liu's report, his two protagonists dissented with the Party and Mao for the cause of the society. It was unprecedented in Communist Chinese literature that approbation for dissidence emerged. Liu projected his protagonists to be loyal to the motherland, the society and even the Party, who fearlessly criticized the Party leadership for their shifting political line not always in conformity with the ideology. Like their literati predecessors, Liu's protagonists wrote letters to the leadership admonishing them for leading the country to disaster: "For the last time I give you most sincere advice.... I think the Central Committee...has committed a series of mistakes, and many of them are mistakes in principle.... The main one is the worship of the individual or what is called the cult of the individual".[38] Directly petitioning to Mao, one of the protagonists said: "you do not permit others to criticize your shortcomings and mistakes...in the course of time, those who will be left around you will be a group of villains holding sway.... I am extremely worried about the destiny of the Party and state. With feelings of utmost sincerity.... I hope you will distance yourself from petty men and bring men of noble character close to yourself".[39] The conclusion reached by Liu Binyan was whereas unquestioning obedience only strengthened a repressive system, sincere criticism of politically engaged intellectuals must expose the injustice that is being done in the name of politics and must speak up for the redressal of people's grievances. In doing so, these intellectuals would show a kind of loyalty that was infinitely more desirable for the welfare of the society, the country and even the Party.

Around the same time as the second controversy on alienation, another formulation that generated debate was Liu Zaifu's views on vulgar sociology. In a series of articles published over late 1985 and early 1986, Liu discussed the importance of individual consciousness and subjectivity in literature and art. Liu Zaifu's arguments were based on the contention that the worth of literature cannot be judged only on the basis of society's economic and political conditions, but, more importantly, in terms of coherence and originality of writers which were products of individual consciousness and subjective projection. He argued that if economic and political conditions became the only parameters of evaluating literature or in other words, if literature was evaluated on the scale of literary theories that concentrated on the external laws, it would amount to subsuming individual consciousness — and that would be anti-art.[40] Liu further argued that people, who are the raw material of literature, are complex in all their contradictory preoccupations, dilemma, obsessions and fantasies and can not be analyzed in a simplistic frame of reference like socio-economic relations and to do so would be nothing but "vulgar sociology".[41] Therefore, to comprehend the complex reality with its innumerable human facets, the artists and writers need to do more than logical reasoning and in this regard inspiration and imagination are relevant and necessary in creative writing. Liu Zaifu, thus, not only struck a powerful blow against Mao's Yanan Forum Talks on literature, but also refused to make any concession to the concept of "socialist realism".

Beginning early 1986, when Liu Zaifu was criticized for his views on "vulgar sociology", there were indications of a campaign in the offing. By September, the Sixth Plenum of the CPC's Twelfth Congress was convened and it passed a set of guidelines for the "construction of socialist spiritual civilization". This probably was the beginning of the campaign against "bourgeois liberalization" which was launched in early 1987, right after a series of student demonstrations in December, 1986. Many leading political and literary figures were severely criticized, and though in much milder terms than in the past during the Mao era, they were upbraided by either resignation, expulsion or removal from editorial posts. Most writers protested by remaining silent and literature, both quantitatively and qualitatively, went into a slide for the whole of 1987.

In the years from 1983 to 1986, the Chinese intellectuals had become intensely interested in Chinese "culture". In the literary realm, it came to be known as a "searching-for-roots fever". The other side of this root-searching was criticism of not only traditional Chinese culture, but also of Chinese national character. The criticism of Chinese national character was embodied in the view held by an increasing number of liberal Chinese intellectuals that the root of China's political problems lies in China's historical tradition. What followed was a conscious need to discover new cultural concepts and ideals that would revitalize China on all fronts. With the ongoing "Open-Door Policy" and exposure to the West, the intellectuals naturally looked for answers in Western concepts and -isms. Their search included philosophy, literature, art and social sciences and came up with a mind-boggling variety. In literature the range was from stream-of-consciousness, modernism, futurism to New Criticism, structuralism, post-structuralism and post-modernism. The whole scene was stimulating, though somewhat superficial.

This culture fever culminated in the creation of a six-part television serial called "*River Elegy*"[42] (*He Shang*). According to this serial, virtually all of China's contemporary problems stemmed from Chinese tradition. Presenting a parable on the past, present and future of China, it argued that the Yellow River, symbolic of Chinese civilization and culture, is dead and advocated that for any further progress of the Chinese people, this inwardly focused Yellow River Civilization must emerge out of its constrained existence and embrace the open Blue Ocean, symbolic of modern Western culture. Though consciously praising China's current efforts of reform, it held China's socialist present, jointly with traditional past, responsible for the drowning of China.

The agenda put forward by "*River Elegy*" was to form a "class" composed of the broad majority of Chinese public, who, with the initiative of a young generation of progressive democracy-minded officials and rational market-oriented entrepreneurs, will drive China forward towards modernity. As the Harvard Professor Tu Weiming sums up:

> 'The River Elegy' was a cultural essay, intended to serve the dual purpose of articulating the impatience of the young and exposing the inertia of the octogenerian orthodox ideologists."[43]

With the commentary written by a team of talented young reformers led by Su Xiaokang, the serial gave way to an anti-traditional wave followed by an unprecedented cultural debate: "Whither China?"

This controversial serial jolted the whole nation. Apart from a common complaint that it "forgot the ancestors" i.e., it took insufficient pride in Chinese tradition, the popular response was generally positive within the obvious limitation of the ordinary masses not being much exposed to intellectual debate and discourse. On the other hand, the officially inspired criticism denounced the wholesale Westernization propagated by the serial. At once, there was a warmth of perplexed and variegated response from the Chinese intellectuals. There was even a schizophrenia in the official reaction with the majority of Party veterans singing disapproval while the Party General Secretary, Zhao Ziyang, was said to be elated. The serial was withdrawn from public viewing for a year, and was re-telecast in 1988. There was so much confusion that Li Zehou, one of the initiators of culture fever, not only dissociated himself from the views taken by "River Elegy", but also indicated a new direction for the search for the roots of present problems:

> " I do not believe that the key problem, as of now, is the so-called culture or "enlightenment", but reform of the political-economic system. Those people who are opposed to "tradition" so vehemently have covered up precisely this point. The implication of their excessive criticism of "culture" is to say that the fault lies equally with all of us. This, in turn, tends to exonerate those who really should bear responsibility. There is no way I can believe that the fault lies more with us than with them. The problem before us is how to reform our extremely irrational, feudalistic, and copiously flawed system."[44]

Another similar epic serial "*Sunrise in the Heart*" was in the making to commemorate the 70th anniversary of the May Fourth Movement, but never saw the daylight in the aftermath of the Tiananmen Square Incident in 1989.

Although quantitatively speaking post-Mao Chinese literature has been dominated by realism of the Deep Realist School (in which Critical Realism has emerged as a force to reckon with), there has been some exciting and stimulating experimentation with technique. Some of these experiments have been successful in that these innovations have enriched and more importantly, managed to create a comprehensiveness in a given literary work consiously balancing between and mutually complementing the theme and technique. There are also works in which the writer has been so preoccupied with technical innovations that they made stiltedly difficult reading. Nevertheless, the exploration itself was path-creating conducive to the enrichment of Chinese literature.

Some of the Chinese literary critics have distinguished between (1) those works which have realistic contents, but has used certain modernist techniques, and (2) works which are more modernist both in terms of content and method.[45]

(1) In this category, modernist techniques like stream-of-consciousness, symbolism and impressionism have often been used by many well-known writers like Wang Meng, Zong Pu, Deng Gang and Zhang Xinxin. This is the category which probably forms the major share of post-Mao Chinese literature that are not within the limits of Deep Realist School. This category has been called the Open Realist School in China.

Wang Meng's experimentation with the stream-of-consciousness technique is remarkable in the fact that it helps to vividly convey the richness and the rapidly changing of life. In "Kite Streamers", Wang Meng describes two young lovers who have nowhere to go, nowhere they can meet undisturbed. The description is given by an outside narrator:

> "Look, look, and a whole night is used up. Our vast and boundless sky and land, our magnificent three dimensional space — is there any corner for the young people to talk, embrace and kiss? We only need a very small place. And you — you have room for towering heroes and earth-shaking rebels, for vermin and villains that besmear heaven and earth, for so many battlefields,...meeting grounds, execution grounds...but you have no room for the passionate love between Susu and Jiayuan: One 160 centimetres tall and weighing 48 kilograms; the other barely 170 centimetres in height and weighing 54 kilograms."[46]

In this humorous description, the writer juxtaposes a series of images and enables the readers to perceive an ordinary aspect of life as an intense subjective experience. At the same time the narrative is rooted in visual images of a typically Chinese setup. Thus, this experimentation is successful because the use of this technique does not make the author lose his grip on the reality of Chinese life. In Wang Meng's own words:

> "When we write about psychology, feelings, and consciousness we have not forgotten that they are reflections of life; we have not forgotten their social significance. It is just that we hope to be able to write with "exceptional insight" and with more depth, more distinctive characteristics, more "flavour". For all these reasons, our "stream-of-consciousness" is not a stream-of-consciousness that urges people to escape reality by an inward flight; it is rather a healthy and substantial self-feeling that urges people to face both the objective and the subjective worlds, to love life and to love human heart."[47]

Similarly Zhang Xinxin's works, which are reminiscent of Western modernism because of the techniques she used, are also rooted in contemporary Chinese urban life. In "*On the Same Horizon*", she has made use of symbolism and imagery to portray the love-hate relationship of a young couple. Through the exposure of social and psychological complexity with the help of such symbolism like a football match, a track race and a boxing contest etc. She mirrrored the ruthless struggle for survival in large cities where not even the near and dear can be trusted.

Writers like Wang Meng, Zhang Xinxin and others, who have used new techniques and innovations of the modernist school, have actually managed to open a new vista in Chinese realist tradition because their borrowing from modernism has been used as means to depict the complex reality of present-day China with deeper insight. Moreover, such techniques have helped to produce literary works that are sociological commentaries of fast-changing China.

(2) This category more or less conforms to the Modernist school. Apart from using modernist techniques and methods, they also reflect abnormal relationships between men and women, the individual and society, material environment and nature, and distorted psychology, pessimism and nihilism caused by such relationships — the concerns which are generally associated with Western Modernist literature. Pioneers in this category are Can Xue, Mo Yan, Liu Suola, Xu Xing and Han Shaogang. Most of these writers are pessimistic and disillusioned with the world they live and the writer's individual subjectivity or subjective impression of their surroundings are represented in symbols and imagery.

The works of Can Xue are remarkable in that the realistic conventions such as characterisation, social setting and plot are not met. Can Xue's images are mostly linked with filth, death, destruction and darkness. For example in her "*Ah Mei in Pensive Mood on a Sunny Day*", Ah Mei notices only pimples and bad breaths of the people around her. The surrounding is depicted as grimy, rickety and infested with worms. Can Xue not only shatters normal human tenderness but also the illusions about many social institutions like family and marriage. Her techniques and her vision of the world and society are mutually suited in that the techniques (e.g., negative imagery and symbols) are not displayed as mere tools, they complement and enhance the depiction of her vision.

On the other hand, in some works techniques and technical innovations are too dominant. For example, in "*You Have No Choice*", the innovations are self-conscious and over-emphasised. As a result, the pictures it projects of some alienated, confused youth sound over-written and insincere. So much so that one Chinese literary critic has to say the following about this work:

> "It satirizes the atmosphere of campus life.... The whole conception is disorderly with casual touches of colour, abrupt dialogue, hysterical screams and such cynical ideas as dropout.... There is neither plot nor typical characters nor events, only a recklessly presented, restless world. The story betrays a marked influence, and one might even say is simply a stylistic imitation, of the American black-humour writer Joseph Heller."[48]

Summing up the Chinese literary scene in the post-Mao period can conclude that in the first place, the New Literature is indicative of fundamental changes in the milieu from which it rises — both in terms of social reality and social consciousness that shape literature. Today problems of alienation, crisis of faith, diminished human value as a result of authoritarian state and orthodox ideology, abuse of power and privilege, problems of social and human relations etc., are all acknowledged social reality. Acknowledged, because they have been publicly discussed at some point or the other and since they are acknowledged they are a part of social consciousness. Some of these problems did exist in the Mao era as well but were never tackled openly either in public discussion and debate or in literature. Secondly, since such social consciousness is being expressed in literature, it can be said, that social conscience is shaping contemporary literature. Literature, in turn, by raising these social issues, is trying to influence social reality from which it emerges — exposing the undesirable and unacceptable trends and calling for change. Thirdly, approach of writers, literary theoreticians and critics towards literature and literary criticism signifies a conscious revolt against old dogmas and Mao's literary doctrines. Because, the people associated with literature are redefining the role of literature, yardsticks of literary criticism and literature itself. In other words, they are striving for true literature (in its variety and sincerity) in contrast with the false controlled literature of the past, which, if analyzed in the framework of Trotsky's literary thought, was so tarnished (with exceptions, of course) that it had ceased to be literature at all. This redefinition, in turn is giving rise to new aesthetic principles and taste. Fourthly, the efforts of this joint body of literary practitioners at redefining the various aspects of the literary process, are significant in reformulating the relation between literature and politics. In post-Mao China, literature is not as subservient to politics as in the past. It can be tentatively said that now literature is serving the cause of society and country, and people who compose of this society both as individuals and as a collective. In this service to the people, literature is sometimes unbridled and definitely unconstrained by orthodox ideology and dogmatic politics. This may be the first hint of universal human culture to be created in distant future. Fifthly, this New Literature, with unprecedented scope, is indicative of a comparatively strong-willed, independent body of writers, who are not so much controlled by official dictum in their creative undertaking. More and more writers today are venturing into areas that are still forbidden. This does not necessarily mean that they are opposed to socialism or want to overthrow socialism. On the contrary, the majority of such writers are stepping across the forbidden line either by being true to reality or by choosing themes that are frowned down upon, because they believe in Liu Binyan's brand of the second kind of loyalty. By acting as the conscience of the system, they are trying to reform, repair and revitalize from within. In other words, rather than starting from political beliefs and ideological convictions which resulted in literature of the socialist realist kind, they are letting the mirror of literature truthfully reflect life and judge the shortcomings of the system.

Notes

1 For proceedings of the Congress and speeches delivered, see *Wenyi Bao* (Literary Gazette), nos.11-12, 1979, pp. 8-26.

2 Zhou Yang, "Our Lessons and Tasks Ahead", *Beijing Review*, no. 50, 14 December 1979, p. 10. This article being the excerpts of Zhou Yang's speech to the Congress.

3 The unofficial press published 84 individual issues of 27 titles of which some 12 titles were published regularly between November 1978 to 4 May 1979.

4 Published for the first time in *Today*, no. 2, p. 6. However, the poem was originally written around 1970/1. Translation taken from David S.G. Goodman, *Beijing Street Voices: The Poetry and Politics of China's Democracy Movement*, London, 1981, pp. 130-31.

5 Published in *Today*, no. 1, p. 267. Translation as in David S.G. Goodman, *op. cit.*, p. 98.

6 Published in *Harvest*, no. 1, p. 267. Translation as in David S.G. Goodman, *op. cit.*, pp. 77-78.

7 Published in *Today*, no. 3, p. 38. Translation as in David S.G. Goodman, *op. cit.*, pp. 115-16.

8 Published in *Today*, no. 3, p. 38. Translation as in William, Tay, "Obscure Poetry": A Controversy in Post-Mao China" in Jeffrey C.Kinkley (ed.), *After Mao: Chinese Literature and Society, 1978-81*, London, 1985, p. 135.

9 Quoted in *Shi tansuo*, 3:49 (1981). Translation taken from Kinkley, *op. cit.*, p. 134.

10 *Shikan*, 10:28 (1980). Translation taken from Kinkley, *op. cit.*, p.136.

11 As mentioned in *Shikan*, 10: 49-51 (1980), Gu Cheng's father Gu Gong testified that Gu Cheng has not been exposed to either Crescent School or Western modernism.

12 *Shikan*, 10:29 (1980). Translation as in Kinkley, *op. cit.*, p. 138.

13 *Shikan*, 10. 28 (1980). Translation taken from Kinkley, *op. cit.*, p. 140.

14 *Xingxing* 1, 1979. As cited in Kinkley, *op. cit.*, p.141.

15 *Wenyi Bao*, 16: 19-20 (August 1981). As cited by Kinkley, *op. cit.*, p. 142.

16 Translation as in Kinkley, *op. cit.*, p.143.

17 *Shi tansuo*, 1:56 (1981) As cited by Kinkley, *op. cit.*, p. 145.

18 *Shikan*, 12: 4 (1980). As cited in Jeffrey C. Kinkley (ed.), *op. cit.*, p. 146.

19 This article was published in *Shikan*, 3: 55-58 (1981).

20 Quoted in *Shi tansuo*, 1: 52 (1981). Translation as cited in Kinkley, *op. cit.*, p. 147.

21 Liu Xinhua, "Shang hen"; *Wenhui bao* 11, August 1978. It has been translated as "The Wounded" in Lee and Barme, *The Wounded* (Hong Kong: Joint Publishing Co., 1979).

22 Though this work is one of the best example of 'scar literature', it was published, much after the initial wave of 'scar literature' in 1980.

23 Helen F. Siu, and Zelda, Stern, *Mao's Harvest, Voices from China's New Generation*, New York, 1983, Introduction, p. xliii.

24 Sha Yexin, Li Shoucheng and Yao Mingde, "*Jiaru Wo shi Zhende*", special issue of *Xiju yishu* (Art of Drama) and *Shanghai xiju* (Shanghai Drama) (Shanghai, 1979).

25 Wang Jing, "Zai shehui de dang'an li", *Dianying chuangzuo* (Film creation), no. 10, 1979, pp. 22-43.

26 Bai, Hua and Peng Ning, "Kulian", *Shiyue* (October), no. 3, 1979, pp. 140-71, 248.

27 Marx & Engels, "On Literature and Art", Progress Publishers, Moscow, 1978, p. 92.

28 Liu Binyan, "Ren Yao Zhijian", *Renmin wenxue* (People's literature), no. 9, 1979, pp. 83-102.

29 The talk by Hu Yaobang has been published in *Wenyi Bao*, no. 1, 1981, pp. 2-10.

30 The Bai Hua case has been discussed in detail in Richard Kraus, "Bai Hua: The Political Authority of a Writer" in Carol Lee Hamrin and Timothy Cheek (ed.), *China's Establishment Intellectuals*, M. E. Sharpe, 1986. Also see "Film and Politics: Bai Hua's *Bitter Love*", in Jonathan D. Spence, *Chinese Roundabout*, W. W. Norton & Co. Inc. 1992.

31 Zhou Yang, "The Path of Our Country's Socialist Literature and Art in China", *Renmin Ribao*, 4 September 1960, pp. 5-7. As cited in Merle Goldman, *China's Intellectuals: Advise and Dissent*, Cambridge, Mass., Harvard University Press, 1981, p. 46.

32 Zhang Xinxin, "Zai tong yi dipingxian", *Shouhuo* (Harvest), no. 6, 1981, pp. 172-233.

33 Zhang Xinxin, "Women zhege nianji de meng", *Shouhuo*, no. 4, 1982, pp. 95-120.

34 Wang Ruoshui's speech, 15 August 1979, published in his collected essays, "Wei rendaozhuyi bianhu" (In defense of humanism), Beijing, 1986, p. 16. As cited in Lowell Dittmer and Samuel S. Kim (ed.), *China's Quest for National Identity*, Ithaca, Cornell University Press, 1993, p. 139.

35 *Ibid.*, p. 13. As cited in Dittmer and Kim, *op. cit.*, n. 36, p. 139.

36 Zhang Xianliang, "Nanren de yiban shi nuren" (The half of a man is woman), *Shouhuo*, no. 5, 1985, pp. 4-102.

37 Liu Binyan, "Dierzhong zhongcheng" (The Second Loyalty), *Kaituo* (Explorer), March 1985.

38 *Zhongguo Baokan* (Chinese Journals), 18 February 1985, in JPRS, no. 86-004, 15 January 1986, p. 36.

39 *Ibid.*

40 Liu Zaifu, "Lun wenxuede Zhutixing" (On Literature's Subjectivity), *Wenxue Pinglun* (Literary Criticism), no. 6, 1985, pp. 11-26; no. 1, 1986, pp. 3-19.

41 Liu Zaifu, "Lun renwude erchong xingge zuhe yuanli" (The Theory of Composition of Forces in Dual Personality), *Wenxue Pinglun*, no. 3, 1984, pp. 24-40, 141.

42 "River Elegy" was a six-part VI feature document first screened in 1987, and again in summer 1988. Transcript of the narration is available in Cui, Wenhua (Ed.), *Heshang lun* (On "River Elegy"), Beijing, 1988.

43 Tu Weiming, "Intellectual Effervescence in China", *Dedalus*, Vol. 121, no. 2, Spring 1992, p. 262.

44 Li Zehou, "Wuside shishifeifei" (The May Fourth Movement: Its Rights and Wrongs As Commentators see), *Wenhui Bao* (Wenhui Daily) Shanghai, 28 March 1989, p. 4. As cited in Dittmer and Kim, *op. cit.*, p. 146.

45 Miao Junjie, "A Preliminary Study of Literary Schools in the New Era", *Chinese Literature*, Winter 1988, p. 180.

46 Wang Meng, "Kite Streamers", *Beijing Wenyi* (Beijing Literature and Art), no. 5, 1980, p. 11. Translation taken from Lee, Leo Oufan, "The Politics of Technique: Perspective of Literary Dissidence in Contemporary Chinese Fiction" in Kinkley, *op. cit.*, p. 167.

47 Wang Meng, "An Open Letter on 'Stream-of-consciousness' " (translated by Michael S. Duke), *Modern Chinese Literature*, Vol. 1, no.1, September 1984, p. 28.

48 Miao Junjie, *op. cit.*, p. 185.

MIRA SINHA BHATTACHARJEA

39

MAO ZEDONG'S VISION: CHINA, THE WORLD AND INDIA

Premier Zhou Enlai, who dominated the international sector of Chinese polity for close on half a century, has been widely credited with the crafting of what is called China's "foreign policy". However, the basic presumption of this article is that for Mao Zedong, foreign policy was an integral part of a holistic strategy for "making revolution". Consequently during the Maoist era, "foreign policy" was not distinguished from "domestic policy", and the compulsions of state and national interests in "foreign policy" were no less amenable to ideas and value change than were those in the arena of "domestic policy".

It is the burden of this exploration that the ideas and perceptions, the methods of analysis, the identification of objectives and the strategies for their realisation that dominated the making and implementation of "foreign policy" (or, what the Chinese call "diplomatic work") were those of Mao. They were derived, as will be discussed later, from the understanding that Mao came to acquire of the objective world of China and of its domestic and external oppression. This understanding provided Mao with the answers he had been seeking to the three linked questions of what was meant by making revolution, who would make revolution, and how it was to be made. From the answers relating to making revolution in China, Mao drew large generalisations about the what, who and how of making revolution worldwide. Even more, the possibilities as well as the fate of the Chinese revolution were, for Mao, linked inseparably with those of the revolutionay forces in the world as the national part of the global whole. In Mao's holistic approach, the revolutionary prospects of the global whole exercised hegemony which, in varied and critical ways, determined the prospects for revolution within China and all other countries.

I

I venture to think that no other leader in the post-war world viewed the interaction between states, the analysis of the global balance of power, or the education of the masses and the training of diplomatic cadres with the same seriousness as did Mao. The corpus of Mao's writings is interspersed with periodic analysis of the "present situation" that Mao undertook in order to identify the state of the world revolution, and the tasks and goals of the CPC in both its domestic and diplomatic work. A constant purpose of such analysis was to assess the alignment and distribution of global power. Each such assessment reaffirmed the Maoist conclusion that the global and national balance was heavily weighed in favour of the reactionary or imperialist forces. Mao was, therefore, constantly aware of the weakness or, of what I have called the minority status of revolutionary forces within China and in the world.[1] He, therefore, made developments in the outer world, the critical determinant of the strategy and tactics, the methods and objectives of "making revolution" even within China.

Yet Mao did not abandon the possibility of or abdicate the domestic and national responsibility and initiative for "making revolution". What he did was to inspire a revolutionary optimism, born of a distinctive perception and a unique mode of analysis, and to innovate the strategy of the united front as a means of transforming present weakness into future strength. Such transformation was, for Mao, a process, not an event. The present therefore acquired great significance: it was the womb and the guarantor of the desired future, as was the insightful identification of objective universal trends. Thus, as the situation in the outer world changed, so did the Maoist style of leadership, his broad strategy and methods of work. The core of Mao's holistic approach, namely, anti-imperialism and the paired objective of making revolution, nevertheless, remained constant, as did his strategy of the united front. What changed was his personification of "imperialism" identified as a particular state and determined by an alteration in its power and policy. Thus, imperialism was first personified in Japan, then the US and in his last years, the Soviet Union.

The above is by way of explaining the title of and the exploration behind this essay. It takes Mao and his perception of the objective world, and his delineation of strategy for making revolution as the founts of China's interstate behaviour and its diplomatic work. Consequently it also takes as credible the Maoist concern with establishing new norms of state behaviour, namely, the *Panchsheel* (Five principles of Co-existence), as well as the attempt to introduce these in the behaviour of the Chinese state.

This essay analyses eight interventions made by Mao in response to developments in the outer world, that brought about a change in Maoist strategy and method. Three of these interventions took place prior to the founding of the PRC and five between 1949 and 1976. In keeping with the title, the essay also examines China's bilateral relations with India to argue that Nehru and India were given a pivotal role in the united front strategy throughout the Maoist era. Consequently, all bilateral Sino-Indian issues were demoted in significance and were not permitted to upset the united front against US imperialism. The 1962 war, from this analytical perspective, had immense strategic and political purposes for Mao, precisely because of India's pivotal role in the united front. The confrontation with India, it will be argued, was intended to forestall a Soviet inspired fundamental change in the agenda of world politics from anti-imperialism to anti-nuclear war, and the consequent re-alignment of world power and forces that would come about. Both the new agenda and the re-alignment of power would, in Mao's perspective, be greatly detrimental both to the Chinese state and to "making revolution".

Though the intervention of 1962 was, from Mao's perspective, largely successful, it was not, however, decisive. It set Mao on the awesome task of substituting, in the world's eye, the USSR — the world's first socialist state — for the US as the contemporary personification of imperialism. To prepare China, the CPC and its leadership, for battling the dangers posed by Soviet revisionism to "making revolution", Mao launched the Cultural Revolution within China. In the mid-seventies he proposed a new paradigm of international politics, contained in the Three Worlds thesis, to explain the distribution of global power after the defection of the Soviet Union to imperialism, as well as the dynamics and trends in the contemporary world. Mao was too old and too feeble perhaps to lead China out of the chaos of the Cultural Revolution and to ensure that future leaders would follow his strategy for making revolution. His last intervention failed and brought to an end the Mao era of "making revolution", together with its unique way of perceiving the interlocking relationships between China, the world and India.

An essential feature of Maoist analysis was the intimate, inseparable and critical relationship he posited between the outer world and the inner world of China. The boundaries of the Chinese nation as he had delineated them in 1939, enclosed the domestic or inner of China as they did for all other states. And, together with the right to sovereignty, they separated the inner world from the outer world of China in seemingly traditional ways. Influenced by Marxism, however, Mao superimposed on this coventional divide, a structure of systemic unity between elements belonging to the traditional domestic and elements belonging to the traditional external. Thus, not Japan but Japanese imperialism was linked to domestic counter-revolutionary forces in an inseparable class pairing. This conjoining blurred the line separating the conventional domestic and external of China, as it did for all other states. It also altered their meaning and concept. For example, from the conventional perspective, all of Japan was the external enemy of all within China's domestic world. At the same time, however, Japanese imperialism had breached the traditional domestic to find a support base within China. This consisted of more than the traitors or collaborators that every war or revolution has known. They were, in Maoist analysis, social groups and classes, the seedlings of domestic imperialism within China — the comprador classes or elements. Together with Japanese imperialism they constituted for Mao, a new non-conventional "outer" of China. As a counterpoint, the revolutionary "inner" comprised the revolutionary anti-imperialist forces within China that, in like manner, had systemic links with similar forces within the conventional domestic of Japan and of other imperialist countries. The balance of forces and the balance of power that existed in both the traditional and non-conventional meanings of the inner/outer world concept became, thereafter, the most critical detriment of the Maoist strategy for "making revolution" both at home and abroad.

Mao's holistic approach and mode of analysis acknowledged with stark realism that the revolutionary forces were in the minority in the world, as were the CPC and the revolutionary forces within China. Mao's awareness of being in the minority in both global and national terms appears to have dominated all his thinking and analysis thereafter. To counter this disadvantage, Mao argued that weakness could be transformed into yet undiscovered advantages or strengths. Mao innovated the appropriate strategy and tactics for bringing about this dialectical transformation in the political and organisational form of the United Front. Both the domestic and international united fronts had the same "principal enemy": Japan or imperialism or fascism. Thus, in the anti-Japanese war, revolutionary optimism meant perceiving the opportunities for alliance and the spaces for political action provided by China's semi-colonial status. In the outer world of China, by carefully differentiating between the competing interests of the various imperialist powers and by aggregating the support of all countries and groups opposed to Japan or fascism. Within the inner world of China, by aggregating the strength of disparate social groups in united resistance to Japanese aggression and by introducing hitherto peripheral groups or people into the calculus of forces. In short, in the outer world, the Maoist strategy attempted to enlarge the space between Japan and all possible constituents of the international united front. In the inner world of China, he attempted to narrow the political space between disparate, often mutually hostile, elements that were to be brought into the domestic united front. The "single spark" thesis explained the possibility of victory in the Chinese anti-Japanese war together with the support that would be provided by the international united front. Later, during the civil war, when both united fronts had broken down, Maoist calculations included intangibles like the inherent weakness of the KMT and the support of the people to anticipate the collapse of the KMT and the victory of the CPC.

It is part of the folklore of the CPC revolutionary history that the Chinese national war of resistance brought about the defeat of Japan in the inner world of China. This defeat was by any reckoning one of history"s critical junctures : it also resolved the central political question that had faced China since the May 4 Movement. In brief, the danger of China becoming a Japanese colony had been averted. Even more, China's role as a frontline state in the global anti-fascist war had finally brought about the end of the unequal treay system and so ended China's century of humiliation. It is one of the ironies of history that China in its time of greatest weakness gained recognition as a great power. It was made a founding member of the United Nations, a permanent veto wielding member of the Security Council.

In an interview with Anna Louise Strong (not made public till 1958), Mao posited a three-way division of the world that interposed a vast intermediate zone lying between the Soviet Union and the United States.[2] It reflected Mao's analytical method and arraigned the world forces in three vertical bands. It, therefore, differed from Stalin"s two bloc — "we" vs "they" — division of the world's forces, the rigidity of which left no political space for "friends" in the Soviet global strategy by discounting the dynamic of nationalism. Mao's intervention, on the other hand, enlarged and created political space between the newly independent countries and imperialism. In short, Mao recognised nationalism as the contemporary global dynamic of political change, emphasised its anti-imperialist, pro-democracy character and created possibilities for the implementation of his broad United Front strategy. In the outer world, this enabled China to make common, though limited, cause with all anti-colonial national liberation struggles, as well as with the newly independent states anxious to protect their sovereignty. This laid the ground for a global international united front so essential for Mao's strategy of making revolution. In the same interview, Mao also attempted to dispel the fear of the nuclear weapon whose terror had been demonstrated in Nagasaki and Hiroshima. He revived revolutionary optimism by describing it, in strategic terms, as a "paper tiger" that could be defied by a resolute people"s struggle. By undertaking and winning the civil war, the CPC was to demonstrate that this could indeed by done.

Months before the PRC was formed, in an essay entitled "On the People"s Democratic Dictatorship" Mao reaffirmed the CPC's commitment to socialism and its membership of the socialist camp. By then, as will be recalled, the fragile war time alliance between the US and the USSR had already broken down to be replaced by the Cold War. Once again, Mao responded to this critical change in the international arena in a manner consonant with his commitment to socialism. As earlier, this was accompanied by a change of pace and strategy at home. In anticipation of the CPC's victory in the civil war and its assumption of leadership of the nation and the revolution, the CPC's commitment to New Democracy innovated in 1940,[3] was upheld but in the significantly new form of a people's democratic dictorship. After the victory, the CPC's organisation of state power would be such as to ensure that the CPC would effectively have the power and authority to undertake the gradual transition to socialism.

All this created a natural and special role for Nehru and India in the Maoist scheme of things. The legitimation and recognition of the force of nationalism appealed to Nehru who had long sympathised with China's fate. Moreover, Nehru was eager to witness the emergence of India and China as well as the rest of the colonised world as proud indepedent states where they would no longer be "the playthings of the west". It was also part of the Nehruvian vision of the future that these countries, having suffered aggression and colonisation, would strive jointly to introduce a new moral pattern of inter-state behaviour. The intermediate zone of Mao's conception could, from Nehru's perspective, help to confirm his rival concept of a non-aligned grouping of countries following a third path in world politics. In the Nehruvian vision as it unfolded, China occupied the same pivotal role as was assigned to India in the Maoist strategy.

II

From 1949 until his death in 1976, except for a brief period after 1957, Mao extended this holistic approach and analytical method to the international arena to arrive at broadly the same strategy and tactics of the United Front that he had adopted both during the anti-Japanese war and the civil war. During this period, Mao intervened on at least five occasions to ensure the continuance of his strategy of making revolution. Each intervention came in response to developments in the outer world, but impacted on domestic policy. Each intervention acknowledged that the balance of forces both globally and nationally continued to be unfavourable. Nevertheless, the course of making revolution could be pursued with cautious optimism if an appropriate strategy was devised to take advantage of the favourable trends. Thus, with each intervention, Mao attempted to create conditions for the constitution of a new united front by redefining its central idea, namely, anti-imperialism. At the time of his last intervention this redefinition that cast the world's first socialist state as the No. 1 imperialist more dangerous than even the United States, was so startlingly unorthodox as to find few sympathisers. Whether his attempt in the mid-seventies to create a new international (and domestic) united front against Soviet imperialism would have succeeded or not, will remain one of history's unanswered questions. Mao was too ill and too old to provide the continuing leadership to do so. His death in 1976 opened the domestic flood gates for an almost complete denial of his holistic approach, his mode of analysis and his broad strategy for "making revolution" by the new leadership.

MAO'S INTERVENTION NO. 1 (1950): BRANDING THE US AS IMPERIALIST

China's decision to enter the Korean War and to confront the powerful United States despite weakness and the tasks of reconstructing a war-torn economy and society is attributed to Mao.[4] It derived from his analysis of the US policy towards the revolution, following the US action in Korea and the June decision of the USA to recognise Chiang Kai-shek regime as the legitimate China, protect Taiwan and isolate communist China. Mao concluded that the US had reached a strategic decision to oppose the Chinese Revolution and overthrow the CPC government. He envisaged a US threat and possible attack against China from vulnerable points along China's periphery: Taiwan, Korea, Indochina and even from far away Tibet. In response to this perceived multiple threat, China, almost simultaneously, took the following actions: it despatched "volunteers" and advisers to North Vietnam; sent "volunteers" to North Korea; claimed sovereign rights to Taiwan and charged the US with the occupation of its territory of Taiwan. The cumulative effect of these actions was to confirm the ideological and strategic confrontation with the US, and to cast the US as the principal threat to China, nationalism and socialism.

MAO'S INTERVENTION NO. 2 (1951): LIMITING THE DAMAGE: PRE-PLANNING THE GROUND FOR A UNITED FRONT

A year later, Mao intervened personally to set in process a policy of damage limitation targeted at India and the colonised world. It was designed to contain and limit the fall-out of the Tibetan events on Nehru and India and to revive the possibility of future political cooperation between the two countries.

In a most unusual and highly symbolic gesture, Mao attended the national day celebrations at the Indian Embassy in Beijing in 1951. His speech called for unity with India in "working for peace".[5] This gesture gave public sanction and legitimacy to China's desire for a special relationship with India in the common cause of "working for peace".

As part of its policy of damage limitation, China proceeded to handle sensitive issues in Sino-Indian relations in a manner that would not be immediately provocative to India. For example, Beijing did not protest independent India's exercise of erstwhile British rights in Tibet. Nor did it end them unilaterally as it had done in the case of the rights that had been exercised by the imperialist powers in China. Taken together, Mao's gesture as well as the sensitive handling of delicate bilateral issues helped to assuage Indian fears of China. Indeed, it was shrewd Maoist understanding of Nehru's personality and politics and of his dominant role in the making of Third World public opinion and Indian national policy, that enabled the policy to succeed. Its success, in turn, revived the political possibility of united action for shared purposes by Mao's China and Nehru's India in the international arena. As the Maoist strategy unfolded, India was cast once more in a pivotal role : as the champion of nationalism and anti-colonialism, and as the natural leader of the newly independent countries. The success of the policy of damage limitation (that also encompassed the armistice in Korea and the Geneva spirit) led to Zhou Enlai's visit to India in 1954; to the India-China agreement on Tibet; and to the Panchsheel as the new universal norm of state behaviour. The momentum was maintained with Nehru's "Roman triumph" visit to China later that year. Within a few months, it led to the Bandung Conference and the emergence of an Afro-Asian grouping that included a Communist China willing to leave future initiative and leadership to India and Nehru.

Bandung demonstrated how successfully the PRC had overcome the grave risks that attended Mao's 1950 decision to enter the Korean War. In fact, it did more. It brought into being the intermediate zone that Mao had envisaged in 1946 as an essential requirement for the pursuance of the united front strategy. Friendship and common cause with India and the newly independent countries of Asia, moreover, helped to project a PRC identity distinct from that of the Soviet Union despite ideological fraternity and treaty partnership. The PRC's new image was that of an Asian country struggling to develop and modernise its economy and society and safgeguard its sovereignty, as were all the newly independent countries, particularly India.

MAO'S INTERVENTION NO. 3 (1957): COMBATING REVISIONISM TO TILT REVOLUTIONARY BALANCE

The Chinese leaders sponsored discussion within the socialist community in 1957 on the dangers of "revisionism". China also declared in Moscow that the balance of power and forces was so delicately poised that it could be made to tilt in favour of global revolutionary forces to end their minority status. The East Wind, Mao said, now prevailed over the West Wind. In short, Mao was arguing the possibility of a strategic shift from the defensive to a seizure of the initiative. For Mao, the two events were interrelated. The strategic shift demanded a recognition that "revisionism", which he saw to be inherent in Khrushchev's 1956 strategy of peaceful coexistence, was enfeebling and would be unable to seize the historical opportunity.

The Maoist intervention of 1957 was not episodic: it continued over many years in which the central issue of debate was revisionism. Its episodic failure of 1957 resulted in grave ideological and political cleavage between China and the Soviet Union, and it dominated Maoist thinking and strategy thereafter.[6]As earlier, Mao initiated new policies within China that divided the CPC leadership and led inexorably to the Cultural Revolution and to the ensuing power struggle. It was accompanied in China's diplomatic work by the temporary abandonment of the United Front strategy. In its place, China supported socialist forces everywhere. It tested the outside limits of the US and the USSR strategic and ideological responses to this initiative during the Qumoy crisis of 1958. India's friendship and Nehru's commitment to "progressive policies" were similarly under test over the India-China boundary issue.

MAO'S INTERVENTION NO. 4 (1962): NOT TERRITORIAL CONCERNS BUT STRATEGIC CONSIDERATIONS

The 1962 border war with India developed ostensibly out of rival nationalisms and conflicting territorial claims. But, it was a major strategic decision designed to alter the Khrushchevian agenda of world politics.

According to this new agenda, detente and prevention of nuclear war, instead of oppositon to imperialism, was the central concern of international politics. Its acceptance by the countries of the Third World — Mao's intermediate zone — would alter the balance of world forces in favour of a revisionist Soviet Union and, therefore, in the Maoist view, of imperialism. In this still transitional phase, India's role acquired signal importance precisely because of its leadership of the Third World and the pivotal role it had been given in Mao's United Front strategy.

The new agenda was seductively attractive for many in the non-aligned world, particularly for Nehru who had long espoused these concerns. Thus a strong, almost ideological, commonality emerged between Khrushchev's USSR and Nehru's India. It was to be reflected in Nehru's support to super power detente and the test ban treaty. Thus from 1959 onwards, there was growing convergence in Indian and Soviet strategic perceptions of China — which opposed both — and its role in the world. Soviet reluctance to support its fraternal neighbour, China, in its territorial dispute with India was a manifestation of this covergence.

The re-alignment of forces that it would lead to would not, in the Maoist analysis, be favourable to China and to making revolution.

China's hardline policies and its "testing" of the responses to its initiatives by the leaders, as it were, of all three zones of Mao's framework, i.e., of the Soviet Union, the US and India, was thus an attempt to deny legitimacy and centrality to the new Soviet agenda. By simultaneously fanning tensions between them, Mao was attempting to create political space and greater manoeuvreability for Chinese diplomatic, state and revolutionary action.[7] The failure of Zhou Enlai in acheiving any result in his visit to India in 1960 shadowed the prospects of arriving at a peaceful settlement with India. For the next two years however, China continued to adopt a dual track policy: it pressed for negotiations or for an agreement to respect the line of actual control and non-disturbance of the status quo. Simultaneously, it strengthened and advanced its position on the ground, as did India.

The Chinese decision to use force in 1962 was once again a calculated high risk policy. Like the decision to enter the Korean War, it revealed China's minority status and possible isolation in world affairs. As in 1950, it also destroyed all possibility of Indian participation in any future united front partnership with China. The year 1962 furthermore compounded China's security concerns for it had, in effect, created three live fronts. The decision to use force was, it must be presumed, not taken lightly. Its importance for Mao's strategy of "making revolution" as also for the Chinese state, may be gauged from the fact that it was taken at a time when China was facing a severe economic and leadership crisis. China's military and diplomatic success, despite these highly adverse factors, can be attributed, once again to a shrewd understanding of Nehru's personality and India's lack of military preparedness, and to a remarkable capacity for innovation.

China's military strategy of conducting a controlled war, limited in time and depth across the length of the entire border, took Nehru, India, and perhaps the whole world, by surprise. It resulted in a humiliating defeat for India, and the exposure of its inability to defend itself even against a Third World country. Diplomatically, it revealed that India did not command the support of all Third World countries.

This intervention was accompanied, once again, by a policy of damage limitation. This time, unlike in 1951, its success relied on demonstrating China's ability to take independent decisions and actions (contrasting India's inability in this regard), as well as on the display and acquisition of sufficient capability for national defence. It also aimed, in essence, at establishing China as an independent power centre. The military success of 1962 was followed by the first atomic test in 1964 and by the more intangible assertion of the national will by the Chinese to defend their country. Like the resort to force in 1962, these were presented to the world as defensive measures forced on the Chinese state.

The war itself had been preceded by a diplomatic initiative that resulted in the conclusion of a series of border agreements with neighbouring countries, most of which were also India's neighbours. These agreements suggested that China's bark was worse than its bite, that China's real territorial demands were reasonable and limited. It was followed by a statement of China's territorial policy and negotiating strategy vis-a-vis India which remained unchanged despite its military victory. By not enlarging the war and by refraining from occupying Indian and disputed territory into which it had advanced in the eastern sector, China gave credibility to its intention of limiting the political damage and keeping the door open for a return to the negotiating table. The Maoist policy of damage limitation was again targeted primarily at India to prevent 1962 from making China the national and strategic enemy of India. Eight years later in 1970, as in 1951, Mao was to personally and publicly articulate China's desire to put the past behind and forge a new constructive relationship with India. This time, however, this gesture was made as China attempted to normalise its relations with the US and as Mao prepared to identify the Soviet Union as the principal imperialist power. Once again, Mao cast India as an important, though no longer, the pivotal player in a putative united front, directed more against Soviet imperialism. At that time, in Maoist calculations, the pivotal player in a re-alignment of world power to counter the Soviet Union was the United States.

Beginning from 1962 till the end of the Maoist era, the policy of damage limitation in relation to India was, in effect, a holding operation. Its underpinning was an undisturbed line of control along the India-China boundary, an unchanged policy position on the territorial issue, and skilful management of its new status as a nuclear weapons power. China relied on the passage of time for the Indian wounds of 1962 to heal, for greater exposure of the Soviet Union's expansionist and interventionist tendencies, as well as for the resurgence of an indian search for an independent and sovereign role in world affairs. This policy began to pay dividends fourteen years after the disastrous war of 1962. In 1976 (the year of Mao's death and after India's first nuclear "implosion"), the two countries raised their diplomatic representation to ambassadorial level. As India withdrew her ambassador first after the 1962 war, she had to be the first to send back her ambassador.

The process of opposing "revisionism" and the new international agenda proposed by the Soviet Union that was initiated by Mao in 1957 was thus advanced further in 1962. It was to culminate in his next major intervention in 1964, accompanied by a profound change in domestic politics, namely, the Cultural Revolution. The objective of which was to weed out "revisionists" from the leadership of the CPC and keep China on the path of "making revolution", and provide an alternative to Soviet revolutionary strategy for revolutionary forces everywhere.

MAO'S INTERVENTION NO. 5 (1964): SPELLING OUT THE MAOIST ALTERNATIVE

The Maoist intervention of 1964 was in response to a development in the socialist world. It followed what was called the systemisation of revisionism at the Twenty-second Party Congress of the CPSU into a general strategy for all socialist countries and parties. In proposing an alternative strategy for the international communist movement and not just for China, Mao challenged not only Soviet strategy for opposing imperialism but also its leadership of the socialist world.

This was as momentous a decision as the 1946 decision to embark on a civil war with the KMT supported and equipped by a nuclear United States and that of 1962 to enter into a confrontation with India. In both the 1946 and 1964 instances, the odds were stacked against Mao and China. If 1962 destroyed the international united front, 1964 split the socialist bloc and communist parties everywhere. In doing so, it marked the end of a pattern of international politics that had existed since 1945. Consequently, it initiated a process of re-alignment and readjustment of world forces that eventually wrought the collapse of the Soviet Union and the communist bloc.

In the mid-seventies, Maoist China began to resume interaction with the international community. China was no longer an international outcast: the PRC finally occupied the China seat in the UN, received US President Nixon in Beijing, and exchanged diplomatic recognition with those countries which had refused to do so until then.

Accordingly, Mao prepared to revert to his holistic approach, analytical method and strategy of making revolution in the PRC's interaction with the outer world. As was his style, Mao offered a fresh assessment of the global balance of power and forces, and of the dominant or universal trends in world politics. Having firmly placed the Soviet Union in the imperialist camp, it is not surprising that he found the balance to be grossly disadvantageous to the revolutionary cause and to the Chinese state. In his perception, however, the states of the world could still be divided in three ways but not, as earlier, into three broad horizontal zones of countries distinguished by their ideological proclivities. Mao's new paradigm was triangular, seemingly similar to the traditional hierarchical ranking of states in terms of power. It differed, however, in that it clubbed countries together to create new unities, or three worlds, distinguished by the degree of combined economic and political power each commanded. Significantly, Japan was not placed in the First World as an economic super power. But, largely because it lacked independent military capability, it was placed in the Second World of developed countries.

At the apex of Mao's paradigm were the two super powers, constituting the First World. The Second World was that of the middle ranking developed countries that was not expected to play the role of the intermediate zone of Mao's earlier formulation. The developing countries together formed the Third World. The Maoist paradigm rested on the assumption that the era of anti-colonialism had ended with the emergence into nationhood of the colonised territories. The dominant trend as he identified it, was the pursuit of economic and technological development by all states, whether capitalist or socialist. The universal dynamic, however, was still identified as being nationalism.[8] Thus, in Mao's perception, the international arena continued to be marked by interstate struggle that could be moulded into an inter-world struggle which, in turn, would lead to fresh possibilities of creating a united front against imperialism, now conceived as hegemonism. The possibility flowed from two fault lines that Mao perceived within the international system: one created by the resistance of Second and Third World states against the thrust of hegemony by either or both of the super-powers. The other by the spontaneous and natural rivalry that he saw as existing between the two super-powers and their friends and allies. Both fault lines also created large areas of possible unity among states on the other side of the line. Thus, a united front against "hegemony" directed against one or both super-powers, at any given time, became plausible. The differentiation between the three worlds based as it was on economic and political power, reduced the Third World to playing the role of the poor peasant, oppressed by the rich, the developed and the powerful. Consequently, countries of the Third World and India in particular continued to play a revolutionary but no longer a pivotal role in bringing about an alteration in the world balance. That role was now assigned to countries of the Second World and in particular to Japan. China on its part stood alone and apart from the Third World, not within it — a lone socialist country ploughing a lonely furrow as exemplar. The world, as perceived by Mao in the mid-seventies, was a far more complex one than that of two decades earlier. It was spontaneously less revolutionary, more likely to succumb to the sugar coated bullets of the super-powers and to the goals and fears of conventional nation states.

Consequently, when Mao's Three Worlds thesis was boldly pronounced at the UN General Assembly in 1974, it was accompanied by a long list of what China — as exemplar of a revolutionary state — would or would not do in its international behaviour. Ironically, this pronouncement was made by Deng Xiaoping, recalled for this purpose from political exile when illness struck down both Mao and Zhou Enlai. Four years later, after Mao's death in 1976 and his being waylaid again, Deng Xiaoping emerged as China's strong man and leader. As he consolidated his power, Deng, once the second most important target of Mao's Cultural Revolution, put forward a long-term strategy of modernisation. He advocated integration with the world economy, and the opening of China to foreign investment. Five years after Mao's death, the Cultural Revolution was severely condemned for having obstructed and delayed China's economic and technological development, and for the cleavages it had introduced into both its inner and outer worlds. Soon thereafter, the Three Worlds thesis was given an unceremonious burial together with the approach and the method of analysis for making revolution unique to Mao.

Notes

1. See *Selected Works of Mao Tse-tung,* Vol. I (Peking : Foreign Languages Press, 1967), p. 162.
2. "Talk with the American Correspondent Anna Louise Strong August 1946", *ibid.*, pp. 99-100.
3. "On New Democracy", *ibid,* Vol. II, *op. cit.*, pp. 339-82.
4. *Diplomacy of Contemporary China* (Hong Kong : New Horizon Press, 1990), p. 49.
5. *Ibid.*, p. 213.
6. Stanley Karnow, *Mao and China — From Revolution to Revolution,* (New York : Macmillan, 1972), pp. 92-109.
7. See Mira Sinha, "India China Confrontation — A Re-Interpretation", *China Report,* Vol. VI, No. 3, May-June 1970, pp. 1-15.
8. The Three Worlds thesis was propounded in a speech to the UN General Assembly by Deng Xiaoping, leader of the Chinese delegation, on 10 April 1974. For an analysis of this thesis see Mira Sinha, "Strategic Rediscovery of the Third World", *China Report,* Vol. X, No. 3, May-June 1974, pp. 44-45.

GIRI DESHINGKAR

40

THE NEHRU YEARS REVISITED

"Nationalism is good in its place but it is an unreliable friend and an unsafe historian. It sometimes distorts the truth, especially when it concerns us or our country."[1]

—Jawaharlal Nehru

Relations between the two Asian giants, India and China were at their best, at least on the surface, during the Nehru years. They came to be at their worst also, at the end of the Nehru years. How did this come about? Indian historians and analysts generally attribute the best of motives to Nehru and they are convinced that China had the worst of motives vis-a-vis India. When elaborated through examples, it almost becomes a genetic theory of behaviour. If Nehru is criticised, it is for his innocence and gullibility and, of course, for listening to wrong advice. If the Chinese are "praised", it is in the same perverse way as some Arabs may praise the Israelis, for their cunning, ruthlessness and perfidy. In contrast to the almost uniform Indian view, the view from the Chinese side is not so clear cut. Nehru is seen as a bourgeois leader, no doubt, to be dealt with wary circumspection. But his motives are not central to Chinese thinking; they are one factor among many. The British imperial legacy, the US designs against China, Soviet machinations in the later period and the internal power struggle in China itself become equally important factors.*

Some caveats when discussing the relations between the two states of India and China are in order. Jawaharlal Nehru was only one actor, albeit the most important one. The others included his peers such as Vallabhbhai Patel, S. Radhakrishnan, Moraji Desai, Govind Ballabh Pant and Krishna Menon. Then there were the invisible actors: B N Mullik, the head of the Intelligence Bureau, and officials of the Ministry of External Affairs, the military chiefs and the ambassadors accredited to China. Above all, there were the files of the British Raj which Nehru must have consulted from time to time.

During Nehru's initial years in power he was more or less the sole maker of China policy. But after 1958, in addition to the different views of his colleagues within his own party, he was subjected to increasing pressures from the opposition leaders as well as the news media. The role played by such foreign powers as the United States, Britain and the Soviet Union must remain largely in the realm of speculation until the documents on foreign affairs are released for scholarly examination. In fact, the denial of access to all archives pertaining to China from 1911 onwards, far beyond the conventional thirty year rule, makes analysis of India-China relations very tentative. The situation for scholars looking at the Chinese side is much worse; even secondary sources are scarce.

Vallabhbhai Patel's view on China stood in stark contrast to Nehru's. He was not ony a nationalist, but also a staunch anti-communist, hence he saw a conflict with China as inevitable. In fact, he clearly conceived China as India's national enemy (in addition to, of course, Pakistan). Some of Patel's concerns must have been shared by Nehru because he took steps to extend India's security perimeter to the northern borders of Nepal, Bhutan and Sikkim. He also immediately started pushing Indian

---

*In this essay, I refer primarily to the perceptions of the leaders of the People's Republic of China. The leaders of the rival Chinese regime on Taiwan did not take an ideological view of Nehru or India but they remained convinced of the Chinese case on Tibet and on the India-China border question. They blamed the "Chinese Communist bandits" for being aggressive but approved their action in "defending" the border against India's "expansionist" acts.

administration right up to the McMahon line and sent military aid to the new government in Burma to fight communist insurgency in its northern part which bordered on India. But Patel died in 1950 and thereafter foreign policy became almost exclusively Nehru's domain.

While the other leaders became active only in the late fifties when Nehru's China policy ran into difficulties, Mullik, Chief of the Intelligence Bureau (IB), carried forward Patel's legacy. Mullik was uncompromisingly anti-communist. He had direct access to Nehru, perhaps as a result of his work done in Kashmir. He took Pakistan and China as India's direct enemies and persuaded Nehru to accept them as such as far as intelligence work and covert actions were concerned.[2] He fought his own private war with China through Tibetan refugees, through the rebellious Khampas inside Tibet and through the establishment of IB posts along the border.[3] As far as published accounts go, not once did Nehru disagree with Mullik's intelligence assessment, nor did he ever object to the IB's overt and covert actions.[4] Nehru's talks to the intelligence community, as reported by Mullik, carried an entirely different message from the Asian "bhai-bhai" stance he adopted in public.[5] The Kongka Pass incident of 1959, which became the turning point in India-China relations was engineered by Mullik; his Army and External Affairs Ministry colleagues frontally accused him and the IB of "aggression" and "expansionism".[6] But this did not deter Mullik at all; he pursued his private war with China until the two armies clashed in 1962. Although a mere civil servant, he must be counted as a major contributor to the making of Nehru's China policy. In fact, it is difficult to say whether the tail was wagging the dog or whether Nehru had a split-level approach towards China.

This essay does not allow enough space to discuss the contributions of Nehru's collegues in the government and the party nor can it discuss the role of his critics in the Opposition and the media.[7] But the importance of files pertaining to "frontier affairs" must be mentioned however briefly. It is through these files (and partly through Mullik's mindset) that the British imperial legacy lived on during Nehru's years and well beyond. Nehru made some departures from the imperial legacy such as giving up British Indian rights in Tibet. But, while not exactly playing the "Great Game" (which emphasised the north-western frontier), he nevertheless accepted the British imperial view that the defence of India began at the topographical frontier, i.e., the Himalayan high crest in the north. This is why despite his respect for nationalism, soon after the Chinese communists came to power he concluded treaties with Nepal, Bhutan and Sikkim which reaffirmed the British imperial arrangements.[8] He also viewed Tibet as a buffer state just as the British did. Hence the distinction between "suzerainty" and "sovereignty"; it meant nothing to the Chinese and only made them suspicious. And hence the importance given by Nehru to "autonomy" for Tibet when he would have rejected outright similar autonomy for the north-east or Tamil Nadu.

As the imperial legacy claimed more and more of Nehru's imagination, it got reflected in Indian official cartography. The 1950 new Indian map showed the McMahon line as "undemarcated"; for the middle and western sector, the legend said "boundary undefined". In that map, Nepal, Sikkim and Bhutan were shown outside India. But in the map published in 1954, the McMahon line was shown as a firm boundary and so were the boundaries in the middle and western sectors. In this map, Sikkim and Bhutan were shown within India's northern border with a legend explaining that they were so by "special treaty". These changes were not discussed in Parliament;[10] we do not know whether they were discussed within the Cabinet. By 1959, the Indian boundary claim in the western sector had become as firm as the McMohan line but this time after Parliament's approval. Now it was a matter of officially and overtly filling out the boundary with Indian armed presence. It looked to the Chinese that the British imperial "Great Game" had been resumed.

There were glaring asymmetries in the way India and China looked at each other. Perhaps as a result of Western scholarship, English educated Indians had developed an "orientalist" view of China. To Western scholars, the "Orient" or Asia was a cultural continuum, particularly because of the Buddhist connection. In the English educated Indian mind, however, it became "Indianisation" of China. This perspective gave a distorted picture of India's place in China's world-view. In reality, Buddhism started on the periphery of the Chinese society and by the time it acquired a large number of adherents, it had become so transformed that it ceased to be Indian. Politically, Buddhism was strongly opposed by the Confucian mandarins who thought it subverted Chinese values. The much talked about "missions" were from and to the peripheries of both societies and by the early fifteenth century they had stopped altogether. But westernised consciousness in India took such contacts to be between nations.[11] Hence the myth of India and China being Asian sister-countries[12] a myth given currency not only by Nehru but many others.[13]

The Chinese communists also adopted the myth during the "bhai-bhai" days.[14] But their ancestors rarely ever showed any interest in India whatsoever except to acknowledge the remote origins of Buddhism in the "Western Heaven".[15] Until the early fifties, Chinese scholars had not produced a single work on India as a country.[16] "India" entered Chinese consciousness as the land from which soldiers of the British Indian Army came to loot and kill; it was from where opium came.[17] All state-to-state contacts were with British India where Indians were not the decision-makers. They saw Indians in China as "zou gou" (running dogs) of the British. Through translated works, they came to know that Buddhism had disappeared from India, that India had first gone under Islamic rule and then western "barbarian" rule.[18] Public affairs, which were central to Chinese thinking, were mismanaged by Indians. Chinese thinkers when debating the Western challenge to China cited India as a negative example. They would deal with the West in their own way, decidedly not as India had done.[19]

Such asymmetries formed the psychological substratum of Indian and Chinese leaders when state-to-state contacts began in the late forties. Jawaharlal Nehru's view of China had three principal latent characteristics: He nursed a pan-Asian sentiment ever since his student days in Britain. He felt proud when he heard the news in 1905 that Japan, an Asian country, had defeated Russia, a European country. His pan-Asian sentiment, particularly with regard to China, was exuberantly expressed at the Brussels Conference of 1927 and twenty years later at the Asian Relations Conference of 1947. In Brussels, he wanted Indians to follow the "notable example" of the Chinese.[20] And at "the New Delhi Conference, he repeatedly spoke of "we Asians", "fellow Asians" advancing together.[21]

Unfortunately for Nehru, however, the leaders of other Asian countries and colonial territories were barely conscious of Asia as anything more than a geographical term; they certainly did not share any sentiment of "Asianness". No eminent Chinese leader, communist or non-communist, ever did. Nehru probably did not realise that for East Asians particularly, Japan was not an Asian brother but a deadly enemy even before the turn of the century.[22] Apart from Nehru no other Asian leader seems to have thought of holding a pan-Asian meeting.

The second element in Nehru's thinking was India as the bridge between the East and the West. At the Asian Relations Conference, he described India as the "meeting point" between the West and East.[23] The perception came about undoubtedly as a result of his westernised upbringing and western education to be later fused with his Indian nationalism. His personal feeling that he was a man of both worlds made him believe that India, too, was a bridge between those worlds because of its geographical location, the history of having received Islamic and Western cultures and also having "sent" Buddhism to the rest of Asia. Nehru's perception of India's role made him offer himself as a mediator between the US and China. He sought to interpret Chinese policies to American leaders and vice versa. Despite resistance from both ends, he doggedly pursued the mediatory role. He did this during the Korean War and then during the Vietnam conflict after 1954.[24]

But the perception of India's role among the Chinese leaders was quite different. They used India only as a channel of communication with the US; the only other channel available to them was the Soviet Union but its efficacy depended on US-Soviet relations at any given point of time. That is why they used India to convey the warning to the US that China would enter the Korean War if the US threatened to carry the war beyond the Yalu river. But when they realised that the warning conveyed through India did not carry credibility in Washington, they became more cautious about using the Indian channel. Later, during the Korean Armistice negotiations they often expressed their dissatisfaction with India's mediation. While Indians tried their best to appear neutral to both sides, the Chinese, often suspected Indians to be partial towards the US.[25] They appeared to trust Indians more later since they accepted India as the Chairman of the Control Commission over Indo-China. But India never earned China's complete trust as a mediator.

At the Bandung Conference in 1955, Nehru decided to adopt a low profile for himself and to promote Zhou Enlai and the new Chinese state on the international scene. It is doubtful if Zhou saw it that way. He was too sophisticated to reject Nehru's helping hand but he proceeded to behave as a leader in his own right and to establish direct contacts with other leaders, including those of Pakistan.[26] China, Zhou indicated, did not need any one to mediate for her.

The third aspect of Nehru was his strong streak of unilateralism. Just as he was unilaterally pan-Asian and "unilaterally" often a self-appointed mediator, his views on the India-China border question were declared as the final truth without conceding any legitimacy to the Chinese views or actions. Without a Chinese surrender on major issues Nehru was not prepared to consider even minor concessions. In his eyes the McMohan line became "final", "map or no map". Later, the boundary in the western sector also became final.[27] The depiction of the Himalayan states on Indian official maps, too, was a unilateral decision. His pronouncements on Tibetan autonomy also bore the same mark. Nehru's unilateralism was not just limited to China. In his other policies, too, he seldom bothered to consult his cabinet colleagues; the unreserved support he extended to Krishna Menon and his request to the US for an "air umbrella" are glaring examples of his unilateralism.[28] It is doubtful whether he consulted any of his colleagues when approving Mullik's covert actions.

The Chinese on the other hand, always recognised that the border was not a settled issue; they wanted negotiations and suggested mutual concessions. On Tibet, they took Nehru's view into consideration when signing the 1951 agreement with the local government of Tibet. Whatever else may be said about Chinese evil motives, bad faith, duplicity, etc., they did not adopt a unilateralist stance even after 1959.

Of these three latent elements, Nehru's pan-Asianism suffered rapid erosion after he came to power. Already at the Asian Relations Conference he had become aware of the fact that there was little Asianness shared by the participants. Each country had its own preoccupations. They could agree about decolonisation but little else. The Chinese delegate (of the Kuomintang government) strongly protested against Tibet being shown as an independent country on the Conference map; that map had to be withdrawn. Most countries remained suspicious of Japan. Nehru's pan-Asian sentiment must have suffered a blow.

During the subsequent years, as the Cold War progressed, there was nothing to encourage Nehru's sentiment. Asian countries were deeply divided by ideology and irridenta. This became all too apparent at the Bandung meeting. Both the New Delhi and Bandung meetings were held at India's initiative; no other country in Asia carried forward the idea. A second Bandung was never held. Nehru no longer spoke of Asianness; he probably ceased to believe in it.

Simultaneously with the erosion of his pan-Asianism, Nehru began to pay more attention to *realpolitik.* He consolidated the northern border, occupied Tawang and concluded treaties with the Himalayan states. He rejected the notion of a plebiscite for Kashmir. Despite his earlier dislike of communism in the Soviet Union, he dramatically improved relations with that country, perhaps in response to the new alliance relationship between Pakistan and the US. It is this change from idealism to *realpolitik* which made him more receptive to the advice tendered by Mullik of the IB.

While the above mentioned latent elements underlay Nehru's thinking and style of diplomacy, his explicit foreign policy framework also had three elements: nationalism, non-alignment, and peaceful co-existence. He sought to fit the new Chinese state into this framework.[29] But once again, there was asymmetry in the understanding of all these concepts. By nationalism Nehru meant the new nationalism of the decolonised countries; he thought that his new nationalism would be free of the European inheritance of war, rivalries and blocs. New nations would spontaneously opt to be non-aligned vis-a-vis the Cold War participants in the Old World; non-alignment did not submerge national independence and sovereignty as the alliance system did. As for peaceful co-existence, Nehru believed that modern wars were caused by rival universalist ideologies like capitalism and communism. New nationalism like China's would rise above the extra-Asian communist ideology, just as India would rise above capitalism. Together the two would show the Old World and America how to co-exist peacefully despite differences in social systems. Together, India and China would reshape the world order.

To Nehru, the Chinese appeared to acquiesce to his framework. But, in reality, they perceived things quite differently. Whatever the substratum of Chineseness in the thinking of the communists (which they never articulated), they perceived everything in ideological terms. Indian bourgeois nationalism under Nehru could, for them, become a component of the "United Front" against imperialism and colonialism. The bourgeoisie was always double faced and wavering; its anti-imperialist face was acceptable.[30] Non-alignment did not make any sense to them; they believed that in the titanic struggle between imperialism and socialism, it was necessary to "lean to one side". At the same time it was necessary to win over as many countries as possible in the front against imperialism. The non-aligned group offered an attractive target; they would reserve their differences with its members and seek common ground. Peaceful co-existence made even less sense. War and peace for the Chinese were class issues. So long as international class struggle existed, war was inevitable. When war between the two systems came, the new bourgeois nationalists would appear in their true colours.[31] Until then, their anti-colonialism would serve the United Front.

At the articulated level, it was a remarkably crude ideological analysis. But the innate Chineseness of Zhou Enlai took away much of its edge when it came to diplomacy and negotiations.

Nehru thought that in recognising the People's Republic of China soon after it was established, he was acknowledging the new nationalism in China, not its communism. So he ignored China's professed ideology and the crude negative ideological statements about India and himself. He translated all Chinese ideological rhetoric in nationalist terms. Its sharpness, he believed, stemmed from the fact that Chinese nationalism was misunderstood and isolated by the rest of the world. He would reduce that isolation by befriending China and mediating between China and its ideological adversaries.

But the Chinese leaders never forgot that Nehru was a bourgeois leader. They never admired his nationalism but thought that his anti-colonialism only temporarily concealed his own colonial impulses towards Sikkim, Nepal, Bhutan[32] and Tibet. Buddhism having disappeared from India, the argument about "cultural affinity" between India and Tibet, sounded absolutely spurious to Chinese ears. For Chinese leaders, the Indian revolution was yet to come and Nehru was an impediment in its path. Nehru showed his true colour in his counter-revolutionary policy against the communist revolutionaries in India. He was opposed to the socialist transformation of Tibet and chose to join the US imperialists and Kuomintang reactionaries to counter it. Nehru was, the Chinese eventually concluded, the true heir to the British imperialist legacy.[33]

Even so, it may be said that the Chinese leaders did not frontally challenge Nehru's foreign policy framework; otherwise the challenge would have come immediately. After Patel's death Nehru adopted a political, not legal, approach towards China. This gave him much flexibility in dealing with bilateral issues.[34] His initial belief was that Chinese communism was radically different from the European variety.[35] Its sinification could be hastened by reducing China's isolation. So, he refused to brand China as an "aggressor" in the Korean War and promoted the case of China both in the United Nations and in the non-aligned group. Against this background the Chinese had no difficulty in acquiescing to his overall policy framework.

On the India-China border, Nehru did not take a legal stand until 1959. While he unilaterally declared that the McMahon line was India's border, he never explicitly claimed that it was a legal boundary, that it had been accepted by the Chinese or that it was legally binding on China. He was more ambiguous about the western sector; he did not initially say that the line there was "firm", "identifiable" or "non-negotiable". This is perhaps why, despite the knowledge that China had built a road through Aksai Chin, he did not lodge any diplomatic protest. (Even at their talks in 1960, Nehru did not raise India's claim over Aksai Chin.) In fact, up to 1958, India and China went on consolidating their control over areas in the eastern and western sectors respectively, and neither objected to what the other was doing.[36]

During all these years the Chinese maintained that there was no territorial dispute with India. Such statements are taken by Indian historians as examples of Chinese duplicity. Perhaps because Nehru also thought that the time was not yet "ripe" to adopt a legal approach to the whole issue, he too did not press for any clarifications from China. (K M Panikkar has been blamed for this but the ultimate decision was always Nehru's). So China did not need to confront the problem. It is not that China had a border policy which it wanted to conceal from India to mislead Nehru. China had no border policy at all vis-a-vis any of its neighbours. The Kuomintang government of China had a clear policy which it maintains even today; had that government been in power the border problem would have arisen right away. But during the first decade of their rule, the communists had yet to make up their minds about China's historical claims precisely because they claimed theirs to be a revolutionary government.[37] Theirs was a political, not a legal approach. By the time they came to power, Outer Mongolia, Korea and Vietnam were already independent states. The disputed areas along the Sino-Soviet border were under the control of their Soviet ally. The Chinese leaders were very uncertain as to what to do about pre-revolutionary historical claims.[38]

Under the circumstances, they seem to have decided to accept accomplished facts of history, but as *de facto* control, not as legal claims. This is why while tacitly accepting India's *de facto* control up to the McMahon line[39] and also the *de facto* independence of Outer Mongolia, they did not recognise the validity of the Simla convention. They took their time to recognise the juridical independence of Outer Mongolia and delayed the conclusion of border treaties with Burma, Nepal and Afghanistan. All this was a radical change from the traditional Chinese position but Nehru does not seem to have comprehended it. On the other hand, the Chinese hastened to extend control over what were not accomplished facts of history; the independence of Tibet had not been recognised by any state and the western sector of the India-China frontier had remained a no man's land.

The adoption of an explicitly legal stand by India in 1959 forced China to make legal counter-claims. The rebellion in Tibet in the same year also made ambiguity very dangerous from the Chinese point of view. Above all, in the Sino-Soviet ideological dispute China decided to take the mantle of Marxism-Leninism-Stalinism away from the "revisionist" Soviet Union. China could no longer even tacitly accept such concepts as nationalism, non-alignment and, more particularly, peaceful co-existence. "Soviet revisionism" was openly endorsing Nehru's concepts and both had to be exposed. This probably explains the crudeness of the Chinese attacks on India. Nehru became a "reactionary", a "compradore", a "running dog of imperialism" and his entire foreign policy framework was challenged by Beijing. By 1960, the Chinese were convinced that Nehru wanted to keep the border dispute alive by escalating both territorial claims (now in the western sector) and preconditions (China must withdraw first).[40]

Chinese ideological crudity was matched by Nehru's racial-cultural explanations of Chinese behaviour. If Mullik is to be believed — no one in authority in India has yet repudiated him — Nehru was stressing China's "imperialistic tendencies" as early as 1950.[41] In fact, he asked Mullik not to be misled by the open professions of his own government vis-a-vis China. In 1952 Nehru told Mullik that China had "always been an aggressive country". He had added that the "war between the two cultures was not over ... and would go on for a long time".[42] Friendship with China was an expedient until India was strong enough to take on China. Chinese economic power combined with its large population, Nehru said in a briefing to the IB, was an "explosive" missile; it would become a danger to the whole world in the next couple of decades.[43] By 1960, he was saying all this publicly. China now became a "danger to the whole world". It was an "aggressive, arrogant and expansionist neighbour". After the 1962 war, he spoke of "Chinese-ism" as the "tradition of expansionism"[44].

Nehru's colleagues, most opposition leaders and the media were even more unsophisticated; they resorted to outright racist slurs. All the Western steriotypes of "Mongoloid hordes", "human wave tactics", "cheapness of Chinese life" gained currency in India. Chinese food habits were derided as barbaric. The Chinese were described as "sly, wily, untrustworthy", etc.[45] Later, as the tension mounted, a law was passed in India declaring all persons of Chinese extraction, regardless of their nationality, as enemy aliens. (It possibly stands in the books even today). Some Chinese in India were rounded up and detained in camps.

After 1959, it is difficult to say who formulated India's foreign policy. It was, at any rate, no longer Nehru's exclusive preserve. Nehru came to be constantly accused of "appeasing" China and was forced to adopt an increasingly hard stand. Whether he intended it or not, his tough stance vis-a-vis China earned him US support and financial aid.[46] He was aware of the intensity of the Sino-Soviet dispute and reasonably confident of Soviet neutrality in the India-China dispute. His reading was that China had become a pariah state, devoid of any friends whereas India could count on several powerful ones. His persistent judgement that China would not resort to war, that it would not dare, was not altogether wrong, given Nehru's assumptions. He always maintained that an India-China war would be a world war, even a nuclear war.[47] This judgement made him test the Chinese resolve. It made him issue even intemperate statements about "throwing out the Chinese". The victory in the war over Goa also reinforced his confidence. Moreover, he knew that China was passing through extremely difficult times because of the failure of the Great Leap Forward, the three drought years of 1959, 1960 and 1961 and the withdrawal of the Soviet aid. The morale of the Chinese Army was low. China was at its most vulnerable point. It was simple *realpolitik* to press one's advantage.

Nobody pointed out to him the other side of the coin. China had taken the great risk of entering the Korean War when it was very vulnerable. It had once again taken such a risk at the time of the Quemoy Crisis. China had also defied the Soviet Union at perilous risk to its own economy. Nobody told Nehru either that the Indian Army was not prepared to take on China, that it was incompetent even if better equipped than the Chinese People's Liberation Army.

Chinese acts appeared very aggressive to India while China thought it was merely resisting India's "forward policy". But at that time, China felt severely threatened "from all four sides". During the fifties the US had encircled China all around its southern perimeter. The Soviet Union, too, threatened from the north. India could become a possible opening. Hence, the Chinese leaders were actively thinking of adopting as conciliatory a line towards India as was possible. The proposal to do so came from Wang Jiaxiang, an important official connected with foreign affairs, in February 1962, as war clouds were gathering thick and fast. Wang's proposal vis-a-vis India is worth quoting:

"As for the India-China border question, ... we should continuously and endlessly repeat: that China and India must be friends; that there is no objective basis at all for any conflict between India and China; that the India-China border dispute is the troublesome legacy handed down from the time imperialism ruled over both China and India in the past; that the border dispute must be solved on the basis of mutually empathetic understanding and through negotiations; and that it can indeed be solved.

If we say so and also act accordingly, it means that we hold high the banner of China-India friendship, hold high the banner of the Five Principles of Peaceful Coexistence and hold high the banner of resolving the China-India dispute through negotiations.

Of course, relations between countries are not determined purely by the subjective efforts (of only one side). In the final analysis, they are determined by the nature of each country, by the class to which the power holders belong, the policy line of that social stratum, the relationship between the strengths of the countries and the benefit and harm (arising out of this) as well as the nature of the contentious debate and its scope and so forth ....

However, we should never underestimate (Chinese) subjective initiative; otherwise it will do us no good. It seems that there will be advance and there will be retreat, there will be attack and there will be defence, there will be contention and there will be yielding, reins will be tight and they will be loose. It seems all these are methods which will not be found wanting in external struggle."

This internal and secret proposal, part of a much larger proposal on Chinese foreign policy initiatives, was circulated among the leaders of the Chinese Communist Party. After two of Wang Jiaxiang's senior colleagues had endorsed it, the proposal was sent to Zhou Enlai, Deng Xiaoping, Chen Yi and Liu Shaoqi who did not disagree with anything said in it. The proposal was then circulated to members of the party's Secretariat. Finally, it reached Chairman Mao Zedong who also did not think that there was anything the problem with it.[48]

Could the war have been avoided? Around 1976 Mrs. Indira Gandhi, when reminiscing about India-China relations seemed to think so. Once again, a full quotation which the Chinese publishers have chosen to reproduce, is in order:

> "In 1953, we visited China. We saw Zhou Enlai and Mao Zedong. Mao had never been to India; I heard later on that he was waiting for an invitation to him from us. If we had invited him to visit India, a lot of things, perhaps, would have been quite different. Had we known then that he had such thought, he would have become the most welcome and respected guest in this country.
>
> I liked Zhou Enlai. He was extremely knowledgeable. He was the only person we met in China who had travelled abroad. He was extremely experienced and mature in foreign affairs. He was a cut above the others in understanding matters."[49]

Whether or not she was right, there is no doubt that during the mid-fifties, more consultations between India and China, rather than unilateral assertions and actions, could have given a very different turn to the course of India-China relations. An agreement extremely favourable to India in the eastern sector (without bringing in the McMahon line or the Simla Convention) was a distinct possibility.[50] But the opportunity was missed. Similarly, by 1956, the Chinese had been implementing their 1951 Agreement with the Tibetan local government. China had already withdrawn 9 per cent of Han cadres from Tibet and also some troops from Lhasa. China was considering the withdrawal of all troops from Tibet if there was internal peace there.[51] But Khampa rebel attacks started and escalated from that year. Nehru surely knew — Mullik certainly knew — the American CIA and the nationalist regime on Taiwan were aiding the rebels. He did nothing to stop them; he certainly did nothing to curb the anti-communist activities of the Tibetan refugees in India. After 1959, India's support to the Tibetan rebels was all but open. But all this did not achieve any purpose. It did not lessen the suffering of the Tibetans because Chinese oppression was stepped up. It also harmed the cause of Tibetan autonomy.

It would seem that even if we grant all the compulsions on the Indian side once the border dispute became open and bitter — Nehru's publicly committed positions, pressure from the Opposition, the ferocity of Indian public opinion — there was enough room to cool tempers without appearing to be appeasing.[52] The new posts set up in the western sector during March-April 1962 and which led to firing by Chinese troops were not necessary at the time. It is not that Nehru was left with no flexibility. He was prepared to negotiate but chose to impose too many preconditions; almost in all instances he wanted the Chinese to withdraw first as a price for talks. He did so in the belief that when it came to a show down, China would make the concessions Nehru so badly needed vis-a-vis his domestic critics. The Chinese probably did not understand Nehru's domestic compulsions. Even if they did, they looked at the whole Indian government; Nehru was not central to their thinking.

As Wang Jiaxiang's proposal shows, there were no compulsions on the Chinese side to go to war. Indeed, the opposite was the case. Military preparations were, of course, made by the military professionals as a contingency exercise but the decision to initiate action rested with Beijing. According to Wang Jiaxiang's memories, there was only one person, Kang Sheng, who opposed Wang's proposal. However powerful Kang may have been, he could not have overruled others. So, the only conclusion one can come to is that all the signals from New Delhi were interpreted in Beijing as a determined preparation for war against China. Once that conclusion was reached, the Chinese decided to take pre-emptive action. And when one dose of such action in October 1962 did not produce results, they administered a second one in November.

It is quite extraordinary that until the war actually came, Nehru refused to believe that China would go to war. But once it had taken place, his judgement came exactly to the opposite conclusion; he did not believe that the ceasefire declared by China would last; he thought the war would go on for several years.[53] Chinese withdrawal to the McMahon line was assessed as temporary because of climatic and extended supply lines. (Actually, the Chinese supply lines in the western sector where there was no withdrawal were just as extended and the weather was just as cold). Military actions were interpreted in purely military terms; their political import was not comprehended in New Delhi at all. The Chinese message was: China accepts the Indian claim in the east; India should accept the Chinese claim in the west. That remains the broad Chinese position even today.

Granting the worst of motives to the Chinese leaders, Nehru's China policy must be reckoned as having failed. He could not solve the border problem with China nor could he avoid armed conflict with that country. At the end of his tenure, his tacit assumptions lay in ruins. There simply was no Asianness outside the westernised segment of Indians, waiting to be tapped for friendship and cooperation. India was never accepted as the bridge Nehru thought it was destined to become. Instead, it was India which was seeking the mediation of the Colombo Powers in the India-China dispute after 1962. Nehru died a broken-hearted man but without realising that he had been self-righteous. He admitted to having lived in a world of his own making but that was a protestation of innocence in the face of Chinese perfidy. He believed that his practice of *realpolitik* was wholly moral; the Chinese practice of the same craft was wholly immoral.

Asian nationalism during the Nehru years turned out to be no different from nationalism of the Old World; it was, in fact, much worse, because of territorial disputes, internal repression and adherence to universal ideologies, often for selfish ends. Non-alignment gathered many adherents from among the newly independent countries but in the context of the India-China dispute, they became non-aligned vis-a-vis both. Nehru's judgement that one could not be non-aligned vis-a-vis China sounded bizarre; it made sense for India but not for the entire non-aligned group. In any case, when the military situation became serious, Nehru turned to the West (and even Israel!) for military support. He almost took India into the Western military bloc. That he resisted from doing so showed his strong personal faith in non-alignment but other Asian and African countries drew their own lessons. After Nehru's death, the concept was transformed into vaguely defined "Third Worldism"; member states could now belong to one military bloc or the other.

The first joint declaration on *Panchsheel*, the Five Principles of Peaceful Co-Existence, Nehru believed, committed China to the third element of India's foreign policy i.e., peaceful co-existence. What is more, Nehru found an ally in Nikita Khrushchev who also supported it. However, there was a tremendous difference of interpretation between Nehru and Khrushchev on one side and the Chinese on the other. Nehru and Krushchev took the term to mean peaceful co-existence between the capitalist and the socialist systems worldwide whereas the Chinese interpreted the term much more narrowly. For one thing, peaceful co-existence was only one among the Five Principles and it applied only as long as the four other principles were also applied faithfully. Moreover, it applied between countries, particularly neighbouring countries, not social systems. This is why China made such joint declarations with only its neighbours. Nehru thought that with that declaration "all problems" between India and China were "solved". In Chinese eyes, the problems could be solved by working out mutual benefits (mentioned in Panchsheel) but they were not actually solved. China took Nehru's unilateral stance on the border and Tibet as a violation of two principles : mutual respect for territorial integrity and sovereignty and mutual non-interference in internal affairs. But what really determined the fate of peaceful co-existence was China's ideological dispute with the Soviet Union. In any case, Nehru too had come to the conclusion that peaceful co-existence with an "imperialist and expansionist" China was impossible.

Committed nationalist scholarship has its uses; it helps the process of nation - and state-building and it can help mobilise and people for defence and development. But as Nehru has himself pointed out in the quotation cited at the beginning of this essay, it distorts truth. In India-China relations, truth was distorted on both sides. Jawaharlal Nehru left behind two legacies : friendship with China and bitter enmity towards China. India and China cannot live in enmity forever. Distorted truth becomes an impediment in the solutions to problems. If Nehru's former legacy is to be restored, we must reorder India-China relations once again on the basis of all the Five Principles of Peaceful Coexistence. Recently, a beginning seems to have been made by both India and China in that direction.

Notes

1. See his *Glimpses of World History* (Delhi : Oxford University Press, 1982), p. 443.
2. B.N. Mullik, *My Years with Nehru The Chinese Betrayal* (Bombay: Allied Publishers, 1971). pp. 84-85.
3. *Ibid.*, pp. 178.
4. *Ibid.*
5. There are scattered references to this throughout Mullik's book.
6. *Ibid.*, pp. 240-45.
7. A very substantial body of literature is available on this subject. Most such writings started around 1959 and the stream tapered off only towards the end of the sixties.
8. He made it clear that an attack on Nepal would be regarded as an attack on India. See Sarvespalli Gopal, *Jawaharlal Nehru: A Biography*, Vol.. II (Oxford University Press, 1984), p. 68. We do not know if he got the concurrence of the Nepal government before making such a statement.
9. Nehru asked China not to send troops into Tibet. *Ibid*, p. 105.
10. See Mira Sinha, "China: Making and Unmaking of Nehru's Foreign Policy", *China Report* (Delhi), Vol. 15, No. 2, March-April 1979, pp. 51-64.
11. For an extended discussion of the Buddhist connection, see K.P. Gupta. "The Making of China's Image of India", pp. 39-40.
12. See Jawaharlal Nehru, *op. cit.*, pp. 28, 328.
13. Prominent among them was the poet Rabindranath Tagore. He established the Cheena-Bhavana for researches into India-China historical relations at the Visvabharati University, Santiniketan during the twenties.
14. They constantly spoke of "2000 years of friendship" between India and China. But it was a political construct, not a historical fact.
15. The region of India was also called "*Tian Zhu*" or The Land of Heavenly Bamboo but it was neither a geographical nor a political expression.
16. See Yuan Chuanwei, "Indian Studies in China" (unpublished paper).
17. Literature on the opium trade is extensive. Most textbooks on the history of Modern China also discuss the deployment of Indian soldiers during the Opium Wars and the Boxer uprising.
18. See, F.W. Drake, *China-Charts the World. Hsu Chi-yu and His Geography of 1848* (Cambridge : Harvard University Press, 1975), p. 102.

19. Ssu-yu Teng and John K. Fairbank, *China's responses to the West* (1975), pp. 152-53. Kang Youwei, who had spent some time in India, was particularly contemptuous of India and Indians.

20. See his speech at the Brussels Congress, *Selected Works of Jawaharlal Nehru*, Vol. II (Delhi Orient Longmans, 1972), p. 272-76.

21. See *Jawaharlal Nehru's Speeches* (New Delhi: Publications Division, 1967), pp. 297-304.

22. Nehru sympathised very much with China's struggle against Japanese imperialism. Hence the despatch of the Indian medical team to China. But he did not understand how bitterly the Chinese disliked the Japanese.

23. See, *Jawaharlal Nehru's Speeches, op. cit.*

24. S. Gopal cites numerous examples of Nehru's attempts at mediation between not only the US and China but also between the US and the Soviet Union. See his *Jawaharlal Nehru : A Biography*, Vols. II and III.

25. *Ibid.*, Vol. II, pp. 138-75.

26. *Ibid.*, pp. 227-43.

27. He made a number of such statements. For a sample see *Lok Sabha Debates*, 2nd Series, Vol. XIX, pp. 4629-32.

28. John Kenneth Galbraith, *Ambassador's Journal* (London : Hamish Hamilton, 1969), pp. 408-551. All these chapters covering the border war and thereafter are extremely illuminating.

29. For the following analysis of the framework of Nehru's foreign policy, I draw largely on Mira Sinha's article cited in note 10 *supra.*

30. The literature on the concepts of the United Front both in the domestic and the international context is too extensive to be quoted. But specific references to Nehru are found, after he ceased to be a reliable partner in Chinese eyes in two major articles. See Editorial Department of the *Renmin Ribao* (People's Daily), "Revolution in Tibet and Nehru's Philosophy", *Renmin Ribao*, 6 May 1959 (trs. New China News Agency); and "More on Nehru's Philosophy in the Light of the Sino-Indian Boundary Question", *Renmin Ribao*, 27 October 1962 (trs. *New China News Agency*).

31. These views are laid out in extenso in *The Great Polemics* (Peking: People's Publishers, 1965).

32. India's unhappiness about the development of independent Chinese relations with Nepal was very well known to China.

33. See *Renmin Ribao*, 24 April 1959.

34. See Mira Sinha, *op. cit.*

35. He expresses this belief at the Brussels Congress. See *Selected Works, op. cit.* See also, S. Gopal, Vol. II, *op. cit.*, p. 64.

36. Mira Sinha, *op. cit.*

37. They probably were thinking of imitating Lenin's policies immediately after the Bolshevik Revolution.

38. Zhou Enlai's statement about Chinese maps being old Kuomintang maps and the new government not having had the time to revise them is quoted by Indian scholars as yet another example of Chinese cunning. It seems to me that they genuinely did not know how to go about revising them.

39. S. Gopal, citing an unpublished document, says that Zhou Enlai told the Burmese leaders that China would accept the McMahon alignment as a *de facto* boundary. See, S. Gopal, Vol. III, *op. cit.*, pp. 33-40.

40. Interview with Neville Maxwell, *The Sunday Times* (London), 19 December, 1971.

41. B.N. Mullik, *op. cit.*, pp. 84-85. Mullik repeats this throughout his book.

42. *Ibid.*, pp. 178 ff.

43. *Ibid.*, p. 243.

44. See his interview to *The Saturday Evening Post*, 19 January 1963.

45. A daily programme, "India and the Dragon", on All India Radio gave currency to such views. The Indian newspapers were full

of such articles and news items.

46. This becomes abundantly clear from Galbraith's journal, *op. cit.*

47. S. Gopal, Vol. III, pp. 204-14.

48. My working translation from Chinese. The ellipses are as in the original. See, Wang Zhongli, *Liming yu Wanxia* (Daybreak and evening twilight), (Beijing: Publishing House of People's Liberation Army, 1986), pp. 394-95.

49. My working translation from the Chinese translation. Emphasis is mine. The implication of what Mrs. Gandhi is saying is that things went wrong somewhere after the mid-fifties and neither Mao nor Zhou were to blame for what happened. See, Ya Nanze, *Gandi Furen Zishu* (My Truth), (Bèijing : Contemporary Publishers, 1985), p. 72.

50. See note 39, *supra.*

51. See G. Ginsberg and Michael Mathos, *Communist China and Tibet* (The Hague: Martin Nijhons, 1974), pp. 113-15.

52. Zhou Enlai was determined not to go back to China without achieving some agreement. But he was decisively rebuffed in Delhi.

53. S. Gopal, Vol. III, *op. cit.*, pp. 237-39.

S.K. BHUTANI

41

RETRACE INDIAN STEPS IN THE AGRICULTURAL SCENE IN CHINA 40 YEARS BACK

As early as 1927, Mao Zedong realised the revolutionary potential of China's peasants. In the Yanan period, he developed new agrarian policies, which helped win the the support of millions of peasants in the war against Japan and then, during the civil war in the forties. When the Communist Party led by him united the country and came to power in 1949, he set about on a wholescale reform of China's agriculture.

The establishment of agricultural cooperatives became the key factor of development. The Chinese leaders believed that transforming small peasant holdings into large collective farms by itself would lead to higher production because it would permit better organisation of farming operations, hasten adoption of new techniques and make available large labour power for intensive cultivation.

To create a favourable environment, the government established institutions to purchase farm products at prices notified in advance of the harvest. This ensured the amount of income available to the farmer. Institutions were set up to supply consumer articles to the farmer — this stimulated greater effort on the farm. Credit cooperatives stimulated his savings which were supplemented by the credit made available by the state institutions.

Agriculture was collectivised in a short span of five to seven years in distinct stages. After the absentee landlords were deprived of their landholdings, all farmers became peasant proprieters. They were placed in three categories — rich, middle and poor. The latter two were persuaded to set up mutual aid teams and then elementary cooperatives where size of landholding in addition to labour, counted for income. Intense propaganda and discreet use of monopoly sale, purchase and credit institutions were utilised for this purpose by the Party and state authorities. Soon these were followed by cooperatives of the higher type of collectives where payment was based on labour alone and the landholding was no longer relevant. By mid-1956, ninety-two per cent of the farmers had joined the cooperatives; nearly sixty-two percent belonged to the higher type, where not only the land but draught animals, large tools etc. were handed over to the cooperatives. It was claimed that the cooperatives, by themselves, had increased the productivity of the farm by fifteen to twenty percent. The target for the first five year plan ending in 1957 was an increase of a little over twenty-three per cent.

In some respects, condition of agricuture in India resembled the condition in China. A limited quantity of land supported a large population. The size of farms was small. The farmer relied on higher productivity to raise his income. The success of cooperatisation in China stimulated interest in India. The second five year plan of India postulated that a large proportion of agricultural land would be farmed on a cooperative basis and this would be achieved over a decade or so. At Indian request, China agreed to receive two delegations to study the development and role of cooperative institutions and to study the programme and methods of raising agricultural productivity in China. The latter delegation was at the ministerial level and included senior officials dealing with agriculture and planning. Both delegations arrived in China in the summer or 1956.

The two delegations met Premier Zhou En-lai. He was much concerned with the increasing population of China and showed interest in the family planning programme in India. Concerning agriculture, he ruled out large scale mechanisation since this would be expensive and displace labour. Productivity of land would be increased through use of manpower and animal power. He insisted on the need for careful experimentation and not to be carried away by enthusiasm alone.

Premier Zhou was asked about the relative merits of large and small cooperatives in the context of motivation of the farmer, which was an important consideration since the productivity of land was based on the farmer's effort and not on mechanisation. He accepted that the question was valid — the cooperatives allowed cultivation of small individual plots by farmers, whose produce was sold in the open market. Further, he did not envisage a farm labour surplus in the near future as there was considerable scope for building infrastructure in the villages, e.g. roads, water conservancy works. (The establishment of communes two year later did not correspond with his ideas expressed at this time.)

The Indian agricultural delegation was intrigued by the methods of collection of data relating to farm size and production. The methods relied on visual survey and peasant memory. The delegation felt there was an unwitting bias towards overstating the results, especially since the countervailing methods like crop cutting sample surveys were not used. This bias influenced fixation of planned targets of production too. Despite this, the delegation felt that agricultural productivity had indeed increased. India could introduce some of the techniques in its agriculture even though collectivisation on the Chinese model was not envisaged. India was committed to peasant ownership of land.

Spring and summer of 1958 saw a massive mobilisation of all sections of society to build water conservancy projects in the countryside of China. About fifty kilometres from Beijing, in the vicinity of the tombs of the Ming emperors the soldiers of the Peoples Liberation Army launched a project to build a reservoir. Soon, they were joined by the workers from factories and shops in Beijing. Staff of the government and members of the Communist Party volunteered in the effort. The mood of the country was electrified when Chairman Mao Zedong took part in the voluntary labour. The Afro-Asian diplomats did not want to be left out and requested the Ministry of Foreign Affairs to arrange for their participation. On the appointed day, the trip was suddenly cancelled since appropriate arrangements could not be made. It is unlikely the project suffered a delay in completion due to our non-participation.

About this time, there was an occasion when help of the diplomatic corps was actually sought. The Chinese authorities were much concerned at the loss of foodgrains due to the depredations of the pests. Sparrows were considered to be a pest. It was discovered that the sparrows died if they did not rest after flying a certain number of hours. The citizens of Beijing were mobilised to prevent resting space to the sparrows so that they were forced to fly until death resulted due to exhaustion. The Ministry of Foreign Affairs summoned a meeting of the representatives of the dipomatic missions to request that the sparrows be denied refuge in the diplomatic compounds! This was an unusual request. Some representatives were sceptical and were convinced only when they personally saw a senior Vice-Minister standing on the roof of the Ministry shooing off the sparrows. Not all the missions were wholly cooperative. Unknowingly they helped by saving some sparrows — it was soon discovered that the sparrows played a role in eliminating some insect pests.

The main centre of action was in the rural areas which saw frenetic activity that year. In early September, the Ministery of Foreign Affairs invited the diplomatic corps to visit Mi Yun, the site of a resevoir under construction, north of Beijing, and to the east of the Great Wall. The reservoir was being constructed at the confluence of two rivers and envisaged construction of eleven dams. It was a tremendous effort centred on the mobilisation of peasants who were going to be the main beneficiaries. A fortnight later, the Ministry organised visit to a commune.

The organisation of communes had received official approval in August. The seeds had been sown earlier when several collectives had pooled their manpower and other resources to jointly build water conservancy works. The commune which was shown to the diplomatic corps was also in the vicinity of Beijing. We were shown the community dining hall, the kindergarten and the experimental rice plot, where five thousand kilos of rice per mou (a sixth of an acre) were being produced. This was an incredible achievement.

The reservoir and the commune had been visited by the Indian Ambassador, Mr. G. Parthasarathi. After consultation within the Embassy, the Government of India were asked to send a group of experts to study the technique of raising the farm yield, the mobilisation of rural labour to build irrigation and drainage works, and to study the methodology of amelioration of land lying uncultivated. The Government of China readily agreed to receive the experts who arrived in late January, 1959 and were in China for nearly forty days. The Ambassador had me included in the group.

The group travelled nearly five thousand kilometres by air, over three thousand kilometres by train and half that by road. The group visited agricultural exhibitions, agricultural colleges, research and training institutes, experimental centres, newly completed projects, construction sites and several communes. Most of these visits were concentrated along the Beijing-Guangzhou axis. The study of communes per se was not on the agenda since the approaches of the two countries to peasant proprietorship were different. Yet, a study of agricultural practices could not be divorced from some knowledge of the communes.

One of the largest communes was located in the vicinity of Tianjin. It had eighty-thousand members. Of whom, sixty-four thousand were able-bodied. The rest were old or sick and able to perform light duties only. The members elected a representative board of two hundred and fifty. In turn, the board elected a managing committee of thirty-three members, including thirteen leading cadres, director and his deputy. The director was paid by the state.

Nearly half of the total income of the commune was expended on capital construction and procurement of seeds, fertilisers and machinery. The remainder was used to supply food, clothing etc. to the members and their families. The food was supplied by the communal kitchen releasing women for labour in the fields. The sick and the old could receive food at home. The members also received a cash supplement averaging five yuans per month. The quantum depended on the nature and quality of work. Men received two and woman four holidays a month.

The commune also provided free education and medical aid. It ran schools, hospitals and maternity homes and paid the staff employed for this purpose.

The primary activity in this commune was farming. At the next commune, in Guan Shan in Henan province, the accent was on preventing soil erosion in a hilly, coal-mining area and providing irrigation facilities. The commune had a population of about sixty-thousand. On the other hand, the commune in Chusan village had a strength of four thousand members only. They were divided into working groups. The commune had organised a special construction brigade of seventy workers, which was engaged in afforestation as part of soil conservation work. At the Bo Hu Xiang commune, we were explained the advantages of deep ploughing, i.e. ploughing to a depth ranging from forty centimetres to more than a metre. The wells were the source of irrigation in this commune. Their number had increased from twenty-three thousand in 1956 to nearly thirty-eight thousand in 1958. The data on irrigated area related more to potential created than to what was actually achieved.

Still in Henan province, the Jiliyan commune of twenty-thousand people, owned and managed a hydro-electric station with a fall of three metres and three turbines. The commune had a large cotton growing area and proposed to set up a textile mill!

The Ankou county had three hundred and ninety villages with over ninety-two thousand peasant households. The total arable area was nearly nine hundred thousand *mu*. The land was irrigated by wells, both deep and shallow. The average yield of foodgrains had increased from two hundred and thirty-two kilos per *mu* in 1957 to seven hundred and twenty-seven kilos per *mu* in 1958 as a result of implementation of the eight point charter. The eight points were Irrigation; Use of Manures and Fertilisers; Deep Ploughing and Improvement of Soil; Seed Selection and Seed Breeding; Close Planting; Plant Protection; Reform of Tools; Farm Management.

The villages of the county were grouped into eight people's communes. Out of the total population of four hundred and twenty-seven thousand, only one hundred and eighty-three thousand were able-bodied men and women, i.e., within the age group of eighteen to fortyfive. Persons between fortyfive and sixty were classified as semi-able received no specific tasks. Ten percent of the able-bodied were employed in local industry and the remainder in farming and related activities. In the following year, 1959-60, only fifty percent were to be engaged on farm-related work, the remaining fifty percent to be employed in industry, i.e., iron and steel, machine building, electrical industry, etc. (A campaign had been launched to build iron and steel furnaces in the backyard in the rural areas. This quickly proved to be a failure. The visit of an Indian team to study this programme was cancelled.)

Construction programme of the Cheng Ho reservoir in Hubei province provided an example of the mobilisation of labour on a large scale. Twenty-four communes located in five counties took part in construction. Eight out of these twenty-four communes were from Quemoyi county, which was the main beneficiary. One hundred thousand workers were engaged on the project. Construction was to be completed in two winters and two springs, i.e., during the slack farming period. The communes were responsible for provision of food and lodging to the labour. The commune members were to build their own lodgings with materials supplied by the commune. Medical personnel were provided by the communes. Medicines were provided by the government, which also provided construction machines. The labour brought its own small tools and implements. While the tools and implements were transported on trucks provided by the government agencies, the workers came on foot, in some cases from as far away as two hundred kilometres.

Cha Kao commune in Guangdong province provided an example of utilising water power. The commune with over ten thousand families had constructed three electricity generating stations, seventeen water power and electricity generating stations and seven water power stations. The commune utilised wooden turbines, pulleys, shafts etc. manufactured locally.

The agricultural experimental stations we visited, were engaged in summing up the "experience of masses" in soil conservation and in increasing the agricultural production. The agricultural exhibitions provided the norm or the ideal for comparing the situation in the field. There was considerable variation between the norm and the reality on the ground. This variation might have adversely affected agricultural production.

The major characteristic of the communes was the ability to mobilise large numbers of local people to construct water conservancy works. Water conservancy was the key element in agricultural production and the government sought to bring all cultivable land under irrigation, hence the mass mobilisation. A small corps of enthusiastic men played a key role in motivating the labour force. For this, objectives were clearly defined and explained. Concentration on water conservancy and soil amelioration, it seemed, affected adversely the normal agricultural operations. There were instances where harvesting of paddy and processing of cotton were delayed, affecting in turn the agricultural operations for the ensuing season.

The group of Indian experts was impressed by the use of local materials and indigenous tools, which could be practised in India too. Similarly, local people could be mobilised for small irrigation works designed by competent engineers. While most elements of the agriculture characters could be practised in India, the group felt that deep ploughing and close planting needed further testing at the experimental stations.

Some of the statistics provided to the group stretched the imagination. It was said that the total area of arable land was 1,600 million *mu.* Upto 1957, nearly thirty-one percent was under irrigation. By 1958, this had increased to over fifty percent. One hundred and fifty-four million *mu* were protected against soil erosion upto 1957. In 1958, an additional area of sixty-five million *mu* had been protected. In the four provinces of Henan, Jiangsu, Hubei and Hunan, the average yield of rice had increased to five thousand catties per *mu* in 1958, the year of Leap Forward, as compared to one thousand catties per *mu* earlier. Consequently, the government was thinking of earmarking only a third of the cultivated area to food crops!

The rapid establishment of communes probably dislocated the rhythm of agricultural operations. The harvest was nowhere near the claimed figures. A subsequent drought led to scarcity of supply of food in the urban as well as rural areas, especially during 1960 and 1961. The Chinese friends spoke about the shortages and consequent hardships, which were shared unevenly. The scale of shortages was however unknown.

The premise that collectivisation by itself would lead to rise in farm output had not been proved by the establishment of communes. Crop failures led to a reversal of the policies. Ownership of land and means of production reverted back to the old cooperative or production team level, with the right to manage resources at its disposal. Communal kitchens were closed down. Family became an important production unit too by means of private plots, domestic rearing of animals, etc. The reversal of the policies was a cause of the schism which later developed in the Chinese Communist Party.

DIPLOMATS' REMINISCENCES

DIPLOMATS' REMINISCENCES

外交使節談往事

42. Interwoven Memories About China
K.P.S. Menon

43. My Tryst with India-China Friendship—A Talk at IGNCA
K.P.S. Menon

44. Diary of an Old China Hand
A.K. Damodaran

45. Delicious Memories—A Talk at IGNCA
A.K. Damodaran

46. Walk out of the Dinner and Eat It—A Talk at IGNCA
Brajesh Mishra

47. Memories of An Indian Ambassador, 1987-1991
C.V. Ranganathan

48. A Young Indian Diplomat in China in the 1960s and 1970s
K.S. Rana

49. How I Arrived on the China Scene
Vinod Khanna

K.P.S. MENON

42

INTERWOVEN MEMORIES*

My father (K.P.S. Menon Senior) went to China in somewhat peculiar circumstances: he first went as Agent General for India. The Chinese and others were aware of the diplomatic ranks, Ambassadors, Ministers, Charge d' Affairs, but Agent General? This was something else again. Some thought it was a military title but, wrote mother, one look at him would have disabused them of any such illusion.

The term derived from the fact that when father was appointed as India's representative, in 1943, India was not yet independent; but father continued in China as Ambassador when the Indian National Congress agreed to form the government in 1946. Father was, in fact, one of the two first ambassadors of independent India, the other being Asaf Ali in Washington. That Jawaharlal Nehru thought it fit to appoint one of these two to China shows the importance he attached to India-China relations.

Whether as Agent-general or Ambassador, father was received with the warmth of genuine friendship. Those were difficult days: wartime Chongqing and then post-war Nanjing. But he was able to travel widely and meet people in all walks of life and he established friendships which lasted throughout his lifetime. Indeed, I was to profit from some of them when I was posted to China forty years later.

The then Chongqing was described as an extraordinarily difficult post. My father's predecessor, Sir Zafrullah Khan, had advised him to have his olfactory nerves removed so that he would be saved from the stench that, he said, prevailed. Fortunately, father did no such thing and was none the worse for it.

What a wealth of life there was even in wartime Chongqing! I visited that Chongqing during my vacations from school and I remember being impressed even at the young age by the sheer *joie de vivre* of the Chinese. The eating-places always seemed full and crowded and noisy, there was much talking and laughter and drinking — and gambling. My impressions, however, were certainly superficial, those of a callow youth, for China was undergoing the most terrible wartime privations. The climate did not help: Chongqing was covered in fog seven months of the year, a fog so thick and opaque that it was said when the sun came out the dogs barked. One of the Ambassadors there, who kept a meticulous record of the sunshine, calculated that in four and a half months it had shone for just three and half hours. I visited Chongqing again years later when I was Ambassador to China. I recollect a kindly official warning me that it would be so hot that it was said the birds dropped dead from the head. I have no memory of that head, but I did notice that the talk and laughter and drinking was as lively as I remembered them — but there was no gambling. I found that Chongqing still retained for me the attraction first seen through the eyes of youth, the dwellings on terraced hillsides, the all seeing, eternal Yangtse on its way to the boundless sea. But I do not recollect hearing again the dolorous fog horns of passing ships nor the plaintive cries of bargemen who, tied to ropes, pulled loads up the Yangtse.

In Chongqing I saw at first hand the efficiency of Chinese record-keeping. I told my guide that if possible I would like to visit the house in which I had lived more than forty years ago. I did not have the address and thought no more of it, thinking it would be well-nigh impossible to trace; but to my amazement he informed me within half-an-hour of the two addresses at which the Indian Representative had lived. So, it was with much nostalgia that I saw the house I had stayed in during a vacation, but from afar because it was now occupied by six families and I did not wish to intrude upon them. I was not so lucky in Nanjing.

*Reprinted from *Indian Horizons* (Journal of Indian Council for Cultural Relations), Vol. 43, Nos. 1-2 (1994), Special Issue "India and China".

There, I knew the address of the house, the then 42, Beijing Road, but it had given way to a new construction.

Father has also recorded, amongst much else, of how he marvelled at the painstaking cultivation around Chengdu, where not an inch of land or drop of water was wasted, and at the ancient irrigation system in Guanxian which I too marvelled at years later.

My parents visited in Chengdu my sister Parvathi, who was studying in Jinling College, presided over by the famous Dr. Wu Yi-fang. Parvathi's room-mates turned out to see them, for they were the first Indians they were seeing. One of them remarked to Parvathi, "Your mother must have a little foreign blood in her" — for my mother has large eyes and a prominent nose — "but your father is all right, he is one of us." Mother remarked that was why father had been chosen to represent India in China.

Parvathi wrote that her room-mates were very considerate towards her. In a dormitory of six double-decker beds they insisted on her having the lower berth and wanted even to make her bed. On one occasion, they told her, still in the most friendly manner, that a hundred years ago India was subject to China. When Parvathi protested, she writes, "They looked so sad that I felt tempted to agree with them, until a more enlightened scholar of history came to the rescue".

Several years later when, as a newly-arrived Ambassador in Beijing, I called on the French Ambassador, he said, "You have two sisters", "Four", said I. "Two of them studied in Chengdu", he said. "Three", I said. It turned out that the Ambassador and his wife had been studying in Chengdu with my twin sisters, the other twin had followed Parvathi there. She studied at Yanjing University in Chengdu. Today Parvathi's daughter teaches Chinese language and history at the Department of Chinese and Japanese Studies in Delhi University and the son of one of the twins, Shivshankar Menon, now heads the Division dealing with China in the Ministry of External Affairs in New Delhi.* He has already been posted twice to China, the second occasion being when I was there. When he was due to arrive on this second occasion one of the Chinese on our staff in Beijing asked my Counsellor whether he was the same Menon who had been there before; and she expressed much happiness at his coming again. It was good to feel this friendship. Shivshankar's wife, too, was, as it were, an "old China hand", for her father, Ram Sathe, was in Chongqing and Nanjing with my father, and was later Consul-General in Kashgar and Ambassador in Beijing in his own right.

Another place my wife, Lalitha, and I visited, which had been visited by father first in 1944 and then, thirteen years later from the Soviet Union in 1957, was Xinjiang and, more particularly, Urumqi, Kashgar and Lanzhou. He had stayed in these places and so did we. In Kashgar he had been accommodated in Chini Bagh, the house so beloved of Lady Macartney, whose husband had spent twenty-eight years there. Ram Sathe had stayed in the same house, as India's Consul-general; but by the time we got to Kashgar the winds of change had converted the house to a transit-shelter for truck drivers.

Father has described the amazing changes that had taken place in the interval of thirteen years since his first visit. It was these changes that we saw. We also saw the remarkable efficiency of the Chinese Foreign Ministry in arranging visits of three plane-loads of diplomats to the awesome Takhlamakan desert and to the surrounding areas of absorbing interest, fabled in history and art, such as the Dunhuang caves. The planning was faultless; and more perfectly organized visits cannot be imagined. But Lalitha and I also experienced an example of pride going before a fall or, rather, as it happened, of pride following a fall. For part of the visit the participants had to ride on camels. We tried to get on to the same camel, to its obvious resentment, and when goaded, it took the simple way out: it gently rolled over on the one side. We were deposited into the gleaming, white sands; and treasure as a memento the photograph of our sprawling discomfiture which the Canadian Ambassador had recorded on his camera. But our pride was salvaged when we were the only diplomat couple to succeed in climbing the sand hill by the side of the beautiful Half Moon Lake, described by travellers centuries ago. Others had done it singly; some had failed altogether.

Father's direct association with China was split into two periods, very different in content. During the first period, from 1943 to 1948, when he was Agent-general and then Ambassador to China, China was in the throes of war and civil war. She was suffering the most terrible deprivations, but there was nothing to cloud the sun of India-China friendship. He found nothing but friendship. He would have appreciated what the writer Robert Payne wrote about him in his China Diaries, 1941-46. "Of all the

*This article was written in 1994. Mr. Shivshankar Menon is now India's ambassador to Sri Lanka — Editor.

foreign representatives in China", Payne wrote, "He is the most beloved... Men loved and admired Eggleston (the Australian Minister). In the same way they love and admire Menon". (Brackets mine).

From 1948 to 1953, father was Foreign Secretary in Delhi and so also had to deal with China. Soon after the first clouds began to appear. This is not the place to go into them. Suffice it to say that it was a constant thread in India's foreign policy, when the new China came into being, in 1949, to hold that it was wrong of the Western community, and some who followed its lead, to try to isolate that China. For instance, India incurred the wrath of the United States of America by taking the lead in an attempt to defeat a Resolution in the United Nations seeking to condemn China for intervention in Korea at the time of the Korean conflict.

Despite the vicissitudes through which India-China relations passed in his lifetime, father always held dear the warm Chinese friendships he had. One of his most cherished memories was of the great Madame Sun Yat-sen, the Soong sister who loved China, coming to the airport to see him off when he was leaving China, and taking the trouble to return to the airport all over again six hours later when the flight was delayed. Several years later, in 1973, he sent her, at the suggestion of a common friend, a copy of his book, "Twilight in China". He hardly expected a reply and was deeply touched when she sent him a most gracious letter.

My own direct association with China was marked by no such cleavage. As Ambassador between 1985 and 1987, I went to a resurgent China, ever growing in confidence. As Foreign Secretary between 1987 and 1989, my relationship was with the same China. Fortunately, the Prime Minister, late Shri Rajiv Gandhi, as also the then Foreign Minister, Shri Narasimha Rao, now Prime Minister, had come to the conclusion that even while border-differences between the two countries were being tackled, with a view to resolving them, progress should be made in other fields. This desire for improving India-China relations was fully reciprocated by the Chinese leadership and, shortly before I left Delhi, it culminated in Rajiv Gandhi's visit to China.

From Madras, Lalitha and I take a continuing interest in happenings concerning China. We were happy to spend a New Year's eve here in the pleasant company of the former Chinese Ambassador, Tu Guowei and his wife. The evening brought back to us the happy hours we had passed in Beijing in the company of Professor Wu Xiaoling and his family, who introduced us to Chinese opera. Equally, we recollected the hospitality extended to us by those good friends of my parents, Ambassador Shen Jian, also a former Ambassador to India, and his wife, and the Yangs — Gladys and Xianyi Yang — opened to us a whole treasure-house of Chinese literature in their translations.

In Madras, too, we were happy to see on the stage of the prestigious Kalakshetra, two flower-like little Chinese girls performing Bharatanatyam and Chinese dances. They came to India in response to an invitation extended by Shri R. Venkatraman, former President of India, during a visit to China, and they were trained in Bharatanatyam by the redoubtable Chinese danseuse, Madame Zhang Jun, a particularly close friend of Lalitha's.

Our memories remain ever green. They will be added to, for, as I have said, there is already a third generation in the family busying itself with matters Chinese.

K.P.S. MENON

43

MY TRYST WITH INDIA-CHINA FRIENDSHIP

(A TALK AT IGNCA ON 13TH SEPTEMBER 1996)

Mr. Chairman, Mr. Joshi, Prof. Tan Chung, our guest from the Chinese Embassy, distinguished participants.

I thank Mr. Joshi and Prof. Tan Chung for the very generous words of welcome and for the guidance that both of you have given us. In fact, I think Prof. Tan Chung's guidance has been rather more accurate and perhaps damaging than we had expected because he described diplomacy, in my view, quite rightly, as a tension-generating activity. We like to think otherwise but it would be an interesting study to see which way diplomacy has gone. This was in fact the other cat that he let out of the bag. However, before I came here, at short notice — that is entirely my fault, because I was travelling about — I had a letter which laid down for me two directives. One was that I was to avoid controversial political subjects, quite rightly in this forum which is well above such mundane things; the second, that I was really to talk from personal memories, reminiscences, as it were, anecdotes, etc. I was happy about that because I had written an article of some length for the *Indian Horizon*, which I find printed here in the folder, and so I immediately told Prof. Tan Chung, well, there's my article, there is nothing I can add now, shall we get going. But I am afraid, he would not permit that. So, I have to speak, but not to repeat what I have already written.

When I went to China, Rajiv Gandhi had been Prime Minister for only a few months. When I called upon him he looked up with his charming smile and said, "What worries you?" I said, "Nothing really, but it seems to me that the official talks have run into dry sands. I don't see any progress coming from them and if you want to make some progress, then we have to think of something else." He replied immediately, "It has been my view that even when we leave the border alone, we try to go ahead in other fields. We should try to make progress with China in other directions.

As the Foriegn Secretary, Mr. Salman Haidar, said just now, this approach was perhaps already introduced in a sense during Mrs. Gandhi's time. What Rajiv had said was an advice dear to my heart. I took it as authorised government policy and felt that I could proceed accordingly in China. I do not remember any time raising the border issue in a substantive, comprehensive way in my talks in China. The reason was that I knew the immediate response would be "What have you got to suggest, what have you got to propose?" And I really did have nothing to propose for a settlement at that time. To the best of my memory, too, no Chinese leader raised it either, in a comprehensive way. Ofcourse, as soon as I reached China and attended the welcoming banquet, one of the Chinese leaders referred in his speach to that old analogy of an eagle from a high point taking a comprehensive view. The implication of that was obvious, but otherwise there was no further discussion. Regrettably, though, the border came in indirectly on several occasions when I had to take up with the Chinese objections to what we thought were their transgressions of the border. I had to do this more than I liked on instructions from Delhi. I felt the Chinese also found it rather irksome that I was taking up sometimes seemingly pettifogging points. But I remember particularly a long talk when the Chinese Director-General spoke at greater length than he normally did, in the course of which he said, "Your border management is better than ours." The phrase was slipped in almost as if in passing and then he went on to other topics. I was glad that I grasped at the time that was really the key phrase in his exposition, judging by the events which followed a few months later. I also thought it important to cultivate the several institutions on international affairs that existed in China and, I must say, I developed a healthy respect for them.

Today we in India have certainly excellent institutions, institutions like the IGNCA, IIC and others. But I thought at the time that the Chinese institutions were very good, very thorough, and they knew what they were talking about. I did find that they, like the Government, always spoke with one voice, somewhat contrary to our own traditions where everyone has his/her own opinion and is only too happy to express it. It was in fact from one of the Chinese institutions that I first heard the suggestion which was pressed upon me, that Rajiv Gandhi should visit China. To the best of my recollection, again, I do not remember it being suggested by the Chinese Foreign Ministry.

When I asked why they wanted Rajiv to visit, the answer was that leaders were meeting all over the world and there was no reason why the Indian and Chinese leaders should shy away from each other. When I said that a visit without concrete results might be worse than no visit at all, the answer I got was that one should not be so pessimistic about this sort of thing. There would be a change, a change in atmosphere that one can see, and the visit should take place. Subsequently I think that the Chinese assessment has proved right, judging from Rajiv Gandhi's visit to China. One of the decisions of that visit was to continue with the working group officials, but it was a different sort of meeting. It was regarded as officials working jointly together rather than as two separate teams, sometimes almost taking up antagonistic positions. During his visit to China, Rajiv Gandhi suggested not only official meetings of that sort but he also suggested that a second tier be created at the ministerial level to hold consultations between the two countries before the issue could mature for final decisions. This, the Chinese were not too keen on. They felt the official level meetings followed by decisions at ministerial level were sufficient. We now see that certain decisions taken at the ministerial meetings on trade and other matters quite helped improve relations.

Besides calling on the Government and the institutions in China, I travelled as widely as I possibly could, not only in pursuit of official duties but also in order to try to see something of that vast land and to gain an insight into her ways and thinking. One's interest in history is often prompted by little incidents. Mine in China had been greatly prompted by readings that I had come across when I was very much younger — things like the Xian Incident when Chiang Kai-shek escaped through the window. These may be trivial incidents, but they created an interest in me. During my travels I had the fascination of seeing the very window through which Chiang Kai-shek had escaped, leaving behind only his concubine (I was told about this by the guide when I visited the site) and his false teeth. Of course, there were many other great episodes of history, the room in Shanghai where 13 persons first formed the Chinese Communist Party, the cemetery of Madam Soong Qingling. I remember also seeing the car, in Chongqing, which had been used by Zhou Enlai during the talks between the communists and Kuomintang being mediated by the US envoy General Marshal.

I happened to be in the war capital several years earlier too, and I remember a young member of the communist delegation coming to our mission and looking at the pamphlets on India strewn on the table. He stood there reading them. He must have known English because he looked at them for a long time and then asked whether he could borrow them. We were very happy to let him have them. I do not know whether the Kuomintang suspected the Indian Mission of being in league with the communists!

Besides this, there was the feel of China. I remember on a trip, after going through a comparatively prosperous area, my wife and I found ourselves in a rural setting. The distant twilight shone upon two buffaloes in a field with a man following them and they were the only creatures in that vastness, providing an atmosphere of pastoral peace. I stopped the car to take a photograph of the scene. The guide looked amazed and he asked my wife: "Why! Haven't you got any buffaloes in India?"

It was also when I was in China that the economic liberalisation had just about begun. What was meant by this economic liberalization? There was fervid speculation in the diplomatic corps some holding the view that economic latitude would in due course bring about political upheaval. I asked the leader, Hu Qili, whether he was afraid of other effects coming in. He then gave me a reply which has since become well used. He said, "If you want fresh air in a room you open the window. With the fresh air you get also insects but you can't do without the fresh air. You will have to get rid of the insects separately." It seems to me that this is what China is doing, because the Chinese people have shown their ingenuity in making use of the changed atmosphere.

It was often emphasized to us that the new motto for China was to get rich quickly. That did seem to happen to a certain extent, and I sensed some excitement in the countryside. I was greatly impressed by the places I toured through, where every house seemed to have a television set as the antennae indicated. In the countryside people told me that they all had, or would have very soon, washing-machines, apart from television, and as they now had motor-bikes, they would soon have cars.

Apart from the personal interest of travelling, of seeing something of China, there was of course the old Indian factor — the places so famous in China's cultural history, Luoyang, Guangzhou, Xian. To this very distinguished assemblage, I need not dwell upon them, but I did come across a statement in a work by a Chinese scholar recently that was unknown to me. The scholar pointed out the great cultural effect and the enhancement of cultural life because of the introduction of Buddhist ritual, Buddhist teaching, Buddhist votaries and so on. But at the same time there were other side effects. For instance, merchants had started dressing in silk and an edict was passed at one time that no merchant should wear silk any more, because it was thought that they were becoming too arrogant and vulgarly ostentatious. Again, some monasteries became extraordinarily rich and began to meddle in politics. Another Chinese scholar has said something which perhaps has occurred to all of us but I was glad to get it from him. While he felt that India gave more to China spiritually, China gave more to India in a material sense.

Of course as an example of this the famous fishing nets of my own part of the country, Kerala, are often quoted. Then the shape and roofs of our Kerala houses. The roof is made in China for the dragon to be entwined in it. There is also in Kerala, "Chinabharani", which is a large earthenware vessel for storage. The name suggests that it was introduced from China. The people of Kerala have adopted it as a container of their daily life. I also recollect another observation, perhaps by a Western scholar which I find of great interest. He compared the different attitudes of the Westerners and the Chinese who visited South India in the early years of interchange. When the Portuguese came, they committed horrible atrocities. They had native pilots nailed to the masts of Portuguese ships and so on. They also sexually abused women in Madras. When the Chinese ships came to Indian ports, there was no such atrocity, while Indians and Chinese treated each other as equals.

I had the privilege of seeing something of China in 1944-45 and again in 1946-47. Later, after a long gap, I went to China as India's Ambassador in 1987. I often had the opportunity of seeing China change rapidly.

China's poverty in 1943 was a byword. It was the most horrendous poverty that you can see anywhere. Yet I remember being amazed of how even at that time, in the midst of poverty and war the Chinese could enjoy themselves. The restaurants were always full. People were laughing, and they gambled merrily. In 1987 it was a totally different China I went to. I didn't see any of that poverty. I was told that the poorest people were the boat people. But I sailed on the Yangtze between Chongqing and Wuhan and I didn't see any great poverty along the river. Maybe their clothing didn't look as bright as elsewhere, but certainly there was not the acute deprivation of poverty that still exists in parts of India. I think many foreigners would like to believe that China's poverty is to be found in her closed cities. There were many closed cities when I went to China in 1987, which were barred to foreigners. But I must say that the number was very greatly reduced in the two years that I was there as Indian Ambassador. I also met two foreigners who had happened to have entered some of these closed cities and they told me that they had not seen any great difference between these closed cities and the China we were allowed into. Why, then, was China so sensitive about foreigners seeing her freely? I don't know; and I think it only tends to give a wrong impression of something being hidden.

I was lucky that I went to China from Japan, because you cannot imagine two societies of greater contrast. I was told in Japan by a foreign ambassador that if I was going to relate a joke I should precede it with a remark, "Now I am going to tell you a joke"! But nothing of the sort was required in China. Chinese reactions seemed so much like ours. They would cry, laugh at the same things. But, of course, there are also differences. I am sorry, Vasant Paranjpe, who has written fascinatingly about China, is not here. I would have liked to hear more from him. I agree entirely with him that the Chinese are more pragmatic than we are. Once they make up their minds they plunge into action. I think we are far more concerned about the next world. For the Chinese, present mirth hath present laughter, enjoy yourself when you can. Is it not Confucius who said, "You know precious little about this world, why bother about the next?" That is totally unlike our attitude. At the same time, I think we are not preoccupied with death, like for instance, Egypt of the Pharoahs. The construction of mausoleums and pyramids is so much concerned with death, providing the dead with the comforts they are accustomed to in life. This sort of preoccupation is not with us Indians.

What is our object in life? Even for a diplomat it is self-realization. This, it seems to me, doesn't bother the Chinese at all. But with all their pragmatism in getting things done, some strange incidents sometimes occur. I have referred to the closed cities. One of my officers went with a group of foreigners to visit an open area. To get to it they had to pass through a closed area. They were stopped. They were told it was closed. The foreigners said they had to pass through to get to the area which was open. The Chinese said they could go to the open area, but not pass through the closed area. The foreigners asked how they could reach the one without going through the otner. It was a catch 22 situation and the argument went back and forth. Finally they did get across. I was amazed at this incident, corning from the very practical Chinese.

I found the new China determined, decisive, purposeful. It knew which way it wanted to go. It was so different from the China of 1943. It was working actively for China's entry into the information techonological society of the 21st century. In our own way, perhaps, we are making similar efforts. But in that endeavor, I sometimes wonder what will happen to the Chinese character, the Chinese who is so familiar to us. There was a great similarity between the Chinese and the Indian, both with a great feeling of humanity, of community. To use an arresting phrase from a Greek writer, "China moves with the rhythm of things." I think that is also very true of India. But in our modern society, we are forcing the rhythm of things. I think the natural rhythm of things is getting quite ignored. That old idea of leisure, a certain way to live and let live, I do not know to what extent all this is being affected. I remember a Danish boy who had been in college with me, staying with me in Delhi in the early 50's. He came back home one day from India Gate, fascinated about seeing so many people just sitting around in the evening and chatting. This, he said, would never happen in his country. In Beijing also, when I went out on a warm evening, walking around the streets, it seemed a kind of benediction to see people enjoying the cool of the evening, all at peace, all at leisure, people sitting on the pavements getting their household chores done. Will this last in the new information technological society? I also remember a Japanese, who was once at Shantiniketan, asking me to keep a room for her in my flat when the time comes for her to die. I asked why. "Because", she said, "I want to die in the peaceful environment of India". I thought she was joking, but it turned out that she was entirely earnest, and she has since repeated this request in writing. Will all such things last in this new aggressive technological society? I do hope India and China cooperate more in economic, cultural and perhaps in political matters but I think also that it is the sociological effect of technological progress that is going to be of critical importance.

I think it most worthwhile that India and China pursue their studies together, and compare their individual studies, on what it means to be a developing society in transition to a technological age. Already, there is some rethinking in China about the one-child norm. They believe it might be making for a society of selfish and self-centered people. What about the citizens of the new technological society? Today you go to a modern bank, press a button, get your money, credit money, you don't need to meet a single soul to do any of these things. In contrast, in my good old-fashioned Indian bank, I sit with the manager, sip a cup of tea, the statement of account comes, it has a mistake, it takes another fifteen minutes to correct, but it is an enjoyable experience. All that is changing and is going to vanish. And what will this mean? Are we not evolving into a dehumanized society? I am sorry to dwell so much on this, but I think it is of extreme importance to countries like India and China with their age-old cultures of humanity and it is here I ardently wish that we can cooperate in our studies and get our scholars together on it.

Returning to my "achievements" in China, as Foreign Secretary Haidar implied, I don't think I achieved anything very much. Of course, I tried to get trade going, talked about coal, steel, etc. I am sure my predecessors had also worked in that direction. I cannot claim that I achieved anything spectacular. But I was happy when the Chinese proposed that we should have meetings of delegations before a UN Session to see what common positions we could take. That I thought was a significant step forward. I do not know whether that had happened earlier, but it happened in my second year in China. They also suggested the visit of a team from India to advise them on auditing. I said, "You don't know what you are letting yourselves in for!" But they insisted on it and the audit team went along. They also asked for a team to advise them on running a civil service, and they repeated this when I was Foreign Secretary in Delhi. I expressed surprise: "After all, the recruitment of a civil service by open competitive examination originated in China, it is you who should teach us." But they said, "That might be, but we have forgotten!" I think they would have been happier if they had forgotten much about auditing and such like things. However, I should not take any more of your time. I am grateful and thank you, Prof. Tan Chung, for your welcome and guidance.

QUESTION-ANSWER SESSION

Dr. Abid Husain *(in the chair)*

I think there are three-four very important points which we should consider. He started with a period when it looked that talks were running into dry sand and then by the time he was leaving certain greener paths became evident, and we have got to see the role of the institutions which played outside the Government in China and a lack of similar institutes in India, which, if developed at that time, could have, perhaps, brought our thinking much closer to each other. The role of Mr. Rajiv Gandhi as mentioned by K.P.S. Menon really opens the door for the solution of problems.

K.P.S. Menon mentioned about the Chinese feeling that border management of India was far better than theirs. I think this is an area we might probe more. The second point is about liberalization. The process had just begun at that time. The doors and the windows were open and the insects and the fresh air both started coming in, and we have got to see how it developed because he told us about an era when motorbikes had started coming in, the television was being seen, the washing machines were working. On trade, he said a beginning had been made without much progress. I am happy that A.P. Venketeswaran is here because by that time a delegation was sent and we were to sign the first agreement at that time but nothing spectacular has happened in that particular point of time. One more area, i.e., the area of professional merit where they started seeking help from India, and I think you did very well in dissuading the Indian auditors going there, because when I was in Fiji, a similar thought occurred to the Fijians. They were advised by some auditors in India and they started taking taxes to stop the rich from becoming richer. When I reached Fiji, the President and Prime Minister said, "Mr. Hussain, do something. We called an Indian expert and he has put us in the soup, what do we do?" I said, "If the auditor was from North India, call another one from the South and it will be corrected". One very important point of K.P.S is the rhythm of things. Now he has compared China, Japan and India, in a sweep just in details, and he says there is a certain commonality between China and India and he describes it as a rhythm of things. Now can we catch that rhythm and get into the swing, when we are approaching the 21st century? Recently I have come back from China and they have repeatedly talked about going back to the glorious years of the 50's. To this I always responded, "Do you want us to advance towards the 50's or do you want to go back towards the 50's." I couldn't get an answer. The psychological contrast between India and China that K.P.S. talked about comparing it with Japan, earmarks also the harmony between us, the sharing of a common vision of a good society, that is a good point he made.

Chari: Mr. K.P.S., I was very intrigued by the advice that Rajiv Gandhi gave to you before you left for China, and as I understood, his advice was that the border question was to be kept aside, and Sino-Indian relations were to be improved in several other directions, do you think that border dispute can be really kept out of consideration and what were the thoughts in the Government of India at that time or when Venkateswaran was there at that time about how they should proceed with the border dispute, just keep it aside for all time or do we have a brief in this regard, do we have any ideas how it should be approached?

K.P.S. Menon: "Kept Aside" in a certain sense. He didn't mean just forget it, because he did say that the border issue should be tackled. He meant let the official talks continue, even if they are not leading to results today, continue with what you can do on the border but don't let it stop progress in other fields. At one time, the Government of India's attitude was that nothing could be done till the border issue was finally settled. I would guess that Government would have liked to see an equitable solution on the border. But at that time, that is, when I saw Rajiv Gandhi before leaving for China, Government had not had the opportunity to consider it in depth. Not only Government, but also Parliament. I cannot say that it was a Government decision to put it aside and certainly not for ever. But the first steps in the attitude was being taken by Indira Gandhi and, later more firmly, by Rajiv Gandhi, i.e., let us see what we can do with China even while the border issue is kept pending.

Mira Sinha Bhattacharjea: The Chinese thought that we had a better border management system than they had, I am intrigued. Some 4-5 years prior to this the Chinese were talking about a border management system even with Mongolia and other territorial neighbours. So what is it they mean by border management?

K.P.S. Menon: He did not use the word "system" at all. He said, "Your border management is better than ours." I think the meaning of ours is clear within the context in which he said it. We were talking more seriously than usual about what we regarded as violations of the border by the Chinese and he was responding with accusations of violations by us. And I think he was making the point "You are able to violate the border more easily than we are able to."

Mira Sinha: Quite different to what I thought. I wanted to ask about China-Pak relations, the two countries of totally different systems, the Pakistan system being anti-communist, and the Communist Party being banned for so long, with very little to hold together and we in this country presume that what brings them together is really an anti-Indian attitude. What is your sense of China-Pak relations.

K.P.S. Menon: When you say they are totally different, I think this frankly does not matter a damn to the Chinese. I think they are very pragmatic and a very practical people, making good relations wherever they can. Besides bettering their relationship with Pakistan also having an economic aspect, it gives rise to suspicion in public opinion in India that they are fundamentally anti-Indian: Why should they help the country which is hostile to India? This is a very difficult question to answer. Is China just improving her relations where she can, or is it that the Chinese are very practical? There are two schools of thought on this. One thinks that it is essentially anti-Indian. This formulation makes it more difficult for us to improve relations with China. The other thinks that it is just China is doing what it thinks is the right thing in International relations, not necessarily directed against India. One can argue it both ways. I can argue that if it is anti-Indian why have the Chinese advised our neighbours to improve relations with India or why did they call off aid to dissenting movements in our border areas etc.

Ram Subramaniam: Sir, I can only rely on newspaper reports. I am not privileged to information which is very secret. Yesterday Mr. Madhavan has written in the *Pioneer* that on the issue of Chinese missiles in Tibet, we never raised it with the Chinese, in the *Times Of India* report of 1988 when Rajiv Gandhi was going to China, it was reported that Mr. Rajiv Gandhi was quoted as saying "Why do we talk about these missiles in Tibet, there are no missiles." could you kindly clarify?

K.P.S. Menon: To the best of my knowledge it was not raised as an issue that there were Chinese missiles in Tibet targeting India. But I cannot give that as a final reply because I would think that if Rajiv Gandhi raised it, he would have done so only in a one-to-one talk.

A.K. DAMODARAN

44

DIARY OF AN OLD CHINA HAND*

It was during an unusually interesting period not only in the history of India-Chin arelations but also of China's interaction with the rest of the world that I happened to be posted in Beijing. I reached there in August 1963 almost a year after the border conflict and left in November 1965 after the very first premonition of the Great Proletarian Cultural Revolution. India had been extremely careful in not breaking up diplomatic relations after what we thought to be the betrayal of 1962. The Chinese were also happy to carry on with a modest but, by no means, unimpressive presence in the Indian capital. There were no Ambassadors and the two missions were headed by Counsellors acting as Charge d'Affairs. At a time when China had *de jure* relations only with some socialist and Afro-Asian countries, the Indian Mission was an important one. The specific conditions in Beijing made the normal diplomatic duties of observation, monitoring and reporting a little more demanding than in normal capitals. The diplomats formed a fairly small closed seminar of sorts exchanging views, conclusions and speculations with a certain amount of exuberance. The Indian Embassy was also free of the normal protocol duties of looking after visitors and arranging the itineraries of official guests. This made the task of political analysis much more exciting than in any other capital I have served, not excluding Moscow. We spent a lot of time in talking to each other and comparing notes of our problems with the Chinese. It was a very limited and unusually serious group of people. It had many young diplomats who would distinguish themselves in their careers later on. One of the Third Secretaries in the British Office (there was no British Embassy, only an office, since there was no full recognition), David Wilson, later on became the Editor of *China Quarterly* and also the Governor of Hong Kong. Most of the Russian diplomats went back to very high levels in the Soviet Foreign Office.

Our relations with the Chinese Foreign Office, *Waijiaobu,* were extremely tense because of the almost continuous series of "incidents" which affected our relations: but they were always very polite. Both the Chinese and the Indians are reasonably civilized people and would not permit the private feelings of the negotiators to affect the negotiations. The diplomatic protocol was scrupulously observed when we called on the Foreign Office on business. The protest letters were read out in a serious solemn voice and frigid exchanges were made. At the end of it all, there was the inevitable cup of delicious Chinese tea. Then we relaxed for a few minutes and discussed the weather and other things. There was only one occasion when there was a breach of this genteel convention. In September 1965, when the Indo-Pakistan War had broken out, the Chinese gave us a rather well-known "ultimatum" accusing us of straying across the Nathu La border between Sikkim and Tibet with 365 sheep. Other "gross" violations of the border were also mentioned like the building of bunkers. Jagat Mehta, the Head of the Indian Mission, said he would like to discuss the problem after the Chinese diplomat had finished reading out his statement. The Chinese official told us that there was no time to waste. The message should be telegraphed to India immediately. Or, else...

That was the only occasion when we did not have our obligatory cup of tea. We used to exchange notes with great enthusiasm those days, notes about land and air violations on the border. All these protest notes have been printed in the White Papers and they seem a little trivial now compared with the major developments which were happening in the relations of China with the world outside of which we were beginning to be aware. The Vietnam conflict was beginning and the great Afro-Asian diplomatic crusade of Zhou Enlai was initiated at the end of 1963. The Afro-Asian idea had caught the imagination of the Chinese as a possible alternative to Non-alignment. Behind all this, slowly inevitably, the fuse was burning in the Sino-Soviet dispute which

*Reprinted from *Indian Horizons*, Vol. 43, No. 1-2.

had come out into the open well before the end of 1963. China's relations with Pakistan were warm as also was her special equation with Sukarno's Indonesia. Burma was happy to be friendly with her difficult neighbour.

In India-China relations, it was a period of mild inactivity after the diplomatic excitements of third-party negotiations initiated by the Colombo Powers. The Chinese gave us some indications about this time of their willingness to improve the relations marginally without any commitments about the substantive issues in the conflict. The war prisoners had returned home; a few Chinese expatriates had gone back to China, all in 1963. There were really no serious problems on the border itself even though peace continued to be fragile. However, there was eyeball to eyeball confrontation and there were also small incidents, mercifully without casualties, across the undemarcated border. Considering the fact that a major war had taken place only a few months earlier, it was a stable enough situation. That stability was shown by the manner in which the Chinese indicated to us their willingness to return to something of the status quo ante not on the border, but in the general, wider, relationship, about the end of 1963. This is an interesting enough diplomatic episode to recall at this distant time.

Our Charge d'Affairs, P.K. Banerjee, was due to leave Beijing. He had been incharge throughout the border conflict and later, and had a special personal rapport with many senior members of the Chinese hierarchy. However, it was something of a surprise to us when we were told that the Prime Minister, Zhou Enlai, would himself receive him for a farewell call. I was one of the officers who accompanied the head of the mission. It was a memorable occasion by any standard. Zhou Enlai had a lengthy conversation with Banerjee and repeatedly expressed his hope that the present uncomfortable period would be over soon. He was at his delightful best. One thing he said has stayed with me all these years as an example of what might have been if the domestic situation in China and the Sino-Soviet relationship had not changed totally during the next two years making it necessary for Beijing to put India-China relations on the back burner. Zhou Enlai told us that as Prime Minister he had to read and scrutinize every single bit of diplomatic correspondence between the two countries. "Can't we stop this war of words"? he said. He went on to talk generally on the relations between the two countries but was careful enough to avoid all the details of the border dispute. It was a very important signal. This request at the highest level was followed up a few weeks later when the new Charge d'Affairs, Jagat Mehta, arrived in Beijing. In an unusually warm gesture reminiscent of earlier days, he was invited for a special dinner by the Director of the Asian Division of the Foreign Office, Zhang Wenjin. It was a happy coincidence that the host and the chief guest had an earlier association. They had prepared the officials' report on the border together. Zhang Wenjin seemed to be anxious to repeat Zhou Enlai's signals at his own level. We were all happy and mildly optimistic.

But things went wrong during the next few months. The Sino-Soviet dispute and the India-China alienation intersected in our sponsorship of the Soviet Union as a member of the proposed Second Afro-Asian Conference. This was in April 1964. A few weeks later came Prime Minister Nehru's last, sensible offer to clarify a point of contention in the Western Sector. In Bombay, during the third week of May, he suggested that instead of the two sides nagging each other about the number of posts in the disputed region, a sensible solution would be to have no posts at all. China's response was unpleasantly quick and negative. Within a few days Nehru passed away. The Afro-Asian idea also vanished from history without a trace inspite of China's anxious campaign in several capitals. The Sino-Soviet dispute and the Vietnam War entered the centre of the stage effectively preventing an earlier solution of subsidiary problems.

Panditji's death on May 27, 1964 provided yet another occasion for the exercise of Zhou Enlai's charm. As is the practice on these occasions, we had arranged a condolence book in the Embassy, to be signed by local dignitaries and diplomats. All the foreign diplomats had come and gone but there was still no sign of the Chinese. Towards the end of the second day, just before the time was due to end, we received a message from the Foreign Office that an important visitor would be coming. It was Zhou Enlai accompanied by senior Foreign Office officials. After signing the condolence register he stayed back to talk to us for about ten minutes about his long and extremely eventful association with Jawaharlal Nehru. There was not the slightest hint of acrimony. It was a very graceful gesture. He could have left it to a comparatively junior official to carry out the minimum protocol obligations. But he had a remarkable capacity for being nice and generous.

The other memories I have of Zhou Enlai in those years is his unique personality as distinct from that of his colleagues. He had an easy relationship with large crowds very much like Nehru's. Whenever a foreign delegation came to Beijing, there was a ceremony at the airport to which a large number of students and other young people had been brought. Before the chief guest got down the plane, the group of Chinese dignitaries, Liu Shaoqi, Chen Yi, the Foreign Minister, and some times Zhu De and other senior ministers would move towards the tarmac. Zhou Enlai would suddenly get away from his companions and go to the crowd who would be excited at being greeted by him. Only Zhou Enlai could get away with this sort of behaviour on any occasion. I remember how two years later, when the Cultural Revolution was celebrated by a huge rally in Beijing attended by Mao Zedong, Lin Biao and Zhou Enlai, we were shown the official film about the rally in the Chinese Embassy. Here again, while Mao looked tired and distant, and Lin Biao made an unimpressive speech, it was Zhou who was happiest with the crowds.

The Foreign Office was full of Zhou Enlai's personal recruits. Zhang Wenjin had been his interpreter during the Chongqing years. When we knew him, this polished and handsome diplomat never spoke to us in English. The absolutely rigid rule was to have always the use of the interpreter. Marshall Chen Yi and Zhou Enlai divided the Foreign Office functions between them without any apparent difficulties. During the violence of the Red Guards in 1968, Zhou Enlai protected Chen Yi. From our point of view, an equally important diplomat was Zhang Tong, former Military Attaché in India, who was Deputy Director in our time. Later on, he became Director when Zhang Wenjin was promoted as Assistant Minister.

In spite of our great difficulties, thus, our official relations continued to be correct and even friendly. During the tours of the provinces of China, arranged for the diplomatic corps by the Foreign Office, the Indians did not have any occasion to feel isolated. I remember going on two of these tours. It was a uniquely Chinese convention. We got an opportunity to visit communes and also factories. We had occasion to see the Beijing Opera and the shadow plays apart from climbing up tall hills in search of non-functioning monasteries. Each diplomatic tour lasted about ten days and included visits to at least three provinces. The diplomats and their wives were both welcome and the chief hostess was the utterly charming Madame Chen Yi.

Apart from these tours we could, with the friendly assistance and also surveillance of the Chinese authorities, visit some permitted cities of the country on our own. I had a very interesting visit to Shanghai to return the buildings of the former Indian Consulate General to the Chinese authorities. We got a rather angry note from the Foreign Office saying that the premises of the consulate had not been well maintained. We got the whole thing cleared up very soon with the help of the small Indian community of Sikhs and their Chinese wives in the city. They were wonderful people — these last remnants of the old Indian community in the foreign concessions. Most of them belonged to the old police force in the British concession; when the arrangement ended in 1945, some of them decided to stay back and turn their gifts to the dairy industry. They stayed on until the middle sixties when during the Cultural Revolution all of them left for Hong Kong. There was only one rather elderly gentleman, Mr. Das from Calcutta, who was a wholesale merchant in bay leaves. We helped him to sell to the State his remaining stocks and return to India via Hong Kong. These are desultory impressions. Looking back 30 years later, what one can recapture most is the ease and comfort with which we used to go about Beijing in those politically difficult days. The ordinary people of China, the merchants, the shopkeepers, the servants, the Chinese staff in the Embassy were not hostile to us inspite of the enormous political resentment on both sides. India meant to most of them a distant but friendly western country and Indians were never made to feel unwelcome. This is the reason why so many of us, who were posted in Beijing, look back to our days there with nostalgia.

A.K. DAMODARAN

45

DELICIOUS MEMORIES

(A TALK AT IGNCA ON 13TH SEPTEMBER 1996)

I am merely going to have a straight forward frank indulgence in nostalgia along memory lane. Thirty years ago, I and Kishan Rana who shared with my China experience on his first posting there. The difference between me and the others who spoke in the morning was that I was at the worm's eye level not at the bird's eye level, and I was at the functioning level in the embassy. It was a fascinating period and before I begin with the most eloquent testimony to the presence of the Chinese material in the Indian spirit is in Kalidasa's "Sakuntala". Please remember that beautiful line in "Sakuntala" when Dushyanta goes away after meeting Sakuntala for the first time and then he says: "the body goes in front but the mind goes backwards like the 'Chinbhatambra' ". He was depicting the Chinese silk, fluttering in the breeze. It is important for us to recognize this reality, if not mere sentimentalism. It's a fact and this is what Nehru meant when he went on repeating these things. Please remember that six weeks after the India-China conflict, in December 1962, Jawaharlal spoke at the convocation of Visva-bharati about China in the same passionately affectionate manner, he did not allow temporary difficulties to affect his picture of China.

My stay in Beijing between 1963-65 was a fascinating period. Our troubles had just been over, and by the time we left China, she herself had begun her Great Cultural Revolution. It was from the point of political analysis and diplomatic study, in retrospect, an extremely fascinating period. The interesting thing was the diplomatic corps in Beijing had about 13 missions, and out of these 13 missions, 15 or 20 young men like Kishan Rana, were extremely charming people who also knew Chinese. I remember Krishan, who was the first in our Embassy who thought the change in the tone about the inheritors of the revolution. Late 1963 and early 1964 in our actual daily life there was not the slightest reflection, in our relations with ordinary people into whom political problems had not penetrated. The word, "India", was a known word in Chinese history "western land", they did not know much about Pakistan. This small diplomatic corps was very much concerned about the biggest change that was happening at that time, and that had nothing to do with India — the Sino-Soviet dispute. It was coming up and so we had this fascinating experience of watching China through Soviet eyes, through Romanian eyes. This made us extremely sensitive to things that were happening. The type of interactions which we noticed between the great Chinese leaders from the distance was very great. Zhou Enlai was comfortable in his countenance, Mao was a recluse and Liu Shaoqi was a very shy person. These differences made our diplomatic work extremely interesting. This had a dramatic consequence 18 months later, in May or June 1965, suddenly in the papers there was news of the swimming episode in which both Chairman Mao and Chairman Liu had participated in the Shisanling (Ming Tomb) reservoir. This story came 6 months after the National People's Congress (NPC) which had registered the period of readjustment of Liu Shaoqi and Deng Xiaoping and which had really put Mao's position in the back. We reported to Delhi and we were convinced that this was something of great importance, of course the story was projected probably by Liu Shaoqi's side.

The Chinese are a very hospitable people. Their wonderful diplomatic tours, every embassy sent two people, and there were about 60 people in the group which was usually led by a worthy person no less than the Foreign Minister Marshal Chen Yi and Madame Chen Yi. The first trip was to Nanjing, Hangzhou etc. and all the beautiful places. The discussions we had with the Chinese during that time had nothing of our bilateral political problems, unhappy thoughts were not allowed to intervene in our conversation. It was a very important way of interaction. The second trip was to Changsha and Mao's birth place Shaoshan. Then we went to Guangdong, the place where the second (economic) revolution was going to flower exuberantly i.e., prosperity backed by the investment from the overseas Chinese.

In our excitement, we overromanticized the Chinese situation. I remember my first report to Delhi, in December, 1963. I got excited. It was Mao's birthday and I wrote in the report: "Mao is Lenin gifted with longevity", I did not realize that within two years the Mao fraternity in the Chinese leadership will splinter into many parts. I thought the solidarity was permanent since the founding of People's Republic of China in 1949, a phenomenon so happily demonstrated in China.

One political memory. In 1965 October/November before I was leaving, I thought I should take a final tour in China, I first went to Wuxi and Suzhou and then went back to Beijing via Shanghai. In Shanghai the Chinese guide asked me what I would like to see. I said I would like to see a play based on Lin Biao's great victory at Pingxingguan in North China in 1937 against the invading Japanese army. One day later, Lin Biao's voice was blared out from the radio again and again. That was the great occasion of another "people's war", the beginning of another great chapter in Chinese history — the Great Cultural Revolution. Such an exciting place of politically sensitive people cannot be duplicated in any other part of the world.

I will end on a mildly optimistic political note. We have talked about the problems remaining between India and China — the border dispute. I have watched the India-China relations from near and from afar, from all over the world. The fact that this troubled border between the two countries had only three incidents in thirty years suggests that this is one of the quieter borders in the world. Secondly, although India-China bilateral obsession is very interesting but the world is not interested. All the books about Chinese foreign policy written by Americans do not count the India-China border dispute at all. Thirdly, at no point, during the 1960s or during the 1970s, either China or India played the zerosum game on non-bilateral problems. At the global level, throughout this period we were on the side of the havenots in their struggle with the haves. After the Chinese became member of the United Nations India and China cooperated well in the UN despite of earlier expectations or speculations about some frictions and troubles. Why? Unobtrusively, with no fuss made about it, these positive things should be noted at this point, the resumption of diplomatic relations since 1976 and the visit of Rajiv Gandhi in 1988 were merely representing the expression of the general feeling of an absence of crisis, whatever our seminarists and professional commentators might like to say.

I personally would not hurry, the famous formula of 1961 July when R.K. Nehru and Zhang Wenjin has evolved in their talks that, "Either solve the problem immediately by official talks or leave it to the politicians to discuss, if that is not enough, leave it to the shelf and let destiny decide". That I think is a sort of attitude which we can take, we are two large nations, made not to worry about one momentary episode in our long histories.

BRAJESH MISHRA

46

WALK OUT OF THE DINNER AND EAT IT

(A TALK AT IGNCA ON 13TH SEPTEMBER 1996)

I was in New York in 1968 when instructions came that I was to go to Beijing, I was to be the Charge d' Affaires (CAD), and, the posting had perhaps something to do with the fact that in 1960-61, I was Deputy Secretary (China) at headquarters. Perhaps it also had something to do with the political family to which I belong. I remember after my posting was announced, one newspaper, *(The Patriot)* wrote that there must be something deep in the posting of Brajesh Mishra to China. Perhaps says *The Patriot*, Mrs. Gandhi wants to improve relations and knowing that Brajesh Mishra is the son of his father, she thinks that she will get political support for improving relations with China. I don't think Mrs. Gandhi had anything in her mind about my pedigree before posting me to China, but she certainly wished to improve relations with China. In fact, when I called on her before leaving for Beijing, she instructed me in one sentence. She said: "I am in a box so far as relations with China are concerned, and I want us to get out of that box." And then we talked about other matters so her intention was quite clear and this was in 1969 when she had not yet established her supremacy in the Congress Party. It was going to happen later that year and yet less than seven years after the 1962 War, she was conscious that the two countries had to at least normalize the relations even if they could not go back to the earlier days. So, I got to Beijing in April 1969, somebody from the embassy came to Hong Kong to escort me to Beijing. As we crossed the border this gentleman who came to escort me from Beijing, who knew Chinese, apparently heard the border gaurds saying: "This is the man". Those were very bad days in our relationship with China. In my four and half years in Beijing, I was received only once by the Vice-Minister of Foreign Affairs in charge of Asia, Han Nianlong, and that too in 1971, i.e., two years and many months after my arrival in Beijing. Kishan Rana had joined me by that time, China had gained her right for a place in UN, Indira Gandhi wrote letters to heads of state of government explaining our case in regard to the problems in East Pakistan, and there was a letter for Premier Zhou Enlai, which I delivered to Han Nianlong. That was the only time he received me. Those days of a lot of propaganda against India I used to go very often to the Chinese Foreign Office to be received either by the Deputy Director or for a few months by the Director, who later became Ambassador to Turkey. We used to engage in discussion about India-China relations, and how to improve them. This went on for about a year when on the 1st of May 1970 the heads of mission were lined up on the ramparts of the Tiananmen and to our surprise Chairman Mao was present there. So there we were lined up in order of precedence, and I was virtually the last one just after the British CAD. Chairman Mao went to each head of mission, shaking hands. Then he came to the British CAD, who congratulated Chairman Mao on the satellite which the Chinese had sent up then Chairman Mao replied, "My greetings to the Queen, and we wish her the same success". Then he came to me and said: "My greetings to President Giri and to Prime Minister Indira Gandhi", and then, he uttered the famous words: "How long can we keep on quarrelling like this?" Then he kept quiet for a moment and said "Let us be friends again". So this was about the famous Mao smile and handshake which all of you know about. There were, of course, many reasons for the expression of the desire to be friends again. There was the international scene, American jets had started bombarding Cambodia in April 1970, but basically I took it to mean that the Chinese Government was reciprocating the desire which I had expressed on behalf of the Government of India to improve the relations. From then on, things began to improve, between the Embassy and the Foreign Office and there was more forthrightness in talking to us and this went on until April 1971. In between, Mrs. Gandhi had gone to elections, she won with a thumping majority. Prime Minister Zhou Enlai, at one party, asked me to send his congratulations to Mrs. Gandhi. And then came the problem in East Pakistan. The way I perceived it, the Chinese stepped back as soon as it became clear that Indo-Pak relations were going to take a nosedive over the problem in East Pakistan. In August 1971, I came to Delhi for consultations, on 9th of August The Indo-Soviet Treaty of Peace was concluded. Obviously all this had an effect upon Chinese thinking. But I want to share an open secret. Even at that time, despite the lukewarm attitude in Beijing and despite the corresponding negative thoughts in the Foreign Office in Delhi, Mrs. Gandhi was quite clear that the effort to improve relations must continue. In 1971 during one of my meetings with Mrs. Gandhi I got a clearance from her to propose exactly the same thing. I went back to Beijing in September 1971, the Lin Biao incident had taken place, the leadership was busy with the aftermath and there wasn't much of a response. Then by October things had hotted up between India and Pakistan, China had become a permanent member of the Security Council, and obviously that was not the time, so far as the Chinese were concerned, to think of exchange of Ambassadors between India and China.

So, during the Indo-Pakistan War, the situation was tense, and there was apprehension that the Chinese might intervene and we spent two weeks and more wondering as to what was going to happen. But in this connection, I must go back before the War. About a week before the war began I had a conversation with the Direction of the Asia Division, the gentleman who became China's Ambassador to Turkey afterwards. We had a long discussion, with myself explaining what was happening in East Pakistan etc. and towards the end, he said to me: "Mr. CAD, you should understand, that China will act in accordance with international law." I don't know what kind of expression I had on my face, I probably gave him the impression that I hadn't understood what he was saying, so as we came out he walked up to the gate to see me off, he repeated that sentence. So there was a feeling I gathered that China was not going to intervene, militarily at least, in the conflict. The war was over by 16th December and on 17th December, I was called to the Foreign Office, and handed over a note of protest against Indian troops crossing the Sikkim border. We wondered as to why this kind of note because the Indian Army was engaged in various fronts and would not be foolish enough to cross the Sikkim border. But Kishan told me not to bother, this is just a show of solidarity with Pakistan. This note we sent to Delhi.

After the war, it took a long time for the Chinese to make up there mind that the time was ripe for the process of normalisation to begin. I had left by that time, but I must recount another incident which touched me quite a lot. November, 29 used to be the Albanian Day and Albania was the most important friend of China during that period. The Albanian Ambassador was the most important diplomat and a reception was organized by him in the Peking Hotel. I was there, the normal practice was that after the second course, the host would make a speech and the Chinese would reply. After the second course, no speech, it was only after the ice cream was served that the speeches began, and of course the Chinese guest attacked India on Indo-Pak conflict and I walked out. This kept on happening from the 29th November till the 16th December. I must have attended four or five banquets during that period, and no speech was made when the second course was served. Speeches took place only after ice cream. Later on, a Pakistan diplomat told me that the Chinese had indicated that they would like the Indian CAD to complete his meal before he walked out. So, I would enjoy the courses plus the ice cream and then had my walk out — my wife following suit with a full stomach.

I have dealt with this India-Pakistan-China triangle because even today, it bedevils our relationship with China. I wanted to tell you as to how it affected the improvement in Sino-Indian relations even at that time. Since it is a long standing problem, this triangle has to be looked into. It's not going to be easy to normalize relations without finding a solution to this problem. The border question has to be settled, the level of trust and confidence necessary between two friends will not be there finally, until the border question is settled fairly and equitably. But we must not forget that the other problem which faces us is what is perceived in India as China's support to Pakistan against India. May be our perceptions are wrong, may be there's another side to the story, but this is the perception in this country by and large. And I believe having worked for more than four years in Beijing trying to mend the relationship, trying to begin the process of normalization, I believe that this full normalization is not going to be possible until this [Sino-Pak collaboration] problem is taken care of. Either India accepts the point of view of China, or China modifies its stand. This is not to say that the process of normalization in other spherers should not continue, it must of course. May be that process of normalization would bring about a situation where it would be easier to solve the border question, and to deal with India-Pakistan-China triangle. May be the intervention of trade, economic relations, other kinds of cooperations would help us in arriving at a normal situation and we must pursue it. After all let us not forget that we are saying the same thing to Pakistan and Bangladesh, we are saying to Pakistan that of course we must discuss Kashmir, but let us also proceed in other spheres, and we are saying to Bangladesh that of course we must have a satisfactory agreement on sharing of river water but let us also proceed elsewhere. We in India, need also to recognise that China has become a global player, economically and politically, therefore, we need to recognize that China has certain other preoccupations, and we need to recognize that in those other preoccupations there could be a question mark in China's mind as to what India's attitude would be.

C.V. RANGANATHAN

47

MEMORIES OF AN INDIAN AMBASSADOR: 1987-1991

I was assigned to Beijing for the second time in my career in 1987. My previous posting there was as First Secretary in the Embassy from 1965-68. I understood then what the proverbial Rip Van Winkle must have felt when he woke up to find his world transformed after a 20 year sleep!

The hundreds of portraits and statues of Mao Zedong had given way to just one at the Tiananmen Square. Some old messengers of the Embassy who joined in Red Guard demonstrations against us in 1967 received me warmly at the airport. Shiny skyscrapers overshadowed stodgy Soviet-style structures. Air hostesses went out-of-the-way to make passengers comfortable instead of thrusting red-books at their faces. The last Indian diplomatic walk-out from a Chinese-hosted Reception receded more than a good 15 years. Many models of Japanese cars plied the streets where traffic jams were common. Foreign tourists crowded the Friendship Store. So many signs of a China which was so different from the sixties. While it was evident that China had changed, I had the confidence that things could also change for the better in Sino-Indian relations.

Two days before I arrived in May 1987, Mr. P.N. Haksar came as special envoy of Prime Minister Rajiv Gandhi accompanied by Mr. V. V. Paranjpe. The evening of my arrival we were invited to a fabulous dinner by the late Prof. Wu Xiaoling, a close friend of Mr. V.V. Paranjpe and a great Sanskrit scholar. During the dinner Mr. Haksar and Prof. Wu Xiaoling recited verses from Kalidasa's *Meghdoot* in Sanskrit. Mr. Haksar had by then finished rounds of discussions with then Premier Zhao Ziyang and senior Chinese officials. The message conveyed by Mr. Haksar was that India was prepared to be forward-looking, that India did not consider China to be an adversary and that both countries must make efforts to put the past behind. A clear signal of India's desire to work towards better understanding and improved relations with China and thus conveyed at an authoritative level.

Within two weeks of this visit, there was the transit halt in Beijing of the then Minister of External Affairs, Mr. N.D. Tiwari, on his way back to India from Pyongyang. Discussions with the Chinese Vice Foreign Minister Liu Shuqing took place after the evening banquet. The background to the visit was the situation created on the ground over the previous two years in a small section of the Kameng frontier in Arunachal Pradesh, over which there was a measure of mutual dissatisfaction. Indian and Chinese troops had stationed themselves in close proximity to each other in an action-reaction sequence. There was wide publicity given to each side's viewpoint thus leading to speculation in domestic and international circles that India and China were headed in the direction of an escalation of tension along the border, if not an armed conflict. Discussions during the Tiwari visit led to a lowering of public disputation and the determination that differences over the territorial question would not impede the development of relations over a wide gamut of subjects.

In December 1997 came the visit to India of the Chinese Vice Foreign Minister Liu Shuqing with a formal invitation to Prime Minister Rajiv Gandhi to visit China. The Prime Minister's immediate acceptance of the invitation came as a big relief to the Chinese side. It was a concrete sign that India meant to follow-up on the messages conveyed during the Haksar mission.

My familiarity with Chinese language and an earlier assignment in Beijing were not the only factors which helped in my becoming fully acclimatised to the China which was so different in the eighties when compared to the sixties. The Embassy was staffed with officers, all of whom knew Chinese, were excellent students of China and who enjoyed a wide network of contacts with the China that had "opened up". Led by Counsellor Shivashankar Menon, they briefed me thoroughly in each area of their operations and assisted me in all my calls on senior Chinese officials. Amongst the vastly expanded diplomatic and journalist corps, there were atleast three others who knew me from earlier times. Among the Ambassadors with whom I enjoyed discussions was Troyanovsky from the erstwhile Soviet Union. Coming to China after a two-year stint in Moscow I was fully aware of the vastly improved tenor of Sino-Soviet relations consequent on Gorbachev's assumption of office in 1985. Hearing Troyanovsky urging for better relations between India and China was a refreshing contrast from Ambassador Vorontsov's discouraging remarks on this subject, a decade earlier in Delhi. From Troyanovsky one got a good sense of the several areas of political, economic and military interactions which were rapidly re-opening between Beijing and Moscow and the softening Chinese posture over their three problems with Moscow.

1988 was a year of preparations for the Rajiv Gandhi visit. A few delegations from the Congress-I Party visited China and were well received at high levels. They were told that the Prime Minister would be received warmly at the highest level, that his visit would give the momentum so necessary in relations and that it was seen as a foundation-laying exercise from which both India and China would benefit. Similarly a few hand-picked leading journalists were despatched to China to gauge the sentiment in China and to help prepare the public-opinion base in India. A few days before the visit I was interviewed about Indian expectations from the visit by the leading newspaper *Renmin Ribao* (People's Daily), the *Xinhua* Agency and by Radio Beijing. People had forgotten when an Indian Ambassador was last given such positive media prominence in Beijing. The editorial in the *People's Daily* on the day of Rajiv Gandhi's arrival in Beijing, on a cold winter morning in December 1988 was warm and very friendly. The two preparatory visits undertaken by Foreign Secretary, K.P.S. Menon, ensured that the visit itself would pass off smoothly and that the substantive discussions during the visit and the bilateral agreements to be signed would lead to beneficial results.

The visit of the Prime Minister of India to China after a gap of more than three decades, which had seen friendship turning into hostility prior to the gradual normalisation of relations, was of great symbolic and substantial significance. Enough has been said of these aspects elsewhere. Less reported perhaps is the deep impact that the attractive Rajiv and Sonia couple imprinted on the youth of Beijing and Shanghai and the quiet contrasts they drew with the aging Chinese leadership. Their appreciation and identification with the image of an attractive and modern India which the couple reflected was evident in the thunderous applause accorded by the students of Qinghua University, when they were addressed by Rajiv Gandhi. Official talks with State President Yang Shangkun, Supremo Deng Xiaoping, Premier Li Peng, General Secretary of the Communist Party of China Zhao Ziyang were conducted in a warm and friendly atmosphere, with the leaders of both sides carrying on conversations as though there had never been any break in highest level dialogues between India and China. The highlight of the visit to the Forbidden City by the Indian Prime Minister and his party was the first-ever opening of the private chambers and collections of some early Qing Dynasty emperors. The astronomical predictions which guided sowing and other agricultural operations inscribed in stone were explained in great detail at the Temple of Heaven.

Apart from the official programme in Beijing, one of the highlights which pleased me very much was the reception organised by the Embassy for our Prime Minister and party at the State Guest house complex at Villa No. 18 in Diaoyutai. Normally reserved for head of states, kings and queens, the Chinese opened this Villa for our Prime Minister. The Chinese generously allowed the Embassy to use the spacious Reception halls of this Villa for an evening reception, where leading Chinese academic figures and professors who devoted their lives to classical studies on India attended, along with Chinese Ministers, former Ambassadors to India, senior Foreign Office officials, leading representatives of the burgeoning business groups, dancers, musicians and young Chinese scholars who had studied in India. The galaxy included the doyen of Indian studies of Beijing University, Prof. Ji Xianlin, along with the translator of *Ramacharitra Manas*, Prof. Jing Dinghan, an old student from Santiniketan (who happened to be Mrs. Indira Gandhi's classmate) Prof. Wei Fengjiang, Prof. Huang Xinchuan, Director of the Institute of Asia-Pacific Studies (formerly of South Asian Studies), Prof. Wu Baihui, a well known interpreter of Indian philosophical texts and scores of senior associates from the Chinese Academy of Social Sciences and other higher educational institutions like Beida etc. engaged in studies of contemporary South Asia. Each of them presented writings on India to the Prime Minister. My satisfaction with the fullest Chinese cooperation in ensuring the success of this moving event was particularly complete since my proposal to have this reception at the Embassy premises was turned down by the advance Indian Security Party in yet another instance of arbitrary decision-making and interference in the programmes of visiting dignitaries not warranted by a proper appreciation of local conditions.

Rajiv Gandhi's departure to Xian on the morning after the conclusion of the Beijing segment of the visit by special plane was delayed by some three hours on account of foggy conditions in Beijing and Xian. Throughout the delay, I was impressed by the close attention to the details of adjustments to the programme and the up-to-the-minute information that was provided by the Chinese Protocol Department to some of the impatient higher-ups in the Indian Party! The Xian programme consisting of visits to the Terra-Cotta Warriors, the Xian Museum, the Mosque, the ancient City Walls and the evening banquet by the Governor of Shaanxi Province etc. went off smoothly, the only practical adjustment being to the banquet which was delayed by an hour and a half. From Xian the Prime Minister's party flew to Shanghai. An extensive visit was arranged to a suburb of Shanghai to the Malu township in Jiading county. There we saw many Township and Village Enterprises (TVE) (one of the proud hallmarks of Dengist Reforms) and had an insight into the graphic Chinese saying of "Leave land-tilling without leaving the village" (*li tu buli xiang*), and "Enter factory without entering the city" (*jin chang bujin cheng*). Small scale industrial production of consumer requirements, ancillary components of larger industry, food processing units were the features of the TVEs here. As in other parts of China, these enterprises located near urban capitals feed the requirements of the bigger towns and have been the engines of contemporary economic growth in China. The mandatory drive through Shanghai city to view the sights from its days as a British "concession" attracted vast crowds who were blocked in Shanghai's narrow streets by the security authorities to allow the long motorcade to pass unhindered. Chinese media publicity over the previous few days to the visit as much as the blocked roads ensured that hundreds of thousands of enthusiastic public applauded as the motorcade wound its way to the State Guest House. Here Zhu Rongji, then Mayor of Shanghai and now the Premier of China, hosted a luncheon where he spoke eloquently about Shanghai and the proposed Pudong Development Project, the economic prospects of Shanghai and its vast social problems. A few hours after that the Prime Minister and his party left for India.

The Minister-in-waiting Qu Yuanjing and his wife, with whom my wife and I waited on the tarmac till the Air India plane went out of view, turned around and hugged both of us and in an uncharacteristic gesture kissed me on both cheeks. We both obviously were greatly relieved that the visit passed-off smoothly. Since that date not an opportunity is missed by Chinese spokesmen on occasions of high-level exchanges between Indian and Chinese leaders to recall the visit and its historic significance. The impact on the Chinese psyche and the frequent recall of the importance of this visit is a proof positive of its outstanding success, no matter how critics in our plural society view it!

Reference to the Rajiv Gandhi visit would not be complete if one forgot to mention the uncharacteristically large delegation of VIPs who accompanied him. Former Ministers Narasimha Rao, Dinesh Singh, Shankaranand, Natwar Singh were in his entourage. Secretaries to the Government, K.P.S. Menon, Ahluwalia, G.K. Arora, S.K. Misra (Civil Aviation), Veeraraghavan (Culture), Gowarikar (Science) were also there amongst other officers from the Ministry of External Affairs and the Prime Minister's Office. Nearly a hundred Indian journalists came either in the same aircraft or separately. The unsung heroes of the visit were my Embassy colleagues who managed the logistics of separate meetings for practically all of the above VIPs with their Chinese counterparts, in addition to looking after their private requirements of special diet, shopping etc. Ably coordinated by Counsellor S.S. Menon, the officers and staff performed outstandingly and my thank-you Reception for the Chinese and Indian colleagues was small compensation for the grinding demands they made on themselves for over two months in November and December of 1988. My wife went through self-taught crash courses on the Forbidden City, the famous artistic street, Liulichang, and the historic old city of Beijing to guide Mrs Sonia Gandhi on her separate tours.

1989 was remarkable for the Tiananmen Square episode and the Gorbachev visit to China in the latter half of May when the Square was fully and most colourfully occupied by demonstrators. From a couple of days after the former General Secretary of the Party Hu Yaobang's death, the Square began filling-up. Intellectuals, students from practically all the higher institutions of learning were joined by workers in massive demonstrations. The age-old big character posters, leaflets, pamphlets, banners sprouted almost everywhere. The Army which was called in from the outskirts of Beijing to disperse demonstrators was blocked with the public refusing right-of-way to the hundreds of their transport vehicles. Public expression of dissatisfaction to which our avid Chinese readers in the Embassy had access, ranged from the serious to the trivial. The "have-nots" from every layer of society and those who saw no sign of personal benefit from Chinese reforms documented their grievances. Opportunistic politicians sprouted from amongst the youth as well as articulate self-appointed leaders. To one who was witness to the years of the Cultural Revolution, the big difference in the demonstrator's attitude, reflecting the changed environment in China and the world was their readiness to share their grievances, real or alleged, with foreigners. The foreign media played a direct role in the turmoil to a much greater extent than it did on the occasion of the mourning for Zhou Enlai, more than a decade earlier. We mounted a 24-hour monitoring of events in the Embassy and were able to predict the exact moment, where high level internal bickerings would lead to the decision on the use of actual force to disperse the demonstrators. Gorbachev arrived to find the ceremonial welcome in the Square cancelled, no official engagements were possible for him at the Great Hall of the People and the major achievement of full Sino-Soviet normalisation was overshadowed by the happenings in Beijing.

There was a fall-out on our Embassy of the Tiananmen Square event. A very high level delegation of Indian writers consisting of U.S. Anantamurthy, Mrinal Pande and others arrived in Beijing a couple of days before the use of force. Chinese authorities were understandably keen to continue agreed exchanges and important visits with foreign countries in an effort to show that Beijing was normal. Our delegation was put up in a hotel near the centre of student rallies near the university area. Since some of their interlocutors sided with the students, they were not available for planned meetings with them. Worse still, after the demonstrators were dispersed from the Square, communications with our delegation were cut off. Accompanied by my colleagues, I visited them in their hotel on the same afternoon of the entry of tanks into the Square. My ride to their hotel enabled me to see the burnt-out remains of tanks, lorries and trucks which were on their way to the Square. The Indian writers were told that the rest of their programme was cancelled and there was nothing to do except to return to India. The difficulty was in obtaining airline seats for them as the hosts had disappeared.

The other fall-out from these events was more direct, leading to some difficult decisions. For a couple of days after the clearance of the Square of demonstrators, patrolling armed soldiers from armoured carriers shot at random into the high rise buildings where foreigners stayed along the Changanjie — the diplomatic area of Beijing. A few shells dropped into the apartments of foreigners including some of our staff quarters. On one occasion when I was on the phone around noon with the Joint Secretary in the MEA, Vijay Nambiar, he could pick up the sound of light gun fire let-off by Chinese patrolling troops near the Embassy. We decided then that it would be best if for some time till full normalcy was restored in Beijing, wives and children of officers and staff were repatriated to India. This was done soon thereafter. The Indian Writer's delegation was also on the same aircraft. The wives and children returned to Beijing after normalcy returned sometime in late July. Most of the Western, South East Asian and some African Embassies also temporarily repatriated their families. Schools for foreign children in Beijing closed down for 4-6 weeks. Mr. and Mrs. B.K. Nehru visited China as tourists in early June. I packed them off from Beijing two days before the tanks entered the Square to Guilin and Guangzhou. They heard about the events only 4 days after, when they reached Hong Kong.

Fairly soon after Jiang Zemin's appointment as General Secretary of the CPC, it so happened that Mr Ghulam Nabi Azad, then one of the General Secretaries of the Congress Party, scheduled a transit visit through Beijing on his way back from Pyongyang. This was a good opportunity to be received by the new Chinese General Secretary. My request was met immediately and we became the first foreign delegation to be seen by Mr Jiang Zemin after he became General Secretary. For the rest of my tenure in Beijing I had three other occasions to be received by him when delegations from Indian political parties visited China.

In July 1989, Foreign Secretary S.K. Singh visited Beijing for the first Joint Working Group meeting set up to discuss the boundary and other related bilateral and international questions. He was received by Premier Li Peng. In the discussions, the Premier frankly acknowledged the lack of Chinese expertise in controlling mobs, the bitter memories of the chaos during the Great Proletarian Cultural Revolution and the paramount need to maintain stability as the highest value in society while thanking the Government of India for its understanding attitude when referring to the recent turmoil in China. During the autumn, as in previous years, we participated in the tour engaged for Heads of Missions by the Chinese Foreign Office. This time it was to Jiangxi Province. An important footnote was the picnic at the scenic Lushan mountain where in the stormy meetings of the Politburo of the CPC in 1959, Mao Zedong victimised Marshal Peng Dehuai. Lushan has one of the most attractive botanical parks I have ever visited with trees and horticultural species from all over the world.

In early 1990, Qian Qichen the Foreign Minister visited India when a different government under Mr. V.P. Singh's Prime Ministership was in power and when Mr. I.K. Gujral was the External Affairs Minister. Hearing Mr. Singh's very affirmative remarks about the Rajiv Gandhi visit and its significance, the Chinese Foreign Minister said at a Press Conference that he could see with his own eyes that there was a consensus cutting across all parties on India's relations with China. Through 1990 and till mid-1991 when I left Beijing on transfer for India there was a brisk exchange of official and non-official delegations from various spheres.

I left in May 1991 after a 4-year assignment which saw events fully packed with significance for China and for India-China relations. While it was a privilege to have witnessed some of these events, life in China was very satisfying for a variety of less publicised and therefore perhaps more fulfilling engagements.

Just a few months before the Rajiv Gandhi visit, the Embassy had started a journal, "India Digest" which was the Chinese version of the well acclaimed English version of the same name which my colleague, the then Commissioner in Hong Kong, P.P. D'souza had launched. For the Beijing edition we had added contributions from Chinese scholars on India and a page on comments from our Chinese readers. It was heartening to see how well this publication was received in China and print-orders had to be increased, a small reflection of the more open intellectual atmosphere in China. Like the Annual Children's painting competition held by *Shankar's Weekly*, we too had a similar event in Beijing. Selected school children from Beijing and the Provinces participated along with children of the Indian Embassy. Subjects were allotted by a panel of Chinese judges who adjudicated the competition held in a spirit of enormous good-will and fun. Gifts were exchanged, snacks and drinks consumed and impromptu songs and dances performed.

My several visits to Prof. Ji Xianlin, the doyen of classical scholars on India at Beijing University ("Beida" as we called it) were always very educative. He was instrumental, at Tan Chung's initiative, in getting me to address in Chinese, an international seminar on Dunhuang and Turfan studies organised by the Chinese Academy of Social Sciences. The Embassy organised functions to confer the *Desikottama* award from Visva-Bharati University on Prof. Wu Xiaoling. On another occasion we launched the Chinese translation of volumes of Tulsidas' *Ramcharitra Manas* undertaken by Prof. Jing Dinghan. We presented on more than one occasion, collections of classics and contemporary books from India in English and Hindi to the Beijing Library, Institute of Foreign Languages and Beida.

One of the memorable tours undertaken by my wife and I was to Xinjiang and Gansu. In Kashgar we visited the old "India House" made famous by Lady Macartney's memories, where the Sathes stayed as the last Indian representatives. The old and now dilapitated "India House" and its spacious grounds was dominated by a multi-storeyed hotel, the favourite lodge of truckers and traders from Pakistan. From Urumqi we drove in the company of my Danish colleague and his family to Turfan and then via Hami to Dunhuang. The Chinese guide from the Xinjiang branch of the Foreign Office accompanied us. His family and that of the driver, brought delicious packed food for us, along with bottles of beer and drinks to last us over the three-day drive. With the Tian Shan mountains on one side and the desert on the other, one saw such a variegated landscape. A dip in the famous Kerez (underground springs of delicious freshwater) was most reviving as were the grapes and peaches of Turfan. At Dunhuang, I established contacts with the director of the Museum and Grottoes, Prof Duan Wenjie which were consolidated by Dr. Kapila Vatsyayan and the IGNCA.

The Embassy was provided a gardener, Lao Yu, who was an expert in rose-cultivation. Thanks to his tender and full-time administration, the Embassy won the best "flower-garden category" of the annual competition run by the Diplomatic Personnel Service Bureau. These and scores of other personal memories of travels, of meetings, of chance encounters, some good friendships and dozens of outstanding meals would remain as souvenirs of the culmination of a career connected with China.

KISHAN S. RANA

48

A YOUNG INDIAN DIPLOMAT IN CHINA IN THE 1960s AND 1970s

I went to China on my first substantive Foreign Service assignment in July 1963, well before I completed the 2-year Chinese language programme at Hong Kong University. I packed off from the relative comfort of a familiar academic environment, thanks to an on-the-spot decision by Foreign Secretary M.J. Desai. A couple of months earlier, while transiting through Hong Kong airport he had heeded a complaint voiced by the Head of Mission at Beijing P.K. Bannerji, who had lamented that he did not have a single Chinese-speaking officer. "Take one of these youngsters", he replied, pointing to Bhupat Oza, then in the first year of his language studies, and myself in the second year. Before I knew what was happening, I was posted to China! Quite a distant cry from the styles of Foreign Service Board meetings, and the structured formalities of decision-making on personnel issues! This was the first of my encounters with chance, a powerful force which took me on a career full of excitement and discovery.

I travelled from Hong Kong by train, with senior colleague A.K. Damodaran and his family. He was moving from Bonn to take up his assignment as the First Secretary (Political) and the No. 2 in the Indian mission. He became in time a valued elder brother, graced as he has been with a particularly calm and generous temperament, and a degree of concern for others, which is a rarity in any profession, much less in our Service. That day as we progressed through the measured formalities of crossing into China, walking across the famous bridge at Shenzhen, which marked the separation of the British colony from the mainland, it was difficult to restrain my enthusiasm. One was finally getting to the country which has been such a parallel – and contrast– to India, the other Asian giant embarked on its own drama of human and social engineering.

In Beijing I found that life in the Indian Embassy was one of camaraderie and immersion in a collective enterprise. It was only much later, when I served and observed elsewhere, that I understood the extraordinary character of our Mission and its special *esprit de corps.* The India-China Border War of 1962 represented for all Indians a huge trauma. For someone immersed in Chinese language studies at that time at Hong Kong University's Language Institute, it became a routine humiliation to study in class an editorial from a mainland or Hong Kong journal, scorning India's case, or to listen to comments form a Chinese perspective on the unfolding events. Living in that environment one felt even more sharply the disbelief of most Indians that things could go so wrong, so fast. It put under cloud one's fascination with China and the saga of its nation-building. But on reaching Beijing I found that it did not extinguish one's admiration. If anything, it sharpened curiosity and the quest for personal understanding, as a "beginner China-watcher". And truthfully, it also at times engendered a kind of "schadenfreude", some glee at China's own troubles, an attitude of "it serves them right!". Thus the little Indian community in the Chinese capital, made up exclusively of the diplomats and staff, found its own equilibrium in a cocktail of emotions. There was a collective sense or purpose at being located in a country at whose hands, we sensed, our nation had suffered. For myself, the other dominant mood was of excitement at living in a place where things were happening, not all of them clearly discernible; where information was at a premium. Among the small number of foreign diplomats and even fewer journalists, there was a special affinity, and friendships came easily. For the handful of us who spoke Chinese — or as non-Chinese would call it, the Mandarin dialect — there was direct access to local people, despite the severe restraints which were then enforced for the most innocent of such contacts. It may seem hard to imagine today, but for foreigners, China of yesteryear practised the most stringent internal controls, hardly in any after place found. In that environment the Indian Embassy came to win a reputation for professionalism, which has endured over the decades.

It was a privilege to be on such a team.

In the early 1960s there were barely 35 diplomatic missions in Beijing, and just around 5 international correspondents. Besides the twice daily staple of the English language Hsinhua (Xinhua) News Agency bulletin, there were the 4 national dailies in Chinese, and a handful of weeklies and other periodicals. Those in the Embassy who travelled to Hong Kong on weekly courier duty with the diplomatic bag (and all of us took turns, from the Charge d' Affaires downwards) could liven up the boring 30 hour journey by scrounging for local newspapers, simply unavailable in the capital, for little nuggets of local information. That journey was rather more adventurous than most would have preferred, starting off from Beijing at 6 o'clock in the morning in a Russian IL-14 or IL-18 aircraft (country-cousins of the World War II vintage Dakota and the like), with refueling stops at 3 cities before reaching Guangzhou, for an overnight halt in a hotel, and the next morning a train to the border, the walk across the bridge, and on to the cornucopia of consumerism which the Crown Colony represented even then. Bad weather at any point on the air journey meant an unscheduled halt at Changsha or Wuhan, when fellow-travellers — the odd diplomat or businessman among the passengers — learnt the virtues of bonding!

Right up to the 1970s when I came back to China as a First Secretary and second-ranking diplomat in the Mission, travel by resident foreigners was limited to a radius of 20 km. from the centre of the capital, the Forbidden City, the 3 permitted exceptions being the Great Wall and the Ming Tombs — both located to the west, at a distance of 45 and 40 km. respectively, and the airport to the east. All other trips required the specific authorization of the Foreign Ministry, and in the usual course, only the "open" cities could be visited — Shanghai, Hangzhou, Nanjing and the like. The list expanded gradually, when places like Chongqing in Sichuan were made accessible. The travel privileges first went to the "friendly" countries, in a subtle political hierarchy of favour-dispensation. One could say that for China, this was no more than the traditional way of dealing with foreigners.

For someone who spoke Chinese, travel was a special joy, because one had direct access to new experiences, and could learn a bit about the provinces and the far-flung regions which were not accessible as a matter of course. Sometimes there were unexpected encounters with people one could not meet in the tightly regulated conditions of life for foreigners in China.

I vividly recall a journey made from Beijing to Shanghai by train sometime in 1964. In the "soft" class 4-berth sleeper I had only one travelling companion — a professor of some sort (as I made out from his conversation with his wife and teenage daughter who had come to see him off at the railway station). After the train started we began a conversation and I was delighted to have a distinguished academic as a companion. We had dinner together in the dining-car, quite a fine meal. The professor gradually disclosed that he had in fact visited India and knew Gandhiji's secretary Mahadeo Desai, whom he had met in Poona. Respecting the circumstances and the context, I steered clear of political or sensitive issues, but got along very well with him. The next morning when I woke up I found that sometime during the night we had acquired a third travel-mate, a rather loud person who turned out to be an army officer. He engaged in a noisy conversation with the professor on international affairs, speaking of unspecified "reactionary countries" and how China would deal with them. I ignored him, and some time later, when we were alone in the train corridor, the professor said in a soft voice that some people had not liked the idea of his conversation with an Indian diplomat, and it was better if we did not have lunch together on the train before it reached Shanghai. I replied that I understood, and hoped I had not inadvertently created difficulty for him. He laughed and said that it was a small matter. There is a footnote to that chance encounter. When I narrated the incident later to one of our senior China scholars, he said that the professor had been his teacher, and that he was also one of the distinguished India experts in the Chinese Academy of Sciences (later the Chinese Academy of Social Sciences). The professor had been too discreet to speak much about himself. It was inconceivable at that time that open and friendly contacts could be sustained between the Embassy and such personalities.

Another such chance meeting took place during my second China assignment, in early-1971, during the course of a tour for the diplomatic corps to the historic cities of Luoyang and Xian. As we visited a museum devoted to stone tablets commemorating the deeds of historical figures of the Song dynasty, I paused to admire an inscription in Chinese and Sanskrit – quite rare – recalling the journey of Faxian to India. One museum staff member, with whom I had been in conversation volunteered the observation: "With such a shared history, how can we persist in our existing problems!". It was good to learn that even in the harsh climate of what then was the last phase of the Cultural Revolution, there were some who made private gestures to affirm that our relationships should be rather different.

In early 1964 Jagat S Mehta took over as the Head of Mission, the de facto ambassador but officially carrying the title of "Charge d'Affairs ad interim", in keeping with the formally reduced level of representation in the two capitals, which was to persist till 1976. He provided strong leadership to the Embassy, and became for many of us a persuasive role model. For the junior-most diplomatic official, as I remained till fellow China-specialist, Bhupat Oza, arrived on the scene a year later, it meant working on a series of essays and studies on specific themes, ranging from aspects of China's economy, to the education system and the pattern of basic technical education and culture. Under Jagat, the pattern was established, which was to persist for many years, that the Embassy would devote energy to as much in-depth reportage as was possible, given the scarcity of data and independent information. The goal was thematic analysis covering the internal scene, with the object of understanding the complex nation, and disseminating our reports within the governmental system in Delhi and to other Indian Missions. This was the classic mode of dispatch-writing, modelled in style on the British diplomatic method. I recall particularly well the papers written on China's "part-work part-study schools", a bit akin to vocational schools in other countries, as also the early notes on the intense debate which was emerging on cultural issues around early 1965. For instance, little could anyone imagine that the controversy which suddenly erupted in mid-1965 over a sensitive film, "Early Spring" (which some friends and I managed to see in the few weeks it was screened, before being banned), would herald the storm of the Cultural Revolution. No one could then decipher the complex and indirect signals. But even for those who were ignorant of the master-plan saw that an artificial controversy was being generated. Cultural objects like that film were being offered deliberately as scapegoats. The ulterior purpose was invisible till the time I ended my first tenure in China in September 1965.

It was in 1964 that some of us took the initiative to set up a lunch club, consisting exclusively of Second and Third Secretaries — the foot-soldiers in every embassy. The first meeting took place in my home with the 6 founders, and the group soon expanded to 12, which we set as the outer limit. New participants were admitted only when someone left on transfer, or was promoted — in the latter case, the person was ceremoniously thrown out after a farewell lunch. When the lunch sessions became too convivial, ending at 4 P.M. or so Jagat Mehta expressed a bit of displeasure, and gave us the sobriquet "The Tails of Mission Lunch Club". The name stuck, and the group was in vigour at least till the mid-70s when I was invited to the monthly meetings as one of the founders!

In the diplomatic missions (other than the socialist embassies of that time), there were a handful of Chinese-speakers. Roping in some Chinese personnel who either worked in embassies, or were teachers to diplomats learning the language — and were thus permitted to have contacts with these foreigners — some of us cobbled together a "club" where we could practise speaking skills, and enjoy the cultural and culinary ambiance of the capital. The socialist embassies had a phalanx of language-specialists, but not all of them spoke English, and in addition the Westerners had their inhibitions in dealing with them. We, on the other hand, straddled both camps. Clearly, from the perspective of the Chinese authorities who kept us under scrutiny, this was a "permitted" contact network, perhaps useful from their perspective in giving an insight into the diplomat fraternity. Special care was exerted by all the participants of what we came to call the "Yenjing Club" (after one of the historical names of Beijing) to steer clear of any issue which might embarrass our Chinese friends, or worse, lead to the end of that experiment. We met every couple of weeks, either in the home of a diplomat-member, or by preference, in one of the 140 restaurants that operated in the city, sometimes after a visit to the Beijing Opera, or one of the many regional operas, or to a film or the circus. Friendship developed, even within the constraints of cautious conversation, and we learnt a little of the fun of Chinese life, like the wine-drinking games. And we were zealous in our search for varied and exquisite cuisine — which was then outrageously inexpensive. Of course such a club could not survive the Cultural Revolution, and when I got back to China in 1970 such open contact, however innocent, was unthinkable. I cherish the frayed navy-blue club tie which David Wilson — then fellow-member and now Lord Wilson — had obtained from Hong Kong for each of us, inscribed all over with the Chinese characters "Yan Jing".

One great institution of our China experience was the diplomatic tour, an annual event which brought to the fore the great organizational talent of the Chinese system. The traditional pattern was that the Head of Mission and spouse were invited by the Foreign Ministry as guests, together with one other diplomat to accompany them. Under the latter provision, junior officers had their chance to visit far places, including some not on the list of "open" cities of that time, in the course of what was usually a week-long excursion. Sometimes the tour covered places which in those days were completely inaccessible, save under special arrangements — such as the lengthy car journey which took one group to the "national model" agricultural village of Dalian. This was also the opportunity to practise and utilize language skills. It was a challenge for the language-speakers to ferret out some local information which hopefully added to one's fund of knowledge, or gave a special insight, even while this was resented by the Protocol Department "handlers" who were usually watchful to see that this particular segment of their charges did not stray too far. *The group travelled mainly by special train, accompanied by a Foreign Ministry Vice Minister, the Chief of Protocol*, and a bevy of officials. The hospitality was lavish, and the provinces vied with one another in offering to the "foreign guests" the best of the local cuisine specialities. If Lawrence Durrel had been around, he would have found a treasure trove of amusing anecdotes and ego jousts within the Diplomatic Corps, given the fact that a shared journey of a week or more brought out some of the rivalries and petty jealousies, already accentuated in the hot-house atmosphere of a restricted diplomatic post. During the car trips the Foreign Ministry took scrupulous care to ensure that the assignment of vehicles were in the correct protocol order, with the Dean of the Corps in the lead, seated naturally in Car No. 1. This led me once to wonder as to the vehicle number of the car in which the Vice Minister travelled, since he seemed always to be ahead, besides, of course, the escort and security convoy. His car bore No. 0 — a perfect compromise!

In 1964 one such trip took us to the fabled Huang Mountain of Anhui province. This mountain range, dotted with Buddhist temples, accessible only by steep foot-track and arduous series of steps, is a place of remarkable scenic beauty and has inspired much Chinese painting and poetry. It also became the revolutionary base of Marshal Chen Yi in 1927, after the collapse of the short-lived co-habitation between the Kuomintang (KMT) and the Communists in Shanghai. In 1964, the Marshal, in his role as China's Foreign Minister, joined us for that particular segment of the trip, his very first return to a region which had many memories for him. As we scrambled up the seemingly endless gradients and steps — much like our own mountain places of pilgrimage — and were lodged in what must have originally been spartan dormitories for the travellers, we caught glimpses of him and wondered at the panorama of emotions which he must have experienced. The photographs I took of the mountain peaks in the early dawn, and of the pine trees along the many perpendicular crags, are a souvenir of a memorable and exhausting journey.

One might ask, did life in the Chinese capital give any special insight which might otherwise not have been available? Of course, one gained some flavour on matters of detail, in the ways narrated above. On the really big hidden events, it gave partial information, which could not always be interpreted fully. For instance, those who lived in Beijing through the hardest years of the suffering and deprivation of the Great Leap Forward, knew that the situation in the interior provinces was hard. But none could fully estimate the scale of the self-inflicted agricultural crisis which unfolded after 1958, immediately following the much-acclaimed initial phase. I recall attending a lecture by the noted Cambridge economist Joan Robinson at Delhi University in 1959, in which she had waxed eloquent about the Great Leap, to an audience composed mainly of students like myself, who could not possibly imagine that a person whose textbooks were mandatory reading, could be so wrong. The impact of the Leap persisted for many years, and was evidenced in the 60s in the efficient system of food coupons and travel permits which enforced tight rationing and also ensured that the cities — which were much better off — did not become magnets to a population exodus. Winston Churchill's memorable phrase describing Russia could equally apply even more forcefully to China: "A riddle, wrapped in a mystery, inside an enigma". Often it took hindsight to interpret the events that took place right under ones' nose. An incident vividly underscores this factor.

In the days of my first assignment, I was a bachelor and shared a rather comfortable house within the Old City with another bachelor officer — it had originally housed our Counsellor, a post left vacant after the post-1962 scaling down in diplomatic representation. We had a couple of good friends who enjoyed dropping in on Sunday mornings, for coffee and conversation. One of them was a young colleague from an Asian country which enjoyed significantly better relations in China than we did, and he was a useful source of information. One morning, probably in early 1965, when this friend came and narrated this experience of a visit by their education minister, who ended his substantive programme with a meeting with Chairman Mao, customary for foreign visitors of that road in those days. Mao asked the visitor about his travels and his impressions. The visitor responded with fulsome praise of the things he had seen, the institutions visited and the education system in general. To this Mao gave a curious reply, saying that the visitor should not believe everything he had been told, and that things were not as good as apparent outwardly. This was said in the presence of the Chinese Education Minster, and we could not figure out what the Chairman had meant. It seemed to go beyond the typical expressions of Chinese politeness, when after the foreign guest who offers fulsome praise is told, in phrases which are part of the ancient syntax, that the praise is not merited. We could not believe that Mao was profoundly dissatisfied with the shape of the education system. Or that the entire polity needed a sharp cleansing action, to usher in a "permanent revolution" as subsequently claimed during the Cultural Revolution. As in the case of the artificial — or rather guided — debate on culture which unfolded at around the same time, we simply did not see the master design of the Great Helmsman.

Another good friend in those days was the journalist Jacques Marcuse, a Belgian who represented AFP in the Chinese capital in the 1960s. At a time when the Western media were represented only by Reuters and this agency, he was a familiar figure, distinguished by his monocle, and his sardonic humour. He had lived in Shanghai in the late 1930s, and knew some of the leading figures from that time; this made him a cynic and sometimes rather sharp in his judgments. Jacques also had a fund of jokes, most of which he swore were true stories. His book "Peking Papers" contains many of the outrageous stories which I had heard first-hand from him — not always to be taken literally, but poking fun at some officials and others who were excessively serious. An example was his habit of inventing his own so-called sayings of Confucius — Jacques claimed that there was no one who ever responded that the "saying" cited was bogus, or that he did not recall any such statement by Confucius. Jacques was admired by his friends for another reason; at the bar at Beijing Airport, he had a standing arrangement to have "his" bottle of *Maotai.* Friends were welcome to dip into it as they awaited delayed flights — all one had to do was to call for Mr. Marcuses' bottle!

When I came back to China in mid-1970 with a family, a wife, two children of 3 and 1 and a nanny in tow, the country had been through the trauma of the Cultural Revolution, though the likes of Lin Biao and Jiang Qing were very much in power, and the curtain would really come down on that particular experiment of Mao only some years later. In many ways contacts between foreigners and the Chinese were even more difficult, but the presence of the children usually gave rise to friendly comment and gestures of natural affection, which tempered a little the alienation which arose in those artificial circumstances. This was particularly true of the outings to the parks, and the shopping forays for souvenir-hunting to which all diplomats fell prey in Beijing. For a Chinese-speaker, it was a particular joy to listen to the children prattle in the bell-like tones of perfectly spoken Beijing dialect, which they picked up so effortlessly from the Chinese cook and maid. Alas, they lost the language with equal speed when we left after a two-year stay.

Diplomatic life was a bit changed from that of the 1960s, with the number of embassies more than double the earlier figure, and the presence of many more African and Arab missions, besides the Western nations which set up representation in one large surge, after the French recognition of the People's Republic of China in 1964 (the French came with the zeal of new converts, to "interpret China to the world"). A second surge more or less coincided with the Nixon visit of 1971, Canadian recognition of the PRC, and the stationing of a shoal of Japanese correspondents, as a prelude to Japan's recognition of its great neighbour. All this made for a much larger number of diplomats, journalists and business visitors, changing the intimacy of the former period for a more "normal" major capital. In other ways, life was less interesting than before, since the performing arts were still to revive from the decimation of the Cultural Revolution, and one encountered only the standard fare of revolutionary art, drama and music. The number of restaurants was also much reduced from the earlier numbers, and many of the fabled places – like the "San Jwor" of the inner city with its memorable dishes of fresh-water eels – were gone! The subsequent period saw a gradual revival, of cuisine and of the arts, but I left China in September 1972, much before the real "normalization" of the post-Cultural Revolution life of China.

Living in China in those years enabled one to observe a complex political process, the shaping of a great, but secretive, Asian power. The early 1960s coincided with the intense ideological debate with the Soviet Union, and the early 1970s with the terminal phase of Mao's last major social experiment. We said in those days that one sometimes wrote an analysis of China in the first 6 weeks of arrival, when the first encounter gave what seemed to be definitive insights. The alternative, especially for those who were not short-term visitors, was that one realized the limitations of one's understanding, and chose the gradual unraveling of the many areas of ignorance, before venturing forth in print. It was rather like Einstein's response to a gushing admirer who praised his vast fund of wisdom; he replied: "What I know is but a fraction of what I do not know!". In the 1960s the air was thick with heavy polemical debate between the two communist giants, whose bilateral relationship deteriorated progressively. The smaller communist states were proxies in the debate, or were drawn into the vortex through their geo-political compulsions. Beijing was a useful observation point also for the evolution in these inter-relationships, ranging from the ultra-privileged status of Enver Hoxja's Albania (which received massive material support in exchange for its total identification with China), to the fence-sitters like North Korea and North Vietnam of that time. The behaviour of the diplomatic missions of these countries in the rarefied atmosphere of Beijing became a side drama for outside observers like ourselves. Yugoslavia (in whose name the entire Sino-Soviet debate had first commenced, when the "Peoples' Daily" thundered in 1961: "Is Yugoslavia a Communist Country?") was for us the coolest of the lot, both on account of the uniform high professionalism of their diplomats, and because of our natural empathy and proximity to them. I was not in China in the difficult period of 1966-68, when the Cultural Revolution was at its climax, and when diplomatic missions were attacked by mobs manipulated by Jiang Qing and her ilk; the Beijing Diplomatic Corps showed its weakest face at that time through disunity, and currying of favour by a few embassies who believed that this was their road to narrow advantage. This is a small sad foot-note to that era.

Immediately after the India-China border war of 1962 which ended with a unilateral cease-fire and partial withdrawal of Chinese troops to their pre-war claim-line, China took the high road of urging negotiation and freezing of the difficult issue, pending improvement of relations on other fronts. This was sound strategy from their perspective, but overlooked the extent of injury to India. In the treatment of the Indian Embassy in Beijing this sometimes took the form of petty pinpricks, combined with a few gestures of special consideration for about a year immediately after the war. This coincided with the remaining term of P.K. Banerjee as the Head of Mission, who was summoned to meetings with Premier Zhou Enlai from time to time, almost invariably at no notice at all, and usually at night – since this legendary Zhou of the time (and almost the only one to have kept his repute intact) kept an owl's hours, and commenced his work after sunset! My only personal encounter with him occurred in late-1963, when P.K. Banerjee was given the special favour of a personal farewell call, and took with him 5 of his embassy colleagues. Premier Zhou was suave and smiling, essentially repeating the message loudly proclaimed by China to Asia and to the world, that China sought a negotiated border settlement, that it was prepared to wait till India was ready for this, and that in the interim the two countries which had so much in common should improve relations in other areas. At that meeting we had a taste of Zhou's renowned alertness and charm. At one point he said something humorous, and noticing that I had smiled before the interpretation was completed, he immediately remarked that I spoke Chinese. After inquiry as to where I had learnt it, he complimented me on my accent! It should be said in parenthesis that the accent business is very serious for foreigners learning Chinese. At the same time, among the Chinese themselves, the range of accents is so vast that other than the few born in the immediate vicinity of the capital — which is where the Oxford accent of Chinese is located — speak in tones which betray their places of origin, even to the extent of incomprehension. Thus Mao's Hunan accent was so strong that he needed interpreters to make himself understood to his own compatriots not used to him. Lin Biao was another one whose accent tested the limits of one's comprehension range. While at the Language School at Hong Kong we cultivated several North Chinese friends, through lunch clubs and the like, to get speaking practice. One example was Steve Chou, a good and generous friend to many generations of Indian students. I once mentioned to one of my teachers that Steve's Beijing dialect was superb. How can that be, she responded, since he was born in Tianjing (150 km. away from the capital) and moved to Beijing only when he was 10 years old!

During the years I spent in China, there was no real India-China dialogue. After the Border War it was simply too early for India. In the 1964-65 period there was some gentle probing of intentions, given Jagat Mehta's easy equation with the then Director of the Asia Division Zhang Wenjin, his counterpart in the futile "Official Talks" held in 1959-60, (he later became China's Ambassador to the US, and Vice-Foreign Minister; a member of the Premier Zhou's top team). But this led to nothing, while preventing further downslide in relations. Some petty slights were received by the Indian Embassy, but for the main part the relationship was correct and the attitude of senior officials was constructive. When Asian or other diplomatic groups were received jointly, we were handled with perceptible coolness, but never in discourtesy. The Middle Kingdom has long practised a finely-tuned method of subtle differentiation, and these habits were a great deal deeper than the patina of communism. Seen with detachment, the Chinese manner of handling foreigners was a delight to watch, rooted as it has always been in profound self-confidence and a holistic vision of content and form.

My second sojourn began just after Chairman Mao's deliberate gesture of reconciliation to the Indian Charge d'Affairs Brajesh Mishra at the top of the Tienanmen rostrum at the May Day parade of 1970, when he said directly to our envoy that "the two countries had long been friends and we could not go on quarrelling". We know now through diverse sources that this was a calculated gesture bearing Mao's personal stamp, and was meant to be taken seriously. And this was precisely the manner in which it was interpreted by the politically astute Head of Mission. One suspects that the premature manner in which the move was leaked to the Indian media, just at the time when Mishra was in Delhi to help in full assessment, and the gesture was even held to mild ridicule through its characterization as "the Mao Smile", bore the stamp of our domestic pro-Soviet lobby. Further, we were even then probably not ready to move towards that window of opportunity.

1971 saw the build-up to the Bangladesh crisis and the 19-day war of December in the same year, and again the view from Beijing was revealing. China did not support the actions of Pakistan in its then Eastern wing, and clearly counselled caution, while making pro-forma expressions of support as the events moved to their denouement. The Indian brief was clearly to keep China informed of the increasingly impossible situation and the very limited goals of Indian policy, i. e. containment of the crisis. Brajesh Mishra played the vital role as the dialogue partner in this communication link, and was responsible for the accurate assessment that China would make public expressions of support to Islamabad but would stay out of any conflict. Thus the Embassy's task for virtually the entire year was to manage this issue in a complex environment, and it came to dominate the bilateral relationship. It took China several months after the creation of Bangladesh to begin to come to terms with the realities of South Asia, and this produced an amusing incident.

As the Bangladesh crisis escalated, increasingly open criticism of India became the norm in Chinese speeches delivered at national day celebrations of various embassies and state banquets in honour of visiting foreign delegations. By local custom the diplomatic receptions took the form of sit-down dinners, while the Chinese banquets were even more formal, and again by local custom included all Heads of Missions in the guest-list. Mishra made it clear from the outset that he would not sit through direct criticism of India, and would walk-out. It soon became our internal and deliberate Embassy practice to inform the Chinese chauffeur of the flag-car that he should stand by with the car at the main entrance, in anticipation of likely walk-out. This worked well. Sometimes the speeches were delayed till the meal was over — rather than delivered at the beginning as per Chinese custom — and this provoked comment in the diplomatic corps that it was to ensure that the Indian Charge finished his meal before making his exit! In the event, there eventually came the reception around the middle of 1972 when contrary to form, India was not criticized in the Chinese dignitary's speech, marking the end of that particular phase. As it happened, the Soviet Union was attacked in that same reception speech, and the Soviet envoy, accompanied by his bloc phalanx staged a walk-out — much more impressive in sheer numbers. The effect was spoilt when the group came down the steps of the huge Palace of the People complex and were met by the Indian flag-car, tricolour and all, but alas not their own vehicles. They were not amused at the delay in mobilizing their transport to go home!

The Bangladesh war also produced for us the melodrama of assisting the then Pakistani diplomats of Bengali origin to establish contact with their own new government-in-the-making, since in the politically charged atmosphere of Beijing there were none but the most formal contacts with Pakistani diplomats — mainly I should add at the preference of the latter, who may have found that even routine courtesies, or return of courtesies to Indian counterparts, detracted from their self-image of victims of Indian machinations. This was my only exposure to the cloak-and-dagger style, as roundabout means were mutually used to make soundings and first contacts, often via the spouses, since the latter often had their own friendships and equations! The establishment of these first links with the Bangladeshis, who became major players in their new nation, was a heart-warming experience. It also provided relief and counterpoint to the tension generated by the war. We celebrated the signing of the surrender documents by the Pakistani generals in Dacca with champagne — the first and only time that my wife cultivated a high-class hangover. As we drove home she wondered why there were so many people on the road that late hour; I responded that they were just the early morning shift going to work!

A small instance of the quality of the evolving India-China relationship of 1970 was the visit to the Embassy by the renowned Mao biographer Edgar Snow, who was on what represented his last visit to China. I had met Snow a couple of years earlier, at the home of Professor Gilbert Etienne in Geneva (inviting me to that lunch meeting Gilbert had warned me not to get into an argument with Edgar Snow over India-China relations; I had replied that one could not argue with a legend!). Reading in the Chinese press around October 1970 that he was in Beijing as Mao's personal guest, I tried to phone him and failing in that, sent him a note seeking a call. He telephoned some weeks later and said that he had been travelling in the provinces, and that he would come and meet me at the Embassy. He turned down my offer to call, and some days later drove up in his official limousine, for about 40 minutes of general conversation. He was too wily to give away any hard information and spoke in general terms of his positive impressions of the changes in the country. He also pumped me for information on some new document which had emerged in the Hong Kong press about events on the mainland, relating to Chinese personalities, if I recall correctly. There was nothing of substance in the meeting. The significant aspect was that it took place at all, and that Snow made it a point to visit the Indian Embassy. It was a straw in the direction of normalization.

Another encounter with an author, perhaps a year later, had more in content. On the way back from a routine courier trip to Hong Kong I travelled with a Chinese-speaking American academic, who seemed interesting and we got into a conversation. She gave her name as Roxanne Witke, and she spoke of her interest in meeting Chinese leaders — rather a difficult task for an unknown visitor. A couple of weeks later I read in the Xinhua news bulletin that she had met Jiang Qing, someone who seldom met foreign visitors. I tracked her down at the then premier lodging in the capital, the Beijing Hotel, and invited her to join my wife and myself for dinner at the Mongolian restaurant on Hou Hai lake, at the back of the Forbidden City. She accepted and, over the meal, she proceeded to unfold her extraordinary experience. This is narrated in her biography of that complex and, of course, controversial leader of the Cultural Revolution. The difference was that she spoke fresh from her first meeting with Madame Mao, at a point when Witke did not know that on her way out of the country through Guangzhou (still the only viable entry-exit point, even though direct flights to Shanghai from the West and Addis Ababa had commenced), she would be summoned back by the imperious lady for a series of additional meetings. The story of how later on attempts were made in the mid-70s to stop the publication of her book, at a time when Jiang Qing was under political attack and headed for downfall, are well-known.

The striking aspect for me in that dinner-meeting with Witke was the tale she unfolded, and her unerring prescience. She had earlier met Deng Yingchao, the spouse of Premier Zhou Enlai. Witke narrated the meticulous manner in which she had to prepare herself for the audience with Jiang Qing, listening to unpublished speeches where she could take notes but not see the text or record the reading on tape. She recounted that Jiang was truly concerned that she was not viewed with sympathy by the outside world, and felt that Witke could help in depicting a more human picture of her. Witke remarked that someone was trying to make her into a latter day Edgar Snow, and perhaps she was not displeased at the prospect. Jiang told her that Premier Zhou had urged her to go ahead with this meeting. Witke also spoke of the thorough investigation made into her academic and family background, plus the ways in which different Chinese interlocuters made known their knowledge of this. Then she went on to add her initial conclusion based on that first meeting, that someone was giving Jiang a long rope to hang herself. Witke also felt that she had unwittingly become enmeshed in China's internal politics, and might be used in the manoeuvring by various personalities. This proved to be remarkably close to the truth, as the world learnt subsequently, when some of the inside stories on the events in China of the Mao era began to emerge. But to go back to that evening in the Mongolian restaurant, Hoxanne Witke told a story which gave deep insight into the inner workings of a land of enormous secrecy, and she seemed credible just for the reason that the account was vivid in personal detail.

My account of an Indian diplomat's life in China some decades back, perhaps looks disjointed and sketchy. It describes some events and people that stand out in memory. It is intended to evoke some of the flavour of that time, and to underscore the wonder of one's first start in a service career. Truly, it was a privilege to be exposed to China at a young age. It imprinted on me the enormous will and courage which this Asian giant mobilized, in its successful efforts to pull itself up by its own bootstraps. The circumstances of India are so different that direct comparisons are hard. But there is a great deal in the Chinese model which is relevant for us. The goals of democracy and freedom are absolute, and should not be compromised for economic achievement. A full 50 years after Independence when the basic needs of our people are yet to be met, in education and health, in three square meals per day, in shelter and jobs, and even in drinking water, it can legitimately be asked — is this freedom? China's record, evident in the excesses of the Great Leap and of the Cultural Revolution, suggests that it has swung in cycles of normalcy and extremes. The post-1978 economic reforms of Deng Xiaoping have brought great achievement and prosperity. But the tension between political and economic freedom, the contradictions and disparities between coastal and interior regions, and the restraints on individual freedom are among the issues which may pose for China its future challenges. Is individual liberty possible without the satisfaction of basic needs? Each society gropes for its own answers to these dilemmas. The comparable features and circumstances of India and China provide a basis for stronger cooperation, particularly in functional areas like agriculture or applied researach. As we move to the next millennium, we must put aside the past, and seek out new ways of working together.

VINOD KHANNA

49

HOW I ARRIVED ON THE CHINA SCENE

Like many other contributors to this book, I have spent a very large part of my working life, diplomatic and academic, dealing with China. When Prof. Tan Chung invited me to record my "Reminiscences and Impressions" I thought that I might try to recall what China had meant to me before I entered it for the first time on 1st July 1966. While each individual has his own unique intellectual and emotional background, perhaps the perceptions of China with which I began my career were shared in some measure by many others of my generation.

As far as I can remember my first encounter with China was as a child in early 1940s in the shape of something very beautiful: a roll of exquisite silk bought by my family in Lahore from a bicycle-borne Chinese vendor. A little later I saw V. Shantaram's popular film *Dr. Kotnis ki Amar Kahani* (The immortal story of Dr. Kotnis) which dealt with the heroism, romance and death in China of this young Indian doctor. He had gone there as a member of the Indian medical team led by Dr. Atal sent by the Indian Congress in 1938 to assist the Chinese in their struggle against the Japanese invaders. If such experiences in one's childhood leave a lasting impression on one's mind, I began with a decidedly positive image of China: a country which produced lovely things, a country for which our leaders, still fighting for India's own independence, had great affection and sympathy, a country which was cruelly treated by the Japanese.

In my youth as a student in Bombay I became an ardent and almost unquestioning admirer of our first Prime Minister, Jawaharlal Nehru. We looked at the outside world largely through his eyes. As far as foreign policy was concerned, what he said almost defined for us what any patriotic Indian should believe in. I was too young to react to the birth of People's Republic of China (PRC), or to China's "liberation" of Tibet. However, I was old enough to follow keenly the visit to India in 1954 by Premier Zhou Enlai (whose name we spelt as Chou En-lai then and for years thereafter till overwhelmed by the Peking/Beijing-ordained Pinyin standardization) and that of Nehru to China later in the same year. Not all my schoolmates took much interest in these matters but those of us who did were thrilled by the realization that these were representatives of two most populous nations of the world, two of the most creative ancient civilizations, two neighbours who had never gone to war with each other through history, two Asian giants — now masters of their own destiny. Each time one thought of India's foreign policy, two words seemed enough: Non-Alignment and Panchsheel. The latter, it will be recalled, was the name given to the Five Principles of peaceful co-existence first formulated in the preamble to the agreement between India and China in regard to Tibet which was signed in April 1954.

However, even at the height of our youthful immersion in the *Hindi-Cheeni Bhai-bhai* fervour, there was an element of ambivalence in our attitudes. We developed early a dislike for the non-liberal elements in Soviet and Chinese communism. In a sense, therefore, one might say that the deterioration of Sino-Indian relations which set in towards the late 1950s resulted in greater harmonization in our perceptions respectively of Mao's China and his party, the Communist party of China (CPC).

In college I did a course on the modern political history of East Asia. This gave me a better understanding of the background to the triumph of Mao in China. One read with revulsion about the Opium War, the shameful imposition of unequal treaties on China and the brazen carving up of areas of influence by the imperialist powers. I read with admiration about the revolutionary activities of Sun Yat-sen and his ideas as incorporated in the Three Principles of the People: nationalism, democracy and socialism. It was interesting to see that just as all Indians (or almost all) hailed Mahatma Gandhi as the Father of our nation, all Chinese, whether the Kuomintang (KMT) or the Communists, revered Sun as the "Father of Modern China". I liked to play with such speculative — and, in a sense, meaningless — games as to what would have been the shape of the Chinese revolution if Sun had not died in 1925. The KMT-CPC conflict over the subsequent 25 years made absorbing reading. Accounts of two events, in particular, left a lasting impression: first, the awesome endurance embodied in the Long March led by Mao and Zhu De and, secondly, the speed with which the forces of Chiang Kai-shek collapsed during the final stages of the civil war (1947-49) in the face of the much smaller, relatively ill-equipped but better led and motivated People's Liberation Army (PLA) whose greatest strength clearly lay in the increasing popular support it enjoyed.

At a student of political philosophy, first in Bombay and then at Oxford, I naturally read a certain amount of the original writings of Marx, Engels and Lenin, but none of Mao.

In October 1961, I returned to India as a lecturer in the Department of Politics of my old college in Bombay. I found myself being swept into the mounting national anger both against the perceived foreign aggressor and the Indian government for failing to deal with it effectively. I was in the midst of the U.P.S.C. examination for entry into government service when the India-China war broke out in October 1962. Many thought we would be conscripted. Depressed by the accounts of reverses on the battlefronts and disconcerted by the newspaper accounts about the "human wave" tactics, which it was said were being used by the Chinese Army to overwhelm the Indian troops, we found it difficult to concentrate on our examination papers. A few months later, along with the rest of the country, I wept unabashedly on hearing Lata Mangeshkar's famous musical tribute to the fallen soldiers.

Soon after appointment to the foreign service, every Indian Foreign Service officer is allotted a foreign language which he has to study and in which he has to pass an examination. We were asked to indicate our preferences and I had selected French and German. As we were awaiting Ministry of External Affairs' decision while undergoing training at the National Academy of Administration in Mussourie, a friend of mine coined his favourite term of abuse: "May you be allotted Chinese". This was a reference to both the known difficulty of the language and the unwelcome prospect it held out of a posting in "Peking" (its Indian image in 1963) rather than Paris or Bonn. My first reaction to the news that I (along with my batch-mate Ranjit Sethi) had indeed been allotted Chinese was of pure dismay. It was, however, only a passing emotion. Very soon I found myself looking forward to the challenge. In any case, the blow was softened by the information that the language was to be learnt not in Beijing but in Hong Kong which appeared to be a very much more attractive first foreign assignment.

We were the first batch of IFS probationers whom Jawaharlal Nehru (who was not only the Prime Minister but also the Foreign Minister) did not meet. This gave us an indication of how frail his health had become. When he died on 27 May 1964, like the rest of the country I was grief-stricken and convinced that his death had been hastened by the shock of what we all regarded as betrayal by the Chinese.

Being a Chinese language probationer I was attached for a few weeks to the East Asia Division, or to be precise, to C.V. Ranganathan, the then Under Secretary (China). Rangi (that was how we called him) who, by a series of happy coincidences, was to become my senior colleague in China-watching through most of my career, asked me to prepare a paper on the impact of the Sino-Soviet dispute on the Indian communist movement. This meant, of course, first trying to understand what the Sino-Soviet confrontation was all about. It was intellectual fun reading about Chinese reaction to Khrushchev's de-Stalinization speech and his views on non-inevitability of war, the possibility of a non-violent transition to socialism, and the idea of peaceful co-existence. It was fascinating that the Chinese attributed greater significance to Soviet sucesses in launching the first ICBM and earth satellite, than did the Soviet Union itself. It was my first exposure to Mao's genius in coining such striking phrases as the "east wind prevails over the west wind" and "the atom bomb is a paper tiger" — a heady mixture of ideological conviction and determined pursuit of very concrete objectives.

I commenced the study of Chinese language (Mandarin as it was called, but academically designated as "Modern Standard Chinese") at Hong Kong University in October 1964. I do not have a talent for learning foreign languages, being not blessed with those skills which make some people natural linguists. I realized early that I could never be as good a speaker of the four-tone Mandarin as some of my colleagues. Of the Chinese speaking foreigners there was none more proficient than our own V.V. Paranjpe, then a First Secretary in our Commision in Hong Kong. I sought to compensate to some extent for the inadequacy of my spoken Chinese skills by concentrating on acquiring as much competence as possible in reading and writing. Learning a couple of thousand characters (totally inadequate for true literacy), each involving several strokes, was tough but frankly I enjoyed it. I had a slightly ambivalent attitude to the simplification of characters by the Chinese government. I was relieved that it made easier the task of learning to read (not, alas, what was being published outside China as Hong Kong and Taiwan refused to adopt what was regarded as a sacriligious move) but some of the characters did look more meaningful — and beautiful — in their original complex shape.

Language study apart, Hong Kong provided an opportunity to take a preliminary look at some facets of the magnificent Chinese culture. I was eager to acquire some knowledge, no matter how elementary, of the famous schools of Chinese thought. The recommended introductory text was Fung Yu-lan's *A Short History of Chinese Philosophy.* I shall never forget the opening lines of the book, "The place which philosophy has occupied in Chinese civilization has been comparable to that of religion in other civilizations. In China, philosophy has been every educated person's concern. In the old days, if a man was educated at all, the first education he received was in philosophy."

Confucianism appealed to me greatly because of its humanistic ethic independent of revealed religion. The *Analects* became one of my favourite books. It is full of pithy sayings encapsulating perennial wisdom. "A gentleman" says Confucius, "in his judgement of the world, has no predilections nor prejudices; he is on the side of what is right." Elsewhere, he advises, "Do not be concerned that you are unknown, but do something to deserve a reputation." Naturally, living and teaching as he did around 500 B. C., he spoke from within the feudal politico-social setting of his day and it would be strange if we were to fault him for the non-applicability of some of his ideas today.

I also made an attempt to understand the aphorisms and paradoxes in *Daode Jing* (or spelled as "Tao-te ching") attributed to Laozi (or Lao Tzu). This small book, according to the introduction in the copy which I acquired (with English translation) had had as great an influence on the Chinese mind as all the Confucian classics put together. Repeated encounters in conversations and other readings with the multifaceted concept of *Tao*, led to the realization that like *Dharma*, this word (though generally translated as the Way), has no precise equivalent in English. To quote the philosopher Zhuangzi (Chuang Tzu) : "*Tao* cannot be conveyed by either words or silence. In that state which is neither speech nor silence its transcendental nature may be apprehended." One could not help but be struck by a sort of affinity with some of our *Upanishads.* Some thirty years later, serendipitously, a Taiwanese friend presented me with a scroll on which was written the character "Tao" in splendid calligraphy.

We were taught that a really good Chinese painting, with its lightening brushstrokes and seductive suggestiveness, was a particularly vivid manifestation of *Tao.* My wife Gita and I became very fond of the work of Chi Pai-shih (or Qi Baishi, in Pinyin). The painter in our family is Gita. In Hong Kong she found a good teacher to introduce her to Chinese brush-painting and this has become her life-long passion.

I had not read much Chinese poetry before coming to Hong Kong. Now it became one of my favourite pastimes. I could not wait till I acquired sufficient competence in Chinese and so turned to translations. Fortunately, thanks to Arthur Waley, Ezra Pound, and other outstanding translators, classical Chinese poetry has long been accessible in English. The very first major work of Chinese literature, the *Book of Songs*, was an eye-opener. Tradition attributes its compilation to Confucius himself. Whether or not that is true, this belief testifies to the antiquity of these songs and ballads. They capture with engaging simplicity and lucidity an amazing range of human experiences. To quote just a couple of memorable lines:

"My sad heart is consumed, I am harrassed
By a host of small men."

Almost a millennium later came the great Tang poets. (I am not suggesting that there were no great poets in the interregnum but I am just concentrating on some of my own favourites). Reading Li Bai (Li Po) and Du Fu (Tu Fu),was a very special aesthetic experience. Hailed as two of China's greatest poets, they were dramatically different: Li was a happy-go-lucky Taoist who loved his drink; Du was a serious and sober intellectual.

At the Hong Kong University, my priority — for purely professional reasons — was to acquire the ability to read Chinese newspapers of the *People's Daily* variety. However, I did manage to reach the stage of being able to read — with the help of our teachers and the famous *Mathews' Chinese English Dictionary* — some writings of a few famous modern Chinese authors. I recall in particular Lu Xun's (Lu Hsun) biting satire *The True Story of Ah Q*, Cao Yu's (Tsao Yu) powerful indictment of contemporary social ills in his play *Thunderstorm* and Lao She's novel *Rickshaw Boy.*

Naturally one had to get down to trying to understand Mao's political thoughts. Stuart Schram's book, with excerpts from Mao's more important writings, provided an excellent starting point. As far as I can remember the first Maoist tract which I read in original Chinese was his "Report of an Investigation into the Peasant Movement in Hunan". This confirmed what one had heard about Mao's deep first-hand study of the peasant question in his country. But there was also another lesson which I learnt from this exercise which came in handy in later China-watching. When reading any Chinese communist tract one had always to note the year of the publication. This essay, like so much of Mao's work, was updated for political correctness. References to the leading role of the working class and the Communist Party were added later in order not to bring into too bold a relief his deviation from the German Marxism-Russian Leninism's relegation of the peasantry to a secondary position in the revolutionary process.

On the whole Mao, quite rightly did not seem to have much inhibition in Sinifying Marxism. Thus in his report to the Sixth Plenum of the Sixth Central Committee, October 1938, published as *On the New Stage* he has this to say [in Schram's translation], "A Communist is a Marxist internationalist, but Marxism must take on a national form before it can be applied ....If a Chinese Communist, who is a part of the great Chinese people, bound to his people by his very flesh and blood, talks of Marxism apart from Chinese peculiarities, this Marxism is merely an empty abstraction. Consequently, the *Sinification of Marxism* — that is to say, making certain that in all of its manifestations it is imbued with Chinese peculiarities, using it according to these peculiarities — becomes a problem that must be understood and solved by the whole party without delay ...." I suppose today we would use the word "characteristics" in place of the awkward "peculiarities".

I remember reading with keen interest what Mao had to say on the problems of a socialist society, particularly his views on the question of "Correct handling of Contradictions among people". It seemed that there was considerable flexibility in defining the terms "enemy" and "people", and, therefore, of the terms "antagonistic" and "non-antagonistic contradictions" leaving sufficient scope for the Party (or the Great Leader) to move a person, and the classification of the "contradiction" with him, from one category to the other.

It was only on reaching Beijing in the summer of 1966 that I acquired and ploughed through most of the 4-volume *Selected Works of Mao Tse-tung*. It took more than a decade before the political situation was found propitious enough for the release of the fifth volume.

Mao, one discovered to one's pleasant surprise, was a reasonably good poet. There is, for instance, his rather touching tribute to his first wife, Yang Kaihui. Entitled "The Immortals" it is addressed to a woman whose spouse, like Mao's had been killed by Chiang Kai-shek's regime:

> *"I lost my proud poplar, and you your willow,*
> *Poplar and willow soar lightly to the ninth heaven."*

(Mao has resorted to a pun to refer to Yang as the name can mean "poplar".)

Mao's writings are replete with classical allusions. One repeatedly encounters strong evidence of how well-versed he was in classical Chinese culture. The vulgarity and philistinism of the Cultural Revolution therefore came as an even greater shock than it may otherwise have done.

I studied in a general way the developments which had taken place in China since 1949 though I cannot now remember what were the books and other sources I relied on. "Hundred Flowers Campaign" gave one an insight into one facet of Mao's vision as well as into his tactics in dealing with domestic dissent. I did not agree with those who felt that Mao had deliberatly lulled the intellectuals into revealing their true views in order to suppress them. I got the impression that he had genuinely miscalculated. I had much greater difficulty trying to comprehend what had actually happened during the Great Leap Forward. Looking at the history of Chinese Communist Movement, I was impressed by the fact that one had to take into account both ideas and personalities. The conflicts within the Party seemed to be a blend of ideological and power struggles.

As Hong Kong was at that time the Mecca of China-watchers, I was able to supplement my reading with discussions with experts of various hues. In the Indian Commission itself, besides Paranjpe, with his superb knowledge of Chinese history and personalities, there was Sivaramakrishnan (alas no more) who did not know Chinese language but had an incisive mind. One batch senior to us were the fellow-probationers, K. Raghunath and Kiran Doshi. Talking to the highly cerebral Raghu was always a stimulating experience and laid the foundation for very close cooperation later in Beijing. Kiran was my guru in chess and bridge, the games which were to provide much joy during the long evenings in Beijing of the Cultural Revolution. Many of the very well-informed staff members of the *Far Eastern Economic Review* became good friends. It was a real pleasure having as one's fellow students of Chinese language, the very bright British diplomatic colleagues all of whom became my colleagues in Beijing during the Cultural Revolution. Leonard Appleyard (later their Ambassador in Beijing), John Weston (their Permanent Representative in New York) and Roger Garside who left the diplomatic service to become the author of much-acclaimed writings on China. The Americans, who at that stage did not have an Embassy in Beijing, posted some of their most outstanding China experts in Hong Kong and with one of them (Nick Platt, now the President of the New York-based Asia Society) I am still in touch.

But not all the members of the Hong Kong-based China-watching tribe were equally intelligent; worse, many of them clearly lacked objectivity. There were some who were convinced that China, and in particular Mao, could do no wrong; at the other end of the spectrum of prejudice were those who indulged perpetually in unthinking condemnation.

Among the starry-eyed admirers of Mao there were those who still spoke in glowing terms of the Great Leap Forward. They hailed it as one of Mao's spectacularly bold moves beyond the comprehension of his slow-witted critics. They accepted Maoist statistics of the Great Leap Forward's achievements and the Maoist alibi for the economic disaster which it generated. (In 1988 I sat in a classroom in Harvard listening to Prof. Amartya Sen presenting with precision and objectivity an account of the millions who died of starvation thanks to Mao's quixotic vision.) I was, therefore, more amused than impressed when these same people became ecstatic about "the bold vision" which inspired Mao's Great Proletarian Cultural Revolution. On my visit to Hong Kong from Beijing towards the end of 1966, one of them, a well-known writer, dismissed my eye-witness accounts of brutality and chaos as being a misunderstanding (I suspect she meant 'slander') of a genuinely revolutionary movement because of my bourgeois background. By the same token, I learnt to take with a grain of salt the observers who saw every Chinese foreign policy move as an expression of its alleged incorrigible expansionism or a step in a grand global revolutionary strategy.

We soon realized the necessity of learning how to pierce the opacity of official media as that was about the only source of information available. Sometimes one felt that the language was the least of the barriers. And I soon discovered that even those observers who were deeply versed in Chinese history and politics were often totally foxed. One thing was obvious enough: the official propaganda was not to be taken literally. *People's Daily* always spoke with an air of supreme self-confidence and certainty. But from the twists and turns in Chinese policies both domestic and foreign from 1949 onwards, it was obvious that there was no reason to take China's course at any given moment as permanent, or to believe that Chinese leadership was gifted with some unique omniscience that would insure them against making grevious mistakes.

Useful training was provided by the study of the campaign against Wu Han's historical play *Hai Rui Dismissed from office.* Gradually, it became clear that this was no mere academic debate about an ancient personality but something with serious contemporary political implications. This lesson about political uses of historical allusions came in very handy in subsequent years. But I was somewhat discouraged by the realisation that decoding the precise significance of any allusion would require something more than a passing knowledge of Chinese history, culture and literature. One would have to possess in-depth knowledge of how Chinese themselves saw their past. And often the references would be beyond the comprehension of even learned Chinese, without elucidation by those in the know of the actual political objective behind a particular allusion.

During my days at Hong Kong University, I took only a passing interest in day-do-day happenings in India-China relations. There was one significant exception. The curious manner in which China sought to intervene in the Indo-Pak conflict of September 1965. After having initially scoffed at China's ineffectual moves giving India an ultimation to demolish certain structures on the Tibet-Sikkim border and to return 800 sheep and 59 yaks that Indian troops had allegedly taken away from Tibetans across the border, I realized that it would be difficult in future to think of Indo-Pakistan strategic equation without factoring in Sino-Pak relations.

I was disappointed when I was asked to proceed from Hong Kong to Beijing in summer 1966 full three months before the completion of my Chinese studies in Hong Kong University. However, I was soon to realize that fate had conferred a very special favour on me because it enabled me to witness the Cultural Revolution from almost its inception.

I cannot say that on the eve of my departure for Beijing I had any idea that we were about to witness a political explosion of inconceivable magnitude. But then I do not recall that any of the veteran China-watchers had predicted with any semblance of accuracy the eventual incredible scope of the "Great Proletarian Cultural Revolution". Of course, it was clear that the Beijing Party Committee of CPC and its formidable first secretary, Peng Zhen (P'eng Chen) were in trouble but I do not think that anybody at that early stage quite understood the significance of the broadcast over Beijing Radio on June 1, 1966, of Nieh Yuan-tzu's (to be romanized now as Nie Yuanzi) big-character poster.

On 1st July I crossed on foot the border between the British colony and the People's Republic of China, along with Gita and our 7 month-old first born, Rohit......

THE FOLLOWING YEARS

So many memories come flooding into my mind when I reminisce about my China-related experiences in the subsequent three decades that initially I was disinclined to try to put them down in a single article. However, on Prof. Tan Chung's urgings, I am attempting what he calls an "epilogue" in which I shall gallop though these years. This is not meant to be a detailed historical account and even less a serious analytical piece but merely a brief personal memoir.

On July 27, 1968, Mao told a group of student representatives who were complaining about "the black hand" using the workers' groups to control the disruptive activities by students that he himself was that "black hand"! This in some ways marked the end of the Cultural Revolution. By coincidence I left Beijing on transfer barely two weeks later. China of the period 1966-68 was not always a very pleasant place for diplomats. Many of us were subjected to a treatment which even the Chinese do not defend today. But I find myself looking back on those two turbulent years as professionally a very exciting period. It was a unique opportunity to witness and study an amazing and a very complex phenomenon. And if life was sometimes hard, it was infinitely more comfortable than what the great majority of Chinese were enduring. I shall never forget the sight of a group of boys and girls barely into their teens lashing an aged woman with bicycle chains simply because she had a picture of Buddha in her house. The British diplomats suffered much more than we did. The Indian Embassy at that time was headed by R.D. Sathe as the CDA. As far as I am aware, no other Indian diplomat has spent as many years in China as him, going back to the days of the Agent-General's Office in "Chungking" (to be spelled Chongqing now) in 1945! It was his able leadership — invariably calm, unprejudiced and in control — which was greatly responsible for the outstanding performance of the embassy through these tumultuous years when political chaos in China coincided with intense hostility in India-China relations.

A three year stint as Under Secretary in the East Asia division of the Ministry of External Affairs (1968-71) gave me an opportunity to make a more careful study of the events leading up to the 1962 conflict. I found myself looking at India-China problems with more objectivity and less emotion. For me the tone was set by the remarks of Prime Minister Indira Gandhi at a press conference on January 1, 1969. Asked whether India would not any longer insist on the Chinese acceptance of the Colombo proposals she replied, "That is not what I meant. What I meant is that we are stuck up in a particular position. That does not solve our problem with China. We should try to find a way of solving this problem." When the persistent questioner demanded "a straight answer", she replied, "Unfortunately straight answers are not possible. They come from the wrong ones (questions)." When a journalist referred to the continuing harshness of Chinese media attacks on the Indian government and on her personally, she responded, "That is their language. It is not our language. I think we should ignore it." But the time was not yet ripe for a major break-through. There was naturally much unhappiness at Chinese behaviour in many areas of concern to us. And to some extent, inevitably, India-China relations were influenced by the international situation. As a lowly Under Secretary not yet admitted to higher counsels of deliberation nor given access to files with top secret classification, I did not come to know all the facts about some of the episodes like the famous "Mao smile" (actually it was more than a mere smile) bestowed on our CDA Brajesh Mishra on May 1, 1970 on the Tiananmen rostrum.

I was able to continue China-watching to some degree in my next assignment (1971-74) which was as First Secretary in our Embassy in Tokyo. For geo-political, security, economic and historical reasons, China always looms very large in Japanese perceptions. This particular period saw a specially intense focus on China. There was the much-hyped trauma which came when they came to know of Kissinger's secret visit to China followed by Nixon himself. But it was fascinating to see how the "Nixon Shokku" was used by the Japanese to free themselves from the past shackles and to move with electrifying speed to put their own relations with China in order. Tanaka was elected prime minister in July 1972 and by September he was in Beijing signing the Tanaka-Zhou agreement.

Not surprisingly the Sinologists of Japan are among the best-informed in the world. Speaking to the China experts in the Japanese government, academic institutions, media and business world was always an educative and, indeed, a humbling experience. It was also interesting to see a very wide range of attitudes. There were those who were somewhat overwhelmed by a sense of guilt for what Japan had done to China in modern times, a country to which they owed such a huge cultural debt from ancient times. But there were others who saw no reason why Japan should feel more apologetic than other imperial powers, and who in particular resented guilt being transferred to the new generation.

I was back in Delhi and the East Asia Division in April 1978. It was now a new stage in India-China relations. Mrs. Gandhi had in 1976 resumed the exchange of ambassadors. In an inspired move, she had selected Shri K.R. Narayanan for the job in Beijing. Then, we had the Janata government in power. It was clear that despite the positions taken by them in the past, Prime Minister Morarji Desai and the External Affairs Minister Atal Bihari Vajpayee were keen to proceed further towards improvement of relations with China.

It will be recalled that Mr. Vajpayee had to postpone his visit to China, scheduled for October 1978, on medical advice According to the original programme a tour of China by an Indian cultural delegation was to take place to coincide with the minister's visit. The minister directed that the cultural troupe should proceed as planned in order to emphasize that there were no political reasons behind the postponement of his visit. As this was the first such delegation to be visiting China after a lapse of more than two decades during which much had happened in India-China relations, it was decided that I should accompany them as some sort of an adviser. Fully conscious of the significance of the event, Dr. Kapila Vatsyayan had put together a very impressive 50-member delegation composed of three dance groups: Darpana Academy of Performing Arts, Kadamb and the Kerala Kalamandalam. Among them there were some of the country's most talented Bharata Natyam, Kathak and Kathakali dancers (some of the younger ones were to go on to acquire much-deserved fame in subsequent years). The delegation was led by Mrs. Mrinalini Sarabhai who did a superb job, handling the crucial public relations with great dignity and charm. The Chinese hospitality was overwhelming. During the four week tour, performances were held in five cities (including Shijiazhuang, the city of Dr. Kotnis) to full houses, rave reviews and very substantial TV coverage. The enthusiastic response of the Chinese audiences was truly astonishing. This was both a recognition of the quality of the performances and the fact that the Chinese had been culturally starved during the Cultural Revolution.

Equally exciting for me was an opportunity to see a China closed to me by the hostile and turbulent political environment during my earlier two-year posting in Beijing. Besides the mandatory — and, from a professional point of view, very useful — visits to model factories and farms, we were able to visit universities and art institutions to meet scholars and artistes. They spoke with pain and sorrow of the oppression and humiliation by the Gang of Four. But the abiding impression I gained was that of their resilience, their indomitable spirit. Particularly memorable was the visit to the famous Beijing University and meeting with the great scholar Prof. Ji Xianlin who told us of his work on translating Valmiki's Sanskrit *Ramayana* into Chinese. On a visit to a prestigious dance school I watched with amazement as a famous Chinese dancer, Dai Ailian, (much persecuted during the Cultural Revolution) gave a brief performance of a Bharata Natyam piece learnt some 25 years ago during a visit to Madras. There was also the simple joy of being able to speak to people in the street. Some of us, for instance, walked unannounced and unescorted, into a small school somewhere deep in Changhsha to be greeted with much affection and excitement by the school principal who spoke nostalgically about seeing, ages ago, the Hindi film *Do Beegha Zameen* and expressed the fervent hope that there will be close friendship again between our two countries.

The next few months back in Delhi were dominated by preparations for Foreign Minister's visit to China now scheduled for February 1979. Foreign Secretary Jagat Mehta, who himself had a long experience of dealing with Chinese, laid down the guidelines for us. The burden naturally fell primarily on the East Asia Division now led by my old friend Rangi. Thanks to the phenomenal work put in by all the colleagues in the Division we were able to prepare an extraordinarily comprehensive set of briefs covering every significant facet of our relationship with China.

At that time many Indian foreign policy analysts — both within and outside the government — still painted a fairly demoniac picture of China. It was, for instance, argued that the Chinese expressions of goodwill were merely tactical ploys, designed to trap us into some suicidal foreign policy moves. Still bearing the scars of 1962, they saw the Chinese policy-makers not only as harbouring diabolical designs but gifted with some sort of fiendish cleverness which their Indian counterparts would not be able to match.

The fact that the Chinese decided to launch their attack on Vietnam even before Mr. Vajpayee had left the Chinese territory was a most depressing experience. The critics of the government's China policy had a field day. But the long-term impact of the minister's discussions in Beijing was certainly positive.

I for one was not surprised when Mrs. Indira Gandhi on return to power made it clear that she intended to proceed ahead with the normalization process. The new Foreign Minister P.V. Narasimha Rao, soon after taking over, sat down to a conscientious study of the outstanding problems in India-China relations. In the meanwhile my old boss, Mr. R.D. Sathe, had become the Foreign Secretary. If and when MEA throws open to public its secret files of this period, students of India-China relations may find it interesting to study how various options were prepared under his guidance for consideration at political level. They will, in particular, be able to fill an important lacuna in the usual accounts of the normalization process: the visit to Beijing in June 1980 of a two-men team led by Secretary (East) Eric Gonsalves. (I was the second member.) If I remember correctly it was meant to be a secret visit squeezed in between the publicly acnowledged visits to Pyonyang and Tokyo, but G.K. Reddy of the *Hindu*, with his unfailing contacts at the top level of government, got wind of it. The importance of the talks which we had with the Chinese can be gauged from the fact that the Prime Minister met us not only before our departure for our trip but also immediately after our return. There was a particular poignancy about the second meeting as it took place soon after the death of Mrs. Gandhi's son Sanjay in a tragic air-crash.

While I was in Beijing I received a message that I had been appointed to succed Rangi as the head of the East Asia Division. By now we had a clear-cut political decision to continue developing mutually beneficial relations with China in as many fields as possible, while trying to look for a satisfactory resolution of the most important outstanding issue between the two countries — the border question. In August 1980 there was a little hiccup. A small Indian army unit on patrol duty on the border lost its way and wandered into Chumbi valley. Successful negotiation with the Chinese of the safe and smooth return of these men was a small but significant step in the evolution of mutual trust so essential if we were to have peace and tranquillity on the border.

My last active involvement in official India-China exchanges during my years at the headquarters came with the visit of the Chinese Foreign Minister Huang Hua in June 1981. Actually I had already handed over charge of the division to my batchmate Ranjit Sethi and was about to leave for an assignment abroad, but the Foreign Secretary instructed me to stay on to assist in handling this visit. Among the results of the visit was an agreement between the two Foreign Ministers to initiate regular official-level talks on the boundary question and further improvement of bilateral relations. The first round of these talks took place in December 1981. But by then I was in Cuba on my first ambassadorial assignment.

Naturally China was somewhat remote from one's concerns in Havana but it certainly was not so in Jakarta where I served as Indian's Ambassador from 1985 to 1988. It was yet another stage in one's perpetual learning process. I felt I now had a better understanding of how Indonesia, the largest member of ASEAN, saw China's role in Southeast Asia. Another theme which fascinated me was the overseas Chinese community in Indonesia. Their position is full of contradictions on which much has been written.

It was only when I got to Bhutan in 1989 that once again my involvement with China was not confined to observation and study. Sino-Bhutanese relations are obviously of great strategic interest to us. Not surprisingly, Sino-Indian relations were also of very great concern to Bhutan. China, therefore, figured, rather prominently in my discussions with the Bhutanese government.

I particularly value the opportunities I have had to look at China in academic settings: a year as a Fellow at the Centre ("Center" as they spell it!) of International Affairs at Harvard University (1988-89), two years as "Visiting Ambassador" at the Department of Chinese and Japanese Studies of the Delhi University (1992-93), and my continuing association with the Institute of Chinese Studies.

The year at Harvard enabled me to meet and attend lectures by not only some of America's leading Sinologists but visiting experts from all over the world including the People's Republic of China and Taiwan. I also experienced at first hand the "love-hate" cycle in the often wildly fluctuating American attitudes towards China, a phenomenon so brilliantly analysed by Harold Isaacs. I shall never forget the transformation in one particular eminent Sinologist. When I arrived in Boston in September 1988 she had just returned from her trip to China and spoke to me with admiration bordering on adulation of Deng Xiaoping. A few days before my departure in June 1989 I was in the auditorium as she denounced Deng with all the passion of a betrayed love. It was, of course, the Tiananmen incident which made the difference.

My assignment at Delhi University as "visiting ambassador" was jointly sponsored by the Ministry of External Affairs and the University Grants Commission (UGC). The idea was to forge a closer link between our ministry and the academic community. This was the first time that such a concept was being tried out. Given my background it was felt that the Department of Chinese and Japanese studies would be an appropriate place for the experiment. Two successive heads of the Department, Profs. Sharma and Gupta were both most supportive. The main responsibility entrusted to me at Delhi University was to join Prof. Mira Sinha Bhattacharjea in teaching a course on Chinese Foreign Policy to M. Phil. students. Mira, of course, is a more genuine authority on the subject than I am.

During this period one of the activities which gave me special satisfaction was a two-day seminar on "China and South Asia in the post-Cold War World" which I was able to organize on behalf of the Department of Chinese and Japanese Studies and the India International Centre. The idea was that a paper on China's relations with each of the South Asian countries would be prepared by an academic expert and the discussant on the paper would be a former diplomat with professional experience relating to that country. The papers later appeared as a special issue of the *China Report* Vol. 30 No. 2 the journal of the Institute of Chinese Studies. Unfortunately it was not possible to cover in that issue the highly stimulating discussions which the papers generated.

From my Hong Kong days I have been greatly attracted by Chinese calligraphy. I find it perfectly understandable that, through the centuries, excellence in calligraphy has been regarded by the Chinese as a hallmark of a truly cultivated man. One of the more memorable moments in my two years with the Department was the opportunity to hear and see in action the President of the Chinese Calligraphy Society who came to give a lecture-cum-demonstration.

Thanks to a UGC grant I was able to visit China for a week in November 1993. I had discussions on China's foreign policy and security concerns with experts in the China Institute for Contemporary International Relations, the China Institute for International Strategic Studies and the Shanghai Institute for International Studies. I had also a long session with the President of the Chinese People's Institute for Foreign Affairs. It was refreshing to find that most of them had junked ideological jargon and now spoke in terms recognizable by students of international affairs everywhere. Further, though all adhered in broad terms to the official line of the day, significant variations would emerge when we got down to detailed analysis, attributable often to the different background of each of these institutions. But all the presentations by my interlocutors reflected China's growing self-confidence arising from the fact that while the Soviet Union had collapsed China had not only held together but had achieved impressive economic growth. Asked about China's current threat perceptions they pointed out that China today had a better security environment than at any time since the Opium War, and that for the first time since 1949 they did not have hostile relations with any of their neighbours. They spoke in sobre terms about the complexity of their relations with USA and Japan. All of them were sanguine about the future of India-China relations.

A meeting with economists in the Shanghai Academy of Social Sciences and Fudan University as also a visit to the ambitious new Pudong project and the spectacularly successful city of Wuxi (harbour city on the Yangtze which according to its officials had more than 2,000 joint ventures with foreign investment of over US $ 2.5 billion) gave me a better idea both of the undoubted economic achievements of Dengist reforms and of the social problems generated by the abandonment of the Marxist-Maoist egalitarian vision.

After voluntarily retiring from government service in March 1994 and a brief but fruitful stint as the Director of the Institute of Chinese Studies in Delhi I accepted an invitation to proceed to Taiwan as the first Director General of the India-Taipei Association in March 1995. My professional responsibility was to promote trade, investment and tourism and I hope I did not do too bad a job of it. But what gave me real pleasure was the fact that my wife and I could now savour many facets of Chinese culture of which we had up to now only read or heard.

Visits to the National Palace Museum in Taipei never ceased to thrill us. It houses in an imposing complex the richest collection of Chinese art in the world — a treasure that came in 4,800 cases from the mainland on the eve of the communist truimph. I was able to spend an occasional holiday admiring at a leisurely pace the fabulous bronzes, ceramics, paintings, and jade pieces. I used to feel sorry for the tourists who had to rush through the museum in an hour or so but I must confess that every now and then I enjoyed the lightening tours in the company of volunteer guides who were full of insightful comments and amusing anecdotes. Through their help one discovered the symbolism of exquisitely carved animals with three themes dominating: longevity, fertility and aspiration to climb up the bureaucratic and social ladder.

On 28 September 1995 I joined the teachers and students gathered in the courtyard of the Confucius Temple in Taipei to pay homage to the sage on his birthday which is celebrated in Taiwan as Teacher's Day.

One of the memorable experiences was an opportunity to see a master painter in action. Prof. Ho-nien Au's bold and swift strokes brought alive, in a matter of minutes, a stunning landscape on a blank paper.

Another intriguing aspect of Chinese culture into which I was able to get a glimpse in Taipei was the Chan (Zen/Dhyana) School of Buddhism. As is well known, according to Chinese tradition, this Meditation School was brought to China from India by Bodhidharma, that extraordinary monk whom the faithful regard as an incarnation of Buddha or Bodhisattva Avalokitesvara, and whose arrival in Canton (Guangzhou) in the 6th century is one of the seminal events in the history of India-China cultural relations. Before leaving Taiwan I was able to call on Master Sheng Yen who had the reputation of being one of the foremost living masters of the Chan tradition. One of my precious possessions is a scroll bearing the single character 'chan' presented to me by the Master in his own calligraphy.

With China in one way or another occupying so much of my adult life there is an endless reservoir of memories. Naturally one responds to a phenomenon like China at many different levels. Students of international affairs cannot afford to harbour any illusions. However, I would agree with what the then Foreign Minister Vajpayee had said in Parliament after his return from his visit to China: "Just as I would caution against euphoria, I would also urge a measure of self-confidence that any effort at improvement in relations need not mean the sacrifice of our national interests and aspirations." Further, no matter what the state of India-China relations at any given time, or indeed of any other facet of Chinese contemporary behaviour, all members of the human family can take joy and pride in the great achievements of Chinese civilization.

BETTER UNDERSTANDING

BETTER UNDERSTANDING

增進瞭解

50. How to Understand China?
V.V. Paranjpe

51. How to Understand Deng Xiaoping's China?
C.V. Ranganathan

52. Positive Agenda for Positive Action: Better India-China Understanding
Eric Gonsalves

53. Indian Policies Towards China—A Talk at IGNCA
Salman Haidar

54. Looking at China Across the Border
Dipankar Banerjee

55. India-China Relations: A Military Perspective
V.R. Raghavan

56. Three Agreements and Five Principles between India and China
Swaran Singh

57. Building Confidence with China
Swaran Singh

58. China Becoming a Superpower and India's Options
Sreedhar

59. Surjit Mansingh
The Importance of Understanding China

V.V. PARANJPE

50

HOW TO UNDERSTAND CHINA?*

There is supposed to be a Chinese curse which condemns men to live in "interesting" times. perhaps one should call it a boon.

I went to China in mid-1947 and lived ten long and "interesting" years in Beijing (Peking) — years which witnessed the freedom of India in 1947, collapse of the KMT rule in China in 1948 and the "awakening of the Chinese giant" under Mao in 1949, followed by a sudden but unfortunately short-lived bloom of Sino-Soviet and Sino-Indian friendships.

I reached Beijing at the end of July 1947, tasted the rigours of a coal-less and therefore bitter winter of 1948 when Beijing was besieged by the communist armies and the University's coal supply lay inacessible to us outside the city walls. The siege fortunately lasted only about a month and on 22nd January 1948 we were "liberated". The University continued to function in a desultory manner. I finally left Beijing in June 1950 ending my student career — only to return to Beijing a year later, in October 1951, as a member of independent India's Embassy in Beijing.

Beida

In those days to be a student of Peking University (more commonly known by its short name "*Beida*") was a great honour. Because Beida symbolised the Chinese renaissance which began in 1919 and in which Beida students led the battle for "Science and Democracy" under the inspiring and patriotic leadership of great men like Tsai Yuan-pei (Cai Yuanpei), Hu Shih and Chen Tu-hsiu (Chen Duxiu). In 1947, Dr. Hu Shih had again returned to Beida as its President and he had gathered a galaxy of Chinese scholars around him.

I thus had the opportunity and priviiege of learning Chinese under scholars like Lo Changpei, Tang Lan, Zheng Zhenduo, Wu Xiaoling and Ren Jiyu at Beida. In addition, I attended classes of Professors Chen Mengjia and Yu Min in Yen Ching (Yanjing) University, of Professor Qi Gong in Furen University and of Professor Zhou Yiliang in Tsing Hua (Qinghua) University. Beida in those days was in its original location in the heart of the town, while Yen Ching and Tsing Hua universities were several kilometres outside the town, and I used to cycle there for my lectures.

Two Beijings

Beijing in 1947 and Beijing today are two different things. Then, it was like a sleepy village which did not initially impress you except with its imposing city walls and watch-towers. But it grew on you with time, because it had character — a very Chinese city with single-storeyed Chinese style houses having many courtyards and red gates. The Forbidden Palace stood out with its shimmering yellow-blue-green tiles. (These tiles are called "liuli" in Chinese which is a transliteration of the Sanskrit word, "vaidurya"). Like other old capitals of China it had a symmetrical design with East-West and North-South lanes. Today's Beijing, in contrast, has become a concrete jungle of high-rise apartments and criss-crossing flyovers like any big Western town. The old city wall is gone; the narrow "hutongs" (lanes) have made way for broad streets and the old historic landmarks of the city have virtually disappeared.

All embassies — and there were not many — were then situated in Dongjiao Minxiang, the erstwhile Legation Quarters.

*Reprinted from *Indian Horizons,* Vol. 43, No. 1-2

The Indian Embassy itself was housed in the Hong Kong-Shanghai Bank building, and I served under three successive Indian Ambasadors — Panikkar, Raghavan and R.K. Nehru — the last being the most successful.

As the only officer who knew Chinese in the Embassy, I became involved in all the VIP visits and talks between Indian and Chinese leaders including Pandit Nehru, Mao Zedong and Zhou Enlai.

Nehru and Mao

It was 40 odd years ago that Nehru visited China in 1954. It was a landmark event in Sino-Indian relations. Sino-Indian friendship reached its high point. Nehru was a sinophile and he had nothing but admiration for Chinese culture. Even the events of 1962 did not change that faith. He was the first leader to make friendship with China a cornerstone of free India's foreign policy.

The Chinese leaders really unrolled the red carpet for Nehru and the massive arrangements for his welcome were overwhelming in their impact. Upon Nehru's return to India it created a cloud-burst of friendly feelings for the Chinese all over India. No wonder, during his return visit to India in 1956, Zhou Enlai received a tumultuous welcome with skies reverberating with the lilting notes of "Hindi Chini Bhai Bhai". This was perhaps the golden period of India-China relations. In Beijing, Indian Embassy received favoured treatment, bettered only by that shown to the Soviet Bloc countries. The degree of Chinese attention to India could be gauged from the number of occasions on which Mao met Indian delegations and graced the Indian Embassy with his presence.

There were at least five different occasions when we had long sessions with Mao. The first two long discussions between Mao and Nehru were during Nehru's visit; then at a dinner in honour of Nehru at Xinqiao Hotel graced by Mao. Even after Prime Minister Nehru's return to India, Mao accepted an invitation for a private dinner with Ambassador R.K. Nehru, a cousin of the Prime Minister. Mao came with Chen Yun and spent nearly four hours at the Embassy chatting away and watching the film "*Jhanak Jhanak Payal Baje*" which had been specially flown from India for the occasion.

The last time I saw Mao was when Ambassador Nehru paid a farewell call on Mao in Canton in January 1957 and Mao, who was accompanied by Tao Zhu, entertained us to a private dinner with a special Chinese wine, called "snake spleen wine" (*shedan jiu*), strongly recommended by Mao for making the eyes "shining and bright". During the dinner Mao spoke about his decision to relinquish Chairmanship of the Republic, and handing over power to his younger colleague Liu Shaoqi.

Mao's poetic farewell to Nehru

My most unforgettable memory of Mao was when he bade goodbye to Pandit Nehru. We were in Zhongnanhai at Mao's place. It was late in the evening, and the moon had come out. Mao escorted Nehru all the way to his car. While shaking Nehru's hand, he suddenly came out with two lines from the Chinese classical poet, Qu Yuan. Quoting him Mao said:

> "There is no greater sorrow than the sorrow of departing alive.
> There is no greater joy than the joy of first meeting."

Alcohol in banquet

During Nehru's visit another memorable thing happened. At Nehru's return banquet for nearly 800 Chinese leaders at the Beijing Hotel, alcohol was served at an official function for perhaps the first and only time in recent times.

Nehru had put me in charge of the banquet arrangements, and it was decided to have a proper Chinese banquet with nearly fifteen courses. Since the Chinese guests were not teetotallers, I thought it would be appropriate to serve liquor, but the Indian governmment practice forbade it and Prime Minister Nehru himself disapproved of it. The then Indian Ambassador Raghavan did not dare raise the subject with the Prime Minister. However Mrs. Indira Gandhi agreed with me that alcohol should be served, and Nehru had such a soft corner for his daughter that it meant half the battle was won! Through a very delicate manoeuvre, we got him to agree to serve drinks — but only mild ones like sherry. So, we served Chinese Yellow wine at all tables.

However, Zhou Enlai, who was the chief guest, preferred Maotai (which is stronger than whisky), and Nehru agreed that we serve it but only at the head table. Needless to say, the dinner was a great success and Pandit Nehru was quite pleased about it.

Zhou-Rajaji dialogue

During Zhou Enlai's visit to India in 1956 his meeting with Rajaji in Madras was a memorable occasion. Rajaji came to call on him at Guindy and there ensued a very lively conversation between the world's two sharp-witted leaders.

While Rajaji strongly advocated India leaving the British Commonwealth, Zhou Enlai, surprisingly argued, and more convincingly too, in favour of India's remaining in the commonwealth.

Zhou on Gandhiji

I believe it was 2nd October 1957; a large Indian Communist Party delegation led by Mr. E.M.S. Namboodiripad was in Beijing. Ambassador Nehru had organised a meeting to commemorate Gandhi-Jayanti. Zhou Enlai himself came to the function. Namboodiripad made a rambling speech. Zhou Enlai spoke briefly but forcefully. Contrary to Soviet assessment, he lauded Gandhiji in eight words paying tribute to Gandhiji's great spirit of simplicity, dedication and capacity to suffer hardships.

Zhou Attends Dr. Atal's Cremation

Dr. Atal, leader of the Aid-China Medical Mission sent by the Indian National Congress and a distant relation of Nehru came to China for a visit and unfortunately died in Beijing. In his last days Zhou Enlai not only made repeated enquiries about his health, but saw him at the hospital and finally even attended his cremation. There were very few people at the electric crematorium. Ambassador Nehru, Zhou Enlai with an aide, and I. There was no Indian priest available. Because of my knowledge of Sanskrit, I had to officiate as a priest. I read a few verses from the Second Chapter of Gita and the ceremony ended.

Travails of an Interpreter

Good interpretation is always a difficult job but when it comes to political topics, it becomes even more so. In the case of the Chinese language, difficulties are compounded by dialectical differences and by the meaning of words being obscured by homonyms. Mao spoke with a very strong Hunan accent which was often difficult to decipher. I remember Mao's telling an Indian delegation to "HO" with Pakistan and his interpreter was stuck because the Chinese sound "HO" stands for two different words, one meaning "peace" and the other meaning "to merge" or "unite". The Chinese interpreter was naturally at a loss to decide whether Mao meant to say "Be at peace with Pakistan" or "Unite and merge with Pakistan". Fortunately, Zhou Enlai, who was present, saw the difficulty and came to the rescue and wrote down the correct Chinese character, which meant "peace".

While watching a Shanghai opera in Huairentang hall inside the Forbidden City, I also incurred Nehru's displeasure because I told him that I could not understand the dialect of the opera. Nehru turned in disgust to Zhou's Chinese interpreter, Mr. Pu Shouchang, and asked him, but the latter also pleaded ignorance and sought Chen Yun's assistance, only then was Nehru pacified.

The second occasion was in Shanghai, when the Mayor held a special musical evening in Nehru's honour. Before the commencement of the programme, the announcer talked at length about a young and talented musician who had returned from the US, and was giving the recital in Nehru's honour. The announcer referred to the musician by the Chinese third personal pronoun "Ta", which is the same word used for "he", "she" or "it". Not knowing the musician, I translated "ta" as "he", but soon the curtain went up to reveal a very pretty female musician. Nehru, hardly able to contain his anger, turned to me and said "You have been referring to the musician as a man, actually it is a woman. What kind of Chinese do you know?" I explained to him that the word "ta" in Chinese did not differentiate the gender and I suggested that he might ask the Mayor if he did not believe me. Nehru did so but the Mayor could not understand what the fuss was all about, and just smiled.

"Standard Indian"

It is only recently that Indians and Chinese are getting to know each other. For hundreds of years there was virtually no contact. Even in the first half of this century, not many Indians had met a proper Chinese. They knew China only from the

Chinese shoemakers and restaurateurs in Calcutta or hawkers who went around with bales of silk cloth on their backs and spoke pidgin English.

Similarly the Chinese apparently remembered Indians only from the bearded burly Sikhs who were brought in by the British as policemen in old concessions of Shanghai, Canton (Guangzhou) and Tientsin (Tinjin). So when I first went to Beijing in 1947, one of my Chinese hostel mates quizzically looked at me and asked "who are you?" I said "I am an Indian". He laughed and said "But you are not the Standard Indian". To him only a Sikh was a standard Indian, while a tiny, beardless weakling like me was not a proper Indian — perhaps a substandard one at best!

A professor in Peking University who came from Shanghai told me how the Chinese mothers in Shanghai used to put their babies to sleep by threatening them: "sleep quickly, otherwise I will throw you to the red-headed devil" (*Hongtou Asan*) meaning the Sikhs.

The Bond of Buddhism

As India and China have been the central theme of my life and career, my mind cannot stop reflecting on things that bind us and things that separate us. A correct appreciation of both would seem essential.

Buddhism has been our strongest bond. It brought India and China together nearly 2,000 years ago.

How the relatively insular Chinese, proud of their own cultural tradition and identity, came to accept a faith like Buddhism — totally foreign to Chinese idiom of thought and life — is in itself a small miracle. Buddhism not only found acceptance and took root in the whole of China but, over the centuries, it became an integral part of the Chinese psyche and social fabric.

It became so, evidently because it filled a vacuum in Chinese life and had something in it for each section of the population — from the plebeian to the poet to the prince. During many Chinese dynasties, Buddhism virtually enjoyed the status of a state religion.

Buddhism brought to China not only its own philosophy of evanescence and emptiness but the whole gamut of Hindu thought and ideas, Hindu social practices and superstitions like idol worship, concepts of heaven and hell, the doctrines of karma and rebirth, an organised order of monkhood, Jataka stories, the story of Hanuman and the Siddhis (or magical powers of sages) and vegetarianism.

To the common Chinese, idol worship (of Buddha) perhaps offered an easy way to enlist divine aid to fulfil their dreams and desires and to end their worries and problems through the inexpensive means of burning an incense! The ingenious doctrine of karma offered a plausible and satisfying explanation for the disparities of wealth in the world; the Jataka stories narrating the exploits of Buddha with some music thrown in, the story of the flying monkey (*Hanuman*) and the *siddhis* (magical powers of sages) all provided colourful entertainment diverting the plebeian mind from the boredom and hardships of daily life.

Buddhist metaphysics with its doctrines of evanescence and illusion (*Maya*) probably fascinated the poetic and the elite.

Chinese imperial rulers, many of whom were men of dubious origin, probably saw in Buddhist monks, willing helpmates who could bestow on them divine blessings and anoint them as "sons of heaven", while Buddhist faith helped divert the minds of their subjects from the harsh realities of their oppressive rule to otherworldly concerns and channelise rebellious thoughts into non-violent ways.

But Buddhism would also seem to have done some real service to the people by bringing to China Ayurveda (Indian system of medicine) which bases its diagnosis on *Naji-Pariksha* (examination of pulse) and *Tridhatu* (Three primary elements in the body viz. phlegm, bile and wind). These two also became the basic principles of Chinese medicines. Indian monks also carried Indian medicinal herbs to China as evidenced by texts of the Chinese *Tripitakas* and the Chinese work called "*Bencao Gangmu*" (or Herbal Pharmacopeia).

Since Buddhistic metaphysical thought came close to Taoist thought, it easily fused with it to create the school of "Qingtan" during the post-Han period from the third century onwards.

If Indian monks did succeed in spreading the gospel of Buddha throughout China and making it virtually a Buddhist country, China, in a way, had it back on India by Sinifying Buddhism to an unrecognisable extent! Indian monks used to live in stone caves; the Chinese Buddhists built beautiful wooden monasteries with Chinese architectural designs. The Chinese virtually eschewed the intricate metaphysical dogmas of Indian Buddhism and stuck to more simple and often Tantric forms of worship. They converted Sanskrit adjectives of Buddha, like Amitabha (one of infinite lustre) and Avalokitesvara (Lord of all he surveys) into proper nouns and made them into separate Gods. Mistranslations and change of gender posed no problem for the Chinese. The most popular Chinese Buddhist idol *Guanyin* is a mistranslation of the original Sanskrit word *Avalokitesvara* (Chinese scholar Xuanzang corrected the translation into "*Guanzizai*" but it failed to gain currency). He was made into a God of Mercy and since Mercy is more fittingly an attribute of women only, Guanyin became a female Bodhisattva! This transformation of gender was a Chinese masterstroke which would have left many orthodox Indian Buddhists dumb-founded. According to the Buddhist canon, no woman can aspire to become a Buddha or Bodhisattva unless she is reborn as a male and even then Buddhahood would be a far cry. In a way China had returned the compliment!

All this is not to say that the dissemination of Buddhism in China was all smooth sailing. It had its ups and downs and its followers often faced persecution. Many Chinese (particularly Confucian) scholars found fault with the philosophical ideas and social implications of Buddhism.

As early as the end of the fifth century, Fan Zhen challenged the idea of soul or spirit having a separate identity apart from the body. He maintained that the spirit is to the body what sharpness is to a knife. No knife, no sharpness. No body, no soul.

In Late Tang (8-9 Century A.D.) there was the famous memorial of Han Yu asking the Emperor to "Turn these monks into men and burn their books" (Buddhist monks being unproductive members of society, were not men).

The most recent and trenchant criticism came at the begining of this century from the veteran Chinese scholar, Dr. Hu Shih, who remarked "Buddhism brought to China not only eighteen heavens but thirty-three hells".

Understanding China

There is a great deal of talk about building closer Sino-Indian friendship which is undoubtedly desirable and necessary. Yet, over the past four decades, we have failed to establish a true or lasting friendship. One of the main reasons, to my mind, is our very inadequate understanding of China and the Chinese people. Granted that it is not easy to understand a country of China's magnitude, antiquity, complexity and cultural richness, serious effort seems to be lacking on our part and ignorance will not promote understanding and without understanding there can be no friendship — in fact, only mishaps!

Moreover, we tend to take Sino-Indian friendship for granted and only remember and harp on the common points, namely that we are both Asians, both are a warm and hospitable people who respect age and learning. But even two brothers can be very different and there are important differences in the ways of thought and expression of Indians and Chinese. Only if we take these differences into account and fashion our behaviour, then can we avoid the pitfalls and misunderstandings which have marred our relations in the recent past.

We are generally aware that the Chinese are a polite but proud and pragmatic people who attach importance to reason; that the Chinese, like the Vedic gods of yore, prefer the indirect to the direct.

Hindus, on the other hand, tend to be emotional, idealistic, voluble, rather vague and a little brash.

But these are only external manifestations of more basic differences rooted in our different world outlooks.

Since ancient times, Hindus were fond of metaphysical speculation and they speculated about reality and life beyond death and put forward the concepts of *Atma* (individual soul) and Brahman (cosmic soul), and the ideal of *Moksha* (emancipation of the soul) or *Amritattva*, (immortality or deathlessness) as the ultimate aim of life.

The Chinese, on the other hand, confined themselves to the mundane affairs of this world, that is to say, the conduct of an individual in society. So, while Hindus produced intricate metaphysical dogmas, the Chinese confined themselves mainly to ethics and etiquette.

Hindus thus became more other-worldly treating this life as a mere preparatory platform for the next.

The Chinese, on the other hand, were firmly bound to this world. For them, there was hardly a world beyond. They lived in the present for the present.

The ideals of life also differed. To a Hindu, the main object of life is immortality or salvation of the Soul — which can only be attained through renunciation of all worldly desires and non-attachment. It cannot be attained by wealth or progeny.

Women and wealth thus became an anathema. Buddhism echoed the same sentiment when it called woman "*Visattika*" (poisonous).

The Chinese did not aim at any salvation of the Soul. In fact, they had hardly a word for soul and there was no soul without a body. So the body was more important. It was a sacred gift from the parents which must be nurtured with care. Body needs food, drink and sex. So these were accepted as the normal and natural urges of man.

To a Hindu the body was an impure appendage which impedes the emancipation of the Soul by imprisoning it. So the body is better despised or even discarded rather than decorated. Hindus thus believed in various *Bratas* (vows) to emaciate the body. Some Bratas prescribe penance wherein one sits among four fires under the blazing sun!

To a Hindu, the spirit is more important than the form; and intention, more important than expression. Thus a Hindu often tends to be informal to the extent of shoddiness. Although a Hindu feels thankful, he would think it too formal to thank some one in so many words. Expression would seem to devalue intention. Curiously enough, many Indian languages derived from Sanskrit had no word for "thank you" -- "Dhanyawad" etc. are modern coinages.

The Chinese have at least three or four different words to express thanks. To a Chinese, the form is as important, if not more, than the spirit. The Chinese tend to be sticklers for protocol and form. They are a more formal people and tend to be tidy and neat.

The Chinese seem to observe a strict reciprocity in human relations. If a Chinese works for you and is paid by you he will try to give you full worth of the money paid to him. The Chinese will not keep a dinner or a gift unreturned. What is received must be returned.

This Chinese reciprocity also works in a vicious way. When it comes to war or feuds, it is eye-for-eye and tooth-for-tooth. As Confucius says "if injury is rewarded by kindness then what is the reward for kindness?" As Mao Zedong said: "If someone attacks me I must counter attack. If someone does not attack I do not attack him either". The Chinese are evidently good friends but bad enemies.

Hindu attitude, on the other hand, tends to be more casual and tolerant. Indians may not be too meticulous in returning visits or gifts, not because of any lack of intention but due to a general laxity. Yet, he is willing to forgive and forget. And he seems to be lukewarm in both friendship and enmity.

A Chinese accepts responsibility for his actions and consequences thereof without "bearing a grudge to heaven or man".

Indians seem prone to find an excuse or pass on the responsibility to some one else. Hindu religiosity may have played a part in it. For centuries the Bhakti cult in India encouraged an escapist attitude to life and society by transferring all responsibility to God. All that an Indian was asked to do was to repeat the name of God ad infinitum. God was there to do everything and shoulder all the burdens while man did nothing.

Hindus seem to have excessive faith in the efficacy of the written word and tend to be legalistic. Written word seems to give them a greater sense of security than the oral one. Indians regard word of "*shabda*" as a valid means of knowledge and elevate it to the status of a cosmic force (*Shabda-Brahma*).

To a Chinese, oral assurance is enough. Vice-Foreign Minister Zhang Hanfu was fond of telling us: "We mean what we say". 19th century European traders described how all their big deals with the Chinese in Shanghai etc. were oral and yet there never was any default in payment. In the last days of KMT when inflation was sky-high I found our grocer sticking to the price quoted by him in the morning, although we were making the payment in the evening when the Chinese Yuan had gone down by 50 per cent.

The Chinese are long-term planners and are deliberate in action. Indians seem often swayed by short term benefits and seem to react to situation as they come up and then act in haste.

In negotiations Indians would lay all their cards on the table; the Chinese take a much longer time to reveal their true hand. In fact as in Urdu poetry the real kick and twist comes last. In negotiating with China you need patience and perseverence.

As a mediaeval Chinese author has observed: "the Chinese are good with their eyes, Indians, good with their ears". The Chinese are good at painting and handicrafts. Indians excel in music. The Chinese music is relatively simple and as Hirabai Badodekar once observed to me, "the Chinese music seems to have only two Ragas; Bhupa and Durgam". It is said that Indian monks were the first to discover the tonal character of the Chinese language.

This is not a complete catalogue but only some tentative observations which are open to correction. I havenot gone into the faults or failings of each side. That would be a bigger and perhaps more bitter exercise.

C.V. RANGANATHAN

51

HOW TO UNDERSTAND DENG XIAOPING'S CHINA*

This paper is the result of an experience-based study of China acquired through long years of working in and on China as a diplomat in the service of India. Its conclusions are more intuitive than empirical, more practical than conceptual. Some random thoughts are put together in an attempt to underline the need for Indians to develop the habit of an independent assessment of recent developments in China rather than depend on borrowed judgements made from different strategic viewpoints. The paper is therefore an attempt to put domestic and external developments relating to China in a context which would suit India's interests in the several changed circumstances witnessed in contemporary times. It is a plea for "understanding" various developments in China from an Indian perspective rather than from a borrowed one.

A starting point for our discussions on understanding China could begin with the domestic evolution of China since the death of Mao Zedong which in turn is inextricably linked with Deng Xiaoping. There can be little doubt that in these last few years of the 20th Century Deng can be considered one of the world's pre-eminent leaders, the impact of whose actions will be felt into the next century as China looms as the world's next super-power as a result of his reform.

Deng pursued many goals during his lifetime, but none more persistently than strengthening the Chinese nation-state. As a staunch nationalist in the tradition of other great Communist leaders of China he sought to restore China's wealth and power. This quest is a consistent refrain during the 19th and 20th centuries: creation of a modern industrial base; transformation of China's agrarian social structure; attainment of a materially comfortable standard of living for the populace; reclaiming national independence, dignity and freedom of manoeuvre in foreign relations; a strong national defence and maintenance of territorial integrity and attainment of great power status. However while he may not have been the first leader with these goals, he was the most successful in realising them to a substantial degree.

Deng inherited from Mao a stagnant economy, alienated society and a paralysed polity. He will bequeath to his successors a robust economy and rejuvenated society, although a political system which is common to the few surviving Leninist Party States. In this Deng was a true Leninist. But unlike Mao who assaulted the commanding heights of the Party/State, Deng sought to rebuild it. Deng believed like other Chinese reformers before him that a strong state which monopolized political power was essential to economic development. His views were reinforced by the East Asian developmental model.

In 1989 when the Tian An Men incident took place Deng faced a paradox; his economic reform programme and the autonomy from State control that he created for Chinese from many walks of life inevitably decreased the Party's previous hegemony. But the brief attempt at subjecting society to propaganda and economic austerity since those events only brought home the realisation that these instruments had dulled as a result of the 1980s reforms. From the collapse of Communist regimes across the globe in 1989-91 Deng drew the lesson that only material gain can ultimately save socialism. Of course tight political control and the loyalty of the armed forces and security personnel were important, but without achieving further material gains, continuing survival of the Party's dominance would increasingly be called into question. Consequently in 1992 Deng reignited radical economic reform. The results were impressive indeed: 12.8 per cent GNP growth in 1992 and a pouring-in of Foreign Direct Investment at unprecedented levels.

---

*Paper presented to the 1995 Seminar on "India and China Looking at Each other"

Deng Xiaoping ruled very differently from Mao Zedong. He did not rely on charisma or ideology. He preferred to rule through formal Party institutions and Leninist norms. But later in his career in 1991-92, like Mao, he circumvented his chosen successors and those who were for a slower pace of reforms, by taking his case for accelerated reforms directly to the people during his famous tour of southern China.

However unlike Mao, Deng trusted in the entrepreneurial spirit in Chinese culture and did much to remove state strictures from public lives. Getting the government "off-the-backs" of average Chinese, in order to free their commercial instincts will be one of Deng's enduring legacies. He rolled back much of the intrusive apparatus that had intimidated a vast nation and provided the stimulus for the realisation of the Napoleonic prophecy of the awakened Chinese giant. His lasting contribution was to stimulate the revolution of rising expectations but like other successful reformers in history, who satisfy people's needs in a significant measure, his reforms created new desires, which he chose not to attempt to fulfil.

The success in China of seeming adherence of economics and politics to different rules, such that there is openness in one and controls in the other can be explained by the background circumstances under which Deng became the "Paramount Leader" and the very traditional Chinese political culture of which he is a distinguished heir. Let us examine this a little further since it provides, albeit very partially, an approach to the conundrum of why "liberal democracy" has not accompanied economic growth.

Deng's rise to power was facilitated by the situation in which China found itself after Mao's death. The decade of the Culural Revolution horror had shattered illusions the Chinese public had about the potency of ideology and left them profoundly cynical about Marxism. Yet equally it reinforced the Chinese cultural dread of the reality of anarchy and disorder. They wanted an end to ideological politics but remained fearful of unpredictable change. This distinctive combination of attitudes provided the basis for legitimacy for the Deng era. The people had enough of grand collective visions and were ready to focus on private concerns but at the same time they wanted public stability and public order. It is no coincidence that the Chinese Government used the bitter memories of the Cultural Revolution decade of anarchy and disorder to justify the use of military force in 1989 at the Tian An Men square. Deng resumed a leadership position in the late seventies when all Chinese wanted to rid themselves of the memories of the Cultural Revolution.

When reforms were initiated by Deng he did not seem to be operating from a given set of plans. Rather he was primarily responding to the universal desire of the Chinese people to escape from the effects of Mao's rule. Much of the change associated with Deng's elevation to power came about because he was willing to tolerate what once had been taboo. The idea that some sections of the population could get rich first was revolutionary only because it so blatantly contradicted the norms of Mao's China. Quite a few changes sought by Deng actually repeated earlier formulas or policy attempts, but this time they were allowed to achieve fruition. His reform measures came at a moment in history when China had to break out of its isolation, abandon an ideological rhetoric and let in some common sense. If the timing of Deng's assumption of power after the disastrous years of the Cultural Revolution in China was suitable, so was his assumption of the mantle of traditional Chinese political culture most natural. For politicians who live by the principle that the name of the game is public exposure it is dificult to understand a political environment in which leaders consciously shun the limelight, do not take advantage of modern communications like radio and TV, and take the utmost precaution to escape prying eyes. Chinese political culture traditionally operates on the premise that omnipotence lies in the mystery which invisibility evokes. The working of the world of the mandarinate were hidden from the eyes of commoners. The Chinese tradition is the greater the leader the more invisible the personage contributed decisively to the relative failure of the Chinese. They did not develop the art of oral persuasion and oratory as nurtured and admired first in Athens and Rome and then in Parliaments or Congresses. Deng's refusal to mount the political stage as Chairman of the Party, Prime Minister or President in the late seventies when he could easily have assumed any office of his choice and thus exploit the powers of modern mass media technologies, thus conformed to a long standing tradition. It was however not just the Chinese people who have assumed that, even though they had little to go on, they in fact did know all that was necessary to fathom Deng's goals, values and political methods. China watchers all around the world also claimed to understand this non-public man!

Following another Chinese political tradition, Deng was the master of the insider's art of personnel management. As a quintessential administrator he understood that power lay in the management of officials. Yet he was almost unique among

Chinese leaders in his understanding that it was possible to delegate responsibilities while staying in command. He rarely intervened in details, except in making personnel appointment. Although both his chosen nominees Zhao Ziyang and Hu Yaobang fell from his political grace, much of the specifics of economic reforms can be credited to the former and the cultural opening and rehabilitation of Cultural Revolution victims to the latter. The mastery shown by Deng as a behind-the-scene administrator showed an extraordinarily self-confident and secure personality. The question whether s stable political succession to Deng has been achieved, continues to be raised after his death, although the transition to Jiang Zemin has been relatively smooth. This again is a non-issue as events since Deng's death have proven.

Another speculation, following the spectacular economic growth of parts of China, is that China faces separation or its Chinese counterpart in warlordism. If one looked at Chinese history, even at the height of the warlord period not a single warlord declared independence. All of them in one way or another flew the banner of fealty to a unified China. What they sought was power in their own backyard. In any event, the conditions that led to warlordism in the early 20th century no longer exist in China. You do not have, as you did then, divisions or larger bodies of troops comprised exclusively of men from the same province. There is a national army in China with units whose personnel are thoroughly mixed and who come from all over China. There is not much possibility now of a military commander building the kind of independent military force needed to sustain his power against the centre.

There has also been tremendous explosion in the geographical mobility and educational level of the Chinese people as well as vast improvement in transportation and communications — things that help tie China together. While it is certainly true that in recent years the Central Government has lost power and the provinces have gained greater autonomy, one should view this as an unstructured devolution of power from the Centre. The last time China had a strong Central Government under Mao and that produced disaster for China in his last years. What we are seeing now is more in keeping with the traditional form of Chinese government.

The dangerous implications of the disparity of incomes -- the difference in living standards between the advanced south and east coast and the backward interior of China is referred to as a dangerous flash point for Chinese politics. True there are real differences. However, the differences between the regions are not as important as how people judge their circumstances in terms of their own experience. The differences say between Guangzhou or Shanghai and rural Gansu are enormous. What counts to the Gansu family is not how the folks in Guangzhou or Shanghai are getting along, but rather how life is now in comparison to the past. And for the average family in Gansu, life — while still extraordinarily hard in any terms — is noticeably better now than it was 15 years ago.

Having looked at the political evolution of China in the Deng era and made some speculations, it must be recognised that as the country rushes headlong towards modernization and consumerism and with communism being abandoned almost everywhere, there is anticipation that the emergence of a civil society can impel the country forward. Old structures of power and ideology structures and groups have taken over functions previously monopolised by the Party-State. While a weakened Party-State remains strong enough to prevent people from blatant violations of official policy, it can no longer manage society as actively as it did in the past or expect the same degree of compliance.

While major transformations in the mode of governance are not imminent while the first generation of revolutionaries remain in power, changes are taking place which are inherent in the situation China faces both externally and domestically. China's involvement in the international community and its search for great power status force the government to atleast adopt postures which attenuate if not modify domestic policies. In order to maintain access to international credits and trade, concessions are made to human-rights concerns and concerns relating to the international trade regimes. The domestic scene also imposes contexts that cannot be ignored any longer: the rise of a bureaucratic technocracy, limited leadership institutionalisation, autonomous private organisation, coastal zones open to foreign influences and the appearance of new social groupings.

However, to determine how far China has moved towards a civil society depends in part on definition and perspective. Despite ineffective attempts to re-centralise control to reassert the primacy of the post-1989 Party-State there seems little prospect of successfully arresting the evolutionary trends towards privatisation of behaviour and acceptance of autonomous associations. Although very large sections of Chinese life and culture are now not subject to state interference on a *de facto* basis, the Chinese government has yet to acknowledge the *dejure* rights of civil society. Social autonomy has therefore weak institutional bases and confined to non-political activities. Such social autonomy can flourish as long as the Four Principles evolved by Deng are not challenged.

The yardstick of the emergence of "civil society" to judge the quality of political life in a developing country however may be an artificial attempt at forcing an equation between Western and Chinese experiences. What we have in China today is an empirical paradox of marketisation and civil associations without multi-Party democratic development. The presence of markets is supposed to signal the imminent arrival of other parts of the "capitalism" compound, like private ownership and democracy. If those other parts do not follow, they nevertheless should. From there it is but a short step to the conclusion: If only the Chinese leaders were not so reluctant to abandon socialism for capitalism, the desired developments would be sure to follow. This kind of reasoning for sure has its echo in China on the opposite side of the spectrum : Given markets, the rest of the undesirable elements of capitalism must certainly follow. Therefore the integrity of socialism must be reasserted against incipient capitalism.

It is time to leave such arguments behind. Rural China before 1950 saw six centuries of private ownership and a market economy, but remained underdeveloped, with the vast majority of the population tied to subsistence-level food production. For rural China to return today to the pre-1950 economic organisation would probably mean even greater problems than those faced earlier: The population is twice as large, and the easy advances and tractor plowing have already been made. It is difficult to see how the market could work its supposed transformative magic against such odds.

The collectivist approach of the 1950s through the 1970s should similarly be left behind. Under that approach, total crop output workday stagnated. The majority of the rural people remained at a bare subsistence standard of living. It makes as little sense today to persist in that appraoch as to return to the pre-1950 economy.

What then? The first task of scholarly research in this area, it seems to me, is to explain why the rural economy developed so vigorously in the 1980s when such development has eluded both the free-market-cum-private-property rural China of 1350-1950 and the planned, collectivist rural China of the 1950s to the 1970s. What was it about the paradoxical mixing of collective ownership by villages and townships with a marketised economy that helped to generate dynamic rural industrialisation?

China's revolutionary history is distinctive for the very large role played by her villages and townships. Those were the loci of Communist organising and revolutionary power. Through collectivisation in the 1950s, villages and townships also became the basic units of ownership of land and other means of production. The permanence and stability of their constituent populations were next ensured by the extraordinary population registration policies enforced from the late 1950s on. Then, they served as the basic units of organisation for massive efforts in water control, public health, and education, greatly elaborating in the process their administrative apparatus. All these changes gave these communities a role in rural change that is exceptional from the standpoint both of developing countries and socialist countries. Finally, in the 1980s, under the twin stimuli of increased autonomy and market incentives, they became the primary units for rural industrialisation. Their crucial role in the resulting development raises the question: Has an empirical reality emerged in China that represents an alternative path to rural modernisation that fits neither of the simple models of socialism or capitalism?

The early nineties witnessed three developments in the international sphere which caused the Chinese to reassess foreign and security policies. One was the downfall of communism almost everywhere. This graphically illustrated the true relationship between modemisation and revolution in the 20th century: Revolution now meant anti-socialist economics, and pro-democracy and marketisation, and economic development was now a pre-requisite to political modemisation, not the reverse. The end of global communism impacted directly upon Chinese foreign policy. The party realised that its time in power would be short unless it reconstructed itself, that marketisation was its only economic altemative, that the influence of personality on politics would have to be limited, that ideology would have to be replaced by a mixture of nationalism and traditionalism. Also that foreign policy would have to include the inputs of new groups in Chinese society and thus that China would not always speak with one voice that China would have to repair its relations with the market democracies and then keep in their good stead for a considerble period. Further, that the door to investment, trade. and technology transfer would have to be kept open wide enough to admit foreign cultural and political influences. For all these reasons, a long-term centrist foreign policy would have to be maintained. This is also the background to Deng Xiaoping's visit to South China in 1992 when he called for a speed-up in opening-up of the

Chinese economy. Another was the definitive end of the Cold War, signified not only by the anti-communist revolutions in East Europe and the subsequent withdrawal of Russian forces from that region but also by the downfall of communism in the Soviet Union itself and the consequent breakup of that country. The strategic triangle-based international system was replaced by a loose arrangement among five power centes — North America, Greater Europe, Russia, China and Japan with very different characteristics: partial substitution of formal alliances by an ad hoc concert-of-Europe; power centered in the Group of Seven-plus-One adding Russia, with China on the outside; domination of marketisation, democratisation, interdependence, and near-universal attention to domestic problems; technology as the most important driving force for change; and the rise to prominence of global issues. Together, these meant that China would have to cooperate in loose international arrangements if it wished to exert its influence abroad. Economics would replace security as Beijing's central concern for the foreseeable future. And its Asian and Global power-status would derive mostly from its rate and level of GNP, per capita income, and technological prowess and much less from military power, population, extent of land, and quantity of production.

The Gulf War was the third systemic change. Not only did it symbolize the replacement of one international era with another. It demonstrated the integral power of the market democracies and reinforced China's need to re-establish a foreign policy derived from reform and the open door. It also showed that a high-technology-based military was China's only military option and that construction of such a force would take considerable time, effort and domestic change. If so, China would have to take the low road in foreign policy, compromising with former or potential enemies, and biding its time (unless unavoidable, direct threats intervened) until its relative power allowed it to achieve its expanded list of international goals. It would be best, therefore, to settle disputes with its Asian neighbours, not engender new disputes or exacerbate old ones, and place as much emphasis as possible on acquiring the new elements of powor as quickly as possible through continuing the prior emphasis on rapid economic development. That meant, in addition, coming to terms (if possible) with the United States or at least not so ruining relations with Washington as to jeopardige Beijing's fundamental economic and security goals. Moreover, China would have to hold constant, or improve if possible, its relations with the other major Asian powers — Japan, Russia and India. It meant, further, doing what was within China's capability to cool down and perhaps help solve a range of regional security problems or at least not delibertely exacerbate them. These included the North Korean nuclear weapons question and associated Korean Peninsular matters, the Spratly Islands issue, reversion of Hong Kong, the possibility of Burmese implosion/explosion, the Kashmir question, and above all relations with Taiwan. Finally, it meant moving toward, if not enthusiastically embracing, the notion that China should work together with other relevant Asian powers to construct a new regional and trans-Pacific political, economic and security order through cooperative invention of new institutions in these three arenas. Rapid economic growth and a rising GDP has enabled China to spend more on its military modernisation, bringing about significant increments in its power thus raising a debate in China's neighbourhood and in the West about how the Chinese would in future deal with a force projection capability. The answer to this question must keep in perspective several factors. China cannot afford to break with the USA which still plays a predominant role in the Asian security scenario and in its economy. Beijing cannot afford to be perceived by its Asian neighbours as threatening, lest they band together and clamour for American leadership. Even a single Chinese foray against one of them would be regarded as proof of a China threat. Together with Europe and USA these states, particularly in South East and East Asia, are the sources of markets, technology and investment without which China's growth would nearly cease.

Experts evaluate that full military modernisation dependent on economic growth would itself take China two decades to accomplish. China needs to balance a desire to expand military influence commensurate with its new economic power and international position and the need to retain markets, sources of supply and international good-will. Thus there is a gap between the country's military capabilities and intentions on the one hand, and its military policies and involvement, on the other.

Account must be taken also of a variety of domestic factors. China, like any other large developing society, has its share of problems inspite of its rapid and impressive growth rate. Inflation, too rapid urbanization, loose controls on population growth, maldistribution of social product, a slow-down in agricultural growth and a speed-up of that in the cities, worsening rural-urban differences, lack of macro-tools of indirect control of the economy, massive infrastructure problems, rising crime and corruption and speculation, a huge "floating" population etc. are some of the ills Chinese society faces and Deng's successors will have their hands full in dealing with these problems.

Turning to the future and the prospect of India-China relations, the first ingredient or requirement in India is the sturdy retention of our independence of judgement about the rapidly changing world around us which we were taught to practise in the first decade of our independence with respect to China, with respect to Non-Alignment and with respect to the process to which we made significant contributions of working for a plural world where there would be a multiplicity of actors. Such an approach was in keeping with our own complex society where diversity, tolerance, secularism, rule of law and respect for different faiths were enshrined in our Constitution. It is ironic to note that economists from the West have today made it a cottage industry to compare India more favourably as an investment destination than China. It seems they see merits in us, which our Indo-pessimism misses. Economists from the same sources were doing exactly the opposite from the mid-fifties to the late eighties! This underlines the need for us to maintain the independence of judgement about developments in our biggest neighbour.

To this we must add the element of self-confidence in our political system together with all its faults, and the Indian genius of seeking consensus-based cooperation from the people. To the admirers of the use of coercion in bringing about Family Planning one could pose the success of the Kerala and Tamil Nadu models in India in this field.

In particular the state of Kerala does provide an interesting comparison with China, since it too enjoys high levels of basic education, health care, and so on. Kerala's birth rate of 18 per thousand is actually lower than China's 19 per thousand and this has been achieved without any compulsive measures. Kerala has a better record than China in factors which help voluntary reduction in birth rates. Kerala has a higher adult female literacy than in every Province in China (86% to 68%). Male and female life expectancies at birth in China are 68 and 71 years. The 1991 figures for Kerala are 69 and 74 years respectively. These commendable results in Kerala are achieved with none of the adverse effects noted in China — heightened female mortality, the dangers of the "one-child" male-oriented family etc. Even with the advantages of coercive methods the Chinese fertility-rate has fallen more slowly than in Kerala. Tamil Nadu has recorded an even faster fall of fertility rates, from 3.5 in 1979 to 2.2 in 1991. Needless to add the Kerala and Tamil Nadu examples have to be contrasted with UP, Bihar, Madhya Pradesh and Rajasthan where the levels of female education, and of general health care are much lower and all have high fertility rates between 4.4 and 5.1.

Now that relations between India and China have acquired a degree of strategic stability following the visit of two Indian Prime Ministers to China and one to India by the Chinese Premier between 1988 and 1993 and one by President Jiang Zemin to India in 1996, the task remains of adding significant substance to the overall relationship such as would make an impact on each of the countries and an impact on the changing world at large. This task is easier said than done sine the habit of intensive search for complimentarities — political, economic, social and cultural — is yet to take root in both societies.

In the way in which our Continental-sized population and their economies have operated in the past, with changes coming in the direction of globalisation setting in only recently, much work needs to be done in both countries. The habit of dependence on the two Governments alone and their agencies will have to be replaced by non-governmental institutions and by the societies at large.

Signs for closer overall relations and closer understanding and cooperation between India and China are propitious. Our two peoples have deep respect for each other as there has been no historical legacy of exploitative relations post our Independence. There is admiration for our long history of cultural interactions from ancient times which extends to this day even though the medium of interaction is not lofty Buddhist philosophy but the popular medium of films and pop culture. Both our peoples feel uncomfortable with the new international disorder which characterises the post-cold war world. Both want to maximise resources and the access to lucrative markets and are wary of "conditionalities" that impede their products from reaching these markets. Both adopt similar stances in international negotiations which have a bearing on technology and financial flows. Above all both have an aversion to the dangers posed to large countries by ethnic or religious extremism. Lastly several agencies from each of the countries — both at Governmental and non-Governmental levels — have increased their interactions and the immediate effect is felt on two-way trade which has seen a commendable increase in recent years.

References

Deng Xiaoping - Portrait of a Chinese Statesman, Edited by David Shambangh. Clarendon Paper-backs. Especially the contribution by Lucien pye.

State and Society in China: The Consequences of Reform, edited by Arthur Lewissenbaun. Especially the introduction by A.L. Rosenbaun.

ERIC GONSALVES

52

POSITIVE AGENDA FOR POSITIVE ACTION: BETTER INDIA-CHINA UNDERSTANDING

The 21st century has been advertised as the Asian century. Asia has made enormous progress in the last fifty years in every dimension — economic, social and political. Yet the promise can only be fulfilled if Asian governments demonstrate sufficient will and capacity. On the one hand, in the new world of globalisation and interdependence this would require independence of judgement and resilience to maintain it under pressure. On the other hand, it also means abandoning the luxury of unabashedly pursuing national interest. Competition must continue but within certain limitations of transparency and teamwork imposed by common Asian objectives. Ultimately Asia and the rest of the world would benefit as this is not a zerosum game.

The key players would have to include Japan, the world's No. 2 economy and China a potential great power. It should also include India once she is able to complete internal reforms and achieve her potential to be another great power. Without a degree of harmonisation of attitudes between these key players and the regional groupings the Asian dream is not attainable. India and China have improved relations in the last two decades but much more can be done.

After 1949 India-China relations after experiencing a high went down to a nadir in 1962 and remained frozen thereafter. The facts are well known. In-depth analysis may still have to wait till the motivations of the Chinese leadership are uncovered by historians. A new phase of gradual improvement started with the exchange of Ambassadors in 1976, and the first high level Chinese visit in 1978. This trend was concretised by Foreign Minister Vajpayee's visit in February 1979 and has continued till today despite some temporary setbacks. It is no coincidence that Deng Xiaoping had then just emerged as the unchallenged leader in China. The measure of improvement can be appreciated if one takes the negative areas in the relationship that have been eliminated or reduced to manageable proportions. Even by the time Foreign Minister Huang Hua paid a return visit in 1981 official level discussions had put many issues in perspective notwithstanding public diagreement over Afghanistan and Cambodia. These have crystallised into firm agreement in succeeding years. The challenge for the future is moving the dialogue into positive areas.

The humiliation suffered in the 1962 conflict and occupation of Indian territory earlier resulted in an understandable emotional Indian reaction. For a long time any attempt to find a compromise solution for the boundary dispute was regarded as surrender and anti-national. Yet even Indian scholars are now beginning to accept that neither the Indian nor Chinese boundary lines were as sanctified by history and tradition etc. as the two sides so confidently stated. Hence a negotiated settlement remains the only way out. But this was unacceptable to both leaderships in the 1960s and later. Prime Minister Zhou Enlai during his visit in 1960 suggested some adjustments which the Indian side rejected. No progress could be made at official level talks in 1961. Then came the border war and relatively frozen relations, although courtesy was gradually restored. Deng Xiaoping in his meeting with Vajpayee hinted at a compromise based on existing ground realities which again could not be accepted by India. The proposal was placed on record a little later by Deng in an interview with an Indian journalist. The public Chinese position was that problems left over by history could be kept aside while the climate was improved. During Huang Hua's visit, the gap between the two positions was partly bridged by the Chinese accepting the need to give public priority to resolving the boundary question and India accepting the need to simultaneously improve other relations.

Since then the boundary has been discussed at the official level in a series of meetings and very gentle progress has been recorded. It is however important to note that both governments have implemented their stated intentions to maintain peace and tranquillity along the line of actual control. Minor trangressions by either side a few times in the last 35 years have never been allowed to escalate out of control even after the Sumdurongcho incident. During the conflicts with Pakistan in 1965 and 1971, despite diplomatic rhetoric China did not seek to influence Indian strategy by moving forces. The withdrawals of Indian forces from the border for use in difficult times in Punjab, Kashmir and Sri Lanka have not been taken advantage of. India too has never really taken advantage at times of Chinese weakness in Tibet. In 1993 and 1996 formal agreements were signed which provided for consultations, and to reduce military forces along the line of control and above all, renouncing the use of force.

Emotion in India would now accept a compromise once it demonstrated that honour is uneffected in the Western Sector. Chinese security concerns about Tibet have also been largely satisfied. The time now appears ripe to move towards working out a final agreement on the boundary taking into account the present ground position including the accession of Sikkim to India and the real security requirements of the two parties.

Another major area of concern on both sides was interference in domestic affairs and support to anti-national groups. In the early years, the export of revolution was seen as the bounden duty of all Communist States. Even with the loud cheers of "Hindi Cheeni Bhai Bhai" in the air, material and moral support was being given to dissident groups in India. This caused India grave problems in dealing with the tribal groups in the North East. India too was an active or passive participant in Western efforts to destabilise China through Tibet. By 1980 both governments had realised that the national interest did not benefit from these manoeuvres. In official level discussions held during that year it was confirmed that official support to each other's insurgency was at an end. This position has remained unchanged till now. By the mid-1990s both governments have separately discovered the need to publicly castigate cross-border activities by fundamentalists, militants etc. Common action is now necessary in this area and also to control the menace posed by drug-trafficking and arms smuggling. An agreement on drug traffic was signed during Jiang Zemin's visit to India in 1996.

Tibet remains a very sensitive issue for China. India accepted Chinese sovereignity in the 1954 Treaty. China's more forceful exercise of control and the consequent departure of the Dalai Lama for exile in India in 1959 put India in a delicate position just as the boundary dispute was escalating from clashes towards conflict. The post-1962 clandestine operations and their end are mentioned above. Following Vajpayee's visit India's pilgrims were allowed access once more to Kailash and Mansarovar. China also began to search fitfully for a modus vivendi with the Dalai Lama. This effort has so far proved unsuccessful. Suspicions about India's intentions on Tibet are still voiced from time to time and protests lodged about the sincerity with which the Dalai Lama is made to refrain from political activity. Yet it would seem that China does not feel it is seriously threatened in Tibet by India. Extending the doctrine of "one country two systems" used for Hong Kong and Taiwan to Tibet might work better than the present policy of forcing Tibet into the existing Chinese political system. The Dalai Lama and most Tibetans would be quite satisfied with such a half-way house. China's present attitude causes a dilemma for India between two cherished principles of maintaining pluralism while resisting self determination. The earlier this difficulty is removed the better.

Third country relationship have bedevilled India-China relations. South Asia has provided the longest lasting friction. For Pakistan and China to make common cause over the former's problems with India was normal real politik, but to India which has espoused China's case in world fora against strong western pressure this seemed gross ingratitude. Sino-Pak military-collaboration was seen as the major security threat and also became one of India's most serious diplomatic preoccupations. Pakistan did benefit enormously from the supports of weapons and the transfer of technology especially nuclear technology. Support to Pakistan over Kashmir, to Bangladesh, to the Nepalese call for a zone of peace and independence and over almost every other contentious issue to subcontinental neighbours against India further embittered relations. China's diplomatic support emboldened India's neighbours to take a tough line vis-a-vis India. It must be accepted that India too was unreasonable in certain matters and made it easy for China to join in the chorus against India's "hegemony".

By the 1980s the refrain began to change. In line with Deng's thesis that developing countries needed peace to concentrate on development, the tenor of Chinese statement was to urge South Asian countries to resolve their problems among themselves while reassuring them that the bilateral relationship with China would not be affected by the improvement of Sino-Indian relations. This attitude was taken a little further during the recent visit of President Jiang Zemin to South Asia in 1996 during which developing a relationship with South Asia as a single entity was given pride of place. By this time China had also acquiesced to U.S. pressure by stopping the transfer of nuclear technology to Pakistan. India must find ways quickly to give greater substance to a China-South Asian relationship. There are still important elite groups in China and India who have to realise the inevitability of regional cooperation in the context of globalisation. India and the smaller South Asian states have already understood the value of regional cooperation. The China card is no longer in play. To make China and other neighbouring regional groups economic partners of SAARC is the next logical step. Energy, environment, water resources, transport and infrastructure are among the areas that can provide for fruitful cooperation. It would also reinforce the inevitability of South Asian regional cooperation to Pakistan.

India's earlier interaction with China was mainly in the Asian arena. India helped bring about and implement the Korean Armistice and Indo-Chinese Peace Accords. China entered the world stage at the Afro-Asian conference at Bandung in 1954 on a fraternal note. But Asian developments soon established the divergence of policies. China supported revolution in Malaysia, Sukarno's fight against neo-imperialism and hoped to shape the ideology and attitudes of newly emergent Afro-Asian countries according to Mao's ideas. By 1965, this effort had largely failed as the army displaced Sukarno and South East Asia began to stabilise; the 1965 Afro-Asian Conference never materialised; and the Cultural Revolution isolated China. Meanwhile the Non-Aligned Movement with India as a leader was becoming the standard bearer of the Third World.

Today's situation is very different awhich portends against taking anything for granted. China has reversed herself on almost all policies, and is accepted as a important power and major partner in the Asia-Pacific Region. India has become an outsider mainly because its economy has stagnated and its indifference in taking more than minimal interest in Asia. India will have to work hard and emerge as a credible partner for South East and East Asia if it is to become a player in the Asian system.

The evolution of the cold war had its fallout on India-China relations. In its early days when everything was black and white India's efforts to play peacemaker and to push China's claims in the U.N. etc. got her dubbed as a fellow-traveller in McCarthy's America. The inevitable improvement of relations with the Soviet Union after Pakistan joined American-sponsored alliances raised doubts in China at a time when the Soviet Union's revolutionary credentials were being questioned by Mao. The Soviet Union after some hesitations leaned towards India after 1962. Ironically China's objections to detente were speedily set aside when the opportunity came in 1971 to establish relations with the USA. Pakistan was the conduit. When India was about to face a major confrontation with Pakistan over Bangladesh coupling with Pakistan's getting closer to China and the U.S.A. it was necessary to formalise India's linkage with the Soviet Union in the Indo-Soviet Treaty.

Bangladesh was liberated and recognised. India's threat perceptions diminished and the Indo-Soviet Treaty's utility also diminished. There was a brief flurry of concern when the Soviet action in Afghanistan seemed to revive earlier concerns. But they faded away soon enough. Despite the efforts of a section of the Indian leadership it became clear that Soviet and Indian interests over China did not necessarily coincide.

Indo-China and Vietnam also posed a source of friction. China did not support North Vietnam as whole heartedly as they did North Korea. China and Vietnam are historical rivals. Further, the Chinese establishment -- and Deng in particular -- developed a strong antipathy to the Vietnamese leadership. The leading Soviet role in supporting Hanoi could have played its part. For India on the other hand, supporting Vietnam was a cardinal principle of her non-aligned policy. China's police action against Vietnam in 1979 during Vajpayee's visit, and India's recognition of the Vietnamese-installed Heng Samrin Government in Cambodia caused temporary polemics. However they did not really impede the process of normalisation between India and China after 1979. One obvious conclusion is that China is callous and India over-sensitive to third country interests.

Most contentious issues have been eliminated by chance or effort from the India-China agenda by now. The major remaining question, i.e. the boundary, can now be settled if the two governments so desire and show the will. Tibet is not really an issue for India and she would be relieved if China and the Tibetans are able to find an accommodation. On South Asia the common ground is growing. There still remains the removal of overall suspicions caused by the hangover of threat perceptions and security concerns over the last 35 years. A limited dialogue between senior military officials has begun and there has been exchanges between think-tanks. However, there is no sign of any attempt to begin a substantive dialogue on military postures and threat perceptions including nuclear threats. Both sides appear to be unwilling to take this up for reasons which are unclear but can be surmised, i.e. existing vested interests. However, they should seriously consider that their basic premise of ensuring peace for development requires transparency and confidence building on security. The more so as it is clear from the 1996 Border Agreement that there is nothing to gain from conflict. This would require that the shadow-boxing whether India is or is not a nuclear power should cease. There could be the further bonus that this would give a fillip to confidence building between India and Pakistan.

There has been a procession of significant high level visits which have helped to improve relation culminating in the visit of Jiang Zemin in 1996. It is important to note that they have covered the broad spectrum of the leadership in the two countries. There is an effective dialogue on economic, cultural and intellectual exchanges. However the level of such exchanges is not commensurate with the existing potential. Trade had quadrupled in this decade and can certainly be expanded many times further if the will is there and the effort is made to study and penetrate markets. Opening up border trade has promise and could ease conditions inside Tibet.

Greater understanding of the other country has to be pursued. China does undertake fairly systematic studies into the Indian polity, economy and society in specialised institutions. Indian scholarship on China which had been commendable has suffered in recent years from a lack of resources and support. It needs to be strengthened. There must also be much larger process of exchanges than at present between experts in social sciences, physical sciences, technology etc.

Both countries are grappling with an immense task of developing an economy and a society with a very large population which makes them unique. Chinese economic reform would have many lessons for India as it started at least 10 years earlier. The evolution of the Indian political system may similarly provide some guidelines as the Chinese seek to modernise their society. Perhaps in the past both have been affected by the "middle kingdom" complex of believing that they know best. Mao's China and Nehru's India were probably the last manifestation of this superiority complex. But today we know only too well that everyone commits mistakes which can be very costly in terms of progress. A greater willingness to undertake comparative studies could be of mutual benefit.

The external environment is of increasing relevance in the era of globalisation. As developing countries dealing with the industrialised world the two countries share a common agenda. The U.S. and its allies will try to retain the existing unipolar system. India and China need an international system with multipolarity, i.e. more democratic decision-making. Should they not share views and concert action to greater effect? No one wants to confront the U.S. rather to convert it from unilateralism to partnership.

In the current post-cold war world, China, Russia and India do have parallel interests in stability in Central Asia. The sooner they start taking concrete action the better. Chinese actions in Myanmar have roused some suspicions about her intended role in the Indian Ocean. However, at present her attitude is unlikely to diverge materially from that of India and the rest of the Indian Ocean Region in wishing to preserve stability there. A direct dialogue is obviously called for to ensure this.

The need is for a positive attitude towards a positive dialogue. It should be substantive and would in time expand itself. No time should be lost in getting it off the ground. What a better India-China understanding requires is positive agenda for positive action.

SALMAN HAIDAR

53

INDIAN POLICIES TOWARDS CHINA

(A TALK AT IGNCA ON 13TH SEPTEMBER 1996)

When I came in here this morning, I thought I must have arrived at a wrong place, the world of culture, arts, liberal thoughts, as the publications in the next room testify, and my sense of bewilderment has been reinforced by Prof. Tan Chung's observations about a holistic perspective, art and culture, messages of love from Guanyin and Krishna and so on. The quotedian world of diplomacy seems far remote from these higher ideas and greater aspirations. Nevertheless, I have to persist and try to say a few words, let me say, couple of preliminaries. I see my colleagues from the East Asian Division*, like me they might be somewhat more inhibited in what they might say in a seminar of this nature. But I have my very distinguished friends and colleagues who were senior to me from the Foreign Service who are extremely knowledgeable about China and who might be in fuller flow than those of us who are still serving in the Ministry.

I am also intimidated by what I am told about the fact that our observations are to be recorded. Well, I hope that this won't be held against me at any rate about others and furthermore I doubt very much if I can say anything of real substance or anything worth recording. But anyway let me take up some of the points that perhaps can be offered at this stage. We have been engaged for quite some time in repairing and restoring and developing relations with China after a period of strain and tension. I need not go into what was done at the time of Mrs. Gandhi, the fact is that we did develop an approach that did not give primacy to the areas of discord without wishing to turn away or without pretending that they did not exist, and we chose instead to seek for areas of mutual benefit and where we could infact develop our relations. Obviously, this has been productive but it requires a will, a settled purpose on the part of the leadership in both countries.

Prof. Tan Chung did refer to this and quite rightly he made a perfectly valid observation. We have been urging others, our neighbours, to adopt a similar approach in handling the problem, not to permit disputes to dominate, but to seek areas of mutual benefit. The fact that we have not got very far on all fronts underlines the relevance and the importance of this long standing approach that we have adopted on bilateralities with China. Now, there was a steady process of exchange, on border and other issues which was steady but also very slow, and through the first part of the last decade. I think it important to recall that in the middle of the last decade, there was a period of renewed difficulty, when it appeared from both sides that activities were taking place on the border, particularly certain sections of the border that brought India trouble, when there was a build up from both sides and an introduction of alarm, (perhaps, "alarm" is not too strong a word), certainly a great deal of watchfulness and a deterioration in our relationship. Owing to this situation what did happen thereafter was a very notable and a bold step taken by the Indian Prime Minister Rajiv Gandhi who, in 1988, took the step of going to China notwithstanding the fact that there had been a military build up along the border. His visit to China in 1988 to which many of those who are present here in this room contributed in signal measures, brought about a new complexion in relations, which did mean that diplomatically, a negative condition was converted into a positive. It was a kind of rebound from the situation of difficulty, and a momentum was created towards a positive process of discussion on border dispute and other questions. And this process has been in effect there since then. A number of meetings of the joint working group which was strengthened and revitalized and given another name on that

*Mr. Salman Haidar was the Foreign Secretary of Government India when he delivered this talk. He was accompanied by officials of East Asian Division of the Ministry of External Affairs.

occasion and the discussions have been purposeful, being accompanied by a number of confidence building measures on the border. I have had, as many others in this room, the oppurtunity for being engaged in these joint working group meetings, and we have, in fact, been able to make slow but steady progress. And with the confidence building measures that have been instituted, there is a measurably improved atmosphere along the border.

There has been some thinning out of military forces as we are informed. This is not a negotiated thinning out, but there has been some voluntary action which bears witness to a more relaxed situation on the border culminating in a climax during Mr. Narsimha Rao's visit to Beijing in 1993 when a border peace and tranquillity agreement was signed which gave a stamp on this process and gave momentum for further developments. Since then, the last meeting of the joint working group has resulted in a small withdrawal from both sides of various posts which were within close range and thereby constituted a potential for confidence building. And this has underlined the point that efforts are made on both sides to render the border tranquil, to remove causes of strife and to reduce physical confrontation along the border.

Another point I would like to say is that from what we can see at least when we talk to the standing committee of the Indian Parliament or when the matter is raised in Parliamentary committes or discussions at the Parliamentary level in various ways, there is a consensus that it would be useful and helpful to the country to make progress in sorting out the border problem with China. This is the broad sense of it. I would say that there is a lot of watchfulness, a lot of careful approach to this matter which is recognized as a matter of great complexity and one that has to be tackled with due care and preparation. The broad trend of opinion is, at least in what I am able to see along the lines, what I have just indicated. With that there has been a development in bilateral economic exchanges. Our trade is around $1.2 billion, is increasing rapidly. $1.2 billion is not a dramatic, but quite substantial and measurable increase and is much more than what it was a few years ago. There is a good rate of growth.

In addition to trade, there are a few joint ventures. In this I must say the Chinese have been more active than we have, in selling technology, in finding partnerships in India, and actively engaged in India. But Indian entrepreneurs and business people are also active now in China. In pharmaceuticals recently, a joint venture was set up and there is a sense of substantial potential in this field. We have been hearing many years ago that India and China are essentially competitors in the world and the complementarities are few. But I think that this is not the view that is being sustained by the experience of the business community on both sides. They have been able to find openings in each other's countries and there is a sense that there will be further openings available. Border trade has opened in a couple of places, though nothing very much has happened, this benefits small isolated communities, which had all along been trading along the border, and they are now able to revive trade which is useful and encouraging. We are hopeful that this process can be expanded, there are some proposals from each side for additional points of border trade and let us see how soon we can get this going.

I do see a couple of points on the border trade worth noting. I see that some businessmen in Kathmandu are quite interested in exporting Indian products to Tibet. So, instead of going directly across the Sino-Indian border, the trade can be routed through Nepal. One recalls, I don't know how good my recollection is, that this was a traditional route, until some time at the end of the 18th century, when the tolls demanded by the new Gorkha regime in Kathmandu became excessive and then the British started looking for alternatives through Sikkim and also through Bhutan which was not so welcoming. But Sikkim then provided a reasonable access. So, it's interesting that we have come back to that situation, at least that possibility is once gain a useful one to look at. And on the other front, the development of communications between India and Myanmar, and the development of the border trade and the fact that Myanmar does have considerable access to Chinese goods of various kinds, means that another possibility of fairly modest trade, at this stage, along the border, has been created.

Once again, there are historical precedents in this case, I believe, going back to the Tang Dynasty. But I am not too clear about the details of that. Let me refer to one or two more points before I conclude. Recently, for the first time, India took part as a dialogue partner in the ASEAN post-ministerial conference in Jakarta and we were also part of the ARF dialogue, this Asian regional forum, which addresses security issues. It was our first exposure to this forum, which is a broad one that includes China, among many countries. There is a number of non-regional and regional countries that are present in this ASEAN Regional Forum.

I draw attention to this because it is one grouping in which India and China find themselves favourably placed. Some of the concepts, some of the ideas for stabilising the broader arenas, for promoting co-operative endeavour or at least co-operative thinking, if not actions, have been unfolded at this stage. An exploration of each other's views, that is what such fora excel, can bring our two countries closer.

I don't know whether this points to the larger vision that Prof. Tan Chung alluded to, but it certainly is a broader basis for exchanges, between the countries of the region, including India and China. And I personally believe that there is a considerble potential for looking at each other bearing this perspective. I think that I would like to stop here and also strongly advise Prof. Tan Chung not to either record or print my remarks but that is entirely his decision. I must also thank him and IGNCA for this opportunity. I really come here more in a spirit of solidarity, both with the Indira Gandhi National Centre for the Arts and with the distinguished representatives here, in order to express Ministry of External Affair's abiding interest in the subject and my desire to be associated with it.

DIPANKAR BANERJEE

54

LOOKING AT CHINA — ACROSS THE BORDER

The early morning sun attempted to peep out, but quickly gave up and hid behind the clouds. A blanket of snow covered the earth below my feet as I trudged slowly to the observation post. I was trying to familiarise myself with my company's area of operations located physically closer to the gods than I would have liked. Soon I stood next to the sentry and through the bunker loopholes had my first fragmented view of China. It was somewhere in Sikkim in the mid 1960s. The vista was one of high mountains and rolling hills, as far as the eye could see. All was peaceful in a transcendental way. It was my tentative version of "looking at China". This is how most Indian military officers of my generation have looked at our northern neighbour over the years. In some ways I have been more fortunate than my colleagues. Over the years I have looked at China from many directions and angles, from inside and outside. And have had the opportunity to share my views directly or indirectly with countless others in the military's training institutions and other civilian academic and research establishments.

But on that day I could not but reflect that elsewhere on the same mountain where blood had flowed only a few years ago even though all was tranquil now. What is it that divides people and civilizations? Is it mere hills and mountains? Formidable though they may seem, no physical barrier has ever separated people. Iron bars by themselves never made a prison. It must be something else. Perhaps it is a more intangible fear. A fear of the unknown leading to anxieties, uncertainties, and suspicion. That day I decided that I needed to break through this invisible barrier, for my own understanding.

The first step must necessarily be to "look at each other". Not merely with our two open eyes, but also with our inner eye. The eye that provides a deeper view and a degree of understanding. How have we looked at each other? What have we seen? What have we understood? An honest examination of these and other questions can help us to know better, what in military terms is referred to as the side across the hill.

Officers of my generation were deeply affected by the India-China war. In a way it was intensely emotional. And of course it changed our lives totally in many substantial ways. Twentieth October 1962 was a defining moment. A question we often asked each other was where we were on that fateful day? I was far from any scene of action. Less than ten per cent of the Indian Army came into contact with the Chinese forces and I was not amongst them. I was alone commanding a remote post in Jammu & Kashmir. The world came to me only through a portable transistor radio, a proud personal possession and an inseparable companion. What we heard that day made a deep impact on every one of us. The overwhelming feeling was one of betrayal. Not merely by China, but our own leaders who had unknowingly and, we thought criminally, led us up a path from where there was to be no return. For many of our close comrades of several years, it was indeed to be the end of the road.

It is important to understand the depth of our feelings and our hurt. Well over three decades have past since then. The bitterness has gone and time has healed many wounds. But suspicion still lingers. How far can we go in normalising relations with our northern neighbour? What lies ahead along the road that we need to travel together? Can we proceed confidently trusting each other? Many layers of mistrust perhaps still remain to be removed, step by step. A process has indeed begun over several years, but we have many miles to go.

The aftermath of the 1962 War was significant. Official interactions between India and China remained frozen. Ambassadors were withdrawn, though diplomatic relations continued at a low key. Encouraged by our estrangement and helped greatly by the resultant improvement in their bilateral relations, Pakistan initiated two wars against us. The 1965 War was a blatant attempt at exploiting the perceived weakness of the Indian military. Field Marshal Ayub Khan apparently discussed the strategy with Zhou Enlai. The latter saw through the fundamental weakness of the plan and did not encourage its pursuance. However, he did little to dissuade Islamabad either. The September War was a severe set-back for Pakistan, even though it had the advantage of first strike.

China provided all manner of diplomatic and political support, including accepting Pakistan's position of plebiscite over Kashmir. But it refrained from any military assistance. We in the military, however, felt sure that without China's tacit support and promise of diversionary efforts, Pakistan would hardly attempt a war as major as this. Most of us did not follow the diplomatic manoeuvrings behind the scene. For in March 1965 when Ayub visited Beijing he did not receive the categorical assurance that he hoped. Even Marshal Chen Yi, whose position in 1962 was strongly anti-India, did not provide anything more than fulsome expression of Chinese friendship. When the Chinese ultimatum came on 17 September, I was in command of a company with my battalion in the Sialkot Sector. Beijing demanded dismantling within three days all "aggressive military works" in Sikkim. To be sure the warning was late in coming and was in no way as threatening as it might have been. But to most of us still involved in the war with Pakistan it was a reminder of the continuing strategic relationship between the two countries. We were of course prepared for any eventuality this time. But were then not sophisticated enough to realise that this statement was at best a face saving gesture on the part of Beijing. Neither global conditions, nor internal situation within China were conducive to direct involvement.

The mid-60s were a turbulent era for India. Amidst political uncertainty in the country there emerged left extremist movements in many parts of eastern India and insurgencies in the northeast. All of us who were involved with these internal security operations realised the degree of Chinese influence over many of them. While in some cases these were only ideological, in the northeast there was overt Chinese involvement. The malaise of course lay mainly within. As these conditions were dealt with effectively the internal situation improved. Not in the northeast though, where China's support till the late 1970s was a major factor for continuing instability.

The next war with Pakistan in 1971 was a result of internal contradictions in that country, but with major consequences for India. The oppressed East Pakistan finally exercised its political right through the ballot. But this was not acceptable to a power-crazy elite in Islamabad led by the Army. The subsequent brutal military crackdown led to one of the major holocaust of this century and a demographic invasion of India in the east. This transformed what might have been an internal question for Pakistan into one of external aggresion of India. The inevitable war in December was started by an air bombardment by Pakistan in the west. Chinese position in the conflict was of concern to India. As early as April 1971 Zhou Enlai expressed steadfast commitment to Pakistan's territorial integrity and expressed the view that the situation in East Pakistan was an internal matter for Pakistan. The "secessionists" were termed a mere handful of individuals, rather than what they actually were, a majority in the nation.

Ultimately China did nothing in tangible terms. Though it continued to express solidarity with Pakistan in the United Nations Security Council. A number of developments, such as the Sino-Soviet clash on the Ussuri River two years earlier, emerging Sino-US detente and the after-effects of the Cultural Revolution, may all have contributed to this restraint. Besides, winter ensured that passes remained blocked in the north. We were by now also more aware of China's limitations. Still the friendship treaty with Russia came as a welcome reassurance. No strategic planner in India could look with equanimity at a two-front war. These fears were to be compounded by the opening of the Karakoram Highway in 1978 which provided for the first time a direct usable road-link between China and Pakistan. Its strategic implications were indeed far too obvious.

None of us really understood the internal dynamics of China's transition and the political convulsions of the last years of Mao's rule. Even serious China scholars were somewhat ignorant of the implications of these developments. Else we would have known the many contradictions within China. Beijing has yet to come to terms with this era in its recent history. Just as India needs to closely examine many issues relating to its China policy in the 1950s and 60s. Beijing also needs to do the same for the same period.

The next time I personally came face to face with China again was in the mid 1970s in Arunachal Pradesh. It fell on me to study in detail the Chinese offensive in that sector in 1962, as part of a small team of selected officers. Meticulous research revealed many aspects of the conduct of these operations which till then were somewhat hazy. We expanded our search to include the wider dimension of understanding China's strategic thoughts. One appreciated the manner in which the People's Liberation Army (PLA) had imbibed the teachings of Sunzi and other military strategists of ancient times. Blending these with modern military thinking of Zhu De and Mao it evolved a military strategy with Chinese characteristics, further modified to suit the needs of modern war. The professionalism of the PLA stood out. Also their determination and the long and meticulous preparation for the conflict. With understanding came respect. But by the mid-1970s we were a much self-assured Army and entirely confident of our ability to handle any contingency.

One incident during this time stood out and remains imbedded in my memory. It was the Tulung La incident of September 1974. A small detachment of the Assam Rifles while on a routine border patrol, well south of the watershed and clearly within the Line of Actual Control, was ambushed and savagely killed. This was quite pointless and utterly unnecessary by the accepted concepts of border domination. Yet, about five years later a larger Indian patrol in Sikkim when it strayed across the Line on a misty day was treated with utmost civility and returned in very good order.

I had other occasions to look at China across the border, in areas as diverse as Bhutan and Ladakh. They provided sharp contrasts and some similarities. Both areas had Buddhist populations astride the Line. There had been much to and fro throughout history. Cutting-off contacts since 1962 have harmed the people on both sides greatly. Artificial boundaries have kept the people apart. The earlier route from India to Bhutan lay through Yatung in Tibet. Now it had to follow a much longer and more difficult way. Flying by helicopter along much of these borders one was always struck by the fact that seen from high boundaries drawn by man were indistinguishable. The land looked the same whether in Tibet or India. Standing on the observation post at Demchok, one could on a clear day look west for two hundred kilometres and east for another six hundred. Mansarovar beckoned in the distance, holy to all Hindus and in recent years much frequented by pilgrims.

For the first thirty years of my army career I saw no Chinese soldier except at some distance and often through the lens of a binocular. But I had experienced the loud sound blasts of powerful speakers across the mountain passes in Sikkim that both sides inflicted on each other with telling effect. It was meant to be propaganda. The only effect it has was on our ear drums, but that was severe enough even at some distance. It was one dimension of surreal "looking" that I could surely have done without.

An enormous gap persisted in our thinking on China. Officers of my generation learnt about it from popular fiction, vague ideas of the past and in recent years from media reports that confront one from every other international journal. This view is not real. No second hand perception can ever replace personal experience. Especially in the case of China which attracts such widely divergent and often partisan views. Yet, reportage such as this provides a strong impression and often colours our thinking. This is particularly true of the military whose direct access to foreign countries is especially restricted. It was only after the restoration of Ambassadorial relations in 1976 and the beginning of the Deng Xiaoping era two years later that it was possible to resume direct people-to-people contacts. But even then the Armed Forces remained out of it. Contact between the Indian Armed Forces and the PLA was resumed only in 1990.

Major General Fu Jiaping was an apt emissary from the Midle Kingdom. A pleasant well mannered gentleman more in the mould of a Confucian scholar, he usually wore a disarming smile. He was the first Chinese general to visit India in a long while and also the first whom I met at close quarters. Director of the Foreign Affairs Bureau of the Ministry of Defence, one of his responsibilities was foreign military relations. I clearly remember the reception for him at the Army Mess at Delhi. His speech made a major impact on me. Swinging his right hand on a vertical plane to emphasise his point, he said that the PLA would never attack India across the mountains. He repeated that his superiors had asked him to convey this very clearly, that the PLA would never launch an offensive against India.

Six months later I was a member of a two-men delegation from the Indian Army to visit China at the invitation of the PLA. This was the first visit from India after a gap of 34 years. It was memorable in many respects. It at last enabled me to actually "look at China" and in particular the PLA, totally unfettered and without blinkers. General Fu Jiaping received us at the airport and immediately made us at ease. There were many memorable moments during the visit and looking back it is not easy to highlight any out of several substantial features. One of them was our discussions with Major General Xiong, a sharp and highly competent professional soldier. General Xu Xin received us for a formal meeting. He was then the First Deputy Chief of the General Staff of the PLA. My first visit to the National Defence University and first discussion with my friend Major General Cheng Mingchun, the head of the Strategic Studies Department. His clear thinking, eloquent expression and a warm sense of humour always made our discussions a special delight. Then there were our visits to the Command and General Staff College at Nanjing and a day spent with the 54 Infantry Division.

But without doubt what made the most impact on me was the spontaneous and warm hopitality that we had received everywhere. There were no reservations, no want of sincerity and nothing artificial about the way we were treated. A phrase that featured repeatedly was that, there were five thousand reasons why China and India should be friends and not even one why we should be enemies. The visit itself was totally open. We were explained the conduct of computer war games at the Staff College against an imaginary enemy. And on a field firing range, in the divisional area, its complete fire power and its other major warlike tasks were demonstrated in seventeen separate activities.

My next visit to China was two years later. It was when I led a delegation of the Institute for Defence Studies and Analyses for a bilateral dialogue with the China Institute of Contemporary International Relations. This time my meetings were entirely with various research institutes at Beijing, Chengdu and Kunming. It also allowed me to renew my acquaintance with friends made earlier and meet many officials dealing with policy towards India. We exchanged ideas freely and frankly on a whole range of issues of interest as well as concern. Our discussions were conducted with frankness and goodwill.

This visit also enabled me to see a little more of the country. We could experience the enormous progress that was taking place all round. The large numbers of buildings and roads under construction, ports being developed, industries sprouting everywhere. The countryside was humming with activity as well, with light industries and agriculture booming in the new environment. We also experienced the rich heritage of the nation and its history, that flowed in a continuum for over 6,000 years. Only by my visit could I appreciate that this rapid progress and improvement in material living of well over a billion poeple could not be held hostage by the threat of, or even worse, the outbreak of conflict.

My last visit was in mid-1996. I was a member of a high level delegation from India. A two-day seminar addressed the possibilities of bilateral cooperation between our two countries in a whole range of areas. Our Chinese hosts brought together senior officials who had dealt with India past and present. Senior Indologists, officials, former Ambassadors and scholars from many institutes gathered together. We were entirely of one mind that the future held many possibilities. In the interest of our two countries and prosperity in Asia and the world, it was incumbent on us to find modalities for cooperation. We frankly discussed these possibilities. We bared out all our doubts and none lay hidden under the carpet. We decided to resolve all problems that we could and set aside the thorny ones, so that they did not interfere with the many opportunities that lay ahead.

Many others from the Indian Armed Forces have visited China in the last five years. One delegation was led by the Defence Minister Sharad Pawar, and another by the Chief of the Army Staff, General B.C. Joshi. Finally, Admiral Shekhawat, then Chairman of the Joint Chiefs of Staff, visited in 1996. The Indian National Defence College has been sending a delegation every alternate year since 1990. As these visits have intensified so is the range of understanding expanded. Today there are a fairly significant number of military officers who can grasp with China much beyond the view from the observation bunker.

There are many officers from the PLA who have also had opportunity to "look at India". General Xu Huaizi, the First Deputy Chief of the General Staff of the PLA, came to India. I was impressed with his vast operational experience. Currently he heads the Academy of Military Sciences, a major think tank of the PLA. Next was General Chi Haotian the Defence Minister. A very distinguished soldier, he had a very sharp appearance and a fine bearing. A senior delegation from the National Defence University, a high level Air Force delegation and a senior team of officers from the Chengdu Military Region were among the others.

Slowly the barriers have fallen and earlier suspicions are beginning to give way. A perspective for cooperation is developing on both sides albeit among a minority of officers. There is obviously a need to widen our ability to "look at each other".

I am often called to lecture on China either at formal courses of instruction spread across the country to officers whose commissioned service range from 5 to 30 years or, military formations during their study periods. The former study China as a part of their larger area studies or professional curriculum. The latter are often merely interested observers. I have tried to gauge how they look at China.

Younger officers between 5-15 years of service and below 35 years of age have a distinctly different view than their more senior colleagues. Younger officers are more detached and perhaps a shade more objective. They have no hang-ups and do not carry the baggage of the past. In particular, there is an admiration for China and its recent economic progress. They appreciate China's firm nationalistic stand on international issues. Chinese sportsmen and their performance around the globe also attract them. In general there is a desire to know more about that country. Of course they too have many serious concerns.

Amongst the older generation, especially those bred in the Army of the 1960s there is a clear difference. These are the officers in the highest rung of decision-making and who will remain there for some time in the future. Most of them vividly recall the relations immediately prior to the 1962 War and the conflict itself. There is great wariness regarding China and its future intentions. The defence budget of the PLA is carefully noted. Its growing military capability and its force projection ability, limited though they actually are, is often exaggerated. Both capabilities and intentions are scrutinised and discussed. Finally, there is always a doubt about the willingness of Beijing to resolve the border question.

I attempt to put across in as objective a manner as I possibly can, based on what I have seen and studied and tried my best to convey what I have "looked" and found personally from my visits and understandings. It is not easy. Some misgivings and suspicion are too deep-rooted to overcome. Barriers once erected by emotion cannot be crossed through logic. Yet, I always become wiser through such interactions.

My Chinese friends too have raised a number of issues with me. These reflect of course the views of a small group of research scholars and experts to whom I have had access. I am particularly struck by the total absence of the burden of the past in their thinking. Their perception of the events of the late 1950s and early 60s is vague and ill-informed. They are overwhelmed by so many profound developments within China that the Sino-Indian conflict is out of their minds. They view it only as a minor incident of an earlier era but put blame squarely on Indian irrationality. The unprovoked attack by the PLA on India is termed as a "self defence counter-attack" and entirely justified. They are totally oblivious of the psychological hurt that the Indians felt over the entire episode. Such a perspective has its own problems and hampers understanding.

We need to reconsider the whole question of threat perception. It has not yet been fully accepted in India that in today's world assessing military threats to a nation is not the best way of planning for national security. Today the approach has to be more sophisticated. The objective has to be rooted more firmly on enhancing national interests, and defending the core values of a nation with a greater orientation towards economic issues. The emphasis must be to enrich the population and rescue them from poverty and ill health. Our long-term goal is to ensure the nation's respectable place in the comity of nations as a stable polity and a strong economic power. In the last nearly two decades China has been more purposive and determined than India in this respect.

Therefore, it is wise to refrain from considering a nation or even a group of nations as a threat, unless there is a possibility of a near term hostile intention. This is pragamatism. Over exaggerated threat perceptions may be good secret military contingency planning but a mis-guided self fulfilling calculation. This is precisely what any sane strategic planner must avoid.

With a right perspective, let us consider the outstanding problems that agitate the minds of both sides. From the Chinese perspective the only thorn is the problem of Tibet and Dalai Lama. An underpopulated peripheral deeply religious province, its possibility of secession from the mainland is one of the worst case scenarios that must be of serious concern to any responsible person in China. For it also has the potential to unravel the state. In the absence of democratic institutions to cushion popular discontent it is a matter of concern.

From the Indian viewpoint the litany is long. The unresolved border, past support to ethnic insurgencies, China's large stockpile of intermediate range nuclear weapons that may only target countries on its periphery, its high defence expenditure and political and military support to India's neighbours, are some of them. While articulating these concerns the positive developments are usually overlooked. There is an agreement to maintain peace and tranquillity on the borders. Support to insurgents stopped in 1978. China's nuclear policy of no first strike, no use against non-nuclear powers, positive and negative security assurances and willingness to eliminate nuclear weapons if all states did the same are discounted. There can be many views on China's defence expenditure and in any case it is really not excessive for a country of China's size and length of borders. A case that India itself often makes in justifying its own defence spending. That leaves the question of China's support to India's neighbours, especially Pakistan, very high amongst India's concerns.

It is not the objective here to discuss the merits of these issues. It is really a question of perception and how one views these situations.

Today we are coming to the end of a millennium and entering the threshold of another. There is a whole era that has passed. A new epoch is begining. This is a juncture of opportunity though also of challenge. Our aim must be to set our eyes on the new millennium and strive for a better world for all our citizens. In this interdependent world and fast shrinking spaces and distanced narrow mindsets and frog-in-the-well views are out of order. We in India are looking east -- a east that has entered a dynamic period of growth and opportunity. To shape any role in the area we have to establish a relationship of cooperation with all its members. China is surely the most important of them.

It is in this way that we must address our relationship with China. But to do that with effect and impact we must understand China. It is in developing this process of understanding that we must first learn to "look at each other" and share our experiences with each other.

V.R. RAGHAVAN

55

INDIA-CHINA RELATIONS: A MILITARY PERSPECTIVE

It is never less than a challenge to attempt to understand the cultural factors which influence a nation's conduct in the international arena. When that nation is China and the subject of introspection is its relations with India, such an endeavour can at best be fraught with far too many variables. The two have had the longest uninterrupted existence as nations. Their combined size and population makes them the largest geographical and human resource mass on the planet. India and China have had cultural, religious and trade links going back centuries in history. They also came into being as nation states almost simultaneously in this century. They also share a past of colonial and imperialist subjugation from which freedom had to be won with a major struggle. Paradoxically enough, the two countries fought a war with each other over disputed frontiers. That conflict episode, the continuing border dispute between the two countries and China's rapid growth in military power, not unsurprisingly create anxieties about the future relationship. China's aggressive foreign policy postures also do not encourage a benign view of it. There are enough strategic thinkers in India who reckon China to be the major future threat to India. This short essay attempts to focus on the military perspective of Sino-Indian relations.

The means adopted to secure freedom by China and India provide some indication of the approaches adopted by them to cope with the international order. They explain the methods the two nations brought to bear on their responses to the geo-political situations. The basis of relationships established by the two states bilaterally with other states were also founded in that historical context. China had won its freedom through an armed struggle of epic proportions. Its military was unlike any in history in its struggle against overwhelming odds and its commitment to an ideology. Its military leaders were living legends, but they were also simultaneously ideological and political leaders. Marxist-Leninist revolutionary thought provided the underpinnings to much of China's post independence policy. The notion of military power as an instrument of internal and external policy, formed a not insubstantial part of the Chinese policy framework. This was not an entirely new element in Chinese political management. China had a long history of strong military involvement in the management of political issues. The Marxist theology provided a perfect patina for a widespread and traditional military content in China's national life.

India chose the route of non-violence and of political struggle through constitutional means to wrest freedom from colonial rule. Its leaders brought to bear on the freedom movement a long tradition of negotiation and debate instead of armed struggle. There was no military content to the freedom movement other than stray incidents of bomb throwing and use of explosives. The better part of the struggle for independence was guided by the insistence on non-violent means and adherence to constitutional norms. As for the Indian military, its leaders were expressly advised by the political leadership to keep well out of the freedom struggle that was being waged. There was no military content in India's highly successful mass mobilisation against the British rule.

In the post-independence period, China preferred to use military power extensively in pursuit of its geopolitical aims. A confrontationist and belligerent image of China was therefore inevitable. China's choice of the military option in a series of cases confirmed the image of a militarist state willing to use its power to settle issues by force. Formosa (Taiwan), Korea, the conflicts on the Sino-Soviet borders, the war with India in 1962, China's open espousal of the Pakistani cause during 1965 in what was a purely bilateral conflict, China's actions in the South China Sea, its role in Vietnam-Cambodia-Laos make a very long list of contributive factors compounding the image. China's assistance over decades to sub-national and ethnic groups with ideology, funds, and weapons, retarded the progress of newly independent states in her neighbourhood. Its acquiring of nuclear weapons capability has evoked admiration but has not reduced concerns about its future employment, given China's record in managing international relations. The image is not made any less adverse by the continuing growth and modernisation in China's military capabilities during the last decade.

The Indian picture over the same period is a contrast in many ways. India was tireless in its support to China's cause in the international arena from the very beginning. India's attempts to grapple with the enormous task of nation building, of social and distributive justice, of security against external military and terrorist threats, of economic development through democratic processes, were monumental in size and in the investments required. These were not helped by China's support through the decades of the 1960s and 1970s to insurgent groups. They were made positively worse by China's assistance programme to Pakistan in nuclear and conventional weapons. It is ironic that China which willingly embraced the concept of Panchsheel in the 1950s with India and other newly independent states, discarded its principles so soon and so comprehensively.

Attempts have been made to view the contrasting positions, postures and processes used by China and India through the lens of cultural history. The ancient cultural contacts between the two nations were through a transfer of religious thoughts. Intrepid travellers of ancient times carried images of India to China. There is little to indicate that a reverse flow of images, religious beliefs and learned treatises occurred. There is also inadequate evidence of images about India and its thoughts and beliefs influencing the policy choices of the ruling elites in China. It is useful to remember that much of the India-China interaction took place through geographic areas in the western reaches of ancient India and which no longer form part of India. Trade between India and China formed a very small part of the totality of their relationship. In military terms, the two nations shared no commonalities in doctrine and organisational concepts. Perhaps the only shared military experience between India and China was the Mongol invasions of their territories.

The pre-eminent written texts on national policy and security in the two nations were the *Arthashastra* written by Kautilya in India, and *Art of War* or *Bingfa* by Sunzi (Sun Tzu) in China. The latter is more widely known in the western translations as "On War". A comparison of the two provides some fascinating insights in the two nations' approaches to state policy. The differences become apparent early in the titles given to the books. While *Arthashastra* literally means the science of wealth (or of economy, in modern parlance), *Bingfa* focuses on the ways of gaining victory in battles. Notwithstanding their titles there are commonalites. The former effectively emphasises the importance of military means in ensuring the safety and well being of the state. The latter even as an emphatically military treatise gives importance to the loyalty and well-being of the people, if wars are to be won. On the other hand, the former dwells at length on matters of state-craft, economic resources, political and other relations with other states, and the military component forms only a part of the whole gamut of chapters. The latter is emphatically militarist with a focus on conquests, victory in battles, the techniques of achieving victories through surprise, strategems and so on. In its philosophical foundation the *Arthashastra* is strong on defensive modes, e.g., forts, and safe borders, while the *Bingfa* is vehement on the need for offensive action.

The two justly famous texts were products of their times. The *Arthashastra* is attributed to about the middle of the second century AD, while the *Bingfa* is estimated to be from around 500 BC. Traditional thoughts run deep in civilisational responses. Consequently, they indicate through the approaches and emphasis of state policies, a deeper and psychological national preference. The Indian text leans heavily on the defensive while the Chinese emphasises on the offensive. As Kautilya saw it, the army was only one amongst seven major elements of the state's power. He recommended alliances and coalitions as the means to stabilise the state's security. Sunzi saw war as "a matter of vital importance to the state ...". He warned the ruler against allowing the state into fighting a protracted war.

Indian responses to internal and external policy stimuli were a continuation of the cultural traditions. The initiative on Non-Alignment, the choice of the UN as a forum to settle the Jammu and Kashmir issue even when it was winning the war, the restraint in the nuclear weapons field, the initiatives on SAARC, are indicative of the underlying Indian belief in negotiation and tolerance as the essential element of state policy. The Chinese approach stands out in contrast. It is of victory by use of force in pursuit of its objectives, an unwillingness to tolerate dissent in internal policies, of using protracted wars in other countries through encouragement to dissident groups and the preference for demonstrated military strength in its neighbourhood. *Arthashastra* and *Bingfa* provide the clues from the past to the two nation's policy preferences of the present. One might even say that China has been the true "Realist" state and India the "Idealist" in the use of power to further national interests.

At the turn of the millennium, the world is changing through information technology, and economic interdependence. India and China both realise the need to adapt to these tectonic changes, if they hope to develop as economically stable and politically lasting entities. The leadership in both states is aware of the need to ensure the social and economic well-being of their peoples. In that lies real security and stability, the two essential conditions for development. They realise that autonomous behaviour in internal and external relations is no longer feasible in international arena. The need to assure neighbours of their interests through confidence building measures, placing ancient disputes in correct perspective, reaching for consensus instead of conflict resolution by force are the need of the day. India and China both realise the need for military strength commensurate with their security and the anxieties of neighbours. The reality after the Cold War is of a world order based on equity amongst states and constructive engagement through trade and economic development. Even as some hegemonic and other similar mindsets are still to be seen, the future of inter-state relations is well set on the course of cooperation. China and India realise the need for cooperation and for moving away from old animosities through mutual agreements. They have resolved to find solutions to their disputes through negotiations. Indian initiatives in South Asia and Chinese efforts in finding solutions to its issues of contention with Russia, Japan, USA and in the Asia Pacific are evidence of their new awareness. In some ways China is adding a healthy dose of "Idealist" balance to its policies. India on the other hand is introducing an element of "Realist" pragmatism to its policies. They are in the process going beyond the culture constraints of the past. Kautilya and Sunzi would have both approved of such a reorientation.

In the military perspective, the best way to remove the prospect of war remains the removal of the bone of contention. There has never been a better time than the present to take cooperation between India and China to the levels they are capable of reaching. The need of the time is to formally and finally resolve the disputes between the two giant sized states. The conflicts of the past between China and India were not of nations but between states following different policies to secure themselves. Now that the two states are in a better environment of "Realist-Idealist" mix, specific measures can be looked at. The border dispute should now be formally and finally settled. This will need accommodation from both sides and that should not be an insurmountable problem given the new circumstances. The larger issue of weapons rivalry between the two states and through either of them into the region is another issue which requires urgent attention. If these two vexing issues are taken in hand, the way ahead in the 21st Century would be free from the compulsions of the past and pave the way to a stable future. If that is achieved, the military perspective which so dominated the India-China relations in the last 50 years would be balanced by the larger contexts of economy, trade, and international cooperation. China and India would then be partners in providing a lead through the principles of Panchsheel and in moving the world away from military conflicts. It would be a condition which both Kautilya and Sunzi would have approved.

SWARAN SINGH

56

THREE AGREEMENTS AND FIVE PRINCIPLES BETWEEN INDIA AND CHINA

As suggested by Prof. Tan Chung, I have composed the following as a separate article to be the reference point to my ensuing piece on India-China confidence building measures. The word "Panchsheel" (also spelled as "pancasila") denoted "Five Taboos" in the ancient Buddhist scriptures governing the personal behaviour of Indian (later Chinese and other foreign) monks. This was taken from the holy books by India's first Prime Minister, Jawaharlal Nehru, to be applicable to international behaviours of the modern states. When Nehru proposed to make *Panchsheel* enshrine the first India-China agreement in 1954 as the Five Principles of Peaceful Co-existence, the Chinese Premier, Zhou Enlai, readily agreed. Thus, these five principles have become the joint India-China invention.

All inter-state interactions, especially their written agreements, surely make their contribution towards evolving an environment of mutual security and mutual confidence yet some remain more directed towards this motive than others. In that context, this essay consists of only the three most important agreements which have laid the foundations and defined the perimeters of confidence and security building measures (CSBMs) between India and China. These include the *Panchsheel* Agreement signed in Beijing on April 29, 1954, Agreement on Maintenance of Peace and Tranquillity along the Line of Actual Control which was signed in Beijing on September 7, 1993 and the Agreement on Confidence Building Measures in the Military Field along the Line of Actual Control signed in New Delhi on November 29, 1996. All three agreements have been duly ratified by both sides. Below, I present to our readers the three documents each with an introductory note explaining the context and historical significance of them.

1. The Panchsheel Agreement

Popularly known as the *Panchsheel* Agreement, this was basically a trade pact between China and India streamlining their bilateral trade operations in Tibet and, therefore, at the time of signing it was not visualised as a CSBM agreement, though without saying it in so many words, it intended to serve the same objectives as the latter two CSBM agreeements of 1993 and 1996. The negotiations for this agreement were held in Beijing between December 31, 1953 and April 29, 1954 at the end of which this agreement was finally signed in Beijing.

The lasting significance of this agreement lies in the fact that this was the first document where both India and China enunciated the famous "Five Principles" (*Panchsheel*) of peaceful co-existence which today form the centrepiece of their current CSBMs. And being the basis in defining the code of inter-state relations, even after 43 years *Panchsheel* remains an extremely valid framework. In practical terms, however, China was the immediate beneficiary of this agreement. India, on the other hand had felt satisfied with its intangible gains. At least that was how Jawaharlal Nehru repeatedly explained it to his people. In terms of its concessions, it meant that for the first time, India recognised China's complete control over Tibet. In this agreement India voluntarily gave up its military, communication and postal and other rights which New Delhi had inherited from the British in accordance with the Anglo-Tibetan Treaty of 1904. It is strange why India did not demand any reciprocal concession? In retrospect, this presented a rare opportunity to resolve the rest of the border dispute which is the only basic problem between these two countries today.

India's non-insistence on reciprocal concessions while recognising China's suzerainty over Tibet by India has, of course, to be understood in the context of the "Hindi-Chini Bhai Bhai" spirit of 1950s where China's leaders swore of "eternal peace and friendship" and Indian leadership felt satisfied having got a written guarantee of good behaviour from China in terms of *Panchsheel* being a part of this Agreement's Preamble. Also, such an Indian response has to be understood in view of Nehru's personality and beliefs. He had been India's sole spokesperson on foreign relations and following the death of Gandhiji (1948) and Sardar Patel (1950) Jawaharlal Nehru had clearly emerged as the single most important leader of the monolith Indian National Congress. Defending this Agreement in Indian Parliament, he said: "It was the recognition of existing situation there. Historical and practical considerations necessitated the step." In April 1954, Nehru was still a man who sought security in peace and trusted China's friendly gestures.

Going by the tenor of Nehru's arguments, this agreement was clearly seen as geared towards generating mutual trust and confidencebetween two newly liberated and strongly nationalistic republics. Thus, in retrospect, this can be safely described as the first Sino-India CSBM Agreement. Whatever may have been its reasons, had Dalai Lama not left Tibet and sought asylum in India, this Agreement would have stood the test and been maintained as a momentum towards greater understanding. And here, Dalai Lama's arrival in India in 1959 was perhaps the one most important factor that changed the entire spirit of Sino-Indian relations. Prime Minister Zhou En-lai who during his earlier visit to New Delhi had assured Nehru of his support in China's recognising the MacMahon Line as the Sino-Indian border. He, however, wrote in his famous letter to Nehru later, saying that China had never recognised the McMahon Line. This portended for a downward trend, gradually resulting in deteriorating their relations and later leading to the 1962 war. This completely changed the context in which this Agreement had been signed and their relations remained frozen for the next two decades or so. Below is the text of this agreement as also of the notes exchanged between the two delegations:

AGREEMENT BETWEEN THE GOVERNMENT OF THE REPUBLIC OF INDIA AND THE GOVERNMENT OF THE PEOPLE'S REPUBLIC OF CHINA ON TRADE AND INTER-COURSE BETWEEN TIBET REGION OF CHINA AND INDIA

The Government of the Republic of India and the Central people's Government of the People's Republic of China:

Being desirous of promoting trade and cultural intercourse between the Tibet region of China and India and of facilitating pilgrimage and travel by the people of China and India;

Have resolved to enter into the present agreement based on the following principles:

(1) Mutual respect for each other's territorial integrity and sovereignty;
(2) Mutual non-aggression;
(3) Mutual non-interference in each other's internal affairs;
(4) Equality and mutual benefit; and
(5) Peaceful co-existence

and for this purpose have appointed as their respective plenipotentiaries:

The Government of the Republic of India:
H.E. Nedyam Raghavan, Ambassador Extraordinary and Plenipotentiary of India accredited to the People's Republic of China,

The Central People's Government of the
The People's Republic of China:
H.E. Chang Han-Fu, Vice-Minister of Foreign Affairs of the Central People's Government,

Who, having examined each other's credentials and finding them in good and due form, have agreed upon the following:

ARTICLE I

The High Contracting Parties mutually agree to establish trade agencies:

(I) The Government of India agree that the Government of China may establish trade agencies at New Delhi, Calcutta and Kalimpong.

(II) The Government of China agree that the Government of India may establish trade agencies at Yatung, Gyantse and Gartok.

The Trade Agencies of both parties shall be accorded the same status and same treatment. The Trade Agents of both parties shall enjoy freedom from arrest while exercising their functions, and shall enjoy in respect of themselves, their wives and children who are dependent on them for their livelihood freedom from search.

The Trade Agencies of both parties shall enjoy the privileges and immunities for couriers, mail bags and communications in code.

ARTICLE II

The High Contracting Parties agree that traders of both countries known to be customarily and specifically engaged in trade between the Tibet region of China and India may trade at the following places:

(1) The Government of China agree to specify (1) Yatung, (2) Gyantse and (3) Phari as markets for trade; the Government of India agree that trade may be carried on in India including places like (1) Kalimpong, (2) Siliguri and (3) Calcutta, according to customary practice.

(2) The Government of China agree to specify (1) Gartok, (2) Pulanchung (Taklakot), (3) Gyalima-Khargo, (4) Gyanima-Chakra, (5) Ranura, (6) Dongbra, (7) Pulling-Sumdo (8) Nabra, (9) Shangtse and (10) Tashigong as markets for trade; the Government of India agree that in future when in accordance with the development and need of trade between the Ari district of the Tibet region of China and India, it has become necessary to specify markets for trade in the corresponding districts in India adjacent to the Ari district of the Tibet region of China, it will be prepared to consider on the basis of equality and reciprocity to do so.

ARTICLE III

The High Contracting Parties agree that pilgrimages by religious believers of the two countries shall be carried on in accordance with the following provisions:

(1) Pilgrims from India of Lamaist, Hindu and Buddhist faith may visit Kang Rimpoche (Kailash) and Mavam Tse (Mansarowar) in the Tibet region of China in accordance with custom.

(2) Pilgrims from the Tibet region of China of Lamaist and Buddhist faiths may visit Banaras, Sarnath, Gaya and Sanchi in India in accordance with custom.

(3) Pilgrims customarily visiting Lhasa may continue to do so in accordance with custom.

ARTICLE IV

Traders and pilgrims of both countries may travel by the following passes and routes:

(1) Shipki La Pass
(2) Mana Pass
(3) Niti Pass
(4) Kungri Bingri Pass

(5) Darma Pass, and
(6) Lipu Lekh Pass.

Also the customary route leading to Tashigong along the valley of Elek Gatasangpu (Indus river) continue to be traversed in accordance with custom.

ARTICLE V

For traveling across borers, the High Contracting Parties agree that diplomatic personnel, officials and nations of the two countries shall hold passports issued by their own respective countries and visas by the other party except as provided in paragraphs 1, 2, 3, and 4 of this article.

(1) Traders of both countries known to be customarily and specifically engaged in trade between the Tibet region of China and India, their wives and children, who are dependent on them for livelihood and their attendants will be allowed entry for purposes of trade into India or the Tibet region of China, as the case may be, in accordance with custom on the production of certificates duly issued by the local Government of their own country by its duly authorised agents and examined by the border check posts of the other party.

(2) Inhabitants of the border districts of the two countries, who cross borders to carry on petty trade or to visit friends and relatives, may proceed to the border districts of the other party as they have customarily done heretofore and need not be restricted to the passes and route specified in Article IV above and shall not be required to hold passports, visas or permits.

(3) Porters and mule-team drivers of the two countries who cross the border to perform necessary transportation services need not hold passports issued by their own country, but shall only hold certificates good for a definite period of time (good for three months, half year or one year) duly issued by the local agents and produce them for registration at the border checkpost of the other party.

(4) Pilgrims of both countries need not carry documents of certification but shall register at the border checkpost of the other party and receive a permit for pilgrimage.

(5) Notwithstanding the provisions of the foregoing paragraph of this article, either Government may refuse entry to any particular person.

(6) Persons who enter the territory of the other party in accordance with the foregoing paragraphs of this article may stay within its territory only after complying with the procedures specified by the other party.

ARTICLE VI

The present agreement shall come into effect upon ratification by both Governments and shall remain in force for eight years. Extension of the present agreement may be negotiated by the two parties if either party requests for it six months prior to the expiry of the agreement and the request is agreed to by the other party.

Done in duplicate in Peking on April 29, 1954, in Hindi, Chinese and English languages, all text being equally valid.

Plenipotentiary of the Central Government of the People's Republic of China — CHANG HAN-FU

Plenipotentiary of the Government of the Republic of India — N RAGHAVAN

TEXT OF NOTES EXCHANGED

BETWEEN THE DELEGATIONS OF INDIA AND CHINA

Peking, April 29, 1954

Your Excellency, Mr. Vice-Foreign Minister,

In the course of our discussion regarding the agreement on trade and intercourse between the Tibet region of China and India, which has happily concluded on Thursday (April 29) the delegation of the Government of the Republic of India and the delegation of the Government of the People's Republic of China agreed that certain matters be regulated by an exchange of notes. In pursuance of this understanding, it is hereby agreed between the two Governments as follows:

(1) The Government of India will be pleased to withdraw completely within six months from date of exchange of the present notes the military escort now stationed at Yatung and Gyantse in the Tibet region of China. The Government of China will render facilities and assistance in such withdrawal.

(2) The Government of India will be pleased to hand over to the Government of China at a reasonable price the post, telegraph and public telephone services together with their equipment operated by the Government of India in the Tibet region of China. The concrete measures in this regard will be decided upon through further negotiations between the Indian Embassy in China and the Foreign Ministry of China, which shall start immediately after the exchange of the present notes.

(3) The Government of India will be pleased to hand over to the Government of China at a reasonable price the twelve rest-houses of the Government of India in the Tibet region of China. The concrete measures in this regard will be decided upon through further negotiations between the Indian Embassy in China and the Foreign Ministry of China which will start immediately after the exchange of the present notes. The Government of China agree that they shall continue as rest-houses.

(4) The Government of China agree that all buildings within the compound wall of the Trade Agencies of the Government of India at Yatung and Gyantse in the Tibet region of China may be retained by the Government of India; and the Government of India may continue to lease the land within its agency compound wall from the Chinese side. And the Government of India agree that the Trade Agencies of the Government of China at Kalimpong and Calcutta may lease lands from the Indian side for the use of the Agencies and construct buildings thereon. The Government of China will render every possible assistance for housing the Indian Trade Agency at Gartok. The Government of India will also render every possible assistance for housing the Chinese Trade Agency at New Delhi.

(5) The Government of India will be pleased to return to the Government of China all land used or occupied by the Government of India other than the lands within its Trade Agency compound wall at Yatung.

If there are godowns and buildings of the Government of India on the above-mentioned land used or occupied and to be returned by the Government of India and if Indian traders have stores or godowns or buildings on the above-mentioned land so that there is a need to continue leasing land, the Government of China agree to sign a contract with the Government of India or Indian traders, as the case may be, for leasing to them those parts of the land occupied by the said godowns, buildings or stores and pertaining thereto.

(6) The Trade Agents of both parties may, in accordance with the laws and regulations of the local government, have access to their nationals involved in civil or criminal cases.

(7) The Trade Agents and traders of both countries may hire employees in the locality.

(8) The hospitals of the Indian Trade Agencies at Gyantse and Yatung will continue to serve personnel of the Indian Trade Agencies.

(9) Each Government shall protect the person and property of the traders and pilgrims of the other country.

(10) The Government of China agree, so far as possible, to construct rest-houses for use of pilgrims along the route from Pulanchung (Taklakot) to Kang Rimpoche (Kailash) and Mavam Tse (Manasarowar), and the Government of India agree to place all possible facilities in India at the disposal of pilgrims.

(11) Traders and pilgrims of both countries shall have the facilities of hiring means of transportation at normal and reasonable rates.

(12) The three Trade Agencies of each party may function throughout the year.

(13) Traders of each country may rent buildings and godowns in accordance with local regulations in places under the jurisdiction of the other party.

(14) Traders of both countries may carry on normal trade in accordance with local regulations at places as provided in Article II of the agreement.

(15) Disputes between traders of both countries over debts and claims shall be handled in accordance with local laws and regulations.

On behalf of the Government of the Republic of India, I hereby agree that the present note, along with your reply, shall become an agreement between our two Governments which shall come into force upon the exchange of the present notes.

I avail myself of this opportunity to express to you the assurances of my highest consideration.

N. Raghavan
Ambassador Extraordinary
and Plenipotentiary of the
Republic of India

29 April 1954

Peking, April 29, 1954

Your Excellency Mr Ambassador

I have the honour to receive your note dated April 29, 1954 which reads:

(text omitted — **Editor**)

On behalf of the Central People's Government of the People's Republic of China, I hereby agree to Your Excellency's note, and your note along with the present note in reply shall become an agreement between our two Governments, which shall come into force upon the exchange of the present notes.

I avail myself of this opportunity to express to Your Excellency, Mr Ambassador, the assurances of my highest consideration.

Chang Han-Fu
Vice Minister
Ministry of Foreign Affairs,
People's Republic of China

29 April, 1954

2. The CSBM Agreement of 1993

This was the first document which was so clearly focussed on evolving a framework of CSBMs between India and China. In the context of the post-Cold War era of disarmament, this also became Asia's first major agreement on conventional military disengagement which has resulted in effecting actual disarmament (not just arms control) between two former adversaries and that too without any role played by third countries.

This new spirit towards expanding mutual understanding and cooperation had resulted following the historic visit in December 1988 to Beijing by Prime Minister Rajiv Gandhi which was followed by a spate of other high-level visits from both sides including visit by Chinese Premier, Li Peng, to India in December 1991 and by Indian President, R. Venkataraman, to China in May 1992. This was followed by the visit of Prime Minister P.V. Narasimha Rao to Beijing in September 1993 during which this agreement was initialed by both sides along with various other agreements. This agreement has since resulted in generating new enthusiasm in the working of Sino-India Joint Working Group on Boundary Question which during its Eighth Round in New Delhi (August 1995) agreed to dismantle four closest military posts on the border and setting up four border trade ports as also four meeting points between their military personnel on the border. Expansion in their interactions in the border region can be cited as another positive result of mutual confidence that this agreement has generated during these last few years. In fact, the second CSBM agreement signed in November 1996 has been described as continuation of this positive process initiated by this first CSBM agreement of September 1993. Below is the text of this agreement:

AGREEMENT BETWEEN THE GOVERNMENT OF THE REPUBLIC OF INDIA AND THE GOVERNMENT OF THE PEOPLE'S REPUBLIC OF CHINA ON THE MAINTENANCE OF PEACE AND TRANQUILLITY ALONG THE LINE OF ACTUAL CONTROL IN THE INDIA-CHINA BORDER AREAS

The Government of the Republic of India and the Government of the People's Republic of China, (hereinafter referred to as the two sides), have entered into the present agreement in accordance with the five principles of mutual respect for sovereignty and territorial integrity, non-aggression, non interference into each others internal affairs, equality and mutual benefit and peaceful coexistence and with a view to maintaining peace and tranquillity along the line of actual control in the India-China border areas,

Have agreed as follows:

ARTICLE I

The two sides are of the view that the India-China boundary question shall be resolved through peaceful and friendly consultations. Neither side shall use or threaten to use force against the other by any means. Pending an ultimate solution to the boundary question between the two countries, the two sides shall strictly respect and observe the line of actual control between the two sides. No activities of either side shall overstep the line of actual control. In case personnel of one side cross the line of actual control, upon being cautioned by the other side, they shall immediately pull back to their own side of the line of actual control. When necessary, the two sides shall jointly check and determine the segments of the line of actual control where they have different views as to its alignment.

ARTICLE II

Each side will keep its military forces in the areas along the line of actual control to a minimum level compatible with the friendly and good neighbourly relations between the two countries. The two sides agree to reduce their military forces along the line of actual control in conformity with the requirements of the principle of mutual and equal security to ceilings to be mutually agreed. The extent, depth, timing and nature of reduction of military forces along the line of actual control shall be determined through mutual consultation between the two countries. The reduction of military forces shall be carried out by stages in mutually agreed geographical locations sector wise within the areas along the line of actual control.

ARTICLE III

Both sides shall work out through consultations effective confidence building measures in the areas along the line of actual control. Neither side will undertake specified levels of military exercises in mutually identified zones. Each side shall give the other prior notification of military exercises of specified levels near the line of actual control permitted under this Agreement.

ARTICLE IV

In case of contingencies or other problems arising in the areas along the line of actual control, the two sides shall deal with them through meetings and friendly consultations between border personnel of the two countries. The form of such meetings and channels of communications between the border personnel shall be mutually agreed upon by the two sides.

ARTICLE V

The two sides agree to take adequate measures to ensure that air intrusions across the line of actual control do not take place and shall undertake mutual consultations should intrusions occur. Both sides shall also consult on possible restrictions on air exercises in areas to be mutually agreed near the line of actual control.

ARTICLE VI

The two sides agreed that references to the line of actual control in this agreement do not prejudice their respective positions on the boundary question.

ARTICLE VII

The two sides shall agree through consultations on the form, method, scale and content of effective verification measures and supervision required for the reduction of military forces and the maintenance of peace and tranquillity in the areas along the line of actual control under this agreement.

ARTICLE VIII

Each side of the India-China Joint Working Group on the Boundary Question shall appoint diplomatic and military experts to formulate, through mutual consultations, implementation measures for the present Agreement. The experts shall advise the Joint Working Group on the resolution of differences between the two sides on the alignment of the line of actual control and address issues relating to the redeployment with a view to reduction of military forces in the areas along the line of actual control. The experts shall also assist the Joint Working Group in supervision of the implementation of the Agreement, and settlement of differences that may arise in that process, based on the principle of good faith and mutual confidence.

ARTICLE IX

The present Agreement shall come into effect as of the date of signature and is subject to amendment and addition by agreement of the two sides.

Signed in duplicates at Beijing on the 7th September, 1993 in the Hindi, Chinese and English languages, all three texts having equal validity.

For the Government of
the Republic of India

For the
Government of the
People's
Republic of China

3. Extending CSBMs to Military Field

Signed on November 29, 1996, during the historic visit by President Jiang Zemin to New Delhi, this agreement has been generally described as one that marks the completion of the positive process of evolving Sino-Indian CSBMs. Commentators from both sides have described this document as the first "No War" Pact between China and India. The strength of this agreement lies in its being very specific in pointing out their areas of agreement, something which is generally not possible amongst former adversaries who continue to have major disagreements on their boundary question. Also, the fact that this agreement was signed in the context of the historic visit by China's President, Jiang Zemin to India which was the first visit by a Chinese head of State in the history of these two ancient civilisations of over 5,000 years has revived the spirit of cooperation that was initiated by their earlier agreement in 1993 and it is this spirit of cooperation that today appears to be the salient feature of their multifaceted interactions. The agreement has since been ratified by both sides and the Instruments of R1atification were exchanged by both sides during the Tenth meeting of Sino-Indian Joint Working Group in New Delhi in August 1997. Apart from signalling the completion of basic framework of CSBMs, this agreement also marks the beginning of major initiatives in actually resolving the border dispute and initial steps towards this have been incorporated in the document. The agreement reads:

AGREEMENT BETWEEN THE GOVERNMENT OF THE REPUBLIC OF INDIA AND THE GOVERNMENT OF THE PEOPLE'S REPUBLIC OF CHINA ON CONFIDENCE BUILDING MEASURES IN THE MILITARY FIELD ALONG THE LINE OF ACTUAL CONTROL IN THE INDIA-CHINA BORDER AREAS

The Government of the Republic of India and the Government of the People's Republic of China (hereinafter referred to as the two sides),

Believing that it serves the fundamental interests of the peoples of India and China to foster a long-term good-neighbourly relationship in accordance with the five principles of mutual respect for sovereignty and territorial integrity, mutual non-aggression, non-interference in each other's internal affairs, equality and mutual benefit and peaceful co-existence,

Convinced that the maintenance of peace and tranquillity along the line of actual control in the India-China border areas accords with the fundamental interests of the two peoples and will also contribute to the ultimate resolution of the boundary question,

Reaffirming that neither side shall use or threaten to use force against the other by any means to seek unilateral military superiority,

Pursuant to the Agreement between the Government of the Republic of India and the Government of the People's Republic of China on the Maintenance of Peace and Tranquillity along the Line of Actual Control in the India-China Border Areas, signed on 7 September 1993,

Recognising the need for effective confidence building measures in the military field along the line of actual control in the border areas between the two sides,

Noting the utility of confidence building measures already in place along the line of actual control in the India-China border areas,

Committed to enhancing mutual confidence and transparency in the military field,

Have agreed as follows:

ARTICLE I

Neither side shall use its military capability against the other side. No armed forces deployed by either side in the border areas along the line of actual control as part of their respective military strength shall be used to attack the other side, or engage in military activities that threaten the other side or undermine peace, tranquillity and stability in the India-China border areas.

ARTICLE II

The two sides reiterate their determination to seek a fair, reasonable and mutually acceptable settlement of the boundary question. Pending an ultimate solution to the boundary question, the two sides reaffirm their commitment to strictly respect and observe the line of actual control in the India-China border areas. No activities of either side shall overstep the line of actual control.

ARTICLE III

The two sides agree to take the following measures to reduce or limit their respective military forces within mutually agreed geographical zones along the line of actual control in the India-China border areas:

(1) The two sides reaffirm that they shall reduce or limit their respective military forces within mutually agreed geographical zones along the line of actual control in the India-China border areas to minimum levels compatible with the friendly and good neighbourly relations between the two countries and consistent with the principle of mutual and equal security.

(2) The two sides shall reduce or limit the number of field army, border defence forces, para-military forces and any other mutually agreed category of armed forces deployed in mutually agreed geographical zones along the line of actual control to ceilings to be mutually agreed upon. The major categories of armaments to be reduced or limited are as follows: combat tanks, infantry combat vehicles, guns (including howitzers) with 75 mm or bigger calibre, mortars with 120 mm or bigger calibre, surface-to-surface missiles, surface-to-air missiles and any other weapon system mutually agreed upon.

(3) The two sides shall exchange data on the military forces and armaments to be reduced or limited and decide on ceilings on military forces and armaments to be kept by each side within mutually agreed geographical zones along the line of actual control in the India-China border areas. The ceilings shall be determined in conformity with the requirement of the principle of mutual and equal security, with due consideration being given to parameters such as the nature of terrain, road communications and other infrastructure and time taken to induct/deinduct troops and armaments.

ARTICLE IV

In order to maintain peace and tranquillity along the line of actual control in the India-China border areas and to prevent any tension in the border areas due to misreading by either side of the other side's intentions:

(1) Both sides shall avoid holding large scale military exercises involving more than one Division (approximately 15,000 troops) in close proximity of the line of actual control in the India-China border areas. However, if such exercises are to be conducted, the strategic direction of the main force involved shall not be towards the other side.

(2) If either side conducts a major military exercise involving more than one Brigade (approximately 5,000 troops) in close proximity of the line of actual control in the India-China border areas, it shall give the other side prior notification with regard to type, level, planned duration and formations participating in the exercise.

(3) The date of completion of the exercise and deinduction of troops from the areas of exercise shall be intimated to the other side within five days of completion or deinduction.

(4) Each side shall be entitled to obtain timely clarification from the side undertaking the exercise in respect of data specified in Paragraph 2 of the present Article.

ARTICLE V

With a view to preventing air intrusions across the line of actual control in the India-China border areas and facilitating overflights and landings by military aircraft:

(1) Both sides shall take adequate measures to ensure that air intrusions across the line of actual control do not take place. However, if an intrusion does take place, it should cease as soon as detected and the incident shall be promptly investigated by the side operating the aircraft. The results of the investigation shall be immediately communicated, through diplomatic channels or at border personnel meetings, to the other side.

(2) Subject to Paragraphs 3 and 5 of this Article, combat aircraft (to include fighter, bomber, reconnaissance, military trainer, armed helicopter and other armed aircraft) shall not fly within ten kilometers of the line of actual control.

(3) If either side is required to undertake flights of combat aircraft within ten kilometers from the line of actual control, it shall give the following information in advance to the other side, through diplomatic channels:

(a) Type and number of combat aircraft;
(b) Height of the proposed flight (in meters);
(c) Proposed duration of flights (normally not to exceed ten days);
(d) Proposed timing of flights; and
(e) Area of operations defined in latitude and longitude.

(4) Unarmed transport aircraft, survey aircraft and helicopters shall be permitted to fly up to the line of actual control.

(5) No military aircraft of either side shall fly across the line of actual control, except by prior permission. Military aircraft of either side may fly across the line of actual control or overfly the other side's airspace or land on the other side only after obtaining the latter's prior permission after providing the latter with detailed information on the flight in accordance with the international practice in this regard.

Notwithstanding the above stipulation, each side has the sovereign right to specify additional conditions, including at short notice, for flights or lands of military aircraft of the other side on its side of the line of actual control or through its airspace.

(6) In order to ensure flight safety in emergency situations, the authorities designated by the two sides may contact each other by the quickest means of communications available.

ARTICLE VI

With a view to preventing dangerous military activities along the line of actual control in the India-China border areas, the two sides agree as follows:

(1) Neither side shall open fire, cause bio-degradation, use hazardous chemicals, conduct blast operations or hunt with guns or explosives within two kilometers from the line of actual control. This prohibition shall not apply to routine firing activities in small arms firing ranges.

(2) If there is a need to conduct blast operations within two kilometers of the line of actual control as part of developmental activities, the other side shall be informed through diplomatic channels or by convening a border personnel meeting, preferably five days in advance.

(3) While conducting exercises with live ammunition in areas close to the line of actual control, precaution shall be taken to ensure that a bullet or a missile does not accidentally fall on the other side across the line of actual control and causes harm to the personnel or property of the other side.

(4) If the border personnel of the two sides come in a face-to-face situation due to differences on the alignment of the line of actual control or any other reason, they shall exercise self-restraint and take all necessary steps to avoid an escalation of the situation. Both sides shall also enter into immediate consultations through diplomatic and/or other available channels to review the situation and prevent any escalation of tension.

ARTICLE VII

In order to strengthen the cooperation between their military personnel and establishments in the border areas along the line of actual control, the two sides agree:

(1) To maintain and expand the regime of scheduled and flag meetings between their border representatives at designated places along the line of actual control;

(2) To maintain and expand telecommunication links between their border meeting points at designated places along the line of actual control;

(3) To establish step-by-step medium and high-level contacts between the border authorities of the two sides.

ARTICLE VIII

(1) Should the personnel of one side cross the line of actual control and enter the other side because of unavoidable circumstances like natural disasters, the other side shall extend all possible assistance to them and inform their side, as soon as possible, regarding the forced or inadvertent entry across the line of actual control. The modalities of return of the concerned personnel to their own side shall be settled through mutual consultations.

(2) The two sides shall provide each other, at the earliest possible, with information pertaining to natural disasters and epidemic disasters in contiguous border areas which might affect the other side. The exchange of information shall take place either through diplomatic channels or at border personnel meetings.

ARTICLE IX

In case a doubtful situation develops in the border region, or in case one of the sides has some questions or doubts regarding the manner in which the other side is observing this Agreement, either side has the right to seek a clarification from the other side. The clarifications sought and replies to them shall be conveyed through diplomatic channels.

ARTICLE X

(1) Recognising that the full implementation of some of the provisions of the present Agreement will depend on the two sides arriving at a common understanding of the alignment of the line of actual control in the India-China border areas, the two sides agree to speed up the process of clarification and confirmation of the line of actual control. As an initial step in this process, they are clarifying the alignment of the line of actual control in those segments where they have different perceptions. They also agree to exchange maps indicating their respective perceptions of the entire alignment of the line of actual control as soon as possible.

(2) Pending the completion of the process of clarification and confirmation of the line of actual control, the two sides shall work out modalities for implementing confidence building measures envisaged under this Agreement on an interim basis, without prejudice to their respective positions on the alignment of the line of actual control as well as the boundary question.

ARTICLE XI

Detailed implementation measures required under Article I to X of this Agreement shall be decided through mutual consultations in the India-China Joint Working Group on the Boundary Question. The India-China Diplomatic and Military experts Group shall assist the India-China Joint Working Group in devising implementation measures under the Agreement.

ARTICLE XII

This Agreement is subject to ratification and shall enter into force on the date of exchange of instruments of ratification. It shall remain in effect until either side decides to terminate it after giving six months' notice in writing. It shall become invalid six months after the notification.

This agreement is subject to amendment and addition by mutual agreement in writing between the two sides.

Signed in duplicates in New Delhi on 29 November, 1996 in the Hindi, Chinese and English languages, all three texts being equally authentic. In case of divergence, the English text shall prevail.

For the Government of
the Republic of India

For the Government of the
People's Republic of China

Conclusion

Having presented these three historic Sino-Indian CSBM agreements, the single most important element that comes to the fore lies in the sustained mutual commitment from both these countries towards the sanctity of what is known as the *Panchsheel.* These Five Principles of peaceful co-existence not only represent the very soul of Sino-Indian friendship and understanding but also form the common thread that provides continuity and joins these three agreements together. *Panchsheel,* therefore, can be safely described as the very core and the very essence of these three agreements that represent the successful termination of two different phases of flux and friction in Sino-Indian relations. These Five Principles have since been adopted not only in various other Sino-Indian agreements and other bilateral documents but have also been presented to the world as an ideal framework for peaceful and stable inter-state relations. During the historic visit by Prime Minister Rajiv Gandhi to Beijing in December 1988, China's paramount leader Deng Xiaoping had, in fact, proposed that both China and India should work together and present Panchsheel as the basic framework for defining the new world order of post-Cold War world.

Seen individually, the 1954 Panchsheel Agreement formed the cradle of these historic Five Principles of Panchsheel. To start with, the Agreement had sought to put behind some of historical entanglements of the Sino-Indian ties, albeit incomprehensibly. By invoking the spirit of Panchsheel — which also have cultural connotations for being the integral core of Buddhist preaching — this agreement had once emerged as the strongest force in combining the people of these two civilizational-states of China and India. However, despite the fact that there was nothing wrong in the formulation of this agreement's letter and spirit, the attack on it came, as I have alluded to earlier, from a deteriating atmosphere not generated from this agreement itself. For one thing, both the young republics were intoxicated in copious patristic nationalist alcohol. For another, there was the cold war developing from strength to strength, and India and China were unwittingly sucked into its whirlpool.

Although the Agreement lapsed, in 1962, it has stood as a shining document with an immortal guiding principle in international affairs.

The 1993 and 1996 agreements have closed a chapter which had been the most unpleasant in the history between the two countries. They have ended the eyeball to eyeball confrontation over the Himalayan peaks, have stopped making the holy range a hot spot in international conflict. Here, too, the spirit of *Panchsheel* was brought to play.

Apart from various other factors like historical legacies, evolved conventions, and mutual perceptions, treaties remain the most widely accepted and most legitimate legal instrument that defines and determines the code of conduct for inter-state interactions. These three agreements assume special significance when signed by two nation-states which may be either widely different in terms of their histories, languages, cultures, political systems or levels of development or which may have fallen prey to unfavourable atmospherics generated by their not-so-friendly or conflictual relations. In fact, treaties have always had a special place in terminating inter-state wars or in resolving other inter-state disputes. Though, such a tradition of treaty-making can be traced back to the ancient times yet, the two World Wars and the consequent emergence of the League of Nations and United Nations have particularly clauses and principles, it soon fell prey to the difficult ground realities and unfavourable circumstances. The 1954 Agreement was allowed to lapse at the end of its 8-year life because the bilateral atmosphere in 1962 was too unfriendly to extend its existence. It was precisely because of this change in the ambiance in which this agreement was conceived that it could not bear fruition. Nevertheless, in looking back, it has stood as one most shining document in the historical times and its Five Principles of Panchsheel have found their place of pride in various other international treaties and other inter-state documents. This agreement has also continued to be the guiding force for all the latter Sino-Indian initiatives towards renewing their friendship and building confidence.

The other two CSBM agreements of 1993 and 1996 mark the continuation of the first Sino-Indian Panchsheel Agreement, both in letter and spirit. In the same manner, they also mark the success of Sino-Indian *rapprochement* that has been so assiduously evolved since the mid-1970s. These two agreements finally have closed the sad chapter in Sino-Indian ties which had witnessed the longest freeze in post-independence diplomatic relations as also an actual shooting war followed by incidents of eyeball-to-eyeball antagonism making the Himalayan gap not only insurmountable but also one of the dangerous international boundaries on the earth. But more than that, these two CSBM agreements underline important steps agreed mutually to guide Sino-Indian relationship towards the goal of greater friendship, more transparency and a future pattern of mutual trust, peace and friendship between the two Asian giants. However, sceptics have continued to describe them as only pious and good intentions and complain that these have not been followed by action. This argument does remain valid to a certain extent. But considering the magnitude of complications that engulf Sino-Indian ties, even good intentions obtain special significance once put on paper in black and white. In the end, therefore, despite their limited and slow pace of success, these agreements definitely have much greater historical significance than what meets the eyes at a first glance. They also initiated a spirit of looking at each other in the bilateral relations setting up rules and regulations that govern the operations for the ground activities. Lately, with rapid developments in the fields of science and technology, rising inter-state awareness, synergy and interdependence have tremendously increased the significance of what have come to be known as the confidence building treaties. These treaties, as a first step, seek to contain (not eliminate), the possible chances of inter-state conflict, especially those that may be completely unpredictable in their nature, timings and magnitude. And here, though, all inter-state agreements, in a way, make contribution towards evolving an environment of mutual security and mutual confidence yet some of these remain more clearly directed towards this motive than others.

Considering that Sino-Indian ties present one of the most complicated examples of inter-state relations, treaties signed by these two countries have been repeatedly subjected to varied debates and interpretations. By presenting my introductory piece to the volume which is dedicated to an overall improvement of atmosphere between the two contries, my humble submission is to draw attention from the ruling elites and the wider circles of India and China to the flowering and function of mutual trust and good will that have been achieved against the backgroud of enormous misunderstanding and inexperienced handling of the bilateral problems bequeathed by history.

It is significant to note that both the 1993 and 1996 India-China agreements quoted the five principles of the 1954 Agreement verbatim without invoking the name "Panchsheel". This is tantamount to the partial resurrection of the historic 1954 Agreement. This is further proved form the attempts of the two agreements of the 1990s to revive border trade which was one of the central cencerns of the 1994 agreement. The two 1990s agreements, thus, like their 1954 predecessor, served to put behind a portion of irritants and misgivings between the two countries in the interim period of four decades.

SWARAN SINGH

57

BUILDING SECURITY AND CONFIDENCE WITH CHINA

Except for the brief period of confrontation between 1959-1962 and the diplomatic freeze that followed for next few years the relations between China and India had never been conflictual in nature. But because of the complicated colonial legacies — which were further compounded by the Cold War dynamics and by the border war of 1962 — mutual distrust and threat perceptions have continued to undermine all efforts towards building confidence. One may ask why confidence and security building measures (CSBMs) between India and China are so critical to the evolution of their multifaceted and multilayered *rapprochement*? The one line answer would be that these CSBMs present a perfect barometer for any crystal gazing into the future of these two Asian giants. However, this answer remains far too simplistic to explain the complexity of Sino-Indian ties. And it is in this context of complications that this essay tries to examine and highlight Sino-Indian CSBMs in terms of their being the first significant step forward untying the knots in the bilateral relations and mutual perceptions.

Firstly, to deal with the theoretical elements of Sino-Indian CSBMs, it has been unjustifiably fashionable to view Sino-Indian CSBMs essentially in the framework of western ready-made models. If anything, the CSBMs in the Asian context have far preceded all western models and, therefore, are neither borrowed from nor identical to those leading to the Final Act of the Helsinki process of the Conference on Security and Cooperation in Europe (CSCE) that was concluded in 1975. Beginning from the Joint Defence Council of 1948 that effected the division of assets and armed forces between India and Pakistan to the Sino-Indian *Panchsheel* Agreement of 1954, and later the Indo-Pak Simla agreement of 1971, various formal and informal agreements had already effected these CSBMs like "non-use", or the "selective use" of armed force and created various other mechanisms. Therefore these CSBMs had been institutionalised in Asia far earlier.[1] Besides, these were also far more broad based than the Western CSBMs, including those that were later incorporated the Document of the Conference on Disarmament in Europe held in 1986 at Stockholm (Sweden).[2]

Coming to the salient features of what can be described as the Asian CSBMs that distinguish the Sino-Indian CSBMs from most of their comparable Western models, one sees the near absence of a subjective feeling in the Asian context of an imminent threat which is so central to all those Western conceptions of CSBMs.[3] In Asia's rather lose polycentric situation, nations had never been so clearly divided as are the communist and liberal democratic traditions that characterise the bipolar division of the West. Similarly, the second basic condition of equality of the military strength between the potential parties to the conflict, again seems very much a Eurocentric feature of CSBMs and is generally missing in the Asian situation.[4] China, India and Pakistan can themselves be cited as ideal examples of this asymmetry of power. Nevertheless, CSBMs have continued to evolve amongst these three countries. Thirdly, the inter-state boundaries which form the basic element of European CSBMs are itself a major problem and therefore the very objective towards which most Asian CSBMs seek to provide solutions. Also, Asian CSBMs are generally backed by ever widening network of measures like state sponsored people-to-people contacts which are aimed at expanding mutual trust and understanding between the entire social elite on both sides.

Nor should we regard the Asian CSBMs in general and the Sino-Indian CSBMs in particular as the byproduct of the post-Cold War peace dividend although the global factors have surely been much more influential in moulding the European CSBMs than those between Asian countries. This is because unlike Europe, (a) the conflicts in Asia were never seen to be vital to the national interests of both the super powers; and, (b) the middle ranking powers like China and India have become increasingly independent from the regimented bipolar world order of the Cold War years. To give two most apt examples, contrary to Cold

War trends, India had initiated its CSBMs during the mid-1970s and India's Foreign Minister, Atal Behari Vajpai, paid his first visit to Beijing at the time when China was launching its war against Vietnam and the Soviet forces were about to enter Afghanistan yet, despite India's closeness to Moscow, the new Cold War of the early 1980s did not disturb the smooth evolution of Sino-Indian *rapprochement.* Similarly, following the June 1989 Tiananmen Square incident, while most of world powers had imposed sanctions thus completely isolating China, the relations between China and India not only continued to be smooth but experienced a greater momentum: the period from the second half through 1989 and 1990 saw 10 high-level visits between the two countries that included visits to New Delhi by Vice Premier Wu Xueqian in October 1989 and by Foreign Minister Qian Qichen in March 1990.[5] The credit for this goes to (a) this unique Asian way of trial and error which, therefore, lends some sort of originality of these Sino-Indian CSBMs, and (b) to the political leadership of both the countries who were able to take and stand by such bold initiatives.

If anything, it is their expanding interactions at various levels that has been the greatest single factor behind the evolution of Sino-Indian CSBMs. (see Table 1) Starting from their exchange of Ambassadors in 1976, these expanding official and business interactions can be divided into three major phases. The first phase (1976-1988), was characterised by both *China and India looking at each other* simply gauging the potential for expanding mutual goodwill and trust. Second phase (1988-1996), which witnessed five formal summits interspersed by hectic initiatives and agreements towards evolving and consolidating CSBMs. Then having established this strong network of CSBMs the recent four agreements signed during President Jiang Zemin's visit to New Delhi in November 1996, Sino-Indian *rapprochement* has now entered into its third and final phase where the two are expected to take concrete decisions on more difficult issues like the boundary question.

A quick glance through this evolution from freeze to fervour shows how, though no breakthrough has yet been achieved on the crucial boundary question quite a substantial progress has been made considering the complicated and knotty ground realities. The historic 1988 visit to Beijing by Prime Minister Rajiv Gandhi had worked as a catalyst in facilitating a U-turn in Sino-Indian relations.[6] Especially, considering Indian sensitivities vis-à-vis China, this visit itself was an extremely bold initiative. But more than this, in the Joint Communiqué at the end of this visit India agreed, for the first time, to dropping its earlier policy stance of asking for settlement of the border as a precondition for any improvement in relations in other fields. Secondly, India not only agreed to describe Tibet as an integral part of (not just an autonomous region) of China but also expressed "concern over anti-Chinese activities by some Tibetan elements in India" — a proviso which was criticised by some as a clear sell-out of the Tibetan interests.[7] India's over-reaction towards Tibetan protesters during the visit by Premier Li Peng in 1991 was another demonstration of India's resolve in not letting Tibet become a problem in the way of Sino-Indian *rapprochement.* All this meant that, Rajiv Gandhi's visit had finally abandoned India's discredited forwards policy and, at least during the interim, accepted China's long-standing demand for the maintenance of tranquillity on the line of actual control (LoAC).

There were also some legal hurdles to this visit. The historic November 1962 resolution of Indian Parliament had bound successive Indian leaders from making any move towards improving Sino-Indian ties until they had obtained every inch of India's sacred land claimed or taken by the Chinese. But this December 1988 visit by Rajiv Gandhi to Beijing became possible because of another major resolution that was passed by the All India Congress Working Committee on November 5, 1988 urging the government to seek a settlement through "peaceful negotiations" based on "mutual interest" and "acceptable to the peoples of both countries" even if it took time.[8] Apart from minor objections, no main national political parties raised any hue and cry against these "concession" by Rajiv Gandhi. This was because (a) the Congress Party, at this time, had an overwhelming majority in Indian Parliament and (b) the earlier major initiative towards building peace with China had been taken during the Janata Party government in February 1979. Moreover, eight rounds of border talks (initiated during Foreign Minister, Huang Hua's visit to New Delhi in 1981) had already created some sort of favourable backdrop. (see Table 2).

Apart from these interactions at the political level, Rajiv Gandhi's visit also opened avenues for direct military interactions. Because of the 1962 war, any interaction between the military personnel or on defence related matters remained a taboo until the early 1990s. The first exchange in this direction was made by the senior serving officials of the National Defence College (New Delhi) and the National Defence University (Beijing) respectively visiting each other in 1990 and 1992.[9] The two have also since been considering undertaking an arrangement for an institutional exchange wherein at least one officer could attend the other's training courses. The military-to-military dialogue was taken to a higher level by India's Defence Minister, Sharad Pawar's visit to China in July 1992.[10] This opened the way and was followed by Vice Chief of China's People's Liberation Army, Lt. General Xu Huizi, visiting India in December 1993 followed by a visit by their Defence Minister, Chi Haotian's visit to India during September 7-13, 1994. From the Indian side, Chief of Army Staff, General B.C. Joshi and Chief of Naval Staff, Admiral V.S. Shekhawat paid reciprocal visits to various defence facilities in China during July 1994 and March 1996 respectively. This increasing interaction and transparency between the two military establishments has surely contributed to the building up of mutual confidence.

Once again, just like the lack of interactions and other historical legacies had coloured their visions during the earlier years, increasing information and confidence has led to revision and rectification of various policies on both sides. One good example of this spectrum of biases in perceptions can be seen in the way various China watchers interpreted the incident when in May 1992 China detonated a 150 megaton nuclear device just hours after President R. Venkatraman arrived in Beijing. While some called it an act of intimidation, others described it as an expression of China's solidarity with India in their strategic defiance of Washington. However, with persistent efforts from both sides, a relatively more objective understanding of each other has started to emerge during the 1990s. Observing the tenor of policy pronouncements from both sides there appears to be an obvious shift of emphasis away from the assertion of huge territorial claims or high moral principles increasingly towards "mutual concessions" and "accommodation" from the Chinese side and on historical, legal, geographical realities from the Indian side with both now calling for a "fair, reasonable, and mutually acceptable" compromise solution to their boundary question.[11]

Also both sides today have far greater mutual understanding on various issues ranging from global *problematic* like the US nuclear non-proliferation to regional and bilateral contentions like Kashmir, Tibet, and border. As a result, while owing to their ideological systems and methods of operation the two had appeared to be dramatical opposites during the 1950s, over the years the two sides have begun to appreciate and emphasise on their similarities and evolved common approach on certain issues like nuclear disarmament, trade and human rights. On the nuclear question, for example, while China has sought to keep its own nuclear build-up completely insulated from the ongoing disarmament debates between Moscow and Washington; yet, Beijing has also generally kept a low profile on India's nuclear and missile programme and, in fact, assisted India by supplying heavy water at a crucial stage in January 1995.[12] Nevertheless, there still exist differences of approach on various issues and inspite of substaintial improvement, India has continued to be deeply concerned about China's supplies of nuclear components, materials and knowhow to other countries in India's neighbourhood. This is especially true of China's indulgence with Pakistan. Yet, in the end, all this has never discouraged India from making efforts at improving ties with both Beijing and Islamabad.

From the Indian side, these efforts for *rapprochement* had all started as early as late 1960s. Later, starting from Sardar Swaran Singh's (then Foreign Minister) offer in August 1970 "to settle all matters...peacefully through bilateral negotiations," India not only became the first one to take many major initiatives but also became the first one to declare and actually resume its Ambassadorial level diplomatic relations with Beijing.[13] Besides, India also made many other goodwill gestures towards China like installing telex links in each other's embassies, supporting China's candidacy for the Manila-based Asian Development Bank, inviting China to a regional UNESCO conference in New Delhi, and Prime Minister Mrs. Indira Gandhi herself making a personal gesture by visiting and signing the book of condolences in the Chinese embassy in New Delhi as mark of respect for the late Premier Zhou Enlai. The first feelers from the Chinese side came in May 1980 and April 1981 from then Vice Premier Deng Xiaoping who revived Zhou Enlai's 1960 proposal for a package deal on the boundary question.[14] Here, Deng proposed Chinese recognition of the McMahon Line in the eastern sector in return for Indian acceptance of the status quo along the LoAC in the western sector. In fact, according to Mrs. Gandhi's foreign policy Advisor, G. Parthasarthy, Mrs. Gandhi had even agreed to accept the Chinese package deal only that, with the Chinese assent, the formal announcement had been postponed until after December 1985 general elections.[15] Soon the assassination of Mrs. Gandhi in October 1984 and later the Sumdorong Chu valley incident in July 1986 completely rocked this spirit of accommodation and delayed major initiatives by few more years.[16]

A clear shift in China's South Asia policy, however, began to occur from late 1980s when Beijing gradually gave up its earlier post-1962 tactics of providing moral and material support to India's smaller neighbours which was aimed at: (a) tying New Delhi down to the South Asian region and, (b) trying to offset India's preeminence even in this smaller region. In 1989, for example, China not only refused to supply weapons to Nepal and gave only muted response to India's peacekeeping in Sri Lanka, it even told General Ershad of Bangladesh to expect no more Chinese support on their river water dispute with New Delhi.[17] This has since resulted in improving India's relations with both Bangladesh and Nepal. Putting an end to its dilly-dallying of late 1980s, the Rao-Li joint statement of December 1991 clearly told China's closest ally Pakistan that Beijing now regards Kashmir as a bilateral issue between India and Pakistan. Since then China's position on Kashmir has also undergone a marked change on at least two basic counts: (a) by describing it as a bilateral issue between India and Pakistan that should be dealt not under UN resolutions of 1954 but the 1972 Simla Agreement, and (b) by broadly agreeing to underline the fear from "islamic fundamentalism". In the second case, the Joint Statement did not directly mention either India's Kashmir or China's Xinjiang yet, as both these provinces share common borders with Pakistan, the statement has clear implications for Islamabad.[18] But nothing perhaps stands comparison to the first Magna Carta on Sino-Indian CSBMs that came two years later and was a part of the next Rao-Li Joint Statement from Beijing.

By any standards, this nine-point "Agreement on Maintenance of Peace and Tranquillity along the Line of Actual Control (henceforth MPTA), signed between two Prime Ministers Narasimha Rao and Li Peng at Beijing's Great Hall of the People on September 7, 1993 has been the corner-stone of Sino-Indian CSBMs. Though already in vogue since the Rajiv Gandhi visit to Beijing in 1988, it was this agreement that formally institutionalised the process of Sino-Indian CSBMs.[19] Picking up strings from India's first CSBM agreement of April 1954, the MPTA reiterates its faith in *Panchsheel* and asserts that these Five Principles of Peaceful Coexistence should form the basis of all inter-state relations. But unlike in the earlier Sino-Indian *Panchsheel* agreement where India unilaterally made major concessions, the MPTA clearly represents equality of two nations and lays out various CSBMs that should further buttress Sino-Indian rapprochement.[20] This business-like spirit is crystal clear throughout its concise text that details on number of specific points.

Article one of MPTA starts by highlighting the consensus where both sides wish to resolve the boundary question "through peaceful and friendly consultations" and where both undertake to "strictly respect and observe the line of actual control" and never to "use or threaten to use force" and whenever necessary "jointly check and determine the segments" of their border. Article Two makes a far more concrete recommendation asking the two sides to keep their border military presence "to a minimum level compatible with the friendly and goodneighbourly relations" and to further agree "to reduce" them "in conformity with the requirements of the principle of mutual and equal security." Taking off from here, Article Three talks of evolving "effective CBMs" and asks each side not to "undertake specified levels of military exercises in mutually identified zones" and to "give the other notification of military exercises" along the border. Articles Four and Five speak about their agreement to create mechanisms for dealing with intrusions and other exigencies while in Article Six both sides clarify that despite these resolutions nothing in this treaty shall "prejudice their respective positions on the boundary question." To actually kick off initiatives Article Seven asks both sides to start by specifically defining the "form, method, scale and content of effective verification measures", and Article Eight initiates this process by asking each side to "appoint diplomats and military experts to formulate, through mutual consultations, implementation measures for the present agreement", and this setting up of an Expert Group can be easily described as the greatest achievement of this pact in terms of building Sino-Indian CSBMs. Finally, Article Nine gives its date of coming into effect and declares all its versions — Hindi, Chinese, English — as equally valid.

The second CSBMs agreement was signed during President Jiang Zemin's visit to New Delhi in November 1996. This is a 12 Article document that partly fulfils the agenda of their first CSBM agreement of 1993 and it further seeks to extend the CBMs to more specific and sensitive areas in the military field.[21] Going by its first Article that reads "Neither side shall use its military capability against the other side", it virtually stands out as a No War Pact and both sides have also projected it in that light. The agreement begins with (Article II) recognising that both have "different perceptions" on certain segments of border for which the two have agreed "to speed up the process of clarification" and under Article X both sides agree "to exchange maps indicating their respective perceptions... as soon as possible." It is this businesslike approach to these sensitive questions that gives hope for the future as it depicts their growing mutual confidence on the current pace of their *rapprochement.*

As regards evolving CBMs in the military field, the agreement makes a serious attempt at effecting reductions in their military manpower and equipment deployed in the border areas. There had been major confusion as China does not consider their deployments in Tibet as being open for mutual reductions where India believes that Chinese forces on the Tibetan plateau have clear one-to-ten advantage against Indian forces. Accordingly, Article III provides that keeping with "the principle of mutual and equal security" all future ceilings are expected to be based on "perimeters such as the nature of terrain, road communications and other infrastructure and time taken to induct/deinduct troops and armaments." Article IV clearly categorises certain type of offensive weapons withdrawal of which will be given priority. These include combat tanks, infantry combat vehicles, guns (including howitzers) with 75 mm or bigger calibre, mortars with 120 mm or bigger calibre, surface-to-surface missiles, surface-to-air missiles and to start with the two sides will "exchange data on the military forces and armament" that are to be reduced. It also exhorts the two sides to "avoid holding large scale military exercises involving more than one Division (15,000 troops) in close proximity to the LoAC" and to inform the other side on "type, level, planned duration and areas of exercise" in case it involves more than a Brigade (5,000 troops) and about deinduction "within five days of completion." The other side is free to seek any number of clarifications as it deems necessary.

Taking a major step forward, the two agree that no combat aircraft which "include fighter, bomber, reconnaissance, military trainer, armed helicopter and other armed aircraft" shall be allowed to fly "within ten kilometers" of the LoAC "except by prior permission" from the other side (Article V). Similarly, Article VI prohibits any use of "hazardous chemicals, conduct blast operations or hunt with guns or explosives within two kilometers" of the LoAC unless it is "part of developmental activities" in which case the other side shall be informed "through diplomatic channels or by convening a border personnel meeting, preferably five days in advance." Then to "strengthen exchanges and cooperation between their military personnel and establishments" Article VII provides that the two sides shall (a) increase "meetings between their border representatives at designated places, (b) expand "telecommunication links" between these border points, and (c) establish "step-by-step medium and high-level contacts between the border authorities" of the two sides. Should any land or air intrusions take place "because of unavoidable circumstances like natural disasters" the other side is expected under Article VIII to "extend all possible assistance to them" and the two shall exchange information and have consultations to work out "modalities of return of the concerned personnel." And finally, as soon as the Sino-Indian Joint Working Group on Boundary Question starts "mutual consultations" (Article XI) for "detailed implementation measures", each side shall have (Article IX) "the right to seek clarification" regarding the "manner in which the other side is observing the agreement" or on any "doubtful situation" in the border region. Finally, under Article XII though all Hindi, Chinese and English versions are "equally authentic", but "in case of divergence, the English text shall prevail." This agreement has since been ratified by both sides and instrument of ratification were exchanged at the JWG's tenth meeting in New Delhi in August 1997.

These two agreements apart from being a major take-off point for many fresh initiatives, have also provided a major boost to existing "mechanisms" for their border related CSBMs. The Joint Working Group on Boundary Question has been one most effective and generic forum for implementing Sino-Indian CSBMs. (see Table 3) To begin with, the JWG has institutionalised regular meetings of military commanders from both sides at the following four points: Bumla and Dichu in the eastern sector, Lipulekh near Pithoragarh (U.P.) in the middle sector and Spanggur near Chushul in the western sector. These meetings are organised and conducted by these area commanders from the two sides to establish facts on the ground and can also be held more than once in case of any exigencies. Besides, commanders on both sides are now provided with "hotline" links to ensure consultations in case of any intrusions or other emergencies. Advance notices of proposed military manoeuvres on one side is provided to the other and mechanisms for handling possible intrusions on either side are put in place. The high point of these JWG meetings occurred during its eighth meeting during August 1995 at New Delhi where the two sides agreed to actually dismantle four border posts in the Wangdong tract where troops had been deployed at an alarming proximity to each other. Apart from their land-based troops, the two air forces have also been building ties and officers of the People's Liberation Army-Air Force (PLAAF) have already visited India's Air Force bases in 1995.[22] Similarly, the two navies have also been working together allaying each other's doubts about Chinese naval presence in Myanmar or India's maritime capabilities at its Fortress Andaman. India has offered to China's envoy to visit Indian naval base at Port Blair in Andaman and Nicobar. At a certain stage there were even reports of China and India preparing for joint military and naval exercises which, however, was denied by the Chinese side.[23]

Then there are various other bold initiatives that come about from outside the framework of JWG. (see Table 4) Within less than two months of the MPTA, for example, a Chinese ship "Zheng He" made a port visit to Bombay, which was the first of its kind in last 35 years. Before this only *INS Mysore* had visited Shanghai in 1958. Also, working on the basis of Chinese *guanxi* (personal contacts) principle, exchanges between other opinion makers and members of strategic research institutions (like Institute for Defence Studies & Analyses, United Services Institution of India, Centre for Policy Research, and Rajiv Gandhi Foundation from India and China Institute for Contemporary International Relations, China Association for Friendly International Contact, Fudan University etc. from China) have also been increasingly formalised. Similarly, *Xinhua*, *People's Daily* and *Beijing Review* have their accredited correspondents in India and India's *Press Trust of India* has a resident reporter in Beijing. The agreements on exchange of scholars (between the Indian Council for Social Science Research and Chinese Academy of Social Sciences signed at New Delhi in January 1992) and their Agreement on Radio and Television Cooperation (signed in Beijing on September 7, 1993) have broadly contributed to expanding mutual awareness. The Festival of China was staged in India in 1992 and Festival of India was held in China in April 1994. In fact, the Communist Party of China now has direct links with the Indian National Congress, the Bharatiya Janata Party and the Communist Party of India (Marxists). The two had also tried opening up direct flights between New Delhi and Beijing and now have telecom lines between various cities of the two countries. Contact have also evolved between various NGOs like trade unions and woman organisations, stimulating a great deal of interest and confidence.

In the de-ideologised post-Cold War world, trade has come to be perhaps the most durable CSBM which raises stakes in mutual security and peace amongst states. Though compared to their size and total foreign trade, the volume of Sino-Indian bilateral trade remains still very small yet, more than what is visible in terms of statistics, their border trade has substantially increased the traffic of goods and people in their border regions thus consolidating their border related CSBMs.[24] Garbyang (in Uttar Pradesh) was the first border port to be opened in February 1991 followed by Gunji (in Uttar Pradesh) in 1992 and later Shipki La (in Himachal Pradesh) in 1994. A fourth border point agreed upon in principle is yet to be opened. India has suggested an eastern route originating in Sikkim on which China has been evasive as it means recognising Sikkim's accession to India. As an alternative, a route from Kalimpong in Darjeeling District in West Bengal, passing through Sikkim to Yatung in Chumbi Valley, is likely to be agreed upon. Amongst its other intangibles, in 1994, India became China's largest trading partner in South Asia overtaking China's long-standing close friend and ally Pakistan. This obtains for India a greater leverage and psychological advantage vis-a-vis Sino-Pakistan ties. And finally, talking of statistics, according to a recent study by US based Centre for Global Trade Development that monitors trade patterns of 220 countries, has predicted that trade between China and India may cross $ 25 billion by the year 2000. According to the study, this is possible because at their current rate of growth India's total annual exports are expected to reach $ 90 billion and that of China (plus Hong Kong $ 225 billion after 1997) to $ 425 billion per annum.[25] The Sino-Indian Joint Business Council has, however, put the figure at a much moderate level of $ 5 billion by 2000.

During these last twenty years of rapprochement Sino-Indian trade has risen from mere $ 2.5 million in 1977 to $ 1.16 billion for 1996. This expansion in trade has been possible because of persistent efforts on the part of Indian and Chinese trading and business communities, especially during these last ten years. In 1984 the two had signed protocols replacing their differential tariffs by granting each other the most favoured nation (MFN) trading status and since then their annual protocols continue to enumerate expanding list of items for their bilateral trade. The two sides have also ocassionally been signing other trade related agreements. For example, on July 18, 1994, during his third visit to New Delhi, Foreign Minister Qian Qichen signed another trade agreement on "avoidance of double taxation", which is expected to create further favourable conditions "to encourage business, scientific, cultural as well as personal exchanges in the future."[26] Though the Reserve Bank of India and the People's Bank of China signed an MoU for resumption of direct banking links allowing their banks to set up representative offices in each other's country in October 1994, there has been no reciprocal action except that the State Bank of India has opened one branch in Beijing.[27] As much of the trade is in private hands, lack of infrastructural facilities like telecommunications, shipping and banking channels as also the differences of language and business culture have stood as important barrier.[28] Nevertheless, complementarities are gradually coming to the fore, pushing them closer together. China, for example, has enormous need and is ambitious to emerge as world's largest producer of steel by year 2000 and will thus increasingly require India to supply high grade iron ore. The first Sino-Indian joint venture in this regard was already launched in Orissa (India) between India's Mideast Integrated Steels Limited and China's Metallurgical Import Export Corporation (CMIEC) in January 1993.[29] And here, their two agreements of November 1996 on (i) maritime shipping that (a) provides MFN to each others' sea-borne trade commodities and ships and, (b) puts in place the double tax avoidance mechanisms; and (ii) agreement on combating smuggling of narcotics and arms and other economic offenses on the Sino-Indian border will both go a long way in expanding the Sino-Indian trade ties.

As regards exploring collaborations for future, India's growing expertise in computer software can strengthen China's hands in dealing with its Intellectual Property Rights (IPR) problems with the United States. Other uncharted areas for future cooperation can include joint development and manufacture of aircraft and systems (for civilian needs to start with), ship-building and repairs, railway equipment etc.[30] China, for example, has already shown interest in participating in India's Light Combat Aircraft (LCA) project.[31] Similarly, there were also reports about China, India and South Korea jointly working for developing a 100-seater civilian aircraft.[32] In fact, apart from these joint ventures, reviving other network like direct flights between various Chinese and Indian cities and re-building the old Burma Road (and ancient Silk Route) should now be reopened to serve the larger and necessary purposes of trade and transit.[33] This will completely transform the entire communication and trade profile of Sino-Indian ties. But in the long-run, it is their greater understanding as also their cooperation in more basic fields like agriculture and population control that will go a long way in helping them to fulfil their common desire for peace and development.[34]

As the preceding discussion shows so clearly a genuine process of Sino-Indian CSBMs has not only picked up momentum of their own but even reached a certain level of maturity where the two sides are even willing to exchange sensitive information on their military manpower and equipment, and to partake training with each other's officers and men as also to show them each other's defence facilities and establishments. Yet, at the same time, there are issues that have neither been ignored nor completely resolved and they continue to be cause of concern and even occasional friction between the two countries. But then considering the magnitude and complexities of Sino-Indian relations it will also be perhaps patently absurd to expect a perfect harmony between these two civilizational states and pragmatism demands that the best they can do is to be aware of both their strengths and difficulties and both should keep their eyes open to these advantages as well as pitfalls as they start evolving their working relationship in the future which will unfold its own challenges and opportunities.[35]

To first deal with the pitfalls, the boundary question remains the most central and toughest of all issues and slow progress here will continue to delay (if not block) the overall progress in Sino-Indian *rapprochement*.[36] The ramifications of this problem have to be understood in the context of their historical and geographical realities. Firstly, until the modern times, both China and India had never been in full knowledge or control of these far flung territories. Secondly, the areas involved cover over 90,000 square kilometres of land and this generally consists of thousands of miles of deserts, snow capped mountains and dense tropical forests which means that much of it has never been inhabited, making it difficult to examine counter-claims by both sides in the absence of definite details, even local histories or folklore. This also makes it extremely difficult to obtain workable details of these world's youngest and still growing mountain range where both its size and terrain pose serious technical difficulties, let alone evolving a political understanding which is further complicated by their domestic sensitivities. Though lot has been done during the eighteen rounds of Sino-Indian official border talks, with number of border related CSBMs put in place, the border issue remains mired in various bilateral and domestic compulsions and contradictions on both sides.

India, for example, has long been suggesting that steps be taken towards accurate assessment of existing force levels and a freeze should be effected on present troop strength with an expectation of subsequent reductions.[37] Analysts, in fact, believe that during early 1990s, India has unilaterally withdrawn about 35,000 troops from its eastern sector.[38] On the other hand, the PLA maintains a force between 180,000 and 300,000 soldiers and has directly ruled Tibet from 1950 to 1976, and indirectly thereafter.[39] Besides, unlike in the 1950s, Tibet today is connected to other military regions through four-lane highways and strategic roads and Beijing's capability to airlift troops from its other neighbouring military regions has advanced very far from its comparative inability to use air force in 1962. The Gordian knot, therefore, can be cut only at the political level, and for that the Indian side should be clear in its own mind as to what that bottom line is that will be acceptable to the Parliament and the people.[40] China has continued to argue that their troops levels in Tibet are not relevant to the subject of Sino-Indian CSBMs though they have assured India about their commitment to downsizing their military presence in Tibet. Surely then, in the western sector India has not been able to realistically envisage any troop reduction. But here again, the November 1996 agreement on CSBMs, for the first time, underlines these Indian concerns and under its Article III all future troop ceilings are to be decided "in conformity with the principle of mutual and equal security" keeping in mind "parameters such as the nature of terrain, road communications and other infrastructure and time taken to induct/deinduct troops and armaments."[41] And having already initiated disengagement in the eastern sector, this agreement should also open opportunities for troop withdrawals in the sensitive western sector.

As regards China, apart from their reservations on troop withdrawals from inside Tibet, its Indian connection continues to haunt their imaginations. This is despite the fact that successive governments in New Delhi have made repeated policy statements and given assurances saying that India regards Tibet as an integral part of China and that India will never allow its territory to be used for anti-China activities by its 100,000 Tibetans. However, during the 1990s, due to the increasing focus on human rights in the policies of most Western powers, His Highness the Dalai Lama has received expanding support and publicity for his cause through his increasingly frequent foreign trips and speeches, making China weary of Tibet's expanding international recognition. Besides, even within India, apart from the Tibetans themselves, there does exit a small force of pro-Tibet activists ranging from those seeking Tibet's independence to those who exhort Indian leaders to play the Tibet card in their dealings with Beijing.[42] And here, being a democratic country, governments in New Delhi have not been able to play too harsh against these variety of opinions and activities.

Then, apart from their bilateral ties, China's arms transfers to Pakistan, Myanmar, Bangladesh, Sri Lanka and Nepal have occasionally raised all kinds of doubts in India apprehending encirclement. China's alleged supplies of nuclear designs, components, materials and other knowhow and facilities to Pakistan has been the most sensitive sour-point of Sino-Indian ties.[43] A few years ago, apart from persistent reports on China's supplies of M-11 nuclear capable missiles, media reports tracing to American intelligence agencies and high-ranking officials confirming China's supply to Pakistan of 5,000 ring magnets, and a furnace plant for uranium enrichment to weapons grade. China has reportedly been involved in building a missile factory near Islamabad. Besides, China has been the largest and also the most reliable supplier of conventional weapons to Pakistan; has defence collaborations in almost all major areas, and apart from its alleged clandestine cooperation in building nuclear arsenals, China remains the most ardent supplier and builder of Pakistan's civilian nuclear programme.[44] But given the fact that Sino-Indian rapprochement has resulted in (a)India's becoming the largest trading partner in South Asia and, (b)a marked shift in China's policy on Kashmir, thus giving hope that all these and other irritants of Sino-Indian ties will also be resolved in due course of time.

Then talking about the strengths of the Sino-Indian ties it is this process of evolving CSBMs that forms the solid base. Moreover, the *Panchsheel* principles -- of mutual respect for sovereignty and territorial integrity, mutual non-aggression, non-interference in each other's internal affairs, equality and mutual benefit, and peaceful co-existence -- which were propounded by these two countries in mid-1950s have not only stood the test of time but emerged as major positive element in strengthening their ties. Far from becoming outdated in the post-Cold War context, the essential correctness of these principles has become increasingly visible. In fact, in December 1988, it was formally proposed by Deng Xiaoping to Rajiv Gandhi, that the two countries have a great potential for cooperation in working together "to recommend to the international community to take the Five Principles of Peaceful Co-existence as the norm for international relations."[45] Accordingly, the two countries have already evolved fairly substantial common approach towards various issues like restructuring of the United Nations and other international bodies. Though China remains uncommitted in supporting India's candidature for a permanent seat at the UN Security Council, a favourable sign has been noticed in this regard during the early 1990s. During their October 1995 meeting at the UN 50th anniversary celebrations at New York, for example, Jiang Zemin expressed his understanding of India's aspirations to become a permanent member of the expanded Security Council and said that in this regard "views of the general membership must be listened to in order to achieve a reasonable solution."[46] This ensures that China is certainly not the one that will oppose to India's candidature for the UN Security Council's permanent seat.

India has also been supporting China's entry to the World Trade Organisation (WTO) and China supports India's membership in the Asia-Pacific Economic Cooperation (APEC) forum. Besides, with their increasing interest in the Asia-Pacific region, the ASEAN Regional [Security] Forum (ARF) is another platform which has witnessed both China and India working together to deter western members from becoming the masters of the Asian destiny. In fact, ARF's Inter-sessional Support Group on CBMs has already laid out a long list of CSBMs for its members which will further consolidate the Sino-Indian *rapprochement*.[47] This is also expected to resolve some of Indian apprehensions about China's military modernisation especially in areas like China's defence expenditures which, as yet remain complete mystery for Indian scholars.[48] Then there are other issues like trade and human rights which have lately become the latest instrument in north-south confrontation. But here, the two may not have had identical views on human rights yet lately both have agreed that for the developing countries the most fundamental human rights is the right to subsistence and right for development. The two are particularly opposed to the increasing practice on the part of the developed nations linking economic aid with human rights as an instrument for bringing pressure to bear on certain developing countries. In fact, Sino-Indian cooperation in international forums has often frustrated vested interests amongst the western powers who seek to use similar linkage between nuclear proliferation, human rights and trade to pressurise developing countries like China and India.

That since 1986 Sino-Indian border has not suffered any major disruptions as compared to the incessant firing incidents and infiltration on the Indo-Pak borders, makes the Sino-Indian border almost an ideal example of good neighbourly relations. Sometimes commentators negate the process of CSBMs citing that this has not yet resulted in resolving the Sino-India boundary question. But keeping in mind the magnitude of complexities involved this gradual evolution of CSBMs has not only preserved peace between these two Asian giants but also generated great deal of mutual trust and understanding giving hope to the prospects of final resolution of the border problem. This optimism rests not on euphoria, but on the solid base of growing shared interests and understanding between the two countries. There is a tendency to contrast the slow pace of Sino-Indian CSBMs with China's fast recoveries of CSBMs with her newly acquired friends like Vietnam and Russia. Here, once again, one must appreciate that compared to Sino-Indian interactions, China's links with these two countries have been far more deep-rooted and extensive, and this is further reinforced by their ideological, institutional and cultural similarities. By comparison, friendly relations with India during the 1950 were essentially superficial, and its experience of 1962 devastating. It is in this context that CSBMs have played the critical role preparing both sides to find ways and means of working together. Global changes have also played their roles in further facilitating this process. And as a result, in the 1990s, as both China and India envision their future role in this new expanded strategic spectrum of the 21st century Asia, their CSBMs become an absolute imperative towards achieving their common goals of peace and development. And looking at their track record of last 20-25 years, this gradual evolution of Sino-India CSBMs not only proves that they both quite appreciate this new piecemeal approch to their complicated ground realities but this also gives hope of both these countries gradually coming closer and emerging as friends (may be partners) for the forthcoming Asian century of the next millennium.

Epilogue

Recent decision by New Delhi to weaponise its nuclear option has once again kicked-off debates about the future of Sino-Indian CSBMs. According to most commentators the decision to conduct five nuclear tests in May 1998, and more so India's attemtps at highlighting "China" as being the most important factor behind New Delhi's a difficult choice, have definitely administered a severe blow to the spirit of Sino-India *rapprochement* that has been so assiduously built up during the last two decades or so. I for one who have followed this debate quite seriously, feel that this debate has been purely academic with little substantial bearing on the ground reality.

I feel that apart from some momentary exchange of harsh words on the part of government spokesmen of both countries, and some not-too-pleasant articles appearing in the media, nothing has altered the two governments' commitment to CSBMs. The China-India Joint Working Group on the Boundary Question met as was scheduled for June, and the Military Commanders meeting at the border though delayed for a few days, did take place early June 1998. Similarly, bilateral trade and commerce have been going on normally, and other business and cultural interactions have continued without manifest interruptions. Of course, there is no denying the fact that the deep-seated misunderstanding between the two countries has now brought into sharper focus affecting the atmosphere of mutual goodwill, and it will take a while to recover the pre-Pokhran cordiality. There was an element of abruptness in New Delhi's reversal of her own longest-ever self-imposed moratorium on nuclear testing that enough time was not given to the Indian diplomats to put Indian government's position across the board without causing misgivings from Beijing.

In fact, the Chinese side did display its calm by keeping quiet for nearly 24 hours following India's announcement of the first two explosions on May 11. But, in the wake of India's second series of three more explosions on May 13, followed by the leakage of Prime Minister Atal Behari Vajpayee's letter to President Bill Clinton which described China's nuclear arsenals as also their proliferation to India's western neighbour as the main reason for India going nuclear, Beijing unleashed its tirade and described India as trying to emerged as a "hegemone" in South Asia. This display of displeasure in issuing harsh official statements was then followed by China's taking an active part in the passage of resolution 1172 by the UN Security Council and later in chairing another meeting of the P-5 Foreign Ministers in London on June 4. Then, there was the bilateral Joint Statements on South Asia by President Jiang Zemin and President Bill Clinton on June 27, and later when President Jiang Zemin visited Kazakhstan to attend the third presidential summit of five nations (China, Russia, Kazakhstan, Krygystan and Tajikistan) a similar Joint Statement expressing concern on South Asia implicitly putting the blame on India.

It is understandable that Beijing could not have been undisturbed giving the circumstances of India's nuclear decision and the manner of her announcement of it. China's reactions may have also been provoked by India's not having actively engaged Beijing in the post-Pokhran scenario while the latter was obviously the most affected party of all the happenings. But more than it was perhaps the fact that India's display of its nuclear potential also outsmarted most of the Chinese estimates about India's nuclear wherewithal. Whatever it is, the Indian side has since resumed its attempts towards breaking the ice with the Chinese leaders, and Indian Prime Minister's special emissary, Shri Jaswant Singh, has already opened high-level negotiations with the Chinese Foreign Minister Tang Jiaxuan during their pre-scheduled meeting when the two were in Manila to attend the ASEAN Regional Forum's meeting in July. Speculations have been ripe ever since on Jaswant Singh's impending visit to Beijing. In the final analysis, therefore, Pokhran-II may have temporarily disturbed the process of Sino-Indian CSBMs, but it is just an aberration, and before long the dark clouds over the sky of India-China relations may disappear. Hope my optimism augurs well for the future of Sino-Indian ties.

Appendix: Four Chronological Tables

Table 1: Pathbreaking Interations, 1976-1996

1976: Ambassador K.R. Naraynan presented credentials in Beijing on July 24 and — Chen Zhaoyuan presented credentials in New Delhi on September 20.

1979 February: Atal Behari Bajpai became the first Indian Foreign Minister to visit China.

1980 May: Mrs. Indira Gandhi and Hua Guofeng met during the funeral of President Joseph Tito in Belgrade. This was the first meeting of two prime ministers since 1959.

1981 June: Huang Hua became first Chinese Foreign Minister to visit India.

1988 December: Rajiv Gandhi became first Indian Prime Minister to visit China since 1955.

1989 July: Joint Working Group on Boundary Question held its first meeting in Beijing.

1991 December: Li Peng became first Chinese Prime Minister since 1960 to visit India.

1992 May: R. Venkataraman became first Indian President to ever visit China.

1993 January: First visit to China by a Parliamentary delegation, led by Speaker Shivraj Patil.

1993 November: "Zheng He", China's first naval vessel (a training ship), paid port visit to Bombay Last time Indian cruiser *INS Mysur* had visited Shanghai in 1958.

1993 December: Li Ruihuan, Chairman of the 8th National Committee of the Chinese People's Political Consultative Committee paid his first visit to India.

1994 January: Wen Jiabao, an alternate member of the Political Bureau and member of the Secretariat of the Central Committee paid his first visit to India.

1994 February: The Sino-Indian Expert Group (set up to assist the JWG) comprising high ranking diplomats, surveyors, and military personnel from both sides held its first meeting in New Delhi.

1994 June: China's Foreign Trade and Economic Cooperation Minister, Wu Yi, came on her first visit to India

1994 July: General B.C. Joshi became the first Indian Chief of Army Staff, to visit China.

1994 September: General Chi Haotian became China's first Defence Minister to visit India.

1994 October: K.R. Naraynan, became India's first Vice President to visit China.

1996 March: Admiral V.S. Shekhawat became India's first Chief of Naval Staff to visit China.

1996 May: Justice A.M. Ahmadi became India's first Chief Justice to visit China.

1996 November: Jiang Zemin became first Chinese President ever to visit India.

Table 2: Sino-Indian Border Talks, 1981-1987

First Round: Beijing December 1981	The two sides started talks with their historically held dramatically opposite positions.
Second Round: New Delhi May 1982	Normalisation of bilateral relations facilitating cooperation in economic, scientific and cultural fields and raise in their bilateral trade. Despite Indian protests against the Sino-Pak protocol on the opening of the Khunjareb Pass and Chinese protests over the inclusion of Arunachal Pradesh dancers at the closing ceremony of Asian Games in New Delhi, the tenor and schedule of this official dialogue were not affacted.
Third Round: Beijing January 1983	Failed to find consensus on either Indian insistance for "sector-by-sector approach" or Chinese reiteration for a "comprehensive settlement". No breakthrough appeared possible as (i) India did not have the necessary political incentives for fighting its domestic pressures against making any package deal, and (ii) Chinese leaders seemed quite satisfied with *status quo ante*.
Fourth Round: New Delhi October 1983	Showed some progress as China agreed for a sector-by-sector approach while India agreed to carry forward these talks towards a comprehensive solution. These talks were followed soon by two signing a trade agreement in August 1984 bestowing each other the Most Favoured Nation (MFN) trading status.
Fifth Round: Beijing September 1984	In this improved bilateral understanding the two sides explicitly agreed to the one basic point i.e. "to maintain tranquility on the borders" till a final settlement of the border dispute is reached at. This later evolved into the historic Sino-Indian agreement of September 1993.
Sixth Round: New Delhi November 1985	In changed scenario after Mrs. Gandhi's assassination in India and reports about China's nuclear collaboration with Pakistan as also fears that in the wake of Sino-Soviet border settlement China will trasfer its troops from their Soviet border to Tibet created misgivings and thus vitiated atmosphere for talks.
Seventh Round: Beijing July 1986	By now, on the eve of Sumdorong Chu crisis of 1986-87, each side was already exchanging accusations and counter accusations in the eastern sector thus hardening their further positions.
Eighth Round: New Delhi November 1987	Followed by visit by India's Defence and Foreign Ministers in April and June respectively, the two sides agreed that to break this stalemate on their boundry question there was an urgent need to provide the political thrust which came in the form of Prime Minister Rajiv Gandhi's 1988 visit to Beijing.

Table 3: Joint Working Group on Boundary Question, 1989-1996

First Round: Beijing July 1989	Held in the backdrop of Prime Minister Rajiv Gandhi's historic visit and India's continued yp support Chinadespite Western sanction following its Tiananmen Square crisis, the meeting demonstrated their sincerity towards evolving CSBMs.
Second Round: New Delhi August-September 1990	The two sides started by ascertaining "the principles and parameters" that should "govern settlement of the border issue." It established the first critical "mechanism" that initiated the periodic meetings between Indian and Chinese military commanders to "maintain peace and tranquility" along the borders.
Third Round: Beijing May 1991	With minority government of Prime Minister Chandra Shekhar having just faced disqualification of its Foreign Minister, V.C. Shukla and the general election appraoching (in June 1991) neither side was expecting any major decision.
Fourth Round: New Delhi February 1992	For the first time senior military officials were part of the JWG which decided that military commanders meet at Bumla and Spanggur at least twice at year in June and October. They also agreed for setting up "hotline" links between these commanders.
Fifth Round: Beijing October 1992	Trying to increase frequency of their meetings, the JWG met twice in 1992 which strongly reinforced their mutual understanding of each other leading to some major decisions in their next border talks.
Sixth Round: New Delhi June 1993	The JWG (a) agreed to open two new border trade points at (i) Namgya in India's Himachal Pradesh and (ii) Zhuba in China's Tibet; (b) suggested measures for increased transparancy about mutual military positions and activities along the LoAC; and (c) recommended that the JWG should meet more often.
Seventh Round: Beijing July 1994	Among other things the JWG recommended measures to avoid troop concentration on border and setting up more meeting points between their military personnel on the border.
Eighth Round: New Delhi August 1995	The two sides agreed to dismantle four military posts in the Wangdong area which was the first concrete action in terms of their proposed military disengagement on the border.
Ninth Round:Beijing October 1996	Though clearly overcast with the forthcoming visit to India by the Chinese President, the JWG agreed to expand their CSBMs and recommended for two more points for annual meetings between their military commanders on the border: (i) Lipulekh in the middle sector and (ii) Dichu in the eastern sector.
Tenth Round: New Delhi August 1997	The two sides ratified their Agreement Extending CSBMs to the Military field (signed on November 29, 1996) and exchanged intruments of ratification.

Table 4: Bold Initiatives, 1976-1996

1976 April 15: Foreign Minister, Y.B. Chavan became first one to announce in the Parliament that China and India had decided to restore their diplomatic relations at the Ambassadorial level.

1979 February: During Foreign Minister Atal Behari Bajpai's visit to Beijing, China (a) for the first time acknowledged that there was a border dispute; and, (b) assured to no longer support rebels in India's northeasn region.

1980 June: Deng Xiaoping, (a) revived Zhou En-lai's package proposal of 1960 wherein China offered to recognise McMahon Line in the east for India's abondonment of claims to the Aksai Chin in the western sector; and (b) softened their support to Pakistan on Kashmir describing it as a bilateral issue between India and Pakistan.

1981 June: Foreign Minister Huang Hua during his visit to New Delhi announced that China would be opening two secred sites of Mansoravar and Kailash to Indian pilgrims. This visit also paved the way for beginning of first Sino-Indian broder talks which had eight rounds between 1981-1987.

1983 April: China's resumption of party-to-party ties between Communist Party of India (Marxist) which was later extended to the Congress Party and Bhartiya Janata Party as well.

1984 February: The two sides signed a protocol granting each other most favoured nation status.

1988 December: During Prime Minister Rajiv Gandhi visit to Beijing three agreements were signed on (a) cooperation in the field of science and technology; (b) granting reciprocal overflight rights and; and (c) two year cultural exchanges.

1991 February: On February 2 the two signed agreement for resumption of border trade and on February 6 signed agreement opening Garbyang (Uttar Pradesh) as first border port. More points were later opened at Gunji (Uttar Pradesh) in 1992 and Shipki La (Himachal Pradesh) in 1994.

1991 December: During Premier Li Peng visit to New Delhi the two sides signed five documents (i) on Mutual Establishment of Consulate Generals in Bombay and Shanghai, (ii) on Consullar Affairs, (iii) the Memorandum on Restoring Border Trade, (iv) the Protocol on Bilateral Trade for 1992, (v) the MoU on Scientitic & Technological Cooperation for Peaceful Use of Outer Space.

1993 September: During Prime Minister Narasimha Rao's visit to Beijing, he and Premier Li Peng signed (i) the famous CBMs agreement, and (ii) agreement on cooperation in Radio & Television.

1994 May: India Festival, the first such foreign show in China, had 130-strong group travelling to 16 cities in 51days. It was in response to the Chinese cultural festival in India during 1992.

1995 August: The Joint Working Group (JWG) in its 8th meeting in New Delhi agreed to disengage troops from two posts from each side in the Wangdong tract which is first Asian example of disarmament.

1996 October: The JWG agreed to open two more points (Dichy and Lepulekh) for annual meetings between the military commanders from the two sides.

1996 November: During President Jiang Zemin's visit to New Delhi the two signed four agreements: (i) on extending the CBMs to the military field, (ii) on combating smuggling of narcotics and arms, (iii) on maintenance of Indian Consulate in Hong Kong after July 1997, and (iv) on maritime shipping.

Notes

1. Zhao Weiwen and Giri Deshingkar, "Improving Sino-Indo Relations", in Michael Krepon and Amit Sevak (ed.), Crisis Prevention..., *op. cit.*, p. 227; Sumit Ganguly, *op. cit.*, p. 12.
2. Document of the Stockholm Conference, CSCE/SC 9.
3. Masahiko Asada, "Confidence-Building Measures in East Asia", Asian Survey, Vol.xxvii No. 5, (May 1988), p. 491.
4. *Ibid.*
5. Zhen Ruixiang, "Shifting obstacles in Sino-Indian relations", The Pacific Review, Vol. 6, No.1 (1993), p. 66.

6. Shen-chun Chuan, "Peking's relations with India and Pakistan", Issues & Studies, Vol. 25, No. 9 (September 1989), p. 148
7. Prime Minister Rajiv Gandhi, "India-China Joint Press Communique", Statement on Foreign Policy, (New Delhi: Ministry of External Affairs, External Publicity Division, October 1989), pp. 62-64; also Giri Deshingkar, "Gains from the China visit", The Indian Express (New Delhi), 9 January, 1989.
8. Surjit Mansingh, " India-China relations in the post-Cold War era", Asian Survey, Vol.xxiv, No. 3 (March 1994), p. 289.
9. *Ibid.*, p. 293.
10. Chinese foreign office spokesperson described it as "positively significant in increasing mutual understanding between the two armed forces." See The Statesman (Delhi), 31 July, 1992.
11. n. 8, p. 292.
12. This is, however, not to deny that some of the difference on the nuclear question have also increased during the 1990s. For example, China is now a signatory to the NPT (1992) and an adherent to the MTCR and during CTBT negotiations it, in fact, sided with Washington in asking for India's signatures on the draft treaty. What is more worrying for Sino-India ties is that China has used this newly gained club membership to obtain credibility whereas its assistance to Pakistan's nuclear and missile programme has continued unabetted.
13. "Statement by the Minister of External Affairs on India's policy towards China, 26 August, 1970" in A. Appadorai, Selected Docu ments on India's Foreign Policy and Relations 1947-1972, Vol. 1, (New Delhi: Oxford University Press, 1982), pp. 743-44; also n. 7, p. 142.
14. First during Secretary (in Ministry of External Affairs) Eric Gonsalves' visit to Beijing, Deng mentioned this proposal during an interview to an Indian journalist repsenting the not so well know journal Vikrant. Later Deng revived this proposal again during his discussions with a visiting Member of Indian Parliament, Dr. Subamanian Swamy, saying that "conditions are not ripe now for settlement, then other aspects of normalization can take place." For details see Gyneshwar Chaturvedi, India-China Relations 1947 to Present Day, (Agra: M.G. Publishers, 1981), pp. 161-62; also Surjit Mansingh and Steven I. Levine, "China and India: Moving beyond confrontation", Problems of Communism, Vol.xxxviii Nos. 2-3 (March-June 1989), p. 36.
15. G.S. Bhargava, "Dealing with China", Mainstream (New Delhi), 7 January, 1989.
16. Many scholars have tried to explain this change of early 1990s in terms of change in global scnario where collapse of Soviet Union and Tiananmen Square crisis followed by western sanctions had compelled Beijing to search for friends and allies. But it seems that Sino-Indian rapproachement was still the most important factor and while India had described Tiananmen incidents as China's internal matter, China also made no comments on demolition of Babri Masjid which sent correct signal of change. See Allen S. Whiting, "China's Foreign Relations after 40 Years", in Anthony J. Kane (ed.), China Briefing, 1990, (Boulder: Westview Press, 1990), p. 67; and Hwei-ling Huo, "Patterns of Behaviour in China's Foreign Policy: The Gulf Crisis and Beyond", Asian Survey, Vol.xxxii, No. 3 (March 1992), p. 267.
17. See John W. Garver, "China-India Rivalry in Nepal: The Clash over Chinese Arms Sales", Asian Survey, Vol.xxxi No.10 (October 1991), p.968; and, Abu Taher Salahuddin Ahmed, "Sino-Indian Relations: Problems, Progress and Prospects", BIISS Journal, Vol.15, No. 4 (October 1994), p. 384-85.
18. Mao Siwei, "China and the Kashmir issue", Strategic Analysis (New Delhi), Vol. xvii, No. 12 (March 1995), pp. 1572-97. In fact, according to some experts, it is China's sensitivities about Xinjiang that partly explains Beijing's need to evolve "special relationship" with Islamabad.
19. T. Karki Hussain, "Relations with China", World Focus (New Delhi), Nos. 167-168 (November-December 1993), p. 48.

20. Lt. Gen. K.K. Nanda (Retd), "Promising New Turn in Sino-Indian Relations", Defence Seminar (New Delhi), Vol. III No. 3 (March 1993), pp. 5-7. All subsequent quotations from this treaty are from the text of my preceding article in this volume.

21. Agreement between the Government of the Republic of India and the Government of the People's Republic of China on Confidence Building Measures in the Military Field along the Line of Actual Control in the India-China Border Areas. Signed November 29,1996. All the subsequent quotations from this treaty are taken from this text.

22. Officers of PLAAF have been visiting Indian Air Force bases", The Times of India (New Delhi), 22 December, 1995, reprinted in Strategic Digest, Vol. xxvi, No. 3 (March 1996), pp. 444-45.

23. "Sino-Indian Joint Military Exercises plans denied", Xinhua (in English) printed in Foreign Broadcast Information Service - China (henceforth FBIS-CHI), 4-244, 20 December 1994, p. 12.

24. These 15 items are wool, goat skin, sheep skin, yak tail, yak hair, goat, sheep, horses, salt, borax, China clay, butter, silk, and Szaibel yite.

25. Report stresses trade between India, China", Xinhua (in English), FBIS-CHI-94-103, 27 May 1994, p. 15.

26. Qian, Finance Minister sign agreement", Xinhua (in English) printed in FBIS-CHI-94-137, 18 July 1994, p. 9.

27. Banking, Visa Agreements signed", All India Radio (New Delhi), printed in FBIS-CHI-94-205, 24 October 1994, p. 22.

28. It is interesting to note that over 70 to 75 per cent of foreign investment in China comes from the overseas Chinese who have been generally successful in business in Hong Kong, Taiwan, and much of the Southeast Asia and North America. For reasons of their emotional attachement with the mainland and for being so fimilliar with the ways and systems of this expanding Chinese market most overseas Chinese prefer to invest in China.

29. Beijing Establishes Joint Venture in India", Xinhua (in English), printed in FBIS-CHI-93-013, 22 January 1993, p. 15.

30. Jasjit Singh, "Future of Sino-Indian Relations", Strategic Analysis, Vol.xvi No.11 (February 1994), p. 1512.

31. Vivek Raghuvanshi, "China asks to Develop LCA fighter with India", Defence News, 15-21 August, 1994.

32. India, China and South Korea will form consortium: Plan to build passenger planes", The Times of India (New Delhi), 28 August 1995.

33. n. 31.

34. Zheng Ruixiang and Dong Manyuan, "Developing friendly Sino-Indian relations on the Five Principles of Peaceful Coexistence", Foreign Affairs (Beijing), No.12 (June 1989), pp. 69-70.

35. D. Banerjee, "India-China relations and Chinese military capability", Trishul, Vol.III No.1 (July 1990), p. 66.

36. V.P. Dutt, "India and China: A leap into the future", World Focus (New Delhi), Nos. 167-168 (November-December 1993), p. 51.

37. No. 9, p. 291.

38. Pravin Sawhney, "Massive Troop Pullout from China Border", The Indian Express (New Delhi), 24 December 1992; also Pravin Sawhney, "Chinese Checker: Beijing calls the shots on the border dispute", The Asian Age (New Delhi), 31 August, 1995.

39. D. Banerjee, "India-China Relations and Chinese Military Capabilities", Trishul, Vol. iii No. 1 (July 1990), p. 69.

40. A.P. Venketeswaran, "Indian-China Relations: An overview", World Focus (New Delhi), Nos. 1790180 (November-December 1994), p. 51.

41. n. 21.

42. Batuk Vora, India-China Relations: Importance of the Tibet Card", The Times of India (New Delhi), 5 April, 1996.

43. K. Subrahmanyam, "Sino-Pak Nuclear Deal: New Light on an Old Alliance", The Times of India (New Delhi), 30 August, 1995; also K. Subrahmanyam, "Jiang Zemin Comes Calling: Talking Turkey to the Dragon", The Times of India (New Delhi), 21 November 1996.

44. Kathy Gannon, "Sino-Pakistan nuclear ties to continue: Jiang", The Times of India (New Delhi), 2 December, 1996; also Kathy Gannon, "China to build new N-Plant in Pakistan", The Times of India (New Delhi), 6 December, 1996.

45. Zheng Ruixiang, "Sino-Indian Relations Under a New Situation", Guoji Wenti Yanjiu (Beijing) No. 4 (October 1993), pp. 4-7. [Translated version in FBIS-CHI-93-219, 16 November 1993, p. 12; also Wen Boyen, "China, India and the New International Order", China Report, Vol. 29 No. 3 (July-September 1993), p. 294.

46. FBIS-CHI-95-204, 23 October 1995, p. 17.

47. Raphael Pura, "ASEAN's courtship of Burma makes key allies nervous", Asian Wall Street Journal, 19-20 July, 1996; and Barry Wain, "The ASEAN Regional Forum is moving forward", Asian Wall Street Journal, 19-20, July, 1996.

48. For details see Jasjit Singh & Swaran Singh, "Trends in Military Expenditures", in Jasjit Singh (ed.), Asian Strategic Review 1997-98, (New Delhi: Institute for Defence Studies & Analyses, September 1997), pp. 42-48.

SREEDHAR

58

CHINA BECOMING A SUPERPOWER AND INDIA'S OPTIONS

A general impression going around amongst the Indian strategic community is that the People's Republic of China (PRC) is becoming superpower in the next 20 years. It may even offer a challenge to the US by that time. It is further argued that the People's Liberation Army (PLA) is going to be a formidable force in the years to come because of the ongoing modernisation plans. Some even argue that now is the correct time to resolve the Sino-Indian border question and establish cordial relations as quickly as possible with China. Whatever may be reasons for this Indian mindset, whether it was the 1962 debacle or the 1964 Chinese nuclear explosion, these arguments need a closer examination.

The Wars the PLA Fought

Korean War of 1950-51

Before we examine Sino-Indian relations, the first question that needs to be asked is whether the PLA is really militarily so superior as compared to the Indian armed forces or not? A close scrutiny of the PLA's performance during the past 47 years indicates that at every given opportunity, the PLA flexed its muscle and its performance can best be described as a mixed kitty. During the late Chairman Mao's years, the PLA went into action five times — three times to fight a war with neighbours, once to fight the US "imperialism" and once to occupy the Paracel Islands in the South China Sea. The first was in 1950-51 when the PLA clashed with the US forces in the Korean Peninsula. Whatever may be the claims made by the Chinese, the PLA was defeated and suffered heavy casualties. Many would argue that the technological superiority of the US armed forces played a decisive role in the defeat of the PLA.

Sino-Indian War of 1962

A decade later, after the failure of Chairman Mao's Great Leap Forward Programme, in October 1962, China decided to resolve the Sino-Indian border issue by the use of force. In October 1962, the PLA moved in swiftly, defeated the Indian Army and declared unilateral ceasefire after taking possession of approximately 30,000 sq km of Indian territory. Though no official history of the war from the Indian side has been published as yet, the Chinese official version is that they repulsed the Indian attack on Chinese territory. Various versions of the people associated with that war from the Indian side, however, indicate that the Chinese succeeded largely due to the failure of the politico-military leadership of India to assess correctly the PLA's capabilities. Way back in 1974 itself, people like K. Subrahmanyam, who were associated with China during that crucial period in India's Ministry of Defence, argued that had the Indian Air Force been pressed into action, the course of the Sino-Indian war of 1962 would have been different. In fact, at the time of the war itself elder statesman of India, C. Rajagopalachari, advocated the deployment of the Air Force by India to destroy the supply lines of the Chinese Army.

Nathu La of 1967

Three years later, in 1965, two significant events took place on the Sino-Indian border. The first was the warning issued to India about Chinese sheep not being allowed to graze on their side of the border by India. This happened in September 1965 when the Indo-Pak war was simmering on India's western border.

At the same time, in September-December 1965, the PLA sent probing missions on the entire Sikkim-Tibet border. According to one account, there were seven border intrusions on the Sikkim-Tibet border between September 7 and December

12, 1965, involving the PLA. In all these border incursions, the Indian side responded "firmly" without provoking the other. Though details of casualties of these PLA border incursions are not reported, there were reports indicating that the PLA suffered "heavy" casualties against "moderate" loss by India.

Two years later, in September 1967, in spite of their setbacks in 1965, the PLA launched a direct attack on the Indian armed forces at Nathu La, on the Sikkim-Tibet border. The six-day "border skirmishes" from September 7-8 to 13, 1967, had all the elements of a high drama, including exchange of heavy artillery fire, and the PLA soldiers tried to cross the border in large numbers.

The attack was repulsed at all points. According to an account of this incident, from the details of the fighting available, it appeared the Chinese had received a severe mauling in the artillery duels across the barbed wire fence. Indian gunners scored several direct hits on Chinese bunkers, including a command post from where the Chinese operations were being directed. The Chinese were also known to have suffered at least twice as many casualties as the Indians in this encounter between Indian and Chinese armed forces.

The important point to be remembered in this context is that the late Chairman Mao launched his Great Proletarian Cultural Revolution (GPCR) in 1965 and it reached its peak in 1967 to weed out all "anti-socialist elements" from the Chinese polity. Though many Sinologists would not like to describe the GPCR in any other manner, for an outsider like me, it was essentially a power struggle between Chairman Mao and his adversaries.

However, for the purposes of this essay, three significant things emerged from the Nathu La episode on the Sikkim-Tibet border. First, the Indian armed forces demonstrated beyond doubt that the PLA is not as strong and motivated as it was made out to be. In fact, there were rumours, around September 10, 1967, that the PLA was planning to bring in the Air Force to escalate the conflict. Sensing that the Indians were getting ready for such an eventuality, the Chinese official news agency, Xinhua, denied having any such plans.

Second, the Indian politico-military leadership quickly realised this myth about the PLA. This was clearly reflected in the unconditional ceasefire proposed by India in a note delivered to the Chinese on September 12, 1967, all along the Sikkim-Tibet border from 05.30 hrs on September 13. Though officially, the Chinese rejected this unilateral ceasefire offer by India, except for an occasional salvo by the PLA on September 13, 1967, there was a lull all along the border. Many observers felt India scored a psychological victory over the Chinese for the latter's unilateral ceasefire in 1962.

Lastly, the Indian political leadership also realised that the PLA's behavioural pattern on the border had something to do with the domestic turmoil then going on in China.

Ussuri Clashes of 1969

By March 1969, the GPCR entered its final phase and at that time the PLA decided that it could decide the border with the former Soviet Union by the use of force. On March 2-3, 1969, there were "border skirmishes" in the area of the Nizhnemikhallovka border post on the Ussuri River. The intruding PLA men were confronted by the Soviet Red Army and their attack was repulsed.

Again, on March 15, 1969, the PLA launched a fresh attack with an infantry regiment strength (estimated to be 2,000 men) with support units at Damansky Island on the Ussuri River. According to the details of the war available, initially the Chinese succeeded in penetrating the island under cover of artillery and mortar fire from their side of the river. But a massive retaliation by the Red Army made the PLA beat a hasty retreat.

Like they had to bring in the Air Force to meet the Indian armed forces' challenge, this time too, the PLA is reported to have "activated" their North China Sea fleet, but nothing happened; it turned out to be an empty threat.

Again there were border skirmishes in August 1969 in the Xinjiang sector of the Sino-Soviet border between the PLA and the Red Army.

It is a part of history now that the PLA could not take on the Red Army and the Chinese were forced to come to the conference table to resolve the issue through peaceful negotiations.

Capturing of Paracel Islands in 1974

After the end of the GPCR in 1969-70, it is still a debatable question, whether Chairman Mao eliminated all his adversaries or not, but radical changes came into the structure and hierarchy of the PLA. Apparently the ageing Chairman Mao, in a swift move, ordered the PLA to go and capture the disputed Paracel Islands in the South China Sea. With the ongoing conflict in Indo-China at that time, the Association of South-East Asian Nations (ASEAN) and Vietnam, who also claimed part of these islands, did not offer any resistance to the PLA's occupation of the islands.

Virtually without firing a shot, the PLA had a total success in this operation.

An assessment of these five PLA actions indicates that it had a total success in two operations and suffered defeat on three other occasions. The PLA success story is also due to the timing of the campaign like in the Paracel Islands. Whenever the PLA confronted an adversary without any element of surprise, or an adversary who challenged them, its performance was poor. This was obvious from the Korean war, and the Nathu La and Ussrui incidents. In fact, in the Nathu La and Ussuri incidents, the PLA did not offer even stiff resistance. From all accounts, it made a hasty retreat the instant the adversary offered stiff resistance or acted "decisively".

All these five actions of the PLA also clearly indicate three things: (a) the late Chairman Mao, wanted to consolidate his country's boundaries as quickly as possible, and in that exercise, advantage China should be the guiding principle; (b) also, he pressed the PLA into action, whenever his plans to accelerate the peace of economic developments failed; and (c) in all these wars/engagements, the PLA was not as professional as it was made out to be.

Sino-Vietnam War of 1979

In the post-Mao period, after the initial years' power struggle was over and Deng Xiaoping managed to place himself firmly in the saddle, he too looked to the PLA to resolve the outstanding claims of China on its borders. The first was, of course, the now famous February 1979 war with Vietnam. Deng wanted "to teach a lesson" to the Vietnamese. In that Sino-Vietnam war, the PLA was badly mauled and forced to retreat. The battlehardened Vietnamese with better strategy and motivation were able to take on the PLA and inflict heavy casualties. According to one strategic commentator, "The only thing the Chinese are not interested to discuss is the Sino-Vietnam war of 1979."

Deng realised that there was need to improve the technological superiority of the PLA. Consequently, the military modernisation segment of the Four Modernisations Programme (the other three being agriculture, industry, and science and technology) was acelerated. Accordingly, we notice greater allocations for defence in the Chinese budget since then.

Sumdorong Chu Valley Incident of 1985

Six and half years later, Deng decided to flex China's muscles again with India. In mid-1986, it came to the notice of India that the PLA had built a helipad at Wandung in Sumdorong Chu Valley in Arunachal Pradesh. India reacted swiftly and the PLA had an eyeball-to-eyeball confrontation with the India Army in Sumdorong Chu Valley of Arunchal Pradesh in August 1986. After a week of tense moments both sides mutually agreed to withdraw their forces inside their respective territories and create a no man's land. The Chinese posture at that time clearly indicated that Beijing quickly realised that 1962 cannot be repeated. Afterwards, we saw some writings in the PLA's official organ, *Liberation Army Daily*, about the professionalism the Indian armed forces.

Sino-Vietnam Clashes in the South China Sea

Called the Truong Sa Archipelago by Vietnam, and the Nansha Islands by China, the Spratlys consist of about 150 reefs, sandbanks and islands in the South China Sea, 350 km from Vietnam's coast and 1,000 km from China. They straddle busy shipping lanes and are, therefore, strategically important. In addition, the preliminary geological surveys have shown that this area has vast deposits of crude oil and natural gas.

Both China and Vietnam claimed the Spratlys for centuries, but up to 1987 had been content with a war of words. However, from early 1987 onwards, the Chinese started putting markers on some of these islands, making it clear that they had asserted their sovereignty over them. Simultaneously, the PLA also started strengthening its presence and started conducting naval exercises in and around the Spratlys.

This brought a sharp reaction from Vietnam and in the subsequent protest notes exchanged, both sides accused each other of provocations, and claimed that the other side would bear the responsibility and consequences of its actions.

On March 14,1988, the PLA's Navy clashed with the Vietnamese Navy for the first time. Though it was a very short confrontation, both sides suffered considerable casualties. But the tension continued up to the end of the month. In late March 1988, the war-weary Vietnam proposed bilateral talks with China to resolve the issue. As usual, the Chinese rejected the offer initially, but later agreed to the Vietnamese proposal.

However, fresh tensions erupted in May 1992, when the Chinese authorities leased an oil concession to an American Firm, Creston Energy, for oil exploration in and around the Spratlys, and Vietnam took strong objection to it.

From 1993 onwards, both China and Vietnam realised that they could not resolve the issue militarily and started negotiations.

Invincible PLA?

Like Mao, Deng also tried to use the PLA to settle the border issues by use of force but had no success. With the Deng era coming to an end, what his successors would do can only be a matter of speculation. They may or may not continue this policy of using force to settle the "Middle Kingdom's" boundaries.

But the lessons others can draw from the PLA's past engagements is that the PLA's conventional armed forces are not an invincible force as they are being made out to be by a section of the Indian strategic community. As far as China's nuclear capabilities are concerned, the Chinese have given a solemn undertaking to the international community that they will not be the first to use nuclear weapons. And the doyen of India's nuclear programme, Dr. Raja Ramanna, in October 1996, observed that the country has acquired the nuclear weapon manufacturing capability. In other words, we have the needed nuclear deterrent capability.

The other aspect of the PLA is its equipment. Right from the liberation of mainland China in October 1949, the Chinese strongly believed in self-reliance. At the height of the Sino-Soviet friendship, in the early 1950s, a considerable amount of Soviet technology was transferred to China. One can say that the Chinese arms industry was built on this in the subsequent years. The Soviet technology stopped coming from the mid-1950s onwards. With the embargo and containment policy of the West up to 1971, the Chinese arms industry, it is generally agreed upon by China watchers, remained, more or less, stagnant.

In other words, for about 16-17 years, China had no access to any rapidly changing conventional arms technology in the international arms market. In addition, how much the social engineering experiments of the late Chairman Mao affected the overall technological standards in the PLA and outside is a debatable question. Some Western scholars have observed that the PLA was insulated against the social upheavals created by the late Chairman Mao. Still, at least two generations of young people were affected by Chairman Mao's experiments in the 1950s and 1960s. This must have automatically resulted in a low level of technological base in the Chinese society. It certainly affected the civil sector. We can see this by the low quality of Chinese consumer products. And, therefore, its impact on the arms industry cannot be ruled out.

Whatever may be the actual position, there has been a scramble for weapon related technology since 1971, from the international market by China — how much they are able to absorb is an open ended question and can be debated.

The performance of the equipment the Chinese are selling in the international market leaves much to be desired. For instance, some of the biggest recipients of Chinese arms like Pakistan, North Korea and Iran have bought this equipment as a last choice, when it was denied to them from others or they were cash starved. In fact, the Pakistani arms acquisition pattern over the years indicates that their first preference is arms from the West and the last choice is China. This is in spite of an indepth relationship with China, and the fact that Chinese equipment is cheap and available on easy credit.

In this part of the world, the Chinese equipment saw action in war in recent years only in the Iraq-Iran war of the 1980s. The Iranians used the Silkworm missiles from China quite successfully to confront Iraq, but in the later stages of the war only, when Iraqi ammunition was almost depleted.

Therefore, one need not be unduly alarmed at the technological level of the PLA's weapon systems.

Myth of Economic Miracle

The other myth that is perpetuated by a group of China watchers is that Beijing is likely to become an economic superpower in the next two decades, that is, by about 2015 or so. And to support their argument, the World Bank report on China and the *Economist* (London) are liberally quoted. One is tempted to compare this Chinese miracle with the 1970s' assessments of the West about China's crude oil reserves. There used to be screaming headlines in the mid-1970s in the Western Press saying that China's crude oil reserves are bigger than Saudi Arabia's. We, at the Institute of Defence Studies and Analysis, were the first to question these assessments, and the late Mr. Mirchandani, then General Manager of the United News of India promptly carried it on his wire services. Within a few months, that bubble burst.

The Chinese economy witnessed some spectacular development (but not development in the broad sense of the term, that is economic, cultural, social, etc, which India is attempting) of 10-11 per cent growth in recent years. This has been achieved largely due to heavy doses of foreign investment. Here one should not forget the fact that the foreign investor will continue to make investments only if his profits are assured. One more factor needs to be borne in mind here, international capital has no nationality, and concepts like nationalism and patriotism have no relevance to it. The overseas Chinese who made the bulk of investments in China may not continue to do so. Already reports are appearing in the international media that investors in China are not happy with their returns and are looking for greener pastures. This means that the flow of foreign investments into China is going to slow down in the years to come. And in the long run, the Chinese economy may have to settle down for a 5-6 per cent growth rate. Anything beyond that requires at least a couple of trillion dollars of investments in the next two to three decades. First, that type of capital is not available in the international capital market. The $80 billion foreign investment of the past decade created such regional and social imbalances in China that the Chinese authorities have been forced to take a fresh look at the process of liberalisation of the economy.

Therefore, in these circumstances, China becoming an economic superpower, say in the next 20 years, can at best be described as wishful thinking by members of a China admirers' club. And, in fact, a couple of Chinese scholars with whom I interacted with in 1993 were surprised at these assessments. They said that like in any planned economy, they too fixed some target; and if they can achieve even 50 per cent of those targets, they would consider their planning process successful. This is understandable. In fact, any student of economics will be able to tell that a developing country with a population of one billion plus cannot sustain a 10-11 per cent growth rate for too long.

Indian Policy Options

It is in this backdrop that we must examine India's policy options vis-a-vis China in the short and medium terms. To discuss long term perspectives at this stage is not feasible as there are so many imponderables.

At one level, the current phase of Sino-Indian relations started some time in the early 1980s by the late Indian Prime Minsister, Mrs Indira Gandhi, progressed satisfactorily, except for the 1985 aberration mentioned earlier. In fact, from 1987 onwards, efforts were on from both sides to ensure that 1985 is not repeated. Both sides took a number of confidence building measures, including high level political visits, armed forces to armed forces contacts, dialogue at various levels, etc. The Sino-Indian joint working group has been meeting regularly. Even the bilateral trade which was at a low level, started picking up. In other words, both India and China have engaged themselves in a constructive dialogue which proved to be mutually beneficial.

Can we take this relationship forward? This is the question haunting many policy analysts. In this context, one needs to look into three broad areas. Foremost among them is the border question. This issue has two dimensions. First, some-boundary specialists would argue that at the end of 1994, there were more than 100 disputed boundaries around the world. This is a vexed problem of the international community and there are no fixed ground rules for this. And these experts feel that after the 1958-59 India-China boundary talks, it became clear that this issue has no academic solution.

Second, India is not in a position to cede any territory to others except for a few kilometres this way or that. Therefore, to resolve the vexed boundary issue and establish cordial relations with India, China has to vacate the occupied territory.

In addition, both Jiang Zemin and Atal Behari Vajpayee are new to the centre of power in their respective countries. Neither of them are charismatic personalities like Pandit Jawaharlal Nehru, Mrs. Indira Gandhi , Chairman Mao Zedong and Deng Xiaoping. They have limited political clout in their respective countries. Therefore, to expect the governments of these two leaders to find a solution to the decades-old India-China boundary question is just not possible. Hence, status quo will continue and this may remain as one of the unresolved boundary questions which will be carried into the 21st century.

Second is the economic cooperation between the two countries. Both China and India are developing countries, and each side enjoys some advantage over the other in trade. Incidentally, both are exporters of primary commodities and semi-manufactured goods. At the moment, in the international market, India enjoys a marginal advantage over China, because of its being a member of the World Trade Organisation.

Otherwise, both the economies are competing with each other in the international market. Therefore, the scope for a larger volume of India-China trade is rather slim. The existing volume of India-China trade at around $1 billion may at best grow into $4-5 billion by the turn of the century. In percentage terms of foreign trade of India and China, this is less than one per cent of each country's trade. I am not arguing against increasing trade between China and India. But as I mentioned earlier, the ground realities are different. Any expectation of faster growth of India-China trade is nothing but wishful thinking.

India-China joint ventures in third countries is once again a low feasibility proposition because of the reasons mentioned above.

Therefore, we can assume that in the immediate future, say in the next ten years, both sides should reconcile to the fact that the existing level of economic cooperation cannot be improved dramatically, and efforts to improve upon it may result in some changes, but marginally only. In fact, here one should also note that China is mixing politics with economics to a certain extent. For example, China would prefer the US to India in awarding a contract.

Lastly, the option to improve people-to-people level contacts between India and China. This, undoubtedly, is one area where more interaction can take place between the two countries. But, the spirit of *Hindi-Chini Bhai Bhai* of the 1950s cannot stage a comeback for obvious reasons.

To conclude, for their own strategic interests, both China and India broke the impasse that had set into their relations from 1962 onwards, in the early 1980s, and continued to do so even in the 1990s. The political leadership of both these nations have, over the last 15 years, evolved a mature relationship which is mutually beneficial. To take it beyond this level in the immediate future does not seem possible at this point of time. However, both nations would continue the existing level of relationship in future also in their own interest.

SURJIT MANSINGH

59

THE IMPORTANCE OF UNDERSTANDING CHINA

The assertion that more Indians should study contemporary China should need no justification. But perhaps those who find such a statement self-evident inhabit the somewhat rarified domain where knowledge is the preferred path to wisdom, where people from many countries meet and talk, and where the study of cultures, languages and political systems different from inherited ones is nothing strange. In contrast, it sometimes seems many people avid for information question the need of knowledge, dismiss the idea of studying another country as no more than an academic eccentricity, and laugh at the suggestion that a quest unrelated to consumption is a worthy and enjoyable enterprise.

Perhaps sceptics of the need for Indians to study China could be persuaded by a utilitarian rationale. Without entering into an epistemological ocean we catch the piscine gleam of comparative knowledge as one route to improved self-knowledge and offer it here, along with other workaday, even statist, reasons why more Indians should study contemporary China. These are: China's importance in the world as a great and ancient civilisation as well as a global power today; problems posed by China's proximity to India; China's diplomatic and economic achievements that Indians envy; current threat perceptions in India and the concomitant requirement for a solid base of scholarship capable of making independent assessments of China's capabilities and intentions; India's need to build realistically and knowledgeably on the slowly widening opportunities of cooperative commercial (or other) ventures with China so as to open an exciting new chapter in the age-old encounter between Chinese and Indian civilisations.

First of all, China is today a recognised great power of vast extent — the largest in Asia — and population — the largest in the world. China is a veto-holding permanent member of the United Nations (UN) Security Council (one of the P5) whose support or acquiescence is necessary for any collective action to be taken by that body. Within the P5, Britain and France are closely allied to the United States (US) and Russia is in a relatively weaker position than the former Soviet Union, so that China stands out as an independent centre of power, taking decisions on the basis of possibly different, and certainly non-Western, criteria than the others. We do not now posit China as an opposing pole, or counterweight, to the US in world bodies (though that possibility cannot be ruled out for the future), but merely point out the imperative of carefully studying China in an India desirous of enhancing its own profile in the UN.

China's decisive impact on the economic, military, and political security of Northeast and Southeast Asia has become increasingly obvious and well-publicised by the international media in the 1990s. China's participation was integral to negotiated settlements reached in Cambodia and North Korea. China's claims in the South China Sea and to Taiwan led to international crises in this decade and may well lead to more in the next. The fall-out on China of the recent financial crisis in East Asia is a matter of world-wide concern. India is not, and cannot be, insulated from developments in the rest of Asia where China's role can be decisive. Moreover, China's political and economic dealings with the Central Asian Republics — from border agreements and ceremonial visits, to increasing cross-border trade, feasibility plans for pipelines and, perhaps, undocumented movements of people — have a profound impact on those countries too. As presently projected, India's relationships with Asian countries to its east and to its north will broaden and deepen in the decade ahead, stimulated by trade and common membership or association in regional organisations, and to mutual benefit. India's need to know and understand these Asian countries better than it has done in the recent past will grow correspondingly; so too the need to assess and understand their multi-faceted relationships with China.

The people's Republic of China (PRC) is the present-day manifestation of a great civilisation, which, like Indian civilisation, also flourished in the earliest stages of world civilisation and enjoyed periods of great cultural efflorescence. As in the case of other great civilisations past and present, the difficulties of grasping an unfamilar language, script, art form or philosophical framework, are more than amply rewarded by the aesthetic, emotional and intellectual pleasures of exploring another tradition. Hence the appeal of Sinology. In addition, no civilisation is free of troubles or has an unbroken record of success, least of all civilisations that span several millennia, as do China and India. Study of the troughs is likely to prove as stimulating as study of the heights. Both Sinic and Indic civilisations have grappled with many similar situations and problems over the ages. The list is almost endless but would include the following: the problematic interaction of nomadic and settled peoples, the opposing pulls of centripetal and centrifugal forces, the formation and disintegration of states, the symbolic delineation of imperial space, the legitimisation and exercise of power, the structured stratification of agrarian societies, gender inequality in patriarchal systems, the absorption — or not — of alien groups and religions, subordination by European imperialism — albeit in markedly different degree and form — and the consequent tussle between social reformers and political revivalists in the late 19th century. Each civilisation evolved its own particular responses to similar situations and problems, with costs and benefits that are worth comparing. The experiences of China and India in the 20th century may provide many more contrasts than similarities, but it is evident that one theme common to both is "how a great tradition modernises". Again, there are many lessons that can be learned from each other. Especially important, perhaps, is the more balanced perspective achieved by those who might have thought India is *sui generis* with unique problems, and find that China too considers itself *sui generis* and has similar problems, particularly in these years of rapid change affecting every sphere of life! What is likely to interest such students is how each has tackled — or not tackled — these problems.

In short, the first reason we offer for more Indians to study contemporary China is the cultural richness of that civilisation and the likelihood that China's already significant influence on world events will increase in the rapidly approaching 21st century. In the future, persons knowledgeable about China stand to be at an advantage over those who are ignorant, in much the same way as those at ease with the language and culture of European powers have benefitted in the past and present.

Secondly, China is not only an important civilisation "out there", it is India's largest neighbour "right here". With the military incorporation of Tibet into the PRC in 1950 and the Government of India's oft-repeated official acknowledgement of Tibet as an autonomous region of China, the PRC ceased to be a "distant neighbour" and became as proximate to India as the states of the Indian subcontinent itself. China's close and exceedingly cordial relations with Sri Lanka, Pakistan, Nepal, Myanmar and Bangladesh reinforces this point, as does China's sustained effort (not yet successful) to establish a resident mission in Bhutan as a neighbour (along with India and Bangladesh). Opinion varies in New Delhi circles as to whether the former anti-India content in China's relations with India's smaller neighbours remains high or has diminished, and we do not enter into that controversy here. Suffice it to say that for Indians whose prime focus is South Asia, there is an imperative to study China as well.

Furthermore, whatever be the final alignment of a lineal border between India and China, yet to be defined and demarcated in mutual agreement, its total length is bound to be well over 2,000 kms, as is the Line of Actual Control (LAC) along which the two governments are pledged to maintain peace and tranquillity by an agreement of September 1993. The precise length of the final border will depend on what co-ordinates of longitude and latitude are agreed upon for the western and eastern extremities, and therefore involve agreements with Pakistan and Myanmar, as well as the natural features of the terrain in-between. But the maintenance of peace and tranquillity along the LAC depends on the correct understanding of China's capacity, capabilities and intentions by the Indians responsible for those stationed on duty or living in the vicinity. Sentiment alone is not enough. Confidence building measures initiated in recent years and formalised in November 1996 must be bolstered with constantly upgraded knowledge and communication if they are to facilitate lasting peace and eventual settlement of the border problem to mutual satisfaction.

One barrier to self-confidence and peaceful expectation in India is the psychological trauma suffered in the border war with China in 1962 and carried over to this day. Even without attempting to revisit the controversial events preceding that war, or bemoaning the continuing unwillingness of Chinese officials and scholars to admit any share of blame for it, it is undeniable that Indian decisions taken at that time were **NOT** grounded in adequate, up-to-date, knowledge of what was transpiring within China or the motivations of China's then key decision-makers. Stated briefly, New Delhi failed to decipher what Allen Whiting later termed the "Chinese calculus of deterrence" and India suffered disproportionately. There is no excuse for allowing such a lacuna to occur now or in the future. Every welcome reduction of Indian military forces along the LAC, so often used as living barbed wire, must be fully justified by demonstrated reciprocity of force reduction and intent on China's part, and not rest on mere expressions of intent in joint communiques. China probably will continue to be troubled by unrest in its two western autonomous regions, Tibet and Xinjiang, geographically juxtaposed with the Indian subcontinent. At the very least, India needs to be fully informed of developments there as well as in Beijing so as to frame appropriate and realistic policies of its own, and not be caught unawares with the fall-out of China's repression of what it calls "splitism", as it was in 1959 and after.

Thirdly, China's diplomatic and economic achievements over the last twenty years are nothing short of spectacular. They appear all the more striking when seen against a background of the Tiananmen Square massacre of June 1989, a decade of destructive chaos produced by the Cultural Revolution, the death-dealing famines of the Great Leap Forward years, the long drawn out civil war, and the preceding century of humiliation at the hands of the European and American powers. A natural question arises in the minds of many Indians at the dawn of the 21st century — what accounts for China's success? (The question may well be evoked by India's relatively lagging performance at this moment in time but we refrain from comment on that issue.)

Eminent economic historians such as Dharma Kumar remind us that China's key economic indicators were significantly higher than those of India even in the declining phase of the Qing Dynasty and the first quarter of the 20th century. Historians have found the multivarious effects on a people of indirect colonialism — such as occurred in 19th century China — to be less traumatic or negative than those of direct imperial rule — such as experienced in India. Political scientists might argue that totalitarian, or authoritarian, systems are likely to be more "efficient" than democratic ones, especially in foreign affairs. Anthropologists could refer to the social discipline of Confucianism and the racial homogeneity of the Han people in China, contrasting the exuberant individualism and incredible multiplicity of community in India. Conspiracy theorists might like to point to United States behaviour for explanations. Nevertheless, the question remains, and not even tentative answers can be assayed without study of China's achievements and how they were gained.

Among China's diplomatic achievements that deserve particular note are those relating to relations with the US. The PRC's success in winning American recognition for its own primary objectives, especially the principle of "one China" and derecognition of Taiwan as an independent political entity, has been notable from the time of Henry Kissinger and Richard Nixon's visits to Beijing in 1971 and 1972, through the formal establishment of diplomatic ties in January 1979, to the summit meeting of Presidents Jiang Zemin and Bill Clinton at Washington in October 1997 — less than 18 months after a major crisis and military stand-off over Taiwan in 1996. Only 34 countries presently recognize Taiwan, and this number does not include either the US or Japan — which have close (but informal) relations with Taiwan and arguably would prefer the status quo to an actualisation of China's "reunification", peaceful or otherwise. Moreover, the PRC withstood the western embargoes placed on it after June 1989, countered the American-led campaign against Human Rights abuses in China with a White Paper and pan-Asian campaign of its own against linking trade issues with human rights (as well as a few carefully timed releases of imprisoned dissidents), welcomed Clinton's explicit de-linking of human rights criteria from US grant of Most Favoured Nation status to China in 1994, and won explicit support from Washington for China's membership of the World Trade Organization in 1997.

Furthermore, improvement in Sino-American relations was accompanied by improvement in Sino-Soviet relations in the 1980s leading to the Gorbachev-Deng summit in 1989 and important agreements between China and Russia in the 1990s on their long disputed border, trade, and defence cooperation, with China buying top-line military aircraft as well as the services of several thousand scientists and technicians from Russia. China's ability to consolidate relationships with rival states simultaneously is also visible in its substantial dealings with Israel, Iran and the Arab states, as well as its pursuit of normalisation with India without sacrificing support of Pakistan's nuclear programmes. China's tactful flexibility is noteworthy in Southeast Asia where its claims (and occupations) in the South China Sea and attempted coercion of Taiwan in 1996 certainly heightened apprehension but has not triggered in ASEAN an alarmist retreat from engaging China in a multilateral security dialogue or an attempt at anti-

Chinese collective security.

Without attempting to analyse China's diplomacy here, its skill in using various assets to advantage precisely defined objectives must be stressed. One asset — that can also be a liability — is the role of people of Chinese origin in the domestic political and economic structure of countries, especially in Southeast Asia, with which China seeks closer ties. The diffusion of decision-making power in the US political system, and the influence this gives persons or groups with single-point agendas, has proved to be another asset for China in softening the policy impact of American rhetoric critical of China's human rights and nuclear-proliferation record during the Clinton Administration. Thus, as a result of the Clinton-Jiang summit, Boeing Corporation (located in Seattle) signed a contract to sell China 50 jets valued at US$3 billion, and the ardent pro-Tibet pro-Dalai Lama lobby (particularly strong in Seattle) got only Washington's promise to appoint a "coordinator on Tibet" with undefined duties. Similarly, US nuclear companies were given permission to sell equipment to Chinese nuclear power plants, perhaps to the tune of $60 billion, and China's long presumed assistance to Pakistan's nuclear weapons capability was not mentioned.

But China's greatest asset assuredly is its booming economy, from which no world-class potential investor or salesperson wants to be excluded. Many detailed studies have been made of China's economy since Deng Xiaoping launched his "opening up" reforms 20 years ago, pronounced that "to be rich is to be glorious", and led a quadrapuling of national income in two decades. The World Bank's recent publication, *China 2020,* and other independent reports testify that China has made two major transitions: from a command economy to a market economy (albeit "with Chinese characteristics"), and from a predominantly agrarian economy to a largely urban industrial one (though with a huge force of mobile labour now and an ever present threat of high unemployment). Equally important, the number of people surviving below the poverty level has reportedly declined from about 250 million to about 50 million — no small achievement in a total population of over 1.2 billion — and other indices of human development such as mortality, longevity, literacy, fertility, access to education and health facilities, and even treatment of women, point upward at statistical rates higher than those recorded for India over the same period of time. From the point of view of independence in international dealings, the most significant factors of all are the volume and value of China's foreign trade — accounting for more than 2.5 per cent of world trade as compared to India's 0.6 per cent — and its foreign exchange reserves of nearly US$100 billion — as compared to India's less than US$20 billion. Both factors have been significantly augmented by the addition of Hong Kong, a considerable financial and trading entity in its own right, to China on June 30 1997. On the assumptions that these positive trends would continue, and that resulting social strains would not pull China apart, many experts predicted that China's economy soon would be second only to that of the US.

It is not our intention to engage in a romantic extolling of Deng's (or post-Deng's) China similar to what once was fashionable for Mao's China, much less to suggest that the aforementioned successes are the result of some special "Chinese magic" or genes! Rather, we emphasise the need to decipher which Chinese policies and programmes succeeded internally and externally, and which failed, so as to study their possible applicability in comparable situations in India, for example, in dealings with the US. It may also be possible to anticipate Beijing's actions in future, because there is enough evidence to suggest that Beijing dissects the results of its own various policies quite carefully and is willing to make adjustments for the sake of greater success.

Fourthy, the need to build a strong and independent tradition of China studies in India is a palpable one, well expressed in a Note authored by members of the China Study Group in Delhi published in *China Report* (24: 4, 1988). As they pointed out, Cheena-Bhavana was founded by Rabindranath Tagore at Visva-Bharati in 1937, the Chinese language and area studies programmes at Jawaharlal Nehru University date from its founding, and Chinese studies were introduced at Delhi University in 1964, when *China Report* was also launched, yet the general picture remains gloomy. These programmes are not matched in universities elsewhere in India, not even in Calcutta, and most distressing of all, have not spawned the kind of integrated research programmes that contribute to solid theoretical or empirical progress in the social sciences field or Sinology. To quote the Note cited above, "even though a few notable achievements have been registered in the field by Indian scholars of China, they can be attributed more or less to isolated efforts by individuals." It cites as major shortcomings the absence of a well-led foundational programme or an adequate milieu of Area Studies in any Indian University, compounded by the lack of finance for long-term field research in China or documentary and advanced language training facilities in India. We also observe that the habitual insulation of governmental defence, external affairs and intelligence agencies from the wider intellectual community does not serve India's need for well-researched, well-documented, carefully analysed and independent assessments of China that can assist the process of policy-making as well. To repeat a point made earlier, India cannot afford to misread China or uncritically accept extra-Indian evaluations of China's capabilities and intentions if it is to safeguard national security and advance India's interests in the world. For example, what is the validity of a zero sum paradigm? Does Chinese success automatically threaten India? What can be learned from China's new dealings with Russia or with Vietnam? How will Japan and China manage their relationship in future? At the moment, it is probably easier to use the copious Western analyses of China's developments and intentions available in published form than to generate reliable Indian ones.

Some useful assessments surely will be generated by the 1993 research project "China Into the 21st Century" steered by the Institute of Chinese Studies, that itself grew out of the China Study Group in Delhi. But these papers should be the beginning, not the end, of a process. The objectives of the Institute of Chinese Studies include training a new generation of China scholars, promoting systematic study of China in India, contributing to more regular interaction and wider dissemination of knowledge of China in the public domain, and encouraging greater academic and intellectual exchange between India and China (as well as other international centres of China studies).

These are laudable objectives which need much more support from the University Grants Commission, the internationally minded public and the Indian government than they presently receive. For example, universities with language and area studies programmes on China, such as Jawaharlal Nehru University, Delhi University, also need to provide resources and materials for research (which they do not possess at the moment) if their scholarship is to become profound. Nor should the bolstering of China studies be confined to the scholarly community. To make a start, major Indian newspapers should station correspondents in China, give them language training, and encourage them to report on a variety of subjects including the rapidly growing border trade between China and most of its neighbours. Such reports may well stimulate more thought and action within India than research papers on the same topics! Further, officers of the defence services should be given many more opportunities for multi-dimensional knowledge of China than presently available to them. The 1992 and 1994 exchange of visits between the Indian and Chinese defence ministers led to formal ties between the military establishments of the two countries and subsequent exchanges of visits at high-level. The benefit of increased exchanges at mid-levels as well as good-will ship visits can be more than ceremonial only if the officers detailed for them have a prior base of understanding and evaluation.

A final argument for paying more attention to China studies in India is the mundane one of expanding employment opportunities in commerce and industry. Bilateral trade between India and China has grown over the ten years of revival to a value of close to two billion dollars, and is slated for further growth and diversification. In today's competitive market, no exporter can hope to maximise profits without an accurate profile of his customers. And it is hard to imagine market research being conducted in China without some knowledge of Chinese language and culture! The two governments have established a Joint Group on Economic Relations and Trade, Science, and Technology in 1988, and sub-groups being meeting periodically. But ministers and secretaries to government can only encourage, they cannot actually do the work of trading goods or technology. Those who would do so with an "open" China come from the private sector themselves and must develop contacts and knowledge equal to or better than their competitors from other countries, many of whom are likely to be of Chinese origin!

Some infrastructure will be provided by the broadly based India-China Joint Business Council set up in 1997. In the same year, the Confederation of Indian Industries opened a representative office in Shanghai, and the Federation of Indian Chambers of Commerce and Industry, in collaboration with Wisitex Foundation, organised an industrial and trade exhibition to promote Indian products and technology in China. But one witness to the latter event bewailed the lack of adequate preparation on the part of Indian firms represented there, contrasting that with the exhibition of Chinese products and technology in Delhi held in December 1997 where Chinese representatives arrived with samples and order books in hand and did a brisk business. By the end of 1997 there were approximately 50 Chinese joint ventures in India with an investment outlay of $190 million (much of it in technology and personnel rather than finance), and four Indian joint ventures and two wholly Indian-owned companies operating in China with an investment outlay of $7 million. The desirable and likely expansion of joint ventures, and the success of existing ones, have been stressed at some length at practically every India-China meeting held in the last few years, including those of non-officials sponsored by the Rajiv Gandhi Foundation. But what the chief executive officer of Ranbaxy Laboratories, (the oldest and most successful Indian venture in China manufacturing pharmaceuticals in Guangdong since 1993) had to say on the subject on one occasion, and most forcibly too, was that a good investment in China depended on a thorough training of personnel in Chinese language and social mores.

As more and more educated Indian youth take up careers in commerce, finance, management and industry, and as the economies of both India and China expand in the international as well as the bilateral domains, it will be commonplace for Chinese to study India and for Indians to study China. The assertion that more Indians should study contemporary China becomes self-evident.

CONTRIBUTORS

Adlakha, Hemant

Assistant Professor in Chinese of Jawaharlal Nehru University pursuing Ph.D. research on contemporary Chinese political development.

Bagchi, P.C (1898-1956)

Modern India's first great Sinologist who was also a great authority on Indology. Was Director of Research and Vice-Chancellor of Visva-Bharati, and a visiting scholar sent by the Government of India to teach in Beijing University (1947-49).

Bagyalakshmi

Having pursued an intensive study on Guanyin (the Chinese version of Avalokitesvara) for ten years after she completed her MA in Chinese from Jawaharlal Nehru University, she obtained her Ph.D. degree from JNU, and is preparing for a book on Guanyin to be published by IGNCA.

Banerjee, Dipankar

Retired as Major General of the Indian Army, he was the first Indian Army Officer after 1957 to have visited China at the invitation of PLA in June 1991; served for many years on the India-China border and is an authority on PLA's modernisation and China's defence capability and strategy in the new era. He lectures on these issues extensively in India and abroad and also publishes frequently on these topics in academic journals. He is now co-Director of the centre for peace and conflict studies.

Banerjee, Priyatosh

Studied Sanskrit along with Epigraphy and Numismatics and obtained Ph.D. in History in 1950 from the Patna University, Patna. He was Officer on Special Duty for the Buddha Jayanti Publications in the Ministry of Information and Broadcasting in 1955 and 1956 and officer in charge of the Museum Branch, Archaeological Survey of India in 1957-59. He joined the National Museum, New Delhi in 1960 and had served the Museum in various capacities as Editor, Assistant Director, Director and Consultant till 1980. He has visited all the important Museums in India and abroad. Authored a large number of research papers and several books with a new book in the offing.

Banerjee, Radha

Obtained Ph.D from Delhi University in Buddhist Studies, she was awarded a fellowship by the UNESCO, travelled and visited major museums and historical monuments in China, Central Asia, Britain, France and Germany. She is research associate in the East Asian Programme in IGNCA.

Bhattacharjea, Mira Sinha

Her first career was that of an IFS officer posted in the Indian Embassy in Beijing. After resigning from the office, she was selected by the University of Delhi to the Columbia University, USA, to be trained as prospective faculty members of the newly estabilished Department of Chinese Studies. She joined Delhi University in late 1960, and retired form it as Reader in

Chinese Studies in 1995. Thereafter, she became the Director and Project Coordinator of the Institute of Chinese Studies. She is a leading expert on India-China relations, and has written articles and lectured in government institutions on it on innumerable occasions.

Bhattacharyya, D.C.

Professor of History of Art at the Panjab University, Chandigarh, he has been engaged in teaching and research for about three decades.Ten books and more than one hundred research papers published in research journals have established him as a leading scholar of art history.

Bhattacharyya, Manik

Associate Professor of Chinese and Chairman of the Centre for Chinese and Southeast Asian Languages in Jawaharlal Nehru University, he was educated in Calcutta, Delhi and Beijing and received his Ph.D. from Jawaharlal Nehru University. He also taught Chinese in Banaras Hindu University. He has kept Himself engaged in studies and writing on China particularly on the works of Lu Xun for nearly two decades.

Bhutani, S.K.

Retired from the Indian Foreign Service in 1991, he studied Chinese language at the Beijing University and was a member of the Embassy of India in China from 1957 to 1962. He shows keen interest in observing the current Chinese development, and is a regular participant in the China Forum discussions.

Chandra, Lokesh

A leading scholar in culture and art of India and other Asian countries, he heads the International Academy of Indian Culture. Besides being an active author and lecturer in public meetings, he has also other public interests, and was one time the Chairman of the Indian Council of Historical Research and a member of Rajya Sabha. He has visited China many times, and has a collection of valuable Chinese artifacts and historical materials. Author of many books and research articles on culture and art.

Chakrabarti, Sreemati

Currently Reader in Chinese Studies in the Department of Chinese and Japanese Studies, University of Delhi, she holds double M.A. degrees, one in Political Science from Delhi University and another in East Asian Studies from Harvard University and also Ph.D. in Chinese studies from Delhi University. She was a post-doctoral scholar 1Beijing University. She is working on her second book entitled "Mao, China's Intellectual and the Cultural Revolution".

Coomaraswamy, Ananda Kentish (1877-1947)

Son of a Tamil father and an English mother, and born in Colombo, Sri Lanka, he was a man of prodigious learning, equally at home in Vedic, classical, mediaeval European and Islamic literatures. With a D.Sc. degree from the University of London, he came to the field of art by way of science. Conversant with French, German, Finnish, Sanskrit, Pali, Greek, Latin, Italian, Gaelic and even Icelandic, he was an art critic, a historian, philosopher and metaphysician whose mind encompassed the sum total of the Eastern and Western traditions of learning and thought. An exponent of the Philosophia Perennis — where all traditional philosophies are seen as the dialects of the same spiritual heritage — Coomarawamy has left behind a plethora of writings on philosophy, metaphysics, religion, iconography, music, geology, theatre and the place of art in society.

Das, Sisir Kumar

Tagore Professor of Bengali Literature in the Department of Modern Indian Languages, University of Delhi, he had an excellent academic record in the Presidency College of Calcutta University. Obtained his Ph. D. from Germany he has taught in Delhi University for more than three decades. Apart from being an authority on Bengali Literature, especially on Tagore, he is also a pioneer of Comparative Literature in India. With a large number of books and research papers to his credit, he has made substantial contribution in establishing the chronological studies of Indian literatures.

Damodaran, A.K.

Before starting a full career of indian Foreign Services, he taught English Literature. His rich experience in dealing with China in various capacities from the Beijing Embassy to the China Desk of the Ministry of External Affairs, in addition to his discharging higher responsibilities in the Ministry and in its division of policy planning, has resulted in a special interest and profound insight vis-a-vis China. For some time, he was also Senior Research Fellow (Professor) of Jawaharlal Nehru University.

Deshingkar, Giri

Trained in University of London and Yale University as a China scholar, he was one of the pioneers of Chinese studies in Delhi University, in addition to being the co-founder of *China Report* (one of the only two academic journals in English language specially on China in the world during the 1960s). After teaching in Delhi University, he became a senior researcher and, later, the Director of the Centre for the Study of Developing Saocieties. He was one of the founding members of the Institute of Chinese Studies, and was its Director for a number of years.

Deshpande, M.N.

Former Director-General, Archaeological Survey of India, is an archaeologist and art-historian. He was invited as Visiting Professor and Fellow by the Allahabad University and was Advisor to the Nehru Centre, Bombay for the Discovery of India project and the Aditi exhibition in the Festival of India in USA. Among his publications on cave art, his essays on Pitalkhora, Tabo and Ajanta and book on Panhale-kaji caves are notable. A close associate with IGNCA, he helped to convene the first and second international seminar on "Cave Art of India and China" in 1991 (New Delhi) and 1994 (Dunhuang) respectively.

Duara, Prasenjit

After completing post-graduation from Delhi University, he was sent to USA for higher studies on Government of India scholarship. Completed Ph.D from Harvard University, he began to teach in various US universities and is now Professor of History in Chicago University. Author of many books on China and also winner of Fairbank Award. He has initiated a new discourse on History which strives to break away from the dominent western-oriented opinions.

Gandhi, Mahatma (1869-1948)

Mahatma Gandhi is universally regarded as the "Father of Modern India", as he was the main architect of Indian independence. Not only a man of action but also a sage (hence the title "Mahatma") of noble ideas. Dedicating all his life and energy to the salvation of India from the colonial rule, he is the icon of "non-violence" which has become one of the most powerful political trends of the 20th century. Within India the Gandhian legacy will long endure both inside and outside the circles of Gandhian workers, Gandhian scholars, Gandhian politicians etc.

Gandhi, Rajiv (1942-1991)

Son of Indira Gandhi and grandson of Jawaharlal Nehru, he was the fifth Prime Minister of India and the third generation of leaders whose regimes have gone down the history of independent India as the continuum of a family tradition in Indian politics. His great contribution to India-China relations was his China visit in 1988 which helped inaugurate a new era of positive cooperative partnership, bringing confidence building measures into active play between New Delhi and Beijing.

Gonsalves, Eric

Joined Indian Foreign Service in 1950, he served in various capacities including Counsellor London; DCM Washington, Ambassador to Japan and to EEC, Secretary in the Ministry of External Affairs. Never retires after official retirement, busy as Director of India International Centre (1986-1991), attending international conferences in the UN General Assembly, Commonwealth Summit etc. Received Distinguished Service Award from T.M.A Pai Foundation for outstanding Konkanis 1994. Currently President Indo-German Social Service Society, (funding agency mainly concerned with rural development) and Editor-in-Chief, *South Asia Survey*.

Gupta, S.P.

A Ricardo and Jevon scholar of London University and Hallsworth Fellow of Manchester University, he received education at the universities of Calcutta and London with the final degree of Ph.D. (Econ.), London. Was Adviser of Perspective Planning Division, Planning Commission, Member of the Governing Council of the National Sample Survey Organization, India; Vice-President of the Indian Association for Research in National Income and Wealth, Adviser, Global Modelling, World bank, Washington DC (1971-1987); Professor of Calcutta University on economic theory and Indian economic problems, Senior Lecturer in Department of Econometrics in Manchester University, U.K. for nearly five years. Then, he served as the Director and Chief Executive of Indian Council for Research on International Economic Relations, New Delhi for almost a decade, and is at present the Chairman of the Indian Society for Economic and Social Transition.

Haidar, Salman

Member of the Indian Foreign Service, he was Indian Ambassador to China and many other countries, and retired from the post of the head of IFS, i.e. the Foreign Secretary. After a gap of hardly a few month, he once again assumed diplomatic mission as India's High Commissioner to London.

Joshi, M.C.

An eminent archaeologist, after ending his career as the Director-General of the Archaeological Survey of India, he immediately assumed the duty of Member Secretary of IGNCA. He has specialized in historical archaeology and Indian art including Indo-Islamic architecture; excavated historical sites like Purana Qila, Patna, Mathura, etc. Is also a prolific writer, having contributed a large number of research papers on Indian archaeology, Indian art and culture. He visited China in 1996, and delivered lectures on Indian archaeology at Luoyang and Lanzhou.

Kamal Sheel

Educated in Benaras Hindu University, Taiwan and USA, he was Research Associate of the Department of Chinese and Japanese Studies, Delhi University, then, Lecturer and Reader in Chinese Studies of Panjab University, then Reader, and now Professor of Chinese Studies and Head of Department of Foreign Languages, Benaras Hindu University. Author of many books and research articles and editor of the journal organ *Asia-Prashant* of the Indian Congress of Asia and Pacific.

Khanna, Vinod

During his thirty years in the Indian Foreign Service, he had several opportunities to be involved with China-related work. After retirement he served briefly as Director of Institute of Chinese Studies in New Delhi, and Director-General Indo-Taipei Cultural Centre. Again working as the Director of the Insitute of Chinese Studies currently.

Mansingh, Surjit

She was a member of the Indian Foreign Service, before taking up academic assignments in universities in the US, Italy and India, was Senior Fellow at the Centre for Contemporary Studies, Nehru Memorial Museum and Library, New Delhi, took her Ph.D. in International Relations at the American University, Washington D.C. Presently Professor of International Politics at the School of International Studies, Jawaharlal Nehru University. Is an author of many books and research articles.

Menon, K.P.S.

Entered the Foreign Service in 1951 he had several postings in Delhi and abroad, mostly to do with India's neighbours, and participation in bilateral and international conferences. Head of Policy Planning in the Ministry of External Affairs between 1970 and 1975 was Ambassador/High Commissioner in Hungary, Bangladesh, Egypt, Japan and China. Recalled from China to Delhi in 1987 to take over as Foreign Secretary and Head of the Foreign Service. After retirement pleasantly occupied with advisory groups, seminars, etc.

Mishra, Brajesh

During his career as a member of Indian Foreign Service, and when he was Indian Charge D'affaires in Beijing, he had the distinction of being the recepient of the internationally known "Mao Smile" in 1970. He served as Indian ambassador in many countries and Secretary in the Ministry of External Affairs. He has recently been appointed as the Principal Secretary to the Prime Minister's Office.

Mitra, Sabaree

Assistant Professor of Chinese in the Centre for Chinese and South East Asian Studies in Jawaharlal Nehru University, New Delhi and specializes in contemprorary Chinese Literature for which she was awarded the doctoral degree. Other areas that interest her include Political History, Culture Studies and Gender Studies.

Mohanty, Bidyut

Obtained her Ph.D. from Delhi School of Economics, Delhi University. She is Research Officer at the Institute of Social Sciences directing a programme on Women's Development and Panchayati Raj in India. She wrote several research papers on Famines and Agrarian Structure and edited two books. She has visited China several times, and was a delegate to the Fourth World Congress on Women in Beijing at the NGO Forum in 1995.

Mohanty, Manoranjan

Obtained Ph.D. from the University of California, Berkeley, he is Professor of Political Science and Director, Developing Countries Research Centre, University of Delhi and Co-chaiperson of the Institute of Chinese Studies, New Delhi. Has studied China's rural reforms in Wuxi through many field visits since 1979. He has authored three book, in addition to a forthcoming book on China's rural reforms, and several tens of research papers.

Narayanan, K.R

President of the Republic of India, he had a versatile career as teacher, jounalist, diplomat, Vice-Chancellor (JNU), parliamentarian, ambassador, minister, Vice-President and Chairman of Rajya Sabha. Was the first Indian Ambassador to China after the resumption of full-fledged diplomatic relations between India and China. Author of many books and articles. Recently, winner of the "World Stateman" award.

Nehru, Jawaharlal (1889-1964)

Independent India's first Prime Minister, he was the main architect of the political infrastructure of modern India, and father of India's foreign policy wedded with "Panchsheel", non-alignment and peace and peaceful use of nuclear energy. He loved children, and was affectionately called "Chacha Nehru". His autobiography and *Discovery of India* have become classics, being translated into various world languages. After his death (in office), his legacy was carried forward by his daughter, Indira and grandson Rajiv, both were his successors as Prime Ministers. Perhaps no political leader of any country outside China has been so endeared to China's civilizational grandeur and chequered modern development, and spoken and written so much on China as Nehru. No one has broken his world record of a state leader being greeted on his arrival by from a half million (according to Chinese reports) to a million (according to Indian reports) foreigners on the arrival to a foreign capital in his state visit to a foreign country — in Beijing in 1954.

Oberoi, Patricia

A graduate in Oriental Studies from the Australian National University, Canberra, she has taught sociology in both the University of Delhi and Jawaharlal Nehru University, and is currently Reader in Social Change and Development at the Institute of Economic Growth, Delhi. She started her academic career as a student of Chinese literature more than three decades ago, has never left Chinese studies in between, and is actively organizing lecture programmes for the Institute of Chinese Studies.

Paranjpe, V.V.

An ex-IFS retired from his last posting as Indian Ambassador to Korea, he is known as the best Chinese language user among all Indians in modern times. Beginning his career as a government sponsored scholar studying in Beijing University, he acquired high proficiency in Chinese language and interpreted for Prime Minister Nehru and other Indian leaders in their talks to the Chinese counterparts in the 1950s. Joined Foreign Service and looked after the China desk for a number of years. Still taking a keen interest in promoting understanding between India and China.

Patnaik, Utsa

Is Professor of Economics in Jawaharlal Nehru University, author of many books and research articles. She has been a keen observer of the development of political-economy in China.

Rao, Narasimha

Has a long political career both in his home state, Andhra, and in the central government. Was an important cabinet member and minister during the regimes of prime ministers Indira Gandhi and Rajiv Gandhi. Was elected the President of the Congress Party and the Prime Minister of India after Rajiv Gandhi's assassination. His visit to China in 1993 was a milestone in India-China relations and contributed to the improvement of India-China relations.

Raghavan V.R.

Served in the Indian Army for thirty seven years until he retired as Lieutenant General. Being the Director General of Military Operations from 1992 to 1994, he was closely involved in the formulation of the Sino-Indian Accord on maintaining peace on the borders and in the series of negotiations with Pakistan on the Siachen Glacier dispute. Was Chief of Staff of Northern Army Command, also the Commanding General in the Siachen Glacier during some of the fiercest combat actions in the area. After his retirement his expertise in defence strategy is still treasured by the Indian army, and is a visiting lecturer at the principal defence services college in India. Author of many books and research articles, he is currently a Director in the Delhi Policy Group.

Rana, Kishan S.

Served in the Foreign Service from 1960 to 1995, and describes himself as "a lapsed student of China affairs", 1he served as Consul General in San Francisco, and as Ambassador/High Commissioner to Algeria, Czechoslovakia, Kenya, Mauritius and Germany. He specialized in economic diplomacy, and currently does business advising, free-lance column writing.

Ranganathan, C.V.

Member of the Indian Foreign Service from 1959 to 1993, he began his career by learning the Chinese language in Hong Kong University. Thereafter he served in Beijing twice in the Indian Embassy, from 1965-68 as First Secretary, and from 1987-91 as Ambassador of India. He has also served in New York, Bonn, Hong Kong, Addis Ababa, Moscow and Paris. He is presently a Nehru Fellow for a research project on Sino-Indian relations, and also an active member of the Institute of Chinese Studies, in addition to being the President of India Association of Asia-Pacific Twenty First Century.

Ray, Haraprasad

Retired in 1996 after a long career of four decades first as a linguist with the Government of India and then as Associate Professor of Chinese at the Jawaharlal Nehru University.Author of a book on the maritime trade between India and China during the 15th century, and has contributed to a number of international seminars and scholarly journals in the U.S.A., Great Britain, Germany, France, Hong Kong and China. He is presently a research scholar funded by the Indian Council of Historical Research and engaged in translating materials on South Asia in Chinese historical writings.

Roy, Rammohun Raja (1772-1833)

He studied Bengali in his village home, Persian and Arabic at Patna and Sanskrit at Benares. He started learning English at the age of twenty-two. The phantom emperor of Delhi, Akbar II, appointed him as his envoy to the King of English in 1830 and conferred on him the title of 'Raja'. Well versed in both Indian and Western learnings, he was a great scholar, educationist, and reformer of modern India. Above all, he was the pioneer of the Indian renaissance.

Sengupta, Arputharani

Specialising in the problem of style and identity in the Buddhist Art during the Kushan Period, she teaches in the National Museum in addition to her own research.

Singh, Swaran

A product of Jawaharlal Nehru University, he is a Research Associate in the Institute of Defence Studies & Analyses, New Delhi. He has authored a number of books many articles on strategic topics often pertaining to China.

Sreedhar

A very senior Research Associate in the Institute of Defence Studies & Analyses, and author of many articles and books.

Tagore, Rabindranath (1861-1941)

He had the distinction of being the first Asian, indeed, the first non-white writer to win the Nobel Prize for Literature in 1915, for which his name became a household word among the intellectuals in China during the 1920s. At home, he was Gurudeva to not only the common Indians, but even Mahatma Gandhi and Pandit Jawaharlal Nehru. A versatile genius combining in himself a poet, novelist, drama wright, essayist, musician, painter, choreographer, and also thinker and visionary. His idealism of "universal man" was translated into practice by his "universal university", Visva-Bharati. He was particularly keen in forging a Sino-Indian fraternity, and had a Cheen-Bhavana built on the campus of Santiniketan. He was the most admired, most influential and most translated Indian writer in China.

Tan Chung

Retired (in 1994) from thirty six years of teaching, first, in the National Defence Academy, Khadakvasla, then, in the School of foreign Languages, New Delhi, then, University of Delhi, and, finally, Jawaharlal Nehru University, having served as Lecturer, Reader and Professor, headed the Department of Chinese and Japanese Studies (DU) and Centre for Asian and African Languages and Centre for East Asian Languages (JNU) at different times, he is now Professor-Consultant, IGNCA, author of seven books and innumerable research articles (some form chapters of books edited by other scholars).

Thakur, Ravni

Educated in Jawaharlal Nehru University, Beijing University, and the Netherlands, she obtained her Ph.D. from Holland. Author of a book on gender problems in China, she has also contributed research papers for learned journals.

Vatsyayan, Kapila

Beginning her career as a teacher (taught in both Indian and US universities) with accomlishment in Indian dance as well, she has a versatile career uptill the rank of Secretary of Culture and Secretary of Art in the Government of India. Founder head and presently the Academic Director of IGNCA, she has done seminal research on art, has a great number of publications including two on Folk-Dances of India and Traditional Indian Theatre, in addition to editing various primary texts, is a visualiser of exhibitions and seminars. She is recipient of many coveted awards, including the Padmashree, Campbell Memorial Gold Medal Award of Asiatic Society, Bombay.